MW00804245

A COMPANION TO
THE LATIN LANGUAGE

BLACKWELL COMPANIONS TO THE ANCIENT WORLD

This series provides sophisticated and authoritative overviews of periods of ancient history, genres of classical literature, and the most important themes in ancient culture. Each volume comprises between twenty-five and forty concise essays written by individual scholars within their area of specialization. The essays are written in a clear, provocative, and lively manner, designed for an international audience of scholars, students, and general readers.

A COMPANION TO THE LATIN LANGUAGE

Edited by

James Clackson

WILEY-BLACKWELL

A John Wiley & Sons, Ltd., Publication

This edition first published 2011
© 2011 Blackwell Publishing Ltd.

Blackwell Publishing was acquired by John Wiley & Sons in February 2007. Blackwell's publishing program has been merged with Wiley's global Scientific, Technical, and Medical business to form Wiley-Blackwell.

Registered Office
John Wiley & Sons Ltd, The Atrium, Southern Gate, Chichester, West Sussex, PO19 8SQ, United Kingdom

Editorial Offices
350 Main Street, Malden, MA 02148–5020, USA
9600 Garsington Road, Oxford, OX4 2DQ, UK
The Atrium, Southern Gate, Chichester, West Sussex, PO19 8SQ, UK

For details of our global editorial offices, for customer services, and for information about how to apply for permission to reuse the copyright material in this book please see our website at www.wiley.com/wiley-blackwell.

The right of James Clackson to be identified as the author of the editorial material in this work has been asserted in accordance with the UK Copyright, Designs and Patents Act 1988.

All rights reserved. No part of this publication may be reproduced, stored in a retrieval system, or transmitted, in any form or by any means, electronic, mechanical, photocopying, recording or otherwise, except as permitted by the UK Copyright, Designs and Patents Act 1988, without the prior permission of the publisher.

Wiley also publishes its books in a variety of electronic formats. Some content that appears in print may not be available in electronic books.

Designations used by companies to distinguish their products are often claimed as trademarks. All brand names and product names used in this book are trade names, service marks, trademarks or registered trademarks of their respective owners. The publisher is not associated with any product or vendor mentioned in this book. This publication is designed to provide accurate and authoritative information in regard to the subject matter covered. It is sold on the understanding that the publisher is not engaged in rendering professional services. If professional advice or other expert assistance is required, the services of a competent professional should be sought.

Library of Congress Cataloging-in-Publication Data

A companion to the Latin language / edited by James Clackson.
    p.   cm. – (Blackwell companions to the ancient world)
  Includes bibliographical references and indexes.
  ISBN 978-1-4051-8605-6 (alk. paper)
 1. Latin language–History.   2. Latin philology.   I. Clackson, James.
  PA2057.C66 2011
  470–dc22

                                         2011009293

A catalogue record for this book is available from the British Library.

This book is published in the following electronic formats: ePDFs [ISBN 9781444343366]; Wiley Online Library [ISBN 9781444343397]; ePub [ISBN 9781444343373]; Mobi [ISBN 9781444343380]

Set in 10/12.5pt Galliard by SPi Publisher Services, Pondicherry, India
Printed in Malaysia by Ho Printing (M) Sdn Bhd

1   2011

Contents

List of Illustrations

Figures

Tables

Notes on Contributors

J.N. Adams was Senior Research Fellow at All Souls College, Oxford, from 1998 to 2010. His numerous publications on Latin include *The Regional Diversification of Latin 200 BC–AD 600* (2007), *Bilingualism and the Latin Language* (2003), *Wackernagel's Law and the Placement of the Copula* esse *in Classical Latin* (1994), *The Latin Sexual Vocabulary* (1982) and *The Vulgar Latin of the Letters of Claudius Terentianus* (1977). In 2009 he was awarded the Kenyon Medal for Classical Studies and Archaeology by the British Academy.

Philip Burton is Reader in Latin and Early Christian Studies at the University of Birmingham. His previous publications include *The Old Latin Gospels* (2000) and *Language in the* Confessions *of Augustine* (2007), as well as articles on Latin linguistics and on the reception of Classical Antiquity. He is currently working on an edition on the Old Latin traditions of John (www.iohannes.org) for the Vetus Latina series.

David Butterfield is the W.H.D. Rouse Research Fellow and Lector in Classics at Christ's College, Cambridge, and works primarily upon the textual criticism and transmission of Latin literature. He has co-edited *The Penguin Latin Dictionary* (London, 2007) and *A.E. Housman: Classical Scholar* (London, 2009), and has written various articles on Latin poets (particularly Lucretius) and the history of Classical scholarship.

Anna Chahoud is Professor of Latin at Trinity College Dublin. She is the author of *C. Lucilii Reliquiarum Concordantiae* (1998), of articles on Republican Latin and the grammatical tradition, and co-editor of *Colloquial and Literary Latin* (2010). She is currently finalising a commentary on the fragments of Lucilius for Cambridge University Press.

James Clackson is Senior Lecturer in the Department of Classics at the University of Cambridge. His books include *The Blackwell History of the Latin Language* (2007, with Geoff Horrocks), and *Indo-European Linguistics: An Introduction* (Cambridge, 2007). His research interests include historical and comparative linguistics, the sociolinguistics of the ancient world, and the Armenian language.

Greti Dinkova-Bruun is Associate Fellow at the Pontifical Institute of Mediaeval Studies, Toronto. She has published widely on a range of topics within the field of Medieval Studies. A noted palaeographer, she is responsible for a number of critical editions and translations of medieval texts including the poetry of Alexander of Ashby, *Alexandri Essebiensis Opera Poetica* (2004) and *The Ancestry of Jesus* (2005). Since January 2010 she has been the Editor-in-Chief for the *Catalogus Translationum et Commentariorum* (*CTC*).

Rolando Ferri is Professor of Latin at the University of Pisa. He studied at Pisa, Princeton and London, where he was Momigliano Student in the Arts in the years 1993–1996. He has published books on Horace (*I dispiaceri di un epicureo*, 1993) and Senecan tragedy (*Octavia attributed to Seneca*, 2003), and he has edited books devoted to the Roman school (F. Bellandi and R. Ferri, ed., *Aspetti della scuola nel mondo romano*, 2008) and to Latin lexicography (R. Ferri, ed., *The Latin of Roman Lexicography*, 2010). He now works on the bilingual Greek–Latin glossaries and their value as evidence for the study of Late and Vulgar Latin.

Thorsten Fögen teaches Classics at Durham University and the Humboldt University of Berlin. Among his research interests are the history of linguistic ideas, ancient rhetoric, literary criticism, non-verbal communication and semiotics, ancient technical writers, women in antiquity, animals in antiquity and ancient epistolography. He is the author of *"Patrii sermonis egestas": Einstellungen lateinischer Autoren zu ihrer Muttersprache* (2000), *"Utraque lingua": A Bibliography of Bi- and Multilingualism in Graeco-Roman Antiquity and in Modern Times* (2003), and *Wissen, Kommunikation und Selbstdarstellung. Zur Struktur und Charakteristik römischer Fachtexte der frühen Kaiserzeit* (2009).

Benjamin W. Fortson IV teaches Classical languages and Indo-European philology at the University of Michigan. His publications include articles and reviews on Indo-European and historical linguistics, as well as an introductory textbook in Indo-European (*Indo-European Language and Culture*, 2nd edn, 2010) and a monograph on Plautine metrics and linguistics (*Language and Rhythm in Plautus*, 2008).

Michèle Fruyt is Professor of Latin Linguistics at the University of Paris-Sorbonne (Paris IV) and Director of the Centre Alfred Ernout for Latin linguistics. Her research mainly concerns the following: a description of the Latin lexicon from both a synchronic and a diachronic perspective, focusing on the way elements of the language were perceived by Latin speakers (motivation, de-motivation, re-analysis); semantic issues in the functioning of the language; the structural organization of the Latin lexicon; word-formation; the morpho-syntactic evolution of Latin, including grammaticalization, deixis and endophor, verbal periphrases, etc.

Giovanbattista Galdi holds a PhD in Classical Philology from the University of Bologna (2002). He was scientific co-worker at the *Thesaurus Linguae Latinae* in Munich from 2001 to 2003 and wrote his Habilitation at the University of Trier from 2003 to 2007. Currently, he is Assistant Professor of Latin Language at the University of Cyprus (Nicosia). His main areas of interest lie in the field of Late and Vulgar Latin, epigraphic language and Greek–Latin bilingualism. He is the author of *Grammatica delle iscrizioni latine dell'impero (province orientali). Morfo-sintassi nominale* (2004) and of numerous articles on Latin language.

Bruce Gibson is Professor of Latin at the University of Liverpool. His principal research is concerned with the literature of the Roman Empire, with significant connections with various aspects of Roman history and culture. His work also engages with the transmission of Latin texts in manuscripts and with Renaissance scholarship. His publications include an edition and commentary of Statius, *Silvae 5* (Oxford, 2006).

Hilla Halla-aho works as a researcher at the Department of World Cultures, University of Helsinki. Her main interests are the language of Latin non-literary texts as well as variation and change in Latin syntax. Her publications include the monograph *The Non-Literary Latin Letters: A Study of Their Syntax and Pragmatics* (2009).

Geoffrey Horrocks is Professor of Comparative Philology in the University of Cambridge. His publications include *The Blackwell History of the Latin Language* (2007, with James Clackson), and *Greek: A History of the Language and Its Speakers* (2nd edn, 2010). His research interests include the history and structure of the Greek and Latin languages (including Medieval and Modern as well as Ancient Greek), linguistic theory, and historical linguistics.

Christina Shuttleworth Kraus is Thomas A. Thacher Professor of Latin at Yale University. She works on Latin historiography, primarily on Livy and Tacitus, and is currently preparing a commentary (together with A.J. Woodman) on Tacitus' *Agricola*.

Caroline Kroon is Professor of Latin at the VU University Amsterdam. She is the author of *Discourse Particles in Latin: A Study of* nam, enim, autem, vero *and* at (1995), and co-editor of *Theory and Description in Latin Linguistics* (2002).

Her main research interests lie in the fields of pragmatics, discourse linguistics, and, especially, the linguistic articulation of narrative. She is currently supervising a linguistic-narratological research programme on ancient war narrative.

Matthew McCullagh teaches at St Paul's School in London. He received his doctorate in Classics from Cambridge University, and he has taught both at Cambridge University and at Royal Holloway, University of London. He is currently preparing a monograph on the prehistory of the Greek aorist passive.

Wolfgang de Melo teaches in the Department of Latin and Greek at the University of Ghent and is a Quondam Fellow of All Souls College, Oxford. His book *The Early Latin Verb System: Archaic Forms in Plautus, Terence, and Beyond* was published in 2007. His main scholarly interests are the linguistic aspects of Early Latin; the development from Indo-European to Latin, and from Early to Classical Latin; and the closest relatives of Latin (Faliscan, Oscan, Umbrian, Venetic).

Alex Mullen is Lumley Research Fellow in Classics at Magdalene College, University of Cambridge. She has published on linguistic and cultural contacts in Roman Britain and southern Gaul and is currently co-editing a multi-authored volume on multilingualism in antiquity.

John Penney is University Lecturer in Classical Philology at the University of Oxford and Fellow of Wolfson College, Oxford. His research interests include Indo-European phonology and morphology, the languages of pre-Roman Italy, and Tocharian. He has also published articles on historical aspects of the language of Latin verse and prose.

J.G.F. Powell is Professor of Latin at Royal Holloway, University of London. He has published editions of Cicero's *Cato Maior de Senectute* (Cambridge, 1988), of *Laelius de Amicitia* (Warminster, 1990), and of *De Re Publica* and *De Legibus* (Oxford Classical Text, 2006), has edited *Cicero the Philosopher* (Oxford, 1995), and *Logos: Rational Argument in Classical Rhetoric* (BICS Supplement 2007), and co-edited *Author and Audience in Latin Literature* (Cambridge, 1992), *Cicero's Republic* (BICS Supplement 2001) and *Cicero the Advocate* (Oxford, 2004). He is working on, among other things, a new Latin grammar for Wiley-Blackwell.

Bruno Rochette is Professor of Greek and Latin Language and Literature at the University of Liège, Belgium. He is the author of *Le latin dans le monde grec. Recherches sur la diffusion de la langue et des lettres latines dans les provinces hellénophones de l'empire romain* (1997) and of articles on various aspects of Greco-Latin bilingualism.

Rex Wallace is Professor of Classics and Associate Dean of Personnel and Research for the College of Humanities and Fine Arts at the University of Massachusetts Amherst. His research interests are the languages of ancient Italy and historical/comparative linguistics. He is the author of *The Sabellic Languages of Ancient Italy* (2007), *Zikh Rasna: A Manual of Etruscan Language and Inscriptions* (2009), and numerous articles on Etruscan and Italic linguistics.

Roger Wright is Emeritus Professor of Spanish at the University of Liverpool. He is the author of (*inter alia*) *Late Latin and Early Romance in Spain and Carolingian France* (1982), *Early Ibero-Romance* (1995), and *A Sociophilological Study of Late Latin* (2003). His research interests centre on both the linguistic and the historical aspects of the transitional period between Latin, Romance and the Romance languages.

Abbreviations of Ancient Authors and Works

Accius, *praet.*	L. Accius, *Fabulae Praetextae*
Ael.	Claudius Aelianus (Aelian), *Varia Historia*
Afran.	L. Afranius
com.	*comoediae* as in the *Comicorum Romanorum Fragmenta*
Amm.	Ammianus Marcellinus
Andr.	L. Liuius Andonicus (Livius Andronicus), works as in the *Fragmenta Poetarum Latinorum*
App.	Appianos (Appian)
Sam.	*History of the Samnite Wars*
Apul., *Met.*	L. Apuleius, *Metamorphoses*
Asel.	Sempronius Asellio
August.	Aurelius Augustinus (Augustine)
C.D.	*de Ciuitate Dei*
Doct. Christ.	*de Doctrina Christiana*
Quaest. Hept.	*Quaestiones in Heptateuchum*
Trin.	*de Trinitate*
B. Afr.	*Bellum Africanum*
B. Hisp.	*Bellum Hispaniense*
Caecil.	Caecilius Statius (Caecilius)
com.	*comoediae* as in the *Comicorum Romanorum Fragmenta*
Caes.	C. Iulius Caesar (Caesar)
Civ.	*de Bello Ciuile*
Gal.	*de Bello Gallico*
Cato	M. Porcius Cato (Cato)
Agr.	*de Agri Cultura*
Orig.	*Origines*
Catul.	C. Valerius Catullus (Catullus)
Cels.	A. Cornelius Celsus, *de Medicina*

Cic.	M. Tullius Cicero (Cicero)
Ac.	*Academica*
Arch.	*pro Archia*
Att.	*Epistulae ad Atticum*
Brut.	*Brutus*
Caec.	*pro Caecina*
Cat.	*in Catilinam*
Clu.	*pro Cluentio*
Div.	*de Diuinatione*
Dom.	*de Domo sua*
de Orat.	*de Oratore*
Fam.	*Epistulae ad Familiares*
Fat.	*de Fato*
Fin.	*de Finibus*
Har.	*de Haruspicum Responsio*
Inv.	*de Inuentione*
Leg.	*de Legibus*
Man.	*pro Lege Manilia*
Mur.	*pro Murena*
N.D.	*de Natura Deorum*
Off.	*de Officiis*
Orat.	*Orator*
Phil.	*Philippicae*
Pis.	*in Pisonem*
Q. fr.	*Epistulae ad Quintum fratrem*
Rep.	*de Republica*
S. Rosc.	*pro S. Roscio Amerino*
Sen.	*de Senectute*
Tim.	*Timaeus*
Top.	*Topica*
Tusc.	*Tusculanae Disputationes*
Vat.	*in Vatinium*
Ver.	*in Verrem*
Cod. Iust.	*Codex Iustinianus*
Cod. Theod.	*Codex Theodosianus*
Col.	L. Iunius Moderatus Columella (Columella), *de Re Rustica*
Curt.	Q. Curtius Rufus, *Historiae Alexandri Magni*
Dig.	Digesta
D. S.	Diodorus Siculus
Edict. Roth.	*Edictus Rothari*
Enn.	Q. Ennius (Ennius)
Ann.	*Annales* (ed. Skutsch)
Scen.	*Scenica* (ed. Vahlen)
Trag.	*Tragoediae* (ed. Jocelyn)
Eus.	Eusebius
Vit. Const.	*Vita Constantini*

Fest.	S. Pompeius Festus (Festus), *de Significatu Verborum*
Fortunatianus, *Ars rhet.*	Consultus Fortunatianus, *Ars rhetorica.*
Frontinus, *Str.*	S. Iulius Frontinus (Frontinus), *Strategemata*
Fronto, *Ep.*	M. Cornelius Fronto (Fronto), *Epistulae*
Gaius, *Inst.*	Gaius, *Institutiones*
Galen	Aelius Galenus (Galen)
Libr. Propr.	*de Libris Propriis*
Gel.	Aulus Gellius, *Noctes Atticae*
Hipp. Berol.	*Hippiatrica Berolinensis*
Hor.	Q. Horatius Flaccus (Horace)
Carm.	*Carmina*
Ep.	*Epistulae*
Epod.	*Epodi*
S.	*Sermones*
Hyginus, *Astron.*	G. Iulius Hyginus (Hyginus), *de Astronomia*
Isid.	Isidorus Hispalensis (Isidore of Seville)
Or.	*Origines*
Just.	M. Iunianus Iustinus (Justin), *Epitoma Historicarum Philippicarum Pompei Trogi*
Juv.	D. Iunius Iuuenalis (Juvenal), *Saturae*
Laber.	D. Laberius (Laberius)
mim.	*mimi* as in the *Comicorum Romanorum Fragmenta*
Liv.	T. Liuius (Livy), *ab Vrbe Condita*
Lucil.	C. Lucilius
Lucr.	T. Lucretius Carus (Lucretius), *de Rerum Natura*
Marc., *Med.*	Marcellus Empiricus, *de Medicamentis*
Naev.	Cn. Naeuius (Naevius)
com.	*comoediae* as in the *Comicorum Romanorum Fragmenta*
Nepos	Cornelius Nepos
Alc.	*Alcibiades*
Dat.	*Datames*
Non.	Nonius Marcellus, *de Compendiosa Doctrina*
Nov.	*Nouellae Constitutiones*
Nov. Theod.	*Nouellae Theodosianae*
Novius	Q. Nouius (Novius)
com.	*comoediae* as in the *Comicorum Romanorum Fragmenta*
Onas.	Onasander
Ov.	P. Ouidius Naso (Ovid)
Met.	*Metamorphoses*
Tr.	*Tristia*
Pac.	M. Pacuuius (Pacuvius)
trag.	*Tragoediae* as in the *Tragicorum Romanorum Fragmenta*
Paul. *Fest.*	Paulus Diaconus, *Epitoma Festi*
Per. Aeth.	*Peregrinatio Aetheriae*
Persius	A. Persius Flaccus (Persius), *Saturae*
Petr.	Petronius Arbiter (Petronius), *Satyrica*

Pl.	T. Maccius Plautus (Plautus)
Am.	*Amphitruo*
As.	*Asinaria*
Aul.	*Aulularia*
Bac.	*Bacchides*
Capt.	*Captiui*
Cas.	*Casina*
Cur.	*Curculio*
Epid.	*Epidicus*
Men.	*Menaechmi*
Mer.	*Mercator*
Mil.	*Miles gloriosus*
Mos.	*Mostellaria*
Per.	*Persa*
Poen.	*Poenulus*
Ps.	*Pseudolus*
Rud.	*Rudens*
St.	*Stichus*
Trin.	*Trinummus*
Truc.	*Truculentus*
Plin., *Nat.*	C. Plinius Secundus (Pliny the Elder), *Naturalis Historia*
Plin.	C. Plinius Caecilius Secundus (Pliny the Younger)
Ep.	*Epistulae*
Ep. Tra.	*Epistulae ad Traianum*
Pan.	*Panegyricus Traiani*
Plut.	Plutarchos (Plutarch)
Alex.	*Alexander*
Caes.	*Caesar*
Cat. Mai.	*Cato Maior*
Cic.	*Cicero*
Polyb.	Polybios (Polybius), *Histories*
Pompon.	L. Pomponius (Pomponius)
com.	*comoediae* as in the *Comicorum Romanorum Fragmenta*
Prop.	S. Propertius (Propertius), *Elegiae*
Quint., *Inst.*	M. Fabius Quintilianus (Quintilian), *Institutio Oratoria*
Rhet. Her.	*Rhetorica ad Herennium*
Sal.	C. Sallustius Crispus (Sallust)
Cat.	*Bellum Catilinae*
Hist.	*Historiae*
Jug.	*Iugurtha*
Schol. Juv.	*Scholia in Iuuenalem uetustiora*
Sen.	L. Annaeus Seneca (Seneca the Elder)
Con.	*Controuersiae*
Sen.	L. Annaeus Seneca (Seneca the Younger)
Dial.	*Dialogi*
Ep.	*Epistulae Morales*

Med.	*Medea*
Nat.	*Naturales Quaestiones*
[Sen.] *Oct.*	*Octauia*, attributed to L. Annaeus Seneca (the younger)
Serv.	Maurus Seruius Honoratus (Servius)
A.	*in Vergilium commentarius: ad Aeneidem*
Ecl.	*in Vergilium commentarius: ad Eclogas*
SHA	Scriptores Historiae Augustae
Hadr.	*Hadrianus*
Sept. Sev.	*Septimius Seuerus*
Soran. Lat.	*Sorani Gynaeciorum uetus translatio Latina*
Stat.	P. Papinius Statius (Statius)
Silv.	*Siluae*
Theb.	*Thebais*
Suet.	C. Suetonius Tranquillus (Suetonius)
Aug.	*Augustus*
Claud.	*Claudius*
Gram.	*de Grammaticis*
Iul.	*Iulius*
Ner.	*Nero*
Tib.	*Tiberius*
Ves.	*Vespasianus*
Vit.	*Vitellius*
Tac.	Cornelius Tacitus (Tacitus)
Ag.	*Agricola*
Ann.	*Annales*
Dial.	*Dialogus de Oratoribus*
Hist.	*Historiae*
Ter.	P. Terentius Afer (Terence)
Ad.	*Adelphi*
An.	*Andria*
Eu.	*Eunuchus*
Hau.	*Hautontimorumenos*
Ph.	*Phormio*
Tert.	Q. Septimius Florens Tertullianus (Tertullian)
Theodorus Priscianus	
Eupor.	*Euporista*
Tib.	Albius Tibullus (Tibullus), *Elegiae*
Titin.	Titinius
com.	*comoediae* as in the *Comicorum Romanorum Fragmenta*
Tribonian	Flauius Tribonianus (Tribonian)
Inst. Iust.	*Institutiones Iustiniani*
Turpil.	S. Turpilius
com.	*comoediae* as in the *Comicorum Romanorum Fragmenta*
Var.	M. Terentius Varro (Varro)
L.	*de Lingua Latina*
R.	*Res Rusticae*

Vegetius	P. Flauius Vegetius Renatus (Vegetius)
Epit.	*Epitoma Rei Militaris*
Vet.	*Ars Veterinaria*
Vell.	C. Velleius Paterculus, *Historiae Romanae*
Ven. Fort.	Venantius Honorius Clementianus Fortunatus (Venantius Fortunatus)
Verg.	P. Vergilius Maro (Virgil)
A.	*Aeneis*
Ecl.	*Eclogae*
G.	*Georgica*
Vitr.	M. Vitruuius Pollio (Vitruvius) *de Architectura*
V.Max.	Valerius Maximus, *Facta et Dicta Memorabilia*

Note: Where translations are credited to authors but no further source is given, the translation is taken from the Loeb Classical Library.

Abbreviations of Modern Sources

AAntHung	*Acta Antiqua Academiae Scientiarum Hungaricae*
AC	*L'Antiquité Classique*
AE	*L'Année épigraphique*
AION	*Annali dell'Istituto universitario orientale di Napoli, Dipartimento di studi del mondo classico e del Mediterraneo antico*
AJA	*American Journal of Archaeology*
AJPh	*American Journal of Philology*
AKG	*Archiv für Kulturgeschichte*
ALL	*Archiv für lateinische Lexikographie und Grammatik*
ALMA	*Archivum Latinitatis Medii Aevi (Bulletin Du Cange)*
ANRW	*Aufstieg und Niedergang der römischen Welt*
AntTard	*Antiquité tardive*
BEFAR	*Bibliothèque des écoles françaises d'Athènes et de Rome*
BICS	*Bulletin of the Institute of Classical Studies of the University of London*
BIFAO	*Bulletin de l'Institut français d'archéologie orientale*
BSL	*Bulletin de la Société de linguistique de Paris*
CA	*Classical Antiquity*
CAG	*Commentaria in Aristotelem Graeca.* Berlin, 1882–1909
CB	*Classical Bulletin*
CCC	*Civiltà classica e cristiana*
CEL	P. Cugusi, *Corpus Epistolarum Latinarum, papyris tabulis ostracis servatarum.* 3 vols. Florence, 1992–2002
CGL	G. Loewe and G. Goetz, *Corpus Glossariorum Latinorum.* Leipzig, 1888–1923
CHG	E. Oder and C. Hoppe, *Corpus Hippiatricorum Graecorum.* 2 vols. Leipzig, 1924–1927
ChLA	*Chartae Latinae Antiquiores.* Olten, 1954–

CIL	*Corpus Inscriptionum Latinarum*. Berlin, 1862–
CJ	*Classical Journal*
CLE	*Carmina Latina Epigraphica*. 3 vols. Leipzig, 1895–1926
CLL	*Cahiers de L'Institute de Linguistque de Louvain*
CML	*Corpus Medicorum Latinorum*. Berlin, 1915–
CPh	*Classical Philology*
CPL.	R. Cavenaile, *Corpus Papyrorum Latinarum*. Wiesbaden, 1958
CPR	*Corpus Papyrorum Raineri*. Vienna, 1895–
CQ	*Classical Quarterly*
CR	*Classical Review*
DHA	*Dialogues d'histoire ancienne*
ET	H. Rix *et al.*, *Etruskische Texte. Editio minor*. Tübingen, 1991
FLP	E. Courtney, *The Fragmentary Latin Poets*. Oxford, 2003
GL	H. Keil, *Grammatici Latini*. 8 vols. Leipzig, 1855–1923
G&R	*Greece and Rome*
HLov	*Humanistica Lovaniensia*
HSCPh	*Harvard Studies in Classical Philology*
HSK	*Handbücher zur Sprach- und Kommunikationswissenschaft*
IF	*Indogermanische Forschungen*
IG	*Inscriptiones Graecae*. Berlin, 1873–
IGF	D.-C. Decourt, *Inscriptions grecques de la France*. Lyon, 2004
IGPhilae	*Les inscriptions grecques de Philae*. Paris, 1969–
IGUR	L. Moretti, *Inscriptiones Graecae Urbis Romae*. Rome, 1968–1979
ILAlg	*Inscriptions latines de l'Algérie*. Paris, 1922–
ILLRP	A. Degrassi, *Inscriptiones Latinae Liberae rei publicae*. 2 vols. Florence, 1957–1963
ILS	H. Dessau, *Inscriptiones Latinae Selectae*. 5 vols. Berlin, 1892–1916
JEA	*Journal of Egyptian Archaeology*
JIES	*Journal of Indo-European Studies*
JPh	*Journal of Philology*
JRS	*Journal of Roman Studies*
K-S	R. Kühner and C. Stegmann, *Ausfürliche Grammatik der lateinischen Sprache. Satzlehre*. Revised by A. Thierfelder, 3rd edn. Hanover, 1955
LCM	*Liverpool Classical Monthly*
MedArch	*Mediterranean Archaeology: Australian and New Zealand Journal for the Archaeology of the Mediterranean World*
MH	*Museum Helveticum*
NphM	*Neuphilologische Mitteilungen*
O.BuNjem	R. Marichal, *Les Ostraca de Bu Njem*. Tripoli, 1992.
O.Claud.	*Mons Claudianus. Ostraca graeca et latina*. Cairo, 1992–
O.Max.	Unpublished ostraca from Maximianon (Al-Zarqua, Egypt)
O.Wâdi Fawâkhir	O. Guéraud 'Ostraca grecs et latins de l'Wâdi Fawâkhir,' *BIFAO* 41, 1942, 141–196

OCD[3]	S. Hornblower and A. Spawforth, *The Oxford Classical Dictionary*. 3rd edn. Oxford and New York, 1996
OGI	W. Dittenberger, *Orientis Graeci Inscriptiones Selectae*. 2 vols. Leipzig, 1903–1905
OLD	P. Glare, *Oxford Latin Dictionary*. Oxford, 1968–1982
P.Herc.	*Papyri Herculanenses*
P.Masada	H.M. Cotton and J. Geiger, *Masada II, The Yigael Yadin Excavations 1963—1965. Final Reports: The Latin and Greek Documents*. Jerusalem, 1989
P.Mich.	*Michigan Papyri*. Ann Arbor, 1931–
P.Ness.	*Excavations at Nessana*. 3 vols. London and Princeton, 1950–1962
P.Oxy.	*The Oxyrhynchus Papyri*. London, 1898–
P.Panopolis	L.C. Youtie, D. Hagedorn and H.C. Youtie, *Urkunden aus Panopolis*. Bonn, 1980
P.Ryl.	*Catalogue of the Greek and Latin Papyri in the John Rylands Library, Manchester*. Manchester, 1911–
P.Yadin	*The Documents from the Bar Kochba Period in the Cave of Letters*. Jerusalem, 1989–
PCPhS	*Proceedings of the Cambridge Philological Society*
PL	J.-P. Migne, *Patrologiae cursus completus. Series Latina*. Paris, 1844–
PLLS	*Papers of the Liverpool Latin Seminar/Papers of the Leeds International Latin Seminar/Papers of the Langford Latin Seminar*
PSI	*Papiri greci e latini*. Florence, 1912–
QUCC	*Quaderni Urbinati di Cultura Classica*
REI	*Rivista di Epigrafia Italica* (published as part of *Studi Etruschi*)
REL	*Revue des Études Latines*
RenQ	*Renaissance Quarterly*
RH	*Revue historique*
RhM	*Rheinisches Museum*
RIB	*The Roman Inscriptions of Britain*. Oxford, 1965–
RIDA	*Revue internationale des droits de l'Antiquité*
RIG	*Recueil des inscriptions gauloises*. Paris, 1985–
RLM	C. Halm, ed., *Rhetores Latini Minores*. Leipzig, 1863
RPh	*Revue de philologie, de littérature et d'histoire anciennes*
SB	*Sammelbuch griechischer Urkunden aus Aegypten*
SCI	*Scripta classica Israelica*
SEG	*Supplementum Epigraphicum Graecum*, Leiden, 1923–
Sel. Pap.	A.S. Hunt and C.C. Edgar, *Select Papyri*. 5 vols, London and New York, 1932–1934
SIFC	*Studi italiani di filologia classica*
SIG[3]	W. Dittenberger, *Sylloge Inscriptionum Graecarum*. 3rd edn. 4 vols. Leipzig, 1915–1924
SO	*Symbolae Osloenses*
ST	H. Rix, *Sabellische Texte. Die Texte des Oskischen, Umbrischen und Südpikenischen*. Heidelberg, 2002

T.Alb.	C. Courtois, L. Leschi, C. Perrat and C. Saumagne, *Tablettes Albertini. Actes privés de l'époque Vandale.* Paris, 1952
T.Sulpicii	G. Camodeca, *Tabulae Pompeianae Sulpiciorum: edizione critica dell'archivio puteolano dei Sulpicii.* 2 vols. Rome, 1999.
T.Vindol.	*Vindolanda: The Latin Writing Tablets.* London and Oxford, 1983–
Tab. Sulis	R.S.O. Tomlin, 'The Curse Tablets', in B. Cunliffe (ed.), *The Temple of Sulis Minerva at Bath*, vol. 2: *The Finds from the Sacred Spring.* Oxford, 1988: 4–277
TAPhA	*Transactions of the American Philological Association*
TLL	*Thesaurus Linguae Latinae.* Leipzig, 1900–
TPhS	*Transactions of the Philological Society*
Ve	E. Vetter, *Handbuch der italischen Dialekte.* Heidelberg, 1953
WS	*Wiener Studien*
YClS	*Yale Classical Studies*
ZPE	*Zeitschrift für Papyrologie und Epigraphik*
ZSS	*Zeitschrift der Savigny-Stiftung für Rechtsgeschichte*

Symbols Used

*	precedes an element which is reconstructed for an earlier stage of the language or for a proto-language, but which is unattested
**	precedes an element which is unattested or is an impossible formation
< >	enclose an orthographic symbol or symbols (in most cases one or more letters of the Latin alphabet)
[ ]	enclose a phonetic symbol or symbols, representing a particular sound or sequence of sounds
//	enclose a symbol or symbols, representing a phoneme or sequence of phonemes
[β]	a voiced bilabial fricative, like the medial sound in Spanish *beber*
[ð]	a voiced dental fricative, like the initial sound of English *that*
[θ]	an unvoiced dental fricative, like the initial sound in English *thin*
[j]	a palatal approximant, like the initial sound of English *yet*
[ŋ]	a velar nasal, like the final sound of English *sing*
[ʃ]	a postalveolar fricative, like the initial sound of English *shirt*
[x]	a velar fricative, like the final sound of the German name Bach
[ɛ]	a relatively low or open "e" vowel, like the vowel in English *pet*
[ə]	a mid central unrounded vowel (schwa), like the final vowel in English *pizza*
[ɪ]	a close front i vowel, like the vowel in English *pit*
[ɔ]	a relatively low or open "o" vowel, like the vowel in English *paw*
[y]	a high front rounded vowel, like the German vowel written *ü*
[ʊ]	a relatively close back rounded vowel, like the vowel in English *good*
[ɨ]	a close central unrounded vowel, like the second vowel in English *roses*
[ʉ]	a close central rounded vowel
:	written after a phonetic symbol for a vowel sound represents a long vowel
ø	zero/zero morph (indicating the form has no ending)
X→Y	Y is a derivative of X
X>Y	X becomes Y by sound change

Linguistic and Other Abbreviations

abl.	ablative
abs.	absolute
acc.	accusative
ADJP	adjective phrase
ADVP	adverb phrase
agr.	agreement
antipass.	antipassive
C	consonant
Class.	Classical
dat.	dative
Det	determiner
erg.	ergative
fem.	feminine
gen.	genitive
gov.	government
IE	Indo-European
inf.	infinitive
instr.	instrumental
loc.	locative
masc.	masculine
[NEG]	any negative word or phrase
neut.	neuter
nom.	nominative
NP	noun phrase
OL	Old Latin
PIE	Proto-Indo-European
pl.	plural
PP	prepositional phrase

pple	participle
pr.	*praefatio*
rel.	relative
S	sentence
sg.	singular
V	in chapter 9 = verb; in other chapters = vowel
voc.	vocative
VP	verb phrase

CHAPTER 1

Introduction

James Clackson

Latin was the first "World Language" of human history. As the language of the Roman Empire and then the Roman Catholic Church it has spread around the globe, and today well over a billion people speak a language derived from Latin as their first or second language (Portuguese, Spanish, French, Italian, Romanian, etc.). Although there are no native speakers of Latin still alive, Latin has a cultural prestige matched by no other language in the West. In religion, in law, in medicine and in science, Latin terms and phrases are still employed on a daily basis. Latin's position in the modern world reflects its importance as the language of many of the most influential texts written between antiquity and the Early Modern period, from Virgil's *Aeneid* and Tacitus' *Annales* through the works of Augustine and the church fathers, to the use of Latin by Newton, Milton and Spinoza. Despite Latin's enormous cultural significance, this is the first single volume companion to the Latin language, both enabling the reader to access reliable summaries of what is known about the structure and vocabulary of the language, and setting the language in its cultural milieu from its first appearance, in short inscriptions in the first half of the first millennium BCE, to its use as a language of scholarship, of law and of the church in the modern period.

Latin comes after Greek. The initial impetus for this volume was as a companion to Bakker's *Companion to the Greek Language* (2010), and in structure and scope the *Companion to the Latin Language* mirrors its older sister. Indeed, in some areas, the two volumes overlap and complement each other. Just as the *Companion to the Greek Language* combines "traditional" and "modern" approaches to the linguistic study of the language, so does the *Companion to the Latin Language*. This volume attempts to give a comprehensive overview of the Latin language, including aspects of social variation and language change, speakers' attitudes to language and the use of Latin in literary texts.

A Companion to the Latin Language, First Edition. Edited by James Clackson.
© 2011 Blackwell Publishing Ltd. Published 2011 by Blackwell Publishing Ltd.

However, in much the same way that the Latin language has a very different history to Greek, so the structure of this *Companion* also reflects the differences between the two languages. The longer history of Greek (and the continual use of the label "Greek" to describe the language spoken in Greece in modern times) has meant that the written forms of the language have been recast many times. Moreover, the existence of Greek city states in the Classical period, and the emergence of different literary forms through oral and local traditions, have led to the adoption of a range of varieties of the language as written forms (the so-called Greek dialects). In contrast, there is usually reckoned to be only one standard form of Latin, Classical Latin. No dialects of Latin ever reached the status of a literary form, and no later stage of the language ever rivalled the prestige of the Classical standard. The formation of Classical Latin, and the repeated moves to purify or correct the language will be repeated themes of this volume, as will the demonstration that within the apparently monolithic structure of Classical Latin there is room for considerable variation and choice.

The *Companion* is divided into five parts, each of which is built around a different broad theme. Part I deals with the sources of our knowledge of the Latin language. Latin is a corpus language, known only through written documents, and no one who could genuinely be described as a native speaker of Latin has been alive for the last millennium. It is appropriate therefore that the first chapter of this section is devoted to the alphabet that encodes the language. Rex Wallace addresses the question of the adoption and adaptation of the alphabet from the Greeks through Etruscan intermediaries, and his richly illustrated chapter contains the most up-to-date survey of the very earliest Latin inscriptions that survive. He then traces the development of the Latin letterforms, the differing orthographic practices of the Romans down to the imperial period, and the possible connections between and influences from letterforms and orthographic practices among the other literate peoples of Italy. The next two chapters examine the ways Latin texts function as sources for the language. Latin texts have reached us through two principal routes. Either the original written form has survived on a medium such as stone, wood, metal or papyrus, or a text has been copied and recopied in an unbroken chain of manuscript transmission. In general, texts in the second category comprise literary works, and those in the first all other forms of documentation (although there are instances where literary works are recorded in inscriptional texts, such as Augustus' *Res Gestae*, or where manuscripts preserve sub-literary material). James Clackson presents a discussion of some of the pitfalls for the linguist who uses inscriptional and documentary material to research the Latin language, including the vexed problem of attributing "authorship" to an ancient inscription. This chapter also includes a description of the range of such material available for the ancient world and explanations of some of the editorial conventions used. Bruce Gibson addresses the question of how literary texts have been handed down through the centuries. He shows how a modern editor of a text reconstructs a manuscript tradition, and how scholars have addressed the problems of variant readings, non-standard orthographies and different sources for a single text, presenting (among other examples) a test case of a manuscript page of Catullus and the modern reading. Roger Wright concludes Part I by looking at the use of a very different sort of source for the Latin language, the medieval and modern languages which have descended from spoken forms of Latin. As he shows, in order to understand this topic it is important to distinguish first between what counts as Latin and what counts as

Romance, and the chapter includes a discussion of this topic, before a systematic review of the evidence of Romance for our knowledge of spoken Latin.

Wright's chapter is also the first point in this volume where the term *Vulgar Latin* is used, and it is worth pausing to consider this term, which been the most discussed in the study of Latin, and is widely used in modern published work. Many readers will expect to find a chapter, if not a section, on Vulgar Latin in a *Companion to the Latin Language*, and will want to know why this volume does not include one. Part of the reason is the ambiguity inherent in the term. Wright (p. 63) reports József Herman's definition of Vulgar Latin as a collective label for features of the language which we know existed but which were not recommended by grammarians, a usage which is observed by Adams in his chapter (pp. 263–265). Adams notes that the term would then have to include the linguistic behaviour of individuals such as the Emperor Augustus, and as such is at odds with a prevalent understanding of Vulgar Latin as the variety or varieties spoken by the uneducated and illiterate populace. For the sake of avoiding confusion, the writers in this volume generally restrict their use of the term Vulgar Latin to Herman's definition, where they use it at all, and the other senses in which the label is used are defined in their own terms.

Part II aims to provide an overview of the linguistic structure of Latin, concentrating largely on the synchronic grammar of the Classical form of the language. Matthew McCullagh shows how we are able to reconstruct the phonology of the language accurately, to isolate the meaningful sounds of Latin (the phonemes), and, in most cases, specify their phonetic value. Benjamin W. Fortson IV expands the discussion of the sound of Latin by looking at what we can learn about the language from the metres the Romans used, and what we can learn about the metres from comparative and linguistic investigation. Fortson concentrates on three particular problems: the Saturnian metre and its background in inherited verse types of the Indo-European family; the adaptation of Greek metres by the Latin comic playwrights and their nativisation; and the interaction between verse beat (ictus) and the native Latin word and phrasal stress. Inflectional morphology and the selection of the Classical Latin exponents from a range of varieties are then covered by James Clackson. For many people who learnt Latin at school, the memory of lessons on syntactic constructions such as the ablative absolute or the gerundive is enough to provoke winces of pain; experienced teachers are frequently able to answer the question "How?" but rarely the question "Why?" Geoffrey Horrocks, in his chapter on Latin syntax, goes beyond the traditional listing and cataloguing of different constructions and uses modern syntactic theory to give an answer to the "Why?" question, introducing theoretical notions such as "control" into the study of Latin grammar for the first time. The Latin lexicon is the subject of the next two chapters by Michèle Fruyt. In any language, the vocabulary is formed from a combination of inherited, borrowed and derived lexemes. In the first of her two chapters, Fruyt considers the basic vocabulary of Latin, the organisation of the semantic structure of the lexicon, and the means by which the language incorporates words borrowed from other languages, with particular focus on the reaction to, and the reception of, Greek words. In the next chapter, she looks in more detail at the processes of lexical morphology, including the formation of compounds and the derivation of new words from existing lexical items, with detailed consideration of individual affixes and affixation processes, as well as agglutination and recategorisation (the process whereby words are transferred from one lexical class to another with the addition of no overt affix). To round off this section, Caroline Kroon's chapter tackles a linguistic topic that is generally absent from traditional works on Latin, the grammar of discourse. Recent work on pragmatics, the study of language in use, has shown how speakers and writers of different languages employ particles and other text-marking devices in various ways in order to give order and structure to units of communication longer than a sentence. Kroon shows how familiar Latin particles have a more nuanced, and more precise, use in context than is apparent from bare English translations.

Part III is devoted to presentations of Latin through history, from its Indo-European origins to its use in the modern world, detailing the distinctive changes and features for each period, as well as recording the spread of the language. Benjamin W. Fortson IV looks at Latin in the context of the Indo-European language family, and details the major changes which Latin has undergone, and also gives details on its relationship to Oscan and Umbrian and the other Indo-European languages of Italy. John Penney examines in detail the language of the earliest Latin texts up to the end of the second century BCE, including commentary on selected early inscriptional texts, noting changes in language and orthographic practices. The next chapter, by James Clackson, covers Classical Latin, principally the language of the late Republic and the first two centuries of the Roman Empire. This chapter includes extensive discussion of the debates about what constituted *Latinitas,* probably best translated as "correct Latin", the processes of standardisation, including changes in orthography, morphology, syntax and vocabulary, and the treatment of Greek words in Latin. The next three chapters treat the Latin of later chronological periods. First, J.N. Adams examines the notion of *Late Latin,* and asks whether there are distinctive linguistic features to Latin of this date, and how linguistic change, pressure from the standard language and other factors intertwine in texts written in Late Antiquity and beyond. The last two chapters describe the survival of Latin as a written and scholarly idiom, used alongside various vernaculars, from the Middle Ages to the present day. Greti Dinkova-Bruun discusses Medieval Latin, offering sample texts to illustrate the changes in orthography, grammar, vocabulary and style of Latin texts in the period between the end of antiquity and the Renaissance. David Butterfield looks at the language from the Renaissance to the present, showing the repeated attempts by writers to get closer to Classical models, and detailing the link between teaching Classics and writing Latin prose and verse in the last two centuries.

Part IV of the companion is devoted to presentations of the idioms and styles characteristic of a range of specific Latin literary registers. It is well known to any classicist that Latin poetry employs features such as extreme displacements of word order, or calques of Greek syntax, which are not found in Latin prose, and that a letter by Cicero will differ in style and vocabulary from one of his speeches or his philosophical works. The chapters in Part IV examine both the language of specific literary or para-literary genres and the language which is associated with certain contexts, such as the law court or the Christian church. In all these areas it is of course impossible to give a checklist of features which are obligatory for a certain genre or context, and the chapters here indicate, in different ways, some of the limitations of seeing a simple correspondence between genre and language. Even so, there are many broad generalisations to be made, as well as illuminating discussions of individual features, and the chapters together present a completely new picture of the language of literary Latin. Wolfgang de Melo gives an overview of the language of Roman comedy and mime, showing distinctive features of the Latin of Plautus and later dramatists. Rolando Ferri looks at poetic language, particularly as revealed in epic and lyric works (encompassing also the language of Senecan drama). Ferri sets out ancient theories of poetic language, and demonstrates the ways in which the sound and metre of poetry affected the orthographic and lexical choices authors made. Poetic techniques such as metaphor, hyperbaton and Greek syntactic constructions are placed in context and illustrated by citations from authors ranging from Lucretius to Cyprianus Gallus. Quintilian famously stated that *satura quidem tota nostra est* ("satire is all ours"; *Inst.* 10.1.93). Satire is noteworthy as the only genre of Latin literature which does not have Greek models to follow, and Anna Chahoud's chapter on Roman satire shows how lexical and syntactic choices set this genre apart from other Latin poetry, and how the authorial presentations of the genre in opposition to the themes and language of "high" poetry are brought about in style and diction. This chapter also gives an insight into what constituted "coarse" and colloquial language for a Roman audience.

The literary genres of prose are covered in the next chapters in this section. Jonathan Powell reminds us how limited our knowledge of actual Roman oratory is, and traces the development of rhetoric as a topic of study and debate in the Roman world, while also analysing some of the features of Ciceronian periodic style in his speeches. Christina Shuttleworth Kraus writes on the language of Roman historiography and draws out the similarities and differences between history writing and other genres, including poetry and oratory; she documents the ways in which historians from Cato to Ammianus vary their style according to the subject matter, and make use of annalistic and military language in their works. Hilla Halla-aho dissects the construction of different styles apparent in the Latin epistolary corpus (comprising both the correspondence of Cicero, Pliny and Fronto and documentary material such as the wooden tablets from Vindolanda). She separates out colloquial from rhetorical and formal styles in letters, and her presentation of what constitutes a colloquialism has ramifications beyond the Latin of letters alone. Technical writing is not normally reckoned to be a unified genre per se within literary studies of ancient literature, but, as Thorsten Fögen shows, the modern concept of a specific idiom of *Fachsprache* can lead to interesting conclusions when looking at Roman writing on subjects as diverse as grammar, architecture, medicine, farming and the encyclopaedic *Naturalis Historia* composed by Pliny the Elder. All of these disciplines share similarities in their approaches to the formation of new technical terms, their employment of non-personal styles and constructions, and their reactions to Greek models. Finally, the last two chapters examine the two cultural contexts in which Latin has survived the longest into the modern world: law and Christianity. Jonathan Powell considers the tradition of Roman law from the earliest tables, through contracts surviving on wax tablets from the bay of Naples to the Latin tags employed by professional lawyers and jurists even today. Philip Burton offers a condensation of research on the language employed by Christian writers and Bible translators, and revisits the debates about the special nature of Christian Latin. He shows that Christian authors can encompass a wide range of styles, and how special uses of vocabulary items can reveal their indebtedness to biblical language.

What can broadly be termed sociolinguistic approaches to Latin are the subject of Part V. The four chapters here explore different aspects of language variation in the ancient world. We know that some linguistic variation in Ancient Rome correlated with the social status, age and gender of the speaker, and James Clackson assesses to what extent these social dialects of Latin are accessible to us. By considering whether it is possible to associate the social position of a speaker or writer with variation in Latin, this chapter necessarily overlaps with previous research carried out under the heading of Vulgar Latin as discussed above. It goes beyond the discussion of variation correlated with social class, however, by also surveying the evidence for specific features that can be associated with the gender and age of the speaker. This chapter also discusses the significance of the use of Greek by Latin speakers, and this topic is further expanded and analysed in the contribution of Alex Mullen who examines Latin in contact with other languages (including not only Greek but also a range of idioms now no longer spoken, including Oscan and Gaulish). Mullen considers the topic of bilingualism both at the macro-level of institutionalised bilingualism, and at the micro-level of individual speakers, such as Cicero, and the significance of the choices made between two or more languages. The role of the state and of Roman magistrates and emperors in enforcing or promoting Latin, its complex sociocultural relationship to Greek, and the use of Latin in the Greek world through the Byzantine period are clearly of particular importance in the consideration of the social functions of Latin. This is the subject of Bruno Rochette's chapter. Finally, Giovanbattista Galdi summarises the range of evidence for geographical variations in Latin across the Roman world, in both the republic and the empire. Using the mass of evidence gathered by Adams in his recent book on the diversification of Latin across the Roman world (Adams 2007), Galdi brings out salient features of regional Latin, including an examination of the Latin of the north-eastern provinces of the empire.

Galdi's chapter reminds us of the extraordinary geographical spread of Latin. In the first century of the Roman Empire, Latin began to be recognised as a universal language, as shown by the comments of the Greek author Plutarch (*Moralia* 1010D). In consideration of the question of why Plato said that the only parts of speech were nouns and verbs, Plutarch notes that in Latin there is no definite article as there is in Greek, nor as many prepositions. Parenthetically, Plutarch adds that almost all men use Latin. These comments mark a significant stage in the history of Latin, since it is now that Greeks take an interest in the language, and start to relinquish their own claim to linguistic predominance. Although no longer a spoken universal language, Latin has increased its reach and range since the time of Plutarch. The association of Latin with the Roman Catholic Church, and its use in countless legal constitutions, statutes and codes have resulted in the spread of the language to parts of the world unknown to the Romans. Latin supplies models of correct grammar for language purists, it provides syntactical and morphological meat for professional linguists and it is mined for mottos by states, companies and celebrities. In showing something of the complexities of its structure, history and use, this volume will, it is hoped, enhance the understanding and appreciation of the Latin language.

PART I

Sources

CHAPTER 2

The Latin Alphabet and Orthography

Rex Wallace

"Why is the alphabet in that order? Is it because of that song?"

(Steven Wright, stand-up comic)

Introduction

The alphabet used by Latin-speaking peoples resembles the alphabets used today to write most of the languages of Europe and the Americas.[1] The scripts of these languages have the Latin alphabet as their ancestor.[2]

The Latin alphabet of the late republican period was composed of twenty-one letters (*unius et uiginti formae litterarum*, Cic. *N.D.* 2.93). Table 2.1 is a list of the letters arranged in canonical order. Each letter is in capital form accompanied by its letter name and the phoneme(s) that it represented.

The alphabet presented in Table 2.1 was codified before the end of the third century BCE. The order of the letters, which follows that inherited from the Etruscan alphabet (see below), was remarkably resistant to change. It remained the same, apart from the addition of two letters borrowed from ancient Greek in the first century BCE (see further below), until the end of Roman *imperium*. Even today the order of the letters in the English alphabet and the names for the letters that English speakers teach their children follows the Latin closely.[3]

Arrival of the Alphabet in Italy

The origin of the Latin alphabet begins with the establishment of permanent Greek settlements in southern Italy in the eighth century BCE.[4] Colonists from the Euboean city of Khalkis established an emporium on the island of Pithekoussai (modern Ischia) before

A Companion to the Latin Language, First Edition. Edited by James Clackson.
© 2011 Blackwell Publishing Ltd. Published 2011 by Blackwell Publishing Ltd.

Table 2.1   The Classical Latin alphabet

Form	Name	Phoneme(s)	Form	Name	Phoneme(s)
A	*a*	/a, aː/	L	*el*	/l/
B	*be*	/b/	M	*em*	/m/
C	*ce*	/k/	N	*en*	/n/
D	*de*	/d/	O	*o*	/ɔ, oː/
E	*e*	/ɛ, eː/	P	*pe*	/p/
F	*ef*	/f/	Q	*qu*	/k/
G	*ɡe*	/g/	R	*er*	/r/
H	*ha*	/h/, ø	S	*es*	/s/
I	*i*	/ɪ, iː, j/	T	*te*	/t/
K	*ka*	/k/	V	*u*	/ʊ, uː, w/
			X	*eks*	/ks/

750 BCE and a settlement on the mainland at Kyme (Cumae) a few decades later (*c.* 730–720 BCE). Some members of these communities had become literate in their home city; they were responsible for introducing the alphabet to Italy.

The oldest epigraphic evidence in Euboean Greek is on an impasto flask recovered from a grave at the Osteria dell'Osa cemetery near the ancient city of Gabii situated about eleven miles east of Rome.[5] The flask was incised from left to right with five letters. Ultimately it was deposited in a *dolium* that was buried together with the remains of a woman.[6] The inscription is generally read as *euḷin,* which is shorthand for the adjective εὔλινος, "skillfully spinning," referring to one of the traditional tasks of a woman.[7] More substantive Greek inscriptions in the Euboean dialect have been recovered from southern Italy,[8] including the important metrical inscription on "Nestor's cup," a kotyle recovered in 1954 from a grave in a necropolis on Pithekoussai,[9] and the proverbial sentiment, also possibly metrical, incised on a lekythos from Kyme.[10]

Once introduced to Italy, the alphabet diffused rapidly to native peoples. Etruscans from southern Etruria borrowed the alphabet in the last quarter of the eighth century BCE.[11] Other native peoples of the Italian peninsula adopted the alphabet soon after, generally via Etruscan intermediation.[12] If the dates of attestation of inscriptions are to be trusted as a rough guide to the paths of diffusion and dates of adaptation, we see that the alphabet fans out in all directions from Etruria. Old Umbrian inscriptions date to the seventh century BCE, as do inscriptions in Faliscan and Latin. Inscriptions in South Picene, Oscan, Venetic and Transalpine Celtic date to the sixth century BCE.

Etruscan Origins

The primary source of the Latin alphabet – Greek or Etruscan – remains controversial. Scholars who favor a Greek origin point out that the letters B, D, O and X have roughly the same phonological values in Latin as in Greek. Scholars who favor an Etruscan origin point out that the letter C has the same phonological value in Latin as in Etruscan.

Table 2.2 Spelling of velars in Very Old Latin inscriptions

	/k/	/g/	/kʷ/
Fibula	FHE:FHAKED	–	–
Forum	KALATOREM	RECEI	QVOI, QVOS
	KAPIA(D)		
	SAKROS		
Duenos	PAÇA	VIRCO	QOI
	FEÇED		
	COSMIS		
Kavidios	–	KAVIDIOS, EQO	–
Garigliano	KOM, SOKIOIS	–	–
Tibur	–	KAVIOS	QETIOS
Pulpios	–	EQO	
Corcolle	[D]ICASE	–	–

In Greek the letter C (*gamma*) stood for a voiced velar stop. (Etruscan did not have voiced stops.) In this case alphabetic patrimony is best determined by considering orthographic rules and developments that are so unusual they are unlikely to have arisen independently in different languages' writing systems.[13] Spelling conventions attested in Very Old Latin inscriptions point to the Etruscans as the source of the Latin alphabet.

In Very Old Latin inscriptions the velar stops /k, g/ and the labialized velar /kʷ/ were spelled by C, K and Q (see Table 2.2).[14] This diversity of spelling makes sense if it is viewed as an attempt to carry over into Latin the southern Etruscan orthographic convention whereby /k/ was spelled by means of the so-called C/K/Q-rule. In archaic Etruscan the letter C was written before the letters I and E (CI, CE), the letter K before the letter A (KA), and the letter Q before the letter V (QV), e.g. Etruscan KACRIQV [meaning unclear] (*ET* Ta 2.1).[15] A Latin reinterpretation of this convention is found in the Forum inscription (*CIL* I².1). Consider the spelling of the following words: RECEI /reːgej/ "king"; KAPIA(D) /kapiaːd/ "take"; SAKROS /sakrɔs/ "cursed"; QVOI /kʷoj/ "who." As can be seen from the transcriptions, the Etruscan rule was generalized in Latin to include the stops /g/ and /kʷ/, sounds that were not present in the Etruscan inventory. And there was an additional twist: the letter K was written before O as well as A. (Etruscan had no /ɔ/ or /o/.) Borrowing from an Etruscan source provides some rationale for the spelling of the velar stops in other Very Old Latin inscriptions as well. For example, the person who incised the text on the *Duenos* vase appears to have written FEKED and PAKA and then corrected the letter K in both words to C, FEÇED "made" and PAÇA [meaning unclear] revealing some uncertainty about when to use C and K.[16] The same writer used the letter C to spell /k/ and /g/ before O (COSMIS "kind," VIRCO "girl"), and he spelled /kʷ/ by means of Q (QOI "who") rather than QV.[17] Other writers resolved the issue of how to spell velar stops before the O-letter in a different manner. In the *Kavidios* inscription, K was written before A (KAVIDIOS /gaːwidiɔs/), but Q was written before O (EQO /egoː/).[18]

A second spelling convention points to the Etruscans. The phoneme /f/, which was absent from the phonological inventories of ancient Greek dialects, was present in

ΥΦΧΥↃ>ΨΡΜ↑ο 圉ΨↃ XIⵁᗺΙↃↃↃↃↃ8A

Figure 2.1   Etruscan *abecedarium* incised on miniature ivory writing tablet, Marsiliana d'Albegna (Rix *Etruskische Texte* AV.1). Drawing by Brigette McKenna, University of Massachusetts Amherst.

Etruscan and was written by means of a digraph FH.[19] This convention was borrowed to spell the corresponding labial fricative /f/ in Latin, e.g. FHE:FHAKED "made" (*CIL* I².3); FHĘ[CED] "made" (Peruzzi (1963)).[20]

Scholars who favor a Greek origin for the Latin alphabet counter that B, D and O were "dead" letters in Etruscan, that is to say, were never used to spell sounds in inscriptions. It must be remembered, however, that these letters remained in Etruscan *abecedaria* for over a hundred years after the alphabet was adopted. The Etruscan *abecedarium* incised on the border of a miniature ivory writing tablet recovered from Marsiliana d'Albegna carried the twenty-six letters inherited from Euboean Greek (Figure 2.1). Latin speakers learned an unabridged alphabet of this type, one having the full complement of letters. A clever and innovative scribe resurrected the "dead" letters B, D and O in order to represent sounds in Latin that were not found in the Etruscan phonological system. Direct transmission from Greek does not permit a compelling explanation for the use of the letter C to represent a voiceless velar stop in Latin, whereas borrowing from Etruscan does.

Date of Borrowing and Other Considerations

Determining the date of the origin of the Latin alphabet is problematic. Despite recent discoveries,[21] the inventory of Latin inscriptions that can be reliably dated to the seventh and sixth centuries BCE is very small (see Table 2.3).[22] The number that can be dated to the seventh century BCE is smaller still. Of these, two – the *Vetusia* inscription and the *Fibula Praenestina* (Figure 2.2) – are the subject of controversy.[23] The former is problematic because the inscription is interpreted by some as Etruscan; the latter because some consider the gold fibula and its inscription of questionable authenticity. If these items are part of the Latin corpus, – and I am inclined to think they should be included – the date at which the Latin alphabet was adopted must be somewhere in the first half of the seventh century BCE. If they are rejected, the date of borrowing could be as low as *c.* 650–625 BCE.

The paucity of Latin inscriptions that can be assigned to the seventh century BCE and our inability to date them very accurately make it impossible to say much that is substantive about the point of origin and the diffusion of the alphabet in Latium. But we might speculate that the Etruscan alphabet was passed on by an inhabitant of Caere or Veii, given the proximity of these Etruscan towns to the Latin-speaking communities just south of the Tiber River, and given the material evidence for contact between them. Regardless of the point of origin, however, it is notable that inscriptions appear in many parts of Latium by the end of the sixth century BCE.

The reasons for the acquisition of the alphabet by Latin speakers also escape us. It is plausible to think that writing was borrowed to keep accounts of small-scale trade and

Table 2.3 Very Old Latin inscriptions of the seventh to sixth centuries BCE*

	Findspot	Date	Inscription	Citation
1	Praeneste	*c.* 700–600	*Vetusia* inscription	*ET* La 2.1
2	Praeneste	*c.* 700–600	*Fibula Praenestina*	*CIL* I².3
3	Gabii	*c.* 620–610	*Tita* inscription	Colonna (1980)
4	Caere [Rome]	*c.* 625–600	*Vendia* inscription	Peruzzi (1963)
5	Roma	*c.* 700–500	Forum inscription	*CIL* I².1
6	Tibur	*c.* 700–400	Tibur inscription	*CIL* I².2658
7	Roma	*c.* 600–550	*Duenos* inscription	*CIL* I².4
8	Satricum	*c.* 600–480	*Lapis Satricanus*	*CIL* I².2832a
9	Ardea	*c.* 560–480	*Kavidios* inscription	*CIL* I².474
10	Corcolle	*c.* 550–400	Corcolle inscription	*CIL* I².2833a
11	Lavinium	*c.* 550–400	Madonetta inscription	*CIL* I².2833
12	Garigliano	*c.* 500–480	Garigliano inscription	Vine (1998)
13	Roma	*c.* 560–450	*Pulpios* inscription	*CIL* I².479
14	Roma	*c.* 550–300	*Rex* inscription	*CIL* I².2830
15	Ficana	*c.* 600–500	Monte Cugno inscription	*CIL* I².2917c
16	Aqua Acetosa	*c.* 500–450	*Manias* inscription	*CIL* I².2917b
17	Aqua Acetosa	*c.* 500–400	*Karkavaios* inscription	*CIL* I².2917a

*For the dates assigned to these inscriptions see Hartmann (2005).

Figure 2.2 The *Fibula Praenestina* (*CIL* I².3). Reproduced by permission of The Center for Epigraphical and Palaeographical Studies, The Ohio State University.

exchange, and to serve other modest and mundane economic functions, but we have no evidence to support this idea. If the oldest documents in Latin were of such a nature, they were written on perishable material and have not survived. Two of the oldest Latin inscriptions were incised on luxury items, a silver bowl and a gold fibula, that accompanied

Figure 2.3 The Forum inscription (*CIL* I².1). Reproduced by permission of The Center for Epigraphical and Palaeographical Studies, The Ohio State University.

their owners to the grave. The other two seventh-century pieces were incised on ceramic and were also part of the burial cache of their owners. The custom of writing on *instrumenta domestica* was commonplace among elite Etruscans of the seventh and sixth centuries BCE.[24] Incised objects were often exchanged as gifts for the purpose of cementing social ties, military pacts, and trade alliances. It is conceivable that interpersonal relationships of this sort could have facilitated the acquisition and diffusion of writing. But even if the transmission of writing had its origin in contacts between elite Etruscan and Latin speakers, it was soon used in the public arena. The Forum inscription, although difficult to interpret, may have served a juridical function.[25] The *cippus* on which it was inscribed was set up at the boundary between the Forum and the *Comitium* in the center of Rome (Figure 2.3).

Innovations and Changes

It is almost never the case that the alphabet of one language is entirely suited to represent the sounds of another. As a result, during the initial stages of adaptation, adjustments may be made. For example, the Etruscan letters that represented sounds Latin speakers did not have in their inventory, e.g. *theta*, *sade*, *phi*, and *khi*, were not incorporated into the Latin writing system and at some point – we are not sure when – were eliminated from the alphabetic series. Sounds that occurred in Latin but not in Etruscan were accommodated by reviving letters Etruscans did not use, e.g., B and D in the case of /b/ and /d/, and O in the case of /ɔ/ and /oː/. Latin scribes expanded the scope of coverage of the vowel letters I, E, A, O, V to include both short and long vowels. (Etruscan vowels were not distinguished by length at the phonemic level.) The letters I and V covered even more phonological territory; they were used to spell /j/ and /w/, the non-syllabic counterparts of the high vowels. This convention, whereby the letters for high vowels also represented the corresponding semivowels, must have had its roots in Etruscan spelling where the letter I stood for both the vowel /i/ and the palatal semivowel /j/. The convention was adopted in Latin for the letter I and was then extended to the letter V. In the *Vetusia* inscription the letter F represents the semivowel /w/. It may well be that the analogical spread of this spelling convention is to be dated to before the last quarter of the seventh century BCE. The earliest example of V with non-syllabic value (/w/) is the verb SALVETOD /salweːtoːd/ "be well" on the *Tita* inscription.[26]

Other changes in orthography took place soon after the writing system was in place. The rule whereby the letters C, K and Q were written based on the following vowel letter caused problems for writers/scribes early on. The requirements of this convention, if followed strictly, would have led to "allo-graphemic" spellings in the paradigms of words whose stems ended in velars. Consider the following paradigms in which the letters C, K and Q alternate depending on the form of the following vowel letter: FHEFHAKAI "made," FHEFHACISTAI, FHEFHACED, FHEFHAQOMOS, etc.; DEIQO "say," DEICES, DEICET, DEIQOMOS, etc. Toward the end of the Very Old Latin period – and perhaps earlier for some writers/scribes – C was selected to stand for /k/ and /g/.[27] The letter K was gradually phased out of use; it survived in the spelling of a few names and a few common lexical items, e.g., *Kaeso* (*praenomen*) and *Kalendae* "Kalends."[28] Q, primarily in combination with V, was assigned the values /kʷ/ and /gʷ/, e.g. QVOI "who."[29] Once the letter G was added to the inventory (see below), it was used also as the first part of a digraph to spell the voiced labialized velar /gʷ/.

Another example of an early change in orthography involved the simplification FH, the digraph that spelled the /f/ phoneme (FHE:FHAKED "made"). No later than the first half of the sixth century BCE H was dropped from this combination, e.g. FECED "made" (Figure 2.4). As a result, the phonological value that F had in Etruscan, namely /w/ (**venel** "Venel" /wenel/), was transformed completely in Latin.[30]

A glaring gap in the spelling of Latin stop consonants was the lack of a letter for the voiced velar /g/. In the third century BCE the letter C was modified by adding a vertical bar to the bottom of its curved stroke thus creating a new letter G (see Figure 2.5).[31] It may have been the invention of the Greek freedman of Spurius Carvilius Ruga.[32] His school would have provided an ideal channel for the dissemination of the letter. But regardless of who was responsible for the letter's invention, it must have been introduced soon after the middle of the third century BCE because it had gained widespread currency by the beginning of the second century BCE.[33]

The letter Z remained part of the alphabetic series until the third century BCE even though it seems to have been used sparingly – if at all – in Very Old Latin and Old Latin inscriptions.[34] In the earliest Latin *abecedarium* (Figure 2.6), which can be dated to the beginning of the third century BCE, Z appears in its proper position following F.[35] The inventor of the letter G was probably also responsible for the elimination of Z from the

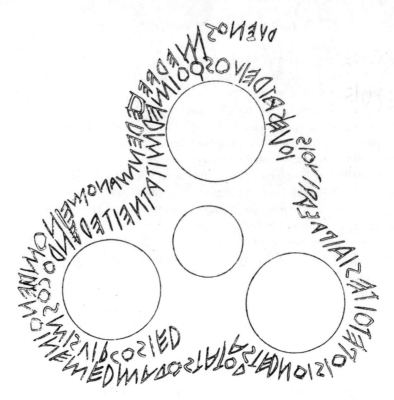

Figure 2.4 Sketch of the *Duenos* inscription showing the letter F in FECED (top left) (*CIL* I².4). Reproduced by permission of The Center for Epigraphical and Palaeographical Studies, The Ohio State University.

Figure 2.5 Inscription showing the letter G (first word, line 2). Sarcophagus of Scipio Barbatus (*CIL* I².7). Reproduced by permission of The Center for Epigraphical and Palaeographical Studies, The Ohio State University.

Figure 2.6 Latin *abecedarium* incised on ceramic plate, Monteroni di Palo. Drawing by Brigette McKenna. Reproduced by permission of Rex E. Wallace, University of Massachusetts Amherst.

abecedarium. He placed G in the position held earlier by Z presumably because it (Z) was a "dead" letter.

During the first century BCE the Greek letters Y and Z were borrowed (re-borrowed!) in order to represent the sounds /y, ȳ/ and /z/ in ancient Greek loanwords, e.g., (EVRYSACVS *CIL* I².1203).[36] When these letters were incorporated into the alphabetic series, they were placed at the end following the letter X.

The last alphabetic reform – though ultimately unsuccessful – was made by the Emperor Claudius (41–54 CE). He introduced three new letters. We know the form of two because they appeared in inscriptions published during his reign as emperor.[37] Ⅎ (reversed, upside-down *digamma*) stood for the semivowel /w/; Ⱶ was used in place of the letter *ypsilon* in Greek names. Its phonological value is unclear.[38] A third letter, which is reported to have stood for the cluster /ps/, has not yet been found in an inscription. Its precise form is uncertain; the Latin grammarians cite several possibilities.[39]

Old Latin Orthography

The rules for spelling during the Old Latin period (fourth to second centuries BCE) were different in some respects from the rules of the Classical period. Some differences reflect aspects of Old Latin phonology. For example, in the third century BCE the diphthong /oj/, which was on the way to becoming a simple long vowel /i:/ in word-final position, had reached the stage /e:/ (a bit higher in vowel space than /e:/) and this new sound was variously spelled as EI or E (QUEI, *CIL* I².7; PLOIRVME *CIL* I².9; FALERIES, Zimmermann (1986)). Some differences in spelling may be attributed to the fact that there was no written norm or standard to which writers, particularly those outside of Rome, might appeal. Other differences arose as writers responded to infelicities that remained in the writing system, most notably the lack of letters distinguishing long and short vowels. Important features of Old Latin orthography are described below.

1 Word-final S and word-final M were not consistently spelled in Old Latin inscriptions, e.g. CORNELIO (*CIL* I².8), cf. Classical Latin *Cornelius*; OINO "one," DVONORO "good," OPTVMO "best," VIRO "men," SCIPIONE (*CIL* I².9), cf. Classical Latin *unum, bonorum, optimum, uirorum*, and *Scipionem*. This spelling reflects the phonological developments of these consonants in word-final environments.

2 N was often omitted before S, e.g., COSOL "consul," CESOR "censor" (*CIL* I².8), cf. Classical Latin *consul, censor*. Once again this reflects a phonological development.

Nasals were lost before fricatives and the preceding vowel nasalized and lengthened. Even so, the spelling of the nasal consonant was retained in Classical Latin.

3 Latin had phonologically long consonants. They were not spelled as such until the end of the third century BCE.[40] One of the earliest examples, HINNAD, which is found in an inscription that dates to 211 BCE (*CIL* I².608), is a transcription of the Greek toponym Ἔννα. The oldest datable examples of native Latin words with long consonants indicated by double spelling of the consonant letter belong to the early part of the second century BCE, e.g. CAVSSA "for the sake of" (*CIL* I².612, 193 BCE), ESSENT "should be" (*CIL* I².614, 189 BCE). For the next hundred years long consonants were sometimes spelled as such and sometimes not. Occasionally, double writing and single writing of long consonants are found within the same inscription.[41] After 100 BCE double writing became the norm.

4 From the mid-second century BCE the digraphs EI and OV, which earlier spelled inherited diphthongs, spelled the long vowels /iː/ and /uː/ respectively, regardless of their etymological source, e.g. [V]EIVAM /wiːwam/ "living" (*CIL* I².1837), COVRAVERVNT /kuːraːweːrʊnt/ "oversaw" (*CIL* I².1806).

5 After *c.* 150 BCE the long vowels /iː, eː, aː, oː, uː/ were sometimes spelled by double writing of the vowel sign, so-called *geminatio vocalium*.[42] The earliest example is found on an inscription from the island of Delos, AARAM "altar" (*CIL* I².2238); it is dated to 135/4 BCE. The double writing of long vowels in most instances is limited to the initial syllable of a word, e.g., PAASTORES (*CIL* I².638), though there are exceptions, e.g., ARBITRATVV (*CIL* I².584). The convention is also restricted in large part to the vowel A, though a fair number of examples of E and V are attested. Only one or two cases of double writing of I and O have thus far come to light, e.g., VIITAM (*CIL* I².364), VOOTVM (*CIL* I².365). A large number of words with *geminatio vocalium* are found on inscriptions from areas that were originally Oscan-speaking and it is generally assumed that the Latin convention was inspired by the one used by Oscans.[43]

6 At the close of the Old Latin period the long vowel /iː/ was occasionally spelled by a tall I, the so-called *i longa*, e.g., FELICI *cognomen*, VICVS "village" (*CIL* I².721). The origin of this sign is uncertain.[44]

7 Another strategy for indicating vowel length, the apex, appeared at the end of the Old Latin period. The apex was a diacritic mark of varying shapes – sometimes an acute bar, sometimes a hook – placed over the vowel sign. It is first attested in an inscription dated to 104 BCE (MV́RVM, *CIL* I².679).[45]

8 /h/ was lost between vowels in Latin, but educated speakers continued to write it in intervocalic position, e.g. *veho* /weoː/ "transport." On occasion the letter was employed to mark vocalic hiatus. Consider AHENVM /aeːnʊm/ "of bronze" (*CIL* I².581) and AHENA (*CIL* I².2093).

Some Old Latin orthographic practices continued to be used sporadically during the Classical period and beyond. The apex was written in dipinti and graffiti at Pompeii (NERÓNIS, *CIL* IV.3884). The double spelling of vowels may be found as late as 300 CE.[46] Even in the most illustrious of imperial inscriptions, the *Res Gestae* of the Emperor Augustus, one finds examples of the apex, *i longa*, H marking hiatus, and the digraph EI spelling long /iː/, e.g., GESTÁRVVM, (*Res Gestae*, preamble), AHENEIS (*Res Gestae*, preamble), EXPVLI (*Res Gestae* 2), EMERITEIS (*Res Gestae* 16). Other Old Latin spelling practices

Table 2.4 Comparison of archaic Etruscan and Latin letterforms

Archaic Etruscan letterforms		Archaic Latin letterforms
A	alpha	A A
—	beta	not attested
Ɔ ٦	gamma	C
—	delta	D
Ⴙ	epsilon	Ɛ
٦	wau	F
I	zeta	not attested
ᗐ	heta	ᗐ ᗐ
⊗	theta	—
I	iota	I
Ж	kappa	K
Ⅎ	lambda	L
ᛘ ₩	mu	₩ M
ᛘ ᛘ	nu	ℕ Ν
—	omicron	O
٦٦	pi	Ր Ր
M	san	—
Ọ	qoppa	Ọ
ᗡ٦	rho	P
⟨ ⟩ ⟨	sigma	⟨ ⟨
Τ	tau	Τ
Υ V	upsilon	Υ Υ V
Χ +	xi	+
Φ	phi	—
Ψ	khi	—

became moribund. In public inscriptions issued during the Classical period it was the norm to spell word-final /s/ and /m/. In the case of /s/, the spelling reflected the fact that this sound was analogically restored in most educated varieties of Latin. In the case of /m/, the spelling served as an orthographic feature by which morphological distinctions might be made even though phonologically, word-final vowel + M represented a long, possibly nasalized, vowel.

Letterforms

The style of writing and the shapes of the letters in Latin documents depended on various factors: the medium used to carry the message, the implement used to write it, the occasion for writing, and the skill of the writer/scribe or stonemason. Letters changed their form over time, reflecting the differences between more formal and less formal styles of writing, outside influences, and the personal preferences on the part of writers/scribes and stonemasons.

The shapes of the letters on seventh- and sixth-century Latin inscriptions are in many respects similar to those on Etruscan inscriptions of the same time period (Table 2.4).[47]

Table 2.5 Variation in Very Old Latin letterforms

inscription	M	S	V	direction
Fibula	Ⱳ	⟩	V	←
Vetusia	—	⟩	V	←
Tita	—	⟨	Y	→
Vendia	Ⱳ	⟨	Y	→
Forum	Ⱳ Ⱳ	⟨	Y V	⇄
Duenos	Ⱳ	⟩	V	←
Lapis Satricanus	Ⱳ	⟨	V	→
Tibur	Ⱳ Ⱳ	⟨ ⟨	Λ	↻
Corcolle	Ⱳ	⟨	V	→

Figure 2.7   The Tibur inscription (*CIL* I².2658). Reproduced by permission of The Center for Epigraphical and Palaeographical Studies, The Ohio State University.

They show much the same variation in form as Etruscan letters on inscriptions from Caere and Veii, a fact that may point to continued Etruscan–Latin contact and cross-fertilization.

Table 2.5 is a synopsis of letterforms extracted from Very Old Latin inscriptions. The letters in the table illustrate some of the diversity of form at this early period.

The Tibur inscription stands apart from other Very Old Latin inscriptions in terms of paleography (Figure 2.7). The letters v and l were written upside down. The letter o has the form of a smallish dot. The letter p is like no other in the corpus. It has a snail-like appearance; the vertical bar is missing entirely. The orientation of the letters v and l could be due to the difficulties encountered by the stonemason as he cut the

Figure 2.8   Dipinto with cursive E and F on fragment of krater (*CIL* I².358). Reproduced from *La Collezione epigrafica del Museo Nazionale Romano alle Terme di Diocleziano* (Milan, 2001) by permission of the publishers, Mondadori Electa.

inscription in a circle around the side of the pedestal, but o in the form of a dot is unique in Latin. Interestingly, it resembles the form of the o on South Picene inscriptions. Inverted v and l are also found in South Picene. These similarities make it tempting to think that the person who composed the text or the stonemason who incised it was familiar with features of the South Picene orthographic tradition (see also the section on letterforms below).[48]

By the beginning of the fifth century BCE some of the variation in Very Old Latin letterforms was eliminated, perhaps signaling a growing independence from Etruscan writing practices. The letterform Y lost ground to V. ⸁ with three bars became the norm; it ceased to be written in retrograde direction. Substantive changes in the forms of some letters also appeared. Five-stroke Ｍ was in competition with a "new" four-stroke version Ｍ, e.g., *Lapis Satricanus*, Tibur inscription, Corcolle inscription. Ultimately, five-stroke M was ousted by the four-stroke version, but the five-stroke form survived as an abbreviation for the name *Manius* (Ｍ', *CIL* I².647).

Changes to the letters P (Ρ Ρ Γ) and R (Ρ) appear to have developed in synch. As the length of the hook of the letter P increased and approached the vertical bar, similarities with the letter R increased. R may have been written with an oblique tail, at first perhaps a very short one (Ρ → Ρ → R), in order to increase its formal distance from P. Fully closed P, which then assumed the form of Very Old Latin R, did not appear in inscriptions until the middle of the second century BCE and is not very common until the imperial period.[49]

Distinctive variants of letterforms developed during the Old Latin period. The most recognizable are the so-called cursive forms of E and F (Figure 2.8).[50] The letter A also developed some striking forms. One such form was written with its medial bar detached from its oblique bars and standing vertical, e.g., Λ. The letters O and Q had variants in which the very bottom of the letter remained open, e.g. ᴼ. The tail of Q was no longer vertical; it was an oblique bar that shot out from the bottom of the letter in the direction of writing, e.g. ᵠ. In the hands of some stonemasons it is nearly horizontal.

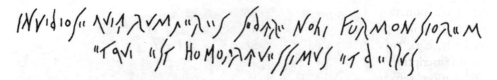

Figure 2.9 Graffito from Pompeii. Drawing by Brigette McKenna. Reproduced by permission of Rex E. Wallace, University of Massachusetts Amherst.

Styles of handwriting developed alongside epigraphic styles and there was some interplay between the two, particularly as regards cursive letterforms.[51] Unfortunately, most handwritten texts were on perishable materials and very little from the republican period has survived.[52] More substantial evidence for the range of styles of handwriting is available from the first three centuries of the imperial period.[53] Several Latin papyri from Herculaneum were written in a style known as the capital; the letters are similar to epigraphic capitals.[54] This script was most suitable for literary papyri. The writing on wax tablets, on the ink tablets from Vindolanda, and on the ostraca from Bu Njem in Libya was less formal.[55] These styles, whether written in ink or incised with a stylus, are usually grouped together under the rubric of Old Roman cursive. The writing of the graffiti from Pompeii and the writing on curse tablets from Rome and elsewhere also belong here (Figure 2.9).[56] The evolution of the letterforms in handwritten styles, particularly the cursive, is more difficult to discern,[57] but the shapes of the minuscule letters that appear in the documents of the early fourth and fifth centuries CE can be traced back to the earliest inscriptions.

Direction of Writing and Punctuation

The earliest Latin inscriptions were written from right to left (*Vetusia* inscription, *Fibula Praenestina* (Figure 2.2)) and from left to right (*Tita* inscription, *Vendia* inscription). Right to left was the standard direction of writing in Etruscan, but left-to-right direction was in vogue for a short period of time at the Etruscan towns of Veii and Caere at the end of the seventh century BCE and this style may have influenced the direction of writing for the Latin inscriptions mentioned above. Two Very Old Latin inscriptions reflect writing practices that may be due to contact with non-Latin writing systems. The Forum inscription was written in a boustrophedon style in which the direction of writing ran alternately from the right and then the left, perhaps in imitation of an Etruscan or Greek model (Figure 2.3).[58] The Tibur inscription was written in a spiral (Figure 2.7). The layout resembles that found on several funerary stelae erected by South Picenes.[59] By the middle of the republican period, however, writers had settled on left-to-right direction as the norm, and almost all Latin inscriptions after this date are written in this manner. Inscriptions in other formats, such as boustrophedon, appear rather infrequently.[60]

Most Latin documents, regardless of type, had very little in the way of punctuation. Very Old Latin inscriptions were often written *scriptio continua*, that is to say, without any word breaks or any punctuation between words, e.g., *Duenos* inscription (Figure 2.4), Tibur inscription (Figure 2.7), *Lapis Satricanus*, Garigliano inscription. In inscriptions that were punctuated, interpuncts separated words. The most common forms of punctuation in Very Old Latin documents were two or three interpuncts arranged vertically, e.g., two interpuncts: *Fibula Praenestina* (Figure 2.2); three interpuncts: Forum inscription (Figure 2.3), Corcolle inscription, Madonetta inscription. Although punctuation separating words becomes a common feature in Republican Latin inscriptions, it is unusual to find it separating sentences or metrical lines. The dashes that divide the Saturnian lines of the epitaph of Scipio Barbatus (*CIL* I².7) are an exception (Figure 2.5). Even more rare is punctuation that separates a document into sections or chapters. The Forum inscription may be unique in this regard, particularly for a Very Old Latin inscription; it appears to have been divided into three units by means of punctuation in the form of circular incisions (Figure 2.3).[61]

In Latin of the imperial period interpuncts were used less regularly to mark the boundaries between words and so writers developed other functions for punctuation. Several notable uses may be illustrated from the Vindolanda writing tablets.[62] For example, interpuncts are occasionally used to group together preposition and dependent adjectives and nouns, e.g. · AD VOCASIVM · (*T.Vindol.* II.315), and to group together verb and following indirect pronoun, e.g. · MISI TIBI · (*T.Vindol.* II.345). The phrases reflect the enclitic character of prepositions and pronominal indirect objects. Of some interest also is the use of interpuncts as clausal dividers. The following are examples of two co-ordinate clauses set off by interpuncts: · NON ẙTẙṆTVR EQVITES · NEC RESIDVNT BRITTVNCVLI (*T.Vindol.* II.164). The features of punctuation described above are found also in ostraca from Wâdi Fawâkir, a Roman military outpost in the eastern Egyptian desert. It appears that soldiers who were trained to write by the Roman military may have been taught similar methods for punctuating texts regardless of where they were stationed.[63]

Abbreviations

One of the most notable features of Latin writing from the third century BCE on is the frequency of the abbreviations. For the most part, abbreviations are restricted to aspects of personal nomenclature, especially the personal or individual name (*praenomen*), e.g., M = *Marcus*, names for familial relationships, e.g., F = *filius*, N = *nepos*, names of months and parts of months, e.g., K = *Kalendae*, SEPT = *Septembris*, and names for political and military offices and titles, e.g. COS = *consul*, IIVIR = *duumuir*, IMP = *imperator*. In some cases, most commonly in lists of consular and triumphal *fasti*, names were abbreviated by omitting the inflectional endings, e.g., Q PETRONI = *Q(uintus) Petroni(us)*. These abbreviations were devised in order to save space and labor, and therefore expense.

Letter Names

The origin of the letter names used by the Romans is a mystery. The evidence is late and not entirely reliable.[64] It is certain, however, that the Etruscans or the Romans (Latins), or perhaps both, made changes to the names for the letters because they no longer resembled their Greek and Phoenician antecedents.

The names for all Latin letters consisted of a heavy syllable, either a long vowel or a syllable closed by a consonant (see Table 2.1). The names for vowels were, as might be expected, the letter itself, e.g. A /aː/. The letter names for stop consonants had CV structure; the default vowel was /eː/, except for the letters K and Q, which were pronounced with the vowels with which they were most often written, namely A and V. The fricatives – with the exception of H – the nasals, the liquid, and the rhotic had VC structure. The name of the letter X /ɛks/ ends in a cluster because Latin phonotactic rules did not permit *ks*– to stand at the beginning of a syllable (word).

The pronunciation of the letter names lies at the heart of an Old Latin spelling convention that is first attested in inscriptions of the third century BCE. This convention, which is known as "syllabic notation" or "abbreviated writing," permits the spelling of a syllable by means of a consonant.[65] For example, the name *Petronius* is sometimes spelled PTRONIO (*CIL* I².239), the pronunciation of the initial syllable being determined by the letter name *pe*. Although there are questions as to the syllables in which this convention may be found as well as to its geographic distribution, it provides some support for the idea that the names of the letters had been reformed by the third century BCE.

Diffusion of the Latin Alphabet

Roman expansion was accompanied by the spread of Latin and the Latin alphabet. The Roman policy of colonization, by which military strongholds and citizen foundations were established in conquered territory, successfully introduced islands of Latin-speaking inhabitants amongst non-Latin-speaking natives. The Latin and Roman *coloni* shared the same political, religious, and legal order; they operated under the same administrative framework. Non-Latin speakers who were admitted into colonial settlements found it advantageous to speak Latin: traders and craftsmen for economic reasons; members of the elite classes for this reason too and for the social advantages that speaking and writing Latin afforded.

The evidence for bilingualism and language shift amongst diverse populations is not sufficient to give us a clear picture of the means by which the Latin language and its alphabet replaced native ones.[66] However, tantalizing pieces of evidence, in the form of bilingual inscriptions and of native Italic inscriptions written in the Latin alphabet, permit us to say that the prestige of Latin must have been such that its alphabet became the alphabet of choice. Oscans in the city of Bantia in the first century BCE incised their civic regulations using a Latin alphabet (*ST* Lu 1 = TB). At roughly the same time Umbrians, who had a century earlier copied the rituals of the Atiedian brotherhood of Iguvium using their native alphabet, now issued a version written in the Latin script (*ST* Um 1 Vb–VII). In Etruria, members of the same family sometimes had their epitaphs incised in Latin, sometimes in Etruscan, depending on whether they wished to highlight their Roman or Etruscan identity. The Latin–Etruscan bilingual epitaph from Pisaurum, which is dated to the beginning of the first century BCE, expresses the subordination of Etruscan visually and linguistically.[67] The Latin inscription was incised in large capital letters across the top of the stone. The Etruscan version was incised in smaller letters beneath the Latin.

In some cases the Latin alphabet was modified in order to bring it into line with other languages' phonological systems. For example, Umbrian scribes who recorded the Iguvine rituals using the Latin script spelled the palatal fricative /ʃ/ by placing a diacritic in the form an acute bar over the letter s, thus ś. Oscans who wrote the *Tabula Bantina* incorporated a z into the script, perhaps under Greek influence, in order to spell the medial fricative /z/, e.g. EGMAZUM "affairs." The Roman alphabet, carried by military personnel, traders, and adventurers, penetrated into the alpine regions of northern Italy in the second and first centuries BCE. A bilingual funerary inscription from Voltino (*CIL* V.4883), which was written in Latin and Celtic, illustrates the fascinating phenomenon of mixed alphabets.[68] The Latin text was written with the letter *san* (transcribed as ś) appropriated from the Lugano alphabet. The Celtic text was written in a native alphabet – almost certainly a Celtic one – but several Latin letters are part of the inventory of signs.[69]

During the height of Roman *imperium* Latin was spoken and – more importantly for our purposes – written in Europe, southern Britain, Northern Africa, the Balkan region as far south as Greece, and portions of the Middle East. The results of the spread of the Latin alphabet are with us today in the form of the script used to compose the chapters that make up this volume.

FURTHER READING

The transmission of the Euboean Greek alphabet to Etruscans in Italy is discussed in Cristofani (1972) and (1978b). Wachter (1987) chapter 2 is an in depth discussion of the origin and development of the Latin alphabet. Wachter (1987) chapter 2 also tackles the thorny issue of the relationship between the Latin and Faliscan alphabets. Lejeune (1957) remains a good introduction to the orthographic adaptations and alphabetic reforms made by native peoples of Italy who borrowed the Etruscan alphabet. For the paleography of Very Old Latin inscriptions see Hartmann (2005); for Old Latin see Cencetti (1956–1957). Vine (1993) discusses an array of problems in Very Old and Old Latin paleography and orthography. For an overview of issues and problems with Latin letter names see Gordon (1971).

NOTES

1 I use small capitals to transcribe Latin words cited from the *Corpus Inscriptionum Latinarum* (= *CIL*) and *Inscriptiones Latinae Liberae Rei Publicae* (= *ILLRP*). Latin words from other sources are in italics. I also use small caps when I refer to letters of the Latin alphabet. For the forms of letters, I use an archaic Latin font. Words in native Italic alphabets are printed in bold. Faliscan words are cited from Giacomelli (1963); Sabellic words are cited from *ST*; and Etruscan words are cited from *ET*.

2 For a short but informative survey of fate of the Latin alphabet after the collapse of Roman *imperium* see Sampson (1985) 110–119.

3 See Weiss (2009) 30 and nn. 36 and 37.

4 Ridgway (1992).

5 Bartoněk and Buchner (1995) 204–205 and Watkins (1995a) 38–42.

6 Bietti Sestieri and De Santis ((2000) 53) describe the burial in detail. Compare the discussion in Holloway (1994) 112.

7 See Watkins (1995a) 38–39 for the reading *euḷin* and for the interpretation of the word as an adjective form.

8   The Euboean Greek epigraphic evidence is published in Bartoněk and Buchner (1995).

9   Watkins (1995a) 41–42. Watkins (1976) is a more detailed exposition of the inscription's metrical structure.

10 Cassio (1991–1993) interprets the inscription as Greek, but does not think it is a metrical text. See Watkins (1995a) 44–45 for an analysis of the metrical structure.

11 The transmission of the Euboean alphabet to Etruscans is discussed at length in Cristofani (1972) and (1978a).

12 For the diffusion of the Etruscan alphabet to other peoples of ancient Italy see Cristofani (1972) and (1978b), and Lejeune (1957).

13 See Wachter (1987) 14. Wachter (1989) 29–34 is a discussion of the difficulties involved in determining alphabetic patrimony.

14 There is no evidence for the spelling of the voiced labialized velar /gʷ/.

15 For a comprehensive treatment of this topic see Wachter (1987) 14–24.

16 See Gordon (1983) 78.

17 The spelling of velars in the *Duenos* inscription appears to be a development of an earlier spelling system similar to that found on the Forum inscription. The spelling of /kʷ/ by means of Q is probably to be seen as a simplification of QV.

18 We might then recognize several sub-systems for the spelling for the velars: (1a): CI, CE, KA, KO, QV (Forum inscription); (1b) CI, CE, KA, QO, QV (*Kavidios* inscription); (2a) CI, CE, CA, CO, Q (*Duenos* inscription); etc. A similar set of sub-systems may be found in Very Old Faliscan inscriptions, e.g., Giacomelli (1963) text 1: **soc[iai]** "friend," **ceres** "Ceres," **arcentelom** "of silver," **porded** "offered," **karai** "dear," **f[if]iqod** "made," **eqo** "I" = CI, CE, KA, QO, (QV); Giacomelli (1963) text 2: **eco** "I," **quton** "drinking cup" = CO, QV; Giacomelli (1963) text 3: **sociai** "friend," **kaios** "Gaius," **kapena** "Capena," **kalketia** "Calcetia" = CI, KA, KE; Giacomelli (1963) text 4: **eko** "I," **kaisiosio** "Caesius" = KA, KO.

19 In south Etruscan inscriptions, primarily those recovered from Caere and environs, the signs spelling the fricative /f/ were frequently written in the order HF, e.g., **θihvaries** "Thifaries" (*ET* Cr 2.7).

20 The spelling FH is found in words incised on two Corinthian vases dated to the first quarter of the sixth c. BCE, one found in south Etruria (!), the other in Attica. Given that the earliest Etruscan examples date to the first quarter of the seventh century BCE (**θavhna** "cup," *ET* Cr 2.5) and the earliest Latin example (FHE:FHAKED "made") to the seventh century I am not inclined to see the Corinthian examples as evidence for the Greek origins of this convention.

21 The language of inscription *REI* 58 from Satricum (La Ferriere) cannot be determined. The text is too fragmentary. But see the short article by Colonna and Beijer (1993) 316–320 who consider the inscription to be Latin.

22 Table 2.3 does not include fragments of inscriptions or *sigla*. See Colonna (1980) 53–69. For the inscriptions in the table see Hartmann (2005).

23 Hartmann (2005) 37–106 provides an extensive discussion of the difficulties presented by these inscriptions. He argues that the *Fibula Praenestina* is authentic and that the *Vetusia* inscription is Latin.

24 For discussion of Etruscan, Latin, Sabellic and Venetic inscriptions incised on *instrumenta domestica* see Agostiniani (1982). Cristofani (1984) examines Etruscan inscriptions on sumptuary objects.

25 See Eichner (1995) for an overview of the linguistic difficulties involved in interpreting this inscription.

26 Earlier examples of the letter V spelling /w/ may be attested in Faliscan (**ui[no]m** "wine," **prauios** "Prauios," **douiad** "give") if Giacomelli (1963) text 1 is to be dated to the middle of the seventh century BCE.

27 In southern Etruria in the second half of the sixth century BCE Etruscan writers/scribes selected *gamma* to spell /k/ and eliminated *kappa* and *qoppa* from the spelling system. It may

be possible to see the selection of C as an areal development encompassing southern Etruria and Latium.

28 The spelling KA is found in Imperial Latin, e.g., KARISSIMO "dearest" *CIL* IX.552 [Aeclanum]; KAPUT "head," *CIL* IX.1175 [Venusia].

29 The spelling QV for /ku/ is found with some frequency in late Republican Latin, particularly in the word for "money," e.g., PEQUNIAM "money," *CIL* I².587; QURA "care," *CIL* I².1202. It is also found sporadically in Imperial Latin texts, e.g., SEQURUM "free from care," Pighi (1964) 42 (*P.Mich.* VIII 468.8).

30 For the simplification of FH to H in Venetic, see Lejeune (1966) 156–163.

31 It is not clear to me that the letter ɔ (reversed C) found in *CIL* I².60 (PRIMO.ɔENIA "Primogenia") is to be seen as an early, but ultimately failed, attempt to spell /g/. Other words in this inscription that have the voiced velar are spelled by means of C (CRATIA /graːtia:/ "for the sake of"). On the other hand, I find the idea in Giacomelli (1973), that ɔ represented a palatalized /g/, even more problematic, particularly since the phonological distinction, /k/ vs. /g/, was under-represented.

32 See the discussion in Wachter (1987) 324–333.

33 *CIL* I².614 is the oldest securely datable Latin inscription in which G appears (189 BCE). Several words in a Marrucinian inscription (*ST* MV 1) dated to the second half of the third century BCE and written in a Republican Latin alphabet have the letter G (ASIGNAS "uncut portions"?; AGINE "in honor of"?). However, the date of the inscription is based on the shapes of the letters and so must be regarded with some suspicion. In this inscription the letter G has the form of an angled C tilted upward in the direction of writing (ᐸ).

34 The letter Z appears in a late seventh-century BCE graffito (ZKA̠) incised on a fragment of ceramic (Colonna (1980) 63, no. 29). It is possible, as Colonna suggests, that Z was a substitute for S in this graffito. The statements of Varro and several late Roman grammarians do not shed any light on the status of the letter Z in Latin (see Weiss (2009) 28, n. 22). The appearance of the letter Z in ZENATUO (*CIL* I².365) is due to interference from Faliscan orthography.

35 The *abecedarium* was incised in dextroverse direction on a plate found at Monteroni di Palo near the Etruscan city of Caere. The alphabet is a "reformed" type. The "dead" letters for the aspirates (*theta*, *phi*, and *khi*), for *samek*, and for *san* have been eliminated from the script.

36 See Perl (1971).

37 See Gordon (1983) 116–17 (no. 41) and 118 (no. 43) for *digamma inuersum*. Photographs are published in Plate 27, nos. 41 and 43.

38 Oliver (1949) 249–253. Velius Longus (*GL* VII.75) says that the letter represented the so-called "intermediate" vowel, but there is no evidence to support this suggestion.

39 Oliver (1949) 253–254.

40 The name COTTAS (gen. sg.), with double spelling of T, is found on an inscription from Sicily (*ILLRP* 1277). The Cotta of this inscription is usually identified as Aurelius Cotta, consul in 252 and 248, but the inscription may not be as early as some have speculated. See Perini (1983) 148 for discussion.

41 Some examples of variation in double vs. single writing of long consonants may be due to issues of spacing and line placement. See, for example, *CIL* I².614, in which geminate consonants are consistently spelled, save for POSEDISENT, which is at a line end and may have single spelling because of lack of space.

42 The honor of introducing this convention into Latin is usually given to Accius (see Velius Longus, *GL* VII.55.25–6), but Quintilian (*Inst.* 1.7.14) indicates the usage is older.

43 For the latest treatment see Vine (1993) 267–286.

44 According to Oliver ((1966) 159) the earliest example is EIVS, which is found on *CIL* I².585, an inscription dating to 111 BCE. In this example, however, *i longa* stands for a long consonant /ejjʊs/. Oliver's hypothesis about the origin of the letter does not convince (see Oliver (1966) 162–163).

45 Oliver (1966).

46 Weiss (2009) 29 cites the word VII from *CIL* III.4121 [Pannonia] as a late Imperial Latin example, but I am not sure that this reading is correct.

47 See Urbanova (1999 for the paleography of the letters in the oldest inscriptions.

48 For the letterforms on South Picene inscriptions see Marinetti (1985) 47–54. For the form of the letter O, see p. 54.

49 An early example of a fully closed P is found in *CIL* I².626. The date is 144 BCE.

50 See Cencetti (1956–1957) 190–194.

51 See Cencetti (1956–1957) 190–194 and Bischoff (1990) 54 for the use of the cursive letters E and F in inscriptions. Sometimes, the forms of the letters found in advertisements and election-notices, such as those recovered from Pompeii, were imitated by engravers working in stone or metal (Bischoff (1990) 55). *CIL* X.797 [Pompeii] is a good example. The inscription dates to the Claudian period.

52 A few Pompeian graffiti, some curses on lead plaques, and some papyri from Herculaneum belong to the end of the republic. See Fox (1912) for late republican *tabellae defixionum* in the collection at Johns Hopkins University. Kleve (1994) 317 is a list of papyri from Herculaneum of republican date.

53 See the short discussion of handwriting on Latin papyri by Cavallo (2009).

54 See Bischoff (1990) 55–63 and Kleve (1994) 315, 317. Sample scripts are published in Bischoff (1990) 64 and Kleve (1994) 316.

55 For the wax tablets from Pompeii and Dacia see *CIL* IV and *CIL* X. For the tablets from Vindolanda see Bowman and Thomas (1983) 32–45.

56 The paleography of late republican *tabellae defixionum* in the collection at Johns Hopkins University is discussed in Fox (1912) 51–54. Plate VIII is a comparison of the cursive styles in Late republican and early imperial documents (graffiti, papyri, wax tablets, lead plaques).

57 It is interesting to note that even the Romans had difficulties reading the cursive style. The title character in Plautus' *Pseudolus* makes light of the handwriting in a letter by saying that it appears to have been written by a hen (*an, opsecro hercle, habeat quas gallinae manus? nam has quidem gallina scripsit* "Seriously, does a hen have hands? No doubt a hen wrote this (letter)." (Pl. *Ps.* 28–29)).

58 See Vine (1993) 41–50.

59 South Picene inscription *ST* TE 2 is probably the closest in terms of layout (Marinetti (1985) 203–208). For discussion of the layout of inscriptions see Marinetti (1985) 57–58.

60 See *CIL* I².5.

61 See Vine (1993) 41–50.

62 See Adams (1996).

63 Adams (1996) 210.

64 The evidence for the Latin letter names is discussed in Gordon (1971).

65 For syllabic punctuation in Old Latin see Vine (1993) 323–344.

66 Adams (2003a).

67 Lejeune (1962).

68 See Adams (2003a) 70–74 for inscriptions written with letters from two alphabets.

69 Since the letter *san* is found in a non-Latin name, it is possible that the letter was used in the Latin epitaph to spell a sound not found in Latin. For discussion of the Voltino bilingual see Eska and Wallace (forthcoming).

CHAPTER 3

Latin Inscriptions and Documents

James Clackson

Introduction

Our knowledge of the Latin language is based on texts written by those who used or spoke Latin as a native language, which either survive to the present day, or were copied before being lost or destroyed. This chapter covers all such material, except for literary and sub-literary works transmitted through the manuscript tradition, which are covered separately in the next chapter.

There is an astonishing wealth and variety of Latin inscriptions and documents surviving from the ancient world. In total around 220,000 such texts are known today and more are discovered or published each year. The archetypical image of a Latin inscription is a funerary monument carved on stone, such as the epitaph of Scipio Barbatus discussed in chapter 2 and pictured in Figure 2.5.[1] Stone is the medium for the majority of all surviving Latin epigraphy, and funerary epitaphs are the most common of all stone inscriptions. Stone was frequently used for inscriptions marking buildings or public works, for dedications to divinities and for monuments set up in honour of individuals. But Latin is also found written on a huge range of materials other than stone: on bronze, perhaps a table once publicly displayed in a city forum to record a law, or a diploma awarded to a military veteran; on lead, whether a folded strip on which curses were written before being dropped down a well or thrown into a graveyard, or a slingshot adorned with obscene invective, or a water-pipe bearing the date of its construction; on precious metals such as gold or silver; on bone and ivory; on ceramic and glass, used both for household utensils such as dishes, pots and lamps and for luxury goods including perfume jars and medicine bottles; on jewels and gem-stones; and on building materials, ranging from roof-tiles, wooden beams and fired bricks to messages painted on plaster walls or inlaid in mosaic floors or panels. For correspondence,

A Companion to the Latin Language, First Edition. Edited by James Clackson.
© 2011 Blackwell Publishing Ltd. Published 2011 by Blackwell Publishing Ltd.

accounts, contracts, records, lists, and school-exercises the Romans used tablets or documents made from a variety of materials: slate, pottery (called ostraca), wood, papyrus, leather, linen or wax. Usually writing was carved, painted or penned by a professional stonecutter, sign-writer or scribe; but occasionally texts were scratched or scrawled by an individual who had barely mastered the alphabet. Letters could be stamped on tiles or pottery, minted on coinage, moulded onto glass or lead, or formed by affixing cast metal letters to a panel, through piercing holes through wood or leather or by arranging tiny pieces of stone or tile into a mosaic. We know from ancient sources that Romans lovers, like modern ones, carved their names on trees, although no surviving example is known (Kruschwitz 2010b).

Such a vast range of epigraphic material presents the student of the Latin language with opportunities and problems. Inscriptions and other documents give first-hand access to users of Latin, and often the situation of a written text within a controlled archaeological context can provide precise co-ordinates for the time, place and even social milieu of its composition; for the early period they are the best source for our knowledge of the language (see p. 221). Epigraphy covers a geographical and social range which is unparalleled by surviving literary works. For example, there is no known literary composition written by anyone from Britain during the Roman period, but there are inscriptions on stone and other media throughout the time of the Roman occupation, and the recent discovery of large numbers of wooden writing tablets at Vindolanda, and curse tablets from Bath and elsewhere, enables us to construct a picture of the language of the province (see most recently Adams (2007)). On the other hand, epigraphical material is generally limited in subject matter and short in scope; shorter inscriptions may contain little more than personal names, and longer ones sometimes contain only a string of banal formulaic expressions. Only rarely is it possible to ascribe a corpus of ancient documents to a specific individual, and even then the employment of professionals to execute the writing may leave us uncertain whether to locate a linguistic peculiarity with a scribe or stonecutter or the identified author of a piece. In this chapter I shall aim to address briefly certain questions that arise when using epigraphic material to access the Latin language. I shall look at how the material is presented and catalogued and how it can be most easily searched, found, read and understood. Then I will consider what assumptions, if any, can be made about the "author" of an inscription or document. First of all, however, I shall discuss some of the potential pitfalls for linguists in the interpretation of documents and inscriptions.

The Pitfalls of Interpretation

Anyone who uses a published text of any Roman inscription or document is dependent upon the reading of the text's editor. If a good photograph is provided it is possible to check the editor's reading to some extent, although even this may be difficult if a text is written in one of the more challenging cursive scripts. As we shall see below, reliance on photographs may also lead to error or confusion. Some Roman documents present such a challenge to decipher that they have remained unread, or wrongly read, for decades. Two recent examples can illustrate the difficulties of reading ancient texts, as well as the persistence of mistaken interpretations. The first concerns a wooden tablet found outside the boundaries of the Roman Empire, in Frisia in the northern Netherlands. The text was first published in 1917 by Vollgraff, whose reading and interpretation suggested that the document was a contract for the sale of an ox, witnessed by four persons who signed their names on the back of the tablet. The tablet has now been re-edited (Bowman *et al.* 2009) with the benefit of computer image enhancement and a better understanding of the Roman cursive scripts. The new reading is very different from Vollgraff's. For example, the six letters originally read *LBOVEM* and interpreted as *l(icet) bouem* "it is allowed; an ox" are now read as *ad quem* "to whom". The earliest attested Frisian cow thus disappears from the historical record. The document, on the basis of the recent rereading, appears to be a loan agreement concerning a slave girl. Even more striking is the second example, concerning the rereading of a lead tablet found in the hot spring at Bath in England. The tablet was first read and published by Nicholson, after unsuccessful attempts by other scholars (Nicholson 1904). Nicholson interpreted the text as a letter from a man from Wroxeter (Viroconium) to a married woman called Nigra, and the first surviving written evidence for Christianity from Britain.[2] The discovery of more lead tablets from Bath, all of them curse tablets written in cursive scripts, enabled Tomlin to reread the tablet correctly and show that Nicholson's reading was entirely erroneous. Moreover, Nicholson had read the tablet upside down. Both of these examples reveal the importance of comparative material to make sense of ancient documents; familiarity with documents which employ a similar script, format, and vocabulary will enable better reading and interpretation of a new text.

Even a photograph of an inscription may give a misleading impression. The find of the so-called *Lapis Satricanus* (*CIL* I².2832a) in 1977 was one of the sensations of early republican epigraphy of the last century. The two-line text, uncovered in excavations of the temple of the Mater Matuta in Satricum, is of especial significance for the historian of the Latin language, since it shows a genitive ending *-osio*, otherwise unparalleled (see chapters 13 and 14, p. 208 and 227 for further discussion of this text). The beginning of the text is broken, and the stone as now preserved has only the bottom of an upright hasta after the break. However, over fifteen years after the initial edition of the text (Stibbe, Colonna *et al.* (1980)), publication of a photograph taken during the excavation, when the stone was still *in situ*, led Colonna to believe that he could see a further letter at the beginning, on a fragment later lost (Colonna 1996). Thus the opening of the inscription was read as]*VIEI* rather than]*IEI* as before. But can we trust the earlier photograph? The corner of the stone under discussion is covered in shadow, and has roots and plants around it. Microscopic examination of the photograph and, crucially, comparison with other pictures taken at the time of the excavation, reveal that the extra letter is a mirage: "it is not an inscribed character, but the root of a plant curling up from the surface of the stone towards the onlooker" (Waarsenburg 1997).[3]

These examples of misinterpretation of ancient inscriptions are, unfortunately, not isolated. They all show the importance of treating an inscription in context. I use the term "context" here not just to refer to the physical surroundings of an inscription, and its archaeological surroundings and the original excavation details, although these are essential, as is the nature and state of the inscribed object (examination of the actual *Lapis Satricanus* reveals that the break in the corner of the stone is not recent). Context also comprises the wider background to a text, including the existence of similar text forms and parallel objects. Thus a text written on lead and thrown down a hot spring is *a priori* more likely to be a curse tablet than a letter (as early critics of Nicholson's reading of the text from Bath pointed out).

Consideration of the wider class of documents to which an isolated example belongs can also help give the reader better judgement about any linguistic oddity in a text. Kruschwitz and Halla-aho (2007) illustrate this point well from the Pompeiian wall inscriptions. One class of the painted inscriptions (so-called *dipinti*) from Pompeii comprises appeals to support candidates in elections (termed *programmata*). These *programmata* all include the name of the candidate and the office which they are standing for, usually accompanied by the name of the supporter and an appeal to elect him. Their format is regular, and they often incorporate an abbreviation *OVF* standing for *o(ro) u(os) f(aciatis)* "I ask you to elect him". Kruschwitz and Halla-aho (2007) 45 discuss an example of this type of text with a different verb (*CIL* IV.3828):

> Ti. Claudium Verum | IIuir(um) Obelli(us?) cum patre faue scis Vero fauere.
>
> Obellius and his father (recommend): support Titus Claudius Verus for the office of *duumvir*! You know how to support Verus.

The use of the accusative *Claudium* after the verb *faueo*, which normally takes the dative, might be seen as a significant deviation from Classical Latin in this *dipinto*. But a grammatical explanation is unlikely; the writer is able to use the dative after *faueo* in the final clause of the text. In fact, all the *programmata* place the name of candidate in first place in the accusative case. In this example, the writer has changed from the usual verb in these announcements, but he has kept to the formulaic introduction. In order to understand this, one needs an understanding of how these types of document work through a careful analysis of all the comparable examples.

Collecting and Interpreting Ancient Documents

In Greek studies there has been a traditional split between epigraphy and papyrology. Papyrologists have for most of the last century worked on documents written on papyri, which come in the most part from ancient Egypt, while epigraphers study records left principally on stone from Greece and Asia Minor. There are only a tiny number of Latin papyri surviving in Egypt in comparison with the vast amount of Greek material (over 650 volumes of Greek papyri have been published already, and many remain unpublished in collections around the world, to say nothing of the material which has not yet been excavated). Consequently, there has never been a separate tradition of papyrology from epigraphy in Roman studies. The paucity of Latin papyri has meant that no institute or university department specialising exclusively in this field has ever been set up. Scholars working on publications of new Latin documents on materials analogous to papyri, such as wooden or wax tablets, have come from both the disciplines of Greek papyri and Roman epigraphy.[4] Even so, the split between epigraphy and papyri in Greek studies has meant that some of the Latin documents from Egypt written on papyrus and ostraca have been published in separate series from those on stone and other materials, which find a place within the *Corpus Inscriptionum Latinarum*; frequently this material is catalogued and kept separately in libraries and research institutes. Papyrologists and epigraphers have also employed different editorial conventions in the past, and still today employ different abbreviations for published material. For example, the tablets from Vindolanda, published by Bowman and Thomas (1983, 1994 and 2003), are generally referred to by epigraphers as *Tab. Vindol.* but by papyrologists as *T.Vindol.*

The sheer numbers of surviving documents from the ancient world lead inevitably to a confusing publication history. An individual inscription may be published for the first time as the subject for a specific article, or it may be mentioned in passing during the discussion of a sculpture or an archaeological excavation, or it may be included in a museum catalogue. Often groups of inscriptions are published together from the same excavation or museum or private collection. After their initial publication all epigraphical publications (that is, all texts except papyrus) are gathered into *L'Année épigraphique* (until 1965 published as part of *Revue archéologique*, since then as a separate journal), which assigns a number to each text. The number assigned by *L'Année épigraphique* may be used by scholars to refer to the text. For example, the abbreviation *AE* (1931) 212 refers to an inscription which is gathered in that year's number of *L'Année épigraphique*. Rereadings or new discussions of an inscription are also recorded in *L'Année épigraphique*. For some material, other annual collections also record finds; all written material from Roman Britain, for example, has been included in the journal *Britannia* since its creation in 1970.

The life of a published inscription does not end with its inclusion in *L'Année épigraphique*. Many items may then be gathered into one of the corpora comprising all the documents from one region, or of a specific time-span or type. For most inscriptions, the ultimate destination is inclusion in the largest and most comprehensive corpus, the *Corpus Inscriptionum Latinarum* (abbreviated *CIL*). The *CIL* is divided into seventeen volumes, arranged broadly geographically. Thus volume II contains inscriptions from Spain, volume III from northern and eastern provinces of the eastern empire, roughly the quadrant between (and including) Noricum and Egypt. However some volumes of the *CIL* have temporal or thematic limitations: volume I covers all inscriptions before 44 BCE, volume XV contains *instrumenta domestica* from Rome, volume XVI includes military diplomas, volume XVI milestones. Volume VII, containing inscriptions from Britain, is replaced by the volumes of *The Roman Inscriptions of Britain* (abbreviated to *RIB*). Currently, around seventy parts of the *CIL* are published, containing over 180,000 inscriptions, together with thirteen supplementary volumes. The production (and revision) of *CIL* has been an ongoing project since the corpus was inaugurated by Mommsen in 1853, and it stands as one of the chief monuments of classical scholarship. Even so, revision and updating of the corpus is a lengthy process, and for many areas the relevant volume of *CIL* is seriously out of date.

Once inscriptions have been included in the *CIL* it is conventional to refer to them by their *CIL* number, although some inscriptions are also gathered into other selections or collections. These include Dessau's selection *Inscriptiones Latinae Selectae* (commonly abbreviated to *ILS*); Degrassi's handy collection of republican inscriptions *Inscriptiones Latinae Liberae rei publicae* (abbreviated to *ILLRP*; this collection originally replaced the second edition of *CIL* I, referred to as *CIL* I², but itself has been partly superseded by later fascicles of *CIL* I²); Crawford's collection of Roman legal texts surviving in inscribed materials (*Roman Statutes I*, 1996); and a collection of verse inscriptions inaugurated by Bücheler, *Carmina Latina Epigraphica* (abbreviated to *CLE*). However, this means that a single inscription can lead a multiple life under different aliases. For example, a late republican verse funerary inscription of L. Aurelius L.l. Hermia was included both in *CIL* VI.9499 and in *CIL* I².1221, and also appears as *ILS* 7472, *ILLRP* 793 and *CLE* 959.

CIL is intended to have complete coverage of surviving Latin written material, except in two important areas: documentary material (especially, but not only papyri) and coinage. Tracing the publication of much Latin documentary material can be difficult for the novice. Although the first supplement to volume IV of *CIL*, edited by Zangemeister in 1898, was devoted to wax tablets from Pompeii, and wax tablets found in Roman mines in Dacia are included in *CIL* III.2, more recent editions of writing tablets from Pompeii and surrounding areas have been in separate publications, for example Camodeca's edition of the material from Pozzuoli: *Tabulae Pompeianae Sulpiciorum: edizione critica dell'archivio puteolano dei Sulpicii* (abbreviated in this volume to *T.Sulpicii*). As already mentioned, Latin papyri have generally been published in volumes dedicated to the Greek papyri with which they were found or alongside which they are stored in modern collections. However, a collection of Latin papyri, the *Corpus Papyrorum Latinarum* (abbreviated here to *CPL*), was published in 1958 by Cavenaile, incorporating all the material known by that date. Since the discovery of the wooden writing tablets from Vindolanda in the 1970s, and subsequent discoveries in Britain and elsewhere (notably of wooden tablets from Vindonissa, modern Windisch in Switzerland), there has been a growing awareness that the papyrological material and ostraca from Egypt and the Near East need to be studied alongside the documentary texts from the rest of the empire. One volume which combines letters written on different media, including papyri, wood and ostraca, from around the Roman world is the *Corpus Epistolarum Latinarum, papyris tabulis ostracis servatarum* (abbreviated as *CEL*) published by Cugusi and completed in 2002. Coin legends form another group of texts not normally included in *CIL*, although republican coins are included in the first edition of *CIL* I. Coin legends are necessarily limited in length, but they may still be of interest to the linguist; note, for example, the legend *ROMANO* (for classical *Romanorum* "of the Romans") in republican coins from the fourth and third centuries BCE, showing the archaic form of the genitive plural. Published corpora of Roman coins include the following: Crawford's *Roman Republican Coinage* (1974) for the Republican period; for the empire, the ten-volume *Roman Imperial Coinage* (founded by Mattingly and Sydenham); a corpus of provincial coinage of the Roman Empire is also currently under way, entitled *Roman Provincial Coinage*.

The publication of Latin inscriptions and papyri has special editorial conventions, to enable the user to understand the link between the actual written forms and an editor's presentation. Table 3.1 gives an overview of the conventions employed by editors for both inscriptions and documentary material (the so-called Leiden conventions) now followed in all major publications.

Abbreviations abound in Latin epigraphy. Often these are standard and well-know, such as the onomastic formula given above, *L. Aurelius L.l. Hermia*, which can be expanded to *L(ucius) Aurelius L(uci) l(ibertus Hermia)* "Lucius Aurelius Hermia the freedman of Lucius". Abbreviations are often used to fill out conventional phrases or formulae, particularly in later inscriptions. For example, consider *CIL* VI.11818, a funerary monument from Rome of imperial date. The original text reads as follows, with minimal punctuation.

Table 3.1 Editorial conventions for inscriptions and documents

Sign	Meaning
abc[de]	material lost in the original through damage, but restored by the editor
a(bcd)	material abbreviated in the original, and expanded by the editor
a<b>cde	material added by the editor to correct an omission in the original
ab{ab}cde	material in the original which is thought superfluous or mistakenly written by the editor
ab[[xy]]cde	material deleted or overwritten in the original
ab«cd»e	material which is written over deleted material in the original
((sestertios))	material put in by the editor in place of special signs in the original
abcḍe	material which is partly damaged or obscure, but can be read in context
"abc"	material added in antiquity to complete or correct a text
vac.	area left blank in the original
/	beginning of a new line

D · M
ANNIAESATVRNINAE
QVIXIT·ANN·XVII·M·V
D·XII·L·EVHELPISTVS·VXOR
B·M·F·

The only Latin words which are not abbreviated in this short inscription are the names *Anniae, Saturninae, Euhelpistus* and the verb *uixit*. An editor of this text is able to fill out the abbreviations from comparable inscriptions, and insert fuller punctuation and capitals to aid modern readers:

> d(is) m(anibus) / Anniae Saturninae / q(uae) uixit ann(os) XVII m(enses) V / d(ies) XII.
> L(ucius) Euhelpistus uxor(i) / b(ene) m(erenti) f(ecit).

> To the sacred shades of Annia Saturnina who lived for 17 years, five months and 12 days.
> Lucius Euhelpistus made this monument for a well deserving wife.

In order to aid the novice reader of Latin inscriptions, a compilation of common abbreviations and their expansions are available at Gordon (1983) 208–225, with references to more extensive lists elsewhere. Despite the efforts of generations of scholars, the interpretation of a few recurrent abbreviations in Roman inscriptions remains disputed. One example is the abbreviation NP which occurs in inscribed *Fasti* or calendars, most of which date from the first fifty years of the principate. The *Fasti* provide the *notae dierum*, that is a calendar which shows the Kalends, Nones and Ides of each month, and indicates for each day whether it is *fastus* (abbreviated *F*) or *nefastus* (abbreviated *N*), i.e. whether the magistrates is allowed to conduct business (on days marked *en(dotercisi)* business is allowed only in the central part of the day). Various explanations have been offered to explain what *NP* stands for: *nefas piaculum, nefas (feriae) publicae, nefas (feriae) posteriores, nefastus purus, nefas principio* or *nefas parte*, but there is no way of knowing which of these, if any, is correct.

In individual texts the Roman penchant for abbreviations sometimes leads to obscurity, and their interpretation can rely solely on the ingenuity of the editor. The publication of the third volume of *Roman Inscriptions of Britain* (Tomlin *et al.* 2009) provides an example of a very short inscription which only uses abbreviations: *RIB* III.3358 is an inscription of only two letters and a numeral: *H P III*, which occurs as a graffito next to a crude drawing of a phallus found on the undressed side of a quarried slab at Vindolanda. Since the abbreviation *p.* before a numeral can stand for *pedes* "feet" (the unit of measurement), Tomlin reads the complete inscription as a boast of the possessor of the image *h(abet) p(edes) III* "it is three feet long".

The study of Latin inscriptions and documents is changing through the internet which provides an ideal platform for hosting large and complex databases. It is slowly becoming easier to search Latin inscriptions and papyri through online databases and corpora, and there is a very welcome move to include images along with reproductions of documents and inscriptions on the web. Over half of all the inscriptions from Greece and Rome are now available to be searched online (nearly 400,000 texts) and images are now available for all of the inscriptions from Roman Tripolitana and over 23,000 inscriptions from Spain. For documentary material, the online Duke Databank of Documentary Papyri contains most of the Latin papyri from Egypt and all the writing tablets from Vindonissa and Vindonissa, but it does not yet contain the archive of wax tablets found near Pompeii (*T.Sulpicii*).

The Writer of a Latin Text

Few surviving documents from the Roman world were composed verbatim and written by the same individual. Stonecutters carved inscriptions, scribes wrote documents and letters. On rare occasions we may know the name of an individual craftsman; Gordon records that only three known stonecutters can be associated with individual carved stones, and only one of those, Furius Dionysius Filocalus, the official engraver of Pope Damasus (366–384 CE) is known to have carved more than one inscription (Gordon (1983) 39, 43). In the case of Filocalus we also know that he composed verse, but he was probably the exception. Many stonecutters will have taken the wording of an inscription from the person who commissioned the text, whether that was a private individual or an official. However, it is possible that intermediary figures were also involved in the process, such as the so-called *ordinator* (not an ancient term) who sketched out the draft on the stone, in cases where the stonecutter did not do this himself (see Susini 1973 for discussion of the process of the creation of an inscription). Sometimes we can be fairly certain that the text of an inscription is close to that created by a specific individual, for example, the *Res Gestae* of Augustus, inscribed on several copies around the empire, of which the *Monumentum Ancyranum* is by far the most complete, or the speech of the Emperor Claudius recorded on a bronze tablet in Lyon (*CIL* XIII.1668). But when an inscription was commissioned by an individual from lower down the social scale, it is possible that the written text was much further removed from the original wording. Workshops may have had prepared models or inscriptions ready for purchase "off-the-shelf". There certainly were also local preferences and styles in the composition and wording of inscriptions, as well as formulae appropriate to different genres (such as the election *programmata* discussed above) or current among specific groups in society, such as Jews or Christians.

With graffiti and other documents we may appear to be on firmer ground when addressing the question of authorship, since graffiti sometimes bears the name of the individual who scratched it into the wall or plaster. In groups of comparable documents, such as the Bath curse tablets, it is possible to identify different hands and isolate specific individuals. Indeed, the diversity of different writing styles implies that each curse was written out by the person making the curse, a conclusion apparently confirmed by one man, named Docilinus or Docilianus, who wrote a curse-tablet both at Bath (*Tab. Sulis* 10) and at Uley in Hampshire (Uley 43).[5] In both of his written curses, Docili(a)nus employs a phrase which is otherwise unattested in any other curse tablet:

ut [e]um dea Sulis maximo letum [a]digat (*Tab. Sulis* 10.10–2)
that the Goddess Sulis drives him to his greatest death

rogo te ut eos maximo leto adigas (Uley 43)
I ask you that you drive them to their greatest death.

The phrase *maximo leto adigo* "drive to greatest death" (or *maximum letum adigo*, it is not clear whether Docili(a)nus intended an ablative or accusative) is unparalleled in Latin (see Adams (1992) 7–8). Are we then faced with creative use of Latin by the writer? In this case, it seems not, since funerary and building inscriptions were not the only texts that used fixed formulae; they were also prevalent in every other domain of epigraphy (compare the election *programmata* discussed above). In curse tablets, in particular, there is a preponderance of repeated phrases and set figures, and there may well have been ancient "spell-books" in circulation which are now lost. The word *letum* seems to have been limited to the highest levels of Latin literature by the empire, and Docili(a)nus' uncertainty about whether to write an accusative or ablative here perhaps reveals that this is a formula derived from some lost spell-book rather than a genuinely creative use of the language. Since it is likely that only a fraction of all the Roman curse-tablets ever created have been found, the lack of any parallels to this phrase is not a problem for this theory. In the same way, graffiti often employs stock phrases and expressions (much as modern graffiti does). Short poems, obscenities and insults are repeated across the empire; letters and legal documents also make frequent use of formulaic language.

Thus when we are faced with an inscription such as *CIL* VI.11818 given above (which was chosen by Saller (2001) 96 as an inscription "notable only for its typicality") we may conclude that this is a text without any individual author, consisting entirely of abbreviated formulae and of a stock pattern. Can this text tell us anything about the Latin language, despite the absence of an individual author? On its own, probably not. The words are all spelt in the standard forms of Classical Latin, and the text has no grammatical peculiarities. But we cannot conclude from this that Annia Saturnina or Lucius Euhelpistus spoke "correct" Classical Latin, or indeed that anyone involved in the production of the stone did. If there had been a "mistake" in the Latin of this text, for example, if *uixit* had been spelt *bixit* or *uxor* spelt *ussor* (both mistakes are frequent in inscriptions from the later empire), then one might be more tempted to draw conclusions about the speech of the dedicator, but this approach is liable to skew the evidence. The spelling *uixit* tells us that the individual who commissioned the stone, or one of the parties involved in the execution of the memorial, had been taught Classical Latin spelling conventions; the spelling *bixit* reveals that the level of education of the writer(s) was not so high, but does not necessarily entail that the speech habits of any of the parties were substantially different from those who could reproduce "correct" forms. On the other hand, more unusual errors, such as the use of a genitive in -*aes* rather than -*ae* in the woman's name, might be significant, especially if we could link it with prosopographical or onomastic peculiarities.[6]

On this reasoning, Adams (2007) 629–634 has argued against studies which attempt to find out the progress of a linguistic change through the Roman Empire on the basis of statistical analyses of the number of correct and incorrect forms found in inscriptions, pointing out that such studies in fact show the level of adherence to a standard norm rather than any clear results about speaker habits. Adams argues that statistical studies on inscriptions and documents can be useful in constructing a picture of the language if the texts studied form part of a "coherent corpus", meaning by that term "a body of texts about which we know something, (as for example their date, authorship, provenance, educational level) and which belong together in one or more senses (geographically, culturally or in subject matter)" (Adams (2007): 633). Scattered inscriptions which have no certain chronological and geographical unity, or which are not linked by other peculiarities (such as a distinctive iconography of the monument, or origin of the dedicators) are unlikely to tell us anything on their own. On the other hand, as Adams has himself shown in numerous studies, when we do have coherent corpora of inscriptions and documents, it is possible to make small pieces of evidence reveal more than might have been expected. I discuss in later chapters examples of this sort from Vindolanda, both of which were first discussed by Adams (see pp. 247–248 on the evidence for the pronunciation of initial *h-* at Vindolanda, and p. 517 on the use of the form *debunt* for *debent* at Vindolanda).

Conclusion

Most of the languages spoken in the ancient world for which we have any evidence are known only from inscriptions and documentary material. Our grammars and dictionaries of numerous languages, from Accadian to Umbrian, are constructed entirely from original documents without any recourse to manuscript transmission or a continued tradition of teaching and learning. It would be theoretically possible to construct a picture of the Latin language drawing only from epigraphical and documentary sources (of which there is far more than for any other ancient language of the western Mediterranean) and ignoring the precepts of ancient and medieval grammarians or the example of literary texts. How different would the language appear to be if we had no manuscript tradition to rely on? Clearly there would be large lacunae in some areas of our knowledge: for example, for Latin in the third and second centuries BCE, the epigraphical tradition is meagre in comparison with the corpus of Plautine material; inscriptions and documents give a more limited range of examples of complex syntactic constructions and textual discourse than some of the surviving literary works; some of our paradigms would be more difficult to fill out with attested forms; and we would be deprived of the explicit statements of Romans about their language which reveal their language attitudes and judgements. But the grammar and vocabulary of Latin gathered from such an exercise would also remind us of some of the ways in which the traditional grammar of Latin is skewed by literary texts. Orthography and morphology would be revealed as more variable than is apparent from our school-texts, and the syntax less rigid. Latin would be revealed more clearly as a language used across the whole of the Roman Empire, and less closely tied to the elite culture of the city of Rome.

FURTHER READING

Gordon (1983) is still probably the best single-volume guide to Latin epigraphy in English, with a well-chosen selection of texts from the earliest documents to a Christian inscription from 525 CE. Gordon also includes a list of the most common abbreviations to appear in Latin inscriptions. Bérard *et al.* (2010), which has regular updates on the web, is indispensable for help in finding details about publications of inscriptions (both in Latin and Greek, as well as other languages around the Mediterranean) and for much ancillary material. It also gives details of web-sites which include corpora of material. Bagnall (2009) includes excellent chapters on Greek and Latin writing and Greek and Latin language in papyri, as well as surveys of the use of Latin in Egypt and the construction of ancient writing materials out of wood, pottery and papyrus. The *Checklist of Greek, Latin, Demotic and Coptic Papyri, Ostraca and Tablets* (last print edition 2001, but kept updated online, hosted by Duke University, Durham, NC), gives details of all papyrological publications, and includes information about all Latin documents in the papyri.

NOTES

1 Note however that the Scipio epitaph is atypical in republican inscriptions in being carved on the tomb of the interred corpse. Most Romans were cremated not buried during the republic.
2 Nicholson's reading still survives in the published corpora of Latin letters: *CEL* 236.
3 The Colonna reading has however persisted in the literature; it is cited by Hartmann (2005) 142.
4 Note for example the recent republication of a wooden tablet from the Netherlands (Bowman *et al.* 2009), published jointly by Roger Tomlin (by training a Roman epigraphist), Klaas Worp (a Greek papyrologist) and Alan Bowman (originally a Greek papyrologist, but then editor of the Vindolanda documents).
5 This tablet provides a good example of some of the difficulties of referring to published and partly published inscriptions. The inscription is published by Tomlin in *Britannia* 20 (1989) 329–330, as text number 3, but the number 43 refers to the numbering given to it in Tomlin's preliminary report on the lead tablets excavated at Uley in Woodward and Leach (1993), although these tablets have still not been fully published. This tablet has an *AE* reference: *AE* (1988) 487.
6 See Mullen's discussion of *RIB* I. 1065, at pp. 543–545 of this volume, for another example of an inscription where the prosopography of an individual who commissioned an inscription can shed light on his use of non-standard Latin forms.

CHAPTER 4

Latin Manuscripts and Textual Traditions

Bruce Gibson

Introduction

As well as texts from the ancient world found on a variety of substances such as stone, metal, and papyrus, a large body of evidence for the Latin language has survived in the form of manuscripts, a term usually found with reference to works that are found in a bound codex, written on a range of substances, but typically on parchment from prepared animal skins. This practice continued even after the slow diffusion of knowledge of paper from the Arabs, who had acquired knowledge of it from the Chinese (Bischoff (1990) 7–19). At the outset, it is important to realise that the current usage of the term "manuscript" in connection with modern practices of publication is not necessarily a helpful one. In our own era, we might expect to hear of an author presenting a manuscript (nowadays most likely a computerised typescript) which might represent a final or near-final text to a publisher for publication. What is different about manuscripts of ancient texts is that they are typically from long after the time of the particular text's composition. And if we set manuscripts alongside other kinds of textual remains from antiquity, what distinguishes materials transmitted in manuscript form from some of the types of evidence covered in chapter 3, such as inscriptions on stone, is that manuscripts come to us as a result of a lengthy chain of transmission, about whose processes and problems we are often uncertain. By contrast, inscriptions, though they too can experience later interventions, and of course often suffer damage, are usually a part or the whole of a text at the moment it was originally composed (although the carver of a stone inscription is admittedly likely in many cases to have worked from a written text). Consideration of the evidence offered by manuscripts to the historian of the Latin language thus requires some awareness of the various processes of transmission.

A Companion to the Latin Language, First Edition. Edited by James Clackson.
© 2011 Blackwell Publishing Ltd. Published 2011 by Blackwell Publishing Ltd.

It is also necessary to remember that, in an ancient context, publication would have represented the decision to circulate an approved version of a particular text, either through booksellers or though the agency of friends, who might also even be asked, as a preliminary stage, to suggest changes to the author (on publication practice in Rome, see e.g. Nauta (2002) 120–141, 280–290). Though such texts might begin their lives under the control of the author, there was of course nothing to stop the production of further copies (and there was no law of copyright), which might also include textual differences, either by accident or by design: the reproduction of an ancient text could of course only be done by hand. There are very occasional examples where ancient authors play on the idea of their text as an autograph copy of their work (thus Ovid, in the opening poem of the first book of his poetry written from exile, draws attention to the blots on the text caused by the poet's tears, *Tr.* 1.1.13–14), and authors also sometimes draw attention to the physical format of texts (see e.g. Catul. 22.5–8, Ov. *Tr.* 1.1.5–12). Within antiquity, there are isolated references to the survival of autograph copies of texts: to give one example, Quint. *Inst.* 1.7.20 claims that he has seen texts written in the hands of Virgil and Cicero which show the older spelling of *s* as double *s* in words such as *caussa* (on this form, see Wallace, chapter 2 of this volume), where later conventional usage would be *causa*. Nevertheless, the surviving manuscript evidence for ancient authors such as Cicero, Virgil and others does not depend on the author's "original" version of a text: the Latin literature of the ancient world has reached us in copies of copies, often the result of scribal work in medieval monastic settings. Indeed, there are in fact examples from antiquity where the danger of unauthorised changes to a text is explicitly raised as a possibility. To give an example from the Bible, the book of Revelation famously ends with a curse imparted on any person who adds or removes anything to the prophecy contained within the work (Revelation 22: 18–19), which is as much a recognition of the possibilities of a text being lost from the control of its original author as a statement of the importance of a sacred text. Similarly, the tradition that Virgil's request for the text of the *Aeneid* to be burned was disregarded after his death, even if it has little or no factual basis (see Horsfall (2000a) 22–23), is another reminder of the lack of control an author might have over his own text.

The examples of Revelation and of the *Aeneid*'s survival in spite of its author's alleged wish to destroy it, point to the possibilities for texts to experience deliberate intervention in the course of their transmission, but equally significant is the fact that the most careful processes of copying can at any point introduce mistakes and changes to the content of an ancient text. Such errors are of many types: not just mistakes in the copying of single words (where errors might include changes to single letters or to larger sections of the word, replacement of a word with another word, which might be a synonym, or even a word with the opposite meaning, the so-called "polar error"), or omissions of material (which might be caused by the scribe's eye jumping to the wrong place in the text being copied), but also interpolations of extraneous material and more complex phenomena such as transpositions of material to the wrong place (especially in verse texts), or the intrusion of what were previously marginal annotations into the text itself. The processes of *textual criticism*, the production of the most accurate text possible on the basis of weighing up the available evidence and identifying and then attempting to correct corruption to a text, were already practised within classical antiquity itself: the scholarship reflected in the ancient commentaries (*scholia*) on the Homeric poems provides invaluable examples of this.

In Latin literature there is also evidence for work of this type. A simple example of such textual criticism occurs in the late fourth-century commentary on Virgil ascribed to Servius. In the first *Eclogue*, one of the characters, Meliboeus, refers to the troubled state of the countryside (Verg. *Ecl.* 1.11–12):

> non equidem inuideo, miror magis: undique totis
> usque adeo turbatur agris.

I for my part am not envious, rather I am amazed: everywhere continually there is disturbance [*turbatur*, literally "it is being disturbed"] in all the fields.

The Servian commentary discusses the reading *turbatur* and whether or not it might be correct:

VSQVE ADEO TVRBATVR AGRIS: *turbamur* ("we are disturbed") has nothing to differentiate it for good or ill. And with a spirit of ill-will he attacks the times of Augustus in a hidden way. Certainly the true reading is *turbatur* ("it is being disturbed"), so that it is impersonal, which pertains to everyone in a general way: for the expulsion of the Mantuans was collective. For if you read *turbamur*, it seems to refer to a few people. (Serv. *Ecl.* 1.11–12)

In miniature, this discussion from late antiquity reflects some of the major issues that arise in textual criticism. In the first instance, Servius is confronted by variant readings in these lines from the *Eclogues*, and observes at the outset that on one level both variants have nothing to choose between them, because neither is obviously wrong. It is not hard to see why *turbamur* might be viewed as a possible reading. In the first place, a change of only one letter is needed to give rise to *turbamur* as a variant of *turbatur*. Secondly, the personal form of the first person plural passive *turbamur* might seem clearer than the third person singular *turbatur*, especially as Servius goes on to explain that the usage of the verb is impersonal, since there is not an explicit personal subject of the passive verb stated here. Servius also defends his choice of reading with the further historical point that when the people of Mantua were removed from their lands it was a collective expulsion, and this is in fact the basis of Servius' choice here, since the reading *turbamur* might suggest that the confiscation affected only a few individuals. We can see from this passage that textual criticism and the study of the texts that are transmitted to us can provide knowledge of the Latin language (in this case comment on the usage of the impersonal passive in the third person singular). At the same time, however, such textual scholarship also proceeds precisely from an understanding of the Latin language. This is reflected in the practice of textual scholarship down to our own time, since editorial decisions on the best text in a particular passage are often supported by appeal to linguistic parallels. In practice, the dangers of circular argumentation in such examples are limited to instances where there are only a few examples of a given linguistic feature, but it is nevertheless useful to remind ourselves that, just as Latin texts transmitted in manuscripts provide a mass of evidence for our understanding of the language, so too is our own knowledge of the language dependent on the accidents of transmission in the texts that have (or have not) come down to us.

The Processes of Transmission

Manuscript evidence for the Latin language should not be assumed to be uniform in character. There is not the scope within the confines of this chapter to offer a detailed treatment of the discipline of palaeography, literally "the study of ancient writing", but it is important to note here that Latin scripts vary substantially over time, and that individual scripts can be associated with particular types of errors when copied by scribes from later periods, which can affect the reliability of the textual traditions presented to us. In the first centuries BCE and CE, Latin scripts, even in a cursive form, were based on the more formal squared capitals familiar from Latin inscriptions; the development of cursive scripts towards minuscule forms (that are the forerunners of modern lower case letters) is likely only to have taken place in the third century CE (Bischoff (1990) 54–66).

   Furthermore, manuscript evidence for classical texts covers an enormous time span. Some of the oldest evidence for Latin texts goes back to antiquity itself, exemplified by the earliest witnesses for the text of Virgil, such as the so-called *schedae Vaticanae*, the surviving leaves of a finely illustrated volume of Virgil from the end of the fourth century CE (Vat. lat. 3225); other, more extensive, evidence for the works of Virgil comes from the fifth and sixth centuries (see discussion in Reynolds (1983) 433–436). It is thus the case that modern editions of Virgil have the benefit of direct evidence from the end of antiquity. Conversely, there are other texts whose transmission depends on surviving testimony from no earlier than the Renaissance. To give a famous example, the text of the poet Catullus appears to have come down to us on the basis of a single manuscript, the now-lost Veronensis, of uncertain date (though see Thomson (2003) 24–25 for the suggestion that it might date from around 1280): the oldest surviving evidence for the corpus of Catullus' poems, however, consists of three manuscripts from the fourteenth century. In some cases, there are texts where it is possible to construct lines of transmission between earlier and later manuscripts, which allows us to speak of a *stemma*, the Greek word also used in Latin to denote a family tree. The text of Catullus, with the exception of one poem which also survives excerpted on its own in an earlier manuscript (poem 62, preserved in a ninth-century *florilegium*, a miscellany of various texts), can be presented in a simplified form (taking no account of later corrections found in the original manuscripts, or of possible intermediate stages of transmission between the Veronensis and the surviving manuscripts) with a stemma as shown in Figure 4.1.

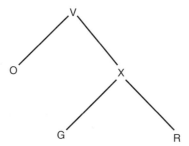

Figure 4.1   Simplified stemma showing the relationship of the principal manuscripts of Catullus.

In Figure 4.1:

V represents the Veronensis, the lost Verona manuscript from which all our manuscripts
   derive
O represents a manuscript from the fourteenth century which is descended from *V* and
   is now in Oxford (Canonicianus class. lat. 30)
X is another lost manuscript, also descended from *V*, which gives rise to two further
   manuscripts:
   G, a manuscript which can be dated to 1375, now in Paris (Parisinus lat. 14137), and
   R, a manuscript now in Rome which is from the late fourteenth century (Vat.
      Ottobianus lat. 1829).

It will be seen that when the readings for particular words found in the three manuscripts
O, *G*, and *R* are in agreement, this allows the inference that we might have the reading
of the lost manuscript *V*. In contrast, occasions when the manuscripts disagree make it
harder to reconstruct the readings of lost manuscripts in a stemma such as this. But it
should not of course be assumed that, even when the reading likely to have been present
in *V* can be inferred, such readings will necessarily be correct.

   The discussion above offers a simplified account of how the three oldest manuscripts
of Catullus form a stemmatic manuscript tradition: it takes no account, for instance, of
recent suggestions that *O* and *X* were not direct copies of *V*, but copies of at least one
intermediary stage of transmission, a lost manuscript referred to as *A* by Thomson in his
recent edition of Catullus (Thomson (2003) 25–28). It has moreover been shown that
the process of reconstructing the readings of the lost manuscript *X* is a more uncertain
task, since the later variant readings found in *G* and *R*, usually denoted as R^2 and G^2,
exhibit a complex relationship to each other, involving a further manuscript, *m*, copied
from *R* and dated to 1400 at the earliest. The readings in *R* in the hand of Coluccio
Salutati *(R^2)* contain not only Salutati's own corrections of the text, but also variant
readings likely to have been copied from the contents of the lost manuscript *X*. By
contrast, the variants found in G^2 are derived from *m* and its variants. The presence of
variants in manuscripts, even in a simple stemmatic tradition such as this, is a reminder
that there is always the potential for contamination (the process whereby the copying of
a manuscript in one branch of a textual tradition might also draw on manuscript evidence
from another part of the tradition), which can blur what appear to be straightforward
relationships between manuscripts (on the relationship between *X*, *R* and its variants,
and *m*, see McKie (1989), Thomson (2003) 35–43).

   Other traditions are more complex. The first decade of Livy's history of Rome, a very
small section of which is documented in a papyrus from the fourth or fifth century CE,
has an elaborate stemma of manuscripts, including several stages of a transmission which
involve hypothetically reconstructed manuscripts. The later stages of this tradition also
include clear instances of contamination from one strand of the tradition to another
(Oakley (1997) 152–327). But there are also many texts whose transmission cannot be
illustrated with even an elaborate stemma, since the various stages of the tradition are
interlinked in too complex a way for relationships between manuscripts to be represented
in this fashion. No convincing stemma can be constructed for the textual transmission of
Juvenal, for example. Although one manuscript, *P*, from the ninth century, is regarded

as the best witness to the text, and closely linked to other related manuscript evidence, there is also another group of manuscripts, of which the earliest are also from the ninth century, that scholars regard as impossible to separate out from each other, such is the extent of contamination between them (Clausen (1959), xii; Reynolds (1983) 201).

There are even texts whose transmission is entirely dependent on early printed editions from the Renaissance, such as Julius Obsequens' *Liber prodigiorum* ("Book of prodigies"), a text first attested in a Venetian Aldine edition of 1508, and without any surviving manuscript evidence at all (Reynolds (1983) 196). As noted above, there is a huge chronological diversity of surviving material which provides us with evidence for the Latin language. Likewise, it should be not assumed that the processes of transmission down to our oldest surviving manuscripts for individual texts were uniform with regular copying of manuscripts over regular intervals down the centuries: sometimes a text would sit in a library unread and uncopied over a period of centuries, which means that the next scribe to make a copy might have great difficulty in reading an unfamiliar script. Moreover, manuscripts vary considerably in their presentation of texts, not only in terms of the kinds of scripts used but also in terms of conventions for abbreviation and for orthography (see Dinkova-Bruun, chapter 17 in this volume, for a full discussion of medieval orthography) which can often reflect current medieval practice. Such considerations are always significant when using the evidence of texts transmitted in manuscript in studying the history and development of the Latin language.

Furthermore, the transmission of many texts is by no means straightforward. Some texts do not survive complete, and are truncated by the accident of damage at some stage in their history. Still others survive only because they have been quoted or summarised (and this is a distinction which can certainly matter to the historian of the Latin language) in other longer and more complete works. There are even some texts which have precariously survived when the parchment on which they were written has been reused, so that, on occasion, we are extremely fortunate to have traces of the earlier text which have survived the process of reuse: such palimpsests, as they are called, include all three of the main surviving witnesses for the works of Fronto, all of which saw the writings of the second-century CE epistolographer written over with Christian material (Reynolds (1983) 173–174).

Sometimes we can combine our knowledge of a text from its manuscripts with material from elsewhere. A simple example of the kind of knowledge that is possible when we are lucky enough to have additional material as well as the direct manuscript tradition of a Latin text is found in the opening of the first poem of Catullus' collection of poetry (Catul. 1.1–2):

> cui dono lepidum nouum libellum
> arido modo pumice expolitum?

To whom do I give my charming new little book, just now polished with dry pumice-stone [*arido ... pumice*]?

Here, *arido* is the reading of the three fourteenth-century manuscripts of Catullus, *O*, *G* and *R*, and is therefore likely to have been the reading found in the lost Veronensis manuscript (*V*). The masculine gender for *pumex*, "pumice-stone", is regularly attested. However, an additional piece of information needs to be considered here as well.

Though *arido … pumice* is not just acceptable Latin but perfectly normal, with *pumex* as masculine, there is also a brief discussion of the gender of this noun in Servius' commentary on Virgil's phrase *latebroso in pumice*, "in the pumice-stone that is full of hiding-places" (Serv. *A.* 12.587):

> "in pumice" autem iste masculino genere posuit, et hunc sequimur: nam et Plautus ita dixit: licet Catullus dixerit feminino.

> But *in pumice* he put in the masculine gender, and we follow him: for Plautus also spoke in this fashion: although Catullus put the word in the feminine.

The explicit evidence offered by Servius here is a sound basis for accepting in the text of Catullus not *arido*, the masculine form of the adjective attested by the oldest direct witnesses to the text of Catullus, the three fourteenth-century manuscripts *OGR*, but *arida*, the feminine form, even though the masculine *arido* is not incorrect or even unusual Latin. It is true that the evidence from Servius does not explicitly relate to this passage, and logically it is therefore possible that Catullus might have used the feminine gender for *pumex* in one passage, and the masculine in another passage of his works. As it happens, unless it is assumed that the feminine gender of Catullus was used in a lost work that is not known to us, *pumex* only occurs once elsewhere in the extant works of Catullus (Catul. 22.8), and in a context where the lack of an accompanying adjective means that its gender cannot be determined. The picture is further complicated by citations of this passage from poem 1 in several ancient texts, such as the seventh-century Isidore of Seville (*Origines* 6.12.3), which give the passage with the masculine gender, indicating that the reading found in the Renaissance manuscripts was also known in the seventh century CE. The issue of whether or not Catullus innovated by making use of the feminine gender of *pumex* in this passage from poem 1 ultimately has to be a matter of judgement for the editor, weighing on the one hand the evidence of the manuscripts in favour of the reading *arido*, other ancient testimonies such as Isidore, and the general usage of the masculine *pumex* elsewhere in Classical Latin, against the explicit testimony of Servius that Catullus used the feminine gender for this noun.

On other occasions, information about the Latin language comes from even more indirect routes. Our knowledge of the Republican Latin poet Ennius, for example, depends on the survival of fragments of his poetry. Though papyrus fragments (*P.Herc.* 21) likely to come from Book 6 of the *Annales* have been discovered at Herculaneum (Kleve (1990)), for the most part our knowledge of the *Annales*, Ennius' epic poem on Rome in eighteen books, depends on the fragments that have been transmitted as quotations in other texts.

A couple of examples from Ennius' *Annales* can illustrate possible difficulties in obtaining certain knowledge of much fragmentary material. I turn first to an example of the kind of summarising evidence that we are sometimes offered, which does not include direct quotation. In his first book, Lucretius (first-century BCE) famously refers to Ennius' dream in book 1 of the *Annales* (Lucr. 1.117–126):

> Ennius ut noster cecinit qui primus amoeno
> detulit ex Helicone perenni fronde coronam,
> per gentis Italas hominum quae clara clueret;

> etsi praeterea tamen esse Acherusia templa
> Ennius aeternis exponit uersibus edens,
> quo neque permanent animae neque corpora nostra,
> sed quaedam simulacra modis pallentia miris;
> unde sibi exortam semper florentis Homeri
> commemorat speciem lacrimas effundere salsas
> coepisse et rerum naturam expandere dictis.

As our Ennius sang, he who first brought down from pleasant Mount Helicon a garland with perennial foliage, which might be spoken of with renown throughout the Italian nations of men; although Ennius in addition shows, as he holds forth in his eternal verses, that there are nevertheless temples of Acheron [a river of the underworld], to which neither do our bodies nor our souls flow, but certain images of us, pale in wondrous ways; from here he narrates that the appearance of Homer who is always flourishing rose out and began to pour forth salt tears in his presence, and to expound on the nature of the world in words.

This passage raises several methodological issues arising from the use of testimonies such as these in the study of Latin texts. In the first place, the general question is raised as to how far we should go in seeing discernible evidence for the text of Ennius amid the works of Lucretius. Scholarship has in the main taken a positive view of this passage: thus Skutsch (1985) 155 suggests, for instance, that the phrase *Acherusia templa* appears to be Ennian, pointing out that the phrase also appears in Ennius' dramatic works: *Acherusia templa alta Orci saluete infera*, "hail temples of Acheron, deep depths of Orcus" (Enn. *Trag.* 98, from the *Andromacha*). However, this ignores the possibility that Lucretius may be recalling two passages from Ennius at the same time, combining a reference on the larger scale to the passage from the *Annales* with a precise verbal reminiscence of a passage from Ennius' dramatic works (*Acherusia templa* is moreover a phrase which Lucretius repeats on two other occasions, at 3.25 and 3.86). Such multiple allusion is a common technique in Latin literature, but the moral from this is that we should perhaps be less confident that the phrase *Acherusia templa* actually appeared in Ennius' *Annales*, even if it is found elsewhere in his works. And in the previous line of this passage from Lucretius, we may come to similar conclusions on the phrase *clara clueret*, and what this can tell us about another passage of Ennius, *Ann.* 12–13 (which also neatly illustrates some of the issues involved in the transmission of direct quotations), lines which are printed thus by Skutsch (1985) 71:

> Latos <per> populos res atque poemata nostra
> <   clara> cluebunt

Our subject and our poems will be spoken of <with renown (*clara*)> <through (*per*)> the broad peoples.

In its original transmission (in an anonymous grammarian) this fragment appears as *latos populos res atque poemata nostra cluebant*, which cannot be fitted into the hexameter metre: the insertion of *per* is thus reasonable. *cluebant*, moreoever, cannot have directly followed *nostra* as the metre would again be impossible: it is thus to be inferred that there is a gap between *nostra* and *cluebant* which would fall in a subsequent hexameter line. Debate over whether to retain the transmitted reading *cluebant* or the future *cluebunt*, a conjecture (which gives a confident expression of hope for future fame), has largely subsided in favour of the emendation *cluebunt*. But what about *clara* in this passage of Ennius? As with *per* in the previous line, the presence of angle brackets indicates that an addition has been made to the transmitted text. But what is the basis for inserting the word? Skutsch (1985) 168 explains in his commentary that the insertion, made by an earlier scholar, is supported by the passage of Lucretius quoted above. But once again, we might choose to wonder instead whether Lucretius' use of the word *clara* necessarily indicates that the word was present in Ennius: it is not, after all, an uncommon pattern of allusion to find a later poet echoing the wording or indeed the thought of a predecessor, but at the same time making changes to the phrasing. Moreover, Lucretius' phrasing *per gentis Italas hominum quae clara clueret* may in any case be another example of simultaneous allusion to another fragment of Ennius, in this case Enn. s*cen.* 366, *esse per gentes cluebat omnium miserrimus*, "was spoken of through the nations as most wretched of all", so that the claim that it is possible to reconstruct Ennius' usage of *clara* in the *Annales* on the basis of Lucretius seems even more difficult. This passage, I hope, shows the difficulties that sometimes arise with indirect testimony for a lost text, and the problems that those addressing the Latin language in such fragmentary material need to confront: before making assumptions about the usages of Latin in early poets such as Ennius, it is always worth considering the nature of the evidence available.

My second example is an instance of direct attestation of a line of Ennius. Enn. *Ann.* 166 is a line of verse which we know of through two later sources, Festus 412 and Nonius Marcellus 226.33. The verse appears as follows in Skutsch's edition of Ennius:

> nomine Burrus uti memorant a stirpe supremo
>
> Burrus by name, from the highest lineage, as they relate.

In this line, there is uncertainty in the evidence that relates to each of the first three words. Thus the word *nomine*, "by name", is found in the line as it is transmitted by Festus, but in Nonius Marcellus' version of the line, the first word is *homines*, "men", which would be a nominative plural subject of the verb *memorant*, "they relate". Skutsch, in his edition of Ennius, rejects the idea that *homines* might be correct on the grounds that this is an intervention from a scribe, trying to provide a subject for the verb *memorant*. Part of the issue depends on whether or not the previous line in Ennius' fragments (*Ann.* 165) joins immediately with *Ann.* 166 or not: there is debate on this issue (Skutsch (1985) 332). Secondly, the nineteenth-century scholar Emil Baehrens considered replacing the word *uti* with genitive *Iouis* ("of Jupiter"), to be construed with *a stirpe supremo*, with *memorant* thus being deemed to be a parenthesis outside the syntax of the rest of the sentence, though the parenthesis makes the syntax awkward. The final problem relates to the second word, *Burrus*. The manuscript evidence of both Festus and Nonius Marcellus would point to a reading *Pyrrhus*, which is the normal form of the proper name of the Epirot king found in Classical Latin. However, there are traces of the form *Burrus* in the Ennius papyrus finds (Kleve (1990) 15), and there is also a secondary piece of evidence from antiquity, found in the works of Cicero (*Orat.* 160):

> Burrum semper Ennius, numquam Pyrrhum
>
> Ennius always says "Burrus", never does he say "Pyrrhus".

What has therefore happened is that, in the transmission of this line of Ennius in later ancient sources, Festus and Nonius Marcellus, the original spelling *Burrus* (also given as an example of the usage of *b*, but without attribution or context, by Quint. *Inst.* 1.4.15) has been overwritten, and has been replaced with the classical form *Pyrrhus*. The normalisation of the surviving manuscripts for Festus and Nonius Marcellus would have left us unaware of what Ennius actually wrote, were it not for the accident of the survival of Cicero's account that Ennius wrote the name as *Burrus*. This single example illustrates how our knowledge of the Latin language is always in a sense filtered through the way in which Latin texts are transmitted to us.

Standardisation

The phenomenon of standardisation does not only occur in the historical transmission of Latin texts, but is also evident in the production of scholarly editions. Thus, in the introduction to his influential edition of the *Annales* of Ennius, Otto Skutsch explained that he had modernised spellings in the text, in order to spare his readers the horror of seeing unfamiliar Latin forms: "As is customary in editing early Latin texts I have in the main used the classical spelling, refusing to shock the reader with *Olumpum* and *sopiam*" (Skutsch (1985) 68).

This practice, which might seem reasonable from the perspective of introducing readers to Ennius who are familiar with later classical epic poetry such as Virgil, shows the difficulties inherent in the use of textual evidence in constructing the history of the Latin language. The tendency of scribes to normalise spellings finds its counterpart in modern editorial practice. Thus Quintilian's evidence, mentioned above, for the double *ss* spelling in words such as *causa* being found in the autograph copies of works by Cicero and Virgil has had little effect on the presentation of such words in modern editions of literary texts: forms like *caussa* are generally very rare (though for an exception, see the discussion of Virgilian orthography in Coleman (1977) 37–40).

Orthography has been a matter of concern throughout the history of classical literature and its reception, both during antiquity and afterwards. Thus a fragment of the second-century BCE satirist Lucilius addresses the issue of assimilation of prepositional elements like *ad* ("to") into compound words and how they might be written (Lucil. 375–6 Marx):

> atque accurrere scribas
> "d"ne an "c" non est quod quaeras eque labores

> And whether you are to write *accurrere* ["to run to"] with a *d* [*adcurrere*] or a *c* [*accurrere*], there is no reason that you should investigate and toil over this.

This line might on the one hand be felt to point towards a happy freedom in the approach to the assimilation of prepositional elements in compound words such as *accurrere* (= *ad* + *currrere*), but at the same time, the fact that Lucilius considers it necessary to make such a claim might suggest that there is anxiety over what the correct forms might be. The point can also be made, as Quintilian would later observe (*Inst.* 1.7.11), that orthography is liable to change according to usage, and is certainly not something which is inflexible.

Against that, we have to set the fact that orthography has often been an area of almost ideological conflict in classical scholarship. Thus, in the late nineteenth century, it is possible to note the demands of scholarly bodies such as the American Philological Association that the spelling of Latin in American texts be regularised, mainly with a view to making reading easier for those learning the language (see "Proceedings for July 1895." *TAPhA* 26 (1895): liv–lv. and "Proceedings of the 28th Annual Session 1896." *TAPhA* 27 (1896): xxii–xxiv.)). These issues were also discussed in British journals in the same era (see, for example, the contribution of an American scholar, Buck (1899) 116–119), and similarly, in 1905, a group of scholars in the United Kingdom appointed by the Classical Association, including A.E. Housman and J.P. Postgate, published a short article in which they called for information from scholars in determining the spelling of various Latin words for which the spelling was uncertain (Conway *et al.* (1905)). The kinds of information which these scholars were appealing for are of interest: they included the spellings of "*good* inscriptions" (original italics), "good manuscripts" and modern discussions of orthography (Conway *et al.* (1905) 6). The use of the word "good", to characterise both inscriptions and manuscripts, is a pointer to the ideological element involved here. It is thus essential to recognise that the phenomenon we see in Skutsch's edition of Ennius, the desire to regularise orthography, not only has its roots in antiquity, but also has a place in the longer history of classical scholarship.

A Sample of Manuscript Evidence

While there is a strong tendency in the editing of classical texts to regularise forms of words, usually to a standard of spelling characteristic of the later first century CE, manuscripts themselves also have their own dynamics in the presentation of texts. It will be useful to give a brief transcription of a section of text as presented in a manuscript, and then to set it alongside the same passage as presented in a standard critical edition.

Figure 4.2 shows a page from the Oxford manuscript of Catullus mentioned above, *O* (Canonicianus class. lat. 30). The page shows part of poem 63, a poem written in the difficult galliambic metre, which deals with the frenzied religious experience of Attis as he castrates himself and abandons his current life for the worship of the mother goddess, Cybele. It will be seen from the (slightly cropped) photograph that the text does not occupy all of the available space on the page, and also that there is extensive use of abbreviations (which have been resolved in the transcription here). Below is a transcription of the last seven lines of the page, where Attis begins to lament his situation, followed by the text of these lines as it is printed in Mynors' Oxford Classical Text:

Transcription of the manuscript

Patria omei creatrix omea genitrix
Ego quam miser relinquens dominos ut herifuge
Famuli solent adide tetuli memora pedem
Vt caput niuem et ferarum gelida stabilia forem
Et earum omnia adirem furibunda latibula
Vbi nam aut quibus locis te positam patriam reor
Cupit ipsa popula atte sibi derigere aciem

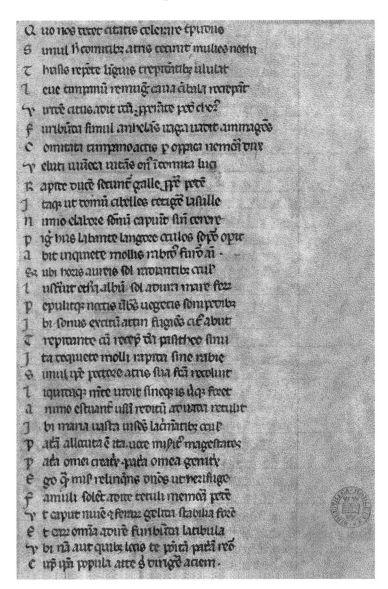

Figure 4.2 MS Canonicianus class. lat. 30, f. 20r., showing Catullus 63.26–56. Reproduced by kind permission of the Bodleian Library, Oxford.

Oxford Classical Text ((Mynors (1958) 56)

patria o mei creatrix, patria o mei genetrix,   50
ego quam miser relinquens, dominos ut erifugae
famuli solent, ad Idae tetuli nemora pedem,
ut aput niuem et ferarum gelida stabula forem,
et earum omnia adirem furibunda latibula,
ubinam aut quibus locis te positam, patria, reor?   55
cupit ipsa pupula ad te sibi derigere aciem,

O homeland that created me, o homeland that is a mother to me, which I am leaving in wretchedness, as runaway slaves are accustomed to leave their masters, I have brought my steps to the woods of Ida, so that I might be amid the snow and the cold shelters of wild beasts, and that I might approach all their lairs in a frenzy, where or in what places can I think of you as situated, my homeland? The very pupil [of my eye] desires to direct its gaze at you for itself, ...

This small passage of text exhibits a number of features which are worth commenting on. In the first place, note the confusion of *stabula*, "shelters", in line 53, with *stabilia*, a form of the adjective *stabilis*. In line 52, the manuscript's *memora*, suggesting the adjective *memor*, "remembering", cannot stand, but is an easy confusion from *nemora*, since it is by no means difficult for a scribe to write an incorrect number of minims (vertical strokes), so that *n* and *m* can frequently be confused. In line 55, the reading *patriam*, with the horizontal line over the final *a* indicating the accusative *patriam* (the very small vertical line over the horizontal line may be an immediate attempt at deletion by the original scribe or a later reader's intervention) shows how a word can be attracted into the grammatical case of an adjacent word, so that the feminine accusative *positam* may have caused a scribe to see the next word as *patriam*, rather than understand *patria* as vocative. And consider the intriguing error *caput*, "head", in line 53, which appears in Mynors' edition as *aput*, an alternative ancient spelling of *apud* (on which see Leo (1912) 248–251). The argument here would be that scribes unfamiliar with the form *aput* wrote *caput*, "head", instead (note, incidentally, that the other two oldest manuscripts of Catullus have the readings *caput* (*G*) and *capud* (*R*), which suggests that *caput* was present in the lost Verona manuscript, *V*, as well). The reading *caput* may well reflect an ancient stage in the transmission, but it cannot be said with certainty that *aput* was the spelling used by Catullus himself. Another detail: note the reading *popula*, which does not make sense as Latin, but is perhaps a psychological corruption of the unfamiliar word *pupula*, "pupil" (of the eye), on the basis of the much more familiar Latin word *populus*, "people". Additionally, the reading *omnia*, which appears in the manuscript and in many editions, has nevertheless been called into question, as has *earum* in the same line (see e.g. Harrison and Heyworth (1998) 104). *Earum* is of particular interest, methodologically speaking, to the student of the language, since an argument which has been used against it is the rarity of the form in verse usage (on which see further e.g. Butterfield (2008a), especially 166–167). It can be seen here that debates over frequency of usage themselves play a part in defining when contested instances of particular linguistic usages are accepted. Finally, I note the adjective *furibunda*, which has occasioned debate about its gender. Is *furibunda* feminine, agreeing with a now emasculated and feminised Attis? This seems the most natural reading. On the other hand line 51 contains the masculine form *miser*, also applied to Attis. Here scholars have suggested that the masculine can be defended, because Attis is referring to his past, but it is also of interest to note that it was suggested by Fröhlich that *miser* might be emended to feminine *misera* (on the issue of the transmitted genders in the poem, see Fordyce (1978) 264)). Can *furibunda* in line 54 be satisfactorily applied to Attis, seen as feminine in spite of the transmitted reading *miser* in line 51? One scholar has even argued that the line should be deleted altogether (see Trappes-Lomax (2007) 165). Our understanding of how the Latin language can be used is thus bound up with our view of what is offered by the manuscripts available to us, even in such an ostensibly "literary" issue as the presentation of gender identity in Catullus' extraordinary poem.

This brief examination of a short passage as documented in the readings of a single manuscript has, I hope, given an indication of the kind of difficulties which can arise in the transmission of texts. It should not, of course, be assumed that all texts present quite such a concentration of problems in so short a space all of the time (and the unfamiliar and difficult galliambic metre of Catullus' poem can hardly have helped scribes), and there are, of course, passages where the reading of a manuscript might be indistinguishable from modern editions, even in texts where there has traditionally been doubt and uncertainty. To give one example from a text which is widely recognised as requiring significant intervention from editors to make sense of a difficult transmission, it is nevertheless the case that a reader of the first ten lines or so of Propertius 1.4 who consults the twelfth-century manuscript *N*, the oldest witness to the text of Propertius, will nevertheless find little to distinguish the readings of the manuscript from those found in a modern critical edition.

Traces of the Unusual

Though manuscripts have a strong tendency towards regularisation of forms, on occasion a manuscript tradition will defiantly preserve evidence of what is rare and unusual. A simple example of this is provided in the text of Aulus Gellius, the second-century CE scholar. At 13.14.1, Gellius quotes a definition of the *pomerium*, the legal boundary of the city of Rome (Marshall (1990) 396):

> pomerium est locus intra agrum effatum per totius urbis circuitum pone muros regionibus certeis determinatus, qui facit finem urbani auspicii.

> The *pomerium* is a place designated with fixed boundaries [*certeis regionibus*] within the countryside demarcated by the augurs [*agrum effatum*] through the circuit of the whole city behind the walls, which makes the boundary of the city's auspices.

Here the manuscripts of Gellius offer various possibilities for *certeis*, "fixed, certain", which in standard Classical Latin would regularly be written as *certis*. Some read *certe is* (O^2N), some have *certe his* ($O^1\Pi$), while another group ($F^2X^2\delta$) reads *certis*, which would represent a normalising reading. However, the reading *certeis* appears to be found in the first hands of two manuscripts, *F* and *X* (F^1X^1), where later hands have, as we have seen, corrected to the more normal spelling *certis*. The reading *certeis* is of particular interest as it may reflect an older orthography, where long *i* is represented with *ei* (on this digraph, see Wallace, chapter 2 in this volume). Curiously, this kind of spelling is discussed by Gellius later on in connection with the orthographical views of Nigidius Figulus (Gel. 13.26.4), but is itself not greatly represented in the extant manuscripts of Gellius himself, in spite of Gellius' own taste for various other kinds of archaising linguistic features. In the present case, the range of evidence points strongly to the older orthography *certeis*: as well as the reading *certeis* found in F^1 and X^1, the other readings *certe is* and *certe his* seem to be attempts to resolve the presence of *certeis* in the tradition by a scribe unfamiliar with this form. The weight of the different readings found here thus points to the validity of the reading *certeis*, and we have here perhaps (especially as Gellius' tendency is not to use the *ei* form for long *i* elsewhere) a reflection of the historical form used in the document that was quoted by Gellius. This example thus both illustrates the tendency for scribes to normalise readings to something more familiar, either by updating spelling or by looking to "correct" difficulties, and shows how, on occasion, a manuscript tradition can still provide a witness to linguistic rarities which have somehow survived the uncertainty of the scribes involved in their transmission.

On occasion, manuscript evidence reflects the older history of the language even when the particular words are confused by scribes. Thus at Prop. 2.26.53–4, many manuscripts offer the following text:

> crede mihi, nobis mitescet Scylla, nec umquam
> alternante uorans uasta Charybdis aqua.

> Believe me, Scylla will grow gentle for us, and vast Charybdis never devouring as the tide changes.

Here, there is a significant problem, as the sense should be that both Scylla and Charybdis, fearful monsters that are associated with the travels of Odysseus in the *Odyssey*, will become gentle. The presence of *nec umquam*, literally "not ever", is problematic, since the negative appears contradictory: the sense should be that Charybdis normally devours her victims, but in these circumstances will not do so. However, as was pointed out by Housman ((1888) 7, cf. (1893) 192, and also discussed by Heyworth (2007b) 228), the reading *uorans* is likely to have been derived from *uocans*, the reading which has now been found in the manuscript *S*. On the surface, *uocans* appears to be a meaningless reading, as it is not easy to understand how Charybdis might never be calling. However, Housman realised that *uocans* could in fact represent an older orthography of the word *uacans*, a word which was originally spelt as *uocans*: with *uacans*, the sense is then "and vast Charybdis, never free from the changing tide [will grow gentle for us]". The corruption from *uocans*, which might have given no sense to a scribe who was unfamiliar with this orthography, to *uorans* is not a complicated one, as it involves a change of only one letter, *c* to *r*, letters which in many scripts might in any case look very similar to each other. Moreover, *uocare* and *uacare* occur as variant readings not infrequently in other texts as well: consider e.g. Gel. 13.13.4, where the Oxford Classical Text presents Gellius' quotation from Varro (*Antiquitates rerum humanarum* bk 21 fr. 3) as follows (Marshall (1990) 396):

> Qui potestatem neque uocationis populi uiritim habent neque prensionis, eos magistratus a priuato in ius quoque uocari est potestas.

> There is also the possibility for those magistrates who have the power neither of summoning the people on an individual basis nor of holding anyone to be called to law by a private citizen.

Strikingly, in this passage, as well as the reading *uocari* ($F^2X^2\Pi NZ$), adopted in P.K. Marshall's Oxford text, we also find the reading *uacari* (F^1OX^1Q). It is very hard to see how *uacari* might be satisfactorily construed here, not just because of the very difficult passive present infinitive, but also because there is no obvious sense even if we emend to *uacare* (construing *in ius ... uacare* as "to be available for a law(suit)" runs aground on the instrumental ablative *a priuato*, which is then left hanging). Nevertheless, note that two of the manuscripts which offer the reading *uacari*, *F¹* and *X¹*, are the same two manuscripts which offer the more historical reading *certeis* in the passage from Gellius we have looked at previously. Intriguingly, two manuscripts which were able to transmit a historically older reading of the adjective *certeis* appear to have erred here, possibly in some strange confusion of *uocari* and *uacari* based on a scribe's garbled awareness of the older spelling.

It is useful to recognise as well that there are documented occasions where archaic spellings in manuscripts appear to be have been deliberately introduced at later stages in the transmission: a famous instance is the British Library manuscript Egerton 3027, used by Joseph Scaliger in his edition of Catullus, a fifteenth-century manuscript inscribed by the poet Pacificus Maximus Asculanus (Grafton (1983) 166–167). There is also an equivalent danger in looking to introduce archaic forms which may not be needed: thus at Catullus 55.22 *dum uestri sim particeps amoris*, "provided that I might share in your love", Scaliger suggested that the variant reading *nostri*, "our", in his manuscript was concealing the older form of *uestri* ("your"), *uostri*, but while this would of course be a simple corruption, it is also the case that confusion between Latin *uester* and *noster* is in any case extremely common (especially when the words are abbreviated, as noted by Housman, (1894) 253, citing an example at Catul. 71.3), so that *nostri* cannot with any certainty be said to be a corruption of *uostri* as opposed to *uestri* (Grafton (1983) 174–175).

Punctuation

"The punctuation of a classical text involves the imposition of modern conventions upon an alien environment" (Heyworth (2007a) liii). As with orthographical practice in modern editions of classical texts, so too is punctuation an issue where it is salutary to remind ourselves that the printed texts used as regular points of reference today are punctuated with a view to modern readers and their experience of punctuation in their own native languages: indeed Heyworth goes on to explain that his Oxford text of Propertius will be punctuated "in the style that is most familiar to me as a writer of English" (liv). It is perhaps useful at this point to say a little about the conventions of punctuation which developed over the history of the transmission of Latin texts.

During antiquity various practices in the marking of texts can be observed, so that it is difficult to speak in overall terms of Latin punctuation as if it can be understood in monolithic terms. Nevertheless, some major features can be mentioned, such as the use of interpunction (the insertion of a point between words; see further Wallace, chapter 2 in this volume), which can be seen not only in surviving Latin papyri from antiquity but also in inscriptions (though it is worth noting that the practice of interpunction appears to have gone into decline from the second century CE onwards; see further Anderson, Parsons and Nisbet (1979) 131–132). But there is also a range of ancient evidence for other kinds of marking (and uses of space) of Latin texts, which have more in common with modern punctuation as a means of marking different kinds of pause, typically at the ends of grammatical constituents. These marking practices can be linked to ancient treatments of pauses, such as the discussion of how to read the opening lines of the *Aeneid* offered by Quintilian, who considers where one might use *distinctio* ("separation"), a pause which might be followed by a new thread in the sense, and two kinds of lesser pause (*Inst.* 11.3.35–8; see further Habinek (1985) 42–88).

If we turn to the presentation of punctuation in manuscripts, a complex picture emerges, with considerable variation occurring over time. The demise of interpunction within antiquity, even in long texts written in capital scripts, can be seen as heralding the more widespread problem for readers of manuscripts who may not be sure of where to apply word-divisions. Some of the late antique evidence for the text of Virgil includes early attempts at providing punctuation: thus the Medicean manuscript of Virgil (*M*), written in rustic capitals dating from the fifth century, uses dots for punctuation in three positions after words, high, low and medium, with the high dot corresponding to the strongest pause, Quintilian's *distinctio*, and the other two dots denoting lesser pauses (see further Habinek (1985) 81–87 on punctuation in this and other late antique manuscripts). But significant too is the fact that the manuscript indicates that the text was pointed by Turcius Rufus Apronianus Asterius, consul of 494 CE, since that would imply that the manuscript in its original form did not have any marks of pointing. What follows in later periods, however, is a much more varied picture, with a wider range of marking practice (including no marks at all), as well as developments such as the appearance of the earliest forerunners of the modern question mark (Bischoff (1990) 169–173). More modern punctuation of Latin texts would evolve as a result of developments during the Renaissance, including the arrival of printing itself, which was a strong force in the direction of greater standardisation. Before leaving punctuation, a word is in order about one area of modern punctuation which is perhaps most removed from ancient practice, namely parenthesis, where there is no marked equivalent to the modern use of brackets until around 1400 (Parkes (1993) 48–49). The significance of this for the study of the Latin language is that readers were clearly able to cope with quite elaborate parenthetical structures which did not need to be physically marked as such, such as Catullus 65, where the entire poem is effectively one long sentence, beginning with a concessive clause (lines 1–4) marked with *etsi* ("although"), in which the poet explains his personal difficulties, followed by an explanatory parenthesis (lines 5–14), marked off with dashes in the Oxford Classical Text (Mynors (1958) 74–75), in which the poet talks of the loss of his brother, followed finally by the main clause of the sentence which answers the earlier *etsi* with *tamen* ("all the same", "however"), as the poet explains that he will nevertheless provide the poem's addressee with a translation from the Greek poet Callimachus in order to meet a promise that he has made (lines 15–24). The presence of a parenthesis of ten lines in length in the middle of a single sentence of twenty-four lines which comprises the entire poem is a powerful reminder of the powers of memory one might associate with ancient readers, not merely in terms of their ability to recall texts which had been studied before, but also in understanding the complex syntax with which they could on occasion be presented.

Conclusion

Latin texts transmitted in manuscript form are of course crucial evidence for the understanding of the Latin language. At the same time, it is, however, essential to recognise that manuscripts exhibit their own conventions, which can reflect both the era of their production, and more long-standing tendencies to standardise the Latin language. So too the modern critical editions which furnish our evidence for the history of Latin in literary texts themselves engage in processes of standardisation in areas such as punctuation and orthography. The processes of transmitting and editing Latin texts, even in manuscript, help to define the boundaries of our understanding of the Latin language, but it is also the case that such texts themselves form a major part of our evidence for Latin. It is perhaps useful to conclude with an example which shows on a wider level the extent to which conceptions of the nature of Latin usage in effect become almost ideological, determining our sense of what individual readings within texts might or might not have been.

An issue which arises not infrequently in textual scholarship concerns arguments about the boundaries of acceptable Latin. Naturally, appeal can be made to parallel illustrations of usage and meaning, but on occasion wider debates about the stylistic features of given authors have created problems for editors. The *Siluae* of Statius, for instance, where our knowledge of all the poems found in the five books bar one (*Silv.* 2.7, first attested in a ninth-century *florilegium*) depends upon a fifteenth-century manuscript, *M*, which was copied in 1417 or 1418 for Poggio Bracciolini during a visit he had made to the Council of Constance. This manuscript, which Poggio himself described as having been written for him by a scribe who was "the most ignorant of all living persons (one has to proceed by divination, not by reading)", has occasioned a wide spectrum of responses from textual scholars. Undoubtedly, there are on occasion some serious problems, such as gaps in the text and there are even instances where meaningless words are found, such as *rotagae* at the end of the line at *Silv.* 5.1.82. Considered more broadly, scholars have either been reluctant to emend the *Siluae* or have been ready to propose numerous conjectures. Much of the debate in particular instances has depended on views as to Statius' style and whether or not he has pushed the language to the limits. To give one example, at *Silv.* 5.5.33–34, Statius speaks of his grief at the loss of a child, and his need to take recourse to his poetry. The transmitted text in the manuscript *M* of these lines (barring the fairly minor Renaissance correction of *M*'s error *incomite* to *incompte*) is as follows:

> iuuat heu, iuuat inlaudabile carmen
> fundere et incompte miserum laudare dolorem.

> It helps, alas, it helps to pour out a song that is not to be praised, and to praise a wretched grief in disarray.

Here, there have been attempts to defend the phrase *laudare dolorem*: the German scholar Vollmer, for example, attempted to argue that the song of praise for Statius' grief for his child is put together poorly, and that the song is hence described as *inlaudabile*, "not to be praised" in the previous line (Vollmer (1898) 550–551). Before Vollmer, Gronovius had attempted to connect the transmitted *laudare* with the practice of the *laudatio funebris*, the Roman funeral oration. While in Latin it is possible for *laudo* to be used in such as a way as to refer to a funeral oration of praise (compare e.g. Pliny, *Ep.* 2.1.6 *laudatus est a consule Cornelio Tacito*, "he was praised [in a funeral oration] by the consul Cornelius Tacitus"), it is harder to see how *laudare* with *dolorem* as the object could possibly convey this sense, as Markland observed in the eighteenth century (Markland (1827 [1728]) 406). Subsequent editors of this passage have tended to adopt scholarly conjectures, such as Markland's own suggestion of *nudare* (which gives the sense "to lay bare his grief"), on the basis that *laudare* might have intruded into the text because of the nearby presence of *inlaudabile* (a very frequent type of phenomenon), although a few have retained the transmitted text *laudare*.

The significance of examples such as this for the student of language is that our conceptions of the boundaries of Latinity shape the way in which we can view the manuscript evidence that we have for the Latin language. If we think that Statius is a poet who pushes the Latin language to the limits, then we might be inclined to follow Vollmer and consider *laudare dolorem* as a paradoxical formation that conveys the idea of praising in the midst of grief. On the other hand, if we have a sceptical attitude to difficult phrases like this, we might be inclined to reach for the conjectures of later scholars. The evidence of texts transmitted in manuscript is thus at times conditional in character, and dependent on our existing understandings and views of what the Latin language actually is. Whereas an inscription on stone from antiquity might be felt to give a record of Latin usage at a given moment, the evidence of a text found in manuscript must always be seen as mediated and potentially affected by the processes of transmission.

FURTHER READING

Reynolds and Wilson (1991) is an invaluable general account of textual transmissions in both Latin and Greek, while for more detail on specific Latin textual traditions, see Reynolds (1983). Critical editions of Latin authors published in series such as the Oxford Classical Texts and the Bibliotheca Teubneriana are essential sources for detailed information on the readings provided by manuscripts. On palaeography, Bischoff (1990) gives a useful introduction to Latin palaeography; Thompson (2008), a revision of the original 1912 edition, is a much older work, but offers an extremely extensive collection of photographic examples of ancient and medieval scripts. For a complete facsimile of the Oxford manuscript of Catullus discussed in this chapter, see Mynors (1966).

Useful treatments of orthographic practice and punctuation in Latin are somewhat scattered. The following discussions are, however, indicative of the kinds of work that have been undertaken in this area: Goold (1965), especially 9–18 on orthography and punctuation, Housman (1910), on the forms of Greek names in Latin poetry, Kenney (1986), Parkes (1993) and Tarrant (1998). On textual criticism in general, see Kenney (1974); on Latin textual criticism in antiquity (including Servius), see Zetzel (1981). For an outstanding recent work of textual scholarship, see Heyworth (2007b), a full-length treatment of textual issues to accompany Heyworth's Oxford Classical Text (2007a) of Propertius.

CHAPTER 5

Romance Languages as a Source for Spoken Latin

Roger Wright

Latin and Romance

Latin was the main language of the Roman Empire, all round the Mediterranean, but it only survived as a spoken language in about half of that geographical area after the fifth century. The eastern part of the empire had always been predominantly Greek-speaking and became increasingly so, including Egypt and Cyrenaica on the southern shores of the Mediterranean as well as Constantinople and the Byzantine Empire. In the north, in what is now southern Germany and in the Low Countries, Latin was lost as a spoken vernacular in favour of various newly arrived forms of Germanic; in the British Isles, it gave way to the pre-existing Celtic and the subsequent Germanic. Then in the seventh century, African Latin (or Early Afro-Romance), between Carthage and the Atlantic, began to be overtaken by Arabic. As a result, the surviving Romance-speaking area in the latter half of the first millennium CE was considerably smaller than the Latin-speaking area had been. Subsequently Romance languages have spread to most of the Americas, much of Africa and some of Asia, but between the time of the world-wide language status of Latin and those of Spanish, Portuguese and French, there lies a long period of relatively insignificant prestige. The language was continuously developing all the time; and by the end of the first millennium CE, although not so obviously before, it was noticeably developing in different ways in different places. In due course, natural internal divergence within a multivariant Romance led to the fragmentation into the conceptually separate Romance languages that we can see attested in the twelfth and thirteenth centuries (a fragmentation largely promoted by political agendas rather than linguistic facts on the ground). Essentially the Romance languages are Latin, only later, in the same way as Modern Greek is the same language as Ancient Greek, only later; so it is natural and intriguing to speculate on whether Romance tells us something about the nature of spoken Latin.

A Companion to the Latin Language, First Edition. Edited by James Clackson.
© 2011 Blackwell Publishing Ltd. Published 2011 by Blackwell Publishing Ltd.

It has sometimes proved tempting to believe that Latin acquired a perfect canonical form some 2,000 years ago, and that it has somehow remained essentially the same since the age of Cicero. After all, the Latin which some of us have had to learn in school is essentially the Latin of that time. But we are all simultaneously aware of the existence of the modern Romance languages which developed from Latin; and so for many years the development of the Romance languages seemed to be a problem in need of an explanation. Yet the development of historical linguistics has shown that linguistic change over time is a natural process only to be expected; that is, the fact that Latin changed during the centuries is in itself in no need of any explanation, since that is what always happens, albeit at a faster or slower rhythm in different contexts. The way in which Latin changed into what has come to be called Romance, the way in which Romance has internally diverged and then fragmented into the separate entities now known as the Romance languages, the way in which these entities came to acquire different names, and the way in which even erudite Latin continued into the modern world as a separate entity from Romance, are four complex questions which deserve detailed consideration; but the fact of change itself is unsurprising.

And change was always occurring. The Latin of 2,000 years ago acquired a canonical status as the "best" Latin, but it too was dynamic rather than static. What is attested there is a kind of snapshot of a particular point during the continuous development from what we call Indo-European through what we call Italic, Latin, Romance and then separately the different Romance languages; culturally, and indeed sociolinguistically, it is a period of great significance, but linguistically there is no reason to see the language of that period as in any sense "better" than the stages which preceded or followed it.

We can take nominal morphology as an example here. The system which we are given in modern grammatical textbooks goes back to the morphological characterizations established by Aelius Donatus in the fourth century CE; nouns have six "cases", inflectional suffixes, known as the nominative, vocative, accusative, genitive, dative and ablative, in both the singular and the plural. But in historical perspective this is just one fluid stage in the evolution from earlier times, in which there had been further cases (including the locative), to subsequent periods in which first the ablative and then the other oblique cases were gradually going to stop being used in nouns in speech. Indeed, the locative was still perceptible in texts of this so-called Classical period, and there was already no distinctively ablative inflection in the plural. The nominal morphology is presented as a geometrically neat system in B.H. Kennedy's *Primer* (which ultimately derives from Donatus), but at the time it was in dynamic evolution. It is difficult to see the patterns of that period as preferable to those of earlier or later times; there are many potential methods for explaining the meanings expressed by the locative, ablative, dative and genitive inflections, and the inflections used by speakers of the first century were not necessarily better or worse in any functional sense than the prepositions which increasingly came to be used during the first millennium CE.

If we can accept that the developmental period which came to be chosen as the standard for "correct" Latin by subsequent grammarians, the one to be imitated subsequently by serious literary writers, was chosen for reasons other than the linguistic, then it becomes clear that the subsequent changes should not be regarded as examples of corruption, decay, decadence or barbarism. They often have been, but it makes no more sense to criticize the speech of 800 CE on the grounds of not being the same as the speech of 800 years earlier than it would to criticize Cicero for not using the same kind of language as Ennius, or to criticize Ennius for not speaking proper Indo-European.

The language changes, and if new features seem inappropriately new-fangled for some time, old features also seem inappropriately archaic after a while. That is, Latin was always moving. It may not always be easy for us now to see what was happening, and when, but we can no longer accept the view that Latin only began to develop significantly from its idealized fixed state in the fifth century, as the Western Empire collapsed politically, or in the seventh century, as has sometimes been claimed.

The variation apparently inherent in all linguistic communities existed in Latin. Grammarians were then, and probably always have been, temperamentally inclined to dislike variation; presented with two possible ways of pronouncing the same word, for example, rather than simply saying that there are two such ways, they often prefer to decree that one way is "correct" and that any others, either by implication or explicitly, are "incorrect". The "incorrect" methods are often ascribed to laziness, corruption, or in the Latin case "barbarism", but even if these descriptions have occasionally contained a grain of truth, that does not make them any the less worth investigating. We should try to understand why, for example, the ablative case no longer seemed worth bothering with, and why the use of prepositions deriving chronologically from Latin DE followed by forms of nouns deriving from accusatives came increasingly to appear preferable to the inherited genitives to express possessive and related meanings.

Variation has several facets. Some are sociolinguistic: some groups prefer to speak with these features, while other groups prefer to speak in this other way. The Romans themselves were particularly aware of this as regards the differences between the way country people and city people spoke. These differences can be geographical; people speak this way in one part of the world, but that way in that other area. The Romans realized that as well, as we see in the tales of visitors to Rome, even those who acquired some social status (including one or two emperors), whose speech betrayed the fact that they came originally from Spain or Africa. Such geographical particularities trumped those of social class or levels of education; St Augustine of Hippo (in Africa) suffered such opprobrium in Milan. Variational differences can depend on style or register, both in speech and in writing, even in the same person. Writing tends to be more formal than speech, but this is not a rigid distinction, and in the case of Cicero it seems to be diametrically wrong: that is, his letters are in a less formal style than his speeches, although the latter are really in effect written compositions as well. It is odd to see Cicero regularly held up as the standard of correctness when his letters seem to exemplify details characteristic of a less formal style; individuals vary with themselves as well as with each other.

And some linguistic variation is the consequence of diachronic developments. Features characteristic of an earlier age can gradually fall into disuse overall but still appear for centuries in some styles, registers, geographical areas or social contexts. This fact could worry grammarians, temperamentally wishing to admire the *antiqui* but unsure whether to follow them in their use of, for example, the letter *u* rather than *i* in the middle of *maxumus*. It also means that genitive inflections, for example, can occur in post-imperial documentation alongside the newly spreading prepositional phrases with DE. What seems normal at one period can seem archaic at a later period, but even then the features can take a long time to stop being used altogether; genitives are still there now, for example, in Romance pronouns in some areas. Italian *loro*, developing from ILLORUM, is still a possessive pronoun rather than an adjective; we can tell this from the fact that it is invariant, as in *le loro bottiglie* ("their bottles") in which *loro* is specifically neither feminine nor plural (not **le lore bottiglie*), unlike French *leurs* which has become an inflecting adjective. Documentation of a thousand years ago, in both written Old Romance and Late Latin, still seemed to have no qualms about attesting genitive forms of proper names; *ecclesia Sancte Marie*, for example, "The Church of Holy Mary", was normal, rather than "*de Sancta Maria*".

Any individual diachronic change tends to take a long time to complete, and it may or may not be traceable at the time in written evidence. It is not a single event. A phenomenon describable with hindsight as a "linguistic change" involves at least three separate stages, none of which implies that the following stages are necessarily likely to happen at all. The first stage is the arrival of a new linguistic feature: a new way of pronouncing a word or a phoneme (which might lead to a sound change), or a new suffix or phrase to express a syntactic relationship (possibly leading to a morphological or syntactic change), or a new meaning for an existing word (perhaps leading to a semantic change), or a new word (a lexical change). Not everybody adopts the new usage at once, or at the same time, so it is at first (unless it disappears again) just one of two or more available variants. Thus the second stage involved in a linguistic change is one of variation between old and new; in our sample Latin case, this is the stage when both genitive inflections and the use of DE with the same meaning are available, acceptable and comprehensible in all parts of the community; or, similarly, when intervocalic /-t-/ could be represented as either (old) [t] or (new) [d] in words such as that written VITA; or when the old synthetic future tense forms (such as *cantabo*) coexisted with new futures composed with an infinitive and a modal auxiliary (such as *habeo cantare*); or when new and old words coincided with the same meaning, such as (older) *equus* and (newer) *caballus* for "horse". This variation stage can be long, and need not ever end (indeed, EQUA in the feminine is still there in Spanish *yegua*, "mare"); and if indeed it does end, it is not necessarily the case that the older variant is the one that drops out and the newer variant is the one which survives. There was, for example, a move to combine *con* (< CUM) and *elo* (< ILLUM) as a single word *cono* in tenth-century northern Spain, which was thus then in variation with the older two-word phrase *con elo*, but the latter, older, alternative is the one that survives in Castilian (as *con él*). What we call in retrospect a "linguistic change" has only occurred once the third stage has been reached, in which the older feature falls out of usage, if it ever does. If all we do is compare first-century (Latin) and thirteenth-century (Romance) usage, as handbooks tend to do, we can declare that, for example, [-t-] > [-d-] in several areas, but that ignores and elides the long period of variation between [-t-] and [-d-] for /-t-/ that must have intervened at some time (even if we have difficulty in dating it precisely).

For many reasons, then, it is impossible to answer the question "When did Latin change into Romance?" Changes are not single datable events; there are many different factors involved which do not coincide chronologically. Indeed, it seems unnecessary even to try to distinguish Latin from Romance as metalinguistically separate entities until we approach the end of the first millennium CE, which is when the speakers first hesitantly and inconsistently began to make that kind of distinction themselves; and even then, at first the label "romance" was only used to refer to new modes of writing, rather than of speaking. The only reason that modern Romanists make this distinction on their behalf is that the "correct" Latin usage came into general consciousness as a result of the activities of the grammarians, who described several features in their works as being part of Latin and thereby by implication suggested that the features that were not mentioned in the grammars were in some way "incorrect" Latin, or indeed not Latin at all. The most influential of these writers in later times was the fourth-century teacher Aelius Donatus (who trained Jerome), whose *Ars Minor* eventually went onto the Carolingian educational syllabus as the initial teaching primer. In the fourth-century context, Donatus was concentrating on explaining how to understand the writers of three centuries earlier, and hardly considering speech at all. Much of his *Ars* details nominal morphology, presumably because much of it was gradually falling out of use at the time and his readers and students needed this advice. Naturally, in cases where variation existed in the fourth century, he concentrated on variants that were respectably antiquated. As time went on, the *Ars Minor* of Donatus changed status, from descriptive (implying "this is what happened in the respected ancient texts") to prescriptive (taken to imply "this is how you ought to be writing now"). Thus the way in which trainee scribes were taught to write increasingly implied a need to imitate features current in the distant past, and this in turn led to writing and speaking becoming increasingly different from each other, to an extent which it is not simple for us to reconstruct now.

The phrase "Vulgar Latin", coined in the nineteenth century by Hugo Schuchardt, is unfortunate, but has come into common usage among scholars. József Herman defined Vulgar Latin as a collective label for those features of Latin which we can be sure did exist, but which were not recommended by the grammarians. It should not be, although it often has been, envisaged as being a separate language (or "system") co-existing with "Classical" Latin. Both terms are ambiguous, and probably best avoided: all the styles and periods might as well be included under the umbrella of "Latin", *tout court.*

"Romance" is no clearer a word when applied to these centuries. The word is sometimes used as an alternative label for what others call Vulgar Latin, implying that Latin and Early Romance were then, and are now in retrospect, clearly distinct simultaneous entities. This perspective could only command adherence before the development of sociolinguistics which has made clear that variation is normal within a single language, and we need not assume that the existence of synonymous variants (such as DE and genitives, or AMABO and AMARE plus an auxiliary) implies that they each belong to a different language (or "system"). It is true, of course, that by the second millennium CE it had become normal to distinguish, at least in some contexts, Latin and Romance as separate entities; but it now seems anachronistic to postulate such a mental distinction as existing before the seventh century, and probably (for reasons there is no room to go into now) before the Carolingian "Renaissance" of *c.* 800 CE. Attested features in writing of the period preceding this separation of Latin and Romance may well therefore be direct evidence of the spoken usage of that time (inasmuch as written evidence can be taken to attest speech anywhere): e.g. when St Benedict of Nursia in the sixth century CE used both *manducare* and *comedere* to mean "eat" in his Monastic Rule, it is reasonable to take that as evidence for both words being used at that time and in that area; but it is a pointless argument to discuss whether these uses attest sixth-century southern Italian "Latin" or "Romance", as if that had been a real distinction in St Benedict's context. It makes it awkward for us, but we need to realize that calling the spoken language of pre-Carolingian post-imperial times (*c.* 400–800 CE) "Latin" (or "Late Latin" or "Vulgar Latin") or "Romance" (or "Early Romance") is only a terminological distinction. There was just one language there, however variable it was in increasingly elastic and complex ways.

The word *romance* (from ROMANICE, and variously spelt) was first used as a linguistic label (that is, as a noun, rather than as earlier an adverb) to refer to the newly written modes which we see now as being the initial textual evidence for its existence. Earlier, *romanice* and *latine* seem to have been essentially synonymous terms, even in the writings of ninth-century Carolingians. It has thus been tempting to deduce that it is only with the arrival of undisguised written Romance texts, composed and written down in the second millennium by intellectuals consciously breaking free of the Donatan grammatical tradition in which they had been trained, and consequently deliberately representing spoken features in both the orthography and the morphology, that we have clear evidence of what Romance actually was. But it has not always been sufficiently appreciated that spoken word order and vocabulary had always been represented in unpretentious texts in every period; the final break came with the decision to abandon the old spellings and nominal inflections. Thus it was that the practitioners of Romance reconstruction, most notably Robert A. Hall Jr. in the USA and Robert De Dardel in Europe, felt justified in ignoring all the textual evidence produced between the end of the Roman Empire and the elaborations of written Romance, on the grounds that those who wrote these texts may well indeed have been speaking Romance but were writing Latin, envisaged within this scholarly perspective as being a separate language throughout. There is a grain of truth in this, of course, because many writers deliberately imitated the past, sometimes using exaggeratedly convoluted techniques (e.g. many of the writers from Visigothic Spain); but others were less determined to disguise their own speech habits. The reconstruction scholars were inspired by the apparently successful techniques used by the investigators into Proto-Indo-European (PIE); we think we know a great deal now about the ancestor of the Indo-European languages, as spoken 5,000 or 6,000 years ago, long before the invention of writing, because of the reconstruction techniques based on arguing backwards from the written evidence of several millennia later. There was no alternative available; there is no other evidence; without reconstruction, we would get nowhere in the PIE case. But this does not mean that the specialists deliberately ignore any new written evidence that is turned up by the archaeologists; if the Romance reconstructors really wished to follow the example of the investigators into PIE, they would as avidly study the many texts which survive from the first millennium. But these scholars ignored those and based their analytical techniques on the earliest undisguisedly Romance texts instead, apparently on the assumption that these indeed did directly and in reliable detail attest the language of their time and place. This confidence betrays an exaggerated vision at the other end of the same spectrum, because written language has never been an exact photographic counterpart of all the features of speech, not even in the thirteenth century, but for their purposes it sufficed.

Phonology and Phonetics: Vowels

Despite all the criticisms that can be and have been levelled at Robert Hall and his colleagues, they achieved something important. Looking back from the several Romance languages as attested a millennium later, they discovered genuinely valuable details about spoken Latin, particularly as regards pronunciation. They thought that they had discovered a separate linguistic entity, which they called "Proto-Romance", in effect misdiagnosing a normal state of variation for one of bilingualism, and this misconception is still able to lead occasionally to confusions; but on the whole most of their phonetic reconstructions are generally accepted as valid for the spoken Latin of at least the later period of the empire. These include the general loss of phonemic length distinctions for vowels, deducible, for example, from the fact that no Romance variety seems to have made any difference between the evolution of Latin short [a] and long [aː]. The other vowels show geographical differences; in Sardinia and Africa, the other four vowel phonemes lost length distinctions in the same way as [a], as for example [e] and [eː] merged as [e], and [i] and [iː] as [i]; but in the rest of the Romance area, [eː] and [i] merged as [e], [iː] survived as [i] and short [e] as an open [ɛ]. These reconstructable differences led these analysts not only to postulate that a Proto-Romance existed as a separate language alongside Latin, but that it split at an early period into separate Proto-Romance languages such as Proto-Italo-Romance, Proto-Hispano-Romance and Proto-Gallo-Romance. This needless proliferation of separately nameable metalinguistic entities was dated to a chronologically astonishing early time; Proto-Sardinian Romance was even said to have emerged in the third century BCE. This implausible dating annoyed the Latinists, given that there is no historical evidence nor, indeed, evidence in contemporary texts to suggest that Sardinians were not part of the same general wide Latin-speaking community as everybody else. It has never been made clear how the Proto-Romance analysts dated their discoveries; the postulated vowel developments are real enough, but their postulated existence as the sole phonetic realization of the phonemes concerned, as opposed to being new co-existing variant alternatives, is not. The dating of the definitive loss of the old length distinctions from speech, which undoubtedly happened at some point (since they do not exist at all in Romance), need not have happened at all soon after the initial manifestations of speech styles which lacked them. Dating a change is difficult, as we have seen above; roughly dating the arrival of the new is often possible, usually depending on a textually attested *terminus ante quem*; but even roughly dating the loss of the old from speech is almost impossible, given authors' propensity to wish to imitate the *antiqui*. Metric composition, based on the vocalic length distinctions, never died out, despite the rise of the so-called "rhythmic" verse (which was more often based on syllable counts than on rhythm, in the event); but it could be that this remained possible after the loss of the length distinctions precisely because the grammarians, and the commentators on Virgil in particular, were there to tell aspiring poets how it could be done. Twentieth-century schoolboys in various countries could still compose metric Latin verse without knowing such length distinctions in their own native languages for essentially the same reason.

So it makes sense to ignore the reconstructionists' datings while accepting their discoveries. We can accept, therefore, that there came a time at some point when Sardinian and African speakers failed to merge [eː] and [i] while most or all speakers elsewhere were doing just that. The chronological evidence for the differentiation can be deduced by Latinists looking at contemporary written evidence, particularly in this case the African epigraphy, which has led Adams to the conclusion that African Latin did not merge [eː] and [i] at the same time that the vowels were confused by speakers in Gaul (Adams (2007) 636–649). The Latinists could in theory carry on this research independently of the Romanists, but it is inevitably helpful to all concerned if their conclusions can coincide, or at least refrain from being incompatible. Philip Burton's analysis of the language of the Vulgate, for example, shows that it is hardly "vulgar", but his analysis has benefited greatly from a knowledge of the main lines of Romance evolution. The more that Latinists and Romanists meet and discuss the data of mutual interest, the better for us all.

Still in the area of vowels, the Romance evidence suggests that Latin diphthongs had variant single vowel realizations from as early as the empire; thus the original [aj] diphthong found in a word such as QUAERO must have developed to an open [ɛ] in time for it to diphthongize again in stressed position to [jé] in the regular way in Castile (QUAERO > Spanish *quiero*, as the [ɛ́] of TERRAS > *tierras* did, etc.). Dating of these developments is even less clear than it is in most cases; the [aj] > [ɛ] one could have been the earliest (and the consequent confusion in spelling between *ae* and *e* is common from an early date), but [oj] > [e], as in POENAS > Spanish *penas* may not have been far behind. The reason for suggesting that [oj] became [e] rather than [ɛ] is simply that these words did not go on to rediphthongize in the way that [ɛ] did, including in words where [ɛ́] developed from [aj]. Thus the data allow us to argue with some certainty for a sequence [áj] > [ɛ́] > [jé] in such words as *quiero* < QUAERO, implying that the monophthongization process was mainly completed before the new diphthongization process got under way, which in turn allows us to suggest that the first development spread long before the end of the empire; but absolute dating is impossible on this evidence alone, and needs, when it is available, assistance from datable epigraphic data, from comments by grammarians, and (in the case of vowels) from the rhythmic, metric and rhyming habits of poets and versifiers of various kinds. One other monophthongization whose initial stages are attributable to the imperial centuries – that is, both the newer and the older realizations could have been available then in some places or styles – is that of [aw], which in most Romance regions became [o] and did not subsequently rediphthongize (so presumably becoming closed [o], rather than the more open alternative which did indeed diphthongize: as in e.g. BONUM > Italian *buono*); but in Portugal it remains diphthongal as [ow] written as *ou* (e.g. AURUM > Portuguese *ouro*, compared with Spanish *oro*).

These diphthongizations of the open mid vowels varied from place to place in the Romance world, which suggests that the main spread of the phenomenon happened later than the end of the empire. Such a dating is probable rather than provable, however. The effects of syncope and apocope vary even more; the different trajectories of e.g. the word for "thirteen", TREDECIM, which became monosyllabic French *treize*, disyllabic Castilian *trece* and trisyllabic standard Italian *tredici*, show how the effects of vowel-dropping could eventually vary widely geographically. Even so, it is likely that the initial examples occurred during the empire, particularly in cases where the resulting consonant clusters were already phonotactically acceptable (unlike the cluster [-dk-] resulting from losing the middle vowel of TREDECIM), such as the [-kl-] in the many words ending in the suffix which was written -ICULUM but often pronounced [-íklo] without the first [u]. The pronunciation of unstressed /i/ and /e/ as semivocalic [j] when immediately next to another vowel, in words such as FORTIA [fórtja], was probably also widespread.

Phonology and Phonetics: Consonants

Consonantal developments from standard Latin were mostly conditioned, varying according to their position in a word and the nature of the following vowel or consonant. But it seems likely, given the rules of elision in metric verse, that [h] was not pronounced in imperial times in any case, regardless of the spelling; HOMO gives Italian *uomo*, and

HOMINEM French *homme* and Castilian *hombre*, but the French and Spanish spellings with initial *h-* were erudite inventions of a much later age; Old Castilian, for example, had the written form *omne*, and French *on*, from the same lexical etymon, still has no *h-*. The only case of a general consonantal development that happened regardless of a sound's position in a word is that of the palatalization of the velar plosives [g] and [k], but even this only happened before a front vowel, [e] or [i], and semivocalic [j]. Thus a word such as GEMMA came to be pronounced with an initial palatal affricate similar to both consonants in the English word *judge*, as it still is in standard Italian *gemma*; this may well have occurred relatively early, but the subsequent deaffrication to the sound of French *gemme* (and the subsequent revelarization to [x] in Castilian *gema*) are much later. The unvoiced [k] also palatalized before front vowels; in this case the difference between the palatal affricate [tʃ] (as in both consonants in the English word *church*) found in Italian *cielo* < CAELUM and the more forward alveolar [ts] found in the Old French and Old Castilian pronunciations of *ciel* and *cielo* respectively, might possibly have already been incipiently audible in the fifth century.

Otherwise, Romance consonantal evolution depended mostly on the sound's position in the word. Initial consonants, other than the velar plosives followed by front vowels already mentioned, usually remained as they were; a notable exception is the apparent [f-] > [h-] development found in Old Castile and a few other regions. The use of [h-] in the Romance of Basque-speaking bilingual areas has led to some strange analyses; the explanation may be that the Latin /f-/ of e.g. FACERE had an aspirated (less occluded) allophonic variant from the earliest times of Roman settlement in that area, perhaps similar to [pʰ], and the Basque-speakers preferred to generalize that, not having at that time words with initial [f-] (although they do now). Since Latin-speakers further east tended to adopt Greek words with [ph] as Latin [f] there was certainly a perceptible connection of some kind, but the regularity of the [f] resolution in such words as Italian *filosofia* suggests that [f] for /f/ was the most common allophone, although perhaps it only became the default case in the late rather than the early empire. Other initial changes in Romance, including the palatalization of [ka-] in northern France in words such as *chat* < CATTUM and *chien* < CANEM, happened later; there is no sign of this development elsewhere, and CATTUM even developed its initial sound in a different and unexpected direction in Italy (*gatto*) and Spain (*gato*).

Word-final consonants, on the other hand, often disappeared in spoken Early Romance, with the exception of [-s] in more western and northern areas. Italy, indeed, seems to have been more enthusiastic than elsewhere in this respect: thus POST lost the [-t] everywhere, leaving *pues* in Castilian (which still has the [-s], despite changing its meaning) and *puis* in France (which had [-s] in Old French, but has lost it now), but *poi* in Standard Italian, where [-s] > [-j] was a common development. EST became French *est* (which has no consonants at all now, despite the spelling, but did in Old French), Spanish *es* [es] and Italian *è* [e]. An interesting variant on this theme occurs in third-person plural verb morphology, with e.g. CANTANT becoming monosyllabic French *chantent* (still written with a "silent" *-ent*), disyllabic *cantan* in Castile (where originally final [-n] dropped, as in NON > *no*, but originally penultimate [n] survived), and eventually trisyllabic Italian *cantano*, preserving the [-n] but then also satisfying the Italians' apparently insatiable desire not to have word-final consonants at all by adding the etymologically peculiar but phonotactically satisfactory [-o] which seems so natural now to Italians and so odd to other Romance-speakers. It seems from all this that the existence of a weakened or even absent variant allophone of word-final [-t] is fairly early, but the subsequent developments must be too late to be attributed to imperial times. The loss of [-t] took a long while to become definitive everywhere, in any event; the spelling of French, modern as well as medieval, suggests that the /-t/ was still there in some phonetic guise in at least some verb forms as spoken by at least some people in France only 1,000 years ago.

Initial consonant clusters usually remained in Romance; e.g. French *traire* < TRAHERE, Italian *breve* < BREVEM, etc. But there are two notable exceptions. The first concerns the initial clusters of [s-] followed by a consonant. Early Romance seems to have developed a rule whereby a preconsonantal [s] could only be syllable-final. Word-internally, there was no problem; whether such clusters as [-st-] had originally been heterosyllabic or not, they could be phonologically reclassified that way, even in cases of vowel-final prefixes (such as the RE- of RESPONDERE). Word-initially, the consequence seems to have been the unwitting adoption of an additional epenthetic front vowel. In Late Antiquity this vowel was even sometimes written down, as both *i-* and *e-*; some of St Isidore of Seville's etymologies (of the early seventh century) only work, for example, if this vowel is seen as integral to both words etymologically connected in his analysis. The most startling example of this concerns two words said to be related to ESCA ("bait"; or more generally "food"): ISCURRA ("parasite", *Origines* 10.152) and ESCARUS ("a kind of maritime fish", *Origines* 12.6.30), words more normally written as SCURRA and SCARUS. Such words as *espacio* < SPATIUM, *espada* < SPATAM, still have initial [es-] in Castilian Spanish, where modern borrowings such as Anglicisms even now require this epenthesis; hence Spanish *estrés*, from English *stress*, is disyllabic, with both its syllable-final [-es] sequences sounding identical. The epenthetic vowels survived as either [es-] or [e-] in vernacular French (*espace* < SPATIUM, *épée* < SPATAM), which still have the initial [e-] even though for the last 500 years French-speakers have had no problem in coining neologisms with [sC-]; Old Italian usually used the [i-] variant (e.g. *ispazio*), but then reversed the tendency to such an extent that not only are *spazio* and *spada* normal, with initial unvoiced [sC-], but there are also now Italian words with initial voiced [zC-] clusters unknown to both Latin and most other varieties of Romance, such as the [zb-] in *sbaglio* and the [zdr-] in *sdrucire*. It is tempting to date the initial arrival of variant pronunciations manifesting this epenthesis to two or three centuries earlier than Isidore, but direct manifestations of its existence are not obviously that early, and there is no sign of it in the poetry of the empire.

The other remarkable Romance development involving initial clusters concerns words beginning with [pl-] and [kl-]. In standard Italian, [pl-] develops to [pj-] and [kl-] develops to [kj-], as in PLENUM > *pieno* and CLAVEM > *chiave*. In Castile, both [pl-] and [kl-] became the palatal lateral [λ] (as in English *million*): *lleno* < PLENUM and *llave* < CLAVEM. In Portugal, the change went even further: both became the palatal sibilant fricative [ʃ], as in PLENUM > *cheio* [ʃéju] and CLAVEM> *chave* [ʃáv]. In France and Catalonia the clusters remained unchanged, as in French *plein* and *clef*, Catalan *plę* and *clau*. This distribution might suggest that the southern developments were post-imperial, but in this case the Romanian evidence is interesting: in Romania, PLENUM > *plin* (unchanged) but CLAVEM> *cheie*, which seems to imply both that the [kl-] clusters developed first and that the [kl-] began to palatalize before the late third century CE.

Intervocalic unvoiced single consonants (and [-Cr-] clusters) to the north and west of Tuscany usually become voiced; thus APRILEM > French *avril*, Portuguese, Castilian and

Catalan *abril*, but Italian *aprile* and Romanian *aprilie*. In the same areas, voiced intervocalic consonants fricativized and often, though not always, disappeared, especially in France; thus BIBERE > French *boire*, Catalan *beure* and (northern) Italian *bere*, but Portuguese and Castilian *beber*. The disappearance of the intervocalic voiced consonant is not predictable; the Italian and western Iberian results opted the other way round in CREDERE > French *croire*, Castilian *creer*, Portuguese *crer*, Catalan *creure* and Italian *credere*. Alveolar intervocalics, and [-m-], usually remained unchanged, although in Portugal [-l-] and [-n-] eventually tended to disappear also; thus LANAM > Castilian and Italian *lana*, Catalan *llana*, French *laine*, but Portuguese *lã* (with a nasal vowel).

Intervocalic geminates, in the same northern and western Romance regions, became single, while remaining geminate further east. French spelling sometimes obscures this development; in Italian *gemma* < GEMMA, for example, the -*mm*- spelling indeed represents a geminate pronunciation [-mm-], but French *gemme* is not geminate, being pronounced with [-m-] (as is Castilian *gema*); neither is French *battre*, which has [-t-] as Castilian *batir* does, rather than the [-tt-] of Italian *battere*.

The relative and absolute chronology of the intervocalic consonantal changes have been much debated. There is clearly some connection between the degemination of geminates, the voicing of the unvoiced, and the potential disappearance of the voiced, in the western areas. The fact that the degeminated unvoiced consonants, such as the [-t-] < [-tt-] in the old Romance words deriving from Latin MITTERE, CATTUM, GUTTAS, etc., never then progressed to become voiced, implies that the voicing process was effectively completed before these degeminated single [-t-]s turned up as potential input; nowhere in the Spanish-speaking world, for example, is the word for "cat" **gado or the word for "put" **meder. The newly voiced intervocalics did eventually fricativize, but that fricativization was chronologically secondary, happening long after the first change of e.g. [-d-] > [-ð] in words such as CREDERE. This seems to imply a chronological sequence in which the change [-d-] > [-ð-] was largely over by the time that [-t-] > [-d-] got going, and then that voicing process in turn was largely complete before the degeminations built up steam. The apparently required chronological leeway is such that the initial stage in the sequence, ([-d-] > [-ð-]), and possibly also the first manifestations of the second stage (i.e. /-t-/ acquiring a sociolinguistic variant [-d-]), probably need to be assigned to the time of the empire. A drag-chain of this type, in which /-d-/ vacated the [-d-] slot in the phonetic structure, leaving it available for /-t-/ to exploit, and subsequently the [-t-] slot was similarly left vacant and available for /-tt-/ to use, is generally considered to be more plausible a scenario than a push-chain would be (and the existence of push-chains may just be a myth anyway).

Those intervocalic clusters in which the consonants were not tautosyllabic tended to simplify via the loss of the initial component of the pair, since that was by definition syllable-final. Thus [ns] became [s], and definitely did so in imperial times, as shown by numerous attestations in the epigraphic data (such as COSUL for CONSUL), including reverse hypercorrections such as HERCULENS; also [ps] > [s], as in IPSAS (> Castilian *esas*), etc. Some cases in which the second, syllable-initial, component was [n] became palatalized; this happened to the cluster [gn], which is why in France and Italy the letters *gn* came in due course to be used to represent the palatal consonant. Similarly, [ks], represented in Latin by the letter *x*, tended to lose the [k] and palatalize the sibilant, leading to [ʃ] (as in Italy LAXARE > *lasciare*); in Castile, [-kt-] and [-lt-] preserved the [t] to end up as [tʃ] (e.g. LACTEM > *leche*), but that is a good example of a localized development which is so local that it cannot have happened earlier than the time of definitive divergence. Similarly, the semivocalic [j] which developed from unstressed [e] and [i] in hiatus with another vowel was probably heard in imperial times, but the Romance developments in which it changed the nature of an adjacent consonant needed the [j] to have arisen first, so are unlikely to have been widespread already then.

A stress accent certainly existed in the later part of the empire, and maybe all the way through; the Latin grammarians who used the model of Greek grammars to claim a pitch accent for themselves are now widely thought to have misunderstood their exemplar, and in addition modern scholars might well have misunderstood their Latin forebears. A pattern whereby one syllable in any word of two syllables or more was pronounced louder than the others, with the stress being allocated on fairly clear general principles, seems a secure deduction for the fourth century and probably much earlier (with the likely complicating factor of the presence of clitic words that were not stressed at all); this pattern survived in essence in modern Romance apart from eventually in northern France, where a different accentual pattern arrived much later. Very few words in Romance have changed the syllable which is stressed. But there may well have been words which were sometimes phonetically unstressed and other times stressed, with no difference in their written representation to manifest this now, as happens in English (compare the clitic pronouns in [əsóːhɪm] and stressed pronouns in [ájsohím], both written as *I saw him*); the fact that subsequent Romance languages, unlike Latin, distinguish graphically and phonologically between atonic and tonic pronouns (e.g. French *me* and *moi*, Italian *mi* and *me*) has led some Romanists to believe that Latin had no clitic pronouns; but that is likely to be an overstatement.

Similarly, the facts of elision in quantitative metric verse, and the regular and apparently deliberate avoidance of the possibility of elision in qualitative rhythmical verse (which was more often based on syllable count than on rhythm), suggest that sandhi was a feature of Latin colloquial speech as it is almost everywhere else. But sandhi was always a variant, in that word-final vowels always needed to be pronounced before a following word beginning with a consonant, which remained the majority. Compound-internal sandhi, and in particular the assimilated variants of prefixes, could provide another source of variation, and indeed conscious disagreement among grammarians, with reference to both speech and writing; should one elide, for example, the [-n] of CONLOQUIUM as [l], and/or write *colloquium*? The phrasing of such dilemmas seems to imply that the [n] was almost never audible in such cases, whatever the orthography advocated.

Overall, then, we can be certain that the pronunciation of spoken Latin continued to change at all times, and we know quite a bit from the subsequent vicissitudes of Romance concerning the nature, and sometimes the relative chronology, of the changes; but absolute datings on the basis of the Romance evidence would be hard to achieve.

Nominal Morphology

The morphology of the Early Romance languages in general varied greatly from that of Latin in nouns and adjectives, in that the nominal inflections disappeared; and also in the verbs, even though those inflections continued in use, because new paradigms were formed to supplement the many that continued from before. There may well have been some kind of direct connection between the phonetic developments and the collapse of the main systems of nominal inflection; in the first declension, for example, the loss of [-m] and of the phonological distinction between long and short vowels meant that the forms written as ROSA, the nominative, used to express the sentence subject, originally [rosa] with a short [a], ROSAM, the accusative, used to express the direct object, originally [rosam], and ROSA, the ablative, used mainly after prepositions, originally [rosaː] with a long [aː], all came to have [-a]; and since ROSAE, originally [rosaj] but in due course [rose], was already multiply ambiguous between the genitive singular used to indicate possession, the dative singular used to indicate the indirect object, and the nominative plural (and the vocative also, should that ever have arisen), the potential ambiguities were ever increasing. Similar awkwardness could apply also to the second-declension nouns, and the masculine forms of adjectives, such that accusative singular BONUM and dative and ablative singular BONO came to represent the same pronunciation in the many areas where short [u] and long [oː] developed to the same sound, [o], and similarly nominative singular BONUS and accusative plural BONOS coincided (creating a homonymic clash still operative in Old French); and in third-declension forms where nominative singular CIVIS and plural CIVES came to be pronounced the same way after the loss of the distinction between [i] and [eː]. There were, however, also a number of nominal inflections whose phonetic distinctiveness remained, even if the precise pronunciation changed; e.g. the first- and second-declension genitive plural forms in -ARUM and -ORUM remained distinctive even after they came to be generally pronounced [-aro] and [oro], as did their dative and ablative plurals in -IS ([íːs]), and their third-declension equivalents in -IBUS even after these were generally realized as [-eβos]; but despite their phonetic distinctiveness, all the ablative, dative and genitive forms all fell out of use eventually, probably in that chronological order rather than all at once.

This long drawn-out process surely began in the imperial period, and, indeed, was no more than a continuation of an on-going centuries-old process of replacing inflections with prepositions. In any event, prepositions came to be used more and more with the originally accusative forms of the noun to indicate the meaning previously embodied in the inflection. The ablative inflections could be dropped anyway without serious consequences, having little meaning of their own. The preposition AD (usually phonetically [a]) was increasingly used in preference to the dative. DE, originally meaning "down from", came to replace the genitive, although for a long time both uses could co-exist in the same text. In some places, AD OR PER came to be used to indicate the direct object, although in France and Italy this option was not pursued and the relative word order was the feature which came instead to have the function of indicating which noun phrase was the subject of a sentence (that in the preverbal position) and which was the direct object (post-verbally). The gradual result of all this, whether precipitated or merely assisted by the phonetic developments, was an increasingly less fluid word order, at least in France and Italy, in Romance than in Latin. A simple sentence containing a subject, a verb and an object, could have any of six possible word orders in Latin; although some orders were commoner than others, the choice seems to have been made on pragmatic rather than grammatical grounds, and none were unacceptable. Much the same applies to modern Castilian, where subjects are often placed after the verb and objects sometimes preposed, with any potential ambiguity averted by the use of *a* before the object; but not in France or Italy. It seems likely, however, that the use of this object-marking *a* only spread at all widely in the second half of the first millennium, so the situation in the fifth century may have been more or less the same geographically over all the Romance speech community, with the subject and the object being statistically likely, but not necessarily, placed respectively preverbally and postverbally as their default positions.

The loss of the subject forms of nouns and adjectives in the Iberian peninsula, and then of many direct object forms in Italy, probably post-dates that stage; France even maintained the distinction between subject and object morphology well into the second millennium CE. But it would be a mistake to deduce from this that the morphological system itself had disappeared from the speakers' competence, because (apart from the ablative) it survived in the pronouns. For example, subject EGO, direct object ME and indirect object MIHI (and the other personal pronoun forms) continued in use, with the further sophistication of developing a contrast between tonic and atonic forms. Clitic pronouns are the most complicated part of modern Romance grammar to analyse. Subject pronouns are now both optional and tonic in most of Romance (e.g. Italian *io* and Castilian *yo*, from EGO, which do not have to be mentioned along with *canto* to mean "I sing") but, in great contrast, obligatory and atonic in France (where *je* has to be included in *je chante*, "I sing"). The reflexive third-person forms derived from SE and SIBI also survive, with wide additional functions, adding to the complexity. Multiple pronoun sequences can occur, in which each has a separate unambiguous function: Spanish *yo te lo mandé* or *te lo mandé yo*, both meaning "I sent it to you", are both unambiguous. The *yo* here can precede or follow the rest, and is optional anyway, but the order of the component parts of *te lo mandé* is as fixed and inseparable as the Latin inflections were, which has led many Romanists to see the *te* and the *lo* in such cases as intrinsic parts of the verb in the same way as the *-é* is, rather than as one or two separate noun phrases. This interesting result must have been still in the future in the first millennium, though, since the pronouns, much used in the texts of all periods, can usually turn up almost anywhere, preverbal or postverbal, either immediately attached to the verb or not, and must still have been noun phrases of their own.

The development of [-s] as a plural marker happened first in the Iberian peninsula, where the accusative forms were usually the only ones to survive, and as a result the only formal difference between singular and plural was a consistent one: in e.g. *rosa* < ROSAM and *rosas* < ROSAS, *bueno* < BONUM and *buenos* < BONOS, *noche* < NOCTEM and *noches* < NOCTES, the only formal difference was the use of the [-s] in the plural. Before long, this identification was so great that originally neuter nouns such as *cuerpos* < CORPUS changed semantically to become plurals, leading to the invention of [-s]-less singulars such as *cuerpo*; they even invented a plural of *quien* (< QUEM) as *quienes*, QUOS having disappeared. This can only have happened post-imperially; in Latin there were so many singulars in [-s], particularly nominatives but also third-declension genitives, and plurals without [-s], again particularly nominatives but also genitives, that it needed the previous reorganization of the morphology to lead to the idea of [-s] indicating plural.

The gender system was also simplified in the nouns, but less so in the pronouns. The neuter category disappeared from the noun system, a process which was probably under way in the later empire; but most of the forms themselves did not. Most neuter singulars came to be reclassified as masculine, given that both their nominative and accusative inflections were often identical to the masculine in -UM ([-o]); thus LIGNUM, neuter, survives as Italian *legno* and Castilian *leño*, masculine; but the neuter plurals ended in [-a] in both nominative and accusative, and these usually became reclassified as feminine singulars, often with a collective meaning and without a further plural form of its own in [-s], as LIGNA became both Italian *legna* and Castilian *leña*, "firewood". This has led to remarkable subsequent complications in Italy, but in imperial times these still lay in the future. Some neuter singulars in -US were reclassified as Romance plurals, as we saw above; but some others ending in [-e] were not obviously destined to be either masculine or feminine, and there will have been some vacillation, a vacillation which is still not fully resolved in the case of Spanish *mar* < MARE, which can be both masculine and (particularly in the usage of actual sailors) feminine.

The use of prepositions rather than inflections has been interpreted as being a part of a more general tendency to move grammatical indicators from after to before their lexical unit; there are several such moves in verb phrases (see below), and another lies in the decreasing use of the comparative and superlative inflections *-ior* and *-issimus*, with a corresponding wider use of either *magis* or *plus* before the adjective. This tendency was probably growing during the imperial period, but it was a slow process. The -IOR ending stopped being productive, and regular formations in -IOR dropped out of use, but the irregular ones such as MELIOR (that is, formally unconnected to the base adjective, BONUS) are still there in Western Romance, having always existed as separately lexicalized entities; French *meilleur*, Italian *migliore*, Portuguese *melhor*, Spanish *mejor*, Catalan *millor*; but Romanian prefers to use *mai bun* (< MAGIS BONUM), and Spanish *más bueno* seems to be an increasingly viable variant, so we may here just have one very long operating change which began in the empire and is not over yet. There is, of course, no reason why the advent of a new alternative should necessarily lead to the total loss of the old.

Verbal Morphology

The development of the verbal morphology was markedly different from that of the nominals. Some paradigms were lost, and others invented, but much of the novelty occurred later than the main changes in the nominal system did, and may have only had a slight presence as variants in the fifth century. The changes have often been presented as symptoms of an increasing general preference for analytic over synthetic forms, although this is only approximately true; one good example concerns the synthetic passive forms, including all those ending in -UR, which in due course disappeared and may have no Romance descendants at all. This tendency seems to have been noticed by Late Antique grammarians and pedagogues who, to judge by the increasing presence of semantically inexplicable *-ur* forms without passive meaning in written texts, seem to have told their apprentice scribes that to add *-ur* to a written verb is a way of elevating the style, rather than conveying any semantic content. But this could also be interpretable as a Late Antique flowering of the category of deponent verbs; if this were true, it would be an unusually clear case of a distinction between written and spoken grammar, given that the deponent category did not survive at all in Romance (which seems to some analysts, including myself, to be a good reason for doubting that this is the explanation).

The synthetic passive forms were only able to disappear because of the increasing presence of semantically acceptable equivalents. The finite synthetic forms were only found anyway in the present, future and imperfect tenses (e.g. AMATUR, AMABITUR and AMABATUR, as compared with the equivalent active forms without the -UR); the growing tendency for the originally past passive participle (in this case, AMATUS) to be used as either a past or as a passive but not as both at once, meant that uses of this participle with the auxiliary SUM, a combination which originally had specifically past passive meaning, preserved the passive semantics but could increasingly come to be used with present reference; that is, AMATUS EST or EST AMATUS, which meant the past passive "he was loved" originally, despite the fact that the auxiliary itself was neither passive nor past, came to be used to mean "he is loved" in the present. This development was helped by the inherent temporal ambiguity of the participle, which could be interpreted either as verbal (in which "the window was broken" refers to an action, e.g. "by Fred, with this brick") or adjectival (in which "the window was broken" refers to a resultant state, e.g. "still not mended, after having been smashed six months earlier"); which means that the construction could be understood with either tense anyway. The result was that when used with SUM these participles lost any inherent tense reference at all, with the tense being indicated instead by the tense of the auxiliary; in this way AMATUS EST came to be semantically present passive, AMATUS ERIT the future, and AMATUS ERAT the imperfect; and in due course the combination AMATUS FUIT (which was not unknown previously) came to be the normal unmarked form for the preterite, which had originally been expressed as AMATUS EST. Written uses with the past of the auxiliary are a good indicator that this change was well under way. The later Romance results have the auxiliary usually preposed: French *il est aimé*, Italian *è amato*, etc.

This was not all. At the same time grammatically reflexive uses of SE, in which the direct object referred to with SE co-refers with the verbal subject, were extending their range to situations which were not semantically reflexive; that is, it was no longer necessarily the case that the referent was both an agent and a patient. This had always been possible in Latin, though a minority usage, with some combinations such as SE HABERE being lexicalized, and even used insouciantly by grammarians who denied its possibility. These cases involved inanimate subjects, and could usually have been rephrased as passives. Thus here there was another already available alternative for speakers who disliked the -UR forms. The particularly Romance development is said to be the use of such expressions with non-agentive animate subjects; as in the modern Romance terms for getting unintentionally sunburnt, such as *se brûler* in France, *bruciarsi* or *abbronzarsi* in Italy and *quemarse* in Spain. Yet this non-agentive human reflexive use is found in Petronius, in the phrase *nec medici se inveniunt*, "and no doctors are to be found", although it is true that it does not find itself being used widely in writing until much later, when it was to spread itself particularly widely in the Iberian peninsula; here it is now the commonest way of expressing simple passive meaning (e.g. *aquí se habla inglés* < SE FABULAT, "English is spoken here", literally "here English speaks itself"). The isolated case in Petronius suggests that this phenomenon existed, and was intelligible, even then; maybe such a vestigial existence applied to many of the morphological and syntactic phenomena which were later to spread and be thought of as Romance (rather than Latin) by modern grammarians.

The development of an auxiliary which could be used in all passive paradigms is not the only such case. Romance languages also have perfect auxiliaries; one or both of the words deriving from HABERE and ESSE accompany the past participle in the modern constructions, creating a regular paradigm with no direct counterpart in the original Latin. Romance languages now vary widely in the formation and the use of these perfects, but older stages of these languages tend to coincide in using the derivative of HABERE for transitive verbs and of ESSE for the intransitive. The origins can again be found in Latin: if HABEO EPISTULAM SCRIPTAM, "I have the letter written", comes over time to imply that the letter has been written by me, qua subject of HABEO, as seems to have happened, the trajectory of SCRIPTAM from adjective to intrinsic part of an analytic verb form is unsurprising. The use with intransitives is more surprising in that these participles were in origin passive (as we have seen above), and intransitive verbs by definition have no passives; but here we are meeting the other half of the decision taken not to keep the originally past passive participles as both past and passive simultaneously. In a transitive verb such as AMARE, EST AMATUS came to be passive but no longer past; in intransitive verbs such as EXIRE ("to go out"), new participles could be analogically invented if they had never existed (often being the same as the already existing supine), being past but not passive, to lead eventually from e.g. EST EXITUS to Italian *è uscito*, "has gone out". The resultant ability to express the perfect unambiguously is a consequence of the spread of such auxiliaries once they were potentially available for such exploitation, and (like the spread of SE) represent a good argument in favour of the view that the development of Romance grammar led to a wider range of expressive options rather than to any kind of decay or corruption; for Latin had originally had no such clear paradigm, and grammars tend to say simply that e.g. AMAVI had both meanings (that is, both "I loved" and "I have loved"). The -AVI forms survived, but as preterites alone, without the alternative perfect semantics.

Latin future tenses also disappeared in the end, to be replaced by analytic forms involving the infinitive and an auxiliary. In Romance, the auxiliary eventually preferred was again HABEO; French *je chanterai*, Italian *canterò* and Spanish *cantaré* all derive from (EGO) CANTARE HABEO. Other auxiliaries were available in several areas, including DEBEO and VOLO, and during Late Antiquity it may only have been in Africa that HABEO had become the sole such auxiliary. The auxiliary eventually chose definitively to follow the infinitive, although there may well at first have been no fixed order for the two constituents. Subsequently the two have fused into syntheticity again, and the cycle has restarted (that is, French *je vais chanter*, Italian *vado a cantare* and Castilian *voy a cantar* have developed as auxiliaried alternatives since). The reason for losing the original synthetic forms such as AMABIT may have lain in a potential homonymic clash with the past tense AMAVIT, but the clash would only have been operative in some first-conjugation forms, and this is likely to have been a contributory rather than a primary cause.

HABEO had tenses of its own, and this led to the development of possibilities previously unenvisaged; the so-called Romance conditional, such as Italian *canterebbe* and Spanish *cantaría*, is usually taken to have developed from CANTARE HABEBAT and/or HABUIT. These are translatable as either "would sing" or "was going to sing", the future as seen from the past. The only clear way of rendering this meaning previously would have been with a future active participle and a past auxiliary (ERAT CANTATURUS); the future participle disappeared from speech, and there may have been some kind of causal relationship between its disappearance and the preference for the less unwieldy conditional paradigms.

The spread of auxiliaries also led eventually to something else quite unknown before; double, or even treble, auxiliaries, such as HABERE HABEO plus participle to mean "will have" (the past as seen from the future), a combination which was in due course preferred to the synthetic future perfect, whose forms survived but as future subjunctives (e.g. Portuguese *cantares* < CANTAVERIS); and this too had a past tense, so "would have sung" would be expressed in Romance in due course by e.g. Spanish *habría cantado*. "Would have been loved" has three: Spanish *habría sido amado*. These possibilities increased further the greater expressive possibilities of Romance as compared to Latin, but were still in the distant future in the fifth century.

The Latin imperfect subjunctive also fell out of use, to be replaced by past subjunctives which had originally had pluperfect semantics: thus Italian past subjunctive *cantasse* comes from CANTAVISSET. This semantic promotion was probably related to the spread of the auxilary form HABUISSET to form pluperfect subjunctives, as in Italian *avesse cantato*, leaving the form *cantasse* available for other uses; as usual, the advent of one form and the loss of the other with the same function presumably did not coincide, and took place via a lengthy period in which the meaning could be expressed either way. This process may have started by the end of the empire.

Latin had four regular verb conjugations; some Romance languages have no more than three. A number of third-conjugation verbs (those with infinitive -ERE, having the stress on the stem) survived as members of the second (-ÉRE) or fourth (-IRE) conjugation, and in Spanish the third category disappeared entirely; e.g. SCRÍBERE > Spanish *escribir* ([eskriβír], as compared with Italian *scrivere* [skrívere]) with analogically adopted regular -*ir* morphology such as preterite *escribió* (that is, no longer being an irregular verb; cp. Italian *scrisse* < SCRIPSIT), and proparoxytonic PÉRDERE > Spanish oxytonic *perder* [perdér] with regular -*er* forms, compared with Italian proparoxytonic *pèrdere* and French paroxytonic *perdre*; there are textual signs in Late Antiquity of the change in the Iberian peninsula. But there had anyway been a number of Latin verbs which were apparently able to belong to both the second and third conjugations at once; it seems plausible to argue that often this ability represented a transitional stage in which both the older (third-conjugation usage, in this case) and newer (second) paradigms could be used and unproblematically understood with the same stem, such that this too is a change well under way in the empire itself; this could have been the extended lexical diffusion of a single morphological change.

Verbal inflections themselves suffered phonetic changes in the same way as all other words, naturally. Romance was to see a number of further analogical developments here, such as the adoption by all Spanish third person singular past indicatives (except *fue* < FUIT) of the inflection [o] or [ó], attributable in the many otherwise etymologically inexplicable cases (such as DIXIT > *dijo*) to the force of analogy based on the regular development of -AVIT > [ó]. But it seems probable that these processes began at a later date than the paradigmatic changes mentioned so far.

Syntax

Compared with the startling developments in morphology, the differences between original Latin and Early Romance syntax were not great. Word order became on average less free as time went on; the separate components of a noun phrase (most obviously, noun and adjective) increasingly came to be found together in written texts, and the verb tended increasingly to come earlier in the sentence, than was normal in the imperial period, but these tendencies had probably characterized speech in any event. They also aided comprehension rather than causing any problem. The best-known development concerns the decreasing use of accusative and infinitive constructions, with a concomitant increasing preference for finite tensed clauses introduced by a complementizer; but these changes are merely statistical, since *quod* clauses for indirect speech were found in Latin, with particular pragmatic implications, and verbs of perception still operate even now with accusative and infinitive constructions; e.g. Italian *ci vede venire*, "she sees us arrive". The statistical tipping-point is dated by József Herman to about 500 CE, when the uses with the conjunction came to be the default construction; *ut* disappeared altogether, but probably later than this.

Latin is said not to have had articles in the way that Romance does. But Romance definite articles developed from the demonstratives ILLE and IPSE, which could be used with an attenuated demonstrative force barely distinguishable from that of a definite article (hence the word "articuloide" sometimes used by Romanists); similarly, the indefinite articles descended from UNUS, of which the meanings "an" and "one" are not always separable. Indeed, most of the syntactic and morphosyntactic developments which are said to be characteristic of Early Romance involved the increasing use for a different purpose (we could say "grammaticalization", if that fashionable term were not currently losing all clarity) of normal words which already existed; they were semantic changes, in effect, in such words as ILLE, UNUS, SE, AD, HABEO, SUM and QUOD. These changes necessitated absolutely no change in orthographic practice, since these words already had a standard written form that could be used regardless of their function; consequently their use is not impossible to find in textual data, and it may overall be reasonable to deduce that the early stages of all or most of these developments were to be found as variants in imperial times. We need not believe a theory that Latin had no clitics or articles, for example.

Modern linguistic theory has placed more stress on the centrality of syntax than it deserves; compared with morphological and phonetic (and even semantic) developments, strictly syntactic changes from Latin to Romance were negligible.

Semantic and Lexical Changes

Semantic changes, in which existing words acquire new meanings, and lexical changes, the arrival of new words, happen all the time in all languages in a mostly atomistic fashion, without obvious general tendencies. Even so, semantic changes can happen in a drag-chain, participating in a chronologically lengthy sequence of cause and effect; for example, the semantic movement of Latin BUCCA from "cheek" to "mouth" (as in French *bouche*, Italian *bocca*, etc.) led to a wide variety of subsequent Romance changes to fill the ensuing lack of of an unambiguous word for "cheek". There are three main mechanisms for filling such potential gaps, and Romance used them all: semantic change, such as happened in Spain where MAXILLA shifted its reference from "jaw" to "cheek" (modern *mejilla*), derivational morphology, such as happened in Portugal, where *bochecha* with a distinguishing and essentially meaningless suffix means "cheek", and lexical borrowing from another language, such as in Italy both *guancia* from Germanic and *ganascia* from

Greek; chronologically, it seems clear that only the initial stages of the change in BUCCA happened in imperial times, with the Romance developments, different in different places, coinciding with each other chronologically later.

Semantic change rarely plays a starring role in handbooks on Romance development; but that is a historical accident of the discipline, for it is not in itself a small area of study so much as one which it has not yet been fashionable to investigate within either historical linguistics or semantics. Even a cursory glance at an etymological dictionary shows us what a large number of words have changed meaning, even if only slightly, over the years. These can at times be explained by extralinguistic cultural changes; for example, the advent of technical Christian vocabulary from the fourth century led most notably to borrowings of words from Greek (such as ἄγγελος), but also to semantic specializations in many already existing words (such as SPIRITUS).

New words were often coined via existing lexemes and affixes. Spoken Latin probably exploited this possibility more enthusiastically than written Latin did, but the increasing use of diminutive suffixes without evident diminutive meaning is quite well attested. The Romance results include such words as French *soleil* (< SOLEM + -ICULUM, no smaller than the Italian *sole*) and the various words for an "ear" of any size (AURICULUM > French *oreille*, Portuguese *orelha*, Spanish *oreja*, Italian *orecchio*, Catalan *orella*, Romanian *ureche*) whose ubiquity implies an early arrival into the lexicon. The suffixal expressivity available to Romance speakers is another symptom of its greater versatility as compared with the standard Latin of grammarians, but the grammars almost certainly obscured the common existence of such formations in spoken Latin reality; this is a good example of where Romance evidence can take priority over Donatus. Suffixes could even be borrowed from Greek, such as the increasingly common causative suffix -IZARE; and free words could become bound affixes, as MENTE "mind" eventually became the adverb-forming suffix -*mente*, "-ly", whether mental activity was involved or not.

Some pairs of near-synonyms saw one of them eventually drop out of usage and the other take over, but these are very often slow developments, with both words surviving a long time even if the distributional statistics changed markedly, or with geographical variation. Thus EDO "I eat" fell out of use, to be replaced by both its prefixed alternative COMEDO and MANDUCO. Modern French *mange* and Italian *mangio* derive from the latter and Iberian *como* from the former, but (as we saw above) both words occur in texts from all over the former empire in Late Antiquity; so the handbooks which tell us that the replacements for EDO were different in different places are at best oversimplifying. The conclusion to be drawn is that often such cases of apparent substitution are prime examples of lengthy variation in practice; e.g. both IGNIS (destined to disappear) and FOCUS (destined to survive everywhere in Romance, as in French *feu* and Italian *fuoco*) were both used to mean "fire" until well after the end of the imperial period; similarly EQUUS and CABALLUS, and other standard cases.

Foreign words used in Latin were almost certainly common during the initial period after the colonization of a new area; but after a couple of generations most such words would fall into disuse as the Latin language became a first language with native speakers in that region, unless there was no alternative word with that meaning in Latin. Thus surviving words tended to be used to refer to local phenomena (geographical, flora and fauna, mining techniques, etc.) and in consequence remained not only local but of obscure etymology, given that many such pre-existing languages fell out of use. Speech would have used more such lexical items than appear in our written data, not least because they did not have a fixed written form. This is most problematic for us in place names, which are often the main, or even the only, evidence for the details of a pre-Roman language, but which are also tantalizingly uncertain in their etymological interpretation and also, as a consequence, prone to remodelling under the influence of popular etymology. Thus the Andalusian town of Cabra (meaning "goat" in Spanish) has a heraldic shield proudly featuring two goats rampant, but that is a historical reinterpretation made in the ninth century of a form deriving from its Latin name IGABRUM, which is well attested epigraphically, of probably "turdetano" origin; and the trail runs cold there, since we cannot know if that was a motivated name in that language, nor for sure how it was then pronounced. But it seems that the Romans tended to preserve an existing name if there was one, although new settlements naturally acquired new toponyms.

Conclusion

The study of Romance languages leads to a number of conclusions concerning the nature of spoken Latin. Widespread features found in Romance probably already existed as variants in speech during the Roman Empire, but this does not mean that the previous features which the Romance ones may seem in retrospect to have neatly replaced had yet fallen into disuse. Written textual data from all periods can be used as a valuable source, so long as the analyst is aware of the natural and necessary differences between speech and writing and indeed reading, since reading (aloud or not) a language which we know nearly always proceeds logographically, by recognizing the word and giving it its normal sound, rather than phonographically, letter by letter. The particular value of the textual data under this perspective, if used with care, is chronological, since features cannot normally appear in writing before they exist in speech (with the possible exception of foreign words being used by an untypically polyglot writer). But above all, the fact that in due course the language changed its name from Latin to French, Spanish and so on should not obscure the fact that the study of Romance languages and the study of Latin are essentially the same research field.

FURTHER READING

Books which cover the development of the Romance languages from Latin include Elcock (1975), R.A. Hall, Jr. (1976), Harris and Vincent (1988), and Wright (1982 and 1996). Adams (2007), Burton (2000), Herman (2000), Vainio (1999), Wright (2002) and the papers in Wright (2008) deal with aspects of Latin pertinent to Romance studies. Janson (2002) and (2004) give readable overviews of language change and the history of Latin. Specific studies on individual Romance languages include Ayres-Bennett (1996) and Lodge (1993) on French; Maiden (1995) on Italian; Harris-Northall (1990) and Penny (2000) and (2002) on Spanish. The external history of the Romance languages is the subject of R.A. Hall, Jr. (1974), for which Ward-Perkins (2005) chapter 7 is also relevant.

PART II

The Language

CHAPTER 6

The Sounds of Latin: Phonology

Matthew McCullagh

Reconstructing Latin Phonology

One popular misconception about corpus languages such as Latin is that, given the absence of native speakers, we can have little or no clear idea of their phonology. The truth, however, is quite different: in fact we have a wide range of evidence for Latin phonology that, in most cases, allows us to reconstruct the sounds of Latin with an impressive degree of certainty and precision. The most important sources of evidence are the following: (1) statements of Latin grammarians and other authors about the pronunciation of Latin; (2) puns, word play and ancient etymologies; (3) representation of Latin words in other languages; (4) later developments in the Romance languages (French, Spanish, Italian, etc.); (5) spelling conventions of Latin, e.g. "mistakes" made by scribes or inscribers; (6) the internal structure of Latin itself, e.g. its metrical structure; and (7) comparative historical evidence from other Indo-European languages.

Reconstruction of the individual sounds of Latin involves combining evidence from two or more of these sources to determine their likely phonetic value, with the particular combination of evidence varying from sound to sound. We can also make use of our extensive modern knowledge of the typical phonological patterns and developments found across languages. By careful use of these various sources of evidence, it has been possible to build up a generally accepted account of Latin phonology, even if a few areas of uncertainty remain.

This chapter will focus on outlining the phonology of educated speakers of Latin during the Classical period. However, our evidence also allows us to recover the main changes that took place during the history of the language, as well as at least some of the synchronic variation in non-standard varieties of Latin, e.g. regional or socially less prestigious varieties. Such non-standard varieties were important for the later history of

A Companion to the Latin Language, First Edition. Edited by James Clackson.
© 2011 Blackwell Publishing Ltd. Published 2011 by Blackwell Publishing Ltd.

Table 6.1 The consonant phonemes of Classical Latin

Manner of articulation		Place of articulation							
		Bilabial	Labiodental	Dental	Alveolar	Palatal	Velar	Labiovelar	Glottal
Stop	Voiceless	P /p/		T /t/			C, K /k/	QV /kʷ/ (?)	
	Voiced	B /b/		D /d/			G /g/	GV /gʷ/ (?)	
	Voiceless Aspirate	[PH /pʰ/]		[TH /tʰ/]			[CH /kʰ/]		
Nasal		M /m/		N /n/			G, N /ŋ/ (?)		
Fricative	Voiceless		F /f/		s /s/				H /h/
	Voiced				[z /z/]				
Trill					R /r/				
Approximant						I /j/		V /w/	
Lateral approximant					L /l/				

the language, as they would ultimately develop into the Romance languages. The more important of these diachronic and synchronic differences in phonology from standard Classical Latin will be mentioned in the discussion below.

The Latin Writing System

The Latin alphabet is ultimately based on the western Greek Euboean alphabet, probably borrowed via an Etruscan intermediary; it underwent a number of modifications during its history (see chapter 2 for details). In general, standard Latin orthography provides an efficient system for representing the sounds of Latin and is close to having a single symbol for each phoneme. The main areas of ambiguity are in the representation of the vowels. Long and short vowels are not distinguished; e.g. <A> represents both /a/ and /a:/ (Latin letter signs are given as small capitals throughout this chapter). However, in this chapter we will follow the practice of most modern handbooks in using the macron (e.g. ā) to mark long vowels. The other main area of ambiguity is that <I> and <V> are used to represent both the approximants /j/ and /w/ and the vowels /i/ and /u/.

Consonants

The consonant phonemes of Classical Latin are set out in Table 6.1 (square brackets indicate phonemes borrowed from Greek).

Double consonants

Consonant length is distinctive in Latin, e.g. *ager* /agɛr/ "field": *agger* /aggɛr/ "mound". Double consonants are written single in early Latin inscriptions; double writing starts to appear around 200 BCE, but is not completely generalised until the end of the century.

Plosives: velars

In early Latin writing systems, <C>, <K>, <Q> are used to represent both voiceless /k/ and voiced /g/. The three symbols loosely follow a system of using <C> before front vowels, <K> before consonants and /a/ and <Q> before back vowels. A similar distribution is found in Etruscan inscriptions from southern Etruria, and the lack of distinction between /k/ and /g/ may also come from Etruscan, since Etruscan lacked a contrast between voiced and voiceless consonants. Subsequently, <C> was generalised to represent /k/ in all positions; <K> was retained only in a few conservative spellings, e.g. *Kalendae* "Kalends"; and <Q> was kept only in the digraph <QV> (see below). In order to distinguish the voiced velar plosive, <G> (i.e. <C> with a line) was developed, and is first found in the third century BCE.

Latin also has the symbol <X>, which represents the cluster /k/ + /s/; this is sporadically written as a digraph on inscriptions (<CS>, <XS>, <CX> and other variations).

Plosives: labiovelars

It is disputed whether the digraphs <QV>, <GV> represent single phonemes, voiceless and voiced labiovelars [kʷ] and [gʷ] respectively, or clusters [kw] and [gw]. None of the arguments that have been advanced on either side seem to be conclusive. For instance, in metrical texts a short vowel before <QV> is normally treated as belonging to a light syllable (see below on syllable structure), thus implying syllabification of, e.g., *liquidus* "liquid" as [lɪ.kʷɪ-]. However, we occasionally find such syllables scanned as heavy, which may indicate syllabification as [lɪk.wɪ-] etc., although this is disputed. Another argument is that Latin <QV> normally continues the IE labiovelar *k^w, which was almost certainly monophonemic. However, since Latin <QV> can also develop from clusters, and, in any case, it is common for a single phoneme to become two (e.g. IE *g^w > English *kw*) and for two phonemes to become one (e.g. IE *tw > Greek *s*), the evidence would actually be compatible with either articulation (see Devine and Stephens (1977) 13–104).

The articulation of <GV> is also disputed, and it is not certain that it necessarily represents the voiced counterpart of <QV>, particularly since the sequence is highly restricted, occurring only after /n/, e.g. *lingua* "tongue", "language".

Plosives: voiceless aspirates

The digraphs <PH>, <TH> and <CH> are first found around 150 BCE, being used to represent the Greek aspirates <φ> ([pʰ]), <θ> ([tʰ] and <χ> ([kʰ]) in loanwords, e.g. *chorus* "chorus". Earlier borrowings transcribe the Greek aspirates as the corresponding voiceless plosive.

From *c.* 100 BCE, aspirates also start to be written in a number of native Latin words instead of earlier voiceless plosives, normally in the vicinity of /l/ or /r/ (e.g. *pulcher* "beautiful"). The explanation for this may be that the voiceless plosives had aspirated allophones in this position, which started to be written with the aspirated digraphs once these had become available to represent Greek borrowings.

Fricatives

/z/

The sign <z> was borrowed during the first century BCE to represent Greek <ζ> in Greek loan-words. It is likely that Latin <z> represents single [z] in initial position and double [zz] medially.

/h/

/h/ has a restricted distribution and shows a tendency to disappear at all periods, to different degrees depending on position in the word and the particular variety of Latin. It is rare word-internally between vowels and after consonants is only found in a few compounds (e.g. *ad-hibeō* "add to"). It does occur word-initially before vowels, and is marginally distinctive (e.g. *hōs* "those" (acc. masc. pl.): *ōs* "mouth"), but seems to have been weakly articulated even here; e.g., in metrical texts final vowels are elided before words beginning with /hV/, exactly as before initial /V/.

Initial /h/ started to be lost in sub-elite varieties at an early date, and was subsequently lost completely. Its loss seems to have caused a period of uncertainty about its correct usage and subsequent "hypercorrection", where words which had always started with a vowel were mistakenly pronounced with initial /h/ (e.g. Catullus 84 mocks a certain Arrius for saying *hīnsidiās* for *īnsidiās* "ambushes" (acc. pl.)).

Nasals

/m/

Word-finally, the bilabial nasal /m/ seems to have been reduced to nasalisation (with lengthening) of the preceding vowel; e.g. *decem* "ten" reflects [dɛkẽ]. The effects of this can be seen in metrical texts, where the final syllables of words ending in /V/ + <M> are treated in the same way as those in final /V/, being elided before a following initial /V/.

/ŋ/

The velar nasal /ŋ/, which occurs only at syllable codas, is written as <G> before /n/, e.g. *agnī* [aŋni:] "lamb" (gen. sg.) and <N> before labials and labiovelars, e.g. *quīnque* "five" [kʷi:ŋkʷɛ]. The writing of this sound could be taken to show that it is simply an allophone of /g/ or /n/, but the fact that some contrastive triplets can be cited (e.g. *amnī* "river" (dat. sg.) ~ *annī* "year" (gen. sg.) ~ *agnī* [aŋni:] "lamb" (gen. sg.)) suggests that it is at least marginally phonemic.

Approximants

/j/ and /w/

The signs <I> and <V> represent both the approximants /j/ and /w/ and the vowels /i/ and /u/. In Indo-European, and possibly also in Early Latin, /i/ and /j/ were allophones, as were /u/ and /w/. However, by the Classical period, the vowels and consonants are separate phonemes; cf. *iambus* [ɪam-] "iamb": *iam* [jã] "now", *uoluit* [-lʊɪt] "he/she/it wanted": *uoluit* [-lwɪt] "he/she/it rolled".

/j/ mostly occurs either word-initially before a vowel or medially between vowels. It does not normally occur after a consonant, except in compounds, e.g. *con-iungō* "join together"; thus, e.g., *medius* "middle" is pronounced [mɛdɪ-], not [mɛdj-]. In intervocalic position, <I> normally stands for a double consonant /jj/; e.g. *maior* "greater" was pronounced [majjor]. This can be seen in metrical texts, where the preceding syllable in such cases is treated as heavy, even if it contains a short vowel. In poetry, vocalic /i/ and consonantal /j/ are occasionally interchanged for metrical purposes (e.g. *Iūlius* can scan either as a trisyllable or a quadrisyllable).

/w/ is less restricted in occurrence than /j/: it can stand word-initially before a vowel, medially between vowels or after liquids (/l/, /r/), and can also appear in the cluster /sw/, and possibly /kw/ and /gw/, although it is not certain that these sequences are clusters (see on the labiovelars above). After other obstruents, it is found only in compounds, e.g. *ad-ueniō* "approach". As with /j/ and /i/, /w/ and /u/ are sometimes interchanged in poetry; e.g. *genua* "knees" is normally trisyllabic, but in poetry can be treated as disyllabic [gɛnwa].

Lateral approximants

/l/ has two main allophones: dark (velarised) before consonants and word-finally (e.g. *facultās* "ability", *facul* "easily") and clear elsewhere (e.g. *facilis* "easy").

Vowels

The following section sets out the main features of the Latin vowel system: basic monophthongs, marginal monophthongs and diphthongs.

Monophthongs

The basic monophthong system consists of five short vowels /i e a o u/ and their long equivalents /iː eː aː oː uː/. Vowel length is distinctive for all five vowels, e.g. *anus* [anʊs] "old woman" vs. *ānus* [aːnʊs] "ring, anus" etc.

Short /a/ and long /aː/ seem to have been qualitatively similar, but the long close and mid vowels seem to have been significantly closer than their short equivalents. Thus, on the front axis, /i/ was probably phonetically realized as [ɪ], but /iː/ as [iː], and /e/ as [ɛ], but /eː/ as [eː], making short /i/ actually closer in quality to long /eː/ than to long /iː/. Similarly, on the back axis, /o/ was probably realized as [ɔ], but /oː/ as [oː], and /u/ as [ʊ] but /uː/ as [uː].

This difference in height between the long and short close and mid vowels had important consequences for the sub-elite varieties of Latin from which the Romance languages ultimately developed. In later Latin, vowel length was lost as a distinctive feature, becoming an automatic feature of stressed syllables, and long and short vowels merged. The loss of phonemic length distinctions had the effect of making the originally secondary qualitative distinctions more important, and the short vowels merged with the qualitatively most similar long vowels to create a new system based on qualitative distinctions. In stressed syllables, short /a/ and long /aː/ merged as /a/, but in most areas of Romance original short /i/ merged with long /eː/ as a new close-mid front vowel /e/, long /iː/ developed to new /i/, and original short /e/ developed to a new open-mid front vowel /ɛ/. This produced a new three-way distinction on the front axis between /i/, /e/ and /ɛ/. Similarly, on the back axis, short /u/ and long /oː/ generally merged as a new close-mid back vowel /o/, long /uː/ developed to /u/, and original /o/ developed to /ɔ/, producing a new contrast between /u/, /o/ and /ɔ/.

Other monophthongs

Classical Latin uses <Y>, which was adopted in the first century BCE to represent Greek <υ>, a front rounded vowel [ü], with long and short variants, e.g. *crypta* "crypt". Earlier borrowings use <V> to represent this sound. Although educated speakers in the Classical period may have borrowed the Greek sound as well as the letter, its writing as <V> in sub-elite inscriptions suggest that it was pronounced as [u] in non-standard Latin, as in the earlier period. Borrowings into later Latin also write this sound as <I>, which develops in Romance in the same way as /i/.

We can also reconstruct an "intermediate" vowel. This vowel occurs in medial light syllables before a labial consonant, e.g. *optimus* "best". Short vowels in medial light syllables are usually raised to /i/ by a process known as "vowel weakening" (see on accent below), but before a labial the vowel in question is written in Early Latin with <V>, but later normally with <I>, e.g. Early *optumus* vs. Classical *optimus*. This vowel may have been a short close central vowel [ɨ] (and possibly its rounded equivalent [ʉ] at an earlier period).

Classical Latin also has a set of nasalised vowels: /ĩ ẽ ã õ ũ/. These are inherently long, and do not contrast with short nasalised vowels. They are restricted to: (1) word-final position, where they are written <IM>, <EM>, <AM>, <OM>, <VM> in standard orthography, having arisen from earlier clusters of /Vm/; and possibly (2) before the clusters / ns/ and /nf/.

Diphthongs

A number of distinctive diphthongs are found in Early and Classical Latin. There was a tendency at all periods of Latin towards monophthongisation of diphthongs, although this process shows some differences according to position in the word and the variety of Latin.

Early Latin has the following diphthongs: /ei/, /ai/, /oi/, /au/, /ou/ and /eu/ (/eu/ occurs only in a single inscription). These had mostly become monophthongs by the Classical period. The full details are quite complex, but in general: (1) /ei/ > /iː/; (2) /ou/ and /eu/ > /uː/; and (3) /oi/ > /uː/ word-internally, although in a few words it is kept as /oe/ (e.g. *poena* "punishment"), and /oi/ > /iː/ word-finally and after /w/. The other diphthongs are maintained: /ai/ normally develops to /ae/, /au/ is usually kept and /oi/, when not monophthongised, was kept as /oe/. Classical Latin also has the rare diphthongs /ui/ (weakened from earlier /oi/), /eu/, /ei/ and /ou/, the last three all resulting from contractions.

In sub-elite Latin, and later more generally, the process of monophthongisation went further. /ae/ monophthongised and merged with original /e/ as the new vowel /ɛ/ and the few remaining cases of /oe/ monophthongised, merging with original /eː/ and /i/ as the new vowel /e/. On the back axis, /au/ also started to monophthongise in non-standard varieties at an early date, merging with original /oː/. However, this process was never as widespread as the monophthongisation of /ae/, and, although /au/ has monophthongised in some parts of Romance, in certain areas (e.g. Romanian) it has been preserved up to the present day.

Syllable Structure

Latin syllables can be classified as either *light* or *heavy*. The distinction is important, since it determines the position of the word accent and is the main principle in Classical Latin versification. A light syllable is an open syllable containing a short vowel, i.e. followed by not more than one consonant (a single following consonant belongs to the following syllable, e.g. *pe-cus* "cattle"). A heavy syllable either contains a long vowel, in which case it is automatically heavy (e.g. *pō-tus* "drunk"), or a short vowel in a closed syllable, i.e. followed by two or more consonants (at least the first then belongs to the preceding syllable, e.g. *pec-tus* "chest"). Sequences of plosive plus liquid (/l/, /r/) are exceptional. A syllable containing a short vowel followed by plosive and liquid may be syllabified as: (1) an open, light syllable (e.g. *pa-trem* "father" (acc. sg.)); or (2) a closed, heavy syllable (e.g. *pat-rem*). Early Latin poetry shows only (1), but in Classical verse, either (1) or (2) is possible, with (2) being imitated from Greek practice.

Accent

In prehistoric Latin, the word accent seems to have been a stress accent on the initial syllable of the word. The main evidence for this comes from the behaviour of short vowels in non-initial (i.e. unaccented) syllables. Short vowels in medial and final syllables tend to be either raised, a process known as "vowel weakening", or lost completely (syncope). The full details of this process are quite complicated, but the clearest set of developments involves short vowels in medial syllables: in open syllables, /e/, /a/, /o/, /u/ all generally raise to /i/, while in closed syllables /a/ raises only to /e/ and /o/ to /u/; e.g. *faciō* "make", "do", with compounds such as *reficiō* "remake", *refectus* "remade". In some cases, short vowels in non-initial syllables are lost completely by syncope, e.g. *dexter* "right (hand)" < *deksiteros*.

By the Classical period, however, a different system had developed. Word accent, with a few exceptions, follows the "penultimate law": in polysyllabic words, the accent falls on the penultimate syllable if this is heavy, and the antepenultimate if the penultimate is light.

Although the position of the accent in Classical Latin is clear, there has been some disagreement about its nature. Most modern scholars view it as a stress-based accent (as in prehistoric Latin). The Roman grammarians, however, generally describe it in terms of pitch, like the accent of Classical Greek. Despite the grammarians' statements, though, a stress accent is much more likely. For instance, we know that the prehistoric Latin accent was stress-based, as discussed above, and developments in later Latin also show extensive vowel loss that points to the effects of a stress accent: it seems more probable that the Classical Latin accent was also stress-based, rather than shifting from stress to pitch back to stress again. The statements of the Roman grammarians could then be explained as the result of their close imitation of Greek models.

FURTHER READING

On our evidence for Latin phonology, see Allen (1978). For general surveys, see Sturtevant (1940), Kent (1945), Leumann (1977), Allen (1978), Sihler (1995), Meiser (1998), Clackson (2004), Touratier (2005), which have been the main sources for this chapter. On historical changes, see Leumann (1977), Sihler (1995), Meiser (1998), Herman (2000), Clackson and Horrocks (2007), Weiss (2009). On regional and social variation, see Herman (2000), Clackson and Horrocks (2007), Adams (2007).

CHAPTER 7

Latin Prosody and Metrics

Benjamin W. Fortson IV

Rather than providing a generic list of Latin metrical forms and descriptions, of a type readily obtainable elsewhere in greater detail (e.g. Raven (1965); Crusius (1967); Drexler (1967); Halporn (1963); Halporn *et al.* (1994); Boldrini (2004)), this survey explores a small set of partly interrelated issues in the historical and linguistic study of Latin metrics. We first examine the native background of Latin poetry in its Italic context, with emphasis on the Saturnian. From there we move to the meters of Roman comedy, noting how certain of their characteristics may reflect native poetic practices and how others provide a window onto details of the prosodic and rhythmic organization of spoken Latin. In the last section we provide an overview of the ictus/accent question and Roman recitational practices, especially in the context of the comic iambo-trochaics and Classical hexameters.

Italic Background, *Carmina*, Saturnian

Among the inscriptions that have come down to us in the fragmentarily preserved Italic languages Oscan, Umbrian, South Picene, and Paelignian are a number of religious or solemn character, including prayers, curses, and epitaphs. These stand out stylistically in having distinctive poetic features. The oft-cited South Picene epitaph from Bellante (*ST* Sp TE 2) consists (except for the first word) of bipartite alliterative phrases **postin viam videtas tetis tokam alies esmen vepses vepeten** "Along/Behind the road you see the 'toga' (covering?) of Titus Alius buried (?) in this tomb"; simultaneously it can be divided into three seven-syllable (2 + 2 + 3) cola, **postin viam videtas / tetis tokam alies / esmen vepses vepeten**. Bipartite alliteration is found also in e.g. **fakinss fangvam** "deeds (and) words (lit., tongue)" from an Oscan curse; *sacaracirix Semunu* "consecrator

A Companion to the Latin Language, First Edition. Edited by James Clackson.
© 2011 Blackwell Publishing Ltd. Published 2011 by Blackwell Publishing Ltd.

of the crop-gods" from a Paelignian epitaph; and *futu fos* "be propitious" in Umbrian prayers from the Iguvine Tables. These prayers are the longest such texts, and feature not just alliteration but also other types of assonance, together with grammatical parallelism, repetition, and *figurae etymologicae*. These stylistic figures are also characteristic of the Latin *carmina* – solemn utterances like prayers, oaths, and legal formulae in the Roman world. Taken together, all these texts constitute the basis of our knowledge of native Italic poetry.

There is some uncertainty whether to call the longer texts "poems"; though they consist of recurring strophic and smaller units, it is not clear that they are genuinely metrical, and "rhythmic prose" is the term often applied instead (cf. Williams (1992) 54–55; for analytic studies of *carmina* see e.g. Thulin (1906) and Watkins (1995b)). But the important point for the continuity of the Roman poetic tradition is that they utilize the same species of verbal artistry that the Romans felt was suitable for use when writing later in Greek meters. This strongly suggests that they occupied at least some of the same linguistic-cultural "space" as later poetry, regardless of what one chooses to call them.

The dawn of attested Roman literature in the third and early second centuries BCE occurred at a time when Greek influence on the arts was increasing, and native meters would soon be abandoned in favor of the Greek ones, especially for extended poetry. Those meters have disappeared without a trace except for the Saturnian (on the *versus quadratus* see further below). This is usually agreed to be a survival of an indigenous Italic poetic form (the arguments of detractors like Williams (1992) 57 who posit a Greek source are very weak, and Fraenkel's (1951) identification of a model type in the Cretan hymn of Zeus Dikte is a grasp at straws). Introductions to the Saturnian typically enshroud it in great mystery, and it is true that in spite of innumerable attempts no descriptive model adequate for all the remains has yet found universal approval. But the majority of Saturnians do share a common pattern: verses consisted of two hemistichs, each further divisible into two quarter-verses by a caesura (the *caesura Korschiana*) usually before the last three syllables. The cadence of both hemistichs is normally a trochaic or spondaic – × (or ′×, depending on whether one uses a quantitative or stress-based description, see below); the first-hemistich cadence is typically preceded by another – × sequence; and the second hemistich normally begins – ×. The commonest verse-type consists of a three-word, seven-syllable hemistich (2 2 | 3, just as in the South Picene epitaph above) followed by a two-word hemistich of six syllables (3 | 3), as in the famous opening line of Livius Andronicus' *Odyssey: Virum mihi | Camena || insece | uersutum*. The problem has always been how to bring this common type under the same hat as less typical exponents like Andr. 3: *mea puera quid uerbi ex tuo ore supra fugit*. Additionally bedeviling the picture is the constant specter of corruption in the manuscripts.

Whether the meter was stress-based, quantity-based, or some combination of the two is still not agreed upon (see the useful survey of representative approaches in Beare (1957) 14–31 and Mercado (2006a) 7–35). Quantitative models, which represent the bulk of the hypotheses, fail because of the immense variety of quantitative patterns needed to account for all the verses; such models have tended to be highly complex, excessively flexible, and in the end not terribly credible as learnable or appreciable metrical schemes. Accentual models have fallen victim to disagreements over the nature and position of Latin accentuation. Since the Classical Latin penultimate stress rule does not yield a coherent and consistent rhythm across all the surviving Saturnian fragments, some scholars have tried to deduce from those fragments other positions of the accent that may have obtained instead; but that approach begs the question.

The most recent in-depth treatment of the Saturnian and its place among the other native Italic meters is Mercado (2006a), a very important work that provides a minutely detailed and skillfully argued analysis based on a novel combination of stress and syllable-count. In Mercado's view, there are two basic cola, a six-syllable second hemistich (A) with two word-stresses and a seven-syllable first hemistich (B) with three. Each of these has a large number of variants which he derives via acephaly and anaclasis (inversion). Commonest are his type A.1.2 ($'\times\times\times \mid \times \,'\times\times$), with 50 "secure" exponents, and B.1.3 ($'\times\times \,'\times\times \mid \times \,'\times\times$), with 66. Combining the two produces the best-attested type of Saturnian verse noted above. Mercado also offers several new and stimulating observations on the connection of the Saturnian to other Italic meters, with interesting speculations on the antiquity of stress-based Indo-European poetry.

Though a published version of this thesis is still in preparation, it has already achieved some well-deserved notice and circulation, and so a brief critical reaction may not be inappropriate, subject to the usual caveats. Much of Mercado's overall scheme seems to work well, and it is admirable that he is able to make this disparate-looking corpus look regular. But the ability of any theory of the Saturnian to convince will depend on how cleanly it does this and on the degree to which it avoids (or appears to avoid) arbitrary application of licenses and multiplication of verse-types. On these two scores its success will probably lie in the eye of the beholder. With the acephaly and anaclasis noted above, a full 13 A and 14 B subtypes are generated for what are only about 130 secure verses. This sort of thing is unavoidable for theories of the Saturnian that seek to derive each specific attested pattern from one or two underlying ones. Though prompted on internal grounds by key features common to most of the extant specimens (e.g. the nearly universal Korschian caesura and cadence patterns), this approach could well benefit from more critical scrutiny (cf. Beare (1957) 24–25). That is to say, our surviving Saturnians could be like our surviving hexameters and all be examples of the same meter; or they could be like our surviving body of glyconics, pherecrateans, hagesichoreans, hendecasyllables, and phalaecians – different meters belonging to the same family and sharing certain structures. In either case, entities must be multiplied and Occam's razor must be violated; absent outside controls, it amounts to a matter of taste which set of entities one is more comfortable multiplying.

Like everyone else who posits templates that contain a set number of syllables, Mercado too has to resort to the usual metrical first-aid kit of resolution, elision, hiatus, and synizesis in order to make verses with ostensibly the wrong number of syllables fit. He does suggest constraints on the use of some of them (as in the case of resolution; cf. also Cole (1969) 30–31) and is judicious in their application; but his procedure does not free him from inconsistencies any more than his predecessors were free of them. For example, he assumes hiatus before the caesura in Andr. 24 *tópper cíti* | *ad aédis* (plausible on linguistic grounds if the prepositional phrase *ad aedis* was set off by a prosodic break across which elision was not licensed); simultaneously he allows elision across the caesura in order "to avoid recourse to hiatus, resolution, or both" (112), as in 34.3 *múlta áli⌐a ‿ in ísdem*, where elision is posited in exactly the same environment as in the preceding example with hiatus (and hiatus is posited between *multa* and *alia* to avoid the stress-clash of *múlt(a) ália*). In e.g. *CIL* I² 10.1 *quei‿ápicem‿insígne* | *Diális* elision is posited after *-m*, but not in Naev. 25.1 *postquam avem | aspexit* or Andr. 11 *pártim érrant | nequínont*, which he stipulates is an example of "liaison" or resyllabification of the coda *-m* as the onset of the next syllable (113). This would be descriptively, but not explanatorily, adequate. The underlying issue here is whether one expects the meter to have essentially demanded elision when possible (as is normally the case with the quantitative meters), in which case all instances of hiatus should have a coherent linguistic explanation; or whether one posits elision as the marked situation, in which case hiatus becomes the default and elisions need justification.

Much more fruitful discussion will surely ensue once the revised work is published; even now, no researcher of ancient Italic metrics can afford to ignore it. In particular, since Mercado is mostly interested in providing a synchronic account of the Saturnian, many questions remain about its diachrony (in spite of Mercado's chapter on comparing it with other Italic poetic remains). In this light the analysis of Coleman ((1998) 1090–1093) is of interest (mentioned in passing by Mercado, p. 18). Although his programmatic treatment leaves the reader to connect a number of dots, Coleman's basic approach is to regard the synchronic variability of the meter not as the result of a set of optional metrical derivational procedures, but as the diachronic product of successive re-analyses of the meter that resulted from the historical shift to the penultimate stress rule. Thus in the original prehistoric Saturnian, each stressed position corresponded with the beginning of a word; after the stress system changed, the stress template remained but new possibilities of word-distributions were opened up, themselves leading to further re-analyses and the creation of verse types with greater or lesser numbers of syllables. These and other remaining issues will insure that the scholarship on this meter is far from being exhausted.

There is no evidence that the preliterate Italic peoples possessed any tradition of extended oral poetry of the Greek or Sanskrit type (in spite of Romantic-era claims of oral historical "lays," see Williams (1992) 56), and in fact the Sabellic poetic styles described above are much better suited for the short compositions we see them in like epitaphs and curses. It is probably the case that the Saturnian was also restricted to such genres, which makes sense in light of its probable cognacy with some of the Sabellic verse-forms (Mercado (2006a) and (2008)). When Livius Andronicus and Naevius used it for longer compositions, they were innovating. A striking difference should also be mentioned between the Sabellic material and the extant Saturnians, namely a rarity of contiguous alliteration in the latter (alliteration is an "occasional ornament," Beare (1957) 125). Within the preserved corpus, a line like Naev. 6.1 *eorum sectam sequuntur multi mortales* or a run of second hemistichs consisting of bipartite alliterative phrases like in the epitaph *CIL* I² 1531: *asper afleicta / ... / ... leibereis lubentes / ... maxsume mereto / ... crebro condemnes* is exceptional. Commoner are instances like Naev. 20.1: *blande et docte percontat* || *Aenea quo pacto*, where the alliteration serves to demarcate structural points in the verse (Mercado (2006a) 33).

On the whole, though, alliteration is much more characteristic of Latin poetry than it is of Greek (cf. Williams (1968) 693), which is surely rooted in the native tradition. And if one knows where to look, it is possible to find seven-syllable sequences combined with bipartite alliteration; note Plautus, *Capt.* 903: *quanta pernis pestis ueniet, quanta labes larido*, which has two bipartite alliterative phrases embedded in seven-syllable (2 + 2 + 3) sequences, *pernis pestis ueniet, quanta labes larido*. Compare also traditional phrases like *kalo Iuno Couella* "I call (thee), Juno Covella" that was intoned on the

Calends (Fortson (2003) 73 with n. 35). Again, there is always the possibility that such resemblances are due to chance, but the matter deserves investigation. Faliscan, now widely considered a dialect of Latin (see most recently Bakkum (2009)), has in the famous inscription **foied vino pipafo cra carefo** "today I will drink wine, tomorrow I will do without" also a seven-syllable clause or colon followed by a shorter one that has often been cited in connection with Saturnians, though Mercado ((2006a) 199 and preceding discussion) is skeptical of any equation of the two.

Comic Meters

Some aspects of the native poetic tradition that we have been discussing probably shine through in the poetry of Plautus (traditional dates 254–183 BCE), whose works form the largest surviving corpus from the early period of Roman adaptation of Greek meters. Plautus' metrical technique differs considerably both from that of his Greek models and from that of subsequent Roman authors, and opinions have varied widely on how to interpret these differences. Some have maintained that, since Plautus was one of the pioneers in using Greek meters, his generation was still relatively unskilled in this practice and therefore he frequently made mistakes from the Greek point of view. Others have averred that the many "licenses" reflect genuine pronunciations current in the colloquial Latin of the time. A third approach (which complements the second), not so frequently found, is that some of the deviations reflect native poetic compositional tendencies. We obviously stand to gain much more from pursuing the second and third approaches than from dismissing deviations from Greek practice as due to error or incompetence.

   Let us now document some of the differences. We may first note that the treatment of the feet is much looser than in Greek. Here we will focus on the commonest meters in Plautus, the iambic senarius (derived from the Greek iambic trimeter) and trochaic septenarius (derived from the catalectic trochaic tetrameter); in spite of the nomenclatural difference, the former can be thought of as the latter with the addition of a cretic at the beginning. Below are two ways of comparing them from right to left: the first shows the identical location of the caesura (||), the second shows division into metra or dipodies:

iambic senarius	˘ — ˘ — ˘ ‖ — ˘ — ˘ — ˘ × ‖
trochaic septenarius	— ˘ — ˘ — ˘ — ˘ ‖ — ˘ — ˘ — ˘ × ‖
iambic senarius	˘ — ˘ — | ˘ — ˘ — | ˘ — ˘ × ‖
trochaic septenarius	— ˘ — | ˘ — ˘ — | ˘ — ˘ — | ˘ — ˘ × ‖

Whereas the Greek iambic trimeter limited the number of allowable substitutions, especially of light syllables with heavy ones or their resolutions, in Plautus such substitution is free except in the line-final iambic cadence. The same applies, *mutatis mutandis*, to the trochaic line. A senarius consisting underlyingly of six iambs could therefore theoretically surface with anywhere from 12 to 22 syllables (though the attested maximum is 18). Many have wondered how it was possible for the Romans to perceive or project an even trochaic or iambic rhythm in lines where the feet can have such uneven lengths and where the only guaranteed "pure" leftover iambic rhythm is at the end of the line. As Gratwick ((1993) 55–56) has shown, however, we must distinguish between the odd and even short positions (or, put another way, the first and second short positions of each dipody): the replacement of a short by a long is far commoner in the odd positions than in the even positions (and, as per above, forbidden in the last even position). Statistically speaking, then, an iambic rhythm still shines through, but primarily as a cadential rhythm (in the second foot of a given dipody) rather than as a rhythm characterizing the line as a whole. The Roman comfort with anisochronicity in the first five feet of a senarius (or the first six and a half feet of a septenarius) coupled with strict respect for the cadence is of course immediately reminiscent of what we saw with the native style that was flexible in the number of syllables and quantities per metrical unit, though one would be hard-pressed to prove such influence. A similar freedom obtains also in some of the lyric meters in Plautus, where there is on average much greater freedom than in Greek in substituting longa (or their resolutions as two shorts) for short positions (see further below).

Second, there are frequent apparent mismatches in Plautus between actual syllable weight and the weight that a given metrical position demands. The most familiar of these results from the process called iambic shortening or *brevis brevians*, where the heavy second syllable of an iambic sequence (either a full iambic word like *homō*, an iambic sequence at the beginning of a longer word like **modestus**, or a phrase-initial iambic sequence across word-boundary like **sed ostendere** or **quod ad uos**) must scan as light. Iambic shortening was a linguistically real phenomenon in the history of Latin (whence the short ultima of such words as *mihi tibi bene male*); disputed has been whether all instances of it in Roman comedy are to be attributed to linguistic factors or whether some of them are artificial poetic licenses. Concerning its appearance specifically in Plautus, the most likely theory in this writer's view is that iambic shortening is linguistically real and affected iambic strings that were destressed or whose stress was subordinated to that of surrounding material, whence its most typical appearance in pronouns, particles, sentence adverbs, and strings of clitics (Fortson (2008) ch. 7, building on Devine and Stephens (1980); note that, contrary to usual descriptions, the heavy syllable itself can be underlyingly stressed, as in *modéstus* above and in numerous other examples that are difficult or impossible to emend out of existence). The residue of full-content (and therefore typically fully stressed) lexemes exhibiting the phenomenon becomes more tractable when likely effects of pragmatic foregrounding/backgrounding on sentence prosody are considered. In a study of iambically shortened nouns (Fortson (2008) ch. 8), it was tentatively proposed that nouns expressing "old" (thematic) information were more likely to be shortened, evincing prosodic subordination to new or contrastive information that received greater emphasis. (Similar ideas were adumbrated at least as long ago as Lindsay (1922) 52–65, and cf. also Drexler (1969) *passim*) The fit is, however, not perfect, and many cases still require further investigation; but if the approach is correct, this example of a Plautine metrical "license" can allow us to recover (in a valuable and perhaps unparalleled way) the prosodic effects of information flow in a dead language.

Many other phenomena in Plautus, especially the metrical "laws," shed further light on sub-phonemic details of Latin pronunciation and phrasal organization. When a longum is resolved into two shorts, no word boundary may intervene (the law of the split resolution or Ritschl's law); but if the word-break occurs inside a clitic group (type *ut opiniōne*), the split resolution is licensed. This may provide evidence for resyllabification of coda consonants in clitic groups (Fortson (2008) 7–8), resulting in a phonetic juncture that for the purposes of the meter was indistinguishable from that between syllables within one and the same word. The final position of the first and second dipody of the senarius (and equivalent positions in the septenarius) could be filled by a *brevis in longo* or light syllable counting as heavy (Jacobsohn's law); these *breves in longo* typically come before a syntactic boundary and presumed prosodic break and might provide evidence of phrase-final lengthening effects or lack of resyllabification of coda consonants at the ends of prosodic phrases (Fortson (2008) 86ff.). Other phenomena are discussed in Ceccarelli (1991), Questa (2007), and Fortson (2008) (with some necessarily speculative conclusions).

The most frequent meter in Plautus is the trochaic septenarius. It has often been averred that this meter is not merely the Roman adaptation of the Greek catalectic trochaic tetrameter, but also continues the so-called *versus quadratus* or "square verse" attested in popular and military songs. This consists of four trochaic metra (type *Postquam Crassus | carbo factus, | Carbo crassus | factus est*); compare a literary example, Pl. *Men.* 1015: *uos scelesti, | uos rapaces, | uos praedones.:: | Periimus* (offered in Gratwick (1982a) 92). However, not all are agreed that the *versus quadratus* is a native form, since similar material is found in Greek and could have diffused into popular oral culture early on, and all the attested examples are from later periods. See Gratwick (1982a) 92–93 and Coleman (1998).

Requiring separate treatment are the lyric or *canticum* meters of Roman comedy. (Technically *cantica* include all meters besides the iambic senarius, the only meter that lacked musical accompaniment, but in Plautine studies the term usually also excludes the "recitative" trochaic septenarius.) The scansion and colometry of some *cantica* are still imperfectly understood due to problems in the manuscript transmission and the high degree of polymetry, which brings with it greater than usual uncertainty in when to invoke exceptional scansions like iambic shortening. (We are, however, on considerably surer footing overall than in the days of Leo (Leo 1905) and Lindsay, thanks in part to Cesare Questa's efforts, culminating in Questa (1995).) The sources of Plautus' lyric meters are not fully clear. Probably they originated with meters used in Atellane farce, which themselves may ultimately go back to the lyric meters of Greek Old Comedy as brought to Italian shores in earlier times. The New Comedies that Plautus based his plays on had almost no songs and did not use most of these meters; this has led to the widely held theory (Sedgwick (1930) 102ff.) that his early comedies (e.g. *Miles Gloriosus*, *Asinaria*), with their smaller number of songs and less metrical variety, follow the Greek models more closely, and that only as he matured did he add more original polymetric song and dance of a peculiarly Roman flavor. In infusing his works with more song than their models, Plautus was not alone: Plautus' successor Caecilius did the same, as did Ennius in his tragedies (Williams (1968) 361–365, 693; Gratwick (1982a) 116, 133). With the more reserved Terence, however, we return to the aesthetic of Greek New Comedy: his six plays contain a total of only 25 verses of song (Duckworth (1952) 380).

In the *cantica*, too, there are considerable deviations from Greek practice. First, the combinations of different metrical types are in many cases without antecedents in Greek. Plautus is quite fond of what are basically pairs of verses whose second member is a short colon of some kind, and one wonders again if there is any echo of a Saturnian-like aesthetic in this. Second, strophic responsions are extremely uncommon. Third, *cantica* contain many typical features of the traditional Latin *carmina*, such as assonance, parallel phrases, repetition, and alliteration (Williams (1968) 361–365, 693). Because of their metrical challenges, the *cantica* have tended to be neglected, and a full investigation of them with an eye to identifying native poetic inheritances would doubtless be revealing.

Perhaps the most widely discussed issue concerning the relationship between Plautine metrics and spoken Latin is the interplay between the supposed verse-ictus or metrical beat and word-stress. This topic actually extends beyond Plautus, and we turn to it next.

Stress, Ictus, Recitation

As a modern scholarly issue the verse-ictus dates back to Richard Bentley's prefatory Σχεδίασμα *de metris Terentianis* to his edition of Terence (1726). In this work, among other things, he took schoolmasters to task for two practices. The first was reciting hexameters with stress on the beginning of each foot; Bentley contended that the natural word-accents should be maintained instead. His second complaint was in regard to schoolmasters' neglect of Terence's verses, which he said were actually easier to teach pupils because they closely resembled English iambo-trochaic verse. In this way, ironically, the very thing Bentley militated against in the case of hexameters was applied to comic iambo-trochaics – a regular stressed verse-ictus on the English model. Subsequent scholars extended this to include the hexameter (more or less reversing Bentley's suggestion), and ultimately came to embrace all Latin and even Greek poetry. Soon a doctrine arose summarized by Kapp (1941) 87 as "the assumption that Greek and Latin poets composed their lines for singing or reading with a stressed accent at definite points in each metrical line." Once an emphatic verse-ictus had been postulated, its frequent conflict with the position of word-stresses turned into a scholarly problem. (Bentley himself was quite aware of this already in the case of Terence but was not overly troubled by it.)

Not often does a problem costing so many scholars so many years of toil turn out to be founded on false premises and therefore illusory: the theory that there was a verse-ictus, never universally accepted, has by now been conclusively discredited. The most recent discussion is Zeleny's ((2008) 1–32 and 60–82), who adds some additional textual evidence and arguments to those already forwarded by Madvig, Tamerle, Beare, Stroh, Soubiran, and others. As has been remarked on, the debate often took on a nationalistic cast: with some notable exceptions, English (/American) and German scholars, speaking languages with strong stress-accents, were its most ardent supporters; the opposing camp was primarily Italian and French. In what follows, we will review a modest selection of the evidence and arguments and then briefly summarize the prevailing view that stress-patterns and word-shapes alone (i.e., independent of quantity alternations) were decisive for line-construction and to the Romans' sense of rhythm.

Ancient authorities attest clearly to beating (the real meaning of the term *ictus*) metrical rhythm of Latin verse with the feet or hands, by snapping the fingers, or by elevating the voice (see the *testimonia* collected in Beare (1957) 63–65). But this was an analytic or pedagogical device and not part of performance practice. Stroh, in a famous study ((1990) 107–108), concluded that originally such physical gestures had nothing to do with recitation per se, but were simply accompaniments to make podic units perceptible visibly or physically during the analytic (not recitational!) practice of scansion. In scansion, the line was broken up into feet; if pronounced out loud, the feet were spoken as separate units with no regard for the real word-breaks. A Roman, if reading these out loud, would unconsciously apply his native stress rules to each of these sequences of syllables, resulting in, e.g., *Ármaui rúmqueca nóTro iaéqui prímusab óris.* In Late Antiquity, after phonemic quantity had broken down in the living language, a stress on the beginning of each foot became a necessary expedient for determining proper versification (cf. Sergius *GL* IV.522.25ff. on how scanning can help determine which syllables are long by nature). Our calling this an "ictus" is also a misnomer: as Stroh shows elsewhere ((1979) 13–18), our modern notion of reciting Latin poetry with a strong and regular metrical beat (of the kind that Bentley protested for the hexameter) was not established until around 1600, and only after that did our understanding of "verse ictus" come to encompass stresses of this kind.

Modern scholarship agrees with the original Bentleyan position concerning the hexameter – that during recitation, words kept their regular stresses and the quantitative alternations were not highlighted (see the references in Becker (2004) 316 with n. 13). Direct evidence for this has been seen in the fifth-century Oxyrhynchus papyrus *PSI* 1.21 (= *CPL* 11), which contains two passages of Virgil where all but one of the word-stresses are marked with accents and there is no indication of any ictus. One should also add *P.Ness.* 2.1 (= *CPL* 8), a group of papyri unearthed in 1937 at Auja el-Hafr (present-day Israel; see Casson and Hettich (1950)) containing passages of Virgil arranged columnarly (normally one word per line) with facing Greek glosses; word stresses are sporadically marked throughout. Several passages from Cicero (most recently treated in Zeleny (2008) 68ff.) show that marking metrical rhythm was absent from performance and only distinctions in quantity were perceptible to an audience. All the other ancient reports are consistent with this.

Supporters of the theory that recitation of verses could shift stresses from their natural positions to metrical ictus positions have pointed to a comment by the third-century grammarian Sacerdos (*GL* VI.448.20ff.): "while beating out (*percutientes*), that is, scanning, verses, from time to time we pronounce accents differently from when we place them on words individually"; he offers the example of *toro* and *pater* in *Aeneid* 2.2 (*Inde toro pater Aeneas sic orsus ab alto*), which are stressed *tóro* and *páter* normally but (he says) *toró* and *patér* when scanning this line. Though something is awry with his ictus on *patér* (see Zeleny (2008) 63–64 with n. 152 for four possible interpretations), it is clear that Sacerdos is referring to scansion, not recitation. Remarks by Quintilian (*Inst.* 1.5.28) and Sergius (*GL* IV.484.2) have also been adduced regarding the penultimate stress placed on, respectively, *uolúcres* (*A.* 4.525) and *latébras* (*A.* 2.55) when reading these lines, as opposed to normal antepenultimate stress. But this also has nothing to do with a verse ictus. Ordinary *uolucres* and *latebras* had tautosyllabic *muta cum liquida* (*uo. lu.cres, la.te.bras*) as per the usual syllabification rules, resulting in antepenultimate stress because the penults were light. But in poetry these clusters could optionally make position and be heterosyllabic (*uo.luc.res, la.teb.ras*) in order to fit the last three positions of the line; the alternative syllabification naturally attracted the accent to the penult. (Some have interpreted the scansion as reflecting poetic lengthening of the penultimate vowel, which would have had the same accentual effect.) See Kabell (1960) 28 n. 25.

The question of ictus/accent agreement and clash found its chief battleground in the pages of Plautus. Agreement of (surmised) ictus and accent is considerably more common than clash here, leading a long line of scholars to claim that he strove for coincidence wherever he could and to devise sometimes desperate hypotheses explaining away the clashes. In Terence, matches are even more frequent (Gratwick (1982a) 124). At the ends of lines, clash was essentially unavoidable; the line-final ictus can never coincide with a word-accent except when the final position was filled with a heavy monosyllable, which it only rarely was. For longer words at line-end (type *ēuenit* with stress on the antepenult), one common claim was that there was a secondary stress on the final syllable, rendering the clash illusory. Evidence from syncope of medial syllables (type *caldus* < *calidus*, Spanish *niebla* < *nebula*) provides some support for this notion, but the explanation fails in the case of the many lines ending in an iambic word (over a third of the total, a number that only increased in later writers; Soubiran (1988) 431). These and practically all other mismatches were accounted for under a much grander theory, promulgated in particular by Fraenkel (1928) but adhered to by several others (e.g. Sturtevant (1940) 183), that the ictuses actually reflect re-accentuation or shifting of word-stresses within phrases. Although certain stereotyped, prepositional, and univerbated phrases unquestionably or arguably did undergo such stress-shifts (whence e.g. *ádmodum* < *ad módum*, *ílico* < **in (st)lócō*), there is no inner-Latin or cross-linguistic support for a productive process of stressing whole phrases according to word-level stress rules. (At most, there is some evidence, from iambic shortening, of *subordination* of certain lexical accents relative to others within a larger phonological phrase, but no evidence of any wholesale shift in the position of stresses; see Fortson (2008).)

In the hexameter, ictus/accent agreement is the rule in the last two feet, while clash is the rule especially in feet two through four (agreement is more common in the first foot, Sturtevant (1940) 184). This led to a widely repeated claim that conflict earlier in the line was intentional: the poets are said to have desired a movement from clash and tension early in the line to peace and resolution at the end. According to Sturtevant ((1923) 52), many words that because of their shape could only ever receive an ictus on an unaccented syllable (e.g. *deōs*) were relegated to the beginning of the line so as to save harmony for the end; the poets "thereupon made a virtue of necessity and actually preferred clash in the earlier part of the verse, in order to give their poetry the air of aloofness from common speech which was traditional in heroic verse." This is extremely implausible (note Zeleny's pithy critique, (2008) 74 n. 174).

It is still worth issuing the reminder that the observed distribution of stresses in the hexameter is largely epiphenomenal. Stressed monosyllables were avoided at the end of a line after Ennius, meaning the second-to-last syllable was almost always the (stressed) heavy penult of a two- or three-syllable word. (Line-final stressed monosyllables were not avoided so as to prevent ictus/stress clash, but because they upset the typical cadential stress pattern – a pattern increasingly favored over time, see below. There are at any rate not many full-lexical monosyllables in Latin and even fewer appropriate for poetry. Unstressed line-final monosyllables were equally inappropriate because they are mostly proclitic, and Latin poets from Plautus on – except for the satirists; Raven (1965) 102 – avoided ending lines with proclitics because of the natural prosodic break that line-end entailed.) Working backwards, this means the initial longum of the fifth dactyl is usually a stressed heavy penult or antepenult as well.

The placement of the caesura is largely responsible for the lack of agreement earlier in the line. From Ennius' time on it occurs by far most commonly after the first longum of the third or fourth foot (penthemimeral or hephthemimeral caesura). The penthemimeral is also called "masculine," in contrast with the "feminine" caesura – ˘ | ˘; Skutsch ((1985) 46) in fact names the high proportion of masculine caesurae over against Homer as Ennius' most striking departure from epic practice (80 percent masculine as compared with less than 45 percent in Homer). To be sure, the general trend in Greek hexameters from the fifth century BCE onwards was a sizable increase in the use of masculine caesurae (West (1982) 153), but Callimachus, the major post-Homeric influence on Ennius, bucked this particular trend (rate of feminine caesurae 74 percent). The presence of a penthemimeral caesura has repercussions farther back in the line: the second half of the preceding foot must be filled either with the heavy penultimate or the light penultimate and antepenultimate syllables of the same precaesural word; in either case, the word stress would fall in this part of the foot. That in turn means the preceding strong time of the foot would be filled by a word-end (or by an unaccented ante-antepenultimate syllable).

Instead of poets striving for particular relationships between word-stresses and the nonexistent ictus, what we see instead is the favoring of particular patterns of stressed and unstressed syllables; over time these patterns became in some cases canonical. The evolution has nothing to do with Greek models, but was home-grown on Roman soil and "largely bound up with the accent" (West (1982) 189). This is most obvious in the cadence. In Ennius, lines ending in trochaic or spondaic disyllables or trisyllables with light penult were strongly preferred, which greatly constrained the variety of accent-patterns: 92.5 percent of his lines end with a word-stress on the beginning of the fifth and sixth feet (the familiar adonic clausula translated into a stress pattern). This rate only rises as one moves into the first century BCE and subsequent periods, to 99.5 percent in Virgil, 99.6 percent in Ovid, and ultimately even 100 percent at times in the Silver Age (certain books of Lucan and Statius); see Sturtevant (1923) 57. Thus line-ends of the type *ígnis máre férrum*, with a different stress pattern from the norm, become more than ten times rarer in Lucretius and Virgil than in Ennius (Humphreys (1879) 52; Sturtevant (1919) 383; Wilkinson (1940) 35). In other meters besides the hexameter, we see similar tightening of practice: ending pentameters with a disyllable rises from 39 percent in Catullus to 100 percent in Ovid (Wilkinson (1940) 38) which restricted the cadence to a dactyl–trochee–iamb stress pattern (type *córpus ináne rógo*, *mórs adopérta cáput*).

It is not surprising that stress was so important in Latin poetry (even if not in quite the same way that supporters of the ictus/accent theory imagined): all the linguistic evidence strongly indicates that Latin had a strong expiratory stress-accent throughout its history (not just in its prehistory and in later Antiquity, contrary to a longstanding view), quite probably secondarily accompanied by change in pitch-contour relative to unstressed syllables. It was at any rate not a melodic accent as in Greek.

We do not want to oversimplify the poets' technique; regard for accent was not the only factor that influenced the evolution of the cadence. Several verse-end types used by Ennius and Lucretius having the favored dactyl–spondee stress pattern were all but abandoned later. Thus Ennius freely ends lines with quadrisyllables of the shape *opulentae*, which Virgil strongly avoids doing; but, as Leumann ((1977) 250), following Nougaret, points out, Virgil avoids such words in general if they would have followed a stressed monosyllable or longer elided word with stressed ultima (types *dī genuērunt, aeu(om) agitābant* Enn.). Quintilian (*Inst.* 9.4.64) tells us that words filling two feet were felt to be effeminate at sentence-end; perhaps *dī genuērunt* was considered equivalent, but this goes only so far in explaining the line-internal avoidance. What might be relevant is the word-break after the first position in the fifth foot which was generally avoided; of the three types of line-ends noted by Wilkinson as only "occasional" in Latin hexameters ((1940) 35), two have a word-break there; of the 15 "rare" and unattested types (35–36), fully eight have a word-break there (one of which has an elided syllable, *ment(em) animumque*). Why a word-break after the fifth long was perceived to make the cadence improper or at least inferior is what really needs explanation, especially since a "feminine" caesura within the second half of the foot was perfectly licit (types *arma requirunt, nocte per umbras*).

It is this insistence on a regular and predictable cadence that shines forth as the most salient feature of all the hexametrists and that provides the meter, especially in the context of the variability of the early part of the line, with its true Roman stamp. This was ably emphasized by Engelbert Tamerle in vol. 1 of his *Der lateinische Vers* (1936) 21, *non vidi*, quoted in Zeleny (2008) 26 n. 31), who pointed out the important additional fact that these cadential rhythms and word-shapes are specific to the cadence – they are not typical of other two-foot sequences in the line or met with at (line-internal) sentence-ends. Tamerle also attributes the increasing desire to begin lines with dactyls to distinguish line-beginnings from line-ends (*apud* Zeleny (2008) 225 n. 408). In all respects these practices differ markedly from those of the Greeks. (Absolutely regular stress every four moras was strongly avoided, probably as monotonous, whence the rarity of a line like Lucr. 1.674: *dé nihilóque renáta uigéscat cópia rérum*, cited in Zeleny (2008) 18.) We have seen this same cadential strictness in the other meters discussed above – both Plautine iambo-trochaics (though the Greeks also prohibited substitutions in the last two positions of the line, it was only here that their strictness was adhered to by the Romans, not earlier in the line, as we saw above) and the Saturnian, and if any native practice is still reflected in the hexameter, this may well be where we see it. (Coleman (1998) 1094–1095 has suggested that certain hexameters with five stresses, such as Ennius' *matronae muros complent spectare fauentes* or Virgil's *Italiam fato profugus Lauinaque uenit*, are attempts to incoporate a Saturnian aesthetic. Though an intriguing idea, at least in the case of Ennius, the claim seems odd given his scornful rejection of the Saturnian at *Ann.* 206–207. Not all will even agree that the Virgilian examples sound like Saturnians. Though both authors are in many ways indebted to certain aspects of native Latin poetic technique, these particular similarities are probably coincidental.)

Conclusion

When immersed for too long in the sometimes dry business of metrical analysis and distributional percentages and quantity patterns, one can lose sight of the art and the beauty of these cultural monuments, which were the poets' primary creative purpose. The danger exists today as much as it did when Wilkinson opined ((1940) 33) that Virgil did not start the *Aeneid* by writing **Arma uirumque cano qui Troiae primus ab oris* because he "was at pains to make ictus and accent conflict in the fourth foot where there was a choice." No reader of this survey needs to be told the degree to which such a statement trivializes the artistry of this most famous of Roman poem-openings – how essential it is that *Troiae* be clause-initial to balance its sentence-final mate *Romae*, which is simultaneously the destination of the journey traced by the sentence as well as the city that must be equated with Troy (compare *altae moenia Romae* with *Troiae sub moenibus altis* in line 95, cf. Morwood (1991) 212). Our greatest challenge in analyzing these meters is the fact that the corpus is not mechanically rule-generated output. Great art breaks rules. But this fact is not incompatible with modern analysts' desire for cut-and-dried, testable frameworks, as the artists were not also unprincipled. As we get closer to understanding their technique, we can set into relief the greatness of their achievement whenever they left the pedestrian in pursuit of the empyrean.

CHAPTER 8

The Forms of Latin: Inflectional Morphology

James Clackson

Introduction

Declinatio inducta in sermones non solum Latinos, sed omnium hominum utili et necessaria de causa: nisi enim ita esset factum, neque discere tantum numerum verborum possemus (infinitae enim sunt naturae in quas ea declinantur) neque quae didicissemus ex his, quae inter se rerum cognatio esset, appareret.

Declinatio has been introduced not only into the Latin language, but into the speech of all mankind, for a useful and necessary purpose; for were this not so, we could not learn such a vast number of lexical items (for the structures into which they are derived and inflected are infinite in number), nor would it be at all clear on the basis of those words which we had learnt, what sort of relationship exists between them. (Varro *L.* 8.3; translation after Taylor (1974) 36)

For Varro, *declinatio* covered what modern linguists would call both inflectional and derivational morphology. The presentation of morphology in this chapter will deal with the declination and conjugation of nouns, pronouns and verbs, but not with the processes of word-formation in Latin, which will be covered separately in chapter 11. Numerous monographs and handbooks have been written on Latin morphology, and the language has furnished theoretical morphologists with a testing ground for their ideas (note for example Matthews (1972), Aronoff (1994) and Halle and Vaux (1998)). Ideas on how to frame Latin morphology have changed, but Varro's arguments for the importance of the topic in Latin still stand.

A Companion to the Latin Language, First Edition. Edited by James Clackson.
© 2011 Blackwell Publishing Ltd. Published 2011 by Blackwell Publishing Ltd.

Nominal Morphology

Latin nouns are inflected for number (singular and plural) and case (nominative, vocative, accusative, genitive, dative, ablative and, for certain place-names and nouns of location, locative). The case traditionally called the ablative has a larger array of uses than the name suggests, being the result of syncretism with an earlier instrumental and, in part, locative (the term *ablatiuus* for this case is first attested at Quintilian *Inst.* 1.4.26, who is aware that it has wider uses, but the name probably goes back earlier; Varro refers to the case as the *sextus* "sixth" case or the *Latinus*, since it is unattested in Greek).

Latin nouns are traditionally grouped into five morphologically distinct declensions. All nouns are either masculine, feminine or neuter in gender. Neuter nouns are only attested in the second, third and fourth declensions, and do not alter between the nominative and accusative case. Nouns in the first declension are mostly feminine; masculine nouns in this declension are largely restricted to compound terms such as *agricola* "farmer", *indigena* "native", or loans such as *nauta* "sailor" (from Greek ναύτης) or *Spurinna* "name of a Roman gens" (from Etruscan *spurina*, *ET* AS 1.184), or *verna* "male or female house-slave" (or uncertain origin). Nouns in the second declension are predominantly masculine or neuter; the feminine nouns in this declension are largely restricted to place-names, terms for trees, and loanwords with some terms which can be either gender referring to natural sex, for example: *lupus* "male or female wolf" (*lupa* exists, but can also be used to refer to a prostitute), *turdus* "thrush" (Varro, *L.* 9.55 says that *turda* is not used) or *puer* "child", normally masculine in Classical Latin but used as feminine in early Latin poetry (Livius, Naevius) and epigraphically. Most nouns in the fourth declension are masculine, although the very frequent *domus* "house" (which has many second-declension forms as well as fourth-declension) and *manus* "hand" are feminine. Nouns in the fifth declension are all feminine, except for *dies* "day", which can be either masculine or feminine, and is usually feminine when referring to a specific or appointed day. A few other Latin nouns also show variation in their gender. Sometimes the variation in gender occurs diachronically, for example *aluus* (second declension) "belly" which is masculine in early authors, feminine in Classical Latin but masculine again in post-Classical Latin. For other nouns, such as *callis* "path, track" there is variation in all periods, even within a single work.

A special type of gender variation involves the small set of nouns that alternate between the neuter and masculine (and the smaller number which vary between the neuter and feminine), since this also involves variation in the form of the nominative singular and nominative and accusative plural cases. Thus the noun *locus* "place" has a plural *loci* and an alternative form *loca*; *acinus* "grape" has plurals *acina* and *acini* (as well as a neuter singular *acinum* and a feminine *acina*); and *iocus* "joke" has both *ioci* and *ioca* as plurals, the latter of which seems to be paralleled in the Umbrian word for "prayers" *iuka* or *iuku*. It is difficult to draw any conclusive semantic distinction between the masculine and neuter forms in the Latin texts we have, but it is possible that the alternation continues an inherited process in which originally the neuter plural denoted a collective ("region", "badinage", "bunch of grapes") and the masculine denoted a count plural ("places", "jokes" and "grapes"), a distinction found in other early Indo-European languages (see Eichner (1985)).

Table 8.1 Representative paradigms of the main declension classes of Latin

	I	II	IIIa	IIIb	IV	V
	mēnsa	lupus	rēx	turris	manus	rēs
	table	wolf	king	tower	hand	thing
Singular						
Nom.	mēnsa	lupus	rēx	turris	manus	rēs
Voc.	mēnsa	lupe	rēx	turris	manus	rēs
Acc.	mēnsam	lupum	rēgem	turrim	manum	rem
Gen.	mēnsae	lupī	rēgis	turris	manūs	reī
Dat.	mēnsae	lupō	rēgī	turrī	manuī	reī
Abl.	mēnsā	lupō	rēge	turrī	manū	rē
Plural						
Nom.	mēnsae	lupī	rēgēs	turrēs	manūs	rēs
Voc.	mēnsae	lupī	rēgēs	turrēs	manūs	rēs
Acc.	mēnsās	lupōs	rēgēs	turrīs	manūs	rēs
Gen.	mēnsārum	lupōrum	rēgum	turrium	manuum	rērum
Dat.	mēnsīs	lupīs	rēgibus	turribus	manibus	rēbus
Abl.	mēnsīs	lupīs	rēgibus	turribus	manibus	rēbus

Table 8.2 Paradigms showing distinctive neuter endings

	II	IIIa	IIIb	IV
	iugum	genus	rēte	genū
	yoke	kind	net	knee
Singular				
Nom.-voc.-acc.	iugum	genus	rēte	genū
Gen.	iugī	generis	rētis	genūs
Plural				
Nom.-voc.-acc.	iuga	genera	rētia	genua
Gen.	iugōrum	generum	rētium	genuum

Representative paradigms of the different declension classes of the Latin noun are given below in Tables 8.1 and 8.2; note that the third-declension class has two main sub-types, here labelled IIIa and IIIb. Nouns of neuter gender, which are given in Table 8.2, only occur in declensions II, III and IV. Their case endings are the same except in the syncretic nominative-vocative-accusative, and the table only gives these forms and the genitives for the different paradigms.

In early Latin and in substandard Latin of all periods there is ample evidence for other endings occurring in place of the ones given above. For example, the genitive singular of the first declension originally took the form -*ās*, preserved in the juxtapositions *paterfamiliās* "head of the household" and the term for his wife, *māterfamiliās*, and a handful of times in early poetry (Livius Andronicus, Naevius and Ennius). This ending was replaced by disyllabic -*āī*, the combination of the stem vowel -*ā*- with the ending of the second declension, which is better attested in all verse of the republican period Lucretius, but only used four times in the *Aeneid*. The contraction of disyllabic -*āī* to a diphthong, originally spelt -*ai* but from the early second century BCE also -*ae*, also took place early enough to figure in Plautine verse. From the late Republic on, there is also abundant epigraphical evidence for a genitive form -*aes*. Originally, this is virtually restricted to *gentile* names of freedwomen who also bore a Greek cognomen: a contamination of the inflection of the nomen in the genitive -*ae* and the cognomen in -*es* (= Greek ης) led to the ending -*aes*, which subsequently spread to other names and occasionally more widely (see Adams (2003a) 479–483).

Occasionally, variant endings became specialised in Classical Latin with certain words. The best example of this is probably the old genitive plural ending -*um*, replaced by innovatory -*ōrum* (itself already attested in the Early Latin epitaph of Lucius Scipio, son of Scipio Barbatus) in the standard language. But, as was noticed by Cicero (*Orat.* 155–156) and Varro (L. 8.71, 9.85), -*um* was retained in certain contexts: as a poetic variant, in various formulae such as the exclamation *pro deum fidem* "good heavens!", in expressions of money, weights and measures after numerals, and finally in the declension of juxtapositions of the type *decemuir* "body of ten men".

The second declension has two sub-classes: the first, masculine nouns which have -*r* before the stem vowel, which have nominative singular ending in -*(e)r* as *puer* "boy", genitive *puerī*, *uir* "man", genitive *uirī*, and *ager* "field", genitive *agrī* (note that other nouns and adjectives with stem-final *r*, such as *erus* "master" decline like regular second-declension nouns); and the second-declension nouns ending in -*ius* or -*ium*. In the Republican period these are found with a genitive singular in -*ī*, as *collēgī* from *collēgium*, and a vocative -*ī*, as *Memmī* "o Memmius" and *fīlī* "o son". Analogy led to the creation of a genitive singular -*ii*, first in adjectives ending in -*ius*, but soon spreading to nouns (note for example *magister conlegii* in Augustus' *Res Gestae*). Although an analogous vocative *fīlie* is already attested in Liuius, this ending never caught on until after the end of the imperial period; instead Roman writers tended to avoid using the vocative of nouns ending in -*ius*, except for *fīlī* and in names (Dickey 2000).

In the third declension there is considerable overlap between the type given above as IIIa, originally stems ending in a consonant, and IIIb, which were originally formed with a stem vowel *i*. The overlap partly reflects sound changes that took place within the history of Latin, which eroded the distinctions between the two types. By the classical period, one can find original *i*-stems, such as *mōns* "mountain" or *mēns* "mind" which appear the same in the nominative singular as original consonant stems, such as *ferēns* "carrying", and original consonant stems, such as *canis* "dog", *mēnsis* "month" which look the same as inherited *i*-stems such as *sitis* "thirst" or Greek loans which follow this declension, as *turris* "tower". In Classical Latin, generally the genuine *i*-stems have a genitive plural -*ium*, the genuine consonant stems have a genitive plural -*um*. The majority of cases are explained by the school-book rule that third-declension nouns have a genitive plural which is a syllable longer than their nominative singular, although in Classical Latin genitive plural forms such as *montium*, *mentium*, *canum* and *mēnsum* do not follow the rule owing to the particular history of these forms. Even so, the participle forms show genitive plural -*ium* (except for a few exceptions in early verse) and also the *i*-stem neuter plural ending -*ia*. The *i*-stem ablative singular in -*ī*, accusative plural -*īs* and accusative singular in -*im*, are even more lexically restricted than the genitive plural ending, and were subject to variation. Varro (L. 8.66) states that some people say *ouī* and *auī* for the ablative singular of the words for "sheep" and "bird", others use *oue* and *aue*, some people use accusative plural *montēs*, others *montīs*; later grammarians gave more hard and fast rules (e.g. Charisius pp. 112–113 Barwick). The ablative singular -*ī*, genitive plural -*ium* and neuter plural ending -*ia* (but not the accusative singular ending -*im*) are generally used in third-declension adjectival forms, even where these are of consonant origin, such as *fēlīx* "lucky" (exceptions to this rule include some adjectives with stem-final -*r*, among them comparatives in -*ior*, *pauper* "poor", and the antonym of *pauper*, *dīues* "rich"). The adjective rule helps explain a syntactic peculiarity: present participles in absolute constructions have ablative in -*e*, as *me praesente* "in my presence", but used as adjectives they have ablative in -*ī*, *sine praesentī periculo* "without current danger".

The fourth and fifth declensions are much more lexically restricted; in the classical period loan-words do enter these declensions, and the inflection of Greek names after the fifth declension is given up; no adjectives inflect in these declension types; there is only one productive suffix in the fourth declension (-*tus*), and none in the fifth declension. It is consequently unsurprising that both these declension types disappear in the spoken language and neither is preserved in the Romance languages. Already in the Classical language there are examples of overlap between these declensions and respectively the second and first declensions, and some uncertainty about the formation of some oblique case forms.

Most adjectives fall into two declension patterns. The first distinguishes three different genders, incorporating second-declension forms for masculine and neuter and first-declension forms for the feminine, as *longus*, *longa*, *longum* "long". In the second type, the feminine is not distinguished, and the third-declension *i*-stem type is followed (IIIb above), as *facilis*, *facile* "easy". Adjectives and adverbs have an additional category of gradation, so that alongside the unmarked "positive" degree of an adjective such as *longus* "long" there are also paradigmatic forms for the comparative *longior*, *longius* "longer, too long" and a superlative *longissimus*, *longissima*, *longissimum* "longest, very long"; the adverb *longē* "far off" similarly forms comparative *longius* and superlative *longissimē*. Adjectives ending in the masculine nominative singular -*er*, whether of the first or second type of declension, form superlatives in -*errimus*, as *celer* "swift" (genitive *celeris*), superlative *celerrimus*. A handful of adjectives ending in -*lis*, including *facilis* "easy" and *similis* "similar" form superlatives in -*illimus*, as *facillimus* "easiest".

Pronouns

The Latin pronominal system has the same categories as the nominal system. Personal pronouns are marked for number and case, and demonstrative, anaphoric, interrogative and relative pronouns are marked for number, case and gender. Pronouns do not have a vocative case; the personal pronouns use the nominative in place of the vocative.

The declension system of personal pronouns in Latin is synchronically anomalous as the paradigms in table 8.3 show (note that there is no third person pronoun other than the reflexive *sē*, oblique forms of the anaphoric pronoun *is*, *ea*, *id* are used to supply the deficiency).

Table 8.3   The Latin personal pronouns

	"I"	*"You" (sing.)*	*"We"*	*"You" (pl.)*	*third person reflexive*
Nom.	ego	tū	nōs	uōs	
Acc.	mē	tē	nōs	uōs	sē
Gen.	meī	tuī	nostrī	uestrī	suī
			nostrum	uestrum	
Dat.	mihi	tibi	nōbīs	uōbīs	sibi
Abl.	mē	tē	nōbīs	uōbīs	sē

Table 8.4   The Latin pronoun *hic, haec, hoc*

	Singular			**Plural**		
	Masc.	*Fem.*	*Neut.*	*Masc.*	*Fem.*	*Neut.*
Nom.	hic	haec	hoc	hī	hae	haec
Acc.	hunc	hanc	hoc	hōs	hās	haec
Gen.	huius	huius	huius	hōrum	hārum	hōrum
Dat.	huic	huic	huic	hīs	hīs	hīs
Abl.	hōc	hāc	hōc	hīs	hīs	hīs

For the genitives of the plural pronouns, two variants are given, and these correspond to different functions in the Classical language: *nostrum* and *uestrum* are used as partitives, *nostrī* and *uestrī* in the objective functions of the genitive. Although Latin has no morphological distinction between accented and clitic forms, it is likely that the personal pronouns could either carry the stress accent or not, depending on context and emphasis (see further Adams (1994a)).

Classical Latin has a fairly rich system of demonstrative and anaphoric pronouns. There is a three way deictic contrast between the demonstratives *hic, haec, hoc* "this" (indicating proximity to the speaker); *iste, ista, istud* "that" (indicating proximity to the hearer); and *ille, illa, illud* "that" (indicating distance from both speaker and hearer). The declension of these pronouns shows two principal peculiarities: they have a distinct ending for the genitive singular in all genders, *-ius*, which does not correspond directly with any nominal genitive ending, and most show a final *-d* in the ending of the neuter nominative/accusative singular. The pronoun *hic, haec, hoc* "this" is reproduced in its Classical paradigm in Table 8.4, and this displays the addition of a deictic particle *-c* (earlier *-ce*) to some of its forms. In Early Latin the particle is found on other forms, such as accusative plural masculine *hōsce*. Note that the neuter singular *hoc* is generally scanned long, although the vowel is short, since the final *c* here represents a double consonant, reflecting original *hod-c(e)*.

The anaphoric pronoun *is, ea, id*, given in Table 8.5, does not have any deictic particles added. There is, however, a wide variety of alternative forms and spellings found for this pronoun. Some of these reflect phonological developments or orthographic uncertainties,

Table 8.5 The Latin pronoun *is, ea, id*

	Singular			Plural		
	Masc.	*Fem.*	*Neut.*	*Masc.*	*Fem.*	*Neut.*
Nom.	is	ea	id	iī	eae	ea
Acc.	eum	eam	id	eōs	eās	ea
Gen.	eius	eius	eius	eōrum	eārum	eōrum
Dat.	ei	ei	ei	iīs	iīs	iīs
Abl.	eōc	eā	hōc	iīs	iīs	iīs

Table 8.6 The Latin relative pronoun

	Singular			Plural		
	Masc.	*Fem.*	*Neut.*	*Masc.*	*Fem.*	*Neut.*
Nom.	quī	quae	quod	quī	quae	quae
Acc.	quem	quam	quod	quōs	quās	quae
Gen.	cuius	cuius	cuius	quōrum	quārum	quōrum
Dat.	cui	cui	cui	quibus	quibus	quibus
Abl.	quō	quā	quō	quibus	quibus	quibus

for example the nominative plural masculine is spelt *i, ii, iei, eei, iI* and *I* (using I to represent inscriptional *i longa*) on inscriptions, and the dative-ablative plural is spelt *eeis, ieis, iis, iIs* and *is*. The genitive singular is normally written in Classical texts as *eius*, but scanned as a trochee (heavy-light); ancient grammarians recommend the spelling *eiius*, which also occurs epigraphically, revealing that the weight of the first syllable is due to the gemination of the following *i*, not written in modern texts. The dative singular could represent a disyllable, /ejjī/ (as suggested by inscriptional *eiei*) or a monophthong /ei/. In Plautine comedy the form is scanned as both (and as a iamb), but since the form is largely avoided in classical poetry, it is difficult to be certain which form is correct for the later language.

Latin relative, interrogative and indefinite pronouns derive from two originally distinct paradigms, one an *i*-stem, the other an *o*-stem. In the nominative singular, the distinction is still made in the Classical language between the *i*-stem *qui(s)* (masculine and feminine), *quid* (neuter), which serve in the interrogative and indefinite functions and in compound forms such as *aliquis* "someone", *quisque* "each", and the *o*-stem *qui* (masculine), *quae* (feminine) and *quod* (neuter) which function as relative pronouns, and are also generally used for adjectival interrogatives and indefinites, hence *quae mulier?* "which woman?" and *aliquod ius* "some law". In Classical Latin the forms outside of the nominative singular (and nominative/accusative neuter) are the same for interrogatives, indefinites and relative pronouns, with the relative declined as in Table 8.6.

However, in earlier stages of the language there is evidence for further forms from the original two paradigms, such as dative-ablative plural *quīs*, and for a greater overlap of function between the two forms (which is continued in the Classical language in the use of both *quis* and *qui* as the adjectival interrogative "which?").

Table 8.7   The interrelationship between tense, mood and verb stem in Latin

Tense	Mood		
	Indicative	*Subjunctive*	*Imperative*
Present stem			
Present	Present indicative	Present subjunctive	Present imperative
Imperfect	Imperfect indicative	Imperfect subjunctive	
Future	Future indicative		Future imperative
Perfect stem			
Perfect	Perfect indicative	Perfect subjunctive	
Pluperfect	Pluperfect indicative	Pluperfect subjunctive	
Future perfect	Future Perfect indicative		

Verbal Morphology

Latin finite verbs are marked for person, number, tense/aspect, mood and voice. There are three persons and two numbers, singular and plural. There are six tenses of the indicative and four of the subjunctive, built from two separate stems, here termed the present stem and perfect stem. Table 8.7 represents the interrelationship between tense and mood and the two stems of the Latin verb. There are three indicative tenses, two subjunctives and two imperatives regularly formed from the present stem, and three indicatives and two subjunctives formed from the perfect stem.

The array of tense and mood formations presented in Table 8.7 applies equally to the two "voices" of the verb, active and passive. Active and passive forms are built on the same present stem, but the perfect passive is always periphrastic, formed from the perfect passive participle and auxiliary verb *esse* "to be". Accordingly, in the perfect passive verbs also encode the gender of the subject, as well as the number and person.

The non-finite verb system is less orderly. There is a present and future participle active, and a perfect participle passive; the present participle is formed from the present stem, but the future participle is generally formed from the same stem as the perfect passive participle, even where the verb is suppletive. A future passive participle, denoting necessity or obligation, and termed the "gerundive" in traditional grammar, is also formed from the present stem. Thus *ferō* "I carry" has a present participle *ferēns*, and gerundive *ferendus*, -*a*, -*um*, but a future active participle *lātūrus*, -*a*, -*um* and perfect passive participle *lātus*, -*a*, -*um*. There are six tense- and voice-marked infinitives, of which three – present active, perfect active and present passive – are synthetic while the others are periphrastic – the future active infinitive = future active participle + *esse* "to be"; the perfect passive infinitive = perfect passive participle + *esse* "to be"; and the future passive infinitive, made through the curious periphrasis of the "supine" (on which see below) + *īrī*, the passive infinitive of *eō* "I go". There are also two defective verbal nouns: the first, traditionally called the "gerund", is in form identical to the neuter singular forms of the gerundive and provides the oblique cases to the present infinitive active; the second, the "supine", also has active meaning and is formed from the same stem as the past participle passive and has two distinct forms (originally case forms) -*um* (thus *lātum* from *ferō*) and -*ū* (*lātū*). In Classical

Table 8.8   The four regular Latin verb conjugations

	Conjugation I	*Conjugation II*	*Conjugation III*	*Conjugation IV*
	amāre "to love"	spondēre "to pledge"	regere "to rule"	uenīre "to come"
Present indicative				
1 sg.	amō	spondeō	regō	ueniō
2 sg.	amās	spondēs	regis	uenīs
3 sg.	amat	spondet	regit	uenit
1 pl.	amāmus	spondēmus	regimus	uenīmus
2 pl.	amātis	spondētis	regitis	uenītis
3 pl.	amant	spondent	regunt	ueniunt
Present subjunctive				
1 sg.	amem	spondeam	regam	ueniam
2 sg.	amēs	spondeās	regās	ueniās
3 sg.	amet	spondeat	regat	ueniat
1 pl.	amēmus	spondeāmus	regāmus	ueniāmus
2 pl.	amētis	spondeātis	regātis	ueniātis
3 pl.	ament	spondeant	regant	ueniant
Future indicative				
1 sg.	amābō	spondēbō	regam	ueniam
2 sg.	amābis	spondēbis	regēs	ueniēs
3 sg.	amābit	spondēbit	reget	ueniet
1 pl.	amābimus	spondēbimus	regēmus	ueniēmus
2 pl.	amābitis	spondēbitis	regētis	ueniētis
3 pl.	amābunt	spondēbunt	regent	uenient

Latin the -*um* supine is only used as an optional means of expressing purpose clauses after verbs of motion (for example, *spectātum ueniunt* "they come to watch") and the -*ū* supine is used after certain adjectives (for example, *mīrābile dictū* "amazing to describe").

The formation of the different tense and mood paradigms and personal endings is the same for all verbs conjugated in the perfect system, but in the present system there are four main conjugation classes which differ in personal endings and in the formation of the future tense and present subjunctive. Table 8.8 presents the present indicative, present subjunctive and future indicative of the active for the four conjugations.

Note that there is also a sub-class of conjugation III of the type *facere* "to do", which forms present indicative *faciō* and *faciunt*, and subjunctive *faciam*, *faciās*, etc., future *faciam*, *faciēs*, etc. As can be seen in the present indicative, the four conjugations share the same set of personal endings, which are basically those of conjugation III but differences arise from fusion of the endings with stem vowels in conjugations I, II and IV. In the subjunctive the personal endings are the same except for the first person singular, which is marked by -*m* rather than -*ō*. These two endings are a survival of a much more pervasive system of differentiation of primary (= non-past, non-subjunctive) and secondary (= either + past, or + subjunctive, or both) endings, which is more widely attested in some Early Latin texts. The distribution of the -*m* and -*ō* morphemes is still largely governed by the original primary/secondary distinctions, except in the future

Table 8.9 Other present stem formations of the verb *amō*

Imperfect indicative	amāb -am, -ās, -at, -āmus, -ātis, -ant.
Imperfect subjunctive	amār -em, -ēs, -et, -ēmus, -ētis, ent.
Imperative I	amā, amāte.
Imperative II	amātō, amātō, amātōte, amantō.

Table 8.10 The Latin perfect conjugation

Infinitive	amāre	spondēre	regere	uenīre
Perfect stem	amāu-	spopond-	rēx-	uēn-
	(suffix -u-)	(reduplication)	(suffix -s-)	(long vowel)
1 sg.	amāu -ī	spopond -ī	rēx -ī	uēn -ī
2 sg.	amāu -istī	spopond -istī	rēx -istī	uēn -istī
3 sg.	amāu -it	spopond -it	rēx -it	uēn -it
1 pl.	amāu -imus	spopond -imus	rēx -imus	uēn -imus
2 pl.	amāu -istis	spopond -istis	rēx -istis	uēn -istis
3 pl.	amāu -ērunt	spopond -ērunt	rēx -ērunt	uēn -ērunt

indicative. For this tense, not only is there a difference in the first person singular morpheme in conjugations III and IV from conjugations I and II, but there is also a radically different stem formation. The other present stem tense and mood forms of the verb *amō* are given in Table 8.9.

In the imperative paradigms there is no form for the first person and the forms given are respectively second singular and plural for the imperative I, and second singular, third singular, second plural and third plural for imperative II. In the second person there is consequently a difference between two different imperative forms. This is not a difference of aspect but rather one of relative tense. Where the two forms are used in conjunction, the future imperative is used to refer to an event following the present imperative – note for example the following commands from Plautus' play *Pseudolus* (line 18):

cape hās tabellās, tūte hinc narrātō tibī

Take these tablets and find out for yourself from them.

Cape, present imperative "take!", refers to the initial action, and *narrātō*, future imperative "tell!", refers to an action consequent on this, reading what is written on the tablets.

The perfect stem is generally marked over against the present stem, either through the addition of a suffix (-*s*- or -*u*-), reduplication of the initial consonant or consonant cluster of the root syllable, change (usually lengthening) of the nucleus of the root syllable, or through suppletion; however, one class of perfects has equivalent stems to the present. The perfect is further marked by a special set of personal endings in the perfect indicative. As examples of the different types of perfect formation and the endings, Table 8.10 gives the perfects of the four verbs featured in Table 8.8.

Representative examples of perfects formed through suppletion, and the perfect with unchanged stem, can also be added: *ferō* "I carry", perfect *tulī*; *bibō* "I drink", perfect

Table 8.11   Other perfect stem formations from the verb *amō*

Future perfect	amāuer -ō, -is, -it, -imus, -itis, -int.
Pluperfect	amāuer -am, -ās, -at, -āmus, -ātis, -ant.
Perfect subjunctive	amāuer -im, -is, -it, -imus, -itis, -int.
Pluperfect subjunctive	amāuiss -em, -ēs, -et, -ēmus, -ētis, -ent.

bibī. Some Latin stems show variation between two or more different means of forming a perfect. For example, *pangō* "I fix" has a regular perfect *pepigī* in Classical Latin, with occasional attestations of *pānxī* and *pēgī*, but the compounds of *pangō*, *compingō* and *impingō* have perfects *compegi* and *impēgī*.

The third plural ending *-ērunt* of Classical Latin probably represents a conflation of two competing morphs *-ēre* and *-erunt*. All three endings are attested in Early Latin verse (Lucretius has all three endings, and a contracted form within three lines at 6.3–5: *recreāuērunt, rogārunt, dederunt, genuēre*), and *-ēre* seems to have been marked in Classical Latin as an archaism. In poetry, *-erunt* with short *e* is the least frequent ending in Classical hexameters, but that may be because many of the resulting scansions would have been unmetrical. It is difficult to be certain when *-erunt* with short *e* was used outside of poetry, but this is the form which survived into Romance and which lies behind the contracted forms of perfects of the first declension, such as *rogārunt* for *rogāuerunt*, which are found in most Classical Latin texts (but avoided by Sallust and Tacitus) and which become the predominant form in, for example, the sub-literary documents from Vindolanda (Adams (2003a) 544). Contracted forms of the second person, as *amāsti* and *amāstis* are also widely attested (even in Sallust and Tacitus); third-person forms, such as *inritāt* for *inritāuit* at Lucretius 1.70, are difficult to identify since in most circumstances they can be taken as historic presents.

Other conjugations also show contracted forms in the perfect at all periods. Most frequently this effects verbs which form the perfect with the marker *-u-*, hence forms such as *plesti* "you filled" and *plerunt* "they filled" from *pleo* "I fill" and its compounds are widely found. Syncopated forms of perfects made with a marker *-s-*, such as *dixti* "you said" from *dico* "I say" are less widely attested, and seem to have been largely avoided in Classical prose, although Quintilian comments on Cicero's use of the form *dixti* at *Pro Caecina* 82 (*Inst.* 9.3.22).

The remaining tenses and moods of the perfect stem take either the secondary endings found in the present system or, in the case of the future perfect, the primary endings of the present system, as sketched out in the examples from the verb *amō* given in Table 8.11.

In Early Latin the future perfect and perfect subjunctive were better distinguished, since the perfect subjunctive showed a long vowel in the ending, *amāuerīs, amāuerīt*, etc. Parallel to the contracted perfect indicative forms *-asti, -astis -arunt* alongside *-auisti, -auistis* and *-auerunt*, we find contracted forms *amārim*, etc. for *amāuerim*, and *amāsse*, etc. for *amāuisse* (again, Sallust and Tacitus avoid contracted forms which result in *-ar-* but admit forms with *-as-*).

A large number of verbs ("deponents") only show passive morphology of finite forms but are not semantically passive. Many of these correspond to middle or reflexive verbs

Table 8.12　Passive forms of the verb *amō*

Present indicative	amor, amāris, amātur, amāmur, amāminī, amantur
Present subjunctive	amer, amēre, amētur, amēmur, amēminī, amentur
Future indicative	amābor, amābere, amābitur, amābimur, amābiminī, amābuntur
Imperfect indicative	amābar, amābāre, amābātur, amābāmur, amābāminī, amābantur
Imperfect subjunctive	amārer, amārēre, amārētur, amārēmur, amārēminī, amārēntur

Table 8.13　Perfect passive forms of the verb *amō*

Perfect passive indicative	amātus sum, amātus es, amātus est, amātī sumus, amātī estis, amātī sunt.
Perfect passive subjunctive	amātus sim, amātus sīs, amātus sit, amātī sīmus, amātī sītis, amātī sint.

in other languages, thus *īrāscor* "I become angry", *ūtor* "I use", *reor* "I think" and *morior* "I die". Deponent verbs do not have separate active paradigms, but they do use some non-finite active forms, such as the present and future participles; note also that the gerundive of deponent verbs is semantically passive. In all periods of Latin there was some variation in the assignment of certain verbs to the deponent class: *assentiō* and *assentior* are both found with the same meaning, "I assent", or "I approve", and Varro (*ap.* Gel. 2.25.9) credits Sisenna with promulgating the active form in place of the deponent.

As discussed above, the present system of the passive is formed from the same stem as the present active system. Thus for the verb *amō* "I love" the passive present indicative, present subjunctive and future indicative are given in Table 8.12.

In the second person singular, the old indicative form ending in -*re*, as *amāre*, functions only as the passive imperative in the Classical language, but could also be used as an indicative in earlier Latin. The -*re* forms were retained in the other moods and tenses, however, being slightly more frequent in Cicero than forms in -*ris*, but thereafter began to fall out of use in prose.

The perfect stem of the passive is different from the perfect active stem, and all moods and tenses are formed through periphrasis with the perfect passive participle and present stem forms of the copula verb *esse*. The perfect passive indicative and subjunctive of *amō* are given in Table 8.13 for illustration (in all persons the forms agreeing with a masculine subject are given; agreement for a feminine or neuter subject would be different).

FURTHER READING

The standard school grammars of Latin (Gildersleeve and Lodge (1894), Hale and Buck (1903), Greenough *et al.* (1903), all with many reprints and revisions, and the last widely available on the web) give more amplified presentations of the synchronic inflectional morphology, including paradigms of irregular forms. The fullest presentation of the forms that are found in texts and inscriptions is Neue and Wagener (1892–1905). Weiss (2009) gives a very good overview of the diachronic morphology of Latin, and includes discussion of many early Latin forms. The most comprehensive reference works are Kühner *et al.* (1976) and Leumann (1977). Matthews (1972) has been influential in modern theoretical studies on morphology.

CHAPTER 9

Latin Syntax

Geoffrey Horrocks

Introduction

Sentences are usually taken to be the largest linguistic structures for which syntactic rules can be stated; rules for constructing combinations of sentences, such as paragraphs or chapters, are clearly of a different kind, being essentially informal guidelines of a pragmatic, rhetorical or narratological nature.

Since the grammatically well-formed sentences of any language are infinite in number, and most have therefore never been written or uttered, a syntactic description requires the identification of the underlying structural patterns (constructions) that collectively characterize *any* sentence. Accordingly, a typical grammar lists the permissible parts of sentences and formulates rules for combining and arranging these, with examples to illustrate the rules' requirements. For a language like Latin, with no native speakers to interrogate, the grammaticality of syntactic structures can be established only by reference to data preserved in a textual corpus. Ordinarily, a syntactic description of such "corpus languages" is judged satisfactory to the extent that sentences it characterizes as well formed correctly replicate the grammatical properties of output data taken to be well formed by native speakers in earlier times. But Latin remained in creative use down into the Middle Ages and beyond, continuing to evolve long after it had ceased to have native speakers. Once the intuitive grasp of individuals who acquired Latin naturally can no longer be appealed to, even indirectly via texts they created, the issue of what is grammatical becomes more problematical. Priority is therefore given here to the Latin of the ancient world, and specifically to the "Classical" language used in literary texts and official documents from the first century BCE until the fall of the Roman empire in the west, though even this increasingly standardized written variety was never homogeneous

A Companion to the Latin Language, First Edition. Edited by James Clackson.
© 2011 Blackwell Publishing Ltd. Published 2011 by Blackwell Publishing Ltd.

(usage differs, for example, according to period, genre and individual preference), and any general syntactic account must abstract away from this stylistic variation in some degree.

Focusing on elite written Latin in this way brings two clear advantages: first, the surviving corpus is large, exemplifying a wide array of sentence structures as a basis for analysis; secondly, usage at this level was carefully considered and subject to revision, so we may reasonably assume that the surviving material properly reflects the grammaticality judgements of educated native speakers to a high degree. We should not forget, however, that elite Latin was a rather contrived medium, subject to class-driven "refinements" and the influence of a higher education system involving exposure to both the Greek and Latin literary traditions. Even allowing for discrepancies in the volume of available evidence, any syntactic description based on Classical Latin texts will be significantly different from one describing the more natural usage of the average speaker-hearer of the period.

For reasons of space, what follows will necessarily focus on general principles and on a small selection of illustrative phenomena that raise interesting questions of analysis. For a comprehensive treatment the reader is referred to the full-scale grammars and studies listed in the bibliography (Hofmann and Leumann (1965–1979), Kühner, Stegmann and Thierfelder (1976), Pinkster (1990a), Woodcock (1959)). Baldi and Cuzzolin (2009) offers some interesting perspectives on various issues raised here.

Meaning and Sentence Structure

It is commonly argued that the meanings of declarative sentences are the situations or states of affairs they are used to describe. Typically, situations are classified into states (e.g. as denoted by a sentence like *she is cold*), activities (e.g. as denoted by a sentence like *she ran fast*) and accomplishments (e.g. as denoted by a sentence like *she cleaned the car*). Any situation has both essential and accidental properties. In any situation involving "giving", for example, it is necessarily the case that an agent (the giver/source) deliberately transfers something (the gift/patient) to a third party (the recipient). On the other hand, though an act of "giving" is also normally located in time, and may optionally be characterized by further content (e.g. the place of giving, the manner of giving, the reason for giving, etc.), none of this additional material is intrinsic to the action per se.

Individual situations are often characterized formally as "complete semantic predications". These make explicit the circumstances required within the relevant framework of reference (e.g. this world, the world of a novel, etc.) for a given sentence to be paired with a given situation as its meaning. The essential components of a complete semantic predication are a core relational element ("the semantic predicate") and those participants unavoidably involved in the relationship in question (its "arguments"). Semantic predicates are classified as one-place (e.g. "being cold"), two-place (e.g. "cleaning"), etc., according to the number of their arguments: predicates with up to three arguments are not uncommon (e.g. "giving", "putting"), those with four probably represent the maximum (e.g. "[someone] betting [someone else] [a sum of money] [that something will happen]"). Such representations of situations are intended to be non-language specific: i.e. sentences in two or more languages that denote the same situation are taken to be synonymous. See Cann (1993) for a clear introduction to formal semantics.

Unsurprisingly, the grammatical properties of sentences across languages partly reflect the semantic content of the situations they describe, though this is far from being a mechanical correspondence (translation, for example, clearly involves a great deal more than vocabulary substitution into otherwise universal structures). None the less, a semantic predicate is prototypically denoted by a verb (intransitive, transitive or ditransitive according to the number of arguments to be represented grammatically),[1] and each of its arguments by a nominal expression (i.e. a noun, with or without further modification); and when a complete situation functions as an argument, the regular grammatical correspondent is a subordinate clause (e.g. *Caesar dixit [se felicem esse]*, literally "Caesar said [himself happy to-be]", i.e. "Caesar said he was happy").

But the syntactic structures in which these grammatical elements appear also have properties that do not follow from semantic considerations. Indo-European languages like Latin, for example, have a syntactic rule that obligatorily assigns structural prominence to just one of the argument-denoting nominals of a semantic predicate by distinguishing a "subject" from the remaining sentence structure consisting of a verb plus the representations of any remaining arguments (i.e. its "objects", etc.). This latter element is traditionally known as a "(syntactic) predicate", and the term "(syntactic) predication" is used to describe the relationship between subjects and their (syntactic) predicates.[2] Since subjects and objects are regularly identified formally through the assignment of different grammatical cases (viz. nominative for the subject of a sentence with a finite verb, i.e. one that can be inflected for person and number, and accusative for the direct object of a transitive verb), languages like Latin are often called "nominative-accusative languages".

Note that the notion of a subject is a purely grammatical one, with no connection to any specific semantic role or property. The subject of a sentence, for example, may denote an agent (e.g. in *Caesar inimicos interfecit* "Caesar killed his enemies"), a patient (e.g. in *Caesar mortuus est* "Caesar died"), a recipient (e.g. in *Caesar donum accepit* "Caesar received a gift") or an experiencer (e.g. in *Caesar dolorem passus est* "Caesar suffered anguish"). So strong is the rule enforcing the presence of a subject that there are sentences in which the subject denotes no argument at all, cf. the meaningless "it" reflected in the third-person inflectional morphology of weather verbs like *pluit* "it's raining" or impersonal passives like *itur*, literally "it-is-gone", i.e. "people go". The absence of a straightforward syntactic–semantic correlation is particularly clear in active–passive pairs such as that in 1. When the passive agent is specified, the two sentences describe the same situation (i.e. are broadly synonymous), but in the first the subject denotes the agent and in the second the patient:

1 (a) coniurati$_{nom}$ Caesarem$_{acc}$ interfecerunt$_{3pl}$
        conspirators Caesar killed
        the conspirators killed Caesar

  (b) Caesar$_{nom}$ (a coniuratis$_{abl}$) interfectus$_{nom}$ est$_{3sg}$
        Caesar (by conspirators) having-been-killed is
        Caesar was killed (by the conspirators)

Correspondingly, while direct objects often represent patients, patients are by no means necessarily represented by direct objects.

There is nothing inevitable about this way of doing things. For example, the "ergative-absolutive" system of case marking used in Basque and many languages of the Caucasus, North and Central America and Australia, ordinarily treats the nominal expression denoting the patient argument of a two-place predicate and that denoting the single argument of a one-place predicate in the same way, i.e. both elements receive the absolutive case reflecting the fact that both combine with the verb to form the grammatical nucleus of a sentence. Other nominal elements are peripheral to the nucleus and are marked with cases more closely reflecting the semantic roles of the relevant arguments: thus peripheral nominals representing agents are marked with the ergative case (the case of the "doer"), and peripheral expressions representing patients are marked with an oblique case often called the dative (the case of the person/thing that something is done "to" or "for").

Sentences containing what would be transitive and intransitive verbs in a nominative-accusative language, e.g. *kill* and *arrive*, therefore take the following (schematic) forms:

2 (a) [kill Caesar$_{abs}$] the conspirators$_{erg}$
        i.e. there is a killing involving Caesar – by the conspirators
  (b) [arrive Caesar$_{abs}$]
        i.e. there is an arrival involving Caesar

The sentence type in **2a**, however, may be restructured by a rule of "anti-passive", which internalizes the representation of the agent and marks it absolutive, thus pushing the representation of the patient to the periphery, where it receives dative case:

3 [kill$_{antipass}$ the conspirators$_{abs}$] Caesar$_{dat}$
    i.e. there is a killing involving the conspirators – to/for Caesar

Furthermore, in at least some of these languages the sentence type in **2b** has a peripheral ergative in place of the internal absolutive whenever the corresponding argument is clearly an agent:

4 [run] Caesar$_{erg}$
    i.e. there is a running – by Caesar

Taking **2–4** together, it is clearly impossible to identify any structural elements that function systematically in the manner of Latin-style subjects and objects. The sentences of ergative-absolutive languages are more akin to nominal expressions of the type *the destruction of the city (by the barbarians), the love of the barbarians (for the city), the arrival of the barbarians, the attack (by the barbarians)*, etc., where an internal "genitive", whether denoting a patient or an agent, combines with a noun to form a structural nucleus, and any additional/peripheral material is marked with semantically transparent prepositions. See Dixon (1994) for an accessible introduction to ergativity.

Constituency and Discontinuity

As will now be clear, syntactic rules often refer to abstract grammatical notions like subject, object and predicate. Any reasonable account of the active–passive relationship exemplified in 1, for example, must make a connection between the direct object of a transitive verb in an active sentence and the subject of the corresponding passive sentence. But the items functioning as subjects, objects and predicates have no fixed linear positions, are of variable length, have no consistent superficial properties,[3] and in Latin may sometimes be represented by sets of words that are in part non-contiguous (see the discussion of 5 and the first clause of 7 below). It is clear, therefore, that the items associated with such functions cannot be identified in a satisfactory way by simple examination of the sequences of words that overtly "realize" the more abstract structures underlying sentences (e.g. as "the first *n* words", "the *n* words after the first word", etc.).

A simple but effective way to identify the "sets of words" within a string that constitute grammatically significant entities is to organize each such set into a single structural building block (or *constituent*) at the level of analysis where underlying constructions are made explicit (i.e. the level relevant to construal, at which one necessarily talks about things like subjects, objects, etc.). Each of these larger constructs belongs to one of a limited set of types that serve as higher-order constituents of sentences; each type can be shown to occur in a characteristic set of "structural", as opposed to linear, positions (its *distribution*), and each structural position can be associated with a determinate function. Nouns and verbs, for example, are the word-level constituents of higher-level noun phrases (NP) and verb phrases (VP), both of which may contain further material (e.g. demonstratives, adjectives, relative clauses, etc. on the one hand, adverbs, objects, subordinate clauses, etc. on the other). But while verb phrases have only one structural position (co-constituent of a subject noun phrase within a sentence) and one function (syntactic predicate), a noun phrase can serve *inter alia* as a subject or a direct object according to whether it appears alongside a verb phrase as a co-constituent of a sentence, or alongside a verb as a co-constituent of a verb phrase. According to this constituency model of sentence structure, syntactic rules must (i) regulate the internal structure of all phrase types, (ii) stipulate the distribution of each phrase type within sentences, associating each structural position with an appropriate grammatical function, and (iii) specify any optional or obligatory "realizational" divergences from the underlying constructions so described, involving the reordering or dismemberment of constituents. See Adger (2003) for an up-to-date introduction to syntactic theory.

With regard to this last function, it is clear that constituents may or may not be assigned fixed positions relative to one another according to their function, and that their structural integrity may or may not be reflected in the contiguity of their component parts within particular linear realizations of a given construction. Using English and Latin as examples of different practice, English plainly allows fewer realizational discontinuities than Latin (attributive adjectives, for example, cannot easily be separated from the nouns they modify), and unlike in Latin constituent order is fixed, with subject noun phrases in declarative sentences preceding verb phrases, and transitive verbs preceding their objects. These differences follow from the fact that in Latin, the invisible/inaudible syntactic relationships that bind elements together into constituents are made manifest through the imposition of specific requirements on morphological form: an attributive adjective, for example, is part of a noun phrase by definition, but may, for pragmatic or stylistic reasons, be separated structurally from the noun it modifies because overt morphological agreement reveals the existence of the underlying relationship regardless of positioning. In the "poetic" example in **5** the two relevant pairings of discontinuous adjective and noun are picked out in italic and bold:

5 et *liquidum* **spisso** secreuit ab **aere** *caelum*
   and *bright*$_{sg.neut.acc}$ dense$_{sg.masc.abl}$ he-separated from atmosphere$_{sg.masc.abl}$ heaven$_{sg.neut.acc}$
   and (god) separated the bright heavens from the dense atmosphere (Ovid, *Met.* 1.23)

Within this specific realization there is clearly no way *liquidum caelum* "the bright heavens" or *a(b) spisso aere* "from the dense atmosphere" could be represented as the constituents they plainly are at the more abstract level relevant to construal. Similarly, the words of the sentence:

6 puella patrem osculatur
   girl$_{nom}$ *father*$_{acc}$ *kisses*$_{3sg}$
   the girl is kissing her father

may in principle appear in any order (again with stylistic/pragmatic differences), though each of these orderings realizes the same underlying construction, namely that of an NP (subject) with a VP (predicate) consisting of a transitive verb and an NP (direct object).[4] This information is recoverable, regardless of order, from the cases overtly assigned to the noun phrases (nominative to the subject, accusative to the direct object) and the overt agreement of the verb with its subject. In English, by contrast, where the rich array of morphological marking available to Latin has been largely lost, satisfactory identification of constituents depends very largely on their retaining their structural coherence (e.g. *peaceloving Romans never attack Gauls* cannot mean "Romans never attack peaceloving Gauls", contrast **5**), and correct interpretation of grammatical functions requires the relative ordering of constituents to be syntactically fixed (e.g. *the Romans attacked the Gauls* cannot have the same meaning as *the Gauls attacked the Romans*, contrast *puella patrem osculatur*, *patrem puella osculatur* both of which convey the information that the girl is kissing her father).

We should not, however, exaggerate the extent to which ordinary Latin prose permits the kind of scrambling of constituents seen in **5**. Such breaking up of constituents, occasionally carried to extremes, is a striking characteristic of Latin poetry but it represents a marked deviation from "normal practice". In prose texts major sentential constituents, while allowing considerable freedom in the internal ordering of their component parts, mostly retain their overall structural coherence. The only regular exceptions involve the obligatory preposing of material for grammatical reasons (e.g. in interrogative and relative clauses, see below) and the optional focalization or topicalization of material, again by preposing, for reasons of emphasis/contrast or backgrounding (again see below).

To illustrate, consider the complex sentence in 7, where every multi-word noun phrase (NP), prepositional phrase (PP) and adverb phrase (ADVP) has been bracketed together as an uninterrupted unit:

7 Quae precatus [$_{PP}$ a dis immortalibus] sum, [$_{NP}$ more institutoque
   which-things having-prayed from gods immortal I-am with-custom convention-and
   maiorum] [$_{NP}$ illo die] quo auspicato [$_{NP}$ comitiis centuriatis] [$_{NP}$ L.
   of-ancestors that day on-which having-taken-auspices at-comitia centuriata Lucius
   Murenam] consulem renuntiaui, ut [$_{NP}$ ea res] [$_{NP}$ mihi fidei magistratuique meo,
   Murena consul I-declared, that that thing for-me for-faith for-magistracy-and my,
   populo plebique Romanae] [$_{ADVP}$ bene atque feliciter] eueniret, eadem
   for-people plebs-and Roman well and happily might-turn-out, the-same-things
   precor [$_{PP}$ ab isdem dis immortalibus] [$_{PP}$ ob [$_{NP}$ eiusdem hominis] consulatum
   I-pray from same gods immortal for of-same man consulship
   [$_{PP}$ una cum salute] obtinendum], et ut [$_{NP}$ uestrae mentes atque sententiae]
   together with safety being-obtained, both that your minds and judgements
   [$_{PP}$ cum [$_{NP}$ populi Romani] uoluntatibus suffragiisque] consentiant, [$_{NP}$ eaque res]
   with of-people Roman wishes votes-and may-agree, that-and thing
   [$_{NP}$ uobis populoque Romano] [$_{NP}$ pacem, tranquillitatem, otium, concordiamque]
   for-you people-and Roman peace, tranquillity, leisure, harmony-and
   adferat.
   may-bring.

> What, in accordance with the customs and conventions of our ancestors, I requested of the gods that day when, after taking the auspices, I declared Lucius Murena consul at the *comitia centuriata*, that this matter might turn out successfully and well for me, my good faith and my magistracy, and for the people and masses of Rome, those same things I request of those same gods in the interests of this same man entering into his consulship in safety, both that your intentions and judgements may concur with the wishes and votes of the Roman people and that this matter may bring peace, tranquillity, quiet and harmony to you and the Roman people. (Cicero, *Mur.* 1)

This is the regular state of affairs in even the most artistic Latin prose. Note that simple linear separation of syntactically related items within a constituent does not of itself constitute discontinuity, which always entails actual structural dismemberment, as in **5**. For example, the complex PP *ob eiusdem hominis consulatum una cum salute obtinendum*, literally "for the-same man's consulship together with safety being-obtained", has the internal structure illustrated in **8**, in which the hierachical arrangement of constituents has been made explicit in the form of a "tree diagram".[5] The clause-like status of the accusative NP dependent on *ob* (i.e. *consulatum obtinendum*) follows from the fact that the ADJP, containing a specifically *verbal* adjective (gerundive), is assigned a predicative (VP-like) role in construction with the preceding (subject-like) NP. *Mutatis mutandis,* the agreement of the gerundive with the subject is then parallel to the agreement seen in the regular copular construction [NP [(*esse*) ADJP]]:

8

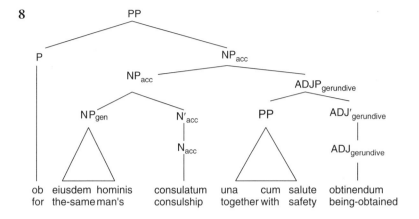

Though *eiusdem hominis* and *una cum salute* intervene in linear terms between pairs of syntactically related items, namely *ob* and *consulatum*, and *consulatum* and *obtinendum*, *eiusdem hominis* is a constituent of the phrase containing *consulatum*, and *una cum salute* a constituent of the phrase containing *obtinendum*. The structural coherence of the PP is therefore unbroken, and the items in construction with one another within it (P and NP, NP and ADJP) remain contiguous at the relevant structural levels.

The sole discontinuity in 7, therefore, involves the words at the very beginning. The direct object relative pronoun *quae* "which-things" has been preposed to clause-initial position in the usual way, but the periphrastic verb form *precatus sum* "I asked for", literally "having-asked-for I-am", has been divided by the PP *a dis immortalibus* "by the-immortal gods". If we assume that *sum* "I-am" remains in the "basic" verb position (i.e. final in its immediate clause in Classical Latin, see below on constituent order), it seems that *precatus* "having-asked-for" has been preposed for reasons of contrast with the following *(eadem) precor* "(the-same-things) I-ask-for", the contrast here being one of time reference rather than lexical content: "what I asked for *then*, I also ask for *now*." As noted, the vast majority of discontinuities in Classical Latin prose involve grammatically driven or pragmatically motivated preposings of this kind, and both can be handled in a simple and systematic way, as we shall see later in this chapter. There is therefore no reason to doubt the basic empirical adequacy of a constituency model of Latin syntactic structure, or to abandon the many advantages this approach brings in terms of clarity and precision of description.

Phrases: Heads, Complements and Adjuncts

Each major word class (noun, verb, adjective, adverb) in Latin is defined by a characteristic set of grammatical categories, and each category has a set of "values" of which only one can be carried by any specific word form within a sentence. So Latin nouns and adjectives, for example, are characterized by *number* (singular, plural), *gender* (masculine, feminine, neuter) and *case* (nominative, vocative, accusative, genitive, dative, ablative), while verbs are associated with *person* (1, 2, 3), *number* (singular, plural), *tense* (present, future, past), *voice* (active, passive) and *mood* (indicative, subjunctive, imperative). The particular values, or grammatical properties, carried by a given word form are indicated partly by its inflectional morphology and partly by its syntactic function in specific contexts: e.g. the noun form *bellum* means ["war" + singular + neuter + nominative/accusative], while *bella* means ["war" + plural + neuter + nominative/accusative]; when these are used as subject or direct object NPs, either nominative or accusative is necessarily selected to the exclusion of the other.

The relationship between the values of grammatical categories and the real world is variable. Gender, for example, is an inherent property of individual nouns (i.e. not a matter of choice) but rarely correlates with definable characteristics of noun denotations despite a tendency for male and female beings to be denoted by nouns of masculine and feminine gender respectively. By contrast, the choice of number is normally determined by the character of the denotation (assuming that the items in question are countable), and that of case may well be (if the case function is adverbial, as with "instrumental" ablatives, etc.), though we have also seen that case can reflect purely grammatical considerations (e.g. the nominative assigned to the subjects of finite verb forms).

In attributive adjectives, by contrast, the values for number, gender and case depend *entirely* on the values of these categories in the nouns they modify, i.e. there are no inherent values and no semantic correlates. As noted in the previous section, the grammatical properties of an adjective merely connect it formally to the noun with whose meaning its own meaning is to be combined, so *saeuum* [singular + neuter + nominative/accusative] *bellum* "cruel war", *saeua* [plural + neuter + nominative/accusative] *bella* "cruel wars", etc. Such *agreement* or *concord* involves the copying of grammatical properties from a controlling element (where they may or may not be semantically motivated) onto a controlled one (where they are not). Obviously agreement can be marked overtly in this way only when the related pairs of items belong to word classes characterized by at least a common subset of grammatical categories.

There is a distinct type of relationship between a controlling element and a controlled one, namely that of *government*. In this case the controlling item does not transfer its own properties to the dependent item, but rather imposes a characteristic "mark" on it, usually in the form of a specific value for a particular grammatical category. Thus prepositions and transitive verbs select specific cases for the NPs that accompany them (e.g. *ad* + accusative "at, to/towards", *in* + accusative "into" or + ablative "in", *amo* + accusative "love", *do* + accusative and dative "give", *utor* + ablative "use", etc.). Similarly, conjunctions govern the choice of mood in a following clause (e.g. *ut* + subjunctive, *ubi* + indicative, etc.), while verbs taking subordinate clauses usually require these to take a specific form, e.g. to contain a subjectless "bare" infinitive (e.g. *conor* "I try"), an infinitive with an accusative subject (e.g. *arbitror* "I think"), or a finite verb with a specific conjunction (e.g. *gaudeo* "I rejoice" + *quod* "that/because") etc.

Agreement and government are the key syntactic relationships involved in the construction of phrases. As we have seen, each word class (noun, verb, adjective, adverb, preposition) can "project" a superstructure above itself, the individual noun, adjective, verb, etc. being the *head* of the relevant constituent in each case, i.e. the indispensable element on which all other elements, if any, depend. Each head represents a semantic predicate, and any additional material represents either its arguments (i.e. items presupposed by the predicate, if any) or its modifiers (i.e. items adding extra information but not required by the predicate per se). The phrases[6] representing semantic arguments of a predicate are the *complements* of the head, and are governed by it. Complements are specific to each individual head and, as grammatical representations of the arguments of the predicate it denotes, obligatory (i.e. if not physically present, something appropriate must be understood from the context). Taking a set of verbs to exemplify this point, *amo* "I love" takes a direct object NP in the accusative, *do* "I give" takes a direct object NP in the accusative and an indirect object NP in the dative, while *dico* "I say" takes a subordinate clause containing an accusative subject and an infinitival predicate, etc.[7] The phrases representing optional semantic modifiers are *adjuncts*, and these agree in all the grammatical categories they share with the head. Adjuncts, like their denotations, are optional, and the array of available options in each case depends on the type of expression being modified: e.g. ADJPs are typical modifiers within NPs, ADVPs within VPs, etc.[8]

Complements attach to heads before any adjuncts as a mark of their close syntactic bond, so that a head X (of any major word class) and its complement(s) form a subphrase of type X′ ("X prime"); X and X′ share all their grammatical properties by definition. In Classical Latin prose verbs normally follow their complements unless the complement is a subordinate clause; heads other than verbs, however, normally precede their complements, with subordinate clauses coming last:

9 Complements (neutral ordering)
   (a) NP/PP < V < S
   (b) X (= head other than V) < NP/PP, S

Other orders are always possible, but these are usually associated with some degree of pragmatic markedness involving contrast or emphasis (see the section below on constituent order in clauses, including the placement of subjects).

Adjuncts combine with subphrases of type X′ to form full phrases of type XP, or with phrases of type XP to form still larger phrases of type XP (see below for further discussion of these two levels of attachment); X, X′ and XP share all their grammatical properties by definition. The placement of adjuncts with respect to X′ is in principle quite free, though relative clauses follow the nominals they modify, and both demonstrative/anaphoric and interrogative/indefinite "pronouns", when used adjectivally with nominals, normally precede, standing before other pre-nominal adjuncts, e.g. *hic (bonus) uir* "this (good) man", *illa mulier* "that woman", *qui(s) senator* "which senator?/some senator", *quaedam puella* "a-certain girl", etc.; these items are *determiners* (Det), i.e. they combine with nominal elements denoting sets of properties, e.g. "(good) girl", to form full NPs denoting individuals characterized by those properties, e.g. "this/which/some/a certain [person who is a] (good) girl" etc. Otherwise, a post-X′ position for an adjunct is more neutral in pragmatic terms than a pre-X′ position. Adjuncts at the XP level, however, are much more loosely connected, and convey rather incidental information, including afterthoughts, clarifications, etc.; accordingly, they typically follow XP:

10 Adjuncts (neutral ordering)
   (a) Det < N′
   (b) X′ < XP/S
   (c) XP < XP/S

Summarizing, each phrase has the schematic structure in **11**, where X represents any lexical category (i.e. noun, verb, adjective, adverb, preposition), and each complement or adjunct (other than Det) is a full phrase or a subordinate clause:

11

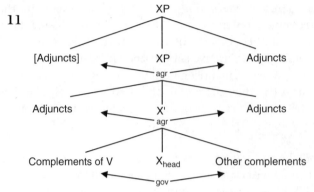

Every head denoting a relational predicate has its own characteristic set of complements to represent the relevant arguments, the head and its complements forming a subphrase X′. All X′ may then combine optionally with adjuncts: e.g. N′ with demonstratives, possessive adjectives, attributive adjectives, NPs in semantically significant oblique cases (descriptive ablatives and genitives), and relative clauses; V′ with various types of adverbial modifier (e.g. certain PPs and obliquely case-marked NPs, clauses with conditional, temporal, causal, etc. functions, and so on). XP may also combine with further adjuncts, albeit adjuncts of a less "connected" character. Independently of **9** and **10**, there is also a tendency for heads and agreeing modifiers to be positioned so as to sandwich dependents of the modifier, e.g. *ceteras rei-publicae partis* "the-remaining of-the-republic parts", *mutati in deterius principatus* "of-the-changed for the-worse principate" (both examples from Tacitus, *Annals* 4.6).

The level of attachment of adjuncts is determined by their modifying range or "scope". In the NP *uir sapiens, quem omnes admirantur* "the wise man, whom all admire", for example, one interpretation is that the relative clause adds information about the wise man. This is reflected in **12**, where the higher and more peripheral position of the relative clause gives it wider scope than the ADJP:

12

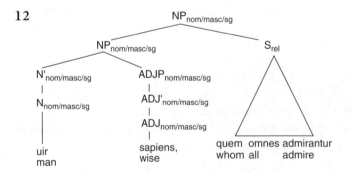

In principle, however, relative clauses may contribute to the identification of a referent by restricting its range (e.g. "the (wise) man whom all admire" rather than, say, "the (wise) man whom his wife despises"); this restrictive type of relative clause, unlike the non-restrictive type in **12**, is never associated with an intonational pause (represented graphically by a comma). The two readings are naturally accommodated, as in **13**, by adjoining restrictive relative clauses at the X′ level and non-restrictive ones at the XP level, where an intonational pause may be assumed:

13

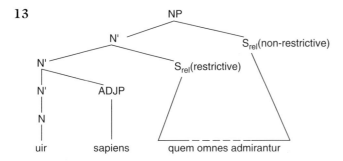

The higher level of adjunction is also useful for distinguishing between attributive adjectives (with ADJP adjoined to N′) and predicative uses of adjunct adjectives and participles. Consider the examples in **14**:

14 (a) urbem ueterem incenderunt
    *city*_{fem.acc.sg} *old*_{fem.acc.sg} *they-burned*
(b) urbem captam incenderunt
    *city*_{fem.acc.sg} *captured*_{fem.acc.sg} *they-burned*

The most natural reading of **14a** is that "they burned the old city", though in a suitably supportive context it might also mean "they burned the city, (it being) old". Conversely, **14b**, with a perfect passive participle *captam* "captured", is less likely to mean "they burned the captured city" than "they burned the city, (it being) captured", i.e. "they captured the city and burned it". Such predicative adjuncts function rather like non-restrictive relative clauses (cf. *they burned the city, which was old/which had been captured*), or even adverbial clauses (cf. *they burned the city because it was old/after it had been captured*). Consider first **15**:

15

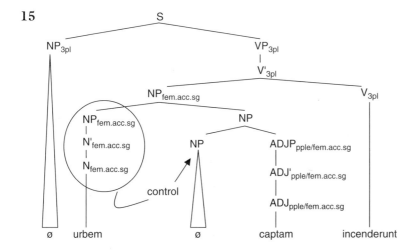

The adjunct containing *captam* is treated here as an NP in apposition to the NP headed by *urbem*, i.e. as occupying the same position as a non-restrictive relative clause and with a very similar function (cf. **12**). Its internal structure is that of the "sentence-like" NP in **8**, i.e. the ADJP headed by a *verbal* adjective (a participle, which would be modified by an adverb if required) again stands in a predicative (VP-like) relation with the preceding "subject" NP. Here, however, the subject is omitted, being automatically understood as "the city"; this linking relationship is marked in **15** as one of "control", whereby the content of the NP to the left is automatically duplicated in the vacant NP position to the right. The direct object NP as a whole therefore means "the city, (the city) having-been-captured".

The notion of obligatory control introduced here requires further explanation. Note first that such participial ADJPs may in principle have overt subjects of their own, as in the so-called "dominant participle" construction, e.g. *[Caesar$_{nom}$ occisus$_{nom}$] rempubli-cam euertit*, literally "[Caesar having-been-killed] republic overturned", i.e. "the killing of Caesar overturned the republic", where the nominative NP as a whole functions as the subject with a clause-like meaning (more or less equivalent to "(the fact) that Caesar had been killed").[9] Compare now appositive NP structures in which the sole function of the clause-like NP to the right is to supply predicative information about the referent of the left-hand NP, cf. *my brother, the doctor* = "my brother, (my brother (is)) the doctor", etc.; i.e. the left-hand NP and the subject of the predicative expression can never be referentially distinct, making any overt specification of the latter redundant. It is important to appreciate that information cannot be predicated directly of the left-hand NP because that would require a single NP to carry two grammatical functions simultaneously, one within the sentence containing it (direct object in **15**), and the other as subject of the predicative expression. This is by definition a grammatical impossibility. The only solution therefore is to allow for two distinct NP positions, and to link these referentially through the control relation. Control is distinct from simple anaphoric linkage in that a controlled subject position is obligatorily empty, being necessarily understood to share the content and reference of the controlling item: so in **15**, the empty position can only be understood as an NP with the properties [third person, accusative, singular, feminine] referring to the same entity as *urbem*. By contrast, the rules of anaphora link pronouns[10] to possible antecedents, though without ever *requiring* such coreferential readings within a sentence. In **16**, for example, *eum* "him" may refer anaphorically to Caesar, but can just as easily refer to some other previously mentioned individual:

16 Caesarem certiorem fecerunt [Pompeium dixisse [se eum Romam
    Caesar$_{acc}$ more-certain$_{acc}$ they-made Pompey$_{acc}$ to-have-said himself$_{acc}$ him$_{acc}$ to-Rome$_{acc}$
    reducturum$_{acc}$]]
    being-about-to-bring-back
    They informed Caesar that Pompey had said he would bring him back to Rome

Non-restrictive relative clauses and appositive NPs are only loosely attached to their NP hosts, and both are in fact free to appear as independent constituents in a sentence, functioning in these circumstances rather like an adverbial clause. Consider, for example, the non-restrictive relative clause in *Pompeius Caesarem excepit, quem antea spreuerat*

"Pompey$_{nom}$ Caesar$_{acc}$ welcomed, whom previously he-had-spurned", which conveys a nuance of "even though", or the NP containing the predicative participle in **17**:

17 C. Flaminio restitit [NP agrum Gallicum diuidenti]
 Gaius$_{dat}$ Flaminius$_{dat}$ he-resisted ø$_{dat}$ territory$_{acc}$ Gallic$_{acc}$ dividing$_{dat}$
  He resisted Gaius Flaminius, as/while he (Flaminius) was apportioning the Gallic
  territory. (Cicero, *Sen.* 11)

Such discontinuities cause no problems of interpretation because relative pronouns are inherently anaphoric, agreeing with their antecedents in number and gender, while the control relationship between two NPs, as in **17**, requires only that the related items appear within the same clause.

Constituent Order in Clauses

It was noted above that in relative and interrogative clauses the phrase containing the relative or interrogative pronoun (*qu*-word) is routinely preposed to the beginning of the clause in question, regardless of its grammatical function within it:[11]

18 (a) puer [cui donum dedit]
   boy to-whom$_{dat}$ gift she-gave
   The boy to whom she gave the gift
 (b) Cui donum dedit?
   to-whom$_{dat}$ gift she-gave
   Who did she give the gift to?

In the case of relatives, the *qu*-word in this position provides an anaphoric link between the NP described (standing to its left) and the clause describing it (standing to its right). In interrogatives the positioning is more obviously semantically motivated: the preposed *qu*-word is a quantifier-like element binding the variable represented by the empty NP position in the sentence following: e.g. "for which x (a person) [did she give the gift to x]?" In both cases, the phrase in question stands outside the basic clause nucleus, as in **19**, leaving a gap of the same category within it:

19

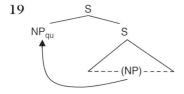

Preposing is also common, though not obligatory, as a means of marking a constituent as a topic (i.e. an element introducing what the rest of the sentence is about) or a focus (i.e. an element indentified as emphatic/contrastive and stressed accordingly). A preposed topic is typically separated from what follows by a brief intonational pause (which may be represented by a comma), while a focus is not. Where there is both a topic and a focus, therefore, the topic is the more peripheral. Consider the examples in **20**:

20 (a) *prouincias*(,) praetores nondum sortiti sunt (Cicero, *Att.* 1.13.5)
   provinces$_{acc}$ *praetors*$_{nom}$ *not-yet drawn-by-lot have*
   As for the provinces, the praetors have not yet drawn lots for them

   (b) *me* Q. Catulus parentem patriae nominauit (Cicero, *Pis.* 3)
   me$_{acc}$ *Q. Catulus*$_{nom}$ *father*$_{acc}$ *of-country named*
   I'm the one that Quintus Catulus named "father of our country"

   (c) *de Tadiana re* (,) *mecum* Tadius locutus est (Cicero, *Att.* 1.5.6)
   on of-Tadius matter me-with Tadius spoken has
   On the matter of Tadius, Tadius has spoken with **me**

Many clause-initial phrases are inherently topical when their function is to effect an anaphoric link to the preceding discourse:[12] a focal element may then follow the topic in the usual way. In **21**, for example, *hic* is just such a topicalized subject, while the ADJP headed by *optimus* (to which the temporal adjunct *illis temporibus* is adjoined as a modifier) has been fronted out of the NP functioning as predicative subject complement, thereby creating a discontinuity, as often when constituent parts of phrases rather than complete phrases are focalized:

21 hic *optimus* illis temporibus est patronus habitus (Cicero, *Brut.* 106)
   this$_{nom}$ *best*$_{nom}$ *in-those times is defender*$_{nom}$ *considered*
   This man was thought the **best** advocate in those times

A further feature illustrated here is the attraction of forms of the verb "to be", and sometimes of other verbs, to emphatic constituents, whether these stand in a preposed position as here, or elsewhere within a sentence (see Adams (1994b)).

It should be noted, however, that variation of constituent order *within* a phrase or clause nucleus is also available as a means of backgrounding and foregrounding information. For example, since verbs normally stand last in V′, placing an object or other constituent after the verb can have the effect of highlighting it, as in **22(a)**, just as placing a subject NP after rather than before a VP may bring it into focus, as in **22(b)**, where the initial/topic position of *abest* "is absent" reflects the continuation of the theme of absence from the preceding sentence:

22 (a) secum habebat *hominem χρηστομαθῆ* (Cicero, *Att.* 1.6.2)
   himself-with he-had man scholarly (Greek)
   He had with him a man who was scholarly

   (b) abest enim *frater ἀφελέστατος et amantissimus* (Cicero, *Att.* 1.18.1)
   is-absent for brother most-artless (Greek) and most-loving
   For the absence is of a brother most artless and loving

Note, however, that verb-initial is a completely neutral order if all the information conveyed by a sentence is new to the discourse, particularly if the sentence has an existential/presentational meaning with an indefinite subject (cf. the subject inversion and the meaningless place-holder *there* in *there appeared a stag on the horizon*, etc.):

23 relinquebatur una per Sequanos uia (Caesar, *Gal.* 1.9.1)
   was-left one through the-Sequani road
   There remained one (other) route through the land of the Sequani

See Devine and Stephens (2006) for a thorough analysis of factors regulating the ordering of constituents.

Clause Structure: Main and Subordinate Clauses

Every well-formed sentence of Latin consists of one or more clauses, each denoting a complete semantic predication. In a multi-clause sentence the meanings of the component clauses combine to form the meaning of the whole, with the required manner of composition indicated syntactically through the co-ordination and/or subordination of the relevant elements.

Main clauses are not dependent on the presence of any other item and can therefore stand alone, though two or more main clauses may always be co-ordinated with an appropriate conjunction, e.g. *et/atque* "and", *sed* "but", *aut* "or". As noted earlier, each main clause consists of an NP subject and a VP predicate, together with any sentence adverbials (i.e. those with scope over the sentence as a whole); the NP is nominative (the subject case associated with finiteness) and the VP contains a finite verb form (whose agreement with the subject in person and number marks the predication relationship). The head of the NP may be a noun or pronoun, but only pronouns that are emphatic or contrastive, including those marking a change of subject, are made explicit. Since verbal agreement morphology itself provides adequate "pronominal" information, repetition in the form of a subject pronoun is normally redundant: omission is therefore routine when the subject is first- or second-person, or when the intended third-person referent is clear in context.

Each main clause may contain one or more subordinate clauses, which may be either complements or adjuncts. Clausal adjuncts containing finite verb forms comprise both adjectival/relative clauses adjoined to an N′ (restrictive) or NP (non-restrictive) and an array of adverbial clauses (i.e. temporal, causal, conditional, concessive, consecutive, final) adjoined to the main clause or to some other subordinate clause. As just noted, however (see the final paragraph of the section on phrases), non-restrictive relative clauses are not always adjoined directly to NPs as simple descriptors, and may instead have the distribution, and in part the function, of adverbial clauses, taking on a range of roles (e.g. final, consecutive, causal, etc.) as determined by the choice of verbal mood and the requirements of the context; the same applies, *mutatis mutandis*, to similarly "detached" predicative participial expressions (cf. **17**). All of this is fully covered in standard grammars and nothing further need be said here.

It is worth adding, however, that both gerunds and supines have related adverbial functions, cf. *hominis mens discendo alitur* "of-man the-mind [by-learning] is-nourished" (Cicero, *Off.* 1.105), *legatos ad Caesarem mittunt rogatum auxilium* "envoys to Caesar they-sent [to-ask-for help]" (Caesar, *Gal.* 1.11.2). Both types of expression involve clause-like NPs headed by *verbal* nouns whose "subjects" are necessarily suppressed (only infinitives among the verbal nouns can assign a case, viz. accusative, to NPs in this position; see below for discussion of the accusative and infinitive construction).[13] In the first example above the missing/"understood" subject is therefore supplied by the rules of anaphora ("the learner" may be "the mind of man" or "people in general"), while in the second it is supplied by the rules of control ("the asker" is necessarily either the "senders" or the "envoys" according to whether the supine is adjoined as a sentence adverbial or a VP-adverbial).

Turning now to complementation, the marking of a complement clause by a lexical head X falls into two main types: (i) government requiring a finite clause introduced by a specific conjunction (along with a specific verbal mood), and (ii) government requiring a non-finite clause containing an infinitive (with or without its own accusative subject), supine, gerund/gerundive, or participle. A given lexical head often allows more than one type of complement, though there may be significant differences of meaning among the options. A representative sample of finite and non-finite complement types is given in **24** and **25** respectively, with some examples of heads taking more than one type of complement provided in **26**:

24 Finite complements[14]
    (a) *ut, ut non* + subjunctive: *accidit* "it happens", *facio* "make", *difficile (est)* "(it is) difficult", *tempus (est)* "(it is) time"
    (b) *ut, ne* + subjunctive: *cupio* "desire", *curo* "see to it", *impero* "order", *persuadeo* "persuade", *munus (est)* "(it is) a duty"
    (c) *ne, ut (ne non)* + subjunctive: *metuo* "fear", *uereor* "fear", *periculum (est)* "(there is) a danger"
    (d) *quod/quia* + indicative: *accidit* "it happens", *facio* "do", *gaudeo* "rejoice"
    (e) [NEG] *quin* + subjunctive: *[non] impedio* "(not) hinder", *[non] dubium (est)* "(it is) [not] doubtful"
    (f) indirect question (subjunctive): *delibero* "deliberate/resolve", *dico* "say", *impero* "order", *rogo* "ask", *dubium (est)* "(it is) doubtful"

25 Non-finite complements
    (a) bare (prolative) infinitive: *conor* "try", *cupio* "desire", *curo* "care", *doceo* "teach", *gaudeo* "rejoice", *impedio* "hinder", *incipio* "begin", *metuo* "fear", etc., *cupidus* "eager", *difficile (est)* "(it is) difficult", *munus (est)* "(it is) a duty", *tempus(est)* "(it is) time"
    (b) accusative + infinitive: *accidit* "it happens", *arbitror* "think", *audio* "hear", *cupio* "desire", *curo* "see to it", *dico* "say", *doceo* "inform", *gaudeo* "rejoice", *persuadeo* "convince", *puto* "think", *uideo* "see", *difficile (est)* "(it is) difficult", *tempus (est)* "(it is) time"
    (c) accusative + participle: *audio* "hear", *uideo* "see"
    (d) gerund/gerundive: *curo* "see to", *cupidus* "eager", *tempus (est)* "(it is) time"
    (e) supine: *difficilis* "difficult", *horribilis* "horrible"

26 Examples of heads taking more than one type of complement
    (a) *accidit*:
        (i) *ut* + subjunctive
            accidit [ut omnes Hermae deicerentur] (Nepos, *Alc.* 3.2)

it-happened that all Herms were-cast-down
It happened that all the Herms were thrown down

(ii) *quod* + indicative

accidit perincommode [quod eum nusquam uidisti] (Cicero, *Att.* 1.17.12)
it-happened very-inconveniently that him nowhere you-saw
It was a very inconvenient turn of events that you didn't see him anywhere

(iii) accusative + infinitive

nec ... acciderat [mihi opus esse] (Cicero, *Fam.* 6.11.1)
nor it-had-happened to-me need to-be
Nor had I happened to have any need

(b) *persuadeo*:

(i) *ut* + subjunctive

patri persuasi [ut aes-alienum filii dissolueret] (Cicero, *Phil.* 2.46)
to-father I persuaded that debt of-son he-might-annul
I persuaded the father to annul his son's debts

(ii) accusative + infinitive

hoc uolunt persuadere, [non interire animas] (Caesar, *Gal.* 6.14.5)
this they-wish to-persuade not to-die souls
This is what they want to convince people of, that souls do not die

(c) *gaudeo*:

(i) bare infinitive

animus [aliquid magnum agere] gaudet (Quintilian, *Inst.* 1.2.30)
soul something great to-do rejoices
The soul rejoices in doing something great

(ii) *quod* + indicative

gaudeo [quod te interpellaui] (Cicero, *Leg.* 3.1.1)
I-rejoice that you I-interrupted
I'm glad I interrupted you

(iii) accusative + infinitive

[quae perfecta esse] ... gaudeo (Cicero, *S. Rosc.* 136)
which-things done to-be I rejoice
I'm glad this has been done

(d) *audio*:

(i) accusative + infinitive

[quem apud se esse] audio (Cicero, *de Orat.* 1.214)
whom chez *himself to-be I-hear*
who I hear is at home

(ii) accusative and participle

[idque Socratem] audio [dicentem] (Cicero, *Fin.* 2.90)
that-and Socrates I-hear saying
And this is what I hear Socrates saying

(e) *cupio*:

(i) (*ut* +) subjunctive

[tu] cuperem [adesses] (Cicero, *Att.* 2.18.4)

you I-would-desire you-were-present
I would long for you to be here
(ii) bare infinitive
[scire] cupio [quae causa sit] (Cicero, *Fin.* 4.19)
to-know I-desire what the-reason is
I long to know what the reason is
(iii) accusative and infinitive
ego [me] cupio [non mendacem putari] (Cicero, *Leg.* 1.4)
I me I-desire not deceitful to-be-thought
As for me, I really want myself not to be thought a liar

(f) *dico*:
(i) *ut/ne* + subjunctive
qui diceret [ne ab exercitu discederet] (Nepos, *Dat.* 5)
who might-tell that-not from army he-should-depart
to tell him not to leave the army
(ii) indirect question
dixit [quid sentiret] (Cicero, *Fin.* 2.3)
he-said what he-felt
He said what he felt
(iii) accusative + infinitive
[omnes sub platano consedisse] dicebat (Cicero, *de Orat.* 1.29)
all beneath plane-tree to-have-sat-together he-said
He said that everyone had sat down together under the plane tree

(g) *difficilis/difficile*:
(i) *ut* + subjunctive
difficile est [ut ad haec studia animus possit accedere] (Seneca, *Dial.* 11.8.3)
difficult it-is that to these studies the-mind be-able to approach
It is hard for the mind to be able to approach these studies
(ii) bare infinitive
erat difficile [opera perficere] (Caesar, *Civ.* 1.50)
it-was difficult the-works to-complete
It was hard to complete the works
(iii) accusative + infinitive
difficile est [ita uersari imperatorem] (Cicero, *Man.* 64)
difficult it-is thus to-behave a-general
It is hard for a general to conduct himself in such a way
(iv) supine
quia locus ... nobis [aditu] difficilis (Sallust, *Jug.* 91.6)
because place for-us in/for-approaching difficult
because the place was hard for us to approach

(h) *mos (est)*:
(i) *ut* + subjunctive
mos est [ut nolint eundem pluribus rebus excellere] (Cicero, *Brut.* 84)

> *custom it-is that they-not-want same-man in-many things to-excel*
> It is their custom that they do not want one man to excel in many
> things
(ii) bare infinitive
> mos est [non humare corpora suorum] (Cicero, *Tusc.* 1.108)
> *custom it-is not to-bury bodies of-their-own*
> It is their custom not to bury their dead
(iii) accusative and infinitive
> mos est [laudari eos qui sint in proelio interfecti] (Cicero, *Orat.* 151)
> *custom it-is to-be-praised them who are in battle killed*
> It is their custom for those killed in battle to be praised
(iv) gerund(ive)
> mos [liberos obiciendi saeuissimis earum] (Pliny, *Nat.* 7.14)
> *custom children of-exposing to-most-savage of-them*
> the custom of exposing their children to the most vicious of them
> (snakes)

While this survey of the range of complementation is by no means exhaustive, some general patterns can be discerned, based on the meaning, and in part the word class, of the lexical items involved. Verbs of "saying and thinking", for example, take an accusative and infinitive, verbs of "direct perception" an accusative and participle, verbs of "ordering and persuading" *ut/ne* + subjunctive, verbs of "fearing" *ne/ut* + subjunctive, verbs of "happening" or "causing to happen" *ut/ut non* + subjunctive, and verbs involving an attempted or actual manipulation of the future a bare infinitive ("try", "force", etc.); complements that are "factive" (= "the fact that S") are normally introduced by *quod*; adjectives alone may take a supine (inflected in the ablative/dative) and nouns alone a gerund (inflected in the genitive), albeit alongside other options in both cases. But there are many overlaps, and some items are associated with a range of meaning(s) that puts them into more than one category: *dico* = "say", for example, regularly takes an accusative and infinitive complement, but when it means "tell" (i.e. "order", a colloquial use) it takes an *ut*-clause; verbs of perception may involve direct observation and take the accusative and participle construction ("I saw/heard her singing"), but may as easily describe a report ("I hear that she divorced her husband") or an understanding/belief ("I see that this may be a problem"), in which case they are classified with verbs of "saying and thinking" and take an accusative and infinitive; verbs of "ordering/persuading" may readily be thought of as involving attempted manipulation of the future, with consequential inconsistencies, so *impero* usually takes a dative object followed by an *ut/ne* clause, while *iubeo* takes an accusative object + bare infinitive. The largely notional categories of traditional grammar therefore provide only rough and ready guidelines to complementation, and the only sure method is to use a dictionary or electronic corpus to check the range of options attested for each head, noting any meaning differences associated with specific choices (not all variety is semantically motivated), identifying which options are routine and which less so, and establishing whether there are differences of style, register or period associated with different selections.

The remainder of this section will be concerned specifically with infinitival constructions, both those with and those without an overt subject. Consider first the examples in **27**:

27 (a) Caesar conatus est [dictator fieri]
  Caesar$_{nom}$ tried dictator$_{nom}$ to-become
  Caesar tried to become dictator

  (b) Caesar Crassum coegit [consulem fieri]
  Caesar$_{nom}$ Crassus$_{acc}$ forced consul$_{acc}$ to-become
  Caesar forced Crassus to become consul

  (c) Pompeio licet [imperatori fieri]
  Pompey$_{dat}$ it-is-allowed general$_{dat}$ to-become
  Pompey is allowed to become a general

Each of these examples involves the use of a bare (prolative) infinitive expressing a potential or actual outcome after a verb whose meaning "looks to the future" in some way;[15] note in particular that *Crassum* in **27b** is the direct object of *coegit* and not part of an accusative and infinitive construction (in which the accusative NP is the subject of the infinitive). None of these infinitival clauses allows for an overt subject to appear (cf. **Caesar conatus est [Pompeium dictatorem fieri]*, "**Caesar tried (for) Pompey to become dictator*", etc.), but in each case a NP bearing a grammatical function in the main clause is necessarily understood to function also as the missing subject of the infinitive; since predicate nominals agree in number and case with their subjects (any agreement in gender is obviously fortuitous), the grammatical case of each missing subject is made apparent. It appears, then, that we are once again dealing with a control relationship in which the grammatical properties of a controlling NP (i.e. the nominative/subject NP *Caesar* in **27a**, the accusative/direct object NP *Crassum* in **27b**,[16] and the dative/indirect object NP *Pompeio* in **27c**) are obligatorily transferred to the "missing" subject NP position of the infinitival subordinate clause.

Control comes into play, as we have seen, when a sentence denotes a situation in which two semantic roles, distributed across two predications of which one is an argument or modifier of the other, are *necessarily* carried by the same individual; e.g. the individual denoted by *Caesar* in **27a** denotes both the "trier" and the one who will "become dictator" if his efforts come to fruition. This situation of obligatory coreference arises here with the infinitival complements of so-called "control" verbs (i.e. those whose meaning entails effecting or allowing some future state of affairs), but it is also characteristic of appositive NPs containing predicative participles (see the discussion of **14** and **15** above) and of adjunct supines (see the beginning of this section).[17] Control is an economic solution for the syntactic representation of such situations, allowing the content and reference of the expression filling the grammatical slot associated with one semantic argument to be automatically understood as simultaneously filling the slot associated with the other.

There are two key syntactic characteristics of the control relation. First, the controller must be a single NP bearing a single grammatical function (i.e. just one of subject, direct object, indirect object). This is necessary to guarantee that a unique set of non-conflicting features can be transferred to the controllee, but it also distinguishes control very clearly from simple anaphora, where the controlling antecedent may well be "split", as in: *[Caesar et Pompeius putant [Crassum credere [(eos) oportere [bellum uitare]]]]*, literally "[Caesar and Pompey think [Crassus to-believe [them it-to-behove [war to-avoid]]]]", i.e. "Caesar and Pompey think Crassus believes they have to avoid war", where the antecedent of *eos* "them" may be "Caesar and Pompey", "Caesar, Pompey and Crassus", or even another group of men altogether. Secondly, control operates only on the *subject* position of *non-finite* subordinate clauses (including clause-like NPs containing verbal nouns and adjectives). This might be explained on the basis that there was no mechanism, at least originally, for assigning a case directly to subject NPs in clauses containing non-finite verb forms, a situation that required this position to be left vacant and its semantic content to be supplied by other means; these naturally "bare" VPs (or predicate-like NPs) had an inherently subordinate function, therefore.[18]

Consider now the examples of impersonal verbs in **28**:

> **28** oportet/decet/piget me abire
> *it-behoves/it-becomes/it-irks me to-go*
> I have to go/it is right for me to go/it is irksome for me to go

These all denote complex situations in which a single individual plays two semantic roles, one in the dominant situation represented by the main clause and the other in the subordinated situation represented by the infinitival complement: i.e. the patient whom "it behoves/becomes/irks" to go is necessarily the agent who may in due course depart. The direct object accusative NP *me* therefore represents the patient argument in the main clause,[19] and the subject position in the subordinate clause is controlled by it in the usual way. It is not at all difficult, however, to imagine a simple re-analysis in which what is necessary/becoming/irksome is still taken to be "my departure", but *me* is understood instead as the *overt* subject of the infinitive, leaving the impersonal verb without an object and the sentences in **28** meaning "it is necessary/becoming/irksome [(for) me to leave]". That such a re-analysis took place is confirmed by examples of accusative and infinitive complements with verbs that take dative objects, where the two arguments are denoted by two different NPs:

> **29** Pompeio displicet [Caesarem abire]
> *Pompey$_{dat}$ it-displeases Caesar$_{acc}$ to-depart*
> "Pompey doesn't like Caesar leaving"

Once it was felt that infinitives could assign accusative case to their subjects independently of the case-marking requirements of the verb in the main clause, the distribution of the accusative + infinitive construction was readily extended beyond the domain of object-control verbs to provide complementation to any verb denoting an activity requiring a complete semantic predication as one of its arguments, i.e. the set of verbs of "saying and thinking" in traditional terms, but also many more:

> **30** dixit [Caesarem abire]
> *she-said Caesar$_{acc}$ to-leave*
> She said Caesar was leaving

Here, of course, there is no possibility of a semantic connection between the subject of the infinitive and the verb in the main clause: Caesar is only the "leaver", and has no role with respect to "saying", making *Caesarem* the subject of *abire*.

Given that this is so, the expected passive form of sentences containing accusative + infinitive complements is one in which the main verb becomes impersonal and the complement remains unaffected. Compare the active–passive pair in **31**:

> **31 (a)** dicunt [Homerum caecum fuisse]
>   *they-say Homer_{acc} blind_{acc} to-have-been*
>   They say Homer was blind
>
>   **(b)** dicitur [Homerum caecum fuisse]
>   *it-is-said Homer_{acc} blind_{acc} to-have-been*
>   It is said that Homer was blind

While the type of sentence in **31b** is certainly not ungrammatical, Classical Latin writers increasingly preferred to employ the "personal" passive, as in **32**:

> **32** Homerus dicitur [caecus fuisse]
>   *Homer_{nom} is-said blind_{nom} to-have-been*
>   Homer is said to have been blind

Semantically this makes no sense, since the personal passive construction apparently treats *Homerum* in **31a** as a direct object NP representing an argument of "saying". Furthermore, *dico* is seemingly treated as a control verb, with the subject NP of passive *dicor* controlling the subject position of the dependent infinitive (cf. the *nominative* predicative adjective *caecus* in **32**), even though there is only one semantic argument position involved, namely that represented by the subject of the infinitive ("the person who was blind"). Homer has no business being where he is!

Since no argument is represented by the subject of the impersonal passive *dicitur* (i.e. the impersonal "it" has no denotation in the situation of "saying"), this position is semantically empty, being provided syntactically only because all sentences have to have subjects (see p. 120). It seems, therefore that the subject of the infinitive has been raised to fill this empty slot, giving the main clause a "real" subject, contrary to the semantics:

33

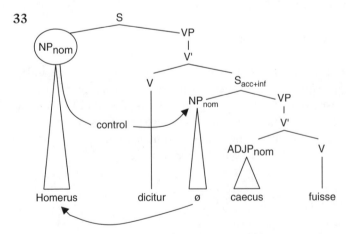

The fact that the active impersonal verbs in **28** do not allow such subject raising (there are no examples of the type *∗pigeo hoc dicere, etc.*, "I-am-disgusted this to-say") suggests that the process was indeed confused in the minds of Latin speakers with passivization, presumably on the basis of the presence of an accusative NP, though not a direct object, in the corresponding active sentence (cf. **31a**). Whatever the motivation, the result is a syntactic structure in which there are two NP positions to be filled with the same content. It is not surprising, therefore, that the control mechanism should be used to refill the empty subject position with the content that it should have retained all along, even if the usual semantic criteria for control do not apply in the absence of two distinct semantic roles.

Conclusion

It was a part of the traditional teaching of Latin in schools to impress upon pupils the "natural logic and clarity" of the language – in comparison, one assumes, with the inherent "sloppiness" of modern languages like English. The case was clearly overstated, as I hope the discussion above has made clear. Written Latin was certainly reduced to relatively rigid rules by those who contributed to the final standardization of the language in Cicero's generation, with many alternative forms and constructions duly becoming stigmatized at the highest levels of discourse in the quest for a variety of Latin that could rival Greek as an official and cultural language. But the insistence on using gerundives rather than letting a gerund take a direct object or the preference for personal over impersonal passives with verbs taking accusative + infinitive complements are simply classroom prescriptions of the "don't end a sentence with a preposition" variety. These certainly affected the written (and perhaps in part the spoken) usage of the educated elite but ultimately had little impact on the natural evolution of the language among the mass of its speakers. In any case considerable variety and uncertainty inevitably remained, while the link between the preferred/elite options and "logic" (assuming this means something like closeness of fit between syntactic structures and the semantic predications they denote) is patently no closer in Classical Latin than in the vernacular, and is sometimes more remote. A major determinant of choice among the linguistic options was, after all, not logic but snobbery, reflecting a desire for distinctive ways of using the language that identified the insiders and excluded the rest (see Clackson and Horrocks (2007) ch. 6).

NOTES

1   This does not preclude other realizations, since semantic predicates are simply sets of properties defining a word's meaning. But not every semantic predicate presupposes arguments. Thus "woman", "tall", etc. in isolation do not (though these may be arguments of a predicate that does, e.g. "[X] be [(a) woman]", "[X] be [tall]").
2   The syntactic predicate is therefore, semantically speaking, a function from individuals to truth values. "Killed the enemy", for example, when applied to the individual "Caesar", creates a

complete semantic predication that is either true or false within the relevant domain of reference.

3   Subjects may be nominative or accusative, for example, according to whether they are the subjects of finite or non-finite predicates; some verbs take accusative objects while others take objects in other cases, etc.

4   Subjects and objects are always NPs, even when they contain only nouns, (i) because there is always the potential for modification, and (ii) because only NPs refer to individuals (i.e. *puella* within an NP = "a girl"/"the girl"), while nouns in isolation denote semantic predicates (i.e. *puella* alone = "(the set of properties involved in being a) girl").

5   For full details of the layout of such diagrams, see the section on constituent order below. N' and ADJ' (read "N prime", "Adj prime") are constituents intermediate between word-level and (full) phrase-level constituents.

6   Both complements and adjuncts are either phrases or subordinate clauses (on the latter see the penultimate section of this chapter); i.e. even though modification by a bare adjective or a bare adverb is always possible, the potential for these to be modified in their own right requires them always to be represented as the heads of ADJPs or ADVPs, etc. (see note 3 above, and cf. *[[$_{ADJP}$ (admodum) clarum] somnium]* "a (quite) clear dream", *[[$_{ADVP}$ (ualde) celeriter] currit]* "s/he runs (exceedingly) fast", etc.).

7   Note that subjects, as an essential component of the predication relation, are not comple-ments of any head, even though they typically represent arguments of the relevant semantic predicate. They are therefore not marked as governed by individual heads, but instead take their case according to the type of predication in which they participate (i.e. nominative if finite, accusative if non-finite).

8   Nouns generally assign genitive case to NPs with which they are in construction regardless of the semantic relationship between the two elements. Partitive (e.g. *pars Galliae* "part of-Gaul") and objective genitives (e.g. *supplicium hominis* "the-punishment of-the-man") are clearly complements, while possessive genitives are adjective-like adjuncts (cf. the possessive adjectives *meus* "my", *tuus* "your (sg.)", etc.), the case here having a clear semantic signifi-cance. The status of subjective genitives is more debatable; though the genitive arguably marks a relationship akin to syntactic predication, this may be no more than an evolved use of the possessive genitive with deverbal nouns that retain an action-like meaning. NPs, after all, do not *require* genitive subjects in the way that VPs do.

9   The "ablative absolute" construction, e.g. *[sole$_{abl}$ orto$_{abl}$] urbem incenderunt*, literally "(with-) the-sun having-risen, the-city they-burned", is a special case of this, in which the NP functions as a "circumstantial" sentence adverbial. Though typically used when the referent of its subject has no role in the action described by the main clause, the ablative absolute may also be employed to emphasize the separateness and importance of the action it describes: cf. *[perfecto scelere] magnitudo eius intellecta est*, lit. "having-been-committed the-crime, the-magnitude of-it understood was" (Tacitus, *Annals* 14.10.1).

10 Anaphoric pronouns are not, however, obligatory, cf. *cum Pompeius Caesarem excepisset, (ei) solacium dedit* "after Pompey$_{nom}$ Caesar$_{acc}$ had-welcomed, (to-him$_{dat}$) solace he-gave". In these circumstances the rules simply treat the gap as an inaudible/invisible version of the overt pronoun. Note, however, that while the immediate context here encourages the reading given, the recipient of the solace might, say, be Pompey's wife (previously mentioned as being in distress), given that the dative form *ei* is neutral with respect to gender.

11 Grammatical rules may reposition constituents under specified conditions: i.e. a phrase in a sentence carrying the grammatical property [+ *qu-*] is moved to clause-initial position for the reasons given immediately below.

12 These include so called "connective" relative pronouns: e.g. *hostes uocare coeperunt: quorum progredi ausus est nemo* (Caesar, *Gal.* 5.43.6), literally "the-enemy to-call they-began; of-whom to-advance dared has no-one", i.e. "they began to call the enemy: but none of them dared to advance". These resemble detached non-restrictive relatives (cf. the final part of the section on phrases below), except that here the pronoun begins a new main clause.

13 The enforced absence of subjects here contrasts with their possible presence in clause-like NPs containing verbal adjectives (i.e. gerundives and participles). A predicative gerund or supine is the head of the NP as a whole, and takes its case from this superordinate element; but a subject can only be supplied indirectly through the control mechanism in the absence of any means of assigning a case directly to an overt NP in this position. In the adjectival types, by contrast, it is the noun in the subject NP that is the head of the NP as a whole, with the ADJP (gerundive/participle) functioning predicatively; the subject NP therefore inherits the case assigned to the superordinate NP, and the ADJP agrees with it.

14 With certain verbs *ut* is regularly omitted before a complement. The corresponding negative is given in each case.

15 Many such verbs also allow non-finite accusative + infinitive clauses and finite *ut/ne* clauses, in which control, as described immediately below, is not involved because both types allow for their subject positions to be filled overtly. Any optional coreference between the clauses in these cases is simply a matter of anaphora (though this becomes obligatory in the case of reflexive pronouns).

16 If there are two potential controllers, as in **27b**, the actual controller is the one that is structurally closer to the controllee. This automatically gives objects precedence over subjects, because a direct or indirect object and the relevant infinitival are always co-complements of V within V′.

17 It might also be extended to verbs of "saying and thinking" when the subjects of the two clauses denote the same person, as in Greek ἔφη [σοφὸς εἶναι] "he-said clever$_{nom}$ to-be", though Latin in fact prefers the option of a reflexive pronoun in an accusative and infinitive construction, cf. *dixit [se sapientem esse]* "he-said himself$_{acc}$ wise$_{acc}$ to-be", which marks the obligatory coreference in a different way (cf. note 15).

18 This limitation remains true of supines and gerunds, while the appearance of overt subjects with predicative participles and infinitives is clearly a secondary phenomenon. Consider the inherent oddness of the "dominant participle construction" (for which see the discussion following **15** above), and see below for the possible origins of accusative subjects with infinitives.

19 That such verbs may take a direct object is confirmed by examples like *me piget stultitiae meae* (Cicero, *Ver.* 1.1.35) literally "me it-irks for-stupidity my", i.e. "I am upset by my stupidity", in which the accusative clearly marks the NP denoting the person affected and the genitive the NP denoting the cause of the emotion.

CHAPTER 10

Latin Vocabulary

Michèle Fruyt

In this chapter, we will describe the main characteristics of the Latin vocabulary in the Classical period. We will first define the fundamental Latin vocabulary, then we will analyse the main types of lexical sets existing in the synchronic organisation of the Latin lexicon. Thirdly, we will describe the role of some of the main semantic phenomena, primarily but not exclusively, lexical metaphor and metonymy. And finally, we will describe the main processes leading to lexical innovation, drawing a clear distinction between those innovations involving a new *signifiant* on the formal level and those involving just the *signifié* of a given pre-existing word on a semantic and referential level.

The Fundamental Latin Vocabulary

Any study of the main tendencies of the Latin lexicon must first of all consider the fundamental words, those that make up the basic vocabulary. These can be of two types: (a) the most frequent words (i.e. lexemes) found in the Latin texts, or (b) those words which denote entities, processes or states of affairs that are of such importance for the speech community that the common spoken language cannot do without them.

The most frequent words in Classical Latin (according to Delatte *et al.* (1981), who used a corpus of Latin dating from the first century BCE to the first century CE) are grammatical words, such as the coordinators *et* "and", which is the most frequent word in the Latin texts, the enclitic *-que* "and", the relative pronoun *quī* "who", the preposition *in* "in", the negation *nōn* "not", the three anaphoric, cataphoric and deictic pronouns-adjectives *hic, is, ille*, and the preposition *ad* "towards".

Even among verbs, adjectives and nouns, the most frequent words are also the most grammatical ones and, therefore, the least lexical ones.

A Companion to the Latin Language, First Edition. Edited by James Clackson.
© 2011 Blackwell Publishing Ltd. Published 2011 by Blackwell Publishing Ltd.

The most frequent verbs are: *esse* "be" as a full verb, which is the second most frequent word in the lexicon, then *esse* as an auxiliary verb, the modality verb *possum* "be able", and *faciō* "do". The high frequency of *faciō* is primarily due to the fact that it is often used as a "weak verb" (e.g. in *curriculum facere* "run" with the same meaning as *currere*; see p. 150) and, secondly, to the fact that it functions semantically as the archilexeme of all kinds of verbs denoting actions (*euoluere librum* "read a book" (Cic. *Tusc.* 1.24); *relinquere* "avoid (a topic)" (Cic. *Brut.* 190); *dare* "give" (Cic. *Fin.* 2.79): *uadem te ... dabis* "you will give yourself as an hostage"), as well as states (*tacēre* "be silent", "not speak about something" (Cic. *Brut.* 157), feelings (*ōdisse* "hate" (Cic. *Fin.* 1.14), evaluation and thought (*pro nihilī dūcere aliquid* "consider something as worth nothing" (Cic. *Tusc.* 5.90)).

The most frequent adjectives also have either a purely grammatical function (e.g. the possessive adjective *suus*) or a lexico-grammatical function such as quantification: *omnis* "all, any", *magnus* "big", *alius* "other", *multus* "numerous, much", *nūllus* "none".

The first noun appears far down the frequency list, in thirty-first position. As could be expected, it is the archilexeme for all inanimate entities and states of affairs: *rēs* "thing". It is followed in the list by its counterpart in human beings: *animus* "mind, feeling, spirit".

The first terms in this list of frequencies with a purely lexical meaning in the verbal category are (in order): *dīcō* "say", *dō* "give", *habeō* "possess, have", *uideō* "see", all of which, we may assume, were also very frequent in ordinary speech. The most frequent noun with a purely lexical meaning, *rēx* "king", is a long way down the frequency list. The fact that *rēx* is the most frequent lexical noun has probably more to do with the subject matter of the selected texts than its frequency in the everyday, spoken language. Then come the generic spatial term *locus* "place" (which was certainly usual in the spoken language), *deus* "god", *pars* "part" as a quantifier (with a partly grammatical function) and *diēs* "day, daylight", which was certainly frequent and an essential part of everyday speech.

We may also consider as fundamental words some of the nouns, adjectives and verbs denoting those structures of society that were important in communication within the speech community: numerals, kinship terms, nouns denoting body parts, domestic animals, seasons, gods, institutions, social, political and military functions, and agricultural terms.

A significant proportion of these words are inherited and have cognates in several IE languages, or involve inherited elements adapted or combined in various ways by Latin:

- The inflection of the relative pronoun *quī* comes from the pronominal stems $*k^wo$- and $*k^wi$- which are used with various grammatical functions in the IE languages.
- The enclitic coordinator -*que* "and" continues PIE $*k^we$ (Sanskrit *ca* "and", Greek τε).

The most usual verbs in Classical Latin generally continue PIE roots, with important examples in:

- "be", both in the *infectum* stem *es-/s-*: *es-se* (PIE $*h_1es$-, Sanskrit *as*-, Greek εἰμί "I am", Hittite *esmi*, Gothic *im*, Modern German *ist* "is", English *is*), and in the *perfectum* stem *fu-*: *fu-ī* "I was" (PIE $*bhew$-H- "be" in the zero grade: $*bhū$-; Sanskrit *bhav-/ bhū-*, Modern German *bin* "I am", English *be*)

- Lat. *dīcō* "say" represents PIE **deyk̂-* "show" (Sanskrit *deś-/diś-* "show", Greek δεικ-in δείκ-νῡ-μι "I show") with the original meaning of "show by speech"
- Lat. *dō* derives from PIE **deh₃-* "give" (Sanskrit *da-dā-ti* "he gives", Greek δί-δω-μι "I give").

The three following fundamental kinship nouns are all inherited:

- "father": *păter* nom. sg. (*patris* gen. sg.), Sanskrit *pitár-*, Greek πατήρ nom. sg. (πατρ-ός gen. sg.), Old Irish *athir*, Gothic *fadar*, Old High German. *fater*, Modern German *Vater*, English *father*, etc.; PIE **ph₂-ter-*
- "mother": *māter*, Sanskrit *mātár-*, Greek μήτηρ (μᾱτηρ), Old Irish *māthir*, Old High German *muoter*, Modern German *Mutter*, English *mother*, etc.; PIE **mā-ter-*
- "brother": *frāter* "brother, cousin", Sanskrit *bhrātar-*, Old Irish *brāth(a)ir*, Gothic *brōþar*, Old High German *bruoder*, Modern German *Bruder*, English *brother*, Greek φράτηρ "member of a religious *collēgium*", etc.; PIE **bhrā-ter-*.

Some Latin numerals have exact cognates in other IE languages: e.g.

- *duo* "2" (Sanskrit *dváu*, Greek δύο, Armenian *erku*, Old Irish *dāu*, Lithuanian *dvì*, Gothic *twai*, Modern German *zwei*, English *two*)
- *trēs* "3" (PIE **trey-es*, Sanskrit *tráyas*, Greek τρεῖς, Modern German *drei*, English *three*)
- *děcem* "10" (PIE **dek̂ṃ*, Sanskrit *daśa*, Greek δέκα, Modern German *zehn*, English *ten*)
- *centum* "100" (PIE **dk̂ṃ-to-m*; Sanskrit *śatam*, Greek ἑκατόν, Modern German *Hundert*, English *hundred*).

Some names of body parts are inherited, e.g.:

- "foot" *pēs* (gen. sg. *pěd-is*) masc.; PIE **pēd-s* nom. sg. (**pěd-*); Greek πούς (pronounced [*pōs*], gen. sg. ποδ-ός); Modern German *Fuss*, English *foot*; Sanskrit *pād-a-* masc. "foot" (with a wide polysemy for the denotation of units in various domains)
- "heart" (centre of thought): *cor* (gen. *cord-is*) neut.; PIE **k̂ēr-*; Sanskrit *śrad* (in *śrad-dhā-* "be confident in"), *hṛd-* "heart"; Greek κῆρ, καρδία; Lithuanian *širdis*; Gothic *hairto*, Old High German *herza*
- "thigh": *fěmŭr* neut., an ancient heteroclitic **r/n* formation with an old genitive *fěm-in-is* and an analogical form: *fěm-or-is*
- "knee": *gěnū* neut., Sanskrit *jānu-*, Greek γόνυ, Modern German *Knie*, English *knee*.

The main domestic animals also have inherited names:

- "bovine, cow": *bōs* (gen. *bǒu-is*) fem. masc. (PIE **gʷōw-s* nom. / **gʷow-*; Sanskrit *gau-s* nom., *gām* acc. masc. fem.; Greek βοῦς masc. fem.)
- "sheep" *ŏuis* fem. masc. (Sanskrit *avi-s* "sheep", Greek ὄϊς "sheep", English *ewe*)
- "pig" *sūs* (gen. *sǔ-is*) masc. fem.
- collective noun *pecu* neut. "herd" (Sanskrit *paśu-* masc. neut., Modern German *Vieh*, English *fee*): since domestic animals were an important source of wealth, this word was used as a suffixation basis for the word meaning "money, currency" (*pecūnia*).

Although the wolf is a wild animal, it must have been very important for a large number of IE speech communities since several cognates exist in the IE languages, even some-times with a specific noun for the female wolf:

Lat. *lŭpus* masc. "wolf" (*lupa* fem. "female wolf"), Sanskrit *vṛka-s* masc. "wolf" (*vṛkī*-fem. "female wolf"), Greek λύκος masc. fem., Lithuanian *vilka-s*, Gothic *wulfs*, Modern German *Wolf*, English *wolf*, PIE **wlkʷo-s*.

Another fundamental word in the lexicon is the neuter name for a way, journey, route:

iter (built on the zero grade of PIE **h₁ey-* "go"), displaying the heteroclitic **r/n* formation.

At least two of the names of the seasons are inherited: *uēr* "spring" and *hiems* "winter", as well as those of other natural elements: *humus* "earth", *terra* "earth" (lit. "the dry one"), *mare* "sea", *ignis* "fire" (Sanskrit *agni-*).

The names of some important social functions are inherited: *rēx* "king" (a root-noun, PIE **h₃reĝ-* "direct, lead"). The feminine -*ī*- morpheme (**-yh₂-*) and the **-nā-* feminine suffix in Lat. *rēg-ī-na* "queen" have cognates in Sanskrit *rāj-an-* masc. "king" and *rāj-ñ-ī-* fem. "queen".

Red is the most salient colour in ancient civilisations and this may explain why it has a common denomination in several IE languages (Greek ἐρυθρός "red"): since its denom-ination was independent of the matter or object on which it appeared, the colour itself was conceptualised. The generic adjective *rŭber* "red" with a short *u* continues PIE **h₁rudh-ro-*, while the full grade **h₁reudh-ro-s* leads to long *u* (*rūfus*) or long *o* (*rōbur* "robustness").

But Latin also widely adapted its inherited lexical material, since inherited words were submitted to Latin phonetic evolution. For example, Latin avoided monosyllabic words ending with a short vowel: therefore the PIE negation **nĕ* (Sanskrit *na*) had to be reinforced in **ne oinom* "not even one" > *nōn*. Occasionally, Latin phonetic evolution involved the merging of two IE roots: e.g. the Latin verbs in -*dō* (-*dĕrĕ*) result from the merging of **dheh₁-* "put" (zero grade, i.e. the short form of the root without medial *e*, in *con-dō*, -*dĕrĕ* "found a city") with **deh₃-* "give" (zero grade; in *trā-dō*, -*dĕrĕ* "hand over"), since in this phonetic environment both IE **-dh-* and PIE **-d-* evolved into Lat. -*d*-. Latin re-enforced the **-ti-* feminine suffix in -*tiōn-*, a productive suffix for process nouns, in order to avoid phonetic accidents where **-tis* would disappear, as in nom. sg. *pars* "part" from **partis* (see chapter 11).

Phonetic evolutions within Latin altered some inherited forms which thus became irregular within their own paradigm. Since there was a strong tendency in favour of regular paradigms with a constant stem (i.e. the same phonemic sequence and the same number of syllables in the whole paradigm), Latin regularised some inflectional paradigms. For this reason IE vocalic alternations usually disappeared in Latin. When, occasionally, they were maintained, they were reduced, as we see with the inherited nouns in the vocabulary of kinship (see above in this section) which contain the kinship suffix **-ter-*, which had three vocalic alternations in Sanskrit and Greek. But these were reduced in Latin to only two (long full grade in the nominative sg. **-tēr* > -*ter*; zero grade **-tr-* for the other cases). In order to avoid irregular forms, other morphological elements were sometimes added in the nom. sg.: e.g. *-ĕx* in *sĕn-ĕx* (gen. pl. *sĕn-um*) "old man" and *-i-* in *iŭuĕn-i-s* "young man" (gen. pl. *iŭuĕn-um*). In these words, the original nominative forms were avoided, since they would have been monosyllabic and the stem would not have been recognised (**sĕn-s >*sēs, *iŭuĕn-s >*iŭuēs*).

Latin developed verbal radicals ending with a consonant in order to preserve the integrity of the radical in front of an inflectional morpheme beginning with a vowel. Hence Latin extended the *-c-* found in the inherited *perfectum* stem *fēc-* (in *fēc-ī*) to the whole paradigm of *făcere* (radical *făc-*). Latin *faciō* "do, produce" continues PIE **dheh₁-* (Sanskrit *dhā-* "put", Greek -θη- in τί-θη-μι "I put"), but displays an adaptation of this root.

The same tendency towards regular paradigms was at work in *ipse* masc. (*ips-a* fem., *ips-um* neut.) "himself". This word comes originally from the agglutination of *is* (an anaphoric and cataphoric pronoun-adjective) and the enclitic reinforcing particle *-pse*. *is* was therefore originally inflected, as is shown by the attestation of *eum-pse* (acc. masc. sg.), *ea-pse* (nom. fem. sg.) in the archaic period. But the fact that the inflectional ending was not situated at the end of the word was abnormal in Latin morphology, with the result that the position of the inflectional element was subsequently regularised and shifted to the end of the word.

The Internal Structure of the Latin Lexicon

The internal organisation of the Latin lexicon is based on various types of sets of words associated with one another according to various criteria (see also chapter 11 for further discussion of several of the lexical sets discussed in this section).

The first type of lexical sets is a lexical paradigm, defined as a group of words denoting the same class of *designata* or extra-linguistic entities. These may have a formal common element, usually a suffix.

The *-or* masculine nouns for physical and natural processes such as temperature (*calor* "heat"), fear (*pauor*), deterioration (*putor* "putrefaction") constitute such a lexical paradigm based on referential and extra-linguistic criteria.

Another lexico-referential set contains the depreciative *-cus* adjectives denoting physical handicap or psychological problems: *mancus* "having only one hand" (*man-* in *manus* "hand"), *caecus* "blind" (perhaps from **kai-* "one"; originally "having only one eye"), *raucus* "hoarse" (*rauis* "hoarseness"), *famēlicus* "starved" (*famēs* "hunger"). This group shows several formal features (two syllables; *a* vocalism; diphthong; *-cus* ending; consonant gemination) that may be realised or not at the same time in a given adjective: the prototypes are *flaccus* "floppy" (of ears) and *raucus*.

The *-tūra* nouns also constitute such a set for objects made by man, as do the *-ārius, -ī* masculine nouns for soldiers and craftsmen, the *-ōn-* masculine profession nouns (*lēnō* "brothel-keeper, slave seller", *com-mīlit-ō* "fellow soldier") and the *-ālia* neuter plural suffix for religious festivals.

When these lexico-referential sets contain a large number of words, the words do not necessarily all have the same suffix: e.g. the names of plants may be considered as a lexical set due to the common extra-linguistic category of the entities they denote. But their formation varies considerably so that there is no one suffix that can be considered as characteristic of plant names. Hyperonyms may also be found within such sets: e.g. *herba* (*-ae* fem.) is the hyperonym for plants with a flexible stem, and *arbŏr* (*arbŏr-is* fem.) is the hyperonym for plants with a strong, more or less wide stem or trunk (*arbor* covers "tree" and "bush").

The second type of word set is the genetic set. The common denominator of the words here is a synchronic radical with a lexical meaning, whereas the suffixes vary. Due to the various functions of the suffixes, the suffixed words are in a complementary distribution. The genetic set defined by the radical *can-* "sing" contains the verb *canere* "sing", its frequentative *can-tāre*, two process nouns *can-tus* masc. and *can-tiō* fem., an agent noun *can-tor* "sing-er" and its feminine counterpart *can-trīx*. Another genetic set is found: on the basis of *inuen-* "find" with *inuen-ī-re*, *inuen-tiō*, *inuen-tor*, *inuen-trīx*, on the basis of *arā-* "plough" with *arā-tor*, *arā-trum*, *arā-tiōnēs*. *Rŭber* belongs to the same genetic set as the state verb *rŭb-ē-re* "be red", the noun *rŭbor* masc. "redness", the adjectives *rŭb-icundus* "suffused with red", *rŭssus* "red with a brownish shade, red-haired", *rūfus* "red-haired". The common denominator is the radical meaning "red", which has several allomorphs (*rŭb-/rūb-/rōb-/rūf-/rŭss-*).

The third type of set may be called lexical micro-systems, in which each word is in a complementary distribution with the others, but the words themselves do not necessarily have a formal common point. They denote entities that have to be carefully distinguished, so that the denominations are also opposed to one another by their semantic features.

The kinship vocabulary and the denominations of human beings according to their gender, age and social function are made up of terms which may be generic (*homō* "human being" masc. or fem.; "mankind" masc. pl.) or specific: *īnfāns* "baby", *puer* "boy" masc., *adulescent-ulus* "very young teenager", *adulescēns* masc. "teenager", *iuuenis* masc. "young man", *senex* masc. "old man"; *puella* fem. "girl", *uirgō* fem. "unmarried girl of marriageable age", *mulier* fem. "woman, married woman", *anus* and *senex* fem. "old woman". The oppositions between the members of these sets may be plurifactoral, with polysemic words such as *uir* "adult male person, man". In the gender contrast, *uir* is in opposition to *mulier* "woman" and, for age, to *puer* "child", *adulescens* "teenager". When meaning "husband", *uir* is opposed to *uxor* "wife" in an antonymy based on a converse relationship. When used as a specific term meaning "one possessing manly virtues (courage)" with a specific laudative connotation, *uir* is opposed to the generic term *homō* "man".

The various denominations of domestic animals are also organised in micro-systems with a generic term (e.g. *bōs* masc. or fem. "bovine animal") and several specific terms according to age, gender, utility: *uitulus* "male calf" masc., *uitula* "female calf" fem., *uacca* "young cow", *taurus* "bull, breeding male", *bōs* masc. "male draught animal". The generic term of such systems (here *bōs*) usually has two functions: it is usually an unmarked generic term (masc. fem. "bovine"), but when it is opposed to another term in the same system, it becomes a marked specific term (*bōs* masc. "ox").

Main Semantic Phenomena

The denominations of natural categories, such as plants, wild animals (birds, fish, mammal), stones and minerals are based on the perception of their salient features. These selected salient features may be expressed in a direct or indirect way.

The extra-linguistic feature selected for a given denomination may be expressed directly by a pre-existing word, such as *rŭber* "red" in *rŭbr-īca* "red ochre" (then "chapter-heading in a book of laws", since it was painted red, and finally the chapter itself), *rōbŭr* "red core of an oak", *rōbīgō* "red deterioration of metals, rust, plant illnesses characterised by a red deposit".

But the salient feature may also be expressed indirectly by a lexical and cognitive metaphor or metonymy. This is a usual situation that drives the polysemy of many terms.

In a metonymic denomination, the name of a given entity is extended to another entity which is contiguous to it in external reality: e.g. *imperium* "supreme power", and hence "empire", the space where the supreme power is exercised. The polysemy of *purpura* may be explained by several successive metonymic shifts: "the shell-fish producing the purple colour", "the little bag inside this shell-fish containing the liquid", "the liquid itself", "the dying liquid as a raw material", "the entity dyed with this liquid, a purple-dyed cloth", "the purple colour itself", "the purple colour as a sign of power".

The meaning of *rōbŭr, -ŏris* neut. "solidity" is due to a metonymic shift from the radical *rōb-* "red": the extra-linguistic feature is the red(dish) colour of the core in a cross-section of the trunk of an oak tree; this dark part is the hardest and is used for timber. The words *Rōbīgus, -ī* masc. "deity supposed to avert rust in crops" (Varro *R.*) and *rōbīg-ālia, -ium* neut. pl. "festival held in honour of Robigus" (Varro *L.*) are derived morphologically and semantically from *rōbīgō* "illness of plants" with a metonymic shift.

Metaphoric denominations are usual when there is no pre-existing word expressing the selected salient external feature. The sword-lily (*gladiolus*) is named from the noun for "sword", since its stem is in the shape of a sword: *gladius* "sword" → *gladi-olus* "sword-lily" with a metaphoric suffix *-ulus* (*-olus*, **-lo-*) (see chapter 11). In such cases, the associated entity used as a standard is well-known to the speech community and its denomination is then used for another entity which is not as well-known. Similarly, Latin may use the name of a body part in order to name a plant: e.g. *Iouis barba* "shrub" (lit. "Jupiter's beard") for a plant with fluffy parts. In order to name a wild animal, the name of a domestic animal may be used: *bōs* "bovine animal" denotes a reindeer (Caes. *Gal.* 6.26.1), a fish (Ov.; Pliny *Nat.*) or an elephant in the lexicalised sequence *Lūca bōs* fem. (Plautus).

Among other important semantic phenomena visible in the Latin lexicon, it is worth mentioning the Latin evolution which continues in the Romance languages in French *avoir faim* "be hungry", *avoir peur* "be frightened". These are the "weak verbs" (French *verbes supports*; German *passe-partout* in J.B. Hofmann's terminology) and in Classical Latin they are mainly represented by *facere* and *dare* "do, produce", *esse* "be" and *habēre* "have", *gerere* "wage" and *agere* "lead, do". A weak verb is a verb that only conveys grammatical morphemes, while the lexical information is conveyed by its complement. It has a very reduced or non-existent semantic value, so that the relevant linguistic unit is then the whole sequence containing the weak verb and its complement. For example, *curriculum facere* "run" has the same meaning as *currere*, *lustrum facere* "perform an expiation" the same meaning as *lustrāre*. Other frozen verbal syntagms with weak verbs are: *uerba facere* "speak" (*uerbum* "word"), *grātiam facere* "give pardon" (*grātia* "indulgence"), *poenās dare* "be punished" (*poena* "punishment"), *dare uiam* "give way" (*uia* "way"), *dare locum* "give way" (*locum* "place"), *dare uēla* "set sail" (*uēla* "sail"), *esse odiō alicuī* "be hated by someone" (functioning as the passive voice of *ōdī* (+ acc.) "I hate (someone)").

Lexical Innovations

Coinage (lexical creation) is usually considered as very innovative, since it involves the creation of a new word. But most new words documented in Classical Latin were already "attestable" words, since they were built in following the rules of existing, productive sets. In all periods, Latin increased the number of its words by reproducing pre-existing patterns and extending its productive groups. Although Petronius coined numerous new words in his freedmen's speeches, these words were, in fact, built on regular models: *ně-săp-ius* "who does not know, ignorant", in Petr. 50.5: *Et ne me putetis nesapium esse, ualde bene scio unde primum Corinthea nata sint* "And so that you don't think I am ignorant, I know very well where Corinthian vases come from" imitates the pattern of *ně-scius* "who does not know" with the replacement of the radical *-sci-* by *-săp-* "know". The co-occurrence in this sentence of *săp-* "know" and *scī-* "know" (in *sciō*) is a clue that we are witnessing the very beginning of a suppletion. In the low-level language of the speaker, *scī-* "know" is partly replaced here by *săp-* (*săpěre*) in its developed meaning "know", which was continued in the Romance languages (French *savoir* "know" < Lat. **sapēre*).

Many of the new words used in building the Christian vocabulary were also attestable words, since they followed the normal rules of suffixation. Authors such as Plautus do, of course, show a high degree of novelty and innovation when coining fancy words for fun which are very distant from the usual patterns found in the lexicon. However, these individual and marginal creations were ephemeral and did not take root in the language.

In many respects, the Latin lexicon was stable and perfectly adequate for the needs of society. In the domain of agriculture (agricultural instruments, cultivation of the vine, tilling the soil, crops, etc.), agronomy (quality of the soil, names of cultivated plants), surveying (land, fields, boundaries, limits), perception of natural phenomena (temperature, humidity, clouds), breeding (denomination of domestic animals), farm construction (building materials, stone, concrete, limestone, lime-kilns), etc., the Romans had at their disposal lexical material that was fully adapted to their needs. The Latin lexicon also provided a precise vocabulary for social links: e.g. in the domain of kinship (kindred, family structure), as we have seen, but also of social relationships (profession denominations), religion (gods, priests, brotherhoods, festivals), law and institutions (decrees, magistrates), and army (soldiers, military ranks, arms). The military vocabulary is particularly impressive in the large number of lexemes involved, and in its very precise divisions and oppositions.

But nonetheless the Latin lexicon did evolve, loosing words and acquiring new ones built on currently productive patterns. Lexical coinage is a continuous process in the language of all dynamic societies.

In Latin, lexical coinage was especially intense in the translation of Greek terms in the scientific domains (philosophy, architecture, the medical and veterinary arts, astrology, etc.) that the Romans took over from the Greeks. The Roman authors complain about the insufficiency of the Latin vocabulary compared to Greek: this deficiency is mentioned by Cicero for the Latin adaptation of Greek philosophy, and by Quintilian and even Aulus Gellius (Gel. 2.26.5) for the denomination of colours. In the learned idiolects of the Classical and post-Classical periods, the texts reflect an intensive activity of lexical creation in order to translate Greek terms.

Various methods were used in Latin for lexical creation. In all cases we have a new *signifié* (meaning) and a new *designatum* (the extra-linguistic entity denoted). But in some cases we also have a new *signifiant* (phonetic and phonemic sequence). (See further chapter 11 for discussion of some of these processes of lexical creation in Latin.)

The most frequent method used for the creation of a new *signifiant* is a new combination of pre-existing Latin elements by the suffixation (and/or prefixation) of a pre-existing productive suffix (and/or prefix) on a pre-existing basis. It is usually an extension of a productive formation: e.g. *aquā-tilis* "aquatic" (Varro, Cicero, Vitruvius, Pliny, *Nat.*) was built on *aqua* "water" with the *-tilis* suffix as a variant of the very productive *-lis* suffix; *aquā-tilis* was then in competition with *aquā-ticus*, since the *-ticus, -icus* suffixes were less productive.

This coinage may also occur under the external influence of a foreign language, especially of Greek. In the translation of Greek words, this process is called a "morphological calque": each Greek morphological element is translated by its Latin counterpart. The Greek possessive (or *bahuvrīhi*) compound adjective μεγά-θῡμ-ος (-ος fem., -ον neut.) "magnanimous" was first analysed in two morphemes related to the adjective μέγας "big, great" and the noun θῡμ-ός (-ου) "spirit"; it was then translated into *magn-anim-us* (-a, -um) from the stems of *magn-us* (-a, -um) "big, great" and *anim-us, -ī* "spirit".

These morphological calques were very much used in poetry, especially during the Archaic period, when the first Latin poets were much influenced by Greek literature.

The Christian vocabulary also used this type of transfer. The verbs in *-ficāre* may translate Greek compound verbs in -ποιέω "make" (*dei-ficāre* is a morphological calque of θεο-ποιέω) or suffixed verbs in -ίζω.

The toponym *Rubrum mare* "the Red Sea" (from *ruber* "red" and *mare* "sea") is probably a morphological calque of Greek ἡ Ἐρυθρὰ θάλασσα "the Red Sea and a part of the Indian Ocean". In Greek, just as in Latin, this denomination is based on the name of the red colour, selected as a salient feature for the sea concerned. In this particular case, the morphological calque is perfect, since the Greek and the Latin terms both display the same morphological structure as lexicalised syntagms joining an adjective and a noun.

The noun *circum-caesūra* "surface outline, contour" in Lucretius (3.219) is a morphological calque of Greek περι-κοπ-ή, the prefix περι- being translated here by *circum-* "around" and κοπ-ή by *caes-ūra* "cutting down". This last term, built with the suffix *-tūra/-sūra*, is the resultative noun associated with *caedō* "cut, strike". In contrast to this formation, *circumcīs-ūra* (Pliny *Nat.*) "a cutting round of trees" was built according to the Latin pattern, as a resultative noun derived from the verbal stem of *circumcīd-ō* "make an incision round".

But Latin was also capable of creating new words with an entirely new *signifiant* (i.e. not a combination of pre-existing elements). These are usually borrowings from another language where the *signifiant* of the Latin word is an imitation of the *signifiant* of the foreign word, with adaptation to the phonemes and phonetic constraints of Latin, by a "grapho-phonemic calque". The meaning and denotation of the new Latin word are usually similar to those of the foreign word, but semantic changes may also occur during the transfer from one language to the other.

Latin borrowed some words from the Semitic languages in the preliterary period for the denotation of concrete entities (usually manufactured objects or raw materials);

saccus "bag" is one of these "civilisation borrowings". For some borrowed Semitic words, Greek was the intermediate language. These words are totally integrated into the Latin vocabulary and they were given Latin suffixal and inflectional morphemes: e.g. *tūn-ica* "tunic", with a Latin suffix -*ica* on the basis of *tūn-*, probably of Semitic origin.

Among the Celtic languages, Gallic gave Latin some nouns denoting wheeled vehicles: *carrus* "Gallic type of wagon", *carpentum* "two-wheeled carriage". Some Latin authors also mention Gallic clothes that were called in Latin by their Gallic names adapted to Latin phonetics and morphology: *brācae* (-*ārum* fem. pl.) "Gallic trousers". The possessive adjective *brācātus* "wearing trousers" was institutionalised in the Latin vocabulary in that part of Gaul called *Narbonensis* (Pliny, *Nat.*) and among its inhabitants.

It is not easy to find Latin words borrowed from Etruscan, since the number of lexical Etruscan words we know is rather limited; the suffix -*erna* in *luc-erna*, *lanterna* may be of Etruscan origin.

An internal -*f*- in a Latin word is a clue for a borrowing from one of the other languages of Ancient Italy (especially Umbrian and Oscan) or for a dialectal origin: e.g. *scrōfa* "sow".

As we have seen, the Latin words continuing the root meaning "red" show several allomorphs: *rŭb-/rūb-/rōb-/rūf-/rŭss-*. Some of these are due to diatopic variations or borrowing from dialectal variations: -*ō*- and -*f*- in *rōbŭr, -ŏr-is* neut. "oak-tree, strength", *rōbus* "red" (for oxen), *rōb-īgō* "rust", *rūfus* "red-haired".

The Latin vocabulary may also contain words borrowed from other unknown languages, which could be the pre-existing languages spoken in Ancient Italy usually called "Mediterranean languages". Such an origin could be possible for the name of the donkey (*asinus*), the olive and olive-tree (*olīua*), and for wine (*uīnum*), although *uītis* "vine" is usually considered as having an IE origin (from a root meaning "be flexible").

But the language from which Latin borrowed the most numerous words is clearly Greek, which had a profound influence on the Latin lexicon, involving the three main kinds of transfer: the "morphological calques" that we have already seen and the "graphophonemic" (i.e. an imitation of *signifiant*) and "semantic" calques both of which we will look at now.

In grapho-phonemic calques, the Latin word phonetically imitates the phonemic sequence of the Greek word with an adaptation of the Greek phonemes to Latin phonemes and phonetic constraints. These borrowed words show various degrees of integration into the Latin lexicon and they differ according to the period and the circumstances in which they were borrowed.

Greek words entered the Latin lexicon very early in the pre-literary period and these words are already totally integrated in the Latin lexicon in the first Latin texts at the end of the third century BCE. They were "civilisation borrowings" denoting concrete entities, manufactured objects or raw material brought by the Greek by sea or land. The denomination was thus borrowed at the same time as the denominated entity. In these periods, the borrowings were oral processes, so that Greek phonemes were adapted to the nearest Latin ones. Since Latin did not have aspirates, the Greek aspirates φ, θ, χ (pronounced /pʰ/, /tʰ/, /kʰ/) lost their aspirate element and were reduced to the corresponding non-aspirate consonant, written <p>, <t>, <c> in Latin. Greek φ was adapted as Lat. *p* in Greek πορφύρα > Lat. *purpura* "shellfish yielding the purple dye". Being completely integrated, these words were subsequently submitted to normal Latin phonetic constraints: Greek ă became Lat. *ĕ* in an internal open syllable before /r/ in *cămĕra* "vaulted ceiling, room" from καμάρα; the final sequence of βαλανεῖον was reduced to -*ĕum* in *balnĕum* "a room for bathing".

Such integration of Greek words also happened during the Latin literary period: e.g. *māchina* fem. (since Plautus) "machine, assemblage" from μαχανά/μηχανή was integrated, as shown by the derived words: an adjective *māchinā-lis* (*scientia* "mechanics" Pliny, *Nat.*) and a verb *māchinā-rī* "invent, devise cunningly" (from which were derived *māchinā-mentum* "machine", *māchinā-tiō* "mechanism").

The noun *scēna* (or *scaena*; from σκηνή) "scene" was integrated into the Latin lexicon and used as a suffixation basis for several adjectives meaning "related to the scene" (*scaenā-ticus, scaenā-tilis, scaen-icus*); *thĕātrum* neut. "theatre" (from θέατρον), used as a suffixation basis in the adjective *theātr-ālis*, has the same status; *pŏēta* masc. "poet" (from ποιητής), *pīrata* masc. "pirate" (from πειρατής) were also well integrated into the Latin vocabulary. Latin speakers did not consider these words as foreign and used them just like any other word since their foreign origin was not relevant in their functioning in the language.

Other Greek borrowings are usual in certain idiolects of Latin, but their Greek origin may have still been felt by some Latin speakers, since they kept spellings that were not Latin: e.g. <ch> in *architectus* "architect" (< ἀρχιτέκτων, -ονος). When Cicero (*Ver.* 2.5.67) used *archi-pīrata* "pirate chief" (<ἀρχι-πειρατής), he certainly knew that *archi-* was borrowed from Greek ἀρχι-.

But some words were still felt to be foreign and used on purpose as xenisms (a technical term borrowed from Greek ξένος "foreign") with a foreign connotation: e.g. the use of the exclamation "*Graphicē*!" "Beautiful!" in Plautus, as the transcription of the Greek adjective γραφικός > Lat. *graphicus* with the addition of the Latin de-adjectival and adverbial morpheme -*ē*. In Lucilius (86), in the Archaic period, *rhētoricōterus, -a, -um* "inclined to speak in an inflated style" is the transcription of the Greek comparative in -ωτερος of the adjective ῥητορικός with Latin inflectional endings. In a later period, Aulus Gellius (Gel. 17.20.4: *Taurus mihi "heus" inquit "tu, rhetorisce"*) mentions the vocative *rhētorisce*, a transcription of a Greek diminutive suffix in: *rhētoriscus* masc. "a young rhetorician" (from ῥητορ-ίσκος).

The noun *rhētor* masc. "rhetorician" is part of the integrated Latin vocabulary, but the verbal suffix -*issāre* is the transfer of Greek -ίζω with a phonemic and phonetic adaptation of Greek -ζ- into Lat. -*ss*-. Thus the verb *rhētor-issāre* "use rhetoric, declaim" (adaptation of ῥητορίζω) probably still conveyed a Greek connotation.

The peregrinisms (a technical term borrowed from Lat. *peregrīnus* "foreign") show an intermediate situation between xenisms and fully integrated words. These words are felt as foreign, but are commonly in use in specialised idiolects, where they sometimes maintained their Greek inflectional endings: e.g. *rhētoricē* (gen. -*ēs* fem.) "rhetoric" (from ῥητορική) in Quintilian (Quint. *Inst.* 2.17.5: accusative -*ēn*). The learned authors, who had a good knowledge of Greek and were usually bilingual, tried to be as precise as possible in the transcription of the Greek words, using the Greek inflectional endings rather than the Latin ones and the signs of the Latin alphabet especially created for the Greek phonemes that had no equivalent in Latin: <y>, <ch>, <ph>, <th>.

In all these cases lexical innovation was represented by a new *signifiant*. But there is also another way of denoting a new entity which does not involve the coinage of a new *signifiant*. A new meaning may simply be assigned to a pre-existing word. Thus the polysemy of the pre-existing word is increased.

The noun *pontifex* "one of the college of priests having supreme control in matters of public religion in Rome" was used in the Christian vocabulary with the new meaning "bishop".

When this process is applied to the translation of a Greek word, it is called a "semantic calque". This is well illustrated in the vocabulary of grammar by *cāsus, -ūs* masc. "event" (process noun of *cădere* "fall"), which takes on the meaning "grammatical case" by alignment on its Greek counterpart πτῶσις "fall" and, metaphorically, "grammatical case". The polysemy of *causa, -ae* fem. "trial, plea, cause, pretext, reason" was also increased under the influence of Greek αἰτία "reason".

It is interesting to note that the constitution of the Christian vocabulary mainly involved two of the processes that we have just mentioned and that it distinguished between them according to the nature of the denominated entities. Grapho-phonemic borrowings involving the imitation of the Greek *signifiant* were used mainly for concrete entities, such as the nouns *ecclēsia* "church" from ἐκκλησία (originally "general assembly") and *presbyter* "priest" from πρεσβύτερος (the comparative of πρέσβυς "old"), alongside the verb *baptizō* "baptise" from βαπτίζω. The semantic calque increasing the polysemy of pre-existing Latin words was used for abstract notions: *grātia* "grace", *dominus* "Lord", *deus* "God", *pietās* "dutiful respect", *spiritus* "(holy) spirit", *trīnitās* "Trinity", *Verbum* "the Word".

Conclusion

The Latin lexicon may be described according to the several internal and external processes underlying its organisation. A significant proportion of fundamental words are inherited, but Latin often adapted this inherited lexical material and it is also important to take into account the various diastratic variations.

Various methods were used by Latin for lexical creation and in all of them we have a new *signifié* (meaning) and a new *designatum* (the extra-linguistic entity denoted). But in some cases we also have a new *signifiant* (phonetic and phonemic sequence) being created, due to the combination of pre-existing elements or to the borrowing of words from a foreign language.

The Latin lexicon is structured by a variety of word sets (essentially lexical paradigms, genetic sets, micro-systems). It is also dependent on the various semantic concepts, some important ones of which we have looked at in detail (metaphor, metonym, weak verbs). A more thorough semantic study would also include polysemy, synonymy, antonymy, and homonymy, all semantic notions which have also driven the lexical (and grammatical) evolution of the Latin language.

FURTHER READING

The best available dictionary of Latin is the *TLL*, which covers all stages of the Latin language, and is still in progress; the *OLD* is the best single volume Latin–English dictionary, although it does not record Christian authors or most works later than 200 CE. Etymological dictionaries of Latin include Ernout and Meillet (1979), Walde and Hofmann (1969) and de Vaan (2008); Benveniste (1969) is also useful for tracking IE origins of Latin vocabulary relating to specific social institutions, and Maltby (1991) records ancient etymologies. Latin borrowings from Greek and from Etruscan are discussed in Biville (1990, 1995) and Hadas-Lebel (2004). There are numerous studies on selected lexical items or lexical areas in Latin, among which it is worth mentioning here Adams (1982a) on sexual vocabulary, Fruyt (2006) on colour terms, and the studies of André (1967, 1985, 1991) on birds, plants and anatomy. The vocabulary appropriate for different genres of literary composition and in technical writings are discussed in Axelson (1945), Coleman (1989a) and Langslow (2000b).

CHAPTER 11

Word-Formation in Classical Latin

Michèle Fruyt

In this chapter, we are going to look at the six main types of word-formation in Latin: suffixation, nominal compounding, verbal compounding, preverbation, agglutination and recategorisation.

Suffixation

Latin used suffixation for the formation of all its grammatical categories: nouns, adjectives, adverbs and verbs. Suffixation was the dominant type for nouns and adjectives. A given suffix may be considered productive in Classical Latin if there is a large number of lexemes in which it appears. If we structure the list of these lexemes in decreasing order of frequency, we will see: (a) a very high frequency for a few of the lexemes at the top of the list, and (b) a large number of hapaxes and lexemes with very low frequency at the bottom of the list.

The presence of a large number of lexemes with the suffix and the very high frequency of a few of them reflect the importance of the formation in the texts, and therefore probably in speech. The presence of a large number of very low frequency lexemes provides a clue to the suffix's potential for extension and its capacity for creating new items. Thus, for a suffix to be considered productive we also need words which are attested only once or twice, or even which are not attested at all but which are "attestable", i.e. lexemes that have the potential to exist, since they could be coined by any speaker according to regular patterns.

Latin suffixes often resulted from an adaptation of inherited elements. Moreover, many words containing inherited suffixes that were not productive any more were still in

A Companion to the Latin Language, First Edition. Edited by James Clackson.
© 2011 Blackwell Publishing Ltd. Published 2011 by Blackwell Publishing Ltd.

use in Classical Latin, since they still belonged to the core of the lexicon and their referential value was essential for the speech community.

A first group of noun suffixes (-*tiō*, -*tus*, -*tor*, -*tūra*, -*bulum*, etc.) involves **suffixes that may occur in a complementary distribution within a "genetic set"**, i.e. a set of lexemes based on the same Latin synchronic radical. A synchronic radical is a lexical morpheme, i.e. a minimal significant unit with a lexical meaning. For example, the lexical morpheme *inuen-* "find" occurs in the verb *inuen-ī-re* "find", in the -*tiō* process noun *inuen-tiō* "action of finding, the thing discovered", in the -*tor* agentive noun *inuentor* "inventor", in its feminine counterpart -*trīx: inuen-trīx*, and in the neuter noun *inuen-tum, -ī* "discovery" (a lexicalised form of the past passive participle of *inuenīre*).

In these genetic sets we also find the nouns suffixed with -*tūra* denoting concrete, inanimate entities created by man and resulting from the craftsman's work, as well as the -*tōr-ius* adjectives (the suffix being the joining of agentive -*tōr-* and relational adjectival -*ius*), and the -*bulum, -ī* neut. instrument nouns, etc.

These organised sets of complementary lexemes were much in use in technical vocabularies: e.g. in medicine, *exulcerā-re* "inflame", *exulcerā-tiō* "ulceration" (Celsus, Plin. *Nat.*), *exulcerā-tōrius* (adj. masc.) and *exulcerā-trīx* (adj. fem.) "bringing ulcers" (Plin. *Nat.*).

Latin makes much use of **process nouns** (also called verbal nouns) in -*tiō* (gen. -*tiōn-is* fem.) denoting the same process as the parallel verb: e.g. the noun *admīrā-tiō* "wonder, surprise" denotes the same process as the verb *admīrā-rī* "wonder", from whose stem it is derived (*admīrā-rī* → *admīrā-tiō*). This kind of formation on an *ā* verbal stem is the most productive for the -*tiō* nouns.

Aside from this quasi-grammatical use, the -*tiō* nouns also show normal polysemy with concrete meanings denoting any entity linked to the process such as the result of the process, the space where the process takes place, etc.; e.g. *ambulā-tiō* "act of walking, walk" is the process noun of the verb *ambulā-re* "to walk", but it may also mean "place for walking, promenade" with a metonymic shift.

-*tiō* was clearly very productive in all periods of Latin and it has survived in some Romance languages (French -*tion*). It did not undergo any semantic restrictions for the processes denoted. Although it was mostly used for actions, it also occurred for non-active processes, especially in Cicero's philosophical vocabulary (where -*tio* is also a characteristic feature for the Stoic philosophers): e.g. *affec-tiō* "state of feeling" (Cic. *Inv.* 1.41) is associated with the verb *afficere* "affect". It is noticeable that *affectiō* is documented in Classical Latin, since, in this referential domain of feelings, -*tus* (-*tūs*) masc. was usual and *affec-tus* "feeling" would have been possible here. This shows the unstoppable progression of -*tiō* at the expense of -*tus* even in areas where -*tus* was usual.

-*tiō* was probably productive in everyday oral utterances and written texts in all diastratic variants. Cicero used numerous -*tiō* nouns in the specialised idiolects of philosophy, agriculture, etc., as did Quintilian, who accumulates -*tiō* nouns in his vocabulary of rhetoric.

On the other hand, -*tu-s* (gen. sg. -*tūs*) masc., from PIE *-*tu-*, was the object of morphologisation in the formation of the supine in -*tum* (grammaticalised from the directive accusative sg. of a *-*tu-* noun: *īre cubitum* "go to bed" Plautus) and -*tū* (from a dative sg.: *difficile dictū* "difficult to say"). This grammaticalisation process is correlated with a loss of lexical productivity for -*tus*.

Some -*tus* nouns in (pre-)Classical Latin have a very high frequency and belong to the core of the Latin lexicon: e.g. *exercitus* "army" (*exercēre* "exercise"), *aduentus* "arrival" (*ad-uen-ī-re* "arrive"), *introitus* "going in" (*intro-īre* "go inside"). But the formation itself was no longer capable of extension and underwent semantic and referential constraints, becoming limited to certain sub-groups associated with motion verbs: *aduen-tus* "arrival" (*aduen-ī-re* "arrive"). But even on this familiar ground -*tus* was threatened by -*tiō* (cf. *discessiō* "action of going away"). The -*tus* nouns were also well documented for noises: *crepitus* "sharp sound made by a door" associated with a verb (*crepāre* "make a sharp sound"), but sometimes they were not associated with a verb: *tumultus* "confused uproar". A small microsystem of -*tus* lexemes denotes the four senses: *uīsus* "sight", *audītus* "sense of hearing", *tāctus* "sense of touch", *gustus* "sense of taste". However, the -*tiō* nouns built on the same bases, on the contrary, were not lexicalised and still functioned as process nouns, e.g. *audī-tiō* "fact of hearing" (*audī-re* "hear").

The -*tiō* formation was productive and potentially capable of extension in all periods of Latin, while, as we have said, the -*tus* formation had already lost its extension capacity in Classical Latin. The only exception is in hexametric poetry, where the -*tus* nouns may be metrical substitutes for -*tiō* nouns on the same basis. Therefore, as a poetic device the -*tus* nouns acquired a connotation with a higher level of speech and this continued into Late Latin poetry and high level prose.

-*tiōn*- fem. is a Latin adaptation of inherited *-*ti*- (following the zero grade of the root in other IE languages, i.e. the short form of the root with no media *e*), phonetically reinforced by *-*ōn*- or *-*iōn*- in order to avoid phonetic disturbances. *-*ti*- is a primary suffix following the PIE root in *nā-tiō* "people who have the same genetic origin" (a concrete collective meaning) from the zero grade of *$\hat{g}enh_1$*- "give birth".

The agentive suffix -*tŏr* (gen. -*tōr-is* masc.) was productive in all periods of Latin and has survived in the Romance languages (French -*teur/-seur/-eur*). Its most productive formation was behind an *ā* verbal stem, e.g. *arā-tor* "plougher" on *arā-re* "plough", or behind a Latin synchronic radical, which may continue an PIE root, e.g. *genitor* "father", *genetrīx* "mother". While diachronically -*tor*- is a primary suffix in *genitor* (lit. "who generates" on *$genh_1$*-), the synchronic analysis is ambiguous: it may be *geni-tor* or *gen-itor*, since both the radical and the suffix display allomorphs (*gen(i)*- and -(*i*)*tor*).

The same suffix may denote women according to their profession: *nūtrīx* "nurse", *meretrīx* "courtesan" with a feminine agentive -*tr-īx* suffix, formed on the masculine -*tor* by the addition of -*ī*- (PIE *-*yh_2*-), a morpheme used for the denotation of female human beings or animals on the basis of the noun denoting the corresponding male: *genitor* "father" → *genetrīx* "mother", *rēx* "king" → *rēg-ī-na* "queen" (Sanskrit *rāj-an*- "king" → *rāj-ñ-ī*- "queen").

Some of these agentive nouns were almost verbal adjectives associated with a verb: e.g. *uictor* masc. "victorious" (*uic-/uinc*-, *uincō* "overcome") displayed a gender agreement in the feminine *uic-tr-īx*; *inuentor* had its feminine counterpart, *inuentrīx* (Verg. *G.* 1.19: *oleae … Minerua inuentrix* "Minerva, who invented the olive tree") and displayed an agreement in the feminine plural for an inanimate entity: *Athenae* "Athens" (Cic. *de Orat.* 1.13: *illas omnium doctrinarum inuentrices Athenas* "Athens, that invented all the sciences") (see below). The -*trīx* suffix is used in agreement with a feminine noun denoting an animal in *can-trīcēs* (*auēs*) fem. pl. "singing birds", *auis* "bird" being of the feminine gender (Varro, *R.* 3.5.14). The feminine form of the suffix is also used for an inanimate entity denoted by a noun in the feminine grammatical gender (Liv. 1.58.5: *uictrix libido*). The adjectivisation of *uictrīx* has been driven even further, since the word shows some occurrences in the neuter gender in poetry (Verg. *A.* 3.54: *uictricia … arma*).

But some other *-tor* words were lexicalised and no longer functioned in association with a verb: *auctor* "guarantor", built on *aug-* (also occurring in the causative verb *aug-ē-re* "increase"), underwent a semantic specialisation in the legal vocabulary that distanced it from the verb. The same kind of lexicalisation occurred in some denominations of magistrates, where the original radical is not synchronically felt any more: *quaes-tor* "quaestor" (*quais-* "look for", *quaerō*), *dictā-tor* "dictator" (*dictā-re* a frequentative-intensive of *dīcere* "say"). This lexical *-tor* set also included nouns of profession built on Latin radicals or verbal stems: *sū-tor* "shoemaker" (*su-* "sow", *suere*), *tonsor* "barber" (*tond-* "cut (hair, beard)", *tond-ē-re*). This profession suffix was extended to noun stems denoting the entity dealt with: *(h)olitor* "producer and seller of vegetables" (on *(h)olus* "vegetable"), *port-itor* "porter" (on *porta* "door").

In this professional area, *-tor* overlapped with the domain of *-ārius* masc. for the denomination of craftsmen and soldiers on the basis of the noun denoting the entity they took care of: *uēxill-ārius* "standard-bearer" (*uēxillum* "military standard") (see below and chapter 10).

The -*tūra*, -*ae* feminine suffix built nouns denoting concrete entities resulting from human activity, especially in the idiolects of craftsmanship, cooking, painting, etc. It was submitted to semantic and referential constraints: *condī-tūra* "method of seasoning, preserving" (*condī-re* "preserve"), *pic-tūra* "painting, picture" (*pig-/pic-* "paint", *pingō* "paint"), *uorsūra* "money borrowing" (*uertere* "turn round"), *cūrā-tūra* "diet, treatment" in the medical vocabulary (*cūrāre* "treat"), *par-tūra* "action of giving birth" (*pariō, -ere* "give birth to") and *stă-tūra* "stature, height of the body in the upright position" (*stā-re* "stand") in the agricultural vocabulary (Varro, *R.*), *mēnsūra* "measure" (*mētior* "to measure"), *iac-tūra* "throwing over board" from a boat (*iaciō* "throw").

The *-tūra* nouns are usually synchronically associated with a verb. Some are built on the stem of the verb, others on the Latin radical which also built the verbal stem.

In this group, the most frequent lexeme in Classical Latin (according to Delatte *et al.* (1981)) is *nā-tūra* "nature" (sometimes personified), where the suffix follows the Latin radical *nā-* referring to birth (*nā-scor* "be born"; allomorph *gen(i)-*). Its original meaning could be "creation, creatures, created beings", the concrete result of *creā-re* "create".

The suffix *-tūra* is a Latin creation, that joined two inherited suffixes: **-tu-* (with a lengthening of *u*) and **-ro-* in the feminine form **-rā*.

Words in *-tūra* are often in parallel with words in *-tiō* or *-tor* built on the same bases: the action is expressed by *-tiō*, the agent by *-tor*, and the concrete result of the action by *-tūra*. In the denomination of the office of magistrate: *praetūra* "office of a *praetor*", *quaestūra* "office of a *quaestor*", *-tūra* is substituted for (and not added to) agentive *-tor*. This is for phonetic reasons: a haplology avoiding the succession of two syllables beginning with the same consonant (**quaes(tōr)-tūra*).

The **instrument suffixes** build neuter nouns, the grammatical gender being correlated with the inanimate feature of the denoted entity, which may be a tool, a place, etc., used by people for their activities. They were synchronically built on verbal stems or Latin radicals denoting the relevant action. Sometimes the suffix was diachronically a primary suffix, directly added to the PIE root, e.g. *stǎ-bulum* "stable" on the zero grade of **steh₂-* "stand".

-*bulum* (PIE **-dhlo-*) was productive in the Archaic and Classical period, while -*trum* (PIE **-tro-*), -*brum* (PIE **-dhlo-*), -*crum* (*lauā-crum*) were no longer productive. -*culum* (PIE **-tlo-*), which is only weakly productive, must be distinguished from the diminutive suffix -*culus, -a, -um* (from **-ko-lo-*), whose basis is a nominal stem (see below in this section). The -*trum* and -*brum* nouns were still motivated when they belonged to a genetic set based on the same Latin radical. These suffixes were then in a complementary distribution with the other suffixes: *arā-trum* "a plough", *arā-tor* "plough-er", *arā-re* "to plough" and in poetry *arā-tiōnēs* pl. "ploughed fields" (result of the process).

The productivity of -*bulum* involved its extension to a substantival basis within a group of nouns denoting containers and vessels (allomorph -*ābulum*): *acēt-ābulum* "bowl for vinegar" on *acētum* "vinegar".

The neuter nouns built with -*měn* (gen. -*min-is* neut.; PIE **-mṇ*, Sanskrit -*ma*, Greek -μα) refer to the inanimate locus where the process denoted by the basis takes place. The entity denoted by *flūmen* "river" is the locus of *fluō, -ere* "flow". These nouns are synchronically associated with a Latin radical that built a verbal stem from the third conjugation (thematic stem *leg-ě-re*): e.g. *flū-men* and *flǔere*, *ag-men* "army on the march" and *agere*, *car-men* "song, poem" and *canere* "sing", *ful-men* "lightning" and *fulgēre* "shine brightly". Their origin is often an **-s-men* sequence leading to the assimilation of the last consonant of the PIE root. The most recent formations are built on an *ā* verbal stem: *certā-men* on *certā-re*, *forā-men* on *forā-re*. But for several words, there is no verb that can be synchronically associated with the -*men* nouns: *nōmen, līmen, ōmen*.

The most frequent word in -*men* in the Classical texts (according to Delatte *et al.* (1981)) is *nōmen* "name, renown", followed by *flūmen, agmen, carmen, crīmen, lūmen, nūmen*, which all belonged to the fundamental Latin vocabulary, occurring in prose as well as in poetry, although some of them occur more often in poetry (*carmen, lūmen, nūmen, līmen, fulmen*).

-*men* was in competition with -*mentum, -ī* neut. (from -*men* reinforced by a collective **-to-*), which became productive mainly on verbal stems (*ornā-re* "ornate"→ *ornā-mentum* "ornament") and survived in the Romance languages (French -*ment*), while -*men* had already lost its productivity in Archaic Latin.

But the -*mentum* nouns are mainly documented in prose and generally avoided in poetry, since they have mainly technical and concrete meanings, as can be seen from the most frequent terms: *tormentum* "rope", *frūmentum* "corn", *impedīmentum* "baggage, obstacle", *argūmentum* "argument", *mūnīmentum* "fortification", *iūmentum* "animal used for carrying, draught animal". The most recently formed terms are built on *ā* and *ī* verbal stems and denote the concrete entity resulting from the process: *mūnī-re* "provide with defensive work"→ *mūnī-mentum* "defensive work".

A second category of process nouns is illustrated by the suffix -*ǒr, -ōr-is* masc. which displays specific cognitive features: the *designata* are extra-linguistic entities or processes belonging to the natural world of physics such that human beings do not have any control or power upon them. When dealing with human beings, these lexemes denote adverse physical and psychological states in which men are paralysed or out of their mind (*stupor* "stupefaction, numbness", *stupēre* "be physically powerless", *stupidus* "physically dazed"), in extreme fear (*pauor* "panic", *pauēre* "be terrified", *pauidus* "terror-struck"), or showing a total lack of strength (*languor, langēre, languidus*; *torpor, torpēre, torpidus*). The *-or* formation also denotes a decaying state of natural entities: rotting, putrefaction, deliquescence, liquefaction (*putor, putēre, putidus*) or undesirable properties aggressive to the senses (*acor, acēre, acidus* with *ac-* "pointed, acid"). These nouns thus acquired a depreciative connotation that was not originally linked to the suffix itself.

Most of them are part of sets of three lexemes built on the same synchronic radical and therefore denoting the same process in different morphosyntactic categories: a noun in *-or* masc., a state verb in *-ē-*, an adjective in *-idus, -a, -um*. This is well illustrated in the domain of temperature with a scalar progression between: *tepor* "mild heat", *tepēre* "be tepid", *tepidus* "lukewarm"; *calor* "warmth", *calēre* "be warm", *calidus* "warm"; *ardor* "fierce heat", *ardēre* "be fiercely hot, burn".

-or is probably a masculine form of PIE *-es-/-os-* documented in the neuter nouns *gen-us* (*-er-is*), *corp-us* (*-or-is*) (Sanskrit *jan-as* neut., Greek γέν-ος). In pre-Classical times, the suffix was still motivated, but no longer productive. The *-or* nouns were usually maintained in Late Latin and the Romance languages, where they became feminine in French, but not in Italian or Spanish (Latin *calōrem* > French *chal-eur*, Latin *tepidum* adj. > French *tiède* adj. → *tiéd-eur* noun).

A residual inherited formation could be defined synchronically as a "zero grade" of suffixation, illustrated in Latin by *rēx* "king", *uōx* "oral utterance", where the inflectional ending immediately follows the synchronic radical *rēg-, uōc-*, without any suffix. Diachronically, these are also root-nouns where the inflectional ending follows immediately the PIE root.

We will now look at **suffixed nouns derived from the stem of a noun or an adjective**. Usually called "quality nouns", they display the feminine gender. The most productive suffixes are *-ia* and its allomorphs *-it-ia, -nt-ia* (*stult-itia, arrogānt-ia/arrogā-ntia*) and *-tās/-itās* (*-tāt-*: *extrēmus* "situated at the end" → *extrēm-itās* "outermost part"). The suffix *-tūs* (*-tūt-*) in *iuuen-tūs* "youth" (from *iuuen-* "young") is residual.

When built on the basis of a noun stem, the suffixed word has a collective meaning: *Sicil-ia* "Sicily" (on *Siculī* "Sicilians"), *cīuitās* "state, city" (on *cīuis* "citizen"), or is the denomination of a magistrate's office: *aedīl-itās* "office of an aedile" (on *aedīlis* "aedile").

When the basis is an adjectival stem (sometimes a lexicalised participle) denoting a quality, the suffixed noun is a quality noun: *inert-ia* "idleness" (*iners* "idle"), *amoenitās* "pleasantness" (*amoenus* "pleasant"). The latter word illustrates the origin of the allomorphy *-tās/-itās* since two synchronic analyses were possible: *amoen-itās* and *amoeni-tās*.

-itās was productive in the (pre-)Classical period as an abstract quality suffix. It was used by Cato (*Agr.* 5.8) as a reinforcement for a noun that was already a synonym: *autumn-itās* "autumn season" on *autumnus* "autumn". *-itās* was usual in the Epicurian vocabulary, as shown by Cicero's character Cotta, who defends the Academic school and mentions *beāt-itās* "supreme happiness" (on *beātus* "happy") as the term used by his addressee, who defends the Epicureanism. Cotta adds the usual common term *beāt-itūdō*:

> ista siue beatitas siue beatitudo dicenda est
> your *beatitas* or the *beatitudo*, whatever name we should give it. (Cic. *N.D.* 1.95)

The diminutive suffix *-culus* masc., *-cula* fem., *-culum* neut. (allomorphs *-ulus* and *-olus*) builds nouns from nouns, maintaining the gender of the basis. Its function is semantic, which may be minoration: *oppid-ulum* "small town" on *oppidum* "town". Several minorative suffixes may then be used recurrently in a row, especially with the allomorph -*ulus* (**-lo-*) for young animals: *porcus* "pig" → *porc-ulus* "young pig" → *porc-el-lus* → *porc-el-l-ulus*; *agnus* "lamb" → *agn-ulus* → *agn-el-lus* → *agn-el-l-ulus*. Some of these diminutive formations are already lexicalised in preliterary Latin: *puella* "young girl" is derived from *puer* "young boy" (*puer-lā).

This suffix is also used with a metaphoric or metonymic value. The metaphoric use is illustrated by the name of the plant *gladi-olus* "gladiolus, sword-lily", so called because of the shape of its strong and straight stem that was associated with that of a sword (*gladius*). It is to be noted that the English denomination for this plant, *sword-lily*, is based on the selection of exactly the same extra-linguistic feature (shape of the stem), itself expressed with a reference to the same entity (a sword).

The diminutive suffix -*culus/-ulus/-olus* also displays some connotative occurrences expressing the speaker's emotions: *mulier-culae* (on *mulier* "woman") in Plautus does not mean "small women", but women for whom the speaker feels pity (since they happen to be in a dangerous situation). Catullus also uses -*culus* as a connotative morpheme expressing pity or affection.

The function of this diminutive suffix changed in Late Latin. Losing its semantic values, it became a mere reinforcement, on the *signifiant* level, of a noun that did not have enough distinctive contrast in its pronunciation: Augustine already uses *api-cula* (from *apis* fem. "bee") with the new meaning "bee" (and not "small bee").

The Latin lexicon also contains many other **fundamental lexemes built with suffixes**. One of the most important of these is -(*i*)*mōnium* neut. (joining -*mōn*- and -*ium* from *-*yo*- neut.), documented within the social and legal vocabulary in *patr-imōnium* "property of a *pater familiās*" (on *pater* (*familiās*) "head of a family"), *mātr-imōnium* "state of being married" for a woman (on *māter* "mother"), *uăd-imōnium* "guarantee that a defendant will appear before the magistrate at an appointed date" (on *uăs*, gen. *uădis* "one who gives this guarantee"). This suffix also appears in the feminine gender -(*i*)*mōnia* in a few quality nouns such as *ācri-mōnia* "pungency" (on *ācer* "sharp"), but it was in competition with -*tūdō* (*ācri-tūdō* "pungency, bitterness") and the productive de-adjectival substantival suffixes -*itās* and -*ia*. Although -*tūdō* is not productive any more in Classical Latin, it is an important suffix since it is documented in some fundamental nouns: *beātitūdō* "happiness", *magnitūdō* "size, greatness" on *magnus* "big", *longitūdō* "length" on *longus* "long".

The Latin **adjectival suffixes** are mainly based on noun stems.

-*lis* (allomorphs -*ālis/-āris/-īlis*) is probably the most productive suffix building adjectives from noun stems, since it is not submitted to any semantic, referential or morphological constraint, being used in all semantic domains, in the social, political, religious and common vocabulary.

It builds relational (non gradable, by contrast with qualificative) adjectives on the basis of nouns. In the social vocabulary, the -*lis* relational adjectives are built on nouns denoting human beings according to gender, age, status: in the feminine gender denoting females, we have *mātrōnā-lis* "of a matrona" (on *mātrōna* "matron"), *uirgin-ālis* "of a uirgo" (*uirgō*, gen. *uirgin-is* fem. "unmarried girl"), *puellā-ris* (*puella* "girl"), *muliebris* "concerning women" (*mulier* "woman" from **mulies-ri-*with *s>b*); for the social status: *ancillā-ris* (*ancilla* "female servant"); in the masculine gender, denoting male humans according to their age: *uir-īlis* (*uir* "man"), *puer-īlis* (*puer* "boy"), *iuuen-īlis* (*iuuenis* "young man"), *sen-īlis* (*sen-ex* "old man"). Two antonyms are based on social status: *er-īlis* (*erus* "master") vs *seru-īlis* (*seruus* "slave").

In the political domain, *-lis* was already productive before the first Latin texts, as shown from the magistrate denomination *aedīlis* "aedile" (on *aedēs* "building", an *i* stem), *consul-āris* "of a consul" (on *consul* "consul", *-āris* being a variant of *-ālis* due to a dissimilation), *līber-ālis* "of or relating to free men" (on *līber* "free man"), *decem-uir-ālis* "of a decemvirate" (on *decem-uir* "decemvir"), *familiā-ris* (on *familia* "family, household"). The productivity of the *-lis* adjectives increased in (pre-)Classical Latin, since *cīuīlis* (*cīuis* "citizen"), *hostīlis* (*hostis* "enemy") replaced *cīuicus, hosticus*. In the religious vocabulary, *-ālis* builds relational adjectives derived from religious functions: *sacerdōt-ālis* "of a *sacerdōs*" (*sacerdōs* "priest"), *augur-ālis* "of an augur" (from *augur*). A productive lexical paradigm is created by means of *-ālia* (neut. pl.) for religious festivals (see chapter 10).

-(ā)lis also occurs in the common vocabulary: *autumn-ālis* "of autumn" (*autumnus* "autumn").

The allomorphs *-ālis, -īlis* result from resegmentations: the final vowel of the basis stem is incorporated into the suffix with a shift of the morpheme suffixal boundary from … *ā-lis* to … *-ālis* (from *matrōnā-lis, puellā-ris, ancillā-ris* to *uirgin-ālis*). In the *i* stems, the shift goes from … *ī-lis* to … *-īlis* (from *cīuī-lis, hostī-lis* to *sen-īlis, iuuen-īlis*) so that the synchronic analysis then becomes ambiguous (either *cīu-īlis* or *cīuī-lis*), while the diachronic analysis is *cīuī-lis* with a lengthening of the short *i* of the stem *cīui-*.

The *-ius, -a, -um* suffix (from **-yo-*) builds important relational adjectives in the social and political domain, e.g. derived from political functions: *rēg-ius* (from *rēx* "king"), *praetōr-ius* (*praetor* "magistrate"), *censōr-ius* (*censor* "magistrate"), *senātōr-ius* (*senātor* "senator"), *quaestōrius* (*quaestor* "magistrate").

Productive *-ius* contributed to the creation of other suffixes: from the resegmentation of *-ius* on the basis of *-tor* nouns was created *-tōrius, -a, -um*; *-ius* reinforced residual *-icus*, creating *-ic-ius* in a sub-group of relational adjectives derived from magistrate denominations: *patr-icius* "patrician" (*patrēs* pl. "senators"), *praetōr-icius* "concerning a praetor" (*praetor*), *aedīl-icius* "concerning an aedile" (*aedīlis*), *tribūn-icius* "of a *tribūnus militum* or a *tribūnus plēbis*" (*tribūnus militum* a military office, *tribūnus plēbis* a Roman magistrate).

The adjectival suffix *-nus, -a, -um* (*-ānus/-īnus/-inus*; from **-no-*) played an important role in the Latin lexicon and is documented in various extra-linguistic domains. Its bases may be kinship terms: *pater-nus* (*pater* "father"), *māter-nus* (*māter* "mother"); or toponyms and denote places: *urb-ānus* "related to the *urbs*" (*urbs* "town" or *Vrbs* "Rome"); or anthroponyms: *Iugurth-īnus* "of Iugurtha" (*Iugurtha*); denominations of animals: *su-īnus* (*sūs* "pig"), *ouīnus* (*ouis* "sheep"). The *-ānus* allomorph resulted from derivations such as: *Rōma* "Rome" (toponym) → *Rōmā-nus* "of Rome, Roman", with a further re-analysis in *Rōm-ānus*, thus allowing the derivation *urbs* "town" → *urb-ānus* "of a/the town", *pāgus* "village"→ *pāg-ānus* "of a village".

An old use of **-no-* is to be seen in some denominations of men at the head of a social unit: *dominus* "master" ← *domus* "house, household" (<**domo/u-no-s*), *tribūnus* "commander of the troops furnished by each tribe" ← *tribus* "tribe" (*tribū-no-s with a lengthening of *u* before a secondary suffix).

The *-inus* allomorph with a short *i* (*iuncus* "rush" → *iunc-inus* "obtained from rushes" Plin. *Nat.*) was in competition with *-eus* (*iunc-eus* Plautus, Columella, Plin. *Nat.*) and was reinforced by the borrowing of Greek adjectives in -ινος.

The adjectival suffix -*eus* (-*a*, *um*) is found on the basis of nouns denoting substances: *aurum* "gold" → *aur-eus* "made of gold", *argentum* "silver" → *argent-eus* "made of silver". Its use was extended to other properties of the same entities, e.g. colour, especially in Pliny's technical vocabulary: *aur-eus* "golden", *argent-eus* "displaying the colour of silver".

The adjectival suffix -*ōsus* is a quantifier with the semantic feature of "great quantity" used for a massive or a numerable entity denoted by the basis: *pretium* "price" → *preti-ōsus* "precious", *pilus* "hair" → *pil-ōsus* "hairy". Productive in all periods of Latin, it was maintained with the same function in the Romance languages (French -*eux*: *pierre* → *pierr-eux*).

The inherited -*icus* (-*a*, -*um*) suffix lost its productivity in the political vocabulary, but was maintained on the basis of toponyms and ethnic nouns (*Gallī* "the Gauls" → *Gall-icus* "of the Gauls", *Germānī* "the Germans" → *Germān-icus* "of the Germans"), and it was reinforced in this function by the borrowing of Greek -ικός adjectives.

Adjectival -*ēnsis* (-*iēnsis*) was productive behind a common or proper noun denotating a place: e.g. the name of a country (*Hispānia* "Spain" → *Hispāni-ēnsis* "of Spain": Cic. *Vat.* 12: *cum illud iter Hispaniense pedibus fere confici soleat* "although this journey to Spain is usually made by road"; *Sicilia* → *Sicili-ēnsis* "of Sicily": Cic. *Brut.* 318: *Siciliensis annus* "the year spent in Sicily"), or the name of a town (*Carthagō* → *Carthagin-iēnsis* "of *Carthago*"), or the denomination of a place familiar to the speech community (*circus* "circus" → *circ-ēnsis* "of the *circus*", *castra* "military encampment" → *castr-ēnsis* "connected with military service").

The diminutive suffix -*culus* (-*ulus*) builds both nouns (see above in this section) and adjectives. As a denotative morpheme, it is a quantifier that reinforces the semantic feature of its basis when the basis denotes a small quantity (*paruus* "small" → *paru-ulus* "very small"), but it moderates and reduces the meaning of its basis when the basis denotes a large quantity. This suffix may also be used as a connotative morpheme: *bellus* "nice, pretty" is the **-lo-* derivative of *bonus* "good" (*bellus* < **dwen-lo-s* and **dwenos* > *bonus*). In Archaic and Classical Latin it is applied only to women, children and statues (but not to men) as shown in the following passage from Plautus:

> bellan uidetur specie mulier?
> Doesn't this woman look pretty? (Pl. *Bac.* 838)

This -*lu-s* suffix, which denotes the emotion of the speaker, may be added twice in a row for intensification in *bel-l-ul-us* "very beautiful":

> edepol haec quidem bellulast!
> By Pollux! This woman is definitely beautiful! (Pl. *Mil.* 989)

Later on in spoken Latin, *bellus* was lexicalised, lost some of its specific semantic features and became the orthonym (i.e. the usual and basic term) which replaced *pulcher* "beautiful".

Latin has some **adjectival suffixes built on a Latin radical or verbal stem**, such as *-bilis*, a modality suffix translated by English *-able* (English *us-able* lit. "which may be used"). It usually has a passive meaning, since it is predicated about the object of the implied verb: *admīrā-rī* "wonder" → *admīrā-bilis* "remarkable" (lit. "which may be admired"), *uendibilis* "that can easily be sold" (*uend-ĕ-re* "sell"). A numerous sub-group is prefixed with the negative morpheme *in-*: *crēdere* "believe" → *in-crēd-ibilis* "un-believ-able", *exōrā-re* "persuade" → *in-exōrā-bilis* "inexorable" (lit. "who cannot be convinced").

In several cases, *-bilis* underwent a haplology (disappearance of a syllable when two syllables in a row begin with the same consonant), which led to an allomorph *-ilis*, e.g. in *hab-ilis* "easy to handle" (from **habibilis*) on the radical *hab-* "hold" (*hab-ē-re* "have, hold").

Adjectival *-bundus* and *-cundus* are added to verbal stems: *mori-bundus* "dying" (*morior* "die"), *uerē-cundus* "restrained by scruples of morality" (*uerē-rī* "show respect for") or to a radical: *iū-cundus* "pleasant" (*iuu-ā-re* "give pleasure to"). The initial *b* may be the remnant of an inherited root (PIE **bhew-H-* "be" in a reduced form) since *-bundus* may have a progressive meaning (*moribundus* "moribund"). These improductive suffixes could, therefore, come from previous second terms of compounds.

Within the heterogeneous category of adverbs, some **gradable adverbs are suffixed and derived from qualitative adjectives**.

They are created from the freezing and lexicalisation of inflected forms of the qualitative adjectives of the first and second declension (*bonus, -a, -um*), mainly in the old instrumental sg. in *-ē*, which is a productive formation: *bonus* "good" → *bene* "well", *malus* "bad" → *malē* "badly", *inurbānus* "not refined"→ *inurbān-ē* "without refinement", *inūsitātus* "unusual" → *inūsitāt-ē* "in an unusual way" (Cic. *Brut.* 260: *inusitate loqui* "speak in an unusual manner"). The same process occurs with the freezing of an ablative-instrumental neut. sg. in *-ō* (*continuō*), or an accusative neut. sg. in *-um* (*prīmum*).

The diminutive **-lo-> -lu-* suffix denoting a small quantity also builds the adverb *paulum* "a little" (where it is lexicalised). It may be repeated several times as an intensifier of the small quantity when the basis already denotes a small quantity: *pau-lu-m* → *pau-l-ulum* "a very little" → *paul-l-ulum* "a very very little". This recurrent diminutive **-lo-* is also documented on the basis of nouns and adjectives (see above).

The usual adverbial suffix built onto adjectives of the third declension (*fortis* masc. and fem., *-e* neut.) is *-iter* (probably originally from … *i-ter*): *fortis* "courageous" → *fortiter* "in a courageous way". It was productive in (pre-)Classical Latin and was widely extended in Late Latin.

Another adverbial suffix is *-itus*, related to Sanskrit *-taḥ* (an ablative sg. and pl. inflectional ending): *fund-itus* "from the foundations" (on the noun *fundus* "bottom"), *rādīc-itus* "from the roots" (on *rādīx* "root"). It was also extended in Late Latin: *dīuīn-itus* "from God" (on *dīuīnus* "divine").

Only a **few verbal suffixes** were motivated and/or productive in Latin. We do not include here the denominative verbs, which we study below on p. 174.

A productive verbal suffix is the frequentative and intensive suffix *-tā-re*: in the archaic period, *pō-tā-re* means "drink a lot" (e.g. in a banquet; radical *pō-* "drink"). Built on the radical *spec-* of *speciō* "watch", *spec-tā-re* has an intensive meaning "watch carefully", as well as *intrō-spectāre* "gaze in" (Pl. *Mos.* 936) on *intrō-spiciō* "look into". The frequentative meaning usually involves the repetition of the same action by the same person or different persons and is often reinforced by words meaning "many people", "often", or by a durative tense (indicative imperfect). But the repetition of unfruitful actions may also lead to a conative value:

> Quintus frater ... Tusculanum uenditat, ut, si possit, emat Pacilianam domum
> My brother Quintus is trying to sell his property at Tusculum in order to buy, if he can, Pacilius's house. (Cic. *Att.* 1.14.7)

This semantic value of *-tā-re* involves a possible accumulation of suffixes: on *dic-* "say" (*dic-tu-s* "said", *dīc-e-re* "say"), the addition of *-tā-re* gives *dic-tā-re* "dictate, recite", where *-tā-re* is lexicalised; but the second *-tā-re* suffix in *dic-t-itā-re* was freely added by the speaker as a frequentative morpheme with the meaning "persist in saying, repeat":

> qui Catilinam Massiliam ire dictitant
> those who repeat that Catilina is going to Massilia. (Cic. *Cat.* 2.16)

In Late Latin, *-tā-re* was de-semanticised and used as a mere *signifiant* tool in order to lengthen some verbs: *canere* "sing" → *can-tā-re* "sing" (> French *chanter*).

The *-scō* suffix is also a productive morpheme in Archaic and Classical Latin. Its function is a purely semantic one, with an ingressive or progressive value for the process denoted by the basis: on the stative verb *alb-ē-re* "be white" (stative *-ē-*) is built *albē-scĕre* "become white". *-scō* is lexicalised in *crēscō* "increase", *nāscor* "be born", *pāscō* "feed (animals)". It was desemanticised in Late Latin and maintained in the Romance languages as a mere morphological element.

The long *e* morpheme denoting a state (*alb-ē-re* "be white" from *alb-us* "white") was productive in all periods of Latin. But some verbs had been lexicalised for a long time: e.g. *uid-ē-re* "see" (on the zero grade of PIE **weyd-* "see, know") must have meant originally "be the recipient of a vision", its grammatical subject referring to the person who was the experiencer, before it became a transitive sensation verb.

The productivity of this stative *ē* involved the decrease of the homophonous causative *-ē-*, which was limited to certain verbs only. These causative verbs kept the inherited *o* grade of the PIE root: *mon-ē-re* "remind", *torr-ē-re* "burn" (of the sun), with the exception of *terr-ē-re* "frighten". In order to fill this causative gap, Latin uses various devices: e.g. verbs such as *cal-ē-faciō* "warm something" (+ acc.) with the causative morpheme *-faciō*.

Nominal Compounding

Nominal compounding is not as developed in Latin as it is in other IE languages, since the prototypical length of Latin words is rather short (one syllable for grammatical lexemes and only two or three for lexical lexemes). Some compounding patterns that were productive in other IE languages are residual in Latin and the productivity of nominal compounding in Latin is restricted to some specific types.

The Roman authors themselves were aware of the fact that nominal compounds were not as usual in Latin as they were in Greek. According to Quintilian, compounding is more convenient for the Greek language than for Latin:

cum κυρταύχενα mirati simus, *incuruiceruicum* uix a risu defendimus
although we admired κυρταύχενα, we can hardly stop laughing at *incuruiceruicum*. (Quint. *Inst.* 1.5.70)

This Greek adjectival compound κυρτ-αύχην "having the neck arched" is a *bahuvrīhi* or possessive compound, from κυρτός "curved" and αὐχήν "neck". Its Latin morphological calque *incurui-ceruīc-us* (from *in-curuus* "curved" and *ceruīx* "neck") is a compound forged by Pacuvius about dolphins (this verse of Pacuvius is quoted by Quintilian in *Inst.* 1.5.67).

The determinative compounds are productive, but limited in the number of elements able to function as the first term of the compound.

First of all, the inherited *in-* negative prefix (from PIE *n-, Sanskrit *a-*, Greek α-; English *un-*) may be freely added as a prefix in front of an adjective or an adverb that fulfils given semantic and referential requirements.

(a) adjectives: *ūtilis* "useful" → *in-ūtilis* "use-less", *ualidus* "strong" → *in-ualidus* "weak; *uendibilis* "that can easily be sold"→ *in-uendibilis* "un-saleable (Plautus).
      Some of these adjectives are only documented in the negative form: *in-tolerāndus* "that cannot be tolerated" (*tolerā-re* "tolerate").
(b) past passive participles: *uīsus* "seen" (*uidēre* "see") → *in-uīsus* "un-seen", *audītus* "heard" (*audī-re* "hear") → *in-audītus* "not heard of (before), new":

uti tu morbos uisos inuisosque ... prohibessis
so that you keep away the known and unkown illnesses [or "the seen and unseen illnesses"] (Cato, *Agr.* 141.2)

non inuisa solum, sed etiam inaudita
not only unseen, but also not heard of. (Cic. *Har.* 57)

Some of these negative participles were lexicalised into quality adjectives: *in-uictus* "un-defeated, invincible" (*uictus* "overcome", *uincō* "to overcome"); *in-tūtus* "un-safe" (*tūtus* "safe"; with the same radical as in *tueor* "protect"). The prefix *per-* expressing intensification is also productive, modifying a gradable adjective or adverb: *magnus* "big" → *per-magnus* "very big". The *prae-* prefix displays the same intensive meaning: *feruidus* "hot" → *prae-feruidus* "very hot". The opposite phenomenon, the disintensification of gradable adjectives and adverbs, could also be achieved by a prefix: *sub-* e.g. with chromatic adjectives: *albus* "white" → *sub-albus* "whit-ish". This prefix could then be combined with the diminutive *-ulus* suffix, which was also used for disintensification: *sub-alb-ulus* "whit-ish".

Nouns displaying the structure of a determinative compound are mainly prefixed with *con-* and *sub-*: *con-seruus* "fellow slave" (*seruus* "slave"), *con-discipulus* "schoolfellow" (*discipulus* "pupil, student"), *com-mīlit-ō* "fellow soldier"; *sub-custōs* "deputy-keeper" (*custōs* "keeper" Plautus). These formations are theoretically productive, but the number of lexemes is limited by the extra-linguistic reality.

In compounds of the *agri-col-a* type, the second term contains a Latin synchronic radical, which usually also occurs in verbal stems. The first term is a nominal stem without any inflectional ending, according to the inherited morphological structure. In Latin, we mainly have a short vowel *i* in front of the compounding morpheme boundary. This short *i* has several possible origins: in the particular case of *agri-col-a*, it may come phonetically from the closing of the thematic vowel *-e/o-* at the end of the first term *agro-*.

In a synchronic analysis, the compound is semantically the denotative equivalent of a verbal syntagm containing the verb and an object: *agri-col-a* could be glossed by *colere agrum* or *colere agros* "cultivate land". The first term of the compound would be semantically the equivalent of the object and the synchronic radical *col-* the equivalent of the finite verb.

This formation generally displays three kinds of morphological elements at the end of the compound: (a) a masculine *-ā-* morpheme: *agri-col-a*; (b) a consonant, which is also the final consonant of the radical in the second term (mainly *-c-*): *auri-fex* (*-fic-is* masc.); (c) a thematic vowel following the radical in the second term: *-dic-u-s* in *causi-dicus* (*-ī* masc.).

This inherited structure is well documented for a few radicals: *-fex* (*auri-fex* "goldsmith"), *-dex* (*iū-dex* "judge", lit. "one who shows the right"), *-spex* (*au-spex* lit. "one who observes the birds"), *-cep-s* (*au-cep-s* "bird-catcher"; synchronically associated with *auis* "bird" and *cap-* "take"), *-ficus* and *-dicus* (*causi-dicus* "solicitor"). The adjectival compounds in *-ger* "bear" (*āli-ger* "having wings"; *āla* "wing"), *-fer* "produce" (*lēti-fer* "bringing death"; *lētum* "death") are productive in poetry where the poets (e.g. Ovid) use them as choriambs, a succession of four syllables (a long syllable + a short syllable ending in short *i* in front of the morpheme boundary + a short syllable + a long syllable).

The possessive compounds or *bahuvrīhi* (a technical term borrowed from Indian grammarians and the prototype for this kind of compound; the literal meaning of this Sanskrit word is: "who has a lot of rice") are well documented in IE languages (English *a blue-eyed girl*). This structure, inherited by Latin, was maintained with a certain variety in poetry, but underwent strong restrictions in the common Latin vocabulary. The first term is mainly a numeral (*bi-*, *tri-*) or a prefix (negative *in-*; for the loss of a pre-existing entity, *ex-*, *dē-*), while the second term is limited to inalienable possession, with the denotation of a body part or a part of a whole for an inanimate entity. In the usual vocabulary, we may have in the first term of the possessive compounds:

(a) a numeral: *bi-pēs* "having two feet (legs)" (*pēs* "foot"); there exists a paradigmatic series, limited by the extra-linguistic reality: *quadru-pēs* "four-legged", *bi-dēns* "having two teeth" (*dens* "tooth"), *bi-corn-is* "two-horned" (*cornu* "horn"), *bi-penn-is* "having two wings or blades" for a bronze axe (Verg. *A.* 2.479) (*penna* "wing")

(b) the negative *in-* bound morpheme: *in-ops* "deprived of wealth" (*ops* "wealth"), *in-ui-us* "not affording a passage" (*uia* "passage"), *im-berb-is* "beardless" (*barba* "beard")

(c) the prefixes *dē-*, *ā-* and *ex-* for the absence or loss of the body part denoted in the second term: *dē-mēns* "mad" (*mens* "thought"), *ā-mēns* "mad", *ex-anim-is* "dead" (*anima* "vital principle"), *ex-sangu-is* "bloodless" (*sanguis* "blood"), *ex-ŏss-is/ex-ŏs* (*ŏs* "bone")

(d)   a spatial relational morpheme: *prae-cep-s*, stem *prae-cipit-* (*caput* "head"), lit. "whose head is placed forward".

But in poetry, an adjectival stem may occur in the first term of the possessive compounds: *clāri-son-us, -a, -um* from *clārus* "loud, sonorous" and *sonus, -ī* masc. "sound", *sicc-ocul-us, -a, -um* (*siccus* "dry" and *oculus, -ī* "eye"). The first term of a poetic possessive compound may also be a noun stem: *auri-com-us, -a, -um* "golden-haired" (*aurum* "gold" and *coma, -ae* fem. "hair"), *angui-man-us, -a, -um* "with snaky hand" (*anguis* "snake" and *manus, -us* fem. "hand"), *tauri-form-is* "having the form of a bull" (*taurus* "bull" and *forma* "shape"). In all these poetic compounds, the second term denotes a body part. Some of them were influenced by Greek, when, overtly or not, the Latin author translated a Greek possessive compound by a morphological calque: *magn-anim-us, -a, -um* is the transposition of μεγά-θυμος, -ος, -ον (from μέγας "great, big" and θυμός, -ου "soul"); *alti-thron-us, -a, -um* (from *altus* "high" and *thronus,-ī* masc. "throne") translates ὑψί-θρονος, -ος, -ον (from the adverb ὕψι "high" and θρόνος, -ου "throne").

These possessive adjectives sometimes became nouns, with the addition of a suffix (often *-ium, -i* neut.) in order to synthetise the lexeme: *bi-sacc-ium* "a double-bag" (*bi-* "two", *saccus* "bag").

Some other compounds contain a preposition in the first term and a noun in the second term, in the same order as a prepositional syntagm and with a similar meaning. These preposition-governing compounds are, theoretically, a productive formation, but they are limited by the extra-linguistic reality: *extra-ordin-ārius* "supplementary (troops)" (on *extra ordinem* "in addition to the normal troops"), *post-līmin-ium* "resumption of civic rights held in suspension during exile, capture" (on *post līmen* lit. "behind the threshold"), *ab-origin-ēs* "pre-existing inhabitants" (*ab originibus* "since the beginnings"), *in-aur-ēs* "ear-rings" (*in auribus* "on the ears").

Reduplicative compounds were productive in preliterary Latin, but only for pronominal and adverbial formations referring to free-choice and indefinite lexemes: *quis-quis* "whoever", *ut-ut* "in whatever way", *ubi-ubi* "wherever", *quot-quot* "whatever numerous". This formation was in competition with the *-cum-que* type: *quī-cum-que* "whoever", *ut-cum-que* "in whatever manner", *ubi-cum-que* "wherever".

Verbal Compounding

There is no productive process using verbal compounding in the usual language of Classical Latin, apart from the verbs in *-fic-ā-re*, containing the synchronic radical *făc-/-fĭc-* with a causative meaning "make, produce". The success of this formation is due to the lack of causative morphemes in Latin, since the inherited causative *-ē-* was eliminated by the homophonous stative morpheme. *-ficare*, being a causative bound morpheme, actually had a tendency to become a suffix. Originally, these verbs may have been derived, with the addition of the verbal morpheme *-ā-*, from the *-ficus* adjectives or the *-fex* nouns.

Some of these -*ficāre* verbs have a noun stem in the first term: *aedi-fic-ā-re* "build" (*aedēs* "building", an *i* stem), while others have a verbal radical: *horri-ficō* "frighten" (Verg.) is a parallel to the causative adjective *horri-ficus* "frightening" (Lucr., Verg.). The first term may also contain an adjectival stem: *ampli-ficare* "enlarge" (*amplus* "large"), a structure developed in the Christian vocabulary, where some -*ficāre* verbs are the morphological calque of Greek verbs: *beāti-ficāre* "make blessed" (Augustine; *beatus* "blessed") translates Greek μακαρ-ίζω; *dei-ficāre* "deify, consecrate" is a morphological calque of θεο-ποιέω, while *dei-ficus* (Tert.) means "who makes God".

The -*ficāre* verbs are also used in specialised technical vocabularies, such as the medical domain: *crassi-ficāre* "fatten (animals)" (Caelius Aurelianus; *crassus* "fat, big").

A few verbs in -*fer-ā-re*, -*ger-ā-re*, -*cin-ā-re* are based on the Latin radicals *fer-* and *ger-* "bear, produce", *can-* "sing, play a music instrument"; but these formations are not very productive. They are often associated with verbal expressions containing a "weak verb" (see chapter 10), of which they represent a synthetic form: *bellum gerere* "make war" is the analytic counterpart of the compound *belli-gerāre* with the same meaning. The same relationship exists between *mōrem gerere* (+ dat.) "regulate one's conduct in accordance with another's wishes, indulge" and its synonym *mōri-gerāri*, and also between *sacra facere* and *sacri-ficāre* "perform a sacrifice".

Preverbation

Preverbation is a very productive process in all periods of Latin and is different from verbal compounding, where the first term is a noun or an adjectival stem. From a diachronic perspective, preverbation belongs to agglutination, since preverbs were previously lexemes or free morphemes that were later frozen in front of the verbs they modified. The remnants of this earlier situation may be seen in Archaic Latin in the few occurrences of *tmesis* (a technical term meaning "a cut", borrowed from Greek and denoting the situation where the preverb is separated from the verb by other words). Preverbs may be lexicalised in a particular word and then demotivated: e.g. *re-* in *respondēre* "answer", originally built on *spondēre* "promise". In this case, the semantic evolution of the preverbed verb separated it from its basis in the synchronic perception of the speech community.

The most productive preverbs have prepositional counterparts (both, preverbs and prepositions, being relational elements): *in-* "in", *ad-* "towards", *dē-* "down, from", *ex-* "from, out of", *ab-/ā* "from", *prae-* "in the front part of", *prō-* "instead of, in front of", *sub-* "up, under", *ante-* "before". But there may exist semantic differences between a given preposition and the associated preverb, since preverbs have a tendency to evolve quicker than prepositions.

A special class of preverbation is the parasynthetic verbs. They derived from a noun with the simultaneous addition of a relational element in the initial position and a verbal morpheme in the final position, so that the whole lexeme is a verb. Among them, we may distinguish two structures.

Some of them are based on a prepositional syntagma (preposition + noun): *ex-pector-ā-re* "banish from one's affections" on *ex pectore* "outside of the heart" (*pectus, -oris* neut. "heart"), *ex-hērēd-ā-re* "disinherit" on *ex* "out of" and *hērēs* (*hērēd-*) "heir". The preverb *in-* "in" denotes the insertion of something into something else: *in-ocul-ā-re* "graft (trees) by budding" in agriculture, on *oculus* "eye", used here in a cognitive metaphor for the part of a plant (in budding, the incision made in the stem for the reception of a bud, and the bud itself); the underlying syntagm could be *in oculum* "in the incision".

In a second sub-class, the noun in the second term denotes the entity on which the action has an effect, while the action itself is denoted by the preverb. *ex-* "out of" and *dē-* "away from" mean that the entity denoted in the second term (generally a body part, a part of a whole in an inalienable possession relationship) is withdrawn, extracted, pulled out or rooted up: *ex-oss-ā-re* "remove the bones from" (Plautus; *ŏs, ŏss-* "bone"), *ex-stirp-ā-re* "root out" (*stirps* "root"), *ē-dent-ā-re* "knock the teeth out" (*dēns* "tooth").

Agglutination

Agglutination is the phenomenon whereby two or more words come together into one and the same lexical item (e.g. English *nowadays*). It represents the freezing and rigidification of a syntactic sequence to form a lexical item; this makes it a type of both lexicalisation and grammaticalisation. Latin used agglutination in all periods in the formation of all its grammatical categories and it is still productive in the Romance languages.

Most of these agglutinated formations were already completed by the first Latin texts and they belong to the Latin fundamental vocabulary. Some are still written as two words, some as one word:

(a) agglutinated nouns: *iūs-iūrandum* "oath", *rēs pūblica* "state, Republic", *pater familiās* "head of a family" (with the preservation of *-ās*, an old no longer used gen. sg. ending), *praefectus fabrum* "office in the Roman army" (originally probably a kind of engineer)

(b) agglutinated adjectives: *uērī-similis* "having the appearance of truth"

(c) agglutinated verbs: *anim-aduertere* < *animum aduertere* "pay attention to", *manū-mittere/manū mittere* "to free (a slave)", *uēn-īre* < *uēnum īre* "be sold" (lit. "go to the sale") vs *uēn-dere* < *uēnum dăre* "sell" (lit. "put on sale")

(d) spatial adverbs may come from the agglutination of a prepositional syntagm: *ob-uiam* in *obuiam īre alicuī* "go and fetch someone". An important group of directive adverbs results from the agglutination of a directive adverb meaning "in the direction of" and a past participle meaning "turned in the direction of": *retrōrsus* < **retrō uorsus* (with *retrō* "backwards" and *uorsus* "turned" as the past participle of *uertere* "turn" or *uertī* "turn oneself towards"), *intrōrsum/intrōuorsus/intrō uorsus* "to within, inside" (lit. "turned towards the inside"). The two frequent adverbs *rūrsum* (*rūrsus*) "backwards", "back again" (in reversal of a motion), "a second time" (in the repetition of an action) and *prōrsum* "forward, straight ahead", "quite" (intensive meaning) are due to this formation, which involves the grammaticalisation of a past participle, frozen in the nominative or accusative masculine singular

(e) various grammatical lexemes with very high frequency involve an agglutination in their formation: *ipse* ("myself, yourself, himself") comes from the anaphoric and cataphoric *is* and the postposed focalising particle *-pse*; *īdem* "the same" from *is* and the particle *-dem* (from *-em*, PIE *-e/om*). The focaliser *quid-em* involves the agglutination of the same particle *-em*.

It is necessary to distinguish this agglutinative type of word-formation from inherited compounding. We can see the difference in the two formations from the different phonemes that appear in front of the morpheme boundary in *agrī-cultūra* fem. "agriculture" and *agrī-cola* masc. "farmer": *agrī-cultūra* is a recent agglutinative formation in Latin (the freezing has been seen in progress in Classical Latin) with a long *i*, which is a gen. sg. inflectional morpheme, whereas *agrī-cola* with a short *i* illustrates an inherited pattern where the first term of the compound is not inflected (see above).

Another class of lexemes also illustrates the agglutination process in Latin: the causative verbs in ... *ē-facio*, e.g. *calē-facio* (+ acc.) "warm (something)" (lit. "make (something) warm"), *tepē-facio* "make (something) lukewarm". These were in contrast with the state verbs in *-ē-*, since they were causative and they denoted a progressive process: *pauēre* "be terrified" vs *pauē-facere* "terrify". The verb *faciō* here maintained its free form (without *ă > i* as in the preverbed verbs: *af-ficiō*) and, moreover, some occurrences showing a separation between the two elements (with a tmesis) or the reverse order of the elements (*facit are* "make (something) dry" for *arefacit* Lucr.) are a clue for the synchronic and probably diachronic status of these verbs as agglutinated sequences. The semantic cover of these verbs is the same as that of the *-or* nouns (physical and natural processes).

The ... *ē-faciō* and *-ficāre* (see above) types are both causatives; the difference is both morphological and semantic. The former represents a case of agglutination with a specific first term and its extension is morphologically and semantically limited. The latter type, however, represents a case of compounding where the first term is less limited.

Recategorisation

Recategorisation is a process of word-formation that does not involve any of the processes we have discussed above (suffixation, compounding or agglutination).

A very productive recategorisation in Latin occurs when an adjective becomes a noun (within the limits of certain semantic and referential constraints): from *bonus, -a, -um* "good" is derived the neuter noun *bonum* neut. sg. "patrimony", "what is morally good", *bona* neut. pl. "goods, patrimony, good fortune", *bonī* masc. pl. "honest people", *bonus* masc. sg. "a good man".

The *-ālis* adjectives also illustrate the productivity of this morphological type, leading to a whole range of neuter plural nouns denoting religious festivals dedicated to a given god(dess) and based on the name of the divinity: *Flōr-ālia, -ium* neut. pl. "festival held in honour of Flora" (Varro), on *Flōra, -ae* fem. "Flora" (goddess of flowers). *Volcān-ālia, -ium* neut. pl. "festival of Vulcan" derives from the adjective *Volcān-ālis* "of Vulcan" (*Volcānus, -ī* masc., god of fire). This formation was so productive that the festival denomination may be usual even if the *-ālis* adjective is not found (the festival denomination is then built directly on the god's name). The most famous name showing this structure is *Bacchānālia, -ium* neut. pl. "festival of Bacchus", on *Bacchus, -ī* masc. (god associated with the vine). The final sequence *-ān-ālia* here is the joining of two suffixes *-ānus* and *-ālis* by analogy with the final sequence of *Vulcānālia* (reanalysed as

Vulc-ānālia). This kind of left-shift of the morpheme suffixal boundary is usual within lexical sets denoting entities perceived by the speech community as belonging to the same extra-linguistic category.

The adjectival suffix -*ārius*, -*a*, -*um* was also substantivised in several ways. In the masculine gender, -*ārius*, -*ī* built professional denominations for craftsmen and soldiers (see above) on the basis of the noun denoting the entity they dealt with: *carbō* (*carbōn-*) "charcoal" → *carbōn-ārius* "charcoal-burner", *uēxillum* "military standard" → *uēxill-ārius* "standard-bearer". In the feminine or neuter gender, the suffix denoted places involved in the activity characterised by the entity denoted by the basis: *argentum* "silver" (metal and currency) → *argent-āria*, -*ae* fem. "bank".

The existence of a symmetrical transcategorisation from noun to adjective is less clear, since in some cases there is no clear-cut boundary between nouns and adjectives in Latin. The agentive -*tor* words are usually considered as nouns: they are definitely nouns in professional denominations, denoting men with the masculine grammatical gender (*senātor* "senator", (*h*)*olitor* "vegetable seller"). But the masc./fem. couples *genitor* masc. "father"/*gene-trīx* fem. "mother" and *uictor* masc./*uic-trīx* fem. "victorious" are not similar: *genitor* and *genetrīx* are nouns, while *uictor* and *uictrīx* may well be adjectives, since *uictrīx* is the feminine form of *uictor* with a grammatical agreement.

Some ethnic names such as *Rōmānī* masc. pl. "the Romans" (derived from the toponym *Rōma* "Rome") show ambiguous relationships with the corresponding adjectives *Rōmānus*, -*a*, -*um* "Roman, of Rome or its people". The noun *Rōmānus*, -*ī* masc. "a Roman" sg., *Rōmānī* "the Romans" pl. could be analysed as the lexicalisation of the adjective, but, conversely, the adjective could also be considered as an adjectivisation of the ethnic name, since it is used both as an ethnic adjective (for persons: *cīuis Rōmānus* "a Roman citizen") and as a ktetic one (for inanimate entities: *mōre Rōmānō* "in the Roman manner").

The denominative verbs are derived from substantival or adjectival stems and they have some productivity in all periods of Latin. The transfer is noticeable morphologically by the new verbal stem and inflection. Most denominative verbs have a stem in long *a* (*nōminā-re* on *nōmen* "name"), the most productive type in Latin of all periods, or in long *i* (*fīnī-re* "to end" on *fīnis* "limit"), a type which was productive in preliterary Latin.

Long *a* and long *i* here have a verbal grammatical role, different from the verbal suffixes such as inchoative-progressive -*scere* or frequentative-intensive -*tāre* (see above on verbal suffixes). This *ī* at the end of the verbal stem may be morphologically explained, e.g. in *fīnī-re* "to end", where it is the lengthening of the final *i* in the noun stem *fīni-* "an end" (*fīnis*); the same lengthening may occur with an adjectival stem in *lēnis* "gentle" → *lēnī-re* "moderate". But in denominative verbs, the *ī* may also be added to a consonant stem: *custōs* "guardian" (*custōd-*) → *custōd-ī-re* "keep safe", or to an adjectival thematic stem: *blandus*, -*a*, -*um* "flattery" → *bland-ī-rī* "flatter", *artus* "tightly-fastened" → *art-ī-re* "fasten tightly" (Cato). The *ā* stem of *ancilla* fem. "female servant" is maintained as the derivation basis of the verb *ancillā-rī* "be a female servant", but the *ā* is added to a consonant stem in *nōmen* "a name" (*nōmin-*) neut. → *nōmin-ā-re* "to name".

There is a link between the denominative verbs and the parasynthetic ones (see above), since the latter may sometimes be derived from the former by addition of a preverb.

Some uninflected words have also been transcategorised into another grammatical category. Although there is no morphological change (they keep the same form since they are not inflected), they then have a new syntactic function: e.g. the modal impersonal verb *licet* (+ subjunctive) "it is permitted" became a usual concessive subordinator "although" in Late Latin prose.

Conclusion

The most productive formation in Latin is suffixation. Agglutination is also productive, but only in specific cases. Nominal compounding is less productive in Latin than in other IE languages (such as Sanskrit, Greek or Germanic) and it is mainly limited to specific structural types. Verbal compounding is mainly represented in the usual non-poetic vocabulary by the causative morpheme *-ficāre*. Recategorisation is widely productive, but only for some grammatical categories (from an adjective to a noun, and from a noun or an adjective to a denominative verb).

Most Latin suffixes are the result of new combinations of pre-existing elements. Inherited elements were usually remodelled according to the constraints and specific properties of Latin.

There is no correlation between the productivity of a given formation and its age: an inherited formation is not necessarily more stable than a more recent one built in Latin itself. Some old formations have totally disappeared in Latin or are residual and only illustrated by a few remnants. Others were maintained, although usually with some adaptation to the changing system of the language.

Finally, it is important to note that the classifications we have used above for the word-formation in Latin only cover those Latin lexemes that we can actually analyse. However, a large part of the Latin lexicon consists of synchronically unmotivated and diachronically obscure lexemes, some of which belonging to the Latin fundamental vocabulary. Nevertheless, this does not appear to have hindered their functioning in the language, showing that a lexeme does not need to be motivated in order to be an efficient communication tool for the speech community.

FURTHER READING

Historical grammars of Latin usually give an overview of the principal nominal and verbal suffixes in the language, and their historical background, see in particular Leumann (1977), Meiser (1998) and Weiss (2009). Books that aim for a general coverage of Latin word-formation, incorporating both diachronic and synchronic considerations include Leumann (1944), André (1971), Fruyt and Nicolas (2000), and Kircher-Durand (2002). Compounding is a particular branch of studies of word-formation, and the following works are specifically devoted to it: Bader (1962), Benedetti (1988), Flobert (1978), Fruyt (2002), Lindner (1996 and 2002), Moussy (2005) and Oniga (1988). In order to give an indication of the number and variety of books and articles on various different derivation processes of Latin it is enough to consider the formation of diminutives, often effected through a suffix containing an *-l-*, which is the subject of Conrad (1931), Fruyt (1989), Gaide (1992 and 2002), Hakamies (1951), Zucchelli (1969a and 1969b).

CHAPTER 12

Latin Particles and the Grammar of Discourse[1]

Caroline Kroon

Introduction: Aims and Key Concepts

In this chapter we will focus on the structure of Latin beyond the level of the grammatical sentence, and on the role particles may play in the complex organization of a discourse. By *discourse* I mean any communicative event that takes place between speech participants (speaker and hearer; writer and reader) in a particular communicative situation. The patterns and meanings of discourse, which may be loosely referred to as the *grammar of discourse*, involve textual segments of varying size, ranging from single words to extensive texts.[2] The word *particle* in the title of this paper is used as a non-technical cover term for all those uninflected words which do not contribute to the propositional, truth-conditional content of a clause, but which help to organize the communication and to integrate the text segment they "act upon" (the *host*) into its particular communicative context. Particles in this sense are function words, not content words, and as such reflect the fact that language is meant for communication.

This is not to say that the notion of particle is in any way straightforward or uncontroversial.[3] As a result of the variety of theories and methodologies employed in the study of particles, we are still in want of a single, generally accepted model for the description of particles in the languages of the world. Accordingly, opinions of linguists differ greatly on terminology and categorization of this group of words, distinguishing, for instance, *focus particles*, *modal particles*, and *pragmatic particles*, the last group of which is alternatively labeled as *discourse particles*, *discourse markers*, *discourse connectives*, or simply *connectives*. In the next section I will return to this terminological confusion in more detail. Examples **1–3** provide some prototypical Latin instances of the main particle categories discerned. *Solum* in **1** is an example of what is often referred to as a "focus particle," *modo* in **2** of a "modal particle," and *nam* in **3** of a "connective particle."[4]

A Companion to the Latin Language, First Edition. Edited by James Clackson.
© 2011 Blackwell Publishing Ltd. Published 2011 by Blackwell Publishing Ltd.

1 ceterae ciuitates suis *solum* incommodis commouentur.
   the other places are roused by their own troubles *only*. (Cic. *Ver.* 2.3.108)

2 fuge *modo* intro, ego uidero.
   just run away indoors, I'll see to [him]. (Ter. *Ad.* 538)

3 is pagus appellabatur Tigurinus; *nam* omnis ciuitas Heluetia in quattuor pagos diuisa est.
   The name of the canton was the Tigurine; *for* the whole state of Helvetia is divided
     into four cantons. (Caes. *Gal.* 1.12.4)

In addition to the issues of terminology and internal categorization, we are also confronted with the problem of demarcating particles in an unambiguous way from other word classes, such as adverbs, conjunctions, and interjections. This problem has led many scholars to the conclusion that particles can only be defined in a negative way (for Latin e.g. Rosén (2009) 327), or not at all (e.g. Zimmermann (forthcoming)). A related problem is that certain invariables, also in Latin, seem to belong to more than one word class, diachronically as well as synchronically, and that the borderlines between them may be fuzzy.

In this chapter I will largely pass over these problems, adopting a line of approach in which I will concentrate mainly on the mechanisms involved in establishing a coherent Latin discourse, and the various ways in which "particles," just like other linguistic devices, may play a role in this process. This means that I do not intend to focus on one or more Latin particles in particular and investigate their whole spectrum of functions, trying, for each item, to detect a "core meaning" or other kind of interrelatedness between the various uses observed.[5] As a result of the perspective chosen, the account will be mainly synchronic in nature, and may be seen as complementary to the mainly diachronic approach of Rosén (2009).

After some brief further remarks, in the next section, on the concept of particle and the more specific type of items under discussion in this chapter, I will first sketch, in a very general way, what a discourse grammar might look like. Next I will narrow my focus to particles with a connective function, and demonstrate how these can fulfill a variety of jobs in establishing a coherent Latin discourse. In addition to this connective group of items, which form the bulk of Latin particles, there is a remaining group of particles which do not point to the specific relationship of their host to another discourse segment, but which rather involve the management of the interaction taking place between the interlocutors, or point to the interlocutors' stances towards the transmitted content. This latter, non-connective type of particles, which I will refer to as "interaction managing," will be addressed in the penultimate section. The final section is reserved for some remaining relevant issues, and for drawing conclusions.

Particles as Pragmatic Markers

Due to the fact that particles cannot be adequately described within a sentence grammatical paradigm based on verbs, obligatory arguments, and optional satellites (adverbials), grammarians for long treated them in the manner of a wicked stepmother.

Particles "are just the kind of thing that tends to escape the net of the grammarian and lexicographer," as Brown and Levinson (1987) 273 put it, and "their very existence was an embarrassment, as evidence that language is, after all, SOMEBODY's language, and that its structure reflects, and is shaped by, the needs of its users" (Wierzbicka (1986) 520).

With the rise of pragmatic and functional approaches to language in the last four decades, and the concomitant introduction of the linguistic discipline called *discourse linguistics* or *discourse analysis*, the interest in particles has considerably increased. The insight that particles are an important cue for interpreting the communicative goals and implications of a transmitted content, together with the availability of new theoretical concepts and heuristic tools, has put particles firmly on the research agenda of linguists all over the world, including those studying Latin. Particularly useful appeared to be the insight that the complexity of discourse organization can only be captured by combining information pertaining to various distinct levels of analysis, for instance a grammatical level, a textual level, and a non-linguistic, situational level. As we will see below (pp. 181–183), recognition of such levels is essential for understanding the contribution of particles to a text.

Thus far I have used the term particle in a quite loose sense, characterizing particles as those uninflected words which are not, themselves, part of the propositional content of a text segment, but rather play a role in structuring the discourse or in managing the interaction between the interlocutors. As they are not defined in terms of a clear set of shared syntactic features, particles cannot, as a group, be put on a par with (nor contrasted to) syntactically defined word classes as conjunctions, adverbs, and interjections. As a matter of fact, items from all these three word classes can have a "particle" use, in addition to one or more other uses. In English, for instance, the particle *well* (in contrast to the adverbial *well*) can, on the basis of its syntactic behavior, be assigned to the word class interjection. But not all interjections in English have a use as a particle: an interjection for expressing pain like *ouch* clearly does not meet the criteria for being called a particle.[6]

To further illustrate the point consider the following examples from Latin, which are also discussed in Risselada (1996) 111–112:

4 (a) ancilla mea quae fuit hodie, sua *nunc* est.
     that maidservant I owned until today, is *now* free. (Pl. *Per.* 472)

(b) (Reaction of Psyche to her sisters, who have warned her that her mysterious
     lover is a horrible beast)
     bestiamque aliquam recte dicentibus uobis merito consentio. meque magnopere
     semper a suis terret aspectibus malumque grande de uultus curiositate
     praeminatur. *nunc* si quam salutarem opem periclitanti sorori uestrae potestis
     adferre, iam nunc subsistite.

     You must be right when you say he is some beast, I agree. He is always
     frightening me from looking at him, and threatening some great punishment
     for any curiosity about his features. *Now*, if you can bring some salvation to
     your sister in her danger, help me right now. (Apul. *Met.* 5.19)

In **4a**, *nunc* is a temporal adjunct which is fully integrated in the syntactic clause, and a constitutive part of the propositional content conveyed by this clause: it refers to the point in time at which the situation described ("to be free") obtains, and is fully comparable in this function with words like *heri* ("yesterday") and *cras* ("tomorrow"). In **4b**, the same word is not used as a temporal adjunct, but as a particle which points to a transition in the discourse structure: from a narrative description of the speaker's situation to a non-narrative request that ensues from it. That *nunc* in **4b** is to be regarded as a discourse-structuring particle rather than as a temporal adjunct, is strongly suggested by the fact that it occupies the first position of the sentence. Moreover, there is a clearly adverbial second *nunc* at the end of the sentence, which makes it quite unlikely that the first *nunc* is a temporal adjunct as well. Although in both cases *nunc* will normally be taken as belonging to the word class adverb, it is used as a particle in **4b**, but not in **4a**. In this respect Latin *nunc* has the same range of uses as English *now*.

The definition of particles as used in this chapter includes, as argued above, the discourse-structuring use of adverbs like Latin *nunc* or English *now*. It excludes, however, the group of words that is commonly referred to as focus particles. Focus particles, like *also*, *even*, *just*, and *only* in English, or *adeo*, *demum*, *etiam*, *solum*, and *tantum* in Latin, are an integrative part of the grammatical structure of the clause. What they do is single out a constituent of the clause in relation to a set of possible alternatives that are available in the described world. I repeat here example **1**, in which the focus particle *solum*, by adding the shade of meaning of exclusivity to the focused constituent *suis*, contributes to the propositional content of the clause as a whole.

1 ceterae ciuitates suis *solum* incommodis commouentur
the other places are roused by their own troubles *only*. (Cic. *Ver.* 2.3.108)

Because of their essentially proposition-internal function, focus particles should best be kept apart from those invariables which operate *above*, rather than *within* the proposition level.[7] Because of this fundamental difference, we might even consider dropping the confusing term "particle" entirely and referring to the proposition-*external* group of words as *pragmatic markers*, as has been suggested by others as well. This has the additional advantage that we can also take on board functionally similar expressions which are less "particle-like" in their form, such as certain adverbs with a clear lexical meaning (see the discussion above on *nunc*), or lexicalized verb forms like *amabo* ("please"), which have a typical interaction managing function, but are usually not referred to as particles.

In the remainder of this chapter I will leave the Latin focus particles aside, unless the items concerned also have a clear use as a pragmatic marker, such as *quidem* (see pp. 184–186 below). I have taken the same decision for the invariables and other particle look-alikes that express epistemic modality (the Latin equivalents of English expressions like *certainly, maybe, no doubt, of course, surely: certe, certo, fortasse, nimirum, plane, profecto, sane, scilicet, uero*, and the like). It is especially here that the categories seem to shade into one another and it is often hard to decide whether the words involved point to the speaker's stance or commitment towards the transmitted content, in which case we might consider them as pragmatic markers; or that the epistemic evaluation is itself a part of the transmitted content, and we should rather speak of a "modal sentence adverb." The Latin epistemic particles, and the problems involved in drawing the dividing lines between epistemic particles and epistemic sentence adverbs, are discussed extensively in, for instance, Pinkster (1972), Orlandini (1997), and Schrickx (in press). Two examples of *uero*, one in which it functions as an epistemic "content word" and one in which it is a clear epistemic particle, may suffice for the moment:

> 5 SCIPIO: quid? domi pluresne praesunt negotiis tuis?
> LAELIUS: immo *uero* unus.
>
> > "How about your residence in the city? Are several persons in charge there?"
> > "On the contrary, in fact only one." (Cic. *Rep.* 1.61)

> 6 nequeo, leno, quin tibi saltem staticulum ... uide *uero*, si tibi sati' placet.
> Pimp, I can't refrain from dancing for you that lovely little dance ... Do see now [*uide uero*], if it isn't rather winsome? (Pl. *Per.* 824–825)

In **5** *uero* expresses the actuality or truth of the situation described (one person is in charge of the house), as compared to a possible alternative event in the same world (more persons are in charge of the house). As such, *uero* can be regarded as a content word here. In the directive speech act of **6**, however, we see *uero* in a conversation-managing role. In instances like this, *uero* emphasizes the sincerity of the speaker's communicative intention. Or stated otherwise, *uero* indicates that the speaker is highly committed to the actual realization of the intended action by the hearer. By virtue of this function, *uero* lends the directive a more urgent character. The more specific communicative effect of adding *uero* to a directive speech act depends crucially on the context and the type of directive involved. The presence of *uero* may, for instance, reveal the irritation of the speaker in a repeated directive; it may have a reassuring or encouraging effect in a granting of permission; it may make a request more urgent and picture the speaker in a supplicatory role; etc.

To conclude this section we need briefly to address the issue of the semiotic status of particles. In what terms are we to describe the "meaning" of this group of function words? In the light of the content word/function word distinction discussed above, it is clear that the items involved do not have a referential meaning themselves, but somehow pertain to the verbal and nonverbal context in which some referential content is conveyed. Pragmatic particles do not, however, describe an aspect of the context, they only indicate that a contextual aspect of a certain type should be taken into consideration in the interpretation process (Foolen (1996) 5). In this sense, particles can be said to have a *deictic* or *indexical* rather than a *referential* meaning. In any case, they are not, as has often been suggested, empty or meaningless fillers, but, as the Renaissance grammarian Tursellinus (1545–1599) puts it, *ad usum magna et plane necessaria* (cf. Hand (1829) x–xi). That particles are not void of meaning, but essential cues in the interpretation process, can be demonstrated by examples like **8** and **9**:

> 8 NAUSISTRATA: mi uir non mihi dices?
> CHREMES: *at* –
> NAUSISTRATA: quid "*at*"?
>
> > "my dear husband, won't you tell me?"
> > "but ..."
> > "What 'but'?" (Ter. *Ph.* 1002–1003)

9 (Cicero to his juridical opponent)

  census nostros requiris, scilicet. est *enim* obscurum proximis censoribus hunc apud
   exercitum fuisse.

  You require our census lists, of course; it is *enim* unknown that he was with the
   army at the time of the last censors. (Cic. *Arch.* 11)

In **8** the second instance of the particle *at* is clearly the focus of Nausistrata's interrupting question ("What do you mean, 'but'?"), which proves that the first *at* is not semantically empty, but a quite important cue for the interlocutor how to interpret the words that will follow (as an objection, that is). In **9** the addition of the consensus particle *enim* ("of course," "as we all know") is essential for grasping the irony of the statement made. What Cicero wants to stress here is the absurdity of his opponent's request: it is a well-known fact that his client's name is not on the census lists because he was absent from Rome when these were made. I will return to the particles *at* and *enim* later.

From Sentence Grammar to Discourse Grammar: The Location of Particles in a Grammar of Discourse

From the discussion above it has become clear that, in order to adequately explain and describe the role of pragmatic particles in a text, we should have recourse to a kind of grammar that also takes the communicative interaction into account. Such a grammar is only one component within a wider theory of verbal interaction, in which the grammar interacts with a number of other, non-grammatical components, such as a conceptual component and a contextual component.

The conceptual component of this theory of verbal interaction accounts for the prelinguistic phase of communication, in which a *communicative intention* is formed, for instance issuing an order or making a statement. In the grammatical component this intention is transformed into a *formulation*. This formulation is, in turn, strongly influenced by the contextual component, which contains not only all information that is known from the preceding discourse, but also information on the actual perceivable setting in which the communication takes place, and of the social relationships between the interlocutors. The way a speaker formulates an order, for instance, will be strongly influenced by the social relationship with the hearer, and the specific setting in which the communication takes place. Within a wider theory of verbal interaction it is assumed, thus, that the formal properties of language are adapted to the communicative intentions and strategies of the language user and the context in which the language is used.

When we now zoom in on the grammatical component of the theory, there are two levels of structural analysis (two types of structures) that have to be accounted for: a pragmatic, *interpersonal* level, dealing with configurations of communicative acts; and a semantic, *representational* level, dealing with configurations of elements which refer to some possible world. Grammars that intend to capture both levels of structural analysis may be referred to as *discourse grammars*.[8] For the description of pragmatic particles, it is especially the interpersonal level of structural analysis that is relevant.

As far as the *interpersonal* level of the grammar is concerned, we may analyze a sentence like **10** below as one single communicative *act* which involves a speaker, an addressee, an illocutionary force (requesting, ordering, asserting, asking a question, etc.; see Pinkster (1990a) ch. 10), and a communicated content. In terms of the *representational* level of analysis, we are dealing with one propositional content, involving two situations in the represented world that are causally related, each with its own configuration of semantic roles.

10 multos cometas non uidemus quia obscurantur radiis solis.
    we do not see many comets because they are obscured by the rays of the sun.
    (Sen. *Nat.* 7.20.4)

The causal relation between the situation referred to in the main clause ("we do not see many comets") and the situation in the subordinate clause ("the comets are obscured by sunrays") is expressed by the subordinating conjunction *quia*. As the causal relationship involved holds in the world described, and the subordinate clause is syntactically integrated in the main clause as a causal adjunct, the conjunction *quia* is clearly not a pragmatic particle here: it signals a relationship on the representational level of discourse.

   In addition to semantic relationships of the type illustrated in 10, discourse also displays relationships of a pragmatic type, which do not hold between situations in the world described, but between communicative acts (or larger communicative units). These relations are known as pragmatic relations or *coherence relations*. For an example consider the invented discourse segment in 11, uttered by one single speaker:

11 I have to go home.   *So* let's make a new appointment.
    ‾‾‾‾‾‾‾‾‾‾‾‾‾‾‾‾‾‾‾   ‾‾‾‾‾‾‾‾‾‾‾‾‾‾‾‾‾‾‾‾‾‾‾‾‾‾‾‾‾
              Act 1   Act 2

In terms of the interpersonal level of discourse, this text segment consists of two communicative *acts* which maintain a pragmatic relationship of conclusion. Together the two acts constitute one communicative *move*. The more specific relationship involved (orientation, preparation, motivation, conclusion, inference, comment, clarification, counter-argument, addition, and the like) may be marked explicitly by means of a pragmatic particle (like *so* in 11, for which in Latin *igitur* would be a good equivalent), or may remain implicit. Most of the pragmatic particles in Latin function as markers of this type of coherence relations. Note that, whereas in 10 the conjunction *quia* links two events in the described world and plays a proposition internal connective role (representational level of the grammar), *so* in 11 is involved in the sequencing of *speech* events (interpersonal level of the grammar).

   The discourse structure of 11 may be represented as follows:

A *move* is an autonomous monological contribution to a communicative interaction and may consist of only one act or several related acts which all may, but need not, have the form of a full grammatical clause. Autonomous in this sense means that the discourse unit is communicatively complete, and in essence opens up the possibility to be countered by a reactive move of an addressee. In monological texts, which form the bulk of Latin literature, reactive moves by the addressee are, of course, only a virtual possibility. If an initiative move of a speaker is countered by a reactive move of the addressee, we speak of an *exchange*. This dialogical type of discourse structure is illustrated in **12**, where Speaker 2 counters the initiative move of Speaker 1 by an objecting reactive move.

12 Speaker 1: I have to go home. *So* let's make a new appointment.
　　Speaker 2: *But* it's only ten o'clock!

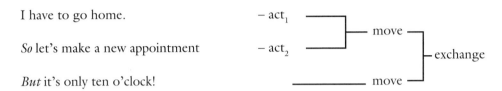

I have to go home.	– act₁		
So let's make a new appointment	– act₂	move	
			exchange
But it's only ten o'clock!		move	

Like the relations between the constitutive acts of a move, the relations between the constitutive moves of an exchange (confirmation, affirmation, rejection, correction, objection, request for confirmation, interruption, and the like) may also be marked by pragmatic particles. In **12** the relation "objection" is explicitly marked by *but*. In Latin, objections are typically marked by the particle *at*, as has been illustrated by example **8** above. Other Latin particles that may play a role in marking the reactive move of an exchange structure are e.g. *ergo* and *immo*.

The discussion above was meant to explain where we are to locate connective particles like *igitur* and *at* in a discourse grammar of Latin. In the next section we will see more examples of Latin particles that may function as markers of coherence relations. In addition, Latin possesses a number of non-connective pragmatic particles which pertain to the relation between speaker and hearer, or otherwise play a role in the management of the conversation. These, too, can only be accounted for on the interpersonal level of the grammar. Two examples of this latter group of particles we have already seen in **2** and **6** above. Latin is not assumed to be particularly rich in such conversation-management particles, especially not in comparison with languages like German, Dutch, or Ancient Greek. Later on we will see, however, that certain connective particles, like the highly frequent particle *enim*, can also be described in terms of a conversation-management function and are sometimes better accounted for in this way.

Connective Particles

Markers of coherence relations: sed, nam, igitur, autem, quidem, *and* at

Sed, nam, igitur

Typical markers of coherence relations in Latin are, for instance, the particles *sed, nam* and *igitur*, as they are used in examples 13–15. For an extensive account of *nam* I refer to Kroon (1995), for *igitur* to Kroon (1989, 2004).

13 magnum opus omnino et arduum, Brute, conamur; *sed* nihil difficile amanti puto.
This is doubtless a great and arduous task, Brutus; *but* nothing, I think, is hard for
a lover. (Cic. *Orat.* 33)

14 mater rure rediit; *nam* uideo Syra astare ante aedis.
my mother's back from the country; *for* I see Syra [her servant] standing in front
of the house. (Pl. *Mer.* 807–808)

15 concedo esse deos; doce me *igitur* unde sint, ubi sint, quales sint.
I grant the existence of the gods; do you *then* teach me their origin, their dwelling-
place, their nature. (Cic. *N.D.* 1.65)

In **13**, *sed* marks a coherence relation of counter-argument between two successive acts. In
example **14**, the act introduced by *nam* maintains a coherence relation of evidence with
the preceding act, rather than a semantic cause–consequence relation with the content of
the prior clause: the situation of the speaker seeing his mother's servant in front of the
house, is, of course, not the cause of his mother's return but the evidence that is adduced
for the prior statement. More generally, we can say that Latin *nam* signals that its host unit
has a subsidiary function with regard to some other, communicatively more central,
discourse unit. Depending on the context, the more specific relationship involved may be
evidence, as here, or justification, motivation, elaboration, explanation, exemplification,
and the like. In **3** above, for instance, *nam* marks a relation of explanation.

The connective particle *igitur* is, in a sense, the mirror image of *nam*: *igitur* marks the
transition to a new central step in the argument or narrative, inferred from, or based on,
some preparatory discourse unit in the prior context. In **15** the first act counts as the
necessary precondition for issuing the directive act that is to follow, a relationship that is
explicitly marked by *igitur*.[9]

Autem, quidem

Slightly different is the use of *autem* and *quidem* as connective particles. Although *autem* is
usually ranged, together with words like *at*, *sed*, and *uero*, among the adversative connective
particles, it behaves markedly different from all of these. In Kroon (1995) ch. 10 I argued
that *autem* is typically used to expressly mark off a piece of information from some other
piece of information in the verbal or non-verbal context. The particle can be applied locally
(within the boundaries of a single sentence), or more globally (between units of discourse
larger than a single sentence). An instance of the former, local use of *autem* is **16**:

16 tu magnus amator mulierum es, Messenio, ego *autem* homo iracundus.
you, Messenio, are a great lover of the ladies, while *I* am a choleric man. (Pl. *Men.*
268–269)

When applied on a more global level of the discourse structure, *autem* can be described
as a marker of thematic discontinuity, as is illustrated in **17** and **18**:

17 hoc here effecit. hodie *autem* in Aenariam transire constituit <ut> exsulibus pollicetur
This was yesterday's achievement. Today *autem* he has arranged to cross over to
Aenaria to promise the exiles their recall. (Cic. *Att.* 10.13.1)

18 NAVTAE coacti fame radices palmarum agrestium ... colligebant et iis miseri perditique alebantur; CLEOMENES *autem* ... totos dies in litore tabernaculo posito perpotabat. ECCE *autem* repente ebrio Cleomene esurientibus ceteris nuntiatur piratarum esse nauis in portu Odysseae; nam ita is locus nominatur; NOSTRA *autem* CLASSIS erat in portu Pachyni. CLEOMENES *autem* ... sperauit ...

THE SAILORS (*nautae*), as food was so short, had to set about collecting the roots of wild palms ... and they tried to keep themselves alive on these. Now CLEOMENES (*Cleomenes autem*) ... spent whole days drinking in a tent pitched on the shore. AND NOW (*ecce autem*), while he was drunk and his men starving, the news suddenly arrived that there were pirate ships in the harbour of Odyssea (because that was what the place was called). Now OUR FLEET (*nostra autem classis*) was in the harbour of Pachynus. Now CLEOMENES (*Cleomenes autem*) ... counted on ... (Cic. *Ver.* 2.5.87)

What makes *autem* different from connective particles like *igitur*, *nam* and *sed* is that it does not function primarily to mark coherence relations of the type conclusion, evidence, counter-argument, and the like. Its structuring role is based on a different coherence principle, that of continuity and discontinuity of the linear information structure. The linear information structure of a discourse naturally evolves along various concurrent thematic strands of information, involving continued reference to, for instance, the same person, location, time, situation, and circumstances. Whenever one of these chains is interrupted and replaced by a new chain, this causes a transition in the discourse structure. *Autem* is typically attached to pieces of information that start such a new thematic chain. In the prior context of the letter cited in **17**, Cicero has described to Atticus what Antony had been doing the day before, a passage which is rounded off by the summary statement *hoc here effecit* ("this was yesterday's achievement"). In the next sentence *autem* marks a transition in the information structure, pointing to a shift in the temporal chain of information: now Antony's achievements of the *present* day will be described. In **18** the thematic chains involved are ultra-short: at the start of every new sentence the narrator shifts his attention to a new person or a new circumstance. As this is not what we expect in a coherent narrative, the narrator repeatedly brings *autem* into action, as a means to help the reader keep track of the quite chaotic information structure of the episode.

   Whereas *autem* signals that a new and conceptually discrete thematic strand is coming up, the particle *quidem*, by contrast, indicates that its host unit is informationally not complete and needs, for its proper interpretation, another piece of information with which it forms a conceptual whole (Kroon (2005, 2009); see also Solodow (1978) 13). In other words, *autem* has to do with conceptual discreteness, *quidem* with conceptual integrity. Signaling conceptual incompleteness, as *quidem* does, seems especially opportune when the component parts of the conceptual whole are divided over separate communicative units, as is the case in example **19**:

19 consul ... suos *quidem* a fuga reuocavit;   act 1
ipse ... missili traiectus cecidit   act 2
      The consul ... did *indeed* rally his men from their flight; but he himself ... fell
         struck with a javelin. (Liv. 41.18.11)

Quidem can be regarded here as a forward-oriented discourse-organizing device. It serves as a warning to the reader that the present discourse unit is conceptually not yet complete, and instructs him to search for a companion unit in the following context, with which the *quidem*-unit constitutes a conceptual whole. It is a warning, so to speak, that for its proper interpretation the *quidem*-unit needs to be considered in the light of a piece of information in the following context.

More often, however, *quidem*'s linking force is backward-oriented, as in **20**, where *quidem* is a signal that its host unit, despite its status as an independent new act, conceptually forms a unity with the preceding act. The reasons for dividing a conceptual unity over two separate acts may be various. In **20** it is clearly the need for emphasizing the wickedness of the deed that has led the narrator to present this manner adjunct as a separate act.

> **20** cupit regnum, et *quidem* scelerate cupit, qui transcendere festinat ordinem aetatis.
>   He covets the throne and *indeed* covets it to the point of crime, since he hastens
>   to leap over precedence in age. (Liv. 40.11.7)

As argued in Kroon (2005, 2009), the alleged function of *quidem* as a marker of adversative or concessive coherence relations is to be described as a contextually dependent side-effect of the particle. *Quidem* itself merely indicates that the content of its host unit can only be interpreted in combination with the content of a discourse unit in its vicinity. In this sense, *quidem* is a clear coherence creating device.

For reasons explained above, I leave the use of *quidem* as a focus particle out of account here. For this use, see Solodow (1978).

At

To conclude this section on connective particles I shall finally discuss some examples of the Latin connective particle *at*, which has already been mentioned above as a typical marker of reactive moves, more specifically of reactive moves with the communicative function of an objection. *At* is, in other words, a particle that marks coherence relations in a dialogical environment, at the level of the exchange.

A prototypical instance of the use of *at* can be seen in **21**:

> 21 eloquere
>   *at* pudet
>   "Go on, tell me"
>   "*but* I'm ashamed to." (Pl. *Cas.* 911)

In Kroon (1995) I observed that *at* has a strong preference for occurring in a dialogical environment, for instance in conversations, but that it is not at all excluded from monologues. As in an overwhelming majority of cases the monologues concerned appear to have clear dialogical "traits," it is, however, possible to describe most of the instances of *at* in monologues in the same way as the unequivocally dialogical instances. In these monological environments it is suggested (rather than formally expressed) that an interactional exchange is taking place, either between the speaker/writer and some implied addressee, or between the internal characters of a narrative. This can be illustrated with examples **22** and **23** below, respectively.

> **22** tu fortasse orationem, ut soles, et flagitas et expectas. *at* ego quasi ex aliqua peregrina delicataque merce lusos meos tibi prodo.
>
> > You expect and demand, perhaps, as usual, an oration. *But* I am going to put into your hands, as if they were some choice bits of foreign merchandise, some of my poetical amusements. (Plin. *Ep.* 4.14.1)

We can describe the monological stretch of text in **22** in terms of a coherence relation between the two constitutive acts of a move. The first act functions as an orientation or preparation with regard to the second, more central act. Together they constitute one single communicative move. This particular coherence relation is not, however, expressed explicitly by a marker. We can also describe the combination of clauses in **22** in terms of a relation between an initiative move and a corresponding reactive move, which together constitute an exchange. The initiative move, albeit *worded* in this case by the "I," essentially contains the embedded voice of the "you." This dialogical interpretation is strongly suggested by the presence of *at*, whose prototypical function is to mark an objecting reactive move in an interactional exchange.

Example **23** illustrates how *at* may be used in the monological environment of a narrative. One explanation why *at* is used here instead of, for instance, *sed* or *autem*, may be that Livy wants to evoke the image of an actual verbal dispute between the two parties, without going so far as to suspend the progress of the narrative for reported speech. The use of *at* gives the text a dialogical touch, so to speak. This interpretation is enhanced by the fact that the imperfect tense is used here (*trahebant*, "they were claiming"), and not the perfect tense.

> **23** priori Remo augurium uenisse fertur, sex uoltures; iamque nuntiato augurio cum duplex numerus Romulo se ostendisset, utrumque regem sua multitudo consalutauerat: tempore illi praecepto, *at* hi numero auium regnum trahebant.
>
> > Remus is said to have been the first to receive an augury, from the flight of six vultures. The omen had been already reported when twice that number appeared to Romulus. Thereupon each was saluted king by his own followers: the one party laid claim to the kingship on the ground of priority, but the other (*at hi*) on the ground of the number of the birds. (Liv. 1.7.1–2)

Latin does not seem to abound in particles which, like *at*, typically mark coherence relations between the initiative and reactive moves of a conversational exchange. We may mention *immo* here, which, as argued by Orlandini (1995), can mark both a coherence relation of correction ("rather"), and a coherence relation of confirmation ("indeed"). Another candidate for indicating coherence relations on the level of the exchange structure is *ergo* which, like *at*, is clearly more suited to "conversational" genres like drama, dialogues, letters, orations, and philosophical discourse, and which is relatively rare in historiography (Krylová (2003) 68). On account of its particular behavior, however, *ergo* might be better described as a non-connective, interaction management particle. In this respect it resembles particles like *uero* and *enim*, which will be discussed below. For *ergo*, see Kroon (1989) 239–240; (1995) 92–93, 369–370; (1998) 48–49 and Krylová (2001, 2003).

Markers of transitions between discourse segments: an illustration from Sallust's Iugurtha

Coherence relations and their markers may be described, as we have seen, in terms of the pragmatic functions of discourse units: a discourse unit may count as an orientation, preparation, motivation, conclusion, inference, comment, clarification, counter-argument, addition, objection, confirmation, etc., with regard to some other unit. Most if not all of the particles that may play a role in marking coherence relations between successive sentences also occur as markers of transitions at major boundaries in the discourse structure. This latter, discourse-organizing use can be seen as an extension of their use as markers of coherence relations. In addition to connective particles like *sed*, *igitur*, and *nam*, there are also many adverbs in Latin that may serve as transition markers. I have already mentioned the discourse-structuring function of the adverb *nunc*. Hilton (1999) and Rosén (2009) 319 draw attention to the discourse-organizing use of temporal adverbs like *tum* ("then"), *deinde* ("next"), and *postea* ("thereafter"), which play a major structuring role in narrative texts.

I will illustrate the discourse-organizing use of Latin particles with an extract from Sallust's monograph on the war with the Numidian king Jugurtha.[10] This text displays a particularly rich variety of transitions and transition markers.

In the context preceding the extract printed in Figure 12.1, the narrator has described how the Roman commander Marius has succeeded in taking an occupied mountain. He now proceeds to tell how, at about the same time, the quaestor Sulla arrives on the African scene, who will be one of the leading figures not only of the rest of the story, but also of later Roman history. This arrival is reported in segment 1, which is introduced by *ceterum* ("moreover," "in addition"), a typically Sallustian word, and the first example in this extract of the discourse-organizing use of a connective particle. *Ceterum* indicates the transition to another episode worth mentioning at the moment of the story where the narration has arrived.

Segment 1 may be considered as an essentially complete communicative unit (a move), which is expected to be followed by a next move in which a related next event on the narrative time line will be told. Before doing so, however, the narrator decides to insert a digression in which he describes the life and character of this important new figure Sulla. Segments 2–5 can be regarded as a complex move which, as a whole, has a subsidiary function with regard to the narrative main line of the story. This main line is resumed not earlier than in segment 6, which is the next central move as far as the continuation of the narrative is concerned. This next central move will turn out to have a complex hierarchical structure itself (not quoted here further). Note that, due to the length of the digression, this new narrative move starts with a resumptive summary of the prior narrative move in segment 1.

1. **Ceterum**, dum ea res geritur, L. Sulla quaestor cum magno equitatu in castra uenit, quos uti ex Latio et a sociis cogeret, Romae relictus erat.

> 2. **Sed** quoniam nos tanti uiri res admonuit, idoneum uisum est de natura cultuque eius paucis dicere.

>> 3. Neque enim alio loco de Sullae rebus dicturi sumus et L. Sisenna, optime et diligentissime omnium, qui eas res dixere, persecutus, parum mihi libero ore locutus uidetur

> 4. **Igitur** Sulla gentis patriciae nobilis fuit, familia prope iam extincta maiorum ignauia, litteris Graecis atque Latinis iuxta atque doctissime eruditus, ...
> Atque illi felicissimo omnium ante ciuilem uictoriam numquam super industriam fortuna fuit, multique dubitauere, fortior an felicior esset.

>> 5. **Nam** postea quae fecerit, incertum habeo pudeat an pigeat magis disserere.

6. **Igitur** Sulla, uti supra dictum est, postquam in Africam atque in castra Mari cum equitatu uenit ...

---

1. **But** during these events [i.e. the attack on the fortress] the quaestor L. Sulla arrived in camp with a large force of cavalry, which he had mustered from Latium and the allies, having been left in Rome for that purpose.

> 2. **But** since the event has brought that great man to our attention, it seems fitting to say a few words about his life and character;

>> 3. for we shall not speak elsewhere of Sulla's affairs, and Lucius Sisenna, whose account of him is altogether the best and most careful, has not, in my opinion, spoken with sufficient frankness.

> 4. Sulla, **then**, was a noble of patrician descent, of a family almost reduced to obscurity through the degeneracy of his ancestors. He was well versed in Greek and Roman letters ...
> And, before his victory in the civil war the most fortunate of all men, his fortune was never greater than his deserts, and many have hesitated to say whether his bravery or his good luck was greater.

>> 5. **For** as to what he did later, I know not if one should speak of it rather with shame or with sorrow.

6. **Now** Sulla, as I have already said, after he came with his cavalry to Africa and the camp of Marius, soon became ...

Figure 12.1   Sallust, *Jug.* 95–96.1

After having analyzed the structure of the extract on the highest hierarchical level, we may now move on to the analysis of the internal structure of the subsidiary move 2–5, the digression on Sulla. The structure of this segment can best be explained by means of the tree-structure in Figure 12.2, which shows how this embedded move 2–5 may, again, be analyzed in terms of central and subsidiary units. The central unit of the digression is unit 4–5, which comprises the actual description of Sulla. The last element in this description calls for a narratorial comment, which is conveyed by the subsidiary unit 5. The description in 4 is preceded by a subsidiary unit 2–3, in which the narrator announces that he is about to interrupt the narrative main line of his story for a character portrayal. This subsidiary unit is a complex unit itself, in that the announcement in

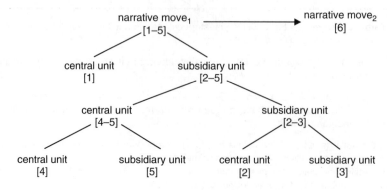

Figure 12.2   Hierarchical structure of Sallust, *Jug.* 95–96.1

segment 2 ("it seems fitting to say a few words about his life and character") is justified in segment 3.[11]

The representation of the text in figure 12.1, with a number of pragmatic markers set in bold face, makes clear that at all major "joints" in the structure there is explicit linguistic marking in the form of a connective particle. Each of these particles seems to cue the reader as to the particular type of transition involved: paratactic transition, embedding, or return.

I already mentioned the discourse particle *ceterum* in segment 1, which signals a transition from one narrative scene or episode to another. At the second major transition, involving a change in text type (the narrative move is interrupted for a descriptive move), we find the connective particle *sed*, which has the function of breaking off the current line of the narration, and of drawing attention to something else. When the narrative is finally resumed in unit 6, this is signaled by the resumption marker *igitur*. The particle is used in the same way in unit 4, where it indicates the start of the actual description after a justificatory "digression."[12] *Enim* in 3 I leave out of the discussion here, for reasons to be explained in the next section.

The description proper, in unit 4, is composed of a series of smaller discourse units of equal communicative status, only the last of which ("before his victory in the civil war the most fortunate of all men, his fortune was never greater than his deserts") calls for a subsidiary remark: the emphatic statement that Sulla's good fortune and industriousness were in balance *before* his victory in the civil war, might leave the reader wondering about this balance *after* this victory, when Sulla had obtained the dictatorship. In the *nam*-segment following segment 4, the narrator justifies the fact that he does not go into this last period of Sulla's career. As a typical marker of subsidiary (i.e. motivating, elaborating, justifying) discourse units, *nam* is an obvious choice in unit 5.

It might be noted that most transitions in the structure of the extract are linguistically articulated in more than one way. In sections 1 and 6, for instance, we observe the use of recapitulating clauses alongside the use of connective particles. Likewise, in sections 4 and 6, the front position in the sentence of the constituent *Sulla* clearly corroborates the function of the connective particles. For a more elaborate discussion of the interaction between the various structuring devices, I refer to Kroon (2009) 150.

Conversation Management Particles

I will end the discussion by providing some more instances of the heterogeneous group of particles that I have referred to above as "conversation-management particles." These particles have in common that they do not, or do not primarily, signal a relation between their host unit and a previous or following unit, but that they somehow point to the relation between the speaker and the hearer, or to the relation between the speaker and the propositional content of his utterance. Particles in this group have to do with speaker and hearer commitment, with epistemic stances towards the content of utterances; with emotional values; with what counts among the interlocutors as controversial or mutually accepted; with the specific illocutionary force of an utterance; and the like. For reasons explained above, I leave out of account here the group of Latin words that express the epistemic stance of the speaker towards the propositional content of the sentence.

Vero, modo, *and other modifiers of directive speech acts*

Two frequently used conversation-management particles in Latin we have already met in the opening sections of this chapter. In **6**, *uero* emphasizes the sincerity of the speaker's intentions in issuing a directive, which results in a quite urgent request:

> **6** nequeo, leno, quin tibi saltem staticulum … uide *uero*, si tibi sati" placet.
> Pimp, I can't refrain from dancing for you that lovely little dance … Do see now (*uide uero*), if it isn't rather winsome. (Pl. *Per.* 824–825)

> **2** fuge *modo* intro, ego uidero
> *just* run away indoors, I'll see to [him]. (Ter. *Ad.* 538)

In **2**, discussed by Risselada (1994) 327, *modo* modifies the directive communicative intention of the speaker by indicating that all that the hearer has to do is run away. The addition of *modo* has a mitigating and reassuring effect here: "don't worry, just go inside, I'll take care." As Risselada convincingly shows, this illocution-modifying use of *modo* is directly related to its use as a proposition-internal "content word," as in the expression *semel modo* ("only once"). Likewise, the illocution-modifying use of *uero* as illustrated in **6** is directly related to its adverbial use, as has been argued on pp. 179–180 above. Other Latin particles that may modify, in various different ways, the directive illocutionary force of an utterance include *age, proinde,* and *sane*.[13]

We may finally mention here the Latin equivalents of English "please" (the lexicalized verbs *amabo, quaeso, sodes*), which all have the capacity to turn the unspecified illocutionary force of an utterance into a directive.

Enim, ergo, nempe

In addition to pragmatic particles that somehow indicate the speaker's own stance towards what he is saying (a phenomenon that is often referred to in terms of subjective modality), languages may also possess linguistic means which shift the responsibility of the content of the utterance wholly or partially to another party (e.g. the addressee), or which otherwise involve other parties in what is being said.

A common example of such a particle in Latin is *enim*, which I have described in Kroon (1995; 1998) as a consensus particle which indicates an appeal to the involvement, cooperation and empathy of the addressee in the communicative event. Good paraphrases in English are *y'know*, *as you know*, or tag questions like *isn't it?* German has a near-equivalent in the particle *ja*. In **24**, taken from Plautus' comedy *Amphitryon*, Mercury apparently uses *enim* for reasons of bonding with the audience. In order to underline the actuality and truth of the content of his statement, he not only uses an epistemic adverb of certainty (*certe*), but also a consensus seeking particle (*enim*, "as you can observe yourself").

> **24** MERCURY (in an aside to the audience, interrupting Sosia's soliloquy):   certe
> *enim* hic nescioquis loquitur.
> Surely (*certe*), someone is speaking here. [*enim* not translated] (Pl. *Am.* 331)

This consensus seeking function of *enim* is highly compatible with the type of coherence relations that is typically indicated by the connective particle *nam* "for" (see above p. 184: explanation, evidence, justification, and the like), but in contrast to *nam*, *enim* does not, or not primarily, express this relationship. At most we could say that *enim* is highly compatible with this type of coherence relationship: on account of its particular function, *enim* may turn a neutral supportive argument into a common-sense argument, which may, of course, strengthen the persuasive power of the argument.

My conclusion that *enim* is not, or not primarily, a connective particle that is more or less synonymous with *nam*, but rather a conversation-management particle which seeks to establish a bond between speaker and hearer, is based on a variety of linguistic and non-linguistic arguments, for which I refer to Kroon (1995) ch. 7. One of the most ponderous arguments is the observation that *enim*, unlike *nam*, can be combined with unequivocal connective particles like *sed*, *et*, and *at*, and can even occur in subordinate clauses, for instance in clauses introduced by the causal subordinate conjunctions *quia* and *quando* ("because"). An example is **25**:

> **25** (Charinus is considering going into exile)
> EUTYCHUS: cur istuc coeptas consilium?
> CHARINUS: quia *enim* me adflictat amor
>
> > "What makes you think of taking such a step as that?"
> > "Because [*quia*] I suffer so from love [*enim* not translated]."
> > (Pl. *Mer.* 648)

The predilection of *enim* for occurring in explanations and other support contexts seems to have led to a widening of the particle's meaning and to a situation in which the particle gives an indication about stances as well as coherence relations. This means that, also synchronically, *enim* may be a conversation-management particle, a connective particle, or both at the same time. In Classical Latin literature, the conversation-management aspect seldom seems to be absent, however.[14]

This same two-sidedness can also be observed for *ergo*, which, like *enim*, combines non-connective, addressee-involving features with a strong tendency to occur with coherence relations, in this case of the inference type. By marking a discourse unit as undoubtedly justified, *ergo* signals that the speaker expects that – on the basis of shared knowledge, general communicative principles and the like – the hearer/reader will also accept the unit as such (Krylová (2006) 96). An illustrative example is **26**. The text quoted contains the last of four instances that Cicero gives of prominent Romans whose houses were destroyed as a consequence of their alleged tyrannical aspirations. Because of this pattern, which is well established at the point of the text where **26** starts, the audience is expected to accept the *ergo*-unit as undoubtedly justified, and as something that they might have concluded already themselves. In this conversation-managing, addressee-involving respect, *ergo* differs from *igitur*, which merely seems to indicate a coherence relation of conclusion.

> **26** M. Manlius ... regnum adpetisse est iudicatus. *ergo* eius domum euersam ... uidetis
> M. Manlius was judged to have aimed at the tyranny. And *therefore* his house was
> razed ..., as you see it to this day. (Cic. *Dom.* 101)

Thus, like *enim*, *ergo* is used as an appeal to the addressee to accept the speaker's standpoint or to identify with his mindset. According to Krylová (2006) 97, *ergo* differs from *enim* in that *enim suggests* consensus, whereas *ergo demands* it. Both particles typically occur in dialogues (for *ergo*, see my remark on p. 188 above), or in monologues with strong dialogical traits.

As a final example of a particle that involves the addressee, we may mention *nempe* (Schrickx (in press) 84–118). A typical example is **27**.

> **27** DEMAENETUS: apud Archibulum ego ero argentarius
> LIBANUS: *nempe* in foro?
> DEMAENETUS: ibi
>
>   "I shall be at banker Archibulus's"
>   "In the forum *you mean?*"
>   "Yes, there." (Pl. *As.* 117)

Here, by using *nempe*, the speaker shifts the responsibility for the content of the utterance to the hearer. The speaker presents the content, so to speak, from the hearer's perspective, and states what the other might have said or thought.

Conclusion

In this chapter I have discussed Latin particles from the point of view of a grammar of discourse, in an attempt to give these words a proper place in the system of the language. A complicating factor turned out to be that linguistic forms that can function as a pragmatic particle typically fulfill other functions as well, either synchronically or diachronically. After having delineated pragmatic particles from uninflected content words, I have sketched the outlines of a discourse grammar, in order to make clear how the Latin pragmatic particles may contribute to establishing a successful communicative interaction. The analysis showed that Latin is rich in particles which indicate, in one way or another, a coherence relation between communicative acts or moves, and also that it has a larger repertory of conversation-management particles than is usually assumed. An extract from Sallust's *Iugurtha* illustrated, moreover, the important role of pragmatic particles as signposts in complex text structures.

I am fully aware that the account given is far from an exhaustive overview, and that much more could be (and has been) said about individual Latin particles, and about the group as a whole.[15] There has been little or no room to go into such interesting matters as the heuristics of studying particles in a dead language;[16] the position of particles in their host unit (first, second, or later); polysemy, diachrony, and grammaticalization;[17] the uneven distribution of particles over various genres and text types;[18] and, especially, the trade-off between pragmatic particles and other linguistic devices in Latin with a function on the level of discourse.[19] All these issues are still in want of more, and more thorough, research, in which use is made of the achievements of modern particle research in general.[20] Studying Latin particles means exploring the realms of discourse. There is still a whole world to be discovered there.

NOTES

1 I thank Mieke Koenen, Harm Pinkster, and Josine Schrickx for their helpful comments on an earlier version of this paper.
2 Discourse may, of course, also include non-linguistic features (gestures) or intonational features (pitch, volume, intonation). Textual discourse may involve both spoken and written language.
3 Already the ancient grammarians had difficulties in assigning the words involved a proper place in the system of the language as they saw it. For the various uses of the term "particle" in the Latin grammatical tradition see Pinkster (1972) ch. 8 n. 2 and, especially, Schenkeveld (1988). An extensive discussion of the treatment of particles (notably conjunctions) by the ancient grammarians can be found in Baratin (1989). For recent discussions on terminology, see e.g. Foolen (1996); Roulet (2006) 119; Hansen (2006) 26–28.
4 All translations have been taken, with few adaptations, from the editions of the Loeb Classical Library.
5 This line of approach can e.g. be found in Kroon (1995) for particular "connective particles," in Risselada (1994; 1998) for certain "modal particles," in Rosén (1994a) and Bertocchi (2001) for the "focus particles" *demum* and *modo*, and in Schrickx (in press) for a number of "epistemic particles." Hand ((1829–1845); 4 vols.) is the only handbook available for Latin particles in general. Although it was written almost two centuries ago, and never reached completion, it still counts as a valuable source of information on Latin particles.
6 For this observation, see Foolen (1996) 6. For the distinction between particles and interjections, see Hansen (1998) 38–41.
7 This is not to say that focus particles cannot have an interaction-managing side-effect. As a matter of fact, focus particles often play an important role in steering the communication in a certain direction, in the same way as evaluative adjectives and adverbs may do. Cf. e.g. the different argumentative directions of the English expressions *a small chance* and *little chance* in the following sentences, addressed by a lawyer to his client: "There is a small chance that we will win the case" and "There is little chance that we will win the case." Although objectively

the chances for the client may be the same, the specific choice of words of the lawyer may strongly influence the decision of the client whether or not to undertake legal action.

8   The account given in this chapter links up especially with the Geneva Discourse Model (see e.g. Roulet *et al.* (1985; 2001); Filliettaz and Roulet (2002)) and with Functional Discourse Grammar (see Hengeveld and Mackenzie (2008; 2010).

9   The type of coherence relations illustrated in **13–15** may also be signaled by such adverbs as *tamen* ("all the same") and *nihilominus* ("nevertheless"). However, as is shown by Pinkster (2004) and Spevak (2006), *tamen* and *nihilominus* differ from *sed*, *nam* and *igitur* in a number of syntactic respects.

10   I have discussed this text earlier in Kroon (1995) 83–88 and (2009) 147–150.

11   The *quoniam*-clause in segment 2 might qualify for independent act status, in which case segment 2 should be split up further into a central and a subsidiary unit. For the sake of clarity I have refrained from pushing the analysis to the level of the individual act, here and in the other sections.

12   Polanyi and Scha (1983) introduced the evocative terms "push marker" and "pop marker" for connective particles that mark digressions and resumptions, respectively. *Ceterum* and *sed* are clear push markers here (shifting the discourse temporarily into a different direction), whereas *igitur* is a typical pop marker (bringing the discourse back to its initial track). For *igitur* as a pop marker, see Kroon (1989; 2004). An example in which the resumptive nature of the *igitur*-unit is made explicit is Cic. *Orat.* 33: *Referamus igitur ad eum incohanum* ("Let us return, then, to our task of delineating that ideal orator").

13   For *sane*, see Risselada (1994; 1998). Other particles that frequently occur in directives are *dum* and *quin*. For a detailed overview of the various uses of *quin*, see Fleck (2008).

14   See however Langslow (2000a) for some observations from a diachronic point of view, and for the different way in which *enim* (and other particles) behave in a corpus of non-literary, technical Latin prose texts.

15   Latin has many more pragmatic markers than I could discuss in this chapter. Rosén (2009) 385–389 lists 120 different particles in literary Classical Latin, including, however, focus particles and epistemic adverbs.

16   See e.g. Kroon (1995) ch. 5; Rosén (2009) 336–350.

17   See e.g. Langslow (2000a), Rosén (2009), and Schrickx (in press).

18   An example is the unequal distribution of *enim* in Cicero's correspondence. In his letters to his friend Atticus, Cicero uses *enim* much more frequently than in the quite formal *ad Familiares*, which are letters to business partners and political connections. Apparently the letters *ad Familiares* lend themselves less well for appeals to involvement of the addressee and to shared knowledge. Likewise, in Caesar's *Gallic War enim* is almost absent outside (in)direct speech, and far less frequent than in his *Civil War*. Here, too, the difference in distribution might be ascribed to a difference in audience and subject matter, but probably also to Caesar's intentionally detached style in the *Gallic War*, which is hardly compatible with an interactional particle like *enim*. See further Kroon (1995) 123–124.

19   A wealth of details on most of these subjects can be found in Rosén (2009).

20   For the state of the art in particle research in general, see Fischer (2006) and Celle and Huart (2007).

PART III

Latin Through Time

CHAPTER 13

The Historical Background to Latin within the Indo-European Language Family

Benjamin W. Fortson IV

Proto-Indo-European: Who, When, and What?

Priscian (*GL* II.455.6–7) called attention to the fact that a number of words in Latin begin with *s-* while their Greek equivalents begin with a *spiritus asper*, like Lat. *sex* and Gk. ἕξ, or *septem* and ἑπτά. In so doing he stumbled upon the principle of the regularity of sound correspondences, which centuries later would form the cornerstone of the modern science of comparative linguistics. The ancients could not draw the same conclusions from these correspondences that we do now; the Romans generally viewed Latin as derived from Greek, rather than both as descendants of a common ancestor. Much later scholars would be aided in their interpretation of these correspondences by the addition of languages about which the Romans knew nothing – principally Sanskrit, which became known to Westerners in the wake of British colonial expansion into India and which provided the crucial third member of the comparison. Nearly two centuries' worth of scientific comparison of Greek, Latin, Sanskrit, and their relatives has garnered us the understanding that they are derived from a common prehistoric ancestor, Proto-Indo-European (PIE), and has allowed us to reconstruct that ancestor in considerable detail. Most linguists believe this language was spoken in the fourth millennium BCE in the steppe region north of the Black and Caspian Seas, though there are a number of alternative views. Gradual expansion and fragmentation of the original population resulted in increasing dialectal divergence, ultimately giving rise to ten branches that have entered the historical record – Anatolian, Indo-Iranian, Greek, Italic, Celtic, Germanic, Armenian, Tocharian, Balto-Slavic, and Albanian. A few poorly attested languages, such as Messapic and Lusitanian, are unaffiliated and may represent additional branches; there may have been others that have vanished without a trace.

A Companion to the Latin Language, First Edition. Edited by James Clackson.
© 2011 Blackwell Publishing Ltd. Published 2011 by Blackwell Publishing Ltd.

The linguistic ancestors of the Romans were among the early Indo-European (IE) groups that moved westward into Europe; probably by the mid-second millennium BCE speakers of Proto-Italic had arrived in the Po Valley from the northeast. This language would ultimately spawn two, possibly three, known branches: Latino-Faliscan, Sabellic (or Osco-Umbrian), and (in many scholars' view) Venetic. Of these, Sabellic became the most widely represented by the mid-first millennium, in terms of numbers of speakers, varieties of languages, and geographical spread; its members (Oscan, Umbrian, South Picene, Paelignian, and various others) were scattered throughout most of central and eastern Italy. Latin and Faliscan (the latter now increasingly considered merely a dialect of the former) were confined to a minor corner of the west, though of course the fortunes of this minor corner would one day vastly outstrip the fortunes of all the others. Venetic, spoken in extreme northeastern Italy, may represent an early hiving-off from the Proto-Italic group whose other members continued moving farther south.

Since a living language does not exist absent a people and culture, the reconstruction of PIE, together with archaeological finds and comparison of the texts in ancient IE languages, has opened a window onto PIE culture. It is generally agreed that the Indo-Europeans had a fairly typical late Neolithic pastoralist economy; were comprised of patriarchal and patrilocal family units; worshiped a polytheistic pantheon headed by a god of the daytime sky; placed especial value on reciprocity in both economic and religious spheres; had a stratified society containing an elite class of warriors and clan-chiefs integrally connected with praise-poets, who also occupied a crucial role in the transmission of warrior-class values and religion; and probably possessed wheeled vehicles and domesticated horses.

Many of these social characteristics are continued virtually unchanged in early Roman culture and in the cultures of related Italic peoples. The Roman *pater familias* in his role as head of the household continues a familiar Indo-European social role. The Roman patron–client system comprises mutually beneficial and interdependent relationships and obligations that likely go back to similar systems of reciprocity in PIE times. The head of the Roman pantheon, Jupiter/Jove, is directly descended from the PIE sky-god (note the older meaning "sky" is still discernible in the phrase *sub Ioue* "in the open air," literally "under Jove" and etymologically "under the sky"). The Roman emphasis on correct ritual procedure and exacting use of formulaic phrases in both law and cultic practice has many analogs throughout the IE world and is doubtless inherited. The aristocratic military elite that were the driving force behind Rome's rise (and many of her ills), with their heady competition for glory and status, were the latter-day version of the PIE warrior who sought "imperishable fame" – one of the complete noun phrases that can be reconstructed for the proto-language (*$\hat{k}leu̯os$ $n̥dhg^{w}hitom$*) and clearly of high cultural importance.

And on the purely linguistic side, Latin itself betrays its Indo-European origins in every paradigm and corner of the grammar. But the two to three millennia separating Latin from PIE have wrought considerable change, and below we will examine all the major developments in phonology, morphology, and syntax. For each of these areas of grammar, we will first present a brief look at the linguistic picture painted for it for PIE, and then follow how that evolved into the descendant Latin system. (A fuller overview of the reconstruction of PIE may be found in Fortson (2010), with references to additional technical literature for the details.) It should be borne in mind that without the hope of our finding any written records in the language, PIE will forever be a hypothesis, and researchers differ on many details. The views outlined below, however, are generally uncontroversial.

The History of the Sounds of Latin

Most of the reconstructed PIE consonants were stops (plosives), of which there were a total of fifteen, divisible into three series according to voicing and aspiration (voiceless, voiced, and voiced aspirated), with each series represented at five places of articulation (bilabial, alveolar [or dental], and three that are collectively termed velar or dorsal: palatal velar, plain velar, and labiovelar). These stops are notated $p\ t\ \hat{k}\ k\ k^w$ (voiceless), $b\ d\ \hat{g}\ g\ g^w$ (voiced), and $bh\ dh\ \hat{g}h\ gh\ g^wh$ (voiced aspirated, also written $b^h\ d^h\ \hat{g}^h\ g^h\ g^{wh}$). The voiced aspirated stops were pronounced with a puff of breath or breathy voice following release of the stop. The palatal velars ($\hat{k}\ \hat{g}\ \hat{g}h$) were pronounced farther forward than the plain velars ($k\ g\ gh$), somewhat like the *k* in the word *kit* as contrasted with the more posterior *k* in the word *karma*. Most branches collapsed at least two of the three velar series, including Italic; for the purposes of Italic historical linguistics there is no need to distinguish original $\hat{k}\ \hat{g}\ \hat{g}h$ from $k\ g\ gh$, but for conventional reasons the distinction will be maintained below in citing PIE forms.

In addition to these stops, PIE had one sibilant, *s*, allophonically voiced to *z* before another voiced consonant; thus **nizdos* "nest," the source of Lat. *nīdus* and Eng. *nest*, was underlyingly **ni-* "down" + **sd-*, a reduced form of the root **sed-* "sit" + the stem-vowel **-o-*, i.e. literally "where (the bird) sits down." (An asterisk indicates that a form is reconstructed.) There were also four resonants, the two liquids *l r* and the two nasals *m n*. These had the important feature of occurring in either consonantal or syllabic value depending on the nature of the surrounding sounds: between other consonants, for example, they effectively acted as vowels and formed the peak of the syllable. In their vocalic role they are conventionally notated with a subscript circle, e.g. **tn̥tos* "held (taut)" > Lat. *tentus* "held" (cp. Gk. τατός "able to be stretched"). This property is shared with two further consonants, the glides or semivowels *i̯ u̯* (or *y w*), whose syllabic allophones were the high vowels *i* and *u*.

Rounding out the inventory of consonants were three of disputed phonetic value, termed laryngeals. (A few scholars posit a lesser or greater number.) These do not directly survive as consonants except in the Anatolian languages, where their reflexes are an assortment of velars or gutturals; elsewhere they sometimes became vowels and sometimes disappeared, but also left many indirect traces. Most agree that they were *h*- or *kh*-like sounds of one kind or another in the proto-language. Given these uncertainties, they are algebraically notated as $h_1\ h_2\ h_3$ (or $ə_1\ ə_2\ ə_3$). Two of their indirect traces are especially important with regards to Latin. A short *e* when directly adjacent to an h_2 was changed ("colored") to *a* already in PIE, while an *e* next to an h_3 was colored to *o*. Thus **$h_2$enti* "opposite, in front of" became **$h_2$anti* > Lat. *ante*; **$h_3$ek^w-* "see; eye" > **$h_3$ok^w-* > Lat. *oc-ulus* "eye." The second important trace came about (a bit paradoxically) as a by-product of the laryngeals' disappearance: if a laryngeal directly followed a short vowel, the vowel basically absorbed the laryngeal and became lengthened as a result (a process termed compensatory lengthening). Thus **dheh₁-* "place, put" > **dhē-* (becoming the first syllable of Lat. *fē-cī*), **steh₂-* "stand" > **stah₂-* **stā-* as in Lat. *stā-re*, **deh₃-* "give" > **doh₃-* > **dō-* > Lat. *dō-num*. The laryngeals also left direct traces when standing between consonants: somewhat analogous to the resonants and glides, in this position they became vocalized or syllabic, probably by sprouting a short prop vowel. These vocalized variants became *a* in Italic (and other vowels in the other branches). Thus Lat. *pater*, Gk. πατήρ, and Sanskrit *pitắ* (stem *pitár-*) all descend from PIE *ph₂tér "father," with the first vowel in each descendant form the respective outcome of a vocalized *h₂*.

We have already seen a few of the PIE vowels – the high vowels *i* and *u*, the mid vowels *e* and *o*, and the low back vowel *a*. These also had long counterparts, *ī ū ē ō ā*. This basic vowel system is continued intact in Latin, though we will see later that there were many changes to individual vowels in particular word-positions. Additionally, the non-high short vowels *e o a* could combine with a following high vowel *i* or *u* to produce the diphthongs *ei oi ai eu ou au*; less commonly, the long vowels could do the same, producing *ēi ēu ōu*, etc. These are not as stable as the monophthongs in Latin, as discussed further below.

Sounds in combination with other sounds often undergo special changes. Two of interest to students of Latin, and already of PIE date, will be mentioned here. The first was regressive voicing assimilation of stops: if two adjacent stops differed in voicing, the voicing of the first assimilated to that of the second. In most of the known examples, the second stop was voiceless and caused devoicing of a preceding voiced stop. The effects live on in Latin forms like *īn-flīc-tus* "struck" from underlying **flīg-t-* (cp. present *flīgō*) and *lāp-sus* "slid" from underlying **lāb-s-*. The second combinatorial sound change occurred in consonant clusters consisting of two dentals. Such clusters were frequent at morpheme boundaries because several important suffixes began with *t* and many roots to which these suffixes were added ended in a dental. Between the two dentals a sibilant developed, whence in the first instance *tst, *dzd, and the like; in Italic, these combinations ultimately developed to *ss*. This is the source of perfect participles like *fissus* "split" alongside *findō*, *fīdī*: the form goes back to *bhid-tos in PIE. By the time of Classical Latin, the *ss* was simplified to *s* except after short vowels, whence e.g. *rōsus* "gnawed" from *rōssus (*rōd-tos, cp. *rōdō*), *caesus* "cut" from *caessus (*kaid-tos, cp. *caedō*), and *pēnsus* "weighed out" from *pēnssus (*pend-tos, cp. *pendeō*).

The Italic branch as a whole underwent significant change to the inherited PIE stop consonant system. As already intimated, the three series of velars were reduced to two, a plain velar series (*k g gh*) and a labiovelar series (*kʷ gʷ gʷh*) – a change found also in Greek, Celtic, and Germanic. More notable was the fate of the voiced aspirates, which in most positions lost their status as stops and became fricatives (spirants). In the Sabellic (or Osco-Umbrian) sub-branch of Italic, the aspirated stops mostly merged as *f* (probably allophonically voiced to *v* or a bilabial fricative β between vowels). In Latin the developments were far more complex, with two basic outcomes: *f* or *h* word-initially and a voiced stop (*b d g* or *gu*) word-internally. Here Latin differs even from its closely related sister language (or dialect) Faliscan, where *f* is found word-internally as well (**carefo** "I will do without" = Lat. *carēbō*, with Fal. **f** and Lat. *b* continuing *bh). See Table 13.1, where in particular the complicated changes affecting *dh are to be noted.

Of significance also are the changes to the syllabic resonants. In most IE branches, these sprouted vowels before them, and this was true in Italic also. Syllabic **r̥* and **l̥* became *or* and *ol* (the latter typically becoming *ul* in Latin), while **m̥* and **n̥* became

Table 13.1   Development of PIE voiced aspirates in Latin

PIE	Latin	Phonetic environment	Example
*bh	f	word-initially	*$bher$- > $fer\bar{o}$ "I carry"
	b	word-internally	*$albho$- > $albus$ "white"
*dh	f	word-initially	*$dheg^wh$- "burn" > $fou\bar{e}re$ "keep warm"
	b	after u	*h_1rudh- "red" > $rub\bar{e}re$ "be red"
		after r	*$\mu erdho$- > $uerbum$ "word"
		word-internally before r or l	*$ghladh$-ro- > $glabro$- "smooth"
			sth_2-$dhlo$- > $stabulum$ ($stablum$) "stable"
	d	word-internally elsewhere	*$medh\mu o$- > $medius$ "middle"
*$gh/\hat{g}h$	$h, \emptyset$	word-initially before vowel	*$\hat{g}hortos$ > $hortus$ "garden"
			*$\hat{g}hans$- > $\bar{a}nser$ "goose"
	g	word-initially before l	*$ghladh$-ro- > $glabro$- "smooth"
	f	word-initially before r or u	*$ghrendh$- > $frendere$ "grind"
			*$\hat{g}hud$-to- > $f\bar{u}sus$ "poured"
	h	word-internally between vowels	*$\mu e\hat{g}h$-e- > $uehere$ "convey"
	g	word-internally after consonant	*$an\hat{g}h$- "tight" > $angustus$ "narrow"
*g^wh	f	word-initially	*g^when- "smite" > ($d\bar{e}$-)$fendere$ "ward off"
	u (μ)	word-internally between vowels	*$snig^wh$- > $niuis$ (gen.) "snow"
	gu	after n	*$sning^wh$- > $ninguere$ "to snow"

em and *en* (though another development *am*, *an* seems to be found in Sabellic in word-initial position). Later in the history of Latin a new set of syllabic resonants was generated after certain sequences of resonant plus vowel lost the vowel (see below).

As noted above, the vocalizations of all the laryngeals became *a* in Italic (most famously in the initial syllable of the word for "father," Lat. *pater* <*$ph_2t\bar{e}r$*; but note also *datus* "given" <*dh_3tos* and Oscan accus. **anamúm** "life," Lat. *animus* "soul" <*h_2enh_1mos*; compare Greek πατήρ "father," δοτός "given," and ἄνεμος "wind," where famously the vocalic reflexes of the three laryngeals were kept distinct). The sibilant *s* remained intact in the first instance, though the voiced allophone *z* was lost with compensatory lengthening of the preceding vowel (besides *nīdus* "nest" above, note also *sīdō* "sit down" <*$sizd\bar{o}$*, originally *si-sd-$\bar{o}$* with the same structure as *sistō* "set up").

In the prehistory and early attested history of Latin itself, many more changes to the consonants took place. Most well-known was rhotacism, whereby *s* between vowels became *r*, whence alternations of the type *es-t* "is" with preserved *s* next to *er-it* "will be" with intervocalically rhotacized *s*. (The older, pre-rhotacism form *esed* is preserved on the Forum Inscription or Lapis Niger from *c.* 500 BCE. See further below for more on the morphology of this form.) Compare also such pairs as *ges-tus* "waged"/*ger-ō* "I wage," *us-tus* "burned"/*ūr-ō* "I burn," and *hones-tus* "honorable, honest"/*honōr-is* "of honor." (Sometimes an *r* that arose by rhotacism spread to other forms by analogy; such is the case with nom. sg. *honor*, which replaced older *honōs*. The original paradigm *honōs honōsem* became *honōs honōrem* by rhotacism and then *honor honōrem* by analogy.) The process was probably completed in Latin by the early fourth century BCE; Cicero (*Fam.* 9.21.2) mentions that L. Papirius Crassus, dictator in 339 BCE, was the first in his family to modernize the spelling of his *gentilicium* from Papisius to Papirius. Classical Latin words containing an *s* between vowels, such as *causa* "reason," *caesus* "(having been) cut," and *uīsus* "seen," go back to forms containing double *s*, as we noted earlier.

The greatest number of changes, however, took place in consonant clusters, which were subject to significant simplifications and other alterations. Chief among these were simplifications of clusters containing an *s* and a resonant and often additional consonants, where the tendency was to lose all but the resonant. From the root **ieug-* "yoke" a pre-Latin noun **iougsmentom* "team of oxen" was formed, attested in the Lapis Niger as pl. *iouxmenta*; the cluster *-ksm-* (written *xm*) was in time whittled down to just *m*, resulting in Classical *iūmentum*. Similarly, the preverb *ex-* "out of" became *ē-* before resonants, whence e.g. *ē-lūcēre* "to shine out" from **eks-l-*. These changes also explain some of the curious alternations seen between diminutive forms and their bases, such as between diminutive *pastillus* "small loaf" and the base *pānis* "loaf": *pānis* was originally **past-nis*.

Also of note was the weakening of the voiced labiovelar **gʷ* to just *u̯* in most positions, e.g. *uīuō* "I live" < **gʷīu̯ō*. (In the Sabellic languages, **gʷ* became *b*, whence e.g. Oscan **biítam** "life" alongside Lat. *uītam*. The general development of the labiovelars to labial stops is characteristic of Sabellic vis-à-vis Latino-Faliscan, and tells us, among other things, that the Latin noun *bōs* "cow" must be a loanword from a Sabellic language since the original initial consonant was **gʷ*. The Romans must have earlier called the animal a **uōs*!) Other changes affected the labiovelars as well; in particular **kʷ* was subject to delabialization, becoming just *k*, when next to a rounded vowel (*o* or *u*) or preceding another consonant. The participle *coctus* "cooked" contains an instance of both changes, as both *c*'s continue earlier **kʷ*- (Italic root **kʷekʷ-* "cook," modified from PIE **pekʷ-*). Note also archaic *quom* "when" becoming Classical *cum*, and forms like *relictus* "left behind" alongside present *relinquō*.

The system of vowels and diphthongs was inherited into Latin nearly intact, the only Italic change of note having been the merger of the diphthongs *eu* and *ou* as *ou*. (That rare inscriptional spellings with *eu* continue unshifted original *eu* is doubtful.) Even the long diphthong *ōi* is preserved in the early Latin dat. sg. spelled *-oi*. (We know this was pronounced as *-ōi* and not *-oi* because it became Classical Latin *-ō*, while *-oi* became Classical Latin *-ī*.) But during the language's attested history, unstressed vowels were beset by an onslaught of reductions, and several of the diphthongs were monophthongized. Latin stress was fixed on the initial syllable to start with (see further the end of this section); thus all syllables after the first were pronounced less strongly and were therefore subject to weakening. (After the changeover to the Classical stress pattern, such syllables could, and did, wind up bearing the main word stress, as in several of the examples below.) The changes are complex, but the general outlines are as follows. In unstressed open syllables, short vowels were reduced to *i*: thus *cōnficiō* "put together" from **cónfaciō*, *contineō* "contain" from **cónteneō*, and *agricola* "farmer" from **ágrocola*. In closed syllables, *a* was reduced to *e*, as in *cōnfectus* from **cónfactos*. Apparent exceptions, such as the *o* in *agricola* or the *a* in *complaceō* "capture the fancy of," are due to analogical influence from the simplex or the root (*colō* "till, cultivate," *placeō* "be pleasing"), or the compound was formed only after the weakening rules had run their course. Quite often the expected outcome has been obscured by other changes caused by surrounding consonants. For example, the compound *ob-* + *celō* is *occulō* "conceal"

Table 13.2　Vowel changes from PIE to Latin

PIE	Latin	Phonetic environment	Examples
i	*e*	word-finally	*$h_2$anti > ante* "before"
		before *r* (also *r* < **z*) in open syllables	**ish$_2$o- > erus* "master" (< **izos*)
	i	everywhere else	**linkʷ- > linquere* "leave"
u	*i*	initial syllables between *l* and labial	OL *lubet > libet* "it pleases"
	o	before *r* (also *r* < **z*) in open syllables	**fuse > *fuze > fore* "to be about to be"
	u	everywhere else	**rupto- > ruptus* "broken"
e	*i*	unstressed internal open syllables	**kontenēs > continēs* "you contain"
		before [ŋ] and sometimes other nasals	**dengua >* OL *dingua > lingua* "tongue" **en > in* "in"
	o	before "dark" *l*	**u̯elomos > uolumus* **u̯elt(i) >* OL *uolt*
	e	everywhere else	**ped- > pedis* (gen.) "foot"
o	*u*	final syllables	**prokos > procus* "suitor"
		before "dark" *l* plus consonant	OL *uolt >* Class. *uult* "wants"
		before [ŋ]	**onkos > uncus* "hook"
	o	everywhere else	**(s)tog-ā* "covering" *> toga* "toga"
a	*i*	unstressed internal open syllables	**kónkapis > concipis* "you perceive"
	e	unstressed internal closed syllables	**konkaptos > conceptus* "perceived"
	a	everywhere else	**kap- > capere* "take"

and not **occilō* because all short unstressed vowels became rounded to *u* (the round counterpart of *i*) before a so-called "dark" *l* (in this case, an *l* preceding a back vowel). Similarly, *ad + tangō* yields *attingō* "touch" rather than **attengō* because of a rule that *e* was raised to *i* before *ng*. These changes cannot be gone into here; see Leumann 1977 and Weiss 2009 for much fuller treatments.

Diphthongs, too, were treated differently when not under the accent. While stressed **ai* underwent a trifling change to *ae* (with slight lowering of the second vowel), unstresssed **ai* was monophthongized to *ī*, as in the compound *occīdō* "kill" from **ób-kaidō* and the first person sg. perfect indicative ending *-ī* from earlier **-ai* (attested in Faliscan *peparai* "I have given birth").

Not all vowel changes were conditioned by the position of the accent. Before a rhotacized *s*, an old *i* was lowered to *e* regardless of the stress: thus *serō* "I sow" comes from **si-s-ō* (a reduplicated present like *sistō* and *sīdō* above, with the internal *-s-* the only remnant of the inherited root for "sow") and the pluperfect indicative active stem *-erā-* comes from **-isā-*, with the same element *-is-* found in the perfect infinitive *-is-se*. For a fuller (if still incomplete) overview of changes to short vowels, see Table 13.2.

The final change to vowels to be discussed was syncope, the deletion of an unstressed vowel. Different syncopes occurred at different times in the history and prehistory of the language. Of special interest was the deletion of vowels in word-final syllables of the type *-rVs*. The resultant sequence *-rs* was syllabified as *-r̥s* (technically "*-r̥₂s*" to distinguish this new syllabic *r* from an inherited IE syllabic *r*), which sprouted an *e* in front of it to yield *-ers*. Subsequently the *-s* was lost. This is the source of the masc. nom. sg. ending of second-declension nouns and adjectives of the type *ager, sacer* from **agros, sakros* (the latter directly attested on the Lapis Niger), and of third-declension masculine adjectives of the type *alācer* from **alācris*. (The fem. *alācris* actually continues **alākrīs*.)

Before moving onto morphology, the Latin stress system should be briefly discussed, for it is substantially different from the one reconstructed for PIE. PIE had a mobile pitch-accent system of the type still attested in Vedic Sanskrit and, with some further changes, in Ancient Greek. Accented syllables were marked by a rise in pitch, and the accent could fall on any syllable of a word. By pre-Latin, and probably Proto-Italic, times this system had changed to one of stress on the initial syllable of all words. (A few indirect traces of the earlier mobility of the accent may survive in the different outcomes of certain vocalic sequences when under and not under the accent, though these are controversial and the subject of ongoing research.) Longer words also received secondary stresses in word-interiors; the familiar Classical stress pattern, whereby the accent falls on the penult if heavy and otherwise the antepenult, appears to have arisen from a reinterpretation of these secondary stresses as primary. This system did not arise until toward the end of the ante-Classical period. There is some evidence that prior to this an ante-antepenultimate stress was possible on words of the type *hominibus*, in which both penult and antepenult were light.

In PIE, full lexical items received an accent under normal conditions. The language also possessed unstressed enclitic particles, including conjunctions like **kʷe* "and" (> Lat. *-que*) and unstressed versions of the personal pronouns. Verbs, too, could be more weakly stressed or destressed in certain contexts; the contraction (aphaeresis) of forms of *esse* "to be" found especially in the early Latin dramatic poets may be related to this, but it could also have arisen independently. In fluent speech in living languages, not all words are stressed equally, but the stresses of some words are subordinated to those of others depending on their position within a phrase or larger prosodic unit. PIE surely behaved the same way, and evidence especially from poetry has shed some light on such phenomena in Latin. Close study of these matters can reveal aspects of prosodic organization and syntactic structure (Fortson 2008, with references to earlier literature).

The Prehistory of Latin Nouns and Adjectives

The morphological system of PIE will be quite familiar to students of the Classical languages. Words consisted of a root (an abstract form expressing a particular semantic concept), usually followed by one or more derivational suffixes, followed by a grammatical ending. Prefixes were rare, though compounding in nouns and adjectives was common; the many prefixes of Latin represent old adverbial elements that used to be free-floating (see further below). Roots are conventionally cited in the form containing the vowel *e* (e.g. **sed-* "sit," **ped-* "foot," **bher-* "carry"), but in specific derivational and inflectional contexts they often took on other guises characterized by a different internal vowel, a lengthened vowel, or no vowel at all. This system of vocalic alternations, called ablaut, was central to the PIE morphological system, being encountered not only at the level of the root but also in derivational suffixes and inflectional endings. It is still clearly discernible in Latin in such word-groups as *teg-ō* "I cover"/*tog-a* "covering, toga"/*tēg-ula* "roof-tile" and *sed-eō* "I sit"/*solium* (earlier **sodium*) "throne"/*sēd-ēs* "seat." (Ablaut is also what lies behind the vowel alternations in "irregular" English verbal paradigms like *sing/sang/sung*, *sit/sat* and nominal derivatives like *song* and *seat* or *soot* [originally "stuff that sits/settles"] – not to mention *ne-st* from the above discussion.) The basic citation form with *e* is called the *e*-grade, alongside which there existed *o*-grade, zero-grade (absence of a vowel), and lengthened *e*- and *o*-grades.

PIE knew two basic types of inflection, called thematic and athematic, found in both nominal and verbal paradigms. Thematic inflection was characterized by the presence of an ablauting stem-vowel (*o* alternating with *e*) before the inflectional ending; athematic words lacked this vowel. The inflectional endings themselves, however, were largely identical in thematic and athematic inflections. Additionally, the position of the accent typically fluctuated within a paradigm in athematic paradigms, but not in thematic ones; and in athematic paradigms, some or all the morphemes exhibited different ablaut grades in different inflectional forms.

Inflectible parts of speech were nouns, pronouns, adjectives, verbs, and the lower cardinal numerals one through four. Nouns and adjectives declined identically, while pronouns exhibited several special inflectional endings. All these parts of speech were inflected in three numbers, singular, dual, and plural. Nominals and pronominals sported nine cases: nominative, vocative, accusative, genitive, ablative, dative, instrumental, locative, and probably an allative or directive case that is still productive in Anatolian but not in the attested histories of the other branches. In accordance with a cross-linguistic tendency, the singular exhibited more overt case-distinctions than the plural and (especially) the dual.

When one includes the vocative, the locative, and forms like the *quī-* of *quī-cum* "with whom" that are old instrumentals, Latin preserves all the eight most securely reconstructible cases of PIE. The disputed ninth case, the allative or directive, has been seen by some to underlie the adverbial *quō* "whither" and similar forms. But though the inherited categories remained, there was much formal renewal and reshuffling, and the rise of formally distinct "declensions" was a significant innovation over against the ancient distinction between thematic and athematic inflection.

PIE formally distinguished animate from inanimate nouns and adjectives in the nominative and (to a lesser extent) the accusative. Animate nom. sgs were usually characterized by an ending **-s*, while inanimate nom. sgs lacked it. Compare Latin animate (masc./fem.) *facili-s* and inanimate (neuter) *facile* (earlier **facili*). Also as in Latin, the nom., voc., and acc. of inanimates were identical. The neuter plurals in *-a* go back to an ending **-eh₂* that was originally a collective plural, referring to a group of entities; such a group could be thought of as a single entity, which is why its descendant in Greek (as well as Old Avestan and the Anatolian languages) takes singular rection with verbs. (This is the traditional explanation, though some new research may lead to a revision of this understanding.) Collective plurals could be formed originally not just to neuters but also to animate nouns; a trace of this is found in the fact that *locus* has both plurals *locī* and *loca*. Compare from Hittite the animate noun *alpaš* "cloud" and its "count" pl. *alpeš* "clouds" alongside collective pl. *alpa* "group of clouds, cloudbank."

The status of the feminine gender in PIE is the topic of much debate (Anatolian, the oldest branch, does not have a distinct feminine gender). For the purposes of Latin, the feminine agrees functionally and morphologically with the same category in most of the other older IE languages.

The thematic declension is continued by the Latin second declension. In PIE, thematic endings consisted of the *o*-grade of the thematic vowel plus a case ending. The only exception was the voc. **-e* (continued unchanged in Latin), formally the bare stem-vowel in the *e*-grade. The *u*-vowel that characterizes the Latin forms *-us* and *-um* has been raised from earlier *-o-*, which is still abundantly found on inscriptions. Directly inherited from PIE are the nominative singulars *-us*, *-um*, and pl. *-a* (the masc. pl. *-ī*, earlier *-oi*, is taken from the pronominal declension and replaced the original nominal ending **-ōs*, which survives in Sabellic); the vocative; the accusative; the dative and ablative singulars (the latter shortened from earlier *-ōd*); and the archaic or poetic gen. pl. *-um*. (The longer *-ōrum* is modeled on the *-ārum* of the first declension.) The PIE genitive singular was **-osi̯o*, surviving only in the name *Popliosio Valesiosio* "of Publius Valerius" on the Lapis Satricanus inscription from the fifth century BCE; the familiar ending *-ī* is also found in Celtic and perhaps a few other European branches. The locative *-ī* is also a direct inheritance, PIE **-ei* or *-oi*. The dative/ablative plural *-īs* is partly a continuation of the PIE instrumental pl. **-ois* or **-ōis* and partly perhaps a continuation of the PIE locative plural **-oisu*.

The other four Latin declensions are historically athematic. Though superficially divergent from one another by Latin times, originally they were all formed by the addition of identical case-endings directly to a consonant or high vowel *i* or *u*. These endings were mostly the same as the thematic endings minus the thematic vowel: sg. nom. animate **-s*, voc. **-ø*, acc. **-m*, gen.-abl. **-(e/o)s* (**-es* became the normal third-declension gen. *-is*; **-os* is found archaically as *-us* in e.g. *nōminus Latīnī* "of the Latin name"), dat. **-ei*, instr. **-h₁*, locative **-(e)i*. (Another so-called "endingless" locative was characterized by "strengthening" of the ablaut grade of the stem-final morpheme, without an overt ending; because of various sound changes it is not clear whether this type is continued in Latin.) In the plural PIE had anim. nom.-voc. **-es*, acc. **-ns*, gen. **-om*, instr. **-bhi(s)*, loc. **-su*, and a desinence beginning with **-bh-* in the dative and ablative. Athematic neuters had zero ending in the nominative, vocative, and accusative singular and **-(e)h₂* in the collective plural.

The stem-vowel *-ā-* of the first declension continues the morpheme **-eh₂-*, which functioned both as an abstract and as a feminine suffix. In the nom. sg., both **-eh₂-* and **-eh₂-s* are reflected in the daughter languages; the latter may be continued in archaic forms like *parricidās* "one who commits parricide." The reason the vowel in Latin nom. sg. *-a* is short is disputed: some believe all final long *a*s were shortened prehistorically (a few instances of long *-ā* in archaic poetry might be survivals of this, but they could also be artificial), while others think that the *-a* is an old vocative that took over nomina-tive function. The genitive was **-eh₂-(e)s > -ās* in the first instance, preserved in the phrase *pater familiās*; this was remodeled using the *-ī* of the thematics to *-āī* (still found in Archaic and archaizing poetry). Classical *-ae* is a contraction of *-āī*, created using the second-declension genitive ending. The dative in *-ae* is from *-āi* from earlier *-eh₂-ei*. The stem-vowel *ā* was regularly shortened before final *-m* to yield acc. sg. *-am*; the ablative was archaically *-ād*, with *-d* imported from the thematic declension already in Italic times. The nom. pl. *-ae* appears to be from *-āi*, a remodeling of the inherited nom. pl. *-ās* on the model of the second-declension *-oi*. The gen. pl. *-ārum*, from *-āsom*, is taken over from the pronominal declension. The original dat.-abl. pl. should have been *-ābos*, which was replaced early by *-āis > *-ais > -eis > -īs*. The occasionally attested examples of *-ābus* (as in *deābus, fīliābus*) are actually analogically created innovations rather than old inheritances.

The bulk of athematic declensional types falls into the Latin consonant stems of the third declension. The lack of an *-s* at the end of some animate nominative singulars is the result of sound change. In the case of *n*-stem nominatives in *-ō* (such as *nātiō* and *testūdō*) and *r*-stem nominatives like *pater, āctor*, the loss of both the *-s* and the *-n* was of PIE date. A nominative like *mīles* was pronounced *mīless* in Plautus' day, from *mīlet-s*. Transparent are e.g. *ferōx* from *ferōc-s, rēx* from *rēg-s*, and *dap-s*.

Forming the other group of third-declension nouns are the *i*-stems. Here the stem alternated originally between zero-grade *-i-* and full-grade *-ei-*. Nom. sg. *-is* is typical of this declension, though the *-i-* was often syncopated in Latin (whence e.g. *mēns urbs*). The acc. sg. *-im* is found still in a few nouns in Latin (e.g. *puppim*), while the abl. sg. *-ī* probably comes from the endingless *i*-stem locative *-ei*. The predicted gen. sg. should have been *-īs* from *-ei-s*, but this was replaced by the *-is < *-es* of the consonant stems. The *i*-stem animate nom. pl. was *-ei̯-es*, which became *-ēs* and was taken over also by the consonant stems, replacing inherited *-es*. The acc. pl. *-i-ns* became *-īs*, and the *-i-* found before the dat.-abl. morpheme *-bus* in all third-declension nouns may have come originally from the *i*-stems.

PIE also had long *ī*-stems that were used to form feminine nouns. In one group, the vowel was normally shortened, as in *neptis* "niece" < *neptī(s)* and in third-declension feminine adjectives in *-is*. (This may be why adjectives like *alacer* have different masculine and feminine nominative singulars; original masc. *alakris* underwent the same change as *tris* "thrice" > *ters* > *ter*, while original feminine *alakrīs* did not and ultimately became *alacris*. But it is also possible that unsyncopated *-is* simply got revalorized as feminine.) The long *ī* apparently survives in the adjective *Laurentīs* "Laurentian" (nom. sg.) in Ennius (*Ann.* 30). In another group, especially feminines to agent nouns in *-tor*, the suffix was extended by a *-k-* of unknown origin, whence the feminine agent-noun suffix *-trīx*.

Parellel to the *i*-stems were the *u*-stems, which yield the Latin fourth declension. The gen. *-ūs < *-ou-s < *-eu-s* is parallel to the expected *-īs* in the *i*-stems mentioned above, but never got replaced. The neuter nom.-acc. sg. *-ū* is of disputed origin, as its PIE forebear was short (*-u*). Both *i*-stem and *u*-stems formed abstract nouns, in *-ti-* and *-tu-*; the former were extended to *-tiōn-* while the latter remained unchanged.

We come finally to the fifth declension, which is a grab-bag of forms that all wound up having a stem-vowel of *-ē-* (there was no *ē*-declension in PIE). The two most common fifth-declension nouns, *rēs* and *diēs*, originally did not resemble each other at all: *rēs* is an old *i*-stem *reh₁-is*, while the paradigm of *diēs* grew up around the old acc. *d(i)i̯ēm*. The original paradigm was nom. sg. *d(i)i̯eus*, voc. sg. *d(i)i̯eu*, acc. *d(i)i̯ēm*, oblique stem *diu̯-*; the noun referred to the daytime sky and was simultaneously the name of the sky-god. The variation between *di̯-* and *d(i)i̯-* was originally conditioned by the weight of the preceding syllable (a phenomenon known as Lindeman's Law), but by Italic times both variants had been lexicalized. In Latin, the monosyllabic voc. sg. *di̯eu* became the *Iū-* of *Iū-piter* (the vocative took over the function of the nominative which is continued as *dius* in *Dius Fidius*, *nu-dius tertius*). The old oblique stem *diu̯-* was remade as *di̯eu̯-*, with the vocalism of the nominative and vocative; this became *di̯ou̯-* in Italic and *Iou-* in Latin.

PIE inflected nouns in the dual number as well; the dual inflection has been lost without a trace except for the forms *duo* (older *duō*) "two" and *ambō* "both," with the inherited *o*-stem dual ending *-ō < *-oh₁(e)*.

Adjectives are marked for feminine gender using the suffix *-a* if the adjective is an *o*-stem, otherwise *-ī(s)*. The latter suffix, as we have already seen, generally lost its length and was folded in with the ordinary *i*-stems. Consonant-stem adjective declension was gradually replaced with *i*-stem declension, though some variation is found in all periods, and present participles were in general more resistant to the change-over.

The comparative degree of adjectives is built using the Latin descendant of the PIE comparative suffix (nom. sg. animate *-i̯ōs*, neut. nom.-acc. *-i̯os*, animate acc. sg. stem *-i̯os-*, oblique stem *-is-*). The long *ō* of the animate nominative was generalized throughout the paradigm and, following rhotacism of intervocalic *-i̯ōs-* to *-i̯ōr-*, the *r* spread to the nominative in the masculine and feminine. (Pre-rhotacized *-ios-* is preserved in forms cited by later grammarians, e.g. *maiiosibus* in Paulus *ex Festo*.) The neuter nom.-acc. remained intact as *-ius* (apart from the regular change of *-os* to *-us* in later Archaic Latin). Though the zero-grade *-is-* disappeared paradigmatically, it is still found in the adverb *magis* "more" and derivative *magis-ter*. The derivative *maies-tās* contains an innovated *e*-grade, analogically after *hones-tās* and such. The productive superlative in *-issimus* is an innovation shared with Celtic, continuing *-is-m̥mo-* (with later so-called "affective gemination" of the *-s-* for emphatic effect). The *-i-* has been syncopated in *maximus < *mag-isamo-*, *pessimus < *ped-isamo-*, and similar forms. Some forms evince a suffix *-t̥mmo-*, as *op-timus*. The variant *-errimus* is regular by sound change from *-C-r-isamo-*, which became *-C-r̥samo- > *-C-ersamo- > -C-errimo-*, just like masc. nom. sg. *ākris > *ākr̥s > *ākers > *ācerr > ācer*. The phonological and morphological details of the histories of some comparatives and superlatives, such as *plūs/plūrimus*, have not been fully cleared up.

The Prehistory of Latin Pronouns, Numerals, Adverbs, and Adpositions

Formally we distinguish personal from gendered pronouns in PIE; the former exhibit many unique declensional features, while the latter differ less markedly from nouns. The high degree of suppletion in Latin (and English) personal pronominal paradigms (three separate roots in the case of *ego mē nōs*, two in the case of *tū uōs*) is a direct continuation of the PIE situation, where the nom. sg. *$eǵoh_2$ "I" was built from a different root from the sg. oblique stem *me- and the pl. root *nes- (o-grade *nos-; the zero-grade *n̥s- is the source of German *uns*, Old English *ūs*, and Modern English *us*). Similarly, the second sg. stem *$t(e)u$- contrasted with a pl. stem *ues-. The reflexive pronoun had a stem *sue-; the glide was lost on the way to Latin.

Latin has significantly refashioned the inherited gendered pronouns and created a number of new ones. *Hic* and *ille* are innovatory; *is* and the first syllable of *īdem* continue a pronominal stem *$(e)i$-, while the second syllable of *iste* contains remnants of the deictic stem *to- that also underlies English *the* and *that* and of which some old case-forms survive as adverbs in Latin (*tam*, *tum*). Traces of the PIE demonstrative stem *so- (the source of the aspirated forms of the Greek definite article – ὁ, ἡ, οἱ, αἱ) are found in Archaic poetry (e.g. fem. acc. sg. *sam*) as well as in the second syllable of *ipse*. (The -p- was originally a secondary transitional consonant that "sprouted" in forms like acc. sg. *eum-se (or *eum-sum), *eam-se (*eam-sam) > *eumps- *eamps-, and then spread to the rest of the paradigm.) Less significantly changed are the Latin relative and indefinite pronouns, which continue the PIE relative-indefinite stems *k^wo- and *k^wi-.

Features typical of the Latin pronominal declension, especially in the singular, are partly of IE origin. Chief among these is the neuter nom.-acc. sg. in -*d* rather than -*um* or -ø which is an inherited feature. The genitive ended in *-so, also peculiar to the pronouns (ironically the distinctive pronominal genitive -*ius* of the Latin gendered pronouns is not originally from a pronominal declension, but probably comes from the nominal o-stem genitive *-osi̯o with an added -s).

The cardinal numerals from one to ten are of good PIE patrimony, continuing *oi-no-, *$du\bar{o}$, *trei̯es, *$k^wetu̯ores$, *$penk^we$ (assimilated early to *k^wenk^we in Italic), *sueḱs, *septm̥, *oḱtō, *neun̥, *deḱm̥(t). Another root for "one," *sem- (the source of the Greek stem ἑν-), is continued in such words as *semel*, *simul*, and *simplex*. "Twenty" (PIE *uīḱn̥tī, usually thought to be a reduced version of *$duih_1$-dḱm̥tih$_1$ "two tens") and "hundred" (PIE *ḱm̥tom, also thought to be a derivative of *deḱm̥(t), perhaps an old substantivized ordinal *$d(e)ḱm̥tom$ "the tenth (ten)") are likewise inherited. Latin *mīlle* is thought by some to be of IE origin but this is very uncertain. The ordinals have been separately refashioned in each branch, though the suffixes *-to- (*quārtus*, *quīntus*, *sextus*) and *-(m)o- (*septimus*, *decimus*) have a long history; *-to- also underlies the English ordinal suffix -*th*.

There does not appear to have been any special morphological means of creating adverbs in PIE. Typically, case-forms of nouns were used in adverbial function, and to convert an adjective into an adverb little needed to be done besides using the neuter accusative, as was still the case much of the time in Latin (hence Virgil's *horrendum strīdēns* "horribly shrieking"). The Latin adverbial suffix -*ē* used with first- and second-declension adjectives is an old instrumental (*$-eh_1$) that was reinterpreted prehistorically as an ablative (whence archaic forms like *rected* with ablatival -*d*). Another instrumental survives in *quī* "how" (*k^wih_1), and *quō* "whither" may be an old allative or directive, as noted earlier. Adverbs of the type *statim*, *partim* are of course old *ti*-stem accusatives; less clear are the pronominal *im*-adverbs like *illim*, *hinc* (*him-c(e)), *in-de*, whose origins are disputed, but appear to have analogs in Anatolian. Ablatival adverbs in -*tus*, e.g. *caelitus* "from heaven," continue a non-paradigmatic PIE ablatival suffix *-tos.

The Prehistory of Latin Verbs

Verbs in PIE were conjugated in three persons in all three numbers and in a variety of tenses and moods built to as many as three tense-stems. From the present stem were formed the imperfective or noncompleted present and past tenses, usually called present and imperfect; the aorist stem formed the perfected or completed past tense, the aorist; and the perfect stem formed a resultative past tense and/or stative called the perfect. (In reality, the perfect was probably not a real tense in the first instance.) There may have been a pluperfect or past of the perfect. To each of these three tense-stems could be formed also a subjunctive and an optative. There was no future tense per se, though the subjunctive could be used as a future and one of the several types of derived presents, the desiderative, could act as a quasi-future and evolved into a proper future tense in some of the daughter branches. Besides distinctions in tense and mood, there was also a distinction in diathesis between active and middle voice. The middle endings doubled as passives; there were no morphologically distinct passive inflections, though certain nonfinite forms, such as the verbal adjectives in *-to- and *-no-, were passive when formed to transitive roots. Verbs could also form imperatives, participles, and a variety of verbal nouns (functioning as infinitives, among other things). Mention has already been made of the so-called derived or secondary presents; apart from desideratives, these included causatives, denominatives, and statives (besides the perfect).

Just as the orderly establishment of five distinct declensions in Latin differs from the PIE situation, so too does the orderly establishment of four discrete conjugations. In PIE, there was a considerable variety of ways of forming present stems, some of them athematic and some of them thematic. Athematic presents included root presents, formed by the direct addition of personal endings to the root with no additional morphology; reduplicated presents, like root presents but with a prefixal syllable consisting of a copy of the initial consonant of the root plus the vowel e or i; and nasal-infix presents, formed by the insertion of a morpheme *-n(e)- before the final consonant of the root. Athematic presents ablauted, such that the ablauting morpheme (the root in the case of root and reduplicated presents; the nasal infix otherwise) appeared in the e-grade in the indicative active singular and in the subjunctive, and the zero-grade elsewhere. Thematic presents were characterized by the addition of an ablauting theme vowel before the personal endings; the vowel appeared as o in all numbers of the first person and in the third pl. active, and as e elsewhere. The source of this alternation is not fully clear. Thematic presents included simple thematic presents (e-grade of root plus thematic vowel plus ending), reduplicated thematic presents, and a variety of presents formed with suffixes ending with the thematic vowel, such as *-i̯e/o- and *-sḱe/o-. The language also possessed a suffix *-eh₂- used to form factitives from adjectives, and a suffix *-eh₁- used to form statives; these appear to have been extended early to *-eh₂-i̯e/o- and *-eh₁-i̯e/o-.

By the time Latin and the other Italic languages are attested, a combination of vowel shifts and morphological revamping had caused the following changes to the picture just drawn. Almost all athematic presents had been remade as thematics and wound up in what would ultimately be called the third conjugation. Thus an old athematic nasal-infix present like sg. *i̯u-ne-g-ti "yokes," pl. *i̯u-n-g-enti "they yoke" first generalized the stem allomorph *i̯u-n-g- from the plural and then thematized it to *i̯ung-o/e-, the source of Latin *iungō*. Reduplicated athematic presents like sg. **si-steh₂-ti* "stands," pl. **si-sth₂-enti* "they stand," also generalized the zero-grade allomorph **-sth₂-* from the plural; after loss of the laryngeals, this became simply *-st-*. After the verb became thematic, the ultimate result was Latin *sistō* "I set up." These, too, became third-conjugation verbs. Verbs that had the plain thematic vowel *-e/o-* to begin with, as well as those with the suffix **-sḱe/o-*, also wound up in the third conjugation.

More complicated were **i̯e/o*-presents. When this suffix was added directly to a root ending in a consonant, the resulting form either became a verb of the third-*iō* conjugation or of the fourth conjugation, depending on the weight of the root syllable. If the root consisted of a single syllable ending in a short vowel plus single consonant, the result was a third-*iō* verb (type *capiō* < **kap-i̯e/o-*). Otherwise, the result was a fourth-conjugation verb (type *audiō* "hear" with diphthong in the base, *prūriō* "itch" with long vowel, *sentiō* "feel" with two root-final consonants, *sepeliō* "bury" with two syllables). This had to do with an early Italic sound change whereby **i̯e* was reduced to *i* after a light syllable but extended to **ii̯e* after a heavy syllable; this latter sequence later contracted to *ī*. Though traditionally the two types of third-conjugation verbs are grouped together, historically the *i* of a form like *agit* "does" and the *i* of an *iō*-verb like *capit* "takes" are not the same: *agit* continues **aget(i)* while *capit* continues an already Common Italic **kapit(i)* from earlier **kapi̯eti*.

The suffix **-i̯e/o-* was also used very productively to derive verbs from other parts of speech (especially nouns, whence the term denominative verb). Since nouns by the Italic period tended to have stems ending in *-o/e-*, *-ā-*, or *-i-*, and since *i̯* was lost intervocalically in early Italic, the resulting denominative stems underwent contraction. Denominatives to *ā*-stems contracted to give a stem vowel *-ā-* and wound up in what would later be called the first conjugation (type *causāre* "to cause"); similarly, denominatives to *i*-stems got a stem vowel in *-ī-* and became fourth-conjugation verbs (type *fīnīre* "finish"). Denominatives to *o*-stems are more curious: some are in the fourth conjugation (type *seruīre* "to serve") while others are in the first conjugation (type *fūcāre* "to dye" from *fūcus* "seaweed, dyestuff"). Neither is easy to explain as stemming from either **-oi̯e/o-* or **-ei̯e/o-*. The *ā*-type may result from the analogical extension of another major source of first-conjugation verbs, namely the factitives. These are built from adjectives using the suffix **-eh₂-i̯e/o-*, which likewise contracted ultimately to *-ā-* (type *nouāre* "to make new"); and indeed *-ā-* did become an all-purpose denominative suffix, being added to athematic nouns too (e.g. *rōrāre* "to shed moisture" < *rōr-* "dew"). But the *ī*-type has so far resisted attempts at explanation.

The verbs discussed above form the bulk of the sources of the first, third, and fourth conjugations. The second conjugation consists of two main historical types, the causatives and statives. Causatives were formed in PIE by the addition of the accented suffix **-éi̯e-* to the *o*-grade of a root; thus to the root **men-* "think" was formed **mon-éi̯e-* "cause (someone) to think." This suffix contracted to *-ē-*, whence *monēre* "to warn." Another large group of second-conjugation verbs comes from forms derived using the stative suffix **-eh₁-*. One important group of these verbs is deadjectival: *calēre* "be hot," *līuēre* "be bluish," *liquēre* "be clear," *stupēre* "be struck dumb" and so forth. They form part of a larger derivational network that includes adjectives in *-idus* (*calidus* "hot," *līuidus* "bluish," *liquidus* "liquid; clear," *stupidus* "dumbstruck") and abstract nouns in *-or* (*calor* "heat," *līuor* "bluish discoloration," *liquor* "a liquid," *stupor* "stupor").

The interchange of nominal and verbal suffixes added directly to roots of adjectival or stative semantics is known as the Caland system and is well attested in other branches of the family, especially Indo-Iranian and Greek. Another subtype of stative is deverbal and consists of a wider variety of forms, some of them transitive: *sedēre* "sit," *habēre* "have," *uidēre* "see."

The only verbs that still inflect to some extent athematically are *sum* "am" (*tes-t*, *es-tis*, without intervening vowel), *uolō* "wish" (*uul-t*), *eō* "go" < **eiō* (thus also *īs* "you (sg.) go" < **ei-s*), and *edō* "eat" (thus *ēs*, *ēst*). *Ferō* "carry" would seem to be athematic also, to judge by *fers*, *fert*, *fertis*, but this is uncertain: it may have arisen by syncope of the thematic vowel (the verb is a simple thematic present in most of the other branches), unless it is a dereduplicated present going back to the same ancestor as Sanskrit *bíbharti* "carries."

The first sg. *-m* in *sum* is the sole present indicative descendant of the PIE athematic primary first sg. ending **-mi* (which lives on more prominently in the "μι-verbs" of Greek). The *-m* in past tense and subjunctive forms (e.g. pluperfect *-eram* and subjunctives in *-am -em -im*) continues the secondary first sg. ending **-m*. Primary endings were used in the non-past indicative tenses, while secondary endings were used elsewhere (except the perfect; see below). They differed from each other primarily in the presence or absence of the so-called "hic et nunc" particle *-i*: primary **-mi* (or *-oh₂* in thematic verbs, whence Lat. *-ō*) **-si *-ti *-mos* (?) **-tes* (?) **-nti*, secondary **-m *-s *-t *-mos* (?) **-te* (?) **-nt*. This *-i* has disappeared in Latin, though one instance of it may be preserved in the form *tremonti* in the Carmen Saliare. The distinction between primary and secondary third sg. **-ti* and **-t* did have a phonological consequence: the former simply dropped the *-i*, while the latter was weakened to *-d*, as in the future *esed* (originally subjunctive; see below) from the Lapis Niger, and in the perfect *deded* "he gave" on a variety of archaic inscriptions. This *-d* was replaced by the other variant *-t*.

The four Latin conjugations represent only one way in which the ancestors of the Romans imposed an organizing grid on the verbal system. A second way in which this was done was by creating a system consisting of a present, past, and future imperfectum that exactly balanced a present, past, and future perfectum, yielding six tenses in the indicative. The present and perfect continue the inherited present and perfect (the latter with some admixture of the PIE aorist, especially in the stem forms; see below), while the future is actually the continuation of the PIE subjunctive (the Latin "subjunctive" is historically the PIE optative). The Latin imperfect is a new creation, as are the pluperfect and the future perfect. Let us now look at these formations in more detail.

The imperfect suffix *-bam -bās*, etc. and the future suffix *-bō -bis*, etc. derive from reduced forms of the root **bhuH-* "be" (*H* is the cover symbol for a laryngeal that cannot be further specified), which in Latin gave rise to the various *fu-* forms in the paradigm of *esse*. The regular development of **bh* word-internally was to *b*; thus the imperfect and future were originally a periphrasis combining a verbal stem with a preterital or future form of "be." The source of the imperfect stem-vowel *-ā-* is not clear. The stem-vowel of *-bō -bis* was simply **-e-*, which is the inherited subjunctive morpheme (see below); we reconstruct **-bh(u̯)-ā-* and **-bh(u̯)-e-*, exactly parallel to the imperfect and future (historically, the old subjunctive) of the other root for "be," *es-*: imperfect *er-ā-* (< **es-ā-*), future *er-i-* (< *es-e-*, attested in third sg. *esed* of the Lapis Niger). Sabellic (Oscan **fufans** "they were") also attests a **-bh(u̯)-ā-*, but a comparable future is lacking.

Another future formation, preserved in archaic texts, is the *s*-future, type *faxō, faxis* "I/you will do," *amāssō* "I will love." These forms exist alongside subjunctives in *-sim*, like *faxim, amāssim*. The *s*-future is historically older than the *b*-future, being found also in Sabellic (where, however, it is athematic, e.g. Osc. *deiuast* "(s)he will swear"). Disputed is whether the Latin *s*-future is an old *s*-aorist subjunctive or an old desiderative subjunctive; in favor of the latter is the fact that the Sabellic formation must be an old desiderative, and it seems best to take the Latin *s*-forms as not an entirely separate entity from the Sabellic ones.

The future of the third and fourth conjugations in *-am -ēs -et*, etc. is, with the exception of the first sg., simply the inherited thematic subjunctive. The PIE subjunctive was formed by adding the thematic vowel to the relevant tense stem; in the case of a thematic verb, this resulted in a double vowel (*ag-e-e-ti*) which contracted. The expected long *ō* in the first pl. and third pl. (cf. Gk. φέρωμεν φέρωσι) was replaced by the *ē* of the second sg., third sg., and second pl. The first sg. was replaced by what is synchronically the present subjunctive (historically an optative or replacement thereof, see below), one assumes because the inherited subjunctive in *-ō* would have been the same as the first sg. indicative. (The related question – why did the inherited subjunctive get replaced in the first and second conjugations by the *b*-forms? – has a similar answer: the contraction products of *-ā-įe-e-*, *-ē-įe-e-*, etc. would not have differed from the corresponding indicatives.)

The perfect system represents the formal and functional melding of two original tenses and tense-stems, the aorist and the perfect. Formally, perfect morphology is retained in most of the personal endings and in stem-forms containing reduplication or *o*-grade (with deredUplication), while the aorist is reflected by other stem-forms (especially those going back to *s*-aorists) and perhaps by parts of certain personal endings. Semantically, the perfect as combining simple, completed past with present-perfective semantics reveals its double origin as both an aorist and a perfect. The inherited PIE endings were first sg. *-h_2e*, second sg. *-th_2e*, third sg. *-e*; third pl. *-ēr*. These would have become in the first instance *-a *-ta *-e *-ēr*. At some point the "hic et nunc" particle *-i* was added; presumably it was attracted to the perfect because of its partial role as a stative and a present and resultative perfect (referring to an event started in the past but continuing into present time or whose results continue into the present). This resulted in *-ai *-tai *-ei *-ēri*. These forms are directly continued by Latin first sg. *-ī*, second sg. *-tī* (preceded by an element *-is-* of uncertain origin), and third pl. (poetic) *-ēre*. The third sg. *-it* scans as long in archaic poetry; the long *ī* continues the old *-ei*, to which the more typical third sg. ending *-t* has been added. (The alternate form *-ed* that we saw above in inscriptional *deded* is the aorist ending, PIE *-et*.) The exact prehistories of the first and second pl. are less certain, since these persons have not been reconstructed with confidence for PIE. The usual Classical third pl. *-ērunt* is a cross between inherited *-ēr(e)* and a more typical third pl. *-unt*, which probably came from the aorist. A short-vowel *-erunt* (< *-is-ont*) is found occasionally in the early poets, and the Lapis Satricanus attests an ending *-erai*, which is a refashioning of *-ēre* under the influence of the first and second singulars.

The less productive perfect stem-types are inherited. Chief among these are the *s*-perfects, which formally continue *s*-aorists (type *uēxī* "I have conveyed," *gessī* "I have waged") though the formation did enjoy an early efflorescence in Italic and many Latin *s*-perfects are not inherited *s*-aorists. Another type is the reduplicated perfects, which formally continue true perfects (type *pepulī*, archaic *memordī*). A number of so-called long-vowel perfects could represent dereduplicated perfects in the *o*-grade (type *fūgī* "I have fled," which could continue **(bhe-)bhoug-*).

But the majority of Latin perfects are *v*-perfects, which are a Latin innovation that partly replaced the old *s*-aorist. The source of this formation is disputed. Given its affinity with long stem-vowels, some view the *-v-/-u-* as cognate with the *-u* that optionally ends the first and third singulars of long-vowel Sanskrit perfects (*dádā* or *dádāu* "I have/he has given"). The starting point under this view was *(g)nōuī* "I know," seen as being formally directly cognate (minus the reduplicating syllable) with Sanskrit *jájñau* "I knew." However, this Sanskrit form is not attested until after the Rigveda and could be a later analogical formation. Another school of thought sees the *-v-/-u-* as originally a stem-final segment that got reinterpreted as a suffix; the starting point under this view was *fuī* "I was" or its immediate ancestor **fouī*, archaic *fūī*.

The pluperfect and future perfect contain an element **-is-* (rhotacized and lowered to *-er-* before a vowel) followed by the same preterite morpheme *-ā-* of the imperfect and the subjunctive (ultimately future) stem-vowel *-e-*, respectively. The source of the **-is-* is not certain, but may somehow contain the old *s*-aorist morpheme preceded by a union vowel. It is probably not the same element as the *-is-* appearing in both numbers of the second person perfect. The original third pl. **-erunt* of the future perfect has been analogically replaced by the *-erint* of the subjunctive.

So much for the active indicative. The passive personal endings in the present system are mostly characterized by an element *-r* that, according to the most widely held view, was originally a marker of the middle voice in primary tenses (i.e., analogous to the "hic et nunc" particle *-i* in the active voice). This **-r* was added to what were the "real" middle endings **-h₂o *-th₂o *-o* third pl. **-ro*. But little trace of these original endings survives in Latin because of influence from the active. The "short" second sg. *-re*, for instance, continues **-se* or **-so*, which replaced **-th₂o* in several branches under the influence of active **-s(i)*. (The more common *-ris* is this **-se* recharacterized by the addition of active second sg. *-s.*) Third sg. and pl. *-(n)tur*, archaic *-(n)tor*, is *-r* added onto **-(n)to*, which replaced **-o* and **-ro* under the influence of active **-t(i)* and **-nt(i)*. For the first sg. we must distinguish *-or* (*-ōr*), standing alongside active *-ō*, from *-r* standing alongside active *-m*. The former could actually continue original **-o-h₂o-r*, while the latter is analogical. The second pl. *-minī* is innovative and usually thought to go back to a middle participial form **-menoi* (masc. nom. pl.) that came to be incorporated into the verbal paradigm. (This participial morpheme otherwise only survives in a few nominalizations such as *alumnus* < **alomenos* "nurtured" and *fēmina* < **dhē-menā* "one being suckled/giving suck.")

In PIE, whether a verb conjugated as an active or as a middle was lexically determined; this situation is continued by Latin and Greek, where the so-called "deponent" verbs are simply middle verbs from the PIE point of view. As a group the middle verbs do have some semantic features in common; they tend to refer to states, changes of state, speaking, motion, and other "internal" activities. However, many verbs that conjugate as actives also refer to such things, and quite a few others in the older IE languages conjugate in the active in one tense and in the middle in another (familiar from Greek in pairs like present active μανθάνω but future middle μαθήσομαι, or present active φημί but imperfect middle ἐφάμην). This type has become virtually extinct in Latin, the only vestiges being the tiny handful of semi-deponent verbs. Several Latin deponents have exact middle cognates elsewhere; a good example is *sequitur* "follows" = Gk. middle ἕπεται = Old Irish middle *seichithir* = Sanskrit middle *sácate*.

The Latin subjunctive employs no fewer than three distinct morphemes: *-ē-* in the present first conjugation and in two past subjunctives, the imperfect and pluperfect; *-ā-* in the present outside the first conjugation and in irregular forms like *fuam fuās fuat*; and *-ī-* in the perfect and in some irregular presents like *sim sīs, edim, duim*, and in archaic *s*-subjunctives like *faxim*. Only the third of these (*-ī-*) has a clear PIE origin, which confusingly was an optative suffix and not a subjunctive suffix at all. (The category called "subjunctive" in PIE, Indo-Iranian, and Greek is not the same as the subjunctive in Latin; as we saw above, the ancient subjunctive became the Latin future.) In PIE, the optative suffix alternated between full-grade *-i̯eh₁-* in the sg. active and *-ih₁-* elsewhere; this is faithfully reflected in Archaic Latin *siem siēs siēt*, pl. *sīmus sītis sient* (where the *-e-* in the last form is actually part of the desinence, PIE *h₁s-ih₁-ent*). The *ā*-subjunctive is found also in Celtic, which shares an important feature with Archaic Latin in sporting present subjunctives formed directly to the root rather than to a present stem, of the type subjunctive *attigat* (*-tag-ā-*) alongside indicative *attingit*. But its ultimate origin is disputed. The same is true of the *ē*-subjunctive, which cannot be traced outside of Italic with any confidence.

The Latin imperatives are for the most part of good Indo-European patrimony. The bare stem seen in the sg. (*am-ā* "love!" etc.) was characteristic of all thematic forms. Athematic verbs utilized a suffix *-dhi* which has vanished in Latin. The plural ending *-te* is inherited. PIE also had a "future imperative" in *-tōd* that was originally indifferent to number. Latin fleshed this out by creating a second pl. in *-tōte* and a third pl. in *-ntōd*, as well as passive forms in *-tor* (*-tō* plus middle *-r*) and a second pl. passive *-minō*, which combined the second pl. passive ending *-minī* with imperatival *-ō*.

Of the Latin participles, two go straight back to PIE: the *nt-* or present participle, and the perfect participle in *-to-*, which continues the PIE passive verbal adjective (which was active or neutral in diathesis when formed from an intransitive root). The future active partciple in *-tūrus* is a Latin innovation (no such formation is known from Sabellic), while the gerundive is found also in Sabellic and presumably represents a Common Italic innovation.

The Latin active infinitives are formed with a morpheme *-se* (rhotacized to *-re* after vowels, and assimilating to a preceding resonant in *uelle* and *ferre*) that probably continues an old locative *-si* of an *s*-stem abstract noun. The passive infinitives in *-ī*, *-rī*, and *-(r)ier* are of uncertain origin. None of the Latin infinitive formations is found in Sabellic.

The supines in *-tum*, *-tū*, and occasionally *-tuī* are case-forms of verbal nouns in *-tu-*. The accusative supine is apparently of PIE date, as it is found also in Indo-Iranian and Balto-Slavic. The form in *-tū* is traditionally labeled an ablative, but is really an old dative (the Classical dat. *-uī* is a replacement of earlier *-ū* in animate *u*-stem nouns).

Verbs in Latin are frequently compounded by the addition of one or more prefixes or preverbs. A few traces survive of an earlier stage where such preverbs were not – or at least not obligatorily – joined to their verb, as in the sacral formula *ob uos sacro = obsecro uos*. Called tmesis, this separation of preverb from verb is known also from Archaic Greece (Homer), Indo-Iranian, Anatolian, Celtic, Germanic, and to some extent in Baltic, and is thought to have been the norm in PIE. In many of these branches, it becomes difficult to tell the difference between preverbs and prepositions, which also had greater freedom of movement originally. Some are in fact inclined to believe that PIE did not have a category of true prepositions (or adpositions), but rather just a set of free-floating adverbs that could function equally as preverbs or adpositions.

Syntax

While the reconstruction of PIE phonology and morphology is a relatively straightforward undertaking in its essentials (if not in many of its details), the reconstruction of PIE syntax is beset with many special problems. Syntactic rules are only deducible from connected speech – phrases, clauses, and sentences. A few phrases can be reconstructed for PIE (such as "imperishable fame" mentioned at the outset), but otherwise connected speech has not been recoverable for the proto-language, and even for the few reconstructible syntagms we are in the dark about what the unmarked word-order was and what transformations of it were licit. It is usually thought that the basic PIE clause was verb-final and that word orders were subject to permutation at the hands of syntactic movement rules, such as topicalization, focus movement, and wh-movement. These rules normally caused clausal material to be fronted to the beginning of clauses, and are still fully alive in Latin. The evidence of the daughter languages further suggests that PIE possessed a number of clitic particles, many of which were placed second in their clause; these included oblique forms of the personal pronouns, conjunctions, connectives, and probably particles used for a variety of pragmatic functions such as emphasis, contrast, and so forth. The second-position placement of such forms has been called Wackernagel's Law, after Jacob Wackernagel, who first systematically documented the phenomenon in 1892. Inherited Wackernagel particles in Latin are the conjunctions -*que* and -*ue* and the question particle -*ne*; later creations include the "postpositive" particles like *autem* and *igitur*.

Determining how much of Latin syntax is inherited is difficult for other reasons as well. For one thing, adequate theoretically informed accounts of synchronic Latin syntax have not been not thick upon the ground (a recent exception is Devine and Stephens 2006, but the framework within which they operate is only one of several possible). But in spite of such difficulties, several syntactic phenomena have close analogs in the other older IE languages and are doubtless inherited. Aside from Wackernagel's Law, these include relative-clause constructions in which the relative clause precedes the main clause and contains the antecedent within it (well known from Anatolian, Vedic, and elsewhere), and the ability to render phrases discontinuous (as in the so-called *magna cum laude* construction, among many others).

The attested ancient IE languages also evince a variety of phenomena whereby the pronunciation of the "edges" of words was altered under the influence of immediately neighboring words (so-called sandhi phenomena); such phenomena are often sensitive to syntactic structure (compare liaison in French). Doubtless words in their grammatical context underwent sandhi rules in PIE also, but it is difficult to recover any.

Lexicon

Much of the Latin core lexicon is inherited from PIE morphologically intact, with most of the rest also of PIE stock but with various refashionings. In what follows, emphasis will be based on inherited *words* (with or without minor changes such as entrance into a different stem-class) having retained largely the same meaning, rather than later innovations derived from inherited roots. The sample lists below, while fairly extensive, are by no means complete (see also the discussion of the inherited vocabulary in chapter 10). All the predictable basic semantic categories are represented, such as kinship terms (*pater māter auus frāter soror nepōs neptis nurus gener leuir socer socrus uidua*; of interest is the replacement of *suHnu- "son" and *dhugh₂tēr "daughter" by *fīlius* and *fīlia*, though these are also built to a PIE root, *dhei- "suckle, give suck"), the cardinal numerals 1–10, 20, and 100; dozens of basic verbs including *sum fīō dō uolō ferō uehō agō dūcō dīcō canō poscō sīdō sistō eō ueniō nō habeō capiō*; function words (*ab ambi- ante cum ex per prō sub super ego/mē tū nōs uōs sē is alius quis et -que -ue*); body parts (including *caput auris oculus nāsus ōs dēns lingua barba cor iecur umerus ulna palma coxa natis clūnis genū pēs ōs cornū uncus mēns*); various basic adjectives (e.g. *albus niger ruber nouus grauis leuis breuis mollis tenuis suāuis ācer saluus uīuus līber cārus iuuenis plēnus caecus*); animals (e.g. *canis equus pecū bōs ouis agnus lāna haedus lupus fiber porcus sūs aper taurus ursus uulpēs mūs auis turdus coruus merula anas ānser uespa uermis anguis piscis fera*); plants (e.g. *fāgus quercus ulmus ornus cornus corulus alnus far grānum acus hordeum faba flōs glāns*); natural world, features, phenomena, and substances (e.g. *sōl diēs nox aurōra uesper tenebrae mēnsis hiems uēr uentus tonitrus nebula imber nix mare mōns collis plānum ager fundus rūs ignis aqua fūmus sal argentum aurum*); man-made structures and technologies (e.g. *domus forēs āra pōns rota arātrum iugum stabulum crībrum nāuis mālus axis uīcus hortus clāuis*); and many miscellaneous other terms (e.g. *hostis genus opus onus rēs iūs dōnum damnum somnus uēnum rēx nōmen mel uir uīs animus deus hostis*).

FURTHER READING

The most up-to-date historical-comparative grammar of Latin is Weiss 2009. Because of its outline format, it does not strive for complete lists of, e.g., examples of particular sound changes or words containing a particular suffix. More complete in this regard is the still indispensable Leumann 1977, whose companion volume (Szantyr 1963) treats syntax. Also useful is Meiser 1998 and Sommer and Pfister 1977 (historical phonology only). An up-to-date etymological dictionary is a desideratum; the recent de Vaan 2008 (encompassing all of Italic) has a good bibliography but contains numerous minority views. The standard dictionaries are still Walde and Hofmann 1938–56 and Ernout and Meillet 1979. For basic Indo-European linguistics, see Fortson 2010, Tichy 2006, and Clackson 2007; for cultural and archaeological material, see Mallory and Adams 2006. Studies on individual aspects of Latin historical grammar are legion; the reader is referred to the bibliographies in Weiss and de Vaan above.

CHAPTER 14

Archaic and Old Latin

John Penney

The earliest remains of Latin are dated to the seventh century BCE; by the middle of the first century BCE, Classical Latin had become established as the dominant prestige variety. The language of the six pre-Classical centuries is sometimes labelled as a whole "Archaic Latin" or "Early Latin" or "Old Latin", and a single term has the advantage of acknowledging that there is a continuum, but a division into periods has also been proposed by some scholars and these same labels (and others) may then be applied in narrower senses, which may unfortunately vary from author to author. For instance, Meiser (1998) 2 distinguishes between *Frühlatein* ("Early Latin"), from the first attestations down to 240 BCE and the first literary productions, and *Altlatein* ("Old Latin") from 240 down to the first half of the first century, and is happy to use *Archaisches Latein* ("Archaic Latin") as an all-embracing term. Weiss (2009) 23 makes a similar division between "Very Old Latin" (down to the third century and the first literature) and "Old Latin" (third and second centuries). Clackson and Horrocks (2007) adopt an alternative division between the language of the first inscriptions, down to *c.* 400, which is labelled "Archaic Latin", and the language from *c.* 400 to the first century, which is labelled "Old Latin"; there is virtually no evidence for Latin in the later fifth and early fourth centuries which makes 400 a convenient dividing point. The usage of Clackson and Horrocks will be broadly adopted in this chapter, out of deference to the editor, but the terminological divergences and disagreements should not be allowed to obscure the fact that the development of the language continues seamlessly throughout the whole period, and indeed on into Classical Latin.

A Companion to the Latin Language, First Edition. Edited by James Clackson.
© 2011 Blackwell Publishing Ltd. Published 2011 by Blackwell Publishing Ltd.

Sources

The best evidence for Archaic Latin comes from inscriptions, few and brief though these are. Most of them are dedications or indications of ownership; the text on a badly mutilated cippus from the Roman forum (*CIL* I².1, from the early sixth century) seems to be a more public document but it is too broken to be readily comprehensible. Only two or three inscriptions containing more than a few letters come from Rome itself, the rest from other parts of Latium, which raises questions about the possibility of dialectal variation that the scanty evidence does not suffice to answer. The dating of these inscriptions is not always easy – for many of them there is no archaeological context – but diachronic variations in letter shapes provide some help (see Hartmann (2005)). The only other available material for the Archaic period comes from fragmentary texts cited in later authors: prominent amongst these are the *Laws of the Twelve Tables*, traditionally dated to the mid-fifth century BCE, but preserved in a spelling that certainly does not reflect the original orthography.

Inscriptions remain important for Old Latin too, even after the appearance of the first literary texts, since they have the enormous advantage of being contemporary documents, and they provide essential evidence for tracking orthographical and phonological changes. Literary texts, or old documents and texts preserved in later authors, were to a large extent subject to modernisation in these respects from antiquity onwards; that is to say they were adjusted to conform more closely to the Classical norms. The epigraphic evidence must, however, be used with some caution: ingrained spelling habits are hard to shift and there is often a marked delay in the acceptance of new spellings that reflects changes in pronunciation, especially in bureaucratic circles (it is noticeable that private inscriptions often lead the way in representing phonological changes). Old Latin inscriptions have been found throughout Italy, in Spain, on Delos and elsewhere: the distribution mirrors the expansion of Roman power. There are funerary inscriptions, which include a number of epitaphs in verse; numerous dedications to various deities by individuals, magistrates or guilds; building inscriptions; ownership marks and makers' signatures; etc. There are also a number of longer texts: a few documents regulating behaviour at religious sanctuaries (*leges sacrae*), some public edicts (pride of place goes to the *Senatusconsultum de Bacchanalibus* of 186 BCE (*CIL* I².581), laying down restrictive rules for the conduct of Bacchic worship), and legal documents such as the lengthy record of the resolution of a dispute over land between two communities in north-west Italy, the *Sententia Minuciorum* of 117 BCE (*CIL* I².584). It is possible to date a certain number of Old Latin inscriptions from historical circumstances (consul dates or the career of named magistrates, for instance), but for many others the only clues are palaeographical or linguistic, with the attendant danger of circularity if linguistic changes are dated according to when they first appear in inscriptions and inscriptions are dated according to whether or not a given linguistic change seems to have taken place. Fortunately there are enough inscriptions with a secure date to allow the establishment of a reasonably reliable relative chronology. The question of dialectal diversity arises again, all the more forcefully given the wider spread of evidence in this period, and there are some signs of this: for instance, the change of the diphthong [ai] to a long vowel, written E, seems to have taken place quite early outside Rome and so shows up in second-century forms like CEDITO (Class. *caedito*) "he is to cut" at Spoleto (*CIL* I².366) or FORTVNE "to Fortune" (dat. sg.) at Tusculum (*CIL* I².48), and this fits well with Varro's statement (*L.* 5.97) that in rural Latium the form *hedus* is used for "kid" but *haedus* at Rome. (A full discussion of all the possible evidence for regional diversity in this period, both from inscriptions and from Roman authors, can be found in Adams (2007) 37–113.)

From 240 BCE, the onset of the career of Livius Andronicus, there are literary texts to enrich our knowledge of Old Latin, but many of these are only known from citations in grammarians or other ancient authors. Some early verse texts are in the Saturnian metre, the translation of the *Odyssey* by Livius Andronicus and the narrative poem on the First Punic War by Naevius, from both of which we have only stray lines; the only complete Saturnian poems, but very much shorter, are found in inscriptions, such as epitaphs of the Scipio family from the third and early second centuries or some mid-second century dedications (see Kruschwitz (2002) for a complete collection of the epigraphic material). When so few lines survive to be analysed, it is perhaps not surprising that the nature of the metre is still a matter for debate (for recent discussion see Parsons (1999); Clackson and Horrocks (2007) 132–138; Mercado (2006b)), and the evidence that it might provide for early Latin phonology remains tantalisingly elusive.

Dramatic works in Latin, based on Greek models and using Greek metres, were first composed by Livius Andronicus, but again we have only fragments, as is the case also for the slightly later authors Ennius, Accius and Pacuvius. The only complete texts to survive are the comedies of Plautus and Terence, and the language of these authors, especially Plautus, provides the fullest representation that we have of Old Latin at the close of the third century and in the first half of the second (see de Melo, chapter 19 of this volume). The Homeric dactylic hexameter was introduced into Latin verse by Ennius in the early second century in a long narrative poem, the *Annals*, but despite the importance of this work as a model for later poets, especially Virgil, only some 600 lines have come down to us in citations. The meagre fragments of all these early verse compositions, however, are not without value for the history of Latin: very often a line is cited because it contains an unusual grammatical form or an obsolete item of vocabulary and this can make a valuable contribution to our knowledge of the early language.

Latin literary prose begins with Cato (234–149 BCE). He was a renowned orator and many of his speeches were still available to be read with admiration in Cicero's time, though we now have only fragments attested in citations. Likewise fragmentary are the remnants of Cato's *Origines*, a ground-breaking historical work, the first of its kind in Latin. Other early orators and historians have fared no better, and the only complete prose work to have survived from the Old Latin period is Cato's *de Agri Cultura*, a book of instruction and advice for owners of estates. The generally plain style of this work seems to have been determined by the subject matter, for the fragments of the speeches show a more elaborate and elevated style, influenced by Greek rhetorical teaching, and it is clear that already differences in language according to literary genre can be recognised (see Courtney (1999) 41–91).

Orthography and Phonology

The Greek historian Polybius, writing in the second century BCE, famously remarked (3.22.3) on the difficulty of understanding early Latin texts (in particular a treaty between Rome and Carthage from 509 BCE) because the language was so different from contemporary Latin. Certainly the Latin of the earliest inscriptions can have a bafflingly unfamiliar appearance, largely due to the different orthographic conventions adopted and to the appearance of forms that have not yet undergone later phonological changes, although allowance must also be made for morphological developments and the use of vocabulary that later dropped out of the language. The following selection of orthographic and phonological divergences ranges beyond Archaic Latin in order to illustrate that the processes of change continued across the different periods.

Spelling conventions

One of the most striking orthographic features of Archaic Latin is the use of the so-called C/K/Q-convention. This was a spelling convention (taken over from the Etruscans) according to which the sound [k] was written with different letters according to the following vowel: C before [e] and [i], K before [a], Q before [o] and [u]. This convention was never very faithfully followed but there are clear examples such as sixth-century KAPIAD for Classical *capiat*, and it has left later traces in the letter names *cē, kā, qū,* in fossilised Classical spellings like *kalendae* "kalends" and in the restriction of the use of Q to the sequence QV. In most environments C was generalised very early, whence Classical *capiat*.

The letter C continues the Greek letter *gamma*, whose original value was [g]. In Etruria this had been pressed into service as part of the convention for writing [k], and this had been possible because in Etruscan there was no phonological distinction between [g] and [k]. Latin does make such a distinction but once the C/K/Q-convention had been adopted, there was no longer a separate sign for [g], a deficiency not remedied until the third century BCE when the letter G was invented (for details see Wachter (1987) 324–333). So, for instance, in the sixth century we find RECEI as the dat. sing. of "king", Class. *rēgī*, and EQO for "I", Class. *ego*.

The earliest form of the Latin alphabet (reflecting its Greek origins) had no letter for the sound [f]; the Romans took over from the Etruscans a digraph spelling for the sound, FH (as it were [w] + [h], where F continues the Greek digamma), and this is found in two seventh-century inscriptions. After this time, F alone was used – with the consequence that the sound [w] now had to be written with V, originally just a sign for a vowel.

Some other orthographic peculiarities persist into the Old Latin period. Geminates (double consonants) are not represented in writing in early inscriptions, so e.g. *esse* "to be" is written ESE. Double spellings do not appear until the very end of the third century and do not become the universal norm for another century or so. At most periods in the history of Latin vowel length is not indicated in writing. There was a short-lived attempt (*c.* 135–75 BCE) to introduce a marker for long vowels by writing the vowel twice (e.g. AARA for *āra* "altar", EEMIT for *ēmit* "he bought") but it was never consistently applied (see Vine (1993) 267–286).

Phonological changes

Amongst the phonological developments that took place in the Archaic Latin and Old Latin periods a special importance attaches to the question of the accent and its influence on unstressed vowels. In Classical Latin the word accent normally fell on the penultimate syllable if this was heavy (e.g. *dīcátur, Rōmānórum, honéstās, capiēbántur*) and on the antepenultimate syllable if the penultimate was light (e.g. *dícitur, altíssima, refícere*). In the first stages of Archaic Latin, however, there was a strong stress accent falling on the first syllable of each word, which had the effect of preserving the vocalism of the stressed initial syllables pretty well but eventually causing weakening of short vowels in other syllables, the outcome being determined by the phonetic environment. The results of this are still apparent in Classical Latin, even after the later shift in the position of the accent, for instance in compound verbs like *refíciō* beside *faciō*, *percipiō* beside *capiō*, *desiliō* beside *saliō*, *abluō* beside *lauō*, *attingō* beside *tangō*, etc. In the case of open syllables (those ending in a short vowel), the weakening could take the form of actual loss of the vowel (this is known as syncope), although it is hard to frame consistent rules for the occurrence of this: examples of syncopated forms are *ualdē* "greatly, very" beside adj. *ualidus* "strong" and *propter* "near by" < **propiter*, derived from *prope* "near".

The initial stress accent of Archaic Latin is not inherited from Indo-European but finds parallels in other languages of central Italy, such as Etruscan, Oscan and Umbrian, languages that show extensive syncope of internal syllables, and is probably a regional feature that spread through contact. Vowel weakening in Latin seems to have taken place during the fifth century: there are still unweakened forms in the earliest inscriptions (e.g. FHEFHAKED "he made" from the seventh century) but by the time that inscriptions start to become more plentiful at the end of the fourth century the familiar forms with weakened vowels are found. The dating fits well with the fact that early borrowings from Greek – perhaps mainly sixth century – are affected by the process, cf. (Doric) *mākhanā* becoming *māchina*, *talanton* becoming *talentum*, etc. The shift to the Classical pattern of accentuation is thought to have occurred during the fourth century, and we can thus recognise here a major difference between Archaic Latin and Old Latin.

Another fourth-century change marking the transition from Archaic to Old Latin is rhotacism, the change of intervocalic [s] to [r]. This resulted in numerous alternations between related forms that still survive in Classical Latin as evidence for the rule, e.g. *queror* alongside *questus*, *erat* and *est*, *fūneris* and *fūnestus*. The change took place in the fourth century (this is in part known from the fact, reported by Cicero, *Fam.* 9.21.2, that L. Papirius Crassus, dictator in 340, was the first to spell the family name *Papirius* rather than *Papisius*). There are examples of unrhotacised forms in early inscriptions such as NUMASIOI (Class. *Numeriō*) from the seventh century, IOVESAT (Class. *iūrat*) from the sixth century, VALESIOSIO (Class. *Valerī*) from *c.* 500; some other archaic forms are cited by Roman grammarians, e.g. *fesias* for *fērias* (Paul. *Fest.* 76).

A number of other developments must be dated later, to well within the Old Latin period. Prominent amongst these is the treatment of the diphthongs that had remained unchanged throughout the Archaic Latin period but eventually became long vowels; cf. from a sixth-century dedication to the Dioscuri the case-endings in CASTOREI (dat.) beside Classical *Castorī* and QVROIS (dat. pl.) "youths" – a Greek loan – beside the Classical second-declension ending *-īs*. In the course of the third century [ei], [oi] and [ou] all underwent this process of monophthongisation.

The diphthong [ou] became [ū]. The earliest evidence for the change seems to be acc. sg. LVCIOM (the praenomen) from original **Loukiom* in one of the Scipio epitaphs from the second half of the third century (*CIL* I². 9). Instances of spellings with OV, however, are still found in the second century, either from old-fashioned habit or as a convenient notation for [ū], cf. LOVCOM (acc. sg.) "sacred grove", Class. *lūcum* (*CIL* I² 366), with an etymological diphthong, and POVBLILIA (*CIL* I². 42) for *Pūblilia* which may always have had [ū] not a diphthong.

The treatment of [oi] varied according to its position in the word. In initial syllables it normally gave [ū], cf. **oinos > ūnus* "one". The diphthong may still be represented in OINO (acc. sg.) from the third century (*CIL* I². 9) but LOIDOS for acc. pl. *lūdōs* "games" in the latter part of the second century (*CIL* I². 364) is an old-fashioned spelling that almost certainly no longer reflects pronunciation. In final syllables [oi] fell together with [ei] quite early on and the only evidence for it comes from sixth-century QVROIS noted above and perhaps a nom. pl. *pilumnoe poploe* (Paul. *Fest.* 224) cited from the ancient *carmen Saliare* but clearly already opaque in meaning to the grammarians.

The treatment of [ei] is worth examining in detail, since it brings out the complex links between spelling and pronunciation and illustrates the care needed in the interpretation of the written forms. Around the middle of the third century, the diphthong [ei] first became a close long vowel [ẹː]: this is indicated by spellings with E, e.g. FALERIES "at Falerii" (Class. *Faleriīs*), PLOIRUME (nom. pl.) 'very many" (Class. *plūrimī*) – both endings originally contained [oi] > [ei] > [ẹː]. This spelling was in competition with the retained spelling EI, a sequence that could now simply be read as a digraph notation for [ẹː] (and this seems to have been the preferred spelling in bureaucratic circles to judge from the consistent EI spellings of the *Senatusconsultum de Bacchanalibus* of 186 BCE). Around the middle of the second century [ẹː] merged with [ī], the change being signalled by the appearance of spellings with I: but as an alternative the traditional EI spelling was still kept, now standing for [ī], and as a notation simply for a long vowel it was used for any instance of [ī], even where there was no original diphthong, so that, for instance, whereas the *Senatusconsultum de Bacchanalibus* carefully distinguishes in second-declension forms between the nom. pl. in -EI and the gen. sg. in -I, late Republican inscriptions can have -I for both or -EI for both.

The diphthongs [ai] and [au] survived longer: [ai] was originally written AI but around the end of the third century began to be written AE (the Classical spelling) but this probably still represented some form of diphthong, at least in urban circles, down to the imperial period; [au] also remained a diphthong except in popular speech (note *Clodius* as the plebeian form of *Claudius*).

The third century also saw another sound change, the disappearance of final [-d] after a long vowel. This principally affected ablative singulars, cf. sixth-century FILEOD "son" beside Class. *fīliō*, and the future imperative in -TOD, Class. *-tō* (*facitō*, etc.). The change had certainly taken place by the middle of the century, when spellings without -D first appear, but final -ᴅ continued to be written well into the second century, e.g. in the conservative orthography of the *Senatusconsultum de Bacchanalibus* (ablatives ꜱᴇɴᴛᴇɴᴛɪᴀᴅ, ᴘᴏᴘʟɪᴄᴏᴅ, ᴍᴀɢɪꜱᴛʀᴀᴛᴠᴅ, etc.).

A similar date seems likely for the change of final [-os] to [-us] (e.g. in the nom. sg. of second-declension nouns) and slightly later, to judge from the inscriptional evidence, of [-om] to [-um], e.g. in the acc. sg. of the same declension. There is a complication here in that final [-s] and [-m] were clearly very weakly sounded in early Old Latin (though not Archaic Latin), as shown by the fact that they were often omitted in writing (cf. third-century ᴏᴘᴛᴜᴍᴏ "best", acc. sg.; Class. *optimum*). In the case of [-m], it may simply be the case that the preceding vowel was nasalised (which would explain why in verse elision over a final [-m] remains possible in the Classical period), and the regular spellings with -ᴍ from the second century on may not necessarily imply the restoration of a full consonant. With [-s] things are different: neglect of final [-s] after a short vowel for the purposes of scansion is condemned by Cicero (*Orat.* 161) as *subrusticum*, and it looks as though a proper [-s] was restored in speech as well as in writing (from the early second century onwards).

Selected Morphological Features

Verbal morphology

Archaic Latin and Old Latin inscriptions show certain verbal forms that are not found in the Classical language. For instance, a distinction is made in Archaic inscriptions between a third sg. ending -ᴛ, found in the present, and a third sg. ending -ᴅ, found in past tenses and the subjunctive, hence present ɪᴏᴠᴇꜱᴀᴛ but subjunctive ᴋᴀᴘɪᴀᴅ. These endings have their origins in Indo-European where there was distinction between so-called primary *-ti* in the present and secondary *-t* elsewhere. At the end of the fourth century ʙᴄᴇ -ᴛ is found as an alternative to -ᴅ and by the early third century it has become the only third sg. ending for all active moods and tenses, whence Classical *-t*.

Well attested in early Latin are sigmatic futures and subjunctives of the type *faxō* and *faxim* to *faciō* "I make, do" (on their function in comedy see de Melo, chapter 19 of this volume). These are by no means confined to literature and must have been standard at one time, cf., from the *XII Tables*, *si im occisit* "if he shall have killed him", *qui malum carmen incantassit* "whoever shall have cast a magic spell" and from inscriptions ꜱᴇɪQᴠɪꜱ ᴠɪᴏʟᴀꜱɪᴛ "if anyone shall have done damage" (*CIL* I².366, early second century). Later these futures were clearly perceived as hallmarks of legal language, as shown by Cicero's use of them in his *de Legibus*. There are in addition several other subjunctive formations, of rather limited attestation, that do not survive into Classical Latin (*duim, crēduās, attigās*, etc.). It may be that all of these unusual forms represent the débris of an originally distinct aorist system, generally lost in the merger with the perfect. (For a full discussion of the forms, their distribution and possible origins, see de Melo (2007b).)

Another form that points in the same direction is Archaic ꜰʜᴇꜰʜᴀᴋᴇᴅ "he made" (or "he had made") on the Praenestine fibula (see below) from the seventh century: this is a reduplicated perfect of *faciō*, standing alongside ꜰᴇᴄᴇᴅ in the sixth-century Duenos inscription (see below), which continues an old aorist form. By Classical Latin the inherited perfect and aorist have completely merged as the Latin perfect, with the selection of just one of the two original stems, but here there seems to be evidence for an indeterminacy that may be an indication that the two categories had not long been combined.

Levelling of a different kind took place in the verb "to be" where it seems that there were once parallel sets of stressed and unstressed forms (Meiser (1998) 221), for instance stressed third sg. *est* v. unstressed *st*, seen in forms like *inauguratumst* for *inauguratum est* "omens have been taken" (Pl. *As.* 259). Such forms are extremely common in the manuscripts of Plautus and Terence (and indeed later authors) and there are similar forms in Oscan, which points to a common Italic development. For the first sg. Varro (*L.* 9.100) cites an ancient form *esum*, which can be explained as the original stressed form beside: an inscription on a pottery bowl, known as the Garigliano bowl (Cristofani (1996)), dated to between the mid-sixth and mid-fifth centuries BCE, begins ESOM KOM MEOIS SOKIOIS ... "I am, together with my companions [presumably the rest of a set of bowls], (the property of....)" and this confirms Varro's report and establishes the Latinity of the form.

Nominal morphology

There are perhaps fewer peculiarities in the nominal morphology of early texts, but one remarkable form is the gen. sg. ending -*osio* of the second declension. A dedication to Mars from Satricum (*CIL* I².2832a), dated to the end of the sixth century, records that the dedicators were POPLIOSIO VALESIOSIO SVODALES "the companions of Publius Valerius". The ending -*osio* is inherited from Indo-European and is attested also in early Faliscan; a later form of it is no doubt to be recognised in TITOIO "of Titus" on a third-century dish from Ardea (Ve. 364a). The familiar Classical ending -*ī* is first attested in the early third century, but it is also found in Faliscan and is also inherited from Indo-European, so there can be little doubt about its antiquity. The Latin evidence does not allow more than speculation about the original function and distribution of the two endings.

From the second century come numerous instances of a second-declension nom. pl. ending -EIS (also found in pronouns) e.g. MAGISTREIS "magistrates" in several inscriptions or Q. M. MINVCIEIS "Quintus and Marcus Minucius" (*CIL* I².584, 117 BCE), the names of two brothers with their family name in the plural (see further below under "Some syntactic patterns"). The origin of this ending has been much discussed and among the preferred explanations are contamination with the third-declension ending -*ēs* or influence from Oscan, where the ending is -**ús**, but there is no obviously correct solution. (For a full collection of the evidence, and a quite different explanation, see Vine (1993) 215–239.)

In several Old Latin inscriptions there are third-declension forms with a gen. sg. ending -VS or -OS. This will continue *-*os*, which can readily be explained in Indo-European terms as a regular variant of the *-*es* that gives the normal Classical ending -*is*. Second-century examples include VENERVS "of Venus", NOMINVS LATINI "of the Latin name", DIOVOS "of Jupiter", KASTORVS "of Castor". Unfortunately the evidence is not sufficient to allow us to determine the original distribution of the variant ending or to make any secure claim for it as a dialectal feature (see the stern remarks of Adams (2007) 40–43).

Lexicon

The limited material from the Archaic period cannot give more than a glimpse of the vocabulary in use at the time, but it is at least possible to identify one or two items that later fell out of use, including two verbs. In two sixth-century inscriptions, including the Duenos inscription (see below), a third sg. form MITAT occurs, from the context obviously meaning something like "gives, presents". It may be related to Classical *mittō* "send" but because it belongs to a different conjugation it would have to be a separate formation from the same root (it cannot be subjunctive like Class. *mittat* because the context requires an indicative and also because the ending for a third sg. subjunctive would be written -D). Also from the Duenos inscription comes a future imperative TATOD, probably "may he steal": a verb *tā-* is otherwise unknown in Latin, but it will be an Indo-European inheritance, with cognates in Old Irish, Hittite, etc.

Evidence for the Old Latin period is far more plentiful, and here the picture is very different. This seems to have been a time of exuberant creativity, with new coinages arising at a remarkable rate. Categories that enjoyed particular expansion included denominal adjectives (Rosén (1999) 53–56) and substantival nominalisations, or abstract formations, where the older language shows an abundance of choice that is severely curtailed in Classical Latin (Rosén (1999) 62–70). For instance, "dirtiness" in older texts may be *squālitās, squālitūdō, squālēs* or *squālor* but only the last survives in normal Classical usage; similarly for "leanness", from amongst the options *macor, macritūdō* and *maciēs* in older Latin the Classical language selects just *maciēs*.

Vigorous variety gave way to Classical purity and precision, but the price paid was perhaps rather high.

Some Syntactic Patterns

Relative clauses

There are scant traces of an early construction in which the relative pronoun functions simply as a determiner of the noun in a nominal phrase. The best examples come from citations: cf. *qui patres, qui conscripti* (Paul. *Fest.* 304) with reference to senators; *diui qui potes* (Varro, *L.* 5.58) "powerful deities", taken from the books of the augurs. This usage is thought to continue an Indo-European pattern (Benveniste (1958)) since there are striking parallels in Greek and Sanskrit. An Old Latin literary example may be *salvete, Athenae, quae nutrices Graeciae* "hail, Athens, nurse of Greece" (Pl. *St.* 649), though some would prefer to see here, and certainly elsewhere in Old Latin a simple ellipse of the verb "to be" (so Lavency (1998) 112–113).

Likewise inherited is a more widely attested Old Latin pattern in which the relative clause, nearly always a restrictive (or defining) relative clause, precedes the main clause, with the nucleus (or head) incorporated into the relative clause and taking its case from its function within that (Lehmann (1979); Hettrich (1988) 467 ff.). The nucleus may be repeated in the main clause, or an anaphoric pronoun may be employed, as in the following examples:

IN AREA TRANS VIAM PARIES QUI EST PROPTER VIAM, IN EO PARIETE MEDIO OSTIEI LVMEN APERITO
in the area across the road, the wall which is near the road, in the middle of that wall he shall make an opening for a door. (*CIL* I².698. 9–11, 105 BCE)

ab arbore abs terra pulli qui nascentur, eos in terram deprimito
the shoots that grow from the tree from the ground, those one should push down into the ground. (Cato, *Agr.* 51)

It is possible to see a further development of this pattern in examples like:

agrum quem Volsci habuerunt campestris plerus Aboriginum fuit
the land that the Volsci occupied, the level land mainly belonged to the Aborigines. (Cato, *Orig.* fr. 7 Peter)

ostium quod in angiporto est horti, patefeci fores
the entrance to the garden in the alley, I have opened (its) door. (Pl. *Mos.* 1046)

patronus qui uobis fuit futurus, perdidistis
you have lost the man who was going to be your patron. (Pl. *As.* 621)

eunuchum quem dedisti nobis, quas turbas dedit!
the eunuch you gave us, what a disturbance he made! (Ter. *Eu.* 653)

These could, however, also be classified as instances of attraction (*attractio inversa*), with regular antecedents taking on the case of the relative pronoun, and this is especially likely to apply in the rare instances of appositive relative clauses following the pattern, e.g.

Naucratem quem conuenire uolui, in naui non erat
Naucrates, who I wanted to meet, wasn't on the ship. (Pl. *Am.* 1009)

or where the nucleus is determined by a demonstrative pronoun, e.g.

istos captiuos duos, heri quos emi … is indito catenas singularias
those two captives that I bought yesterday … put light fetters on them. (Pl. *Capt.* 110–112)

and the rare examples from Classical times are probably best explained as instances of attraction rather than as survivals of the earlier usage. In Late Latin the construction with *attractio inversa* is common and is generally regarded as a colloquial feature. In Old Latin it does not obviously have any such connotation, which it no doubt acquired as a consequence of the strong preference in the Classical language for the regular construction in which the relative clause immediately follows the antecedent (even in Plautus preposed relative clauses are less frequent than other patterns), and often serves simply as a way of marking the main topic of a sentence, as can be seen from several of the examples above. Traditionally the Old Latin relative clauses have been viewed with hindsight from the point of view of the Classical language, but if one takes into account the probable Indo-European inheritance a more illuminating account of the early stages becomes possible, and at all events there is a marked development through time ((Lehmann (1979); Hettrich (1988) 467 ff.; Rosén (1999) 33–35, 164–173).

Genitive and adjective

Another characteristic feature of early Latin that survives in later popular language but was originally probably unmarked for register is the employment of an adjective where Classical Latin prefers an adnominal genitive (see in general Wackernagel (2009) 487–490; Löfstedt (1942–1956) I.107–124). A classic instance is *nostra erilis concubina* "our master's concubine" (Pl. *Mil.* 458) as opposed to *concubina nostri eri*. This usage occurs frequently in Plautus (cf. *erile scelus* "my master's crime" (*Rud.* 198), *seruiles nuptiae* "a slave's wedding" (*Cas.* 68), *facinus muliebre* "the woman's shameful deed" (*Truc.* 809), etc.) but can be found in a wide range of texts. This helps to account for the great productivity in Old Latin of denominal adjectives with purely relational meaning: alongside formations with specific meanings such as *-ōsus* "full of" or *-ātus* "endowed with", which remain productive in Classical Latin, there are countless adjectives in *-āl/ris, -ārius, -icus*, etc. that simply indicate an adnominal relation, and these types lose ground in the Classical period in favour of the genitive (Rosén (1999) 53–56).

The antiquity of this use of the adjective is shown by established titles like *flāmen Diālis* "priest of Jupiter" and *uirgō Vestālis* "virgin of Vesta, Vestal virgin". Temples, on the other hand, are standardly referred to with the deity's name in the genitive, so *aedes Iouis* "the temple of Jupiter", *aedes Vestae* "the temple of Vesta", SVB AEDE KASTORVS "in the temple of Castor" (*CIL* I².586), which may perhaps be explained as an indication of a truly possessive relationship (Löfstedt (1942–1956) I.111–112). A certain fluidity of usage can be found: Plautus in the *Rudens* uses *sacerdōs Veneria* "priestess of Venus" three times (329, 350, 644) but also once *sacerdos Veneris* (430). Other survivals include month names such as *mēnsis Martius* "March, the month of Mars" and place-names at Rome such as *collis Quirīnālis* "the hill of Quirinus" and *campus Martius* "the field of Mars".

One use of adjectives that may aspire to be an Indo-European inheritance, given that there are convincing parallels in Greek, Venetic and elsewhere, is the formation of patronymic adjectives. This process is no longer in evidence as such in Latin (it survives in Umbrian) but it underlies a large number of *gentilicia* or family names. *Tullius*, for instance, was originally an adjective derived from the personal name *Tullus* and meant "son of Tullus", but it came to be applied to descendants in the next generation too and thus became a family name (just as in English *Johnson* ceased to mean literally "John's son" and became a surname to be passed on down the family).

It is interesting to note that in early Latin a *gentilicium* still behaved as an adjective. This explains why the road built on the instructions of someone called Flaminius is known as the *uia Flāminia*, and why a law proposed by someone called Sulpicius is known as a *lēx Sulpicia*. These are old patterns that remained as a model for later times. The adjectival nature of the *gentilicium* is also manifest in one or two Old Latin inscriptions mentioning brothers, e.g. the following from Praeneste, probably early second century BCE (*CIL* I².61):

Q. K. CESTIO Q. F. HERCOLE DONV DEDERO
Quintus and Kaeso Cestius, sons of Quintus, gave this as a gift to Hercules

The form CESTIO here is a nominative singular that has lost its final [-s]; it is singular because of the rule that when an adjective qualifies a number of preceding nouns it agrees with the last of them. In the course of the second century, the grammatical status of the *gentilicium* changed and it became a noun, and this is reflected in another inscription mentioning brothers, this time from the second half of the century (*CIL* I².1531) where we find M. P. VERTVLEIEIS C. F., with the family name in the nominative plural (in -EIS, see above) because it is now in apposition to *Marcus* and *Pūblius* as a noun (Meister (1916) 81–112).

Nominalisations with verbal syntax

The productivity of nominalisations in Old Latin was noted above, but their syntactic behaviour also deserves comment. In this period there are several examples of deverbal nominalisations behaving like verbs in taking direct objects or other complements. Some examples:

> quid tibi hanc digito tactio est?
> How come you are touching this girl here with your finger? (Pl. *Poen.* 1308)

> quid tibi hanc curatiost rem?
> How is this matter any concern of yours? (Pl. *Am.* 519)

> eius crebras mansiones ad amicam
> his frequent stays at his girl-friend's (Turpil. 171–172 com.)

> manum iniect[i]o
> "casting on of hands", i.e. "arrest" (*CIL* I².401)

In the Classical language an objective genitive replaces the accusative, though other forms of complement linger on, cf. Cicero, *Att.* 9.5.1 *mansio Formiis* "staying at Formiae".

Archaic Latin

The language of the XII Tables

Although attested only in citations that have been modernised in their spelling and phonology, the *XII Tables* (for which see Crawford (1996) II. 555–721) nonetheless preserve a certain number of Archaic morphological, lexical and syntactic features. For instance the preposition *endo*, attested also in a sixth-century inscription: this is an enlarged version of **en* (Class. *in*) which appears in nominal phrases such as *endo dies* "per day" and as a preverb in *manum endo iacito* "let him lay hands on (him)" i.e. "let him arrest (him)". This form is later used to provide archaic colouring by Cicero in his deliberately archaising legal language in the phrase *endo caelo* (*Leg.* 2.19); but the usual form in Old Latin is *indu*, cf. Ennius' *induperator* for *imperator* – such alternative forms being especially helpful in dactylic verse but already to be classified as artificial poetic creations.

One instance of *endo* is in *endoque plorato* "and he is to call out" (Class. *implorato*), where the preverb appears in tmesis, separated from its verb by an enclitic conjunction; cf. also *transque dato* "and he is to hand over" (Class. *tradito*). Tmesis of preverbs is a pattern inherited from Indo-European, where the elements that later became preverbs were essentially independent adverbs, but only one or two other examples survive in citations from old prayers: *sub uos placo* for *supplico uos* and *ob uos sacro* for *obsecro uos*, both meaning "I beseech you" (Paul. *Fest.* 402). It is unclear whether later instances such as *de me hortatur* "dissuades me" in Ennius (*Ann.* 371 Skutsch) represent archaic survivals or imitations of Homeric practice (Leumann (1977) 562; Weiss (2009) 463–464).

A striking syntactic characteristic of the *XII Tables* is the absence of any indication of the frequent changes of subject, which makes for a certain rugged concision: the most famous example (I.17 in Crawford's edition) is *si nox furtum fa<x>it, <ast> im occisit, iure caesus esto* "if he (A) shall have committed theft by night (and) he (B) shall have killed him (A), he (A) is to be lawfully killed". To be noted here also are the archaic verbal forms in *-s-*, still used in conditional clauses in Plautus but only as deliberate archaisms thereafter (see de Melo (2007b) 171–190) and the future imperative, which became a regular feature of legal language, as Old Latin inscriptions and Cicero's archaising legalese make clear.

Samples of Inscriptions

To illustrate how features such as those selected for comment above combine to give Archaic Latin a distinctive appearance, two short inscriptions may be cited in full.

The earliest Latin inscription (probably from Praeneste) is on a gold brooch and is dated to the seventh century BCE (*CIL* I².3): this is the *Fibula Praenestina* (see Figure 2.2, p. 13). Its authenticity has been challenged, but there are good arguments for accepting it as genuine (see Hartmann (2005) 67–106; Poccetti (2005)).

> MANIOS: MED: FHE:FHAKED: NUMASIOI
> (*Manius me fecit Numerio*)
> Manius made me (or "had me made") for Numerius

Noteworthy are the following points:

- nom. sg. [-os] remains unchanged
- MED for acc. sg. "me" beside Classical *mē*, shows a final [-d] intact after the long vowel (the source of the [-d] is not altogether clear, but it is the standard archaic form)

- FHE:FHAKED provides the best example of the FH spelling for [f], with punctuation of the reduplication that can be paralleled in an early Faliscan inscription (PE:PARAI), and with the expected final -D in a past tense; for the stem, see under "Morphological Features" above
- NUMASIOI, dat. sg., shows no internal vowel-weakening and no rhotacism, in contrast to the Classical equivalent *Numeriō*, and has a final diphthong, probably [-ōi] eventually becoming Classical [-ō].

More puzzling in content, at least in part, is an inscription written round the outside of a group of three small conjoined pots, found at Rome and to be dated probably to the mid-sixth century (*CIL* I².4), the *Duenos* inscription (see Figure 2.4, p. 16). There have been claims that the inscription is in verse.

IOVESATDEIVOSQOIMEDMITATNEITEDENDOCOSMISVIRCOSIED

ASTEDNOISIOPETOITESIAIPACARIVOIS

DVENOSMEDFECEDENMANOMEINOMDVENOINEMEDMALOSTATOD

The inscription does not mark division into words, but there is broad agreement amongst modern scholars on the analysis of the first and third lines, the second being almost entirely unintelligible; the meaning of the phrase EN MANOM EINOM in the third line is disputed. Most of the forms have Classical equivalents:

IOVESAT DEIVOS QOI MED MITAT NEI TED ENDO COSMIS VIRCO SIED
iūrat deōs quī mē (dōnat), nī tē in cōmis uirgō sit
…
DVENOS MED FECED EN MANOM EINOM DVENOI NE MED MALOS TATOD
bonus mē fēcit in (…(um) (…)um) bonō, nē mē malus (clepi)tō
He who gives me swears by the gods, if the girl is not affable towards you …
a good man made me … for a good man: let not a bad man steal me"

Noteworthy points that have not already been addressed:

- ENDO (see above) seems here to be used a postposition, governing acc. sg. TED
- SIED, with third sg. -*d* in the subjunctive, conforms to the original pattern of vowel alternation between singular and plural in this paradigm, with e.g. second sg. *siēs* but second pl. *sītis*, the plural stem eventually being generalised to give Classical *sim, sīs, sit* (the usual forms in Plautus except in certain metrical positions)
- DVENOS is the direct ancestor of *bonus* with regular sound changes.

Old Latin: On the Threshold of the Classical Language

In marked contrast with these Archaic texts, we may consider an inscription securely dated by its content to 241 BCE: it is on a bronze cuirass that was part of the booty from the capture of Falerii in that year (Zimmermann (1986)):

Q. LVTATIO. C. F. A. MANLIO. C. F.

CONSOLIBVS. FALERIES. CAPTO

Captured at Falerii under the consuls Q. Lutatius C. f. and A. Manilius C. f.

This shows a number of changes that herald the Classical norms:

- final [-d] has been lost from the ablative singulars
- [-os] has become [-us] in the ending -IBVS
- the spelling CONS- has replaced the COS- that was standard a little earlier (whence the abbreviation *cos.* for *consul* that survived into the Classical period), presumably with nasalisation of the vowel
- rhotacism has taken place in FALERIES < *Falisiois*, cf. *Falis-cī*.

Residual early features are:

- the second O of CONSOLIBVS (Class. *cōnsulibus*), cf. also TABOLAM (Class. *tabulam*) "tablet", acc. sg. in the *Senatusconsultum de Bacchanalibus*
- the E in the ending of FALERIES (a definite change from Archaic Latin but not yet the Classical vocalism – see above)
- the spelling CAPTO, with no indication of the final nasal and no change to the vowel of the final syllable (Class. *captum*).

One can see from this inscription that by 240 Latin was rapidly approaching its Classical state, at least as regards orthography and pronunciation. The changes to come were relatively minor, e.g. the regular change of vowel in *uoster* to *uester* "your (pl.)", *uorsus* to *uersus* "towards", *uotō* to *uetō* "forbid": this took place around the middle of the second century, the older forms remaining well enough known to be used as deliberate archaisms by later authors. The voiceless aspirates of Greek ([th], [ph] and [kh]) were at first ignored in Greek loanwords and these sounds were represented in inscriptions with T, P and C just like the unaspirated stops, cf. BACANAL in the *Senatusconsultum de Bacchanalibus* of 186 BCE as opposed to Class. *Bacchānal*; but around the middle of the second century greater care was taken to represent the aspiration in writing, and no doubt in pronunciation too, since aspiration seems then to have spread to some purely Latin words, perhaps initially as an affected pronunciation, e.g. *pulcher*. The transition may be seen in a dedication by L. Mummius following his destruction of Corinth in 146 BCE which contains both the phrase ACHAIA for Greece (perhaps the first example of the new spelling style) and abl. sg. CORINTO for Corinth with the older neglect of the aspiration.

FURTHER READING

This period in the history of Latin is well covered in chapters 4 and 5 of Clackson and Horrocks (2007) 90–182. On the origin and development of the Latin alphabet see Wachter (1987) esp. 7–54, 324–333 (on the date of the invention of the letter G); Wallace (1989). The most convenient collection of early Latin inscriptions is *ILLRP*; Warmington (1940) offers a wide selection with English translations; Wachter (1987) is indispensable for discussion of epigraphical matters and also linguistic features; Vine (1993) deals with one or two individual inscriptions and has chapters on various points of orthography, phonology and morphology, with many acute observations; Flobert (1991) gives an overview of what the earliest inscriptions contribute to our knowledge of the history of Latin; the limited evidence for dialectal variety in the inscriptions is treated by Adams (2007) 37–113. A good selection of prose texts, mainly literary, with a helpful commentary, can be found in Courtney (1999). (For the language of comedy, see de Melo, chapter 19 of this volume.) Phonological and morphological changes during this period are presented within the general context of the history of Latin in various handbooks, notably Leumann (1977), Sihler (1995), Meiser (1998), and Weiss (2009). Rosén (1999), showing how Classical Latin developed out of the older language, discusses numerous points of morphology and syntax.

CHAPTER 15

Classical Latin

James Clackson

Introduction

The term Classical Latin can be used in two different senses.* Firstly, it may refer to a chronological period in the history of the Latin language, from roughly 100 BCE to 200 CE, the period during which the majority of the Latin texts traditionally studied in schools and universities were composed. Secondly, Classical Latin can be used to refer to the standardised form of Latin, the variety which is enshrined by dictionaries and grammars as "correct Latin", and so understood by speakers and writers. In the first sense Classical Latin can be opposed to Early or Old Latin, Late Latin, etc. (as in the surrounding chapters in this volume); in the second sense it is opposed to designations for non-standardised varieties of Latin, sometimes labelled Sub-elite Latin or Vulgar Latin. This double usage of the term reflects the fact that it was during this period that the standard form of written Latin crystallised, and the authors of this time, in particular Cicero and Caesar, have been used as the models of Latinity ever since the first century CE. In this chapter I will attempt to trace the process by which Latin during this period became Classical Latin, and use as illustrations some of the debates about what was correct Latin and what was not. I will then move on to discuss the features that became identified as Classical Latin forms.

The Creation of a Standard

The idea that there were correct and incorrect varieties of Latin has a long history. In the early period of Latin, some texts show an interest in demarcating Latin, that is, in separating out which varieties of the language constituted Latin and which did not.

A Companion to the Latin Language, First Edition. Edited by James Clackson.
© 2011 Blackwell Publishing Ltd. Published 2011 by Blackwell Publishing Ltd.

Already at this time there was an awareness of regional and diachronic variation: in Plautus' *Truculentus*, a character from Praeneste is mocked for his different pronunciations of Latin words (Adams (2007) 119–121), thereby implying that a Roman audience stigmatised accents from outside the city. The epitaph of the poet Naevius (fl. 235–204 BCE), reputedly written by himself, concludes that at his death *obliti sunt Romae loquier lingua Latina* "men at Rome have forgotten how to speak Latin", which suggests that linguistic change was seen as detrimental to the language. However, it is only in the middle of the second century BCE that we see direct evidence for the adoption of a Greek grammatical tradition that included ideas about correct language and contained specific terms to classify linguistic "faults". Unfortunately, there are no Roman grammatical treatises surviving from this period, but the term for a fault of grammar, *soloecismus*, a borrowing from Greek grammatical terminology, is first attested in Lucilius (fr. 1100 Marx, there declined with a Greek inflectional ending), and other fragments of Lucilius show concern with orthography and usage. The incorporation of Greek ideas of grammatical correctness and a search for linguistic purity at this time fits in with the tradition reported by Suetonius (*Gram.* 2) that Crates of Mallus, grammarian and envoy of the King of Pergamum, instigated Roman interest in grammar when he was waylaid in Rome after falling in the Cloaca Maxima and breaking his leg. The debt to Greek ideas on language, and to the Hellenistic models of correct language, even including debates on pronunciation, is apparent throughout the history of Classical Latin.

By the beginning of the first century BCE we know of several Romans writing and discussing Latin orthography and grammar: Cicero sets his dialogue *de Oratore*, which includes discussion of correct language and pronunciation, in the year 91 BCE, and other sources give information on orthographic reforms attributed to the poet Accius (*c.* 170–85 BCE) and of the linguistic prescriptions of the stoic Aelius Stilo Praeconinus (154–90 BCE). The earliest surviving definition of what constitutes *Latinitas*, literally translated as "Latinity", but including within it the idea of "correct Latin", dates to around this time also. It appears in the anonymous treatise, *Rhetorica ad Herennium* (4.17, see Müller (2001) 249–250 on the Greek antecedents to this passage):

> Latinitas est quae sermonem purum conseruat ab omni uitio remotum. uitia in sermone, quo minus is Latinus sit, duo possunt esse: soloecismus et barbarismus. soloecismus est, cum in uerbis pluribus consequens uerbum superius non adcommodatur. barbarismus est, cum uerbis aliquid uitiose efferatur.

> It is Correct Latinity which keeps the language pure and free of any fault. The faults in language which can mar its Latinity are two: the Solecism and the Barbarism. A Solecism occurs if the concord between a word and one before it in a group of words is faulty. A barbarism occurs if the verbal expression is incorrect. (Translation by H. Caplan)

The definition of *Latinitas* given in the *ad Herennium* stresses two connected features: *sermo purus* "pure speech" and "avoidance of error" *ab omni uitio remotus*. This approach accords well with the surviving evidence for the activity of other thinkers on language from the first century BCE, who display a parallel concern with linguistic purity and the absence of faults. How to achieve these goals could be a matter for debate, and the two aims may not be consistent. Thus one possible approach was to insist on purity through the maintenance of features recorded in earlier texts, without the taint of any outside influence. Hence the drive for *Latinitas* could lead to the rejection of any innovatory forms. For example, Varro (*L.* 6.59) records that Aelius Stilo avoided the form *nouissimus* "newest", with the meaning of "last" (*extremus*), on the grounds that *nimium nouum uerbum quod esset* "it was too new a formation". Doubtless the example of *nouissimus* being *nimium nouus* is partly a grammarian's joke, but it is also programmatic, reflecting Stilo's concern to keep to the language of earlier times. The insistence on correct language through avoidance of the novel, the unusual and the recondite is taken up by other prominent figures in the next hundred years, and it is most memorably expressed in Julius Caesar's injunction *tamquam scopulum, sic fugias inauditum atque insolens uerbum* (cited by Gellius (1.10.4)) "you should avoid an unheard and unusual word as (a sailor avoids) a reef".

However, the definition of *Latinitas* given in the *ad Herennium* also encompassed a different view of correctness. It might be thought, for example, that the need to avoid any fault sanctioned the creation of new linguistic forms in place of existing ones that were judged incorrect. By this view, correctness consists in regular formations bound by rules, and anomalous formations needed to be purged from the language. An example of an attempt to construct *Latinitas* in this way may be provided by a surviving pronouncement of Cornelius Sisenna (whose work only survives in fragments, but whose career in the first half of the first century BCE is studied by Rawson (1979)). Sisenna is reported by Varro (recorded at Gellius 2.25.9) to have used the active *adsentio* "I assent" in place of the traditional, formulaic, deponent form *adsentior*, in the Senate, presumably on the grounds that the uncompounded verb *sentio* was active rather than deponent in form, and the compound should show a parallel formation.

Sisenna's decision to say *adsentio* rather than *adsentior* may be seen as an example of the precepts of *analogia* "analogy", that is, the theory that correct language is constituted through *ratio*, regularity and rules. It is impossible to tell from these anecdotal accounts whether figures such as Sisenna and Stilo had consistent positions on what constituted correct language, or whether they were part of a larger division between purists and innovators. One important source could be read to indicate that they were: in Books 8–10 of the *de Lingua Latina*, written probably in the 40s BCE, Varro opposes analogy to *anomalia* "anomaly", the theory that language is ad hoc and follows usage (*consuetudo*). Only five of the twenty-five original books of the *de Lingua Latina* survive but, in the absence of other extant works devoted specifically to language from the Republican period, it remains a vital source for the linguistic attitudes of the period. Much has been written about the analogy and anomaly debate as it occurs in Varro (see Matthews (1994), and Blank (2005) for discussions), and it remains unclear whether the arguments that feature in Varro's account were actually current in Rome in the late Republic or Empire; Aulus Gellius, who had a low opinion of grammarians in general, is able to show up some of the fallacies of grammarians after Varro who attempted to impose a normative usage on the language, and ignored the authority of earlier Latin writers (Holford Strevens (2003) 172–192). Although it may be tempting to arrange individuals on either side of the anomaly and analogy divide, numbering Stilo, for example, among the anomalists and Sisenna among the analogists, we cannot know for certain. It may be significant that Varro nowhere specifies any single Roman as an analogist or anomalist, but rather refers generally to the two positions as ideal poles. Indeed, his presentation of the debate casts both the analogist and the anomalist as straw men, whose arguments necessarily lead to ridiculous conclusions, and between whom Varro can position himself as a reasonable and realistic occupant of the centre ground. In the absence of clear evidence, we do not know of any individual who employed a *Latinitas* constructed entirely and consistently on theoretical principles. It is possible that different writers and speakers used whatever arguments came to hand to justify the variety of Latin that was used by them and their immediate social groups, presenting a justification of their own linguistic practice through the support of whatever theory best suited.

This conclusion derives some support from the evidence of Cicero's writings, as we shall see below. Indeed, in comparison with the information available for the first decades of the first century BCE, there is a comparative wealth of material for the middle of the century to show how Romans decided between different linguistic varieties, principally because of the survival of Cicero's reflections on language in his dialogues, philosophical works and letters, together with the surviving portions of Varro's *de Lingua Latina*. The concentration of information from Cicero and Varro can make it appear that the debate on language was restricted to a small number of individuals, but given the highly competitive spirit of the late Republic, it is likely that many leading Romans used language to position themselves and to disparage others. The anecdote about Sisenna's use of *adsentio* given above is telling in that it refers explicitly to speech in the Senate, and furthermore Quintilian (*Inst.* 1.5.13) reports that many once followed Sisenna in the employment of the active form.

The reliance on features of speech as a mark of social position and education can be seen from debates over pronunciation of individual words, corresponding to part of the second area associated with faults in language in the *Rhetorica ad Herennium*. Fortunately, in one case we have two surviving pieces of evidence from the late Republic that discuss the same "barbarism", the use of the aspirated allophone of voiceless stops ($p\ t\ c$) in some words. Firstly, Catullus, in epigram 84, ridicules a certain Arrius for pronouncing the words *commoda* "advantages" as *chommoda*, as well as inserting unetymological *h* word-initially in utterances such as *hinsidias* for *insidias* "ambush". These speech errors clearly reflect hypercorrections, that is attempts by speakers to upgrade their language to incorporate a feature which they do not have in their own dialect, and inadequate knowledge of the words in which the feature is found. The use of the aspirate with the consonant *c* in *chommoda* reflects the pronunciation of Greek loan words with aspirated consonants, here extended to a non-Greek word. Catullus notes in the poem that Arrius' uncle was a freedman, thereby linking the linguistic fault with a lower-class origin.

In his rhetorical treatise *Orator* (159), Cicero also mentions the aspirated pronunciation of consonants, but this time the emphasis is different:

quin ego ipse, cum scirem ita maiores locutos ut nusquam nisi in uocali aspiratione uterentur, loquebar sic ut pulcros, Cetegos, triumpos, Cartaginem dicerem; aliquando, idque sero, conuicio aurium cum extorta mihi ueritas esset, usum loquendi populo concessi, scientiam mihi reseruaui.

Indeed, I myself, since I knew that our ancestors did not employ the aspirate except before a vowel, I used to say *pulcer* ("beautiful" – for later *pulcher*), *Cetegus* (a Roman cognomen, for later *Cethegus*), *triumpus* ("triumph" for later *triumphus*) and *Cartago* ("Carthage" for later *Carthago*), but after some time – a long time in fact, the true pronunciation was wrested from me by the protest of my ears, and I gave way to the people in the way of speech, and kept my learning to myself.

Here the same linguistic feature that is stigmatised in *commoda* by Catullus is adopted in other words by Cicero, since to avoid using the form appears pedantic and reactionary. The words chosen by Cicero cannot be identified as Latin through their make-up, unlike Arrius' *commoda*, which is clearly a compound involving first element *con–*. Cicero avoids the two extremes of appearing over-punctilious or uneducated, and by keeping to the middle ground finds favour with the largest number of speakers. Usage trumps tradition, but only if enough people agree on the usage.

In a culture that was so imbued with the merits of following the *mos maiorum*, it is striking to see how often an innovative form is preferred to one that appeared to the Romans to be more archaic. Other passages from Cicero show a similar rejection of linguistic features that had a good Latin pedigree. Firstly, two other examples from *Orator*: at 157 Cicero discusses the third person plural ending of the perfect, and prefers the form -*erunt* to -*ere* although acknowledging that the -*ere* form is attested in Ennius; at 161 he refers to the loss of final -*s* after a short vowel which was practised by earlier poets, such as *qui est omnibu' princeps* "who is prince in all things" (for *omnibus princeps*), which *iam subrusticum uidetur, olim autem politius* "now seems rather rustic, although once was more polished". The third example, from the dialogue *de Oratore* (3.44–6) is perhaps more telling. Here, Cotta is said to pronounce the vowel represented in contemporary orthography with the digraph *ei* as a very broad *e*, but he fails to sound like the *oratores antiqui*, the orators of former days, but instead like a farmhand. There is insufficient evidence to know the exact linguistic details, but Cotta seems to have aimed for a pronunciation of [e:] where urban Latin speakers used [i:]. Although this pronunciation may have been in use at an earlier date in Rome, it was certainly marked as a rustic feature by 100 BCE (indeed, it is one of the dialectal features which is ridiculed in Plautus' *Truculentus*). It seems that one prized aspect of correct Latinity was the ability to distinguish the speech of the elite from the rest; aristocratic speech of one generation may not be so distinctive in the next generation, since the accents of all speakers change over time. It is noteworthy also that at *Brut.* 259, Cicero mentions that the same Cotta's accent resulted from his attempt to make his speech sound less Greek: those who attempted to avoid the influence of Greek ended up speaking like rustics. The connotations of *rusticus* "rustic" during the first century BCE may also be important: Joseph and Wallace (1992) have argued that demographic change, in particular rural depopulation and the move into Rome of many of the lower classes from the surrounding countryside, may have led to the rustic dialects becoming the speech of the urban poor.

This is not to say that there was no use of earlier authors to support linguistic choices made in the first century BCE. Several different sources suggest that one favoured model was provided by the speakers and poets associated with or patronised by Cornelius Scipio Aemilianus Africanus. Indeed Scipio himself is a byword for elegant language, and even more so his friend Laelius, mentioned along with Servius Galba in Cicero's dialogue *de Oratore* (1.58) as the orators *quos constat dicendi gloria praestitisse* "who are agreed to be exceptional in their fame in speaking"; furthermore, Laelius avoids the criticism Galba receives elsewhere in the *de Oratore* for harshness. Laelius' eloquence was such that it was held to have been communicated to his daughter (Cicero *de Orat.* 3.45, Quintilian *Inst.* 1.1.6), and to be reflected in the plays of Terence. Indeed, Terence was reckoned to stand apart from the other early Latin comic playwrights on account of his purity of language, a purity which is advertised in the prologue to the *Hautontimorumenos*: 46 *in hac est pura oratio* "in this play there is pure language". In the search for pure and correct Latin, Terence's vocabulary choice provided a model for authors to follow (Müller (2007)), and both Julius Caesar and Cicero wrote verses in praise of Terence's purity of language, perhaps (Courtney (2003) 155) at the instigation of their teacher, the grammarian Antonius.

A passage in one of Cicero's letters to Atticus (*Att.* 7.3) illustrates the recourse to Terence in order to settle a disagreement about correct usage. Cicero and Atticus are debating the right way to say "to Piraeus". The following options are discussed:

1   preposition and Latin ending *in Piraeum* (Cicero's eventual favourite);
2   preposition and Greek ending *in Piraeea* (which was Cicero's first attempt);
3   no preposition and Greek ending *Piraeea* (which Atticus offered as more correct).

Cicero defends *in Piraeum* on the grounds of reason, *Romanitas*, and authority. Since Piraeus is not a town but a locality, it does not fall under the rule that local prepositions are not used with towns; the Latin form is preferable to the Greek since Cicero and Atticus are Romans. The argument from authority cites Terence, who uses the phrase *in Piraeo* at *Eu.* 539. Cicero confirms the link of Terence with Laelius in his comment *cuius fabellae propter elegantiam sermonis putabantur a C. Laelio scribi*, "whose plays were thought to be written by Gaius Laelius because of the elegance of the language".

By the time of the Principate, new models were available to those wishing to speak and write Latin correctly, and a consensus appears to have been reached over what constituted *Latinitas*. In the discussions of language in Quintilian's *Institutiones* we no longer find any programmatic discussion of "purity". It appears that the work of eliminating the errors of speech had been done by the previous generation, and Quintilian can confidently assert that no one would nowadays use coinages such as *tuburchinabundus* "voracious" or *lurchinabundus* "guzzling" which occur in Cato (*Inst.* 1.6.42). For Quintilian, language is constituted on *ratione uel uetustate, auctoritate, consuetudine* "reason, antiquity, authority and use" (*Inst.* 1.6.1), of which the surest guide is use, which is further defined (*Inst.* 1.6.45) as the *consensus eruditorum* "the agreed practice of the educated". The educated are able to rely on the body of knowledge which is now codified by teachers and grammarians, with textual support from a new canon of authors. Quintilian's detailed account in Book X on the *Institutiones* gives us a clear view of which authors are favoured in the new canon: Virgil for epic, Horace for lyric, Livy and Sallust for history and Cicero and Caesar for oratory (compare the canon of authors given by Vitruvius, 9. pref. 16–17, during the Augustan period: Ennius, Accius, Lucretius, Cicero and Varro). These are the texts the Romans can set alongside the Greek classics as worthy Latin equivalents, and which inculcate among readers the norms of the Latin standard. Quintilian accurately reflects the actual use of these texts in his day, to judge from surviving sub-literary texts from Britain, Palestine and Egypt, which testify to the use of these canonical texts in education across the Roman world: lines of Virgil appear on the back of letters and in school exercises at Vindolanda (*T.Vindol.* II. 118 and II. 452, Scappaticcio (2009)) and in two different locations in Palestine, Masada (*P.Masada* 721) and Auja el-Hafr (*P.Ness.* 2.1) as well as in various locations in Egypt, including a writing exercise in Mons Claudianus, a Roman quarry town in the remote eastern desert (*O.Claud.* 190).

The debates about the selection of "correct" language that survive from the end of the Republic and early Empire can only be the tip of the iceberg. In speeches, in private conversations, in letters and more formal writing, language was scrutinised, criticised and corrected. Indeed, Quintilian records the precept of Cicero (*Inst.* 10.7.28) *nullum nostrum usquam negligentem esse sermonem* "never to be careless about our speech". The interest in language as a social marker which we met already in Catullus is seen across all levels of society in Rome from the later Republic into the Empire. No one was immune from criticism. Suetonius records the linguistic foibles of emperors, and that criticism could be made to their face: the Emperor Vespasian was reproached by a senator named Florus for pronouncing the word for "wagon" *plostrum* rather than *plaustrum* (Suetonius *Ves.* 22; Vespasian's response was to address Florus as *Flaurus* the next day, perhaps punning on Greek φλαῦϱος "worthless") and Tiberius was corrected by the grammarian Pomponius Marcellus for using a new word (Suet. *Gram.* 22), with the memorable quip "you can confer citizenship upon men, but not upon a word". Leading authors were also attacked for deviations from Latinity: Virgil's *cuium pecus* (*Ecl.* 3.1) "whose flock?" (for Classical Latin *cuius pecus?*) was parodied by an otherwise unknown poet Numitorius who declares that this form is not Latin, but *sic rure loquuntur* "thus they speak in the country". Asinius Pollio, who could also find fault with Cicero and Sallust, upbraided Livy for *patauinitas* "Paduanism" rather than *Latinitas* (Quint. *Inst.* 1.5.56, although there are no clearly discernible dialectal features in Livy's language (Adams (2007) 148–149). At the other end of the scale, the unlearned and unlettered could be found out from their solecisms and barbarisms: nowhere is this more clearly set out than in Petronius' *Satyrica* where the speech of the freedmen at Trimalchio's dinner party is satirised, complete with its faults and hypercorrections. The complaint of Messalla, a speaker in Tacitus' *Dialogus*, set in 76 CE, may well have been a commonplace (compare the criticism of "modern education" by the character Agamemnon in Petr. 4–5, or Pliny's lament over forensic speaking in his day at *Ep.* 2.14): clever young men of the day are so badly educated that they show in their courtroom speeches *huius quoque cotidiani sermonis foeda ac pudenda uitia* (32.3) "the vile and shameful faults even of our everyday speech".

This process of linguistic purification, of discussion and debate (which has never come to an end) gave rise to what we now call Classical Latin. The steps on the road to Classical Latin are in accord with the stages identified by modern sociolinguistics in the formation of a "standard" language: the selection of a particular variety of language from among a number of different regional and social dialects; the codification of this form in grammars and its use in schools and education; the development of lexical and syntactic resources to enable the standard to be used in the arenas of public life, in cultural productions and technical writings; and finally the speakers' internalisation of the variety as the correct form of the language, inherently superior to other dialects. The striking features of the standardisation of Latin are two: the absence of a single, centralising body behind the selection of what was to be Classical Latin; and the communication of the standard form of the language throughout an empire without the technical advantages of broadcast media or even printing. Not all linguistic communities rely on an academy or a commission to fix the standard language for the nation, it is true, but the Classical Latin situation also seems different from cases where the language of the court or the centres of religion or education become the standard. In Rome it is not the language of the Senate or the law courts or even the emperor which is adopted as the model for Classical Latin (although these all certainly contributed to the make-up of *Latinitas*), rather, it appears to have been the language of the majority of Romans of the equestrian and senatorial ranks. Indeed, in the history of the standard language, it is striking how many key figures are not members of the Roman nobility: Laelius was the son of a *nouus homo*, Terence a freedman, Accius the son of a freedman, Lucilius, Aelius Stilo and probably also Varro were of equestrian rank, and Cicero was of course also a *nouus homo*. Although the drive for purity of language can be seen as a way of keeping out the urban poor from cultured discourse, correct language could also be a means for an outsider to win acceptance into the elite. It is perhaps this strong urge to use language as a social marker to gain acceptance that explains how Classical Latin could gain its sway over the Roman dominion at such speed and with such thoroughness, without the aid of printing presses or radio. Speakers and writers needed to be above reproach in their language, and therefore took every effort to standardise their own Latin through whatever means available.

It makes sense to think in terms of Classical Latin as an "ideology" as Adams notes ((2007) 17), rather than as a fixed set of words and forms. Speakers and writers aimed to make their own speech conform, but although there was broad consensus about what constituted *Latinitas*, there was always room at the edges for some variation and discussion. It was possible for Latin speakers and stylists to make certain choices within Classical Latin, particularly if their choices were sanctioned by some earlier writer or text. Minor infringements of the strictest grammatical rules could be tolerated; indeed, the cultured speaker should avoid the pedantry of a grammarian. Cicero's decision to follow the crowd and keep his learning to himself (cited above) is reprised in later centuries by Quintilian and Gellius, who dismiss the rules and precepts of grammarians as divorced from the real living language of the cultured classes: in the dictum cited by Quintilian with approval (*Inst.* 1.6.27) *aliud esse Latine, aliud grammatice loqui* "speaking Latin is different from speaking grammatically."

Within the ideology of Classical Latin during the Empire tastes and styles are able to change, and over the course of time, as speech habits change and the Classical idiom becomes more a product of learning and education than a reflection of actual practice, there is an increasing tendency to look for new models from the past. Tacitus' *Dialogus* rewrites Cicero's *de Oratore* for a later age, presenting speakers debating whether the new style of oratory in the age of Vespasian is inferior to that of the age of Cicero. One speaker, Aper, defends those who use the contemporary style, and ridicules the archaists of his day who prefer the style and language of earlier authors to the Classical canon, such as Lucilius to Horace, Lucretius to Virgil, and Sisenna to other historians, with the result that the audience cannot follow them (*Dial.* 23). But the archaising movement was to gain ground in the second century CE, or at least, we have clearer reflections of it in the surviving literature of the period, in authors as diverse as Apuleius and Aulus Gellius. Archaism at this period consisted principally of lexical choices, and the trend can be followed through tracking the revival of words and suffixes that were found in early Latin writers, but avoided in the age of Cicero and Caesar. For example, the -*tudo* suffix, used to derive abstract nouns from adjectives, is frequent in early Latin, and much favoured by Cato. In Classical Latin of the first century BCE the suffix falls out of favour: there are few new creations and only some of the existing words with the suffix are retained in use, such as *multitudo* "multitude", *magnitudo* "size", *consuetudo* "custom" (in Caesar, there are only eighteen nouns with the suffix). But from the Flavian period and later the suffix comes back into favour: Tacitus revives *claritudo* and *firmitudo* in the *Annales* at the expense of *claritas* and *firmitas*, and Apuleius uses thirty-seven nouns in -*tudo* (see Rosén (1999) 62–63 and Langslow (2000b) 309). Tellingly, Gellius looks to second-century BCE authors Cato and Claudius Quadrigarius, rather than to Cicero, to justify his lexical choices of *duritudo* "hardness" over "Classical" *duritia*, and *sanctitudo* "holiness" over *sanctitas* and *sanctimonia* (17.2.19–20).

In the rest of this chapter I will look in more detail at the linguistic outcomes of the formation of Classical Latin, and highlight some of the choices that were made between different lexical and morphological options available in early Latin. It is important first to stress once again the incompleteness of our picture of Classical Latin, and highlight the difficulties of comparing Early and Classical Latin texts. Our Early Latin evidence is skewed heavily by the survival of large amounts of drama, particularly comedy, a genre for which we have no Classical Latin counterpart. Some features of Early Latin may seem to disappear from the Classical language, but their absence reflects rather their incompatibility with the generic conventions of the bulk of surviving Latin texts. For example, take the vocative particle *mi* (probably originally a dative form of the personal pronoun), which is found attached to vocatives in Roman comedy, as in the phrases *mi pater* "father mine", *mi uir* "my husband", etc. In Classical texts the particle largely drops out of use: Dickey (2002) 216 calculates that in Cicero's speeches and philosophical and rhetorical works the particle occurs with less than 1 per cent of vocatives. However, *mi* does occur in Cicero's letters, in the letters of Augustus as reported by Suetonius (*Aug.* 51 *et alibi*), and its use is frequent in the Latin Vulgate. Since the language of Cicero's letters admits of features such as switches into Greek, which are avoided in his work written for publication, and since Augustus' epistolary language is also noted for its non-standard forms, it is tempting to see *mi* as a conversational feature which was deliberately avoided as too informal in Classical Latin, and which appeared only in substandard documents until it receives a new lease of life in the less elevated idiom of the Bible translation. However, as Dickey has shown (2002) 215–217, this conclusion is erroneous; *mi* only appears to be absent from Classical Latin because it is largely restricted to the genre of letters, for which we have few examples other than those of Cicero in the first century BCE. In the letters of Seneca, Pliny and Fronto and their correspondents, *mi* occurs frequently. Moreover, *mi* is rare in the Pompeiian graffiti and in direct speech in Petronius (only 3 per cent of the vocatives in Petronius include *mi*), and completely absent from direct speech reported in Suetonius, but, as we have seen, included in his citations of letters. It appears that *mi* was no longer a feature of spoken Latin in the Classical period, but was a feature of epistolary style. It was not a colloquialism or a non-standard feature, but a feature of Classical Latin which is of restricted occurrence in our surviving texts.

Latin Orthography and Pronunciation

In this section I will consider orthographic changes and changes in pronunciation together (see also the discussion of Roman orthographic practices in chapters 2 and 4). Our knowledge of the pronunciation of Classical Latin is of course partly dependent on our knowledge of the orthographic practices, and Roman grammarians consistently use the term *littera* "letter" to refer to sounds as well as written signs, so a clear distinction between orthography and pronunciation is in any case difficult. Classical Latin orthography was never as fixed as the orthography of modern standard languages. There was no agreed resource specifying "correct" spelling which all writers could rely upon, and surviving documents and inscriptions from the Classical period show considerable variation. A professional scribe or stonecutter may use two different spellings of the same word within two lines of the same document or official inscription (for example, *singulos* at *T.Sulpicii* 7.3.8 and *singlis* at *T.Sulpicii* 7.3.9; *c]laussum* at II 42 of the *Monumentum Ancyranum*, the record of Augustus' *Res Gestae*, and *clausum* two lines later on the same inscription). What is more, orthographic practices could and did change over time, although change was often slow and piecemeal, with archaic spellings retained long after the sounds they represented had developed in all varieties of the spoken language.

The current spelling of most Classical texts, as maintained in dictionaries such as the *Oxford Latin Dictionary*, shows certain later developments from the way in which Cicero would have written Latin. Even so, the *Oxford Latin Dictionary* is closer to Cicero's orthography than older text editions, dictionaries and grammars, such as Lewis and Short (1879), which separate consonantal *v* from vocalic *u*, and consonantal *j* from vocalic *i*, a practice which is unknown in antiquity. In many respects, Cicero's orthography would appear archaic to modern readers. For example, in early Latin a geminate *ss* was written and pronounced after long vowels and diphthongs in words such as *caussa* "reason", *claussus* "closed", but in speech this was simplified to a single *s*, and so spelt in inscriptions already in the second century. However, Quintilian (*Inst.* 1.7.20) relates that the older spelling was used both by Virgil and Cicero, and the inscriptional text of Augustus' *Res Gestae* has the spellings *c]laussum* and *caussa* (although the "modern" spelling *clausum* also occurs, see above). Although Quintilian implies that the spelling is antiquated in his day, scribes at Vindolanda and elsewhere wrote with the double *ss* spellings at the end of the first century CE (Adams (1995b) 89–90); as Adams notes, the Vindolanda scribes who use the double *ss* spelling do so consistently, and also use *xs* in place of *x* and occasionally third declension ablatives in *-i* in place of *-e*. It may be that some writers followed an "archaising school" of orthography.

Another archaic feature which Cicero would have used (as shown in his discussion of Cotta's accent in *de Oratore* cited above) is the digraph *ei* for a sound which was originally a diphthong, but which had changed in speech to a long *i* in the second century BCE. Although the earliest official spelling with *i* for *ei* is attested in a *senatusconsultum*, CIL I².586, dated to around 160 BCE (alongside many examples of the spelling *ei* in the same text) the spelling with *ei* was retained for a long period after this. Lucilius appears to have set down rules for distinguishing second declension nominative plurals and genitive singulars through the writing of *ei* for the first, and *i* for the second (reported by Quintilian, *Inst.* 1.7.15). The use of *ei* is still found in some Pompeiian inscriptions and

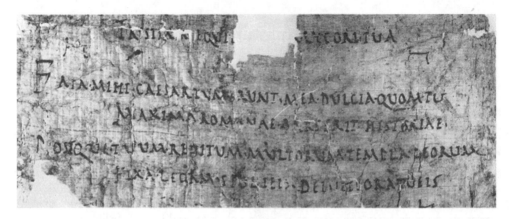

Figure 15.1 Papyrus fragment of Gallus found at Qasr Ibrim. Reproduced from Plate V of *JRS* 69, 1979, courtesy of The Egypt Exploration Society.

in the fragment of Cornelius Gallus found at Qasr Ibrim, which was composed shortly before the assassination of Julius Caesar, and which may reflect Gallus's own orthography (Anderson *et al.* (1979)). There is no evidence for *ei* spellings in the documents found in Britain, but an isolated spelling from a letter of Claudius Terentianus, (*P.Mich.* VIII 469.11) *rescreibae* for *rescribe* "write back!", shows that the spelling is still known in Egypt as late as 110 CE. Long vowels other than long *i* were also marked by some writers of Latin in this period. The doubling of letters to represent a long vowel, as *paastores* for *pastores* "shepherds", associated with the second-century writer Accius, largely falls out of use as an inscriptional habit during the Sullan period (but see Oliver (1966) 155 for later inscriptional examples), but the use of an apex to mark long vowels (other than *i*), as *pástores*, is not uncommon during the Classical period, particularly in manuscript documents, although it is never used to mark every long vowel in a text of more than a few words.

Several other spellings which reflect pronunciations or spelling rules of the second century BCE survived into the first century AD, including final *-os* and *-om* in words where the stem ended in *-u-*, as *seruos* and *equom* for *seruus* "slave" and *equum* "horse", and the writing of *quo* for *cu* in the words *quom*, *quoius* and *quoi* for *cum* "when, since", *cuius* "whose" and *cui* "for whom", and the writing of the medial vowel of *maximus*, *optimus* with *u* for *i* (these seem to be attempts to represent a sound which is halfway between [u] and [i], as Quintilian suggests at *Inst.* 1.4.8). Quintilian noted (*Inst.* 1.7.7) that Latin compound words could be written with "etymological" spellings, showing the origin of the different elements, such as *conlega* for *collega* "colleague", or phonetically, reflecting the pronunciation, as *apsens* for *absens* "absent", although ancient writers were no more consistent in applying an etymological or phonetic approach than the orthography of the *OLD*, which favours *absens* and *collega* —the *Monumentum Ancyranum* has *conlega* but *apsens*.

The choice between various different "archaic" and "modern" spellings enabled literary authors to present individual orthographic styles. The papyrus fragment of Gallus mentioned above, and reproduced as Figure 15.1, demonstrates this well. The text is as follows (interpuncts between words are noted as periods, and large caps represent the larger letters at the beginnings of the lines):

Fata . mihi . caesar . tum . erunt . mea . dulcia . quom . tu
　　Maxima romanae. [pa]rs eri<s> historiae.
Postque . tuum . reditum . multorum . templa . deorum
　　Fixa . legam . spolieis . deiuitiora . tueis.

My life will then be sweet for me, Caesar, when you become the greatest chapter of Roman history; and when, after your return, I will read about the temples of many gods adorned and enriched with your trophies.

As we saw, Gallus uses *ei* for long *i* (*spolieis, deiuitiora* for *spoliis, diuitiora*) but not in the closed syllable *fixa* (nor later in the text in the closed syllable *digna* "worthy"), or in the final syllable of *mihi*. Gallus prefers the modern spelling *maxima* for *maxuma*, which Varro (according to Cassiodorus, *GL* VII.150) credits Julius Caesar with inventing, and *tuum* rather than *tuom*, but uses archaic *quom* for *cum*. In a later fragmentary line he writes *Kato* with initial *K* following a spelling rule prescribing *k* for *c* before *a* which is preserved by the grammarians (Donatus 605 in Holtz (1981)), and which goes back to our earliest Latin inscriptional texts (see Wallace, chapter 2 in this volume), but which never found widespread currency except for proper names (but note *Caesar* not *Kaesar* in the lines cited above). Gallus' lines, although few in number, are important since they represent the only example from the Classical period of a literary manuscript close enough in time and place to its author to have a chance to represent the original orthography. They consequently give a glimpse of some of the orthographic variation that must have been present in ancient literary texts, a phenomenon which we only know otherwise from comments in ancient sources such as Quintilian and Suetonius.

　Changes in pronunciation which took place later than around 100 BCE, or which were not taken up by all members of the elite, are generally not reflected in Classical Latin spelling. For example, the monophthongisation of the diphthong *ae* to a vowel [ɛː] is attested in various areas outside Rome in the second century BCE, and is lampooned as "rustic" in a verse of Lucilius (fr. 1130 Marx) *Cecilius pretor ne rusticus fiat* "don't let Caecilius become the 'rustic' praetor" (Adams (2007) 78–88). By the first century CE, however, the pronunciation seems to have been general in spoken Latin (Adams (1995b) 87–88) and by the age of Servius it was accepted in the spoken Latin of the erudite (Coleman (1993) 5, cited by Adams). However, scribes and stonecutters were generally aware of when to write the diphthong *ae*, and the Classical spelling was largely maintained, except by those with little education. Similarly, knowing when to write in final -*m* and -*n* in Latin became a matter of learning by the end of the first century CE, when both had dropped out of speech (Adams (1977) 22–23).

　Thus, although orthography was capable of changing alongside changes in spoken language, as these examples show, in the first century it appears that there was a growing gulf between the Latin pronunciation of the majority of speakers and the learned orthography. Orthographic habits that might reveal a less than certain command of the learned language were stigmatised and avoided. Doubtless there were those like the Emperor Augustus who felt that Latin should be spelled as it was pronounced (Suet. *Aug.* 88), but few could rely as securely as he could on his position in society. A simple dictation error from the Vindolanda tablets can reveal something of the distance between speech and written Latin at the end of the first century CE. At *T.Vindol.* II. 234, Flavius Cerialis, prefect of the Ninth Cohort of Batavians, writes to an equestrian officer, September, dictating his letter to a scribe. At one point the scribe writes *et hiem*– "and winter–", then erases it and writes *etiam* "also", the correct word in context. The best explanation for this correction is that Cerialis uttered the word *etiam*, but the scribe initially thought that what Cerialis meant was *et hiem–*, before hearing enough of the rest of the sentence to work out *etiam* was intended. In order for this to happen, the scribe must have been familiar with Cerialis' habit of dropping the *h*– from the beginning of words, and must regularly have written *h*– in, even when it was not pronounced. In other texts from Vindolanda, *h*– is always written "correctly" at the start of the word, that is, in the places where other Classical sources and grammarians indicate that it should be (Adams (1995b) 90).

Morphology

In Classical Latin there is a reduction in the possible variants for inflected endings, and near loss of certain morphological formations. In early Latin there were several areas of morphological variation. In nominal declensions, for example, there was variation in the formation of certain case forms: the genitive singular of the first declension could be -*as*, disyllabic -*ai* or a diphthong -*ae*; the genitive plural in the second declension could be -*um* or -*orum*; the genitive singular of the fourth declension could be -*us*, -*uos*, -*uis* or -*i*; and the genitive singular of the fifth declension -*es*, -*ei or* -*i*. Verbal conjugations also showed different possible forms: the third person plural of the perfect varied between -*ērunt*, -*ĕrunt* and -*ēre*, with possible contracted forms such as *amarunt* in place of *amauerunt*; the second singular of the passive/deponent could be of the form -*re* or -*ris*; passive/deponent infinitives could end in -*i* or -*ier*. Some verbs also showed what de Melo (2007b) has termed *extra-paradigmatic* forms, alternative forms that do not fit into either of the two stems of *infectum* or *perfectum*, which were used with future or subjunctive meaning, such as *faxo*, *faxim* from *facio* "I make" and *duim* from *do* "I give". Other verbs exhibited a range of different possible perfect or present forms: for example *pango* "I fix" has a by-form *pago*, and alternative perfect forms *pepigi*, *pegi* and *panxi*; *soleo* "I am accustomed" could have a perfect *solitus sum* or *solui*. In the Classical period, much of this variation was lost, except for survivals in poetry or specifically archaising language or contexts. Thus Virgil uses the genitive ending -*ai* in four places in the *Aeneid*, for which he receives the accolade *amantissimus uetustatis* "very fond of antiquity" from Quintilian (*Inst.* 1.7.18); there is no surviving example of the form used by a poets later than Virgil during the Classical period. De Melo (2007b) 336–364 tracks the survival of extra-paradigmatic forms in Classical Latin. The only form to be used with any frequency during the Classical period is *faxo*, and this principally occurs in legal language or archaising contexts: Livy, for example, uses inflected forms of *faxo* (and *defixit* from the compound *deficio* "fail") only in speeches and prayers, and never in narrative. Even where writers on language recommend the retention or employment of a certain form, that may not be enough to save it: thus Varro (*L.* 9.107) recommends the choice of *solui* as the perfect of *soleo*, but it does not survive after Sallust, and Varro himself uses *solitus es* at *R.* 3.1.6.

It is worthwhile considering the fate of the perfect third plural ending in a little more detail. We have already mentioned Cicero's preference for the form -*erunt* above. The spelling -*erunt* can however represent either a form with long vowel, -*ērunt*, or with a short vowel -*ĕrunt* (two morphs seem to have been inherited into Latin, -*ĕrunt* and *-ēre*; *-ērunt* is the conflation of the two). Verse writers availed themselves of the different variants in Latin from the earliest times, and Lucretius shows all three endings, and a contracted form, *-ārunt* (from *-āuerunt*) within three lines at the opening of Book 6 of the *de Rerum Natura*:

> Primae frugiparos fetus mortalibus aegris
> *dididĕrunt* quondam praeclaro nomine Athenae
> et *recreāuērunt* uitam legesque *rogārunt*
> et primae *dedĕrunt* solacia dulcia uitae,
> cum *genuēre* uirum tali cum corde repertum,
> omnia ueridico qui quondam ex ore profudit.

It was Athens of illustrious name that first in former days spread abroad the corn-bearing crops amongst unhappy mankind: Athens bestowed on them a new life and established laws; Athens first gave the sweet consolations of life, when she brought forth a man endowed with such wisdom, who in past days poured forth all revelations from truth-telling lips. (Translation by W.H.D. Rouse)

Although the ending *-ĕrunt* occurs twice in these lines, more generally it is the least frequent ending in Classical hexameters, but that may be because many of the resulting scansions would have been unmetrical. The only second-century prose writer of whom we have extensive remains, Cato, used both *-erunt* and *-ere* in the *Origines*, but only *-erunt* in the *de Agri Cultura*. The effect of the classicising movement is clear in the works of Cicero and Caesar; the first usually, the second always, avoids the *-ere* form in his writing, and *-erunt* becomes the standard written Latin form in technical authors such as Vitruvius (it is impossible to say whether the prose forms spelt *-erunt* actually have long or short *e*; Coleman (1999) 44 notes that some Ciceronian clausulae scan better with short *e*). But in historians and others seeking an archaic flavour, such as Sallust or Tacitus in the *Annales*, the *-ere* ending was widely employed. It is difficult to be certain when *-erunt* with short *e* was used outside of poetry, but this is the form that survived into Romance and that lies behind the contracted forms of perfects of the first conjugation, such as *rogārunt* for *rogāuerunt*. Contracted perfects of this type are found in most Classical Latin texts (but notably avoided by Sallust and Tacitus) and this becomes the predominant form of first conjugation perfects in, for example, the sub-literary documents from Vindolanda (Adams (2003a) 544). It may be significant that the verses about Julius Caesar reported by Suetonius to have been sung around Rome after Julius Caesar's admission of foreigners to the senate, scan with a short *e* in *sumpserunt* "they took" (*Iul.* 80). Grammarians of the fourth century stigmatise the form *-ĕrunt* with a short *e* as a *barbarismus*, and this may reflect a wish to separate out the correct and learned spoken form from that of the mass of the populace.

Syntax and Textual Structure

Roman writers on language devote comparatively little space to debate which syntactic constructions and text-structuring devices were disfavoured and which were preferred, in contrast with the amount of surviving discussion on other aspects of language, such as morphology and vocabulary. It is telling that when Aulus Gellius cites a long passage of the historian Claudius Quadrigarius' *Annales* (written *c.* 100 BCE), describing the duel between Manlius Torquatus and a Gaulish giant, he does not comment on any pre-Classical features of syntax, such as the use of the preposition *cum* in place of the plain ablative in *cum maxima uoce* "with a very loud cry", but notes an archaic genitive form *facies* "appearance". This is not to say that syntax was completely avoided in discussion; the short passage presented in the *Rhetorica ad Herennium* as an instance of the *exilis* "thin" or *inliberalis* "mean" style (4.16), said to be far from the model of correct and well-chosen speech, is interesting for its presentation of several features which were later avoided in Classical Latin (see further Marouzeau (1921) 137–138, and Ferri and Probert (2010) 21–22):

> nam istic in balineis accessit ad hunc. postea dicit: hic tuus seruus me pulsauit. postea dicit hic illi: considerabo. post ille conuicium fecit et magis magisque praesente multis clamauit.

> For this chap came up to this other one in the baths. Then he says "This your slave struck me." Then the other one says to that one, "I will look into it." Then that one made a protest and shouted louder and louder with a lot of people present.

An obvious syntactic solecism in this passage is the phrase *praesente multis* "with many people present", with *praesente* used as an adverb or preposition, and not in concord with *multis*. This use of *praesente* (and its opposite, *absente*) as a preposition is found in Plautus, Terence, Accius and other early Latin dramatic writers (indeed, the style of this passage may be a deliberate echo of the language of comedy, see Adams (2007) 379–380), but does not recur in Classical Latin, and seems to have been stigmatised. Equally striking in this passage is the repetitive style, the extensive reliance on pronouns, and the lack of subordination. Similar speaking styles are given to the freedmen in Petronius' *Satyrica*, who generally avoid longer complex sentences in favour of short paratactic clauses and direct rather than reported speech, and who rely heavily on banal connective particles, such as *nam* "for" and *et* "and", and on demonstrative pronouns and finite verbs. Authors writing in Latin in the Classical period attempted to inject more variation into their sentence structures and paid more attention to textual coordination and cohesion, while restricting opportunities for syntactic ambiguity or overlap. Throughout the Classical period, literary authors deployed a wider range of subordination procedures, including complex participial constructions, in order to arrive at longer complex sentences. Word order, relative pronouns and passive verbs are used, together with a range of connective particles, in order to ensure that larger chunks of text avoid abrupt changes of subject or repetition of words or endings.

Classical Latin prose was thus marked out from contemporary speech patterns through the complexity of its syntactic structures; it also stands apart from Early Latin prose, as can be seen by comparison of passages of pre-Classical Latin with Classical Latin. The practice of direct comparison of roughly equivalent extracts of prose from Classical authors with their predecessors goes back to antiquity, as is shown by Gellius' overt comparison of two speeches of Gracchus with a passage of Cicero's *in Verrem* (see further Marouzeau (1921) and Rosén (1999) 33–34), and indirectly by his citation of the passage of Claudius Quadrigarius for which there is a parallel passage in Livy's history

(7.9.8 ff.). Several modern scholars have analysed the differences between Claudius Quadrigarius and Livy (listed in Oakley (1998) 114, to which add Courtney (1999) 144–150). Claudius Quadrigarius avoids the banality of the "thin" style cited in the *Rhetorica ad Herennium*, but he does produce markedly less complex sentence structures than Livy. The longest sentence (discounting cases where a modern editor has separated out two syntactic units with a semi-colon) in Quadrigarius is twenty-six words, the second longest nineteen; the parallel passage in Livy includes four sentences of over thirty words. Where Livy has short sentences, they are varied in word order through initial placement of the main verb or by contrast with surrounding sentences; Quadrigarius tends to place all main verbs at the end of the clause, all adjectives following their head noun, and avoids hyperbaton. Compare the parallel descriptions of the arming scene:

> Quadrigarius: scuto pedestri et gladio Hispanico cinctus contra Gallum constitit.
> Armed with a infantry shield and a Spanish sword, he stood against the Gaul.

> Livy: pedestre scutum capit, Hispanico cingitur gladio ad propriorem habili pugnam.
> He takes an infantry shield, he puts on a Spanish sword, adapted to hand-to-hand combat.

Even though the vocabulary is largely the same, the use of asyndeton in Livy, and the interruption of the phrase *Hispanico gladio* with the verb *cingitur* make the syntax varied while retaining the immediacy of the action. In the passage as a whole Livy employs a wider range of subordination techniques, including twelve present participles in the passage, in contrast with the two present participles (both in short ablative absolute clauses) in Quadrigarius. Livy also makes use of his longer sentence structure to avoid repetition of the names of the protagonists in the fight, and makes less use of pronominal forms. Thus in the description of the actual fight scene Quadrigarius mentions Manlius by name twice, and *Gallus* "the Gaul" four times, and further refers to the Gaul with the pronoun *is* twice. Livy only mentions *Gallus* once, refers to him a second time as *hostem* in the fight scene, and makes no use of the pronoun *is*.

It may be argued that these differences between Livy and Quadrigarius are largely stylistic rather than linguistic, but the development of the techniques used to construct the longer periodic sentences frequently involves expansion or innovation of existing syntactic patterns. For example, present participles in cases other than the nominative are not found with direct object complements in Plautus, and Early Latin absolute constructions tend to consist only of noun and participle. Classical Latin authors, no doubt heavily influenced by models of Greek participial syntax, greatly extended the range of possible constructions with present participles up to the point where they can take the same array of complements as full finite verbs, whatever case they are in (Coleman (1989b) 362). Future participles appear in Classical Latin authors for the first time in absolute constructions, whereas they had earlier been restricted largely to periphrastic constructions with parts of the verb "to be".

Alongside this expansion of various syntactic and discourse devices, other features were lost from Classical Latin. These include the use of indicative verbs in certain types of indirect questions at the expense of the subjunctive. In early Latin it was possible to use the indicative in indirect questions as well as the subjunctive (Bennett (1910–1914) I.120–123). Indicatives are still found in indirect questions in the beginning of the period, e.g. in the *Rhetorica ad Herennium*, but by the Classical period the subjunctive became the default mood of subordination (on this change see Stephens (1985), Bodelot (1987), Bolkestein (1995)). The formation of prohibitions affords another instance where Classical Latin decreases the possible range of constructions available to earlier authors. In Early Latin there are a number of different ways in which it was possible to tell someone not to do something: *ne* with the imperative (as *ne fac* "stop doing!"); *ne* with the present subjunctive, as *ne facias* "don't do"; *ne* with the perfect subjunctive, as *ne feceris*; *ne* with an extra-paradigmatic form, as *ne faxis*, or *ne duis* or *ne duas* "don't give"; *noli* with the infinitive, as *noli facere*, and *caue* with or without *ne* followed by present or perfect subjunctive, as *caue (ne) facias/feceris* (see de Melo (2007b) for discussion of these forms). It appears that *ne fac* originally had an inhibitive meaning, to stop an ongoing action, and the *caue* type was preventative, to prevent a future action, but there is no clear semantic or aspectual distinction between the other constructions. In Classical Latin the types *ne feceris* and *noli facere* survive, with no difference in meaning (Cicero also uses the *caue* construction only once in a letter), and some authors preferring one to the other: thus Pliny uses *noli* consistently, but Tacitus favours *ne* with the perfect subjunctive (Rosén (1999) 114).

Vocabulary

Vocabulary forms a particularly salient area of language for speakers. All speakers are conscious of changes in vocabulary in a way that they may not be about shifts in pronunciation or syntax. Puristic movements in language in modern times have often focused on vocabulary items as particular shibboleths, as for example the move to avoid English loanwords in French spoken in France and in the Canadian province of Quebec, or the British English interest in U- and non-U vocabulary in the 1950s and 1960s (even though in this case the original trigger for the interest in U- and non-U, Ross (1954), was concerned with a range of features, not just vocabulary, discussion of which occupies only four pages in a forty-five-page article). Writers and speakers of Latin were also highly conscious of lexical choices that they made, and the search for *purus sermo* brought about a special interest in vocabulary. During the Classical Latin period a number of words and word-formation devices drop out of sight from the literary language. At the same time, a number of new words are created in the language, particularly for calquing Greek technical terms in the arts and sciences, and others lexical items expand their use and meaning.

It is possible to track the fate of the Latin vocabulary during the Classical period in some detail: there is abundant evidence for the Latin vocabulary in the surviving literary records, and the vocabulary of the Romance languages allows the linguist to identify which words were retained in the spoken language or increased their semantic scope in ways which are not reflected in the literature. A single case-history will be helpful to show some of the complexities involved. Consider the word *colaphus* meaning "blow" or "thump". This word is originally a loan from Sicilian Greek, and probably entered Latin with the import of slaves from the south (Adams (2003a) 351 n. 100). It is used in Plautus and Terence and other comedians principally to describe beatings given to slaves, but is avoided by Cicero and all other writers in the first century BCE, who use other terms such as *ictus* or *plaga* when describing violence. When the word reappears in literary texts in the next century, it is initially also associated with lower-class or unrefined characters or situations: Quintilian uses the term (*Inst.* 6.3.83) only once, when citing a bad-taste joke of the sort which is *indignum ... homine liberali* "unworthy of a gentleman", in which someone says to an inferior *colaphum tibi ducam* "I will thump you", and it also occurs with reference to striking a slave in the narrative section of Petronius (Petr. 34.1). However, when Seneca discusses punishing a slave at *de Ira* 3.24 he avoids the term *colaphus*. It is evident that the word had also developed a wider sense in the spoken language, a sense that survives as the standard word for "blow" in French (*coup*) and Italian (*colpo*), by the time of Petronius, since he puts a derived verb-form in the mouth of the freedman Ganymede, *percolopabant* "they were hitting" (Petr. 44.5) where the meaning now has been extended to any sort of striking, rather than specifically blows to slaves (see Adams (2007) 439).

This example is telling in various different ways. Firstly, it shows the reluctance to admit "low" words to literate culture, a reluctance also apparent in, for example, Tacitus' avoidance of the Latin word for "spade", *pala*, instead employing a periphrasis at *Ann.* 1.65 *per quae egeritur humus aut exciditur caespes* "that by which earth is tilled or turf is cut" (Palmer (1954) 142, but see the doubts of Goodyear (1972) 343; or in Housman's observation that Latin poets do not use *asinus* for "ass", instead preferring the diminutive *asellus* or a Greek term (Housman (1930)). Secondly, it underlines the fact that the spoken language and the literary language were part of a single continuum; there was not an unbridgeable gulf between Classical and "Vulgar". *Colaphus* was not unknown or entirely avoided in its restricted sense, of cuffs given to slaves, but authors do seem to have avoided the wider sense applied to any strike or blow, and it is perhaps a reluctance to appear to use the word in its wider sense that led to its avoidance. In much the same way a word such as *bucca* is restricted to meaning "cheek" in Classical Latin, but the meaning "mouth" (which survives in French *bouche*, Italian *bocca*, Spanish *boca*, etc.) is attested already in early comedy. In the Classical period *bucca* means "mouth" only in the speech of a freedman in Petronius and it is recorded as a solecism in Augustus' letters (Suetonius *Aug.* 76); in Cicero's letters *bucca* "mouth" occurs solely in the proverbial expressions *in buccam uenit* "come to mind". Thirdly, the example of *colaphus* is significant since it involves a word borrowed from Greek, and the attitude towards Greek loans and Greek terms is particularly complex in the Classical period.

Latin had borrowed words from Greek from the earliest stages of the language. The presence of large numbers of Greek loan-words in Plautus and other writers of comedy, and their concentration among slaves and low-class speakers has been frequently remarked upon (Karakasis (2005) 83). Already in the second century BCE there seems to have been a move against the wholesale importation of Greek terms. As often, a surviving fragment of the satirist Lucilius (frag. 15 Marx) gives a tantalising glimpse of the debate, even though it is not certain whether he is approving of the cited Greek terms (which are largely avoided in later Latin literature) or, as is more likely, sneering at them (see Chahoud (2004) for fuller discussion of this passage):

porro clinopodas, lychnosque ut diximus semnos
ante pedes lecti atque lucernas
Then we said *clinopodes* and *lychni* solemnly [Greek σεμνῶς] instead of bed-feet and lanterns.

The borrowing *lychnus*, here inflected with Latin endings, recurs in Roman literature to refer to a luxury style of lamp, in both poetry and prose, but *clinopus*, which here is given the Greek inflection of accusative plural in *-as*, is found only in this passage. As Chahoud notes, this term κλινόπους does not occur in literary Greek either, and part of the point of this passage may be the contrast between the pretension of the language and the mundanity of the object.

The debate about the use of Greek words in Latin, which appears to be reflected in the Lucilius fragment, was to continue until imperial times, as reflected by the anecdotes recorded of Tiberius' reluctance to permit Greek words in the Senate or in Senate decrees (Suet., *Tib.* 71). Augustus avoids some current Greek terminology in the *Res Gestae*, preferring to use a circumlocution *naualis proeli spectaculum* rather than the Greek loan *naumachia* "sea-battle", *praedones* rather than *piratae* for "pirates" and *Hadrianum mare* rather than *Hadriaticum mare* for the "Adriatic sea", although other terms such as *amphitheatra* and *athleta* are admitted (Gelsomino (1958)). In the late Republic and early Empire there appears to be a reluctance to admit Greek words that have not previously had the sanction of occurrence in high literature into specific genres, although verse was always more tolerant of grecisms than prose (in the words of Marouzeau (1946) 176 "le mot grec est devenu en latin une sorte d'ornement poétique"). When Cicero does use Greek words in his philosophical works, he usually paraphrases or flags up the word in some way, as for example at *Tusc.* 1.7 *ut iam etiam scholas Graecorum more habere auderemus* "so that we can now dare to have leisure in the Greek style", where the phrase *Graecorum more* alerts the reader to the importation of the Greek word *schola*. Romans were aware of Greek borrowings, even though over time loans may nativised, as Cicero's says of the word *aer* "air" (*N.D.* 2.91) *Graecum illud quidem sed perceptum iam tamen usu a nostris; tritum est enim pro Latino* "the word is indeed Greek, but it is now after long use understood by our countrymen, since it is employed as a Latin word". Even so, the word is more frequently declined in Latin with a Greek accusative, *aera*, rather than Latin *aerem*, and it usually retains its Greek prosody (with two long vowels) in verse (*TLL s.v.*); the word does not occur in Roman historians and only rarely in Cicero's speeches. The decision whether to assimilate Greek words to Latin declensions or to retain Greek endings was clearly a matter of debate at one stage, as is shown by the remarks of Varro (*L.* 10.70–71) and Quintilian's discussion of the precepts of a *grammaticum ueterum amatorem* "archaistic grammarian" on the practice (*Inst.* 1.5.58–64). However, the debate no longer seems to be alive in Quintilian's time, when usage had settled on the preservation of some Greek endings and declensions (such as in names of the type *Aeneas* not *Aenea*) but not others, with licence for poets to use Greek inflectional endings, particularly in the declension of proper names.

Latin authors and writers avoided the wholesale importation of Greek terms through the creation of new Latin vocabulary to fill the need for technical and scientific terms. Often this was achieved through *calquing*, a term which describes the process of rendering Greek suffixed or compound words into Latin through the translation of the separate constituent morphemes. To take examples from the field of grammar, the Greek word for the category of grammatical case, πτῶσις, which is derived from the verb meaning "fall", is calqued by a Latin derivative of *cado* "I fall": *casus*; the Greek name for the nominative, ὀνομαστικός formed from the base noun ὄνομα "name" is matched by with a Latin derivative of *nomen* "name", *nominatiuus*; and the Greek term for the accusative, αἰτιατικός is calqued by *accusatiuus,* which seems to be based on an erroneous equivalence of αἰτία "cause" and Latin *causa* "cause, law-suit". Latin calques of Greek terminology have become familiar as the basis for the scientific and technical terminologies of many modern European languages (such as the words *case, nominative* and *accusative* in English) but calquing was by no means the only method employed for extending or enlarging the native lexicon. Roman writers also sought Latin equivalents for Greek terms through extension of the semantics of existing Latin words (a "loan-shift"), or through construction of a periphrasis. Grammar can again furnish examples: for a loan-shift, the Latin term for "tense", *tempus,* more generally means "time", reflecting the different senses of Greek χρόνος "time, tense"; for periphrasis, Quintilian's definition of the Greek term περίφρασις can suffice, *περίφρασιν uocant, circuitum quendam eloquendi* (*Inst.* 8.6.59) "they call a *periphrasis,* a certain roundabout way of speech". As with the other areas of Classical Latin vocabulary, the different approaches to the incorporation of Greek technical vocabulary was an area of debate and experimentation. A recent study of medical vocabulary, Langslow (2000b), has shown in detail the different techniques which were employed by Celsus and Cassius Felix for enriching the word stock of Latin, from wholesale borrowing of Greek terms to the creation of Latin periphrases, in different times and circumstances.

Conclusion

Classical Latin became a model of the standard literary language for a number of later cultures, including English, French and German. It also became a model for itself, as the chapters on Late Latin and Neo-Latin in this volume reveal. Classical Latin's success as a model of correct and pure language belies the picture of the language as it emerges from the surviving texts written during the Classical period. Authors writing between the beginning of the first century BCE and the end of the second century CE did not have the resources of modern scholars in which they could easily check their orthography, grammar and syntax. The statements of ancient writers and grammarians on language reveal a far more nuanced attitude to the Classical language than is sometimes supposed. It is easier for them to point out incorrect language than it is to elaborate what exactly constitutes correct language. The authorities that are appealed to for justification of a word or construction change from age to age, even from writer to writer, and there was doubtless further variation, particularly in the first century BCE, which is concealed by the skewing of our evidence towards the survival of so much of the work of Cicero in comparison with anyone else from this period.

FURTHER READING

Adams (2007) ch. 1, especially pp. 13–17, is an excellent brief overview of some of the issues of standardisation. Clackson and Horrocks (2007) chs 3–6 discuss the background to the standardisation of Latin in the light of modern sociolinguistic research in more detail, and give some detailed discussion of texts and testimonia. The discussion of Marouzeau (1949) and Palmer

(1954) are also still useful. Rosén (1999) treats aspects of the selection process of Classical Latin with regard to word-formation, morphology and syntax in depth. The works of Fögen (2000), Müller (2001) and Ferri and Probert (2010) are all illuminating on the attitudes towards language of Roman writers, and contain useful accounts of the different linguistic labels (such as *Latinitas* and *sermo plebeius*) used in ancient works.

NOTE

* I wish to thank J. N. Adams for reading and commenting on an earlier version of this chapter, and Katherine McDonald for proof-reading assistance.

CHAPTER 16

Late Latin

J.N. Adams

Introduction: The Term "Late Latin"

The term "Late Latin" is associated particularly with the Swedish school of Latin philology, which flourished in the first half of the twentieth century. Three of the monographs by Löfstedt (1907, 1908, 1959), two by Norberg (1943, 1944) and one by Svennung (1932) have "Late Latin" in the title. Most of the writings of these scholars concentrate on miscellaneous usages that happen to be attested late, and say little to justify the use of the term, though the more general book of Löfstedt (1959) is an exception.

The term is easy to criticise. Linguistic periodisation of this type is unsatisfactory (cf. the remarks of Fredouille (1996)), partly because the history of a language may be seen as a continuum, with diachronic changes running across any chronological divisions that one cares to set up, and particularly because many of the changes that were eventually to alter the shape of Latin and contribute to its Romance outcomes (such as changes to the system of gender, the spread of prepositions for plain case usage, the loss of deponent verbs) can be traced back to an early date. It is arbitrary to fasten on to any "late" period, say CE 200–600, with blinkered vision, and may create an expectation that there will be identifiable within that period a host of new usages belonging exclusively to it.

The adjective "late" also tends to imply decline or decadence. Latin could only be said to have deteriorated over time if it were argued that Italian and French are inferior languages to Classical Latin. Both languages are simply Latin as it is spoken in two different parts of the former Roman world a millennium or two on from the Roman Republic. Their divergences from Classical Latin, and such divergences as there may be of Late Latin itself from Latin of an earlier period, are the result of changes over a long time, not of a lurch into decadence. Nevertheless decadence has come into the narrative of later Latin. Pirson (1906) 402, for example, writing on the syntax of the verb in the

A Companion to the Latin Language, First Edition. Edited by James Clackson.
© 2011 Blackwell Publishing Ltd. Published 2011 by Blackwell Publishing Ltd.

Mulomedicina Chironis, concluded that the reflexive "passive", which has an important role in the Romance languages, particularly Italian and Romanian, was already a *fait accompli* "dans le latin de la décadence", at least in the third person singular and when the subject was inanimate. The idea behind this account is familiar: one must look for anticipations of Romance constructions in the "vulgar texts" of late Antiquity, with the *Mulomedicina* regarded as a prime example of such a work. It is a view that may lead to neglect of the evidence from earlier periods and different registers, as was so in Pirson's case.

A Specimen of Late Latin

Since the term "Late Latin" is open to objections in theory, it may be worthwhile to begin with a practical question, whether it is possible to identify a piece of Latin of known late date as late purely on internal linguistic evidence. If the answer were yes, there would have to be some substance to an entity Late Latin, and one might attempt to define some of its features, and set out some of the limitations that such definitions might be subject to. On the other hand tradition, that is the imitation of earlier models, was so powerful an influence on any writer that talking about Late Latin in practical terms might turn out to be futile.

The following passage has been chosen at random from the *Peregrinatio Aetheriae*, a text dated to the end of the fourth century. Could it be dated, or assigned more generally to the late period, on linguistic grounds alone?

> nam proficiscens de Tharso perueni ad quandam ciuitatem supra mare adhuc Ciliciae, que appellatur Ponpeiopolin. et inde iam ingressa fines Hisauriae mansi in ciuitate, quae appellatur Corico. ac tertia die perueni ad ciuitatem, quae appellatur Seleucia Hisauriae. ubi cum peruenissem, fui ad episcopum uere sanctum ex monacho, uidi etiam ibi ecclesiam ualde pulchram in eadem ciuitate. et quoniam inde ad sanctam Teclam, qui locus est ultra ciui-tatem in colle sed plano, habebat de ciuitate forsitan mille quingentos passus, malui ergo perexire illuc, ut statiua, quam factura eram, ibi facerem. ibi autem ad sanctam ecclesiam nichil aliud est nisi monasteria sine numero uirorum ac mulierum. nam inueni ibi aliquam amicissimam michi, et cui omnes in oriente testimonium ferebant uitae ipsius, sancta diaco-nissa nomine Marthana, quam ego aput Ierusolimam noueram, ubi illa gratia orationis ascenderat. (*Per. Aeth.* 23.1–3)

The usages discussed here will be divided into four groups (for a summary see the conclusion to this section).

1 Some of the features of this text might look non-Classical but on closer inspection are not straightforwardly late. A phenomenon that becomes common in Late Latin may have started to appear even in the literary language of the Classical period.

In the last clause *gratia* precedes the dependent noun *orationis*, whereas the Classical order was genitive + *gratia*. But the order here is well established in Quintilian (Wölfflin (1884) 174), who cannot be classed as a late writer. Preposing is mainly late but not a criterion for a late dating.

The core part of the first sentence, *proficiscens de Tharso perueni ad quandam ciuitatem*, has several suggestive items:

The phrase *proficiscens de Tharso* has, first, a preposition with the name of a town, and, second, *de* rather than *ex* or *ab*. Prepositions with the names of towns go back to Plautus (*in* + accusative indicating motion to and *ex* motion from: Bennett (1910–1914) II.237, 289) and were also used, according to Suetonius (*Aug.* 86.1), by the emperor Augustus, but in this context a preposition would not be abnormal even for Republican Latin: a preposition may be used to indicate starting point when destination is also expressed: see Hofmann and Szantyr (1965) 102, citing e.g. *CIL* I².638 *uiam fecei ab Regio ad Capuam*, Cic. *Att.* 15.11.2 *proficisci … in Asiam … ab Antio*.

As for the preposition itself, *de* marking separation (= "from") was to oust both *ex* and *ab* in later Latin (see Löfstedt (1911) 103, Adams (2003d) 567 with bibliography). The preposition is not, however, in itself diagnostic of lateness. *De* was starting to encroach on *ex* and *ab* even in the Classical period (see also below p. 266). In a specimen of *descriptio* at *Rhet. Her.* 4.51, a text of the first half of the first century BCE, there are first the expressions *e cauea leo emissus* and *belua soluta ex catenis*, and then a few lines later *eicite eum de ciuitate* (in conjunction with a verbal compound in *ex-*, as in the first example; for *ex* in this expression see *TLL* V.2.305.48 ff.). The expressions *e medio* and *de medio* with verbs of removing and the like are both attested in the Classical period (see e.g. Landgraf (1914) 54). Change happens gradually and may take centuries to establish itself fully in the literary language, and that is why we should not expect to find many sharp distinctions between Classical and Late Latin.

The one feature of *de Tharso* that is probably late is that it is the name of a town that is governed by *de*. In republican Latin *ex* (and *ab*) are attested with the names of towns (see above on Plautus and the inscription), and *de* is attested with common nouns, but to judge from *TLL* V.1.46.37 ff. *de* is not used with names of towns. By contrast in later Latin it is commonly so used (Adams (1976) 56).

Another feature of the verb phrase is that the present participle *proficiscens* is perfective, denoting an act that precedes in time that of the main verb *perueni*. The perfect use of the present participle becomes common in Late Latin (Hofmann and Szantyr (1965) 387, Adams (1976) 60), particularly in biblical texts or texts influenced by the Latin Bible, where it is an attempt to imitate past-tense active participles of Greek. But even in Classical Latin there are present participles that can be given a perfective sense, and *proficiscens* itself has that sense in Cicero (Laughton (1964) 40).

Finally there is *ciuitas* in the sense "city, town". *Ciuitas* survives in Romance in this meaning, whereas the two Classical terms *urbs* and *oppidum* disappeared. There are late texts in which both of the latter are lacking (or in which *urbs* occurs occasionally, but in reference to Rome or Constantinople: Adams (1976) 103) and *ciuitas* is common. *Ciuitas* is used to mean "city, town" seventy-six times in the *Per. Aeth.*, whereas *urbs* and *oppidum* never occur (Väänänen (1987) 140). Again the usage itself would not guarantee that the excerpt was late. The *OLD* s.v. 3b allows this new meaning from Seneca onwards. Löfstedt (1911) 175) cites an even earlier instance, in Dolabella ap. Cic. *Fam.* 9.9.3, and refers also to Nepos and

Petronius. The example in Dolabella is merely transitional, and Shackleton Bailey (Loeb) translates "community". There is probably the same transitional character to most of the earlier examples, and it is only in later Latin that the word ousts the others in some texts and is used unambiguously and often (cf. Adams (1976) 103). A single unambiguous example would not establish a text as late. In this short excerpt, however, there are five examples. The difference between earlier Latin (i.e. in this case of the first century CE) and later Latin is here one of degree rather than of kind. The meaning "city" is not exclusively late, but it is only in late texts (of the fourth century and beyond) that it occurs in abundance. The five examples to the exclusion of synonyms would support a late dating, but the meaning itself would not. Many of the identifiable features of Late Latin are of this kind: it is the frequency of occurrence of a phenomenon, not so much the phenomenon itself, that may be taken as a sign of late composition (see the next section). New usages that are beginning to appear in the literary language in the Classical period may only become entrenched much later.

2 Some other usages that one may be tempted to consider late, not least because they seem in type to anticipate Romance developments, can, like the phenomena in (1), be traced well back, sometimes as far as the early Republic, but they differ from the usages in the first section in one respect: they had not intruded into the high literary language by the late Republic or early Empire. Their distribution suggests that that they had long been current in spoken varieties but were stigmatised by the educated and excluded from the written language. Later they may have risen in respectability.

Fui ad episcopum belongs in this category. Here a past tense of the verb *esse* is used with a directional expression, implying motion ("I went [immediately] to the bishop"), a construction with parallels in many European languages and surviving in Romance, especially Spanish. It is well represented in the *Per. Aeth.* but is not late, as it is also attested in Plautus (for details see e.g. Löfstedt (1911) 171–173, Hofmann and Ricottilli (1951/2003) 338, Petersmann (2002–2003), Adams (2007) 348). In the intervening period it turns up from time to time in sub-standard and colloquial texts, such as a speech by a freedman in Petronius (42.2), and one or two idioms. It is not the sort of construction admitted in the early literary language, but would not be a criterion for dating the excerpt.

Apud is used with the name of a town (*Ierusolimam*) where a locative would have been expected in Classical Latin. Such a usage is loosely of proto-Romance type, in that prepositions are used in Romance with town names, but this foreshadowing of the later norm does not make the expression late. *Apud* + name of town is already used by Plautus (*Epid.* 53 *id adeo argentum ab danista apud Thebas sumpsit*) (see Löfstedt (1911) 252), just as he uses *ex* and *in* + accusative with names of towns (see p. 259 above, [1]). Here is one of those non-standard usages that must have existed for centuries at a sub-literary level. Cf. *Per. Aeth.* 17.1 *apud Edessam*.

In this category may also be put the use of the static adverb *ubi* in the verb phrase *ubi cum peruenissem*, expressing "motion towards" and equivalent to Class. Latin *quo* (*ubi* sixteen times thus in the *Per. Aeth.* (van Oorde (1929) 209), whereas *quo* is not so used; cf. Eng. "come here" alongside the stilted "come hither"). This usage is not in Classical Latin, but neither is it (unlike *fui ad* and *apud*) in Plautus. A parallel is the use of locative place names with verbs of motion instead of the accusative (*Romae* for *Romam*). This last usage is early imperial, occurring in a freedman's speech in Petronius (62.1 *Capuae exierat*) in the first century CE and in the letters of Claudius Terentianus of the early second century (*Alexandrie* for *Alexandriam*, often, particularly in the letter *P.Mich.* VIII.471, and indeed at lines 14–15 with the same verb [*exiturum*] as that in Petronius above; see Adams (1977) 38, (2003b) 13). Both of these texts are sub-standard. The earliest clear-cut case of *ubi* for *quo* (the only one cited by the *OLD*) is in Apuleius (*Met.* 9.39 *ubi, inquit, ducis asinum istum?*), but it is in direct speech. Indeed it is put into the mouth of a soldier in a scene "de ton volontairement populaire" (Callebat (1968) 196). Such a context matches those in which *Romae* and *Alexandrie* are attested, and the date of the Apuleian example is not far removed from that of the letters of Terentianus (another soldier). The encroachment on directional by static adverbials with verbs of motion had taken place at least as early as the first century CE, but in popular speech. There was a resistance to such usages in the literary language, a resistance attested to by a grammarian (Caper *GL* VII.92.1 *haec uia quo ducit dicemus, non ubi*, cited by Callebat (1968) 196).

It follows that a "late" usage, found, for example, for the first time in literary texts of the fourth century and beyond, might not have been so late at all. Its late attestation may reflect not the date of its appearance in the language, but the date by which it became acceptable in educated writing, after, conceivably, centuries of currency in more popular spoken varieties. Our heavy reliance on literary texts as evidence for linguistic developments may give a false impression of the chronology of changes.

3 Next there are usages, syntactic or lexical, that are attested only in Late Latin, though it is possible that their attestations may in some cases (but not all: see particularly the next section) give a false idea of their age.

Pompeiopolin, an accusative in the predicate of a passive naming-construction, reflects the fossilising in the accusative of place names in -*polis*, a phenomenon of Late Latin (see Norberg (1944) 52–53). *Perexeo* is late word (*Vetus latina* onwards, but found particularly from the fourth century: *TLL* X.1.1344.65 ff.). It occurs five times in the *Peregrinatio*. Sometimes, as here, it has the sense "*potius motum continuantibus, pergentibus*" (*TLL* 1345.25–26), and one may suspect a semantic contamination with *pergo*. Some forms of the present are similar to forms of the perfect of *pergo* (e.g. *pereximus, perreximus*). The impersonal use of *habet* anticipating e.g. Fr. *il y a* is attested only from the fourth century onwards (see Svennung (1935) 475). The feminine (singular) use of the original neuter *statiua* (followed by *quam*) is late (Löfstedt (1911) 134), though from Early Latin onwards there are examples of neuter plurals shifting into the feminine, such as *castra* in Accius (*praet.* 16).

4 Finally there are Christian lexical items, uses of words that are not attested in the period covered by the *OLD* and belong to the third century or later: *oratio* in the sense "prayer", *ecclesia* "church", and the repeated use of *sanctus* as an epithet of Christians of standing, or places with sacred associations. Christian technical terms are decisive for assigning a text a late date. The majority of such terms were components of the special register of Christianity and did not enter the language in general and pass into Romance. *Oratio*, for example, did not produce the Romance terms for

"prayer". *Ecclesia* by contrast achieved wide currency, and a few parallels might be cited, of terms that had a life beyond the special language of the Christians (e.g. *feria* for days of the week in some areas (Adams (2007) 347–348), *parabola* in the sense "word" (Löfstedt (1959) 81–84)).

Also belonging here is the suffix *-issa* in *diaconissa*. Words with this suffix, which is also found in Greek, are exclusively late. This one is attested from the fourth century (see André (1971) 107–109). Cf. e.g. *abbatissa* (sixth century), *fratrissa* (sixth century), *prophetissa* (third century, from Tertullian; Greek has only προφῆτις: see André (1971) 108), *sacerdotissa* (sixth century?). There are twelve such words attested in Latin over four centuries, nine of them on Greek roots. In the corresponding period there are thirty-one forms in *-issa* in Greek (André (1971) 109). The formation became common in medieval Latin, and was productive in French, Italian and Romanian (André (1971) 110).

Some conclusions

Our initial question may be answered in the affirmative. The passage is identifiable as late, and could not have been written before about the third century CE.

What features of lateness, on the strength of this single piece of Late Latin, might one expect in texts of the third century and beyond? It is in the lexicon only that one is likely to find sudden changes of the type allowing a text to be assigned to a period. The lexicon responds immediately to cultural, scientific, religious and social changes. As scientific developments occur new technical terms are coined, and they gain immediate currency within scientific circles and sometimes beyond. The new religion, Christianity, introduced a flood of special usages, and since many late texts were written by Christians these are much in evidence in writings from the third century onwards. Their presence in a text is a good dating criterion. Syntax is a different matter. Change tends to be very gradual. Signs of a new usage may be found centuries before it is grammaticalised and replaces an older equivalent. An attestation of the usage in a text cannot in itself establish the period of the text. Its frequency, however, may be an indication of date. *De* in the sense of *ex* or *ab* (for example complementing a compound verb with the prefix *ex-*) occurs only occasionally in Classical writers such as Cicero and Caesar, but if we encounter a work in which it has displaced *ex/ab* that work is likely to belong to the second century CE or later. The greatest difficulty in identifying syntactic usages as late lies in this, that a change may take place and become entrenched in speech long before it is accepted into the written standard, and we can rarely be sure that a "late" construction is late at all.

It is worth summarising these features of a late text as set out above. There may be:

1   usages (mainly syntactic) (such as *de* for *ex*) that were making their first appearance in Classical Latin but only became established late; some of these merely provided the seeds of later developments without achieving their Romance functions
2   usages (mainly syntactic) that were old but were long submerged in spoken varieties of the language; they may have surfaced in significant texts occasionally between the time of Plautus and the later empire, but were only accepted into the written standard at a late date

3 usages (syntactic or lexical) for which there is no evidence, direct or indirect, in early or Classical Latin, and which may be late in the strictest sense (e.g. *habet* = *il y a*)
4 late lexical items, particularly technical terms, which could not have occurred in the senses in question before the third century CE or beyond; one should also include here loanwords from languages with which Latin had had little contact in the Republic or early Empire.

Types 1 and 2 are late only in the sense that they become common at a late date, but they may be as old as the recorded language itself.

Some Important Developments, and the Notion of "Vulgar Latin"

It is out of the question here to attempt a comprehensive account of Late Latin (see Clackson and Horrocks (2007), ch. 8 for a wide-ranging discussion of Latin in Late Antiquity). Instead I deal with five features that set apart the Romance languages from Classical Latin. The different categories of lateness just elaborated will be kept in mind. It will become clear that to treat the late period (from say 200 to 600) as somehow distinctive, or as the decisive era in generating the structures characteristic of the Romance languages, would be to oversimplify. It is not acceptable to look for signs of change only in an arbitrarily defined late period. It will also be suggested that one should not overplay the importance of developments of the second type in the above list. Though the normative efforts of grammarians had some influence in retarding change among the literary classes, not all change can be located exclusively, or be said to have begun, in submerged varieties. To put it another way, the developments that show up in the Romance languages cannot be put down *en masse* to changes that occurred principally in a spoken entity "Vulgar Latin".

Prepositions and case usage

Introduction

In the history of Latin it is possible to see a movement from synthetic forms of expression, with syntactic functions conveyed by bound morphemes, to analytic expressions, with independent function words taking over or reinforcing the role of bound morphemes. This development is nowhere clearer than in the transition from plain case inflections to prepositional expressions. Classical Latin expressed a variety of case functions by case endings alone, whereas in the Romance languages these functions are expressed by prepositions, and the endings of the oblique cases were lost. Instrument, possession and indirect-object functions, for example, conveyed in Latin by the ablative, genitive and dative, were passed to prepositions.

It is questionable whether there is much explanatory power in merely setting up a generalised linguistic change, "from synthesis to analysis", working inexorably and consistently across the case system (for reservations about the traditional distinction between synthetic and analytic in the context of Romance see e.g. Vincent (1997)). Nor is it convincing to see the change as having a neat single cause, such as attrition of case endings determined by phonetic developments. A switch to prepositions is attested long before the phonetic changes usually cited in this connection (loss of final *-m* and *-s*, shortening of long vowels in final syllables) took place. A study of different manifestations of the increased use of prepositions turns up a diversity of individualistic cases, with different chronologies, belonging to different registers, and possibly with different determinants. An attempt will be made to bring out this diversity here.

Directional expressions

Signs of a shift towards prepositions are not exclusively late. It has already been remarked that in Plautus names of towns are often accompanied by *in* (+ acc.) and *ex*. Prepositions are used by Plautus particularly with less familiar place names (e.g. *Bac.* 591 *in Elatiam, Poen.* 94 *in Calydonem*), whereas the plain accusative and ablative are regular with place names familiar to Romans at the time (*Athenas, Syracusas, Carthaginem* and others), a distinction which implies that the old unaccompanied case function was under threat (in ordinary speech?: see p. 265 below) but being kept alive by frequency of use in names that came up often. Plautine Latin is not unique in using prepositions with names of towns. The paucity of evidence for the phenomenon itself has something to tell us (see below).

Three centuries after Plautus Quintilian (*Inst.* 1.5.38) found fault with the expression *in Alexandriam* as a solecism: ... *ut fiat adiectione "nam enim", "de susum", "in Alexandriam", detractione "ambulo uiam", "Aegypto uenio", "ne hoc facit"*. The expressions castigated here are all, as far as we can tell, genuine (*ne* for *ne* ... *quidem*, for example, is found at Vindolanda, and *de susum* turns up after this in the *Vetus latina*), and it has to be assumed that *in* + accusative was a sub-standard usage heard in speech throughout the period between Plautus and Quintilian. Non-literary texts are throwing new light on the matter. That Plautine practice was not simply aberrant is shown by the attestation of the *in*-construction on ostraca from Africa and Egypt of the imperial period: *O.BuNjem* 68 *missi in Hyeruzerian Iulius Rogatianus Iulius* ..., *O.Max.* inv. 254.13 (see Bülow-Jacobsen *et al.* (1994) *qui cibaria ferunt in Mys Or(mum)*). For an imperial example of the *in*-construction, see also Russell (2001) I.144 n. 46). This type of phrase is also common in the *Peregrinatio Aetheriae*, where the place names are usually exotic (van Oorde (1929) 103–104). The circumstances motivating the preposition thus replicate those in Plautus (see p. 259 above): unfamiliar place names are more likely to generate a preposition. When the writer expresses motion to a town with a familiar Greco-Latin name, she does not use *in* but the plain accusative: e.g. 3.8, 9.6 *Alexandriam*, 17.3, 23.8 twice *Constantinopolim*.

In Romance languages prepositions are used to mark "motion towards" (also "motion from", which I leave aside here), but these are reflexes not of *in* but of *ad*. It is therefore of interest that the grammarian Pompeius, writing probably later than Aetheria, illustrates like Quintilian before him the same type of "error", but uses not *in* but *ad* in his example: *GL* V.252.21 *non debeo dicere ad Karthaginem uado sed Karthaginem uado*. It follows that the shift to a preposition in this syntagm was early, but that the use of *ad* rather than *in* was late, a nice illustration of the complexities of lateness.

This case prompts some observations about the controversial term "Vulgar Latin". The evidence of Plautus, of an educational theorist, of some new non-literary texts and of a late text known for not adhering to the educated standard makes it certain that there was a largely submerged use of *in* with place names current for centuries. The usage was concealed because it was frowned on by grammarians and purists, and kept out of the literary language. A remark by Suetonius (*Aug.* 86.1), that Augustus used prepositions with names of towns, is also relevant here, because it must be read in the light of another of his observations (*Aug.* 88), that Augustus rejected the rules of grammarians. Many Latin phenomena known to us only from stray pieces of evidence such as that for *in* above must have been suppressed in this way. If one wishes to label these phenomena as "Vulgar Latin", for want of a better word, there is no harm in that, as long as one accepts the limitations of the term. We know little about the details of spoken Latin. The term becomes problematic if it is given a purely social definition in keeping with its etymology. If the emperor Augustus used prepositions with town names the usage cannot be unequivocally described as a usage of the common people, and indeed there are other ways of expressing "motion towards" attested in non-literary texts by writers of limited education, such as the plain accusative itself and the locative (*Alexandrie uenio*: above p. 261). There was a usage approved by purists (the accusative), and other usages kept at bay by them (*in/ad*, the locative) with some but not total success, but the social distribution of the latter and the systems into which they may have entered are a closed book to us. Another problem with the term "Vulgar Latin" and with overlapping terms such as "vulgarism" is that they tend to be used willy-nilly of any phenomena that may look non-Ciceronian, even if these are attested only in literary texts and cannot be located in sub-literary varieties in the manner of the above use of *in*. Hence there arises the phenomenon of the "vulgarism" admitted by educated writers, which may be nothing of the sort but a reflection of a general change in the language. But the least satisfactory aspect of the expression is that it is associated with a view that the submerged varieties were constantly changing but the literary language almost fixed: any linguistic change that was to have an outcome in the Romance languages must begin in Vulgar Latin. It will be shown in this section that this view cannot be accepted.

Prepositions with compound verbs

The antiquity of the tendency for prepositions to encroach on plain cases may be illustrated from constructions of the type *castris egredior* versus *e castris egredior*. This is a case that will also show that the distinction seen above (p. 264), between a prepositional syntagm considered substandard by purists and a plain case considered suitable to the literary language, does not always exist. *Castris egredior* is that type of phrase in which the prefix of a verb determines the case of its nominal complement, as in an expression at Cato *Agr.* 141.2: *agrum terram fundumque meum suouitaurilia circumagi iussi*. Here the case of *agrum ... meum* is determined by *circum-*, and *suouitaurilia* is underlying object of *ago*. This example is from a prayer, and is of very old type. Alongside this construction there is already in Early Latin that in which the noun depends on an independent preposition (*e castris*). There follow some statistics from various republican texts (Plautus, Terence, Caesar, the ps.-Caesarean works, and the speeches of Cicero) showing *ex* versus plain ablative with the two verbs *exeo* and *egredior*. In these texts, all embodying varieties of the high literary language, *ex*-expressions with *egredior* and *exeo* predominate over the ablative by 51:4; there are also three case of the emerging *de*-construction (for which see p. 259 above). The ablative complement was no more than an occasional relic; the prepositional construction for its part had good literary credentials. The language as a whole had moved over to the prepositional construction by the earliest recorded Latin. One should not expect a uniform distinction between the plain case as educated form and the preposition as substandard, and equally one should not expect the prepositional expression to be uniformly, or mainly, late. The shift to prepositional expressions has a variable chronology.

Three texts from a different genre (historiography) present a different picture. In Sallust *egredior* is used five times with the ablative (omitting instances of *domo* and *Roma*) and never with *ex*. He does not have *exeo*. In Livy there are more than forty examples of *egredior* with the plain ablative, but only a handful (about nine) with the preposition *ex*. The historians (Tacitus could be added) must have had a sense that the ablative construction was old, and they adopted it as an archaism.

Ad *marking the indirect object and the dative*

The dative was eventually replaced by reflexes of *ad*. A conventional view of the history of this use of *ad* is that it was already present in Plautus ("in popular Latin"), and survived through to Romance beneath the level of literature (see e.g. Lindsay (1907) 20, 83). There is nothing implausible about such a narrative (cf. on *fui ad episcopum* and *in* + acc. above), except that it misrepresents the use of *ad* in Plautus. From Plautus onwards through Classical and into Late Latin there are uses of *ad* that appear superficially to be replaceable with a dative of the indirect object, but these fall into two classes and are distinct from the dative.

The first, with verbs of announcing, or referring to the dispatching of letters, implies motion across space. At Pl. *Capt.* 360 *dice, demonstra, praecipe / quae ad patrem uis nuntiari* and *Capt.* 400 *numquid aliud uis patri / nuntiari* the prepositional expression *ad patrem* and dative *patri* are in identical collocations and seem to have the same function, but the similarity is misleading. The recipient of the message need not be in the presence of the sender, and the message may have to be transported some distance; *ad* has an idea of destination/motion. *Ad* is not quoted from Plautus with, say, *dico*, or *do* when the indirect object is a person and present. A revealing example is at *Capt.* 384 *quae nuntiare hinc te uolo in patriam ad patrem*. Here *in patriam* shows that the message is to be carried some way.

Second, *dicere* (*et sim.*) *ad* is used, often in formal contexts, in Classical Latin of addressing crowds such as the *populus* (Kühner *et al.* (1976) I.519). The idea is probably that the voice is projected towards the listeners, an act which differs from making a remark to someone in private: see e.g. Ovid *Met.* 15.609 *rursus ad hos Cipus ... inquit*, of addressing a crowd. A slight variation occurs when the addressee is an individual but the address is formal. A remark may be addressed "towards" or "before" the addressee, as if he were at a distance. The usage identified by Kühner, *et al.* recurs throughout Latin.

A feature of the use of *ad* in later Latin is that it is found particularly in texts that are translated from Greek, and particularly with verbs of saying. In later Greek the prepositions πρός and εἰς encroached on the dative (see Jannaris (1897) 341, Mayser (1934)

356–357, 359, Blass *et al.* (1976) 150, 168–169). The profusion of prepositional complements of *verba dicendi* for the dative in Biblical Latin must largely reflect the influence of the original. A case in point is the apocryphal *Actus Petri cum Simone*, where sometimes, but not always, the Latin construction is the same as the Greek (though the Greek version does not fully survive): e.g. p. 83.14 *clamauit ad dominum Iesum Christum dicens,* = 82.20 ἐβόησεν πρὸς τὸν κύριον Ἰησοῦν Χριστόν. Here also is the familiar use of projecting the voice; the existence of this usage in Latin must have facilitated the adoption of a preposition in translation texts with verbs of saying, particularly when the address was formal.

The majority of the expressions with *ad* in the *Actus* accompany the verb *dico* (twenty-eight), and there are five more with other verbs of saying. There seem to be no instances of *ad* with other verbs traditionally taking an indirect object. The dative of the indirect object abounds in the text with many other verbs, e.g. *adaperio, communico, demonstro, distribuo, do, enarro, expono, laudem perfero, monstro, nuntio, offero, ostendo, polliceor, porrigo, praebeo, praesto, reddo, refero, respondeo, restituo, trado, tribuo.* Such a distribution would not favour the possibility that the *ad*-construction was generally making inroads into the dative of the indirect object, late as the text is (sixth century or even beyond). Rather there is seen here a continuation of the old address use, which may have had an equivalent in (later?) Greek. The origin of the Romance construction must lie in this use, which presumably suffered a weakening, such that the idea of projecting the voice was eventually lost, leaving the way open for the construction to be extended to other types of verbs, such as verbs of giving. These developments seem to have been very late. It is misleading to speak of the change as exclusively a manifestation of an inexorable trend (beginning with Plautus) towards analytic forms of expression; it was rather a specific idiom that generated the construction. Even in some medieval texts (such as the *Chronicon Salernitanum*) *ad* is found mainly with verbs of saying. There the "dative as an indirect object is very seldom replaced by *ad*" (Westerburgh (1956) 243), but for *ad* with *verba dicendi* see e.g. p. 21.2 Westerburgh *inquid ad suos* (same phrase 21.11, 84.17), 55.13 *inquid ad uirum,* 96.17 *ad Guaiferium protinus Lando ait,* 121.23 *asserens ad suos quia.*

With verbs of granting, giving, conceding and so on (*do, reddo, praesto, trado, delego*) *ad* is not uncommon by the time of the Merovingian documents discussed by Vielliard (1927) 201.

Genitive *and* de

The Classical Latin genitive disappeared almost without trace, and reflexes of Latin *de* became one of the main exponents of possession and also of an objective relation (= the objective genitive), though not in all Romance languages. There are other types of construction that would come into a full presentation of the Romance "genitive". The possessive and objective uses of *de* belong to Late Latin, but again the roots of the new construction lie in Classical idiom, and developments can be derived from the sense "from" that the preposition has from Early Latin onwards. In Classical Latin *de*-expressions may sometimes seem to be interchangeable with the (partitive or possessive) genitive, but always *de* can be given its basic separative force.

Note for example Varro *R.* 1.41.5 *potius in seminariis surculos de ficeto quam grana de fico expedit obruere. Grana de fico* might seem to be translatable as "seeds of the fig".

The seeds are part of the whole (= partitive genitive), or they "belong" to it (possessive). But the parallel phrase *surculos de ficeto* suggests that the role of *de* is not quite the same as that of a genitive. *Ficetum* does not mean "fig tree", but is a fig plantation or orchard. "Shoots of a fig plantation" is not as appropriate a translation as "seeds of the fig" had been in the other case because, whereas seeds are an intrinsic part of a fig, shoots are not a necessary part of a fig plantation. They may be found there, but not all the time. The force of the *de* is to stress separation or source: shoots "acquired/taken from" a fig plantation.

De porco at Anthimus p. 10.12 (*renis de porco penitus non expedit manducare*) is classified by Liechtenhan (1963) 55 under the heading "gen. possessiuus", but equally the kidneys of the pig are part of the whole and the expression might be classified as partitive. However, the kidneys of a pig (as at p. 10.12) used for culinary purposes have been removed from the animal, and the preposition is local ("kidneys from the pig").

The *de*-expression moves closer to a possessive/partitive-genitive equivalent when in turns up in similar expressions (dependent for example on anatomical terms), but with the idea of separation, removal or extraction not so clearly present. Such uses occur at least as early as the fourth century. Note e.g. Pelagonius 217 (cf. too 150, 218) *si ualidius doluerint, uenae de inguinibus soluuntur* (the veins which form part of the groins are opened for bloodletting, but they are not separated from the groins): see Adams (1995a) 434). Cf. Ven. Fort. *Vita Martini* 2.363 *et manus alma pedes de peccatore luebat* (partitive/possessive). The feet of the sinner are not detached from him.

It is only in very Late Latin that *de* starts to appear as an equivalent of the objective genitive: e.g. *Edict. Roth.* 197 *si quis mundium* ["guardianship"] *de puella libera aut muliere habens eamque strigam, quod est mascam, clamauerit, excepto pater et frater, ammittat mundium ipsius* (note the alternation with the genitive).

As in the case of *ad* expressing indirect object, the Romance-type use of *de* emerges over centuries from the gradual widening of an idiomatic Classical usage, and not because of a sudden shift from synthesis to analysis. Even in Late Latin the Classical Latin genitive remains current.

Instrumental use of de

The genitival uses of *de* above derive from an adnominal use of *de* expressing source or separation. An instrumental use of *de* derives from an adverbial use of the preposition again originally expressing source. Väänänen (1981) 113 cites the proverb at Cic. *Fam.* 7.29.2 *sine eum errare et putare me uirum bonum esse nec solere duo parietes de eadem fidelia dealbare* and translates the last clause "blanchir deux murs **avec un même pot** de chaux"). Shackleton Bailey (Loeb), however, catches the force of *de* more precisely: "Let him go on thinking me a man of honour, not one to cover two walls **from the same pot** of whitewash." The whitewash is taken from a pot, and the preposition has local force. It might be possible to translate loosely as if the *de*-expression were instrumental ("whiten with …"), but that is to suppress the literal meaning.

In technical treatises such uses abound. See Adams (1995a) 435–436 (with the bibliography at 435 n. 10), noting that

> [numerous] examples of *de* in technical works, though loosely classifiable as "instrumental", are in fact markedly pregnant, with various ideas present. The instrumental idea is no more than implied by the context; it is not the primary force of the preposition. Pel(agonius) 456,

for instance ("*cum de posca prius pedes lauaueris*"), literally means "when first you have washed the feet *from* the *posca*", with *de* expressing source. The full implication of the passage might be expressed "when you have washed the feet (with) (some *posca*) (taken) from (a larger amount of) *posca*". While the notion of source is explicitly expressed, partitive and instrumental ideas are implied. There is a quantity of *posca*, from which some is taken, and by means of that the feet are washed.

Such *de*-complements underwent a semantic widening. *Posca* above indicates a substance from which a part may be removed. *Fidelia* indicates a container part of whose contents may be removed. The ideas of source and separation are present in both cases. On the other hand if the complement indicates an implement from which nothing is removed the idea of source is weakened and the instrumental force may come to the fore. This point may be illustrated from a comparison of two passages of Pelagonius (see Adams (1995a) 436). At 448.1 (*ure sicca usque ad uiuum et de penna cauteri eundem locum circumcidito*) the *penna* is part of a cauterising instrument (*cauterium*), possibly the extremity (see *TLL* X.1.1090.46–49 and 1091.35–37), used for cutting. The phrase is instrumental and without any clear notion of separation. On the other hand at 468 (*postea melle de penna inungito*) the *penna* (literal rather than metaphorical in this case) is used to apply something ("smear with honey **from** the feather"), and, although there is a secondary instrumental idea, separation is again apparent.

The phrase *de penn(ul)a* recurs in technical treatises, usually used as Pelagonius uses it in the second passage, with separative force: cf. e.g. Marc. *Med.* 6.16 *de pinnula capiti inlines* (cited by Beckmann (1963) 64 as instrumental, but it is separative). On the other hand there is another instrumental use of *de pinna* at Soran. Lat. p. 52.14: *adipes anserinos uel gallinacios illic missos et solutos de pinna super tollant*. The fat is lifted from a container with a feather.

Such cases of *de penn(ul)a* in similar verb phrases but with two distinct functions suggest that the spread of an instrumental use of *de* cannot simply be explained from the sudden acquisition by *de* of a new function, or from a movement away from synthesis to analysis. Rather *de* came into use in collocations where its local force was still present. Once certain phrases (e.g. *de penna*) became commonplace they were liable to be transferred to contexts in which the local force was less obvious and the instrumental became prominent. These examples illustrate a process described by Pinkster (1990b) 202 as follows: "Another mechanism is the spread of an adpositional [i.e. in this context prepositional] expression from one context where it is quite appropriate to another where it is at first sight out of place."

The earliest instance with full instrumental force has usually been found at Ovid *Met.* 6.80: *percussamque sua simulat **de cuspide** terram / edere cum bacis fetum canentis oliuae* (see Regula (1951) 166, Kühner *et al.* (1976) I.501). Bömer (1976) 30 takes the phrase to be equivalent to an instrumental ablative, and refers the reader to his note on *Met.* 3.260 (1969) 517): "usu vulgari, pro Abl. instrum. vel modi vel praepos. per, oft dichterisch, nicht bei Vergil". *Met.* 3.260 runs: *grauidamque dolet de semine magni / esse Iouis Semelen. De semine* is not, however, instrumental but indicates source: she is pregnant "from the seed". There is nothing vulgar about such a usage: see *OLD* s.v. *de* 11 for comparable expressions from literary Latin (e.g. Lucr. 3.750 *canis Hyrcano de semine*). It would be inappropriate to take *de cuspide* in Ovid above as an isolated vulgarism.

Reservations have been expressed about the instrumental interpretation by Beckmann (1963) 55–56. The verb is passive, and the idea may be one of receiving a blow "from" the sword point. Other supposed early examples of instrumental *de* are also open to different explanations (see e.g. Beckmann (1963) 56), and caution is needed in assessing the evidence. *TLL* V.1.62.18 ff. under the heading "pro ablat. instrumenti vel modi sive praepos. per" brings together disparate examples, by no means all of them instrumental (see Beckmann (1963) 54 and his discussion).

In Late Latin instrumental *de* is not used freely in literary prose until Gregory of Tours, but is found mainly (where concrete expressions are concerned) in low-register texts (see the remarks of Beckmann (1963) 59–60). There is, for example, just a single case in the literary stylist Ammianus (29.3.8 *de fustibus caesi*, but some editors have assumed a lacuna after *de*: see Beckmann (1963) 60). By contrast, one technical text in which there are clear-cut examples is the *Mulomedicina Chironis* (see Ahlquist (1909) 78, Salonius (1920) 103, Beckmann (1963) 64). Note 19 *de ipsis locis uenarum sanguis a pectus detrahitur de sagitta* (the blood is not taken away from the *sagitta*, but from the veins with a *sagitta*), 399 *de pedes feriet terram* (the source of this passage is extant [Apsyrtus]: *Hipp. Berol.* 43.1, *CHG* I.214.5 τῷ ποδὶ τύπτει τὴν γῆν the prepositional construction is Chiron's own).

Some conclusions

It is as well to dispose of some misconceptions.

First, even the selective evidence discussed here is enough to show that the shift to prepositions cannot be explained simply as a move to resolve the potential ambiguities of the Classical case system where, for example, the ablative combined the functions of three earlier cases, ablative, instrumental and locative, such that a form like *Athenis* might express two different ideas, "at Athens" or "from Athens". The prepositional usages seen here, and others that might be added, are far from forming a neat system with ambiguities or polysemy eliminated. A single preposition might take on several different case functions, just as the old case endings were multifunctional. We have seen *de* encroaching on both the genitive and the instrumental. Nor was there a single preposition for a single case function. Instrument is expressed in Late Latin (and to some extent earlier) not only by *de*, but by *cum*, *per* and *ad*.

Second, the adoption of prepositions where an unaccompanied case form might have carried the same function cannot be put down straightforwardly to phonetic changes, such as the loss of various final consonants. Prepositions were encroaching on case forms long before phonetic developments might have played any part in undermining the Classical case system.

Prepositions in directional expressions belong to category 2 in the list on p. 262 above: the phenomenon goes back to the earliest period but was stigmatised and suppressed in the literary language. The one late change seen here was the shift from *in* + acc. to *ad* with names of towns. Earlier there was a distinction, with *in* implying entry into the town (possibly through city gates), i.e. arrival, whereas *ad* could mean "in the direction of".

The use of *de*, with its separative sense lost, as either a possessive or objective genitive, or as an instrumental, might be put in category 3 (late), but these usages did not suddenly emerge. They derive from much earlier uses of the preposition, uses that underwent widening. The same is true of the use of *ad* for the dative of the indirect object, but here the idiomatic old usage (with verbs of saying, of formal address or address of crowds) was very persistent, and it is difficult to find clear-cut cases where *ad* marking the indirect object accompanies other verbs, such as verbs of giving.

Specialised early uses of these prepositions thus provided the starting point for their later assumption of various case functions. The earlier uses were generalised or extended. There seems little point in attempting to find causes of these developments, though it is not impossible that the phonetic changes referred to above had some influence at a late date. These various case studies suggest again that Late Latin cannot be regarded as a discrete entity.

Gender

A major change between Latin and the Romance languages was the loss of the neuter. No Romance language has a morphologically separate neuter, though most have remnants of old neuter morphology that has taken on new roles. Most Latin neuters passed into the masculine, an unsurprising merger given that in the singular second declension neuters were hardly distinct from the masculine. Other neuters, usually via the plural form in *-a*, became feminines. The question to be addressed here is whether the loss of the neuter was late. Are there signs of its receding at an early date?

In Plautus there are instances of what look like masculines for neuter, such as *corius* (*Poen.* 139) and *dorsus* (*Mil.* 397), but there are also neuters for masculine, such as *nasum* (*Am.* 444, *Men.*168, *Mil.* 1265) and *uterum* (*Aul.* 691). Some apparent "masculines for neuter" may reflect not an early shift from neuter to masculine but the fact that the original gender was masculine. *Collum*, for example, was a neuter from the Classical period (Cicero) onwards, but in Early Latin the term (*collus*) was regularly masculine (Neue and Wagener (1892–1905) I.795). There are also some feminines for neuter in Plautus and Early Latin, such as *labeae* (plural: e.g. Pl. *St.* 723a) alongside *labia*, *fulmentae* (plural only: *Trin.* 720) alongside *fulmenta*, and *ramenta* (singular only: *Bac.* 513, 519b, *Rud.* 1016) alongside *ramentum*. There are as well Greek neuters in *-a* that have been reinterpreted as feminine (singular) (*glaucuma* at *Mil.* 148, *schema* at *Am.* 117, *ostreae* at *Rud.* 297). Here is evidence for a popular tendency to reinterpret neuters in *-a*, whether plural, or in the case of Greek, singular, as feminines, and that tendency may be loosely related to later Romance developments (cf. e.g. Fr. *voile* < *uela*, *joie* < *gaudia*). However, there is more to be said about some of the Plautine evidence. Transitions from neuter to feminine were not necessarily generated by form alone, as in some instances there seems to be a semantic determinant. In Plautus in both *fulmentae* and *ramenta* the feminine (plural or singular) is particularising, and contrasts with the neuter, which is collective (see Perrot (1961) 307, 308).

Any connection between Plautine gender and later developments is weak indeed. Gender in Plautus is very variable, and it is not only the neuter in relation to other genders that is affected. More than fifty terms in Plautus are of abnormal or variable gender, and there is more variation between masculine and feminine than between neuter and another gender (details, not all of them accurate, in Hodgman (1902). Numerous factors might be invoked to account for the variability, but here it need only be said that in Plautus there is a lower degree of gender standardisation than in, say, Cicero (though Varro is a different matter: he retains some of the variability of Early Latin).

The first hints of the neuter suffering perturbation are in Petronius. There are about thirty instances of gender change in Petronius, all of them involving the neuter (see Smith (1975) 221; also Heraeus (1937) 131–138). Every single case is in the *Cena Trimalchionis*, and in speeches by freedmen. *Stragula* at 78.1 in the narrative may be excluded, as it derives from ellipse of *uestis* in the common phrase *uestis stragula* rather than from a transfer into the feminine of the neuter *stragulum* (plur. -*a*). Particularly common is the masculine for neuter in second-declension words, such as *fatus* (42.5, 71.1, 77.2), *uinus* (41.12), *caelus* (39.4, 39.6, 45.3) and *uasus* (57.8). There are fifteen such usages, most of them in the nominative singular form -*us*. The distribution of these cases of aberrant gender must be significant. Petronius had noted a feature of non-standard speech, and he made it a prominent element of the freedmen's speeches.

However, special determinants, as distinct from a generalised tendency towards loss of the neuter, have to be allowed even in Petronius. The entity normally designated by a neuter seems sometimes to be personified (on this question see Stefenelli (1962) 61), with the sense of animacy determining the shift to masculine. This is especially clear of *fatus*, as e.g. at 77.2 *hoc mihi dicit fatus mihi*. The personification of *fatum* (in the form *fatus*) is not a peculiarity of Petronius, but is found in funerary inscriptions, from Rome (Konjetzny (1908) 301), Africa (Kübler (1893) 173) and the east (Galdi (2004) 300–301). Petronius must have noticed this usage. 71.1 *etiam si illos malus fatus oppressit* is very similar to *ILS* 5262 *hunc fatus suus pressit* (see Heraeus (1937) 34).

The freedmen often use the neuter correctly, and it would be wrong to say that at this date the decline of the neuter was well advanced. Speakers of lower educational level were maintaining against educated practice some feminines derived from Greek neuters (e.g. 44.8 *schemas*), or more interestingly switching from neuter to masculine in the second declension, especially if there was a personification, but here we see merely the start of a long process.

It is only in much later Latin that there are real signs of the neuter in decline. In the Oribasius translations (of about the sixth century) as analysed by Mørland (1932) 64–66) nominative singular forms in -*us* of original neuters abound, in phrases and terms in which personification is out of the question (e.g. *adiutorius* "remedy" as subject of *est*, *impedimentus* likewise, *malus* for *malum* + *terrae* in a gloss with "be" understood, *plumbus*, *ossus* accompanied by *lesionem* ... *habens*, *periculus* as subject of *sequitur* or *est*; many other examples). There is a difference in kind between the Petronian examples, where personification is marked, and those from this late text, which suggests that, if one early determinant of the shift from -*um* to -*us* was personification, later such forms became banal. The material in Oribasius is further along the line towards the Romance state of affairs.

The Merovingian documents (the *Formulae Marculfi*) analysed by Uddholm (1953) present a further stage in the loss of the neuter. The material collected there (64–65) shows that almost all neuter nouns in -*um* have shifted to the masculine. The same seems to be the case in the royal diplomas and private documents of the Merovingian period discussed by Vielliard (1927) 133.

Since our sources for Late Latin are written, and since writing is conservative, there are inevitably texts even of a very late date in which the decline of the neuter is successfully resisted. However, there is enough evidence from lower down the educational scale to betray what was happening in speech. The loss of the neuter was late, but the seeds of change are to be seen much earlier, particularly in the low social dialects portrayed by Petronius (types 2 and 3 at pp. 262–263 above).

Phonology

Distinctively late phonological developments are hard to find. Many changes started early but are hardly in evidence in written texts through the Classical period because of the conservatism of spelling. For example, the loss (or nasalisation) of final -*m* can be placed well back in the Republic (Allen (1978) 30–31). If omissions of -*m* in writing do not occur in profusion until later Latin, that does not mean that the loss itself was late, but only that bad spelling is better attested in the late period. Another final consonant, *s*, was weakly articulated or lost in Early Latin after short vowels and before consonants, but there is evidence for its restoration by the Classical period, before it was again lost in the eastern part of the former empire at a date that cannot be determined (for details of the earlier period see e.g. Allen (1978) 36–37, Adams (2007) 51–52, 74–75, 104 n. 319, 140–141 with n. 74, Butterfield (2008b); see in general Väänänen (1981) 67–68). Late non-literary texts show little sign of its loss (see Adams (1994a) 107). Another early phenomenon was the monophthongisation of *ae* (< *ai*). In the early Republic it is in evidence outside Rome (Adams (2007) 78–88, 109–110), and the monophthong had a reputation as well in the late Republic for being rural (Adams (2007) 79). Monophthongisation must have been widespread by the early Empire (see e.g. Väänänen (1966) 23–25, Adams (1990) 230–231), and even in those texts of this period in which *ae* is mainly written correctly there may be signs that spelling skills were concealing the state of the spoken language (for Vindolanda see Adams (1995b) 87–88, (2003d) 537). One should not descend on a late text in which *e* for *ae* is constant (e.g. the *Tablettes Albertini*: see Väänänen (1965) 27–28, Adams (1976) 43–45) and find there a feature of Late Latin: what is late is the near-total abandonment of the digraph in writing.

Vowel system

Of greater interest are developments in the vowel system. Here we have the evidence not only of misspellings but also of testimonia, and from the latter it is possible to observe in the late period a contest in progress between the language developing inexorably along certain lines and grammarians attempting to resist change and maintain what they saw as the Classical system. A contest of this sort was played out in other areas of the language too, and there is sometimes evidence that eventually grammarians gave up the struggle. A case of this sort will be considered below, after some remarks about the vowel system.

In most Romance languages in stressed syllables there were mergers both in the front vowels and the back vowels, of long *e* and short *i* to produce a close *e*, and of long *o* and short *u* to produce a close *o* (see e.g. Herman (2000) 31–34). The result was a system of seven vowels (see ibid. and particularly 34 on the greater degree of confusion in unstressed syllables), with two degrees of aperture in the *e*-vowels, and two in the *o*-vowels. There are some regional differences in Romance, which are not of concern here (see ibid.).

The qualitative similarity of long *e* and short *i* may go well back into the Republic, because there are spelling confusions in early inscriptions, with *e* sometimes written for short *i* (see e.g. Allen (1978) 49).

A related development was the loss of phonemic distinctions of vowel length, which were the very basis of the Classical system. This loss shows up in late versification and elsewhere in two complementary tendencies, for short vowels under the accent to be lengthened, and long vowels in unstressed syllables to be shortened (see e.g. Adams (1999a) 114–117, Mancini (2001)).

The following passage from Augustine shows that grammarians were still trying to resist threats to the system of oppositions of vowel length:

> itaque uerbi gratia cum dixeris cano uel in uersu forte posueris, ita ut uel tu pronuntians producas huius uerbi syllabam primam, uel in uersu eo loco ponas, ubi esse productam oportebat, reprehendet grammaticus, custos ille uidelicet historiae, nihil aliud asserens cur hanc corripi oporteat, nisi quod hi qui ante nos fuerunt, et quorum libri exstant tractanturque a grammaticis, ea correpta non producta usi fuerint. (*de Musica* 2.1.1)

> And so for example when you say *cano* or happen to put it in verse, in such a way that you either lengthen in speech the first syllable of the word or place it in a position in the verse where it (the first syllable) should be long, the grammarian, that well known guardian of tradition, will find fault with you, giving no other reason why it should be short, except that those who have preceded us, and whose books are extant and dealt with by grammarians, treated it as short rather than long.

The passage concerns the tendency for short vowels which are stressed to be lengthened (as in the first syllable of *cano*). Augustine notes that the grammarian, the "guardian of tradition", will not only correct those who scan the *a* as long in verse, but will pick up those who lengthen it in speech. The grammarian was fighting a rearguard action, in that the implication of Augustine's remarks is that he does not approve of such pedantry. Nevertheless there must have been speakers, such as some grammarians themselves, who tried to preserve the old system in speech, and if so there would for a time have been two vowel systems coexisting, that of careful speakers and that of those speaking naturally. Another grammarian, Consentius, possibly in the fifth century, finds fault with both of the above tendencies, describing them as African *uitia*:

> ut quidam dicunt "piper" producta priore syllaba, cum sit breuis, quod uitium Afrorum familiare est ... ut si quis dicat "orator" correpta priore syllaba, quod ipsum uitium Afrorum speciale est. (*GL* V.392.3, 392.11)

> Just as some people say *piper* with the first syllable lengthened, when it is short, a vice which is characteristic of Africans ... As if anyone were to say *orator* with the first syllable shortened, which vice is particular to Africans.

These comments tell us things about Late Latin that misspellings in inscriptions cannot. In the fifth century change in the vowel system was still a living issue, and there was possibly a two-tier system, with purists setting themselves apart from everyone else. The above is not the only passage in Augustine of relevance. He also notes that the uneducated cannot distinguish *ōs* from *ŏs*, and that suggests that since the vowel in both was under the accent the distinction of length had been obliterated. Again Augustine is liberal in attitude, favouring a stigmatised form for "bone" (*ossum*) to guard against ambiguity:

> cur pietatis doctorem pigeat imperitis loquentem ossum potius quam os dicere, ne ista syllaba non ab eo, quod sunt ossa, sed ab eo, quod sunt ora, intellegatur, ubi Afrae aures de correptione uocalium uel productione non iudicant? (*Doct. Christ.* 4.10.24)

> Why should a teacher of piety when speaking to the uneducated have regrets about saying *ossum* ("bone") rather than *os* in order to prevent that monosyllable (i.e. *ŏs* "bone") from being interpreted as the word whose plural is *ora* (i.e. *ōs* "mouth") rather than the word whose plural is *ossa* (i.e. *ŏs*), given that African ears show no judgment in the matter of the shortening of vowels or their lengthening?

There is again an implication of a difference between the practice of the educated and that of the uneducated. The educated might be able to pick up a distinction between the two monosyllables because they were taught to keep them apart, but such a distinction would be lost on the uneducated because their speech would have no such contrast.

In the above passages Augustine, in contrast to the grammarian, adopts a *laissez-faire* attitude to a linguistic change. But sometimes it was the grammarians themselves who were tolerant of change. It has to be assumed that the passing of time made a change acceptable, and it is possible that a study of grammarians' attitudes in specific cases would show resistance followed later by tolerance. In a passage on the palatalisation of *t* and *d* before yod (to [ts] and [dz]) Pompeius (*GL* V.286.6–33; see particularly the text of Kramer (1976) 70) goes beyond mere tolerance and finds fault with the unpalatalised pronunciation. Note particularly 286.12–15:

> Quotienscumque enim post ti uel di syllabam sequitur uocalis, illud ti uel di in sibilum uertendum est. non debemus dicere ita, quem ad modum scribitur Titius, sed Tit<s>us; media illa syllaba mutatur in sibilum.

> For whenever a vowel follows behind a syllable *ti* or *di*, *ti* or *di* should be turned into a sibilant. We should not say *Titius* as it is written but *Titsus*; the middle syllable is changed into a sibilant.

On this passage and grammarians' attitudes on such matters see the discussion of Wright (1982) 61–62. Examples of such misspellings may be found in Svennung (1936) 9, Sturtevant (1940) 172, Battisti (1949) 147, Kiss (1972) 55–56 and Väänänen (1981) 53–54. Note e.g. for original *ti* the diversity of spellings:

CIL VIII.9927	*Terensus = Terentius*
T.Alb. VII.24	*Monsius = Montius*
CIL XII.5250	*Tersia = Tertia*
CIL VIII.21751	*Inocensa = Innocentia*
Audollent (1904) 253	*ampizatru = amphitheatro.*

"Confusion" of B *and* V

A development that does not show up until the imperial period is the confusion in writing of *B* and *V*. It becomes very common in later inscriptions. The phonetic developments lying behind the misspellings remain problematic.

Classical Latin had a semivowel /w/, represented in writing by *u* (or *v*, in capitals). When the Germans took over wine from the Romans, perhaps during the Republic, they borrowed the Latin word as well, and the loanword *wein* (< *uinum*) in Gothic shows the original /w/. But misspellings start to appear quite early, suggesting that the original [w] had changed its phonetic value, at least in some dialects or sociolects. *V* representing original /w/ comes to be replaced sometimes by *b*. The spelling confusion is usually explained (speculatively) as due to a merger of /b/ and /w/ as a bilabial fricative [β], which could not be represented precisely in the Latin script and was rendered now with the one letter now with the other (see e.g. Väänänen (1981) 50), though the issue is complicated by the fact that the spelling *b* for *v* is far more common than *v* for *b*, as has often been noted. This continues to be so in new corpora. This is not the place to go into detail, as it is the chronology that is of concern here.

There are examples of *b* for *v* in the early first century CE in the archive of the Sulpicii from Pompeii, in a text precisely dated to 15 September 39: *T.Sulpicii* 68, scriptura interior 12 *Iobe*, 13 *dibi*. There also seem to be examples of *b* for *v* in Pompeian graffiti (first century CE) (see Väänänen (1966) 50), e.g. *CIL* IV.4380 *Berus* = *Verus*, but the interpretation of at least some of them is uncertain (as Väänänen's treatment makes clear). Various handbooks refer to cases from this period. Sommer and Pfister (1977) 129 cite *CIL* III.7251 (Tegea CE 49–50) *lebare*. The earliest examples of the misspelling *b* for *v* cited by Sturtevant (1940) 142 are from the first century CE. In the first decade of the second century the letters of Claudius Terentianus have fourteen instances of *b* for *v* (Adams (1977) 31). In the middle of the second century there is a Latin legal text written in Greek letters by a Greek, Aeschines Flavianus of Miletus (*SB* III.1.6304 = *CPL* 193), in which the semivowel *u* is represented by *b* both initially and intervocalically: βιγεντι, βετρανε = *ueteranae*, βενδιδιτ, Ραβεννατους. The only exception is in the writer's name, Φλαουιανός, of which he had probably been taught a traditional spelling. He also uses β to represent Classical Latin /b/, and there is thus a hint that *u* and *b* had fallen together: but in Latin as he heard it pronounced by native speakers, or in Latin as he pronounced it himself, as a Greek? The phonetic value of β in Greek at this period is not certain (despite Gignac (1976) 68).

Several monographs and articles have discussed the *b/v* confusion in imperial inscriptions, usually with the aim of finding regional variations. There is a discussion of these works and their findings by Adams (2007) 624–683), where it is concluded (see 647) that the phonetic change behind the misspelling was earlier in Africa than it was in Gaul.

There was a degree of falling together of the original /b/ and /w/ in the Romance languages, but with variations across the former Empire. The treatment of the two phonemes also varied according to their position in the word. In general the reflexes of /b/ and /w/ remained distinct in initial position, but merged intervocalically. There are some regional differences, but this is the overall pattern (for summaries see e.g. Politzer (1952), B. Löfstedt (1961) 151, Herman (2000) 46).

Conclusions

A systematic account of phonological changes in Latin would be beyond the scale of this chapter, but some distinctive developments of variable lateness have been noted (palatalisations, loss of phonemic distinctions of vowel length, merger of *b* and *v*).

Other changes that were to leave their mark on Romance (such as the monophthongisation of *ae*) go well back into the Republic and underline a point hinted at earlier, that to attempt a grammar of Late Latin would be futile because the language does not fall into discrete periods. Nor should change necessarily be regarded as mainly a feature of vulgar speech. Grammarians who attempted to preserve the quantitative vowel system could not have been resisting changes exclusive to lower-class speech. Changes known to have affected the speech of the educated sometimes are classified as vulgar in handbooks because scholars fail to make a distinction between speech and writing. A text which drops *n* before *s* in words such as *insula* and *consul* may sometimes be treated as containing a vulgarism, yet we know that Cicero himself did not pronounce the *n* in words such as *foresia*, *Megalesia* and *hortesia* (Velius Longus *GL* VII.78.21–79.4). The vulgarism is one of spelling alone, with the phonetic development a feature of all social levels of speech.

Future Tense

There were some radical changes, particularly morphological, between Classical Latin and Romance, and the question arises in each case whether the start of the change falls in the Late Latin period, or earlier, or beyond. The complicated history of the loss of the neuter was discussed above. Equally striking was the loss of the synthetic passive and its replacement by periphrastic and reflexive forms, but that is a subject too extensive to be dealt with here. A third change concerns the future tense.

The Classical Latin future disappeared without trace by the time of the Romance languages, an event which represents one of "the most striking morphological discontinuities between Class. Latin and Romance" (Maiden (1995) 158). In Italian and French a formation deriving from a Latin periphrasis of the type *cantare habeo* supplied the future (for details of the French type see Buridant (2000) 265–271), though in large parts of southern Italy not only the Classical type but also *cantare habeo* itself is missing. Note Maiden (1995) 158–159: "In dialects south of a line between Viterbo and Ancona, the morphological future tense is lost, and future time is usually expressed by present tense forms, although an analytical construction, usually of the form *avere* + *a* + infinitive, is also deployed to express future time, often with an overtone of obligation or necessity." The use of the present to refer to future time is already well established in Latin in Plautus (see Sjögren (1906) 5–56).

The construction *habeo* + infinitive goes well back in Latin, but in its earliest manifestations was not an exponent of futurity (see e.g. Coleman (1971)). Usually it expressed something akin to possibility (Cicero onwards: *TLL* VI.2–3.2454.12 ff. = *posse*) or obligation/necessity (Augustus onwards according to *TLL* VI.2–3.2454.53 ff. = *debere*). From about the third century (Tertullian onwards, according to *TLL* VI.2–3.2455.65 ff.) it turns up in contexts in which it may be given a future meaning, but that is usually secondary to the modality obligation/necessity. This ambiguity may be illustrated first by some examples from the grammarian Pompeius (for further details see Adams (1991)). Some remarks must also be made about the sense in which obligation/necessity is to be understood. On the modalities of the *habeo*-constructions see particularly Kooreman (1995) and Bourova and Tasmowski (2007).

Into the category obligation/necessity falls on the one hand deontic modality, on which see, for example, Lyons (1977) 843: "deontic necessity and possibility are usually understood to originate in some causal source: i.e. if someone is obliged or permitted to carry out some course of action, it is generally, though not necessarily, assumed that some person or institution has created the obligation or permission."

An instance of the *habeo*-construction in Pompeius that may be given such an interpretation is at *GL* V.253.15 (see Adams (1991) 151–152) *si autem neque in us neque in um, sed aliter, puta Baiae Athenae, iam secundum datiuum adsumere habes*, "if (nouns end) neither in -*us* nor -*um* (in the nominative) but otherwise, e.g. *Baiae Athenae*, then you have to form (the locative) on the model of the dative". Rules are stated for the ending of the locative. It will be the same as the dative if the nominative does not end in -*us* or -*um*. The source of the obligation or necessity is the prescriptive grammarian, who lays down rules. But as well as the deontic sense a future interpretation is possible (note Lyons (1977) 824: "there is an intrinsic connexion between deontic modality and futurity").

Alethic modality may be distinguished from deontic. On the former see Lyons (1977) 791): "What are traditionally described as necessary truths (i.e. propositions which … are true in all logically possible worlds) may now be referred to as alethically necessary propositions." The source of this modality lies in mathematical, physical or natural laws, or beliefs that have the status of absolute truths, such as beliefs about divine predestination.

The *habeo*-construction may be used to express this modality, but at the same time may be ambiguous between that and a future interpretation. Note Pompeius 129.26 (Adams (1991) 148): *si enim sustuleris istam tertiam, remanere habent duae*, "for if you take away the third (last syllable of *Romulus*), two (syllables) have to/will remain." Three take away one is two, which is a mathematical law.

Uses of the construction (from the third century CE onwards) approaching the meaning of futurity are found mainly in Christian writers and also some grammarians, and mainly in Africa (this latter feature being a theme of Thielmann (1885) 48–89). Bourova (2005) 304 gives statistics showing the regional distribution of constructions of the type *habeo* (in whatever tense) + infinitive. Of her electronic corpus of 655 examples, half are from Africa, a quarter from Italy, 5 per cent from northern Gaul, 3 per cent from southern Gaul and 3 per cent from Spain. There is no proof here that the usage was in any sense an Africanism (see Adams (2007) 727–728). Most of these texts were learned rather than low-register, and the contexts in which the construction occurs are more typical of learned discourse than of the colloquial. It seems to have had a particular place in logical argument, and often occurs in the main clause of conditional sentences (see Adams (2007) 728). Such contexts are not suggestive of those usages that the educated sometimes introduced from lower registers or social dialects to impart a discordant tone to a passage. On the contrary, the periphrasis seems to have had some currency among the educated as an exponent of deontic and alethic modalities when it was convenient to convey an ambiguity, with an idea of futurity also present.

This view of the learned status of the construction would seem to be at variance with its widespread survival in Romance, and with the conventional idea that Romance usages tended to originate in Latin from down the social scale. Did it also have a life beneath the surface of the literary language in lower social dialects? That assumption has sometimes been made. Pinkster (1987) 214 suggests that "in sub-standard Latin *habere* +infinitive was much more frequent than in our texts", and he puts down the lack of variation in the construction after Tertullian to the education system (213–214). Fruyt and Orlandini (2008) 233, remarking that infinitive + *habebam* was the origin of the French conditional, one of the functions of which is to express future in the past (e.g. *il disait qu'il viendrait*), suggest that "this sequence must have existed in the spoken language", and that Tertullian chose to use it for his specific needs. On the other hand, they cite Thielmann (1885) 48–89 in a note (233 n. 5) as holding that the usage originated from a high level of speech and was generalised later on.

Is there any evidence about the matter? The *habeo*-construction, at least as expressing something approaching futurity, is missing from certain archetypal low-register texts. It does not occur in the *Mulomedicina Chironis*, a work in which the future tense is constant. Van Oorde (1929) 87 cites just three instances from the *Peregrinatio Aetheriae* (a work in which the present tense is several times used with future reference, and in which there are some examples of the ordinary future), giving all of them the meaning *debere*. Two of these are not relevant because *habeo* is in the imperfect tense (2.1, 4.5). The other expresses deontic modality and futurity is out of the question: 24.6 *et at ubi diaconus perdixerit omnia, quae dicere habet, dicet orationem primum episcopus et orat pro omnibus*, "and when the deacon has said everything which he has to say, the bishop first says a prayer [*dicet* here is present not future: see Väänänen (1987) 58] and he prays for everyone". In the letters of Claudius Terentianus futures are quite common but *habeo* + infinitive does not occur.

There is however one relatively early instance of the Latin periphrasis in a significant text, one of the letters on ostraca from Wâdi Fawâkhir dated to the second century and bearing the name of Rustius Barbarus. For the text see *O. Wâdi Fawâkhir* 4, *CPL* 306, *CEL* 76. The expression is *adferre habes* (the first word written *ad.ferre*), but the context is fragmentary and there are no surrounding words. It is however difficult to see how, in an epistolary context, *adferre habes* could express anything other than a directive, "you have to/will bring", i.e. "bring", with the periphrasis ambiguous between deontic modality and futurity. Cugusi (1992) II.70 takes it that way, comparing *scribes* at line 10. See also in the same corpus the directive futures 3.3 *scribes mi …*, 3.11 *quae mi mittes ut possim …* This is an interesting example, given its early date. It is in a small corpus in which the conventional future is well attested (1 *faciam, mitam, scribam*, 2 *mittes*, 3 *scribes, mittes, afferam*), but on the above interpretation the periphrasis was encroaching on its territory, perhaps introducing a greater urgency. No other periphrases with *habeo* are found in *CEL*. The above example would suggest that the construction with a deontic, even future nuance was not confined to the upper reaches of the language, but it is unfortunate that the text is fragmentary.

The evidence for *habeo* + infinitive in low social dialects is slight indeed, but it is tempting to suggest, tentatively, that the construction belonged to the Latin language in general, not to one particular social level. It certainly cannot be concluded from the evidence that it was predominantly a usage of Vulgar Latin.

Conclusions

The periphrasis with *habeo* approaching a future meaning belongs to later Latin (second/third century), but the construction itself goes back to the Republic, after which it was subject to semantic shifts (type 2, p. 262 above). The analytic future of the

Classical period continues to be fully current even in very Late Latin, and there is no text extant in which infinitive + *habeo* has been grammaticalised as a future tense. The history of exponents of futurity in Latin raises a typical imponderable of Latin linguistic history: was the construction grammaticalised only very late, in the proto-Romance period, or had it already been grammaticalised in the Latin period but at levels of the language rarely surfacing in literature?

Reported Speech

Speech may be reported in Latin by direct quotation or by the accusative + infinitive. The latter construction developed a considerable complexity in literary and legal Latin. In lower registers, as for example in non-literary letters found on writing tablets of the early Empire from Britain, Egypt, Africa and elsewhere, or in special texts such as the *Cena Trimalchionis* of Petronius, there is a far more rudimentary use of the accusative + infinitive, with the subject accusative (often a pronoun) attached directly to the higher verb, a minimum of infinitives in any one construction (usually only one), and an absence of subordination (see Adams (2005b)). Such texts also make liberal use of direct speech.

The main feature of Late Latin in the reporting of speech lies in a proliferation of clauses introduced by *quod*, *quia* or *quoniam* standing in an object relation to the higher verb (e.g. *dico*) (for details see e.g. Herman (1963) 32–44, (1989), Coleman (1975) 119–121, Cuzzolin (1994)). This "late" development is mainly of type 1 in the list above, p. 262. The origin of the *dico quod* construction can be traced back to the pre-Classical and Classical periods, in literary Latin. From non-literary texts of the type mentioned above it is absent. Here was a usage that developed in the literary language, not, as far as we can tell, in submerged varieties, and certainly not exclusively there. It is the increasing frequency of the construction that may be described as late, and also the spread by analogy of the alternative subordinators, *quia* (from Petronius: see p. 281 below) and particularly *quoniam* (late, but precise details unclear: see Svennung (1935) 504 for texts from the *Vetus latina* onwards that have it).

This type of construction was the forerunner of the Romance constructions such as *dire che/que*, though in most it is (*dicere*) *quid*, the latter supplanting (*dicere*) *quod*, that is reflected (Rohlfs (1969) 188–190, Maiden (1995) 206). In Sicily, Calabria, Puglia and parts of the Abruzzo reflexes of *quia* by contrast provided the complementiser with verbs of perception and assertion (Maiden (1995) 226 n. 12, Rohlfs (1969) 189).

Quod = "the fact that" introduces noun clauses regularly in Classical Latin. By definition such clauses stand in a subject or object relation to a higher verb, and they may be interchangeable with an accusative + infinitive, which is often a noun clause.

Note e.g. Pl. *Aul.* 226: **uenit hoc mihi, Megadore, in mentem,** *ted esse hominem diuitem.* The primary subject of the verb phrase *uenit in mentem* is the pronoun *hoc*, but this serves merely to introduce the accusative + infitive, which syntactically is subject of the same verb phrase. A *quod*-clause might have been used instead, as at Gel. 13.30.6: *ecce autem* **id** quoque **in mentem uenit, quod** *etiam Plautus in Poenulo "faciem" pro totius corporis colorisque habitu dixit.* Here again there is a pronoun (*id*) as subject, but this time it anticipates a *quod*-clause that is (appositional) subject of the verb.

Quod-noun clauses may also be object of a verb. As early as Terence *addo* is used with a *quod*-clause as object without a supporting pronoun: *Ph.* 168 *ut ne addam quod sine sumptu ingenuam, liberalem nactus es*. It is no great extension when *quod*-clauses turn up as object of *verba dicendi*, something that happens in the Republic: *B. Hisp.* 36.1 *dum haec geruntur legati Carteienses* **renuntiauerunt quod** *Pompeium in potestate haberent*. The construction continues in the literary language of the early Empire, as for example in Tacitus: e.g. *Ann.* 14.6.1 (with a verb of thinking) *illic reputans se fallacibus litteris accitam ..., quodque litus iuxta ... nauis ... concidisset* (in alternation with the accusative + infinitive). As was noted above, the *dico quod*-construction is absent from the non-literary writing tablets and the like that we now have from scattered parts of the Empire, in which the accusative + infinitive in simple forms abounds, and quoted direct speech is also common. In the conspicuously sub-standard Latin of the freedmen in Petronius it is also not to be found, and it seems possible that here is a syntactic development that was taking place particularly in higher registers. There are two apparent exceptions in the freedmen's speeches, but both notably have *quia* as complementiser, not *quod*, and the *dico quia*-construction is definitely not a component of literary Latin at this period. Note Petr. 46.1 *ego illi iam tres cardeles occidi, et* **dixi quia** *mustella comedit* (cf. 45.10). *Dico quia* is an extension by analogy of the *dico quod*- construction, but the path by which it got into non-standard Latin in the first two centuries of the Empire in unclear.

Such object clauses do become a feature of Late (literary) Latin but they remained in a minority compared with the accusative + infinitive. Herman (1989) 134–135 notes that for five or six centuries their frequency remained constant (at about 10 per cent of the cases where one might expect an accusative + infinitive). Even a text as late as the *Anonymus Valesianus* II (sixth century) has only four instances, compared with twenty-four of the accusative + infinitive (Adams (1976) 94). Some principles of selection between the two constructions have been noted. Herman (1989) shows that the *quod*-type construction is almost always after the verb (a preposed *quod*-clause might be taken as causal, and ambiguity is avoided by flagging the construction with an initial *verbum dicendi*), and he also suggests that the frequency is highest when the agent of the subordinate clause is not the topic. In the *Anonymus Valesianus* most *quod*-type clauses follow the higher verb but are separated from it (Adams (1976) 94), whereas the accusative + infinitive is usually juxtaposed with the higher verb. It has also been shown that in much Christian Latin *quia* is preferred as the subordinator to *quod* and *quoniam* (see Herman (1963) 40–41, and also Salonius (1920) 325 on the *Vitae patrum*), though Herman (1963) 41–42 finds signs of a regional variation, with *quod* favoured in Gaul and *quia* in Italy.

Conclusions

As was stated above, the *dico quod*-construction was relatively early (and not confined to low-register texts), but it only became common from about the third century. The *dico quia* construction made its appearance slightly later, and at first seems to have been in use further down the social scale.

General Conclusions

There is no neatly defined period within which Late Latin might be deemed to fall. We have seen developments that first appear in the early Empire (locative of place names for accusative, *ubi* for *quo*, the *B/V* confusion), and others that show up much later, such as full genitival and instrumental uses of *de*, the loss of phonemic distinctions of vowel length and lexical novelties (e.g. the displacement of *oppidum* and *urbs* by *ciuitas*). But the concept of lateness is made more complicated by the tendency of the educated classes to stigmatise some phenomena and to keep them out of the literary language (e.g. *in* + acc. of place names), such that we have no idea of their chronology. Also many usages that become a marked feature of later Latin have their roots in much earlier Latin. There are as well major developments that are known from the Romance languages to have occurred but are not fully established in any text extant, such as the loss of the synthetic passive, the loss of the future and the use of *ad* as a full-blown replacement of the dative of the indirect object. The history of such changes within Latin itself remains obscure. The result of these complications is that it is hard to offer generalisations about features of Late Latin. If, for example, Classical Latin is compared with Romance languages, it would have to be said that there was a movement from synthesis to analysis in the case system, but the details of this change turn out to be messy, with variable chronology and special determinants from case to case.

New developments in the later period cannot be attributed en masse to lower social dialects. Some of the phenomena discussed above are found mainly in low-register texts, but educated varieties of the language were subject to change too.

New influences on the language came into play in the later Empire. Latin was in contact with numerous vernacular languages, some of which left a mark. Romans had long had dealings with Germanic peoples, but at a very late period these had more impact on the language. The Franks introduced Frankish terms into their law codes, written in Latin (see e.g. Adams (2007) 317–318, 321–322, 323–326), and other borrowings came in via the army (see e.g. Adams (2003a) 274–279). In North Africa some Punic or indeterminately "African" terms entered the local Latin (Adams (2007) 529–532); these occur for example in the *Tablettes Albertini* (Adams (2007) 556–558). Reduced forms of Latin as written by foreigners with imperfect command of the language make an appearance (see Adams (2003a), index s. vv. "learners' Latin", "reduced languages").

The Latin Bible (*Vetus latina* or Vulgate) was imitated by some as a model for literary writing, particularly narrative, and this imitation produced texts stylistically quite unlike texts based on Classical models. In the *Peregrinatio Aetheriae*, for example, a present participle, frequently with perfective meaning, is often placed early in the sentence, and this practice is probably mimicked from the *Vetus latina* (see Klein (1958) 253–257 on biblical influence on this text).

But the Bible was not the only stylistic model even among Christians. Jerome himself, who was responsible for the Vulgate, used very different models when it suited him. The three *Vitae sanctorum* which he composed draw on a wide range of Classical literature from Plautus through Cicero and Sallust to Tacitus and beyond to e.g. Florus (see the notes in the edition of Leclerc *et al.* (2007)).

FURTHER READING

The classic treatment of the general issues is Löfstedt (1959). Clackson and Horrocks, (2007) have two chapters on Late and very Late Latin, and the last two chapters of Weiss (2009) provide a succinct resumé of the main changes between Latin and Romance. On this last subject a mass of detail is packed into Väänänen (1981) which has recently been translated into Italian with supplements (Väänänen (2003)). Several books on specific texts go far beyond their stated subject and discuss many major features of Late versus Classical Latin, notably Löfstedt (1911), another work that has been translated into Italian with supplements, and Svennung (1935). The latter work deals with features of technical prose alongside wider developments in the language, and that is a theme also of Adams (1995a), and Langslow (2000). Books about Latin of the sixth century and beyond (and thus to some extent about the relationship between Late Latin and Medieval Latin) include Bonnet (1890), several of the works of Norberg (1943; 1944), Löfstedt (1961) and Adams (1976). A notable book on much the same theme but with a Romance perspective is Wright (1982). Finally the ongoing conference series, *Latin vulgaire – latin tardif*, which has reached its ninth volume, has many papers of interest.

CHAPTER 17

Medieval Latin

Greti Dinkova-Bruun

Introduction

The term "Medieval Latin" is widely used in a variety of contexts. Yet, similarly to "Late Latin", this is a problematic denomination. The problems arise on a number of levels. First, the term "Medieval Latin" suggests that we are dealing with a distinctly defined language which was taught as such during the Middle Ages and which possessed a set of fixed rules that were systematized into a kind of grammatical primer to be used by teachers in the schools. This plainly is not the case, as Latin instruction in the Middle Ages was based on the grammars of Aelius Donatus (fourth century) and Priscian (early sixth century), which obviously expounded the rules of Classical Latin. What happened to these rules after they were taught in the medieval classroom is a different story all together, and the later departures from the norms could be both signs of philological development and examples of somebody's "bad grammar" (Rigg (1986) 354). The point is that Medieval Latin, with all its peculiar syntax, strange orthography and unusual vocabulary, is still in its core the same literary language that was written in the Classical period. How people spoke in both periods would inevitably influence what they wrote, but the pull towards correctness and grammaticality would always be strong, particularly in later times. Imitators of the Classical elegance of expression, as well as authors striving towards linguistic virtuosity abound in the Middle Ages, but so also do the ones whose grasp of the grammatical rules was obviously tenuous.

Second, talking of Medieval Latin in general terms obscures the chronological and geographical peculiarities of the medieval written idiom. Texts from the earlier Middle Ages (especially before the reforms implemented by the Carolingian scholars) look and read differently from the ones in the later centuries when Latin was transformed into an artificially learned construct. Also, works from the British Isles will exhibit features that

A Companion to the Latin Language, First Edition. Edited by James Clackson.
© 2011 Blackwell Publishing Ltd. Published 2011 by Blackwell Publishing Ltd.

distinguish them from contemporary texts that originate in various regions on the continent. "Hiberno-Latin" and "Anglo-Latin" are well-known terms in the scholarly discourse, whereas the other localized varieties of the language have not been identified by such easily recognizable designations. "Continental Latin" has been used in some publications (Sidwell (1995)) but the term is hardly specific enough.

Third, and this is true for all the stages in the history of Latin, we have to be aware of the different styles of writing which are heavily influenced by the conventions of the genre to which the written text belongs. A document is very different from a commentary on the Bible, a private missive does not resemble a papal letter, an epic poem is quite unlike a liturgical hymn. This rather obvious observation is nonetheless important because it accounts for some of the "otherness" readers feel when they are confronted with medieval texts. Many new literary forms developed in the Middle Ages, all closely connected to the study of the Bible and the celebration of the Christian liturgy, a development which inevitably engendered new ways of expression, new vocabulary, new sentiment. It is important to remember that the relationship between form and content is a fraught one and that Medieval Latin is different not only because of grammar, but also because of spirit.

Finally, what does "medieval" mean anyway, and how long do the Middle Ages last? Since the medieval period is commonly outlined as covering the span from the fifth to the fifteenth century, it is evident that in linguistic terms the beginning of "Medieval Latin" would overlap with so-called Late Latin (see chapter 16 in this volume), whereas its waning years would touch upon the development of Neo-Latin (see chapter 18). The changes and developments occur slowly in any case, and clear boundaries are difficult to set.

Tools for Learning Medieval Latin

The development of the Latin language in the Middle Ages has intrigued numerous scholars in the twentieth and twenty-first centuries. Since it is impossible to provide a comprehensive overview of the vast literature that deals with the various aspects of Medieval Latin, only the most significant studies and compilations will be included here. In general, the works on the subject can be divided into three groups:

1 Philological compendia that collect and organize the features of medieval grammar and style, exemplifying them with excerpts and short Latin phrases rather than providing self-contained passages or entire texts for sustained reading. The crowning study in this category is Peter Stotz's *Handbuch zur lateinischen Sprache des Mittelalters* (1996–2004), which in four volumes (the fifth one contains the bibliography and the various indices) represents a treasure trove of information on lexicography and vocabulary (vol. 1), semantics and word formation (vol. 2), phonology and phonetics (vol. 3), and finally morphology, syntax and figures of speech (vol. 4). In this context two more studies should be mentioned: Karl Strecker's classic *Introduction to Medieval Latin* (written in 1929, translated by Robert B. Palmer in 1957 and reprinted several times) and A.G. Rigg's insightful essay "Latin language" in the *Dictionary of the Middle Ages* (1986).

2   Anthologies, or readers, that contain selections of prose and poetic medieval texts. This is by far the richest and most varied group. It encompasses old favourites, such as Charles Beeson's *A Primer of Medieval Latin* (1925) and K.P. Harrington's *Medieval Latin* (1925), as well as more recent compilations by Dag Norberg (1968), Keith Sidwell (1995), and Pascale Bourgain (2005), to mention only a few. All of these textual compilations contain introductions on the grammatical and lexical peculiarities of Medieval Latin, even though these vary in length, focus and detail. The selections of texts are also quite divergent, as are the approaches exhibited. A noteworthy example is Bourgain (2005). Apart from a very useful introductory study, which is no fewer than 130 pages long, the author organizes the material both chronologically and according to style, provides translations into French and appends copious explanatory notes. Among many others, especially interesting for the student of Medieval Latin is the case of Ademar of Chabannes who in the eleventh century copied and corrected the eighth-century's *Liber historiae Francorum* in accordance with the linguistic realities of his own time (Bourgain (2005) 163–168). Many more examples of Medieval Latin anthologies are enumerated in Strecker (1929/1957) 19–20, esp. n. 29.

3   Textbooks for teaching Medieval Latin to beginners. In contrast with the numerous course systems available for Classical Latin, the primers for Medieval Latin are only a handful. The two course books that come to mind easily are *A Primer of Ecclesiastical Latin* by John F. Collins (1985) and *Apprendre le latin médiéval* by Monique Goullet and Michel Parisse (1996), which the authors later supplemented with a compilation of texts and exercises called *Traduire le latin médiéval* (2003). These manuals represent useful attempts to fill the void of textbooks and formal grammars of Medieval Latin but they are the exceptions rather than the rule.

The picture that emerges here is fascinating. It is apparent that the textual anthologies are the tools that are used most frequently for teaching and learning Medieval Latin today. It is commonly expected that before they begin their instruction in Medieval Latin, the students should have learned already the normative rules of the language by taking a course in Classical Latin. In this, our pedagogical approach follows in the footsteps of the medieval grammar teachers who also started with the Classical norm as presented in Donatus and Priscian before moving to the next step which involved reading various canonical texts and commenting upon them. It is no wonder then that despite the large scholarship produced on the matter and the protestations of several philologists, Medieval Latin is still generally perceived as a deviation and corruption of Classical standards.

Medieval Latin and Its Characteristics

The phenomena that characterize medieval Latinity are closely related to those observed in so-called Late Latin. In fact, the tension between written literary idiom and spoken "vulgar" expression continues to dominate the linguistic reality of the Middle Ages. The situation is complicated further by a third stream of influence coming from the Latin of the Church Fathers and from Jerome's Vulgate translation of the Bible commonly referred to as "Christian Latin" or "Ecclesiastical Latin" (see among many others, Blaise (1955); Mohrmann (1958–1977); Strecker (1929/1957) 22–26, esp. n. 3 for further bibliography). The interplay between these three linguistic forces underlies the unique nature of Medieval Latin which, while striving to preserve the grammatical rules of Classical Latin, absorbs the vocabulary of Christianity and does not shy away from nurturing the colloquialisms that will give birth to the Romance languages.

It is beyond the scope of this chapter to present an exhaustive register of all features of Medieval Latin. By necessity what follows is an overview of general developments that encompasses four main areas: (1) vocabulary, (2) orthography, (3) morphology and (4) syntax. Unfortunately, it is impossible to accommodate the geographical, temporal and individual dimensions of Medieval Latin in such a broad summary. When dealing with a medieval text, the modern reader should never forget that many of its characteristics will depend on when, where and by whom it was written. Excellent in this regard is Norberg's concise history of Medieval Latin (see Norberg (1968)).

Vocabulary

The lexical rejuvenation of the Latin idiom begins in Late Latin and continues unabated during the Middle Ages. The new vocabulary develops in order to fit the changed demands of medieval society, be they religious or educational, administrative or professional, military or juridical, botanical or zoological. In the following I shall examine two general tendencies: first, the entry into the language of loanwords and the creation of new Latin words in specific cultural or material contexts, and second, the semantic shifts that occur in some of the inherited Classical lexis. However, for more detailed examination of the specific lexicological phenomena that characterize the medieval formation of neologisms, the excessive use of diminutives (i.e. *basiliculla* [tiny church], *caverniculla* [minute cavity], *pompula* [small parade], *geniculum* [knee, with no diminutive connotations], *soliculum* [sun], *clericellus* [student at a cathedral school], *homullus* = *homo*, etc.) and the predilection for compound forms (i.e. *altiloquus* [loud], *flammiuomus* [belching flames], *protoplastus* [the first man], *contraluctans* [fighting against], etc.), the reader should consult the studies whose priority is to expound these matters (see for example, Stotz (1996–2004) vols. 1 and 2).

New words

New words enter into Medieval Latin through different channels and from different spheres of life, for example:

1   An entire class of novel vocabulary was adopted in order to accommodate the new Christian reality. This tendency was in full force already in Late Latin and its prominence never waned. Very influential in this context of Christianization was the language of the Latin Bible, through which a number of Greek and Hebrew words became a permanent feature of Ecclesiastical and Medieval Latin: *anathema* (cursed thing, curse), *angelus* (angel), *apostolus* (apostle), *baptisma* (baptism), *ecclesia* (church), *eleemosyna*

(alms), *gazophilacium* (a place where the offerings are put; treasury), *laicus* (common, and later layman), *amen* (true, truly, truth), *Behemoth* (biblical beast), *ephod* (priestly linen garment), *gehenna* (hell), *Sabaoth* (one of the names of God translated as "Lord of Hosts"), *sabbatum* (Sabbath), *synagoga* (synagogue), etc. Furthermore, ecclesiastical institutions and hierarchy also were originally known by Greek names, which were adopted unchanged in the medieval idiom: *abbatissa* (abbess), *catechumenus* (catechumen), *clericus* (clergyman), *clerus* (clerical order, clergy), *diaconus* (deacon), *dioecesis* (diocese), *episcopus* (bishop), *presbyter* (priest), *papa* (bishop, but from the seventh century denoting the bishop of Rome, the Pope), etc. Thirdly, new "Christian" Latin lexemes were created by following the regular rules of Latin word formation, which is probably the most effective way of expanding the new vocabulary: *beneplacitus* (pleasing), *clericatus* (clerical office), *confessor* (confessor of Christianity, father confessor), *cooperator* (co-worker), *corruptrix* (female corruptor), *evangelizare* (to evangelize), *incarnatio* (incarnation), etc. Finally, the special vocabulary that pertains to the liturgical celebrations of the Church also needs to be mentioned here. It contains both Greek and Latin technical words which denote the various liturgical ministers (ordained and not ordained), their postures and gestures, vestments and books, as well as the liturgical vessels, furniture and rites: *missa* (mass), *eucharistia* (eucharist), *casula* (chasuble), *breuiarium* (breviary), *missale* (missal), *lectrina* (lectern), *ceroferarius* (candle-bearer), etc. (Sheerin (1996)).

2   Another large group of new words originated in the intellectual context of medieval education in the later Middle Ages. This technical vocabulary, which developed in full in the later Middle Ages, has been studied for a number of years now by the Comité International du Vocabulaire des Institutions et de la Communication Intellectuelles au Moyen Age (CIVICIMA) under the leadership of Olga Weijers. Between 1988 and 2003 ten volumes have been published as a result of the activities of the Comité containing a number of important articles on the terminology used in the Middle Ages to describe the organization of the medieval teaching institutions (both schools and universities), their administrators and teaching techniques, their students and accreditation procedures, as well as the making, editing and circulation of books in the university towns. Only a handful of words from this rich vocabulary shall be listed at this point, many of which are still in use today: *universitas, collegium, facultas, administrator, rector, vicerector, professor, temptator* (examiner); *bursarius* (holder of bursary), *baccalarius* (bachelor), *doctoratus* (doctorate), *licentiatus* (licentiate); *stationarius* (bookseller), *peciarius* (the master who inspect the copies sold by the booksellers; from *pecia* (piece), because the textbooks were copied by the students section by section), *exemplator* (copyist who creates an exemplar). For many more terms, see Weijers (1987). In the university environment in Oxford towards the end of the Middle Ages we also find a number of words that denote the professional activities of the people who were in charge of the day-to-day practical needs of the institution and its fellows: *barbitonsor* (barber), *elemosinarius* (almoner), *lotrix* (laundress), *maltmannus* (maltman), *pincerna* (butler), *pandoxator* (brewer), *tegulator* (tiler), *valectus* (groom), etc. (Fletcher (1993)).

Another influx of new vocabulary in the university context can be observed in the twelfth and thirteenth centuries when numerous works were translated from Arabic. These translations contain intriguing examples of Arabic words, which were accepted into Latin in order to denote scientific ideas and instruments that were unknown before. Some of these terms were Latinized and some were not, for example, in the medical treatises we find both *siropus* (liquid mixture) and *siphac* (membrane); in the astrological tracts we have both *alfardaria* (period allotted to each planet) and *cehem* (astrological "lot"); and in the musical expositions we see both *elmaurifa* (referring to the specific shape of musical notation) and *rebec* (instrument with three strings). For these terms and many more, see various essays in Mantello and Rigg (1996) as well as Stotz (1996–2004), vol. 1.

Finally, we need to mention the philosophical vocabulary, which develops in the twelfth and thirteenth centuries in relationship to the Latin translations of Aristotle's philosophical corpus, i.e. *Physica, Metaphysica, De anima, Ethica*, etc. Aristotle's treatises arrived in the West with commentaries by Greek, Arabic and Jewish thinkers such as Simplicius, Themistius, Avicenna, Averroes, and Maimonides, whose influence should also be kept in mind. The translations of the works of all these men were the reason for the appearance in Medieval Latin of a large technical vocabulary related to the discipline of philosophy. Some of the terms were newly coined following the rules of Latin word-formation (similarly to what we have already seen in the Christian context), for example: *anitas* (whetherness), *quaritas* (whyness), *talitas* (suchness), *nihilitas* (nothingness), *quidditas* (quiddity, essence), *corporeitas* (corporeality), *cognitivus* (cognitive), *virtualis* (virtual), *totalis* (total), *habitualiter* (habitually), *mentaliter* (mentally), *connotatio* (connotation), etc.; but many other Classical words simply acquired a wider semantic range, for example: *ratio, mutatio, motus, natura, persona, similitudo*, etc. (Brown (1996)).

3   Medieval Latin borrowed liberally from the vernacular languages, especially in the spheres of administration and daily life, including farming, hunting, warfare, seafaring, measures, minting, milling, trading, craftsmanship and food. If Greek and Arabic were the languages, from which predominantly religious, literary and philosophical vocabulary was adopted, the medieval Germanic languages, English and Old French mostly provided the more mundane and "barbaric" terminology. Some examples of these *realia* of medieval ordinary day-to-day life introduced into Latin throughout the Middle Ages include: *baco* (bacon), *bannus* (proclamation, ban), *barellus* (barrel), *bolla* (bowl), *brunia* (body armour), *burgensis* (of a town), *bussellus* (bushel), *cargaria* (cargo, provisions), *cuva* (kettle, cauldron), *fatta* (vat), *foresta* (forest), *gambesio* (quilted military garment, gambeson), *hamellus* (hamlet), *hida* (hide), *leporarius* (greyhound for hunting hares, *lepores*), *lottum* (share of taxation), *mallus* (juridical assembly), *marescallus* (marshal), *mundiburdus* (patron, defender), *namium* (goods seized), *oplondinum* (upland), *shopa* (shop), *wanti* (military hand protection), *warda* (ward, guard), etc. A few words entered daily-life usage from other languages as well. Especially in the language of commerce we see words from Spanish – *morabetinus* (morabetin, maravedi – a Spanish coin); Arabic – *dogana/doana* (customs duty), *galega* (auction), *magasinus* (storehouse), *avaria* (customs duty), *zuccarum* (sugar) – and Greek – *hentica/entica* (capital, investment), *taxegium* (commercial voyage). For more detailed discussion, see Pryor (1996) and Bourgain (2005).

An excerpt from the Domesday Book (also known as the *Liber de Wintonia* [The Book of Winchester], written in 1086) serves as an example of how some of the local

Anglo-Norman vocabulary was Latinized and used in administrative context (Sidwell (1995) 190, lines 7–10):

> Ipsa comitissa [i.e. Godeva] tenuit in Aderestone III **hidas**. Terra est V carrucis. Ibi sunt XI **uillani** et II **bordarii** et I seruus cum IIII carrucis. Ibi VI acrae prati. Silua II **leuugas** longuitudine et II **leuugas** latitudine. Valuit XL libras, modo LX solidos.

So Countess Godiva held three hides in Atherstone, a "hide" being a land measurement, usually 80–100 acres. On this piece of land live eleven villagers [*villani*], two smallholders [*bordarii*] and one serf [*servus*] with four ploughs [*carrucis*; those were counted for tax purposes]. There is also a forest on the lot, which is two leagues long and two leagues wide [*II leuugas*]. The value of the property is 40 pounds [*libras*] and 60 ·shillings [*solidos*].

In addition, a passage from the inventory of the papal riches in Avignon compiled in 1369 provides illustration of the great enrichment of the medieval vocabulary with words describing the material culture of the period (Bourgain (2005) 208, lines 7–16):

> Primo 6 **cupas** seu **ciphos** aureos cum **cooperculis** et pedibus emaltatas et elevatas, ponderantes 46 m. 5 u.
>
> Item 6 **pintas** et 1 **ayguaderiam** auri esmaltatas tam in toto quam in parte, ponderantes 48 m.
>
> Item 1 **conquetam** auream cum 2 **ansis seu manillis** et cum esmalto in medio cum armis Anglie, ponderis 47 m. 2 u.
>
> Item 12 **scutellas** et 12 **grasaletos** ac 2 **platellos** auri planos, ponderis 71 m. 1 u.
>
> Item 12 **tacee** cum esmaltis in medio, 1 **dragerius cum cloqueari suo** esmaltus, 1 **olla elemosinaria** et 1 **turribulum** cum 1 **pomello** auri esmaltato, ponderis 40 m. 7 u. 1 q.

A bewildering number of interesting words are used in this text to indicate various intriguing objects: bowls (*cupas* or *ciphos*), bottles (*pintas*), a jug (*ayguaderiam*), a vase (*conquetam*), plates (*scutellas*), dishes or grails (*grasaletos*), platters (*platellos*), cups (*tacee*), a drageoir or box for sweets with its spoon (*dragerius cum cloqueari suo*), a box for alms (*olla elemosinaria*), a censer (*turribulum*). Many of these valuable items are made of gold (i.e. the six bowls, the jug, the vase, the two platters) or covered fully or partially in enamel (*esmaltatus, esmaltus*), which also was an expensive material in the Middle Ages. Some pieces have lids (*cooperculis*) or handles (*ansis seu manillis*), and the censer has a knob handle (*pomellum*). The weight of each item is provided as well – in marks (m.), ounces (u.) and quarter ounces (q.). In short, the presence of all this specialized vocabulary makes the Avignon papal inventory an invaluable witness of the huge lexical development of the Latin language during the later Middle Ages.

Old words

In addition to the completely novel vocabulary, which develops during the medieval period and which makes reading Medieval Latin difficult, some of the Classical words that continue to be used expand their semantic range in order to accommodate new linguistic and cultural realities. Four general tendencies can be outlined here:

1 Some words acquire a new meaning because the old reality they represent has disappeared in the medieval context, for example, *consul* (Class. Latin: consul, Medieval Latin: municipal official); *praesul* (Class. Latin: leading dancer; Medieval Latin: bishop), etc.

2 Some words develop new meaning through homonymic formation, others through linguistic jumps of signification. The obvious examples for homonymic confusion are words such as *dolus* (Class. Latin: deceit; Medieval Latin: pain, because of *doleo*) and *iterare* (Class. Latin: to repeat; Medieval Latin: to journey, because of *iter*). The jumps in signification are exemplified by *necare* (Class. Latin: to kill; Medieval Latin: to drown), etc.

3 Numerous words add a medieval meaning to their Classical one, and both the usages are attested in the medieval sources: *comes* can mean both "companion" and "count"; *dux* = leader and duke; *fidelis* = faithful and Christian; *miles* = soldier and knight; *pontifex* = high priest and archbishop; *scriptura* = writing and Holy Scripture, *breue* = short and letter, "brief", etc. Here of course also the philosophical terms, which were discussed above, should be included.

4 Some words are preferred to others, i.e. *caballus* is sometimes used instead of *equus*, and interestingly the word *equus* is not preserved in the Romance languages; *bucca* is prefered to *os*, *coxa* to *femur*, *ambulare*, *camminare* and *uadere* to *ire*, *fabulare* to *loqui*, *manducare* and *comedo* to *edo*, *portare* to *ferre*, etc.

It is important to stress at this point that the linguistic developments outlined above are not absolute. Because of the normative nature of Latin and its varying registers of expression, the Classical vocabulary continued to be used on par with the new medieval one.

Names

Before concluding the section on medieval vocabulary one last observation needs to be made, namely, that the medieval Latin lexicon was hugely expanded by numerous novel proper names. On the one hand we have names of people, be they biblical heroes, historical personages or literary writers, and on the other there are the names of countless newly founded towns and villages. The best tool for identifying the various places found in the medieval sources is the geographical lexicon *Orbis Latinus*, the first edition of which is now available on-line and the revised edition is currently available in print form (see Graesse *et al.* (1972)). As for personal names, the rather limited stock of Classical *praenomina* was enlarged considerably, first with names borrowed from the Bible (i.e. Petrus, Mattheus, Thomas, Simon, Andreas, Jo(h)annes, Maria, Anna, Elisabeth, etc.) and second with Latinized or non-Latinized versions of vernacular names (i.e. Hildebertus, Henricus, Edmundus, Ethelredus, Guillelmus, Serlo, Adelperga, Hrotsvitha, etc.). Despite this proliferation of names, there were still too many people carrying the same *nomen*, so an appellation could be added to the personal names in order to distinguish the various personages. Often these additional appellations were connected to a location, either the place of birth of the persons or the place where they held an important office, for example: *Hildebertus Cenomanensis* (Hildebert of Le Mans), *Laurentius Dunelmensis* (Lawrence of Durham), *Guillelmus de Conchis* (William of Conches), *Guillelmus Malmesburiensis* (William of Malmesbury), *Guillelmus (de) Ockam* (William of Ockham), etc. Some appellations are actually akin to nicknames, as can be seen in *Notker Balbulus* (Notker the Stammerer), *Robertus Grosseteste* (Robert Bighead), *Albertus Magnus* (Albert the Great), *Gilbertus Universalis* (Gilbert the Universal), *Saxo Grammaticus* (Saxo the Grammarian), *Petrus Cantor* (Peter the Chanter), etc. It should be stressed here that several of these names represent our naming practices and may have never been used by the medieval contemporaries of the people in question, especially when nicknames are concerned (see Bruun (1999) on Notker).

Phonology and orthography

One may imagine that morphology or syntax would present the next greatest challenge to students of Medieval Latin. In my experience, however, the second area, where the students encounter most difficulty, is the way Medieval Latin appears on the page. The obvious reason for this is the fact that medieval spelling is notoriously inconsistent. Numerous words are written differently not only across various manuscripts and works but even within the same ones. This is a vexing situation for the editors of medieval texts who are constantly faced with difficult decisions regarding the orthographical variants that need to be selected for the final version of the printed text. As a rule, the spelling practices of the medieval author are examined carefully, and the editor follows the predominant tendencies they exhibit. The result is that a number of different spellings of the same word appear in the editions of medieval works, and these various forms would all be acceptable. Thus, one cannot learn to spell "correctly" in Medieval Latin. The "proper" forms, if we agree that those are the ones found in Classical literary Latin, exist during the medieval period only as "Platonic" ideas, which manifest themselves in a number of closely related variations that are shaped by specific pronunciation. This might seem a difficult situation to reckon with but at least in such cases the established Classical spelling provides a starting point for deciphering the transformed medieval graphemes. In contrast, no help what so ever exists with the new words, which, as we have already seen, enter into Medieval Latin from numerous other languages.

This fluidity of medieval orthography makes the use of a dictionary difficult for a novice Latin student. Dictionaries are normative by nature, and their aim is to impose convention and canonicity. In order to find a word in a dictionary, one needs to know how it is spelled. Then what is to be done when the spelling is not standardized? Helpful tools in this regard are wordlists like Latham (1965), which list spelling variants with useful cross-references. For example, in Latham, on p. 313 we find *nipulus*, see *knipulus* (knife), on p. 358 *pondicitas*, see *ponticitas* (brininess), and on p. 451 *stapha*, see *staffa* (stirrup), etc.

Apart from simply creating strange-looking forms, medieval spelling is also responsible for complicating the understanding of the text. This is especially evident in the well-known phenomenon of diphthong collapsing, which results in forms such as *ille* corresponds to both *ille* and *illae*; *pene* to both *poenae* and *paene*; *fere* to both *ferae* and *fere*; or *cedo* to both *cedo* and *caedo*, to mention only a few. This confusing situation requires a firm grasp of Latin grammar, an additional difficulty for the modern student, particularly a beginner.

The peculiarities of medieval orthography are of course representative of the changed pronunciation (eminently localized) of Latin in the medieval period. One can even say that medieval orthography is the written manifestation of the phonological changes that occur in the Latin language. Many of these shifts can be observed already in the Classical spoken idiom (for example the tendency towards monophthongization), but during the Middle Ages the phonological changes continue to multiply and in some cases clearly become the predominant norm.

An exhaustive enumeration of all characteristics of medieval spelling is impossible here; only the most prominent features will be presented below together with some textual examples. For a full treatment of the topic, see vol. 3 in Stotz (1996–2004).

Reduction of the ae *and* oe *diphthongs*

The reduction of the diphthongs is one of the most common peculiarities of medieval spelling, being a graphic expression of a phonological shift that already existed in Vulgar and Late Latin. The examples of this phenomenon are virtually innumerable but a quotation from the *Breuissima comprehensio historiarum* written in the early thirteenth century by the Anglo-Latin poet Alexander of Ashby represents a good example (see Dinkova-Bruun (2004) 52, vv. 599–604):

> Seleuco Babilon datur, **Egiptus** Tholomeo
> Hiique mouent in se **prelia** dira diu.
> Heres **predicti** Tholomeus erat Tholomei
> Cui transfert libros legis **Hebrea** manus.
> Post **hec** Anthiocus **Asie** rex turbat **Hebreos**,
> Sed Iudas ualido Marte tuetur eos.

Babylon was given to Seleucus, Egypt to Ptolemy: for a long time these two fought fierce wars against each other. The heir of the already mentioned Ptolemy was this Ptolemy, for whom the Jewish hand translated the books of the law. After these events Antiochus, the king of Asia [sc. Antiochus IV Epiphanes], began to harass the Jews, while Judas [sc. Judas Maccabeus] defended them courageously.

All the words in bold in this short excerpt from Alexander's versification of the biblical *Book of Maccabees* show a number of reduced diphthongs: *Egiptus = Aegyptus, prelia = proelia, predicti = praedicti, Hebrea = Hebraea, hec = haec, Asie = Asiae,* and *Hebreos = Hebraeos.* Clearly both *ae* and *oe* diphthongs have disappeared here, be they present in proper names *(Hebrea, Egiptus, Asie)*, prefixes *(predicti)*, case endings *(Asie)* or simply as part of the word's root *(hec, prelia)*. For somebody who is familiar with Classical Latin, these spelling variations are not likely to create a huge problem; for a beginning Latinist the situation is rather different.

It is worth noting at this point that, even though the general tendency observed in medieval writing is towards monodiphthongization, a classicizing trend exists as well, especially prior to the twelfth century. In addition to other features, the classicized spelling manifests itself in the use of *e-caudata*, which generally appears in the places where a diphthong is expected. Hypercorrections are often in evidence, revealing a shaky knowledge of accurate diphthong orthography because of its lacking support in pronunciation. Some examples are seen in the following quotation from the eleventh-century anonymous poem *Liber generationis Iesu Christi filii David filii Abraham*, vv. 16–24 (Dinkova-Bruun (2005) 29–30):

> Hi duo preclari dicuntur significari
> Per geminas antes pro templi limine stantes,
> **Quę** bis senorum sunt funiculo cubitorum
> Istis **aptatę**, typica racione **ligatę**.
> Funiculi **spirę**, si uis mysteria **scirę**,
> In duodenorum numero stant discipulorum,
> Dogmata sunt quorum promissis iuncta duorum,
> Tempus ad hoc per **quę** pater auctoratur uterque
> Prolis **promissę** decursa stirpe **fuissę**.

These two excellent men [i.e. Abraham and David] are said to be signified by the two pillars that stand in front of the Temple. The pillars, measuring twelve cubits [in circumference] are aptly linked to those two by typological reasoning. If you wish to understand the mystical meaning of all this, the coils of the measurement stand for the number of the twelve disciples, whose teachings are joined to the promises made to the two [i.e. Abraham and David], through which promise each of them is guaranteed to be a forefather of the promised offspring [i.e. Jesus], after the ancestral line has run its course down to this time [i.e. the Incarnation].

The startling forms in these rhymed Leonine hexameters are the infinitives *scirę* and *fuissę*, which definitely do not need the *e-caudata* at the end but have acquired it in correlation with *spirę* and *promissę*.

Vowels

Some of the more common alternatives attested in vowel usage are between *i* and *y* (i.e. *himnus = hymnus, ymus = imus, misterium = mysterium, styrps = stirps, sydus = sidus, typus = tipus, ymber = imber*, etc.), *u* and *o* (i.e. *iocundus = iucundus, ponire = punire, fabola = fabula, capitolum = capitulum, robor = robur, apostulus = apostolus, tempure = tempore*, etc.), and *i* and *e* (*cremen = crimen, didit = dedit, semilis = similis, domenus = dominus*, etc.). An example of the *i* and *y* confusion and vowel syncopation is found again in Alexander of Ashby's *Breuissima comprehensio historiarum*, vv. 633–636, where we see *mirram/mirra* for *myrrham/myrrha*, and *mistica* for *mystica* (Dinkova-Bruun (2004) 54):

> Ad Christum uenere magi, stella duce, Christo
>   Aurum, thus, **mirram** – **mistica** dona – ferunt.
> Thure Deus, **mirra** mortalis, rex patet auro:
>   Talia sunt tali munera digna dari.

Guided by the star, the magi came to Christ, bringing him mystic presents: gold, frankincense, and myrrh. In the frankincense he is revealed as God, in the myrrh as Man, in the gold as King. Such are the gifts worthy to be given to such a man.

The *i/e* and *u/o* confusion is represented excellently in the so-called *Joca monachorum*, a compilation of short questions and answers used for mnemonic purposes and dated to the period between the sixth and eighth centuries (Bourgain (2005) 155, lines 12–16):

Cuius **curpus** non pertinet in terram?	**Oxoris** Lot.
Qui semul natus et **bes mortuos**?	Lacarus.
Quid bis natus et semul **mortuos**?	Noae.
Quis tribus diebus et tribus **noctebus**	
orauit ne celum uidit nec terram tetigit?	Jonas in uentre **citi**.
Quis est uiuus sepultus, uiuit et sepulcrum ejus?	**Junas** in uentre **citi**.

Whose body does not belong to the earth?	That of Lot's wife.
Who was born once but died twice?	Lazarus.
Who was born twice but died once?	Noah.
Who prayed for three days and three nights without seeing the sky and without touching the earth?	Jonah in the belly of the whale.
Who was buried alive in a living grave?	Jonah in the belly of the whale.

Double variants, such as *Jonas* and *Junas* and *bes* and *bis*, make it evident that *o* and *u* as well as *e* and *i* must have sounded the same at the time when this text was written. Interesting is also the form *curpus* for *corpus*, which is a case of inverted orthography with no phonetic support. In addition, *citi* stands for *coeti*, *celum* for *caelum*, and *quid* for *quis*. Finally, one should observe the presence of initial *j* for *i* (i.e. *Joca, Jonas, Junas*), which suggests that before a vowel the *i* was probably pronounced as in "justice". The situation attested in the *Joca monachorum*, even though typical for the early Middle Ages, is rather extreme. After the Carolingian reforms many of these aberrant spellings disappear. For the remaining oddities of this text, see the explanations in Bourgain (2005) 156–157.

Consonants

As with the vocalic system, only the most salient features of medieval treatment of Latin consonants will be illustrated in this essay with some representative passages from medieval texts. There are three major tendencies, which need to be discussed here: assibilation, aspiration, and the confused use of double and single consonants.

1   Assibilation – when followed by another vowel the syllable *ti* is assibilated and begins to be written as *ci* to fit the pronunciation "tzi" and later also *si*. This early phenomenon, which is attested in late-antique inscriptions, becomes ubiquitous in the medieval period, thus the forms *nacione* = *natione, gracia* = *gratia, iusticia* = *iustitia, leccio* = *lectio, apcior* = *aptior, gencium* = *gentium, uiciis* = *uitiis*, etc. For an example see the prologue of Alexander of Ashby's *Comprehensio* (Dinkova-Bruun (2004) 7, lines 52–54):

> Carnalis autem animus in **inicio** sacre **erudicionis** tripliciter turbari solet.
> Prima **turbacio** est de obscuritate **significacionis**, secunda de uarietate
> **exposicionis**, **tercia** de **mutacione** personarum.

However, in the beginning of sacred instruction the carnal soul is usually troubled on three counts; the first anxiety regards the obscurity of meaning, the second the variety of expression, and the third the change of speakers.

2 Aspiration
   (a) Being already weak in Classical Latin, the *h* created uncertainty about its usage.
        Thus we see it both omitted and added either in the beginning or in the middle
        of words. Some examples are:
        • omissions: *erba* = *herba, actenus* = *hactenus, exibere* = *exhibere, onestus* = *hon-
           estus, trait* = *trahit, coors* = *cohors, uei* = *uehi,* etc.
        • additions: *habundare* = *abundare, honeribus* = *oneribus, exhorare* = *exorare,
           perhennis* = *perennis,* etc.
   (b) *ch ↔ c, th ↔ t,* and *ph ↔ p* or *f.* Again the examples are numerous:
        • *ch ↔ c: monacus* = *monachus, Cristus* = *Christus, achademia* = *academia,
           archanus* = *arcanus, charus* = *carus, archa* = *arca,* etc.
        • *th ↔ t: baratrum* = *barathrum, tesaurus* = *thesaurus, cathalogus* = *catalogus,
           thentorium* = *tentorium, thutus* = *tutus,* etc.
        • *ph ↔ p: triumpauit* = *triumphauit, palanx* = *phalanx, Olymphus* = *Olympus,
           Philatus* = *Pilatus,* etc.
        • *ph ↔ f: falanga* = *phalanga, blasfemus* = *blasphemus, prophanus* = *profanus,
           nephas* = *nefas,* etc.

Some of these tendencies are attested in a passage on the well-known herb *apium*
(parsley) included by Bartholomaeus Anglicus in his thirteenth-century encyclopaedia *De proprietatibus rerum* (see Ventura (2007) 45, lines 20–21 and 27–33):

Apium risus dicitur ab effectu, quia purgat **melancolicum**	=	melancholicum
humorem, ex cuius superabundantia fit tristitia. …	=	umorem
Apium **emoroidarum** est dictum, eo quod eius puluis	=	haemorrhoidarum
uel cinis superpositus fluxum sanguinis desiccat.		
Apium autem commune splenis et **epatis opilationem**	=	hepatis, oppilationem
aperit, calculum frangit, ictericiam soluit, **ydropicis** subuenit.	=	hydropicis
Freneticis convenit, si eius succo cum oleo rosaceo mixto	=	phreneticis
et aceto caput patientis sepius inungatur.		

The "laughter" parsley is called so by its effect because it purges the melancholic humour,
the abundance of which causes sadness … The hemorrhoidic parsley has its name from the
fact that its powder or dust dries the flow of blood when put on top. The regular parsley,
however, opens up the obstruction of the liver, breaks a kidney stone, dissolves jaundice,
and aids people who suffer from dropsy. It also suits frenetics, if its juice, mixed with rose
water and vinegar, is applied often to the head of the patient.

3 Confusion in the use of double and single consonants, meaning that single consonants are doubled unnecessarily or double consonants are reduced to single ones, for
   example: *ocasio* = *occasio* and *peccunia* = *pecunia; suplex* = *supplex* and *dupplex* = *duplex;
   adere* = *addere* and *traddidit* = *tradidit, baptissma* = *baptisma* and *gresu* = *gressu;
   mittis* = *mitis, maniffesta* = *manifesta,* etc. Two examples of this type of confusion are
   seen in the passage from Bartholomaeus quoted above: *emoroidarum* = *haemor-
   rhoidarum* (haemorrhoids) and *opilationem* = *oppilationem* (obstruction).
4 Assimilation and dissimilation of consonants, i.e. *battismo* for *baptismo, peccoris* for
   pectoris, russus for *rursus, nessio* for *nescio,* etc. Especially frequent is the dissimilation

of prefixes, so we see forms such as *conpatitur*, *inpetrat*, *inponit*, etc. At the same time a tendency towards non-assimilating some prefixes is also apparent; thus the forms *obprimit*, *obprobrium*, *subrepta*, etc.

None of the spelling peculiarities presented in the section above would create by itself an insurmountable difficulty in the understanding of the text, but the combined presence of many of them in a given medieval source would result in a clear sense that one is confronted with an idiom that is quite unlike both the literary language of Classical Antiquity and the classicized Latin of the humanist Renaissance. Thus medieval orthography, like the rest of Medieval Latin, seems to be caught between the fixed standards of two normative periods. On the one hand it is perceived as bastardization of Classical rules and on the other it has become the orphan of the Renaissance efforts of standardization.

Morphology

There is relatively little to be said about the morphology of Medieval Latin. It is true that some nouns change their gender, number, and declension and a few verbs alter their conjugation or become deponents, while some of the original deponent verbs lose their deponent nature, but these transformations are neither overwhelmingly numerous nor do they impede the understanding of the texts as long as the changed forms fit properly into the syntax of the sentence. Generally, the attested morphological variations exhibit a tendency towards modifying the difficult or potentially confusing Classical forms, but the trend is not consistent, and old and new forms coexisted happily. The reasons for this relatively stable situation are two: first, morphology was codified in the treatises of the ancient grammarians, which could be easily consulted, and second, morphological rules are the first to be mastered by the student and the easiest to correct by the teacher. Everybody can learn the noun and verb paradigms; how to use this knowledge to build a correct sentence requires a completely different level of comprehension. A detailed exposition on the different morphological characteristics of Medieval Latin is found in vol. 4 of Stotz (1996–2004). The most common phenomena are:

1   Change of gender, number and declension
  (a)   The neuter Greek words of the type *dogma*, *dogmatis* are sometimes perceived as being feminine and belonging to the first declension, i.e. *dogma*, *dogmae* f. Other such words are: *schema*, *diadema*, *anathema*, *phantasma*, *chrisma*, etc.
  (b)   Words in the plural neuter are occasionally understood as being feminine singular, thus leading to forms such as *capitas*, *carminam*, *pecorarum*, *iumentae*, etc.
  (c)   There is some confusion between nouns of the second and fourth declension, for example: *grados* for *gradus*, *cornuis* for *cornibus*, *genuorum* for *genuum*, *fructi* for *fructus*, etc.; or between nouns of the third and second declension, for example *pauperorum* for *pauperum*.
  (d)   The somewhat difficult words of the type *aduena*, *aduenae* m. could be modified into second-declension nouns in harmony with their natural masculine gender; thus we see: *advenum* for *advenam*, *agricolorum* for *agricolarum*, *nautus* for *nauta*, etc.

(e) Some of the specifically pronominal forms are sometimes replaced by the easier first- and second-declension forms, i.e. *illum* is used instead of *illud, alium* instead of *aliud, illo* instead of *illi, alio* instead of *alii, alterutrae* instead of *alter-utri* etc.

2 Change of conjugation

   (a) first-conjugation verbs become second-conjugation, i.e. *congregendum* for *con-gregandum, salueret* for *saluaret*, etc.

   (b) first-conjugation verbs become third-conjugation and vice versa, i.e. *adiuuis* for *adiuuas, rogitus* for *rogatus, uocitur* for *uocatur* or *addans* for *addens, sternare* for *sternere, lambaret* for *lamberet*, etc.

3 Deponent verbs

It is obvious that the deponent verbs are counterintuitive and thus difficult to master. They also produce forms that can be confusing, such as the imperative, and difficult to understand, such as the participles. All these reasons contribute to the tendency of some of the Classical deponents to turn into regular active verbs, even though the opposite is attested as well, probably as a result of hypercorrection or analogy. This is an early phenomenon, found in the Classical vulgar parlance (i.e. in Plautus and Petronius), but in the medieval period it becomes even more pronounced. Some examples are: *minat* for *minatur, adgrediebant* for *adgrediebantur, paciebat* for *patiebatur, mirares* for *mirareris, morabant* for *morabantur*, etc. The opposite is seen in *celerari* for *celerare, pernoctari* for *pernoctare, penetrabatur* for *penetrabat* (perhaps under the influence from verbs such as *peregrinari, rusticari* and *proficisci*).

Naturally, all of the medieval forms enumerated above coexist with the Classical ones.

Syntax

In Medieval Latin the clearly defined and logical rules of Classical syntax break down on both the micro and the macro level, i.e. within the smaller units that make the sentence (for example, altered case and preposition usage) and between the sentences themselves (for example, conjunction changes and misconception of the rules of the sequence of tenses). The catalyst for these syntactical developments is the spoken idiom. The pressure this great force puts on the syntax of Classical Latin is enormous, leading to a number of idiosyncratic constructions, many of which have their beginnings in Vulgar and Late Latin, but develop fully only during the Middle Ages when they migrate from the world of orality into the realm of literature. The general tendencies are towards simplification of the complex Classical turns of phrase and the creation of a more straightforward expression, but the phenomena are so numerous and varied that only a few will be presented in the following, mainly concerning the verbs, the tenses, the emerging forms of the definite and indefinite articles, and the structure of subordinate clauses. The changes in these syntactical relationships are most likely to cause consternation for the readers of Medieval Latin because of the defining role the verb plays in the majority of the Latin sentences. For additional aspects of Medieval Latin syntax, see Rigg (1986), volume 4 in Stotz (1996–2004), and Bourgain (2005).

Changed regimen of verbs

The nature of government in general and verb government in particular was one of the important topics for grammatical discussion during the Middle Ages (Reynolds (1990)). The *regimen* of the verb is especially important in syntactical discourse because it is the underlying force in sentence formation, even when the verb is missing. The most obvious connection between the verb (*regens*) and the part it governs (*rectum*) is expressed in the idea of transitivity and intransitivity, as well as in the fact that some verbs are accompanied by objects in specific cases, for example, verbs of remembering and forgetting are followed by genitive of memory, verbs of plenty and want by ablative of plenty and want, and verbs like *utor* and *fruor* by ablative of means. Another important relationship between the verbs and the part that accompanies them is the verb + infinitive bond, and finally, in a larger syntactical context many verbs trigger a particular clause subordination, such as, for example, *hortor* and *impero*, which require the use of the *ut*–sentences, or the verbs of speaking and thinking, which are followed in Classical literary Latin by an accusative + infinitive construction.

All of these manifestations of syntactical interconnectedness were affected in one way or another during the medieval period. Transitivity and intransitivity are often confused, with a strong pull towards prepositional uses (i.e. *timere ab aliquo* for *timere aliquem* [to fear somebody], *redimere ad VI solidos* for *redimere VI solidis* [to purchase for six shillings], *uictus a prece pauperis* for *uictus prece pauperis* [prevailed upon by the appeal of the poor man], etc.); in the verb–object binary link the accusative case seems to be preferred to other cases in a number of instances (i.e. *caruit praesentem uitam* for *caruit praesenti uita*, *fruere celestia* for *fruere celestibus*, *me nocebit* for *mihi nocebit*, *te persuadeam ut uenias* for *tibi persuadeam ut uenias*, etc.); subordinate clauses are attached to verbs, which traditionally require only an infinitive and vice versa (i.e. *iurauit ut daret*, *do bibere*, *impetrauit implere*, *noli timere accipere*, etc.)

Typical in this context, but not exclusively medieval, is the treatment of indirect or reported speech. Probably under the influence of the language of the Vulgate, the common Classical accusative + infinitive construction tends to be replaced by a subordinate clause introduced either with the conjunctions *quod*, *quia*, *quoniam* followed by verbs in both indicative and subjunctive or with *ut* + subjunctive of the type *putare ut*, *legere ut*, *auditus sum ut*. This of course does not mean that the accusative + infinitive falls in complete disuse, especially in works belonging to the higher register of literary accomplishment. Sometimes the two constructions are used side by side in the same text (Karlsen (2001)). Examples:

Et ut **uidit** Ugo **quod** non haberet terram, cepit de caballarios Toarcinse XLIII ex meliores. (Anonymous, the *Conventum*, c. 1030; see Bourgain (2005) 187, lines 1–2)
As Hugh saw that he did not have the land, he took from the Thouars cavalrymen, forty-three from the best ones.

Audiui ego a multis qui ibi fuerunt **quod** uiginti Turcos et amplius de ponte sumptis spondalibus in flumine obruissent. (Raymond of Aguilers, *Historia Francorum qui ceperunt Iherusalem*, c. 1100; see Sidwell (1995) 227, lines 16–17.)
I heard from many who had been there that twenty or more Turks had fallen into the river since the parapets [*spondalia*] had been removed from the bridge.

Alia uice **dixit quod** uidit in hostia sicut puerum Christum, sed uidebatur esse magnus.
(Angela de Foligno, *Memoriale*, before 1300; see Bourgain (2005) 196, line 19)
Another time she said that she saw in the consecrated host as though the child Christ, but
he seemed to be grown up.

Analytic tense forms and other periphrastic expressions

Many tenses are expressed by analytic forms composed with the verbs *sum* and *habeo*
used as auxiliaries, and some of these constructions become the precursors of the
Romance system of tenses (especially *b* and *c* below). Examples:

(a) periphrastic present and imperfect, in which the present and imperfect of *sum* are
     joined with the present participle, i.e. *sum amans* for *amo*, *erat cupiens* for *cupiebat*,
     tres erant ambulantes for *tres ambulabant*, or *erat exspectans* for *exspectabat*. Many
     of these periphrastic expressions are influenced by the language of the Vulgate.
(b) periphrastic future, which can be expressed in many ways: first, by the construction
     infinitive + *habeo* (i.e. *dicere habeo* for *dicam* or *dare habes* for *dabis*); second, by the
     expression *uolo* + infinitive (i.e. *uolo ire* for *ibo*), and third by *debeo* + infinitive (i.e.
     debet mori for *morietur*).
(c) periphrastic perfect, which is formed by *habeo* + passive past participle, i.e. *epis-
     copum inuitatum habes* for *episcopum inuitauisti*. Sometimes also *coepisse* + infinitive
     was used to represent the perfect tense, i.e. *ille coepit cogitare et respondit*, which
     clearly needs to be understood as "he thought and said".

Equally worthy of mention is the appearance of passive periphrastic forms of the type
amatus sum for *amor* and *amatus eram* for *amabar*. Because of this development, the
passive of the perfect, pluperfect and future perfect begin to be constructed with the
passive past participle and *fuisse*, i.e. *laudatus fui* for *laudatus sum*, *laudatus fueram* for
laudatus eram and *laudatus fuero* for *laudatus ero*. Forms of the type *laudatus fui* were
extant already in Classical Latin, which could have been the reason for the rethinking of
laudatus sum as present. In any case, the shift is clearly attested in the following excerpt
from the inquest of the suspected heretic Pierre Espérendieu held in Toulouse in 1325
(see Bourgain (2005) 204, lines 29–31):

> Item quando fratres **citati fuerunt** [= citati sunt] ad curiam Romanam post per octo dies
> **sequitus fuit** [= secutus est] hos et uni de dictis fratribus citatis misit unum florentinum, et
> predicta omnia coram dicto Germano et non infrascripta **confessus fuerat** [= confessus
> erat], sicut dixit.

> Also when the brothers were summoned to the Roman curia, he followed them for eight
> days and sent a florin to one of the already mentioned brothers who were summoned;
> according to his words, he had confessed all of what was said above to the already men-
> tioned Germanus, but not what follows below.

Definite and indefinite articles

One of the well-known difficulties in translating Latin is its lack of articles. In Medieval
Latin, *ille* began to express the definite article "the" rather than a demonstrative pronoun

"this", whereas *unus* was often used to represent the indefinite article *a* rather than the numeral "one". *Quidam* could also play the role of the indefinite article. An excellent example of this trend is seen in Hygeburg of Heidenheem's *Vita sancti Willibaldi* written sometimes after 778 (see Sidwell (1995) 113, lines 33–41):

> Tunc **illis** in carcere commorantibus **unus** homo de Ispania uenit et loquebat cum illis in carcere et diligenter ab illis inquisiuit, quid essent aut unde essent. Et **illi** dixerunt ei omnia secundum ordinem de sua itinere. **Ille** Ispanus homo habebat fratrem in palatio regis, qui fuit cubicularius regis Sarracinorum. Cumque **ille** preses, qui eos in carcere mittebat, ad palatium ueniebat, et **ille** Ispanus, qui cum illis in carcere loquebatur, et **ille** nautor in cuius naue fuerant, quando pergebant de Cypro, omnes simul uenerunt coram rege Sarracinorum cui nomen Myrmummi.

> Then a man from Spain came to the ones detained in the prison and spoke with them there and asked them carefully who they were or where they came from. And they told him everything about the course of their journey. The Spanish man had a brother in the palace of the king who was a chamberlain of the king of the Saracens. Then the priest, who sent them to prison, came to the palace, and also the Spaniard who spoke with them in the prison, and the sailor too, in whose ship they travelled when they departed from Cyprus – all came together in the presence of the king of the Saracens, whose name was Emir al Mumenin.

Clearly, in the expression *unus homo de Ispania* "unus" is superfluous and the correct translation should be "a man from Spain", while the phrase *ille nautor in cuius naue fuerant* means "the sailor in whose ship they had been" (observe also the word *nautor* for *nauta*). Some additional medieval features are the uncertainty in the usage of deponent verbs (i.e. *loquebat* for *loquebatur*, even though the correct form is used later in the passage), the change in the gender of words (i.e. *de sua itinere* for *de suo itinere*), the orthography (i.e. *Ispania, Ispanus, Sarracinorum, preses*), the confusion in the endings of cases (i.e. *in carcere mittebat, in cuius naue, coram rege*), etc.

Subordinate clauses

Two major syntactical changes can be observed in several subordinate clauses; first, they begin to be introduced by a different set of conjunctions, and second, the indicative is preferred to the usual subjunctive. Even when subjunctive is used, the rules of the sequence of tenses are frequently disregarded. The most striking divergences from Classical norms are observed in indirect questions, result clauses, purpose clauses and fear clauses. In the indirect questions the conjunction *si* is often used instead of *utrum* and the double indirect question is construed with *si ... uel* rather than with *utrum ... an*; *quod* replaces the result *ut*; purpose clauses are sometimes introduced by *quo* even without the presence of a comparative adjective or are simply turned into purpose infinitives (i.e. *abiit quaerere*, *aduenit postulare*, etc.); fear clauses are mostly reduced to complementary infinitives (i.e. *timemus subiugari*, which is much easier to construe than the Classical *timemus ne subiugemur*). It seems apparent that the multi-functionalism of the conjunctions *ut* and *ne* was perceived as semantically confusing and an impetus for substitution. A passage from Angela of Foligno's *Memoriale* written before 1300 provides an excellent example of the medieval syntax of indirect questions and result clauses (see Bourgain (2005) 196, lines 13–18):

Item dixit quod aliquando uidet hostiam alio modo, scilicet uidet in hostia duos oculos splendissimos ita grossos **quod de hostia uidentur** remanere tantummodo ora. "Sed quadam uice non in hostia, sed in cella ostensi fuerant mihi oculi cum majori pulchritudine et in tantum delectabili **quod non credo** inde perdere leticiam de cetero, sicut de gula. Sed nescio **si fuit dormiendo uel uigilando**, sed reinueni me in maxima leticia et ineffabili; et fuit tam magna **quod non credo** eam perdere deinceps."

Also, she said that sometimes she sees the consecrated host otherwise, meaning that she sees in it two very bright eyes which are so large that only a rim seems to remain from the host. "But once it was not in the host but in my cell that these eyes were shown to me; they were of such great beauty and so delightful that I do not believe that I would ever lose this joy in the future, that is, the joy of eating [the host]. I do not know whether this happened while I was asleep or awake, but I found myself in a state of extreme and unutterable joy. And this joy was so great that I do not believe that I would ever lose it from now on."

This short excerpt is so rich with various medieval features that it seems to be the perfect example, with which to conclude this essay. We see here medieval orthography (*leticia*), vocabulary (*de cetero* – from now on, *hostia* – consecrated host, *grossos* – big, *cella* – monastic cell); case usage (ablative of quality with preposition, i.e. *cum majori pulchritudine*); periphrastic perfect tense (*ostensi fuerant*); use of present tense instead of past (*uidet* for *uidit* and *uidentur* for *uidebantur*); reported speech with *quod* (*dixit quod aliquando uidet*); result clause with *quod* + indicative (*ita grossos quod de hostia uidentur*); indirect question with *si ... vel* + indicative (*nescio si fuit dormiendo uel uigilando*); word order (*aliquando uidet hostiam alio modo, scilicet uidet in hostia duos oculos splendissimos* or *in maxima leticia et ineffabili*). No reader would ever believe that this text was written in any other period but the Middle Ages; and yet, despite its strong non-Classical character, this is perfectly understandable Latin. In fact, the medieval developments show that during the Middle Ages the language was not dead but very much alive. Alive not as a mother tongue, that is true, but as an acquired language, which served as means of both literary and oral communication for many centuries and on many levels of the medieval society.

CHAPTER 18

Neo-Latin

David Butterfield

Introduction

The fate of the Latin language after the late medieval period can be briefly summarised by two words: purification and decline. This chapter aims to sketch the process of refine-ment that the Latin language enjoyed from the Renaissance onwards and to outline the general decrease in its employment throughout the subsequent centuries to the present day. It will be seen that these two developments went hand in hand: as Latin became increasingly the closely guarded intellectual province of a small stratum of society, and ever more the domain solely of the educated elite, a steady process of standardising and re-classicising of the language occurred, thereby narrowing the broad diversity that had characterised the widespread use of Latin in the medieval period.

Neo-Latin, sometimes called New Latin, is the term typically applied to the use of Latin as a language for original composition, translation or occasionally general com-munication from the period of the Italian Renaissance up to the modern day. The breadth of the use of Latin over these last six centuries is enormous, although its use has decreased markedly since the mid-eighteenth century. As a result, the task of treating its manifold manifestations within the scope of one short chapter necessarily requires a somewhat fragmented approach.

We may begin with some initial observations about the nature of Neo-Latin as a lan-guage. Its most defining feature is that, since it never represented the living tongue of a given speech community, Neo-Latin lacked in many ways the traditional patterns and traits of development that are generally associated with spoken languages. Instead, from the Renaissance onwards it was strictly a *Kunstsprache*, a language skilfully crafted – largely in writing, and almost entirely by men – as a vehicle for clear communication by scholars both within and amongst a wide swathe of European countries (save areas under

A Companion to the Latin Language, First Edition. Edited by James Clackson.
© 2011 Blackwell Publishing Ltd. Published 2011 by Blackwell Publishing Ltd.

Turkish rule), and in due course the various colonies. Lacking as it did any firm roots in the regular spoken exchanges of a unified society, the language had to formalise itself by reference to existing Latin texts, whether fixed in script or print, or standardised in the formulae of a given institution. It was thus a language that required learning through reading, not (excluding a few exceptional cases) aural acquisition. Such written texts determined the grammatical and syntactical rules and patterns, vocabulary and, to a lesser extent, style within which such writers composed their own Neo-Latin. We shall see that these reference-points shifted in focus from the early Renaissance onwards, continually reshaping the contours of the language in its form and content. Further, we must observe at the outset that Neo-Latin, being a general umbrella term, does not stipulate a completely uniform language with fixed parameters: notwithstanding the artificial crafting of the language according to certain ideals fixed in the past, Neo-Latin did allow some scope for linguistic novelty and served as a medium for a most diverse range of output, both in traditional forms of literature and in wider areas of society.

A New Dawn: Latin and the Italian Renaissance

Our survey of Neo-Latin begins with the resurgence of interest in the literature and culture of the Ancient Roman world that the Italian Renaissance nourished from its dawn in the mid-fourteenth century. Latin in its late medieval phases had developed into a jargonised, scholastic language, more simplified in syntax and more particular in vocabulary than Classical Latin, but differing markedly amongst its various specialised spheres of application. The Renaissance infused early Humanist scholars with a new passion for re-establishing close links with the perceived prior glories of the Roman Republic and early Empire, which duly induced them to supplant the inelegant Latin of recent and contemporary authors with the form of the language at its supposed zenith in the ancient world. As a result of this spirit of classicolatry, the palpably debased form of scholastic Latin led Humanist scholars scornfully to brand it as *Latina barbara* or *gothica*, the sorry and much-corrupted descendant of a once-beautiful tongue. Early scholars of the Renaissance sought to conform their own Italian identity with the great age of their history (i.e. Rome at its height in cultural fecundity and imperial power during the Classical period), and in order to corroborate this association they sought to harmonise their own linguistic employment of Latin with that of ancient practitioners. Indeed, freshly imbued with this new historical consciousness, Humanists identified purifying the Latin language and paring it back to its Classical roots with regaining for contemporary Italy the faded splendours of the lost Roman Republic: the closer the deliberate and precise imitation of Classical Latin, the stronger the perceived links with their linguistic and cultural inheritance from the ancient world.

Under the influence of such influential early Humanists as Francesco Petrarch (1304–1374), Coluccio Salutati (1331–1406), Niccolò Niccoli (1364–1437) and Poggio Bracciolini (1380–1459), such a self-conscious project to reintroduce a Latin style that satisfied the canons followed by the primary Latin writers of Antiquity soon gathered speed. Welcoming Quintilian's doctrine that *aliud est Latine, aliud grammatice scribere* ("it is one thing to write grammatically, but another thing to do so in a Latinate manner"), significant advances were made in understanding and explicating the fields of

Classical Latin grammar and lexicography by Lorenzo Valla (1407–1457), Giovanni Tortelli (1400–1466) and Niccolò Perotti (1429–1480), among others. Important reforms in Humanist education, as pioneered by Guarino of Verona (1374–1460), and developed by figures such as John Colet (1467–1519), Thomas More (1477–1535) and Petrus Ramus (1515–1572), served to instil knowledge of the language in a newly rigorous manner, less governed by the study of logic than that propounded by medieval grammars and lexica, such as the infamous *Doctrinale* (1199) of Alexander de Villa Dei and *Catholicon* (1286) of Giovanni Balbi.

In moving away from the barbarous neologisms and grammatical solecisms that characterised Latin of the medieval period, pervasive in most contemporary writings and certainly entrenched in the language of the Roman Catholic Church, attention had to be refocused upon the great luminaries of the ancient world. The literary figure that came to serve as the primary model for lapidary prose was, not unsurprisingly, the man traditionally heralded as chief of orators, Marcus Tullius Cicero. Although he had been singled out as the supreme rhetorician already in Antiquity (as Seneca the Younger, Quintilian and others bear witness), Cicero also had a great virtue in the sheer scale of his output: given that his varied speeches survived in abundance (augmented by a number of significant manuscript discoveries in the late fourteenth and early fifteenth centuries), ample scope was available for the Italian literati to imitate the particular features that distinguished Cicero's style (*consuetudo*) in his celebrated orations. These include an ornamentally arranged periodic structure, the careful selection of suitably nuanced vocabulary, his keen ear for rhythm and sound, and his own grammatical vagaries. As a result, this new and polished form of Latin was set clearly apart from the despised dress of scholastic Latin; most notably, the concepts of *elegantia* and *Latinitas* – elegant expression through refined Latinity – were actively pursued, with attention to a lucid and rhetorically engaging style, as well as musicality of sound. The drive to emulate Cicero in particular, and thereby to purify Latin of its contaminating accretions and mutations over the centuries, arose from an explicit admission that the optimum form of expression had already been achieved in the language. Accordingly, retrospective imitation (*imitatio*) of the writings of the man generally agreed to be its best practitioner was deemed the most effective means of approaching that necessarily unsurpassable peak.

Innovation through Imitation: The Case of Ciceronianism

The practice of Ciceronianism, the passion for emulating the orator's style, manner of expression and lexicon with as much exactitude as possible, was an exercise in carefully nurtured uniformity, despite the diverse and novel tasks to which such Humanist writers, inspired by their new sense of individualism, were often employing Latin: these scholars were creating afresh a broad body of literature ranging far beyond theology and philosophy, a spectrum for which the variety of extant Classical literature provided a formidable blueprint. Humanists thus sought to strive forwards by looking backwards, forging their own progress by taking directions from Antiquity.

The vogue for Ciceronianism, to which the closest European historical analogue is perhaps the devoted Atticism of the Second Sophistic and Byzantine ages, grew in its influence as the advent of mechanical printing in the mid-fifteenth century spread knowledge of the orator's works wider, not to mention the primary publications of the leading Ciceronians, which served as attractive literary *exempla* of the new and esteemed literary style, which any intelligent person had the potential to emulate. The doctrinaire and dogmatic cult of Ciceronian *aemulatio*, practised in many circles with a remarkable religiosity, soon spread to the primary Italian universities, and in due course schools and other professionalised spheres throughout the country; although it became something of a transalpine development during the late fifteenth and early sixteenth centuries, it failed, for the most part, to revolutionise intellectual practices in all European quarters.

The peak of Ciceronianism was reached around the turn of the sixteenth century and can be seen most strikingly in the writings of Paolo Cortesi (*c.* 1465–1510), Pietro Bembo (1470–1547), Jacopo Sadoleto (1477–1547), Christophorus Longolius (1488–1522) and Romulus Amaseus (1489–1552). Their avid devotion to Ciceronian purity of vocabulary and expression eventually came to attract the scorn of other European Humanists, particularly those outside Italy, who dismissed this rigid and narrow conception of "good" Latin as the slavish imitation and perfunctory aping of but one ancient exponent of the Latin language, a banausic process relying heavily throughout on repertories – particularly Mario Nizzoli's *Thesaurus Ciceronianus* (1535) – as compositional crutches. Desiderius Erasmus (*c.* 1466–1536), the great Dutch scholar and reformer, satirised in his famously polemical Latin dialogue *Ciceronianus* (1528) this conservative orthodoxy embodied by scholars of the Ciceronian school. Despite his setting the dialogue in contemporary Netherlands, there is no doubt that Italian Humanism in particular was the prime butt of the attack, as opposed to the new species of Christian Humanism that Erasmus and others strove to practise, which welcomed by contrast wide and engaged reading of Latin from all periods to allow natural Latin composition "*uno impetu*" ("in a single impulse"). Such a liberal attitude to the language had, however, brought him the denigratory appellations of *barbarus* and *Batavus* from Italian Ciceronians. The protagonist of this barbed dialogue is the haggard figure of Nosoponus ("one diseased from toil", "Workmad"), a man so devoted to the task of writing in the most perfect Ciceronian style that his rate of composition could not exceed a sentence per night. This pitiful wretch ardently desires to be accepted by the influential judges of Latin style (i.e. prominent Italian scholars) as a true Ciceronian, a mistaken passion of which Bulephorus ("Counsellor"), the effective mouthpiece of Erasmus himself, and his friend Hypologus ("Back-up") succeed in disabusing him, not least by means of the *reductio ad absurdum* of showing that Nosoponus could not, on his own terms, accept *any* author after Cicero as sufficiently Ciceronian! The central tenet of Bulephorus' argument against adopting an ultra-Ciceronian style was simply anachronism: because the world had changed in a myriad number of ways since the days of Cicero, it was misguided folly to attempt to describe contemporary society and events in a linguistic dress manifestly not created for the task. The narrow scope of this objection demonstrates that the field of vocabulary was considered by Nosoponus to be of paramount importance in attaining a truly Ciceronian style, a doctrine analogous to Caesar's famous dictum: *ut tamquam scopulum, sic fugias inauditum atque insolens uerbum* ("you should avoid as you would a rock a new and unfamiliar word").

Erasmus no doubt availed himself of satiric hyperbole in his depiction of Nosoponus but he drew his origins from the genuine Ciceronian fanaticism exhibited by some contemporaries. The character most probably satirises the Belgian Humanist Longolius, who is reputed to have read nothing but Cicero for a five-year period in order to purify his Latin style sufficiently of all external contamination, an exertion alleged to have brought his early death (at thirty-three). In a letter to Nicolaus Draco, Longolius defended this choice to imitate Cicero alone as follows:

> Etenim si Latina lingua non iam domestico aut forensi ullo usu, sed tacita quadam mutorum doctorum consuetudine percipienda est, cui nos tandem potius ad discendum demus, quam illi qui omnium aetatum iudicio habitus sit omnium eruditorum eloquentissimus, eloquentium eruditissimus? (*Christophori Longolii Epistolarum Libri Quatuor* (Florence, 1524), 150ᵛ)

> For, if the Latin language must be learned not through any employment of it either at home or in the market-place but through the silent habits of mute scholars, to whom then should we rather devote ourselves in order to learn it than to that man who has been judged by all ages to be the most eloquent of all learned men, and of eloquent men the most learned?

Yet, notwithstanding his avid devotion to the cause, Longolius' writings have been shown in recent scholarship to employ a number of features that cannot be legitimately defended as Ciceronian (see Thomson (1986) 98–100, Tunberg (1997)). To cite but a few instances, we find in his published orations the words *canicula, desipientia, grassari, perceleber* and *uerticosus*, all unattested in Cicero's lexicon and therefore anathema to Longolius' explicit literary principles. In syntax we find other deviations from Ciceronian usage, not only *quamquam, quando* and *postquam* with the subjunctive, but even *esto* (i.e. the third singular present imperative of *esse*) as a subordinating concessive conjunction. Ciceronianism could therefore set the aspiring Humanist up for a very public fall, if the rules of the game were broken.

Alongside Erasmus, numerous scholars within Italy – Angelo Poliziano (1454–1494) and Gianfrancesco Pica della Mirandola (1469–1533) – and without – Petrus Ramus and Marcus Muretus (1526–1585) – came to prominence in attacking such misguided Ciceronianism; by contrast, the influential figures of Julius Caesar Scaliger (1484–1558) and Stephanus Doletus (1509–1546), despite their being based outside the confines of Italian intellectual circles, keenly defended the primacy of Cicero's style. Partly as a result of this vigorous debate, whose ramifications implicitly touched upon methods of education and research, not to mention religious affiliations, such ardent Ciceronianism clearly began to fade around the middle of the Cinquecento. Nevertheless, the movement enjoyed prolonged influence by virtue of Cicero's selection as the primary writer upon which the Jesuit educational system (*ratio studiorum*) based its linguistic focus. Indeed, centuries after the controversy, as late as 1834, the German scholar Johann Krebs felt compelled to produce his massive reference work for Ciceronian-infused Latin, *Antibarbarus der lateinischen Sprache*, a publication much reprinted and thoroughly revised by Joseph Schmalz.

Yet how, we may ask, could a scholar aspire to write in an elegant Neo-Latin style, if he disagreed in principle with embracing Ciceronianism? It so happens that, even within Italy during the Renaissance, various other schools for writing Latin existed as viable alternatives, providing greater dynamism in the use of language, albeit within the parameters fixed by Antiquity. Two primary methods that can be distinguished are eclecticism in compositional style, and the close imitation of another author in Cicero's stead.

The first method, employed by Erasmus and Guillaume Budé (1467–1540) *inter alios*, which by its nature can hardly be termed a school, was to make free use of the whole repertory of ancient Latin as a valid source for formulating grammatical and syntactical strictures, as well as the selection of the most appropriate words that could be found amidst the full extant *copia uerborum*, whether from the third century BCE or the fifth CE. Such catholicism in the writing of Latin, sometimes termed Quintilianism owing to the similarly eclectic attitude of the ancient scholar, was a natural consequence for writers who were infused with the spirit of the Renaissance but saw no purpose in the blinkered imitation of a single writer. The open attitude of this method to using all available building blocks for Latin composition, the *stile a mosaico* of apposite words and phrases, suggests a genuine belief in the language's vivacity, treating it as medium that could develop into the future rather than as a museum showpiece.

A second option, as an alternative to such simple eclecticism, and one often explicitly anti-Ciceronian in its nature, was to look for different writers to imitate. This attitude was embodied by the Latin style of the Fleming Justus Lipsius (1547–1606), who favoured prose writers of the Silver Latin period, with a particular predilection for Tacitus. As a result of this particular focus, the Neo-Latin of Lipsius and similar practitioners tended towards a starker, more dense form of expression than Ciceronianism, one better suited to neat aphorisms and *sententiae*, which highlighted through its studied brevity pointed juxtapositions and paradoxes. Yet more extreme in his employment of a style to rival Ciceronianism was Philippus Beroaldus the Elder (1453–1505), who keenly sought to write in the fashion of the consciously archaising Apuleius (an author whom he influentially edited in 1500), with the result that his Latin style remains harsh and difficult to read. Other figures also strove, through a similar scholarly *curiositas*, to produce archaising prose, such as Hermolaus Barbarus (1454–1493) and Johannes Baptista Pius (*c.* 1476–1542), embracing not only convoluted syntax but also the deployment of abstruse Graecisms.

In many cases, allegiance to these widely divergent schools of composition was more dependent upon the intellectual circle prevalent in a given city (e.g. Ciceronian Rome and Venice, eclectic Florence, archaising Bologna) rather than a scholar's personal tastes. Such alternative schools, however, were exceptions to the widely practised custom of adopting Cicero as the primary basis for compositional imitation. His prevalence has had wide-reaching effects that still infiltrate the world of Latin scholarship: most grammars of the Latin language have based their strictures primarily upon Ciceronian usages (and indeed Stephanus' great *Thesaurus Linguae Latinae* (1543) took much of its origin from Nizzoli's Ciceronian lexicography), defining variations in other authors' styles as (implicitly inferior) anomalies; that the *Oxford Latin Dictionary* (1968–1982) employs 200 CE as a *terminus ante quem* is not entirely uninfluenced by the vestiges of Ciceronianism; the perception of Latin as a language given to a rhetorically intricate and periodic language became pervasive among European scholars; finally, most specimens of contemporary Latin prose still base themselves, whether expressly or tacitly, upon the august model of Cicero's orations, and this seems likely to remain the case for as long as scholars continue to compose in Latin.

We do not here have scope to tackle the changing tastes in Renaissance poetics. Suffice it to say that the poet widely heralded as the greatest of the ancients, Virgil, was the standard basis for poetic composition (of which Politian (Poliziano) and Michael Marullus (*c.* 1453–1500) were outstanding early practitioners). Accordingly, hexameters were the primary metre for imitation, the prime *exempla* being the *Aeneid* for epic and narrative compositions, the *Georgics* for didactic and scientific works (if not Lucretius' *de Rerum Natura*) and the *Eclogues* for pastoral; for amatory verse, by contrast, the elegist Ovid was the most inspiring figure for emulation.

The Linguistic Nature of Neo-Latin

At this point we may turn to discuss some of the primary features that characterised Neo-Latin as a language. By virtue of its inherently retrospective nature and the keen desire of its practitioners to restore the defining features of Classical Latin as far as was possible, Neo-Latin generally exhibits very few discrepancies with, and deviations from, literary Latin of the Classical period. It cannot be regarded, therefore, despite the artificially crafted nature of its formulation, as a natural, linear development of the Latin language from any given period of its history. The principles of Neo-Latin morphology and syntax were explicitly based upon those that could be elicited from the extant canon of the core Classical authors (often, as we have seen, with a firm bias towards certain figures to the scornful neglect of others); the touchstone for the selection of viable vocabulary was typically the extant lexicon as presented by these selfsame writers. Accordingly, those variations from the Classical language that can be found in Neo-Latin texts are usually to be deemed partial misapprehensions of ancient usage or *lapsus memoriae* of the author in question rather than genuine reflections of a linguistic novelty peculiar to them.

Although matters of accidence and grammar were necessarily predetermined as correct and acceptable, or rather as incorrect and despised, there was scope for innovation in a field of paramount importance, namely vocabulary. Additions to the lexicon of Neo-Latin can be evidenced from its earliest stages. Given the myriad developments and inventions that had been made since the fall of ancient Rome in matters such as politics, medicine, academia, the institution of the Church, arts, science, technology, trade, warfare, and the ever-widening field of knowledge about the natural world and its geography, the introduction of new terms (typically nouns) that had no analogue in Classical Latin was unavoidable. To render such entities only by convoluted periphrases that employed pre-existing Latin vocabulary, thereby avoiding the introduction of a short-hand term, would soon have proved to be unworkably verbose. Efforts therefore had to be made to offer new terms for these concepts, ideally founded according to Classical principles upon a solid Latin or Greek etymological route and formalised in the language as the most obvious noun-type (or, for instance, verbal conjugation). Innumerable instances of such words could be cited here but it will suffice to record that it is England, appropriately enough, that gave to Neo-Latin around 1500 a neologism for football, *pedipililudium*, i.e. the addition of the concept of the foot to *pililudius*, a player of a ball-game (cf. *CGL* 5 608,27 (a gloss attributed to Isidore), where it is defined as one *qui pilotello ludit*, "who plays with a small ball"). The process of creating a new Latin word on sound etymological bases was generally deemed a more attractive option than appending a Latinate inflection to an already existing term in a country's vulgate language. Neologisms in technical parlance often favoured the adoption of Greek roots (e.g. *nostalgia, typographia, pantheista*), and this remains the case today with the nomenclature of entities in medicine, pharmacy, zoology and other areas of natural science. In certain instances, however, a direct transliteration from the vernacular was favoured: for example, *parlamentum* (parliament), *medo* (mead), *artilleria* (artillery) and the term *humanista* (Humanist) itself. One often finds the term flanked by *quod* (etc.) *uulgo dicunt* ("which people commonly call") alongside such informal adoptions, or a parenthesis such as *ut uulgo dicitur* ("as it is commonly called"), although such an expression could rather highlight the employment of a word used in more casual Latin but not acceptable in the strictly classicising style employed in a published work. For a partial repertory of the varied vocabulary of Renaissance prose writers, see Hoven and Grailet (2006) and Ramminger (2009), although much work still remains to be done on the lexicography of Neo-Latin from its origins to the nineteenth century.

Since Neo-Latin has come to be employed in certain small circles with reference to all aspects of current society, for instance in the varied business of the Vatican, in the broadcasts of *Nuntii Latini*, the weekly Finnish-based radio programme, and on *Vicipaedia*, the Latin version of the open-access encyclopaedia *Wikipedia*, terms have been invented for entities and concepts unknown to the ancient world, from factors of climate change (*emissiones dioxydi carbonici*) and revolutionary methods of electronic communication (*interrete* and *tela totius terrae*) to masticatory matter (*gummis saliuaria*), cigarettes (*fistulae nicotianae*) and electronics (*compactus discus*). For repertories of more recent Latin neologisms, see especially Bacci (1963) and Egger *et al.* (2003).

To turn back to the early Humanist scholars, we may note that they were very swift to remove much of the *barbaries*, i.e. the more solecistic elements of medieval scholastic Latin, from their writings: for instance, the otiose, and strictly ungrammatical, combinations of prepositions with adverbs (*a longe, e prope, abinuicem*); the employment of *ens* as the present participle of *esse*; the use of *li* (often *ly* or *le*) as a stand-in for the absent definite article, for which the Greek neuter definite article (τό) came to be deployed by later scholars. A number of these impure features can be found in the Latin written by contemporary scholars of northern Europe who were outside the primary Italian Humanist movement and were therefore slow to adopt the linguistic reforms from the south, such as Charles de Bovelles (1479–1553) and Martin Luther (1483–1546). Even in works of major intellectual importance, such as Copernicus' *De Revolutionibus Orbium Cælestium* (written in the 1530s, published 1543), we find a host of constructions and choices of vocabulary which would have not satisfied the purity of leading Humanists (see Blatt (1977) 66–71).

Renaissance Neo-Latin also purified matters beyond vocabulary: in syntax, we find a preference in indirect statements for the accusative and infinitive construction, markedly more common in Classical Latin, instead of *quod*-clauses followed by the simple indicative, which dominated more recent Latin texts; relative clauses oust the unwieldy accumulation of participial clauses; the use of the so-called *pluralis maiestatis*, that is the employment in singular contexts of *uos* for *tu* and related forms, was gradually phased out, since it followed mannerisms of contemporary vernacular languages rather than Classical Latin expression; the use of the infinitive in its role as a gerund in oblique cases also ceased, particularly the employment of *esse* as "being".

Nevertheless, despite the ever-present desire of Neo-Latin to harmonise seamlessly with the defining features of Classical Latin, a number of tendencies exhibited in its early phases that set it apart from its model can be outlined. Indeed, imitating an author so closely as to speak with his voice and spirit, as Ruhnken once claimed Muretus could do, was not a process that could be learned or mastered quickly, particularly with the limited tools available in the

Renaissance. Given that close and prolonged study of good manuscripts or editions of Latin authors, which may themselves mislead through corruption, was required in order to attain a truly purified Latin style, it is understandable that errors could occur through an insufficiently thorough understanding of the language in its ancient context. Much of one's refinement of Latin linguistic acumen occurred not through "bottom-up" instruction about matters of Classical grammar and syntax but rather through the devoted collection of apposite phrases and *loci* from Classical authors to serve as mnemotechnical aids to composition, a method propagated by the reformed educational system of the Humanists that moved away from bare grammar, dialectic and rhetoric.

Such a process, however, afforded ample scope for making errors, even in more polished styles of Latin. A particular area of difficulty for early Neo-Latin authors was the sequence of tenses, which is unable to be fully formulated by rules in its Classical form but was at that time barely understood. Outside this particularly thorny area of syntax, we may focus on a few characteristic features of Renaissance Neo-Latin that show only a mild deviation from its Classical counterpart: *unus* was often employed in the sense of the indefinite article (as if *quidam*), a sense barely paralleled outside early scenic comedy; an erratic, and often superfluous, employment of negatives; the use of *absque* as if *sine*, and *nec* as if *ne ... quidem*; the use of *annon* with simple interrogative clauses, as if *nonne*; the confusion of *parum* with *paulum*, *totus* with *omnis*, and the employment of *cum* and *dum*; errors regarding the correct use of *suus*, *sui* and *eius* were rife, a problem that required explicit treatment by Valla in his *Elegantiae Linguae Latinae* (1446, printed 1471); the otiose use of *minus* or *plus* with a comparative adjective; the accidental creation of unattested active forms of verbs which, on extant evidence, were solely deponent in Classical Latin. A preference for iterative verbs and diminutive forms that exceeded the practice of Classical authors is also evident in many Renaissance writings, although this could equally be a result of the language's application in many new and different contexts. In certain instances corruption in manuscripts could mislead early Humanists: for instance, we find *applausor* ("plaudit") used by various Neo-Latin authors on the basis of the incorrect decision of early editors to print this term in Pliny the Younger (*Pan.* 46.6, for *plausor*), and *stultescere* ("to grow stupid"), found in the works of Erasmus and others on the basis of the form *stultescis*, which was incorrectly printed in early editions of Plautus (*Mos.* 965, for *stultus es*) (cf. Ijsewijn (1998) 383–385). These features, which much be considered as errors given the circumscribed period that Neo-Latin strove to emulate, were eradicated *gradatim* over a period of centuries. The writing of Latin prose, indeed, did not reach a fully "purified" state until the late nineteenth century, influenced primarily by German grammarians, with some support from British scholars and the great Dane Johan Madvig.

We should therefore note that, despite the passionate devotion of many to pure, Ciceronian-infused prose, slips could be made by even the best of scholars. To take one example, Dionysius Lambinus (1520–1572), ranked among the very greatest Latinists, and one explicitly devoted to Ciceronianism, could use the Late Latin construction of *consulere* with the dative in the sense *consilium dare*, seemingly unaware of its lack of Classical pedigree. As demonstrated by Tournoy and Tunberg (1996) 153–155, however, Lambinus was in this case misled by various Renaissance lexicographers (including Balbi, Perotti, Valla and Calepinus). Similarly unclassical vocabulary discovered in his works includes *ingratitudo* and *subodorari*. To turn to the eighteenth century, the greatest British Classical scholar, Richard Bentley (1662–1742), who wrote in a lively but nonetheless classically focused Latin style, was taken to task by the Nottingham schoolmaster John Ker on a point of Latinity. The latter landed a blow by objecting that Bentley, when he claimed that the Latin of his Horatian commentary (Cambridge, 1711) exhibited *sermonis puritas* ("purity of speech"), forfeited his claim to that very purity by employing the noun *puritas*, which was not used by Roman authors before the *Scriptores Historiae Augustae* (third cent. CE). Yet Ker's attack was misconceived: for Bentley, the Latin language was not something bound by the shackles of a narrow Ciceronianism: "Bentley wrote Latin as he wrote English, – with racy vigour, and a wealth of trenchant phrases; he was not minutely Ciceronian" (Jebb (1881) 134).

We may also observe that, notwithstanding the best efforts of scholars to base Neo-Latin on classically validated expressions to the exclusion of later solecisms, some small evidence exists for the influence of the vulgate language upon individual authors' syntactical habits. Nevertheless, in many such cases it cannot be proven with certainty that such inter-linguistic influence did occur, since the ingrained practices of late Medieval Latin could often have been responsible for these diversions from the Classical norm. It is typically prudent, therefore, when analysing such abnormalities in Neo-Latin to look for alternative explanations rather than to suppose the presence of linguistic calques (see Tournoy and Tunberg (1996)).

With the new interest in the minutiae of Classical Latin, and the closer attention paid to better manuscript sources for ancient literature, an improved understanding of orthography was attained. Despite increased exertion in this field, correcting the spelling of Latin to Classical standards was not a central area for scholarly attention; not only could there be significant variation in the spelling employed by members of a closely knit intellectual group but even the same author could employ different orthography of the same word, either through carelessness or disinterest, in different parts of a given work. An area particularly requiring correction was the misapplication of *ae* for *e*, or vice versa, a long-standing area of confusion since the pronunciation of the diphthong and the long vowel had coalesced in late Antiquity; similarly difficult was the matter of when a prevocalic *c* should be aspirated by a following *h* or not, a source of doubt that often inspired false Graecisms. Other egregious spelling mistakes, such as *michi* (*mihi*), *nichil* (*nihil*) and *capud* (*caput*), and the incorrect dittography or haplography of consonants, though very common in medieval manuscripts, were swiftly expelled from polished Neo-Latin compositions. The pervasive miswriting of *caeterum* for *ceterum* (and other various forms) can be traced at least as far back as Tortelli's *De Orthographia Dictionum e Graecis Tractarum* (*c.* 1449, printed 1471), which argued, with ingenious but unfounded learning, that the word was a Latinisation of Greek καὶ ἕτερον ("and the other") and should therefore be spelt with the diphthong, a misconception that took centuries to correct. Indeed, a few mistakes lingered on in Neo-Latin well into the nineteenth century, where *coelum* in lieu of *caelum*, *lac(h)ryma* for *lacrima* and *sylva* for *silua* can still be found. A number of such mistakes can still be seen in the use of Latin phrases in modern languages, for instance *coda* (not *cauda*) in musical parlance and (ironically enough) the name of the undergraduate Classics course at Oxford University, *literae* (not *litterae*) *humaniores*.

The French Humanist Petrus Ramus is credited with the adoption, at least in typographical form, of the use of *j* and *v* as the consonantal forms of *i* and *u*; previously, *j* had been used for the latter member of the pair *ii*, and *v* indiscriminately for consonantal and vocalic *u* in initial position, *u* being employed elsewhere. For the most part, the use of *j* had been removed from Neo-Latin texts by the early nineteenth century. In many cases, *v* still has not been erased from the modern employment of Latin, not only appearing in many contemporary compositions but still unjustly riddling supposedly modern and authoritative edited texts of ancient works, as well as the majority of dictionaries. This continued use of the letter *v* serves as a good example of a feature being recognised as non-Classical but nonetheless commonly retained owing to the clarity it can provide for the modern reader. The same can be said of the lectoral aids of word division, punctuation, diacritics (common in Neo-Latin until the eighteenth century) and the colometry of texts into paragraphs, all of which lack Classical precedents.

Although Neo-Latin encouraged a general uniformity of expression, its pronunciation was quite a different matter. Most educated Europeans, who had learnt the Latin tongue from their very early years, were disposed to pronouncing it, whether in its scholastic form or its purified Neo-Latin guise, in a traditional fashion not markedly distinct from the pronunciation of their vulgate tongue. Accordingly, Neo-Latin pronunciation varied in many details around Europe and the wider world. In a number of particulars almost all countries differed from the Classical pronunciation: for instance, the palatalisation of *t* and *c* before front vowels was pervasive, as was the fricative pronunciation of consonantal *u* (*v*); variations occurred from country to country in the pronunciation of consonantal *i* (*j*) and *z*. It was only with the arrival in the mid-nineteenth century of more refined philological investigations into the sound and orthography of Classical Latin that devoted attempts were made to restore the reconstructed pronunciation of the language in its ancient form. This Reformed Pronunciation was slow to take hold but has now been acknowledged as correct, at least in its major details, by academics; still, however, some countries (such as Italy and Spain) pronounce Latin in a way more analogous to their own vernacular language, and the wholesale removal of pronouncing consonantal *u* as [v] not [w] has a long way yet to go.

This survey is not the place to tackle the prosody of Neo-Latin. It will suffice to say that, as knowledge of ancient prosody became more refined (particularly during the sixteenth century), and as this information became disseminated more widely, Neo-Latin poetry adopted these improvements eagerly. Yet, given that prosodic knowledge was often preserved through individuals' memorising a large array of verses from Classical poetry, progress in this field was slow going. For instance, prolonged uncertainty is evident regarding matters such as the length of final -*o* (no doubt complicated by its correption in certain circumstances by various authors of the late first century BCE and thereafter), the legitimacy of *productio in arsi* at the hephthemimeral caesura, and, as a hangover from Medieval Latin, the prosodic influence of *h*-. As with the imitative nature of Renaissance prose, there was no desire for actual innovation in metrical and prosodic matters.

Diffusion and Diversity:
Neo-Latin after the Renaissance

The empowering intellectual influence of the Renaissance across Europe and, in turn, its colonies not only encouraged the aforementioned purification of Latin but also spurred on its use as a vehicle for literary endeavours in a wide array of fields. The widespread knowledge of Latin among educated society in Western Europe, and its dominant presence within the Church and academic communities, continued from the fifteenth up to the eighteenth centuries. The *renatae litterae* of Neo-Latin continued to provide a potent medium for displaying a writer's own erudition in a way that the employment of a given vernacular simply could not. It accordingly served as the written and spoken language for diplomatic correspondence throughout many regions of the world populated by Europeans, precisely owing to its generally fixed vocabulary and the fact that it enjoyed a wider cognisance among the intellectual elite than any single spoken language. Accordingly, once Neo-Latin in its refined form had come to international prominence, it served as the primary language for most scholarly productions until the early eighteenth century, whether the prospective audience was situated within one's own country or throughout the wider *Respublica Litterarum*. Not only was this the case for the great astronomical writings of Nicolaus Copernicus, Johannes Kepler and Galileo Galilei, and the medical treatises of Andreas Vesalius, William Harvey and Thomas Sydenham, but it also served as the vehicle for the cutting-edge physics of Isaac Newton and the ground-breaking biological researches of Carl Linnaeus; as late as the 1820s, the mathematician Carl Gauss still elected to write his treatises in Latin. Turning to the field of philosophy, it is beyond doubt that many of the most influential works from the Early Modern periods (i.e. to the turn of the nineteenth century) are written in Latin, including the great books of Francis Bacon, Thomas Hobbes, René Descartes and Baruch de Spinoza.

This widespread use of Latin as the language of scholarship began to decline in many areas of Europe from the early eighteenth century onwards, as French, English and German in particular gained greater ground in their respective countries, inspired through the Enlightenment with a desire to present new learning more intelligibly to a broader audience. For such a mission one's native tongue was naturally more efficacious than the polished Latin understood by only a small subset of society. The shift from Latin to the vernacular occurred in each country at different times and under the influence of a varied matrix of factors but most saw the change, whenever it came, develop with surprising speed. Save for certain specific fields, including botany and zoology (especially in cladistics), Latin had become by the turn of the nineteenth century largely defunct as a vehicle for original contributions to scientific, literary and philosophical learning, leaving its vestiges only in the tags and phrases that still intersperse the jargon of most areas of scholarship.

The decrease of the use of Neo-Latin as a scholarly language was inevitably self-perpetuating and effectively irreversible. No text has ever been written in the language for a truly popular audience, since sufficient knowledge of Latin has never been the province of the majority throughout Europe or her colonies. Therefore, as the number of works in Latin decreased, so did the perceived importance of learning the language to engage with the New Knowledge, if much of it appeared in modern vernaculars; as the potential audience skilled enough to read Latin decreased, so did the incentive for scholars of all disciplines to embark upon the more difficult task of composing in Neo-Latin rather than their own spoken tongue. It is now impossible to envisage the return of Neo-Latin as the universal language of scholarship.

The sphere of Ecclesiastical Latin, guarded by the generally static nature of the religious community, has nevertheless served as an oasis for the survival of Neo-Latin, albeit within the Catholic Church, and primarily at the Vatican. It has in recent times given little scope for original composition or scholarship in the field, however, and the great majority of Latin employed in its business has been formalised for decades, or often many centuries. Outside the Church, its employment in original compositions, whether literary or otherwise, decreased markedly from the mid-nineteenth century, although it still exists as a viable language into which vernacular texts can be translated. The numerous major works of twentieth-century fiction that have passed through publishing houses in Latin translation, from A.A. Milne's *Winnie the Pooh* to J.K. Rowling's *Harry Potter* series, are rather surprising, although most such works are explicitly written either for pedagogical purposes or for the translator's own private amusement.

An area that has given continued productivity to the use of Neo-Latin in the last two centuries is Classical scholarship. Not only in academic work upon the Ancient Roman world and its literature, but also in the study of varied material from Ancient Greece and other cultures, scholars continued to employ Latin as a significant language of scholarship. Indeed, it served as the standard medium for a scholarly commentary upon Greco-Roman literature until the mid-nineteenth century in Britain, France and Italy, and until the early twentieth century in Germany, Holland, Scandinavia and various countries of Eastern Europe; continental doctoral theses in the subject could be written in Latin until as late as the middle of the century. Although the Neo-Latin that was employed necessarily involved the use of some post-Classical terms (e.g., for the pluperfect tense – (*tempus*) *plusquam-perfectum* – or printed books – *libri impressi*) and the necessary inclusion of modern names of scholars (often, but not always, Latinised into a given declension), the form of the language remained largely Classical. The twentieth century saw the use of Latin in scholarship decline almost to a complete absence in lieu of the vulgate (or, as has become increasingly common, English employed as a more universal language), although a number of Classical journals still accept submissions in Latin, and some small-scale journals are published entirely in the language (e.g. the Vatican's *Latinitas* and Saarbrücken's *Vox Latina*).

In two areas in the subject, however, Latin is still the standard language employed: firstly, the technical introductions to the manuscript transmission and editorial history of Classical texts (primarily for the Teubner, Oxford Classical Texts and Paravia series); secondly, as the condensed, and often jargonistic, language of the critical apparatuses that provide information regarding manuscript variants and scholarly conjectures at the foot of edited texts, whether in Latin, Greek or another ancient language possessing an analogous form of transmission. This language has allowed itself a good number of post-Classical accretions (e.g., the univerbation *manuscriptus*, or *unci* in the sense of parentheses) and is typically employed in a very abbreviated fashion (e.g., *m.r.* = *manus recentior*, *ci.* = *coniecit*, *s.u.l.* = *si uera lectio*) but remains lucid in its concise simplicity.

Almost nothing has been said with regard to the spoken application of Neo-Latin. There are multiple reasons for this comparative silence. Firstly, except in a very small number of circles (the Roman Church, early university, and sometimes school, education in its more formal dress, certain legal spheres), Latin was not used as the general form for spoken interchange amongst even the most educated Europeans who could speak the same vernacular language. Secondly, by virtue of the transient nature of the medium, and the late arrival of audio-recording equipment, the great majority of evidence regarding such oral delivery of the language when it did occur has been irrevocably lost, and what survives can only give a minute and fragmented picture of affairs. Thirdly and finally, given the artificial construction of Neo-Latin as a polished *Kunstsprache*, it was not a particularly suitable vehicle for impromptu dialogue, and therefore, if used at all, it necessarily differed in its nature from the written form in various particulars and therefore should require separate treatment. Indeed, varied anecdotal evidence survives to suggest that many Renaissance Ciceronians shunned speaking Latin, for the extempore nature of the exchange led them into the potential pitfalls of improper usage or employing a syntactical structure unworthy of Cicero's written eloquence. (The oral delivery of an address written in advance was, of course, a very different affair.)

Despite this general rarity of the employment of the language in quotidian speech, it was the typical medium for educating students, in Latin as well as other subjects, in many European countries until the eighteenth century, most particularly within Jesuit institutions. Although this wholesale employment of Latin was very rare in the nineteenth century, we may note, as a curious development, the reprisal of spoken Latin through the radical implementation of the so-called "Direct Method" in certain British schools during the early twentieth century. The keenest proponent of this demanding form of Latin teaching, in which no other language was employed to mediate the pedagogical progress, was W.H.D. Rouse, sometime Fellow of Christ's College, Cambridge, and long-standing headmaster of the Perse School in the same city. The odd results of this form of teaching – certainly Classical in grammar and syntax but rather stilted in quick-fire dialogue – can be seen in a number of Rouse's publications (e.g., Rouse (1935)). Not surprisingly, it seems that the method, which never won widespread acclaim, was inherently divisive, allowing the more advanced pupils to thrive but leaving the others drifting deep into incomprehension.

In the wake of Latin's decline as a viable language for general academic endeavours, there was nevertheless a marked rise in its use as a medium for pedagogically related compositions in schools, universities and analogous educational institutions. The nature of this burgeoning field of work in Latin was primarily translation-based. Such compositions enjoyed a particularly British following, and the tradition of prose and verse composition still survives in the United Kingdom more than in any other modern country. Given the increased didactic focus of writing in a Latin prose or verse style that closely imitated a given ancient author, the primary purpose of the exercise concerned translation from the vulgate language (English or otherwise) into polished, Classical Latin. Accordingly, Neo-Latin developed into a yet more artificial mode of language, serving not as a vehicle for original composition (as was the case even for the most ardent Ciceronians) so much as for mere translation. If the task was solely translation, due focus could rest upon imitating the given author to the most minute detail of language, expression and, where necessary, prosody. Cicero was once more the central figure for imitation in prose writing (although the styles of Sallust, Seneca, Tacitus and occasionally Livy were also emulated); in verse, Ovid was chosen as the most appropriate basis for imitation in elegiacs, Virgil in hexameters, Catullus in hendecasyllabic and iambic metres, and Horace for sapphics and alcaics. With regard to all of these authors, clearly fixed rules for imitation had been published in handbooks by the end of the nineteenth century. A huge array of poetic translations, and to a lesser extent original compositions, was produced in Latin verse throughout the nineteenth century and well into the twentieth, not only in Europe but also both Americas, Africa, Australasia and a few corners of Asia (India, Sri Lanka, Japan). Certainly more than two hundred people world-wide continue to practise the art-form actively, although publication in print is now markedly more rare.

An interesting corollary of this keen focus upon close imitation was a marked scholarly advance with regard to research into the minutiae of various Latin authors' employment of the Latin language. Increased scrutiny into matters of vocabulary, word order, clausulae, prosody, metrical practices and stylistics brought new insight into the intricacies of the Classical language. These developments, of course, once discovered and duly disseminated in print by scholars, served only to polish and refine further the nature of Neo-Latin as it was employed in the nineteenth and twentieth centuries. Even outside the confines of translation among students, professionals and amateur practitioners in wider society, this furtherance of knowledge in the field came to influence Neo-Latin when occasionally used for original composition, driving it ever closer to its Classical roots. Resplendent examples of this refinement can be seen in the compositions produced by the Public Orators for the Universities of Cambridge and Oxford, and Trinity College, Dublin, whose levels of technical perfection are typically extraordinarily high, and in many respects more classicising than the very "best" Renaissance compositions.

Conclusion: The Difficult Path Ahead

Neo-Latin currently finds itself in something of a quandary: never has more knowledge about the intricacies of the Classical Latin language been available in print, whether specific to a given author or diachronic in its focus, and never have the texts of the Classical authors been more readily available in a more purified state, yet never perhaps has the global knowledge of Latin been at such a low ebb. As a result, the application of the language has become remarkably rarefied, typically practised and read by a small subset of scholars who specialise professionally in teaching and/or researching linguistic matters concerning the Greco-Roman world. The vast resources of scholarship upon Classical Latin allow the best practitioners of Neo-Latin to produce truly remarkable compositions but the general rarity of practising the art-form has also led to an embarrassing series of debased forays into Latin composition. Yet, since it will forever lack a true speech community, Neo-Latin can safely be judged as enduring in its form, relatively impermeable to change or decay. The primary hope is that it can continue to serve future generations of Classical scholars as the most concise, lucid and elegant means of conveying knowledge about the ancient world.

FURTHER READING

The volume of published Neo-Latin literature is so large and varied that further investigation into the field can appear daunting and haphazard. Very useful for seeing the bigger picture is the most wide-ranging introduction to the study of Neo-Latin to-date, Josef Ijsewijn's two-volume *Companion to Neo-Latin Studies* (Ijsewijn (1998), which covers much of the language's development and diffusion from the Renaissance to the early twentieth century. The best introductions to Renaissance Ciceronianism are Sabbadini's classic treatment (Sabbadini (1885)) and the lucid article of Tunberg (1997), although Erasmus' *Ciceronianus* (1528) remains as informative in this field as it is amusing. The great work on the history of Neo-Latin verse composition remains to be written but useful material is available on its development in Britain was gathered by Bradner (1940) and Money (1998). The annual journal *Humanistica Lovaniensia*, based in Leuven, and its supplements, are the primary vehicle for new research in Neo-Latin. An *Instrumentum Bibliographicum Neolatinum*, which records the myriad threads of current research in the field, has been published in issues of *Humanistica Lovaniensia* since 1974. Also useful repertories of varied studies under the aegis of Neo-Latin are the triennial *Acta Conventus Neolatini*.

Since the grammar and syntax of Neo-Latin are explicitly Classical, no large-scale work has sought to tackle these topics in isolation. In the more interesting area of vocabulary, the repertory of Hoven and Grailet (2006) and the website maintained by Johann Ramminger (2009) serve as good introductions to the lexicon of Renaissance and early modern Neo-Latin. David Morgan, of Furman University, has been engaged for many years in an English–Latin dictionary of words attested from CE 700 to the present day; although copious results are available online, its prospective date of publication is unclear.

PART IV

Literary Registers of Latin

CHAPTER 19

The Language of Roman Comedy

Wolfgang de Melo

Introduction

Roman comedy is not a uniform genre. The type that is best attested is the *fabula palliata*, "comedy in Greek dress", named after the *pallium*, a Greek cloak which some of the actors wore. Its most significant exponents are Titus Maccius Plautus (died in 184) and Publius Terentius Afer (*c.* 185–159), the only comic playwrights of whom complete plays survive.[1] In addition we have fragments of Lucius Livius Andronicus and Gnaeus Naevius, both of them predecessors of Plautus; and of Caecilius Statius (died in 168), a contemporary of Terence, whose style closely resembles that of Plautus rather than Terence.[2] All *fabulae palliatae* were based on Greek originals; in a few cases we are fortunate enough to be able to compare Greek fragments with their Latin counterparts.[3] The *fabula togata*, "comedy in Roman dress", is a spin-off of the *fabula palliata*. Some of the actors wore togas, the Roman national dress, and the plays were set in Italy. Not many fragments survive.[4] The most important authors are Titinius, probably an older contemporary of Terence, Lucius Afranius, who belongs to the late second century, and Titus Quinctius Atta, who died in 77. A third type of comedy is the *fabula Atellana*, named after the Oscan town Atella. The genre remained oral for a long time. We have about 300 lines from a scripted version of it by Lucius Pomponius and Quintus Novius, both from the early first century BCE.[5] A genre related to comedy is the *mimus* or "mime", consisting of the performance of improvised sketches. Mime became literary only in the late Republic. Its best-known authors, Gnaeus Matius, Decimus Laberius and Publilius Syrus, all lived in the first century BCE.[6]

Plautus is an author of whom we have complete plays as well as fragments coming down to us mainly through the grammarians. Interestingly, the language of the two sources does not correspond closely. The reason is that grammarians cite Plautus for his

A Companion to the Latin Language, First Edition. Edited by James Clackson.
© 2011 Blackwell Publishing Ltd. Published 2011 by Blackwell Publishing Ltd.

grammatical oddities, which mostly do occur in the directly transmitted comedies as well, but much more rarely. If we had only the fragments, our picture of Plautus would be distorted. Consequently, we cannot form a fully reliable picture of the language of the fragmentary playwrights either, and our main focus has to be on Plautus and Terence.

The language of Plautus and Terence is by no means uniform. There are diachronic differences between the two authors. Moreover, within each author individual character types like old men or soldiers have different speech patterns. There are also different literary genres within comedies, again with different linguistic characteristics, for instance letters, prayers or of course dialogue. And finally, there is an important distinction between spoken passages in senarii, recited passages in "long verses" (trochaic septenarii, etc.) and sung passages in other metres.[7] Especially in Plautus the long verses and sung passages are marked by a higher incidence of certain figures of speech and archaisms.[8]

In what follows, I shall examine the language of Roman comedy, beginning with spelling, phonology and metre. After that, I shall turn to morphology and then to syntax. Lexical aspects will be discussed last.

Spelling, Phonology and Metre

We know surprisingly little about how Plautus and Terence spelled and even less about other writers, whose fragments are transmitted only indirectly through grammarians, lexicographers or literary scholars. The spellings in the manuscripts of Plautus and Terence do not reproduce the spellings the authors would have used themselves.[9] The manuscripts going back to Late Antiquity, that is the Ambrosian palimpsest for Plautus and the Codex Bembinus for Terence, reflect conventions in Varro's day. For instance, the digraph *ei* is commonly used for what in Classical Latin was pronounced as long *i*, regardless of whether we are dealing with an original long vowel or an original diphthong. In Plautus the two were still distinct in pronunciation and spelling, the former being written <*i*> and the latter <*ei*> or <*e*>.[10] Plautus would thus have said *captiuei* or *captiue* (both nominative plural), but the acrostic argument of the *Captivi*, written a few centuries later, has nine lines because it uses the pseudo-archaic spelling *capteiuei*.

Plautus and Terence rendered the Greek letters υ, ζ, φ, θ, χ as *u*, *s* or *ss*, *p*, *t*, *c*, while Varro and the ancient manuscripts used the modern *y*, *z*, *ph*, *th*, *ch*. Aspirate spellings made their first appearance in the middle of the second century,[11] and unaspirated pronunciations persisted well into the first century BCE (Cic. *Orat.* 160).

The final consonants of prefixes were commonly assimilated to the initial consonant of a word stem in pronunciation, though perhaps not for every prefix.[12] This enables Plautus to pun on *adsum/assum* "I am here" as if it were a form of *assus* "roasted" in Pl. *Poen.* 279. But whether Plautus and Terence wrote *adsum* or *assum* is a different question. Inscriptions of the period use both spellings, and Lucilius 375–376 Marx states that one can write *accurrere* "run towards" as well as *adcurrere*. It should also be noted that Plautine manuscripts frequently write *obsonium* for *opsonium* "provisions"; as the word goes back to Greek ὀψώνιον, the spelling with <*b*> is the result of a false etymology involving the Latin prefix *ob-*.

Medieval manuscripts of Roman comedy have undergone further modernization in spelling. Often copyists were at a loss when confronted with older spellings. Thus at

Pl. *Cas.* 71 we find the post-Classical spelling *aio* "I say" in the palimpsest and the Codex Londiniensis, while other manuscripts have *alio* or *alia*, both "corrections" of the older spelling *aiio* (attested for Cicero by Quint. *Inst.* 1.4.11).

Modernized spellings can also obscure older morphology. In the first declension, Plautus had a dissyllabic genitive in *-ai* and a monosyllabic one in *-ae* (possibly also written *-ai* at this time[13]). In the manuscripts the spelling is *-ae* throughout; *-ai* is only transmitted in *Poen.* 51, though other spelling corruptions pointing to earlier *-ai* can be found.[14] Similarly, it is quite likely that Plautus and Terence mostly wrote *siet* rather than *sit*, even where the latter was intended in pronunciation. The manuscripts were modernized inconsistently, resulting in a certain amount of confusion. Where we still find the spelling *siet*, it must be old, even where the metre demands a monosyllable. Where we find *sit*, we can assume that the authors wrote *siet* if metre demands two syllables; but if the metre demands a single syllable, we cannot know what Plautus and Terence had written.

To the linguist, the metres of Roman comedy are important because they make many deductions about earlier pronunciations possible.[15] In Plautus, the shortening of long vowels in final syllables ending in consonants other than *s* has not yet begun; in Terence they are mostly long as well, but in Ennius long and short vowels already alternate according to metrical necessity:

1 Noenum rumores ponebat ante salutem. (Enn. *Ann.* 364)
   He did not put people's talk before the good of the state.

2 Volturus in siluis[16] miserum mandebat homonem. (Enn. *Ann.* 125)
   The vulture ate the wretched man in the woods.

1 only scans if *ponebat* still has a long vowel in the final syllable, while the same morpheme in *mandebat* in **2** must contain a short vowel.

Plautus and Terence have also kept final geminate consonants, which persisted into the Classical period only in monosyllables (*hocc* < **hod-ke*):

3 Miles impransus astat, aes censet dari. (Pl. *Aul.* 528)
   The soldier stands around without lunch and thinks he'll be given the money.

This verse is an iambic senarius. It only scans if the final syllable of *miles* is heavy. Since that syllable has always had a short vowel, the syllable can only be heavy because there is still a final geminate consonant (*miless* < **milet-s*).

Final *-s* is often lost after a short vowel if the next word begins with a consonant. This phenomenon, also attested in archaic inscriptions, occurs more frequently in spoken than in sung verse (Dressler (1973)). Iambic shortening means that a sequence of a light and a heavy syllable counts as two light ones; the originally heavy syllable may not bear the word accent, but may have a long vowel and/or be closed. We seem to be dealing with a fast-speech phenomenon (Devine and Stephens (1980), as this occurs more often in senarii than in sung verse; however, iambic shortening is particularly frequent in anapaests, where the rationale is different: every metrical element has to be two moras long, which can often only be achieved by unusual shortenings.

Finally, it should be noted that prodelision in comedy can take place more freely than in Classical poetry. Vowel-less forms of *es* "you are" and *est* "he is" can be attached to words ending in -*us* etc., which is no longer allowed later on.

Morphology

The morphology of Roman comedy often looks archaic to the Classical scholar, especially that of writers before Terence. However, we have to distinguish between what is archaic from a Classical perspective and what is archaic from the perspective of the writers of comedy. An example can make this distinction clearer. In the fourth conjugation Classical Latin has futures like *sciam* "I shall know" and imperfects like *sciebam* "I knew". In comedy we find the alternatives *scibo* and *scibam* as well.[17] To a speaker of the Classical period these forms looked archaic. In Plautus and Terence, however, the situation is more complex. The Classical future *sciam* goes back to an old subjunctive and is in fact older than *scibo*, which is an innovation based on futures like *amabo* "I shall love" or *monebo* "I shall admonish". By contrast, the Classical imperfect *sciebam* is an innovation, while *scibam*, with -*ba*- added directly to the stem, is the original formation. *Sciebam* arose when -*eba*- rather than -*ba*- was analysed as imperfect suffix in forms like *monebam* "I admonished".

The status of the two formations is not the same in Plautus and Terence. In the imperfect, the forms in -*ibam*, -*ibas* etc. are still common.[18]

As can be seen from Table 19.1, the imperfect in -*iebam* is still rare in Plautus and Terence, with five tokens altogether. The forms in -*ibam* are the norm and certainly not yet archaic from the perspective of these writers.

The situation is different in the future tense, as can be seen from Table 19.2.

The future in -*ibo*, archaic from the Classical perspective, is already rare in Plautus and even rarer in Terence, although it still occurs occasionally at a later date (e.g. *uenibo* "I shall come" in Pompon. *com.* 65). We can go further. Of the 46 tokens in -*ibo* in Plautus, 21, that is almost half, belong to the verb *scire*. *Scire* is a frequent verb, but among the futures in -*iam* it is not nearly as predominant (43 of 184 tokens, less than a

Table 19.1   Imperfects in Plautus and Terence

	-*ibam*	-*iebam*	Total	-*ibam* (%)
Plautus	17	3	20	85.0
Terence	13	2	15	86.7

Table 19.2   Futures in Plautus and Terence

	-*iam*	-*ibo*	Total	-*iam* (%)
Plautus	184	46	230	80.0
Terence	72	11	83	86.8

quarter). The future in -*ibo* is thus undergoing a process of fossilization before its ultimate demise. In this case, what is archaic from the Classical perspective is also archaic from the archaic perspective.

There are few forms which are archaic from the Classical perspective, but unmarked in comedy. The ending of the second person singular passive/deponent in the forms of the *infectum*-stem belongs here:

> **4** PHAE: Obloquere. PAL: Fiat maxume. PHAE: Etiam taces? (Pl. *Cur.* 41)
> PHAE: That's it, interrupt me.
> PAL: Yes, by all means.
> PHAE: Won't you be quiet now?

Phaedromus uses *obloquere* as the second person indicative of *obloqui*, but Palinurus deliberately misunderstands him and takes the form as an imperative. The Classical indicative *obloqueris* has an ending that was influenced by second person active forms.[19] Plautus predominantly uses the older form in -*re* and Terence does so exclusively, though the absence of any forms in -*ris* is presumably due to chance rather than to deliberate avoidance.

Similarly, Plautus and Terence still have a stylistically neutral, adjectival possessive *quoius, quoia, quoium* "whose" (*quoia* in Ter. *Eu.* 321). This is one of the few genuine archaisms that remained in Spanish (*cuyo, cuya*) while dying out elsewhere; in Virgil the use is already an archaism (*cuium pecus* in *Ecl.* 3.1).

Among the forms which were already archaic in Plautus and Terence we have to distinguish between those which are merely doublets of their Classical equivalents and those which cannot be "translated" into more modern forms. Nouns and pronouns with morphology that was already archaic in Plautus always have Classical equivalents. We have already seen an example in the first-declension genitive -*ai*. A similar case is the genitive of the fourth declension. Here there is also much variation in inscriptions. Plautus has the genitive *senati* twice, both times in the phrase *senati columen* (*Cas.* 536, *Epid.* 189), while the *Senatusconsultum de Bacchanalibus* (*CIL* I².581.8) contains the form *senatuos*.[20] The word is not attested in Terence, so we do not know which form he would have used, but he also has a non-Classical fourth-declension genitive *anuis* "of the old woman" (*Hau.* 287). In the fourth declension the genitive in -*i* seems more common than that in -*uis*; *quaesti* "of gain" also occurs in Caecilius (*com.* 130) and Titinius (*com.* 26), while Turpilius has a form *tumulti* "of the tumult" (*com.* 154). In the second declension, the genitive plural ends in -*orum* in Classical Latin, an ending developed by analogy to the genitive plural -*arum* of the first declension.[21] The older ending in -*um* mainly survives in terms for currency.[22] In comedy the ending -*um* is still more widespread (*deum* "of the gods" in Caecil. *com.* 211) but actually not yet the only one used with words for currency:

> **5** Quin ego nunc subigor trium nummum causa ut hasce epistulas
> dicam ab eo homine me accepisse quem ego qui sit homo nescio. (Pl. *Trin.* 848–849)
> Yes, for the sake of three coins I'm now forced to say that I received this letter from someone I don't know.

6 Erat ei de ratiuncula
   iam pridem apud me relicuom pauxillulum
   nummorum. (Ter. *Ph.* 36–8)
   I owed him a trifling amount of coins on a trivial account.

In the first example from Plautus we find the old form *nummum*, which eventually
became standard; in the second example from Terence we find the innovated form
nummorum, which gradually dropped out of use again. This innovated *nummorum*
already occurs in Plautus (*Trin.* 152). Yet on the whole the old forms in -*um* are rare in
comedy and the artificially archaizing over-use seen in tragedy and remarked on by
Cicero (*Orat.* 155) does not occur:

7 … consilium socii, augurium atque extum interpretes.
   Postquam prodigium horriferum, portentum pauos … (Pac. *trag.* 81–82)
   … partners of counsels, interpreters of auguries and entrails. After the fear of hor-
   rifying signs and omens …

In this short passage from Pacuvius we find six genitives in -*um* where Classical Latin
would have -*orum*. Such extreme usages are alien to comedy and could only occur in
parodies of the tragic style.

The original ablative singular endings were -*ad*, -*od* and so on. The old ablative forms
of the personal pronouns were *med*, *ted*, and *sed*, and in Latin these forms came to be
used as accusatives as well. As the vowels before the final consonants are long, the final
consonants got lost early on. Terence has no traces of the final -*d*. In Plautus it occasionally remains in the monosyllables *med* and *ted* (still *ted* in Titin. *com.* 65). We are dealing
with metrical licence here, as is obvious from two facts. First, the manuscripts preserve
the forms *med* and *ted* or corruptions thereof only before vowels, which indicates that
they were used only in order to prevent hiatus. And second, while we have many instances
of *med* and *ted*, there is no accusative/ablative *sed* in Plautus. The reason for this is that
there was no need to use the archaic *sed* because there is a reduplicated form *sese* beside
the simple *se*, and this reduplicated form has the same effect as *med* and *ted*: if it stands
before a vowel, we are left with one complete syllable of the personal pronoun.

The last pronominal forms I wish to discuss are those of *ipse*. In comedy we find an
alternative nominative *ipsus*, modelled on the nominative of the second declension. But
perhaps more interesting than these nominatives are forms with internal inflection:

8 Quia te adducturam huc dixeras eumpse, non eampse. (Pl. *Truc.* 133)
   Because you'd said you'd bring *him* along, not *her*.

Internally inflected forms occur only thirty-seven times in Plautus,[23] whereas the Classical
forms are attested almost 300 times. Terence has not preserved internally inflected forms
at all. The internally inflected forms are older (*is* + particle -*pse*); the Classical forms arose
because internal inflection is a synchronic anomaly. Often it is not clear why Plautus uses
internally inflected forms; in our example the reason seems to be that there is a contrast
of gender and that internal inflection allows the speaker to keep the regular word accent
while still putting the stress on the contrastive morpheme.

Not all verb forms which are archaic in Plautus and Terence have Classical equivalents. The ones that do not are special future and subjunctive forms.[24] In comedy we still find *s*-futures of the type *faxo* "I shall do" and *amasso* "I shall have loved". In Plautus such forms are relatively frequent, whereas in Terence it is practically only *faxo* that survives. Some of the forms seem to go back to old aorist subjunctives, but many, incidentally including *faxo* and *amasso*, must be innovated forms.[25] Their distribution pattern is highly unusual. In main clauses we only find fossilized *faxo*, usually combined with a clausal rather than a nominal object, and this clause is mostly in the future indicative or present subjunctive. The meaning of *faxo* is that of a simple, perfective future, although in some instances it seems to have lost its verbal force and to have become a mere marker of certainty:

9 Atque ob istanc industriam etiam faxo amabit amplius. (Pl. *Men.* 791)
And because of your officiousness he'll certainly make love to her even more.

Here the speaker is an old man talking to his daughter who has been too domineering and controlling; the old man warns her that because of her behaviour her husband will turn to prostitutes even more. *Faxo* cannot mean "I shall do/bring it about", because not even in Roman comedy are fathers as harsh as such a statement would entail. Also of note is the consistent absence of the subordinator *ut*, which in fact occurs only once (Pl. *As.* 897, of course with the subjunctive rather than the future).

The fossilized, perfective simple future meaning in main clauses seems to be original. In subordinate clauses, where we find a variety of verbs in all persons and numbers, this future has acquired future perfect meaning (future anteriority). The type is particularly common in conditional clauses, probably in imitation of archaic legal style; and the forms in subordinate clauses are deliberately employed to mark an elevated register, whereas main clause *faxo* still seems to be stylistically unmarked.

The *s*-future has an *s*-subjunctive beside it (type *faxim*, *amassim*). The *s*-subjunctive goes back to old aorist optatives and always has non-past meaning like the present subjunctive. It occurs in wishes, but especially frequently in prohibitive clauses and never in commands, where other subjunctives are common. This distribution pattern is shared with the perfect subjunctive, which is also found in prohibitions, but never in commands, an old survival of aorist usage. While the perfect subjunctive has past meaning in most other contexts, the *s*-subjunctive is always non-past, which seems to be the original state of affairs for the perfect subjunctive as well;[26] the perfect subjunctive acquired past meaning only by association with the perfect indicative.

Two other types of subjunctive pattern like the *s*-subjunctives: the type *duim* "I may give", which has special stems and the subjunctive morpheme -*i*- that we also find among the *s*-subjunctives, and the type *attigas* "you may touch", which contains old aorist stems and a subjunctive morpheme -*a*- that is of unclear origin.

Many archaic verb forms in comedy are just doublets of the Classical forms. In general, the Classical forms are already the norm and the archaic forms mostly employed for metrical reasons. A case in point are the medio-passive infinitives in -*ier* (type *fabularier* instead of *fabulari* "to speak"). Compared with their Classical counterparts, such infinitives are rare and, equally importantly, almost entirely restricted to iambic line ends, where the Classical forms are metrically impossible. In Caecil. *com.* 263, for instance, we find *amari* "be loved" and *expeti* "be sought" within the line, but *arcessier* "be fetched" at line end. Much the same can be said about the present subjunctive forms of *esse*. The inherited paradigm is *siem, sies, siet, simus, sitis, sient*, with the full grade of the subjunctive (originally optative) suffix in the singular (-*ie*-) and the zero grade in the plural (-*i*-).[27] Again, the Classical forms *sim, sis, sit* and *sint* have almost replaced their older counterparts, which are much rarer and almost entirely restricted to iambic line ends.

The third person perfect indicative is more complex. The standard ending in comedy is already -*ērunt* (*fecērunt* in Pl. *Epid.* 32), which is a contamination of the older -*ĕrunt* (*fecĕrunt* in Pl. *Men.* 586) and -*ēre* (*fecēre* in Pl. *Mer.* 318). The ending -*ĕrunt* is very rare in Classical Latin and mainly used for metrical reasons (e.g. *profuĕrunt* in the pentameter in Tib. 2.3.12); but it survived on a sub-literary level and has Romance reflexes.[28] In comedy it is rare and seems to be stylistically unmarked. The ending -*ēre* is typical of Classical epic poetry; in comedy it is rare and restricted to contexts where the register is elevated.

Syntax

Roman comedy is entirely in verse. The greatest influence metre exerts on the syntax of Classical poetry concerns word order patterns. Word order in Classical prose is less syntactically and more pragmatically determined than in most modern European languages. In Classical poetry, the influence of pragmatics does not increase, but that of syntax further decreases in favour of metrical forces. The two most common metres of comedy, the iambic senarius and the trochaic septenarius, can relatively freely substitute heavy syllables for light ones and two light syllables for a single heavy one. Does this greater metrical freedom lead to a more prosaic, syntactically determined word order?

Comedy follows the most fundamental word order rules in the same way as prose. Thus Wackernagel's Law fully applies: unstressed connective elements like *autem* "but", but also non-contrastive personal pronouns like *ego* "I" or *mihi* "to me" are placed in second position in their clauses.[29]

In de Melo (2010) 72–80 I have studied the position of possessive pronouns with regard to their head nouns in Plautus. Studying the position of possessive pronouns has several advantages over studying the position of other determiners. First, their meaning is simple: they merely indicate that there is a connection between the head noun and another entity (which is often, but not always, a possessor). Second, while they can be focus constituents like adjectives, their pragmatic functions are easier to determine than those of adjectives: they are focal if contrastive (*my own* rather than just *my*), but non-focal otherwise. And third, they do not all scan in the same way: on the one hand the first and second person plural pronouns scan in the same way, and on the other hand all remaining possessives go together.

I have counted all possessive pronouns in Plautus and put them into four groups: "position 1" means that the possessive stands before its head and is separated from it by constituents that are not part of the noun phrase (pre-modifier hyperbaton); "position 2" means that the possessive stands immediately in front of its head; "position 3", that it follows its head immediately; and "position 4", that it follows its head and is separated from it (post-modifier hyperbaton). Table 19.3 presents the figures.

Table 19.3 The position of possessives in Plautus

	Position 1	Position 2	Position 3	Position 4	Total
meus	195 (15.97%)	469 (38.41%)	404 (33.09%)	153 (12.53%)	1,221
tuos	155 (18.17%)	297 (34.82%)	279 (32.71%)	122 (14.30%)	853
suos (sg./pl.)	56 (13.37%)	133 (31.74%)	141 (33.65%)	89 (21.24%)	419
noster	42 (19.53%)	93 (43.26%)	60 (27.91%)	20 (9.30%)	215
uoster	19 (19.79%)	46 (47.92%)	22 (22.92%)	9 (9.38%)	96
Total	467 (16.65%)	1,038 (37.02%)	906 (32.31%)	393 (14.02%)	2,804

The table ought to be read as follows: there are 1,221 forms of *meus*; of these, 195 are in position 1, that is, in front of their heads and separated from them; and these 195 tokens constitute 15.97 per cent of all first person possessives.

Several interesting facts emerge from this table. First, in general the most frequent position of the possessive is immediately in front of the head noun (37 per cent of all tokens). Placement immediately after the head noun is also frequent (32 per cent). What is astonishing is the overall frequency of hyperbaton (31 per cent). In early Latin prose, hyperbaton, especially with an intervening verb, is still rare and a feature of elevated registers (Adams (1971)). In Plautus, hyperbaton is so frequent that within the genre of Roman comedy it must be considered stylistically unmarked. It may well be an artificial feature of Plautine *Kunstsprache*, but because of its frequency it does not make sense to try and explain every single instance with stylistic reasons.

Two additional observations can be made. First, even though all possessives behave in roughly the same way, *meus*, *tuos* and *suos*, when compared with *noster* and *uoster*, seem to have a slight preference for positions 3 and 4, that is, a preference for following their head nouns. And second, in the case of *suos* the preference for position 4 is stronger than for *meus* and *tuos*. Since these preferences cannot be accounted for semantically or pragmatically, they seem to be metrically determined.

But is it correct to speak of a displacement of *meus*, *tuos* and *suos* rather than of a displacement of *noster* and *uoster*? I believe it is, because there are certain phrases, most notably with *causa* "for x's sake", where the possessive regularly precedes, but where in Plautus it can follow its head for metrical reasons. In Plautus *causa* is only attested with singular possessive pronouns. He has the type *mea causa* twelve times and the type *mea … causa* ten times. The type *causa mea* occurs thirteen times and only for metrical reasons, as it is practically restricted to iambic line endings.[30] In addition, we have the unnatural order *causa currendo tua* in *Mer.* 151, where *tua causa* would be impossible at line end and where *currendo causa tua* would violate Meyer's Law.[31]

With regard to my second observation, the higher frequency of *suos* in position 4 compared with *meus* and *tuos*, I have no real explanation. But at least the displacement is not completely random: as one might expect, many of the forms of *meus* and *tuos* in position 4 are at line end (69.45 per cent, 191 out of 275 forms), but with *suos* this tendency is even more pronounced (83.15 per cent, 74 out of 89 forms). Why Plautus should make greater use of it in the case of *suos* remains unclear, but at least it is clear that we are dealing with metrical licence, not with displacement for linguistic reasons.

Table 19.4 Focus and the position of possessives

Position 1	Position 2	Position 3	Position 4	Total
207 (44.33%)	317 (30.54%)	147 (16.24%)	43 (10.94%)	714 (25.47%)

We have observed two phenomena. First, hyperbaton, rare in early prose, is so common in Plautus that it is an unmarked feature within Plautine *Kunstsprache*. And second, while metre is important for word order in Plautus, it is not of such importance as to distort the regular speech patterns entirely, otherwise there would not be such an astonishing agreement in the placement of *meus, tuos* and *suos* on the one hand and of *noster* and *uoster* on the other.

The main factor that seems to exert influence on the position of possessive pronouns is their focal status, as shown in Table 19.4.

This table should be read as follows: there are 207 emphatic, contrastive possessive pronouns in position 1 (pre-modifier hyperbation).[32] These make up 44.33 per cent of all possessive pronouns in this position. What this table shows is that while we cannot predict on the basis of focus alone where Plautus would place a possessive pronoun, there are clear tendencies. Focal possessives are most likely to be in position 1, less likely to be in position 2, even less likely to be in position 3, and least likely to be in position 4.

Metre does indeed have an influence on word order in Plautus, but it is not an influence that is so great as to obliterate the syntactic and pragmatic rules determining word order in prose.

But let us now turn to other features of syntax.[33] As with morphology, a phenomenon that is archaic from the Classical perspective need not yet be archaic for the writers of comedy. Plautus and Terence regularly use the indicative in *quom*-clauses:

10 Praesagibat mi animus frustra me ire, quom exibam domo. (Pl. *Aul.* 178)
    I had a feeling I was going in vain when I left the house.

In Classical Latin the subjunctive is used when such clauses have causal or other nuances in addition to the purely temporal meaning. When Cicero quotes this passage (*Div.*1.65), he accidentally uses the subjunctive *exirem*; for him, the indicative was archaic in such contexts, while in Plautus and Terence the subjunctive could only occur because of attraction of mood. In later comedy, the subjunctive is reasonably well attested in *quom*-clauses; for instance, we find *quom emerem* "when I bought" in Afran. *com.* 233.

A clear instance of a construction that is unmarked in comedy, but used as an archaism in the Classical period, is *ne* + present imperative. As Vairel-Carron (1975) has shown, in Plautus and Terence the meaning is always inhibitive ("stop doing"); the action prohibited has already begun:

11 MEN: Eheu!
    CHR   Ne lacruma. (Ter. *Hau.* 83–84)
    MEN: Poor me!
    CHR   Stop crying.

Here Menedemus is already wailing when Chremes tells him not to. Such inhibitive prohibitions can of course also be expressed lexically, for instance with *desine / desiste* + infinitive, which may be the reason why *ne* + present imperative fell out of use. It is taken up again in Classical poetry, but there it is simply an archaism, without inhibitive force:

> 12 Equo ne credite, Teucri. (Verg. *A.* 2.48)
> Trojans, do not trust the horse.

Here *ne credite* can hardly mean "stop trusting", as the Trojans, or at least some of them, do not yet believe that the horse is a genuine gift.

Roman comedy, like Classical Latin, also contains many instances of the prohibitive type *ne* + perfect subjunctive. It is usually said that the perfect subjunctive continues old aorist usages which have parallels in Greek (μή + aorist subjunctive) and Sanskrit (*mā* + aorist injunctive). Some Latin perfect stems continue old perfect stems, others continue old aorist stems. What is interesting is that the type *ne* + perfect subjunctive is excluded if the perfect is reduplicating and thus continues an old perfect (Magariños (1939)); this restriction no longer applies in the Classical period. Equally important is the fact that this type is also avoided if the perfect is a *u / v*-perfect (types *monui* "I have admonished" and *laudaui* "I have praised") (de Melo (2007a)); this restriction indicates that we are also dealing with old perfects here.[34]

A feature which has sometimes been classified as colloquial,[35] but on closer inspection turns out to be an archaism, is the use of the present infinitive in accusative and infinitive constructions where Classical Latin demands the future. This usage is an archaism only from the Classical perspective; in Plautus and Terence it is still quite normal, although we can observe a certain diachronic decline of the construction when we compare the two authors.[36] Strictly speaking, the "future" infinitive indicates posteriority, not future tense as such, and the "present" infinitive mostly indicates simultaneity, also with past events, and not present tense as such; but I will retain the traditional terminology here. The two infinitives, both with future reference, can be seen side by side in the following passage:

> 13 TRA: Dic te daturum, ut abeat. THEO: Egon dicam dare? (Pl. *Mos.* 633)
> TRA: Say that you will give it, so that he goes away.
> THEO: I should say that I'm giving it?

In de Melo (2007c) I have examined the accusative and infinitive constructions in Plautus and Terence after twenty superordinate verbs like *dico* "I say" or *iuro* "I swear". It appears that the most important factor influencing tense choice is telicity. This concept can best be illustrated with two English examples:

> 14 I ran home.
> 15 I ran.

The first example is telic because it contains a natural endpoint. The second example is atelic and contains no such inherent endpoint, although of course no one would assume that the running continues for good. A simple interruption test can make things clearer:

> 16 I stopped running home. → I have not (yet) run home.
> 17 I stopped running. → I have run.

Table 19.5 Telicity and tense in the accusative and infinitive construction

	Future infinitive	*Present infinitive, future meaning*	*Total*
Telic	111	74	185
Atelic	98	6	104

If a telic event is interrupted, the endpoint has not been reached, so in **16** the speaker has not reached home. On the other hand, if an atelic event is interrupted, there is no inherent endpoint, so the event can already be predicated as in **17**.

In Plautus and Terence, the present infinitive with future meaning is almost restricted to telic events, see Table 19.5.

If an event is telic, both future infinitives and present infinitives with future meaning can be used. If an event is atelic, the present infinitive with future reference is very rare and the future infinitive almost obligatory.

These patterns make sense from a diachronic perspective. The future infinitive is a fairly late creation in the history of the Latin language; earlier, the present infinitive was a true non-past infinitive and could be used with present or with future force. But when the future infinitive was created, it gradually ousted the present infinitive with future force.

But why did the future infinitive oust atelic present infinitives with future force before it ousted telic ones? Again some English examples can make things clearer:

18 I'm writing you a cheque.
19 I'm going to write you a cheque.
20 I'm dreaming about my next holiday.
21 I'm going to dream about my next holiday.

Under the right circumstances, the first two sentences, both of which refer to telic events, can be used interchangeably. The present progressive can indicate that I have already begun to write a cheque, while this is less likely with the *going to*-future. But in neither case has the cheque already been written; in both sentences the final conclusion of the action is still outstanding. The second pair of sentences cannot normally be used interchangeably. The event is an atelic one. With the present progressive the action is in full swing and even if it is interrupted, some dreaming has already taken place. With the *going to*-future the event has not yet begun.

We can thus see that the distinction between present and future is much clearer among atelic events. This is the reason why in Latin the future infinitive became obligatory here first, not among the telic events where such a distinction is much more difficult to draw.

We have now examined several syntactic features which set the language of early comedy apart from Classical Latin, yet are still unmarked in pre-Classical Latin. But Roman comedy also contains features that were already archaic when the plays were staged. One of these is the use of *quisque* to introduce generalizing relative clauses ("whoever"):

22 Nam meum est ballista pugnum,[37] cubitus catapulta est mihi,
umerus aries, tum genu ad quemqu' iecero ad terram dabo,
dentilegos omnis mortalis faciam, quemque offendero. (Pl. *Capt.* 796–798)

For my fist is a stone, my elbow is an arrow, my shoulder is a battering ram, and I'll knock to the ground anyone I direct my knee at. I'll make all mortals tooth-collectors, whomever I meet.

In this passage we have two instances of *quemque* where Classical authors would have used the generalizing *quemcumque*. Interestingly, the old man overhearing this talk says in line 811 that our speaker is issuing decrees. This usage of *quisque* does indeed seem to be at home in legal or at least formal language. In Plautus we also find it in *Mer.* 20 in a formal prologue, and in the *Miles* in lines 156 and 160, both in a mock law, in line 460 in a threat, and also in line 1391, where no such a rationale seems to apply. Terence has the same usage twice, in *Hec.* 65 and 386, both of them in neutral dialogue.

Syntactic colloquialism is more common in comedy than syntactic archaism.[38] Some constructions associated with formal language are rare in comedy, except in highly marked passages. The ablative absolute, for example, is restricted to battle reports, prayers and the like.[39] The construction already shows certain signs of fossilization in Plautus: we find *praesente nobis* "in our presence" in *Am.* 400, with irregular number agreement (singular participle and plural pronoun), presumably formed on the basis of fossilized *me praesente* "in my presence". Similarly, Pomponius (*com.* 168) has *praesente testibus* "in the presence of witnesses", with singular participle but plural noun. In general, comedy avoids complex sentences; clauses are shorter than in formal prose or poetry and subordination is rarer.[40] This goes hand in hand with a relatively low frequency of passives since there is less need to maintain clarity by keeping the same subject in one main clause and several subordinate ones.[41]

This shows that a construction which is not restricted to any one register may nevertheless be a stylistic marker if it has a high or low frequency in a specific text type. Other constructions have been considered colloquial in themselves, but not always on good grounds. Among them are anacoluthon, "confusion" between accusative and ablative, and pleonastic strengthening of possessives:

23 Tu si te di amant, agere tuam rem occasio est. (Pl. *Ps.* 659)
    You, if the gods love you, there's an opportunity to do what's good for you.

24 Numero mihi in mentem fuit
    dis aduenientem gratias pro meritis agere atque alloqui? (Pl. *Am.* 180–181)
    When I arrived, it didn't occur to me too quickly to thank the gods for their good turns and to address them, did it?

25 Suo sibi suco uiuont. (Pl. *Capt.* 81)
    They live on their own juice.

In 23 there is a clear anacoluthon: the speaker begins with a nominative pronoun, as if he wanted to say "you can do", but then switches to an impersonal construction after the conditional clause by saying "there's an opportunity". Anacoluthon is more at home in spoken than in written language because in speech there is less time to plan an utterance. However, dangling nominatives are not necessarily always colloquial. At least sometimes they do have the pragmatic function of emphasizing the agent, as is the case here. In **24** we find *in mentem fuit* instead of *in mente fuit* or *in mentem uenit*, in other words, we find the accusative of direction with a verb that is not normally regarded as describing motion. Here, however, *fuit* must mean "it came" rather than "it was". As Adams (2007) 348 points out, the phenomenon is well known from English as well, where we can say *I've been to America*, combining a past tense of *to be* with a prepositional phrase indicating direction.[42] Petersmann (2002–2003) 99–100 shows that in Plautus this construction is restricted to lower-class speakers like slaves. The same construction existed throughout the history of Latin in colloquial registers; Spanish went one step further: *fui* is the simple past of both *soy* "I am" and *voy* "I am going".[43] In **25**, *sibi* does not modify *uiuont*. The reflexive pronoun strengthens the possessive *suo* and gives it particular emphasis ("their own" rather than just "their"). This construction type is often regarded as colloquial. It is better classified as unmarked in Plautus and Terence, even though later on a purist like Cicero avoided it.[44]

Irregular agreement patterns are more likely to occur in spoken language or imitations thereof than in written forms, but not everything that looks irregular is the result of confusion between two grammatical patterns. A case in point is *uterque*, which in comedy sometimes takes plural verb agreement. The Classical rules are straightforward: *ambo* means "both" and thus always takes plural agreement, while *uterque* means "each of the two" and takes singular agreement because it looks at two entities separately. The plural *utrique* is possible if each of the two entities consists of several persons or things, and in that case the verb has to be plural. In comedy, the singular *uterque* can also take plural agreement simply because two entities are involved; but in some cases this plural agreement is in fact unavoidable and can hardly be called a feature of colloquial speech:

> **26** Curemus aequam uterque partem. (Ter. *Ad.* 150)
> Let us each look after our fair part.

If *uterque* refers to the third person, the singular is expected and the plural looks unusual from the Classical perspective. The reason is that the third person singular is inherently vague and without further specification can refer to anyone other than speaker or addressee. But the first and second person singular each refer to one single, specified person, the speaker or the addressee; any other participant is excluded. If *uterque* is used for the speaker plus someone else, or the addressee plus someone else, there is no choice but to use plural verb agreement. In such cases the plural verb agreement can hardly be considered a colloquialism.[45]

If we now look at *uterque* with a third person verb form, we have to exclude all cases where the verb is in the singular and the two entities are things rather than persons, because even in co-ordinations of the type *x et y* singular agreement is the norm here. This leaves us with eight tokens of *uterque* in Plautus and five in Terence where the reference is to humans. Plautus has singular agreement in four cases and plural agreement in the other four; Terence has singular agreement in three cases and plural agreement in the remaining two.

What about plural forms like *utrique*? If we have *utrique* as subject, the verb is of course always in the plural. But is *utrique* always used in the Classical way, with reference to two entities, each of which consists of several persons or things? The answer is no, but that does not mean that the unclassical usages are colloquial:

27 Deinde utrique imperatores in medium exeunt. (Pl. *Am.* 223)
    Then the two commanders come forward into the centre.

Here there are two commanders, one on each side, so the Classical construction would be *uterque imperator ... exit*. But the passage as a whole can hardly be classified as colloquial; it is from an elaborate, highly stylized battle report. Apart from this instance, we find plural forms like *utrique* where Classical prose would contain the singular in Pl. *Mos.* 1137 and Ter. *An.* 287–288. The Classical usage is followed in Pl. *Truc.* 152 and Ter. *Hau.* 394 (twice).

Another alleged colloquialism is the ellipsis of the subject accusative in the accusative and infinitive construction. However, on closer examination it turns out that this kind of ellipsis is equally frequent in tragedy and formal prose. In fact, ellipsis seems to be favoured by factors other than register because it is particularly frequent if the infinitive is in the future active or the perfect passive.[46] Here the explanation has to do with the morphology of the infinitives in question. The future active and perfect passive infinitives both contain participles, and participles are marked for the gender and number of the subject accusative, which makes it easier to retrieve if it is left out.

Pleonasm, the use of more words than necessary to convey a concept, is extremely common in comedy. Plautus uses *propere celeriter* "fast (and) quickly" (*Rud.* 1323) and *nemo ... homo* "nobody" (*Am.* 566) (lit. "nobody man"), among many others. The latter is remarkable because historically speaking, *nemo* is a contraction already containing a form of *homo*. In Caecil. *com.* 273 we find *oscitans hietansque* "gaping and opening the mouth", and Terence also uses this stylistic device. Alliterative pleonasm is particularly common. Pleonasm is often colloquial, but not always, especially when alliterative: it is also a feature of Roman religious language, where *asyndeton bimembre*, the co-ordination of two synonyms (or antonyms) without co-ordinator, is frequent.

Roman comedies are adaptations of Greek plays, and sometimes they render the Greek fairly closely. The question naturally arises if there is interference from Greek syntax in the Latin. It seems that on the whole the answer is negative. There is one clear instance in Plautus where it could be argued that the Latin syntax is modelled on the Greek:

28 Argenti uiginti minae med ad mortem appulerunt,
    quas hodie adulescens Diabolus ipsi daturus dixit. (Pl. *As.* 633–634)
    Twenty silver minas have driven me to my death; young Diabolus said he'd give them to her today.

After *dixit* "he said" we normally get the accusative and infinitive construction. The accusative is commonly left out, but the participle constituting the non-finite element should be in the accusative. Instead, it is in the nominative, as is customary in Greek when the subject of the finite verb and the subject of the infinitive are the same. There is a similar case in Catullus:

> 29   Phaselus ille quem uidetis, hospites,
>   ait fuisse nauium celerrimus. (Catul. 4.1–2)
>   That pinnace you see, my friends, says she was once the fastest of ships.

As Catullus consciously imitates the language of Hellenistic poetry, the nominative with infinitive is hardly surprising, but the phenomenon is unexpected in Plautus.

It should also be noted that *phaselus* is masculine in Catullus, as in Greek. In comedy words for "ship" can also be feminine, as was common throughout Latin; compare *lembi … duae* "two ships" in Turpil. *com.* 98. Comedy also has a tendency to nativize Greek adjectives, as in *columnas monolitas* "monolithic columns" (Laber. *mim.* 38); in Greek this adjective has no separate feminine endings.

Elsewhere Greek influence can be detected, but it is perhaps better not to speak of interference as the Latin syntactic rules are not violated. Adams (2003a) 518 remarks that demonstrative pronouns, mostly *hic* "this" and *ille* "that", are unusually frequent in the delayed plot narration of Plautus' *Miles gloriosus* (from line 88 onwards). Typically they are combined with nouns indicating character roles. This is in accordance with Greek usage: in Greek plays characters typically have standard names associated with them, which is why prologues generally mention the roles, in combination with the articles, rather than the actual names of the characters. Plautus seems to have translated the Greek article with demonstrative pronouns. However, these demonstratives have not lost their deictic force: in the prologue *hic* is still used for people near the speaker and *ille* for those further away.

Lexicon

In the same way that much of the syntax of Roman comedy is neutral and stylistically unmarked, most of its lexicon is shared with other genres. However, as with syntax, we can distinguish three particularly obvious areas that are not neutral and stylistically unmarked: Grecism, colloquialism, and archaism. In addition, women's speech is in many respects lexically differentiated from men's. Sexually charged words will also need to be looked at briefly.

The use of foreign words in comedy deserves special attention. If we except Greek, it is remarkable how little use is made of foreigners' speech as a source of entertainment. In Plautus' *Poenulus* we find a Punic passage in lines 940–949[47] and some individual Punic words and phrases later on. The Punic language parts were clearly not understood by many in the audience, but at least the content of the longer passage must have been obvious to the listeners because of what precedes and follows and of course because of the acting. Interestingly, Plautus does not use the Punic language as a source of amusement, only the slave Milphio's ignorance of it and the subsequent misunderstandings.[48]

The only other foreign language used extensively in comedy is Greek. Terence uses it far more sparingly than Plautus. However, the Greek words in these authors do not seem to be taken directly from the Attic originals, even where they are in the Attic dialect. For instance, Plautus uses *apage* "go away" and *euge* "hurray", both of them Attic words.

Yet *apage* also occurs in Afranius (*com.* 383), a writer of *comoedia togata*, a genre not based on Greek texts, even though there may be indirect influence from Greek plays via the *fabula palliata*; and *euge* is also attested as an expression of surprise (Pl. *Bac.* 991), a usage alien at least to Attic Greek. The Greek of comedy often has Doric characteristics and thus reflects the Greek spoken in Italy; in addition, Plautus' Greek also contains idiosyncratic features not belonging to any real Greek dialect.

The Greek in Plautine comedy is not the Greek of the originals he adapted but rather the Greek spoken in Rome and the rest of Italy, and its connotations are not prestige and education but servile status and frivolity.[49] Thus the word for trick is *machina* in Plautus, not the Attic form *mēchanē*. The vowel weakening in the medial syllable shows that this word was not a Plautine borrowing, but goes back some way. Similarly, the Acheron, a river in the underworld, masculine in Greek and Classical Latin, is called *Acheruns* by Plautus, has an unexplained heavy first syllable and is feminine (*Capt.* 999). This word may have come into Latin via Etruscan; the feminine gender in Plautus may have to do with the fact that he treats the word as a place name rather than a river.[50] Such adaptations are common: at Pl. *Persa* 394 the word for "witticisms" is *logi*, with the Latin ending rather than Greek -*oi*. "Blows with the fist" are transmitted as *colaphos* (accusative plural) in *Capt.* 88, again with a Latin ending. This word, incidentally, originated in Sicily and spread from there to Greece on the one hand and Italy on the other.[51] The spelling in our editions nicely corresponds to Greek κόλαφοι, but we should not forget that the Greek aspirate was probably pronounced as a plain stop in Plautus (and certainly written -*p*-), a state of affairs reflected in Italian *colpo* "blow". Plautus is also fond of the Greek verbal suffix -ίζειν, rendered as -*issare*. Some of his coinages look quite Greek, for instance *cyathissare* "ladle out wine" (cf. *Men.* 303), while others are clearly formed by Plautus himself, such as *graecissare* "assume Greek airs" (cf. *Men.* 11); Greeks did not refer to themselves as *Graeci* when speaking Greek. Plautus can also adapt Greek adjectives and adverbs and give them Latin endings. The Greek adjective βασιλικός "royal" has βασιλικῶς as its adverb, but Plautus prefers the Latin endings and says *basilicus* and *basilice*. The semantic shift of this word in Plautus is remarkable. In *Persa* 462 *exornatu's basilice* means "you're dressed up magnificently", not as a king, but as a Persian merchant. And in *Epid.* 56 *interii basilice* means "I've perished completely", with the adverb being little more than an intensifier. Such usages have no parallels in formal Greek. Fraenkel (2007) 130–132 points out that they are typical of slaves, Plautus' favourite role, and that we therefore seem to be dealing with a purely Plautine mannerism.

Plautus also makes up his own Greek puns. In *Mil.* 436 Philocomasium, pretending to be her own twin sister, calls herself Dicea,[52] that is, Δικαία, "the just one". Sceledrus does not believe her and says:

30 Ἄδικος es tu, non δικαία (*Mil.* 438)
　　You're unjust, not Justine.

Other jokes are truly bilingual. In *Ps.* 210–211 the pimp speaks of *oliui* δύναμιν which must mean "a vast amount of oil". But δύναμις does not have the meaning "vast amount" in Greek. The puzzle can be solved if we translate into Latin: δύναμις normally means "power" and in this sense corresponds to Latin *uis*, but the Latin word also means "vast amount", and this is what is behind the Greek δύναμις here. Another case of translator's Greek can be found in the *Pseudolus*:

31 PSEVD: quis istic est? CAL: Charinus. PSEVD: Euge! Iam χάριν τούτῳ ποιῶ.
    CHAR: Quin tu si quid opust mi audacter imperas? PSEVD: Tam gratia.
           (Pl. *Ps.* 712–713)
    PSEUD: Who is that?
    CAL: Charinus.
    PSEUD: Goodness! Now *je dis non, merci à lui*.
    CHAR: Why don't you command me boldly if you need anything?
    PSEUD: Thanks, but no thanks.

In this passage, Calidorus brings Charinus as a helper for Pseudolus, who is unimpressed. His Greek exclamation *euge* can hardly mean "hurray" here, as it would in real Greek; Pseudolus is surprised and disappointed. His exclamation is followed by a phrase of translator's Greek, combined with the Latin *iam*. χάριν τούτῳ ποιῶ does not mean "I am grateful to him" (a phrase which in Latin would contain the verb *habere* or *referre*), but the same as *gratiam alicui facere de aliqua re*, "to decline someone's offer with thanks", a phrase found in *Mos.* 1130 and repeated in a shortened version in the next line here. While this wrong use of a Greek phrase is likely to be facetious, not all usages deviating from the standard language are intended as humorous: *andron* means "men's quarter" in Greek, but in Vitruvius (6.7.5) it is a technical term in the meaning "corridor", a usage alien to Greek, but not intended to amuse.

Particularly interesting are concepts for which Plautus uses both Latin and Greek words.[53] For instance, Plautus refers to a banker as either *argentarius* or *tarpezita* (Greek τραπεζίτης), and to a sword as either *gladius* or *machaera* (Greek μάχαιρα). At first sight, one could think that the Greek terms have been taken directly from the Greek plays. But the situation is more complicated. The Plautine Greek word for "banker" is *tarpezita* (probably spelt *tarpessita* by Plautus), not *trapezita* or *trapessita*, as one might expect from Attic τραπεζίτης. Presumably the Plautine form comes from Italian Greek. Plautus uses this Greek form to give his plays a Greek atmosphere, whereas *argentarius* occurs in passages in which Plautus talks about Roman life.[54] *Machaera* (an Attic form) is used by Plautus to refer to the sword of Greek mercenaries,[55] while *gladius* is used elsewhere.[56] Nevertheless, Plautus seems to have taken this word from the Greek he heard in Italy rather than from the Greek comedies he was adapting, for the word for sword in Greek comedy is σπάθη (borrowed later as *spatha*, with Romance reflexes[57]).

Plautus, but not Terence, also mocks non-Roman Latin. In *Trin.* 609 the phrase *tam modo* "just now" is called Praenestine, and while an overt value judgment is not made, the tone seems to be mocking, as people from Praeneste are not appreciated; in *Bac.* 21 for instance they are described as boastful, and Naev. *com.* 21–24 pokes fun at the inhabitants of Praeneste and Lanuvium. The eponymous hero of the *Truculentus*, who uses the absurd form *rabo* for *arrabo* "part-payment", also justifies this usage on the grounds that the inhabitants of Praeneste say *conea* instead of *ciconia* "stork" without a first syllable (lines 688–691).[58] The character Truculentus is in fact an interesting source of malapropisms not used by any other figure. For instance, he replies to the greeting *salue*

Table 19.6   *Seruos* and *seruolus* in Plautus and Terence

	seruos	*seruolus*	*Total*	*seruolus (%)*
Plautus	267	12	279	4.03
Terence	23	7	30	22.22

"be well" with the words *non salueo* "I'm diswell" (line 259, considered unidiomatic by Sacerdos *GL* VI.433.7–8).

Roman comedy is a good source for lexical colloquialisms, but one has to look at each word individually rather than at entire classes of words, otherwise erroneous conclusions are unavoidable. For instance, interjections are frequent in comedy, but not all of them are colloquial. At least some types are also frequent in tragedy. They seem to be a feature of dialogue rather than intrinsically colloquial. Similarly, it is often said that diminutives are colloquial. Table 19.6 counts the tokens of *seruos/serua* "slave" and *seruolus/seruola* "(little) slave" in Plautus and Terence.[59]

Even if we were to say that all diminutives are colloquial, we could not say it of a great number of tokens. The instances in Plautus amount to an almost insignificant percentage, and while the percentage of diminutives is higher in Terence (almost one-quarter), the absolute figures are low. Still, Terence does seem to favour the diminutive. But diminutives can only really be colloquial if they are equivalent to the non-diminutive forms. If a *seruolus* is a small or young slave, for instance, the usage can hardly count as colloquial. This is not the case in any of the tokens in Plautus and Terence. But usages derived from the meaning of small size are not colloquial either.[60] If the term is used affectionately or contemptuously, we cannot speak of a colloquialism. The following two examples show a contemptuous usage and one where the diminutive is equivalent to the non-diminutive form:

32 Nam mihi quidem hercle qui minus liceat deo minitarier
populo, ni decedat mihi, quam seruolo in comoediis? (Pl. *Am.* 986–987)
Why should I, a god, not be allowed to threaten people if they don't get out of my way just as much as some paltry slave in comedies?

33 Modo eam reliqui ad portum in naui et seruolum.
Sed quid currentem seruom a portu conspicor? (Pl. *Mer.* 108–109)
I just left her and the slave at the harbour on the ship. But why am I seeing my slave coming running from the harbour?

In the first example, Mercury clearly despises human slaves, which is why he uses the diminutive. In the second example, on the other hand, the same person is once referred to as a *seruolus* and once as a *seruos*; the diminutive form seems nothing more than a metrically convenient variant at line end. Half of the twelve diminutives in Plautus and four of the seven in Terence seem to have a nuance of contempt of one sort or another. This leaves us with barely any tokens that could be colloquial. The figure is too low to draw reliable conclusions because where we have a diminutive and a non-diminutive, it is not always the former which is colloquial. Housman (1930) demonstrated that the refined word for "donkey" is the diminutive *asellus*, while the more rustic word is *asinus*. In Plautus, *asellus* occurs only once, in a formal speech (*Aul.* 229), while *asinus* occurs twelve times; and in Terence only *asinus* occurs, found thrice, each time as an insult.

In the Romance languages there is a tendency to continue frequentative verbs rather than the Latin base verbs; thus French *chanter* "sing" comes from *cantare*, not *canere*. Again, one has to be careful not to regard the frequentatives in Roman comedy as inherently more colloquial; many of them still do have the original frequentative function.

Many words in comedy are quoted by later grammarians and lexicographers as archaisms. Naturally some of them were still unmarked in Early Latin. Nouns like *floccum* or *naucum* had gone out of usage before Plautus,[61] but the phrase *aliquem non flocci/nauci facere* remained common and unmarked. Of course this does not mean that the original lexical meaning of such words was still clear; in fact, there is evidence that it was not:

> **34** Qui homo timidus erit in rebus dubiis, nauci non erit;
> atque equidem quid id esse dicam uerbum nauci nescio. (Pl. *Mos.* 1041–2)
>
> Someone who is timid in emergencies will be worth naught; and I don't know what I should say the word "naught" means.

In other instances the lexemes employed in Roman comedy were already archaic at the time of writing and their use is intended to create a more solemn, or mock-solemn, atmosphere. In Plautus we find the word *mactare* eleven times. Originally this was a religious term meaning "to honour someone with something". In Plautus it is only used mock-solemnly, in phrases like *mactare aliquem infortunio*, "endow someone with a beating". Interestingly, Novius has both the religious meaning and the other in *com.* 39.

Terence uses certain lexical items that are still unmarked in Plautus to characterize old men, a clear sign that they were going out of fashion; *satias* "sufficient amount" and *praestolari* "wait for" belong here.[62] *Prognatus* "begotten/son" is already archaic in Plautus. He uses the term in jocular phrases (e.g. *Epid.* 35) or when there is genuine pathos reminiscent of tragedy (e.g. *Rud.* 217).

Imitations of tragedy are in fact not infrequent. One feature of Roman tragedy is the frequency with which complex compounds are employed. This feature was taken over from Greek tragedy. Latin is a language in which compounding follows severe restrictions; the freedom with which Plautus uses often absurd compounds like *sandaligerula* "sandal-bearer" (*Trin.* 253) has nothing to do with natural tendencies of the Latin language and everything to do with artificial, mostly jocular imitation of Roman tragedy.[63]

Most lines of Roman comedy are spoken by men. Where women make an appearance on stage, their speech is clearly differentiated from men's.[64] Adams (1984) examined the use of certain oaths with emphatic functions, among other things, and noted that only men use *hercle* and *mehercle* "by Hercules", while only women use *ecastor* and *mecastor* "by Castor". By contrast, *pol* and *edepol* "by Pollux" are used by both sexes. Women also use more markers of politeness than men, for instance *opsecro* "I beg you". *Amabo* "please" (literally "I'll love you") is almost exclusively employed by women. Similarly, women are far more likely than men to modify a vocative by adding the intimate *mi* "my dear", a tendency which is especially noticeable with personal names.

I shall end this chapter with a few remarks on sexual vocabulary.[65] Roman comedy is not averse to obscenities. Plautus contains far more than Terence, who is rather tame in this respect. But both the *palliata* and the *togata* avoid words considered indecent, which are found commonly in the *Atellana* and in mime:

> **35** Continuo ad te centuriatim current qui penem petent. (Pompon. *com.* 149)
> Immediately a large number of people will run to you seeking out your penis.

> **36** *A:*   Numne aliter hunce pedicabis? *B:*   Quo modo?
>   *A:*   Video, adulescenti nostro caedis hirulam. (Laber. *mim.* 34–35)
>   *A:*   Are you going to bugger him in another way?
>   *B:*   How do you mean?
>   *A:*   I can see you're cutting our young fellow's intestines to pieces.

These two examples, from the *Atellana* and mime respectively, illustrate vocabulary that is avoided in the more refined genres; neither Plautus nor Terence use the words *penis* or *pedicare*, although they do have more oblique ways to express the same concepts.

FURTHER READING

Roman comedy, especially the *fabula palliata*, has received much scholarly attention in recent years. The sheer amount of publications can be rather confusing. A good starting-point for anyone interested in Roman metre is Questa (2007), a lucid and detailed introduction. Moore (2008) discusses the question which types of verse were accompanied by music. Haffter (1934) remains the best study of the influence of verse type on register. Another good source of information for register variation is Hofmann (1951/2003). The clearest introduction to syntax in comedy is Lindsay (1907), even though certain views entertained there are no longer tenable. Bennett (1910–1914) is a standard work on early syntax, but best used as a reference book. In de Melo (2007b) I discuss verbal morphology and syntax at length. Lexical questions are handled admirably by Shipp (1955), where the use of Greek words is treated, and Adams (1982a and 1984), where sexual vocabulary and female speech are discussed. Fraenkel (2007) is a classic on Plautine translation and adaptation techniques; the book is best read in conjunction with Handley (1968), where a Menander fragment of some length is compared with its adaptation by Plautus.

NOTES

1   The standard editions are Leo (1895–1896) and Lindsay (1904–1905) for Plautus and Kauer and Lindsay (1926) for Terence.

2   Ribbeck (1897–1898) contains the fragments of all comic and tragic dramatists, but for genres other than the *palliata* newer editions exist.

3   Gellius (2. 23) compares three passages from Menander's *Plocion* with Caecilius' adaptation; for the sixty lines of Menander's *Dis exapaton* and the Plautine adaptation in the *Bacchides* see Handley (1968).

4   Edited by Daviault (1981) and Guardì (1985).

5   Edition by Frassinetti (1967).

6   Fragments in Bonaria (1965).

7   See Moore (2008) for ancient evidence.

8   See Haffter (1934) and Happ (1967).

9   For details see e.g. Redard (1956).

10 This last spelling reflects a long closed monophthong whose quality was in between original long *i* and original long *e*.

11 Biville (1990–1995) I.139.

12 Details in Leumann (1977) 193–195); for an ancient testimony see Quint. *Inst.* 1.7.7.

13 In the funerary poem in *CIL* I².1211.2 we find the phrase *pulcrai feminae*, "of a beautiful woman", which contains two genitives with monosyllabic case endings, despite the difference in spelling.

14 Details in Leo (1912) 342–343.

15 The best introduction to early prosody and metre is Questa (2007).

16 Thus Priscian and others; Skutsch puts the corrupt *in spineto* from Charisius and others into the text.

17 Third-conjugation futures in -*bo* are rare innovations that never caught on. An example is *uiuebo* "I shall live" in Novius *com.* 10.

18 Data from de Melo (2009). I am leaving out of the discussion forms like *aibam* and *aiebam*, which historically speaking belong to a different conjugation class. They are also discussed in de Melo (2009).

19 See Meiser (1998) 218.

20 In *CIL* I².365 (*c.* 150 BCE) we also find the form *zenatuo*; the script is Faliscan, but the language almost standard Latin.

21 This ending in turn comes from the pronouns.

22 See Gerschner (2002) 77–80 for details.

23 The attested forms are *eapse* (nominative and ablative), *eopse*, *eumpse* and *eampse*.

24 Discussed in detail in de Melo (2007b).

25 The inherited aorist stem of *facere* survives in the Latin perfect stem *fec-*, and the geminate -*ss-* in *amasso* can hardly be an original aorist marker.

26 See Wackernagel (2009) 316.

27 Despite appearances, the third person plural does not have the full-grade suffix -*ie-*; it has the third person ending -*ent*.

28 Italian *fecero* and French *firent* are both reflexes of Latin *fecĕrunt*.

29 On personal pronouns see Adams (1994c) and (1999b).

30 The only exception is in the middle of *Cur.* 150, a cretic tetrameter; since this metre is relatively rigid, it does in general not allow for much freedom in word order.

31 On Meyer's Law see Questa (2007) 393–413.

32 Obviously, it is often difficult to judge what was intended as focal and what was not. With possessive pronouns the task is slightly easier because focus is only possible if there is a contrast involved.

33 Lindsay (1907) is still a useful introduction.

34 If Rix (1992) is correct, this Latin perfect type developed through univerbation of perfect active participles and the copula.

35 E.g. by Kühner *et al.* (1976).

36 Also noted by Hofmann and Szantyr (1965) 358.

37 For *pugnum* see *GL* V.587.12; the Palatine manuscripts have *meust … pugnus*.

38 For a clear discussion of the problems associated with colloquialism and with special emphasis on Plautus see Hofmann (1951/2003).

39 Data in Bennett (1910–1914) II.368–372.

40 Interestingly, Plautus has a far greater tendency to let verse end and clause end coincide than Terence (Deufert (2007)).

41 For Terence see de Melo (2007d).

42 Similarly in Dutch, where a literal translation of this sentence is perfectly grammatical (*Ik ben naar de VS geweest*).

43 The opposite phenomenon occurs in the type *in lustra iacuisti* (Pl. *Cas.* 242), "you lay in the brothel". Here we might expect the ablative, but *iaceo* effectively functions as the passive of *iacio* "throw".

44 See de Melo (2010) 84–87. Apuleius, the great imitator of Plautine diction, is unusually fond of the construction, but uses it as an archaism and often without the emphasis it always has in early Latin.

45 This is the only instance in Terence. In Plautus the situation occurs four times (*Bac.* 755, *Cas.* 371, *Epid.* 259, *Men.* 1105).

46 For data see de Melo (2006).

47 For details see Gratwick (1971); lines 930–939 possibly constitute a later adaptation or correction of lines 940–949, which had become obscure in the process of transmission; and lines 950–960 are probably also a later translation of the Punic.

48 By contrast, fun is made of an African's (possibly a Carthaginian's) language in Plautus' *Caecus uel Praedones* (fr. x Lindsay).

49 Shipp (1953) 112.

50 The Greek name *Ganymedes* also came into Latin via Etruscan *Catmite*. In Plautus, *Catamitus* can still be a personal name (*Men.* 144), while later on the word usually indicates a catamite or the passive member in homosexual intercourse.

51 Shipp (1979) 326–327.

52 The scansion is *Dicĕa*, despite the Greek form. In the same way we get *Pellaeo* "from Pella" (*As.* 397) next to *Pellĕo* (*As.* 333).

53 The best discussion of this is in Shipp (1955).

54 *Argentarius* also occurs in the post-Plautine prologue to the *Casina* (l. 25); the reference is specifically to the bankers the Roman audience has to deal with.

55 In *Bac.* 887 a Greek soldier is said to have a *machaera*.

56 The phrase *uorsis gladiis* (*Cas.* 344) comes from gladiatorial (and thus Roman) fights; it refers to putting away the blunt display weapons and taking up the ones for the real fight.

57 Italian *spada*, Spanish *espada*, French *épée*.

58 On the distinctive vocalism of *conea* see Adams (2007) 111.

59 The feminine forms are rare because the normal word for a female slave is *ancilla/ancillula*.

60 The same holds true if the diminutive is used for disambiguation, as at Pl. *Cur.* 316, where *uentulum* (acc.) "little wind" is used in order to make clear that the speaker meant the noun when he said *uentum*, not the participle of *uenire* "come".

61 Naevius (com. 105) can still say *eius noctem nauco ducere*, "book a night with her for virtually nothing".

62 More examples in Maltby (1975) 237–238.

63 For compounds in comedy see Oniga (1988).

64 A useful collection of ancient testimonia regarding differences in speech between men and women is Gilleland (1980).

65 The best discussion of this semantic field is in Adams (1982a).

CHAPTER 20

The Language of Latin Epic and Lyric Poetry[1]

Rolando Ferri

Theories of "Poetic Language" in Greek and Roman Critics

There is no ancient treatise devoted to "poetic language" as such, but several ancient critics, most famously Aristotle, but also Philodemus, Dionysius of Halicarnassus and the so-called "Longinus," dealt with poetry, and its effects.[2] Aristotle, in particular, in both *Poetics* and *Rhetoric*, made some influential observations as to what he viewed as qualities of the "poetic language," mostly the use of compound and "strange," "defamiliarized" words on the one hand, and of metaphors and rhetorical figures generally (mostly in *Poetics* 1457–1459 and, even more clearly, in the third book of the *Rhetoric* 1404a–b, where he uses the expression ποιήσεως λέξις for "the language of poetry," 1404a 29). For Aristotle, however, in *Poetics* at least, the distinctive feature of poetry was, to put it simply, the "plot."[3]

A later Greek theoretician living in the age of Augustus, Dionysius of Halicarnassus, in περὶ συνθέσεως ὀνομάτων ("On arrangement of words"), gave more emphasis to the "arrrangement" or "order" of the words. Both these Greek scholars downplay the role of meter; on the contrary, the Latin grammatical and scholarly tradition would emphasize metrical constraints in analyzing linguistic usage in poetry.[4]

Our Latin sources do not appear to employ a general definition of *lingua poetica*, or *lingua poetarum*, although close is Cic. *de Orat.* 2.61, *poetas ... quasi alia quadam lingua locutos* "the poets almost speak a different language" (from the orator's viewpoint). Later grammarians who use the expression *poetica elocutio*, or *poetica licentia* never use it in a general sense, but refer to a precise poetic passage which seems to them irregular or removed from either the general usage or the written standard.[5] We must also keep in

A Companion to the Latin Language, First Edition. Edited by James Clackson.
© 2011 Blackwell Publishing Ltd. Published 2011 by Blackwell Publishing Ltd.

mind that, for Roman scholars, to elaborate the concept that there was a distinct language of poetry was more difficult, because, contrary to what had happened in Greece, no real or stylized version of a Latin regional variety or dialect had shaped the language of poetry in a recognizable way.

Roman critics who come closest to the notion of an idiolect of poetry, foremost among them Quintilian and Cicero, are teachers of rhetoric, and this has the implication that poetry is always observed as a term of comparison, often setting the limit which the good speaker will not trespass. Among the few Roman writers who discuss poetry in its own right is Horace, both in *Satires* and in *Epistles* 2.3, the so-called *Ars Poetica*. Horace is strongly under Aristotelian influence, yet says relatively little on poetic language as such.[6]

I take as a start a passage from Quintilian which is indicative of a somewhat reductive approach to the language of poetry, ascribing most of the linguistic particularities of poetry to the *metri necessitas*.

1 Meminerimus tamen non per omnia poetas esse oratori sequendos, nec libertate uerborum nec licentia figurarum: genus ostentationi comparatum, et, praeter id quod solam petit uoluptatem eamque fingendo non falsa modo sed etiam quaedam incredibilia sectatur, patrocinio quoque aliquo iuuari: quod alligata ad certam pedum necessitatem non semper uti propriis possit, sed depulsa recta uia necessario ad eloquendi quaedam deuerticula confugiat, nec mutare modo uerba, sed extendere corripere conuertere diuidere cogatur. (Quint. *Inst.* 10.1.28)

Let us remember that the orator should not follow the poet in everything – neither in his freedom of vocabulary nor in his licence to develop figures – and that poetry is designed for display. Quite apart from the fact that it aims exclusively for pleasure and pursues this by inventing things that are not only untrue but also unbelievable, it also has a special defence for its licence, namely that it is bound by metrical constraints and so cannot always use the literal expressions, but is driven by necessity off the straight path and into certain byways of language; it is obliged, therefore, not only to change words, but to extend, shorten, transpose, and divide them. (Trans. D.A. Russell)

Poetry offers pleasure and nurtures the imagination, and deploys to this end "new words," and a "licence to develop figures." The poets' linguistic "freedom" is excused also by the "necessities" of verse.

The more current view is that poetry "arouses" feelings, in order to persuade and give pleasure. It was not, however, lost on all that poetry also "gives expression" in unique manner to feelings and sentiments, sometimes even a character's most deeply buried ones, as in

2 Est emphasis etiam inter figuras, cum ex aliquo dicto latens aliquid eruitur, ut apud Vergilium: "non licuit thalami expertem sine crimine uitam degere more ferae"; quamquam enim de matrimonio queritur Dido, tamen huc erumpit eius adfectus ut sine thalamis uitam non hominum putet sed ferarum. (Quint. *Inst.* 9.2.64)

Emphasis may be numbered among figures also, when some hidden meaning is extracted from some phrase, as in the following passage from Virgil (*A.* 4.550–551): "Might I not have lived, from wedlock free, a life without a stain, happy as beasts are happy?" For although Dido complains of marriage, yet her true feelings emerge so powerfully that she declares life without wedlock as no life for man, but for the beasts of the field. (Trans. H.E. Butler).

This is perhaps not what Dido was saying in that couple of lines, but the comment is interesting as it comes close to modern definitions of poetry as a probe into the subconscious (*latens aliquid eruitur ... erumpit eius adfectus*), as Quintilian states that Dido's stifled desire for love is given away by her assertion that life without marriage is unworthy of human beings. Readings such as this had no influence on any ancient theory of poetic language, but it is interesting to point out that the idea was at least once expressed.

Another of Quintilian's observations on the "language of poetry" is also interesting from a modern literary-critical viewpoint, and regards the redundant or pleonastic nature of poetic language, something related to what modern critics sometimes call its "overdetermined" character. An element of poetry's "defamiliarized" use of language is seen in its use of adjectives, which sometimes purely add a connotative element not immediately active in the context:

> **3** namque illis satis est conuenire id uerbo, cui adponitur, itaque et "dentes albos" et "umida uina" in his non reprehendemus: apud oratorem, nisi aliquid efficitur, redundat. (Quint. *Inst.* 8.6.40)

> Poets employ it with special frequency and freedom, since for them it is sufficient that the epithet should suit the word to which it is applied. Consequently we shall not blame them when they speak of "white teeth" or "liquid wine."[7] (Trans. H.E. Butler)

Roman grammarians, following Greek precedent, made a distinction between incorrect usage in the spoken language and prose (*uitia orationis, barbarismi, solecismi*) and *metaplasmi*: the former were caused by ignorance of correct usage, whereas poets incurred the latter intentionally, both under metrical constraint or for the sake of ornament. *Metaplasmus*, in extant discussions of grammatical writers, extends to very different categories of poetic language, but centers mainly on phonetic and morphological archaism, and it is not elaborated into any theory of poetic language as such. *Metaplasmus* is based on ancient precedent and authority, is intentional, and aims at formal beauty and ornament. It is likely that the issue of the difference between "incorrect" and "poetic" usage arose first in discussions of prosodic and morphological features which were too archaic or affected to be employed in formal prose and oratory, such as the genitive -*ai*, some forms of synizesis, syncope of verbal forms, and so on. *Metaplasmus* was categorized on the basis of extrinsic, mechanical criteria, such as "omission of initial letter," "omission of final letter," "omission of medial letter or syllable," and no other linguistic consideration; explicit concern in grammatical quarters over how to teach that poets did not make the same mistakes as low-education speakers must also have been part of the theory, but explicit comparison between comparable phenomena in "vulgar" and in poetic Latin is found only in the fifth-century grammarian Consentius.

The Sounds of Poetry. Prosody and Recitation

Classical Latin poetry is based on repeated patterns of heavy (or long) and light (or short) syllables, formed into *feet* and subdivided into *elements* (*elementa*), in which syllabic and, by implication, vowel quantities play a structural role. Comparison with early drama, especially comedy, shows that hexametric poetry and tragedy, especially of the imperial period, was less sensitive than comic meter to the prosodic realities of connected speech in informal or everyday language.[8]

To take just one example, syllabic value in the spoken language was influenced by contextual prosodic factors, causing sometimes phonetic and syllabic reductions within a word or a word-group. Typically, words of iambic quantity in comedy, especially non-lexicals such as adverbs or prepositions, or iambic sequences in polysyllabic words, were subject to reduction to pyrrhic sequences (double short): for example the word *uoluptatem*, ⌣–––, was scanned as ⌣⌣––. This phenomenon, called "iambic shortening," largely disappears in epic and tragedy, from which it seems reasonable to infer that these higher genres adopted a more stylized performance and delivery style, in which the syllabic value of an element within the foot was fixed and determined solely by etymological vowel quantity and by the structure of the syllable. A famous example can help to clarify the distinction between the phonetic reductions of connected speech and the more deliberate style of verse.

> **4** Cum M. Crassus exercitum Brundisii inponeret, quidam in portu caricas Cauno aduectas uendens Cauneas clamitabat. Dicamus, si placet, monitum ab eo Crassum, caueret ne iret; non fuisse periturum, si omini paruisset. (Cic. *Div.* 2.83)

> When Marcus Crassus was embarking his army at Brundisium a man who was selling Caunian figs at the harbour, repeatedly cried out "Cauneas, Cauneas." Let us say, if you will, that this was a warning to Crassus to bid him "Beware of going," and that if he had obeyed the omen he would not have perished. (Trans. W.A. Falconer)

In this Cicero anecdote, a street-seller tries to attract new customers recommending his Caunian (i.e. from Caunea, a region of Asia minor) figs by repeated loud calls. The speaker is from Brundisium but the passage gives no indication that his cry was other than what normally expected from someone of this status and situation. What Cicero reports implies that the elliptic phrase *Cauneas (meas, ficus attendite)* "try out my Caunian figs," could have sounded, to Crassus about to embark on an expedition fated to end disastrously, as the warning "not to go," *caue ne eas*. If this is so, the homophony of *Cauneas* with the complete imperative phrase *caue ne eas* implies that in connected informal speech, possibly without exaggerated sociolectal implications,

1. the final, etymologically long imperative ending -*e* of *caue* was fully eliminated (by apocope) before a consonant-initial *ne*, also owing to grammaticalization;[9]
2. that there was coalescence of same timber vowels in *ne* and *eas* (the former being etymologically long, the latter short, on which more later);

3   that word boundaries between what were three different words according to formal
    grammar were blurred, and the word-group was pronounced with one main stress
    on the first syllable, *cáuneas*, probably [kawneaːs] and possibly even disyllabic by
    synizesis of word internal -*ea*-. This phonosyntactic treatment of the word group
    caue ne eas would be inconceivable in Classical poetry. The etymologically correct
    iambic measurement of *caue*, presumably obsolete by the time of Plautus, is only
    rarely preserved (more commonly the word is scanned as a double short) owing to
    the extension of iambic shortening in the common language: apocope, however, is
    not found before a consonant, for this word. Even synaloephe of the long monosyllable
    ne into a same timber but prosodically short vowel or syllable is unparalleled in epic
    and tragedy at all periods.

Another phonetic aspect for which the diction of poetry appeared more formal than current speech was the treatment of vocalic encounters. These were of course normal in
speech, between words and word-internally: speakers probably tended to reduce them
by consonantization, or pausing between words. Writers on rhetoric recommend avoiding hiatus, except when hiatus is sought for special effect.[10]

In Classical poetry vocalic encounters were subject to great restrictions. Hiatus, for
example, in which the two vowels preserve their phonetic independence, is as good as
absent, except, mostly, to emphasize the foreignness of a proper, mostly Greek, name.
Metrical analysis shows that the encounter of two vowels was treated as forming one element, in which the two word-final and word-initial vowels coalesce. The phonetic reality
of such coalescence is not entirely clear (in some cases elision, that is disappearance of the
first vowel, is a possibility), but, as shown for *ne eas*, some types were clearly avoided (for
example long into short) or impossible (monosyllabic long into short); moreover, in all
post-Virgilian poetry, we see that vowel encounters are increasingly avoided – an extreme
development of the abhorrence against hiatus in formal speech, and clearly a phonetic
factor which made even just the *sound* of poetry fundamentally different from informal,
casual speech, and aiming at a sort of "euphonic" unhampered word flow.[11]

Verses were shaped by the occurrence of word-ends at regular positions within the lines,
called *caesurae* (after the third, the fifth, and the seventh element, mostly). Sometimes
caesurae corresponded to recitation pauses, at least to judge from the occasional
co-occurrence of lengthening, or, more correctly, by the retention of syllable implication.
Short of that, the line was pronounced as a phonetic *continuum*, a string of phonemes in
which processes of resyllabification took place. For example in Virgil's line (*A.* 1.4) *ui
superum, saeuae memorem Iunonis ob iram* ("by the will of the gods, by cruel Juno's
remorseless anger") the last three words were resyllabified as *Iu-no-ni-so-bi-ram*, thus
"opening" at least two syllables which in isolation were closed (i.e. -*nis* and *ob*). Similar
processes took place also in normal connected speech, as we saw for example in *cauneas*.
However, in ordinary speech, resyllabification took place in word-groups determined by
semantic or syntactic factors, rather than metrical, as seems to have happened in poetry.

Another case in which syllabification in poetry diverged from that of the spoken language was that of the consonant cluster of plosive + liquid or nasal, also known as *muta
cum liquida*. Words such as *uolucres, tenebrae* were syllabified in spoken Latin as *uó-lu-cres*,
té-ne-brae, as shown by Romance reflexes presupposing an open medial syllable. In Classical
(but, significantly, not early) poetry, such consonant clusters are sometimes treated as

heterosyllabic, providing a close (or heavy) medial syllable, *uo-luc-res, te-neb-rae*. That too was an element which added to the more formal and "estranged" diction of poetry.[12]

About the actual delivery or recitation style we only have vague information. Typical is the following extract from Quintilian:

> **5** Sit autem in primis lectio uirilis et cum sanctitate quadam grauis, et non quidem prorsae similis, quia et carmen est et se poetae canere testantur, non tamen in canticum dissoluta nec plasmate, ut nunc a plerisque fit, effeminata. (Quint. *Inst.* 1.8.2)

> his [the pupil's] reading (*here*: of poetic passages) must be manly, combining dignity and charm; it must be different from the reading of prose, for poetry is song and poets claim to be singers. But this fact does not justify degenerating into sing-song or the effeminate modulations now in vogue. (Trans. H.E. Butler)

Quintilian's extract describes two manners of delivery, one affected, the other correct, but neither very clear in prosodic terms, except that both are described as kinds of "song." All in all, we must admit that the exact effect and sound of Classical Latin poetry is not recoverable for us. At best we can say that the description of poetry as a *canere* reveals the estrangement felt before poetic meter, planned and regular, and without the variety of rhythmic combinations of informal speech,[13] though it is impossible to deny that some kind of special intonation was adopted, in formal recitation of poetry, in which an element of voice raising and pitch was adopted and recognized as "poetic."[14]

The "estrangement" of poetry must have become more and more conspicuous as time went by, because we have fairly reliable information that vowel quantity as a linguistic productive feature must have been in retreat already in the Classical period, as suggested by the shortening of all closed syllable vowels at word-end. Explicit information that vowel quantity was learned at the grammarian's school occurs only in the fifth century,[15] but widespread metrical errors in epigraphic poetry, and the faulty metrical analyses of some grammarians[16] suggest we should ante-date the process to at least the third century. By then vowel quantity had ceased to be a productive linguistic feature in Latin, to which "all ears" were alive.[17] It is from this period, roughly, that we must date the traditional scanning of Latin poetry by stressing not the normally accented syllable of a word, but the so-called *arsis*, or strong element, of each foot.[18]

Phonetics, Spelling, and Morphology

Latin poetry of the higher genres was written, mostly, for the upper classes, and adopted naturally standard features of educated Latin. However, the category of higher genres covers a long time, from the third century BCE to the fifth CE, and in the course of this long period what was regarded as "standard," especially in pronunciation and phonetics, varied to some extent.

One significant example of this adaptation to the changing standards of the language is provided by the treatment of final -*s*. Tragic and epic poets of the earlier period (third to first century BCE), down to Lucretius and (in one isolated case) Catullus, show in their versificatory practice that they did not consider -*Vs* before a following consonant initial word as syllable closing, from which it is deduced that they did not pronounce -*s* in that position.[19] However, later poets, such as Horace, Virgil, Ovid, and Seneca, treated final -*s* before consonant initial words as syllable closing, and a passage in Cicero famously describes omission of final -*s* as a linguistic trait once regarded as "refined," but in his time fallen out of usage, indeed censored.[20]

A sign of poetry's adherence to the standard is the retention of etymological final -*m*, which had ceased to be pronounced in popular Latin from a relatively early date, but in poetry is consistently treated as syllable closing, before consonant initial words: this was probably in line with what happened in educated speech, in which a nasalized pronunciation of the vowel preceding the -*m* was adopted, presumably with concomitant vowel lengthening.

Other phonetic variants adopted in poetic language were closer to the more colloquial register, especially syncopated forms, which were adopted in metrical positions where the longer form would not have been usable. This is the case for *periclum* (from *periculum* "danger"), *uinclum* (*uinculum* "bond"), *saeclum* (*saeculum*, "age"), all with parallel reductions -*cul*-, -*tul*- > -*cl*-, -*tl*- in the lower registers and spoken Latin (*auricula/auricla*, *uetulus/uetlus*). But syncope occurs also in verb forms, most typically with perfect formants and endings -*ue*-, -*ui*- and -*is*- (*portarunt* for *portauerunt*, *dixti* for *dixisti*, *erepsemus* for *erepsissemus*). Both Virgil and Horace have *noris*, *nosti*, *noras* for *noueris*, *nouisti*, *noueras*, where we happen to have explicit information that the syncopated form was considered normal even in educated speech (Cic. *Orat.* 157).[21] There are even stranger cases, for which we are in no position to identify or reconstruct parallels with the lower levels of the language, such as Hor. *Carm.* 1.36.7–8 *memor/actae non alio rege puertiae*, "remembering a boyhood spent under the self master," for *pueritiae* (cf. however, the existence of byforms *coercitio/coerctio*; *aperitio/apertio*).

Another prosodic feature which reveals a limited concession to more colloquial phonetic realizations is the fluctuating treatment of -*i*-/-*u*-, followed by a vowel, sometimes fully vocalic, sometimes semiconsonantic. Thus in Virgil's *Aeneid* the ablative *abiete* (from *abies*, "fir-tree") occurs four times, always as a trisyllable and in the same metrical position. The phenomenon, called also synizesis, reflects a tendency of the spoken language to reduce word internal hiatus in all positions: high poetry appears to have availed itself of this linguistic option.[22] Some combinations are apparently shunned by high poetry, especially yodisation after -*t*- or -*c*-: trisyllabic *ratjonem* occurs in a substandard metrical inscription in Pompeii, and was probably pronounced [*ra'tjonem*] or even [*ra'tsjonem*];[23] similar is *otiosis* scanned as a trisyllable, for [*o'tjosis*], also from Pompeii. The reverse phenomenon is also found, for example in Hor. *Epod.* 13.2 and *Carm.* 1.23.4, where *siluae* is trisyllabic (˘ ˘ –): its isolated occurrence in Horace, however, suggests that this was an affected "drawl" rather than a colloquial form.

Yet, on the whole, the most outstanding phonetic and morphological features of poetry of the higher genres were archaisms rather than colloquialisms or "vulgarisms." In epic especially, firmly anchored in a long prestigious tradition and narrating past deeds, phonetic and morphological archaisms are relatively well established.

One of the most striking examples is the retention of originally long vowels in final closed syllables which had shortened in the common language. We find thus words such as *honor*, *amor*, *arbor* scanned as with a long final *ō* (editors sometimes introduce a spelling distinction, writing -*s* when the vowel is long: *honos*, *arbos*): cf. Verg. *A.* 11.323 *considant, si tantus amor, et moenia condant*, "let them settle, if their desire is such, and build their city."

Amongst the most conspicuous morphological archaisms are the dative pronominal *olli* for *illi*, the genitive disyllabic ending in *-ai*, free alternation between *i-* and *e*-stem endings in the third declension (for example *montis* for *montes*, even in the nominative plural where it was not etymological), with the former set representing what was probably the more obsolete set of variants, and was chosen, apparently, for euphonic reasons.

We do not know to what extent archaism was represented in spelling, too. The standardization of orthography of Latin was a very long and never fully accomplished process. Quintilian records that he had seen autographs of Cicero and Virgil in which the, in his time obsolete, spelling with geminate *-ss-* after a long vowel or diphthong in words such as *causa, promisi* was still found.[24] Even a common word such as *natus* "son" was sometimes spelled with initial etymological *gn-, gnatus*. Since poetic texts are almost always transmitted by MSS much later than the original date, we cannot reach certain conclusions on the poets' own spellings, not to mention that the poets themselves may not have been always consistent.

The Lexicon

Latin poetry of the higher genres adopts a relatively restricted approach to the lexicon. This is an outcome of different factors, technical, thematic, and of poetics.

The technical element has always been emphasized since antiquity, that is the constraint, *metri causa, metri necessitate*, to avoid particular words, and consequently experiment with periphrases, change singular to plural, adopt more archaic forms or metrically more convenient variants of a common word (*periclum* at line-end, *periculum*, in other positions), which is what Quintilian alluded to in **1** with his claim that poetry is sometimes forced to *mutare ... uerba*, which he exemplified with *extendere corripere conuertere diuidere*.

The commonest of the metrical systems employed by high poetry in Latin (epic, didactic poetry, satire) was the hexameter. It was impossible for the dactylic hexameter (whose basic pattern was – ˇ ˇ) to accommodate tribrach (ˇ ˇ ˇ) or cretic-shaped words (– ˇ –) such as *gaudium, nuptiae, militum* (as the genitive plural of *miles*), or words including such sequences (e.g. *imperator* "commander," and *continere* "to hold"); there were also various restrictions determined by minor euphonic rules, such as avoidance of elision of words of particular metrical shape, above all the cretic-shaped words.[25] A most striking example is the intractable *arbores* (long-short-long), in the place of which Roman poets adopt *arbusta*, literally "bushes"; the singular *arbor* is of course acceptable, as well as naming an individual plant as the sense requires. Many perfect forms were unusable, e.g. *pertulerunt* (– ˇ – –), especially because the variant ending with short *e* (inherited by the Romance languages) was felt as too colloquial: an appropriate substitute was often found in the pluperfect, in this case *pertulerant*. A passage like Ov. *Fast.* 2.737–8

6 pertulerant dominos. regalia protinus illi / tecta petunt

[the horses] bear their masters to the journey's end. The royal palace first they seek. (Trans. J.G. Frazer)

shows how necessity was effortlessly turned into virtue, as the elliptical paratactic phrasing neatly emphasizes the thoughtless impetuosity of the young Tarquinius rushing on towards Lucretia. A plainer prose version could start with *postquam*, or *simul ac* before *pertulerant*: "no sooner had the horses brought their masters to destination than they lost no time to ..."

On the whole, the role that *metri necessitas* played is easily overstated, at least in the sense that Roman poets found easy and inventive means to go round the main hurdles. However, it would be impossible to deny that (1) some words did not match the meter, and (2) the established practice to have word-ends (*caesurae*) in at least two, if not three or four regular positions within the line, in hexameter poetry and even in tragedy, led to some avoidance of polysyllabic words, and especially words longer than four syllables are very rarely found. That put a severe limit on the greater part of the abstract and technical vocabulary of Latin.

Yet, thematic and ideological reasons weighed most in the shaping of the Latin poetic vocabulary. The vast majority of Latin poems of the higher genres deal, in fact, with heroic deeds set in a remote past. Thus epic poets avoid certain more usual sets of words, such as *uxor* for "wife," preferring *femina* and *coniunx*. Other words preferred in the more elevated genres are *ensis* for *gladius*, *famulus* for *seruus* ("servant"), *uirgo* for *puella* ("girl"). A predominantly poetic flavor was also attached to words such as *haud* (for the negative, *non*), *iubar* ("radiance"), *latex* ("liquid" for *aqua*), *polus* ("pole" for *caelum*), *pontus* ("sea," for *mare*), *gressus* ("strife," "walk"), *genitor* (instead of *pater*).

To say, however, that *uirgo, famulus, ensis* were preferred words need not imply total exclusion of *puella, seruus*, or *gladius*. As well analyzed in Watson (1985), a desire to avoid repetition, as well as restraint in the use of anaphorics and pronouns in general (see below) justify some pointed exceptions. Beside, the criteria for exclusion or inclusion in this "canon" of poetic words are often difficult to grasp in full. Some words were felt as more archaic, more alien from common usage, more appropriate for representing a remote world; for example *famulus* or *minister* conveyed a more indefinite notion of "attendant, servant," including different degrees of subordination, while *seruus* conjured up an actual, perhaps too life-like and discredited, social figure. *Puella* was probably too loaded in emotional terms, at least for epic purposes: it was too much of "my girl-friend," or "a little child," to become suitable to describe a young woman of marriageable age in a heroic setting.[26]

As the last example suggests, lexical selection was different in the lesser genres, namely love elegy, satire, and even to some extent lyric poetry. Here poets described everyday situations, and lexical selection is less restrictive. Satire is the most innovative, expansive genre, and draws on a larger store of vocabulary.

What has been said up to this point on the matter of lexical choice is not completely irreconcilable with the claim, made in recent times, that much of the vocabulary of Roman poetry is "neutral," that is it drew on linguistic resources available to all speakers with no register connotations, and that it is not true that technical and everyday vocabulary was shunned per se.[27] Even high poetry was indeed receptive to occasional expressive or color-ful technical words, but on the whole, the general impression is not one of inclusiveness.

To sum up these considerations from a more schematic viewpoint with the words of Cicero (*Orat.* 201), the linguistic usage of poets distinguished itself from that of rhetors mainly on three points of language of which they make more frequent and freer use: the use of *uerba prisca, noua*, and *tralata*.[28]

Morphological and phonetic archaisms have been touched on above. In the lexicon, too, archaism was checked within close bounds, and, in epic, almost restricted to formulaic usage: the most striking archaisms are *fari* for *loqui*, "talk," and, in Virgil only, *adorare*, with the same meaning, the adverb *actutum* "at once," the prepositions *pone* (for *post*, "after"), and *ergo* (*A.* 6.670–671 *illius ergo / uenimus* "we came on his account"). But if Virgil makes some openings to lexical archaism, Seneca's tragedies avoid almost entirely the vocabulary of tragic writers of the early period (Ennius, Accius, Pacuvius).

Neologisms are not numerous, and mostly unobtrusive in the types of formation. Poets of the earlier period had imitated their Greek models in coining longer nominal compounds made of two independent parts, for example a noun and a verbal, mostly participial, element such as *arquitenens* (on the model of τοξοφόρος). Poetry of the classical period inherited some such compounds, but on the whole new coinages are limited to forms with the suffixes *-fer*, *-ger*. Equally commonly, Greek compound adjectives such as εὔρροος, χρυσόκομος and the like are replaced by "appositive ablative" constructions, such *fluuio amoeno*, *radiante coma*, on which see below.

A particularly interesting procedure for introducing new words were ad hoc created forms with intensifying prefixes, such as *inaccessus* ("unapproached," from *in-* and the past participle of *accedo*), *exsaturabilis* ("that may be satiated," from *ex-*, the adjective *satur* and the suffix *-bilis* indicating possibility), *inlacrimabilis* ("unmoved by tears," from *in-*, *lacrimae*, and *-bilis*). These new formations are particularly abundant in Virgil, but Horace, Ovid, Seneca, and later poets too used this linguistic resource.[29] For example, in Ovid *Met.* 6.478, a new word is the verbal form *praecontrectat* (from *prae* "before" and *contrecto*, an intensified form of *tracto* "to touch"), used to express the impatient, luscious gaze of Tereus at the sight of Philomela:

7　spectat eam Tereus praecontrectatque uidendo

> Tereus gazes at her (Philomela), and as he looks feels her already in his arms. (trans. F.J. Miller)

Innovation, more than in the invention of new words or the resumption of obsolete ones, was sought in semantic lexical shift and new word collocations. This crucial point was already recognized by ancient critics, and lies under what Cicero calls *tralata* in *Orator*, which does not refer exclusively to metaphors, but includes a great variety of word collocations and rhetorical figures. In this way, the available lexicon, if limited by metrical constraints, and by some ideological and even puristic scruples (for example a relative avoidance of Greek loanwords),[30] was greatly extended thanks to an inventive application of, especially, metonymy and synecdoche, whereby endless lists of synonyms could be formed by semantic shift. These semantic shifts were established early on in the tradition, and practically by the time of Virgil it was common lore that, for example, words for, simply, "ship" were *ratis* (in origin a "raft"), *carina* ("keel"), *puppis* ("stern"), and so on; for *amor* there were *ignis* ("fire"), *aestus* (lit. "heat, boiling, fervor"), *ardor*, *cura* ("anxiety")[31]; words for *mare* were *sal* ("salt"), *pontus*, *marmor* ("marble"), *aequor* ("plain"), *freta* ("billows"), *uada* ("shallows"); the "arms" were *bracchia* (one of the "admissible" Greek words), *umeri* ("upperarm"), *ulnae* ("elbow"), *lacerti* ("upper arm, muscle"). All these words, in poetry, sometimes lose the original meaning (as is the case, mostly, for the anatomical words replacing *bracchia*), sometimes retain an element of their *proprium*. *Aequora*, for example, is mostly used of a "calm sea" – yet Horace, *Carm.* 1.5.6–7 has the beautiful *aspera / nigris aequora uentis* "seas roughened by black storms."

Some of these points can perhaps be best illustrated by use of a longer example. In *A.* 1.174–179, Aeneas and his followers have only just survived a terrible sea storm, which has cast them off their intended course. With only seven remaining ships, Aeneas takes shelter on the Lybian coast, near Carthage, and disembarks with his men:

8   ac primum silici scintillam excudit Achates
                    succepitque ignem foliis atque arida circum
                    nutrimenta dedit raputque in fomite flammam.
                    tum Cererem corruptam undis Cerealiaque arma
                    expediunt fessi rerum, frugesque receptas
                    et torrere parant flammis et frangere saxo.

> At once Achates struck a spark from flint, caught the fire in leaves, laid dry fuel about, and waved the flame amid the tinder. Then, wearied with their lot, they take out the corn of Ceres, spoiled by the waves, with the tools of Ceres, and prepare to parch the rescued grain in the fire, and crush it under the stone. (Trans. H.R. Fairclough)

Achates, Aeneas' chief attendant, endeavors to make some fire; other sailors take out the grains from water-soaked sacks, roast them in some vessel, and grind them (to make meal). The action is in principle realistic, but the description is couched in general, fairly vague terms. What are the *Cerealia arma*, "Ceres' tools" and how does the action of preparing flour and bread proceed? The fourth-century Virgil commentator Servius notes that Virgil "tries to avoid all lowliness and he has therefore ennobled a humble action with decorous language, as he does elsewhere, where, to avoid using the homely *lucerna*, says *testa cum ardente uiderent scintillare oleum*." (*G.* 1.390, "seeing the oil sputter in the fiery lamp").[32] In other words, just as Virgil in the *Georgics* avoided the everyday *lucerna* for "lamp" but used instead the synecdoche *testa*, literally "sherd," Virgil refrains now from mentioning the real tools Aeneas' companions use to make flour from the wheat, for example a wooden scoop to take the grains from the sacks (*popia, trula*), a pan for roasting them (*testum, rutabulum*), pestle and mortar for crushing (*pistillum, mortarium*) or a portable mill or quern, if this is what *saxo* means. The language of Servius is strongly connoted in social terms (*uilia, dignitas, honestas*). This indefiniteness was for Virgil a poetic strategy, a *sfumato* suggesting the remoteness of the stories he sang.

As mentioned earlier, a second crucial area of semantic extension in the language of poetry was that of word collocation, a heading under which both ancient and modern scholars include several different rhetorical figures, metaphor primarily, but also enallage, brachylogy, hendiadys, hyperbole. This is possibly what Horace called *iunctura*: "you'll speak most happily, when skilled juxtaposition renews a common word" (Hor. *Ep.* 2.3.48).[33] A typical procedure is that of replacing an established verb-object collocation with a new object from a different semantic field. See for example

9 uulnera derigere et calamos armare ueneno

> aiming wounds and arming shafts with venom (Verg. *A.* 10.140 trans. H.R. Fairclough)

But "wounds" are not "directed," or "thrown out," or "aimed" in ordinary Latin, and one expects *sagittas* "arrows": the figure employed here is perhaps enallage, or brachylogy (a fuller phrase would be *derigere sagittas ad infligendum uulnera*).

Similar to the previous example is

10 rumpitque hanc pectore uocem (Verg. *A.* 3.246)

> breaks forth with this cry from her breast (trans. H.R. Fairclough, adapted)

where *rumpit ... uocem* is probably suggested by more usual phrase *erumpit in haec uerba*, but clearly aimed at creating a new effect (the commoner metaphor was *rumpere silentium*, "to break silence").

Among the most famous lines of Latin poetry is this description of Dido's love in Verg. *A.* 4.2:

11 uulnus alit uenis et caeco carpitur igni

> [she] feeds the wound with her life-blood and is wasted with fire unseen (trans. H.R. Fairclough)

where we find an aggregate of different metaphors: first Dido metaphorically "nurtures" (*alit*) her passion, but this is complicated by yet another metaphoric substitution, *amor* with *uulnus* (a passion which is her undoing), then the synecdoche *uenis* for "in her whole being," or *mente*; in the second half-line, perhaps more innovatively, Dido is "plucked" by passion (*ignis*), blind, because unseen, with a reversal of the usual meaning from active ("he who does not see"), to passive ("who is not seen").[34]

This striving for new collocations and effective new phrases is not limited to transitive verb-object phrases, but extends to prepositional constructions. See for example

12 superosque in uota fatigant / Inachidae (Stat. *Theb.* 2.244–245)

> The sons of Inachus weary the gods with vows. (Trans. J.H. Mozley)

where *in uota fatigant* literally means "weary the gods (so much that they turn their attention) towards the objects of their prayers": a more usual construction would have been with a simple ablative, *uotis fatigant*.

Syntax (Nominal, Verbal, Periodic)

The longer extract from the *Aeneid* (8) leads naturally to the transition to analysis of poetic syntax in Latin. Poetic Latin is primarily characterized by a use of the nominal cases slightly different from that found in written prose of a formal register.[35]

Let us have a look at some of the other short phrases describing the action of making some fire to dry the soaked provisions: Achates strikes a spark from or with the flint. Logically the spark is generated from repeated rubbing of the flint on a piece of iron or on another flint – it is the friction which generates the spark. Here conceivably a more precise Latin description would have been *Achates lapidem cum altero lapide atterens scintillam excudit*, or *ex attritu lapidum scintillam excudit*. However, Virgil sees the action as a "striking a spark *to the flint*," with the dative (*silici scintillam excudit Achates*). The dative makes the flint almost a sentient object – it almost "yields" or loses the spark to Achates. This use of the dative as a more dramatic case has been studied especially by the great Swedish scholar E. Löfstedt.[36]

In poetry, the dative encroaches on prepositional constructions in many compound verbs expressing movement, union, sometimes even separation, such as *infero* (e.g. Lucr. 5.976 *sol inferret lumina caelo* "when the sun brought its lights on to the sky"), *adlabi* (Ov. *Met.* 14.243 *terris adlabimur illis* "we arrive at this land"), *appellere*, *accingere*, and so on. It is common also with simple movement verbs such as *ire* (*it clamor caelo*).

Back to example **8**, *Cerealia … arma* is also worthy of comment not only for the rhetorical use of metonymy, but from a syntactical standpoint, as it exemplifies the common practice of replacing a genitive by a possessive adjective. This appears to have been a syntactical archaism. Originally, there was a difference between a generalizing adjective indicating pertinence or origin and a genitive indicating possession: this difference can be exemplified by the distinction between the expressions *bellum ciuile* "a civil war," and *bellum ciuium* "a war of the citizens." Poets however blur this distinction. So, in poetry we find *Thesēa carina* for "the ship of Theseus" (from disyllabic *Theseus*, with the derivative formant -*ēus*, parallel to -*eius*), in Prop. 1.3.1 (*qualis Thesea iacuit cedente carina*, "just as (Ariadne) lay asleep when Theseus' ship receded"); in Ov. *Met.* 10.3 *Orphēa … uoce uocatur* means "invoked by Orpheus' voice," not "by a voice resembling Orpheus's," and so on.

The genitive, too, is found in poetic Latin in constructions alien to current or even correct prose usage. A first class is the genitive depending on adjectives expressing deprivation or its opposite, in connection with which an ablative was expected. In **8** we read *fessi rerum*, but examples are very common. Among the most famous such phrases is Horace's *sceleris … purus* ("unsoiled from guilt") in *Carm.* 1.22.1. Another typically poetic extension of the genitive is when it is governed by verbs expressing deprivation, removal from (*egeo, inuideo, abstineo, desino*), and also verbs expressing authority (*regno*). Such constructions are sometimes argued to be native to Latin, but synchronically they were certainly perceived as imitations of Greek practice:[37]

13 neque ille / sepositi ciceris nec longae inuidit auenae (Hor. *S.* 2.6.83–84)

   he grudged not his hoard of vetch or long oats. (Trans. H.R. Fairclough)

14 tempus desistere pugnae (Verg. *A.* 10.441)

   It is time to stand aside from battle. (Trans. H.R. Fairclough, adapted)

In example **8** line 175 *succepit … ignem foliis*, "catches the fire in the leaves," exemplifies another poetic mannerism, the preference for omission of prepositions: in this case *foliis* is either a locative or an instrumental ablative, though the former is more likely. On the other hand, it would be mistaken to believe that poetry does away with prepositions in search of indefiniteness, archaism, or simply *metri causa*. Prepositions abound in poetry, and struck some ancient critics[38] for their marked, emphatic, determined employment:

> **15** Idem Cyclopa cum iacuisse dixit "per antrum," prodigiosum illud corpus spatio loci mensus est. (Quint. *Inst.* 8.3.84)
>
> Vergil, when he says that the Cyclops lay stretched "throughout the cave," by taking the room occupied as the standard of measure, gives an impression of the giant's immense bulk. (Trans. H.E. Butler)

In this case Quintilian remarks on the effectiveness of *per* instead of the expected locative construction *in antro* in Verg. *A.* 3.631 (*iacuitque per antrum*), perhaps even exaggerating the implications.

In poetry, the use of unconstrued ablative nominal complements becomes especially frequent in descriptive periphrases which can be described in traditional grammatical terms as "attending circumstances," or sociative ablative. See for example:

> **16** (anguis) tumidumque nodis corpus aggestis plicat
>   cogitque in orbis. (Sen. *Med.* 689–690)
>
> (a serpent) knots its swollen body into writhing folds,
> and settles them into coils. (Trans. J.G. Fitch)

where there is no difference, in referential terms, between the ablative *nodis ... aggestis* (*plicat*) and *cogit ... in orbis*.

Another famous example is

> **17**   fluuio Tiberinus amoeno
>   uerticibus rapidis et multa flauus harena
>   in mare prorumpit. (Verg. *A.* 7.30–32)
>
> the Tiber, with a pleasant stream, leaps forth to sea in swirling eddies and yellow with plenteous sand. (Trans. H.R. Fairclough)

where the phrase *fluuio ... amoeno* is in fact amounting to "the Tiber with its lovely river," and the construction is sometimes called "appositive ablative."[39]

The classic type of poetic use of the cases in Latin is the so-called accusative of respect, or "Greek" accusative, dependent on adjectives and passive verbs, typically participles. In the following lines from Horace describing school pupils in his native town Venusia,

> **18**   ... qui macro pauper agello
>   noluit in Flaui ludum me mittere, magni
>   quo pueri magnis e centurionibus orti
>   laeuo suspensi loculos tabulamque lacerto
>   ibant octonos referentes idibus aeris. (Hor. *S.* 1.6.71–5)

[my father], who though poor with a starveling farm, would not send me to the school of Flavius, to which grand boys used to go, sons of grand centurions, with slate and satchel slung over the left arm, each carrying his eightpence on the Ides. (Trans. H.R. Fairclough)

the word-group *loculos tabulamque* exemplifies this type, here governed by *suspensi*, literally "hung." This accusative is called "of respect" in traditional grammatical accounts of Latin syntax because it signifies an object, or part of the body, "with respect to which" the subject is affected by the action of the verb.

The passage permits us also to add some observations about the nominative, especially frequent in appositive and predicative phrases (*macro pauper agello*), often participial. In poetic language adjectives are often used to replace adverbs, generally avoided, or other modal expressions. In **8** we found *fessi rerum*, which stood vaguely for "exhausted as they were," or "dragging themselves." This too becomes a familiar mannerism of high poetry.

In the area of verbal syntax, the most remarkable innovation of poetic language in opposition to prose was the greatly extended use of infinitives, partly in imitation of Greek usage, partly as a native feature:

19 utimur et uerbo pro participio: *magnum dat ferre talentum*, tamquam "ferendum" … interim etiam dubitari potest, cui uitio simile sit schema, ut in hoc: *uirtus est uitium fugere*: aut enim partes orationis mutat ex illo "uirtus est fuga uitiorum," aut casus ex illo "uirtutis est uitium fugere," multo tamen hoc utroque excitatius. (Quint. *Inst.* 9.3.10)

We can also use a verb for a participle: "he gives him a great talent to carry (Verg. *A.* 5.248)," where *ferre* replaces *ferendum*; … One may sometimes indeed doubt what the error is to which the figure corresponds: in "it is a virtue to escape vice" (Hor. *Ep.* 1.1.41) the writer either changes his parts of speech (making a variant on "virtue is to escape from vice") or his cases (making a variant on "it is a mark of virtue to escape vice"), but, whichever it is, the figure is more vigorous than either of the alternatives (Trans. D.A. Russell)

Only the first example appears pertinent, where the infinitive *dare* has the function of a consecutive clause.[40] The encroachment of infinitival constructions on participials, which oust the more cumbersome -*nd*- forms (gerunds and gerundives), was probably motivated by the need for concision. This extended use of the infinitive was commonly perceived as an imitation of Greek syntax, but it appears to have been shared by lower registers of the language. This was a source of some concern for grammatical writers (see above on *metaplasmus*). The second example offered by Quintilian, from Horace's *Epistles*, in which an infinitive, *fugere*, has a nominal function, appears to us "normal" Latin: Quintilian's predicament suggests that there was a doubt about the correct Latinity of using a verb as a noun. Quintilian himself is uncertain whether the poet is using a rhetorical figure, or merely committing an error: he concludes, interestingly that the infinitive is "more vigorous."

Last, periodic syntax.[41] Periods in poetry are mostly shorter than in prose, though it is impossible to reduce individual usage to a general formula. Typical of Virgil is the recourse to short parallel cola (*dicola abundantia*), in which the same idea is repeated with a slight variation (also called "theme and variation"), but Virgil himself, and others, are capable also of more complicated sense-structures, and do not exclusively rely on parataxis. Indeed, passage **18** from Horace shows the deployment of one of these more complicated structures to create subtle effects of narrative suspense. We encounter here first a relative clause (*qui noluit*) governing an infinitive (*me mittere*); on this depends a further relative (*quo ...*), in which three participial clauses are embedded (*orti, suspensi, referentes*), two of them before we finally identify the verb of the relative, *ibant*. In particular, the descriptive participial phrases (*orti, suspensi*) allow Horace to lay out some fine humorful strokes before we reach the verb *ibant*, finally releasing all syntactical tension.

Cohesion and Word-Order

At the level of textual cohesion, the most outstanding feature of "poetic Latin" is the marked avoidance of most pronominals (personal pronouns, demonstratives, possessives).[42]

The fourth-century poet Cyprianus Gallus transcribed in poetic style the first seven books of the Old Testament, the *Heptateuchus*. This poetic version, or "paraphrasis," affords us a rare chance to compare poetic Latin with its exact prose source. This is particularly significant because the source, in this case the Latin versions of the Old Testament, were composed in plain, unpretentious Latin, with many colloquial and spoken elements.

> **20**
>
> forte domum uacuam solumque ut repperit, instat
> consertumque manu cogit decumbere secum.
> exilit ille alacer uestemque a corpore demit
> atque inter dominae geminas dilabitur ulnas.
> femina proclamat uiresque a crimine sumit,
> uociferans praedulce decus temerasse pudoris
> fidentem forma iuuenem, dum lubricus aeuo
> feruet et erilem molitur scandere lectum. (1198–1205)

> One day, as she found him alone, and the house was deserted: she pressed him, and forced, grasping his hand, to lie with her. But Joseph, nimbly, ran away, losing his garment in the attempt and slipped away from the arms of his lady. The woman raised a loud cry, her shame gave her strength: a lament she raised, that the youngster, made bold by his beauty, had soiled her preciously guarded honor – his passion roused by the seething of age – and that he had dared to rise to his master's couch. (Trans. Ferri)

Cyprianus Gallus' lines are a paraphrase of chapter 39 of Genesis, in which the story of Joseph and Potiphar's wife is narrated. Potiphar's wife fell in love with her husband's young servant, Joseph. The woman approached him several times, to no avail. One day, the woman found him alone (*solum repperit*), and urged him (*instat*); she took him by the hand (*consertumque manu*) and tried to force him in bed with her (*cogit*). Both in the above translation from Latin and in the English paraphrase, I have used several anaphorics, especially *him*. Yet, in the Latin poetic version, almost no pronominals are found: reference to Joseph is conveyed by the adjective *solum* and the conjunct participle *consertum*. He is also called *puer* (before the extract), then *iuuenem*; Potiphar's wife is *domina, femina*. Comparison with the Vulgate version (**21**) shows that use of anaphorics such as *ille, eius, eos, eum* was common in simple Latin. In the poetic passage **20**, even possessives are entirely absent; not so in the prose narrative: *in manibus suis, domus suae*. In **20** even the nominatives *ille, illa* are avoided: thus Potiphar's wife is *dominae* in line 1201 (cf. the Vulgate *in manu illius*) and *femina* in the following. Only at 1200 do we find *ille*, to mark a shift of focus on a different participant (*exilit ille alacer*): now it is Joseph who takes the initiative, and the new turn in the narrative is signified by a marked word-order, with the verb in the emphatic first position, *exilit ille*.

The perception of pronominals as "unpoetic" was probably one of the factors leading to the vast recourse to semantic lexical shift in Latin poetry, a device thanks to which a number of near-synonyms can be deployed to designate an identical referent in a passage without being repetitious.

> **21** accidit autem ut quadam die intraret Ioseph domum et operis quippiam absque arbitris faceret et illa adprehensa lacinia uestimenti eius diceret: "dormi mecum." qui relicto in manu illius pallio fugit et egressus est foras. cumque uidisset mulier uestem in manibus suis et se esse contemptam uocauit homines domus suae et ait ad eos "en introduxit uirum Hebraeum ut inluderet nobis. ingressus est ad me ut coiret mecum." (Vulgate Genesis 39:11–14)

> But one day, when he went into the house to do his work and none of the men of the house was there in the house, she caught him by his garment, saying, "Lie with me." But he left his garment in her hand, and fled and got out of the house. And when she saw that he had left his garment in her hand, and had fled out of the house, she called to the men of her household and said to them, "See, he has brought among us a Hebrew to insult us; he came in to me to lie with me." (From the *Revised Standard Version*, adapted)[43]

Another frequent connector between phrases found in high poetry is the connecting relative:

> **22**   cum uidet exstinctos fratres Althaea referri.
> quae plangore dato maestis clamoribus urbem
> inplet. (Ov. *Met.* 8.446–447)

> ... when she saw the corpses of her brothers carried in. She beat her breasts and filled the city with woeful lamentation. (Trans. F.J. Miller)

Typically, connecting relative pronouns are extracted from a subordinate clause, often temporal (*cuius ut, qui postquem, quem quoniam*), in which they really belong:

23   redditus orbis erat; quem postquam uidit inanem …
        Deucalion lacrimis ita Pyrrham adfatur obortis: (Ov. *Met.* 1.348, 350)

> The world was indeed restored. But when Deucalion saw that it was an empty
> world … he burst into tears and thus addressed his wife … (Trans. F.J. Miller)

Relative connections and relative pronouns generally came to be seen as markers of the
high style so much that they are overused in stylistically poorer examples of epigraphic
poetry, mostly sepulchral, where attempts at imitation of higher models are sometimes
not successful:

24   lector, fatum miserabile cernis:
        Parcae nam inpubem quem rapuere mihi
        maeret cara soror, quae fratrem luget ademptum. (*CIL* VI.10226)

> reader, you see a lamentable end:
> he whom the Parcae took away from me before manhood is
> wept for by a beloved sister, who laments her brother snatched
> away. (Trans. Ferri)

Cohesion was also obtained by the meticulous deployment of coordinating and other
particles, typically pleonastic -*que*, but also *nam, enim, at.*

Discussion of cohesion leads naturally into the problem of word-order in Latin poetry.
Latin had no syntactical word-order and separation of syntactically linked constituents,
the so-called hyperbaton, was a pragmatic feature of the language, as amply shown in
chapters 9 and 12 of this volume. It is however evident that high poetry (for example in
comparison with comedy, where hyperbaton is moderately used) resorted to an artificial
separation of syntactical constituents, to the extent, sometimes, that we may wonder
whether even educated native speakers had difficulty in understanding certain poetic passages at an aural level, for example during recitation,[44] which in the imperial age was very
popular. Roman critics found this an especially extreme case:

25 synchysis est hyperbaton obscurum, ut "tris notus abreptas in saxa latentia
   torquet, / saxa uocant Itali mediis quae in fluctibus aras, /dorsum inmane maris
   summi"; cuius recta compositio est talis, tris notus abreptas in saxa torquet, quae saxa
   mediis fluctibus latentia Itali aras uocant. (Charisius, *Ars grammatica* p. 363 Barwick)

> synchysis is the name of a more obscure type of hyperbaton, as in *tris notus abreptas*
> *in saxa latentia torquet, /saxa uocant Itali mediis quae in fluctibus aras, /dorsum*
> *inmane maris summi* (Verg. *A.* 1.108–110), "The south wind catches three, and
> whirls them onto hidden rocks (rocks the Italians call the Altars, in mid-ocean, a vast
> reef on the surface of the sea)" where the normal order would be *tris notus abreptas*
> *in saxa torquet, quae saxa mediis fluctibus latentia Itali aras uocant* (Trans. Ferri).

In this example, which was quoted also in Quintilian, what was perceived as *obscurum* is
explained by the prose paraphrasis: it was the embedding of the relative pronoun four
words after the beginning of the clause.

From Ovid we can see the following "difficult" type of discontinuous word order:

26   hac agit ut pastor per deuia rura capellas
                  dum uenit abductas et structis cantat auenis. (Ov. *Met.* 1.676–677)

> With this [the *uirga*, i.e. his magic staff, or *caduceus*], in the character of a shep-
> herd, through the sequestered country paths [Mercury] drives a flock of goats
> which he has rustled as he came along, and he plays upon his reed pipe as he goes.
> (Trans. F.J. Miller)

In this passage, in which Mercury is setting up a trap, of which his disguise as shepherd
is an essential part, *agit* is separated from his object *capellas* by two nominal constituents,
ut pastor and *per deuia rura*. In this case, a Roman listener (and reader) might have
found some challenge in the fact that, in terms of text pragmatics, the only link with the
previous lines is the staff, which Mercury retains to complete the shepherd's set-up, but
on the whole, with the appropriate intonation and pauses, the text was not difficult to
follow: *hac agit – ut pastor – per deuia rura – capellas – dum uenit abductas.*

Satire too, generously deployed hyperbaton, sometimes as a compensating device,[45]
since its subject-matter and vocabulary were perceived to be lower:

27   nec magis huic, inter niueos uiridisque lapillos
                  sit licet, hoc, Cerinthe, tuo tenerum est femur aut crus
                  rectius (Hor. *S.* 1.2.80–82)

> yet not softer or finer are a woman's limbs amidst snowy pearls and green emeralds,
> than yours, Cerinthus. (Trans. H.R. Fairclough, adapted)

Here the construction is even more complicated and interlocked than in the Virgil
passage censured by Charisius: *nec huic* (the rich matron), *licet sit inter niueos uiridisque
lapillos, est femur magis tenerum, Cerinthe, quam tibi* (*tuo*, "than yours is"): especially
remarkable is the separation of *magis* from *tenerum*.

28   nunc et latentis proditor intumo
                  gratus puellae risus ab angulo. (Hor. *Carm.* 1.9.21–22)

> and the merry tell-tale laugh of the girl hiding in the farthest corner [the verb is
> supplied by *repetantur*, line 20, *let one seek out*] (Trans. C.E. Bennett, adapted)

In **28** the word-order is heavily interlocked, with a sequence which we can schematize as
bacaBAC (capitals for nouns, lower case for adjectives or predicatives). The first three
words of line 21 are juxtaposed and syntactically loosely related: *latentis* depends on
puellae, *proditor* on *risus*; more importantly, any syntactical interpretation of *intumo* is
suspended till the end of the following line, where *ab angulo* finally clarifies it. However,
listeners in tune with the "code" of this sort of poetry must have been used to memorizing
and then recomposing strings of words like this into a meaningful picture. Being able to
do so was probably part of the effect and pleasure of poetry. Of course, discontinuity and

hyperbaton were more frequent and larger in domain with words of stronger semantic content, which were, in a way, significant even in syntactic isolation, and were easier to remember. Nisbet has convincingly argued that adjectives in hyperbaton acquired an even more emphatic meaning, and that, in the *Odes* at least, certain themes, for example sensuous and erotic images, called for more intricate and interlaced patterns.[46]

In the following example from tragedy,

29   cum *Tyrrhenum* rate ferali
                    princeps captam fraude parentem
                    misit in aequor[47] ([Sen.] *Oct.* 311–312*)

                    when the emperor deceived his mother
                    and sent her out on the Tyrrhene Sea
                    in a death-bound ship. (Trans. J.G. Fitch)

Tyrrhenum is separated from *in aequor* by several words and constituents, including the verb: this was certainly an artificial construction, but relatively easy to decipher, especially because *Tyrrhenum* was a predictable epithet for "sea." Disjunction was of course more frequent with semantically strong words than with weak semantic content and non lexical words, such as particles and pronominals, with which hyperbaton also occurs, but the domain of the dislocation is more limited (there are fewer interposed words):

30 inde Lami ueterem Laestrygonis" inquit "in urbem/uenimus" (Ov. *Met.* 14.233–234)

   "After that" [Macareus] said, "we came to the ancient city of Laestrygonian Lamus." (Trans. F.J. Miller)

31 illa suum, quamuis radice tenetur,/uertitur ad Solem. (Ov. *Met.* 4.269–70)

   Still, though roots hold her fast, she turns ever towards her Sun. (Trans. F.J. Miller, adapted)

FURTHER READING

The most innovative recent treatments of "poetic Latin" in English are Adams and Mayer (1999) and Reinhardt *et al.* (2005), two collections of essays where a judicious combination of modern linguistics and traditional literary and philological analysis has made a significant impact on the subject. The prosody and metrics of Greek, but also, to some extent, Roman poetry, are discussed in Devine and Stephens (1994) from a perspective strongly informed by modern trends in phonological studies. A similarly important discussion of these issues, mostly focused on early Roman poetry, can be found in Fortson (2008). Different views on the relationship between language and metrics in early Latin are put forward in the various essays collected in Danese and Gori (1990). Readers of German and Italian will find much of use, especially on the rhetoric and the vocabulary of Roman poetry, in the earlier but still important anthologies by Maurach (1989) and Lunelli (1988), where

Kroll (1924), Janssen (1941), and Leumann (1959) are translated into Italian and accompanied by a full annotation and bibliographical updates. Many important entries on the language of Virgil and Horace by leading international scholars (all translated into Italian) are to be found in Della Corte (1984–1991) and Mariotti (1996–1998), note especially Bettini (1984). Detailed, sometimes excellent, accounts (in English) of the language of individual Latin poets are typically to be found in the introductions of single-book editions with commentary, for example Harrison (1991), Ferri (2003), or in dedicated chapters of recent *Companion* volume series, for example Kenney (2002) in Boyd (2002) on Ovid and Horsfall (2000b) in Horsfall (2000a) on Virgil.

NOTES

1 Thanks are due to Francesca Lechi and the editor for pointing out to me oversights and factual errors in this chapter.
2 On Philodemus and his sources and antagonists (the "euphonists") see Janko (2001) 120–189. On ancient criticism in general see Grube (1965). On "Longinus" see Russell (1964).
3 For a full analysis of Aristotle's theory of poetic language cf. Janssen, in Lunelli (1988) 79–82. Another very good review of ancient theories is in Lyne (1989) 1–15.
4 Dionysius of Halicarnassus περὶ συνθέσεως ὀνομάτων 21.9 ἐν ποιητικῇ τε διαλέκτῳ καὶ τῇ ἄλλῃ πάσῃ τοῖς αὐτοῖς ὀνόμασι χρώμενοι πάντες οὐχ ὁμοίως αὐτὰ συντίθεμεν. ("in poetry and in all other manner of speaking we all use the same words, [but] we do not put them together in the same manner" (translation mine); cf. also. *CAG* XX1.2 225.19.
5 In Latin the only exception for the use of *poetica dictio* as poetic *langue* as a general category is in the fourth-century grammarian Diomedes, *GL* I.474.31 *pes est poeticae dictionis duarum ampliusue syllabarum cum certa temporum obseruatione modus recipiens arsin et thesin* ("a foot is a measure of poetic language, enclosing two or more syllables and observing a well-defined temporal length. It consists of an arsis and a thesis"). An interesting comment is found also in the fifth-century grammarian Pompeius Maurus, *GL* V.213.15 *haec autem elocutio apta est poetis, apta lyricis, longe remota est a sermone communi* "but this manner of speaking is fitting for poets, fitting the lyric, and far removed from the common speech" (on the phrase *da mihi bibere*).
6 Brink (1971) 132–133.
7 *Dentes albos* source unknown, *umida uina* is from Verg. *G.* 3.364 *caeduntque securibus umida uina,* "they cut out the liquid wine with axes."
8 We do not really know the "prosody" or "sounds" of especially connected speech in Greek and Latin, but for attempts to reconstruct different sides of it, for example word junctures, iambic shortening, resyllabification, vowel reduction, especially in connection with poetry and the evidence which can be derived from it see Allen (1973), Devine and Stephens (1994), Fortson (2008).
9 Fortson (2008) 177.
10 On this topic see Riggsby (1991) 328–343.
11 Allen (1973) 142–150; Soubiran (1966) 559–612, with figures for the reduction of elision, for both epic and tragedy, from the early to the post-Classical periods.
12 Tautosyllabic *muta cum liquida* as a feature of normal Latin: cf. Mánczak, in Petersmann and Kettemann (1999) 81–5. For an updated discussion of the chronology of phonological change in the transition from Late Latin to Romance (especially as regards syllable structure, and including register variants in the syllabification of *muta cum liquida*) see Loporcaro in Wright (2008) 338–339, with references. For a slightly different view, namely that the heterosyllabicity of such consonant clusters was perhaps "a reflection of contemporary

speech variants rather than a contrast between current and archaic metric conventions" see Coleman (1999) 33.

13 We do not know what rhythm was perceived as "natural" in ordinary speech in Latin, even if the sources speak of the iamb as the most frequent rhythmical figure occurring in "natural speech" (e.g. Cic. *Orat.* 189; 196). However, commenting on another passage in lyric meter, bacchiac tetrameters, Cicero (*Orat.* 183–184) complains that, if you remove the original music which accompanied the theatrical performance, both the rhythm and the word-order will strike us as quite prosaic: *quanquam etiam a modis quibusdam cantu remoto soluta esse uideatur oratio maxumeque id in optumo quoque eorum poetarum qui* λυρικοί *a Graecis nominantur, quos cum cantu spoliaueris, nuda paene remanet oratio. quorum similia sunt quaedam etiam apud nostros, uelut illa in Thyeste: "Quemnam te esse dicam? qui tarda in senectute" et quae secuntur; quae, nisi cum tibicen accessit, orationis sunt solutae simillima.*

14 Coleman (1999) 33.

15 Adams (1999a).

16 References in De Nonno (1990) 453–494.

17 Famously, a different view was maintained by Pulgram (1975), who argued that already at the time of Plautus two varieties of the language existed, a high and a low variety, and that distinctive vowel length as a phonemic trait of Latin was only a feature of the high.

18 Explicit evidence from Latin grammatical writers of this method of scanning Latin poetry is collected by Allen (1973) 340–341.

19 This seems however to have been a feature of spoken Latin restricted to nouns of the second declension: see Väänänen (1966) 77–81.

20 *Orat.* 161.

21 On ancient Roman commentaries on "current speech" see Ferri and Probert (2010) 12–41.

22 However, not all examples of poetic synizesis may reproduce, or have had parallels in, phonetically reduced forms of the spoken language: there are strong doubts, for example, on disyllabic *genua.*

23 For discussion of many cases in which Classical poets adopt an allegedly more colloquial morphological variant see Coleman (1999). Full list of cases of synizesis in Virgil, for example, are conveniently assembled in Johnston (1897) 7–11.

24 Quint. *Inst.* 1.7.20 quotes spelling with geminate -*s*- after a long vowel or diphthong as found in Virgil's autographs, for words such as *caussa, diuissio, promissi.* See also Adams (1990) 239.

25 For more extensive lists of such words and a description of the "tricks" developed by Latin poets to go round technical difficulties see the essays of Kroll, Janssen and Leumann in Lunelli (1988) esp. 24–27, 84–86, 160–161, with references to earlier literature.

26 Watson (1985) 433.

27 Adams and Mayer (1999) 3–4; precise figures, for Virgil, in Görler (1985) 262–263. Also important on this point is Lyne (1989) 1–20.

28 The point is repeated also in Quintilian.

29 On neologisms in Virgil see Pascucci, in Della Corte (1984–1991) III.696–701. On neologisms in Horace see Viparelli in Mariotti (1996–1998) II.925–928. The most complete recent study of nominal composition in Latin is Lindner (2002).

30 Görler (1985) 262.

31 Coleman (1999) 75.

32 CEREALIAQUE ARMA *fugiens uilia ad generalitatem transiit propter carminis dignitatem et rem uilem auxit honestate sermonis, ut alibi, ne lucernam diceret, ait testa cum ardente uiderent scintillare oleum.* For a general literal explanation of the *realia* of this passage see Henry (1873) I.476–481.

33 Brink (1971) 132–138.

34 On many aspects of Virgil's style see Conte (2007) 53–128.

35   Coleman (1999) 78–94 is particularly good on poetic syntax and judiciously weighs the balance
      between native and imitative Greek constructions in the development of Latin poetic style.

36   Löfstedt (1942–1956) I.175–237. To exemplify the "dramatic" and thus more expressive use
      of the dative, the great Swedish scholar E. Löfstedt compared two much more dramatic
      phrases: the difference is clear if we imagine the two phrases *equorum crura succiduntur* (*lit*
      "the legs of the horses are cut"), and *equis crura reciduntur* ("the legs are cut to the horses").
      In the latter phrase, the horses become actively and painfully involved, not simply objectified
      and observed as non-patient beings.

37   Extensive discussion in Mayer, in Adams and Mayer (1999) 169–170, with a very full analysis
      of the evidence in grammarians and commentators.

38   Servius, on the contrary, remarked that "poets for the most part make a superfluous use of
      prepositions" (Serv. *A*. 1.307).

39   Examples from Hillen (1989).

40   The passage is well discussed by Mayer, in Adams and Mayer (1999) 165–166.

41   Classic account in Norden (1927) 385–387. An updated discussion in Harrison (1991) 287–290.

42   Cf. Axelson (1945) 70–74 for more precise figures on avoidance against *is*, but also *hic, iste*,
      and the few exceptions.

43   Cyprianus Gallus probably worked from one of the earlier Latin translations of Genesis, of
      which only fragments survive, and which were translated from the Greek of the Septuagint
      (whereas Jerome's *Vulgata* was based on the Hebrew). For present purposes, comparison
      with the Vulgate is sufficient to emphasize the peculiarities of "poetic Latin," though of
      course the Latin of the pre-Jerome version is even plainer in register: the corresponding pas-
      sage from *Vetus Latina* reads [parentheses for supplements] (*erat autem*) *Ioseph decorus
      aspectu et speciosus facie ualde et immisit uxor domini eius oculos suos in Ioseph et ait illi "dormi
      mecum." ille noluit. ... (ille) non audiebat eam. una e diebus ingressus est Ioseph ... attraxit
      illum a uestimentis dicens "ueni, dormi mecum." at ille relinquens uestimenta sua in manibus
      eius fugit et exiuit foras.*

44   Calcante (2000) for the issue of comprehension in a recitation or performance context of
      discontinued syntax in Latin poetry.

45   To judge from Horace's famous statement in *S*. 1.4.54–62.

46   Nisbet, in Adams and Mayer (1999) 138–139.

47   For a discussion of disjunction with weak semantic content words (demonstratives) in
      Augustan and later poetry see Ferri (2003) 413–416.

CHAPTER 21

The Language
of Latin Verse Satire

Anna Chahoud

Introduction

Satire is notoriously difficult to characterise (an "elusive genre": Classen (1988), cf.
Keane (2006) 6). Quintilian's famous claim that *satura* is an entirely Roman invention
(*Inst.* 10.1.93) creates the strongest link between the poetry of Lucilius, Horace and
Persius with the context of its production – Rome. Satire is defined as a native form,
goes by a native name of ambiguous etymology (Diomedes *GL* I.485–486; Coffey
(1976) 11–18; Gowers (1993) 109–111), and is perceived to be free from the
constraints of Greek literary models and representative of characteristically Roman
values: male *virtus*, female *castitas*, and everybody's *pudor*; political and personal *amicitia*; moral and verbal *decorum* and display of educated *urbanitas*; and above all the
élite notion of *libertas*, all the more prominent when freedom of speech is dangerous
(Hor. *S.* 1.4.103) or endangered (Juv. 7.116; 8.264), missing (Persius 4.73) or perverted
(Juv. 2.77). When Horace associates Lucilius with Attic comedy (*S.* 1.4.1–7) and
Hellenistic diatribe (*Ep.* 2.2.60), he has a manner of expression in mind, rather than
the specific diction associated with the communication of a specific kind of subject-
matter that we call "genre". This manner is the unrestrained freedom that characterized Lucilius, the "inventor" of the poetic form in second-century Rome, as it had
characterized the *onomasti komodein* of Eupolis, Cratinus and Aristophanes in Classical
Athens (Hor. *S.* 1.4.5, *multa cum libertate notabant*); in Quintilian's words, Lucilius'
quality was a combination of learning (*eruditio*), aggressiveness (*acerbitas*) and verbal wit
(*sal*). Roman satire evolved through constant referring to this model of authorial voice,
which the three major figures of Roman satire mirrored and reconstructed in their
programmatic statements: Lucilius is the uncontrolled voice of Republican freedom to

A Companion to the Latin Language, First Edition. Edited by James Clackson.
© 2011 Blackwell Publishing Ltd. Published 2011 by Blackwell Publishing Ltd.

Horace (*S.* 1.4.6–13; 1.10.3 ff., 2.1.62–68), the biting censor of prominent individuals to Persius (1.114–115), the epic champion of indignation to Juvenal (1.19–20 and 165–166). Each characterization is mirrored in the language that each author uses to create it for his own purposes: epic imagery for Juvenal's chariot-racing Lucilius (1.165–166 *ense uelut stricto quotiens Lucilius ardens | infremuit*); abrupt apostrophe to the victims of Lucilius' aggressive biting in Persius (1.114–115 *secuit Lucilius urbem | te Lupe, te Muci, et genuinum fregit in illis*); emphatic pairing of mildly disparaging qualifications, gemination of the keyword "writing", and run-over in Horace's portrayal of exuberant, wordy, muddy Lucilius, *garrulus atque piger scribendi ferre laborem, atque | scribendi recte* (*S.* 1.4.12–13).

The tradition as we have it spans the late second century BCE to the early second century CE, with four canonical authors writing at a distance of over half a century from each other, and each one giving the genre his original trademark and distinctive style. Self-conscious experimentalism with linguistic varieties, literary registers, poetic genres and rhetorical techniques is part of each author's poetic programme, the discussion of which has little place here, nor has an evaluation of the metaphorical, metapoetic, or moralizing force of themes in individual texts or in the genre as a whole. This chapter focuses on aspects of Latin usage that may, or may not, account for definitions of Latin verse satire as *sermo*, "conversation". This is what Lucilius and Horace called their own poetry; this is, as modern scholarship insists, what even the most rhetorical works of Persius and Juvenal fundamentally are (if idiosyncratically so: Harvey (1981) 4; Powell (1999) 316 "argumentative conversational discourse").

Satura and *Sermo*

Quintus Ennius, the father of Latin literature, is to be credited with the choice of the word *satura* as a title for one of his collections of miscellaneous, low-key, personal poetry (Gratwick (1982b) 159; Courtney (2003) 7). The twenty or so extant fragments are enough to identify extracts of informal dialogue (e.g. *FLP* 8 Courtney *dum quidquid <des>, des celere*; 12C), including threats (7C *malo hercle magno suo conuiuat sine modo*); first-person declarations (20C *numquam poetor nisi podager*; 19C *meum non est, ac si me canis memorderit*); dramatic cumulation of verbs (10C *restitant occurrunt obstant obstrigillant obagitant*) and wordplay (18C); parody of Ennius' own high poetry (9C *contemplor | inde loci liquidas pilatasque aetheris oras*); animal imagery (23C); proverbs (24C) and fables (17C, 21C) (see Petersmann (1999)). The metre is mostly the iambo-trochaic verse of comic dialogue or the hexameter. Ennius' pioneering experiments with a variety of themes, registers and metres prefigure the main characteristic of the genre; and yet his name left little trace in the tradition of Roman satire, which is constantly associated with the abusive, dialogic and argumentative hexameters of Lucilius: "when [Quintilian] says *satura tota nostra est* he means that the special type of literature created by Lucilius, dominated by a certain spirit, clothed in a certain metrical form, fixed by the usage of a series of canonical writers, and finally designated by a name specifically Latin, is Roman and not Greek" (Hendrikson (1927) 58; cf. Rudd (1960) 44; Freudenburg (2005) 4).

Lucilius did not use, as far as we know, the word *satura*. He called his verse *ludus ac sermones nostri* (1039M). If we are to believe Cicero, he humorously claimed to address an audience of moderate literary refinement (Cic. *de Orat.* 2.25 *dicere solebat ea quae scriberet neque se a doctissimis neque ab indoctissimis legi uelle* "he used to say that he wanted neither the too-learned nor the unlearned to read what he wrote") or limited linguistic competence (Cic. *Fin.* 1.7 *Tarentinis ait se et Consentinis et Siculis scribere* "he says he writes for the people of Tarentum, Consentia and Sicilia"). Horace denied the title of *poeta* to those who, like himself, "write in a style rather close to prose" (Hor. *S.* 1.4.42 *sermoni propiora*), for their poetry "except that it differs from prose in the regularity of its rhythm, it is prose pure and simple" (47–48 *nisi quod pede certo | differt sermoni, sermo merus*; trans. Rudd (1987)). Persius distinguished himself from Muse-inspired poets, choosing a "semi-rustic" mode of expression (prol. 6–7 *ipse semipaganus | ad sacra uatum carmen adfero nostrum*) and proved his point by renaming Hippocrene *fonte … caballino* (prol. 1). Juvenal fashions his writing as outburst of unchecked anger under the pretence of poetic inadequacy (I.78–79 *si natura negat, facit indignatio uersum | qualemcumque potest*).

All these claims are of course poses. The questions we address here do not concern *why* the satirical writers did so – a matter pertaining to, and skilfully handled by, literary criticism – but *how* they did it, and more precisely what features of oral discourse were imported into the verse structure, transformed into characteristic elements of a specific poetic register, and/or recast as individual literary innovations. The artless realism of Roman satire is a literary fiction. But it is a convincing one. Satire is excluded from classic discussions of "poetic diction", on the grounds that its language is too close to "everyday speech" (Janssen (1941/1988) 87), and labelled as "the most unpoetic of all Latin poetic genres" (Leumann (1947)). Writers on language and style in antiquity defined *sermo* as intrinsically dialogic (Var. *L.* 8.64 *sermo non potest in uno homine esse solo, sed ubi oratio cum altero coniuncta* "conversation cannot take place with one person, but it is rather a discourse engaged with another") and eminently informal (*Rhet. Her.* 3.23 *oratio remissa et finitima cottidianae locutioni* "relaxed discourse closest to everyday speech"; cf. Witke (1970) 57–58). What exactly ancient critics meant by "everyday speech" (*sermo cotidianus*) is far from clear, for discussions rarely take into account the linguistic varieties that we would call sociolects, and more often than not concentrate on stylistic matters pertaining to formal rhetoric (Ferri and Probert (2010)). It is extremely difficult to ascertain the precise extent to which *speaking practices* contributed to the creation of a *literary style*, not only because of the difficulties involved in recovering patterns of everyday conversation in a corpus language such as Latin (Dickey and Chahoud (2010)). Oral discourse is marked by inherent faults – "false starts, nonce mispronunciations, abrupt and ungrammatical transitions, anacolutha, rambling pleonasm and banal repetition, not to mention mere noise" – which rarely find their way in a written, let alone, literary record (Coleman (1999) 24–25). Such traits, however, may be exploited for poetic effect, and Roman satire presents itself as a genre aiming to reproduce the expressiveness of the pragmatic, syntactic and semantic characteristics of orality (Hofmann (1951/2003); Koch (1995); Österreicher (1995); Chahoud (2010)). The outline below concentrates first on aspects of the subjective, dialogic, or emotive discourse of Roman satire as "oralité mimetique" (Koch (1995) 126); I then turn to a discussion of register and of distinguishing features of vocabulary selection.

Discourse Organization: Subjectivity

Personal names and personal pronouns

From its inception Roman satire is marked by the presence of the author's own name. A fragment from Ennius' *saturae* (*uar.* 11 Courtney) contains the greeting *Enni poeta, salue, qui mortalibus | uersus propinas flammeos medullitus.* The notion of "verse drawn out of one's depths" is just as important as the reference to the name of the person saluted as *poeta.* In what were perhaps the opening lines of his first collection, written around 131–126 BCE, Lucilius presented his poetry as deeply personal (590–591M *ego ubi quem ex praecordiis | ecfero uersum*) and puts forward his name as emblematic of his non-conventional choice of poetry over public life (671–672M *publicanus uero ut Asiae fiam, ut scripturarius, | pro Lucilio, id ego nolo et uno hoc non muto omnia*): writing satire is, to Lucilius, "being himself". Only fragments survive from Lucilius' thirty books, and context is recoverable for hardly any of them. Yet, in some cases there is little doubt that assertive emphasis on the first person pronoun and proper name aimed to characterize the voice of the first non-professional, free-born writer at Rome, proud (688–689M *fictis uersibus Lucilius, | ...studiose et sedulo*) and disdainful (712M *tu Lucilium credis contenturum?*). The frequency of the name (Lucil. 254, 366, 580, 688, 712, 774, 822M) prefigures the obsessive self-references and self-addresses we read in Catullus (twenty-five times) and, after him, in Ovid (forty-nine times). The authorial "I" dominates the work with its frequent recourse to emphatic *ego* in first position (654M *ego enim contemnificus fieri*, with parodic compound, on which see below; cf. 734M, 937M) or otherwise contrastive (628M *ut ego effugiam, quod te in primis cupere apisci intellego*; 630M *at ego ut dissimilis siem*; 1026M *omnes formonsi, fortes tibi, ego inprobus: esto*).

It is often said of Latin colloquial style that "the overriding concern in conversation is the relationship between the two speakers" (Hofmann (1951/2003) 240–241, § 95). If this is what Lucilius wrote, in 690M *proferam ego iam, uester ordo scelera quae in se admiserit*, with the pronoun following a future verb in initial position, the line amounts to a threat of the type well-documented in comedy (e.g. Pl. *Ps.* 382 *exossabo ego illum*; Ter. *Eu.* 803 *diminuam ego caput tuum hodie*) and demonstrated to be a pattern of informal and formal speech whereby the pronoun highlights the preceding verb, which Catullus adopted in the famous line *pedicabo ego uos* (Adams (1999b) 110). More generally, the placement of the pronoun after a marked term plays a "focusing" function, for example on an emphatic or antithetical term (Adams (1999b) 108). In about half of the occurrences of *ego* in Lucilius' fragments, the personal pronoun sets the speaker against his interlocutor(s). This is true also for oblique forms of the pronoun in clearly non-enclitic position: at the start of the line (675M *mihi quidem non persuadetur pulices mutem meos*) or of the colon (629M *et quod tibi magno opere cordi est, mihi uehementer displicet*); occurrence at the end of the line may be a feature of informal registers (Adams (1994c) 108), but not necessarily so (378M *nihil ad me* "*I* don't care", following bucolic diaresis: cf. Nisbet (1999) 145).

The absence of context in Lucilius forbids certainty as to the identity of the speaker in any given fragment, and in general it does not matter – to an evaluation of diction as opposed to a reconstruction of narrative – whether Lucilius appropriates patterns of conversation to speak *in propria persona* or to characterize one of the speakers of his dialogues. It is not implausible, however, that some of the examples above might have been intended to reproduce authorial pronouncements on poetic choices of subject-matter and style, as correspondences with the later tradition show. Horace and Persius exploit some of the collocational patterns illustrated above to make a programmatic point. The pronoun is contrastive after a verb in Hor. *S.* 2.1.74 *quidquid sum ego, quamuis* | *infra Lucili censum ingeniumque* "whatever I am, and however inferior to Lucilius in rank and talent", and perhaps also in 1.5.48 *lusum it Maecenas, dormitum ego Vergiliusque* "Maecenas went off to take exercise; Virgil and I had a sleep"; there is a dialogic opposition with *tu* in 2.3.235, 2.7.80 (Adams (1999b) 126). Persius underlines his own Stoic stance with an emphatic gemination: 6.22 *utar ego, utar* "For me, it's enjoy what you have" (cf. 18 *discrepet his alius*). Juvenal's exordium, on the other hand, focuses on the "always" which the speaker's silence cannot endure, producing the elliptical rhetorical question: 1.1 *semper ego auditor?* "[Must I be] always a listener [only]?"

The sequence *non ego* deserves special attention. While it offers the hexametrical poet a convenient dactyl, especially in first position, *non ego* was already a favourite of Plautine dialogue, which employs it, with various connotations, forty-five times; notably Terence has only three examples, two of which are with *dico*, "did or did I *not* say" (*An.* 619 *an non ego dixi esse hoc futurum*; *Hau.* 781 *non ego in perpetuom dicebam*, etc.). The collocation does not belong to the lower end of the colloquial register; we read it, for example, in Horace's *Odes* and in Virgil's *Aeneid*. The colloquial flavour it sometimes acquires in Horace derives from its use in elliptical form *non ego* "Not me" (*S.* 1.2.118, 1.5.101, 1.10.76). What matters here is the preferential use of the construction in satirical verse to assert the author's attitude towards a tradition in which he claims a place for himself or his view on a topic central to his subject-matter. In Horace's impatient clarification at *S.* 1.1.103 the contrast is between two excesses, and the pronoun simply highlights the antithesis: *non ego auarum* | *cum ueto te, fieri uappam iubeo ac nebulonem* "when I urge you not to be a miser, I am *not* saying that you should be a rake and a wastrel" (trans. Rudd (1987), my emphasis). In all other instances Horace sets his own personality against somebody else's: "*I* don't" marks Horace's distance from Lucilius in *S.* 1.6.58–59, his preference for a select readership in 1.10.76, his refusal to write abusive poetry in 1.4.69, to entertain superstitions in 1.5.101, or to inflict on himself sex deprivation in 1.2.118 (a rewriting of Lucil. 308M). The single occurrence in Horace's second book of *Sermones* (2.2.116) is put into the mouth of the "countryman Ofellus, an unprofessional philosopher of sturdy common sense" (2.2.3 *Ofellus* | *rusticus abnormis sapiens crassaque Minerva*) – i.e. Horace's alter ego. Just as the two examples in the *Ars Poetica* (234, 351), six out of seven examples of the construction in Horace's *Sermones* make a literary point. The author's definition of his satiric persona, its scope and limits, is more insistently expressed in Book 1, where critics rightly observe that "the 'I' is gradually built up to become a seemingly anonymous inhabitant of a vividly realised world" (Muecke (2007) 106). The force of Persius' claim at 1.45 *non ego cum scribo … laudari metuam* does not lie so much in the first-person statement ("I am not the man to shrink from applause"), but rather in the function of the statement as a corrective to Persius' far more significant elaboration, a few lines earlier, of Horace (*S.* 1.10.74–6 *an **tua** demens* | *uilibus in ludis **dictari carmina** malis?* **non ego**) into a grotesque visualization of the writer as a school set book (Persius 1.30–31 *ten cirratorum centum **dictata** fuisse* | *pro nihilo pendes?*).

But here we step into the realm of poetic imitation, and I refer to the excellent discussion of Rudd (1976) 57–58 = (2009) 110–111.

Contact and amplification

The more dialogic poems of Horace and Persius present devices intended to draw the attention of the interlocutor and call for emotive participation. Alongside interjections and expression of contact such as *age, agedum* "come on" (Hor. *S.* 1.4.38; 1.10.51; 2.3.152, 155, 224; 2.7.92; 2.8.80; Persius 2.17, 22, 42; 6.52) or *quaeso, si uis* "please" (Hor. *S.* 1.10.51; 1.3.14), we note the insertion of expressions such as *certe est* "I am sure", *crede mihi* "believe me", *inquam* "why, I mean". Semantically these expressions add very little to the statement that hosts them; their force is subjective – emotive, illocutive, or otherwise – redundancy (Hofmann §§ 113–115 (2003) 277–280).

The distribution of *crede mihi* (Lucil. 796M, cf. Pl. *Men.* 1088; Ter. *Ph.* 44), or *mihi crede* (dub. Lucil. 1372M, cf. Ter. *Ad.* 101), with its countless occurrences in Cicero's letters and in the personal poetry of Propertius and Ovid, suggests that the appeal to the speaker's credibility was a trait of informal conversation. A notable use of the adverb *certe* and parenthetical *certe est* is the combination with the indefinite *nescio quis*: Hor. *S.* 1.9.67 *certe nescio quid* "I am sure there was something or other"; Persius 5.51 *nescio quod, certe est, quod ... astrum* "*some* star, I am sure, there is". Parallels are found in low-register poetry (e.g. Catul. 80.5, Verg. *Ecl.* 8.107), although not exclusively there (K–S II.491). Monologic *inquam* offers the opportunity for a case-study.

Lucilius uses *inquam* outside dialogue nine times, Horace four times, Persius and Juvenal avoid it altogether. One would be tempted to infer that frequency in satire decreases with the increasingly rhetorical quality of the genre. This hypothesis does not stand up to scrutiny. In two examples in Lucilius, *inquam* is used in conjunction with figures of repetition: polyptoton in Lucil. 38–40M *nam si fluctus... | tollere decreris, uenti prius Emathii uim, | uentum, inquam, tollas* and emphatic gemination in 110–113M:

> uerum haec ludus ibi, susque omnia deque fuerunt,
> susque haec deque fuere, inquam, omnia ludus iocusque;
> illud opus durum, ut Setinum accessimus finem,
> αἰγίλιποι montes, Aetnae omnes, asperi Athones
> But there all this was play and everything as free and easy,
> all this I say was free and easy, play and fun;
> but when we reached the boundary of Setia – *that* was a hard business –
> goat-deserted mountains, all Aetnas and rugged Athoses. (Trans. Warmington)

The passage is noted by Wills (1996) 65 as a rare case of *inquam* marking an emphatic gemination in poetry (another one is Mart. 9.25.3 *nugas, has inquam nugas*). The claim is justified. The phenomenon is extremely common in formal speech, where two traits of orality – emotive interruption of the train of thoughts and pleonasm – are elaborated rhetorically for the sake of pathos (Hofmann and Szantyr (1965) II.809–811, Ricottilli (2003) 180 n.; Kühner *et al.* (1976) II.577). The technique is a favourite of Cicero, who uses *inquam* to highlight the repeated term or phrase in twenty-five out of 133 occurrences of *inquam* in his speeches, eight in the *Philippics* alone (e.g. 2.53, 2.91, 13.41 *tu, tu inquam*; 8.22 *deserti, deserti inquam sumus*; 12.3 *decepti, decepti inquam sumus*); the correspondence shows a far more restrained use (*Att.* 3.155, 4.2.5, 6.2.9, 7.2.6). No occurrence of *inquam* in Horace's *Sermones* (2.3.276, 2.7.21, 2.8.25) has it combined with emphatic gemination except in 1.10.64–65 *fuerit Lucilius, inquam,* | *comis et urbanus, fuerit limatior idem* ...; this isolated case finds a parallel only in the highly stylized *Carmina* (2.8.13 *ridet hoc, inquam, Venus ipsa, rident* | *simplices nymphae ferus et Cupido*). There is no example of this rhetorical elaboration in Persius, who employs emphatic gemination not infrequently (e.g. 3.41–42 *imus, imus praecipites*; list of passages in Harvey (1981) 18), nor in comedy nor in Petronius' *Cena*, where the collocation is often found with imperatives (e.g. Pl. *Mil.* 857 *abi abi*; Petr. 49.4 *uoca uoca cocum in medio*; cf. Hofmann (1951/2003) 178–180, § 59).

The vivid report of Lucilius' journey to Sezze includes the idiom *susque deque* = "of no consequence" (Plautus, Laberius) and Homeric Greek in a parodic alliterative hyperbole (*aigilipoi ... Aetneae ... Athones*). The effect is a progression from realistic colloquialness to mock-epic grandeur (I owe this point to Professor E. Courtney). It may be worth adding that, if at l. 111 one reads *susque et deque* (with Gell. 16.9.3), the redundant connective *et* would point to this passage as the earliest evidence of *-que* going out of currency in speech, to be preserved only in archaizing or otherwise self-conscious literary Latin (Campanile (2008) 353–355); the process is complete by the late Republic, where Horace's *Sermones* supply many examples of the substitution of *et* and even *atque* for postponed *–que*, e.g. *S.* 1.8.34 (Ernout (1946–1965) III.101–102).

Emotiveness, incoherence, brevity

"Emotionally motivated constructions" appear in Classical Latin – not so much so in Early Latin – as a feature of both informal language and artistic stylizations of speech (Rosén (1999) 18). Features of oral discourse such as economy of expression (brevity, ellipse), or incoherent sentence structuring (series of parentheses; anacoluthon) can be fashioned into special effects, so much so that rhetorical theory may raise seemingly imperfect utterances to the dignity of *ornamenta*. *Breuitas* is, of course, also a characteristic of poetic language (Kroll (1924/1988) 47–50). Horace's comic diatribe *S.* 1.2 offers two striking cases in point: (a) omission of *facio* at line 90 *hoc illi recte* "and they're very wise" (Rudd (1987); lit. "and rightly so"), as often in Cicero's letters with such adverbs (e.g. *Att.* 9.10.3, 5.4.2, 13.6.2); (b) anacoluthon at line 101 *altera, nil obstat* "[with] the other one, there's no problem", with focusing "nominativus pendens" (Koch (1995) 135; Adams (2007) 19) bringing the "professional woman", as opposed to the married *matrona*, to the head of the line.

Persius' poetry, with its frequent ellipses, interruptions of the logical sequence of thoughts by sudden apostrophes (e.g. 1.58, 3.35) and series of parentheses, offers good examples in this respect. An extreme one is at 1.8–12:

> nam Romae quis non – a, si fas dicere – sed fas
> tum cum ad canitiem et nostrum istud uiuere triste
> aspexi ac nucibus facimus quaecumque relictis,
> cum sapimus patruos. tunc tunc – ignoscite (nolo,
> quid faciam?) sed sum petulanti splene – cachinno.

Is there any Roman who hasn't – if only I could say it – but I can,
when I look at our venerable hair and that austere demeanour
and all we've been at since we gave up marbles and assumed the wisdom
of disapproving uncles, then – sorry, it's not that I want to –
but what can I do? It's my irreverent humour – I must guffaw! (Trans. Rudd (1987))

Quintilian's warning (*Inst.* 8.2.15) on moderate use of *interiectio*, which "normally obstructs intelligibility unless it is brief" (Marouzeau (1953) 101) finds no application here. The result is broken expression of incoherent thinking. Persius commentators remark on the fluctuations of the poet's mind, most aptly Nisbet: "like Browning, he tries to reproduce the confused movement of thought and conversation, and again like Browning, he never lets the result sound quite like human speech" (Nisbet (1963) 43). Horace's use of parenthetical comments dominates the *Satires* and the *Epistles*, with a frequency three times higher than in the *Odes* and *Epodes* (Bo (1960) 296–297). The *Satires* alone exhibit thirty cases of asyndetic parentheses (e.g. *S.* 1.7.35, type *mihi crede* noted above) and twenty-four parenthetical clauses, more often than not subordinate – with a preference for conditional *si*, *S.* 1.4.14, 2.2.10, 2.5.61, 2.8.4, 2, 8, 21) – but also coordinate, e.g. *S.* 2.3.323 *iam desine*; *hoc etenim* introduces an eleven-line long inter-mission at *S.* 1.7.9–19, all the more remarkable as it follows immediately the resumptive marker *redeo*. Juvenal's notorious tendency to digress (Courtney (1980) 47–48) often resorts to conjunctions signalling the start or the end of a parenthesis or digression (e.g. *sed*: 3.232, 10.185 *et alibi*: see Courtney (1980) 644.

The passage from Persius cited above displays another construction typical of brevity. The first is substantival infinitive, which under the influence of Greek increasingly populates Latin prose (but not historiography: Wackernagel (2009) 343–344): Persius 1.9 *nostrum istud uiuere triste*, 1.27 *scire tuum*; 1.122 *hoc ridere meum*, 3.17 *pappare minutum*, 3.8 *mammae lallare*, 5.53 *uelle suum*, 6.38–9 *sapere* ... | ... *nostrum hoc*. Its use in Plautus, Cicero's letters and philosophical works, Petronius and Martial is regarded as an indicator of everyday use (Wölfflin (1886); Hofmann (1951/2003) 328–329; Kühner *et al.* (1976) I.666, Hofmann and Szantyr (1965) 343–344; Harvey (1981) 17), but generalizations are not advisable. The substantivizing demonstrative or possessive pronoun is a common Latin rendering of the Greek article (Rosén (1994b) 132–133 cites three examples of *hic*, *iste* and *ille* from Cicero's *philosophica*, noting also Varro's preference for *hic* as a "full-fledged substantivising article"). On the other hand, Persius' qualification of the substantivized infinitive by an attribute (1.9; 3.17) is likely to be a poetic appropriation of a usage that will surface in Christian Latin (Wackernagel (2009) 343–344). The effect of 3.17 *pappare minutum* is a vivid concretizing image ("din-din pre-chewed", Rudd (1987)). No less innovative is Persius' use of the substan-tivizing pronouns: the striking combination at 1.9 *nostrum istud uiuere triste* "that gloomy life of ours" results from the juxtaposition of first-person possessive *nostrum* and second-person demonstrative *istud*: whose gloomy life is it? Where is the speaker placing himself? One may contrast 1.122 *hoc ridere meum* (picking up *cachinno* in line 12); 6.38 –39 *sapere* ... | ... *nostrum hoc*.

Particularly well documented in satire is also the use of the infinitive governed by a non-verbal adjective (Hofmann and Szantyr (1965) II.350). The earliest example is in Lucilius, 414M *soluere nulli lentus*. Persius has *artifex sequi* prol. 11 and eleven more examples (1.70; 1.59 *mobilis imitari*; 1.118 *callidus suspendere*, cf. 3.51; 2.54; 5.15, 24, 37; 6.5–6, 23, 24; with comparative 4.16 *melior sorbere*). Horace has ten examples in the *Sermones* (*cautus* 1.6.51, *contentus* 1.10.59, *durus* 1.4.8, 2.7.85, *fortis* twice, *meritus* 1.3.120, *minor* 2.3.313, *piger* 1.4.12, *ridiculus* 2.8.24, to which one may add the constructions with the verbal adjectives *suetus* 1.8.18 and *adsuetus* 2.2.11); but it is a small figure compared to the total eighty-five examples in his lyric poetry (Bo (1960) 263). The usage is characteristic of poetic language, and another case of a pattern of economy which poetic and spoken usage developed independently (Coleman (1999) 83).

Lexicon: Informality and Stylization

All satirists set the tone of their work with a rejection of the language and themes of high poetry in programmatic places. According to Varro *L.* 5.17, Lucilius opened his mature, and entirely hexametrical, collection of satires with an Ennianesque *aetheris et terrae genitabile quaerere tempus* (Lucil. 1M). Horace's address to Maecenas is polemic and prosaic: "How is it (*qui fit*), Maecenas, that no-one (*nemo*) is content with his own lot?" (*S.* 1.1). Persius cites a (most probably parodic) grand line from Lucilius (Persius 1.1 = Lucil. 9M *o curas hominum! o quantum est in rebus inane!* "Ah, the obsessions of men! What an empty world we live in"), only to dismiss it straight away with two lines of comic segmented dialogue (1.2–3 *"quis leget haec?" min tu istud ais? nemo hercule. "nemo?"* | *uel duo uel nemo. "turpe et miserabile." quare?* " 'Who will read this?' 'Are you asking me? Why, no one.' 'No one?' 'Well, perhaps one or two.' 'Disgraceful! Pathetic!' 'But why?' "). Juvenal threatens to retaliate against the harassment of contemporary epic, and does it having recourse to rhetorical questions, ellipse and the mundane *repono* "pay back" (*OLD* s.v. 5) (1.1 *semper ego auditor tantum? numquamne reponam* | *uexatus totiens rauci Theseide Cordi?* "Must I be always a listener only, never hit back, although so often assailed by the hoarse *Theséid* of Cordus?").

A study of satiric diction can hardly be disentangled from a study of satiric themes. The subject matter of satire is the variety of everyday life – politics and war, food and drink, love and sex, friends and enemies, school and entertainment – and the inclusion of themes excluded from other genres, whether high (epic and tragedy) or low (comedy), required the inclusion in satiric diction of formerly excluded terminology. I deal with some specific types in the following sections. My preliminary considerations here concern register, and more specifically the similarity, and the distance, between satire and other mimetic literature. By way of introduction, consider the following passage from Petronius' *Cena Trimalchionis*, which shares with satire a characteristic topic (money), its ranting tone and its linguistic vividness. The speaker is the freedman Ganymedes (Petr. 44.13–15):

> sed quare? habemus aedilem **non trium cauniarum**, qui sibi mauult assem quam uitam nostram. itaque domi gaudet, plus in die nummorum accipit, quam **alter** patrimonium habet. iam scio unde acceperit denarios mille aureos. sed **si nos coleos haberemus**, non tantum sibi placeret. nunc populus est **domi leones, foras uulpes**. quod ad me attinet, iam pannos meos comedi, et si perseuerat haec annona, **casulas meas** uendam.

How come? Well, we've got this two-bit aedile who'd sell us all for a penny. He's sittin' all cosy at home, makes more money in a day than anybody else has got in the family. And now I know where he got that thousand gold denarii, though I'm not sayin'. If we had any balls, we'd wipe that grin off his face. But the people are lions at home and foxes in public. As for me, I've sold every rag I owned just to feed myself, and if prices don't go down I'm going to have to let that little shack of mine go. (Trans. S. Ruden)

Note the use of *alter* for *alius*, prefiguring Romance outcomes (K-S I.139), and the substitution of *foras* for *foris* (Väänänen (2003) 197–198 §245). Morphological variants typical of "vulgar" speech are generally absent from satire (see for Horace, Ricottilli (2003) 472). So are orthographic variants departing from the author's own practice. Characterization purposes motivate Horace's *plostellum* "little cart" (< *plaustrum*, regularly used in *S.* 1.6.42) at *S.* 2.3.247, for that was probably the pronunciation of the word as stereotyped in a children's game (Campanile (1971/2008) 356–357); or Lucilius' derision of *Cecilius pretor*'s rusticity at 1130M (e.g. Adams (2007) 7; Chahoud (2007) 46; Campanile (1971/2008) 359). Switches to non-Latin words such as (if one can believe the fragment's source: Adams (2007) 175–176) Praenestine *tongeo* in Enn. *uar.* 3C or Oscan *sollo* in Lucil. 1318M find a similar explanation.

Ganymedes fears for his *casulae* ("emphatic" plural: Hofmann and Szantyr (1965) II.16). The frequency of this diminutive in Late Latin suggests that the form had a wide currency, although the attestestations in literary Latin of the Classical and post-Classical period are few: in prose the word is found only in Petronius and Apuleius, in poetry in the *Moretum* and in Juvenal. Distribution points to a low register; but Juvenal places it in an alliterative context and pairs it with the equally emotive diminutive for "puppy" at 9.61 *rusticus infans | cum matre et casulis et conlusore catello* "that child in the country with his mother and little cottage and playmate pup"; the surrounding contexts in 11.153 *suspirat longo non uisam tempore matrem | et casulam* "he sadly misses the mother he has not seen for years, and longs to return to the cabin" and in 14.179 *uiuite contenti casulis et collibus istis | o pueri* "remain content, my lads, with those little cabins of yours, and with those hills" have a similarly nostalgic and poetic flavour. The force of these forms has to be evaluated in each of the contexts in which they occur. Horace, for instance, speaks modestly – or so he would have us believe – of his own *uersiculi* at *S.* 1.10.32, and disparagingly of somebody else's at *S.* 1.2.10. Diminutives in general, and diminutive adjectives in particular, tend to have an emotive connotation, be it affectionate or derogatory. The presence of these forms in conversational registers is more accurately described as an oral feature (Koch (1995) 140) than a prosaic one (Axelson (1945) *contra* Ernout (1946–1965) II. The emotive quality of diminutives makes them a productive area of *ad hoc* formations (Hofmann and Szantyr (1965) II.772); to the high number of diminutive adjectives in particular, which are comparatively rare in poetry except for comedy, satirical poets appear to contribute coinages such as *macellus* (Lucil. 242M), *rubicundulus* (Juv. 6.425); *rancidulus* Persius 1.33, Juv. 11.135).

Idiomatic expressions abound in satire but coarse language is generally avoided (see below). As Smith (1975) 111 notes, the slang phrase *si nos coleos haberemus* is found in Persius in more polite form (1.103 *si testiculi uena ulla paterni | uiueret in nobis*), and in Quintilian in high-prose style (*Inst.* 1.10.31 *si quid in nobis uirilis roboris maneat*). The proverbial "not worth three Caunian figs" has comic ancestry (Aristophanes *Pax*

848; Pl. *Poen.* 381 and 463 *homo trioboli*); we find a variation in Persius 5.76 *non tresis agaso*. The proverb "lions at home and foxes on the street" is also comic (Aristophanes *Pax* 1189–1190), drawing on animal imagery, like many of Horace's proverbs (e.g. S. 2.1.52 *dente lupus, cornu taurus petit*, 2.1.55 *neque calce lupus quemquam neque dente petit bos* (in parenthesis); 2.2.64 *hac urget lupus, hac canis, aiunt*). Juvenal substitutes sententiousness for proverbiality: "Horace likes proverbs, which are unpretentious and folksy, like Sancho Panza; Juvenal, like Don Quixote, prefers *sententiae*, which belong to a higher realm of thought" (Highet (1954/2009) 293 n. 27).

Plainness and expressiveness

Certain categories of words are undeniably low-register colloquial. Alongside obscenities (see below), one might mention onomatopoetic and nursery words (André (1978) 60–75) *lallare* (Persius 3.18, cf. Jerome's *Epist.* 14.3), *pappare* (Persius 3.17, cf. Pl. *Epid.* 727), and *papae* (Persius 5.79; Juv. 6.633). A great number of terms and expressions, however, do not have a register connotation per se. There is nothing intrinsically prosaic or poetic about a word like e.g. *oculus* "eye"; there may be an affective connotation in the diminutive *ocellus* in erotic contexts, be it in Plautus or in Catullus; but the grotesque image of Persius 1.18 *patranti ocello* "ejaculating eye" (trans. Gunderson in Freudenberg (2005) 237) is achieved through typically poetic *breuitas* (Kroll (1924/1988) 49 paraphrases: "cuius oculi fracti sunt tamquam eius, qui coitum patrat"). No less creative is Juvenal's absurd juxtaposition of the grand archaism *induperator* and the semantically lowly verbs *gluttio* and *ructo* in 4.28–29 (Powell (1999) 326). Staying with parts of the body, the word *uenter* does make its occasional appearance in the epics of Ennius and Virgil, in place of the recherché synonym *aluus* (Adams (1980) 54); only distribution tells us that *uenter* was the term for everyday use, and the one to carry the connotation of bowel movements: six examples in Lucilius (*aluus* conjectural at 661M), ten in Horace's S. and *Epist.* (*aluus* twice), three in Persius, fourteen in Juvenal (*aluus* once). What satire achieves, for example, is the transformation *pars pro toto* of people into bellies (Lucil. 75M *uiuite lurcones, comedones, uiuite uentris*; cf. Adams (1982c) 42), and the assimilation of bellies and voices, hollow and empty (Persius prol. 11). When register-differentiated synonyms are available, satire chooses the one more fitting to the context: Lucilius, for example, normally refers to the "lips" as *labra* (303, 1004, 1299M), the most common term in all periods and genres of Latinity (Fleury in *TLL* s.v. *labium* VII/2.774.81–84), but goes for erotic *labellum* in an explicitly erotic passage (303M), and for the lower term *labea* in the assault described at 336M. Also at 336M Lucilius describes the opponent's face as a *rostrum* "snout", a slang term here and at 210M; similar transfers of animal terminology to humans occur elsewhere in Roman humour and were passed on to the Romance languages (see Adams (1982b) 102–103; (2007) 254–255 and 82).

Absence or limited usage in high poetry classifies some words as definitely **prosaic**, for example *nemo* and *iste* (Axelson (1945) 71–72; 76). Extensive recourse to plain words (*habere, facere, dare, esse*, etc.) also points towards an informal register, when distribution of examples supports the hypothesis (see Chahoud (2010) 50–53 for plainness as a generally accepted indicator of colloquialism). I offer here merely a few selective remarks. A famously "prosaic" word (Axelson (1945) 94) is *sane*, a "subjective and evaluative" intensifier (Risselada (1994) 334–339): against sixty attestations in Plautus, Virgil – the first to introduce it in high poetry – has only one, with concessive force (*A.* 10.48). In Lucil. 468M *id genus sane* the word emphasizes the literally generalizing phrase *id genus* "that sort", i.e. "and all that" (cf. Hor. *S.* 1.2.2 *hoc genus omne* "and all that lot"). One should differentiate between the use of *sane* as a sentence adverb "certainly; and that's a fact" (*OLD* 3), and its use with adjectives and adverbs, which is an analytical form of the superlative, "quite, decidedly" (*OLD* 2), as in Pl. *As.* 8 *sane breuest* or Ter. *Hau.* 524 *sane bona*. Juv. 9.46 *sed tu sane tenerum et puerum te | et pulchrum et dignum cyatho caeloque putabas* "but you, of course, used to think yourself a pretty young lad, fit to become a butler in heaven" is probably the former construction.

Intensifying adverbs used in satire are *bene, belle, pulchre, male*, with various degrees of informality (Hofmann (1951/2003) 195–207 §§ 69–76): *bene*, like Fr. *bien* (e.g. Lucil. 1070M *bene potus*; Hor. *S.* 1.3.61, 1.9.44, 2.3.74) undoubtedly belongs to "Konversationssprache" (Wölfflin (1933) 138–140), but it enjoys respectability, as is suggested by its occurrence in Ennius' epic (see Skutsch on *Ann.* 32 and 268) and by its humorous or ironic use (Campanile (1971/2008) 382); the offensiveness of *non bene = male* in Priap. 80.1 is not its construction but its contextual reference to a *mentula*. Horace would use *male* in the same way (*S.* 1.9.65 *salsus*, 2.5.45 *ualidus*). More decidedly informal are *belle* "nicely" (Hor. *S.* 1.4.136, Persius 1.49, cf. Cic. *Att.* 6.1.25 *bene curiosi*, and, with ellipsis, *Att.* 5.10.2 *bene adhuc*) and *pulchre* "pretty [good/well]" (Persius 1.44, 49; four times in Petronius e.g. 51.3, 64.2; *pulchre nosse* at Hor. *S.* 1.9.62).

Idiomatic phrases also lend themselves to the satirist's appropriation and possible innovation. This is the case for instance with idioms such as *nihil esse cum aliquo* "I've nothing to do with" (Hor. *S.* 1.2.57–58) or *magnum facere* "to accomplish a great, i.e. difficult task" (Hor. *S.* 1.4.10); but one should appreciate Horace's stylization of *bene facit quod* "it is a good thing that" (markedly colloquial: Hofmann and Szantyr (1965) II.579) at *S.* 1.4.17f. *di bene fecerunt, inopis me quodque pusilli | finxerunt animi, raro et perpauca loquentis* "Thank God for giving me a timid mind with few ideas, one which seldom speaks and then says practically nothing": note the postponement of subordinating *quod*, and the emphatic isolation of the first element of the tricolon *inopis ... pusilli ... raro–loquentis*. Persius, in line with his preference for the conflation of constructions and imagery, gives a coarse twist to the idiom *uenit in mentem* "it came to mind" at 4.48 *si facis in penem quidquid tibi uenit* "if you do whatever occurs to your prick".

If satirical *sermo* approaches and exploits prosaic features, it also distances itself from it by adopting some exclusively poetic characteristics. Expressiveness accounts for the convergence between colloquial and poetic language against the rationalizing processes that lie behind stylized prose (Leumann (1947) = (1959) 134–135; Coleman (1999) 90). I now turn to illustrate briefly an area of word choice and coinage in which satire shares a prominent place with other poetic genres.

It is often stated, following Quint. *Inst.* 1.5.70, that Latin, unlike Greek, did not like **compounds**. More correctly one should say that the productivity of *nominal* compounds in Latin was subject to such constraints as were imposed by the length of Latin words and Latin preference for prefixation and agglutination (Fruyt (2002) 259). It has been rightly observed that "special situations, *away from everyday speech*" (my emphasis) may favour the creation of nominal compounds (Fruyt (2002) 264–265): poetry is one such situation. Greek-based or Greek-influenced formations may take a prosodic form especially suited to the hexameter (esp. choriamb, e.g. *altisonus*); some forms may be productive in the Latin poetic diction, and from there the Latin language, others may be on-the-spot formations serving a purpose in their context (Coleman (1999) 61–63). Just as the most surrealist of Plautus' countless coinages serves a comic purpose, high-style oddities such as Pac. *trag.* 408 *incuruiceruicus* had no other currency than in their own text and possibly in parody, e.g. Lucil. 654M *contemnificus*, in which both elements are verbs, and was clearly intended as parodic of high style (Leumann (1977) 136; Coleman (1999) 61–63; Fruyt (2002) 261). From the wide rage of examples in satire, and in Lucilius in particular, I select a few examples of nominal compounds with the second element verbal, which are notably productive but can also be "whimsical creations" (Fruyt (2002) 265). Some are established features of comic diction, such as *furcifer* (Hor. *S.* 2.7.22), but most are *ad hoc* formations for contemptuous or humorous effect, such as the hapax legomena *cordipugus* "heart-piercing" verse (Lucil. 698M) and *mercedimerus* "wage-earning" legions (Lucil. 13M). The metaphorical sense of *lucifugus* for a "shady" individual (Lucil. 468M) recurs in Cicero and Apuleius, and is the only sense known for the noun *lucifuga* (in Seneca, *Ep.* and Apuleius). This type of compound noun, which defines *nomina agentis*, is also comic in flavour. Compare such comic isolated formations as Lucil. 718M *cibicida* "food-killer" (the first case of a compound –*cida* with active sense: Bader (1962) 74) and Pl. *Mos.* 884 *bucaeda* "ox-slaughterer", or the characterization of bibulous women in Lucil. 302 *uinibua* "wine-drinker" (οἰνοπότις Aristophanes *Thesmophoriazusae* 393, with *bua* = baby-talk for *potio*, Var. ap. Non. 131–132L; cf. Lindner (1996) 206) and Pl. *Cur.* 77 (*anus*) *multibiba atque merobiba* "much-and-unmixed-wine-drinking old hag". All these formations are isolated and evidently intended for comic effect in their contexts. In some cases, however, they may reflect a tendency of spoken Latin, in its informal or lower registers, to create compounds of this kind, such as *seribibi* (*CIL* IV.581) or *piscicapus* (*CIL* IV.826) from Pompeii (Väänänen (2003) 166–168 §196; cf. Biville (2005)). The epithet *pinnirapus* "peak-snatcher" for a gladiator in Juv. 3.158 does remind us of the comic *bustirapus* "grave-robber" of Pl. *Ps.* 361, although one cannot rule out the possibility that the noun might have enjoyed some currency in the technical jargon of gladiators (Courtney ad loc.; *contra* Mosci Sassi (1992) 152–154).

Finally, a note on **Greek words** in early satire. If it is true that Greek words add a touch of foreignness of sound, colour, and dignity to high poetry (cf. Adams and Mayer (1999) 11–12), satirical poetry pursued an altogether different line, appropriating non-literary, rare, or downright vulgar words from the Greek spoken at Rome, as well as loanwords and calques for Greek literary, philosophical, technical terminology. Lucilius, who counted himself among the ranks of *semigraeci* "half-Greek" (379M) introduced Greek vocabulary as well as on-the-spot hybrid formations (e.g. 86M *rhetoricoterus* "more rhetorical" and perhaps 187M *lerodesque* "and rubbish") in his satires on a massive scale, to characterize the speech of e.g. highly-educated orators (84–85M) as well as drunken women (238M), and of course his own (e.g. 184–188M); he even established criteria for the morphology of Greek nouns and adjectives (Housman (1907) 150 = (1972) 687; cf. Petersmann (1999) 300). Characterization purposes, as well as participation in the informal codeswitching practised by the educated Roman élite (Adams (2003a)) – motivate Lucilius' free mixture of Greek and Latin which Horace

(*S.* 1.10.30) would come to criticize and reject as a practice more befitting a bilingual Canusian than a Roman citizen (see, in a wide literature, Korfmacher (1934–1935); Mariotti (1960); Baier (2001); Chahoud (2004). Horace does not lapse from his rule when occasionally adopting Greek literary terms (*S.* 1.10.43 *epos*; 2.3.193 *heros*) or adding a comic touch (e.g. *S.* 1.2.49 *moechor*) or everyday flavour (or Lucilian allusion: *S.* 1.6.126 *lusum ... trigonem*). Juvenal, after Horace, disapproved of Greek vocabulary (3.63), used it sparingly, and even then possibly in a deliberate imitation of Lucilius (Courtney (1980) 46).

Coarse slang

Physicality in general, and sexual practices in particular, have always played a central role in satirical subject matter, and Roman satire is no exception. But while the texts are populated by graphic descriptions of sexual acts and references to bodily functions, the authors' choice of vocabulary does not match Martial's interpretation of *Romana simplicitate loqui* as a taste for what we would call "four-letter words" (Mart. 11.20). Martial, like Catullus and the *carmina Priapea*, allowed the blunt language we read in Pompeiian graffiti to enter his literary works in a way the Roman satirists never did. While generally unseemly, vulgar and coarse words (Quint. *Inst.* 10.1.8f. *parum uerecunda*; *humilia et uulgaria*; *sordida*) might be acceptable and even appropriate in certain contexts, basic obscenities (*foeditates*) – "words that have no other, primary sense to soften their impact" (Adams (1982a) 1) – were not. Cicero's approval of them in a famous exchange with his witty friend Paetus, is a personal statement about *libertas loquendi* that in itself signifies banishment of words such as *mentula* from polite conversation (*Fam.* 9.22).

For all their talk of asserted or perverted masculinity, of wives and prostitutes, the Roman satirists refrain from coarse slang. A significant exception is Hor. *S.* 1.2, where the presence of the words *futuo, cunnus* and *mutto* is motivated, we are told, by the Lucilian tone of the poem. But even if we had had the whole of Lucilius, we would probably see our suspicion confirmed that the obscenity of much of his poetry was very seldom realized by recourse to sexual slang. The surviving fragments exhibit only a handful of examples. We find three instances of possibly vulgar terms for the male and female sexual organ respectively (307 and 1067M *mutto*; 940M *eugium*) and an obscene description of intercourse polluted by bodily fluids (1186M *haec inbubinat, at contra te inbulbitat <ille>*); the reference to buggery at 74M *pedicum*, despite the scholium "*uitium mollitiae*", is dubious. In Lucilius as in the later tradition, obscene subject matter is otherwise handled by suggestive innuendo, metaphorical or metonymic association (Adams (1982a) 221–222). I give examples in my selective inventory of euphemistic substitutes below.

Only Horace's diatribic persona in *S.* 1.2.127 literally "fucks", and it is a comic scene. In the lexical world of satire people "are with" someone (*esse cum*: Lucil. 504M, a time-honoured euphemism since Plautus and Cato (Var. *L.* 6.80); "sleep" (*dormio*: Juv. 6.34, 6.376) or "lie" (*iaceo*: Juv. 6.27) with someone; they simply "do it" (*facere*: Juv. 7.240; see Courtney ad loc. with Adams (1981) 123–124) or specify positions (Lucil. 303–306M; Hor. *S.* 1.2.125 *supposuit corpus*; Juv. 6.334 *clunem summittat*) and movements, either directly (*ceueo*: Persius 1.87; Juv. 9.40; *criso*: Lucil. 330M, Juv. 6.320; cf. Juv. 6.O19 *clunem atque latum discunt uibrare*), or metaphorically ("grind": Hor. *S.* 1.2.35 *permolere uxores*). Whatever sexual assault the speaker contemplates as a punishment for his wife in Lucil. 283M (*uxorem caedam potius quam castrem egomet me* "I'd rather bang the wife than castrate myself with my own hands"), the act is described as one of "striking", although one cannot rule out that the choice of *caedo* over *futuo* or *pedico* might have been determined by alliteration, which Lucilius underlines with chiasmus; but Juvenal too avoids *pedico*, in a far more shocking passage where there is no doubt as to what act is being described (9.43 *agere intra uiscera penem*). Acts of sexual *tractatio* are described in variously graphic terms (Lucil. 1031M *muttonis manum perscribere*; Juv. 6.238 *praeputia ducit*) or figurative ones (Lucil. 307M *lacrimas muttoni absterget*), but no one uses the vulgar verbs *masturbor* (Martial) or *frico* (Schol. Juv.).

Likewise avoided are explicit terms for male and female private parts. The basic term *mentula*, which Catullus and Martial exploit widely, is nowhere to be found in satire. The closest in register, judging from inscriptions and glosses, is *mutto*, which provides both Lucilius (307M) and Horace (*S.* 1.2.68) with the opportunity for personification of the organ; but when Persius, following Lucilius, refers to the "sobbing membrum", he goes for the anatomical term *inguen* (6.72), a favourite of Juvenal's. Otherwise the term is the standard *penis* (Persius 4.48; Juv. 6.337) or the metaphorical *cauda* "tail" (Hor. *S.* 1.2.45 cf. 2.7.49); on the calque *cicer* on Gk ἐρέβινθος in the Oxford fragment of Juvenal (6.O373B) see Courtney ad loc. and Adams (1982a) 228. While Petronius' freedman speaks freely of *colei* (Petr. 44.14, above), the satirists refer to *testes* (e.g. Lucil. 281M, in a word-play with the *testa* that cuts them off), or, with the false diminutive that will give the modern outcomes of the word, to *testiculi* (e.g. Lucil. 534–536M; Persius 1.103; Juv. 6.339, 6.372). The picture is only slightly different for the female parts. Horace's early diatribes count three occurrences of *cunnus* (Hor. *S.* 1.2.36, 70; 1.3.107); in all cases the word is a mortifying synecdoche for "woman" (Adams (1983) 322). The authors offer no less offensive references to the female parts, but they do it figuratively – e.g. *bulga* "bag" (Lucil. 73M) – or metonymically – *uesica* "bladder" (Juv. 1.39, 6.64); *uolua* "womb", recipient of the crude metaphor *inmeio* in Persius 6.73, and subject in Juv. 6.129 to a periphrasis for the obscene word *landica*, which even at his most relaxed Cicero refrained from writing down (Cic. *Fam.* 9.22.2; see Jocelyn (1980) 153–154).

Hubert Petersmann's excellent study of the language of early Roman satire explains the general lack of offensive language in Ennius' medley poetry with the inferior social status of Ennius, a foreigner without Roman citizenship, who addressed his work to free-born patrons and the educated ruling classes in general (Petersmann (1999) 296). This would explain the abrupt change of direction on the part of Lucilius, *eques Romanus*, although, as we have seen, he seems to have exercised considerable restraint in the adoption of sexual slang, while appropriating, or perhaps devising, a series of metaphors for his often risqué subject matter. The fragmentary status of the text does not allow further speculations. The facts as we have them point to Horace as the candidate for the palm of downright vulgar diction (*cunnus, futuo*); and yet he was writing under a patron and reminding everyone of his inferior status as *libertino patre natus* "only a freedman's son" (1.6.6, 45, 46). In addition to the sexual terms noted above, Horace uses *meio* (*S.* 2.7.52; also in Juv. 2.12), *mingo* (*S.* 1.8.38), *caco* (1.8.38), *merda* (1.8.37); *pedo* (1.8.46) and the rare *oppedo* "fart in the face of" (1.9.70). The brutal physicality of Persius' satire is almost entirely figurative, as the shocking image at 6.72–73 aptly illustrates (and Rudd's translation aptly conveys): *cum morosa uago singultiet inguine uena, | patriciae immeiat uuluae* "when the fastidious vein throbs his roving cock, relieve himself into an upper-class pouch". As for Juvenal, Courtney notes that *podex* is "the only essentially gross physical word" used by him (2.12) and by Lucilius before him (1267M); it is very bland coarseness indeed, compared to the semantically equivalent *culus* of Catullus, Martial and graffiti.

Conclusions

In my necessarily selective survey, I have perhaps taken for granted the most obvious characteristic of Roman satire, i.e. its humour. Much of it lies in the comic, derisive, or abusive representation of voices, which matches in its adaptability, if not register, Petronius' sustained characterization of his freedmen's substandard Latin. When satire presents us with appropriations or parodic distortions of literary registers, we have an easier task in identifying them and explaining their function in the texts. When Horace has recourse to the comic word *erus*, he has a Terentian scene in mind (2.3.265; cf. 2.8.16, 43); when one of his speakers utters *moriemur inulti* "we'll die in vain" at *S.* 2.8.34, it is hard not to think, anachronistically or not, of Virgil's *Aeneid* (2.670, 4.659). Likewise representations of speech must have some element of authenticity, or else there would be no point in the adoption of socially, sexually or otherwise differenti-ated expressions. The Latin voice of Roman satire, programmatically conversational and forcefully personal, is capable of dubbing a variety of linguistic registers, of raising the plainness, disjointedness or emotiveness of oral discourse to artful poetry, or vice versa incorporating techniques of poetic diction into its discursive texture. In this sense the definition of satire as *sermo* holds true, in its status of "oralité mimetique" or "parlato scritto" (Koch (1995); Österreicher (1995); Ricottilli (2003)), despite the striking dif-ferences that separate Lucilius' multilingual aggressiveness from Horace's irony, Persius' graphic obscurity from Juvenal's grand verbosity. The satirists' contribution to literary Latin is the creation and development of a genre purporting to represent realities – including the realities of language and literature – and of a genre-specific register that, in different ways, purports to reproduce conversational modes of expression, whatever form the dialogue might take and however realistic, or fictitious, the interlocutors might be. In all this process authors introduce individual elements of stylistic innovation:

> the author of the text, or more precisely his linguistic conscience, *selects* elements or con-structions that he regards as particularly characteristic of the *langage de l'immédiat*. One must then expect an extremely subtle and sophisticated game of phonic, morphosyntactical, lexical and discursive-textual allusions, which succeeds to produce the effect that, in another context, we call *textual polyphony*. (Österreicher (1995) 153; my translation)

FURTHER READING

On the language of the *saturae* of Ennius and Lucilius see Gratwick (1982b) and Petersmann (1999), to be complemented for Ennius with Courtney (2003) and for Lucilius with Mariotti (1960) (in Italian) and Manuwald (2001) (in German). On the "colloquial" in Horace see most recently Thomas (2010) (with bibliography p. 262), to which I add, for readers of German and Italian, Müller-Lancé (1992), Horsfall (1994), and Ricottilli (2003). On Persius' language and style see the commentary of Harvey (1981); illuminating remarks on Persius' style in Nisbet (1963) and Rudd (1976 = 2009). On Juvenal's diction the sections on style and metre in Courtney (1980) 36–55 are as invaluable as his scholarly notes; an important corrective of the view of Juvenal's register as "high" in Powell (1999) and (2001). General on literary genres in sociolinguistic perspective: Cuzzolin and Haverling (2009); on the complex relation between colloquial and literary Latin: Dickey and Chahoud (2010).

ACKNOWLEDGEMENT

I wish to thank Jim Adams for invaluable suggestions and corrections on an earlier draft of this chapter. All translations from Horace, Persius and Juvenal are, unless otherwise stated, Niall Rudd's (1973 and 1991).

CHAPTER 22

The Language of Roman Oratory and Rhetoric

J.G.F. Powell

Tantum inter se distant genere dicendi [sc. oratores] ut nemo sit alteri similis

[Orators] differ so much from one another in their manner of speaking, that none is like any other.

(Quint. *Inst.* 2.8.2)[1]

Oratory, Rhetoric and Real Life

The topic of the language of oratory and its relation to other, more everyday uses of language is not a simple one. When the word "oratory" is mentioned, we are apt to think of the great moments at which a speaker, maybe addressing an audience of hundreds or thousands, appears to soar far above the level of ordinary speech: in such an arena, quite apart from aesthetic considerations, the conventions of ordinary language need to be adapted (especially if no artificial amplification of the voice is available)[2] in order to ensure that the message can be heard and understood at all. What we call a "declamatory" delivery, i.e. loud and clear, with careful enunciation, relatively slow tempo, and enhanced intonation patterns, is just a practical consequence of this necessity, as also are many of the well-known "rhetorical figures" used in composition, especially those involving repetition of words or phrases. But orators also speak to smaller audiences on less grand occasions, using a style much less different (if indeed different at all) from standard conversational language. Notoriously, tastes and fashions in public speaking vary; one generation may prefer its oratory relatively expansive, whereas another cultivates laconic brevity; at one period a taste may develop for ornamentation and figures of speech of various kinds, while the next may distrust such things as being artificial; even the question of what counts as proper use of language in public may be the subject of vigorous controversy, and words or phrases of an insulting or sensitive nature may incur moral or

A Companion to the Latin Language, First Edition. Edited by James Clackson.
© 2011 Blackwell Publishing Ltd. Published 2011 by Blackwell Publishing Ltd.

legal censure. Effective speech may come from art or nature or both; the gift of fluency can cause a speaker to come across as glib and insincere, while over-conscientious preparation or obvious following of rhetorical rules can equally often attract criticism.[3] There may be real or perceived cultural differences in styles of public speaking,[4] while a single culture may embrace a wide range of different styles and levels of competence both in oratory itself and in the rhetorical training that is offered to aspiring politicians, lawyers, or ordinary citizens.[5] In sum, there is seldom if ever just one thing that can be called the "language of oratory".

These generalisations are as true of Ancient Rome as of anywhere else. The Romans in the last two centuries of the Republic took some time to come to terms with what one may call the professionalisation of oratory and with the systematised rhetorical theory and training which they initially imported from Greece; but once they had done so, they cherished their own ideal of the Great Orator, lovingly delineated in detail by Cicero or Quintilian, or summed up by Virgil in the course of a memorable simile near the beginning of the *Aeneid*.[6] A version of this ideal has often informed post-Classical conceptions of Roman culture. It is, however, much easier to grasp the ideal than it is to find out about the reality of Roman oratory at any given period. Scholars may be tempted to use the prescriptions of rhetorical theorists as evidence for what Roman oratory was like, but it is not always easy to bridge the gap between theory and practice. Some of the ancient critics' recommendations for effective speaking are largely a matter of common sense, too generalised to be very enlightening: in the area of language, for example, they tend to emphasise both the need to conform to accepted linguistic usage (implying similarity to ordinary language) and at the same time the need to be ornate and memorable (implying distance from it). In a philosophical context (*Off.* 2.48), Cicero suggests that the category of *oratio* ("speech") can be divided into two, ordinary conversation (*sermo*)[7] and "eloquence" (*eloquentia*) or what we would call oratory.[8] For the latter he adopts the alternative term *contentio*, which implies making an effort to prove a point; it is probably true to say in general that in the Roman view, serious oratory was primarily about arguing a case, either in a political arena ("deliberative" oratory) or in the law courts ("judicial" or "forensic" oratory).[9] It may well be that it was easier for Romans to define oratory by its argumentative purpose and audience, rather than by any particular features of language.

On this basis it might seem that the language of Roman oratory would be identical with the language of either law or politics, depending on the subject-matter. As regards vocabulary, this is no doubt largely true. However, the non-expert nature of Roman political bodies and legal tribunals meant that orators tended to steer clear of excessive technicality, even when dealing with precise points of law or governmental policy. Cicero notoriously set up the image of the orator in opposition to that of the legal expert, maintaining that a rhetorically trained advocate, even with limited knowledge of the law, could win against any jurist. Though the Roman advocate might in practice know a good deal of law, his training (if he had any) was as a public speaker, not as a lawyer.[10] After Cicero's time, a member of the Roman governing class might certainly be a specialist in law, strategy, civil engineering, or some other branch of knowledge, but these were not seen as necessary qualifications for a public career; one could learn on the job.[11] Rhetoric, in time, came to be seen as a more generally necessary accomplishment, and appropriate as a form of higher education; modern readers may initially be surprised at this, but a Roman of the Principate would equally be surprised that modern prospective politicians do not automatically receive training in public speaking before they start their careers, since communication is still such an important part of their business.

It can be argued, indeed, that the qualities of Latin oratory (at least when it is at its best) are precisely the result of the need to hold the attention of an audience not necessarily interested, and to explain matters clearly and explicitly to an audience not necessarily well informed: these are the virtues of the teacher, and in fact Cicero regularly used the word *docere* "teach" to denote the orator's function of informing his audience. One of the terms of approval regularly applied to Latin orators was *disertus*, which literally means "explicit";[12] we might say "articulate". This striving after explicitness is apparent both in argument and in style. While in scholarly accounts emphasis is traditionally placed on the orator's manipulation of the audience's emotions, an equally prominent place is in fact accorded by the Romans, both in theory and in practice, to rational exposition, or at least the appearance of it;[13] sometimes, of course, the appearance of clarity and rationality is calculated to mislead.[14] For example, Cicero is on the whole more addicted than are the Classical Greek orators to forms of argument such as the dilemma.[15] From the Augustan period onwards, the word *color* "colour" – presumably a metaphor from the paintbox – came to be used as a technical term to mean a particular argumentative angle on an issue, especially a striking or unexpected one: it is notable that it came to be so used in reference to argument, rather than to qualities of style as one might initially expect. But the desire to reinforce the message produces stylistic effects as well: in some authors, especially Cicero and his imitator Pliny the Younger, it leads to the pervasive feature known as *abundantia* – saying everything several times with a multiplicity of synonyms. Alternatively, it can lead to a taste for striking rhetorical point, antithesis and epigram, the so-called "lapidary" style seen especially in Seneca and Tacitus, which has its modern counterpart in the slogan-writing of political or advertising campaigns. This tendency spread far beyond the confines of practical oratory or school rhetoric, and in the first century CE threatened to invade almost every genre of literature.

Training in oratory does not, however, necessarily involve learning a particular register of the language; it may just involve learning to use the existing registers more appropriately and with greater facility. But because of the difficulty of codifying the "magic ingredient" of successful eloquence, ancient rhetoric (like other forms of training in public speaking) tended to rely on a repertoire of formulae and clichés that could be codified. Thus rhetorical training often encouraged adherence to traditional patterns, for example in the use or over-use of particular figures of speech (e.g. metaphors, rhetorical questions, exclamations), types of sentence-structure and arrangement of words (e.g. anaphora, parallelism, chiasmus), rhythms (such as the notorious Ciceronian sentence-ending *esse videatur*), and so on.[16] These are not necessarily features of all oratorical style; they are found especially in what was called the "grand" style, and inappropriate grandeur with over-use of rhetorical figures could attract censure then as now. There was also a considerable element of imitation of Classical models and repetition of commonplaces; Cicero himself often found it useful to imitate passages both from the Athenian orators and from his Roman predecessors, probably more surreptitiously than by way of explicit allusion, and in later generations Cicero himself is ever-present as a model to be either imitated or consciously avoided. Once the system of rhetorical training had become established at Rome, its products were doubtless identifiable by their use of a "rhetorical" style, which would thus have developed into a desirable badge of élite membership; by the middle and later Empire it would not be altogether absurd to say that you could tell an educated man by his *clausulae*.[17]

From the second century BCE onwards, some Roman orators started to publish written versions of their speeches as the orators of Classical Greece had done. The relationship between what was said and what was published was already in antiquity, and has remained, a matter of controversy. The question is always raised in modern scholarship in connection with Cicero, less frequently in connection with other Roman orators, although the problems are largely the same. If a text of a speech is prepared in advance, as we know to have been done in some instances, there is no reason why the pre-prepared text should not be put into circulation as it stands, and the text may then provide a reliable enough guide to the language of the actual speech.[18] In a Roman law court, however, while the prosecution could prepare its opening speech in advance, both the defence and any subsequent rejoinders by the prosecution had to be adapted to the progress of the trial and could therefore only be partially prepared. Most of Cicero's written speeches, therefore, are re-creations after the event, although there is less reason than many scholars have thought to suspect that they were much altered in substance, and at least some of the original phrasing may have passed into the written version (from memory or through the use of shorthand). The written versions were themselves presumably designed for oral performance, and therefore can be expected to reflect the broad characteristics of oral delivery even if not the exact original words. Ancient readers, like modern ones, were clearly interested in reliving the occasion, and hence the suspicion that an orator had not in fact delivered the speech as published might give rise to adverse comment.[19] At the same time, the urge to elaborate and extend the text of the speech in the written version, for the sake of its literary impact on posterity, was not always resisted.[20] In all, a due measure of caution is in order. There is no reason to suppose that the texts we have are fundamentally fictitious, but at the same time we need to remember that the surviving text gives us access to the language of the original speech only at one remove.

The Unrepresentativeness of the Sample

When we approach the actual oratorical texts which have come down to us by this means, we find a rather paradoxical situation. On the one hand, it is clear that oratory was important to the Romans and that Roman oratory has been important to subsequent generations; the speeches we have were seen as worth preserving. The Roman Republic produced one orator in particular who had an overwhelming influence on both Roman and later European ideas about oratory and rhetoric: M. Tullius Cicero (106–43 BCE), whom classicising writers in later periods could refer to simply as "The Orator" *par excellence*. Under the Empire, rhetorical training was more central to education than it has ever been before or since in Europe, and probably anywhere else in the world. One might think therefore that there would be a good selection of texts to draw on and that one could generalise about the genre "Roman oratory" as we might, for example, about

Athenian oratory in the fourth century BCE, or English parliamentary or forensic oratory in modern times. But in fact there are remarkably few actual oratorical texts surviving from the Classical Latin-speaking world. We have a reasonably representative selection from the speeches of Cicero, including his most famous performances, the Catilinarians, Verrines and Philippics. But apart from that, there are just two other complete speeches from the period up to 200 CE: Pliny's *Panegyricus* in praise of the emperor Trajan,[21] and Apuleius' speech in his own defence on a charge of seduction by magic. Otherwise, there are pamphlets masquerading as speeches (e.g. Cicero's Second Philippic or Tertullian's defence of the Christian faith); there are practice speeches composed by rhetoricians as illustrations of how to do it ("declamations", such as those attributed to Quintilian); and there are scattered brief quotations from famous orators whose works have not survived.

This rather meagre material can be supplemented by referring to a number of other literary sources, and in particular to the surviving works by Cicero and others on the theory of rhetoric. These are by their nature highly prescriptive in their attitude; and when they do describe the characteristics of actual orators, they are sometimes remarkably pessimistic and disparaging. Historians of Roman literature have often tended to take these evaluations at face value. Cicero, in his dialogue called the *Brutus*, argued that oratory (that is, proper professional-style oratory informed by Greek training) came late to Rome, and this idea is usually repeated by modern scholars. Granted, little now remains of pre-Ciceronian oratory, and what there is of it has often been branded as primitive – perhaps unjustly, as we shall see. Later on, after the brief glory of the Ciceronian age, Roman oratory is held to have fallen into decline: this notion is encouraged particularly by some passages of Tacitus' *Dialogus de Oratoribus*, which express the view that, owing to the rise of professional rhetorical training and the disappearance of popular politics, oratory has been reduced to workaday mediocrity. Altogether, the history of Roman oratory tends to be imagined as a narrow bell-curve with Cicero at the top. This conventional picture is not satisfactory, and in order to see why, the historical perspective needs to be expanded.

Oratory in the Roman Republic

Rome in its origins was a city-state, with institutions that bore a general resemblance to those of many other such states in both Greece and Italy. According to tradition, both the Senate and one form of the popular assembly had existed ever since the reign of Romulus, soon after the foundation of the city. The assemblies of the Roman people were formal legislative or electoral bodies, not arenas for debate; but their sessions were preceded by *contiones* (public meetings), often lively and sometimes raucous, at which the issues would (ideally) be explained and differences aired. Whatever the actual extent of democratic participation at different periods of the Republic, the machinery itself could not function without speechmaking, whether in the popular assemblies, in senatorial debates, or in judicial processes.[22] One could see it even in the layout of the city, with its *Comitium* (assembly area outside the Senate House) and *Rostra*.[23] Furthermore, Roman political and legal convention seems to have inclined towards the making of formal speeches according to set procedure: quick-fire debate (*altercatio*) did happen, but it does not seem to have been the general rule. In the Senate, senators were called upon to speak strictly in turn according to seniority; the fact that filibustering was possible (Cic. *Leg.* 3.40) suggests that they would not normally be interrupted. In the law courts, there were often time limits laid down by statute for each side, which would make no sense unless one side held the floor at a time.

Municipal and provincial life, which replicated Roman institutions on a smaller scale, equally required the making of speeches. Negotiations with foreign communities, too, clearly involved speech-making as a matter of course; diplomacy has of course always relied on formalities, and in archaic Latin the word *orator* was often used specifically to mean an envoy. An important but often neglected consideration in the history of Roman oratory is the encounter with live public speakers from Greece (not just rhetorical theory or the texts of the classic orators), which began as soon as Rome became politically involved with any of the communities of the Greek-speaking world and would have been a reasonably regular occurrence during the later Republic, as a glance at the narrative of Polybius will show. The Roman Senate was apparently impressed, for example, by the philosopher Carneades, who was sent as Athenian envoy to the Senate in 155 BCE: it was allegedly remarked that he came not to persuade, but to force the Romans to do as he wished.[24] Such experiences could hardly fail to invite either an adverse reaction, like the one recorded for Cato the Elder, or an attempt at emulation.

Furthermore, the notion of advocacy was ingrained in Roman social attitudes. It was widely believed that ever since the earliest times, the Roman community had had a system of patronage, in which privileged citizens were expected to speak up, as "patrons", on behalf of those less privileged (whether citizens of lower status or foreign individuals or communities) who sought their protection. Although this view was doubtless over-schematic, it functioned as a myth of origins for Roman orators in historical times, who tended to project a high-minded view of themselves as the champions of the oppressed, whether as advocates or as politicians. At the same time the Roman legal system in the Classical period relied to a great extent on volunteer prosecution, a feature shared with much of the Greek world:[25] hence another side to the orator's role, as the champion of justice and scourge of vice, and hence, also, the stereotype of the malicious prosecutor (*delator*).

This, then, seems to be a world in which speechmaking is important and ubiquitous, and in which different contexts would inevitably have required different styles of composition and delivery. Nor was this true only of the Republic: more features of Republican oratorical culture persisted into the Empire than is sometimes admitted.[26] But as soon as we try to get down to detail, we reach the major difficulty that most Roman speeches were not recorded. Even of those that were committed to writing and circulated, the vast majority have been lost. The Roman oratorical texts we have from the Classical period are a very small tip of a large iceberg, and at least nine tenths of them are by just one orator – Cicero. How then is generalisation possible about the use of language in Roman oratory?

It is tempting to look for material in the Latin historians, such as Sallust and Livy, who often set out at some length what appear to be speeches made by major historical figures.[27] The problem is that, especially when dealing with earlier periods, they themselves probably had no written records of speeches on which to draw.[28] Instead, they would use their imagination to reconstruct how the speeches from past generations might have sounded. So, of course, they imagined them largely in terms of the rhetoric of their own time, perhaps with a little archaic colouring, or – more confusing still – followed the imported literary conventions of Greek historiography, sometimes with little enough concern for realism. Rather than attempt a convincing linguistic characterisation, they imposed their own style: in Sallust in particular, the author's stylistic idiosyncrasies are as apparent in the speeches as elsewhere (just as in his model Thucydides). Even so, certain instances of memorable oratory stand out in the historical tradition. Doubtless, it would be naïve to accept without question Livy's story of Menenius Agrippa pacifying the dissident plebeians *prisco illo dicendi et horrido modo* ("in that old-fashioned and unkempt way of speaking") with the story of the Belly and the Members (492 BCE: Livy 2.32), or of Camillus persuading the Romans to return to their city after the Gallic sack (390 BCE: Livy 5.51–54). Yet the picture the historians give us of the Roman Republic, as a community in which public oral debate is both customary and often decisive, need not be fundamentally implausible. It is just that the speeches in the historians provide evidence primarily for the language of Roman historical writing, not for the language of the original speeches. That these literary evocations of oratory could be seen as high points in the historical narrative is indicated by the fact that from Sallust's *Histories*, only the speeches survive, excerpted from the narrative and preserved without the surrounding context.

For Cicero in the *Brutus* – the nearest thing we have to a connected history of Roman Republican oratory – the history begins only with the first published texts of speeches. Evidently, some texts attributed to orators from the third century BCE were in circulation, though their authenticity cannot be regarded as certain; Cicero says they were preserved in family archives. Of such a kind was Quintus Fabius Maximus' funeral oration on his son, or the senatorial speech of Appius Claudius the Blind who had pulled the Senate back from coming to terms with King Pyrrhus. Others left behind them no written speeches, but a reputation for eloquence, such as Marcus Cornelius Cethegus, whom the poet Ennius described as *suauiloquenti ore … flos delibatus populi, Suadaeque medulla* "with sweet-speaking voice … the choicest flower of the People, and the innermost heart of Persuasion". But in none of these cases has any text survived from which we can judge their sweet-speaking eloquence at first hand.

Cato and Gaius Gracchus

The first Roman orator to publish his speeches systematically was Cato the Elder; texts of some of them were included in his historical work the *Origines*.[29] To Cicero, who claims to have read 150 of them, their language already seemed quaint, as it does to modern Latinists approaching them for the first time. But Cicero rightly points out that it is the Latin language that had changed; Cato was not old-fashioned for his time. It should be added that many of our shorter excerpts from Cato come from grammarians and rhetoricians, who quote them precisely because of their old-fashioned linguistic forms, thus giving the impression that Cato's language was more peculiar than it really was.[30] In the few continuous extracts we have, it is easy to see the differences from the language of Cicero's time, but it is easy also to see the sharpness of intelligence that

Cicero commended in Cato's oratory, as in the following passage from the defence of the Rhodians, which I deliberately quote in English translation to lessen the distance:

> Their most determined opponents can only find this to say against them, that they wished to be our enemies. But is there anyone among you, I ask you, who, when his own affairs are at stake, thinks it fair to be punished because he is proved to have wished to commit a crime? Nobody, I think. Certainly I would prefer that principle not to be applied to me! What then? Is there any law so severe as to say: if anyone wishes to do such-and-such, the penalty shall be one thousand sesterces less than the half of his estate; if anyone wishes to possess more than five hundred acres, let the penalty be so-and-so ... But we all wish to possess more, and we are not punished for it. Again, if it is not right to honour someone because he said he wished to do something good but didn't actually do it, then should the Rhodians suffer because they have not done anything wrong but are said to have wished to do wrong? (cited at Gel. 6.3.36–39)

Cicero's freedman Tiro found a technical term of Aristotelian dialectic (*epagoge* "induction") to characterise this form of argument. It is a fair guess that Cato did not know he was using *epagoge*; he was, however, articulating a good argument in favour of his clients, a little brusquely indeed, but with the skill of an accomplished advocate.[31]

Apart from Cato, the only other significant oratorical fragments we have from the second century BCE are some extracts from Gaius Gracchus. For a long time, taking their cue from ancient critics, scholars tended to regard both Cato and Gracchus as at most a sort of early foreshadowing of the great age of Cicero. Attention has often centred on the difference between their style of narrative and that of the Ciceronian age. Here, this time in the original as well as in translation, is a narrative by Gaius Gracchus, describing the intolerable behaviour of a Roman magistrate on a journey through Italy:

> Nuper Teanum Sidicinum consul uenit. Uxor eius dixit se in balneis uirilibus lauari uelle. Quaestori Sidicino M. Mario datum est negotium uti balneis exigerentur qui lauabantur. Uxor renuntiat uiro parum cito sibi balneas traditas esse et parum lautas fuisse. Idcirco palus destitutus est in foro eoque adductus suae ciuitatis nobilissimus homo M. Marius. Vestimenta detracta sunt, uirgis caesus est. (cited at Gel. 10.3.3)

> Just recently, the consul came to Teanum Sidicinum. His wife said she wanted to bathe in the men's baths. Marcus Marius, quaestor of Sidicinum, was given the task of clearing all customers out of the baths. The consul's wife told her husband that it had taken too long for the baths to be made ready for her and that they were not clean. For that reason, a whipping post was set up in the forum, and M. Marius, the most prominent man in the town, was taken there. His clothes were taken off; he was beaten with rods.

Cicero may have had in mind this passage, or one like it, when he composed the narrative of Gavius of Consa in *Ver.* 2.5.160–162. Comparison will show the obvious difference: Cicero's sentences are much longer. Main verbs are reserved for the most important actions, while others are placed in subordinate clauses or participles; and the narration of events is overlaid with vivid and emotive description. Here is part of Cicero's passage:

> Caedebatur uirgis in medio foro Messanae ciuis Romanus, iudices, cum interea nullus gemitus, nulla uox alia illius miseri inter dolorem crepitumque plagarum audiebatur nisi haec: "Ciuis Romanus sum."

A Roman citizen was being beaten with rods in the middle of the forum at Messana, members of the jury, while in the meantime no groan, no word was heard from that poor man amidst the pain and the sound of the blows, except this: "I am a Roman citizen."

The style of the Gracchan passage is simple and paratactic[32] compared with the greater elaboration of Cicero, and it lets the facts speak for themselves without trying to whip up additional emotion. The combination of relative simplicity with priority in time has suggested an evolutionary hypothesis:[33] Gracchus was primitive; he had not yet sufficiently mastered the techniques of rhetoric to be able to compose a properly modulated pathetic narrative. But there is no difference here that could not be accounted for by the context (of course we do not have the context of Gracchus' speech) and by a difference of personal style or fashion. The rhetorical theorists after all prescribed that the language of narratives should be plain and simple, and there were Greek models to hand, especially Lysias (whom nobody has accused of lack of sophistication); such a passage, delivered with appropriate emphasis, could be highly effective.[34] One comment that can be made is that Gracchus trusts the moral reactions of his audience to condemn the consul's behaviour without prompting: Cicero does not, but finds it necessary to use rhetorical pathos to ensure that they respond as he wants them to.

In any case, it is grossly implausible to suppose that Gracchus was incapable of rhetorical elaboration. Though only a few other fragments of his speeches survive, they are enough to indicate that Cicero might have been right in saying that he had no equal in eloquence. For instance, he attacks Piso Frugi – who according to Cicero did not deserve it – in the following words:

> pueritia tua adulescentiae tuae inhonestamentum fuit, adulescentia senectuti dedecoramentum, senectus rei publicae flagitium. (Cited at Isid. *Or.* 2.21.4)

> Your boyhood cast dishonour upon your manhood; your manhood, disgrace upon your old age; your old age, disaster upon the Republic.

And in the last week of his life, as Gracchus saw the swords of his enemies being sharpened, he made a speech in his own defence that contained these memorable phrases, recalling the tragedy of Medea:

> quo me miser conferam? quo uortam? in Capitoliumne? at fratris sanguine redundat. An domum? matremne ut miseram lamentantem uideam et abiectam? (Cited at Cic. *de Orat.* 3.214)

> Where can I go in my misery? Which way shall I turn? To the Capitol? But it is streaming with my brother's blood. Or home? So that I should see my poor mother lamenting and grieving?

These extracts show both the formal rhetorical elaboration and the passionate engagement characteristic of Classical oratory at its peak; Cicero himself could imitate (in the *pro Murena*) but not improve on the latter passage, and we owe our knowledge of the former passage to Isidore's quotation of it as an example of the rhetorical figure of "climax".

Evidently, there was already debate in antiquity as to how much the orators of the second century BCE owed to formal study of the art of rhetoric. The second-century

CE Roman scholar Aulus Gellius expresses the view that Cato's speech for the Rhodians exhibits "all the weapons and resources of the rhetorical discipline" and further that "all these things could perhaps have been said in a more structured and rhythmical way, but could not have been said more strongly and vividly".[35] Another passage from a Catonian speech quoted by Gellius (*in Q. Minucium Thermum*) exemplifies with particular clarity many of the figures of speech catalogued by the rhetoricians (abundance of synonyms, rhetorical questions, anaphora, and so on).[36] Cicero himself, in the *Brutus*, compared Cato to Lysias, a professional speech-writer who nevertheless contrived always to give the impression that his words came perfectly naturally: like those of Lysias, Cato's speeches are *acuti ... elegantes faceti breues* ("acute, elegant, witty, concise"). Cato, with his famous adage *rem tene, uerba sequentur* ("keep hold of the point, the words will follow"), projected an image of himself as doing everything by native wit and despising everything Greek. But it is improbable to suppose that he was innocent of acquaintance with Greek oratory and rhetoric; and this is all the more true of Gaius Gracchus, who had strong cultural connections with the Greek-speaking world, and refers in one speech to the Athenian orator Demades.

From Cato to Cicero

For the generations between the mid-second century and Cicero's maturity, the *Brutus* gives us a fairly full account.[37] Certain figures stand out as the great advocates of their time. They are often presented in pairs, to illustrate some imagined general distinction of style in oratory or advocacy – Servius Galba and Laelius (forcefulness versus elegance), Crassus and Antonius (intellectual cultivation versus the natural approach, subtle legal argumentation versus effective pleading on the facts), Gaius Cotta and Publius Sulpicius (concision versus amplitude, quiet sincerity versus dramatic elaboration). As has been pointed out by Catherine Steel,[38] the *Brutus* is in one respect highly tendentious in that it leaves out most of the tradition of popular oratory – the Gracchi are there, but there is no word of the oratory of Cicero's townsman C. Marius or of Cicero's enemy P. Clodius. Furthermore, for a reader wanting to find out what any of these orators actually sounded like, it is often frustratingly vague.

The point at issue is sometimes the quality of an orator's Latin, and this reminds us that like other languages, Latin was spoken in a variety of ways. Of the orators mentioned in *Brutus* and *de Oratore*, particular criticism is directed at Lucius Cotta, who deliberately cultivated what Cicero saw as a "rustic" pronunciation (for example opening the vowel *i* to *e*), though Cotta himself may have seen it as traditionally masculine (*de Orat.* 3.42 and 46, etc.). A section of *Brutus* (169–172) is devoted to an enumeration of orators from outside Rome, including some friends and neighbours of Cicero himself (such as Quintus and Decimus Valerius from Sora, a town not far from Arpinum). All of these are said to lack the *color urbanitatis* which, if we were to judge from this passage alone, we would think only genuine native Romans had. But Cicero, who here sets himself up as the arbiter of what is "urban" Latin and what is not, carefully says nothing of his own municipal origins. If a perfect Roman accent had been as hard to pick up as all that, could Cicero himself have acquired one? When Cicero comes to pronounce on linguistic matters in the *Orator*, he takes his own "ears" (i.e. his own usage) as the ultimate court of appeal, and takes it for granted that the linguistic instincts of other educated Romans will correspond with his own. In all this, Cicero emerges as a typical prescriptivist in regard to language, as most of us are by nature and upbringing unless we happen to have studied linguistics. Unfortunately neither Cicero nor any of his contemporaries provides more than isolated remarks on the subject; there are no data that a modern linguist would consider adequate for the study of the varieties of Latin current in the oratory of the time.

As regards vocabulary, Cicero tells some anecdotes of orators who invited ridicule by using peculiar words outside the range of ordinary speech. One such was Sisenna, the historian (*Brut.* 260). Once when defending, he characterised the charges against his client as *sputatilica crimina* (perhaps "spit-at-able charges"). The prosecutor objected: "Unfair practice, members of the jury: you must help me; I have no idea what Sisenna is saying. 'Spit-at-able' – what is that? 'Spit' I know; but what does 'at-able' mean?" Sisenna was after all only doing the same kind of thing as Plautus and Cato the Elder had done before him; but such inventiveness in language was coming to be seen as potentially ridiculous. Cicero contrasts it with the practice of Julius Caesar, very much a purist in matters of language. When languages become standardised and purified, greater elegance may be achieved, but at the expense of creativity.

The *Brutus* also discusses different styles of exposition and argumentation: a number of orators are characterised as Stoic, which presumably means that they had derived a repertoire of forms of argument from study of Stoic logic. In fact, Cicero himself in his younger days had also employed a Stoic philosopher, the blind Diodotus, to give him daily lessons in dialectic, and the effect of this is obvious in his frequent use of such argumentative patterns as the dilemma, which was sometimes a powerful logical tool but at other times little more than a stylistic trick giving the false appearance of a knock-down argument.[39] Cicero also mentions orators whose styles evinced particular literary influences. In particular, there were some who prided themselves on a "pure Attic" style based ostensibly on Lysias: chief among these was C. Calvus (Catullus' friend), whose skill in prosecution led to both wonderment ("clever little so-and-so", said a member of the audience as reported by Catullus) and exasperation ("just because he's so clever, does that make me guilty?" said the defendant on one occasion).[40] On the other hand there was Hortensius, Cicero's older rival, who by all accounts spoke in a style that was florid, rhythmical, and often epigrammatic; unfortunately we have hardly a word of Hortensius' speeches, and it was said[41] that the written versions did not match up to the original occasions, which were also apparently enhanced by elaborate use of gesture. In particular, his style was held to owe a good deal to the Greek oratory of Asia Minor, and it is clear enough that the styles of both Cicero and Hortensius did in fact share a number of features (especially rhythmical preferences) which can also be observed in the sparse literary and inscriptional evidence for Eastern Greek oratory. But neither Cicero nor Hortensius was self-consciously "Asianist" in the way that Calvus was "Atticist", and such stylistic controversies probably affected only a minority of practising Roman orators.[42]

Cicero, then, has given us enough information about Roman oratory in the period from *c.* 150 to *c.* 50 BCE to suggest that there was a considerable variety of styles of speaking, but the picture is often blurred in detail. His account would undoubtedly have been more useful to us if he had included more actual quotations, and if he had not been determined to measure everyone else against his ideal of the perfect orator. The *Brutus* in fact provides an excellent example of the confusion that results when a word is used both in a descriptive and an evaluative sense: of the 200 or so speakers he mentions, only relatively few are held to merit the title of "orator". Some are said to have intellectual gifts but not oratorical grandeur; others are eloquent but not sufficiently acute. Some are damned with faint praise, as being *diserti* or *soluti* ("articulate" or "fluent" respectively) rather than eloquent; while several attract opprobrium as *clamatores* (lit. "shouters") or *rabulae* ("ranters"), terms often applied to popular politicians of whom Cicero disapproved for reasons other than linguistic ones. A typical comment is this one, on a contemporary (L. Lentulus):[43] *satis erat fortis orator, si modo orator, sed cogitandi non ferebat laborem* ("he was a reasonably strong orator, if 'orator' is the right word, but he couldn't manage the hard work of thinking"). Clearly, he does not mean to imply that Lentulus did not speak much in public; the rest of the context makes it clear that he did. Rather, Cicero is voicing doubt as to whether Lentulus was a *proper* orator, an orator in the true sense. The development is like the one that has taken place in our own language with the word "poet": on the one hand anyone who writes verses can count as a poet in the descriptive sense, but on the other hand to qualify as a "(true) poet" in the evaluative sense one must write verses above the common level in quality and inspiration. Similarly, in *de Oratore*,[44] Cicero distinguishes the "orator" from the untrained speaker and insists, for example, that the former always speaks in perfectly controlled rhythms: again, Cicero is talking about his ideal, rather than the reality of Roman oratory.

The Evidence of the *ad Herennium*

More helpful, perhaps, is the rhetorical treatise called *Rhetorica ad Herennium*, once falsely attributed to Cicero, and now generally believed to be a product of the 80s BCE. This is also among our earliest sources for the language of Roman rhetoric in another sense, i.e. the Latin equivalents of the Greek technical terms in rhetorical theory. It is here, for example, that we first find the Latin terms for the three genres of oratory (*iudiciale, deliberatiuum, demonstratiuum* 1.2.2), the five parts of rhetoric (*inuentio, dispositio, elocutio, memoria, pronuntiatio* 1.2.3), the parts of a speech (*exordium, narratio, diuisio, confirmatio, confutatio, conclusio* 1.3.4), and a large repertoire of figures of speech and other rhetorical techniques, "all carefully packed, with the name printed clearly on each". Details of the terminology subsequently changed from time to time and from author to author, but the conceptual framework thus established changed little. The *ad Herennium* also deals under the heading of *inuentio* with the classification of issues developed by the Hellenistic rhetorician Hermagoras, and also found in Cicero's youthful work *de Inuentione*: in both of these texts the term *stasis* "standpoint, issue" is translated as *constitutio* or *constitutio causae*, lit. "setting-up of the case" (the Latin term was presumably chosen partly for its etymological relationship to the Greek). Factual issues are called *coniecturales* "to do with guesswork" because the speaker advances a theory as to what happened; then there are legal issues (*constitutio legitima*) and issues of equity (*constitutio iuridicalis*) with their various sub-types. The partial coincidence of technical terms and classification between *ad Herennium* and Cicero implies not only that Latin rhetorical terminology was already well established, but also that there were already different schools of thought among Latin rhetoricians on how the classification should be done. It is incidentally to be noted (the point recurs also in the history of Latin philosophical terminology) that the Republican authors prefer to create pure Latin equivalents of Greek terms, rather than borrow the Greek words unchanged. Thus, for example, the figure of speech that we now call "anaphora", using the Greek word, is called *repetitio* by the author of the *ad Herennium*.[45] Some of these Latin terms were subsequently abandoned, sometimes for obvious reasons; later writers such as Quintilian were more receptive to Greek borrowings. But the cultural and linguistic nationalism implicit in the Republican approach to rhetorical terminology is notable: rhetoric was no longer to be regarded as a suspect foreign import but was to be thoroughly Romanised.

The *ad Herennium* is noteworthy in particular for its examples of oratorical style. The anonymous author goes to some lengths (4.1.1, 4.5.7–7.10) to explain that the specimen passages are made up for the occasion, and thus exemplify in exaggerated form the features he[46] intends to illustrate (real examples, he says, conceal their art and therefore would be less suitable). Best known are the examples that illustrate the theory of the Three Styles, a doctrine – it has to be said – whose prominence both in Roman rhetorical theory and in modern accounts exceeds its usefulness as a tool for analysing actual speeches; but they do give an idea of the variety of styles that were recognised in the rhetorical schools. The specimen of the "grand" style, ostensibly from a prosecution speech for treason, is a vigorous denunciation using a range of familiar rhetorical techniques; it reads rather like a parody of the more elevated passages of Cicero, but (if the usual view of the dating is correct) must predate them. The example of the "middle" style is a passage of argumentation in the *genus deliberatiuum*: the subject is the alleged revolt of one of Rome's Italian allies and the passage enquires into their motives. Particularly interesting is the example of the "plain" or "attenuated" style, a narrative ostensibly taken from the speech of a complainant in an action for assault. It explicitly reflects "everyday" language (*sermo cotidianus*) and is much more colloquial than even the most informal passages of Cicero's speeches; some of its phrases (such as *ecce tibi iste de trauerso* "and he suddenly comes up, look, and he says …") find their closest parallels in the letters to Atticus.[47] A case of this type, arising out of a fracas in the baths, would doubtless have been a private action and an advocate could be expected to use a style appropriate to the occasion; what this passage tells us is that according to at least one first-century BCE rhetorical teacher, a colloquial register was seen as appropriate in this context. The language of the Republican courts, then, was evidently not all unrelieved formality. The apparent greater formality of Cicero's court performances may reflect either the greater importance of the cases from which he felt it worth while to publish the speeches, or his own determination to embellish the occasion (on the principle, perhaps, that if one makes a case seem important, one is more likely to win). The *ad Herennium* also gives examples of what to avoid, again arranged in a triplet: the grand style, when inexpertly managed, becomes inflated (with inappropriate archaism and poeticism, and an Arabian Nights style of metaphor); the middle style becomes rambling; and the simple style becomes scrappy and incoherent. The author again makes up his own specimen passages, adapting those just given, but a morning spent hanging around the praetors' tribunals would also probably have revealed a good harvest of examples of these faults. Other kinds of stylistic error are criticised: they include over-conspicuous repetitions of particular words or sounds (alliteration was the privilege of poets), clashes of vowels at the end of one word and the beginning of the next, or unintentional double meanings; the tendency to fall into these types of fault is of course not peculiar to Latin speakers.

Oratory and Ordinary Language in Cicero's Time

It is not part of the purpose of this chapter to give a comprehensive account of the language and style of Cicero: a survey with further bibliography may be found in my contribution to the *Cambridge Companion to Cicero*.[48] Here attention is drawn only to some salient points.

Cicero both recommended and practised the principle that the vocabulary of oratory should not diverge far from the middle register of ordinary speech; poeticisms, archaisms, non-Latin words and colloquialisms were equally avoided unless for a special effect in individual cases. But in other areas, especially sentence structure and rhythm, Cicero and some of his contemporaries were to set Latin oratory on a path that sometimes diverged significantly from the everyday use of language. The so-called periodic style became the trademark of the Latin orator, or at least the norm from which other styles deliberately varied. There is no rigorously scientific definition of a "period"; it is just the Greek for "circuit" and is rendered by *circuitus* in Latin. But for practical purposes it may be characterised by the following features: (a) a period is a single sentence of some length, which can be divided into smaller units; (b) the lengths of the subordinate units are carefully regulated by rhetorical devices such as isocolon (parallel clauses of equal length) or ascending tricolon (a set of three units, each longer than the last), and often marked with devices such as anaphora (repetition of the initial word or words in parallel clauses) or antithesis; (c) the sense is felt to be complete at the end of the sentence and there is a clear articulation of sense-breaks; (d) at least the end of the sentence is marked by a definite rhythmical pattern; sometimes this applies also to the intermediate sense-breaks. In Greek this style was associated particularly with Gorgias and his follower Isocrates, and is analysed by Aristotle in the third book of the *Rhetoric*; the particular rhythms favoured by Cicero (based on the cretic, long-short-long) appear to have come above all from the Asian school of Greek oratory.

Here is a typical Ciceronian period, taken more or less at random (*Clu.* 155: Cicero is here arguing that a law which was meant to apply only to senators should not be extended to other citizens as well):

Interea quidem, per deos immortales, quoniam omnia commoda nostra, iura, libertatem, salutem denique, legibus obtinemus, a legibus non recedamus; simul et illud quam sit iniquum cogitemus, populum Romanum aliud nunc agere, uobis rem publicam et fortunas suas commisisse, sine cura esse, non metuere, ne lege ea quam numquam ipse iusserit, et quaestione qua se solutum liberumque esse arbitretur, per paucos iudices adstringatur.

Meanwhile, by the immortal gods, since we obtain all our benefits, rights, liberty, even our very safety, by means of the laws, let us not depart from the laws: and at the same time let us consider how unjust this is, that the Roman citizen body should now be engaged on other business, having committed to your care the commonwealth and its own prosperity; that it should have no worry or fear, that through the decision of a few judges, it will be bound by a law of a kind to which it never itself gave sanction, and by a court from whose enquiries it believes itself free and exempt.

The periodic structure may be brought out as follows:

Interea quidem, per deos immortales,
meanwhile indeed, by gods immortal,
quoniam omnia commoda nostra,
since   all   benefits our
                    iura,
                    rights,
                    libertatem,
                    liberty,
                    salutem denique
                    safety lastly,
                                legibus obtinemus,
                                by-laws we-obtain,
                                a legibus non recedamus;
                                from laws not let-us-depart;
simul et illud quam sit iniquum cogitemus,
at-the-same-time also that-thing how it-is unjust let-us-consider,
populum Romanum
<that> the Roman people
aliud nunc agere,
another-thing now is-doing,
uobis rem publicam et fortunas suas commisisse,
to-you the commonwealth and fortunes its has-entrusted,
sine cura esse,
without worry is,
non metuere,
does-not fear,
ne   *lege ea quam numquam ipse iusserit,*
lest   by-law such-that never itself it-has-ordered,
                    et quaestione qua se solutum liberumque esse arbitretur,
                    and by-enquiry from-which itself exempt and-free to-be thinks,
                    per paucos iudices adstringatur.
                    through few judges it-may-be-bound.

When first presented with a Ciceronian period analysed in this way, one's first instinct may be to think of it as overwhelmingly artificial, and a translator who had any feeling for English rhetorical style would have to change the sentence-structure considerably in order to make it effective. However, for various reasons connected with the structure of the language, it works more easily in Latin. Parallelisms and rhythmical cadences occur almost everywhere in Cicero's writings (except in the most casual of the letters) and it seems evident that this style had become second nature to him. Nor is there any reason to believe that this is an artefact of the written speeches: it has indeed been suggested by modern linguists that this kind of syntactical expansion is characteristic of spoken rather than written language.[49] At the same time it must also be remembered that Cicero could also employ a forensic style using much shorter sense-units, *membratim et incisim* as he himself calls it; an example is the argumentative passage at *S. Rosc.* 73–74, where a number of alternative hypotheses as to how the alleged crime might have been committed are set out in a series of short rhetorical questions.

There is evidence for some reaction against Ciceronian stylistic practices during the latter part of his life. The aforementioned Calvus apparently criticised him for excessive fluency and lack of sinew, while Brutus – if the interpretation I have elsewhere suggested is correct – compared Cicero's rhythmical style to the progress of a limping horse. Though Cicero may have exercised a despotism in the law courts and may have been appealed to as an authority on matters of Latin usage, his style was still just one of many; his status as an icon of Latin eloquence did not develop until some time after his death, through the overwhelming influence of his published works.

The culture of the late Roman Republic embraced extremes of urbanity and elegance on the one hand, and of violence both physical and verbal on the other: this may be a difficult mixture for a modern observer to comprehend fully (though it may be partially paralleled, for example, in the European eighteenth century). No account of Republican oratory would be complete without a mention of the sublimated violence to be found in political invective.[50] Although Cicero made his name chiefly as a defending advocate, his historically most famous speeches are denunciations; and the art of political insult has seldom been more assiduously practised than in Cicero's speech against Piso (one of the consuls of 58 BCE who failed to prevent Cicero from being sent into exile), in his references to his enemy Clodius throughout the speeches of the middle 50s BCE, and in the *Philippics* against Antony (although admittedly the most famous of these, the Second, was only circulated as a pamphlet and not actually delivered). The language of these speeches is unparliamentary not only by modern Western standards, but also by the standards of decorum current in later generations at Rome, as shown by the reaction of Quintilian. One can only conclude that the conventions of the Republican Senate, at least in Cicero's time, allowed an almost unlimited licence both to vividly insulting forms of address, such as *belua* (beast, monster) or *caenum* (mud, filth) and to insinuations of colourful sexual practices – all delivered in perfectly rhythmical and elegant Ciceronian sentences. On another occasion, one senator is said to have reduced another to tears by calling him *struthiocamelus depilatus* (a plucked ostrich). There is little evidence for such modes of address being employed in formal oratory outside the narrow and privileged circle of the Senate; it is not clear, for example, that a case for the prosecution in the law courts would be helped by such means, and one must beware of overschematic generalisations about invective as a genre.[51]

The Early Empire and the Rhetorical Schools

Though popular decision-making died with the Republic, other aspects of oratory survived and, indeed, flourished under the early Empire. The shadow of Cicero did not inhibit the growth of oratory in other styles, and the myth of decline encouraged by Tacitus' *Dialogus* should not be taken too seriously. The attentive reader of Tacitus' *Annals* can catch a flavour of both senatorial and forensic oratory (often, in fact, the same thing, since the Senate by this time often functioned as a court) from Tiberius to Nero: it is not always realised to what extent Tacitus himself writes as a connoisseur of oratorical performance, and many names of orators can be recovered together with some account of their salient characteristics.[52] In condemning the *delatores* who brought prosecutions for treason and other offences under the early emperors, Tacitus thought he had identified the source of a new evil in the state, but forgot (maybe) that prosecutors had always tended to have a bad name, from the sycophants of Classical Athens to the accusers with whom Cicero clashed in court. There is no ground for supposing that the *delator* was really a new phenomenon, nor much real evidence to suggest that he brought with him a new style of oratory.[53] Like other historians, Tacitus gives us no direct access to the words or style of the orators in whose manner of speaking he shows interest: orations in direct speech are included by him as by other historians, and always abbreviated and adapted to the grand historical style; indeed, Tacitus is under considerable suspicion of improving his originals, as in the case of the speech of the emperor Claudius which happens to be preserved (in part) on the Lyons tablet.[54] Tacitus' summary is concise and tightly argued; the original appears as a rambling performance by comparison, and (though this is to some extent a matter of dispute) there is almost no stylistic feature of Tacitus' adaptation which recalls the imperial author of the speech.

The most significant development in this period of Roman oratory was doubtless the rise of the rhetorical schools. In the 90s BCE (the period of Cicero's youth) rhetoricians had been forbidden to teach at Rome: L. Crassus, great advocate and protagonist of Cicero's dialogue *de Oratore*, as censor in 93 BCE closed down a Latin rhetorical school at Rome apparently on the ground that nothing was taught there except impudence.[55] But by the 90s CE most élite Romans attended a rhetorical school in preparation for public life, Quintilian enjoyed an imperially funded salary as teacher of rhetoric, and schools of rhetoric were becoming established in the provinces. The beginning and end of this development are not in doubt; the intermediate stages of it are less easy to reconstruct.

The young Cicero, maybe exceptional in his generation, had gone to Greece in search of rhetorical training and models to follow, and he always maintained that his thorough acquaintance with the art of rhetoric had contributed to his success.[56] At the same time, he distanced himself from the idea that rhetorical success might be just a matter of professional training. For him, the orator's art was no less than complete mastery of the use of language in all its aspects, embracing knowledge of the subject-matter (especially politics and the law), the art of argumentation (derived from the study of philosophy and dialectic), style and composition (involving both correct use of Latin and a wide literary culture), a sensitivity to the requirements of the oral medium including sentence-length, symmetry and rhythm, and the practicalities of performance including pitching the voice, pausing for breath in the right places, gesture and facial expression. Quintilian was much influenced by Cicero when, in the *Institutio Oratoria* (Education of the Orator), he set out in detail a programme of professional preparation for the oratorical career, informed by an encyclopaedic knowledge of Greek and Roman rhetorical theory which probably exceeded even Cicero's, and incidentally including a good deal of detail about the correct use of language. It may be thought that Quintilian's emphasis on forensic oratory, rather than political, reflects the changed circumstances of the Empire: in reality this emphasis is not substantially different from that of earlier rhetorical theory, whether Greek or Roman, and the Roman orator, under the Empire as before, was still first and foremost an advocate, a "patron" who spoke up on behalf of "clients". But first-century rhetorical education did not neglect the deliberative genre either. The mock-parliamentary speeches of the modern debating society had their counterpart in the *suasoria*, an imaginary "speech of persuasion" usually set on some historical occasion.

It is not perhaps surprising that rhetorical education in post-Ciceronian Rome did not always measure up to the high standards set by Cicero or Quintilian. The rhetorical schools leave a peculiar set of traces in Roman literature. It is perhaps the fate of school education to become an object of literary satire, since all writers experience it, and it almost always contains elements that seem to bear little relation to the real life for which it is supposed to prepare one. Thus, for example, nineteenth- and twentieth-century English novelists satirise the unreality of the Classical education of their time. For the same kind of reasons, Roman writers constantly satirise the subject-matter of the exercises used to teach rhetoric, with their far-fetched cases involving tyrants, pirates and poisoners, or their dramatisations of historical events long in the past. But looked at objectively, the Roman system of rhetorical education is not necessarily much odder than some types of modern education, and it seems to have functioned as a reasonably effective system of professional training for public speakers.

A less jaundiced (even if still not perfectly approving) view of the rhetorical schools is found in Seneca the Elder, who wrote down his reminiscences of them towards the end of his life, probably in the 30s CE. The schools were, according to him, a substantially new development within his lifetime: Cicero had practised declamation, but of a rather different kind. The full title of Seneca's work is *Oratorum et rhetorum sententiae diuisiones colores*, and it is indeed largely a collection of *sententiae* (what we might call sound-bites), *diuisiones* (divisions of the subject, or in modern terms sets of bullet-points) and *colores* (lines of argument, see above, p. 386) taken from the practice or demonstration speeches of the orators and rhetorical teachers of his time. A division is apparent between the two professions: there were on the one hand professors of rhetoric who never applied their principles to the making of speeches in the real world, and on the other practising orators who did not do particularly well in the artificial environment of the school – a situation which, *mutatis mutandis*, we could compare with the modern division between practising lawyers and those who teach law as an academic subject. Seneca's collection is entirely devoted to the imaginary cases and set themes for debate that formed the basis of school exercises (hence the titles of its subdivisions, *Controuersiae* and *Suasoriae*); it gives probably a misleading view of the character even of the school exercises, since it contains only memorable extracts and no complete speeches; and it is not possible to extrapolate directly from Seneca's lecture-room extracts to the character of real oratory in the Senate or courts at this time. The same difficulty exists in the case of the more continuous and coherent declamations which survive under the name of Quintilian.

Without doubt, the taste for the sound-bite was widespread also outside the rhetorical schools; its presence in first-century CE Roman literature needs no exemplification, and as for courtroom oratory, we may turn to the satirist Persius. Writing under Nero,[57] he expostulates against advocates who cultivate excessive rhetorical adornment (my translation):

> Does it not shame you at all that you cannot defend a man on trial for his grey-haired reputation, without hoping to hear that tepid "Well said, sir!"? "You're a thief," says the prosecutor to Pedius: what does Pedius say? He weighs the charges in clean-shaven antitheses; he is applauded for including learned figures of speech – "That's pretty!" Pretty? Or is Romulus going weak at the knees? Is that sort of thing to affect *my* verdict? No doubt I would bring out

a penny if a shipwrecked beggar were to sing to me! Do you *sing*, when carrying on your shoulders a picture of yourself in a broken ship? Whoever wants me to bend down and listen to his sad story will have to weep real tears, not ones prepared by midnight oil. (Pers. 1.83–91).

The clean-shaven antitheses, the learned figures of speech, the singing (i.e. symmetrical composition or musical delivery or both), and the tears prepared by midnight oil, indicate an orator who is more concerned about his own performance than about the client's case; perhaps (the satirist doubtless thinks) one who is still mentally addressing a school audience rather than a real jury.[58]

Persius' strictures should be balanced against the remarks given by Tacitus to the character Marcus Aper in his *Dialogus de Oratoribus*. Although Aper's point of view is rejected by his fellow-interlocutors, the author gives him some good points in favour of contemporary fashions in oratory. In Cicero's time, says Aper, the studies of rhetoric and philosophy were new at Rome: now everybody is educated and the orator can accordingly take short cuts. Judges are in a hurry to get to the main point and cannot be expected to sit through long speeches, and they are easily bored; consequently their attention has to be grabbed *aut cursu argumentorum aut colore sententiarum aut nitore et cultu descriptionum* (*Dial.* 20.2): by quick-fire argumentation, colourful epigrams, or splendid and elaborate descriptions. Listeners like to be able to take something home with them, so quotability is at a premium; speeches may be further ornamented by poetic colouring taken "from the sacred shrines of Horace, Virgil and Lucan". Cicero seems long-winded and utilitarian by contrast.

If we wish to know who the good orators were during this period, we may turn to Quintilian, who was by no means easy to satisfy. In his survey of Roman orators in the tenth book of his *Institutio Oratoria*, he recommends his students to read Cicero first and foremost, but also a number of others. From Cicero's time there was Asinius Pollio (criticised for his archaism), Messalla,[59] Caesar, Caelius, Calvus, Servius Sulpicius the jurist. Then, a little later, there was Cassius Severus, who suffered exile and book-burning under Augustus, but his speeches evidently survived until Quintilian's time. He is commended also by Seneca the Elder and Tacitus (though criticised in Tacitus' *Dialogus*, cf. note 53). Of his older contemporaries, Quintilian mentions Domitius Afer and Julius Africanus as by far the best and equal to the ancients, though the former's activities as a prosecutor earned him disapproval at Tacitus' hands. From his own generation, Quintilian names Galerius Trachalus, Vibius Crispus, Julius Secundus; and he remarks that there was a plethora of talent in the forum of his own day. We cannot tell whether the speeches of these men, had they been preserved, would have appealed to us in the same way; but awareness of their presence serves to some extent to undercut the myth of decline.

The Reign of Trajan and Later

Oratory in the reign of Trajan is represented by two great names, both best known to us for reasons other than their oratory: Tacitus and Pliny. We have no speeches by Tacitus, and only one by Pliny, his speech of thanks to Trajan on his consulship, which he wrote up (at greater length than the spoken version) and published; it has survived as the first of a series of imperial panegyrics, the rest of which date from a much later period. Though perhaps too courtly for modern taste, it is of considerable historical interest and is now again beginning to attract scholarly attention. In the second century CE the silence is briefly broken again by the appearance of Apuleius' *Apologia*, in which the author defends himself on a charge of using magical practices to entice a lady called Pudentilla to marry him. The accusation was ridiculous, and Apuleius' published speech rises to the occasion magnificently: this one speech, with its confident manner and its mixture of ridicule and intellectual tour de force, is enough to rebut the notion that there was no worthwhile Roman oratory after Cicero. Apuleius also published a set of declamatory extracts called the *Florida*. He had learned his rhetoric initially in his own province of North Africa, which Juvenal, not without reason, called "the nurse of advocates" (*nutricula causidicorum*). It was also to produce Cornelius Fronto, the tutor of Marcus Aurelius: although he was among the leading advocates and public speakers of his time, we have only fragmentary evidence for his speeches, and his Latin style can now be appreciated only from his correspondence with his pupil, the future emperor Marcus Aurelius. Another North African was Tertullian, among the first of a long line of Christians who turned their rhetorical skills to account in the defence of the new faith. The province of Gaul, which had a reputation for native eloquence already before the advent of Greco-Roman rhetorical learning, embraced it wholeheartedly and some of its schools became famous and influential; in the fourth century the poet Ausonius commemorates the professors of rhetoric at Bordeaux. The wide diffusion of rhetorical education in the provinces is notable: while the grammarians of the empire were responsible for setting standards of correct Latin usage, the rhetoricians taught facility in composition and oral delivery, and it is clear that they contributed to the diffusion of a formal literary standard of remarkable uniformity throughout the empire. Doubtless, spoken oratory (however formal in style and register) would have reflected changes in the pronunciation of the language over time, and may to some extent also have reflected regional variations, but any such differences are usually concealed by the written medium.

The practice of Latin oratory (on public occasions and in the courts), together with the formal study of rhetoric, continued throughout Late Antiquity, although preparation for an advocate's career was no longer a purely rhetorical matter as it had been in the late Republic and early Empire: the balance now began to tip towards law as professional training. The study of Latin rhetoric did, however, survive into the Middle Ages and Renaissance as one of the "Seven Liberal Arts" of the educational curriculum, with the *de Inuentione* of Cicero and the *Rhetorica ad Herennium* as principal textbooks. Many of Cicero's speeches were preserved, some of them by a tenuous thread of manuscript tradition, and provided a model of Latin oratory for successive generations. The making of Latin speeches continued to be valued as an educational exercise. Even in our own day, it is still possible to find ceremonial occasions (largely, but not exclusively, in the university world) at which carefully prepared though usually brief Latin addresses on Classical models are orally delivered. Moreover, the styles of Latin oratory (especially Ciceronian) have often had a large influence on the practice of speechmaking in the vernacular languages; but that topic is probably beyond the remit of a *Companion to the Latin Language*.

FURTHER READING

For recent work on Roman oratory and rhetoric in general, see especially the introductory survey of Steel (2006), and the useful collection of essays edited by Dominik and Hall (2007). Standard works on Roman rhetoric include Bonner (1949) (on declamation and its influence), Leeman (1963), Kennedy (1972), Clarke (1996). Berry (2005) provides a useful overview, with which the material of this chapter unavoidably overlaps in places.

NOTES

1   Unless otherwise stated, translations are my own. I am grateful to Lene Rubinstein for comments and help with the proofs.
2   The sites chosen for oratory in the ancient world sometimes provided natural amplification: of such a kind (in the fifth century) was the Pnyx where the Athenian assembly met, not to mention acoustically planned buildings such as theatres. But the acoustic properties of the Roman Forum are less easy to determine, and hard to investigate without a complete set of surrounding buildings at full height.
3   As for example Demosthenes attracted this criticism from his opponent Pytheas: "[his speech] smell[s] of the lamp and elaborate literary labour, with sharp arguments and with periods precisely measured by rule and compass" (Plutarch, *Praecepta gerendae reipublicae* 802e–f, Loeb translation).
4   Thus Romans sometimes liked to see Greeks as (undesirably) more fluent than themselves, e.g. Juv. 3.73–74.
5   "Rhetoric" meant originally "the skill/art/technique of the orator" (*rhetorike techne*). Some classical scholars insist that it should always be used of the theory as distinct from the practice. But other meanings are well established in modern usage: a composition which exemplifies rhetorical skill can itself be called a "piece of rhetoric"; one may talk of the "rhetoric" of a speech, meaning the rhetorical techniques employed in it; or, very commonly, one may disparage a speech or piece of writing as "empty rhetoric" if one feels that its form is not matched by its substance.
6   *Aeneid* 1.148–154 "if they chance to see a man who has some weight among them for his goodness and services to the state, they fall silent, standing and listening with all their attention, while his words command their passions and soothe their hearts" (tr. D. West). See on this passage Dugan (2009), who correctly understands it as an expression of a Roman (Republican) cultural ideal, not only in terms of its possible application to Augustus as it is usually viewed. It could not work in the latter capacity without the pre-existing associations of the ideal of the (Republican) orator.
7   Both *oratio* and *sermo* also share some of the senses of the English word "language"; and *oratio* of course can also mean "a speech" in the sense of an oration.
8   The distinction seems to be a development from the theory found in the *ad Herennium* which divided oratory itself up into three, *sermo* (conversational style, used for narrations, the giving of information, and anecdotes or jokes), *contentio* (argument or debate), and *amplificatio* (enhancement of emotion), reflecting the *ad Herennium*'s version (not the same as Cicero's) of the doctrine of the Three Styles; see below p. 396.
9   The rhetoricians recognised a third category called "epideictic", a catch-all term that embraced all kinds of oratory not specifically directed towards arguing a case; although some forms of epideictic such as the funeral oration were well recognised at Rome, the Roman critics were slow to recognise it as a distinct category of any importance. Cicero's idea that entertainment

was part of an orator's persuasive armoury, and his fondness in practice for leisurely witticisms and digressions, can be linked with the incorporation of epideictic elements into both political and legal oratory; see Winterbottom (1989).

10 This is not as paradoxical as it may at first seem: presentation skills are of the first importance to an advocate, and advocacy both then and now is often concerned with establishing facts rather than arguing points of law.

11 Thus e.g. Frontinus acquired his knowledge of aqueducts after appointment as *curator aquarum*: cf. Powell (2005b) 224–225.

12 As shown by the use of its adverb *diserte* "explicitly", "expressly".

13 See Powell (2007c).

14 See especially Wisse (2007) on Cicero's *pro Milone*.

15 See especially Craig (1993).

16 For a convenient summary of these features see Kirchner (2007).

17 That is, the rhythmical patterns used at the ends of sentences in rhetorical prose. See *OCD*³ s.v. Prose rhythm, Latin.

18 This is the case with Cicero's *post Reditum in Senatu*, which is also more than usually elaborate in style (cf. Frischer (1996), Powell (forthcoming)).

19 The clearest example of this is in a fictitious speech by a historian – Fufius Calenus' attack on Cicero in Dio Cassius 46.7.

20 Pliny the Younger is candid about having done this in the case of his *Panegyric*; he contrasts the practice of Cicero whose speeches were sometimes published in shortened versions (Pliny, *Ep.* 1.20).

21 Transmitted as the first of a series of imperial panegyrics, of which all the others date from after 289 CE: on this genre of oratory see Rees (2007).

22 Lintott (1999), Millar (1998b), Morstein-Marx (2004), Steel (2006). The size of crowds at *contiones* doubtless varied but could theoretically reach several thousands. The Senate of the late Republic comprised around 600 members of whom only a proportion would be present on any given occasion (200 were required as a quorum for some types of business). Juries in Republican courts were smaller, fifty-one being a regular number, though an advocate would doubtless expect to be audible to numerous other persons present in the area of the (usually open-air) court. One might expect considerable variation in style between these different types of speech, but see on this Ramsey (2007) 134, who makes it clear that – at least as far as Cicero is concerned – there is no significant difference in complexity of style between speeches to the Senate and those to the people: "a Roman orator could speak in just as sophisticated a manner to the man in the Forum as he could to his colleagues in the Senate." At the same time, however, Ramsey reminds us that Cicero's surviving speeches may not be typical of Roman oratory as a whole.

23 The original *Rostra* was supposed to date from 335 BCE (Livy 8.14) and to have been intended as a victory monument, not a speaker's platform, but it was a convenient place from which to address an assembly; it is not clear when it was first used as such. Speakers from the *Rostra* at first faced inwards towards the *Comitium*; the tribune Gaius Crassus in 145 BCE apparently created a stir by facing the other way towards the Forum Romanum, where a much larger crowd could gather (Cicero *Laelius* 96 and my note on the passage in Powell 1990).

24 Aelian, *Varia Historia* 3.17.

25 See Rubinstein (2003).

26 Rutledge (2007) rightly argues for a significant measure of continuity in oratorical practice, and its importance, between Republic and Principate.

27 This aspect of Roman oratory has attracted much scholarly attention; see e.g. Marincola (2007b).

28 Where written versions of speeches did exist, historians sometimes avoided the conventional paraphrase or summary: for example, Sallust in the *Catiline* includes no summary of any

speech of Cicero, but refers readers to the published text of the First Catilinarian, and in his narrative he borrows without acknowledgement from the other Catilinarian orations. On the other hand, full-dress treatment is given to the senatorial speeches of Caesar and Cato, which presumably were not available in their original form. Cf. however below, p. 400 (Tacitus' paraphrase of Claudius' speech on the Gallic senators).

29 As in the case of other oratorical texts, the question arises how accurately the written versions of Cato's speeches represented what was actually said; cf. brief remarks in Sciarrino (2007) 65–66.

30 Cf. Quint. *Inst.* 1.6.39–45, quoting some obsolete words used by Cato (*tuburcinabundus* and *lurcinabundus*, both meaning "guzzling"). "They [the old orators] themselves," says Quintilian, "would not talk like that nowadays."

31 The point made in this extract may seem an obvious one, but the Latin legal usage of *volo* "wish, want" indicates that it did need to be argued. The *Senatusconsultum de Bacchanalibus* of 186 BCE, nineteen years before the Rhodian affair, begins (in modernised spelling) *Ne quis eorum Bacchanal habuisse vellet* "That none of the persons concerned should wish to hold a Bacchanal".

32 "Parataxis" denotes a style composed largely of main clauses placed in parallel; the opposite is "hypotaxis" or subordination. One of the best examples of paratactic style is the language of the Hebrew Bible, especially the narrative portions, which some English translations reflect more accurately than others (the King James version is good from this point of view).

33 Von Albrecht (1989) 37 criticises this approach: "For him [Marouzeau] of course Gracchus is not a real person but a stage in a historical development."

34 See especially Sciarrino (2007) 62–63, stressing the importance of delivery.

35 6.3.52–53, rebutting the opinions of Cicero's freedman Tiro who had criticised the speech unfavourably.

36 Barsby (2007) points out that many of these linguistic features are also found in Roman comedy, and supposes that both Cato and the comedians reflect a native Latin rhetorical tradition – not, presumably, a native Latin rhetorical theory, but a repertoire of stylistic features neither named nor classified but passed on by imitation. Sciarrino (2007) (perhaps less plausibly) links them with the "culture of the Italic *carmen*". For rhetorical figures as cross-cultural features of oratorical performance, regardless of theorising, see Kennedy (1998).

37 See Steel (2007).

38 Steel (2003).

39 See n. 15 above.

40 Catul. 53 *salaputium disertum*; Sen. *Con.* 7.4.6 *si iste disertus est, ideo condemnari me oportet?* I have here used "clever" to translate *disertus* (see above, p. 386).

41 Quint. *Inst.* 11.3.8.

42 On "Atticism" as a literary movement among Roman orators see Wisse (2002) 364–368.

43 *Brut.* 268. Cf. ibid. 182 where an "orator" is distinguished from a mere "shouter" (*clamator*).

44 3.175.

45 Unsatisfactorily, because anaphora refers only to one of several types of repetition.

46 The author speaks of himself in the masculine gender (using the plural of authorship).

47 It even contains an apparent "popular" spelling, *oriculas* for *auriculas* "ears". But we cannot know that this spelling was due to the author rather than the manuscripts; nor can we know how common it was at the time of writing, or how widespread the pronunciation *or-* for *au-* was at this time, or what its precise social connotations were.

48 Powell (forthcoming).

49 See Powell (forthcoming) citing Halliday (2004) 654–655.

50 See Booth (2007); Arena (2007).

51 See Powell (2007b).

52 See Syme (1958) 322–339.

53 This notion, suggested by Syme (1958) and Winterbottom (1964), is based especially on the assessment of Cassius Severus by the character Vipstanus Messalla in Tacitus' *Dialogus* (26.4). The following points may however be made: (a) in Tacitus, the characterisation of Cassius Severus' unkempt and quarrelsome style does not seem to be associated specifically with prosecution; (b) Messalla is a spokesman for a view which idealises the Republic in contrast to what has happened since, and judges the Republic by the formal written speeches of Cicero and others; (c) as Rutledge (2007) 111–113 points out, violence was a conventional attribute of prosecutors and this was true also in the time of Cicero.

54 If we may presume that the speech was prepared in writing in advance, it follows that the text on the tablet probably does represent the actual words that Claudius delivered; but scholarly discussions of Tacitus' adaptation of the speech do not always take due account of the incompleteness of the surviving inscription.

55 *de Orat.* 3.93; Suet. *Gram.* 25 gives the text of the edict.

56 *Orat.* 146 *ego semper me didicisse prae me tuli.*

57 Who himself had decided views on oratory: according to Suetonius he forbade advocates appearing before him to make set speeches at all, but instructed them to argue one point at a time.

58 It should be noted that both a "singing" delivery and nocturnal preparation were traditional compaints against orators in Greece; for the former see Bers (2009) 64–67; for the latter, note 3 above.

59 Probably Cicero's younger contemporary M. Valerius Messalla Niger (cf. *Brut.* 246); Quintilian may be playing on his name when he calls his style *candidus.*

CHAPTER 23

The Language of Latin Historiography

Christina Shuttleworth Kraus

The language of Latin historiography cannot be understood, except superficially, independent of its content. This is true of all literary language: but in the case of history it is especially true. This is a genre that aims at the impossible, to "match deeds with words" (Sal. *Cat.* 3.2, Liv. 6.20.8): not only to rival but to (re)present past experience in language, to create a verbal image of lived events. The language is part and parcel of that picture, just as a painter's brushstrokes and technique are part of an artistic representation. There is a tendency (often unconscious) to regard the historiographical product as somehow only formally related to the language of which it is comprised. The language then becomes a window through which we look at the representation. Though I will focus in this chapter on details of language and style, I hope that by connecting those with content I can make that window as opaque as possible, to direct attention onto the medium that is the message.

Latin historiography developed in response to a number of stimuli: the historical epics of Naevius (*Carmen belli Poenici*, on the first Punic war) and Ennius (*Annales*, from the fall of Troy to the Istrian wars of the 170s BCE); the codification of the Roman past in the form of the *Fasti*, a chronological list of magistrates carved on the temple of Hercules Musarum by M. Fulvius Nobilior after his victory at Ambracia in 189; and the pervasive challenge of literature written in Greek, especially, one assumes, the very recent work of Fabius Pictor and the contemporaneous history of Polybius. The first to write prose history in Latin was M. Porcius Cato the Elder (234–149 BCE), who added to the mix the oratorical skill of a lifetime in public speaking and a highly developed sense of propriety, especially concerning the correct moral and stylistic stance to be taken by a senatorial writer of Roman history.

Roman literature (and its history) love founding figures. As the πρῶτος εὑρετής of Latin historiography, Cato set a standard and a tone for subsequent writers to follow,

A Companion to the Latin Language, First Edition. Edited by James Clackson.
© 2011 Blackwell Publishing Ltd. Published 2011 by Blackwell Publishing Ltd.

challenge, or reject. (Cato was himself strongly influenced by his Greek precursors, of course – but that is another *Companion*.) Though his history – seven books of *Origines* – survives only in fragments, it and the man's reception in later authors, especially Cicero and Sallust, give us some idea of that standard and tone. In Cato's hands, history was to (1) employ a choice style (including vocabulary, syntax, and figures) that was sensitive to generic decorum; (2) be carefully structured both in part and whole; (3) contain narrative and speech (both *oratio recta* and *oratio obliqua*); (4) include military narrative and antiquarian details; (5) give the author a strong, self-reflective voice as actor and/or as author. Though Cato's successors vary in the extent to which they engage with him as a model (or foil), prose was as conscious of the challenge of precursors in a genre, and as engaged in literary *aemulatio*, as was poetry. The five aspects enumerated above, then, will serve as touchstones in exploring the language of Latin historiography as it developed after Cato. For despite its breadth of tone and content – from *commentarius* to fully literary history, from expansive narrative to epitome – *historia* is a genre with its own set of expectations and markers (Adams (2005c) 94).

History and Poetry

History is very close to the poets. In a sense it is a prose poem, and it is written to tell a story, not to prove a point. Moreover, it is wholly designed not for practical effect and present conflicts, but to preserve a memory for future generations and for the glory of its author's talents. It therefore avoids tedium in Narrative by employing more out-of-the-way words and freer Figures [et uerbis remotioribus et liberioribus figuris].

(Quint. *Inst.* 10.1.31, trans. D.A. Russell.)

I begin with word choice, syntax (including sentence structure), and figures of speech and thought (*figurae* or *schemata*). *Historia* was an elevated genre which from Herodotus on advertised its affiliation to epic (Marincola (2007a)), not only because it, too, preserved memory, but also because it was a genre that treated matters of the highest import: war, politics, kingship, time, religion, fate, and power. Those topics call for the stylistic dignity and restraint of (high) poetry, as well as – especially in Rome – an emphasis on the didactic/documentary and the exemplary. In Latin, in the second century BCE, that meant primarily the epic poetry of Naevius and Ennius (on their style see p. 222 in this volume). The fragmentary remains make it impossible to tell how much their narrative technique contributed to the genre of *historia*; even evaluation of Cato's diction and its relation to these historical epics is complicated by his being the earliest Latin prose to survive. It does seem possible to say that, like his epic precursors, Cato affected an archaizing tone (e.g. *Orig.* 32, 126, 78–79) and elevated diction (e.g. *Orig.* 83 *inclutissumae; uerucca*: Briscoe (2010) 157–158), together with a preference for *atque* and choice perfects in *-ere*, that together gave him "the means to write impressively" (Briscoe (2005) 60). It is probably the case that Cato sought out words from the poets, there being no earlier prose writers in Latin from whom to draw (Fronto *Ep.* 56.23, Cato is noted for *uerba industriosius quaerendi*). That tendency to favor the choice continues in his Republican successors, in at least some of whom (especially Claudius Quadrigarius and Sisenna) it looks like a desire "to write history in the way in which it had been written in the past" (Briscoe (2005) 72). And it is abundantly clear from analyses of Tacitus' ever-refining diction (e.g. Syme (1958) 711–745, Adams (1972)) and of Caesar's restricted vocabulary (e.g. Hall (1998)), and from anecdotes about Sallust's using a word-hunter to find him particularly old-fashioned words (*priscorum uerborum adfectatione*, Suet. *Gram.* 10.1, 6 with Kaster (1995)) that such *elegantia* ("careful choice" of diction) continued to be a prized element of historiographical style.

The aspect of historiographical diction most frequently commented on is its incorporation of the choice. Axelson's neat categories have, of course, been long since abandoned, and categorizing expressions as "archaic," "poetic," or "colloquial," is notoriously problematic. The language of *historia* does not segregate one type from another – nor, with the (partial) exception of Caesar, is it particularly restrictive, except in a tendency to favor the solemn or the marked. Even how to decide which words or expressions count as poetic can quickly end up in a circle: for instance, the decision to leave out of account words previously attested only in poetry because they are found in Caesar (so Foucher (2000) 136–137). There are, however, clear trends. (1) Some words are found in extant prose exclusively or overwhelmingly in historiography, such as *celerare, inaccessus, ductor*. (2) Epic, unsurprisingly, is a source for the historians, especially after the *Aeneid: gestamen, crebresco*. (3) There is also a subset of words that cluster in historiography, though they may occasionally occur in other prose: *ingruere, abscedere; incertus* + gen. (an artificial use: Adams (2005c) 83). (4) There is some distinction from other prose, though not necessarily an affiliation with poetry, as in the following: *igitur* put first in its clause; *ceterum* "besides," as a transition; many adverbs in -(*t*)*im*. Overall, the point is both distinction and interest: this is deliberately "thick" language.

Frequent and selective use of figures of speech (especially alliteration, homoioteleuton, poly- and asyndeton, parallelism, chiasmus) contribute to history's elevated style, and reinforce its perceived affinities with epic poetry. Chiasmus is omnipresent. It is never purely decorative but, like anaphora and other forms of parallelism, reinforces meaning by putting elements in counterpoise or suggesting new interpretations of the data by juxtaposition or contrast. In Latin history the device appears with great frequency, both on the local and the global level (Steele (1891)). It may help control lists, contrasting adjacent pairs for emphasis, e.g. Caes. *Gal.* 3.19.3 *opportunitate loci, hostium inscientia, uirtute militum* ("because of the advantage offered by their location, the enemy's ignorance, the courage of the soldiers"). It may highlight a twist in the syntax, as at Just. 1.7.13 *gens … effeminata* (a) *mollitie luxuriaque* (b) *uirtutem pristinam* (b) *perdidit* (a) ("the people, … emasculated by softness and luxury, lost their ancient *uirtus*," where the contrasted units are not of the same case or form, and the design is further complicated by *effeminata ~ uirtutem*. Of its manifold uses, I single out only one more, and that is structuring across a long stretch of narrative. This may result in the expansion of what one could term a "table of contents" such as an introductory sentence or phrase (e.g. Liv. 6.7.3, where *hostem … me … uos* is expanded in the order *hostem…. uos … me*; cf. Virgil's procedure at *A.* 1.1, where *arma uirumque* encapsulates the whole poem, with *arma* corresponding to Books 7–12 and *uirum* to Books 1–6, respectively). Or it may represent form imposed on content to enable closure. So, e.g., the four *orationes* in Sallust *Cat.* are chiastically structured, bringing Catiline's two long speeches into parallel – a parallelism that both closes the monograph with a ring structure and complicates the picture of Catiline the monster, reminding us that the rabble rouser (*Cat.* 20) and the exponent of *uirtus* (*Cat.* 58) are one and the same.

Sallust in particular favored *asyndeton bimembre* (Wölfflin (1900)), a building block of his deliberately abrupt style that became a mark of later historiographical language: e.g. *Hist. 4.34M laborare festinare* (so for Livy see Kraus (1994) on 6.4.10, for Tacitus, Goodyear (1972) on *Ann.* 1.32.2; for Ammianus, Blomgren (1937) 3–16). Livy experimented with *epiploke*, the linking repetition of words that both connects sentences and puts elements into responsion: e.g. 6.32.8 *eques immissus ordines* **turbauit**, **turbatis** *signa peditum inlata* ("sending in the cavalry cast the ranks into confusion; against the confused, the infantry brought their standards"). Livy also cultivated a kind of open-ended sentence, finishing with an unexpected single *-que*, a mannerism picked up by Tacitus, and producing an abrupt finish (Kraus (1992)). Following the lead of earlier historians, Tacitus made an art of avoiding parallelism, luring readers in with the first member of a pair only to refuse the expected second element (Sörbom (1935); for Livy see Catterall (1938)). Figures of speech otherwise eschewed in prose, such as the "Priam figure" (a form of "coordinated polyptoton": Wills (1996) 254–261), together with frequent use of anaphora (Steele (1901)) and hyperbaton (Adams (1971)), among others, build the poetics of the historiographical narrative.

While it is difficult to be certain about the extent of deliberate use of alliteration and rhyming figures (see Goodyear (1972) 336–341), from the reader's standpoint this genre crackles with sound play. That often reinforces or is reinforced by word play, especially etymological (e.g. Liv. 6.32.6 *prosperae spei*, Tac. *Ann.* 4.38.5 *contemptu famae contemni uirtutes*), and even intertextually so (e.g. Amm. 26.10.19 *diuturna carie fatiscentem* with Kelly (2008) 210 and Blomgren (1937) 128–131). A particular area of play is in proper names (Woodman (1998) 219–223, esp. 222 n. 12). And that, in turn, invites consideration of the fitting nature of names and their bearers, and of the relationship of language to the things it describes.

Among figures of thought in history, metaphor is particularly important – and unsettling. Historians use metaphors singly which even without a qualifying *uelut* may be (and certainly have been) regarded as adding "vividness" or "color," but not otherwise obscuring the "transparent" qualities of the narrative (e.g. Liv. 6.22.7 *uirebat* of bodily vigor). But metaphor often plays a much more significant role. As Woodman has shown for Tacitus (e.g. (2006, 2010b)) and Krebs for Sallust (2008a, 2008b), pervasive metaphorical language and imagery are not only illustrative but constitutive of the historian's meaning: "The pattern of the metaphor runs parallel to the pattern of events, the plot; but it does more than enforce the impression made by the events, it interprets them." That quotation does not in fact concern *historia*; it comes from Bernard Knox's classic article on the serpent and flame imagery in Virgil's *Aeneid* ((1950) 381). But it is equally applicable to the extended metaphorical patterns in historical prose, which function in precisely the same way as they do in poetry. The content is not simply decorated, it is determined by such writing (for a focused study see Foucher (2000) 384–432 on battle narratives). What, then, are we to make of a historical narrative that represents past events in such figurative poetic terms?

At least since Aristophanes' *Frogs*, the criticism has been made that when poetry of high genres admits overly technical or overly "ordinary" diction, it forfeits its dignity. Though it is difficult to tell from the extant *Origines* whether Cato consistently avoided or paraphrased the precise and the mundane, it is certain that his successors did: military ranks tend to be approximated rather than exact (on Ammianus, e.g., see Müller (1905)); numbers rounded or qualified; the everyday paraphrased (famously, in Tacitus: implements *per quae egeritur humus* rather than "spades," *Ann.* 1.65.7); and the crude either omitted or disowned (see p. 253 in this volume). That said, the mundane is not always avoided (see especially Goodyear (1972) 342–345 and for Sisenna – who showed a liking for technical detail – Rawson (1979) 334), and it would be more accurate to say that in *historia* avoidance of such expressions, be they *inhonesta dictu* or officialese, depends on the historian's individual stylistic choice, not on any generic rule. Elements of everyday language are also found: e.g., *sermo castrensis* perhaps in Cato (*pedatus, Orig.* 28: Briscoe (2010) 156) and emphatically at Caes. *Gal.* 7.73.2–4, Tac. *Ann.* 1.50.1, Amm. 17.11.1 *et saep.* (Mosci Sassi (1983) 126–127, 129, 98). But here, too, the inclusion or exclusion of these lexical items serves the needs of their narrative context, not a generic requirement.

Perhaps paradoxically, one of the characteristics of *historia* that led Quintilian to describe it as *proxima poetis* is precisely this range available to it in matters of stylistic choice (cf. his *et uerbis remotioribus et liberioribus figuris*, quoted above). This latitude may be further illustrated by considering the annalistic and the comic registers, neither of which is *prima facie* appropriate in an elevated genre.

Cato expressed a preference for not including "what is on the Pontifex's tablet": the examples he gives are the price of grain (*annona*) and lunar eclipses (*Orig.* 77). Resistance to including such material not only shows a feeling for levels of style, but also allows *historia* to work more with themes, causality, and human character than with quotidian details. These are, of course, sometimes deployed to give an *éffet du réal* (or even, perhaps, to reflect "what really happened"): Nabdalsa imprudently leaving an incriminating letter out while he takes a nap (Sallust *Jug.* 71.4), slaves bringing water to extinguish the heavenly fire on Servius Tullius' head (Liv. 1.39.1), the sweaty Alexander bathing in a river (Curt. 3.5.2), a weeping Otho jumping up onto his dining couch (Tac. *Hist.* 1.82.1). But for the most part, ancient historical narrative remains on the level of the typical and the schematic, a practice that brings it closer to what Sempronius Asellio approved of as "proper" history, as opposed to the "daybooks" or "annals" more suitable for the immature (Asel. 1–2). The kind of material that does not please Cato is often known as "annalistic" – the tablets to which he refers were those of the Pontifex Maximus, the so-called *annales maximi*. It does find its way into later historiographical narrative, and often, but tends to be confined to the edges of a textual year (cf. e.g. Oakley (1997) 122–124, with references in n. 71). A historian thus has his cake and eats it too: the annalistic material serves as a guarantee of the work's place in the (traditions of the) genre (McDonald (1957) 155–157, especially 157 on the "official mode of expression" contained in Livy's annalistic sections), while its careful deployment on the one hand testifies to the historian's judgment and taste and, on the other, allows his narrative analysis to explore not "what Alcibiades did and suffered" but what *kind* of actions and character produced Rome's past and contribute to its future.

Another genre that contributes to history's "alembicated style" (Mayer (2001) 29) is comedy. Scraps of dialogue mark scenes as partaking of comic atmosphere, even when that atmosphere is about to turn tragic (e.g. Liv. 1.57.8 *age sane*; 1.58.7 *satin salue?* to Lucretia: Poccetti (2010) 115–117). Details of the quotidian also sometimes accumulate (Tanaquil's window, Liv. 1.41.4; the butcher's knife for Verginia, 3.48.5; the knock that startles Fabia Minor (6.34.6 with Kraus (1994) 273); or Vitellius' unmentionable hiding-place (Tac. *Hist.* 3.84.4) and Constantius II's not rubbing his nose in public (Amm. 16.10.10). These moments that remind us of staged action may mark a scene as a typically New Comic plot, say (Ogilvie (1970) 222, Scafuro (1989)), or signal that a narrative bears comparison with the conventions of tragedy. This technique of adding meaning to a scene by suggesting a parallel with drama, especially with its stock figures, is well recognized in Cicero, who does the same thing in the rhetorical establishment and manipulation of character (Geffcken (1973)). Narrative history, like drama and oratory, takes as its basis the interaction of human beings; so Roman historiography deploys structures conventional in drama, both tragedy and comedy, to shape the stories it tells, and like drama, it uses human beings and their character (*mores*), as revealed through action, to explore causation.

Though not necessarily "poetic," certain syntactical forms are more at home in *historia* than in other prose. Selectively, I give four examples, first from the area of verbal description. (1) The historical infinitive was exploited especially in painterly scenes of emotion and horror, often (but by no means always) in groups of two or more. Its ability to give a flash picture of an unfinished action, especially of battle, may be what endeared it to the historians: e.g. Sallust *Jug.* 51.1 *pars **cedere** alii **insequi**, neque signa neque ordines **obseruare*** (translated below). Though Sallust's use of the historical infinitive remained the most creative – its quickness enhanced his famous *breuitas* – subsequent historians continued to exploit its possibilities (Schlicher (1915) 58, Viljamaa (1983)). (2) All the historians use many different types of clause as forward-moving cola (Spilman (1932); see further below), but the ablative absolute is by far the most favored, and together with short, asyndetic sentences became something like a genre-signal, suggesting a connection with – if not a derivation from – actual military reports to the Senate and a "chancellery" style (Odelman (1972) 130–134, Adams (2005c) 74–76).

Second, engagement with the reader. (3) Historians are fond of the disjunctive *siue ... siue* construction (or *seu ... seu*, sometimes *utrum ... an*) especially when listing possible motives for action. One of the alternatives is almost always unflattering: Caes. *Civ.* 2.27.2 *siue uere quam habuerant opinionem ad eum perferunt, siue etiam auribus Vari seruiunt* ("whether they took their true opinion to him, or whether they were enslaved to Varus' ears [i.e. told him what he wanted to hear]"), Liv. 6.12.1 *seu quia celeritate ad bellum opus erat, seu uictoria triumphoque dictaturae ipsi uires se additurum ratus* ("whether because speed was required for war, or because he thought he would add strength to the dictatorship by victory and a triumph"). Tacitus develops this construction (often known as the "loaded" or "weighted" alternative) to a fine art, and it is associated with him, but it is in fact a characteristic way that Latin history explores causality, by inviting the reader to judge between alternatives. (4) The second person singular is used to remark on what the reader could have done or seen if present, as at *B. Hisp.* 25.2 *existimare posses paratissimos esse ad dimicandum* ("you could have judged that they were very ready to fight"), Liv. 44.34.8 *neminem totis mox castris quietum uideres* ("shortly thereafter, you would not have seen anyone at rest in the whole camp"), Tac. *Ann.* 3.1.4 *neque discerneres proximos alienos* ("nor could you have told apart close family from strangers"). The usage, which brings the reader closer to the imagined events – something akin to breaking the fourth wall in theater or film – allows "a special manipulation of time and person within a continuous narrative" (Gilmartin (1975) 121).

Overall, *historia* is marked by a tendency to innovate syntactically. In many cases these innovations are influenced by Greek literary syntax, but it is often difficult to tell how exclusive that influence is: "Latin writers were careful to introduce literary Graecisms that did not offend the Latin language but rather could be adapted to it" (Calboli (2009) 70). *Historia*, especially from Livy on, experimented with (among other things) the future participle, with the gerund and gerundive, with the infinitive dependent on adjectives, with the dative of the "Ort-" and "Standpunkt," and with constructions such as *mihi uolenti est*. Similarly marked is a tendency toward the choice in nominal syntax (e.g., adjectives + gen. as in Liv. 6.11.3 *nimius animi*), plain cases with compound verbs (Tac. *Ann.* 1.65.2 *paludibus emersum*), internal accusatives (Tac. *Ann.* 4.60.2 *falsum renidens*) and middle uses of the passive with accusative object (e.g. Sallust *Hist.* 3.24 *inulti terga ab hostibus caedebantur*: Courtney (2004) 428).

Lastly, historians use *oratio obliqua* with great fluidity, often moving in and out of indirect constructions without much warning. An easy example, where the accusative + infinitive follows on from the *ut* clause in a mild and common zeugma: Caes. *Gal.* 1.2.1 *ciuitati persuasit ut de finibus suis ... exirent: perfacile esse ... totius Galliae imperio potiri* ("he persuaded his people that they should leave their territory ...: it would be easy ... to get control of the whole of Gaul"). This kind of *oratio obliqua* serves especially to represent group thoughts or crowd noises, as at Liv. 7.38.6–7 *inibanturque consilia ... adimendae Campanis Capuae ...: neque immerito ... in eos uersurum; cur autem ... haberet?* ("and plans were entered into to remove Capua from the Campanians ...: nor was it unreasonable ... to turn against them ... for why should ... [the army] have?"). Blurring the line between discourse that is the "property" of the narrator and that of the character produces remarkable effects, which point the absence of a place from which to view the past clearly, as at Tac. *Hist.* 1.29.1:

> Ignarus interim Galba et sacris intentus fatigabat alieni iam imperii deos cum adfertur rumor rapi in castra incertum quem senatorem mox Othonem esse qui raperetur, simul ex tota urbe ut quisque obuius fuerat alii formidine augentes quidam minora uero ne tum quidem obliti adulationis.

After the *cum inuersum* with dependent accusative in indirect statement, Tacitus gives us *simul ex tota urbe* (no verb and no expressed subject), then *augentes* with no object, and *quidam* with no verb. Translation makes the difficulties patent:

> Meanwhile Galba in ignorance and intent upon his sacrifices was importuning the gods of an empire that already belonged to another, when there came a rumor that some senator was being hurried to the camp, then that it was Otho who was being hurried; at the same time from the whole city, insofar as each had met [him], some exaggerating in fear, others [representing things as] less than the truth, not forgetful even then of flattery.

From *simul* to *adulationis*, the sentence is no longer formally part of the *oratio obliqua* (cf. *obliti*), but it is far from clear whose voice we hear.

In any particular case, the motivation for syntactical innovation in *historia* might come from one or more of several sources; but the trend was toward a more flexible, economical, and expressive syntax, one that could "peel back discrepancies between surface behavior and inner motivation" and become "a vehicle for ruthless wit" and "moral judgements about the protagonists and the times" (Ash (2007) 14; her remarks do not apply only to Tacitus).

Finally, historical prose displays its poetic side by its use of poetry proper. It may quote verse explicitly (Enn. *Ann.* is quoted at *B. Hisp.* 23.3, 31.7 and at Liv. 30.26.9, Verg. *A.* at Amm. 15.9.1); allude to it (Sallust *Cat.* 60.2 *gladiis res geritur* ~ Enn. *Ann.* 268 *ui geritur res*; Curt. 6.9.28 to Verg. *A.* 2.557–558; Tac. *Ag.* 29.4 to Verg. *A.* 6.304); pervasively interweave a poetic intertext (Foucher (2000) 263–331); or use the same techniques. By this last I mean not only shared diction, but the kind of procedure that is clear at Caes. *Gal.* 1.1 *Gallia est omnis diuisa in partes tres.* The play with division via mimetic syntax is obvious; what is less evident is that in this opening flourish Caesar is playing the same poetic games as his contemporary Gallus, whose pentameter on the Scythian Hypanis illustrates the same kind of iconic word order in the same kind of description: *uno tellures diuidit amne duas* of the boundary – here idiosyncratically for the Tanais – between Europe and Asia (Courtney (2003) 263 compares Caes. *Civ.* 3.19.1). Caesar, too, defines the Gallic territories by their bordering rivers – also idiosyncratically (Rice-Holmes (1911) 344). Caesar is not, one presumes, alluding to Gallus; but both reflect the same learned impulse and the same impressionistic technique.

History and Oratory

Do you see how great a task history is for the orator? It may in fact be the greatest task in terms of fluency of diction and variety.

(Cic. *de Orat.* 2.62, trans. J.M. May and J. Wisse (2001))

When Cicero has his character Atticus call *historia* an *opus oratorium maxime* (*Leg.* 1.5) he can be partly understood to be responding to history's rootedness in the traditions of Roman public speaking, beginning with the example set by Cato. (Other public figures who turned, or claimed to consider turning, to history-writing include Calpurnius Piso Frugi, Licinius Macer, Cicero, Caesar, Sallust, Seneca (perhaps the Younger: Woodman (2010b) 58–59), Servilius Nonianus, Curtius Rufus, Tacitus, and both Plinys.) Cicero himself, of course, would say that – and, even though another orator, Pliny the Younger, drew careful distinctions between oratory and history (*Ep.* 5.8), like Cicero he did not doubt that his oratorical skill would give him an edge as a historian. Finally, it has been powerfully and rightly argued that oratory and *historia* share a rhetorical basis in *inuentio* (Woodman (1988)).

Where oratorical technique and style most obviously enter into *historia* is in the speeches that complement and articulate the narrative in nearly all the extant Latin historians. Not everyone agreed on the proper proportion of speech to narrative: too many speeches might push the whole work toward oratory (Cic. *Brut.* 286, D. S. 20.1.1–3), and direct speech (*oratio recta*) was disapproved of by Pompeius Trogus (Just. 38.3.11). Curtius incorporates speech generously; Sallust has few set speeches but long ones (the *Cat.* is nearly 27 percent direct speech). Caesar, Livy, and Tacitus seem as partial to indirect speech (*oratio obliqua*) as to direct; Ammianus has few speeches, preferring instead to interweave his narrative with an abundance of digressions and excursuses. Whether in direct or indirect/reported *oratio*, these speeches are generically close to "proper" oratory in argument, structure, and – to a limited extent – style.

One particular area in which these embedded speeches resemble real ones is in deploying the same kind of schematic arguments (based on topics such as "the just" or "the honorable" or "the useful") as used by orators (Ullmann (1927)). A subset of these arguments comprises the *exempla* or "representative historical precedents" used by a speaker in the text, who may be judged by his use of historical *exempla* not just whether he is an effective speaker, but also how skilful he is in interpreting the past (Chaplin (2000) 73–105). Direct and oblique speeches alike show "oratorical" arrangement, both in sentence structure (see below) and figures. Speeches, for instance, account for 75 percent of the anaphora in Livy's surviving text (Steele (1901) 155); other formal rhetorical devices are proportionately more frequent in history's *orationes* (Adams (1973)). Quintilian is again instructive:

> history, which should move with speed and impetuosity, would have been ill-suited by the halts imposed by the rounding off of the period ... It is however true that *in the speeches inserted by historians* we may note something in the way of balanced cadences and antitheses. (*Inst.* 9.4.18, trans. D.A. Russell, my emphasis)

So at Tac. *Hist.* 1.15.1, we find parallelism with anaphora (*et ... et*), near rhyme (*adsciscere ... adiecisse*), and ring composition bracketing each branch (*mihi ... meos/tibi ... tuae*): *si te ... adoptarem, et mihi egregium erat Cn. Pompei et M. Crassi subolem in penatis meos adsciscere, et tibi insigne Sulpiciae ac Lutatiae decora nobilitati tuae adiecisse* ("if I were now adopting you [as a private citizen], it would be for me exceptional to introduce into my house a scion of Gnaeus Pompeius and Marcus Crassus, and for you a distinction to add to your own nobility the honors of the Sulpician and Lutatian [*gentes*]"). Similar devices are found in Caesar's *oratio obliqua*, including an anaphoric tricolon (*quod ... quod ... quod*), parallelism (*quam rem et ... et; neque ... neque*), ring composition with *uariatio* (*sua senatusque/sua ac senatus*), and *copia uerborum* (*beneficio ac liberalitate*):

> sua senatusque in eum beneficia commemorauit, quod rex appellatus esset a senatu, quod amicus, quod munera amplissime missa; quam rem et paucis contigisse et pro magnis hominum officiis consuesse tribui docebat; illum, cum neque aditum neque causam postulandi iustam haberet, beneficio ac liberalitate sua ac senatus ea praemia consecutum. (*Gal.* 1.43.4–5)

> [Caesar spoke of] his own and the Senate's benefits conferred on [Ariovistus]: that he had been declared king by the Senate, that [he had been declared] friend, that gifts had been most liberally sent [to him]; he explained that this happened to only a few, and was customarily granted by the Romans in return for the greatest services; he [Ariovistus], though he had neither access nor any just cause for claim, had received those rewards through the kindness and generosity of himself [Caesar] and the Senate.

Certain lexical items tend to be found only or primarily in inset speech: for instance, the expression *quod .... attinet* in Livy is four times commoner in the speeches; the particles *enim* and *nam* show a consistent distribution (*enim* in direct speech, *nam* outside it) in Sallust and other historians (Kroon (1995) 181). And though the differences between narrative and speech in a given historian are less appreciable than those among the varying examples of oratorical style concocted by the author of the *ad Herennium* (see pp. 396–397 of this volume), historians could characterize their speakers not only through content but also through form. Tacitus' Tiberius is the best known example (see Wharton (1997) for some cautions), but there are others. The pompous, rebellious Gauls at Caes. *Gal.* 7.1.3–2.2 deploy weighty Ciceronian phraseology; Appius Claudius Crassus favors certain rhetorical devices and word orders (Liv. 5.5.4, 6.40.7, 40.8: Kraus (1994) 311–312, 315); Tacitus' Seneca and his pupil, Nero, do *not* talk like the real Seneca (Woodman (2010a)). Prominent figures are often given snippets of direct speech; in the case of centurions – who feature prominently in military narrative – these tend to be conventionally heroic (so Caes. *Civ.* 3.91.3), but famous characters, too, are given *bons mots* that are either characterizing (so Liv. 1.58.2 with Ogilvie (1970) 20) or traditional (Maharbal to Hannibal, Cato *Orig.* 86, Liv. 22.51.2).

While oratory had to be comprehended aurally, history – despite being performed in *recitatio* settings (Dalziell (1955)) – was primarily a written genre. Its Roman practitioners took to heart the distinction articulated by Thucydides between a performance for immediate pleasure and a κτῆμα ἐς αἰεί ("possession for all time"), not only by pitching their work toward posterity (Quint. *Inst.* 10.1.31, quoted above) and insisting on the social and ethical utility of their work (Kraus (1994) 13–14, Willi (2010)), but also by developing a style that challenged and rewarded an intellectually engaged reader. We know this from ancient critics themselves (Sen. *Ep.* 114.17, Quint. *Inst.* 10.1.32–33). Confirmation (if any were needed) comes from observation of historians' word order and choice of preferred syntactical structures. Tacitus' obsession with *uariatio* makes us read very carefully. In addition, he plays with the traditional placement of structural elements (see below). Sallust, to whom ancient critics ascribed *uelocitas* and *breuitas*, likewise sought effects from unpredictability and roughness. In Ammianus, richness of vocabulary joins choice syntactical structures to build a "jewelled" style (Kelly (2008) 215–226).

Livy explores the range of *uariatio* and comprehensiveness possible in a single period of extended narrative description. One might take here as example part of his description of Hercules' encounter with Cacus, which McDonald saw as "illustrating the principles of 'periodic' composition where a writer's conception of his material bears heavily on the stylistic conventions" ((1957) 166). McDonald's attention focuses primarily on the second sentence of the passage (Liv. 1.7.5):

ibi cum eum cibo uinoque grauatum[1] sopor oppressisset,[2] pastor accola eius loci, nomine Cacus, ferox uiribus, captus[3] pulchritudine boum cum auertere eam praedam uellet,[4] quia[5] si agendo armentum in speluncam compulisset ipsa uestigia quaerentem dominum eo deducta erant, auersos[6] boues eximium quemque pulchritudine caudis in speluncam traxit.[7]

When sleep overtook Hercules, heavy with food and drink, a local shepherd, by name Cacus, a creature of ferocious strength, when he was much taken by the beauty of the beasts and wished to steal them, since if he drove off the herd and forced it into his cave, the tracks would lead their inquiring owner in his direction, he selected the handsomest bulls, turned them around, and dragged them into the cave by their tails. (Trans. A.H. McDonald (1957))

The end of this sentence, McDonald said, is "out of touch with its opening words." In fact, however, he is perhaps misled by an expectation of finding something like oratorical periodicity and subordination here. If the sentence is read linearly, it details a complex action in its narrative order (the phases of which are represented by superscript numbers in the extract above; *quia*, 5, is shorthand for "and then he realized that"). There are no afterthoughts or awkwardly inserted explanatory clauses. And the sentence's end is by design far from its beginning – because in it Livy has taken us from Hercules' falling asleep to Cacus' abstraction of the cattle into the cave, with all the actions in between. This is a kind of sentence characteristic of historiography, a narrative period, in which there is plenty of hypotaxis but very little subordination of thought. Each (numbered) verbal unit ("forward-moving colon") gives a further stage in the action; they may be further elaborated by non-forward-moving elements (e.g. the *quia* clause above, which elaborates the content of Cacus' reasoning). Very different are the (textbook) examples of Ciceronian oratorical periods, in which cooperating sense and syntax come together only at the close of the sentence; or discursive periods in speeches, which describe rather than narrate (e.g. Tac. *Hist.* 1.15.1 and Caes. *Gal.* 1.43.4–5, both quoted above).

Sentence structure in history both answers the expectations of generic decorum and conveys meaning. In discussing the different types of period appropriate to different kinds of writing, Quintilian fastens on history's fluidity (*Inst.* 9.4.129):

> History requires not so much definite rhythms as a certain cyclical structure, for its Cola are all connected with one another ... in the way that men who join hands to steady their steps lend mutual support to one another [*qui manibus inuicem adprehensis gradum firmant, continent et continentur*]. (Trans. D.A. Russell)

The combination of connection (*manibus ... adprehensis*) and movement (*gradum*) perfectly describes a unit like the Livian sentence quoted above.

It is a marked feature of Sallust's style (and that of his imitators) that connection is as often made adversatively as conjunctively. Though Sallust's local effects often depend on surprise, he writes with an eye to communicative structure. In his hands, antithesis and asyndeton become building blocks of text, e.g. at *Jug.* 51.1:

> Ceterum facies totius negoti uaria incerta foeda atque miserabilis; dispersi a suis pars cedere alii insequi; neque signa neque ordines obseruare; ubi quemque periculum ceperat ibi resistere ac propulsare; arma tela equi uiri hostes atque ciues permixti; nihil consilio neque imperio agi, fors omnia regere.

> Yet in fact the whole scene of activity was fluctuating, unpredictable, foul and wretched: separated from their own men, some gave way, others pursued; there was no regard for stand-ards or ranks: wherever anyone was overtaken by danger, there he made a stand and resisted; arms and weapons, horses and men, enemies and citizens were all mixed up; nothing was done according to plan or command: chance ruled everything. (Trans. A.J. Woodman (2007))

Sallust begins with a summary, whose *totius* is picked up in ring composition (with *uariatio*) by *omnia* at the end. Asyndeton, antithesis, and inconcinnity function as con-nectives in *dispersi a suis pars cedere alii insequi*; the next group is held together by poly-syndetic anaphora and an alliterative ending. Correlative, linking adverbs follow, before the passage returns to near list form with *arma tela equi uiri hostes atque ciues permixti*, in which related pairs (the first two asyndetic) are capped up by a descriptive participle. Finally, antithesis (*nihil/omnia*), asyndeton, and an active–passive contrast (*agi/regere*) shape the end, finished off with a totalizing statement (*fors omnia regere*). Rather than being shapeless, despite its lacking anything resembling complex syntax, the passage is tightly connected (for asyndeton and other constructions of "change" as connectives see Mendell (1917) 111–140).

This extract from Sallust also illustrates the variation of sentence length and shape typical of historiographical narrative (though oratory, too, is varied: see particularly the analyses of Gotoff (1979) *passim*). Even the "restricted" Caesar has an extraordinary range, with sentence lengths from one word (or three, depending on how one counts: *milites imperat: mittunt* "he demands soldiers; they send [them]," *Civ.* 1.15) to extended periods with considerable subordination (*Gal.* 3.3.2, *Civ.* 1.64.1–2).

Though Livy's narrative is "so varied and extensive … that it is quite … impossible to produce neat formulae to show when and where he was likely to use a periodic sentence" (Oakley (1997) 134), some patterns are discernible. He likes to begin and end his individual narrative units ("Einzelerzählungen": Witte (1910)) with longer periods, moving to short sentences for the main action; like Tacitus, he will often end a section with an epigrammatic formulation (6.10.9 with Kraus (1994)). He imports clarity by meticulously designating the stages of an action with adverbs such as *primo, deinde, tum* (McDonald (1957) 169), and by keeping a reader's attention fixed on the alternation of action through the use of "headings," often proper names at the start of sentences (Luce (1971) 285–287, Chausserie-Laprée (1969) 18–24).

Tacitus, like Livy, varies the length and type of his sentences; like Sallust, he is famous for his epigrams, which give a spiky, pointed feel to his work (cf. Quint. 10.1.130 on Seneca, who broke up "his weighty ideas in his tiny little epigrams [*sententiis*]"; on Tacitus' technique see Voss (1963)). These epigrams aim at least partly at engaging the reader's wit and judgment, at pinning our attention on a paradox or an outrage. A similar motive is at work with what is perhaps Tacitus' most characteristic sentence shape, in which the main clause comes early and is followed by an "appendix," often participial, in which are examined the motives or reactions to events (Oakley (2009) 205–206), e.g. *Ann.* 4.29.1, where the appendix (*pudore Caesaris*) leads into an extended reason for Tiberius' reaction to the indictment: *Tum accusator Cn. Lentulum et Seium Tuberonem nominat, <u>magno pudore</u> **Caesaris**, cum primores ciuitatis, intimi ipsius amici … accerserentur* ("At that the accuser named Cn. Lentulus and Seius Tubero, to the considerable embarrassment of Caesar, since it was leaders of the community, his own intimate friends … who were being summoned" (trans. A.J. Woodman (2004)). One can usefully compare this with instances where a historian lays out the reasoning for actions before they happen, as at Liv. 36.10.3 *tunc adgredi Larisam constituit <u>ratus</u> uel … uel … uel … non ultra in pertinacia mansuros* ("then he decided to attack Larissa, figuring that the inhabitants would no longer remain stubborn, either because … or because …. or because …"; the attack follows).

The *clausulae* of the literary historians, and their favored patterns, are less well understood than those of Cicero; nor are all Latin historians interested to the same degree in producing rhythmic prose. It is clear that those who are, prefer rhythms different from the Ciceronian favorites precisely in the area of poetic sound: historians are much more likely to use either a dactylic or a spondaic *clausula* than is the orator, to whom those rhythms were too close to poetry. (Among our authors, of course, Ammianus is the exception: though he uses Late Antique *cursus* rhythms, his are heavily influenced by Greek practices: Oberhelman (1987).) At the start of their works, moreover, Sallust,

Livy, and Tacitus all feature prominent dactylic rhythms – in the case of Tac. *Ann.* a complete hexameter – which point toward history's roots in the κλέα ἀνδρῶν of epic.

Antiquarianism

The documents abovementioned … may gratify the curiosity of the antiquary, as well as establish the credit of the history.

(G. White, *The Natural History of Selborne*, "Advertisement", 1788)

One of the first things one reads about ancient history is that it is to be distinguished from antiquarian writing. The two modes are differentiated by their organization (chronological/ topical), style (self-conscious, high/none or inconsistent in register), and purpose (commemoration and exemplarity/catalogue and inventory). Yet history needs what the antiquarian collects. However we imagine historians working, their texts are sprinkled with data: e.g. letters (Sallust *Cat.* 44.5 and Curt. 4.1.10–14); *bons mots*, which form part of the *realia* accruing to historical characters (see above); the text of inscriptions (Liv. 41.28.8–9); topographical detail (Liv. 1.8.5, Tac. *Hist.* 1.41.2); records of art works (Amm. 19.6.12); aetiologies for rituals or law (Liv. 1.26.12–13); even literary (Vell. 1.16–17), legal (Tac. *Ann.* 3.25.2–28.4) or political (Sallust *Cat.* 36.4–39.5) history. This kind of material often gravitates toward the annalistic portions of the text. One particular area, however, is more pervasively integrated with the historiographical narrative: ethnography (together with its congener, paradoxography: Gabba (1981)).

Herodotus made ethnography and paradoxography a fundamental part of history, using such passages as a means of delineating military/political narrative, of going deeper into the nature of the nations in conflict, of holding up a mirror to the Athenians. In Cato's hands, ethnography was an even more important element: the first three books of the *Origines* were apparently structured by *populus* and traveled around the Italian city foundations; these books in turn set up the last four, whose narrative – now based on the *res gestae populi Romani* – assumed a more linear, chronological structure. One can see the remarkable statement that Cato puts into his own mouth in his speech on behalf of the Rhodians (*Orig.* 95), to the effect that one should not judge another before walking a mile in his moccasins, as a product of the ethnographical project of the first books. Readers who had moved around the Italian cities, learning about their individual natures and *mores*, would be prepared for the Roman power to take an interest in – even to the point of trying to understand – foreign city-states. Among the fragments of and *testimonia* to the *Origines*, ethnography plays a large part (including topographical description and *thaumata*: *Orig.* 52, 93, 110).

The interplay between these passages and the "main" military/political narrative is as significant as either element on its own. The boundary between the two modes may mark military advance (so the conventional use of an ethnography at the moment an army crosses into a new territory or a nation begins a major foreign war); or it may put the two into responsion, inviting analysis of self and other (some of the best examples are the so-called "reaction narratives" in Sallust *Jug.*, where Rome reflects Numidia and vice versa). Like other antiquarian details, ethnographical items often draw comment from the historian who thereby confirms his authority as he conquers the chaos of tralatitious data by taking the reader through it (good examples of a firm guiding hand at Sallust

Jug. 17–19 and Tac. *Ag.* 10–12). When the paradoxographical narrative of *miracula* enters in, that often enhances the sense of distance from the center that is "us," challenging ideas of what is human and what is not, bringing the ends of the earth, or the monstrous in the densest forest, into view to be assimilated into Roman inventories.

The ethnographical has its own language, a distinctive structure and diction that signal a change away from political or military narrative. The topic-based organization native to stand-alone ethnographical treatises (e.g., Tacitus' *Germania*) makes cherry-picking interesting or relevant details easy, and correspondingly neat dropping them into an extended, chronological narrative as digressions. Historiography, with its self-describing metaphor of the road, is tailor-made for rest stops (Liv. 9.17.1 *deuerticula amoena*). So, even in extended ethnographical passages (Caes. *Gal.* 6.11–28, Liv. 5.33–35, Amm. 31.2), the topic-based structure is retained (or reproduced), affording the reader a different kind of logical organization and a different mode of thought from the chronological narrative. Under the rubrics of *situs* and *gentes* ("lands" and "peoples": Thomas (1982) 1–7), historians provide myriad ethnographical details: foreign social and political structures, explanations for religious or cultural acts, accounts of military practice (especially the horrible or the novel) – all may be flagged with generic markers such as *ut moris* or *ut mos est*, *ut fit*, or *ut sole(n)t*. The novel and the astonishing, usually characterized in terms of size, are generically marked with words like *miraculum, nouum, atrox, inauditum*: the wonderful phoenix in Egypt (Tac. *Ann.* 6.28 *mirantium*), the remarkable deed of the Philaeni brothers (Sallust *Jug.* 79.1 *egregium atque mirabile*), or the marvelously huge Gallic swine (Cato *Orig.* 39 *crescere*).

But the foreign is not the only thing to submit to the ethnographical gaze. When Rome is its target, ethnographical language tends to be found in the "main" narrative, its generic tags and *topoi* marking places which we are to read as observations of a foreign culture, even if that culture is our own. In the early books, Livy invites us to look at Rome as a kind of foreign society whose customs need explanation: etiology is a strong thematic force, and the historian's relatively detached eye lets him stand back and either criticize precedents (1.28.10, 8.7.22) or present these customs to us as new, for our evaluation (see especially Solodow (1979)). Tacitus, who throughout engages the thematic of the emperor as the attacker of his own city (Keitel (2010)), reserves special ethnographical treatment for Nero, constructing him and his Rome as strange and alien (Woodman (1992)). And as the empire grows and its center moves east, Rome indeed becomes a place not to live in, but to visit, the object of spectacle (Amm. 16.10).

Military Narrative

These things thus being so which also … the impediments having been abandoned …
(R. Baker, "Caesar's Puerile Wars")

One of the traditions about the development of Roman military history was that it emerged as a narrative elaboration of generals' reports to the Senate (see above). Though that story is probably only *ben trovato*, military narrative has commanded attention at least partly because of its (wished for) relationship to real ancient communications. Much has been written about its style. Rather than repeating that material here (for it see

Further Reading, below), I offer an extract from Tacitus' *Agricola* (22.1–2) and comment on its "typical" aspects.

> Tertius expeditionum annus nouas gentis aperuit, uastatis usque ad Tanaum (aestuario nomen est) nationibus. qua formidine territi hostes quamquam conflictatum saeuis tempestatibus exercitum lacessere non ausi; ponendisque insuper castellis spatium fuit. adnotabant periti non alium ducem opportunitates locorum sapientius legisse. nullum ab Agricola positum castellum aut ui hostium expugnatum aut pactione ac fuga desertum; crebrae eruptiones, nam aduersus moras obsidionis annuis copiis firmabantur.

> The third year of campaigns opened up new peoples with the ravaging of the territories up to the Taus [Tay] (that is the name of the estuary). This action so intimidated the enemy that they did not dare to challenge the army, although it was harassed by wild storms. There was even time to spare for establishing forts. Experts commented that no other general selected suitable sites more wisely. No fort established by Agricola was ever taken by the enemy by storm or abandoned either by capitulation or flight. In fact, they could make frequent sallies, for they were assured against long sieges by supplies to last for a year. (Trans. A.R. Birley (1999))

Despite the Tacitean idiom – the ellipse of forms of *esse*, the variation in vocabulary (*formidine territi*), the validating mention of the *periti* ("experts," as at *Ann.* 12.25.2, *Hist.* 3.37.2) – this passage displays many typical elements of a (short) episode in any Latin military narrative. It is the abridged story of a campaign year: the Roman advance into unknown enemy territory, the interaction between Romans and Britons as the Romans establish outposts in the Scottish Lowlands, and the logistical state of the Romans and the mental state of their enemy.

After the organizing heading (*tertius … annus*), the first sentence establishes the action as pathbreaking, the Livian *aperuit* + direct object (of a people) a choice idiom (Tac. *Hist.* 2.17.1 with Ash (2007)); *uastatis … nationibus* may be an example of Tacitus' postponing of an absolute construction ("and devastated"; historiographical narrative conventionally puts this kind of statement before the main clause), or it may be an example of the modal use of the past participle ("by devastating"). In any case, the vocabulary is traditional, as is the topographical detail reinforced by the learned parenthesis. In the next sentence, expressive word order shows the terrified enemy surrounding the harassed Roman army. This contrapuntal, slightly paradoxical relationship of enclosing *hostes* to enclosed *exercitus* is further developed by patterns of word order, interwoven (*territi* (a) *hostes* (b) … *conflictatum* (a) … *exercitum* (b)) and chiastic (*conflictatum* (a) *saeuis* (b) *tempestatibus* (b) *exercitum* (a)). Having room to do something (*spatium*) is frequent in military narrative; but *spatium* + dative is choice.

The judgment of experienced men (*adnotabant periti*) projects onto anonymous observers the desideratum, explicitly called for by Cicero, that "concerning [a leader's] plans, the writer should indicate what he approves" (*de Orat.* 2.63). It is expressed in a verb-initial clause, a punctuating device typical of historiographical narrative (Sallust seems alone in not favoring it: Chausserie-Laprée (1969) 347–356). *opportunitates locorum* is a stock military phrase from Caesar through to Tacitus, and *sapientia* (in the sense of sound judgment) the mark of an ideal general (Liv. 44.22.12, Onas. 21.3, Tac. *Ann.* 1.28.3). When the narrative resumes (if Tacitus is not still focalizing the experts!) it confirms with *nullum ... desertum* the opinion of the experts, again in standard language (*ui hostium, expugnatum*) or language that sounds standard (*pactione ac fuga* only here, but cf. Caes. *Gal.* 2.12.1 *terrore ac fuga*, Sallust *Jug.* 55.7 *fuga atque formido*, Liv. 5.38.2 *pauoris ac fugae*) with balance (*aut ... aut*) and parallel construction. At this point, however, one might notice that the *castella*, which were offensive structures before the *adnotabant* sentence (*castellis*), are now defensive (*castellum*). Tacitus thus hints at the stereotypical contrast of *obsessi* and *obsessores*, found in so many military narratives (see Liv. 6.33.9 with Kraus (1994)), to make a transition to the mental state of the cooped-up Romans (*moras obsidionis*). The transition is further aided by the echo of *ponendis ... positum*, where the outposts move from being to having been established; the elegant connective device, an extended *epiploke*, is common in historiographical narrative. A further repetition, again implying progress, rings the passage: *annus ... annuis* takes us from the (explicitly labeled) third "year" to "yearly," a continuing occupation that needs attention every year and in every territory. The spondaic rhythm of *copiis firmabantur*, with a hint of epic not favored by Cicero (see above), makes an appropriately solid close.

What opens as the third in a sequence of yearly narratives (*Ag.* 20–25) turns quickly from specifics to a general evaluation of the ideal commander, whose praise is at least as important here as his military tactics. Traditional diction is extended by close imitation, producing choice but generically appropriate expressions (this is also a typical Livian move); national characteristics, hinted at here, confirm and predict behavior; while artistic word order and *uariatio* keep the reader's attention and emphasize the importance of this year in the life of the Roman occupation.

The Historian's Voice

I took the ultimate historian's position, the god-like narrator. I then invited the reader to join me at my pinnacle of authority, to reason with me, to be a party to the enterprise.

(Zinsser (2009) 164)

Though an authorial voice may not seem to fall under the rubric of "language," it does contribute substantially to the meaning of a text. Shaped by style (hence by language), the historian's *persona* is perhaps the single most determinative aspect of a text's qualities. Add to this the ancient dictum, *talis ... oratio qualis uita*: in prose as well as poetry, choice and arrangement of words and sentences, with all their manifold possible ornament, project character, which in turn is judged along with the writer's words. As in oratory, language creates a speaker's *persona* that forms part of – indeed, often determines the evaluation of – the act of persuasion, so too in history. It is on its writer's self-reflective and authoritative voice that the value of history primarily rests. His excitable style and fulsomely expressed liking for Tiberius the general have been instrumental in bringing Velleius a reputation for flattery and mendacity (despite the fact that Tiberius was unquestionably a good general); Ogilvie ((1970) 24, 21) supports his judgment of Livy as "a small man, detached from affairs" with the damning evidence precisely of his style, "the full resources of his artistry [with which] he carries on the story with the iridescence of a pageant." And there is still a strand of Caesarian scholarship that takes his narrator's absent presence as signifying the man's unvarnished objectivity. The issue cuts deeper even than the question of an implied authorial character. The historian's *persona* both guarantees and stands in for his written world. It projects (and is projected by) the world that the text creates or re-presents. This is a concept with which we are familiar in poetry: Horace's first book of *Epistles* is a rent-boy (*Ep.* 1.20), Philetas so delicate that he has to weigh himself down to keep from floating away (Ael. 9.14). So also in history. We infer Tacitus' character from his text (dour, expert, insider), then project that authoritative gloom back onto the narrative, endowing it, too, with authority (see Woodman (1988) 43–47 on the persuasiveness of a "critical" voice). *Qualis homo, talis historia.*

One yardstick by which scholars measure the *persona* of a historian is by the degree and kind of presence the writer maintains in the text. Leaving aside our own assessment of what this presence conveys (opinions vary), we can say that, among extant Latin texts, the spectrum ranges from the omnipresent Velleius to the nearly invisible Caesar. Velleius' *persona* expresses itself through rhetorical questions (e.g. 2.75.2), emotional reactions (2.114.1, 129.2–130.2), and explicit judgments on the merits of events and characters alike (2.52.5–6, 100.2). His history is both dedicated and pervasively addressed to M. Vinicius (cos. CE 30, 45). That address contributes substantially to the creation of an *auctor* whose emotional and personal involvement with addressee and text resembles the relationship between a didactic author and his addressee. On the other end of the spectrum sits Caesar, especially in the *Gallic War*. From the genre's beginning, the author of Latin history uses the first person, whether as the narrator (Cato's *non lubet* sc. *mihi, Orig.* 77) or as the actor within the text (Tac. *Hist.* 1.1.1, Amm. 19.8.5–12). Caesar retains the first person for the narrator's super-ego, as it were, deploying it in cross-references (e.g. *Gal.* 4.4.1 *quos supra diximus*) or in scholarly digressions (*Gal.* 6.14.3 *mihi*). He refers to the actor in his story as Caesar, in the third person – a distancing in language and literary style that neatly reduces any possibility of emotional involvement on the part of the historian, whose voice becomes a series of meta-narrative stage directions – standing in, perhaps, for an implied *peritus*, one who writes and judges this historiographical project.

Between these two poles sit the other major Latin historians, Sallust, Livy, Tacitus, Ammianus. Though the frequency of their interventions varies, each is present in his text in various ways: e.g. via asseverations of reliability because an eyewitness or expert (Tac. *Ann.* 11.11.1); evaluation/judgment of sources (Liv. 6.12.2); assertions of the nature and importance of their own project (Liv. pr. 1, Sallust *Jug.* 4.3); declaration of objectivity (Tac. *Hist.* 1.1.3); guide through prosopographical complications (Liv. 2.21); evaluation of the proprieties of historiography (Amm. 31.16.9). It is the level of perceived critical acumen that readers have often used to determine *auctoritas*: so (one assumes) Quintilian judges Sallust to be a *maior auctor historiae* than Livy (*Inst.* 2.5.19). He does not say on what he bases that judgment, but generations of readers have take Livy's declaration of insecurity in his Preface literally, and hence found him to be genial but ignorant of "what history was" (Syme (1939) 486). It is not my brief here to elaborate on the reception of these writers, but to emphasize that their self-presentation directly influences how readers evaluate the nature and quality of their historical project. Cato's legacy was a challenge to his successors to show, in their mode of verbal expression, that they were able to meet the challenges of interpreting the past and of defending that interpretation against critics and *aemuli* alike.

FURTHER READING

For the fragmentary Latin historians see Briscoe (2005) and for Cato, Briscoe (2010); on later imitation of Cato, see Levene (2000). Levene and Nelis (2002), Yardley (2003), and Miller and Woodman (2010) explore the relationship between poetry and history, and should be used to supplement and correct Foucher (2000). Wiseman (1998) is the clearest exposition of the theory that there is actual dramatic performance behind Roman history. For wit and misdirection in historiographical style see Plass (1988), Sinclair (1995), and Kraus (2005); for "style and the man" see especially Gay (1974), with Lakoff and Johnson (1980) on metaphor. Clarke (1999) 1–76 is good on the interwoven nature of history, geography, and ethnography, with the specialized study of Oniga (1995) for Sallust; for the historian's *persona* Marincola (1997) is indispensable.

Utard (2004) discusses indirect speech in the historians; for the general issues raised by quoted speech in historiography see Laird (1999) 116–152. For the various kinds of periodic sentence see Wilkinson (1963) 179–188 and Clackson and Horrocks (2007) 218–221. The first section of Chausserie-Laprée (1969) is an extended discussion of historiographical sentence types. Much of the best analysis of military narrative is found in commentaries, but some useful readings include Witte (1910), Luce (1971), Woodman (1979), Horsfall (1999), Lendon (1999), Kelly (2008) 13–103. Aumont (1996) is a thorough treatment of *clausulae* in the Latin historians. And finally, for inventories and analyses of the styles of individual historians see, for Sallust: Kuntze (1892); for Livy: Kühnast (1872) and Riemann (1885); and for Tacitus, Draeger (1882).

CHAPTER 24

Epistolary Latin

Hilla Halla-aho

Introduction

A considerable corpus of letters written in Latin survives from Roman times.[1] Epistolary Latin is a valuable testimony of the different registers of the Latin language, and offers interesting insights into many aspects of the Latin language that would otherwise be poorly represented in the surviving selection of texts.[2]

We possess three major corpora of correspondence from Ancient Rome, those of Cicero (M. Tullius Cicero), Pliny the Younger (C. Caecilius Plinius Secundus) and Fronto (M. Cornelius Fronto).[3] These corpora have reached us through the medieval manuscript tradition. In addition, Latin letters survive on papyri, ostraca and wooden tablets. Cicero's epistolary corpus is the biggest and the most beautiful in several respects.[4] His correspondence presents a variety of epistolary styles, addressees and subject matters. One thing, however, is common to all: the letters are thought to be genuine, that is, written by Cicero as a means of communication, and not as a literary monument designed for publication. This is a basic difference between them and the letters of Pliny the Younger.[5] The latter (with the exception of book 10) have been thought to be largely "literary" letters, written by Pliny with publication in mind, and thus born as literary texts. What is, nevertheless, clear, is that Pliny himself collected and published the letters in books 1–9, and edited their language and perhaps even contents before doing so (Plin. *Ep.* 1.1). Also Cicero planned to have a number of letters published during his lifetime (*Att.* 16.5), but it is usually agreed that the collection *ad Familiares* (to a variety of friends, politicians and members of family, including many letters written by other persons than Cicero) was published posthumously by Cicero's private secretary and freedman Tiro (as well as the minor collections of letters to his brother Quintus and to his friend M. Brutus). It is not known how the other major collection, *ad Atticum*, saw

A Companion to the Latin Language, First Edition. Edited by James Clackson.
© 2011 Blackwell Publishing Ltd. Published 2011 by Blackwell Publishing Ltd.

daylight, but there is evidence that it was circulating by the time of Seneca the Younger, about CE 66.[6] Cicero himself had in all probability not envisaged the publication of these letters. Pliny's letters in books 1–9 are addressed to various persons, including his wife Calpurnia and the historian Tacitus. Book 10 consists of his letters to the emperor Trajan, and includes responses by the latter. Fronto's epistolary corpus is mainly made up of his correspondence with Antoninus Pius, Lucius Verus and, most importantly, Marcus Aurelius, who was taught by Fronto before he was enthroned.[7]

Letters are communicative documents emerging in real-life situations. However, when written by literary figures like Cicero, Pliny and Fronto, they will inevitably be treated as specimens of creative language use, and one type of literary activity.[8] This dual nature of letters is reflected in the study of epistolary language. To certain extent, it can be argued, this dualism corresponds to the study of "language" on the one hand, and "style" on the other. Studies on letter language have largely concentrated on colloquialisms and distinguishing between "colloquial" and "literary" tendencies,[9] or have used letters as "informants" in linguistic research.[10] Studies on epistolary style are usually concerned with rhetorical language use or literary aspects.[11] In addition, recent studies have amply discussed letters as the author's means of self-representation and letters as a social practice.[12]

On a completely different level, the letter also served as a literary form (for example in Horace, Ovid and Seneca the Younger), but this chapter will not be concerned with the literary manifestations of letters. Instead, in this chapter are included only those letters that were, as far as we can tell, actually sent by one person to another. In Pliny's case, this question is not simple and many scholars have held the view that his letters actually were never sent to the addressee, but present an innovative form of Pliny's literary activity.[13] Seeing all of them as purely fictitious, however, does not seem to be possible (taking into account the size of the collection and the trivial subject matters in many letters), and the best way is perhaps to think that the correspondence as we have it is a collection of different types, both genuine, even if edited, letters, and short essays written in letter form and circulated in Pliny's educated circles (Gamberini (1983) 130–136), in some ways comparable to the philosophical letters of Seneca. Genuine communicative function and elaborate language are not in opposition to each other (De Pretis (2003) 131–134), and when we remember that letters were often read aloud to other people, e.g. members of family,[14] it becomes possible to imagine a context for the literary letters in the correspondence of Pliny, and to understand how they probably emerged as an extension of that practice. For the purposes of this study, Pliny's letters will be viewed as "genuine" enough in order to be included in a survey of epistolary Latin. For Pliny himself, no unambiguous dividing line between genuine and literary probably existed. Cicero was a role model for Pliny, no less in epistolography than he was in oratory (cf. Plin. *Ep.* 4.8.4–5), and this comparison, especially when combined with the lack of true political contest in his own time, sometimes made him lament:

> praeterea nec materia plura scribendi dabatur. neque enim eadem nostra condicio quae M. Tulli ad cuius exemplum nos uocas. illi enim et copiosissimum ingenium et par ingenio qua uarietas rerum qua magnitudo largissime suppetebat. (Plin. *Ep.* 9.2.1–2)

> Then, too, no subject offered itself for further writing, for my situation is different from that of Marcus Cicero, whom you invite me to imitate. He had not only the most abundant talent, but also matched it with the most lavish supply of varied and important topics.[15]

Concerning their context but also their language, the letters to Trajan in book 10 are in many respects different from those in books 1–9.

Pliny explicitly names Cicero as his model but for Fronto the relationship with Cicero was not that simple. Fronto does, it is true, mention Cicero's letters as particularly worth reading: *omnes autem Ciceronis epistulas legendas censeo, mea sententia uel magis quam omnis eius orationes. epistulis Ciceronis nihil est perfectius* (Fronto *Ep.* 104.12–14; "All Cicero's letters, however, should, I think, be read – in my opinion, even more than his speeches. There is nothing more perfect than Cicero's letters"). However, as an archaist he was after rare and old words (*insperata atque inopinata uerba*, "words unexpected and unlooked for"), and did not find them in Cicero's speeches (Fronto *Ep.* 57.16–17; see van den Hout (1999) 51–52).

Latin letters on papyri and related materials constitute an interesting point of comparison with more "literary" letters. They date mainly from the first century BCE to the third century CE, and originate from different parts of the empire (Egypt, North Africa, Britain).[16]

Letters have long been considered to be written in a form of language that, among written texts, is closest to normal speech.[17] This notion was expressed already in ancient times, and it has equally pervaded modern studies on epistolary language.[18] It is used to characterize writers as different from each other as Cicero, Pliny and Fronto. Letters, it is true, were usually dictated to scribes (in all levels of society for all we know) but it would be an oversimplification to think that when an educated person like Cicero dictated a letter, he would have produced colloquial language simply because he was using his vocal organs rather than his hand (cf. Pinkster (2010) 192). Moreover, his letters to Atticus are generally thought to be the most colloquial ones in his correspondence – and it is particularly to Atticus (as well as to his brother Quintus) that Cicero usually wrote in his own hand (e.g., Cic. *Att.* 2.23; 8.13.1).

The following passage from Cicero's letter to his close friend Papirius Paetus establishes a strong connection between (certain types of) letters and colloquial language use:

> uerum tamen quid tibi ego uideor in epistulis? nonne plebeio sermone agere tecum? nec enim semper eodem modo. quid enim simile habet epistula aut iudicio aut contioni? quin ipsa iudicia non solemus omnia tractare uno modo. priuatas causas et eas tenuis agimus subtilius, capitis aut famae scilicet ornatius; epistulas uero cotidianis uerbis texere solemus. (Cic. *Fam.* 9.21.1)

> But tell me now, how do you find me as a letter-writer? Don't I deal with you in a colloquial style? The fact is that one's style has to vary. A letter is one thing, a court of law or a public meeting quite another. Even for the courts we don't have just one style. In pleading civil cases, unimportant ones, we put on no frills, whereas cases involving status or reputation naturally get something more elaborate. As for letters, we weave them out of the language of everyday.

Cicero's letters to Atticus are, according to the *communis opinio*, the best evidence of a colloquial style during the Classical period and, together with the plays of Plautus and Terence, form our best evidence of spoken Latin.[19]

A letter can naturally mean very different types of texts, even within the corpus of one author.[20] The degree of colloquial language, rhetorical language and formal language varies considerably across the genre. One obvious distinction is that between official and private letters but the boundary between them seems not to have been as strict in ancient times as it is nowadays.[21] There are clearly defined categories such as letters of recommendation,[22] letters of consolation and official dispatches to the Senate. But usually variation within the genre is caused by two factors, the subject matter of the letter as well as the relationship between the author and the addressee. A famous passage in Cicero's letter to Curio (Cic. *Fam.* 2.4.1) refers to different types of letters, including *unum illud certissimum, cuius causa inuenta res ipsa est, ut certiores faceremus absentis, si quid esset, quod eos scire aut nostra aut ipsorum interesset* ("the most authentic, the purpose in fact for which letter-writing was invented, is to inform the absent of what it is desirable for them to know, whether in our interest or their own"). That the letter indeed was invented in order to inform absent people about things cannot come as a surprise to anyone, and we do not need Cicero to tell that to us. He also mentions two further types, *unum familiare et iocosum, alterum seuerum et graue* ("one familiar and jocular, the other serious and grave") but, as has been pointed out, the passage should not be read as a reflection of his epistolary theory.[23] The context of this characterization is a lamentation with the "nothing to write" motif, caused by the contemporary political situation and the ruin of the Republic (cf. Pliny's remarks on a similar topic above).[24]

Usually when the ancients themselves comment on epistolary language, for example in the often-quoted definition of Pliny, *pressus sermo purusque ex epistulis petitur* (Plin. *Ep.* 7.9.8; "we look to epistles for language which is compressed and unadorned", where an opposition is established to historical and poetical style), they do so in contexts actually addressing something else, typically oratorical language. So too in the following quote from Quintilian:

> est igitur ante omnia oratio alia uincta atque contexta, soluta alia, qualis in sermone <et> epistulis, nisi cum aliquid supra naturam suam tractant, ut de philosophia, de re publica similibusque. quod non eo dico quia non illud quoque solutum habeat suos quosdam et forsitan difficiliores etiam pedes: neque enim aut hiare semper uocalibus aut destitui temporibus uolunt sermo atque epistula, sed non fluunt nec cohaerent nec uerba uerbis trahunt, ut potius laxiora in his uincla quam nulla sint. (Quint. *Inst.* 9.4.19–20)

> In the first place, formal speech is either bound and woven together, or of a looser texture, like that of dialogues or letters (except when these deal with matters above their normal scope, like philosophy, public affairs, or the like). I do not mean to imply that this looser texture does not have its own metrical feet, which are perhaps even more difficult to master; dialogue and letters do not always deliberately seek hiatus between vowels or absence of marked rhythm, but neither do they have any steady flow or coherence, or make one word bring others with it; consequently, the bonds do exist, but they are looser. (Trans. D.A. Russell)

Quintilian is here writing about composition (*compositio*), the arrangement of words in the most beautiful order, with appropriate figures of speech as well as *clausulae*. Within formal speech (*oratio*), he makes a distinction between a well-composed and a loose style. The latter is used in dialogue and letters, but is also appropriate in less serious legal cases (Quint. *Inst.* 9.4.21). It is relatively easy to see here a reference to a less connected and less periodic style, and it is this paratactic and concise style that Pliny's *sermo pressus purusque* must also refer to. Interestingly, the passage refers to letters that *aliquid supra naturam suam tractant* ("deal with matters above their normal scope"). Quintilian thus recognizes the suitability of letter form to address matters above the ordinary and, in doing so, to accommodate their language for that purpose. This is exactly what we see in Cicero's letters when he writes about his beloved republic.

Fronto's relationship with his imperial correspondent was quite different from that of Pliny. Fronto was, after all, the teacher of Marcus Aurelius. But the assessment of the level of intimacy between Fronto and Marcus Aurelius has varied considerably. Some have seen in it a reflection of true friendship (Portalupi (1989) 149–150), while others have stressed that the correspondence, despite the emphatic expressions of warm emotions, was never free of the feeling of social distance between the emperor and his (former) teacher (Swain (2004) 19). Consisting of exchanges of letters between two persons (Fronto and Marcus Aurelius, Antoninus Pius and Lucius Verus), Fronto's correspondence looks much more like a genuine correspondence than that of Pliny, with its plethora of addressees. Recurring themes in the letters are rhetoric and literature (e.g., 40.11–42.3 on composing a simile), health and expressions of love between Fronto and Marcus Aurelius, e.g., the following:

> tu, Caesar, Frontonem istum tuum sine fine amas, uix ut tibi homini facundissimo, uerba sufficiant ad expromendum amorem tuum et beniuolentiam declarandam. quid, oro te, fortunatius, quid me uno beatius esse potest, ad quem tu tam flagrantes litteras mittis? quin etiam, quod est amatorum proprium, currere ad me uis et uolas. (Fronto *Ep.* 2.19–3.3)

> So without end, Caesar, is your love for this Fronto of yours, that for all your eloquence words are scarcely forthcoming fully to express your love and set forth your goodwill. What, I ask you, can be more fortunate, what more happy than I alone am, to whom you send such glowing letters? Nay, more, and this is peculiar to lovers, you wish to run, aye, to fly to me.[25]

Letters as Colloquial and Informal Language

As was mentioned above, the aspect that has received most emphasis in research on letter language is their colloquial style.[26] To take a simple example of vocabulary, and one that corresponds to Cicero's *cotidianis uerbis texere solemus* ("we weave them out of the language of everyday", Cic. *Fam.* 9.21.1) we may look at Cicero's use of the adverb *belle* "nicely". He uses *belle* eighteen times in his letters to Atticus, three times in the *ad Familiares* and another three in his letters to his brother Quintus; the total for his other works is six (three of which are in the *de Oratore*). Clearly, this adverb (and the adjective from which it is derived) belonged to the more colloquial style, and we have no reason to doubt that it was a feature of informal spoken varieties of Latin in Cicero's time.[27] Letters preserve us much vocabulary that is not attested elsewhere, and there is evidence that the use of creative vocabulary belonged to epistolary language.[28] On the other hand, abundant use of common verbs like *esse* and *facere* in epistolary language is probably a feature of everyday language (von Albrecht (2003) 60).

There are a number of stylistic features that are more or less generally taken to be signs of the colloquial nature of epistolary language. It remains disputable, however, whether all of these should carry the label "colloquial", or should better be called informal written language.[29]

General brevity of expression is one of the most typical features of Latin epistolary language. This rather vague notion includes a variety of different phenomena but the most prominent one of these is ellipsis. Ellipsis means leaving out words that the reader will have to supplement in his mind in order to convey the intended meaning (sometimes better called brachylogy). When ellipsis occurs in a reproduced dialogue it creates an impression of a faithful and lively description of the conversation (a good example (from Dammann (1910) 26) is *Att.* 13.42). Indeed, ellipsis has traditionally been regarded as a genuine feature of actual conversation. Cicero's letters to Atticus are renowned for his often extreme use of elliptical language. But there is great variation within the Atticus letters in the use of ellipsis. An affective context makes Cicero favour elliptical language. Letters written to other friends with whom Cicero was on intimate terms, Trebatius and Papirius Paetus, also contain instances of ellipsis, but it is not a typical feature in letters to his wife Terentia. Omitting forms of *esse* naturally is the most banal type (and makes up about half of the cases), and the infinitive itself can be dropped out in nearly all types of letters. Ellipsis of other verbs, such as *fieri, facere, agere, accidere* together with verbs of thinking and speaking are common in books 12–16 of the Atticus letters but rare in letters sent from Cicero's exile (*Att.* 3; *Q. fr.* 1.3–4; *Fam.* 14.1–4). Typically Cicero leaves out verbs that pertain to the exchange of letters (see below for an example).[30]

Pliny's use of elliptical expression is more moderate than Cicero's (Gamberini (1983) 461–470). The commonest type of ellipsis concerns forms of *esse, facio* or the like.[31] In Pliny, too, ellipsis is seen as a feature of colloquial language, for example in cases like the following: *rectene omnia quod iam pridem epistulae tuae cessant? an omnia recte sed occupatus es tu? an tu non occupatus sed occasio scribendi uel rara uel nulla* (Plin. *Ep.* 3.17.1; "Is all well? Your letters have stopped coming for some time now. Is all perhaps well, but you are fully stretched? Or are you perhaps not fully stretched, but with few or no opportunities to write?"). One should, however, remember that ellipsis of common verbs played an essential role in the historical style of Sallust and Tacitus as well, and was thus not confined to epistolary language.

There seems to be widely held agreement that parentheticals are a feature of spoken language, and appear in letters because of the colloquial register appropriate to this genre.[32] In Pliny's letters, parentheticals appear frequently, but are nearly absent in letters to his wife Calpurnia as well as in book 10 (letters to the emperor Trajan). On the other hand, letters to his good friend Tacitus, the historian, abound in parentheticals (Häusler (2000) 215). There is also more detailed information on Cicero's use of parentheticals in his letters, showing that when an entire clause is inserted as a parenthesis, this will happen before the main focus of the sentence (Bolkestein (1998)).[33] Interestingly, the idea that certain types of parentheticals belong to proper letter style seems to have pervaded further down the social scale. In a letter from Vindolanda, Northern Britain (*T.Vindol.* II.310), the writer apparently set out to insert a parenthesis – *miror quod mihi tot tempus nihil rescripsti* ("I am surprised that you have written nothing back to me for such a long time"; cf. Cic. *Att.* 7.12.1) – in his letter, but in the end did not manage to bring the expression to an honourable end.[34] If the general assumption of the presence of colloquial features is strong concerning Cicero, Pliny and Fronto, it is even more pronounced regarding the non-literary epistolary corpus. It is usually taken as granted that if a feature is found in the non-literary material, and especially if it coincides with a feature in the literary corpus, it can without further considerations be placed in the colloquial bag. However, often in these cases we are in fact dealing with a feature that is typical of epistolary language, that is, a register of written language that one was supposed to use when writing letters.

Furthermore, it should be noted that parentheses are used frequently in Cicero's most elaborate writings, and especially in those orations which were written for publication only, i.e., that were never delivered.[35] It seems questionable whether the insertion of a whole clause into another, especially if it comprises more than just a few words, can be considered to happen often in actual speech. One would not expect longer parentheticals that consist of a whole predication to be especially frequent in natural speech, simply for the challenge they propose for the listener (and speaker, too!).

There most probably is a difference between short ones such as *ut Lucretius ait* (Plin. *Ep.* 4.18.1; "as Lucretius puts it") or *quod abominor* (Plin. *Ep.* 6.22.7; "I pray that this does not happen") and longer ones such as *scis quod iudicium prouinciae illius, quanta sit grauitas* (Plin. *Ep.* 2.13.4; "you are aware of the discernment and high seriousness of that province") and *quid enim prohibet, quamquam alia ratio scribendae epistulae fuerit, de studiis disputare* (Plin. *Ep.* 7.6.8; "there is surely nothing to prevent me making a point about the orator's role, though my reason for writing this letter was different"). It is possible, that shorter parentheses of the type *ut opinor* were indeed frequent in spoken language, but the longer and more elaborate forms must have belonged to stylistically refined written language.

As we have seen, the distinction between colloquial and rhetorical/written features is not always as clear-cut as one might be tempted to think. Another case in point is hyperbaton. This has often been thought to be a feature of Latin which, although not strictly an artificial creation, was at least extensively elaborated in the literary language. But even in this case things are not as simple as that. There is now evidence that hyperbaton is by no means restricted to more literary or rhetorical texts but is used freely by Cicero in his letters to Atticus, even in the more elliptical ones (Powell (2010) 184–186).[36] This observation applies also in the case of those constructions where the two elements belonging together are separated from each other by a number of words ("long-range" hyperbaton in Powell's terms).

Apparently we are here dealing with features (parentheses and hyperbaton) that in at least some form were part of educated spoken language, but also lent themselves easily to stylistic elaboration in less formal (letters) or pseudo-oral (dialogues, certain parts of speeches) contexts (Powell (2010) 188).

An illustration of Cicero's typical ellipsis and brevity when he is writing to Atticus is provided by the following letter (written at Puteolanum in November 44):

> binae uno die mihi litterae ab Octauiano, nunc quidem ut Romam statim ueniam; uelle se rem agere per senatum. cui ego non posse senatum ante Kal. Ian., quod quidem ita credo. ille autem addit "consilio tuo". quid multa? ille urget, ego autem σκήπτομαι. non confido aetati, ignoro quo animo. nil sine Pansa tuo uolo. uereor ne ualeat Antonius, nec a mari discedere libet. at metuo ne quae ἀριστεία me absente. Varroni quidem displicet consilium pueri, mihi non. firmas copias habet, Brutum habere potest; et rem gerit palam, centuriat Capuae, dinumerat. iam iamque uideo bellum. ad haec rescribe. tabellarium meum Kalendis Roma profectum sine tuis litteris miror. (Cic. *Att.* 16.9)

Two letters for me from Octavian in one day! Now wants me to return to Rome at once, says he wants to work through the Senate. I replied that the Senate could not meet before the Kalends of January, which I believe is the case. He adds "with your advice". In short, he presses and I play for time. I don't trust his age and I don't know what he's after. I don't want to do anything without your friend Pansa. I'm nervous of Antony's power and don't want to leave the coast. But I'm afraid of some star performance during my absence. Varro doesn't think much of the boy's plan, I take a different view. He has a strong force at his back and *can* have Brutus. And he's going to work quite openly, forming companies at Capua and paying out bounties. War is evidently coming any minute now. Let me have an answer to all this. I am surprised that my courier left Rome on the Kalends without a letter from you. (Trans. D.R. Shackleton Bailey)

Note the elliptical expression at the beginning (with supplements from Dammann (1910) 35); *binae uno die mihi litterae ab Octauiano* (allatae sunt), *nunc quidem* (scribit), *ut Romam statim ueniam; uelle se rem agere per senatum. cui ego* (respondi) *non posse senatum* (haberi) *ante Kal. Ian.* The letter also has a hyperbaton at the beginning *binae uno die mihi litterae* and Greek words (ἀριστεία and σκήπτομαι). Note the asyndetic sequence in *se et rem gerit palam, centuriat Capuae, dinumerat.* Further, note the extreme brevity and lack of politeness (not needed) in the simple imperative *ad haec rescribe.*

Cicero's epistolary style is known for its frequent use of Greek words and even whole phrases. Similarly to certain other hallmarks of his style, Greek appears most often in letters to Atticus, but is virtually absent in his letters to Terentia, and within the Atticus correspondence, in the letters written during Cicero's exile. Thus, it is another marker of Cicero's epistolary mood, so to speak.[37] This strategy of code-switching is, however, part of Cicero's Latin, and should not be taken as evidence that Greek was used regularly in spoken conversation (Swain (2002) 147; 164–167).[38]

The linguistic identity of Fronto that has most often been stressed is that of an archaist. He is linked to the series of writers with Apuleius and Gellius (recently called linguistic nationalists by Swain (2004) 17) who pursued a strategy of enriching (and elevating) Latin with words and expressions taken from the early, archaic writers (before the time of Virgil and Cicero). Despite views that have seen in Fronto's letters ingredients taken from everyday language (Portalupi (1989)), we cannot escape the conclusion that Fronto's colloquialism is even further removed than Pliny's from living colloquial language. It is artificial and derives "aus der dumpfen Luft des Schulsaals" ("from the dusty air of the schoolroom", Marx (1909) 441) rather than from his own spoken vernacular. Many examples of Fronto's "colloquial" expressions have parallels mainly in Plautus and Terence, a fact that strongly suggests that they were taken up by him as archaisms more than anything else.[39] However, what most contributes to the feeling of colloquial language is Fronto's relatively simple and unadorned syntax, without excessive rhetorical ornamentation as in Pliny, or longer and more complex periods as often in Cicero.

The unity of theme that prevails in Pliny's letters, and sets them apart from Cicero's correspondence, has been taken as further indication of their fictitious nature (see Gamberini (1983) 154–155). In the course of a normal letter, the writer usually changes the topic he is writing about several times. In Cicero, this can be seen in the frequent use of topic-changing expressions, of which the most important are clauses introduced by *quod* and phrases with *de* + ablative, e.g. *nam quod me tam saepe et tam vehementer obiurgas et animo infirmo esse dicis, quaeso* ... (*Att.* 3.10.2; "When you take me to task, as you so often and so energetically do, and tell me I am lacking in fortitude, I should like to ask ...") and *de domo et Curionis oratione, ut scribis, ita est* (*Att.* 3.20.2; "About my house and Curio's speech, it is just as you say").[40] In Pliny's letters, these are mostly absent. Instead, it is possible to look at his letter openings. He often opens the letter with a second person reference, e.g. (in a random sample) *amas Egnatium* (4.12; "You are fond of Egnatius"); *saluum in urbem uenisse gaudeo; uenisti autem, si quando alias, nunc maxime mihi desideratus* (4.13; "I am delighted that you have reached the city safely. Your arrival has come at a time when, if ever, I was most longing to see you"); *tu fortasse orationem, ut soles, et flagitas et exspectas* (4.14; "You are perhaps both demanding and anticipating a speech from me"); *gaude meo gaude tuo gaude etiam publico nomine* (4.16; "Rejoice for me, rejoice for yourself, and for our state"). By referring to his addressee's actions in this way Pliny establishes a connection with his correspondent. On the other hand, in Pliny's letters to Trajan the commonest letter openings are proper nouns and substantival phrases (Gamberini (1983) 344–345), together with participial phrases (usually with first-person reference). The difference between "genuine" and "literary" letters can thus possibly be seen even in letter openings.

Letters as Literature: Rhetorical and Elaborate Language

Alongside colloquial elements, epistolary language has been studied for its use of rhetorical devices. The Latin epistolary corpora stem mainly from highly educated members of the Roman elite for whom the use of rhetorical figures would not have been a matter of adding an artificial touch to their otherwise natural and spontaneous epistolary language, but a reflection of an attitude to writing generally, and a deep-rooted manner of self-expression.[41] The degree of rhetorical ornamentation varies considerably across Cicero's corpus. Carefully written letters showing rhetorical elaboration are, for example, his letter to his brother Quintus (*Q. fr.* 1.1, a long letter on the government of a province), letters to Appius Claudius Pulcher (*Fam.* 3), as well as books 7–8 to Atticus.[42] These letters often show the figure of anaphora (the repetition of the same word) that is typical in those passages where Cicero uses elegant and long periods.

In other cases, the use of ornamentations seems to have been conditioned by an affective context. Cicero seems to have been especially prone to use the chiasmus (*Fam.* 3.10.9 *studiorum similitudo, suauitas consuetudinis, delectatio uitae atque uictus, sermonis societas* "similarity of pursuits, the charm of personal intercourse, the enjoyment of a way of life, the give-and-take of conversation") when he was writing about matters that caused him to feel admiration, anger or pain (Dammann (1910) 22–23). In his light-hearted letters to Trebatius (*Fam.* 7.6–22) there are almost no chiasmi. Similarly, it has been observed that Pliny's use of a more rhetorical style is often motivated by an emotive subject matter (Gamberini (1983) 304–305). Above it was noted that elliptical language also was favoured in affective contexts. Whereas elliptical language supposedly was a feature of actual speech, and can thus easily be connected with affective contexts, the motivating force of emotion is more difficult to grasp in the case of rhetorical figures.

Emotions are uncontrolled, and as such something that we would intuitively place in total opposition to the elaborate language produced with the help of teaching from the rhetorical schools.[43]

An archaist in search of the old and rare, Fronto makes use of rhetorical equipment that is to some degree different from that of Cicero and Pliny. One of his favourite figures is alliteration, a figure that was used abundantly by the early dramatic writers, e.g. the double alliteration *at illi ingenui uapores puri perpetuique sunt, grati pariter et gratuiti* (Fronto, *Ep.* 4.9–10; "The natural heat of the former is at once pure and perpetual, as grateful as it is gratuitous").[44]

At this point it will be useful to quote an example from Pliny. His letter to Pomponius Bassus (Plin. *Ep.* 4.23) serves well to illustrate some of the principal characteristics of his epistolary style:

> magnam cepi uoluptatem, cum ex communibus amicis cognoui te, ut sapientia tua dignum est, et disponere otium et ferre, habitare amoenissime, et nunc terra nunc mari corpus agitare, multum disputare, multum audire multum lectitare, cumque plurimum scias, cotidie tamen aliquid addiscere. ita senescere oportet uirum, qui magistratus amplissimos gesserit, exercitus rexerit, totumque se rei publicae quam diu decebat obtulerit. nam et prima uitae tempora et media patriae, extrema nobis impertire debemus, ut ipsae leges monent, quae maiorem annis otio reddunt. quando mihi licebit, quando per aetatem honestum erit imitari istud pulcherrimae quietis exemplum? quando secessus mei non desidiae nomen sed tranquillitatis accipient? uale.

> I was greatly pleased to discover from friends we share that in a manner worthy of your wisdom you are organizing your leisure and coping with it, living in a most beautiful region, exercising your body on both land and sea, participating in many discussions, listening a great deal, and reading and rereading a great deal, and though you are a polymath, learning something new each day. This is the ideal old age for a man who has held highly distinguished magistracies, commanded armies, and devoted himself wholly to the state for so long as it was fitting. For we must devote our early and middle years to our native land, and our closing years to ourselves; this is what the laws prescribe for us, for they restore a man when he is older in years to a life of leisure. When will I be allowed to conform to this, when will I reach the age at which it will be honourable for me to imitate the example you set of living in most idyllic peace? When will my periods of relaxation away from Rome gain the title of peaceful repose rather than idleness? Farewell.

Brevity of expression as well as asyndetic sequences are reminiscent of Cic. *Att.* 16.9 quoted above, but this letter also serves to show how Pliny develops his epistolary style. He adopts from Cicero brevity and asyndetic expressions but whereas in Cicero these are characteristic of his informal and often very personal letters to Atticus and as such are free of rhetorical ornamentation, Pliny adduces rhetorical figures and questions to produce his typical short and rhetorical expression, making ample use of the symmetry of paratactic sentences (cf. Gamberini (1983) 374). Note further the anaphora with *multum*, and the homoeoteleuton in the set of infinitives in *–are* (and once in *–ire*), the paratactic tricolon in *qui ... gesserit, exercitus rexerit totumque ... obtulerit*, another anaphora in *quando* at the end, employed in a pair of rhetorical questions (that also forms a tricolon) *quando mihi licebit, quando ... erit imitari ... exemplum? quando secessus mei ... accipient?* This letter also gives an idea about the reasons why Pliny's letters have so often been thought to be something other than actual vehicles of communication. He begins with an expression of delight at his friend's retirement to *otium* ("leisure, freedom from business"), but in fact ends it in a somewhat pathetic contemplation on his own situation and his supposed inability to follow in his friend's footsteps because of his pressing duties (a similar theme is treated in a rather similar way in, e.g., Plin. *Ep.* 2.8).[45]

In Pliny's short and paratactic style there are certain passages where a different, more hypotactic and periodic style can be observed. These are often places where Pliny has to address a more delicate subject matter.[46] Even though Cicero's syntax generally is to a much higher degree hypotactic, there are places in which the same tendency of moving into a more periodic style in matters requiring caution and deliberation can be observed. An example of this is a letter to Trebatius (*Fam.* 7.17) where Cicero mildly reproaches his young friend for his inappropriate conduct. This is in contrast with the tone and language in which he usually addresses Trebatius (Fraenkel (1957) 70). Difference of subject matter thus accounts for the difference in syntactic style. Considering the very different nature of the two epistolary corpora, this is an interesting observation.

In Cicero, the frequent use of participles is an indication of a more connected and literary, i.e., periodic, style. For example, in the first seven letters of book 16 of the *ad Atticum*, Cicero is in a relatively happy mood and every now and then gives up the characteristic "staccato style" of the Atticus letters to write in a more fluent and periodic style, and thus uses more participles. After that, however, the style changes considerably as Cicero is in a state of doubt, and does not have anything substantial to write about. This conversational and disconnected style does not make much use of participles.[47]

Sometimes Cicero's sentimentality and vanity mediated in a highly elaborate and rhetorical language seem to stretch the limits of the modern reader's sympathy. However, even these intuitively less charming passages are arguably well-motivated in their own context, and we should see in them something other than mere empty verbiage.[48]

A good example of a somewhat delicate matter addressed in a careful periodic style is Cicero's letter to L. Lucceius where he asks the addressee, a historian, to write an account of his consulship and subsequent events. The request is not an easy one to make (although apparently the issue had been mentioned before, and Lucceius may already have written something, cf. *de qua suauissime quodam in prohoemio scripsisti*), and Cicero puts to use his entire rhetorical and literary skill in formulating the potentially intrusive request in a non-intrusive way.[49] Cicero even ventures to ask that Lucceius would sacrifice the historical truth in order to present Cicero as admirably as possible:

> itaque te plane etiam atque etiam rogo ut et ornes ea vehementius etiam quam fortasse sentis et in eo leges historiae neglegas gratiamque illam de qua suauissime quodam in prohoemio scripsisti, a qua te flecti non magis potuisse demonstras quam Herculem Xenophontium illum a Voluptate, eam, si me tibi vehementius commendabit, ne aspernere amorique nostro plusculum etiam quam concedet veritas largiare. (Cic. *Fam.* 5.12.3)

> Therefore I ask you again, not mincing my words, to write of this theme more enthusiastically than perhaps you feel. Waive the laws of history for this once. Do not scorn personal bias, if it urge you strongly in my favour – that sentiment of which you wrote very charmingly in one of your prefaces, declaring that you could no more be swayed thereby than Xenophon's Hercules by Pleasure. Concede to the affection between us just a little more even than the truth will license.

The request Cicero is making here is somewhat audacious. The verb *rogo* "I ask" is followed by three subordinate object–verb pairs, the first two introduced by *ut* and the third by *ne*: *ut et ornes ea ... et leges ... neglegas gratiamque illam ... eam ... ne aspernere* ("that you both ornate them ... and ignore the laws ... and do not scorn the positive sentiment"). Interestingly, the third subordinate verb *ne aspernere* comes so many words after its object *gratiamque illam* that Cicero feels the need to repeat the object by the anaphoric pronoun *eam*. Although pleonastic anaphoric pronouns are often considered typical of a colloquial style (von Albrecht (2003) 57), this cannot be the reason here, given the context of the request and the highly elaborate language.[50] The example illustrates well the intimate connection between the subject matter and linguistic expression. An exceptional request results in an exceptional expression.

The letters to Atticus represent, generally speaking, a more colloquial register than the other letters, but even within that corpus, and even in one letter, there is room for stylistic elaboration and longer periods. An example of the variety of styles can be found in the long letter *Att.* 1.16 that incorporates both short expression typical of the Atticus letters and longer periods (see Fraenkel 1957). In the first part of the letter Cicero describes to Atticus the trial against P. Clodius and its unexpected outcome. He then proceeds to answer Atticus' queries about the political situation in the republic, and about Cicero's own situation. The topic of the "miserable republic" (perhaps especially when paired with comparison to the writer's own success in saving the republic a couple of years earlier, as here) excites Cicero's mind and gives rise to a different style, with long periods (*Att.* 1.16.7–8) and rhetorical ornaments (chiasmus: *bonorum omnium coniunctiones et auctoritate consulatus mei* 1.16.6; anaphora: *cum religio, cum pudicitia, cum iudiciorum fides, cum senatus auctoritas* 1.16.7; a bold hyperbaton *omnem ... παρρησίαν* 1.16.18; see Fraenkel (1957) 69). After information on subsequent events in the Senate, with a quotation of Cicero's speech and a pointed dialogue between him and Clodius (9–10), and on Cicero's own situation as well as on upcoming elections (11–13), the letter ends with the narration of practical matters in a simple style (14–18).

Above it was pointed out that even the non-literary letter material should be viewed in terms of written epistolary language instead of some "pure" form of the spoken vernacular. The writers of these letters naturally present a whole scale of variation, from very good writers to less-educated ones. The prime example of a good writer is Flavius Cerialis, the prefect of the ninth cohort of Batavians stationed in Vindolanda at the end of the first century CE. Flavius Cerialis opens his draft letter thus:

[G]rattio Crispino redeunte [...] [c. 10] [[non fui mihi]] et .d.[.] [c.7 li]benter amplexus s[um do]mine salutandi te occassionem [d]ominum meum et quem saluom [[habere]] esse et omnis spei [[suae]] compotem inter praecipua uoti habeo. (*T. Vindol.* II.225.4–9)

Since Grattius Crispinus is returning to ... and ... I have gladly seized the opportunity my lord of greeting you, you who are my lord and the man whom it is my very special wish to be in good health and master of all your hopes.

It is easy to see that Flavius Cerialis had received a profound literary education (see Adams (1995b) 126). But the attempt to write as well as one possible can is not confined to the best writers. Even those who had a fluent command of Latin (without reaching the elegant level of Flavius Cerialis) did try to express themselves as well as they could. For the most part, naturally, the non-literary letter material includes texts dealing with practical matters, with frequent requests to send an item, or lists of items that had been sent by the writer to the addressee. It is rather trivial to conclude on these cases that the letters only employ certain epistolary *topoi*, such as asking for things to be sent. These letters were, after all, genuine means of communication between people, and not pieces of literature. However, every now and then these writers too show a tendency of trying to raise the level of their language, usually when there was an immediate need for it, for example, when they wanted to persuade the addressee concerning something. In this motivation, if not the actual means used, they are surprisingly similar to the literary writers. As an example I quote a passage from the letter of a person called Rustius Barbarus who wrote the following appeal on an ostracon in the eastern desert of Egypt, in the latter half of the first century CE:

> quid mi tan inuidiose scribes aut tan leuem me iudicas? si tan cito uirdia mi non mittes stati amicitiam tuam obliscere debio. non sum talis aut tan leuis. ego te non tanquam amicum habio set tanqua[m] fratrem gemellum qui de unum uentrem exiut. (*CEL* 74.3–9)

> Why do you write to me in such a hostile manner, or think that I am as unreliable a person as that? If you do not send me the vegetables as soon as possible, I shall have to forget about your friendship immediately. I am not like that or that unreliable. I do not think of you as my friend but as my twin brother who has been born from the same womb. (Trans. H. Halla-aho)

In whatever way we now evaluate the writer's rhetorical skill, it is not to be doubted that in this passage he, motivated by the need to convince his addressee on the necessity of sending vegetables, raised the level of his language far above the ordinary style of his correspondence.

Formal Letters

We have so far seen that epistolary language varies according to context from more colloquial to less colloquial and more rhetorical (with the allowance that in Cicero colloquial is, as it were, more colloquial than in Pliny). But it is clearly not enough to define language and style in letters along one continuum from informal/colloquial to rhetorical/literary, and to associate the absence of literary colouring automatically with colloquial language. The category of formal letters cannot be placed in either of these groups (or better, at either of the two ends of the continuum). Specimens of formal letter-writing in Cicero are, for example, his official dispatches to the Senate (*Fam.* 15.1–2) as well as his letter to Cato (*Fam.* 15.4).[51] In Pliny's corpus, book 10 consists of letters to the emperor Trajan, written for the most part when Pliny was the governor of Bithynia (Plin. *Ep. Tra.* 10.1–14 are "private" letters to Trajan, written before his Bithynian commission).

The first half of the letter *Fam.* 15.4.2–10 where Cicero reports his actions in Cilicia to Cato is composed in periodic style, equal to that seen in Caesar's *Commentarii*.[52] Typical building blocks of the commentary style include a temporal clause or a participial construction at the beginning, an explicit link to previous context (often by means of the free relative connection) and the main clause predicate at sentence end (sometimes followed by an *ut* clause or the accusative + infinitive). However, even the same topic can be treated in different styles when it is described to different persons (and for different purposes). For example, it has been shown that there is a notable difference in syntactic structure between the two letters, *Fam.* 15.4 and *Att.* 5.20. The three markers just mentioned are used clearly more often in Cicero's account to Cato than they are in the comparable one to Atticus.[53] We thus observe variation within one text type, reporting narrative.[54]

Given the peculiar nature and certain taste of artificiality of the other nine books, the collection of letters in Pliny's book 10 has some special interest, preserving as it does a corpus of undoubtedly genuine letters. The difference in style is remarkable. In clear contrast to the other letters, the ones in book 10 make ample use of hypotactic structures (Gamberini (1983) 341). Even if Plinian hypotaxis is not as complex as we are used to seeing in Cicero's writings, there is a considerable difference compared with the other nine books.[55] In book 10, parataxis is used for special purposes, such as narratives, summaries and descriptions of persons (Gamberini (1983) 481). Typically, a letter in book 10 contains a request for advice on a specific topic, or a request for a permission to begin, e.g., a building project. Trajan's answers are always short. It is of some interest to note, in the context of what was mentioned above on the unity of theme in Pliny's other letters, that the same unity of theme can be observed in his correspondence with Trajan. The great majority of the letters address one single topic. Pliny first introduces his problem and closes the letter by asking for Trajan's advice or a permission to pursue a certain course of action. Often the emperor advises Pliny to do what Pliny himself sees as the best conduct in a given situation, or, as here, gives his advice on the general principle but leaves the details for Pliny to decide:

C. PLINIUS TRAIANO IMPERATORI

pecuniae publicae, domine, prouidentia tua et ministerio nostro et iam exactae sunt et exiguntur; quae uereor ne otiosae iaceant. nam et praediorum comparandorum aut nulla aut rarissima occasio est, ne inueniuntur qui uelint debere rei publicae, praesertim duodenis assibus, quanti a priuatis mutuantur. dispice ergo, domine, numquid minuendam usuram ac per hoc idoneos debitores inuitandos putes, et, si nec sic reperiuntur, distribuendam inter decuriones pecuniam, ita ut recte rei publicae caueant; quod quamquam inuitis et recusantibus minus acerbum erit leuiore usura constituta. (Plin. *Ep. Tra.* 10.54)

Public moneys, my lord, through your foresight and my handling have already been and still are being levied, but I am fearful that they lie unused, for there is no opportunity, or only a most occasional one, of purchasing estates, and none are found willing to become debtors to the state, especially at the rate of twelve per cent, the rate at which they borrow from private individuals. So, my lord, consider whether you think that this rate of interest should be lowered, and suitable debtors enticed by this means, and if even so debtors are not found, whether money should be allotted among the city-councillors, specifying that they safeguard the welfare of the state. Even if they are unwilling and reluctant, this will be less burdensome if a lower rate of interest is established.

TRAIANUS PLINIO

et ipse non aliud remedium dispicio, mi Secunde carissime, quam ut quantitas usurarum minuatur, quo facilius pecuniae publicae collocentur. Modum eius, ex copia eorum qui mutuabuntur, tu constitues. Inuitos ad accipiendum compellere, quod fortassis ipsis otiosum futurum sit, non est ex iustitia nostrorum temporum. (Plin. *Ep. Tra.* 10.55)

I too visualize no remedy, my dearest Secundus, other than that the level of interest should be lowered, so that the public money can be more easily lent out. You must decide on the level, depending on the resources of those who will borrow. It is not in accord with the justice of our times to force men to borrow if they are unwilling, when perhaps the money will remain unused in their hands.

The difference in syntactic composition between this letter and the letter quoted earlier (Plin. *Ep.* 4.23) is striking. The stylistic difference remains even when the letter to Trajan is compared with two letters outside book 10 that are occupied with practical and monetary affairs (Plin. *Ep.* 9.37 and 8.2) but which, nevertheless, show the typical concise, elliptical and rhetorical style of the first nine books.[56] The letter quoted above is one of the few in book 10 that touches upon the question of municipal finances (although that was the main reason for Pliny's appointment), probably because Pliny was perfectly capable of arranging the financial matters himself, without asking Trajan's opinion (Sherwin-White (1966) 553–554). The authorship of Trajan's responses has been debated. This letter is one of those instances where the voice of Trajan himself probably can be heard (and not that of his secretary) in rejecting Pliny's proposal to force people to borrow money from the state and making reference to the *iustitia nostrorum temporum* ("the justice of our times").[57] Another such passage is Plin. *Ep. Tra.* 10.117 where Trajan reproaches Pliny for not making a decision himself: *sed ego ideo prudentiam tuam elegi ut formandis istius prouinciae moribus ipse moderareris et ea constituas quae ad perpetuam eius prouinciae quietem essent profutura* ("But I chose you for your practical wisdom so that you would preside over the moulding of the behaviour of your province, and establish the norms which would be good for the enduring peacefulness of the province".)

The letters to Trajan thus give us a good idea of what a genuine formal letter in Pliny's time looked like. Interestingly, Pliny uses the expression *rogo uelis* ("I ask that you consent") in a letter of recommendation:

illud unum quod propter caritatem eius nondum mihi uideor satis plane fecisse, etiam atque etiam facio teque domine rogo gaudere me exornata quaestoris mei dignitate, id est per illum mea, quam maturissime uelis. (Plin. *Ep. Tra.* 10.26.3)[58]

This one request, which because of my affection for him I do not yet seem to have made in sufficient fullness, I make again and again, and I beg you, my lord, to assent at the earliest possible moment to my joy at the illustrious standing of my quaestor, which through him affects my own.

This same phrase finds a parallel in a letter of recommendation among the Vindolanda tablets *rogo ergo domine ṣị quod a te petieriṭ [u]ẹḷịṣ ẹi subscribere* (*T.Vindol.* II.250.5 "I therefore ask, my lord that, if he has made any request of you, you consent to give him your approval").[59]

Conclusion

Letters are documents that have close ties to their immediate context and the particular situation in which they were written. The remarkable variation of style, register and text type that can be observed within the genre is produced by differences in individual authors, addressees and subject matters. Due to these factors, being context-bound and showing a high degree of variation, letters constitute ideal material for Latin linguistic research, be it on colloquial language, genre-specific phenomena, or aspects of politeness strategies and rhetorical elaboration. One can claim that they remain underused as such material.

FURTHER READING

A good introduction on the style and qualities of letter language can be found in Cugusi (1983), with chapters on each of the major epistolary corpora (including Seneca). For Cicero, the commentaries of Tyrrell and Purser (1904) and Shackleton Bailey (1965–1970, 1977 and 1980) can be consulted for stylistic issues. For many aspects of Cicero's epistolary language, Dammann (1910), though old, is still valid and forms the basis of many later studies. Von Albrecht (2003) offers information on random topics in Cicero's letter style (together with often useful references to earlier literature) but is by no means a comprehensive survey. See particularly von Albrecht (2003) 52–71 on the style of Cicero's letters; 118–119 on the chronological development; 136–138 on the style of his friends' letters; Hutchinson's (1998) enlightening study concentrates on the literary aspects of the letters. For an excellent linguistic study based on Cicero's letter language, see Bolkestein (1998). Other interesting articles on Cicero are Mundt (2004) and Powell (2010). Politeness in Cicero's letters is analysed by Hall (2009). Guillemin (1929) offers information on poetic sources and influences in Pliny. A detailed analysis of rhetorical technique and figures of speech in Pliny, together with many other aspects of his language, is provided by Gamberini (1983). Sherwin-White's (1966) commentary, although concentrating on the social and historical aspects of Pliny's correspondence, is useful on stylistic issues as well. For Fronto, van den Hout's major commentary (1999), and its grammatical and stylistic index form a basis for further linguistic research. An older study on Fronto's archaisms and neologisms is Marache (1956). Portalupi (1989) concentrates on the colloquial tendencies in Fronto's language. Furthermore, there is much interesting discussion on Fronto in Swain (2004). For letters in the non-literary material, see the studies of Adams (1977, 1995b and 2003a).

NOTES

1 A letter is a short text written, and sent, by one person to another as a means of communication. More elaborate discussion on what a letter is can be found in Gibson and Morrison (2007) 1–16.

2 Cugusi (1983) is a general epistolographical study on the most important Latin letter corpora. A recent survey on letters as literature is Edwards (2005). Note also letters written by the emperor Augustus, edited by Malcovati (1969).

3 References to Fronto's letters are by page and line number of van den Hout's 1988 Teubner edition. The translations of Cicero are by D.R. Shackleton Bailey, of Pliny by P.G. Walsh, and of Fronto by C.R. Haines.

4 See Tyrrell and Purser (1904) I.54–74 for a general introduction to Cicero's letters, and Shackleton Bailey (1965) I.3–76 on the Atticus letters.

5 For a general intoruction in Pliny's corpus, see Sherwin-White (1966) 1–84 on books 1–9 and 525–555 on book 10.

6 Tyrrell and Purser (1904) I.60–74 on the publication of Cicero's letters.

7 A useful short introduction to Fronto can be found in van den Hout (1999) vii–xi.

8   See Cugusi (1998) on this aspect.

9   E.g., Häusler (2000), Pinkster (2010), Powell (2010).

10 E.g., Risselada (1993), Bolkestein (1998, 2000), Lavency (2002).

11 Gamberini (1983) and Marchesi (2008) on Pliny; Hutchinson (1998) and Beard (2002) on Cicero.

12 For Pliny, see the articles in the thematic volume *Arethusa* 2003, and Noreña (2007) on book 10; for Cicero, Wilcox (2005) on consolatory letters, and above all, Hall (1998, 2005, 2009) on aspects of politeness.

13 See Gamberini (1983) 130–161 for a discussion of the authenticity of Pliny's letters, and Castagna and Lefèvre (2003) for the context of his correspondence more generally.

14 Cf. Plin. *Ep.* 1.16.6 and Cic. *Att.* 1.16.

15 Similar theme in Plin. *Ep.* 3.20.10–12. See Morello (2003) for the "nothing to say" motif in Pliny, and Mayer (2003) for the search of *gloria* and immortality by means of his oratory and correspondence.

16 On the language of these letters, see Adams (1977, 1994a, 1995b, 2003a) and Halla-aho (2009).

17 This applies to letters generally; see Nevalainen (2004) 183.

18 A famous statement on epistolary language is quoted in the rhetorical treatise *de Elocutione* (223–235), a work of uncertain date attributed to Demetrius of Phalerum. Commenting on the plain style, the anonymous author refers to the view of Artemon (the publisher of Aristotle's letters) that, being the other part of a dialogue, a letter should be written in the same way as a dialogue (*de Elocutione* 223; see Malherbe (1988) 2). For Cicero's letters as "dialogue", see Garcea (2002).

19 See Tyrrell and Purser (1904) I.77–83 for similarities between Cicero and comedy.

20 See Cugusi (1983) 105–135 for classification of Latin letters; see Bergs (2004) for a general discussion on the typology of letters.

21 Noreña (2007) 242–272 on Pliny; Halla-aho (2009) 10 on non-literary material.

22 See Cotton (1984, 1985) together with Trisoglio (1984) on Cicero's letters of recommendation.

23 Malherbe (1988) 3; von Albrecht (2003) 68.

24 Cf. *Fam.* 4.13.1 (written seven years later) where Cicero refers to the *genera epistularum* in a similar context.

25 See Cugusi (1983) 259 on the topics of Fronto's letters.

26 But see Pinkster (2010) for a generally sceptical view that letters are reflections of colloquial (as in spoken) language; see also Halla-aho (2009) 39–40. Note Pinkster's ((2010) 191) remark that, in fact, a letter does not pretend to be spoken language unlike the plays of Plautus or a speech or a philosophical dialogue by Cicero.

27 The usual description of the language of Cicero's friends is that, generally speaking, their notion of linguistic correctness perhaps is not as narrow as that of Cicero himself (Tyrrell and Purser (1904) I.93). Cf. Laughton (1964) 150. The language of M. Caelius Rufus, a young and intimate friend of Cicero, has received some attention (most recently by Pinkster (2010)) because no fewer than seventeen of his letters survive (*Fam.* 8).

28 See Tyrrell and Purser (1904) I.87–90 on Cicero's creativity; Pinkster (2010) 193–198 on that of Cicero's correspondent Caelius; Gamberini (1983) 451–460 on Pliny's vocabulary and *hapax legomena*, and his use of poetic words adopted by post-Augustan prose.

29 See Dickey and Chahoud (2010) on what colloquial is and is not.

30 Dammann (1910) 26–29 and 46–47; von Albrecht (2003) 56–57.

31 Similarly in Fronto's language, the elliptical verb is either *esse, fieri* or *facere* (van den Hout (1999) 168–169).

32 See von Albrecht (2003) 49 and 62 on Cicero; Häusler (2000) on Pliny. For a study of paratactic constructions (that have certain overlap with parentheticals) in Cicero's letters, see Patzner (1910).

33 Bolkestein (1998) 10 "In spoken language the speaker would, so to speak, be 'holding the floor' just a little bit longer by inserting a parenthetical remark at such a point, and his interlocutor would violate politeness rules in taking over before the main focus has been presented."

34 On the language of this letter see Adams (1995b) 129–130, Bowman and Thomas (at *T.Vindol.* II.310) and Halla-aho (2009) 94–98 for this interpretation.

35 Von Albrecht (2003) 18, 49, 62.

36 See Pinkster (2010) 202–203 for hyperbaton in Caelius' letters (*Fam.* 8).

37 Dammann (1910) 18–21; Swain (2002) 149–150.

38 For the use of Greek in Fronto, see Swain (2004).

39 Examples of suggested colloquialisms are easy to find by the help of van den Hout's exhaustive index; see his comments, e.g., on 9.13 (van den Hout (1999) 24) *perge uti libet* with a reference to Ter. *An.* 310 *age age ut libet* and a comment "seems to be colloquial"; see Marache (1956) on neologisms and archaic words in Fronto. From Plautus Fronto also adopted "vulgar" words, resulting in a curious mix of elements (Marache (1956) 98).

40 See Garcea (2003) and Pinkster (2010) 204–205.

41 See Hutchinson (1998) 28; von Albrecht (2003) 66. This, however, does not mean that rhetorical figures would be an element of spoken language, a view endorsed by Melzani (1992).

42 See Dammann (1910) 21–25 and von Albrecht (2003) 66–67 on rhetorical figures in Cicero's letters.

43 Cicero's letters from his exile, although full of certain affect, seem to form a special less casual "register" within his correspondence; see Hutchinson (1998) 28–48 on three letters from Cicero's exile (to Quintus, Atticus and Terentia), and on the different style he uses in addressing three different people.

44 See van den Hout's (1999) index under "alliteration".

45 Generally, Pliny's epistolary language follows the trends of his time, making ample use of words taken from poetry, and exhibiting typical features of post-Classical syntax; see Guillemin (1929) 146–152 on poetical influences and Gamberini (1983) 449–487.

46 See Gamberini (1983) 470 on Plin. *Ep.* 8.10 and 8.11 where a hypotactic opening is used to introduce the difficult theme of Calpurnia's miscarriage.

47 Laughton (1964) 148–150; for an example of the "staccato style", see *Att.* 16.9 cited above. See van Gils (2003) 54–57 on ablative absolutes in narratives (modifying Laughton's views).

48 See Hall (1998 and 2005) on *Fam.* 15.2 and *Fam.* 11.27, respectively, and Hutchinson (1998) 27 on Cicero's seemingly excessive self-pity during his exile: "The Romans, it need hardly be said, were not simply a tight-lipped people who built straight roads and used the future perfect: they often displayed their emotions flamboyantly."

49 For an analysis of the letter, see Hall (1998); cf. Cicero's own impression of his text at *Att.* 4.6.4 as *ualde bella*, "a very nice piece".

50 Similarly, at *Fam.* 13.57.2 *illud quod ... id te nunc etiam atque etiam rogo.*

51 Other letters with a more formal appearance, although not written as a magistrate, are *Fam.* 5.5 to Antonius Hybrida, *Fam.* 5.2 to Q. Metellus Celer, and *Fam.* 3.2–8 to Appius Claudius; see Dammann (1910) 8.

52 *Fam.* 15.4.14 marks a break in the report, as Cicero moves from reporting narrative to personal appeal.

53 Mundt (2004) 261–262; Hutchinson (1998) 86–89.

54 Yet another mode in reporting events is found in the official dispatches that were designed for being publicly recited in the Senate (Mundt (2004) 264–265); see further Hutchinson (1998) 80–87 on the letter of Galba and its "plainness and brevity of language", and van Gils (2003) on different narrative techniques in a speech and a letter.

55 See Gamberini (1983) 481–484. Gamberini raises the possibility that Pliny's syntax in book 10 is generally more Classical.

56 See Gamberini (1983) 188–189 for examples.
57 Sherwin-White (1966) 536–546 and 636.
58 On Pliny's use of the common epistolary address *domine*, see Dickey (2002) 96–97 and Noreña (2007) 247–250.
59 Translation from *T. Vindol.* I.22; see Halla-aho (2009) 98–101. Note also similar wording in the opening salutation of a letter by Claudius Terentianus (*P.Mich.* VIII.467.1–3) and in a letter by Pliny to Trajan (Plin. *Ep. Tra.* 10.1.2, congratulating Trajan on his rise to power).

CHAPTER 25

Latin as a Technical and Scientific Language

Thorsten Fögen

Introduction

The standardisation of Latin, i.e. its development into a fully elaborate language that can be employed for all kinds of societal needs, including many types of highly specialised and technical communication, occurred primarily in the first century BCE and the first century CE. It included the reinforced systematic make-up of technical languages which emerge in the technical treatises of various disciplines such as agronomy, geography, architecture, mechanics, medicine and pharmacology, astronomy, music theory, mathematics and military affairs, further in the fields of philosophy, rhetoric, literary criticism and linguistics.

This overview of the technical and scientific elements of Latin starts with a brief summary of modern definitions of "technical" texts and languages and connects them with ancient approaches to their description. It takes into account the lexical, morphosyntactical, pragmatic and stylistic features of Latin technical texts and devotes particular attention to the role of Greek in the formation of Latin as a language for specific purposes.

Modern Definitions of "Technical" Texts and Languages

"Technicality" and "technical texts": the pragmatic dimension

According to many surveys in modern linguistics and communication studies, technical texts and the languages they use can be distinguished from *belles lettres* first and foremost through a pragmatic criterion: technical texts aim at the transmission of factual information

A Companion to the Latin Language, First Edition. Edited by James Clackson.
© 2011 Blackwell Publishing Ltd. Published 2011 by Blackwell Publishing Ltd.

and they do not pursue any aesthetic or even artistic intentions that other kinds of texts attain through the singularity of their language and style. In other words, they are more concerned with content than form (see e.g. Wilss (1977) 150; further Huxley (1963) and Belke (1973) 31–32). Their factual character is attributed to the lack of affective or emotional elements. The individuality of the author of a technical text is said to recede almost completely into the background (see e.g. Savory (1967) 133–136, 164). It goes without saying that such statements are rather general and cannot be applied to all types of technical writing. They also ignore the fact that there exist different national cultures of technical (or academic) writing (see p. 448).

More fruitful have been attempts in pragmatics and text linguistics for the classification of text types (or, to use the German term, *Textsorten*) within technical literature.[1] This approach analyses texts within concrete communicative contexts. A text is viewed as a complex, thematically and conceptually coherent unit through which a verbal act with a specific communicative meaning is performed. The intention and function of a text is constituted through internal factors, but also through external factors such as addressee, situation, relationship between communicative partners, social background, etc. The problem with this method is, however, that modern pragma- and text linguistics has never managed to develop a fully coherent theory and terminology in the classification of text types and their characteristics and functions. As is the case with a great deal of theories of literary genre, scholars often work with certain prototypes which are suitable enough for a very rough systematisation but rather inappropriate for a system that includes all phenomena on the textual level.

The rather rigid picture that emerges from modern descriptions of the characteristics of technical texts is even less applicable to Greco-Roman antiquity. There are various reasons for that: First of all, the corpus of technical literature in Greco-Roman antiquity is very wideranging. Although one may be inclined to think that generic terms such as εἰσαγωγή, ἐγχειρίδιον, ὑπόμνημα, ἐπιτομή or διήγησις and their Latin equivalents ascribed a specific pragmatic status to technical texts, it is by no means simple for the modern scholar to distinguish such terms precisely enough. The boundaries separating a practical-instructive text (defined primarily on the basis of subject matter) from a literary-aesthetic text (classified primarily on the basis of form) were not so strictly drawn as they are today, as the very existence of ancient didactic poetry demonstrates. The crossovers were much more fluid, and allowed for a broad spectrum of text types in the technical engagement with a subject, including even mixed text formats. Moreover, it is not the case that the characteristics of ancient technical texts and their language could be distinguished strictly along disciplinary lines on the basis of conventionalised linguistic and stylistic patterns which gained currency exclusively in certain fields – one of the exceptions being the "*a capite ad calcem*" organisation of many medical texts. For example, the literature pertaining to agriculture contains not only rather pragmatic prose tracts (Cato's *de Agri Cultura*) and more expressly stylistic renditions of dialogic prose form (Varro's *Res Rusticae*), but also works that combine both didactic poetry and prose (Columella, Palladius). It was clearly observed in antiquity that the didactic poem aims in principle less at instruction (*docere*) than at edification (*delectare*).[2] At the same time, it cannot be denied that ancient didactic poetry is full of technical language.

In conclusion, given the wide range of different types of technical literature in antiquity, it is very difficult, if not impossible, to speak of a pragmalinguistically homogeneous genre of "technical texts". Instead, it seems to be more useful to place ancient technical texts on a continuum that ranges from short and arid summaries, which refrain from any stylistic embellishment (e.g. Dionysius Thrax's Τέχνη γραμματική), to very elaborate and extensive treatises, which intersperse their didactic sections with a number of digressions in order to combine instruction with entertainment (e.g. Cicero's *de Oratore*). Yet, however useful for a general approach, the model of a continuum does not encompass the notion of diversity within one and the same work. To give just one example: in his *Naturalis Historia*, Pliny the Elder presents factual knowledge along with anecdotal material that often has no direct, if any, relevance to the more scientific passages. For long stretches of his work, Pliny subscribes to the compositional principle of variation (*uariatio* or ποικιλία), which is also reflected in the rather heterogeneous language and style of those parts of Pliny's work (see Fögen (2007)). It is therefore problematic to categorise the *Naturalis Historia* as one particular type of technical text: although it cannot be classified as an accumulation of anecdotes or even mere paradoxography, it is not an exclusive collection of scientific material either. Rather, it is a heterogeneous mixture of factual accounts as well as anecdotal and historical considerations, frequently entailing moral issues and political concerns of the Roman Empire (see Fögen (2009) 201–264).

"Technical languages"

From a sociolinguistic perspective, every historical language is understood as a diasystem of varieties which can be differentiated from each other through diatopic, diastratic and diaphasic criteria. A speech community is thus never uniform but has geographically confined dialects, group- and class-specific speech forms as well as situationally motivated stylistic divergences. The plurality of each linguistic community is mirrored in the heterogeneity of the language used in it.

Part of the diasystem of a historical language also consists of those forms which occur in "technical" communication. While it is undeniable that such forms of technical communication can be observed in early pre-industrial societies, a rapid development of technical languages manifests itself from the eighteenth century onwards, thanks to a dramatically increasing differentiation and specialisation in the professional world – a tendency that has continued uninterruptedly until the present. For these technical varieties, modern linguistics uses a number of different terms: in English, "technical languages", "languages for special/specific purposes" (often abridged as LSP), "special languages", "scientific languages" and "technolects" are all rather common; in German, *Fachsprachen* (more or less equivalent to "technical languages") tends to dominate over other terms such as *Sachsprachen, Spezialsprachen, Wissenschaftssprachen, Berufssprachen, Standessprachen* or *Subsprachen*, to name but a few (see Fögen (2009) 13–14). The definition of technical languages as specific varieties of a historical language, as proposed in modern linguistics,[3] has been adopted by some Classical philologists, e.g. by Langslow (1989) 34–35; similarly (2000b) 5:

> Technical languages are *varieties* of a language with their own history, with areas of overlap with non-technical varieties which may have influenced them and been influenced by them. Beside geographically-based dialectal variation within a language we recognise sociolinguistic

variation along several parameters – age, sex, class, race, level of education, etc. Another parameter is surely occupation, each occupation or profession bringing with it its own technical language. Like an age-, sex- or class-related variety, a technical language will be limited in use not only to certain interlocutors but also to certain topics, namely to the relevant technical matters. Like other sociolinguistic varieties ... a technical language may have considerable overlap with the standard language.[4]

The most conspicuous feature of technical languages is their specific vocabulary, the so-called technical terminology. Terms as part of technical communication within highly developed disciplines are greatly conventionalised and standardised; ideally, they are unambiguous and monoreferential, which entails that their meaning within a certain field is independent of any context. Although technical vocabulary is not necessarily invariable and may change over time, it is often assumed that its high semantic precision (its tendency towards monosemy instead of polysemy) guarantees the general avoidance of any terminological doublets, wherever possible (see e.g. Huxley (1963) 13–14; Wilss (1979) 183–184; Schifko (1992) 295–296; Albrecht (1995) 119–120, 137–139).

It must not be forgotten that technical terms do not only occur in strictly scientific or scholarly contexts, but also in many areas of everyday communication in which very specific topics are thematised: repairing a car, filing a tax return, reading the business section of a newspaper, using a computer or even playing football are all situations in which communication can only work if the participants have an approximately similar factual knowledge which they are able to articulate and understand through similar linguistic means.

Technical languages are not exclusively characterised by their specific vocabulary; they also have particular morphological, syntactical and pragmatic features.[5] However, what makes it difficult to generalise across languages is the fact that many such features which can be identified for the technical varieties of one language may not occur to the same extent in another. The tendency to use impersonal (passive) verbs in German academic prose, often described as deagentivisation and *Ich-Tabu*, is far less pronounced in English. The length of sentences in technical communication is another issue that varies across languages.

"Technical languages" vs. *"special languages"* (Sondersprachen)

Unlike the majority of English-language scholarship, modern German linguistics differentiates between *Fachsprachen* ("technical languages") and *Sondersprachen* ("special languages"). Although an absolutely precise definition of the two terms is problematic, a more general distinction may be helpful from a methodological point of view.

In an article published in 1961, the German linguist Hugo Moser identifies as part of the diasystem of a language "group-related and special forms of communication" (*Gruppen- und Sonderformen*), which he subdivides into "technical languages" and "special languages" (Moser (1959–1961) 231). Among technical languages, he ranges on the one hand so-called professional languages (*Berufssprachen*) such as those of craftsmen, hunters or farmers, and on the other hand languages of science and technology. As special languages he defines elevated forms of communication in areas such as religion, politics and poetry, further languages spoken among certain social groups, and finally arcane or even secret languages such as special jargons ("thieves' cant") or student language.

The main differences between technical languages and special languages[6] are located on the lexical level: special languages tend to be less standardised than technical languages and allow for a higher degree of individual creativity and innovation, which in turn makes them less suitable to be understood by a wide range of speakers. Typically, the lexical elements of special languages do not verbalise any new facts or objects, as is so often the case in technical languages; rather, they refer to phenomena for which words have already been established, and often do so in an imaginative, playful and even humorous way. Unlike technical languages, many special languages are restricted to rather small groups of speakers who use them as a symbol of identity and solidarity. Special languages may thus be used to reinforce specific social structures and to exclude certain speakers from in-group communication. However, a rigid separation of technical and special languages is difficult to maintain.

The Characteristics of Ancient "Technical" Texts and Languages

Pragmatic and stylistic features of ancient technical texts

Many ancient technical texts are introduced by more or less elaborate prefaces (see the useful collection of proems to Latin technical writings by Santini *et al.* (1990–1998)) in which their authors provide some information on the style of the treatise. Sometimes they also mention for whom they have written their texts. While such prefaces frequently contain a great deal of rhetorical topoi (especially the display of modesty) and may not always correspond to the actual character of the treatises themselves (see Janson (1964)), they nevertheless represent important documents for ascertaining what kinds of qualities ancient writers regarded as constitutive for a "technical" text.

On the pragmalinguistic level, a characteristic feature that is repeatedly emphasised is the **careful disposition of the material** in which the author of the text claims to have invested a great deal of effort.[7] Sometimes the systematic arrangement of the facts and figures is seen as superior to texts written by other authors who are said to have paid less attention to the structure of their treatises.

Intimately connected with systematicity is the postulate of **linguistic clarity and non-ambiguity**, a feature termed σαφήνεια or *perspicuitas* in ancient rhetoric.[8] In Book 8 of his *Institutio Oratoria* Quintilian expounds at great length how *perspicuitas* can be achieved (*Inst.* 8.2): words ought to be used in their principal meaning (*propria uerba*). Archaisms, neologisms and regionalisms should be avoided, since they are not part of common usage (*ab usu remota uerba*). On the syntactical level, an unclear structure, the extreme length of sentences, hyperbata or long parentheses cannot be regarded as virtues, as they may lead to confusion and semantic ambiguity. In some technical treatises the authors attribute their supposedly plain style to the fact that they write for a less well-educated readership. For example, the agricultural author Palladius defines farmers (*rustici*) as his target group and thus wants to keep the language and style of his work simple and straightforward (*Opus agriculturae* 1 pr. 1 cf. Pliny, *Nat.* 18.24). Sometimes illustrations or graphic sketches are inserted to enhance the precision of the verbal exposition, especially in texts that describe machines, anatomical features or geometrical figures (Fögen (2009) 53–56, with further literature).

Another element that ancient writers find essential for technical texts is a certain **brevity** (συντομία or *breuitas*). In a passage of his *Orator* (117), Cicero explains that the definitions of subject matter can be brief if they are presented in a specialised context where experts are familiar with the background; yet for a broader audience such definitions ought to be more extensive for the sake of a better understanding. It is clear that Cicero here, as so often, follows the rhetorical tenet of what is "appropriate" (πρέπον or *aptum/ decorum*): together with other criteria, the communicative partner (or, to be more precise, the audience) is a decisive factor for the selection of the proper stylistic level. Among ancient technical writers, Galen is perhaps one of those most conscious of his target group. As he points out himself (esp. *Libr. Propr.* pr. [XIX 10–11 Kühn]), his treatises written for beginners differ quite considerably from those intended for more advanced students or experts. That the golden mean between extreme length and excessive brevity is not easy to achieve is underscored by the grammarian Diomedes who wrote the books of his treatise for readers of different ages and knowledge (*Ars grammatica* pr. [*GL* I.299.8–14]). Pliny the Elder warns that brevity should not be exaggerated as it may lead to incomprehensibility and a lack of representativity of the information that is presented (*Nat.* 35.1, 35.53).

In general, technical texts seem to share certain features with the so-called "simple style" (*genus subtile*) among the *genera dicendi* of ancient rhetorical theory (see Lausberg (1990) esp. 519–525). The choice of the stylistic level in ancient rhetoric is determined by, among other things, the topic of a speech. The majority of technical texts focus on instruction and factual information (*docere*) and do not deal with any sublime themes, therefore, there is no need for an elevated style, which would be regarded as inappropriate for the subject matter (see Quintilian, *Inst.* 8 pr. 3; Vitr. 5 pr. 1–2; Frontinus, *Str.* 1 pr. 3; and Theodorus Priscianus, *Eupor.* 1.1).

However, theory and practice do not always overlap. As can be observed in many prefaces to ancient technical treatises, several authors strive to demonstrate their rhetorical skills and transcend the narrow boundaries of a simple style. Vitruvius, for example, adds a carefully composed proem to each of the ten books of his *de Architectura* and uses these texts to display his intimate knowledge of the principles of good style. More importantly, he intersperses his prefaces with anecdotes which are employed to support his self-presentation as a true expert on technical matters, but also as a morally responsible writer (see Fögen (2009) 106–151). Elevated style is thus used to support a series of programmatic statements; it is by no means *l'art pour l'art* or introduced for the mere sake of the edification and entertainment of the reader. At the beginning of Book 3 of his *Institutio Oratoria* Quintilian argues that a more refined style (*aliquid nitoris*) within technical exposition also contributes to a certain amount of pleasure on the part of the reader (*iucunditate aliqua lectionis*) and thus lures him into learning more easily (*Inst.* 3.1.2–4). Hence the avoidance of dryness and of the restriction to bare facts is motivated by a paedagogical impetus. Another case is Marcellus Empiricus' pharmacological treatise *de Medicamentis*, which he wants to make more attractive for the reader by placing a didactic poem at its end. As he points out, this poetic text serves as a reward for the reader who has been patient enough to study through his rather technical prose work (*Med.* pr. 7 [*CML* V, p. 4.16–22]). Centuries earlier, Columella follows a similar strategy (see esp. Col. 10 pr. 2–4), but even his books written in prose are sprinkled with quotations from poetic texts, predominantly from Virgil's *Georgics*, as is suitable for an agricultural treatise written by an author who wants to present himself as a reliable authority whose knowledge reaches far beyond the boundaries of his own discipline.

Lexical features of ancient technical texts

Technical terms are the most conspicuous feature of specialised communication and are therefore frequently discussed by ancient writers. Early medical writers and Aristotle devote a great deal of attention to terminology (see e.g. Louis (1956) and Lloyd (1983) 152–157; (1987) 183–214), as do later representatives of every discipline. In a passage of his *de Finibus* Cicero states that all areas of scholarship and craftsmanship rely upon terminologies that diverge from everyday speech (*Fin.* 3.3–5). Such terms with which not everyone is familiar may hinder the intelligibility and accessibility of oral and written technical discourse – a problem acknowledged e.g. by Vitruvius (Vitr. 5 pr. 1–2). However, the interest in specific terms goes beyond technical writing and can also be found in other literary genres. For example, the historian Tacitus (*Ann.* 1.41.2) mentions that the word *caligula* ("little boot"), the basis for the name of the eponymous emperor who used to wear boots as a child, is a military term (*militare uocabulum*).

In general, technical terms in ancient texts are easily recognisable for the modern reader, since they are often accompanied by definitions or certain indicators such as the participle καλούμενος (-η, -ον) or a relative clause of the pattern *quod x uocatur* or the parenthesis *id est x*. This proves that many ancient writers feel the need to explain the terms which they use and thus to make them as intelligible as possible for their readers. Already in antiquity, there is an awareness of several problems in connection with technical terminology, for example (1) the relationship between technical terms and words occurring in everyday speech, (2) problems with terminological variants, (3) the semantic shift of technical terms, and (4) word formation through metaphors and metonymy.

1   The relationship between technical terms and words occurring in everyday speech

First, the same entity or subject matter can be verbalised through different lexemes in everyday speech and in technical language. Frequently the qualifier *uulgo* is added to the word employed in everyday speech in order to indicate that its use is restricted to non-specialists. Two examples: Isidore of Seville remarks that the non-technical term for the night owl (*strix nocturna*) is *amma* (*Or.* 12.7.42); Caelius Aurelianus contrasts the two technical terms *aurigo* or *arquatus morbus* ("jaundice") with the commonly used word *morbus regius* (*Tardae Passiones* 3.68 [*CML* VI.1.2 p. 720.1–2]).

Second, the same word may occur in both everyday speech and technical languages. As a technical term, it usually has a much narrower meaning. For example, Seneca draws attention to the fact that terms such as *uoluptas* or *gaudium* are more narrowly defined in philosophy and even have a negative connotation in Stoicism, which they do not have in common speech (*Ep.* 59.1–2).

2   Problems with terminological variants

Although lexical monosemy is regarded as an ideal for technical communication, it is hard to implement. Variants are caused by a number of factors (see Wiese (1984) 36–38). Parallel scholarship may lead to the same results, but the terms that have been coined in this process may differ. There may be different motives for terms. Those that have been established for quite a long time will often continue to be used, although scholars have created a more precise or more suitable term (e.g. *German measles* alongside *rubella*). In addition, there may be regional variants, as they are typical of certain special languages (*Sondersprachen*).

Pliny the Elder's *Naturalis historia* represents a rich treasure trove for such phenomena, in particular the sections on zoology and botany. A certain herb called *cynocephalia* has the name *osiritis* in Egypt (*Nat.* 30.18). Pliny lists the three terms *milipeda*, *centipeda* and *multipeda* for the millipede, along with the Greek terms *oniscos* and *iulos* (*Nat.* 29.136; cf. 30.47). Names for diseases are particularly prone to variants: according to Celsus, both *morbus comitialis* and *morbus maior* refer to epilepsy (Cels. 3.23.1); the later Caelius Aurelianus adds further terms, such as *puerilis passio* and *sacra passio*, and explains their motivation (*Tardae Passiones* 1.60 [*CML* VI.1.1 p. 464.1–10]).

However, from a modern perspective, the question is whether such terms were really fully synonymous, and if this was indeed the case, one may ask whether these terms belonged to the same period. In some instances, older words might have been grouped together with much more recent terms, although they were no longer in use or at least about to become obsolete. Such cases are challenges for modern historical linguistics, and all too often a definitive answer as to the actual usage of such words cannot be given.

3   Semantic shift of technical terms

Despite its relatively fixed definition or even standardisation, a technical term may undergo a certain semantic shift. This is to be expected even more for ancient terms, as they were not as firmly codified (e.g. in dictionaries) as they are today.

Technical terms that have been imported from another language are particularly susceptible to semantic shifts. Vitruvius provides an interesting example: in Greek the word ἀνδρῶνες refers to those rooms in a house that are reserved for meals enjoyed by men (cf. ἀνήρ, gen. ἀνδρός "man"); the Romans, however, use it to designate corridors that are located between two courtyards of a house, called μέσαυλοι in Greek (Vitr. 6.7.5).

In other cases, certain technical terms are replaced by others – a phenomenon that often occurs in medicine or in military affairs; for the latter, Vegetius is a rich source (e.g. *Epit.* 2.1.2, 2.8.8, 2.15.5, 3.8.18, 4.15.1, 4.22.6). Sometimes, a term is not replaced by a completely different word but instead modified morphologically, as can be seen from Seneca's discussion of the words for "thunder": he says that the two earlier singular forms *tonitrus* or *tonus* have given way to the plural *tonitrua*, which is now more common (*Nat.* 2.56.1–2).

4   *Word formation through metaphors and metonymy*

The miscellanist Aulus Gellius, a keen observer of linguistic phenomena (see Fögen (2000) 180–220), gives a whole list of terms which are used in the context of military affairs (*uocabula militaria*) to designate the various ways of forming an army: *frons, subsidia, cuneus, orbis, globus, forfices, serra, alae, turres* (10.9.1). He adds that the proper meaning of these terms is rather concrete or graphic and has no technical connotation; their special meaning, transferred to a military context, has been derived from their metaphorical potential (10.9.3: *Tralata autem sunt ab ipsis rebus, quae ita proprie nominantur, earumque rerum in acie instruenda sui cuiusque uocabuli imagines ostenduntur*). Word formation through metaphors is a method that is widely recognised among ancient authors.[9]

In addition, terms can be coined through metonymy, in particular through the usage of proper names. This method is very common in modern technical languages (see e.g. Gläser (1996)); it is particularly widespread in disciplines such as medicine (e.g. *Parkinson's disease*), chemistry and physics (e.g. *Bunsen burner, pasteurise, galvanise*), and botany (e.g. *dahlia, forsythia*). It is a principle that is also used in ancient technical languages, as can be seen from numerous examples. In Book 25 of his *Naturalis historia*, Pliny differentiates between plants that derive their name from certain individuals (e.g. 25.29: *Paeonia … nomenque auctoris retinet*; 25.32: *Heracleon uocant et ab Hercule inuentum tradunt*; 25.62: *ipsi Mithridati Crateuas adscripsit unam, Mithridatiam uocatam*), from peoples (*Nat.* 25.82: *Scythice*; 25.84: *Vettonica*; 25.85: *Cantabrica*), and from animals (*Nat.* 25.89–90: *chelidonia*; 25.92: *elaphoboscon*). As in modern times, proper names play an important role in the technical terminology of ancient medicine and pharmacology (see Langslow (2000b) 130–139). Names of remedies, for examples, often refer to their inventor, their geographical origin or a deity with healing power.

Morpho-syntactical features of ancient technical texts

The morphology and syntax of ancient technical languages have not been analysed as extensively in modern scholarship as the lexical level. However, this is a gap from which ancient Greek and Latin suffer as much as modern languages.

On pp. 449–451 on the pragmatic and stylistic features of ancient technical texts, it has already been shown that many ancient technical writers subscribe to the ideal of clarity and brevity. However general such attributes may be in the end, in theory the goal is to avoid complicated, long-winded syntax that does not easily permit the reader to follow the train of thought. On the other hand, it cannot be claimed that a more artistic prose (*Kunstprosa*) is not practised at all in ancient technical literature. Good style is still an issue for many technical writers; it is not that they do not care about the ways in which they present their material.

Morphological and syntactical features of ancient technical texts are partly influenced by the genre or discipline to which they belong. There are areas such as law (see De Meo (2005) 67–131; Langslow (2005) 294–297), religion (Risch (1979); De Meo (2005) 133–170) and military affairs (Heraeus (1902, 1937); Mosci Sassi (1983); De Meo (2005) 171–207) where forms of communication are highly formalised and heavily indebted to long-established written sources. Therefore texts from these disciplines tend to preserve a number of archaic features that may be difficult to understand even for experts, as can be gathered from some ancient testimonies (see e.g. Quint. *Inst.* 1.6.40–41 and Horace, *Ep.* 2.1.86–87 on the *Saliorum carmina*). According to some sources, the language of jurisdiction is characterised by lexical archaisms and syntactic terseness (Cicero, *de Orat.* 1.186 and *Leg.* 2.18), and is often remote from common usage (Quint. *Inst.* 11.2.41). Another reason for the aloof character of such texts is their specific morphology which diverges from later stages of Latin. For religion and law, it is mainly infinitives ending in *-ier* or specific imperative forms (see Risch (1979)). In addition, the phraseology is not always identical with the syntactical patterns of common speech, e.g. in the special language of soldiers (Paul. *Fest.* p. 407.1–3 Lindsay: *"sub uitem proeliari" dicuntur milites, cum sub uinea militari pugnant*; Augustine, *Quaest. Hept.* 7.56: *Sic enim quod militares potestates dicunt: uade, alleua illum, et significat "occide illum", quis intellegat, nisi qui illius locutionis consuetudinem nouit?*).

Certain fields rely upon invariable syntactical patterns (phrasemes). The army constantly makes use of fixed military commands which often follow a thema–rhema structure (see Fögen (2009) 50–51). The language of Roman law is also characterised by specific phrasemes, especially when the jurisdiction requires a certain formulaic style to underscore the official character of certain crucial legal acts such as the appointment of an heir (see Gaius, *Inst.* 2.116–117; cf. 2.127–134, 3.88–96, 4.11 for other legal procedures). A violation of these formal conventions leads to unpleasant consequences; in the case of a testament, its content becomes invalid.

Another noticeable feature of legal texts which may be counted among their syntactical idiosyncrasies is described by Isidore of Seville in the first book of his *Origines*. Under the heading *de notis iuridicis* (*Or.* 1.23) he thematises various abridgements which are said to have been common in legal writings for a long time. These are shorthand symbols in the form of letters or at least of signs derived from letters, which are supposed to accelerate the process of writing. They replace not only words but also whole groups of words (see e.g. *Or.* 1.23.1: *per unum K "caput", per duo KK iuncta "calumniae causa", per I et E "iudex esto", per D et M "dolum malum"*). It goes without saying that such a code is not accessible to the uninitiated; one is reminded of similar problems in modern technical communication where abbreviations sometimes abound.

In agriculture, knowledge is partly preserved in the form of *oracula*, perhaps best translated as "basic principles" which have grown from long experience (*usus*) and have been transmitted orally before they have been written down. They are usually succinct and concise, and represent authoritative statements as to how to properly handle various aspects of the farmer's duties (see Pliny, *Nat.* 18.25–27, 18.39–40, 18.298, 18.319). Comparable are the so-called *leges*, "prescriptions" or "rules", which are characterised by certain adhortative morpho-syntactical structures such as imperatives of the second person (Pliny, *Nat.* 18.315–316). Cato's *de Agricultura* is the earliest agricultural treatise that incorporates such linguistic phenomena which serve to directly address the user of his manual.

In Roman technical texts, the discussion of the morpho-syntactical characteristics of technical languages frequently occurs in connection with the problem of "translating" Greek knowledge into Latin. This issue will be treated in the next section.

The Role of Greek in the Formation of Latin Technical Languages

The vast majority of Roman technical literature is heavily indebted to Greek models, with regard to concepts and ideas as well as linguistic means. Greek culture and learning had a deep impact upon every aspect of Roman culture, a phenomenon which reveals itself not only in *belles lettres*, but also in the fields of architecture, politics, religion, philosophy and science. The Latin language, as the medium for these fields, is no exception, and both poets and prose writers were completely aware of this fact, as is proven by the numerous reflexive passages in their works (see Fögen (2000) with further literature). Literary genres, models and motifs were taken up from Greek precursors and emulated in Latin, but also modified in order to produce something new and exceptional. On a more general level, it may be argued that the creation of a "national literature" (a term which, admittedly, one might hesitate to apply to the Romans) takes for granted the ability of authors to rely upon a suitable linguistic repertoire. Where these resources are lacking, there exist lacunae that must be filled by linguistic innovations; these are the decisive cases that compel creators of literature to demonstrate their artistry by maximising the complexity and variation within their native language.

This section discusses how various Roman writers transfer Greek knowledge, and also Greek technical terms, into Latin. That the notions bound up today with the concept of "translation" cannot be applied unconditionally to the ancient context is true for technical texts just as much as it is for literary ones. The boundaries between literal translation, freer rendering, paraphrase (report), adaptation, creative emulation, epitome and compilation were blurred in antiquity. Since relatively few Latin renderings of Greek texts can be classified as "translations" in the modern sense, it seems to be appropriate to use the more broadly defined term of *transformation* for all forms of Latinising of foreign-language texts in antiquity (see Fögen (2005)).

Cicero

Cicero has contributed a great deal to the formation of Latin as a standard language, in particular its technical vocabulary. It is one of his major achievements to have developed a complex Latin terminology in the areas of philosophy and rhetoric. Although he does not deny that his own treatises are indebted to Greek thinking, he is one of the first Roman authors to exhibit a hitherto unknown self-confidence that enables him to create literary products of their own value and thus make a significant contribution to Roman culture as a whole. When he claims that there exist no noteworthy, stylistically accomplished and sufficiently precise philosophical texts in Latin before his own time (*Tusc.* 1.5–6), it becomes obvious that Cicero follows a rigorous strategy of self-advertisement. He even goes so far as to say that he was the first to have created a philosophical terminology in Latin (*Fin.* 3.5). This in turn is part of what he calls the extension or expansion of the Latin language (*Fat.* 1: *augentem linguam Latinam*), or, to be more precise, the enlargement or enrichment of its vocabulary (*copia uerborum*; cf. *Ac.* 1.26), which thanks to his personal commitment can now compete with that of Greek and even surpass it (*N.D.* 1.8; cf. *Tusc.* 2.35, 3.8–11, *de Orat.* 2.17–18, *Sen.* 45).

When it comes to the Latinisation of Greek terms, Cicero uses different methods, as he explains in *Fin.* 3.15: it is not the case that there is an exact equivalent in Latin for every Greek term, i.e. a one-to-one relation that permits a literal translation (*exprimere uerbum e uerbo*). Often the Greek word needs to be circumscribed by several Latin words, a method that Cicero defines as *unum uerbum pluribus uerbis exponere* (see also *Fin.* 3.55). If it seems impossible to render the Greek word in Latin, one may use the original term – a method which is particularly appropriate in cases where the Greek term is already well-established in Latin, such as *philosophia, rhetorica* or *dialectica* (see *Ac.* 1.25–26, *Fin.* 3.5, *Div.* 2.11, *N.D.* 2.91).

Cicero's guiding principle for successful translations is common linguistic usage (*consuetudo*): whenever the translation of a term leads to a result that speakers may perceive as awkward, it is unacceptable and needs to be reconsidered. For example, for the philosophical term πάθη, he avoids the rendering *morbi* and gives preference to *perturbationes animi* (*Tusc.* 3.7). In another case, however, he translates εὐδαιμονία as *beatitas* or *beatitudo*, although he is aware of the fact that he has created two neologisms which sound harsh (*durum*) and yet need to find their way into common usage (*N.D.* 1.95); this may be the reason why he does not stick to these two words and elsewhere uses *beatum* (e.g. *Fin.* 5.84, *Tusc.* 5.45) and *uita beata* (e.g. *N.D.* 1.67). Occasionally, usage and euphony overlap as criteria for a good translation: while both *species* and *forma* are in principle suitable enough as equivalents to εἶδος, Cicero argues that *species* is not fully satisfactory, since some of its oblique cases such as the genitive plural *specierum* and the dative/ablative plural *speciebus* are rather complicated and not very elegant. By contrast, *forma* has a much simpler paradigm and thus needs to be favoured, especially as it is semantically identical with *species* (*Top.* 30).

In several instances, there are multiple Latin translations of a Greek term (so-called *Mehrfachübersetzungen*), which indicates that a fixed correspondence to the Greek original has not yet been fully established. Such alternative translations may have identical roots and differ only with regard to their suffixes, i.e. morphologically. Seneca offers the substantive *finitor* and the participle *finiens* as translations of ὁρίζων (*Nat.* 7.17.3); Caelius Aurelianus renders ὄρεξις as *appententia* (*Celeres Passiones* 1.114 [*CML* VI.1.1 p. 86.4–5]), *appetitio* (*Tardae Passiones* 3.33 [VI.1.2 p. 698.6]) and *appetitus* (*Tardae Passiones* 4.32 [VI.1.2 p. 792.15–16]). However, a more frequent type of translation is the rendering by semantically cognate lexemes which do not have the same lexical root. To this category belong cases such as *extremum, ultimum, summum* and *finis* as translation of τέλος (Cicero, *Fin.* 3.26), or *decreta, scita* and *placita* as renderings of δόγματα (Seneca, *Ep.* 95.10). This method of providing a number of Latin alternatives appears to have been applied by the ancients to explain the precise meaning of the Greek word in question in the best possible way; another reason may have been the striving for rhythm and variation (see Puelma (1980) 164). From a modern point of view the use of variants such as those mentioned above is not conducive to the establishment of a fully unambiguous terminology which is supposed to prevent the overlapping of semantic doublets and to assign a single meaning to a single term (see p. 458).

Some translations that may have been perceived as rather daring are introduced by statements such as *quasi* (e.g. Cicero, *Tim.* 47: *crebris quasi cuneolis* for ἀοράτοις, πυκνοῖς γόμφοις) or *ut ita dicam* ("so to speak"), or they are embedded in formulae such as *x non absurde y dicimus* (e.g. Diomedes, *GL* I.324.10–11: Ῥηματικά *sunt, quae a uerbis deriuantur nomina. Haec non absurde uerbalia dixerimus, ut dico dictio*) or *x quod nos y dicere poterimus* (frequently used by Caelius Aurelianus, e.g. in *Celeres Passiones* 2.56 [*CML* VI.1.1 p. 164.18–20]: *catalepsin ... nos apprehensionem uel oppressionem uocare poterimus; Tardes Passiones* 2.79 [VI.1.1 p. 592.1–3]: *medicamina ..., quae anodyna Graeci uocauerunt, nos indoloria dicere poterimus*), which give the rendering the character of something provisional or temporary – a compromise which is only adhered to until a better solution can be found (see also Quint. *Inst.* 8.3.37 on neologisms). Such remarks are not always to be taken fully seriously but are rather to be interpreted as a rhetorical *captatio beneuolentiae*.

The philosopher Seneca

Roman "translators" addressed syntactical problems less often than lexical and semantic aspects in their reflections on the subject. In one of his *Epistulae Morales*, Seneca describes how, during a philosophical discourse on Plato, he came to notice the limited expressive possibilities of his native language, as there were no corresponding words for numerous Greek terms or at least no translations which he deemed acceptable (*Ep.* 58.1). He explains this by referring to the fact that many Latin words which existed in the past are no longer in use; thus language change is simply interpreted as loss of words and reduction of the Latin lexicon (*Ep.* 58.2–5). Although he recognises that neologisms have been introduced by connoisseurs of Latin, he still clings to the opinion that most of these new words are rather clumsy. For example, the noun *essentia* for the Greek word οὐσία was coined by authorities such as Cicero and then also used by Papirius Fabianus, but Seneca still finds it unsatisfactory; he confines himself to the statement that the morphological and lexical system of his mother tongue does not allow for a better solution (*Ep.* 58.6). In his opinion, Latin is not only lacking numerous equivalents for Greek terms and concepts, but certain peculiarities of Greek could not be reproduced in Latin at all. For example, the participle τὸ ὄν ("the being/existing"), which is substantivised by addition of the article and thus conveniently transformed into a most useful philosophical term, falls for him into the latter category; owing to the morpho-syntactical deficits of Latin, the only way of translating this term is by the structurally different relative clause *quod est* ("[that] what is/exists") – a solution that Seneca finds less than satisfying (*Ep.* 58.7). One may wonder how Seneca would have dealt with Heidegger's or Adorno's German.

There may be several reasons for Seneca's rather pronounced negative attitude towards Latin. The most plausible explanation is perhaps that statements like these could be used to display a thorough familiarity with the Greek language and learning, even if at the cost of the denigration of one's native tongue and one's compatriots, who thus appear not to have made sufficient effort to overcome the deficiencies of Latin. In any case, it is obvious

that if one were to accept Seneca's view, one would have to put forward the rather awkward claim that languages are static entities which have no potential to be developed
further on various linguistic levels, including morphology and syntax. It goes without
saying that this position would exclude the possibility of the development of complex
technical languages which often exhibit linguistic patterns that differ from those of common speech. On the other hand, one might also argue that, by criticising coinages such
as *essentia*, Seneca simply wanted to avoid a high number of neologisms and thus to
prevent his philosophical letters from losing a certain literary quality and accessibility (see
Fögen (2002) on translation in Seneca).

Seneca is only one of many Roman authors, with the exception of Cicero, who describe
the alleged deficiencies of their mother tongue in terms of the *patrii sermonis egestas*
stereotype, first coined by Lucretius and taken up even by authors from Late Antiquity
like Jerome, Augustine and Boethius (see Fögen (2000)). Looking back to the two
Latin renderings *essentia* and *ens* for τὸ ὄν, it is noteworthy that they are also criticised
for their harshness by Quintilian in his *Institutio Oratoria* (*Inst.* 8.3.33; cf. Fögen (2000)
162–164). Even much later, in the fourth and fifth centuries CE, these coinages still have
not lost their unusual character in the view of a number of writers (on *essentia* see for
example Augustine, *C.D.* 12.2 [*PL* 41.350], similarly *Trin.* 5.2 [*PL* 42.912]; on *ens* e.g.
Priscian, *GL* III.239.5–9, and Pseudo-Acro, *Scholia in Horatii Artem Poeticam* 48
[p. 316.24–317.3 Keller]).

Roman medicine

In a letter to Pullius Natalis, which has survived together with Marcellus Empiricus' *de
Medicamentis*, Celsus (who may not be identical with the eponymous medical writer; see
Fögen (2009) 68–69) remarks that he has completed the required Latin translations of
two Greek prescription books. Apart from numerous intriguing remarks as to his method
of rendering the Greek original, he addresses a very practical aspect of his translation:
converting the prescriptions' measured medicinal amounts from the *drachmae* customary
among Greek doctors to the *denarii* more readily understood by Roman readers (*Celsi
ad Pullium Natalem epistula* 3 [*CML* V, p. 44.23–27]). This approach would today
entail the conversion of spatial measurements like miles, yards, feet and inches used in an
English technical text to their corresponding specifications in the continental European
units of measurement, namely kilometres, metres and centimetres. Modern translation
research classifies such a process as a compensatory translation strategy, which helps to
bridge the specific socio-cultural gaps between an original text and the translation (see
Wilss (1977) 101, 233–234).

That Greek technical terminology has the advantage of a certain "decency" is a
thought that is brought forward by Celsus in the sections of *de Medicina* which deal
with sexually transmitted diseases. Here he points out that the description of genitalia
was more acceptable in Greek than in Latin, and that the Greek terms were also more
widely used among Roman medical practitioners. In addition, reasons of decorum render problematic the use of such unattractive terms tainted by obscene connotations.
On the other hand, Celsus emphasises that a true representative of his subject could
not shrink away from such delicate subject matter, but instead would have to employ

unambiguous terminology so that everyone, even the non-expert, would be capable of understanding what he meant (Cels. 6.18.1; cf. 7.18.3).

The Latinisation of certain terms in this case proceeds more hesitantly, and demonstrates a clear preference for Greek terminology as a well-established constituent of medical terminology, which affects its user neutrally and less directly than coinages in his native language. This phenomenon suggests a comparison with modern "vernacular" designations in the area of medicine, which in the opinion of many native speakers are much more blunt than the corresponding Greek and Latin terms. One could therefore think of examples which correspond to the circumstance formulated by Celsus, like *mammography* vs. *breast X-ray*, but also of numerous designations for diseases which are not related to sexual organs (*herpes zoster* vs. *shingles*), medications (*fungistatic* vs. *cream for athlete's foot*) and diagnostic methods (*colonoscopy* vs. *screening of the bowel*). Research on technical languages has often emphasised that technical terminology, in particular the use of foreign terms, can serve to neutralise and ostensibly objectify an account, and that it may also be used to downplay and trivialise an issue, or to very crudely distort it with the goal of manipulation, as in politics for example (see e.g. Fluck (1996) 42–44, 78–79).

An anonymous treatise on "physiognomony"

In the introduction to his fourth-century treatise on "physiognomony" (φυσιογνωμονία), its anonymous author states that he resorted to relevant works of three Greek authors – Loxus, Aristotle and Polemon – and in so doing principally included basic and easily understandable excerpts. He adds that he did not translate the difficult passages occurring in these treatises, but preferred to quote these in the Greek original (*de Physiognomonia* 1). Apparently the text is a kind of compilation, a typical format in Late Antiquity for many subjects. What is peculiar about this work is its author's avowed eschewal of the translation of problematic segments.

The passages which the anonymous author included in the Greek original are not long ones, nor indeed even sentences or phrases; instead, he incorporates single lexemes exclusively. Moreover, the cases in which a Greek term appears untranslated or even without any additional technical explanations are very rare. Much more often the author tries to juxtapose the Greek term with a Latin equivalent. This method does not necessarily always entail a one-to-one translation, but could also result in a rendering which semantically replicates the original term by using multiple components. The anonymous author replicates the adjective ὑγρός through the hendiadys *molle et flexibile*, i.e. two equivalent, interchangeable, semantically complementary elements (*de Physiognomonia* 54). In a similar way, he specifies in an ancillary remark how the Greek term is *not* to be understood. The writer endeavours to explain the meaning of the word ὑγρός in the clearest possible way because it first received its character as a technical term in Greek through metaphorical usage ("soft, flexible, supple"; basic meaning "wet, moist, liquid"); he also emphasises that the term would arise more often in the course of the work. It is interesting to note that in each of its four later instances ὑγρός is glossed with the adjective *mollis* alone (*de Physiognomonia* 66, 88, 100, 109). Thus the translator seems to have thought it sufficient for the rendering of a Greek term to offer only once – that is, where it first occurs – a more complex Latinisation which is connected with a thorough documentation of its precise meaning. If the term recurs subsequently in the text, its simplistic translation by just one word is now possible, as the reader has already been familiarised with the semantic intricacies of the term in question and does not require another full-fledged explanation.

The real difficulty for the anonymous author, as for the Roman "translator" in general, lies in the so-called loan-translations, which reproduce the Greek expression element for element in Latin. Even when this process is morphologically unproblematic, the translation of some terms may lead to results which are often insufficiently semantically specific in comparison to their common meanings in everyday language, and therefore not completely recognisable as technical terms. One example is the term *a(d)-spectus* as a translation of ἐπι-πρέπεια (*de Physiognomonia* 45), to which a specification in the form of a relative clause is attached in order to make its specialised technical meaning more easily identifiable.

There are most likely two reasons why Greek terminology goes untranslated only sporadically in the treatise on physiognomony. First, the Latinisation in no way falters in these rare cases due to the inadequate linguistic competence of the translator. From his point of view, it is rather the lack of appropriate (in particular lexical) options in the target language which would guarantee an appropriate degree of semantic precision. The especially problematic nature of designations for colours (*de Physiognomonia* 23 and 25: χαροπός; see also 88: μελάγχλωρον) was obvious not only to the anonymous author and other ancient translators (see e.g. Gellius 2.26; cf. Fögen (2000) 207–209); to this day terms for colours serve as a standard example of the difficulties that interpreters and translators face.

Second, with terminology which belongs to the standard linguistic repertoire of specific disciplines, as in the case of the Greek names for the diseases ἀποπληξία (*de Physiognomonia* 23), ἐπιληψία (§29) and σπασμός (§50), one can assume that these terms were already relatively established in Latin, which made their Latinisation superfluous. For the same reason, Cicero (e.g. *Fin.* 3.5, *Div.* 2.11, *N.D.* 2.91), Seneca (*Ep.* 120.4) and Quintilian (*Inst.* 2.14.4) refrained from translating Greek technical terms of this type. Such familiar Greek words, which were no longer consciously perceived as being of foreign origin by speakers of Latin, were sometimes referred to in terms of a personification: they were said to have been "awarded Roman citizenship".

Some general remarks on the transformation of Greek knowledge into Latin

Often, the Latinisation of technical texts was highly concerned with the appropriate rendering of technical terms and morphological-syntactical peculiarities of the original language. The struggle for terminological accuracy in the transformation of Greek technical texts into Latin is vividly documented by the fact that in Latin technical texts Greek terms frequently occur together with their Latin equivalent, which is supposed to serve as their translation – especially when the Latin equivalent was thought by the translator to have not yet been sufficiently established as a fixed term. In other words: in many instances, using the Latin equivalent alone was considered to be insufficient; to be on the safe side in terminological respects, it was accompanied by the corresponding Greek term in order to ensure a higher level of comprehension on the part of the reader. Such considerations did not carry the same significance for the Latinisation of artistic literary prose and poetry, since their transformation did not require the same degree of semantic precision for the rendering of individual keywords and concepts.

Roman "translators" of technical texts were usually well aware that their task was a complex one: they took into account that simple one-to-one relationships between the original and target language on both the lexical and the morpho-syntactical level, where each lexeme or grammatical form has *one exact* equivalent, tended to be the exception. They also realised that both Greek and Latin are differently organised on various linguistic levels, especially the lexical-semantic. Authors engaged in "translation" repeatedly stated, and considered as an impediment, the absence of direct Latin correspondents for certain elements of Greek. Either the problems which thereby arose were solved by implementing alternative techniques that generated a pragmatically suitable equivalent to the foreign-language entity concerned, or the difficulties of the transformation were bemoaned with reference to the almost insurmountable "poverty" of the Latin language, the stereotype of *patrii sermonis egestas* (see Fögen (2000)).

In certain disciplines such as medicine and philosophy, Greek remains an important medium of communication despite the fact that Latin develops highly differentiated technical languages of its own.[10] References to technical terms derived from languages other than Greek remain relatively exceptional. There are occasional references to Celtic, Hispanic, Gallic or Etruscan words, in particular by authors such as Pliny the Elder or other "encyclopaedic" writers who not only cover a wide range of subjects but also encompass phenomena from a considerable geographical span.

Conclusion

Research on ancient technical languages and texts has seen a welcome revival in recent years. Despite some groundbreaking publications it is hard to overlook the fact that there is still a great deal of pioneering work to be done. This includes even some basic tools such as editions, translations and commentaries, since many Greek and Roman technical treatises are not yet accessible in a way that satisfies modern standards. For scholars studying these texts, an interdisciplinary approach and the knowledge of a variety of languages (including non-Indo-European ones such as Arabic for areas like ancient medicine) will be indispensable.

Latin technical terminology, as developed by the Romans, has had an enormous impact upon modes of specialised communication in later periods. Elements of Latin (and also of Ancient Greek) have been exploited for the formation of technical languages long after Classical Antiquity, and it is no exaggeration to maintain that they still play a major role in modern technical languages and will undoubtedly do so for a long time to come.

FURTHER READING

A valuable general overview of the technical languages used in all major disciplines in ancient Rome is presented by De Meo (2005). Restricted to medicine but important also for other areas of technical communication is Langslow (2000b). With particular focus on the period of the early

Empire (first century CE), Fögen (2009) examines not only the lexical, morphological, syntactical and pragmatic characteristics of ancient technical writing, but also various forms of self-presentation of the authors of these texts and their specific rhetorical strategies. The social and ethical aspects of ancient scholarship are also explored; this includes questions such as progress of knowledge, openness and secrecy in the distribution of information and expertise, as well as the practical use and the political dimensions of knowledge (including ideologies and value systems).

Kaimio (1979) and Fögen (2000) analyse the significance of the Greek language for the development of Latin technical languages, which is intimately connected with problems of translation and language awareness in ancient Rome. Fögen (2005) deals with the "transformation" of Greek scientific knowledge by Roman technical writers. Schironi (2010) provides a succinct overview of Greek technical languages.

Among modern linguistic studies on technical languages beyond ancient Greek and Latin, one may refer to the useful introductions by Sager *et al.* (1980), Hoffmann (1987), Fluck (1996) and Roelcke (1999). The monumental two-volume handbook edited by Hoffmann *et al.* (1998–1999) is indispensable for any serious research.

NOTES

1 See e.g. Kalverkämper (1982, 1983, 2005), Göpferich (1995), Albrecht (1995) 146–148, Kalverkämper and Baumann (1996) and Wolski (1998).

2 Especially Seneca on Virgil's *Georgics* in *Ep.* 86.15: *Vergilius noster, qui non quid uerissime sed quid decentissime diceretur aspexit, nec agricolas docere uoluit sed legentes delectare.* The comments of Cicero on Aratus and Nicander's *Georgica* in *de Orat.* 1.69 are comparable (on Aratus, similarly *Rep.* 1.22), and furthermore the personal testimony of Columella (Col. 10 praef. 2–4; his chapters in prose are laced with quotations of verse, especially of Virgil) and of Marcellus Empiricus (*Med.* praef. 7).

3 See e.g. Fluck (1996) 11–26, 47–59, 193–198 and Roelcke (1999) 15–31; further Wilss (1979) 178–179, 182–184; Sager *et al.* (1980) 1–5, 63–69; cf. 21–22, 38–40; von Hahn (1983) 83–126, Nabrings (1981) 144–160, Möhn and Pelka (1984) 24–28, Hoffmann (1987) 53, 75–76, Schifko (1992) 295–296, and Albrecht (1995) 122, 139–141.

4 For similar definitions presented by Classical philologists, see Cousin (1943) 37–39, Mazzini (1978) 544–545) and De Meo (2005) 9–24, further Callebat (1990) 45 and Poccetti *et al.* (1999) 350–351. See also Willi (2003) 56.

5 On syntactical features see e.g. Sager *et al.* (1980) 184–229, Beier (1979), Nabrings (1981) 153–154), Hoffmann (1987) esp. 183, 215, 230, Fluck (1996) 55–56, 204–207 and Roelcke (1999) 80–84. Among studies in Classical philology, one may refer, for example, to Cousin (1943) 45–52 and Langslow (2005).

6 See e.g. Möhn (1980), Bausinger (1971) and Nabrings (1981) 33–36, 110–113, 130–140, 180–181. Gipper ((1979) 128) offers a helpful distinction: "Fachsprachen zielen … auf emotionslose Sachlichkeit, Sondersprachen eher auf gefühlsbetonte Ausdrucksfülle. In den Fachsprachen herrscht Nüchternheit, sie sind deshalb auch im Grunde humorlos. In Sondersprachen haben Phantasie, Gemüt und Humor Heimatrecht. Hier darf sozusagen gelacht werden."

7 See e.g. Cicero, *de Orat.* 1.188; Vitruvius, 4 pr. 1, 6 pr. 7; Frontinus, *Str.* 1 pr. 2 and 4 pr.; Vegetius, *Vet.* pr. 2–4; Vegetius, *Epit.* 1 pr. 4–6, 1.8.7–12, 1.28.1; Marcellus Empiricus, *Med.* pr. 1 (*CML* V, p. 2.4–12).

8 See e.g. Pliny the Elder, *Nat.* 19.1; Hyginus, *Astron.* pr. 6; Diomedes, *Ars grammatica* pr. (*GL* I.299.6); Caelius Aurelianus, *Celeres Passiones* 1.2 (*CML* VI.1.1 p. 22), 1.6–21 (VI.1.1

p. 24–32), 2.55 (VI.1.1 p. 164); Vegetius, *Vet.* 4 pr. 2; Anonymous, *Commentum de agrorum qualitate* p. 50.2–9 Campbell; Anonymous, *de Controuersiis* p. 72.16–17 Campbell.

9   See e.g. Vegetius, *Epit.* 1.20.11, 2.1.2, 4.14.3–4, 4.16, 4.21.4, 4.46.5, Ammianus Marcellinus 23.4.7, further Celsus, *Med.* 7.19.7 (on the medical instrument *coruus*). Cf. Lloyd (1987) 172–214, Fögen (2000) 91–93, 164–165 and, with reference to medical texts, Langslow (2000b) 178–201 and Schironi (2010) 342–345.

10 On questions of language domains in ancient technical literature see Zgusta (1980) esp. 130–135, 138–139 and Kaimio (1979) *passim*, esp. 195–315, further Dubuisson (1989).

CHAPTER 26

Legal Latin

J.G.F. Powell

Introduction

Roman law is a strong contender for the title of the most enduring and influential legacy of the Latin-speaking people to the modern world. Unlike many modern legal systems worldwide, Roman law was from the start largely a homegrown product.[1] It can, indeed, be counted as one of the successes of the Roman legal system that it was able to adapt itself from a relatively early date to the needs of non-citizens (*peregrini*) as well as citizens (*ciues*), to whom alone at first the "civil" law (*ius ciuile*) applied.[2] But the operation of Roman law throughout the Classical period was inseparable from the use of the Latin language. Translations of Latin legal documents into Greek were made, and some survive in inscriptions, but their language always bears the impress of the Latin original. In the East, it was not until the Byzantine period that Greek acquired equal status to Latin in Roman legal contexts, while in Western Europe, Latin obstinately remained the language of the law throughout the Middle Ages and even later, at a time when the Latin-based vernaculars had turned into distinct and mutually unintelligible languages, and when many of the inhabitants of the former Roman Empire (as for example in Britain and Germany) spoke languages not closely related to Latin.

In many cultures, the law uses a specialised register of the language, and Latin is no exception. Because law operates by the continuous application of rules and definitions laid down at some time in the past, it tends towards conservatism in its modes of expression, and the longer the lifetime of the legal system, the more conservative its language may eventually appear to be. At the same time, as the law evolves in practice, new concepts and distinctions arise which call for new terminology, sometimes replacing but more often supplementing what already exists. It is in the nature of law to develop cumulatively; even where an attempt is made to codify the law once and for all, it may

A Companion to the Latin Language, First Edition. Edited by James Clackson.
© 2011 Blackwell Publishing Ltd. Published 2011 by Blackwell Publishing Ltd.

be impracticable to break away to any great extent from existing legal idiom. Legal terminology, then, is apt to look to the non-lawyer like a strange mixture, with fossilised usages from earlier times (sometimes half understood, or not understood at all[3]) coexisting with neologisms. In some instances, as in English law until relatively recently, legal language develops so far from ordinary usage as to be incomprehensible to the non-specialist.

Undoubtedly, the legal profession has not always had an interest in revealing its secrets to the outsider. However, in Rome in the Classical period there was a countervailing factor. For a significant part of its history, the Roman legal system was operated by a combination of specialists and (comparative) laymen. It was not so thoroughly in the hands of the non-specialist as was the legal system of the Classical Athenian democracy,[4] but it was not professionalised to the same extent as most modern legal systems. There was a recognised group of legal experts (*iurisconsulti*, lit. "those consulted on the law", or *iuris periti* "learned in the law": "jurisconsults" or "jurists"); but the magistrates, judges and advocates of the Roman courts in the Classical period were not primarily drawn from their ranks.[5] Those latter functions were carried out largely by non-expert Roman citizens who acquired (from study or experience) as much knowledge of the law as they needed for the purpose, helped in the case of magistrates by their secretaries and assistants (*scribae* and *apparitores*)[6] and advised by the expert jurists where necessary. A certain amount of legal training was apparently part of general education.[7] We do not know the proportion of senators, equestrians, and other well-to-do citizens who performed some function that we would classify as "legal" at some time in their lives, but it seems likely on general grounds to have been quite high. During the Republic it was even possible for Cicero, in a law-court speech, openly to make fun of the technicalities of the jurists, in a way that would be almost inconceivable in a modern court staffed by legal professionals.[8]

Under the middle and later Empire, one sees an increasing level of professionalisation of the law. By the second century CE the responses of jurists (*responsa prudentium*) were seen as themselves having the force of law, and as binding on (lay) judges; the emperors granted certain jurists authoritative status, and procedures were established for resolving differences where authorities disagreed (culminating in the so-called "Law of Citations"). The law schools[9] came to rival and eventually supplant the rhetorical schools as training-grounds for public life, and especially for advocacy in the courts.

The history of legal Latin, then, is co-extensive with the history of Latin itself. Among the earliest surviving Latin texts are extracts from laws and statutes (see below, pp. 471–472). There is abundant attestation of a special legal register throughout the Classical period, and its influence on Latin literature is constantly to be seen: educated Latin readers and theatre audiences were expected to be able to pick up legal references on the wing.[10] Roman civil law reached its definitive written form in the voluminous *Digest*, compiled at Constantinople at the behest of the emperor Justinian in 527–533 CE. Much Latin or Latinate terminology remains in use (despite some reaction against it) among lawyers in the Western tradition even today, in the English-speaking world as well as in those European countries whose legal systems are historically based on Roman law.

For convenience, the main part of this discussion will be divided into two sections: (a) on terminology, and (b) on drafting.

Legal Terminology

The arrangement of this section is broadly linguistic, not historical: a proper historical survey of the development of Latin legal terminology would require much more detail, as well as more attention to the substantive law to which it gave expression.

The core of Latin legal terminology consists of ordinary Latin words, used in special meanings. Let us start with the Law of Persons, the first of the three branches of the civil law distinguished in the Institutes of Gaius.[11] A *persona*, as every Latinist knows, was originally a theatrical mask.[12] From there it came to mean a "character" in a drama, and thence – because all the world's a stage – a "role" played by someone, and eventually a "character", "personality" or "person". It was probably the lawyers who assisted the last stage of this semantic development. The Latin word *caput* is just the ordinary word for "head"; but in its legal sense it refers to civic status: the phrase *deminutio capitis*, literally "lessening of the head", refers to the loss of freedom, citizenship, or family membership. The satirist Persius (1.83) puns on the legal and literal meanings when he talks of an advocate defending a client's *caput* – and then adds the adjective *cano* "grey-haired". The word *manus* means "hand";[13] we too talk of obtaining a woman's "hand" in marriage, but in legal Latin it refers to a particular kind of marriage in which the wife passed into her husband's family (whereas in ordinary Roman marriage in the Classical period she remained in her father's family). However, *inicere manum* "to lay hands upon" meant to arrest someone formally for debt or for non-payment of a legal penalty. To free a slave was *manu mittere*, "to send from (or by) one's hand"; the phrase, transparent in Latin, gives Roman historians their technical term "manumission".

Civil law had two other branches, the Law of Things and the Law of Actions. "Things", *res*, meant anything that could be someone's property, including both physical objects and abstract, non-material things such as rights over property.[14] (In non-technical usage *res* also means "business", "affair" or even "lawsuit".) To undertake legal proceedings was just *agere*, "to act", hence *actio* "an action". The matter in dispute was *qua de re agitur*, lit. "the thing about which the action is taking place".[15] The justification for one's action was *causa* "reason" and hence "cause, case" (in law); to state one's case, or to defend oneself, was just *causam dicere* "to say the reason". Legal acts were supposed to be undertaken with *bona fides* "good faith", cf. our phrase "bona fide", but if not, there might be an element of fraud or *dolus malus*, lit. "bad trick", in which case the law would grant redress. For an offence to be punishable at law, a criminal had to act *sciens dolo malo* (as we would say: "with malice aforethought"). Many more examples could be cited. This stratum of Latin legal terminology is as down-to-earth as could be wished. In some cases the legal meaning of an otherwise ordinary word was unpredictable: for example the word *pauperies*, "poverty", was used to designate damage caused to property by a domestic animal (the first extant example of the usage is in an opinion of the first-century BCE jurist Alfenus Varus,[16] but it may well be older).

Around this core of ordinary words, there gathered a considerable amount of special terminology with specifically legal meaning, but clearly derived from native Latin roots and in some cases clearly very old. The head of a family, for example, as is well known, is called *paterfamilias*: this is a transparent compound of *pater* "father" and *familia* "family" but the latter word has an old genitive ending -*as*, clearly derived from Indo-European, but found in no other Latin word. His power over his family – originally, as legend had it, including the power of life and death – was *patria potestas*, "fatherly power". If a Roman *paterfamilias* was captured alive in war, he could not exercise his rights over his family and property, but he was entitled to resume them on his return: this resumption of rights was called *postliminium*, deriving from *post* "after" and *limen* "doorstep", because it took effect on stepping back across the threshold.

In English law property is classified into real and personal; Roman law divided *res* into *res mancipi* and *res nec mancipi*.[17] *Mancipium* means etymologically "taking in hand", from *manu capere*. *Res mancipi* are types of property – essentially land and houses held privately within Italy, slaves, and beasts of burden – which Roman citizens could own by an absolute legal title, the "right of the Quirites".[18] It was supposed that in early times they could be transferred only by a form of conveyance called *mancipatio*, a picturesque ritual involving the symbolic weighing out of the purchase price before five witnesses (*per aes et libram* "with bronze and balance"). But there was also a way of acquiring a prescriptive right to a piece of property by unchallenged occupation for a certain period: to do this was called *usu capere* "to take by use", whence the abstract noun *usucapio* (older *usus capio*).[19] Again, the Latin phrase is reasonably transparent (in a way that would not initially appear from the English Roman-law term "usucapion").

One who gave judgment between parties was called *iudex*, from *ius* "law"/"right", and *dicere* "say"; the word is of course the origin of our "judge"; the abstract noun *iudicium* meant both the judgment and the court in which it took place. In "accuser" and "advocate" we have retained the Latin words *accusator* and *aduocatus* "one called in", though in the earlier Classical period an advocate was more commonly called *patronus* "father-figure, patron". The principal accuser in a criminal trial, who signed his name to the indictment, was (*nominis*) *delator* "one who reports (someone's name)". The word for "defendant" was *reus*, possibly a derivative of *res*.[20] Specific offences were of course named, as in modern law, but often defined quite broadly. On the other hand, the Republican principle (abandoned under the Empire) was that there should be special courts (*quaestiones* "enquiries") to try each type of offence; in general, nobody was to be prosecuted for more than one thing at a time. Examples of such offences are *uis publica* (public violence), *res repetundae* (lit. "things to be got back" – extortion and misappropriation by provincial governors),[21] *ambitus* (electoral bribery), or *maiestas*, in full *minuta maiestas populi Romani* ("detracting from the supremacy of the Roman people") which originally covered illegal actions by magistrates in office.[22] False accusation was an offence called *calumnia* (hence our word "calumny"; it seems to be related to an old verb *caluor* "to deceive"); the letter *k*, standing for *kalumnia* in the old spelling, was said to be ominous to prosecutors.[23]

A witness was called *testis*, the origin of "testify" and "testimony". Italic parallels beginning with *trist-* demonstrate that this word came from the roots of *tres* "three" and *sto* "stand" and meant "one who stands third", i.e. a person who, after the two parties to a transaction or dispute had spoken, stood up to confirm the transaction or to give evidence to resolve the dispute.[24] To call a person to witness was *testari*, and the act of "calling-to-witness" or *testamentum* acquired the specialised meaning of "will" (as in "last will and testament"), because the making of a will was one of the most common acts for which witnesses were required.

Contrariwise, neither a witness nor a written record seems to have been essential for a contract between citizens: the orality of early Roman practice, and accompanying insistence on the recitation of set forms of words, has often been remarked on.[25] The oral contract was one of the most characteristic Roman procedures and was called *stipulatio*, "stipulation", which Justinian derives from *stipes* "treetrunk" via an adjective *stipulus* alleged to mean "firm". A stipulation was a formal oral request for a promise (the promise was called *sponsio*), setting out its terms, and including the question *spondesne?* "do you promise?"; once the answer was given, *spondeo* "I promise", the contract was binding on the terms stated. The word *spondeo* is cognate with Greek σπονδαί "truce" and σπένδω "to pour a libation" (calling the gods to witness a treaty or similar); although no such religious sanction attaches to a Roman *sponsio* in historical times, it evidently carried a similar degree of solemnity. A *sponsio* had many functions: it could be the equivalent of a modern bet or wager, the stake being referred to as *pignus* ("pledge"); or it could function as a warranty from a seller to a buyer, as for example in the formula for the purchase of farm animals at Varro, *R.* 2.4.5, where the seller certifies that the animals and the herd from which they come are healthy, that the seller has a good title of ownership, and that the buyer is indemnified against damage.

There are a few – but compared with English legal terminology, surprisingly few – examples of fossilised archaisms, which occurred only in specific legal contexts and were not transparent to contemporary Latin speakers. Of this kind are the old words for dividing up an estate among the heirs. The process was called *erctum ciere*. *Ciere* means "to set in motion", so one must assume that *erctum* means partition, although its etymology is completely obscure. If there was a legal dispute about the division of the estate, there would be an *actio familiae erciscundae*. Neither the verb *ercisci* nor the noun *erctum* exists in Latin outside the legal sphere.

The legal mind loves to systematise and classify, and a developed legal terminology needs a large number of terms for this purpose. Roman legal language is rich in terms of this kind. They may be adjectives, especially those with the characteristically prosaic endings *-arius*, *-orius* and *-icius*; or they may be qualifying genitives, or prepositional phrases used adjectivally (see also below). Here I give just a few examples, selected more or less randomly. An *actio* (legal action) can be either an *actio in rem* "action concerning a thing", directed to establishing the ownership or recovery of property, or an *actio in personam* "action concerning a person", directed to enforcing an obligation. An *actio in rem* can be, among other things, *per condictionem*, for recovery. A *condictio*, in turn, could be *certae pecuniae* (for a specified amount) or *incerti* (for an amount yet to be determined, e.g. the value of a piece of property). There was even a type of action called *condictio triticaria* "recovery of wheat", whose nature is easily explained once one understands that grain was one of the most common forms of security for cash loans (as a glance at the Pompeiian tablets will show). If you claimed that a man was your slave, you could bring an action for *uindicatio in seruitutem*; but your neighbour might anticipate you by claiming that the man was free (*uindicatio in libertatem*). However, a *uindicatio seruitutis* was something quite different: this was an action to assert a right (such as a right of way, or a right to draw water) over a neighbour's property. In English law these rights are traditionally called "easements" but the property that is subject to the right is still called the "servient" property, using the Roman term.[26] The jurist Ulpian further divided this type of action into two. If you were trying to get your neighbour to admit your right over his/her property, it was an *actio confessoria*; if he/she was bringing an action to deny you the right, it was an *actio negatiua*.

The law itself was classified into different branches. The law in general, in the sense of the legal system, is called *ius*, corresponding to French *droit* and German *Recht*. It is classified into *ius naturale* "natural law", *ius gentium* "the law of nations" (i.e. the core of legal concepts supposed to be common to all peoples and which therefore applied to foreigners as well as Romans), and *ius ciuile* "civil law". Within Roman law, the old forms of the *ius ciuile* were supplemented and in some ways superseded by legislation[27] and by the newer *ius honorarium* (law administered by magistrates, especially the praetor).[28] A statute law was called *lex* (pl. *leges*).[29] The earliest *leges* were the religious statutes piously attributed to King Numa Pompilius (the *leges regiae* "royal laws"), and the *leges Duodecim Tabularum*, the code of the Twelve Tables instituted by the Decemviri in 449 BCE, which formed the basis of the civil law. These were supplemented by the legislative acts of the Roman People (see below, pp. 473–474). There were *leges agrariae* (land laws), *leges iudiciariae* (laws defining the rights and procedures of the courts), *leges de imperio* (laws conferring powers on magistrates), and other categories. And because, under the Empire, the *lex de imperio* gave the emperor's decisions the force of law, the category of *lex* also included in due course not only legislative acts of the Senate passed at the instance of the emperor, but also the body of imperial decisions collectively known as *constitutiones* ("decisions") and expressed by edicts, responses to enquiries (rescripts), instructions to officials (*mandata*), and otherwise.

Much of the law is concerned with process, and Roman law developed a large repertory of abstract nouns derived from verbs denoting processes (typically ending in -*io*): we have already seen several examples (e.g. *actio* from *ago*, *sponsio* from *spondeo*, *stipulatio* from *stipulor*). Many of these had already come into existence by the time of Cicero, and could provide a model for the creation of new Latin abstracts in other semantic areas (e.g. rhetoric or philosophy). But they continued to multiply creatively throughout the Classical period.[30] A feature of these abstract nouns is that they retain enough sense of their origin as verbs to be able to take all the qualifying phrases that their parent verbs would have taken. Thus the verbal phrase *agere in personam* "to bring an action against the person" is transformed smoothly, as we have already seen, into *actio in personam*; the verbal phrase *in iure cedere* "to surrender in court" turned into *in iure cessio*.[31] Those who practise the art of Latin prose composition are usually told that it is inelegant to use prepositional phrases to qualify a noun directly, without a verb to hook the prepositional phrase on to, but the law knows nothing of such elegance where verbal abstracts are concerned.

A further form of lexical productivity is the creation of compound words, which sometimes wear a strange look from a Classical Latinist's point of view. The key to understanding them is to realise that they are simply two words run together, the first element being in an appropriate oblique case (dative, genitive or ablative). The type is exactly that of the familiar *senatusconsultum* "decree of the Senate" or *iurisperitus* "learned in the law". Among legal terms of this kind are *fideicommissum* (a trust under a will: *fidei* + *commissum*), *fideiussio* (a guarantee: *fide* + *iussio*), *acceptilatio* (a declaration that a debt has been discharged: *accepti* + *latio*). There are also set phrases, almost compounds, consisting of pairs of words in asyndeton (i.e. with no conjunction), complementary in meaning: *emptio uenditio* "sale and purchase", *locatio conductio* "hire" (the person who offers property for hire *locat*, the person who hires it *conducit*). This is a special case of a more widespread legal habit of asyndeton, involving pairs of words ("asyndeton bimembre") as well as the triplets or longer lists more usual in literary language.[32]

Relatively little of the language of Roman law is borrowed from sources other than Latin. However, in one area Greek terminology made some inroads: that of finance, banking and commerce. Here we find naturalised Greek terms such as *syngrapha* "contract" or "bond", *chirographum* "handwritten contract" (required for certain agreements such as the acceptance of security on a loan), *hypotheca* "mortgage" (i.e. security given for a loan without transferring possession of the security; in Roman law not restricted to land), *anatocismus* "compound interest", *arrabo* (or *arra*) "deposit" or "carnest".[33]

Legal Drafting

Legal language is not just a matter of terminology: there is also the question of the drafting of the sets of rules which make up the law itself, and of the written or oral forms whereby the law is put into effect. Some features of legal drafting in Latin, as in other languages, are not in fact exclusively legal, but appear often in legal contexts because of the need to be precise and explicit, and as far as possible to eliminate possible ambiguities. For example, one grammatical feature tending to explicitness, which is particularly common in legal language, is the repetition of the antecedent noun in a relative clause. An example is Gaius 1.13 *eiusdem* **condicionis** *liberi fiant, cuius* **condicionis** *sunt peregrini dediticii* ("they are to become free on the same conditions as foreigners surrendered in war": lit. "on the same conditions on which conditions foreigners are"). Legal Latin also tends to preserve a few old-fashioned usages, e.g. the use of pronominal adverbs of place such as *huc* "to here", *unde* "from there", etc., to refer not to places but to persons. But these features are not by any means peculiar to legal contexts.[34]

A further trick of legal usage, this time not an archaic one, deserves to be mentioned here: this is the use of the verb *habeo* "have" with the past participle. In the language of the jurists, *porcum emptum habeo* (for example) means literally "I have the pig, it having been bought", i.e. "the pig is mine by purchase".[35] It was clearly useful to the jurists to have a neat form of words that would describe the state of affairs in which one had legally acquired a piece of property and still had it. The construction is found very occasionally, but not commonly, outside legal contexts in Classical Latin. However, at some stage (it is not clear exactly when) the construction was reinterpreted by native Latin speakers as a periphrasis for the perfect tense: "I have bought a pig". Once assigned this new sense, it spread widely, and is found not only in all the Romance languages but also throughout the Germanic family (I have bought, *ich habe gekauft, jeg har købt*, etc.). It is not perhaps certain that the wide distribution of this construction in Western European languages is due just to the influence of Roman legal language, but it does seem as though that influence helped it on its way.

There is a considerable variety of evidence for the way in which legal documents were drafted in the Classical Roman period, and it is convenient to subdivide as follows: (a) the archaic law codes; (b) Republican statutes and court procedure; (c) *senatusconsulta*; (d) the ancient forms of action; (e) praetorian law; (f) contracts, wills and other documents.

(a) Archaic law codes

We have no full text of the *Leges Regiae* or the Twelve Tables, but only quotations in various literary and antiquarian sources, from which scholars have laboured to reconstruct what can be salvaged of the text. The orthography of these quotations has clearly been modernised at some point in the transmission; otherwise, for example, the first clause of the Twelve Tables would have read not *si in ius uocat ito*, but rather something like *sei en ious uokat eitod*. The word for "free" (masc. sing. acc.) occurs as the standard, Classical *liberum*, not as *leiberom* or any other archaic variant. It is clear from Cicero's writings that in his time, texts of these law-codes were available in book form, probably already modernised. What had happened to the original "tables" – presumably inscriptions on bronze tablets – is anybody's guess.

The archaic law codes are strikingly laconic in their formulations, and bear a clear similarity to archaic Greek legal inscriptions. A clause of the *Leges Regiae* (i)[36] is here compared with an extract from a sixth-century Greek inscription from Olympia (tr. C.D. Buck)[37] (ii):

(i) Paelex aram Iunonis ne tangito; si tagit, Iunoni crinibus demissis agnum feminam caedito.
A prostitute is not to touch the altar of Juno; if she does, she is to untie her hair and sacrifice a ewe lamb to Juno.

(ii) ... If he [someone previously mentioned] commits fornication in the sacred precinct, one shall make him expiate it by the sacrifice of an ox and by complete purification.

Few and brief though they are, the surviving clauses of these Latin sacred laws nevertheless contain all the essential features of a legal formulation. Often, a clause starts with a prohibition, expressed with *ne* and the imperative form in *-to*. Latin has two imperatives, the simple imperative (*fac* "do!") and the *-to* imperative (*facito* "you are to do; he/she/it is to do). The former is used for direct commands to be carried out immediately, the latter for instructions to be carried out whenever appropriate; thus it is naturally the second form that turns up mostly in laws.[38] A law which, like a "No Smoking" sign, merely issued a command or prohibition without mentioning a sanction, was called by the jurists a lex *imperfecta* ("an incomplete law").

The sanction was regularly expressed in the form "if anyone shall have done X, Y is to happen".[39] The main clause of a formula of this kind would again be expressed using the *-to* imperative. Usually it would prescribe a penalty or a form of restitution. However, one clause of the *Leges Regiae* prescibes neither, but rather provides for one offence to be treated in the same way as another: *Si qui hominem liberum dolo sciens morti duit, paricidas esto* "If anyone knowingly and with malice aforethought puts a free man to death, he is to be (treated as) a parricide". This suggests that the offence of parricide and its canonical penalty[40] was already defined, and that the scope of the law, as we would now say, was being widened to include murder.

In the *Leges Regiae* and (where not modernised) in the text of the Twelve Tables, the verb of the "if" clause has a special tense-form,[41] characteristic of old Latin, of which some samples follow:

(from *tangere*): *tagit* "shall have touched"
(from *occidere*): *occisit* "shall have killed"
(from *dare*): *duit* "shall have given"
(from *facere*): *faxit* "shall have done"
(from *uerberare*): *uerberit* "shall have beaten"
(from *uindicare*): *uindicit* "shall have claimed"
(from *plorare*): *plorassit* "shall have cried out"

The last vestiges of the living use of these forms are found in the comedies of Plautus (e.g. *faxo* "I shall make sure"); by the late Republic they were confined to legal language, and there are signs of uncertainty as to the correct way to form them. For example, in Cicero's philosophical law code in the *de Legibus*, there occur forms in *-assit* and *-essit* from first- and second-conjugation verbs, but in most other verbs these forms are replaced by the ordinary future perfect: Cicero clearly did not trust himself to invent such forms.

The Twelve Tables[42] as transmitted present a mixture of genuine archaisms, modernised forms, and occasional corrupted or misunderstood older forms. An example of the last category is the form *escit*, supposedly an inchoative form of *esse*, where the latest editors substitute the more plausibly reconstructed archaic forms *esit* (pre-rhotacism form of *erit*) or *essit* (old subjunctive form); but it seems that *escit* was in the texts available in the late Republic. Striking archaic features of the Tables include the following: deponent imperative in *-mino* (corresponding to active *-to*); pronominal accusative forms *em* or *im* "him", *sum* or *sam* "it" (masc. or fem.), *endo* "in", *ast* "and if", *nec* "not" (where *non* would appear in Classical Latin). Apart from this use of *nec*, which became standard in the legal register,[43] later instances of these words are signs of conscious archaism rather than common features of legal Latin. Cicero misuses both *ast* and the *-mino* imperative in his philosophical law-code, and a different but equally unhistorical use of *ast* passed into the poetic register of Virgil and other epic poets.[44]

Many clauses of the Twelve Tables concern civil procedure. In this context, a phrase like *manus inectio esto* does not mean, as it might immediately seem, "let there be an arrest", but rather "let there be a *right* to arrest": this use of the verbal noun in *-io*, plus the verb "to be", is characteristic not only of legal Latin but of old-fashioned Latin in general, as in the Plautine phrase *quid tibi hanc rem curatio est?* "what right have you to take care of this matter?".[45] The verbal noun retains enough of its verbal quality to take an accusative object. This type of formula is still productive in late Republican statutes: *qui uolet petitio esto* "whoever wishes shall have the right to prosecute". Later, the use of nouns in *-io* widened, so that they became straightforward verbal abstracts; later legal language is full of them. The influence of legal language, combined with that of philosophical abstraction, ensured that this category of noun remained productive in Latin and, indeed, is still so in more or less all modern Romance and Germanic languages.

(b) Republican statutes and court procedure

A good deal is known about the language of Republican legislation. A bill (*rogatio*) was presented to the popular assembly by a magistrate,[46] beginning with the words *Velitis iubeatis* "May you will and decree" followed by the text of the proposed law. This was called "promulgation",[47] and a certain time, *trinum nundinum* (three nine-day periods reckoned inclusively, i.e. twenty-four days), had to elapse before the proposal could be voted on. During that time debate could take place in public meetings (*contiones*). At the voting assembly two sets of voting tablets were distributed, one set bearing the letters VR standing for *uti rogas* "as you ask", and the other the letter A, meaning *antiquo* "I vote for the former state of affairs". If passed into law, the text was inscribed on bronze with a brief formulaic preamble recording the name of the magistrate who proposed it, the date it was passed and other details, and the law would be known by the name of its proposer and also often by its topic: e.g. the *Lex Cincia de donis et muneribus* proposed by the tribune Cincius Alimentus in 204 BCE, among other things forbidding advocates to receive payment for their services in court; or the *Lex Tullia de ambitu* passed by Cicero during his consulship, forbidding electoral bribery.

Substantial parts of a number of Republican statutes are preserved, although the only one that has survived in its entirety is the *Lex Quinctia*[48] of 9 BCE (well into the principate of Augustus, but the Republican processes still worked at this date), a relatively minor statute dealing with damage to aqueducts. A reader who turns from the Twelve Tables to any one of these statutes will immediately be struck by one overwhelming feature: their verbosity. The difference between the laconic and the prolix legal styles was noticed by Jules Marouzeau,[49] and it is not primarily a chronological or evolutionary difference, but rather one of intention and context. The maker of legal maxims, such as make up much of the Twelve Tables, will tend to cultivate brevity, so that the principles may be easily memorable and widely applicable; whereas the drafter of a statute typically needs to convey a precise and detailed meaning and to be constantly on guard against the risk of leaving loopholes.

The *Lex Quinctia* just referred to provides a good example of the developed legislative style. Here is a very brief extract:

> Quicumque post hanc legem rogatam riuos specus fornices fistulas tubulos castella lacus aquarum publicarum quae ad urbem ducuntur sciens dolo malo forauerit ruperit foranda rumpendaue curauerit ... is populo Romano HS centum milia dare damnas esto.

> Whosoever after the passing of this law shall knowingly with malice aforethought perforate or fracture or cause to be perforated or fractured or cause damage to any channel or conduit or arch or pipe or tube or cistern or reservoir belonging to the public aqueducts which lead into the city ... he shall be liable to pay a penalty to the Roman people in the sum of one hundred thousand sesterces.

This style has not only survived but flourished in legislative language throughout the Western world. Modern examples can be seen in any Act of Parliament. One may wonder whether the multiplication of synonyms has not gone beyond the point at which it serves a useful practical purpose: its function is as much symbolic as practical, to assure the public that they are fully protected and to let prospective malefactors know that they cannot escape on a technicality. Some of the traditional phrases embody real legal principles: *post hanc legem rogatam*, for example, shows that the law applies to any offence committed after it is passed (but not retrospectively). *Forauerit ruperit foranda rumpen-daue curauerit* makes it clear that damage committed through an agent is treated in the same way as damage done in person; and so on. Most of the language of a statute like this belongs to the normal register of the time, but certain traditional formulae remind us of a more archaic idiom. The phrase *dare damnas esto* "let him be liable to pay" had survived unchanged since the Twelve Tables.[50] A later clause of the statute provides that those who obstruct the aqueduct or build in its neighbourhood are liable to the same penalty as those who cause damage to it, using the formulaic phrase *siremps lex esto* ("let the law be the same": the etymology of *siremps* is completely obscure[51]). The statute ends with a number of clauses protecting existing rights which remain unaffected under the new law: each of these is stated in the form *eius hac lege nihilum rogatur* "regarding that, nothing is proposed in this law". The genitive *eius* "in regard to that" exemplifies a characteristically legal usage which grammarians have christened the *genetiuus forensis* "legal genitive".

One further important function of statutes is to establish who has jurisdiction in the relevant area and how cases arising under the law are to be tried; they are thus one of the main sources of procedural law. Republican statutes dealing with major criminal offences directed one of the praetors to "make inquiry", *quaerere*, and the procedures for doing this were laid down in detail. The fullest indications of how this worked are contained in the *lex repetundarum*[52] (generally identified with the law of Gaius Gracchus, hence dated to 122 BCE) and we also have a rich source of evidence in Cicero's speeches. There were several stages in the procedure, from *postulatio* (asking for leave to prosecute) via *diuinatio* (selection between rival prosecutors), *nominis delatio* (drawing up of the indictment), *inquisitio* (the prosecution's collection of evidence) and *inter-rogatio* (the praetor's formal questioning of the defendant), before the trial itself (*iudi-cium*), which might comprise one or more *actiones* (hearings); one statute (the *Lex Seruilia Glauciae*) prescribed just two hearings separated by an obligatory adjournment (*comperendinatio*, from *perendie* "the next day but one"), while others prescribed only one, but allowed the jury to vote for a further hearing (*ampliatio*) if they wished to hear further evidence and arguments. The members of the jury listened, apparently in silence, and then proceeded to a vote,[53] using tablets which said either A (*absoluo*, I acquit), C (*condemno*, I condemn) or NL (*non liquet*, it is not clear). The praetor then declared the result of the vote in the words *fecisse uidetur* ("it seems that he did it") or *non fecisse uidetur*. In the case of a guilty verdict there was then a separate assessment of the penalty (*litis aestimatio*).

There were also lesser jury courts, the *recuperatores* (literally "recoverers") who heard e.g. cases arising from breach of praetorian interdicts (see below), and the *centumuiri* ("Panel of 100") who dealt with family law; these survived vigorously into the imperial period. Magistrates, assisted by an informal advisory board (*consilium*), had jurisdiction in particular areas, with powers of investigation (*cognitio*) as well as of summary law enforcement (*coercitio*), from which there was appeal (*prouocatio*) originally, at least in theory, to the Roman people, and subsequently to the emperor.

(c) Senatusconsulta

Under the Republic, decrees of the Senate (*senatusconsulta*) were not formally part of the law, but were administrative and advisory. Furthermore, they were often vetoed by the intervention of a tribune (*intercessio*) in which case they were recorded as *auctoritates*, "recommendations". Under the Empire, the Senate assumed the legislative functions that had belonged to the popular assembly. It was then customary for the emperors to introduce legislation by means of a speech in the Senate; the imperial will would then be embodied in the form of a senatorial decree. Such decrees are counted by the jurists among the sources of law. Furthermore, the imperial Senate doubled as a high court, and its judicial decisions were set out in *senatusconsulta*, as in the famous decree discovered in the late 1980s, setting out the judgement on Piso and his family after the death of Germanicus.[54]

In all cases senators were asked to speak in order of seniority by the presiding magistrate. Their speeches were always concluded by a formal proposal (*sententia*) or else an expression of support for an earlier speaker's proposal. These proposals, if accepted by a majority, were incorporated into the eventual decree which would be drafted by a small committee of senators. We have several examples of such decrees, which usually follow a set pattern. Typically, the preamble states that the presiding magistrates (the consuls, or in their absence one or more of the praetors) consulted the senate on a certain day and in a certain place and gives the names of those present at the writing of the decree (*scr. adf. = scribendo adfuerunt*). Then the subject of the decree is specified, usually followed by the abbreviation *D.E.R.I.C.* (*de ea re ita censuere* "about this matter they decided as follows"), and then the substance of the decree is set out as an extended indirect command introduced by *uti* (the old form of *ut*) or *ne*. At the end the word *censuere* ("they decided", abbreviated to *C.*) was repeated, unless a tribune had intervened, in which case that fact was recorded instead. This was the official form in the late Republic, but less formal variants are found in some inscriptions; for example, the well-known *Senatusconsultum de Bacchanalibus*[55] of 186 BCE is actually a message from the consuls to the local community reporting the Senate's decision; only part of the inscription is taken up by the actual *senatusconsultum*.

(d) Ancient forms of action

Under the earlier civil law (until the second century BCE), private proceedings could be undertaken only in accordance with certain set forms of action (*legis actiones*) based on the Twelve Tables and subsequent statutes. The forms themselves were highly ritualised, including symbolic gestures as well as words. By combining the incomplete account of Gaius (4.16) with Cicero's satirical version in *pro Murena* (26), we can reconstruct in rough terms the procedure for the *legis actio sacramenti in rem* in cases of disputed ownership of land. The two parties came before the praetor. The plaintiff described the disputed land in sufficient detail to identify it, claimed ownership of it by Quiritary title, and challenged the other party in the words *inde ibi ego te ex iure manum consertum uoco* ("I call you to join hands there out of court"). The defendant then stated his claim in exactly the same words. The praetor then said "I order you to go there with witnesses present for both sides. Go your way." But the journey was only symbolic; the parties simply crossed to the other side of the court and were then told, "Return by the same road." The plaintiff then said to the defendant, "Since I see you here in court, will you tell me for what reason you have laid claim?" The response was: "I have done right, according as I have laid claim." Plaintiff: "Since you have laid claim unjustly, I challenge you by *sacramentum*[56] in the sum of 500 *asses*." Defendant: "And I challenge you." The praetor then took guarantees (*praedes*) from both parties to ensure payment of the *sacramentum* by the eventual loser. After these preliminaries had been completed, the parties were given notice to appear again in thirty days, when the praetor would appoint a *iudex* to judge the case, and the trial itself was fixed for the next day but one.[57] The judge's verdict was expressed as an instruction to the loser to pay the *sacramentum* because he had claimed unjustly. The winner won, as it were, by default.

(e) Praetorian law: the Edict, formulae, interdicts

The *legis actiones* came to be seen as inflexible, not primarily because of their ritualised formality, but because the set of remedies they provided was limited to the situations explicitly stated in the relevant laws. The best known example given by Gaius (4.11) is of a man who sued his neighbour for cutting down his vines; but the Twelve Tables only provided a remedy *de arboribus succisis* "for cutting down trees"; vines were not mentioned in the law, and consequently the poor farmer got no redress. If you, a Roman citizen, had a piece of property stolen by a foreigner, you could not sue for compensation, as the law only admitted actions against citizens. If a woman owed you money, and married by *coemptio* (a form of marriage in which she leaves her father's family and joins her husband's), she was held to have formally changed her identity and was no longer your debtor at civil law, so you could not sue her for repayment.

By a *Lex Aebutia* passed, perhaps, some time in the second century BCE, the *legis actiones* were largely (not entirely) replaced by the "formulary" system, in which the praetor (or other competent magistrate) was virtually able to grant an action on any *prima facie* case presented to him.[58] The Praetor's Edict, issued at the beginning of each year, contained a list of types of case on which an action would be granted, and this was added to by successive praetors, so that by the Imperial period the Edict covered almost any eventuality that might arise.[59] The new procedure was very simple. A praetorian "formula" is an instruction to a judge setting out the issue to be decided. In a disputed debt, for example, it might read: "You are to be judge. If it seems that Numerius Negidius ought to pay Aulus Agerius 10,000 sesterces, in respect of the matter in dispute, you are to condemn N.N. to A.A. in that sum." (The names are conventional and invented, and would of course be replaced in real life by the names of the parties.)[60] The formula was almost infinitely variable. In particular, it provided for the scope of the law to be extended by treating one set of facts like another, by the simple expedient of the use of conditional clauses, e.g.: "If it appears that the theft has taken place by Dio son of Hermaeus of a golden goblet, whereby, if he were a Roman citizen, he would be bound to make restitution, you are to condemn Dio son of Hermaeus to make restitution to Aulus Agerius." The jurists describe this as a "fiction", as though one had to pretend that Dio was a

Roman in order to obtain a legal remedy against him. But there is no pretence. One simply asks: if Dio *were* a Roman, how would he be treated? Let us, then, treat him the same way.

There were still pitfalls in the formulary system, in which the literal interpretation of the words could override apparent equity. For instance, if you, as plaintiff, obtained a formula claiming that your opponent owed you 20,000 sesterces in respect of the matter in dispute, and the judge found that he only owed you 10,000, you would get nothing at all. This might seem unfair, yet there was some merit in a system that discouraged excessive claims. You would have been better advised to get a formula (supposing the praetor would issue one) saying "whatever amount N.N. owes to A.A. you are to condemn him in that sum." Hence the role of the expert legal adviser was still important, even when the jurist was no longer needed to ensure correct performance of the rituals of the *legis actiones.*

Another aspect of praetorian procedure was the interdict, essentially an order by the praetor to do something or to abstain from some act. Interdicts, again, were strictly formulaic, and were classified according to their opening words. An order to produce a person or thing was called *exhibeas* ("you are to exhibit"); one requiring restitution of property was called *restituas* ("you are to restore"); one forbidding an illegal action was called simply *ueto* ("I forbid"). If a *paterfamilias* grossly mismanaged his property, the praetor could grant an interdict to pass control of it to other members of his family (*interdictio bonorum*). Other interdicts were used to prevent disturbance of possession pending the outcome of judicial proceedings: these were called *uti possidetis* ("as you possess") for real property, and *utrubi* ("wherever") for movable property. Another interdict of the same general kind, *de ui armata*, makes a spectacular appearance in one of Cicero's speeches, the *pro Caecina*. Caecina was claiming possession of a farm from which, he alleged, he had been ejected by force. The case had gone from the praetor to a jury of *recuperatores* and they had failed to make up their minds after two earlier hearings. Cicero makes fun of over-literal interpretations of the words of the interdict, and asks the jury to consider the substance of the issue; then he turns round and produces a literal interpretation of his own – a classic Ciceronian dilemma, which well exemplifies the principle (argued for in *de Orat.* 1.238–239 and elsewhere) that a good orator, who is an expert in the use of language, can outmanoeuvre any legal expert.[61]

(f) Contracts, wills and other documents

The last aspect of legal drafting that we must consider concerns what modern lawyers call legal instruments, i.e. documents drafted in accordance with a set procedure in order to effect some legal act such as the making of a contract or the disposition of property by will. Again, precise use of language was paramount. As we have seen, the old Roman form of contract (and the only one strictly enforceable at civil law) was the oral *sponsio.* Roman legal thinking seems to have been slow to grasp the concept of a written contract: the documents in question always take the form of mere written records of the formal oral agreement which constituted the actual contract. Nevertheless, such written documents were used frequently, especially in commercial contexts where there was influence from Greek practice, and although they recorded Roman procedures and were written in

Latin, they were referred to by the Greek word *chirographum* "handwritten document".
Many examples have been found at Pompeii. Particularly interesting are those written
by Greek slaves and freedmen. Some of the parties concerned were very bad at writing
Latin, and in those cases the original text was accompanied by a second version in
correct spelling. The texts are entirely formulaic, but the misspellings provide valuable
evidence for the pronunciation of Latin (or, more precisely, the way Greek speakers
tried to represent the sounds of Latin) at the time. Here is an example[62] in the authentic
bad spelling, for which I provide an approximate English equivalent. The oath by
Jupiter, Augustus and the current emperor Gaius is presumably an effort to stave off
proceedings for recovery.

> C Nouius Eunus scripssi me debere
> Hesuco C Cessaris Augusti Germanic
> ser Eueniano stertertios mile
> ducentos quiquaginta nummos
> reliquos ratione omini putata
> quos ab eo mutos accepi quem
> suma iuratus promissi me
> aut ipssi Hesuco aut C Sulpicio
> Fausto redturum K Noembribus
> primis per Iobe Optumm Maxu
> mu et nume Dibi Augusti et
> genium C Cessaris Augusti

I Gaius Novius Eunus have ritten that I owe to Hesucus [i.e. Hesychus] Euenianus serv[ant]
of C. Cessar Augustus Germanic. one thousnd two hundred and fiffty sterterces (*sesterces*)
remaining from the tottal account which I received as a lone from him. This summ I have
promissed to retrn either to Hesucus in person or to C. Sulpicius Faustus on the 1st of
Noember next following. I swear by Jupitter Bst and Greatst and the sprit of the Defied
Augustus and the Genius of C. Cessar Augustus.

One further type of legal document should be briefly considered: the will.[63] To be valid
under Roman law, a will generally had to be in writing (though there were exceptions);
it had in the first place to institute an heir or heirs in the form *Titius heres esto* ("let Titius
be my heir), and other formulations such as *Titium heredem esse uolo* ("I wish Titius to be
my heir") were regarded as invalid; it had to dispose of the whole estate; and it had to be
formally signed, using the word *subscripsi* ("I have subscribed") and in the presence of
seven witnesses. Several heirs could share the estate in any proportions; the commoner
proportions were expressed, rather quaintly, by the set of terms used for fractions of the
as (in weight or coinage): *semis* (half), *triens* (third), *quadrans* (quarter), etc. Persons
other than the heirs (subject to statutory regulation) could receive legacies (*legata*): the
distinction between inheritance and legacy was fundamental. Other dispositions could
also be made in a will, e.g. slaves could be manumitted. A freeborn child had to be either
specifically instituted as an heir or specifically disinherited (*exheres*). If the will failed to
follow the proper form it was void, and the estate was then dealt with according to the
intestacy laws. Again, the importance attached to following precise linguistic conventions
is striking.

Legal Latin in Post-Classical Europe[64]

Latin continued to be used as the common written language of public transactions in Western Europe for many centuries after the fall of the Western Empire. The immediate successor states continued to use Roman law and some compilations from that period survive. After Justinian's great codification, the system of Roman civil law survived in Greek adaptation in the Eastern Empire; the *Digest* was translated into Greek in the later sixth century. In the West, the Roman Church used Latin throughout and certain elements of Roman law were incorporated into the canon law (which for example retains the threefold division into Persons, Things and Actions – the third of these however now divided into Processes and Penalties). Some of the Germanic nations to the north had their own law codes (for example the *Lex Salica* and the *Lex Ripuaria*, the laws of the Salian and Ripuarian Franks respectively) which were written in a form of contemporary Latin, certainly not the Latin of Classical jurisprudence, with some of the terms glossed in the local language for greater precision. The communities of Spain and Italy continued to use a system descended from Roman law, and legal records were kept in forms of Latin which reflected spoken usage.[65] In France, Roman law was used in the south, while Frankish customs prevailed in the north; this variation persisted up to the time of Napoleon I who imposed a single Roman-based code, formulated in French but incorporating much Latinate terminology (e.g. *dol* for "fraud", from *dolus*).

In the eleventh and twelfth centuries, with the establishment of the universities, there was a rediscovery of Roman law based on the original texts, and the academic study of law may be said to have begun then; the nations of Europe differed in the extent to which these researches were allowed to affect actual legal decisions. In Germany (the "Holy Roman Empire") and the Netherlands, the deliberate decision was made to adopt Roman law, as transmitted through the universities, as the law of the land (the so-called "Reception"): this decision was made for practical reasons, in order to replace the variety of local customs with a uniform system, and the only developed system conveniently available for this purpose was Roman law. The Roman-based law of Holland was taken to the Dutch settlements overseas, especially South Africa; it also survived in Sri Lanka long after the period of Dutch rule. At least until recently, a knowledge of Latin was considered essential for the study of law in those countries.

English law, despite its non-Roman origins, has been influenced by Roman legal thinking to some extent (Scottish law has been so influenced to a greater extent), and its traditional mixture of languages (English, Norman French, and Latin) reflects its complex history. After the Norman Conquest, the common-law courts used medieval French, but what may be called the civil service was in the hands of ecclesiastics, and therefore used Latin. Hence, for example, the Latin names of writs such as *mandamus* (an instruction from a higher court to a lower one to hear a particular case), *certiorari* (an instruction to have the decision of a lower court re-examined by a higher one),[66] and *fieri facias*, abbreviated to *fi.fa.* (an instruction to the sheriff to enforce payment of a judgement debt).[67] These specialised uses of Latin words reflect medieval administrative jargon rather than Roman law. The Lord Chancellor's (or Chancery) Court dealt directly with petitions on matters outside the scope of the common law, and its principles and decisions gradually developed into the system of "equity".[68] Many of those principles were embodied in pithy medieval Latin phrases or "maxims", such as *uolenti non fit injuria* "no injury is done to a willing party"; *ultra suum posse nemo cogitur* "nobody is compelled beyond his powers"; *de minimis non curat lex* "the law does not concern itself with trifles"; *delegatus non potest delegare* "a person delegated cannot delegate to another"; *qui facit per alium facit per se* "one who acts through another acts for himself". These maxims now tend to appear in English form, but are still better known (and more laconic) in their original Latin. There is a clutch of Latin terms connected with such matters as wills, inheritances, and guardianship, which were within the province of the Chancery Court: administrator *pendente lite* (while a suit is pending), guardian *ad litem* (guardian appointed for the purposes of litigation), gift *inter uiuos* (between living persons, as opposed to one made by will). A further source of Latin phrases is the language of jurisprudence, which has always been influenced by both Roman and canon law: here we find, for example, *mens rea* "guilty intention" and *actus reus* "guilty act", or *ratio decidendi* "rationale for a decision". There are many more.[69]

In English courts there is now a virtual ban on the public use of Latin phrases; this is supposed to make things easier for the ordinary citizen to understand. In reality it makes little difference, because the English terminology of the law is in any case so complex and technical as to baffle the non-specialist. Nevertheless, some members of the legal profession still find the Latin terms and phrases convenient, and regard them with affection. A barrister once told me that he had said in court "If I were allowed to use Latin here, I would say *res ipsa loquitur*"; and the judge did not object.

FURTHER READING

A good account of legal Latin is to be found in De Meo (2005) 67–131; see also Kalb (1888), Pascucci (1968), Powell (2005a). Gradenwitz *et al.* (1903) provide a comprehensive dictionary of Roman legal terms. For general treatments of the terminology and concepts of Roman law see e.g. Schulz (1951), Lee (1956), Nicholas (1988).

NOTES

1   The qualification "largely" is necessary, because the Romans themselves were happy to believe that their legal system was initially formed under Greek influence; the Twelve Tables were supposed to have been drafted partly on the model of the laws of Solon. There are, in fact, many similarities between the language of early Roman law and that of contemporary Greek law (not only or primarily Athenian), and it is tempting to think in terms of a common Greco-Italian legal culture; see e.g. Courtney (1999) 13–14. But the Classical development of Roman legal practice (as distinct from the philosophical theory of law) was doubtless due to native Roman creativity, rather than the adoption of foreign models. A relatively minor exception was the adoption by the Romans of Greek maritime law (the *Lex Rhodia*): the Romans did not become a seafaring people until relatively late, and the Roman civil law had no resources of its own for dealing with maritime matters.

2 It should be noted that "civil law" in this context means simply "the law that applies to Roman citizens", as opposed to foreign or international law. The modern English distinction between "civil" and "criminal" does not exist as such in Roman law, although the difference between public trials (*iudicia publica*) and private actions is in some respects analogous.

3 I recently saw a draft will which ended "In witness whereof I have hereunto set my hand and seal to this my Will". I objected that "hereunto" means "to this" and is therefore redundant; but my solicitor insisted that the wording was right. For misunderstood linguistic forms in Latin legal language cf. p. 472.

4 See e.g. Wallace (2006) 422–423.

5 There was however nothing to prevent a jurisconsult from fulfilling such functions; a legal expert who became urban praetor, for example, as did Servius Sulpicius, would have the opportunity to influence the development of the law embodied in the praetorian edict. See in general Harries (2006).

6 Who almost certainly tended to develop a better knowledge of the law than many of their employers. Cicero, *Leg.* 2.46 strikingly comments "Statute law is whatever our *apparitores* want it to be", presumably because magistrates relied entirely on their assistants to look up the relevant statutes. To be able to look up the right chapter of the right statute implies a considerable familiarity with legal forms on the part of the *apparitores*. It was apparently a public-spirited *scriba* who, in 304 BCE, first thought of publishing the forms of action and the legal calendar, so that citizens could find these things out for themselves (see Cic. *Mur.* 25; *OCD*³ s.v. Flavius, Gnaeus; Harries (2006) 39–40).

7 Cicero implies in the *Leg.* (2.9; 2.59) that both he and his friend Atticus (the latter of whom never made any pretence to legal learning) studied the Twelve Tables in their boyhood, and they both attended the consultations of Scaevola the Augur, the greatest jurist of the early first century BCE.

8 *Mur.* 25–9: the point is not relevant to the law bearing on the case, but is part of an argument to show that the jurist Servius Sulpicius was unlikely to have won the election in which his rival Murena was alleged to have bribed the electors. On the procedure parodied by Cicero see below pp. 475–476.

9 Principally those of Rome, Constantinople, and Beirut (Berytus).

10 De Meo (2005) 70–73. A full study of the influence of juridical language on Latin literature remains to be done.

11 Gaius (known always by this name; his other names are not known) was a jurist of the second century CE and the four books of his *Institutes*, discovered in a palimpsest at Verona in 1816, constitute the only surviving textbook of Roman law from before the time of Justinian.

12 Derived either from the verb *personare* "to sound through", referring to the mask's function as a megaphone (although the long *o* of *persona* is a problem on this hypothesis), or from Etruscan *phersu*, apparently a distortion of the Greek πρόσωπον ("face", "theatrical mask", "dramatic character"). For this and subsequent etymologies see Ernout and Meillet (1979) and De Vaan (2008) (the latter for words of native Latin origin only).

13 Cf. De Meo (2005) 80–82.

14 The latter were classified in the later civil law as *res incorporales*, "non-bodily things" (Gaius 2.12–13).

15 The phrase was used particularly in praetorian formulae, cf. pp. 476–477 below.

16 *Digest* 9.1.5.

17 The use of *nec* instead of *non* in contexts of this kind is an archaic feature, peculiar to legal language in the Classical period, except in the compounds *necopinans* and *necopinatus*; cf. De Meo (2005) 91–93.

18 *Quirites* is the plural of *Quiris* which survived in the singular only in the funeral formula *ollus Quiris leto datus est*, "that citizen is dead". It occurs regularly as a vocative in addresses to the

Roman people as a body, and in the formulaic phrases *populus Romanus Quiritium* and *ex iure Quiritium*. It is presumably connected with *Quirinus*, the posthumous name of the deified King Romulus; ancient etymologies connecting it with the Sabine town of *Cures*, or with an alleged word for "spear", are of doubtful status, and the true etymology remains unknown.

19 *Usus* is presumably a dependent genitive, reflecting the ablative with the verb; contrast the phrase *usus fructus* "usufruct" which is an asyndeton, "use and enjoyment".

20 This is just one of several applications of the word *reus*, whose original meaning was approximately "liable" or "having something at stake". Either party to a private suit was in earlier times called *reus*, whether plaintiff or defendant. One who had made a promise was *reus* until the promise was fulfilled; so also in the case of a vow to a god (*uoti reus*). In Medieval Latin it means "guilty", whence the modern legal terms *mens rea* "guilty intention" and *actus reus* "guilty act".

21 The gerundive suffix in -*undus*, rather than -*endus*, has an old-fashioned flavour and is characteristic of legal Latin, though neither confined to it nor universal in it.

22 A magistrate by virtue of his office represents the supremacy or sovereignty of the Roman people; an illegal act by a magistrate brings the Roman people as a whole into disrepute. The scope of the law appears to have been much extended under the Principate; see *OCD*[3] s.v. *maiestas*.

23 Cicero, *S. Rosc.* 57 "that letter to which you (accusers) are so hostile that you even hate the Kalends of every month".

24 There is no connection with *tristis* "sad" which has long *i* in the first syllable. *Testes* "testicles" and its diminutive *testiculi* are held to be a specialised use of *testes* "witnesses"; Greek medical writers called the testicles *parastatai* "comrades".

25 Cf. De Meo (2005) 75–77.

26 Martin (1990) s.v. "servient tenement".

27 *Legis latio*, i.e. the passing of a law, from *legem fero* "I pass a law"; always two words in Latin.

28 For example, the old civil law rules on inheritance led to injustice because a wife who had not formally joined her husband's family (as most did not) could not then inherit from her husband on his death. The praetor was able to remedy this by granting "possession" to the widow, thus bypassing the older law rather than altering it. The development of the *ius honorarium* bears some analogy to the development of equity within the English legal system (cf. notes 59 and 68 below). The word *honorarium* reflects the use of *honos* to mean a magistracy or public office; not "honorary" in our sense.

29 Etymology uncertain, but – surprisingly enough – neither *lex* nor its French derivative *loi* is related to the English word "law".

30 See Daube (1969) 11–63.

31 An old form of conveyance of title, whereby the seller and buyer appeared before a magistrate, the buyer formally laid claim to the thing concerned, and the seller formally relinquished his claim. One of the main uses of this procedure was in the sale of "servitudes" (cf. above), presumably as an insurance against future dispute.

32 De Meo (2005) 116–120; Powell (2005a) 132.

33 I.e. a down payment of a relatively small proportion of the purchase price. A "deposit" in a bank is *depositum*.

34 See De Meo (2005) 85–98, esp. 88–89 and 94–95; on these two usages outside legal contexts cf. also Powell (1988) 129 and 185.

35 See e.g. *Digest* 9.2.52 *si emptor boues emptos haberet, non debere praestare; sed si non haberet emptos ... etc.* This passage is excerpted in Russell (1990) 79–81 (no. 30) and gives a good impression of the style in which jurists' opinions were expressed. Cf. De Meo (2005) 99.

36 Ernout (1957) no. 148.

37 Buck (1955) no. 64.

38 De Meo (2005) 102–103; Powell (2005a) 127.

39 Cf. Daube (1956).

40 The penalty is well known: the convicted parricide was sewn in a sack with assorted animals and thrown into the sea. Cf. Cicero *S. Rosc.* 70; *Inv.* 2.149; Modestinus in *Digest* 48.9.9. How often it was actually applied is a matter for conjecture.

41 What name one gives this tense seems arbitrary. It is sometimes called "sigmatic future" but this is misleading, as many of the forms did not have -*s*-. The stem (with added -*s*- or -*ss*- in some verbs, simple root stem in others) is fairly clearly in origin an Indo-European aorist; the ending -*it* may be an old optative ending. Republican literary texts distinguish a future and a subjunctive from this stem, with the same endings respectively as the future perfect and the perfect subjunctive. For discussion of these forms see de Melo 2007b.

42 The surviving fragments of the Twelve Tables have been edited many times. The most convenient text with English translation and legal commentary is Crawford (1996) II.555–722. A selection with linguistic commentary in Courtney (1999) 13–26.

43 Note 17 above.

44 See Powell (2005a) 136–137.

45 It also has Greek legal parallels: *praxis esto* lit. "let there be recovery" i.e. let there be a right or obligation to recover a judgment debt.

46 In early times there had been a real difference between laws (*leges*) passed by the *populus Romanus* and plebiscites (*plebi scita*) passed by the plebeian assembly at the instance of a tribune; but by the later Republic the difference was purely formal.

47 The etymology of the verb *promulgo* is obscure, though it has been connected with the root *mulg*- "to milk" in an assumed sense of "extract", "bring out".

48 Crawford (1996) II.793–800.

49 Marouzeau (1959); cf. Powell (2005a) 121–122.

50 *Damnas* may be a syncopated form of the participle *damnatus*. In legal formulae it is treated as both singular and plural.

51 There is an alternative form *sirempse*; the suffix -*pse* may be connected with that found in *ipse*, and *si*- may be connected with *sic* "thus", but even this is speculative.

52 Crawford (1996) I.65–112.

53 The phrase for voting is *ire in consilium* which might seem to imply discussion as in a modern jury, but it is not clear whether this was the implication.

54 See Griffin (1997).

55 Ernout (1957) no. 126.

56 The word normally means "oath", but here it refers to a wager.

57 By the procedure of *comperendinatio*, most familiar from Republican trials for *repetundae*, but clearly it had existed in civil procedure long before that. Why the next day but one? Perhaps because most public holidays were on odd-numbered days of the month, whereas most days available for legal business were even-numbered days.

58 The formulary system is described by Gaius 4.30–60. See *T.Sulpicii* 31 for formulae issued by a local magistrate at Puteoli.

59 The Edict's clauses, whether by accident or design, followed almost exactly the archaic legal form: "Nobody is to do X. If anyone does …". The pay-off line was however not a specific penalty or sanction but a statement of intent on the part of the praetor, such as the following: *animaduertam* "I shall take cognisance" (euphemism for using powers of summary coercion); *cogam* "I shall compel"; *ratum non habebo* "I shall treat as null and void"; *seruabo* "I shall uphold", *dabo in integrum restitutionem* "I shall grant restitution" (i.e. compel the offender to repair the loss or damage; *in integrum* means that things should be put back the way they were before), or most commonly of all, *actionem dabo* or *iudicium dabo* "I shall grant a trial". Many of the clauses were highly generalised, e.g. there was one forbidding *dolus*

malus (fraud) in general terms. Nothing illustrates more clearly than the text of the Edict the almost unlimited powers of the Roman magistrate over ordinary citizens – and, on the other hand, the determination of successive office-holders to define clearly the ways in which they might use those powers and to protect the honest petitioner from injustice. See Kaser (1951).

60   Agerius is the plaintiff (from *ago* "to bring an action), Negidius a recalcitrant defendant (from *nego* "to deny"), cf. the real name Nigidius. Other names similarly used were "Titius" and "Seius", while "Gaia" might be used to substitute for the name of a woman.

61   Cicero's tactic is almost exactly the same as that of Lysias in 10 *Against Theomnestus*. One may, of course, choose to see this as an example of the baleful influence of rhetoric on Republican legal practice.

62   *T.Sulpicii* 68.2.3–14. For the language of the Novius Eunus tablets see Adams (1990).

63   See esp. Gaius 2.99–289.

64   For the history of Roman law in Europe from Justinian to the present day see e.g. Tamm (1997) 191–263.

65   See Wright (1982) 166–171, Migliorini and Griffith (1984) 40.

66   The verb *certiorare* (of which *certiorari* is the passive) is not found in Classical literary texts, which use *certiorem facere* for "to inform", but it is quite frequent in the writings of the imperial jurists.

67   Note that English lawyers traditionally pronounce these words according to English sound-spelling rules; e.g. *certiorari* is, or used to be, pronounced *sir-sher-air-eye*.

68   The English distinction between law and equity (*aequitas* "fairness") is now largely historical, but traces of it survive e.g. in the use of the word "equity" (short for "equity of redemption") in connection with mortgages. A borrower's interest in mortgaged property is "equitable", because it was not originally recognised by the common law: as long as one had not repaid the debt, the lender had a right to the whole value of the property.

69   For an amusing tour of Latin terms in English law, see Laws and Laws (2003).

CHAPTER 27

Christian Latin

Philip Burton

Well, by and by the king gets up and comes forward a little, and works himself up and slobbers out a speech, all full of tears and flapdoodle, about its being a sore trial for him and his poor brother to lose the diseased, and to miss seeing diseased alive after the long journey of four thousand mile, but it's a trial that's sweetened and sanctified to us by this dear sympathy and these holy tears, and so he thanks them out of his heart and out of his brother's heart, because out of their mouths they can't, words being too weak and cold, and all that kind of rot and slush, till it was just sickening; and then he blubbers out a pious goody-goody Amen, and turns himself loose and goes to crying fit to bust.

(Mark Twain, *The Adventures of Huckleberry Finn*, chapter 25)

Supposing we were historical linguists a millennium and a half from now, how far could we use the "king's" speech here as the basis for positing a distinctive form of "Christian English", and for identifying some of its characteristics? If we set the bar high and asked what features of the passage are rarely if ever used outside Christian discourse, we might be left with little more than the word *sanctified*; even *Amen*, and the metaphor of the *sore trial*, being familiar enough outside religious contexts. If we set the bar low, we might allow the phrase *holy tears* and the metaphor of "sweetening". Other linguistic features we might find noteworthy, but defying simple analysis; *dear sympathy* (with its transferred epithet) followed closely by *holy tears* creates a balanced pair which, like the alliterating *sweetened and sanctified* belongs ultimately to the neo-Classical tradition of pulpit rhetoric. To this we might add the anaphora of *trial*, the frigid *heart/mouth* antithesis, and the appended *sententia* of *words being too weak and cold*. The malapropism of *diseased*, however, we might regard a misplaced attempt at a genteelism, linguistically interesting in itself but having little specifically to do with Christianity, except in so far as death has traditionally received its social articulation in Christian terms. All this is arguably more a matter of stylistics than linguistics proper – a distinction which, however,

A Companion to the Latin Language, First Edition. Edited by James Clackson.
© 2011 Blackwell Publishing Ltd. Published 2011 by Blackwell Publishing Ltd.

tends to break down under examination. And further questions of context await us as putative linguists of the future; how far is this a specimen of "Christian English"? Samuel Clemens, we know, took some pains over the representation of different varieties of American English; but this remains a second-hand representation, by a fictional character, of an insincere attempt by another fictional character to pass himself off as a devout believer, in a work published pseudonymously by an author thoroughly acculturated to Christianity but none the less critical of many of its manifestations.

The issues confronting the reader of Christian Latin texts will not, of course, be identical. But there are significant overlaps. The language of Christian Latin texts does tend to differ from that found in non-Christian writings, even though there is a wide diversity of styles and registers within Christian writing.

Christian Latin, Biblical Latin, "Vulgar Latin"

Before proceeding further, we need to consider the nature of the evidence. Latin remains the main language for learned communication in Europe until some time between the sixteenth and eighteenth centuries. In other words, much of the Latin that has been written since around the fourth century has been written by Christians, often writing about Christianity or at least in contexts informed by Christianity. What *termini* do we set?

The starting-point is relatively easy to define. While the New Testament contains a number of Latin loanwords, many are connected with some of the less pleasant aspects of the *imperium Romanum*; examples include κῆνσος "census", κουστωδία "guard, custody", λεγιών "legion" (as collective name for demons), φραγελλόω "to whip". Continuous Christian texts in Latin, however, do not appear before the late second century; the *Acts of the Scillitan Martyrs*, a work commemorating deaths of a band of Christians in North Africa in 180 CE, is generally reckoned to be the first. From around 200 CE we have the works of Tertullian and Minucius Felix, and an unbroken literature from the mid-third century onwards (Heine (2004)). Our earliest biblical manuscripts date from the late fourth century, but it is possible from citations in Christian writers to identify some textual traditions as going back to around the year 250 if not before.

There is no clear cutting-off date for Christian Latin. In its absence, we have considered here nothing written later than the sixth century. Broadly speaking, most Latin written before this date will be written by native speakers of the language, within the territory of the high Empire; after this date a higher proportion of Christian texts are written by non-native speakers, if in many cases entirely fluent writers of the language. It will be clear from this that much of our Latin will overlap with what is known as "Late Latin" and "Medieval Latin" (both also impossible to date objectively; see Adams and Dinkova-Bruun in this volume).

Christian Latin must be located also in sociolinguistic as well as chronological space. It is often stated that Christian Latin reflects popular rather than educated usage. Certainly not all the Latin used by Christians was of the highest literary standard. Augustine in his *de Doctrina Christiana* 2.13, 4.10 (composed around 400) gives several examples of non-standard usages that might be heard among Christians; the transference of *ignosco* ("to forgive") from the Classical third to the second conjugation, the use of the ablative case in the phrase *inter hominibus* ("among men") rather than the Classical accusative (*inter homines*); the use of the regularized paradigm *ossum* (genitive *ossi*) of the word for "bone", as against the Classical *os* (genitive *ossis*). His examples are rather a mixed bag. Transference of verbs from the third to more regular second (or fourth) conjugation is a notable feature of Romance languages, and no doubt *ignoscere* reflects this; but alternation of this kind had operated in Latin for centuries and seems to have been widespread. Likewise *inter hominibus* is "wrong" from the standpoint of Classical grammar, but perhaps not an out-and-out vulgarism; syncretism between the accusative and ablative cases again can be traced back centuries in Latin (Coleman (1976)), though usually to the detriment of the ablative not the accusative; this is perhaps best seen as a hypercorrection, and probably not a feature of daily speech. *Ossum* for *os* is the closest to being a straightforward feature of popular speech, as such imparisyllabic words are often replaced or remodelled.

It is perhaps notable that Augustine's *ossum* is the only one of his examples taken specifically from biblical Latin (Psalm 138:15). We can only speculate on the motives behind the early Latin Bible translators' linguistic choices. However, it seems clear that they were prepared to sacrifice literary usage to the twin values of accuracy and clarity. So, for instance, biblical translators do not often use the verb *fleo* ("to weep"), preferring instead the quite Classical if less high-flown *ploro* or *plango*. Likewise, they will use rare and semi-technical words if they capture the meaning of the Greek best; thus the verb *transfreto* ("to cross a body of water") is rare in Classical Latin, but common in biblical Latin and wider Christian usage. Many features of biblical Latin, then, are probably best identified as belonging to a sort of post-Classical *koiné* rather than to any definitely stigmatized register. For instance, the widespread use of *ciuitas* rather than *urbs* as the standard word for "city" may be seen with hindsight as early evidence for one of the distinctive changes between Latin and the Romance languages; as indeed it is. But the semantic step from the Classical sense "citizenry" is not a long one, and there is no evidence this was perceived as a vulgarism. Similarly the verb "to go" in biblical Latin usually follows a suppletive conjugation which (again) anticipates those of Romance (*uado/uadis/uadit/(ab)imus/(ab)itis/uadunt*) – but because all the individual forms are entirely Classical in themselves, it is hard to imagine a context in which a purist could object.

Christian Latin, then, is occasionally prepared to admit features of the popular language which might be unacceptable in other varieties. Inevitably, there are borderline cases. Augustine's older contemporary Jerome on one occasion censures his ex-friend Rufinus of Aquileia (*aduersus Rufinum* 3.16) for using the verb *comparo* ("to buy") rather than *emo*. But elsewhere Jerome commits the same catachresis himself (*Commentarii in Danielem* 1.2). And Christian protestations that their humble language reflects the humility of their religion should be treated as apologetics rather than sociolinguistics. Typical is the apology offered by another early fifth-century author, Sulpicius Severus "if my speech, perchance ungrammatical, should grate on [my readers'] ears, for the Kingdom of God consists not in eloquence but in faith" (*si is aures eorum uitiosus forsitan sermo perculerit, quia regnum dei non in eloquentia sed in fide constat*) (Prologue 3, *Vita Martini*) – a perfect specimen of mannered Late-Antique prose artistry.

How discrete an entity is this Christian Latin? According to one influential theory, particularly associated with the Nijmegen scholars Johannes Schrijnen (1932) and Christine Mohrmann (1958–1977), the Christian community constituted a "special language" from an early date, and all its literature, including its biblical translations, reflects this language. The second part of this theory is, of course, ultimately unprovable, since by definition we have no direct evidence for any Christian Latin before our first sources. And while it is likely that Latin-speaking communities did exist before extensive biblical translations were prepared – since such translations are unlikely to have been made were an audience not already to hand – there is probably a consensus now that many of the typical features of attested Christian Latin are derived from these biblical translations. Furthermore, the evidence we have is extremely varied: Christian texts from this period include biblical translations, sermons given to the populace, commentaries using developed literary and philosophical models of exegesis, expositions of Christian doctrine or history in the polished forms of Classical verse, acts of the martyrs, narratives of pilgrimage, monastic rules. We would expect considerable variety in their language and style, and that is what we find (Coleman (1987)). However, a number of linguistic features do recur across a range of texts, and these we may loosely label as constituting Christian Latin, though their distribution varies widely.

Such features are found most frequently on the level of lexis, and much of our discussion will be focused on this. However, Christian Latin does contains a handful of syntactic devices which are also used widely in free composition by Christian writers, with a higher frequency than is usual in Classical Latin. Typically these features have close counterparts in the Greek of the Bible, and are carried over from there into biblical Latin, and thence into wider Christian use. These include frequent use of present participles to give the backdrop to the main verb (a Graecism traceable back to Republican Latin; Clackson and Horrocks (2007) 191–192; Calboli (2009) 136–137); frequent use of the infinite of purpose, especially after verbs of motion (Calboli (2009) 130–133); frequent use of *quod*, *quoniam*, and (especially) *quia* to introduce indirect speech (Adams in this volume), rather than the accusative and infinitive. It is a commonplace of the study of syntactic interference that where language *A* is under influence from language *B*, then long-term changes are likely to be felt less in the creation of radically new syntactic devices in language *A* than in the promotion of those existing devices in language *A* which have counterparts in language *B* (Coleman (1975)). These forms of interference illustrate this principle very neatly.

Conversely, there are a few constructions found in biblical Latin which are rare in free composition by Christian authors. For instance, in biblical Greek it is quite common to find "why?" questions introduced with the phrase ἵνα τί, "so that what"; Latin translators often render this literally as *ut quid*, a phrase which seems to have been perfectly comprehensible but which never really gains any currency outside biblical translations. So also one finds instances of the genitive of comparison in biblical translations, which again are not totally incomprehensible to the Latin speaker (it is a short step from the Classical *maximus est illorum*, "he is the biggest of them" to the less idiomatic *maior est illorum*, "he is bigger than them") (Coleman (1987) 40–41). But again, this usage never becomes widespread. So also one finds sporadic instances in biblical translations of Classical *pluralia tantum* nouns in the singular, such as *tenebra* or *insidia*; or of Hebrew-style use of participles to intensify the action of a verb, such as *exspectans exspectaui* ("I waited patiently"; Psalm 39:2), *ueniens ueniet* ("he shall surely come"; Habbakuk 2:3); compare also the nominal *desiderio desideraui* ("I have longed sorely"; Luke 22:15), and the gerundival *praecipiendo praecipimus* ("we charge you earnestly"; Acts 5:28) (see García de la Fuente (1994) 219–220); or of the Hebrew-style genitive of description, such as *uir desideriorum* ("a man well beloved"; Daniel 9:23), or *uir sanguinum* ("a bloodthirsty man"; 2 Regnorum 16:7). It should be noted, however, that the distinction between "free composition" and allusion to another text is not an absolute one, and sometimes these constructions surface in contexts where it is questionable whether or not a biblical reference is present.

The Lexicon of Christian Latin

But it is in lexis that Christian Latin writers are most sharply differentiated from others. The new religion called a new technical terminology to express its concepts. Sometimes this took the form of new words, sometimes of the revalorization of existing Latin terms. Three main processes in the creation of a Christian vocabulary are usually identified: *lexical borrowing*, by which Greek (or occasionally Semitic) terms are borrowed into Latin; *calquing* or *loan translation*, by which new Latin terms are created on the model of Greek terms; and *semantic extension*, by which existing Latin words receive new senses on the model of Greek words they translate (Haugen (1950)). To take a simple illustration of each, *baptizo* ("to baptize") is a straightforward borrowing from Greek βαπτίζω; *glorifico* ("to glorify") is a calque or loan-translation of δοξάζω; and *uirtus* ("miracle") is a semantic extension of an existing Latin term, on the model of Greek δύναμις.

There was no historical inevitability about the way these different processes would interact. One has only to think of the way modern European languages have dealt with similar processes. German provides many of the textbook examples of calquing (*Wolkenkreuzer* for "skyscraper", *Fernsprecher* for "telephone", and so on), while French notoriously has difficulty resisting the tide of Anglo-Saxon invasions (*le weekend*, *le sandwich*). No one process is predominant in Latin; but we can perhaps discern the following trends:

- Lexical borrowing is extremely frequent and successful for *nouns*. This cross-linguistic trend, first identified by the Sanskritist Dwight Whitney (1881), is amply illustrated by Christian Latin: *angelus* ("angel"), *baptismus* ("baptism"), *catechumenus* ("catechumen"), *diabolus* ("devil"), *eleemosyne* ("alms"), and so on. Early attempts to find native Latin equivalents for Greek nouns are often largely abandoned; so *similitudo* ("likeness") is found in some earlier biblical versions and wider Christian writings to describe Jesus' parables, but it is *parabola* which not only wins out but provides one of the most common Romance words for "word" (French *parole*, Spanish *palabra*, Italian *parola*, and so on).
- Among *verbs*, those with the -ιζω suffix in Greek are far more likely to be borrowed than those of other morphological categories: *anathemizo* ("to anathematize"), *baptizo* ("to baptize"), *colaphizo* ("to beat"), *daemonizor* ("to be demon-possessed"), *eunuchizo* ("to castrate"), and so on. The *-izo/-isso* suffix had been familiar in Latin at least since Plautus, so this is largely an extension of an established pattern. It is thus among verbs that calques and semantic modifications are most successful; *glorifico/ honorifico* ("to glorify"), *magnifico* ("to make much of, magnify"), *sanctifico* ("to hallow"), *benedico* ("to bless"). Other Greek verbs are seldom borrowed, and calques or

semantic modifications usually win out. The point may be illustrated by the case of two εὐ- compound verbs and their Latin equivalents. The Greek verb εὐαγγελίζω ("to tell good news") is in some early biblical translations calqued as *benenuntio*. But while this calque remains in use in citations of a handful of biblical verses (e. g. Psalm 95:2), it never really gains wider currency; whereas the loanword *euangelizo* enjoys considerable success. In contrast, the Greek εὐλογέω ("to bless") is always translated as *benedico*, and the loanword is not found at all.

- More generally, the more easily a Greek loanword could be assimilated to Latin morphophonology, the less likely it was have competition from Latin calques or semantic modifications, and vice versa. Thus *misericordia* (in the sense "alms") is relatively successful, due to the rather awkward form of *eleemosyne*, while from Tertullian onwards *trinitas* ("trinity") is the standard rendering of ἡ τριάς.

- As in other technical registers of Latin, Greek may be used either as an insiders' term *or* as a distancing device. Latin-speaking Christians in general clearly feel no embarrassment about using Greek terms per se, but can easily use them for polemical effect in debate with other religious groups, such as Gnostics and Manichees: thus *monas* and *dyas* ("monad" and "dyad") (but not *trias*, "triad, trinity"); *pleroma* ("fullness") as the title of an aeon in Gnosticism, but *plenitudo* when the same Greek term is used in Christian contexts; *aeon* ("aeon") again of the Gnostic concept, versus *saeculum* in Christian use.

- The category of semantic extension is likewise more complex than it may first appear. The case of *uirtus* and δύναμις is relatively straightforward. But we might distinguish at least three other sub-classes of this phenomenon:

  Semantic focus, where part of the semantic domain of a given word comes to particular prominence; so for instance *gentes* and *nationes* gain the specific sense "the heathen, the Gentiles" (based on biblical Greek τὰ ἔθνη, and beyond that on Hebrew *goyim*), while never quite losing their wider sense ("peoples").

  Semantic innovation, where an existing word comes to mean something not obviously related to its previous senses; so for instance *sacramentum* comes to mean "sacrament, efficacious sign", on the model of the Greek τὸ μυστήριον, both words having a lexical root meaning "holy" plus an instrument-noun suffix. This is not transparently connected to its previous Classical senses (most often "military oath"); though the two senses can interact with each other (e. g. as when the sacrifice of baptism is seen as equivalent to a soldier's enrolment in the army).

  Canonized metaphor, where a word comes to be used primarily or exclusively in a metaphorical sense; so for instance *collyrium* ("eye-salve") is common in Christian use of any unpleasant but morally beneficial experience, on the model of Revelation 3:13 (*collyrio inungue oculos tuos ut uideas*, "anoint your eyes with salve, so you may see"); or *flagellum* ("whip" in Classical Latin) in Christian usage often means "scourge, affliction", on the model of Greek μάστιξ (compare Psalm 31:10, *multa flagella peccatoris*, "many are the scourges of the sinner"); or *plaga* ("blow") becomes especially frequent in the sense "stroke of misfortune, divine chastisement" (compare Deuteronomy 28:59, *augebit dominus plagas tuas*, "the Lord shall increase your chastisements"). The last of these metaphors is found in Classical Latin also, but becomes canonical in Christian usage.

Test-case: episcopus

The competing claims of loanwords, semantic modifications, and calques may be illustrated from the Greek ἐπισκοπός ("overseer" in secular Greek, "bishop" in Christian usage) and its Latin equivalents. Although the loanword *episcopus* is not attested in secular Latin, it may well have been familiar in non-literary use, through Romans who used Greek-speaking slaves or freedmen to administer their affairs. It is in any event borrowed very early among Christians; Tertullian, our first major Christian Latin writer, uses it frequently without feeling compelled to explain the term. And despite its transparently Greek origins, it quickly acquires Latin derivational morphology; *episcopatus* "episcopacy" is frequent from Tertullian onwards, perhaps a with semi-humorous reference to such Latin terms as *consulatus, magistratus,* and *principatus*. Other Latin affixes follow: *episcopalis* from Ambrose, even the adverb *episcopaliter* in Augustine. In short, few loanwords establish themselves so early and so widely.

There seems, however, to be a fairly wide awareness of the metaphor implicit in the Greek word – that of an estate manager, responsible to the owner for the governance of the estate but also helping the tenants to farm profitably. For this reason, the bishop is often described by Latin writers as god's *dispensator* ("steward"), a use reinforced by Titus 1:7: "An *episcopus* should be beyond reproach, as being god's *dispensator*." Occasionally also we find other terms used: *praeses* ("person in charge") or some form of *administro* ("to manage, administer"); very occasionally *visitator* ("inspector"). This is an example of what has been called the "penumbra principle" in Christian Latin; a Greek term has one or two more or less recognized Latin equivalents, plus various others which may be used but which are less likely to be perceived as equivalents to the Greek.

We might expect Latin writers to attempt to render it through loan translations, especially early on, but this does not happen on any large scale; Augustine more than once explains the term to his flock with the calque *superintentor* or a paraphrase involving the verb *superintendo* ("to have care over"), but this use does not take off until over a thousand years later, when Protestant writers find it useful for avoiding the ecclesiastical associations of *episcopus*.

From the fourth century we find bishops described by the Classical words *antistes* and *sacerdos* ("(high) priest"). Curiously, and perhaps because of its very specific associations with Roman state cult, *pontifex* takes longer to emerge, and indeed its earliest use is firmly derogatory: Tertullian, *de Pudicitia* 1.27 pictures the Roman Pontiff, Bishop of bishops (*pontifex, episcopus episcoporum*) posting notices on brothel doors proclaiming absolution to their clients. Its rise in frequency, from the late fourth century onwards, may reflect on the one hand the increasing prominence of bishops such as Ambrose or Augustine as civic and religious leaders. On the other, it may suggest a growing confidence in the Christian community, and a sense that terms which were formally taboo because of their pagan associations were now safe to use – or alternatively a sort of cultural cringe, in which Christian institutions felt under pressure to dress themselves up in the language of paganism to assert their respectability.

Further Lexical Phenomena

We have concentrated so far on the creation of new words and the revalorization of existing words as a means to express the new theological vocabulary of Christianity. However, four less obvious features also merit attention:

First, we occasionally find a sort of taboo process operating, by which familiar and potentially useful Latin words are largely avoided by Christian authors. So, for instance, the most frequent word for "prayers" is not the Classical *preces* but rather *oratio* (whose semantic centre of gravity has now shifted from Classical Latin "speech, language"). Likewise *ara* ("altar") is vastly less common than *altare*. Presumably in both cases this avoidance is motivated by a desire to avoid associations with pagan religion; though the taboo is not a strict one, and Christian poets will use *preces* and *ara* freely. This tendency is, however, very arbitrary in its operation, and some pagan religious terms are freely employed; *expio* ("to purify by sacrifice"), for instance, is frequently found, despite its pagan associations.

Second, there is the increased frequency of a number of words and phrases which have little or no obviously Christian semantic content. These include *commoror* and *demoror* ("to stay, abide"), *desiderium* ("longing"), *dignor* ("to deign"), *infans* (in the sense "child, young person" rather than "baby"), *intueor* ("to look into", with the notion of special insight), *deduco* ("to lead, conduct"), *postulo* ("to ask") among others (Burton (2008)). While the examples considered here are sometimes used in contexts which are more or less "spiritual", very often they are not; it is their prominence rather than their mere presence which makes them semi-covert markers of Christian discourse.

Third, there are some subtle changes of construction, or of options for construction. Certain established Classical verbs come to take different cases, often on the basis of their Greek equivalents. Thus *operor* ("to give pains to"), in Classical Latin governing the dative case, in Christian use is regularly construed with the accusative on the model of the Greek ἐργάζομαι (a verb particularly used of divine activity in the Gospel according to John); in Christian use it means little more than "to do". *Benedico* ("to speak well of, to speak kindly to") similarly comes to take the accusative rather than the dative case; in Christian usage it now means "to bless", on the model of εὐλογέω. *Misereor* ("to have mercy on") is often construed with the dative case instead of the Classical genitive, though Greek influence is harder to establish here as the corresponding verb ἐλεέω usually takes the accusative case. Further examples of related phenomena are listed in García de la Fuente (1994) 272, whose focus is, however, on biblical Latin rather than wider Christian usage.

Fourth, there is a tendency to use certain forms which were apparently avoided in Classical Latin. This indeed seems to have been an early feature of Christian Greek usage – it has been plausibly suggested that the Christian use of τὸ εὐαγγέλιον in the singular instead of the vastly more common plural represents an attempt to use language both to act as a group marker and to re-engineer the speaker's view of the world; Christianity representing the "Good New", as opposed to the constant flood of "good news" of imperial conquest or munificence found in public decrees. In Christian Latin usage, numerous plural forms become frequent which are rare in Classical Latin. Perhaps the most familiar example is the opening of the Lord's Prayer, *pater noster qui es in caelis* – literally, "our father, who are in the *heavens*", rather than the more Classical singular *caelo* ("in heaven"). But there are many more. Augustine, commenting on the phrase *erue me de sanguinibus* (literally, "deliver me from bloods") observes: "We all know that in Latin one cannot say *sanguines* or *sanguina* ("bloods"); but because the Greek writer put it thus in the plural simply because that is what he found in the original Hebrew, the devout translator preferred to say something un-Latin rather than something unidiomatic" (*Enarrationes in Psalmos* 50.19.1) – the "idiom" in question being that of the church. This phenomenon is particularly noticeable among third-declension abstract nouns in *-as -atis* and in *-io -ionis*, and most especially so of their dative/ablative plural forms ending in *-ibus*. Forms such as *iniquitatibus* ("iniquities"), *obiurgationibus* ("criticisms"), *quaestionibus* ("questions"), *seductionibus* ("deceits"), *suauitatibus* ("sweetnesses"), *temptationibus* ("temptations"), *tribulationibus* ("tribulations") are attested in Classical Latin scantily if at all, but are not uncommon in Christian writers (see Burton (2007) 116–124). As with the case of τὸ εὐαγγέλιον in Greek, the motive seems to be in part one of group membership, and in part to do with the way these usages reflect the speaker's perception of the world. All the words in this list are either negative per se in their denotations, or have negative associations in a Christian context, often triggered by one or two specific biblical passages. A case in point is *quaestio* ("enquiry, question"); not obviously a negative word, but in Christian use associated with fruitless search for truth in the multiplicities of the sensible world, rather than the unity that is god. We may compare Ecclesiastes 7:30: "God made man simple, and they have entangled themselves in endless questionings" (*infinitis … quaestionibus*). None of this is actively wrong by the standards of Classical Latin, but cumulatively it indicates a willingness to go beyond the unwritten rules of the educated language.

These various linguistic phenomena do not, of course, occur in isolation from each other, neither is their distribution random. To gain a sense of how they interact, it may help to consider two diverse passages of ancient Christian Latin writing, which between them give some idea of the range of possibilities open to Christian writers:

Passage 1 Lactantius, Divinae Institutiones

Our first test case is from Lactantius, *Divinae Institutiones* 2.1. Lactantius (*c.* 240–320 CE) was a distinguished rhetorician, appointed by the emperor Diocletian to the chair of rhetoric at Nicomedia; deprived of his post following his conversion to Christianity around 300, he was subsequently made tutor to the emperor Constantine's son Crispus. The *Divinae Institutiones* were composed around 304–311:

gestio enim conuictis inanibus et hominum inpia uanitate detecta singularis dei asserere maiestatem, suscipiens utilius et maius officium reuocandi homines a prauis itineribus et in gratiam se cum ipsos reducendi, ne se, ut quidam philosophi faciunt, tanto opere despiciant neue se infirmos et superuacuos et nihili et frustra omnino natos putent, quae opinio plerosque ad uitia compellit. nam dum existimant nulli deo esse nos curae aut post mortem nihil futuros, totos se libidinibus addicunt et dum licere sibi putant, hauriendis uoluptatibus sitienter incumbunt, per quas imprudentes in laqueos mortis incurrant. ignorant enim quae sit hominis ratio: quam si tenere vellent, in primis dominum suum agnoscerent, uirtutem iustitiamque sequerentur, terrenis figmentis animas suas non substernerent, mortiferas libidinum suauitates non appeterent, denique se ipsos magni aestimarent atque intellegerent plus esse in homine quam uidetur: cuius uim condicionemque non aliter posse retineri, nisi cultum ueri parentis sui deposita prauitate susceperint. equidem sicut oportet de summa rerum saepenumero cogitans admirari soleo, maiestatem dei singularis quae continet regitque omnia in tantam uenisse obliuionem, ut quae sola debeat coli, sola potissimum neglegatur, homines autem ipsos ad tantam caecitatem esse deductos, ut uero ac uiuo deo mortuos praeferant, terrenos autem sepultosque in terra ei qui fundator ipsius terrae fuit.

For having refuted these empty arguments, and exposed the impious vanity of men, I rejoice, Emperor Constantine, to assert the majesty of the only god, taking up the more salutary and important task of calling men back from their wicked paths, and reconciling them to themselves, and to prevent them from despising themselves (as some philosophers do) so much that think themselves weak, superfluous, worthless, and born quite in vain. This point of view drives many to wickedness. For thinking themselves of no concern to god, or destined to non-existence after death, they give themselves over wholly to pleasures; and, thinking they have license to do so, set thirstily about drinking dry all pleasures – through which they run heedlessly into the snares of death. For they do not know their anthropology; if they would only keep this in mind, they would first and foremost acknowledge their Lord, pursue goodness and justice, and cease to subject their own souls to things fashioned of earth and to seek the fatal pleasures to which their whims lead them; in short, they would consider their own importance, and realize there is more in a human being than is apparent – the vital force of man being such that it can be maintained only by laying aside wickedness, and taking up the worship of the true Parent. Indeed, when I think on the sum of things, as I should and often do, it frequently amazes me that the majesty of the only god should have passed into such oblivion that what should alone be worshipped, is rather alone neglected; and that men have been brought to such blindness that they prefer the dead to the true and living god, and earthlings, buried in the earth, to him who was the founder of the earth itself.

Lactantius' approach is an excellent illustration of the cultural politics of writing Latin as an elite Christian in the early fourth century. Just as Lactantius takes over without major modification Euhemerus' views on the origin of pagan religion, so also he takes over the smooth, consciously rhetorical style of later Classical prose. It is a style drawing heavily on Cicero and the Younger Seneca, and is notable not so much for its distinctly Christian uses as for its continuity with the Classical manner. Trademark features include:

- balanced clauses and constructions; for example, *conuictis inanibus … uanitate detecta, reuocandi homines … ipsos reducendi* (the effect in both these cases heightened by chiasmus)
- periodic sentence construction, with the conclusion to the sentence completing the circuit of meaning; for example, *equidem, sicut oportet … potissimum negligatur*, contrasted with
- judicious use of short, telling sentences, such as *quae opinio plerosque ad uitia compellit*, and
- the characteristic Late-Antique positioning of the verb in the penultimate position, in the sequence modifier–verb–headword; for example, *dei asserere maiestatem, tantam uenisse obliuionem*. This construction has complex roots. It is frequently found in ancient Indo-European languages, and is established early on as a feature of Latin epic diction. When found in Classical prose, it is likely to have been felt as a poeticism; in

later imperial prose, it seems to be little more than a marker of a consciously "literary" style. Notable also are

- occasional Sallustian elements, here exemplified by the studied inconcinnity of the phrase *se infirmos et superuacuos et nihili et frustra omnino natos putent*, where the pronoun is modified first by two adjectives, then by a genitive of value, then by a more complex participial phrase.

Sometimes these elements combine; as, for instance, in the phrase *existimant nulli deo esse nos curae*. Here the predicative dative of *curae* is a construction particularly common in Sallust, and the whole clause is reminiscent of *Jug.* 75.8, *rati sese dis inmortalibus curae esse* ("thinking themselves an object of concern to the immortal gods"). In Lactantius' phrase, the adjective *nulli* may be construed either with *deo* ("they think we are of concern to no god") or with *curae* ("they think we are of no concern to god"). The former understanding is quite possible and perhaps the obvious one; the second has the merit of offering a stylish extended hyperbaton emphasizing the *nulli* ("of no concern at all ...") and an unusual (though quite Classical) use of the predicative dative with a qualifying adjective. It is entirely possible that ancient readers no less than modern are presented here with a choice between a rather prosaic and pedestrian interpretation, and a bolder and more imaginative one. Clearly reading a Christian text need not exclude such cultured games.

The sounds too are important. Notable within this one passage are:

- the general avoidance, or at least comparative infrequency, of rhyme between nouns and their modifying adjectives; for example, *conuictis inanibus, prauis itineribus, tantam obliuionem, tantam caecitatem*; in particular here, the avoidance of the *ibus ... ibus* rhyme
- the studied use of pararhyme elsewhere, as in *reuocandi ... reducendi*, or the sequence *agnoscerent . . sequerentur ... substernerent ... appeterent ... aestimarent ... . intellegerent*, with subtle variation to relieve the effect of mere virtuosity
- selective use of alliteration to highlight key words: for example, *uero ac uiuo, fundator ... fuit*
- anaphora of key words, with polyptoton; for example, *terrenos ... terra ... terrae*
- varied use of the Classical clausula system, with phrases often ending in the cretic + trochee sequence $(-\smile-|-\mathrm{x})$, or the double cretic $(-\smile-|-\smile\mathrm{x})$, or the double trochee $(-\smile|-\mathrm{x})$; for example, *uanitate detecta, sitienter incumbent, mortis incumbent* (all cretic + trochee), or *omnino natos putent, continet regitque omnia, mortuos praeferat* (all double cretic), or *obliuionem, esse curae*, or *negligatur* (all double trochee). These rhythms are further varied through resolution of long elements into shorts, as in *posse retineri* (resolved cretic + trochee).

So far we have considered essentially the formal elements of the composition, with little reference to the content. But again it is notable how strictly Lactantius sticks within the Classical vocabulary; for example:

Singularis Christian monotheism is classically expressed in the formula *credo in unum deum* ("I believe in one god"); occasionally we find also this one god described as *solus* or *unicus*. *Singularis* here is a good Classical word (it occurs 240 times in Cicero), but extremely rare in Christian statements of monotheistic belief (the later fourth-century writer Ambrosiaster actually rejects it as inappropriate to the Trinity). On the semantic level, *singularis* arguably conveys the notion of the qualitative uniqueness of the Christian god more prominently than his ontological uniqueness – it is a statement of monotheistic belief, but couched in terms that do not explicitly exclude a sort of Stoicizing understanding that this is the one true god of which others may be regarded as true but partial aspects. This is not, of course, Lactantius' message; but it leaves open this possibility at least as a sort of bargaining position with the educated pagan reader.

Colo/cultus   Christian writers tend to avoid *colo* when describing Christian worship, preferring a range of alternatives based on biblical Greek models, either calqued outright (e. g. *magnifico* < μεγαλύνω) or with their semantics heavily skewed by the Greek (e. g. *confiteor* < ὁμολογέω, *adoro* < προσκυνέω). The obvious explanation for this is the desire to avoid associations with pagan *cultus*, though this explanation is not fully satisfactory (no term has more pagan associations than *deus* itself). Rather it falls into a category of words which *some* Christian writers are prepared to use of Christian beliefs and practices, while others either decline to do so, or do so only reluctantly. A parallel for this would be *numen*, "divinity", and indeed the two words co-occur revealingly in a passage of Augustine, *Epistulae* 17.5: "Please be aware that among Catholic Christians … none of the dead is worshipped (*coli*), nothing made and created by god is worshipped as a divinity (*ut numen adorari*), but the one god himself, who made and created everything." Augustine's use illustrates perfectly this wider pattern; words such as *colo* and *numen* might be applied by outsiders to Christian beliefs and practices, and such usages are not intrinsically wrong; but they are not usually the preferred terms among Christians themselves.

Parens   Jupiter as supreme god is frequently invoked in Classical Latin as *pater*, "father". But in poetry in particular, we find also the terms *parens, genitor*, sometimes *sator*. There is little practical difference in meaning, but *parens* and *genitor* at least offer more metrical possibilities, along with the general sense of high-flown diction which stems from avoidance of the commonplace. In biblical Latin, and in wider Christian use, god is typically evoked as *pater* alone. By choosing *parens* here, then, Lactantius is able to draw implicit links with non-Christian usage, implicitly stressing the overlaps and continuities between Christianity and the best of the Classical tradition.

Fundator   In biblical Greek, the term usually found to describe god's creative activity is κτίζω ("to establish, create"); in biblical Latin and Christian usage this is generally represented as either *fundo* or *creo*. But while the agent-noun *creator* is found in biblical Latin, and is very widely used in Christian authors, *fundator* is not found in the Latin Bible and (when used of god) only very rarely outside. While the avoidance of the familiar word is a feature of the high style generally, Lactantius may more specifically be taking advantage of the civic association of the term. We are perhaps to think of the world as a city writ large, with god as its cosmic emperor; the emperor Constantine would shortly proclaim himself on his Arch at Rome to be *fundator quietis publicae* ("founder of public peace"), but similar formulas had been common on imperial coin-issues throughout the third century.

Even where Lactantius chooses an unusual word such as *sitienter* ("thirstily"), it is with good Classical authority; Cicero had used it at *Tusc.* 4.17.37. The traditional language of Roman politics and state cult is appropriated as easily as he adopts the Euhemeran critique of traditional religion, or the Stoic notion of the relationship between god and the world. Christian elements in the passage are kept low-key. So for instance the metaphors of the "wicked ways", or the "snares of death", or the "blindness" of the idolater all have biblical prototypes (*laquei mortis*: 2 Regnorum 22:6; Psalm 17:6; Proverbs 21:6; *pravis itineribus*: Proverbs 28:6), but equally all three metaphors may be paralleled from Cicero, despite the relative reluctance of Classical Latin authors to use nouns metaphorically. *Deductos*, on the other hand, we have noted as a semi-covert marker of distinctly Christian discourse.

Passage 2 The Itinerarium Antonini Placentini

The *Itinerarium Antonini Placentini* is the account of a pilgrim to the Holy Land, apparently written shortly after 570 CE, by a follower of Antoninus of Placentia. The work exists in two main recensions; the text given here follows Geyer's edition of the earlier recension, in the *Corpus Christianorum* series:

> Tenui autem theophaniam in Iordane, ubi talia fiunt mirabilia in illa nocte in loco ubi baptizatus est dominus. Est obeliscus factus clausus cancellis, et in loco ubi aqua redit in alueo suo, posita est crux lignea intus in aquam, et gradi descendunt usque ad aquam ex utraque parte marmoris. In uigilias theophaniae fiunt uigiliae grandes, populus infinitus; gallo quarto aut quinto fiunt matutinas. Completo matutinas albescente die procedunt ministeria sub diuo, et tenentes diaconi descendit sacerdos in fluuium et hora qua coeperit benedicere aquam, mox Iordanis cum rugitu redit post se et stat aqua usque dum baptismus perficiatur. Et omnes Alexandrini habentes naues homines suos die illo ibi habent habentes colathos plenos cum aromatibus et opobalsamo, et hora qua benedixerit fontem, antequam incipiant baptizari, omnes fundent illos colathos in fluuium et tollent inde aquam benedictam et exinde faciunt aquam sparsionis in nauibus suis ... Completo baptismo omnes descendunt in fluvio pro benedictione induti sindones et multas cum alias species, quas sibi ad sepulturam servant. (*Itinerarium Antonini Placentini* 11)

I observed the Feast of the Theophany [i. e. the combined feast of the Epiphany and the Baptism of Jesus] on the Jordan, where such miracles happen on that night in the place where the Lord was baptized. An obelisk has been enclosed within the chancel, and in the place where the water returns to its channel a wooden cross is set within the water, and steps go down to the water, made of marble on both sides. At the eve of the Feast there are huge vigils and an innumerable congregation. Matins are held at the fourth or fifth cock. When Matins are completed and the sky is growing light, the attendants go forth into the open air, and the bishop, with deacons in attendance, goes down into the stream; and the moment he blesses the water, the Jordan immediately turns back on itself with a roar, and the water stands still until the baptism is finished. And all the Alexandrian shipowners have their own people there on that day with baskets full of perfumes and balsam, and the moment the bishop blesses the stream, before the baptisms begin, they dip these baskets into the stream and take the water he has blessed, and make from it the water of aspersion for their own ships ... The baptism completed, everyone goes down into the river for a blessing, clad in shrouds and many other such things, which they keep for their own burial.

On the level of morphology, we should note first of all the many sub-literary uses; *gradi* for *gradus*, for instance, *fundent* and *tollent* as present tenses (transferred as often from the third to the second conjugation), the confusion between the ablative and accusative cases in *multas cum alias* and *in uigilias*, especially after prepositions. In such cases, however, there is often manuscript variation, and establishing an original reading or sequence for the variants is often difficult. These features do not belong to Christian Latin as such, but to sub-literary ("vulgar") Latin more generally. Other features in this class include the compound preposition *intus in* (compare French *dans* < *de intus*, or Italian *dentro* < *de intro*); the use of *grandis* rather than *magnus* or *ingens*, the unconstrued ablative absolute *completo matutinas* (compare Classical unconstrued *praesente*); the colloquial-sounding *multas cum alias species* (compare the similar *omne genus* construction in Classical Latin); the use of *pro* rather than *ad* to express purpose; possibly also the use of *rugitus*, if the sense is simply "noise" (compare Spanish *ruido*) rather than the Classical "roaring". None of this is specifically "Christian Latin" at all.

More ambiguous is the case of *hora (qua)* effectively to mean "when". For although *hora* is attested in Classical Latin, it is in prose almost confined to precise expressions of time (e. g. *sexta hora*, "at the sixth hour", and so on); freer use of the phrase is largely a feature of poetry (e. g. *Aeneid* 6.537: *nox ruit, Aenea; nos flendo ducimus horas*, "Night falls, Aeneas, while we stretch out the hours with weeping"). This loanword, then, resists categorization either as a feature of high diction or of everyday language. In biblical Latin, it occurs quite frequent in contexts like this; compare Matthew 24:42, "you do not know the hour when (*qua hora*) your master is coming"; and it is tempting to see this as the model for this usage. But this cannot be proved, and the widespread use of *hora* in temporal adverbs in Romance merely muddies the waters; do expressions such as Italian *ora* or Spanish *ahora* reflect a popular Latin use unrelated to Christianity, or do they represent the spread into popular speech of an idiom originally associated with Christianity?

The syntax too stands in a complex relationship to that of biblical Latin. Several features of this passage are particularly common in biblical Latin, though far from unknown in the wider language. Present participles, whose higher frequency we have noted as a feature of translation Latin, occur in *tenentes diaconi* (though the meaning here is somewhat obscure) and in the rather clumsy *Alexandrini habentes naues homines habent …* *habentes colathos*, where the second *habentes* in particular is reminiscent of the Greek use of ἔχων ("having", but effectively equivalent to "with"). More tentatively, we may suggest that the widespread use of the subjunctive in temporal clauses (*hora qua coeperit/ benedixerit, usque dum perficiantur, antequam incipiant*) may reflect at one remove the Greek use of the subjunctive in temporal constructions with ἕως ἄν or ὅταν ("until such time as" and "as and when") – though this suggestion must be made cautiously. Indeed, even in the modern Romance languages it is notable how much variation there is between speakers in the use of the subjunctive in dependent clauses. Similarly, the use of the inceptive phrase *coeperit benedicere* recalls both the frequent use of *coepi* in sub-literary Latin (often described as aoristic) *and* the use of the same verb in biblical Latin, especially rendering Mark's favoured use of the pleonastic ἄρχομαι. The phrase *induti sindones* likewise has multiple affinities. In Classical Latin, *induo* followed by direct object of the thing put on is typically a poeticism, on the model of the Greek middle voice; in prose the verb would usually be construed with the ablative. Its use here may be regarded as a Graecism, or alternatively as an example of the later-Latin syncretism of the non-nominative cases, reinforced by the reluctance of Latin writers in general to use the *-ibus* ending on Greek loanwords of the third declension (*sindonibus* is not found before the high-mediaeval period). We may, in short, be dealing here with multiple causation. More distinctly biblical is the Hebrew-style qualifying genitive in *aquam sparsionis* (we might expect *faciunt sparsionem aquae* or just *aquam spargunt*); as we have noted, this syntactic phenomenon is relatively uncommon outside biblical citations, and this example clearly echoes *aquam aspersionis* at Numbers 19:9.

It is, however, the vocabulary which is most distinctively Christian. Some features are easily missed, notably the semantic specializations. *Sacerdos* ("bishop") we have already considered. *Dominus* ("the Lord, Master") used *tout court* of Jesus is unsurprising, as no doubt it was when this passage was written, but none the less must originally have been striking. So also *populus* ("people"), used of the Christian population; this use, analogous to the use of λαός of the Jewish people, becomes specialized in the sense of "parish, local community" (Spanish *el pueblo*); its synonym *plebs* undergoes a similar development (Italian *la pieve*). Similarly, we have the elliptic use of the Classical adjective *matutinae*, with a word for "prayers" understood, to mean "Matins". So also *gallus* ("cock, rooster") is used with ordinal adjectives as an expression of time, an idiom which presumably has its origins in Peter's denial of Jesus "before the cock crew thrice"; Classical Latin knows only the idiom *ad cantum galli*, "at cock-crow". In this connexion we might add *vigiliae*, used in both a technical Christian sense, "the eve of a religious festival" (from the Jewish practice of beginning the religious day at sunset) and "vigil". Lastly, we may note *mirabilia* ("wondrous things"), in biblical Latin rendering the Greek adjectival expression τὰ θαυμαστά; where *mirabilia* occurs in Classical Latin it is usually in elevated contexts, but in Christian usage it becomes so frequent that it is re-analysed as a feminine singular, in which form it is found in the modern Romance languages (Italian *meraviglia*, French *merveille*, etc.). All these examples originally involve some change to the idiomatic use of the terms in question; this change is more of a modification or restriction of an existing sense than a semantic extension.

It is, of course, the Greek words that stand out most, and it is tempting to see these as being most typical of wider Christian Latin usage. There is certainly some truth in this view, since (as we have noted) Christian Latin writers do make extensive use of loanwords seldom if ever found in the Classical language. Yet even this claim must be modified, as the Greek words here are mixed bunch. *Hora* we have noted before as a word long established in Latin, which may well have lost any Greek overtones for many speakers. Some of the words belong to the semantic field of luxury goods, where Greek words are often used both for their denotative precision and as a distancing device; in this category we would include *aroma* ("perfume"), *opobalsamum* ("balsam"), and probably *sindon* ("cloak", "winding-sheet"); *aroma* and *sindon*, however, have particular importance for Christian writers because of their presence in the Gospel accounts of Jesus' burial. *Diaconus* ("deacon", "servant"), like *episcopus*, is not attested in Latin before Tertullian, but it is plausible that both words were familiar to non-Christian speakers in their purely secular senses; the role of servant, like that of overseer, being widely undertaken by

Greek slaves or freedmen. *Baptizo* and *baptismus* are early borrowings, the translations *(in)tinguo* and *(in)tinctio* failing to catch on. *Theophania* ("revelation of the divine"), on the other hand, is not a biblical word and is perhaps not attested before this passage.

Conclusions

We began by noting it might be difficult even in a relatively modern passage of English to detect whether and how far particular usages represent a distinctly Christian mode of expression; and that identifying a distinctly Christian form of Latin was likely to be no easier. Most of the features of "Christian Latin" considered here may, in formal terms, be paralleled elsewhere in the language; the use of Greek loanwords, for instance, the semantic development of native Latin words, the extension of various syntactic features on the model of the Greek. None the less, the extent to which Christian writers will depart from Classical norms is striking, and probably not merely a function of the surviving evidence.

Paradoxically, however, this Christian Latin depends for its effect on the coexistence of the Classical variety. For most of the period we have considered, Christian Latin writers seem to feel themselves in dialogue with the traditions of the Classical language; whether their stance is one of accommodation between Christian and Classical norms, as was Lactantius', or they insist on the legitimacy of a distinctly Christian idiom, as Augustine did, there is still a pull from both directions, depending on their individual presuppositions and the audience for whom they were writing. To the extent that this is true, we need to be aware not only of the more obvious features of Christian Latin, but also of the contexts in which they are and are not used.

FURTHER READING

For a recent survey of early Christian Latin literature, see Heine (2004). Studies of biblical Latin were first put on a scientific footing by Rönsch (1869), still a useful collection of evidence on distinctive features of biblical Latin, with a valuable classification of the material. Perhaps the best linguistic study of any early Christian text remains that of Löfstedt (1911). The *Sondersprache* ("special language") hypothesis has its canonical statement in Schrijnen (1932), and is extensively developed by Mohrmann (especially (1958–1977)), who attempts to develop the theory and to show its applicability to a range of other Latin texts; arguably demonstrating instead the weakness of the theory in its more dogmatic forms. For critiques of the position, see especially Marouzeau (1932), Holford-Strevens (1981), and Coleman (1987). Coleman's argument that what unites Christian Latin writers is a shared lexicon rather than any wider suite of linguistic features has influenced the presentation here, though a partial rehabilitation of theory is offered by Burton (2008), who stresses the extent to which the common lexicon goes beyond a set of narrowly "Christian" terms, and who suggests that while the original theory now appears dated and naive in its presuppositions, it may none the less be susceptible of reinterpretation using more sophisticated sociolinguistic models.

For an exhaustive manual of Christian and biblical Latin, García de la Fuente (1994) is extremely useful, though the manual format precludes detailed analysis of the phenomena in question.

Burton (2000) is a narrower and more detailed attempt to locate the language and translation technique of the Old Latin Gospels within the wider context of post-Classical Latin. In this connexion it should be noted that many of the phenomena of "Christian Latin" may be paralleled more widely in later, sub-literary, and technical registers of Latin; publications such as Löfstedt (1959), Väänänen (1981), Herman (2000), Adams (1995a), Langslow (2000b) and Wright (2002) contain much that is relevant.

PART V

Latin in Social and
Political Contexts

CHAPTER 28

The Social Dialects of Latin

James Clackson

Introduction

All languages exhibit dialectal variations. Ancient Greek writers recognised variation of language both over geographical space and between different groups of speakers in the same city: in his comedies *Acharnians* and *Lysistrata* Aristophanes represents speakers from communities outside Athens (Laconia, Megara, Boeotia) speaking in their regional dialects (see Colvin (1999)), and their speech generally accords well with surviving inscriptional evidence. Aristophanes also represents different varieties of Attic Greek that were spoken by women and foreigners in Athens, as well as the speech-styles associated with various technical registers. Indeed, in a famous fragment (706), Aristophanes explicitly refers to different dialects within the city:

> διάλεκτον ἔχοντα μέσην πόλεως
> οὔτ᾽ ἀστείαν ὑποθηλυτέραν
> οὔτ᾽ ἀνελεύθερον ὑπαγροικοτέραν

[him] whose language is the average style of the polis, neither urbane and slightly womanish, nor vulgar and somewhat boorish. (Trans. Willi (2003) 161)

This Aristophanes fragment contains the first use of the term διάλεκτος in something approaching the meaning of the modern word "dialect" (see further below). The choice of adjectives used to characterise the three different grades of Athenian speech show the association of dialects with different social groupings and oppositions; within these three lines Aristophanes contrasts male and female speech (ὑποθηλυτέραν), the language of the free citizen with that of the slave (ἀνελεύθερον), and the town dialect (ἀστείαν) with that of the country (ὑπαγροικοτέραν).

A Companion to the Latin Language, First Edition. Edited by James Clackson.
© 2011 Blackwell Publishing Ltd. Published 2011 by Blackwell Publishing Ltd.

Despite the awareness of both geographical and social variation in fifth-century Athens, the Greek grammatical tradition as it developed in later centuries privileged geographical dialects but not social dialects. Hence the statement of Clement of Alexandria (*Stromata* I 142) "A dialect is a form of speech which shows the individual character of a place … the Greeks say that they have five dialects: Attic, Ionic, Doric, Aeolic and fifth the *koiné.*"[1] Since some of the Greek local dialects were associated with literary compositions of a high cultural status, these were accorded recognition in the Hellenistic and later grammatical tradition, whereas social dialects, which were not associated with literary compositions, were largely viewed as incorrect deviations from the standard. In other words, some sorts of geographical variation in language were canonised, but social variation was not. The Greek grammatical tradition, and in turn the grammatical traditions of the Romans and subsequent scholarship in the West, downplayed the significance of social dialects. It has only been since the inception of systematic study of social dialects and language variation in the mid-twentieth century, spearheaded by William Labov in America in the 1960s, that social dialects have been recognised as a valid area for linguistic study. Even so, non-standard forms are still routinely singled out for criticism and disapproval in contemporary media and in popular works on language.

In Ancient Greek and Roman societies, as in many modern ones, standard languages were associated with education, wealth and social status. Any move away from the grammatically "correct" forms might be an indicator of lower social status and background, and it could also be taken to be a sign of moral degeneracy; in the words of Farrell, throughout Roman antiquity "faulty speech could be equated with deviant sexuality" (Farrell (2001) 82). One expression of this view is given by Seneca (*Ep.* 114.1) *talis hominibus fuit oratio, qualis uita* "as a man's speech is, so is his life". In the same letter Seneca describes Maecenas' *uitia* "faults" in his effeminate dress, his love of luxury and his unrestrained and slack speech, giving an example of how character and diction were thought to be intertwined. If Maecenas can be taken to represent the over-urbane and womanish extreme of language and manner, Petronius provides examples of the boorish and uncultivated speakers in his depiction of freedmen's speech in the *Satyrica* (see further below). Just as the freedmen are depicted to be outside the cultural norms of artistic taste and culinary etiquette, so their language is characterised through frequent grammatical mistakes and anacoloutha.

In a society where deviation from the linguistic norms could be used to prompt ridicule or worse at a speaker, it is no surprise that most literate users of the language attempted to fit somewhere into the spectrum of acceptable Latinity. Those taught to write Latin were taught how to write the standard language. Consequently, surviving evidence for social dialects of Latin is meagre, especially during the Classical period of the language. Authors such as Cicero were aware that there was a range of varieties of Latin (see Fögen (2000) 119–127 for discussion of relevant Cicero passages); however, although Cicero uses terms such as *plebeio sermone* "in plebeian speech" (*Fam.* 9.21.1) to distinguish his epistolary from his forensic style, or *uulgari sermone* "everyday language" (*Ac.* 1.5) to describe the unsophisticated language of other writers on philosophy, these descriptions are not descriptive of social dialects as a modern linguist would understand them, but rather stylistic labels. Cicero's elision of the difference between spoken and written styles is particularly problematic for the modern researcher. We must be wary of making a simple correspondence between written texts and spoken varieties.

The speech of one of the freedmen in Petronius provides an entry point for another aspect of the study of social dialects, and one that can be used to unearth details about varieties for which we have no direct written evidence. Echion, who appears to be one of the less prosperous of the freedmen at Trimalchio's dinner (he is described as a *centonarius*, someone who stitches together mats in order that they can be used to put out fires), accuses another diner, Agamemnon, of looking down at his language: *non es nostrae fasciae, et ideo pauperorum uerba derides. scimus te prae litteras fatuum esse* (Petr. 46.2) "you are not one of our bunch, and so you laugh at the speech of the poor. We know that you are crazy for learning." Echion's speech has clear markers of non-standard Latin: *pauperorum* rather than *pauperum* showing the transfer of the adjective *pauper* from the third to the second declension, and the use of an accusative after the preposition *prae*. But equally interesting for the sociolinguist is the notion of language as a sign of group identity. Agamemnon is taken to use his own learning to enable him to deride the mistakes in Echion's speech, but he is also identified as someone who is an outsider, not a group-member. As Petronius is aware, speakers of non-standard varieties may choose to use them, consciously or subconsciously, in order to gain acceptance within a group, or they may avoid non-standard features in order to show their distance from another social group.

Modern work on sociolinguistics has been greatly occupied with questions of group membership, and the use of language as an indicator of social position. Studies have repeatedly shown that many speakers vary their own speech in different social environments, and as a way to demonstrate different group allegiances. Some speakers attempt to "upgrade" their own speech variety in order to sound closer to the standard language; in sociolinguistic terms this is described as an attempt to gain linguistic *prestige*. Thus, for example, a Latin speaker whose own idiolect does not differentiate between words with and without initial *h*, such as *os* "mouth" and *hos* "those", or who does not pronounce an aspirated consonant in Greek loanwords, such as *amphora* "amphora", may gain linguistic prestige by learning when to pronounce these forms correctly. Of course, it may be that the speaker overdoes the correction, and puts aspirates in words which never originally had any; this is termed *hypercorrection*, and its occurrence is a sure sign of the existence of social dialects. (The example of hypercorrection using aspirates in Catullus 84 has already been discussed in Chapter 15, pp. 239–240.)

Just as those born outside the elite may attempt to gain linguistic prestige through upgrading their language, so speakers within the elite may downgrade their language in order to emphasise their close relationship to the common people, or in order to lessen their apparent ties with the social elite. Such a move is known by sociolinguistics as a quest for "covert prestige". The emperor Augustus provides an example from the Roman world of what may be deliberate downgrading of language in search of covert prestige and popularity with the urban plebs. Several ancient sources remark on Augustus' impatience with the precepts of the grammarians (some are collected at Adams (2007) 16–17), such as his use of prepositions with the names of towns (see pp. 263–265 in this volume) and preference for syncopated forms such as *caldus* in place of *calidus*. These features are likely to have been present among many of the less educated speakers in Rome: certainly they are the features that are continued in Romance. However, the anecdotes about Augustus remind us that sub-standard variants may be present in speakers of all classes.

The Romance languages are themselves another possible source for the sub-elite varieties of Latin. Romance forms go back to spoken Latin forms, and, as will be shown below, many of these also tie in with what is known about the Latin of the uneducated and those with lower status. It has often been noticed, for example, that the language of the freedmen in Petronius' *Satyrica* prefigures the linguistic changes of Romance in certain features: the freedmen show confusions between neuter and masculine gender, and in Romance languages most Latin neuters are transferred into the masculine gender; the freedmen sometimes employ periphrases for the Latin future tense, and in Romance the Latin analytical future is replaced in various ways; the freedmen avoid some Latin lexical items, such as *flere* "weep" in favour of *plorare* or *plangere* and their choices are the words which survive in Romance (French *pleurer*, Italian *piangere*) at the expense of *flere*.[2] However, it would be wrong to imagine that the Romance languages derive from a single variety of Latin (the so-called "Vulgar Latin" of some handbooks). The examples given above show that within the Romance languages there is often considerable divergence, both lexically (note that the French word for "weep" derives from Latin *plorare* but the Italian from *plangere*) and in grammatical and syntactic developments (consider the different periphrastic constructions behind the Romance expressions of the future: a periphrasis of infinitive and *habeo* in most of western Romance, a periphrasis of *habeo ad* + infinitive in southern Italian dialects, *debeo* + infinitive in Sardinian and *uolo* + infinitive in Romanian).

At any one time in the history of Latin there must have been a range of different varieties and speech habits. From the distance of the twenty-first century, and given the nature of the surviving evidence, it is difficult to separate out these dialects clearly, particularly since linguistic features may spread out from one dialect over time. In the rest of the chapter, I shall attempt to isolate some of the possible axes on which languages varied in the Roman world. It will be useful to examine these alongside the principal demographic variables that are used in sociolinguistic studies of modern language variation (and which were already anticipated by Aristophanes): variation between male and female speakers; variation between old and young speakers; variation across social class.

Male and Female Speech

According to a recent survey, the gender of the speaker now occupies a position in sociolinguistics research "where many consider it the main social factor driving variation and change" (Cheshire (2002) 439). In modern studies a correlation between gender and language variation has frequently been observed across different communities all over the world. Indeed, in some societies there are distinct pronunciations or morphological forms associated with male or female speech, and avoided by the opposite gender. Such "sex-exclusive" forms are, however, in most societies of fairly limited application, normally restricted to certain domains, such as language dealing with religious or sexual matters. Much more frequent in occurrence are sex-preferential forms, which are used by one gender more predominantly, although not exclusively. Furthermore, a frequent finding of modern studies is a difference between the ways men and women adjust their language to their environment or interlocutor(s); all speakers will employ a wide range of possible speech-variants, but one sex (typically males) may deviate further from the standard, and use non-standard forms in a wider range of social situations.

Work on the difference between male and female speech in Latin goes back at least to observations by the Romans themselves on the speech of individual females or on practices which were seen to be more prevalent among women. Thus, for example Varro (*R.* 2.4.10) observes that women, particularly wet-nurses, use the word *porcus*, literally "pig", to refer to the sexual organs of girls. Gellius (11.6) notes that men and women use some sex-exclusive oaths, such as *herc(u)le* for men, and *(e)castor* for women in early Roman comedy. In the last half-century these observations have been supplemented by more systematic investigations of Latin literature in order to illuminate salient features of the way men and women spoke. The unpublished thesis of Gilleland (1979) and the article of Adams (1984) both concentrate on the representation of male and female speakers in Roman comedy in the search for information on sex differences in language (see also the surveys of Fögen (2004) and (2010) on more recent work on female speech in Latin and Greek, adding Adams (2005a)). Roman comedy is a potentially rewarding field, since the corpus is large enough to allow the drawing of conclusions that are supported, in some degree, by statistics. Thus Gilleland finds that female characters in Plautus and Terence use fewer Greek words and a higher proportion of diminutives than male characters (figures reported in Dutsch (2008) 10 n. 27). Adams (1984) unearths a larger pattern of the linguistic behaviour of women: women in Roman comedy are more polite, using modifiers more often (and preferring to use *amabo* for "please", a word that tends to be avoided by men), and they employ more affective language, using terms of address and vocative particles more, as well as vocabulary items such as *miser* "unhappy" and its derivatives.

Adams' findings about Roman comedy tie in well with observations about women made in modern studies. Women use a greater number of modifiers, hedging devices and politeness indicators than male speakers. Adams, while recognising the dangers of using male authors' representations of women, argued that the linguistic behaviour of female speakers in Plautus and Terence reflected to some degree the actual speech of women in Rome at the time, owing to the similarity with modern studies on female speech, and the need for the Roman comedians' presentation of women to be sufficiently lifelike to reality to resonate with a contemporary audience.[3]

Since Adams' 1984 paper, it has been difficult to make significant advances on his findings for the distinctive features of women's language, other than by including new evidence (such as women writing in the Vindolanda tablets, see below, or the previously undiscussed work of the Latin medical writer Mustio, translator of Soranus' *Gynaecia* (Adams (2005a)). The reason for this is no doubt the paucity of written evidence from the ancient world composed by women. A recent survey of Latin female poets, which also takes into account epigraphic writings and a number of non-poetical texts (Stevenson (2005), especially 31–58), gives a good idea of the very limited scope of the surviving evidence. Female literacy rates were extremely low in the ancient world, and even where women were able to write, they did so in genres that were predominantly male-oriented in terms of audience and convention. Thus the letters of Cornelia, mother to the Gracchi, and the poetry of Sulpicia preserved among the Tibullan corpus (on which see further below), were exceptions rather than the rule, and analysis of these texts on their own reveal nothing distinctive about female diction or linguistic usage. Indeed, there is debate about which poems in the Tibullan corpus are actually to be attributed to Sulpicia, and whether some might be compositions by male poets assuming a female persona, just as Ovid writes in the guise of female characters in the *Heroides*, for example.

The epigraphic evidence for female writers is similarly limited. Many of the inscriptions composed in the name or on behalf of a woman comprise texts that are either formulaic or banal. A minor exception is found in the tiny corpora of letters composed by women included among the Vindolanda tablets. Among these are three letters composed by Claudia Severa, wife of Aelius Brocchus, to Sulpicia Lepidina, the wife of Flavus Cerialis, prefect of the ninth cohort of the Batavians who inhabited the Roman fort at Vindolanda around 100 CE. Severa's correspondence included personal greetings in her own hand, and was most likely dictated, as other letters from Vindolanda were. Severa's Latin is mostly unremarkable, but she does use the vocative phrase *anima mea* "my soul" twice in her letters to Lepidina, the only time this phrase occurs in the Vindolanda correspondence. The use of this term and its relationship to the issue of "female speech" is discussed by Adams (1995a) 120 and Dickey (2002) 158–159. The address *anima mea* recalls the vocative phrase *anime (mi)* "my mind" which is identified by Donatus as a specifically female form of address, and which is predominantly used by women in Roman comedy. In surviving Latin literature *anima mea* is put in the mouths of female speakers by Phaedrus and Apuleius, but it also occurs in surviving correspondence of Cicero as an affectionate address to his wife and children, and as an affectionate epistolary address from Marcus Aurelius to Fronto. Adams and Dickey both argue that these usages need not negate the identification of *anima mea* as a "female" term, but instead suggest that the category of women's language could be expanded to include the emotional, or intimate, language between speakers even when one or both was a man.

The discussion of the phrase *anima mea* highlights the difficulties around constructing any clear distinctions of what is "female language" and what is "male language", particularly over the long time-scale for the attestation of the Latin language. Moreover, there is a danger of confusing the linguistic behaviour with assumptions of stereotypically gendered attitudes: women may be characterised by ancient authors as more prone to be swayed by emotions, and hence in surviving texts the emotive registers of Latin may occur more frequently in the mouths of female characters. It is possible even that literate women are influenced by earlier texts or the precepts of their teachers, and use more emotional language in their own compositions (see the criticisms of research on "women's Latin" by Dutsch (2008) 12). Even modern attitudes towards the linguistic content of work by women may be undermined by prejudice. The case of the poetess Sulpicia is illustrative. Lowe cites the verdict of Otto Gruppe on the Latinity of the poems he identified by Sulpicia in the Tibullan corpus:

> On close inspection the critic will readily recognise here a *feminine Latin*, impervious to analysis by rigorous linguistic method, but which finds natural, simple expressions for everyday ideas without conscious and artistic elaboration of style, and in which the sense is augmented and assisted by free *constructio ad sensum*. (Gruppe (1838) 49, translated by Lowe (1988) 194)

Lowe (1988) in contrast argues that the sometimes convoluted syntax of individual poems is a reflection of a sophisticated poet wrestling with complex ideas within the limits of the elegiac form.

Attempting to disentangle real "women's speech" from this evidence may be a futile task. In any case, as we have seen from comparative studies, the gender differences in speech may be better tracked by the degrees of variation from the standard, rather than individual lexical items. Some ancient evidence implies that women were more prone to upgrade their speech, or maintain higher register forms, than men: Seneca's 114th letter, as we have already seen, made a connection between over-elaborate language with womanish behaviour; and Crassus, a speaker in Cicero's dialogue *de Oratore*, observes:

> facilius enim mulieres incorruptam antiquitatem conseruant, quod multorum sermonis expertes ea tenent semper quae prima dedicerunt. (*de Orat.* 3.45)

> It is easier for women to preserve the ancient forms of speech, since they always keep those forms they first learnt intact, owing to the fact that they do not speak with many people.

Note that Crassus uses the term *incorruptam* "uncorrupted" for the language of women, thereby signifying that women's seclusion is beneficial to their speech, which avoids the contamination that is liable to affect male diction through constant conversational interaction.

Although women's speech has been much discussed in the scholarly literature, much less attention has been paid to male, despite the massive preponderance of written texts composed by men. Of course, if we do not have a clear idea of how women spoke, it is impossible to reckon what was distinctive about men. However, in some areas we can probably make some generalisations. As already mentioned, men typically depart from the norms of the standard language more freely than women, and it seems likely that this was also the case in Latin. In this respect, it may be significant that, although we have ancient sources commenting on the linguistic peculiarities of men such as Augustus, there is no source which directly cites a grammatical or linguistic solecism of a famous woman. One of the liberties which was associated with many men of the Roman elite, deriving from their exclusive shared educational background, is the use of Greek words and Greek phrases in speech. In comedy Roman women (except for servile or low-born characters) are represented as avoiding Greek words and constructions (Karakasis (2005) 89) and Cicero almost completely avoids code-switching into Greek in letters written to his wife. In the words of Swain, Cicero's use of Greek may encode "advanced male solidarity" (Swain (2002) 164). As Swain notes ((2002) 164–165) Juvenal explicitly disparages women who use too much Greek, something which is seen as beyond the boundaries of *sermo pudicus* "chaste speech" (Juv. 6.188). This then leads on to another licence possible for men but not for women: obscenity. Obscenity was normally discouraged among women or in the presence of women, except in specially sanctioned arenas such as festivals, marriages or in the bedroom (Adams (1982a) 216–217, note also that Greek is seen as appropriate when limited to bedroom conversations by Juvenal). Even so, for men there were restrictions on the employment of the basic obscenities, such as *mentula* "penis", *cunnus* "vagina", *culus* "anus", and *futuo* "I fuck", which in literary Latin occur in epigram, but are avoided in history, oratory, elegy and epic, satire (see pp. 380–382 of this volume) and normally also in medical writings. Epigraphical evidence, and the survival of these vocabulary items into the Romance language, show that these obscenities were more widespread in other registers.

Age-Related Variation in Speech

As language varies with gender roles, so also with the age of the speaker. Older speakers may continue linguistic forms no longer current among the young, and in many languages certain words are recognised to be childish or limited to younger speakers. In a corpus language such as Latin it is often difficult to track the age-dependent variables of speech, owing to an almost complete lack of direct evidence. If the very young have left any written record, it is confined to texts composed or copied in the classroom. However, as with the case of the language of women, the testimonia of ancient authors and their representations of speakers of different ages leave no doubt that there were linguistic registers appropriate to different ages.

For the old, as for women, Roman comedians provide the best source for the representation of a distinctive diction. Maltby (1979) and much of Karakasis (2005) are specifically devoted to the characterisation of old men in the comedies of Terence, but some of their conclusions can also be applied to the plays of Plautus. Some of the linguistic features of the speech of old men reflect ancient stereotypes. Thus, for example, old men were seen as being long-winded, and repetitive, just as Nestor was portrayed in the *Iliad* and as Aristotle noted in the *Rhetoric* (B 1390a).[4] Older characters in the main employ pairs of synonyms or more where a single word will do; they use pleonastic expressions and tend to speak at greater length than other characters. The speech of an anonymous old man in Plautus' *Menaechmi* illustrates some of the features well:

> Vt aetas mea est atque ut hoc usus facto est
> gradum proferam, progrediri properabo.
> sed id quam mihi facile sit, haud sum falsus.
> nam pernicitas deserit: consitus sum
> senectute, onustum gero corpus, uires
> reliquere: ut aetas mala est; mers mala ergost.
> nam res plurumas pessumas, quom aduenit, fert:
> quas si autumem omnis, nimis longus sermost.
> sed haec res mihi in pectore et corde curaest,
> quidnam hoc sit negoti, quod fília sic
> repente expetit me, ut ad sese irem. (*Menaechmi* 753–763)

As my age allows, and as there is occasion to do so, I'll push on my steps and make haste to get along. But how easy it is for me, I'm not mistaken as to that. For my agility forsakes me, and I am beset with age; I carry my body weighed down; my strength has deserted me. How grievous a pack upon one's back is age. For when it comes, it brings very many and very grievous particulars, were I now to recount all of which, my speech would be too long. But this matter is a trouble to my mind and heart. What can this business possibly be, on account of which my daughter suddenly asks me to come to her? She hasn't first let me know what the matter is, or what she wants, or why she sends for me.

The catalogue of the old man's ailments is curtailed in the middle (*nimis longus sermost*), no doubt a joke to undercut the audience's expectations of a long litany (Gratwick (1993) 209). However, despite this, the language still contains many of the stock features of the speech of the aged, including pleonasm: *gradum proferam, progrediri properabo, quom aduenit, fert*; repition of synonyms: *in pectore et corde*; and general tautology in lines 756–758. The language of the old man is at times elevated, particularly in his description of the physical trials of growing old, with the personifications of *aetas* "age" and *pernicitas* "nimbleness"; the phrase *consitus senectute* "beset by old age" does not recur in extant Latin literature. But this is more likely to reflect a parody of tragic language than a recognisable feature of the old, although Maltby and Karakasis do find evidence to suggest that old men are more prone to be represented using archaisms in comedy than other characters. It is clear that there is much that reflects generic convention in the language of the aged in Roman comedy, but some of the features presented as typical of the old man might also have occurred in actual speech. Modern sociolinguistic studies have shown that the idiolects of old men are liable to contain a higher proportion of obsolescent vocabulary items or phonological features (Chambers (2002) 358–367), so the prevalence of archaisms in the dramatist's characterisations of the old may also correspond to a linguistic reality.

For the language of children we are not even aided by stock characters in Roman comedy, and must rely almost entirely on the testimonia of ancient authors. Much of this is uninformative: children's speech is lisping (Horace *Ep.* 2.1.126) or their speech is, like that of their nurses, disjointed (as is suggested by Lucretius 5.230 *almae nutricis blanda atque infracta loquella* "the coaxing and disjointed words of the gentle nurse"). In discussing children's speech it is particularly important to separate out the descriptive from the prescriptive, and read the evidence in context. For example, Quintilian recommends that Roman boys should learn Greek before Latin (*Inst.* 1.1.12–13) and Tacitus comments on the use of Greek slave-women to teach the youth of Rome (*Dial.* 29). It has also been noted that Cicero tends to switch into Greek when adding salutations from his son in his letters to Atticus, e.g. *Att.* 2.9.4 *Terentia tibi salutem dicit* καὶ Κικέρων ὁ μικρὸς ἀσπάζεται Τίτον τὸν Ἀθηναῖον "Terentia sends greetings to you and Cicero junior greets Titus the Athenian" (Adams (2003a) 320). This combination of evidence from different sources may lead to the conclusion that the elite male children were prone to speak in Greek rather than Latin (so Dubuisson (1992), and Dunkel (2000) 128). Yet this conclusion is not justified, as Adams has shown ((2003a) 308–312). There is no evidence that Quintilian's recommendation was ever taken up by the majority of the Roman elite and the speaker in Tacitus' *Dialogus* is making a rhetorical overstatement. Cicero uses Greek when sending his son's greetings to Atticus since he wants to emphasise his son's educational accomplishments, rather than because it was the child's normal idiom.

Evidence for special vocabulary items associated with the language of children seems more likely to be representative of actual speech. Varro was evidently interested in nursery words; he records (reported at Non. p. 81M) *cum cibum ac potionem buas ac pappas uocent et matrem mammam et patrem tatam* "since they [childen] call food and drink *bua* and *pappa* and they call their mother *mamma* and their father *tata*." The terms *mamma* (which can also be used in child-language to refer to a grandmother, wet-nurse or the female breast) and *tata* also appear on Roman funerary epitaphs where they function as labels for the parents of children who died young. Martial (1.100) comments on a woman, Afra, who uses the terms even though herself old enough to be a grandmother. Heraeus collected a number of other items of nursery or child vocabulary (Heraeus (1904)), including some terms for body parts and functions (such as *cacare* "shit" and *dida* "breast" (see also Adams (2005a) on this word)). This vocabulary was clearly not used exclusively by children, but also featured in the language of mothers and nurses who brought up young children (see the Lucretius citation above) and who talked baby-talk with them, and thus the language of the nursery overlaps with some areas of the language of women (as noted by Adams (2005a) 590). Many of these vocabulary items, which barely surface in our Latin texts, were to survive in the spoken language into modern Romance.

Class-Based Variation

The third axis of language variation which I shall consider is variation of language corresponding to social class. Since the first modern sociolinguistic studies undertaken by William Labov in New York and Martha's Vineyard in the 1960s, the importance of social class as a factor in language variation and change in modern societies has been widely recognised. Roman society was inherently more hierarchical than American society in the 1960s, so we might expect to see a greater level of language variation according to the social status of speakers. As always, however, the picture is clouded by the nature of much of our evidence: writing implies education, and education implies expense. The majority of the population were illiterate and those of low social status who were trained to write (for example, slaves employed as clerks, scribes and accountants) were trained in the standardised language of the elite. Some authors commented on linguistic features of the non-elite, or represented their language (again we rely largely on the comedians and Petronius), and some texts appear to have been composed at a level more appropriate to lower-class audiences. Written evidence that corresponds more closely to the actual speech of an individual of lower status (who has not undergone education to a high level) does occur, such as for example the famous letters of Claudius Terentianus or the autograph documents written by the freedman C. Novius Eunus found among the wax tablets excavated at Murecine near Pompeii (see p. 478 for a text and translation of one of these documents), but such material is often limited in scope, and it is not always easy to separate the idiosyncrasies of the individual from the particular sociolect. In the rest of this section I will attempt to draw some general conclusions from the surviving material.

Recent estimates for the proportion of slaves in Italian society at the time of Augustus vary from 15–20 per cent to over a third (Bradley (2010) 626). Across time, and in different parts of the empire that figure varied; in Roman Egypt for example slaves only made up a tenth of the total population. The slaves themselves were heterogeneous: some held positions within a Roman household of considerable power and trust; others in rural settings or mines were little more than human pack animals. At all times throughout the Republic and Empire the stock of slaves was renewed through captives from military campaigns or through the slave trade. Scheidel (2005) estimates an average annual influx of between 15,000 and 20,000 slaves for the last two centuries of the Roman Republic. With such a diverse population, constantly replenished by incomers, many of whom were not native speakers of Latin, it is difficult to make generalisations about the language of slaves. Nevertheless, there are features shared by our two principal representative sources of the speech of slaves and freedmen: Roman comedy and Petronius. In Plautine comedies, slave characters use more Greek loans (Maltby 1995) and they code-switch into Greek more than other characters (Adams (2003a) 351), in Terence slaves and low-class characters use a higher proportion of Greek loanwords (Maltby (1985)) and syntactic constructions (Karakasis (2005) 83–89). One of the freedmen in Petronius' novel, Hermeros, is also noteworthy for his frequent code-switches into Greek, and his use of Greek vocabulary (Boyce (1991) 92). Epigraphical sources may also support the conclusion that Greek was the first language of many of the slaves in Rome; according to the information collected for the city of Rome by Solin (1996), of over 28,000 recorded slave names, 67 per cent are Greek. However, such conclusions should be treated with care. The Roman comedians were writing in a period during which there was a massive influx of slaves from Greek-speaking lands as Roman power extended eastwards, and they need not be indicative of the situation in later centuries. The setting of the *Satyrica* in Campania, an area where Greek remained in use throughout the Empire, means that Hermeros may not be representative of Italy as a whole. Furthermore, Roman slave-naming practices may not reflect the origin of the slaves. The most frequent slave names at Rome, Hermes and Eros, are not in general use as personal names in the free Greek world. In the late Republic and early Empire slave names with Italic origins, such as Statius and Pacius, are found, but these and other barbarian names largely disappear after 100 CE; it is possible that the use of Greek names for slaves reflects a fashion, and is not representative of the ethnic origin (Cheeseman (2009) 515–517).

Even with these caveats, it is likely that some features of servile and lower-class speech came about as a result of Greek influence or contact with Greek. A case in point is the use of the genitive singular -*aes* in place of -*ae*, which is found epigraphically across the Western Empire, chiefly in female nomina, but occasionally also in non-appellative vocabulary in some non-literary documents. Most of the attestations of this form, many in the names of female slaves and freedwomen, suggest that it was "liable to be heard wherever there were Greeks using Latin", although it is also found in non-Greek speaking areas, such as in the Vindonissa tablets from Switzerland (Adams (2007) 674). Borrowings of vocabulary items from Greek also sometimes came about through terms used by or about slaves (see the example of *colaphus* discussed on pp. 252–253 in chapter 15). Other features which are identified as servile, rustic or "low-class" may also plausibly have a Greek origin. One possible example is the spread of aspirated consonants in non-Greek words, also discussed in chapter 15 (pp. 239–240). The republican grammarian Nigidius Figulus stigmatised the overuse of aspiration as a mark of *rusticitas*: *rusticus fit sermo, si adspires perperam* "speech becomes rustic, if you aspirate wrongly" (cited at Gellius 13.6.3). But it seems likely that *rusticus* here refers to non-standard speech, rather than the speech of the countryside (Adams (2007) 174). Indeed, Quintilian relates an anecdote (*Inst.* 12.10.57) about a *rusticus testis* "country witness" who was unable to recognise the Greek name *Amphion* unless the aspirate was suppressed and the medial vowel shortened, suggesting perhaps that rural speakers were not *au fait* with Greek pronunciations.

The language of the free rural and urban poor is also largely accessible only through scattered evidence and surmise. Joseph and Wallace (1992) put forward a theory that the speech of the urban poor in Rome in the late Republic and early Principate showed linguistic features which had previously been found in rural dialects, but which were originally excluded from the city of Rome itself. They reasoned that the increase in the size and wealth of the city of Rome, and the creation of a free corn-dole at the end of the Republic, encouraged the rural poor to emigrate to Rome and leave the surrounding countryside. The non-urban features of the speech of these new city-dwellers were then reinterpreted as markers of the social dialects of the lower classes. Joseph and Wallace identify several phonological features in particular as peculiar to the lower classes of Rome, which had originated in rural areas. These include the monophthongisation of the diphthongs *au* and *ae* to long *ō* and *ē*, the development of the Early Latin diphthong *ou* to *ō* rather than *ū*, the loss of final -*s* after short vowels, and loss of initial *h*-. Unfortunately, the evidence in support of this theory is largely inconclusive; the majority of the features discussed cannot be shown ever to have been specific markers of the urban poor or indeed distinct rural features in origin. For example, the change of earlier *ou* to *ō* is doubtful as a genuine dialectal feature of Early Latin, since the evidence principally consists of two spellings with *o* on a mirror from Praeneste, from where other contemporary texts show *ou* (Adams (2007) 64–66); the evidence for the retention of *ō* from *ou* as a feature of lower-class speech in Rome is restricted to Suetonius' report that the emperor Augustus said *domos* rather than *domus* as the genitive of *domus* (*Aug.* 87.2) which, according to Joseph and Wallace "would have been recognised by the lower classes of Romans as provincial perhaps but clearly on their level" ((1992) 111). It is not impossible that populist politicians may have used identifiably non-standard forms in order to gain "covert-prestige" – indeed Publius Clodius Pulcher's change of his name from Claudius, and Vespasian's use of the term *plostram* for *plaustram* "wagon" (Suet. *Ves.* 22) are usually explained in this way, but there is not enough evidence to be sure that Augustus' *domos* belongs here.

On the other hand, the supposition that there was some element of social variation in the use of monophthongised forms of the diphthongs *ae* and *au* is better supported, since in both of these cases there are recognised hypercorrections, i.e. instances where a word with etymological *ō* or *ē* is replaced by a form with *au* or *ae*, indicating that some speakers felt that they might betray a lack of education if they used a form which appeared to have undergone the monophthongisation, and so upgraded their language to avoid it. Some of the "standard" spellings of Latin words reflect hypercorrections of this sort, such as *plaudo* "I applaud", which replaced original *plodo* (as in the compound *explodo* which escaped the change), and some words of uncertain etymology show both spellings with *au* and *o*, such as *caupo* "innkeeper". The best example for hypercorrect *ae* is probably the word for "stage" *scaena*, originally a borrowing from Greek σκηνή, possibly remodelled since the long open *ē* of the Greek word was of a different quality from normal Latin *ē*, and sounded uncomfortably close to a rural vowel (Adams (2007) 81). Indeed, the change of *ae* to long *ē* is also the best candidate for a change which originated outside Rome, since we have explicit testimony from Varro that *haedus* "goat" was the urban variant next to rural *hedus*, as well as supporting evidence from Lucilius and from inscriptions (Adams (2007) 78–88). Other than this single example, all in all there is insufficient evidence to support Joseph and Wallace's reconstruction of lower-class Roman speech through the urbanisation of the rural poor. Indeed, the make-up of the urban poor of Roman is likely to have consisted of peoples not just from rural Italy, but also from other provinces. Cicero himself (*Brutus* 258) comments on the bad influence on Rome of the language of those who came *ex diuersis locis* "from various different locations". He refers to this influence by the puzzling phrase *barbaries domestica* "a domestic barbarism", which could refer to the influence of Greek (or other non-Latin speaking) nurses on the language of the youth (Adams (2003a) 435).

Features of the speech of the lower classes were often stigmatised in written texts by Romans with education, and became shibboleths to be avoided by those keen to show their own social capital. With hindsight, it is difficult for modern commentators to avoid lumping all the non-standard forms of speech together (as was done by Joseph and Wallace). But the evidence suggests that in reality some speakers may use one sub-standard feature but not another, and that at different times in the evolution of Latin the same feature might belong to different groups of the population, with the elite and non-elite variants existing side-by-side for centuries. Furthermore, some features which were stigmatised by grammarians or purists may have been features of the speech of the upper classes as well (as Augustus' *domos* and Vespasian's *plostrum*, see further below). The monophthongisation of *ae*, for example, would become universal in spoken Latin by the fourth century CE and was prevalent among most speakers much earlier than that, but the monophthongisation of *au* never became generalised throughout the Latin-speaking world (as is shown by the preservation of the diphthong in some varieties of Romance). In the business documents and legal transactions written on wax tablets in the years 37–39 CE by C. Novius Eunus and in the letters of Claudius Terentianus nearly a hundred years later there is widespread evidence for the monophthongisation of *ae*, comprising both the use of *e* in place of *ae* and *ae* in place of Classical *e*, but the diphthong *au* is always preserved.

Note also that spelling mistakes such as those made by Novius Eunus tell us principally about the level of education of a writer, and do not allow us to place the spoken variants exactly on the social spectrum. Many speakers of all classes may have used a long $\bar{e}$ vowel where they wrote *ae* in the first century CE, but the spelling with *e* in place of *ae* may have been restricted only to lower-class individuals lacking in education. Indeed the use of monophthongised versions of the diphthong in speech may already have been found in colloquial speech of the educated at the beginning of the first century BCE; in the example of speech of the "simple style", uttered in *cotidianus sermo* "everyday language", the author of the *Rhetorica ad Herennium* employs the forms *pedagogus* for *paedagogus* "tutor" and *oricula* for *auricula* "ear" (*Rhet. Her.* 4.14) and Ferri and Probert (2010) 20–21 consider it possible that these spellings reflect the colloquial pronunciation of the upper classes already at this time. British English offers a contemporary parallel; the fronting of the interdental fricative [θ] to a labiodental [f] in words such as *think* occurs in non-careful speech of younger adults of all classes, but writings such as *fink* are restricted only to representations of lower-class speech and occasionally used by those with minimal education.

Several other non-standard forms, and not just variant pronunciations, may have been employed higher up the social stratum than is commonly thought. Thus the confusion of the second and third conjugation, as for example *debunt* "they should" in place of *debent*, may appear to be a clear indication of a speaker with little social standing. But, as Adams has shown ((1995a) 131), this form is found in a formulaic expression in the Vindolanda tablets composed by a class of under-officers who are not illiterate. Despite the absence of this linguistic feature in any literary text, we can locate the merger of the second and third conjugations, as shown by forms such as *debunt*, within a social class that was above the mass of the illiterate speakers of Latin, even if it did not belong in the work of the literate elite.

Lists of features of "the speech of the lower classes" (sometimes termed "Vulgar Latin" in the handbooks, see the discussion in chapter 1, p. 3) thus must be treated with caution. Many of these features were more general in speech than is apparent from our written texts, and we cannot be sure that all these features necessarily co-occurred in the varieties of all lower-class speakers. It is rare that we can isolate a feature within a particular social group, as we are able to do with the form *debunt*, owing to the survival of a number of written documents of a similar type within a specific archaeological context. Moreover, even if we can deduce in certain cases that one group of speakers used a particular form, we usually do not know whether it was also present or not in other social classes. Associating all forms which were stigmatised by grammarians and avoided by writers of high literary genres of Latin specifically with the speech of the lower classes is an unjustified move.

However, it is possible to draw up lists of features of "sub-standard" Latin, i.e. forms generally avoided in the work of literary authors during the Classical period, but which nevertheless existed in the language. Sub-standard features exist in higher proportions in texts composed by, or representing the speech of, those with limited access to education. Evidence for the existence of these sub-standard features comes in one of three ways. Firstly, "leaks" into the written standard, i.e. the intrusion of forms usually avoided in Classical texts. Leaks may occur in works with literary pretensions, known through the manuscript tradition, such as the *Bellum Hispaniense*, an eye-witness account of Julius Caesar's campaigns in Spain. Non-Classical forms may also occur in documentary and sub-literary material known directly from papyri, tablets, inscriptions, graffiti or *dipinti* from around the Roman world. In some cases we know enough about the individuals writing or dictating these texts to be certain that they were not part of the upper echelons of Roman society, and, as occasionally for the material from Vindolanda, we can make some judgement about the different social strata of the correspondents involved. New texts, or new readings of old texts, are still being found and published, and our knowledge of the language used by Romans beneath the highest level of society is continually growing.[5]

Secondly, we can make use of representations of, or comments on, the speech of real individuals or fictional characters belonging to a specific class or social milieu. The most famous such source is Petronius' representations of the language of the freedmen (as discussed above), and comparison of this with the new documentary material shows agreement in areas where the evidence is comparable (Adams (2003b, 2005b)). More problematic are the comments of grammarians and other writers stating which forms are "correct" Latin and which are to be avoided or are stigmatised as "rustic". One well-known compilation of non-Classical forms, which frequently appears in the handbooks, is the *Appendix Probi*, the third of five grammatical appendices to the *Instituta Artium* of Probus in a seventh- to eighth-century manuscript now in Naples (re-edited in Powell (2007a)). In this text there are over 200 pairs of words each expressed in the form *a non b*, for example *ostiae non hostiae* (207 in Powell (2007a)) "[the correct form is] *ostiae* not *hostiae*" (in this case referring to the word *hostia* "sacrificial victim" usually represented with an *h-* in Classical texts). Recent work has argued that this work is compiled, at least in part, from Greco-Latin word-lists (Barnett (2007)) and has emphasised that the compilation should not be viewed as a pronunciation manual, but a correction of written errors (Powell (2007a)). The reference to the Baths of Diocletian in one entry means that the compilation dates from the fourth century or later, although some of the observations continue grammatical precepts from as far back as the first century BCE; for example, the comment on *hostiae* recycles the prescription of excessive aspiration given by Nigidius Figulus (Gellius 13.6.3). Even so, it is probably unwise to place too much reliance on the *Appendix Probi* as evidence for spoken Latin of the lower classes during the Empire, particularly if uncorroborated by other sources.

A third main source for the reconstructions of non-Classical features of Latin during the Empire are the modern descendants of Latin. Wright (chapter 5 in this volume) has already addressed the question of what can be learnt about Latin from the Romance languages, and there is no need to recapitulate that discussion here. Many of the sub-standard features of Latin are also shared by Romance varieties, or lie behind Romance developments. However, all or most of the Romance languages also share features which are not found in the ancient evidence, or for which the first documented occurrence occurs after the end of the Roman Empire, as for example the palatalisation of velar consonants before front vowels (i.e. the development which gave the initial consonants of French *cent*, Italian *cento* etc. from Latin *centum*). We have no way of knowing for sure whether the Romance developments which are not paralleled in the ancient evidence were in fact present among some speakers already in the Empire.

Having made the above caveats about the impossibility of ever getting a true picture of the spoken social dialects of Latin, it will be convenient here to list some of the sub-standard features, as revealed principally by documents and texts written by those without the same level of training in the Classical language as literary authors and professional scribes. In the lists given below I have tried to limit the features presented to those for which there is evidence in more than a single a source before 200 CE. (I have not given textual references for features which are widespread in documents and inscriptions, such as the loss of final consonants *m* and *t*, or the confusion of *b* and *u*.) Fuller treatments of the linguistic changes which occur in spoken Latin under the Empire can be found in a number of works, including Väänänen (1981), Herman (2000), Kramer (2007) and Weiss (2009) 503–534.

Phonology

Accent and vowel length

1 In some words there is a shift of accent from the position of Classical Latin, for example *mulíerem* > *muliérem*; in this case (as in others) the accent shifts to the more open vowel when two vowels are in hiatus. The first example of this process may be the spelling *Putolis* for *Puteolis* (i.e. from *Puteólis*) at *T.Sulpicii* 52.3.14 (one of the documents written by C. Novius Eunus).

2 By the fourth century CE, it appears from statements by Augustine and grammarians (collected and discussed in Adams (2007) 260–265), that there was a tendency to pronounce stressed vowels as long, and unstressed vowels as short. This tendency was to lead to the loss of phonemic vowel length in the Romance languages, with subsequent mergers of vowels.

Vowels

1   Short *i* is lowered in unstressed syllables, and in written texts from the first century CE on, writers confuse *i* and *ē* in unstressed and final syllables.

2   Vowels *i* and *e* in unstressed syllables merge as a glide ([j]) before *o u* and *a*, hence *-ia* written for *-ea*, *-iolus* for *-eolus*, etc.

3   Short *u* is lowered in unstressed syllables, and in written texts from the late first century CE on, writers confuse *u* and *ō* in unstressed syllables and final syllables.

4   The diphthong *ae* is monophthongised to an open long *ē*.

5   The diphthong *oe* is monophthongised to a vowel written with *e* and sometimes *ae*, so probably also an open long *ē*.

6   Merger of nasal vowels with equivalent long vowels (both in internal syllables before an original sequence of *-ns-* and in final positions from the combination of vowel with a following nasal *-m* or *-n*).

7   Combinations of two like vowels prone to contraction: compare the contraction of *mihi* to *mi* "to me", which already takes place in Plautus and Ennius, and which takes place in the ostraca from Wâdi Fawâkhir written by Rustius Barbarus sometime in the first century CE (*CEL* 73–78); other examples include *dese* for *deesse* at *T.Vindol.* III.648.

8   The vowels *u* and *o* are sometimes lost or contracted before a following *u* or *o*, for example *quator* for *quattuor* (*T.Sulpicii* 52.3.11), *mortus* for *mortuus* at Pompeii (*CIL* IV.3129).

9   Lowering of *e* to *a* before following *r*, e.g., *petiarit* for *petierit* by Novius Eunus (*T.Sulpicii* 67.2.9), *itarum* for *iterum* in a letter by Claudius Terentianus (*CEL* 142.23).

10 Syncope of short vowels in syllables immediately before or after the accented syllable: for example *uirdis* for *uiridis* "green", or as a substantive "greens" (Adams (2003d) 536–537).

11 Occasional insertion of anaptyctic vowels between consonant clusters, such as *ct*, *mn*, *br*; for example Novius Eunus always uses a form *ominis* rather than *omnis* (Adams (1990) 232).

12 Insertion of a vowel, usually *e-*, in word initial position before consonant clusters beginning with *s-*, as *Ismurna* for *Smyrna* at Pompeii (*CIL* IV.7221).

13 The spelling of *y* in Greek words, and probably the associated pronunciation as a rounded front vowel [y] was dropped, with *u* or *i* used instead; at Vindolanda both *amilum* and *amulum* are found for Classical *amylum* "fine meal" (Adams (2003d) 536).

Consonants

1   Loss of aspirate *h-* in all positions, and merger of aspirated and non-aspirated consonants.

2   Loss of word-final consonants *-m*, *-n*, and *-t*; the loss of the first two consonants was doubtless initially accompanied by nasalisation of the preceeding vowel. Word-final *-s* is also prone to loss.

3 Merger of *b* and consonantal *u*, both in word initial and in word-internal position. In Romance languages the merger generally affects word-internal position not word-initial, but there are enough epigraphical examples of the confusion between *b* and consonantal *u* to be sure that this was also a feature of sub-standard Latin in some regions.

4 Palatalisation of *k*, *t*, *g*, and *d* before [j] (which itself often arises from earlier /i/ or /e/ before a back vowel). The first epigraphical examples of this change are from the second century CE, and Servius and later grammarians comment on the change (passages collected in Kramer (1976) 70–74, see discussion of Adams in this volume, p. 275).

5 Voicing of intervocalic unvoiced consonants between vowels and before *l*; the only good example from the West before 250 CE is the word *triticum* "wheat", which is found written as *tridicum* in separate documents: in Pompeiian graffiti (*CIL* IV.5380, 8830), by Novius Eunus (*T.Sulpicii* 51.3.1, Novius Eunus also uses *tridigi* at 52.3.5), and in ostraca from Bu Njem (*O.BuNjem* 76.6); although the change is more widespread in documents from Egypt, and becomes more frequent later in the West.

6 Simplification of geminate consonants, such as *redere* for *reddere* "to give back" (Bowman *et al.* (2009) 162, *T.Sulpicii* 51.2.7 (*redam* for *reddam*)).

7 Assimilation of consonant clusters, usually to geminate consonants but in documents sometimes only a single consonant is written; for example *isse* for *ipse* "himself" (Pompeii, *CIL* IV.1294), since the combination *-ks-* also developed to a geminate *ss*, the writing of *ipsi* as *ixi* which angered Augustus (Suetonius *Aug.* 88) may be another example of the same process.

8 Omission of *n* before consonants, especially, but not only *s*; frequent in Pompeiian graffiti and in other documents (*T.Sulpicii* 51.3.1, *CEL* 10.2 etc.).

Morphology

Nouns

1 Merger of masculine and neuter gender. Note for example *uinus* for *uinum* "wine", *balneus* for *balneum* "bath" in the speech of one freedman (Dama) in Petronius (Petr. 41, see also the comments of Adams in this volume at pp. 271–273). There was also occasional interchange between neuter plural and feminine nouns, for example the *plurale tantum* noun *castra* "camp" was replaced by *castra, -ae* (which is first attested in pre-Classical Latin in the work of Accius, but avoided in Classical Latin and corrected in *Appendix Probi* 136 (Powell (2007a)).

2 First-declension feminine nouns are found declined with nominative plural *-as*. This seems to be by analogy to the equivalence of nominative and accusative plurals in the third and fifth declensions. Nominative plurals in *-as* are found already in Republican inscriptions (see the examples cited by Weiss (2009) 235).

3 First-declension feminine nouns, particularly female names, are declined with a genitive singular *-aes* in place of *-ae*. Such forms are largely limited to epigraphic examples in the early Empire, except for one example in a letter from Oxyrhynchus of Augustan date (*CEL* 10, see Dickey (2009) 164–166 for discussion of other non-standard forms in this text).

4   A tendency to regularise irregular third-declension nominative forms on the basis of the stem form of the oblique cases thereby replacing e.g. *bos* "ox" by *bouis* (Petr. 62.13).

5   Third-declension ablative singular forms generalised as -*e*, accusative plural generalised as -*es*, and genitive plural as -*ium*. Note that the widespread use of -*i* as an ablative singular in some sub-literary documents, as for example the Vindolanda documents (Adams (1995b) 99), can be attributed to this change. Scribes were aware that they should sometime use -*i* in place of -*e*, but over-generalised the "correct" variant.

Adjectives

1   Some confusion between adjectives of the third declension and the second/first declension, hence *pauper* "poor" taken as a second-/first-declension form on the analogy of adjectives such as *sacer* "holy" (Petr. 46.2).

2   Comparative forms are reinforced or replaced by synthetic constructions involving *magis* or *plus*. Although constructions involving *magis* and comparative are already present in early comedy, they are generally avoided in Classical prose, but note *magis suspensiore animo* "more anxiously" (*B. Afr.* 48.3 (cited by Löfstedt (1956) II.201)).

3   Some superlative forms in -*illimus* and -*errimus* are replaced by -*issimus*, as *miserissima* in place of *miserrima* (*CIL* III.4480, IX.3729); note again that this form is already attested in Early Latin but is avoided in the Classical language.

4   Other constructions are used alongside the superlative suffix, such as *bene*, e.g. *bene magnam manum* "a very large band" (*B. Hisp.* 22).

Pronouns

1   Replacement of anaphoric pronoun *is* by *ille*, as shown by the speeches of the freedmen in Petronius and by the letters of Claudius Terentianus (Halla-aho (2009) 160–163).

2   Creation of new genitive and dative forms of the pronoun *ille*; in Claudius Terentianus' letters there is evidence for the new feminine dative spelt *illei* (representing *illaei*) in place of Classical *illi* (Adams (1977) 45–47).

Verbs

1   Confusion between the present indicative paradigms of the second and third conjugation. The use of *debunt* for *debent* at Vindolanda was discussed above; Rustius Barbarus uses *mittes* "you send" for *mittis* and *debio* for *debeo* "I should" in the same letter (*CEL* 74); the writer of a wooden tablet from Holland dating to 29 CE uses *debo* for *debeo*, as does Novius Eunus (Bowman *et al.* (2009) 162, *T.Sulpicii* 52.2.10).

2   Preference for the form -*erunt* with short *e* in the third plural of the perfect indicative (revealed by the preponderance of contracted forms in documentary material, see Adams (2003d) 544).

3   Formation of a future participle by the suffix *-iturus* (*uinciturum* for *uicturum* at Petr. 45.10, *missiturum* for the non-finite future participle in Claudius Terentianus (*CEL* 142.22).

4   Uncertainty over the correct morphology of the future indicative, and attempts to replace the future with other constructions. Thus in Echion's speech in Petronius (45–46), we find the forms *habituri sumus* for *habebimus* "we shall have", *daturus est* for *dabit* "he will have" and *persuadeam* in place of *persuadebo* "I shall persuade you". Claudius Terentianus also uses *daturus est* in place of *dabit* (*CEL* 147.14–15).

5   Confusion over the conjugation of deponent verbs; evident both in Petronius and in documentary sources (*obliuiscere* for *obliuisci* "forget" at *CEL* 74).

Syntax

1   Simplification of the nominal case system

A number of developments can be interpreted as part of a general drift towards a simplification and restructuring of the nominal case system:

1   There was confusion between prepositions with the accusative and ablative, and use of both cases after all prepositions, for example *cum sodales* "with his companions" and *cum discentes* "with his pupils" (for Classical *cum sodalibus* and *cum discentibus*) already in Pompeii (*CIL* IV.221 and 275).

2   Uncertainty over which verbs were construed with an object accusative and which with other cases led to confusion. For example, the freedman Niceros in Petronius use a dative after *adiuto* "help" (Petr. 62.11) on the analogy of verbs *adsum* "help" and *succurro* "help". Rustius Barbarus uses the accusative in place of the genitive after the verb *obliuiscor* "forget": *stati amicitiam tuam obliuiscere debio* "I should immediately forget your friendship" for Classical *statim amicitiae tuae obliuisci debeo* (*CEL* 74. 5).

3   Overlap of locative and accusative of motion. The use of the locative in Classical Latin was restricted to names of towns and small islands, and a few specific words such as *domus* "home", and in substandard texts the locative was liable to replacement by the ablative (Väänänen (1966) 110). In sub-literary documents of the early Empire there is also a tendency to use the locative in place of the accusative representing the goal of motion, as on a grafitto from Pompeii including the phrase *redei domi* "I went home" for "correct" *redei domum* (*CIL* IV.2246, cited by Mackay (1999) 233, in a survey of examples from the early Empire, see also Kruschwitz and Halla-aho (2007) 42–43, who note that this feature also occurs among the officer class at Vindolanda).

4   Use of the accusative in place of the ablative to express the price at which something is bought or sold (an example from Vindolanda and one in the correspondence of Claudius Terentianus are discussed by Adams (1995b) 116).

2   Word order

Romance languages are mostly "head-first", that is to say that the head of a phrase usually precedes its subject, so that a verb is placed before a (non-pronominal) object, and the noun precedes most adjectives which agree with it (except for certain adjectives, such as those delimiting the scope of the noun phrase). In Classical Latin prose texts one unmarked position is to place the verb at the end of the phrase, that is, following the direct object. In the epistolary material written in Egypt by Rustius Barbarus and Claudius Terentianus there is a preference for the order of verb before a nominal object, indicating that this word-order change may already have been under way. However, in the epistolary material from Vindolanda the majority of instances show nominal objects before the verb (Halla-aho (2009) 131). It is clear that the word-order patterns of sub-literary letters in Latin are also influenced by other factors, such as epistolary formulae, the length of constituents and the choice between "new" and "given" information, but amongst all this it is possible that a "Romance" word-order pattern was one feature of sub-elite speech (see Halla-aho (2009) 130–155 for detailed consideration of the evidence).

3 Subordination

One of the markers of Classical Latin literary prose is a periodic sentence style, with authors able to make use of the syntactic resources of the language to construct an intricate web of subordinate clauses fitted together into an artful whole. Speakers with less education show themselves less ready to attempt subordination on this scale, and are liable to reveal themselves when they do. Thus in both the speeches of Petronius and sub-literary documents there is a tendency towards parataxis and asyndeton; when co-ordination between sentences or clauses does appear it is often effected through a limited stock of particles of fairly neutral meanings such as *et* "and", *enim* "for" or *autem* "then" (Halla-aho (2009) 65–69). Some authors of limited education attempt more ambitious constructions, but the results sometimes reveal contamination of two different constructions, or confusion and incoherence. A notorious example is the letter from Vindolanda written by Chrauttius, *T.Vindol.* II.310 (discussed by Clackson and Horrocks (2007) 244–249, Kramer (2007) 47–58 and Halla-aho (2009) 94–98). The author of the letter, Chrauttius, is only known from this document, but is clearly not of a high social rank, and it is even possible that he is a non-native Latin speaker. Certain constructions, such as the ablative absolute, seem to have been largely avoided by writers with little education.

Vocabulary and Word-Formation

Petronius introduces a number of words into the speech of the freedmen which never recur in Latin literature, and which appear to represent *ad hoc* formations. For example, Echion (45.5) describes a certain Titus with the words *non est mixcix*, probably meaning something like "he is not a flibbertygibbet". The word *mixcix* is a hapax, but the freedmen in the *Satyricon* also show some vocabulary choices which anticipate the lexical items which will survive into Romance (the example of *ploro* for "weep" has already been discussed), and the documentary material sometimes corroborates the evidence of Petronius. Thus *adiuto* is preferred to *adiuuo* both in the letters of Claudius Terentianus and in Petronius for the meaning "help" (Adams (1977) 80). However, we must again be careful to avoid the conclusion that words such as *adiuto* and *ploro* were absent from the speech of the elite: *adiuto* occurs in Cicero's letters, and *ploro* in high-style poetry and oratory. Such words were not inherently "vulgar" or "lower-class" (see also the remarks on *colaphus* on pp. 252–253).

However, just as ignorance of the precepts of grammarians and others about morphology or syntax forms could be an indication of an imperfect education, in the same way some lexical constructions were stigmatised, but leak through into texts. One such was the use of the adjective *paucus* "few" with mass nouns, i.e. words which do not have distinct plural forms and which cannot be counted, such as "money", "wheat" or "speech". The use of the expression *pauco sermone* "with a few words" was stigmatised by the author of the *Rhetorica ad Herennium*, and the phrase *paucum aes* "little money" occurs in the letters of Claudius Terentianus. However, once again we cannot immediately conclude that all uses of *paucus* are associated with the speech of the lower classes; Adams has shown ((2005c) 87) that the same construction is found in the *Bellum Africum* and in Vitruvius, and argues that these works should not be assumed to be "vulgar" or "lower-class". Rather they exhibit some of the diversity of literate prose at the end of the Republic.

The change in vocabulary between Classical Latin and the Romance languages happened over a long period of time, and owing to the complex nature of the evidence it is probably best to avoid giving lists of "Classical" vocabulary and "Vulgar" alternatives (as for example "Classical" *eo* but "Vulgar" *uado* "I go", or Classical *os* but "Vulgar" *bucca* "mouth"; a large compilation of such words is given by Väänänen (1981) 75–84), since such presentations are liable to blur the nuances of meaning and use, and compare late forms with those common in the early Empire. Also problematic is the identification of words that occur in documentary material but not in literary Latin as belonging to the dialect of those beneath the elite. Many words of this type, for example the word *equisio* "groom", which occurs once at Vindolanda in the letter of Chrauttius (*T.Vindol.* II.310, discussed above) and nowhere else in Latin before the fifth century, belong to the realm of technical or military vocabulary, a register largely avoided in Classical Latin texts. For this reason, some of the statements made about the word-formation devices employed in sub-elite Latin need to be treated with caution. The suffix *-io*, used, sometimes alongside the suffix *-o*, to form masculine names and job-titles (for example *equisio* "groom"; *equiso* "groom" is attested in Varro and Valerius Maximus), is sometimes taken as being a feature of non-standard Latin (e.g. Leumann (1977) 364). Yet many of the words with this suffix have no "Classical" equivalent, and relate to the army or military contexts, such as *centurio* "centurion" (first in Lucilius), *optio* "junior officer" and *mulio* "muleteer" (both first in Plautus), *lucrio* "profiteer" (Festus and Petronius), *cocio* "dealer" (Laberius and Petronius); *equisio* would seem to belong in this set, and not be a specifically lower-class form. Similarly, words formed with the suffix *-arius/-um* and diminutive forms may have been widespread in speech of all classes, but filtered out of the literary language.

Conclusion

Attempting to trace the different social dialects of Latin can be a frustrating business. All of our evidence has to be gathered through the film of the written record, itself a product of a minority of the speakers of Latin at any one time. Education was a process of learning to write "correct" Latin, and inculcated a set of forms to use and ones to avoid. Beneath this largely smooth surface of Classical Latin it is possible to get a glimpse of other varieties of Latin, those of women, of children and of speakers without education, although sometimes the picture may be distorted or the glint of isolated pieces of evidence may be illusory. It is important to keep in mind the fact that no language is ever fixed. Individuals vary their own language depending on context, register and addressee, and even Cicero's letters are not a verbatim transcription of a single man's speech, but were themselves "corrected" in the commitment to paper. This chapter has shown some of the possible axes along which spoken Latin may have alternated, has given some of the scope of variation between speakers, and has listed some of the variables in spoken Latin. If speakers of Latin behaved in the same way as speakers of modern languages (and there is no reason to suppose that they did not), these variables may have existed in some degree among the whole speech community, among men and women, old and young and the rich and poor. Speakers of different classes, ages and sexes may have employed these variables to a greater or lesser degree depending on factors such as their interlocutors and the setting of the conversation. Unfortunately, we are now unable to recover that variation in any detail.

FURTHER READING

For general overviews of the problem of approaching social dialects of Latin, see Clackson and Horrocks (2007) and Herman (2000). Many of the papers in Dickey and Chahoud (2010) discuss the overlap between spoken Latin, colloquial Latin and other social dialects, note particularly the papers of Ferri and Probert, and Chahoud. Fögen (2004) is a very full bibliography on works on gender-based variation in speech in the ancient world, and Fögen (2010) covers female speech in Latin as well as in Greek. The discovery of a number of new documentary texts (some of which are presented in Kramer (2007)) has changed our understanding of sub-standard features of Latin. Most of this material has now been extensively studied. For the Pompeiian graffiti consult Väänänen (1966) and Wallace (2005) (see also Kruschwitz and Halla-aho (2007) and Kruschwitz (2010a) for recent surveys of the worth of the Pompeiian graffiti for the linguist, and arguments against the assumption that the Pompeiian material is in any way unified, or that it necessarily represents the language of the lower orders). For Latin documentary material on papyri, ostraca, wooden and wax tablets, principally from Egypt and Britain, Halla-aho (2009) can be consulted for a general overview of the material and work on it (notably Adams (1977, 1995a and 2003d)), as well as a detailed survey of the syntax and pragmatics. The linguistically important copies of legal documents written by the freedmen C. Novius Eunus in Campania in 37 and 29 CE are discussed by Adams (1990).

NOTES

1 Cited from Morpurgo Davies (1987). Morpurgo Davies tracks the attestations and meanings of the word διάλεκτος in the grammatical tradition, as well as the evolution of the notion of the geographical dialect.

2 See Boyce (1991) for comparison of the language of the freedmen and the developments of Romance.

3 Dutsch (2008) 12 takes issue with these conclusions.

4 Karakasis (2005) 62 cites a number of other ancient testimonia for the garrulity of old men following Aristotle.

5 See Bowman *et al.* (2009) for a new reading of a text dating to 29 CE that was signed by a legionary tribune, a soldier and a slave.

CHAPTER 29

Latin and Other Languages: Societal and Individual Bilingualism

Alex Mullen

Introduction

The Roman Republic and Empire were Greco-Roman, bicultural creations, and bilingual, to some extent, from the outset. The Romans themselves frequently debated the nature of their biculturalism and discussed the status and function of *utraque lingua*, "both our languages" (Dubuisson (1981)). Until recently, the focus of modern research has been on elite bilingualism and the literary evidence, and largely restricted to Latin–Greek contact. Over the last decade, seminal works, especially Adams (2003a) and Adams *et al.* (2002), have broadened our view by taking into account the myriad contact languages of the Greco-Roman world and the range of evidence, from graffiti on potsherds to elaborate bronze inscriptions. Furthermore, by applying the theories of modern bilingualism to the ancient evidence, a great deal more sophistication has been introduced into both our identification and description of the phenomena of bilingualism and their interpretation, particularly with regard to cultural contacts and expressions of identity. These advances have fitted well with the direction of research in other Classical disciplines, and current research is exploring the scope for interdisciplinary approaches (Biville *et al.* (2008), Cotton *et al.* (2009), Mullen and James (forthcoming), Papaconstantinou (2010), Wallace-Hadrill (2008)). This survey leans towards epigraphic evidence and reflects recent trends in its approach. Traditional accounts from literary or historical viewpoints are widely available; an excellent starting point is Rochette (2010).

A Companion to the Latin Language, First Edition. Edited by James Clackson.
© 2011 Blackwell Publishing Ltd. Published 2011 by Blackwell Publishing Ltd.

Societal and Individual Bilingualism

The term "bilingual" can be applied to both communities and individuals.[1] Bilinguals and multilinguals outnumber monolinguals worldwide and "the idea that monolingualism is the human norm is a myth" (Thomason (2001) 31). The traditional view of bilinguals as being able to speak two languages equally well, often termed *balanced bilinguals*, has been superseded by a spectrum of definitions (Hamers and Blanc (2000) 6–8). The scale begins with minimal competence in a second language, practised by *dominant bilinguals*, and extends to *balanced bilinguals* who have impressive linguistic skills and deep conversance with both cultures.

Societal bilingualism refers to the use of two or more languages within a community (strictly speaking *multilingualism* should be employed for more than two languages, but the term *bilingualism* tends to be extended). Various factors may affect the levels and patterns of bilingualism in a community: duration of contact between speakers, number of speakers, role of imperfect learning, education, literacy, exogamy, age, gender, relative socioeconomic dominance of the groups, linguistic and cultural similarity between the groups, attitudes of the groups, functions of the languages, level of cohesion in the community and role of language as an ethnic marker (Clyne (2003) 20–69).[2] These factors naturally intersect and a simple linear relationship between them and bilingualism does not exist. It is difficult to assess the extent of bilingualism in the ancient world, especially when we have little information concerning these factors and when the written evidence is partial. However, detailed analyses of the written record, combined with knowledge of better documented societies in the ancient world and information from archaeological and historical sources, may lead to tentative conclusions.

Language contact can entail either *maintenance*, where the languages in contact continue to be spoken, or *shift*, where speakers of one language shift to the other (Fishman (1964)). Language shift may ultimately result in the total loss of the language being replaced. Modern linguistic studies cannot supply a strict set of factors which diagnose whether a language in a bilingual environment might be maintained or whether shift will occur. In general, certain factors recur, but their relative importance is variable (Myers-Scotton (2006) 69–70, 89–106). What is indisputable is that the nature of the languages themselves plays no part in the outcome. It is demonstrably not the case that certain languages are in any way inherently "weaker" or more prone to shift than others. The circumstances of the linguistic communities, rather than the nature of the languages themselves, motivate change. Clackson and Horrocks suggest that the languages surviving the Roman Empire tend to be those "of small populations in inaccessible regions, those of nomadic peoples at the margins of the Empire, and those of large, long urbanized populations with deep-rooted literate cultures of their own" ((2007) 88), for example Welsh, Libyan and Greek.

The function of languages in bilingual societies has always been of particular interest to sociolinguists and indeed may have some impact on whether shift or maintenance occurs. For bilinguals, choice of language can be significant for presentations of identity and intergroup or interpersonal relations. Occasionally the choice of language may be due to idiomatic or lexical gaps in one language, but "the major reason is the symbolic value of speaking that language" (Myers-Scotton (2006) 143). Fishman (1965) defined as *domains* the abstract mixtures of status, role relationships, settings and topics which provoke similar language choices. A handful of regions of the ancient world offer a relatively rich variety of evidence, and a description of linguistic differentiation in certain domains can be attempted, for instance for Egypt and Delos (Adams (2003a) 527–641 and 642–686). Yet it is impossible to reconstruct a complete picture of the language choice for many domains in ancient communities, due to the restrictions of the inscriptional record. For most regions we simply do not have enough evidence and the odd text may hint at relations between language and domain which are now irrecoverable; for instance, the Larzac lead tablets (*RIG* II.2 L-98), written in Gaulish in the late first/early second century CE, may be connected with women and, probably, cultic practices.

Diglossia describes a specific type of societal bilingualism in which the linguistic varieties can be assigned H(igh) and L(ow) values *and are functionally compartmentalized*, a defining example being the diglossic situation in Modern Greek with Katharevousa (H) and Dimotiki (L) (Ferguson (1959)).[3] Many commentators have demonstrated that this concept is inadequate for the Roman world (Adams (2003a) *passim*, especially 537–541, 754–755, Adams and Swain (2002) 9–10). It is impossible to reconstruct the whole picture of linguistic functions using ancient evidence and a strict binary division often does not accurately describe the complexities attested and neglects interpersonal variation. Nevertheless, the notion of H and L linguistic varieties can still be useful in our descriptions, as we can often identify communities with, broadly speaking, varieties of different prestige or function, whether or not they show the strict division into domains as expected under diglossia. We might, for example, view the simplified linguistic situation in inland southern Gaul during the Principate as follows: L1 (first language) Gaulish is spoken at home by the majority of the population and has the status L, whereas L2 (second language) Latin is spoken in domains such as education, trade and the army, and has the status H. Within this broad schema there may have been diglossic regions, communities or individuals, but they will have formed only part of a patchwork of linguistic interactions.

The Ancient Evidence

Literary evidence offers copious information for reconstructing the bilingualism of specific individuals; particularly well-studied characters include Cicero (see pp. 539–543), Lucretius (Sedley (1999)) and Polybius (Dubuisson (1985)). As a result, we can create a picture of Latin–Greek bilingualism in a small section of society, namely the well-educated elite. The overall consistency in terms of bilingual competence across the corpus and the supporting anecdotal evidence suggest that Latin–Greek bilingualism in these circles was widespread and of a high standard. The literary evidence, especially in comedy (which is, of course, heavily dependent on Greek models), also provides us with representations of those beyond this section of society, for example Greek–Latin bilingual slaves in Plautus and Terence (Fontaine (2010), Jocelyn (1999), Karakasis (2005) 83–89, Maltby (1985, 1995), Shipp (1953, 1954)), and sporadic hints of contact languages other than Greek. In some cases ancient grammarians and commentators make specific reference to manifestations of language contact in elite and non-elite situations, but this amounts to relatively meagre pickings.

By extending our evidence beyond the literary sources to the impressive range of non-literary material, both epigraphic and papyrological, we attain greater coverage and more direct access to the numerous communities of the Roman world. But we are still in a much poorer position than modern linguists who study bilingualism. They study speech, and copious amounts of it, all carefully collected and contextualized. In reconstructing the bilingualism of communities in the ancient world, we must remember that we are dealing with written evidence, not the spoken word. Whilst only a tiny section of society composed the literature transmitted to us, the inscriptional record is also restricted, though admittedly to a lesser extent (soldiers, elites and freedmen are particularly prolific, women, slaves and children much less so), so we are plagued by what has been termed "epigraphic bias" (Bodel (2001)). Similarly, the written word generally requires more thought than the spoken and may be affected by standardization, formulaic language, deliberate archaism and linguistic choices based on genre. The choice of language for the epigraphy of a community may therefore not represent day-to-day use of language: some indigenous languages seem never to have been written and we cannot describe accurately the complexity of linguistic choices, motivated, for example, by domains, based purely on restricted written evidence.

Furthermore, we are often confronted with inscriptional evidence which may not be well contextualized, either because it was removed in modern times without any record of context or because it had already been reused in Antiquity or the Middle Ages. We cannot be sure how much written evidence has not been transmitted to us; we may not read the texts correctly; we may date the evidence wrongly and we may be thrown off course by fakes. A particularly thorny problem is trying to identify the author(s). Scribes would have been widely employed for the production of letters and other documents (known mostly from Egyptian papyri); dictation is not always identifiable and, as a result, the origins of the linguistic features may remain obscure. The production of lapidary inscriptions may have involved a veritable team of people.[4] Stone inscriptions could have gone through a commissioning stage (the commissioner may have simply adumbrated some details, perhaps not even in the language of the proposed inscription), a drafting stage, an initial carving stage (outlines) and a final carving stage. The bilingual content may therefore be the product of any of a number of people, who may or may not be named in the inscription, and may even be the result of the use of manuals or the purchase of stones with pre-carved formulae.[5]

Despite these problems, scope for fruitful investigation remains. There are four main sources of evidence for bilingualism in the ancient world, all of which may combine.[6] The first, and most obvious, group contains texts which appear with two versions in two different languages, *bi-version bilingual texts*, for instance the Latin–Palmyrene epitaph which we will discuss later, or sometimes three versions, *tri-version trilingual texts*, which would include the Gallus trilingual (Hoffmann *et al.* (2009)) and several Punic–Latin–Greek trilinguals from North Africa (Wilson (forthcoming)). The versions need not say the same thing and they may provide idiomatic or non-idiomatic versions. The other large group of evidence, *texts displaying bilingual phenomena*, consists of texts ostensibly in one language but which show evidence of bilingual phenomena, as we shall see in the letters of Cicero (see pp. 540–543). A smaller group encompasses those texts, *mixed-language texts*, which involve two languages which are mixed to the extent that it is impossible to assign a matrix language to the text, for example some of the graffiti from La Graufesenque (see pp. 536–539). The final group includes texts that have been transliterated, often a Latin text in Greek script or vice versa (see p. 532).

Studies of modern bilingualism have provided us with the terminological and analytical framework to approach bilingual phenomena in a sophisticated way. The three main bilingual phenomena can be summarized as follows:

1   *Code-switching*: the phenomenon of switching between languages within one utterance or text (Gardner-Chloros (2009)). It can be practised by both balanced and dominant bilinguals (see pp. 537–538 for subdivisions).
2   *Borrowing*: the adoption of any linguistic element into one language from another. The items function in the recipient language as native elements, namely they are used by monolingual speakers, often with some degree of morphophonemic integration.[7] This category includes *calquing* and *loan-shifting*. Calquing denotes the translation of a foreign expression by a new native form which matches the foreign form, e.g. *qualitas* is a Latin calque of Greek ποιότης (Adams (2003) 459–461, Nicolas 1996). Loan-shifting describes the process through which a word undergoes semantic extension on the model of a foreign counterpart, namely when "the pre-existing degree of overlap between A and B facilitates the semantic extension of A" (Adams (2003) 523).[8] For example, in certain Celtic-speaking areas, Latin *ualles* "valley" has undergone semantic shift to include the meaning "stream, watercourse", probably based on the equivalent term in Celtic *nantu/o-* meaning "valley" and "stream, watercourse" (Adams (2007) 300–301).
3   *Interference*: the process through which features from L1 are unintentionally transferred into an utterance or text in L2. "The presence of *interference* phenomena (as indeed code-switching) in an utterance or text implies that the speaker/writer is bilingual, if only imperfectly so" (Adams (2003) 27). The phenomena can be orthographical, morphological, phonetic, lexical, or syntactic.[9]

All three categories reside on a continuum (Myers-Scotton (2006) 253–260) and can be extremely difficult to identify and analyse. Borrowing and code-switching show similarities; indeed it is generally accepted that code-switching may be a precursor to borrowing. For the ancient world, the distribution of the item in the extant literature may give an idea of whether it had been accepted into the recipient language (borrowing), or whether its attestation was *ad hoc* (code-switching or interference). Similarly, some features assigned to interference could easily be assigned to code-switching and borrowing. Adams notes that the best way of assigning the features to either borrowing or interference is the direction of the transfer: L2 to L1 for borrowing or L1 to L2 for interference, though the bi-directionality of borrowing, and to a lesser extent interference, causes problems (Langslow (2002) 42–44). Also essential in identifying bilingual features is an understanding of the extra-linguistic context. Interference is "unintentional and beyond the control of the writer, whereas code-switching ... is often a manifestation of linguistic skill" (Adams (2003a) 28).[10]

Certain aspects of ancient bilingualism do not generally find comparative treatment in modern studies. While they are certainly not unique to the past, they are a much more significant consideration because our evidence is mediated through the written, not spoken, word. One such aspect is choice of script. Sometimes texts are entirely transliterated into the script of another language, often to underline a duality of identity, as in this example from Rome: Αλλονια Μαρκ[ε]λα φηκιτ μαριτο σουο βενε μερετι … "Allonia Marcella made this for her well-deserving husband" (*CIL* VI.15450). At other times the change of script may be used to highlight a specific feature of the text which is deemed to be distinctive, for example, sometimes Greek names will be presented in Greek script in a Latin text, and unusual mixtures of scripts are often found in magical texts in a deliberate ploy to obfuscate or lend potency. Orthographical mistakes made in the creation of certain transliterated texts can suggest that the author may not purposefully have chosen that script, but may have had no choice due to illiteracy in the language of the text (Adams (2003a) 53–63). Bilingualism does not necessarily entail biliteracy.

Another commonly attested phenomenon of ancient bilingualism has been termed *imitation*, the process whereby a feature of a second language is copied in the text of the first language for stylistic or other reasons. A distinctive feature of literary texts, this naturally is not a focus of modern bilingualism theory. Throughout the history of Latin literature the phenomenon of using Grecisms, namely imitating Greek features, has recurred (Coleman (1975), Mayer (1999)). But Adams is also able to give evidence of imitatory features, which were non-literary: deliberate affectation of Greek phonetic features, use of suffixes from Greek on Latin words, e.g. -*ta*, -*tes*, and deliberate imitation of Greek syntactical features.[11] Since imitation is an *ad hoc* phenomenon and not a permanent feature of the language, it cannot comfortably be classed as a borrowing. Equally, it cannot be interference as it is a conscious and deliberate strategy, as contextual analysis demonstrates. Consider, for example, Horace's imitation of the Greek nominative and infinitive construction, as opposed to the expected Latin accusative and infinitive: *uir bonus et sapiens dignis ait esse paratus* "The good and wise man says he is ready to help the deserving" (*Ep.* 1.7.22). The Grecism here is motivated by the reference to Stoic philosophy (Coleman (1975) 139). Imitation can perhaps be best categorized as a distinctive form of code-switching. Modern bilingualism theory helps little with the categorization and interpretation of imitation, or with negotiations of script use.

Latin and Societal Bilingualism

Pre-imperial period

In the pre-imperial period, societal bilingualism involving Latin primarily results from contact in Italy and neighbouring islands. The proximity of the Greek-speaking communities of Magna Graecia, established from the eighth century BCE, to the Latin-speaking centres and the high regard in which Greek culture was held meant that Latin–Greek bilingualism became a feature of the elite society of Rome. Early Latin poetry is imbued with Greek literature (topoi, metre, linguistic and stylistic features). Indeed, the first known epic in Latin was an adaptation of Homer's *Odyssey* by Livius Andronicus (third century BCE). Similarly Greek laws considerably influenced the creation of Early Latin law and the very idea of funerary epigraphy in Latin seems to have been largely inspired by the Greek penchant for this mode of expression.

Nevertheless, these genres were not slavish imitations, native Italic aspects also played a part: it is the mixture of Greek and Italic forms that created Early Latin poetic, legal and epigraphic genres (Clackson and Horrocks (2007)).

Latin–Greek bilingualism was not restricted to elite society. Trade, slavery and inter-marriage meant that both Latin and Greek were spoken at lower social levels in numerous communities. The integration of Greek words into Latin at an early stage is shown by an archaic inscription: *Castorei Podlouqueique qurois* "to the youths Castor and Pollux" (*CIL* I².2833). This inscription on a bronze sheet was found in a shrine just outside the walls of Lavinium (Latium, Italy). The piercings at the four corners suggest that it had originally been fixed to an offering. Written from right to left and containing early letter forms such as the koppa, this text has been dated to *c.* 500 BCE. Though probably conceived as a Latin inscription, only *-que* and the endings are not borrowings from Greek (Biville (2008) 43). It is undoubtedly, however, the island of Delos which offers the most impressive array of early epigraphic evidence (from the third century BCE) for Italo-Greek relations in a trading context: bi-version bilingual inscriptions but also inscriptions in one language displaying the phenomena of bilingualism (Adams (2003a) 642–686, Hasenohr (2007, 2008)). The testimony of loanwords in Latin from Greek can also be illuminating (see Biville (1990, 1995), Rochette (2010) 286–287 and Weiss (2009) 479–483 for summaries). A careful analysis of the type of word borrowed and the context in which it is used can reveal information about the cultural contacts that may have surrounded its borrowing and subsequent use. Indeed, detailed linguistic analysis can distinguish between what have been termed "written" or "learned" and "oral" or "vulgar" borrowings.[12] The former are generally borrowed from Greek literary texts and tend to retain their original form, the latter develop within the language, undergoing relevant sound changes in the host language. The time period in which the borrowings took place, and even the dialectal variety of Greek from which they were taken, can sometimes be identified; for instance, Latin *mālum* and *māchina* have both been posited as "non-Attic-Ionic pre-*koiné* borrowings" (Weiss (2009) 480).

Evidence also attests to the importance of bilingualism between Latin and the other languages of Italy, the Italic languages Oscan and Umbrian and the non-Indo-European language Etruscan in particular (see chapter 2, Adams (2003a) 111–184, Clackson (forthcoming), Hadas-Lebel (2004)).[13] Some of the influence is reflected in the loanwords of Latin, which include, from Italic, *popina* "cook-shop, eating-house, tavern" (equivalent to the native *coquina* "kitchen, cookery") and, from Etruscan, *subulo* "flautist". Several words of Greek origin reach Latin not directly, but through the intermediary of Etruscan. We can identify these loanwords since the voiced stops of Greek appear as unvoiced in Latin, a consequence of the devoicing of these stops in Etruscan, for example Greek θρίαμβος > Latin *triumpe*, Greek ἀμόργη > Latin *amurca* (Biville (1990) 220–221, 233–234).

Bilingual inscriptions involving Latin and Italic languages appear from the second century BCE. One of the most compelling examples of Oscan–Latin bilingualism is found on a terracotta tile from *c.* 100 BCE from the sanctuary complex of Pietrabbondante in Samnium (Rix *ST* Sa 35, discussed at Adams (2003a) 124–125, Clackson (forthcoming), Wallace-Hadrill (2008) 90–92, 137–143). This is evidently not to be viewed as part of the epigraphy of the temple and theatre, which is all in Oscan. It was meant to be positioned in the roof of the temple, and therefore was presumably not destined for human eyes and should perhaps be seen

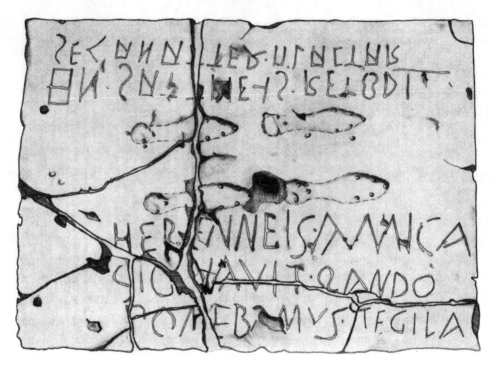

Figure 29.1 Bilingual roof-tile from Pietrabbondante (reproduced from *Studi Etruschi* 44 (1976) by kind permission of Adriano La Regina).

as a rare glimpse of "playful banter" (Wallace-Hadrill (2008) 91) between two workers. Where the tile-making took place cannot be established with certainty, though it is likely to have been local. Before the clay dried two female workers impressed their feet, complete with Samnite shoes (ibid.), into the tile and each left a message, one in Oscan, the other in Latin. The two inscriptions are presented in mirror-image format, making it difficult to decide which comes first and which second, though the Latin inscription is formed with larger letters and takes up three, rather than two, lines, indicating visual primacy (see Figure 29.1).

> OSCAN: **hn. sattiieís. detfri**
> **seganatted. plavtad**
> (Detfri, (slave?) of Herens Sattiis, left her mark with her foot)
> LATIN: Herenneis. Amica
> signauit. qando
> ponebamus. tegila
> (Amica, (slave?) of Herennius, left her mark when we were stacking tiles)

Detfri, a name otherwise unattested, and Amica both appear to be slaves of Herens Sattiis, whose name has been given in Oscan form, even in the Latin inscription (*Herenneis*), where we might expect *Herenni*. The author of the Latin has effectively code-switched from Latin into Oscan for the morphology of the name, in order, perhaps to emphasize her bilinguality and her awareness of the non-Latin identity of the slave-owner. This should come as no surprise: names are deemed important badges of personal identity and attract code-switching. Further evidence of the bilingual environment may be provided by Oscan **seganatted**. This seems to be a denominative verb based on Oscan **segúnú** which is otherwise (at Abella, Cumae and Rossano) only known with the meaning "statue". Untermann suggests that the meaning of **seganatted** attested on this bilingual tile may have been influenced by the semantic content of the equivalent Latin term *signauit* ((2000) 661–662), though our knowledge of Oscan is not secure enough to be certain.

Pietrabbondante reminds us of the complexity of bilingual societies. Oscan was the prime language of the sanctuary complex, but in a workplace nearby, Latino-Oscan bilingualism appears to have been normal. According to Livy (40.43.1), as early as 180 BCE the inhabitants of Cumae, a Greek colony which had been taken by the Oscans in 421 BCE, petitioned Rome for the right to use Latin *publice*.[14] Yet later in the second, or possibly first, century BCE the *Lex Osca Tabulae Bantinae* (Crawford (1996) 271–292) was engraved in Oscan on a bronze tablet already used for the *Lex Latina Tabulae Bantinae*, and during the Social War coins were minted with Oscan legends. Context, in terms of both domain and period, is essential for understanding societal bilingualism.

Imperial period

As the empire expanded, Latin encountered numerous new contact languages (see Neumann and Untermann (1980), Weiss (2009)). In the East, for pragmatic reasons, the *koiné* Greek that had been utilized from Alexander the Great onwards, was retained as the official language in most contexts (H), a situation allowed by the Romans as Greek was already viewed as "the other" of their languages. We can presume that none of the non-Greek indigenous languages (L) would ever have been afforded such an honour.[15] In the same area, Latin played a role, in Adams' terms, as the "super-High" language in specific and highly symbolic contexts, such as coins, milestones and documents pertaining to the army, citizenship and the imperial family (see Adams (2003a) 527–641, Eck (2009), Isaac (2009), Kaimio (1979), Rochette (1997), (2010) 289–290). Traditionally there is thought to have been an increase in the use of Latin from Diocletian onwards. Adams ((2003a) 637, 758–759) urges a re-examination of all the evidence to determine whether the use of Latin in fact increases; he remains unconvinced as to whether Diocletian would have been responsible for such a change. If the change is not a mirage, this is perhaps, at least in part, to be linked to the new imperial residences in the Eastern Empire and the increasing value of Latin in the East for social and career advancement (Rochette (2010) 290–291). After the end of Roman rule, under the Byzantine Empire, Latin continued to be used in specific, official functions (the court, the army, the legal profession) until the end of the sixth century CE when it was superseded by Greek in these functions (Horrocks 2010).

In the Western Empire the sociolinguistic situation in general terms was one of H and L languages, where the H language was Latin (plus "elite" Greek, namely the Greek of the well-educated upper echelons) and the L languages were the indigenous languages (plus "non-elite" Greek, namely the Greek of merchants, traders, slaves). Yet even this non-diglossic H and L schema was probably more complex on the ground. In the absence of a systematic language policy (see chapter 30) or widespread, centrally organized education,[16] the spread of Latin in the West can be compared to that of English today. Latin was not forced upon the inhabitants of the societies in the West, but was rather chosen as having a high cultural, political, legal, social and economic value for its speakers. Many societies entered into a period of unstable bilingualism when language shift towards the H language was taking place, resulting in the death of numerous indigenous languages within three or so generations. However, not all the communities absorbed into the Roman Empire learnt Latin instantly: those in isolated areas may have taken longer and there may have been localized resistance to Latinization in certain communities, different social groups, various professions or by specific individuals. Indeed, some local languages survived the Empire and in some cases we can hear the descendants of indigenous languages spoken today, such as Basque and Welsh.

In the fourth and fifth centuries CE, Goths, Franks and Vandals began to settle in Italy and Spain, France and North Africa, and in 476 the last Roman emperor in the West abdicated. Yet Latin continued to be used as the language of law, administration and literature. Even in private contexts we can still document the desire to write a standard form of Latin, for instance in the *Tablettes Albertini* from late fifth-century North Africa and the slate tablets from north-central Spain in the sixth and seventh centuries (Clackson and Horrocks 2007 (293–295)). Christianity was a key reason for the continued importance of Latin. In the first two centuries CE, Greek had been the language of Christians in both the East and West, but thereafter Latin took over in the West. Over time, the Romance vernaculars steadily diverged from the language of the Church and writing. The result must have been a large amount of bi- and multilingualism (and bi- and multidialectalism) between Latin, the Romance vernaculars and the Germanic, Celtic and other languages of the West (see Russell (forthcoming)).

A unique set of evidence for the complexity of societal bilingualism under the Roman Empire comes from La Graufesenque. Situated on the outskirts of Millau (ancient Condatomagos) in south-western France (Aveyron, Midi-Pyrénées) at the confluence of the Tarn and the Dourbie, this site was first excavated in 1862 and has been the centre of scholarly interest ever since. Archaeologists have uncovered a vast samian-ware pottery, complete with sanctuaries presumably for the community of potters. Only a small proportion of the site has as yet been excavated, but so far it has yielded a phenomenal number of finds (Schaad and Genin (2007)). At La Graufesenque production of samian ware or *terra sigillata* (red-gloss fineware, a distinctive component of the Roman cultural package which spread across the empire) began around 10 BCE, and flourished in the second half of the first century CE, before tailing off in the first half of the second century.

Around 250 graffiti have been uncovered at the site, mostly dating to the second half of the first century CE.[17] These are largely firing lists inscribed onto pottery which was fired in the kiln along with the pottery it recorded, though other inscriptions are attested, for instance a record of the purchase of a slave. The material falls loosely into three groups: inscriptions that are mostly in Gaulish (the Celtic language of Gaul), those that are mostly in Latin, and many which show a mixture of the two languages. These graffiti provide crucial information for analysing the language choices, bilingual phenomena and naming practices of a well-defined bilingual community.

Though many are fragmentary, enough examples of the firing lists exist that the overall structure can be defined. They often open with a heading making reference to the kiln and/or a date. For instance Marichal (1988) text 11, a Gaulish example, opens with a date and *tuθos] allos,* a phrase meaning "the second kiln" *vel sim.*[18] This can be paralleled by Marichal (1988) text 74a, a Latin example, which opens with a date and *furnus secun[dus.* The texts thereafter list the potters' names, followed by the names of the types of vessels which they have placed in the kiln and the number and measurements, using Latin symbols and abbreviations. The differentiation between Gaulish and Latin in the texts is not simply a matter of the heading used. Gaulish features include the ending -*o/-os* (the Celtic nominative of the *o*-declension) for the potters' names, for instance, *MASUETOS catilli DCL* (Marichal (1988) text 19). In Latin the Latin nominative -*us* is employed, for instance, *MASUETUS par (I)(I)(I)* (Marichal (1988) text 17). Other diagnostic features seem to be the loss of final -*s,* which sometimes occurs in the Gaulish examples, but rarely (or possibly never) in the Latin, and the use of -*i* nominative plurals in Gaulish for the names of vessels which are neuter in Latin, for example Gaulish *uinari,* Latin *uinaria.*

Adams summarizes an intriguing aspect of these records.

> The Gaulish record keepers had clearly received rather more than a rudimentary training in a Latin-based literacy. They did not merely know Latin letters, but could also use the Latin numeral symbols up to very high figures, and had been taught Latin sigla. Yet in conjunction with these Latin symbols they used, and were permitted to use, elements of their own language. ((2003a) 697–698)

Indeed, the switching between the languages is such that the categorization of Gaulish and Latin texts along the lines described above is extremely difficult in most cases and many of the texts cannot be easily allocated to either Latin or Gaulish, but seem to be written in a mixture of the languages.

The graffiti provide examples of all of the three main categories of the phenomena of bilingualism, namely borrowing, interference and code-switching. Here we shall consider interference and code-switching. Code-switching can be subdivided into *inter-sentential switching, intra-sentential switching* and *tag-switching.*[19]

1   *Inter-sentential switching* is characterized by a switch in languages between sentence or clause boundaries, e.g. "sometimes I'll start a sentence in Spanish, y termino en español" (English–Spanish) (Poplack (1980) 594). Adams ((2003a) 711–712) cites Marichal (1988) text 30 of the *corpus* from La Graufesenque as possibly exhibiting inter-sentential switching. Marichal's erroneous classification of the text as Gaulish but Latinized was probably influenced by the Gaulish opening word *tuθos.* The text, in fact, seems to show code-switching between a Gaulish heading and a Latin textual body. Alternatively, according to Adams, it might be possible to view *tuθos* as a loan-word from Gaulish into Latin, but this seems unlikely. The apparent equivalent *furnus* appears regularly in the other Latin texts and, perhaps more significantly, the form *tuθos* has not been "nativized", that is Latinized in any way: not only does it retain Gaulish morphology, but the theta would be unexpected in an established Latin loan-word. It possibly represents a code-switch motivated by a conscious decision by the scribe that the translation of *tuθos* by *furnus* was not adequate in this case, or, if unconscious, it may be a case of lexical interference. Adams' proposal that the heading

may have been written in another hand lacks supporting evidence. Unfortunately, the fragmentary nature of the first line hinders the analysis.

2 *Intra-sentential switching* occurs within the sentence or clause boundary, e.g. *Yo anduve in a state of shock pa dos días* "I walked around in a state of shock for two days" (Spanish–English) (Muysken (1997) 361). Adams ((2003a) 702–703) offers a possible example from La Graufesenque (Marichal (1988) text 14). The language of the inscription is predominately Gaulish, but in a Gaulish sentence *extra tuθ* appears, probably a Latin preposition with a Gaulish dependent noun.[20]

3 *Tag-switching*[21] is the insertion of a tag, such as an exclamation or interjection, in a different language from the rest of the utterance or text, e.g. "I mean", "you know". This is not found in the graffiti of La Graufesenque, but is common in the formulaic funerary epigraphy of the empire; for example, several of the Latin epitaphs of Lyon contain the Greek exclamations χαῖρε and ὑγίαινε (*IGF* 148, 149, 150, 151).

The graffiti also contain examples of interference. Phonological interference in the Latin of La Graufesenque may be present in *paropsides* (some form of serving dish), which is found in the probably Celtic form *paraxidi* even in some of the Latinate inscriptions. This almost certainly shows the Celtic sound change /ps/ > /xs/.[22] A similar phenomenon at La Graufesenque may be the form *acitabulum* for the Latin vessel name *acetabulum*, showing the Gaulish merger of *e*: and *i*:, which was represented graphically with *i*. Marichal ((1988) 58) records the former forty-one times, the latter nine, and Adams ((2003a) 710) notes that of the nine attestations, only two are in "Gaulish" inscriptions (Marichal (1988) texts 17 and 93). It seems likely that interference from the writers' L1 (Gaulish) has affected their version of this word in their L2 (Latin), but the authors of 17 and 93 were well trained and cautious enough not to admit this interference in their writing. Indeed 17 and 93 show other features which suggest that the language is "self-consciously Latinate", in fact 93 includes interpuncta and I-longa.[23] This feature, however, serves to illustrate again the difficulties in accurately identifying bilingual phenomena. Adams classifies the *acitabulum/acetabulum* alternation not as phonological interference but as "a form of "orthographic" code-switching" ((2003a) 710). Considering how widespread the feature is, *acitabulum* could perhaps also be classified as a borrowing, namely a Latin word that has been "nativized" in Gaulish.

It is probable that over time in the close-knit community of La Graufesenque bilingual interference features became borrowings and modified the languages spoken there. Presumably, these sort of modifications were the *gentilia uitia* which the fifth-century CE grammarian Consentius warned may occur in the Latin of foreigners, and which should be avoided to preserve *suae linguae puritatem* "the purity of their language" (i.e. Latin) (*GL* V.395) (Adams (2007) 244–250). However, the type of evidence at La Graufesenque is bureaucratic, sometimes based on lists, and highly specialized, and it is improbable that any more than a fleeting glimpse of possible spoken varieties can be attained once we have taken into account sociocultural factors such as literacy and training. However, the fact that both languages are used alternately in the record-keeping of the community suggests that both languages were spoken and understood, to some extent, by the potters of La Graufesenque, and surely the potting community would have used the terminology of pottery amongst themselves and did not reserve it for lists. These graffiti are the product of a group of people working together under the Roman Empire to produce a very distinctive Roman commodity and using Roman literacy to document the process; and yet throughout the lifetime of the pottery both Gaulish and Latin were used in harmony. Indeed, the graffiti serve to remind us of the lack of any rigorous linguistic policy to force Latin on the inhabitants of the empire. The only indication we have of the association of Latin with the H language is that on the stamps on pottery destined for consumers outside the potting community, the language used is Latin, for example *officina, manus, fecit*.[24]

Latin and Individual Bilingualism

Pre-imperial period

A particularly well-known Roman individual has left us a substantial amount of code-switching. Cicero's epistolary code-switching resides firmly in the sector of Latin–Greek elite bilingualism and is generally easier to interpret than, for instance, the code-switching of the potters of La Graufesenque, since we know copious amounts about the individual concerned and have ample context to attempt to interpret the examples found in his *corpus*. A further advantage is that many of the letters are likely to have been dictated and, though subsequent editing may have occurred in some cases, the letters are closer, on the whole, to spoken discourse than, say, epigraphic material or more literary works.

In Cicero's letters we witness the bilingual code-switching of a balanced bilingual, rather than restricted code-switching, though admittedly the two are not necessarily easily distinguishable in textual evidence (Adams (2003a) 305–308). Modern linguistic research, incorporating both linguistic and extra-linguistic factors, has produced theories of the linguistic ability related to various types of code-switching. Data suggest that inter-sentential code-switching is used mostly by dominant bilinguals, whereas balanced bilinguals employ significantly more intra-sentential switching (Poplack (1980) 581). Hamers and Blanc refer to the latter as "a maturational social process" which children learn later "since it requires full development of syntactic rules for both languages" ((2000) 267). Auer notes that "whenever intrasentential code-switching occurs, intersentential switching is a matter of course, but not all code-switching situations/communities which allow intersentential switching also allow intrasentential switching" ((1998) 3). It is generally thought that tag-switching is the form of code-switching which requires the least competence; some researchers do not even consider the phenomenon to be a real instance of code-switching, and it is certainly true that, at least in some cases, the tag can simply be an "emblematic part of the speaker's monolingual style" (Poplack (1980) 589).

Code-switching can also be revealing of speakers' attitudes. Often several factors will be involved in a switch and contextualization is vital to determine these. Generally, intra-sentential is regarded as the most intimate form of code-switching, and tag-switching the least. For instance, in the case of balanced bilinguals who can choose between the two types, an "in-group" interlocutor encourages the former and a "non-group" interlocutor the latter (Poplack (1980) 589–590).[25] Poplack argues that intra-sentential switching should be seen as a "discourse mode", and that what is significant for sociolinguistics is not the exact position of the switch points, which may be relatively random, but rather the fact that the speakers have chosen this discourse mode ((1980) 614), which indicates a duality of identity. Indeed, in some communities, intra-sentential switching is so natural that it can be deemed an unmarked choice (Myers-Scotton (2006) 167).

Following modern sociolinguistics, Adams ((2003a) 297–308) discusses the possible motivating factors for code-switching in the Classical world. He records his uncertainty as to how far we can push the complex analysis of spoken code-switching to fit the ancient evidence and refers to the "futility of relying too much on the jargon and categories of sociolinguistics in analysing a written corpus from a distinctive society" (304). Nevertheless he makes it clear that there is scope for the use of the findings, and whilst code-switching in the written word must be treated as a more deliberate and carefully considered phenomenon than that found in speech, the lack of spontaneity has the advantage of facilitating "deductions to be made about the motives of the writer" ((2003a) 299). Adams selects the following motives as the most common. They are clearly not mutually exclusive; indeed they are highly intertwined, it is hard, for example, to imagine 2 operating without 1.

1 *Expression of identity, perception of self and belonging*: doctors, for example, often use (Ionic) Greek in referring to their profession, soldiers referring to the military use Latin.
2 *Interpersonal, interactional code-switching*: triggered by the perceived taste or character of the addressee. This can involve feelings of solidarity (convergence) or dominance/aloofness (divergence). The accommodation theory of modern linguistics considers this in detail (Adams (2003a) 350–356).
3 *Culturally specific code-switching*: triggered by topics, events, activities, or material.
4 *Stylistically evocative code-switching*: used as a stylistic resource to evoke another world.

In their exemplary discussions of code-switching in Cicero's letters, Adams ((2003a) 308–347) and Swain (2002) were able to add considerable complexity to the above schema, though in fact all the factors discussed can be fitted within the four broad factors.[26] One unifying feature of all the Ciceronian code-switching into Greek is that it appears to be a marked feature of a monolingual discourse (Latin). Though catch-all explanations are neither plausible nor desirable, we can see this marked switching into Greek as part of a game played by educated members of the Roman elite who shared a cultural background (an "in-group"). We need an understanding of Classical literature and the socio-political context in order to interpret many of the switches, and so, presumably, would they. Yet, although this generalization seems to hold true, it needs to be modified in several ways, which serves to highlight the deliberate and marked nature of the phenomenon. Not all the elite Romans with whom Cicero corresponds receive letters containing code-switching and those who do only receive them at certain times. Cicero never code-switches in periods of personal or political trauma, for instance in the aftermath of Pharsalus or his daughter's death. In terms of recipients, Atticus, a Roman of impressive lineage but, as clear is by his name, a well-known Athenophile, and Cicero's brother, Quintus, receive the most. A close friend, Papirius Paetus, however, receives hardly any because he was old-fashioned, pro-*mos maiorum* and, presumably, not comfortable with the practice. Adams concludes that the elite "did not constitute a coherent in-group with a uniform attitude to the second language" ((2003a) 323).

Indeed the sometimes tense and insecure relationship of the Romans towards Greek language and culture meant that even the odd code-switch into Greek could be dangerous and code-switching is largely lacking in Cicero's non-epistolary corpus and his formal letters. We know from his comments in the speech against Verres that he suffered recriminations after addressing the senate in Syracuse in Greek: *ait indignum facinus esse quod ego in senatu graeco uerba fecissem; quod quidem apud Graecos graece locutus essem, id ferri nullo modo posse* "He says that it is an outrage that I addressed a Greek senate; indeed to have spoken Greek amongst the Greeks is something that cannot be tolerated" (*Ver.* 2.4.66). The fact that a Roman addressing Greeks in Greece in Greek could be attacked for having committed an *indignum facinus* demonstrates the delicate sociolinguistic negotiations in play in this period.[27]

Adams ((2003a) 309–312) demonstrates that the heavy reliance of previous analyses of Ciceronian code-switching on the motivating factor of "intimacy" (Dubuisson (1992), Jocelyn (1999)) needs to be tempered. Whilst it is true that many elite Romans would have been taught Greek during childhood (Quintilian *Inst.* 1.1.12), often the language of the code-switches reflects not that of childhood but of advanced education. Similarly, Adams shows examples where intimacy cannot be at stake, particularly in code-switches which have a distancing or euphemizing motivation, for instance, criticism, coding (e.g. Βοῶπις, a Homeric epithet for Hera used to disguise a reference to Clodia at *Att.* 2.9.1 etc.), medical discussion (e.g. περὶ κοιλιολυσίαν γίνεσθαι "*satisfaire à ses besoins*" at *Att.* 10.13.1),[28] endearments or praise.

The following example comes from a letter to Atticus written at the end of 45 BCE. It is a report of a discussion between Cicero and his nephew, Quintus.

> uenit ille ad me "καὶ μάλα κατηφής" et ego "σὺ δὲ δὴ τί σύννους;" "rogas?" inquit, "cui iter instet et iter ad bellum, idque cum periculosum tum turpe!" (*Att.* 13.42)

> He came to see me "right down in the mouth". I greeted him with "You there, why so pensive?" "Need you ask," was the answer, "considering that I have a journey in front of me, and a journey to war, a dishonourable journey too as well as a dangerous one?"

The code-switch into Greek here has often been seen as reflecting the intimacy of familial relations between the interlocutors. However, when we delve a little deeper, it appears that even this innocuous sounding dialogue may be alluding to Menander (Shackleton Bailey (1965–1970) V.397), though this has not been made explicit by Cicero. Our knowledge of Classical texts is restricted to what has been transmitted, and perhaps more of the Ciceronian code-switching may originally have been directly relatable to textual sources. Adams refers to this type of code-switch as a "game which takes place between two members of a self-conscious cultural élite. If there is intimacy here, it is the intimacy of a shared cultural background and not merely of mutual affection" ((2003a) 312).

Earlier discussions of the code-switching also overplayed the associated sense of humour, frivolity and lightheartedness. Whilst certainly a motivating factor in several instances, many letters are humorous throughout and not just at the switch points and many switches are not lighthearted. Earlier scholars argued that the association with frivolity was a reason behind the absence of code-switching at times of crisis. Adams ((2003a) 313) demonstrates that Ciceronian code-switching should not be automatically associated with frivolity, and that code-switching was avoided in times of crisis rather because it constituted an erudite game which was inappropriate in certain contexts.

The next example further illustrates the nature of the game. Cicero writes to Cassius at the beginning of 45 BCE, when Cassius has become an Epicurean. Aware that the group, Cassius' *amici noui*, look directly to Epicurus rather than the Latin versions, Cicero fills the letters with Epicurean words and quotations. The quotations in this case are "unflagged", so Cicero is flattering his reader that he will be able to identify them. Cicero goes even further elsewhere, by leaving unfinished quotations, where to follow his point the reader needs to be able to complete them. When playing around with this sort of erudite intra-sentential code-switching, the game is that Cicero is also showing off his own knowledge and participation in the "in-group". In this particular instance, Cicero is part of the broader elite in-group, but does not want to be part of the specific philosophical in-group in question and appears to be attempting to out-do Cassius, by giving him advice as to the exact use of a certain term.

> fit enim nescio qui ut quasi coram adesse uideare cum scribo aliquid ad te, neque id κατ' εἰδ<ώλ>ων φαντασίας ut dicunt tui amici noui, qui putant etiam διανοητικὰς φαντασίας spectris Catianis excitari. nam, ne te fugiat, Catius Insuber Ἐπικούρειος, qui nuper est mortuus, quae ille Gargettius et iam ante Democritus εἴδωλα, hic spectra nominat. (Cic. *Fam.* 15.16)

> I don't know how it is, but when I write something to you, I seem to see you here in front of me. I am not speaking according to the doctrine of appearances of images, to use the terminology of your new friends, who think that even mental appearances are aroused by Catius' *spectres*. For, in case you have not noticed it, what he of Gargettus, and Democritus before him, called "images" are termed "spectres" by the late lamented Catius, Insubrian and Epicurean.

Without our knowledge of ancient philosophy much of the communication between Cassius and Cicero would be incomprehensible. Interestingly, a few lines later Cicero refers to the εἴδωλον of Britain. This is almost certainly a reference to the sneering rumour flying round Rome that Britain (which Caesar had "invaded" in 55 and 54 BCE) did not in fact exist.[29] Staying abreast of the sociopolitical climate was an essential part of being able to communicate in this form.

The final example highlights another important use of Greek code-switching in sophisticated Latin, namely in what has been called a "metalinguistic function" (Adams (2003a) 323). This includes, in the case of Cicero, comments in Greek to describe his own, or someone else's, speech or writing. That rhetorical and critical terms should come from Greek should not surprise: schooling in rhetoric and grammar at Rome would traditionally have employed a Greek vocabulary. This intra-sentential code-switching can be tied to factors 3 and 4 above (*culturally specific code-switching* and *stylistically evocative code-switching*), but is still part of the in-group dialogue. Certain other subjects, such as philosophy and medicine, could also trigger a switch; sometimes the *mot juste* simply did not exist in Latin. In the final example, Cicero is writing to Atticus again, and performs a code-switch in describing how he will argue, Σωκρατικῶς εἰς ἑκάτερον. In this case the switch has been flagged by the comment in Latin *ut illi solebant* and Cicero is staking his claim to Greek philosophy.

> uenio nunc ad mensem Ianuarium et ad ὑπόστασιν nostram ac πολιτείαν, in qua Σωκρατικῶς εἰς ἑκάτερον, sed tamen ad extremum, ut illi solebant, τὴν ἀρέσκουσαν. (*Att.* 2.3.2)

> I come now to the month of January and *la base de ma politique*. I shall argue thereupon *in utramque partem à la Socrate*, but in the end, according to the practice of the school, shall declare my preference.

Imperial period

Unlike Cicero, most bilingual individuals from the Roman-speaking world express themselves in epigraphic rather than literary terms. One rather intriguing example will serve to highlight the multilingual and multicultural complexity of the Roman Empire and the importance of employing an interdisciplinary approach. At South Shields (north-east England), sometime in the second century CE, Barates, originally from Palmyra (central Syria) set up an epitaph for his wife, Regina, of the British tribe of the *Catuvellauni*. The inscription (*RIB* I.1065) is a bi-version bilingual in both Latin and Palmyrene (the Aramaic dialect of Palmyra).

> D M · Regina · liberta · et · coniuge ·
> Barates · Palmyrenus · natione ·
> Catuallauna · an · XXX ·

To the spirits, Regina, the freedwoman and wife of Barates, the Palmyrene. She was from the tribe of the *Catuvellauni* and lived 30 years.

> RGYN' BT Ḥ RY BR'T' ḤBL

Regina the freedwoman of Barates, alas.

The Latin portion of the text is positioned above the Palmyrene in larger lettering; both are surrounded by borders. The Palmyrene was carved in its native script and takes up one line as opposed to the three occupied by the Latin. The cursive Palmyrene has almost certainly been incised by someone trained in the carving of that script. Though the script contains curves which are not suited to stonework, the result looks fluid and neat. Given that it would have been extremely unlikely for the local workshops producing inscriptions in Britain to have had staff trained in writing anything other than Latin, or possibly Greek, script, this part of the inscription has almost certainly been produced by Barates himself or an associate. The case is not so clear for the Latin. The presence of oddities in the Latin and the fact that "the confident execution of the Palmyrene inscription contrasts noticeably with the erratic lettering of the Latin inscription" (Phillips (1977) 91) have led to the assumption that Barates was responsible for everything. However, it is debatable whether the Latin should be termed "erratic". The epigraphy has an internal consistency and the letters M and G have a certain stylishness about them. Interpuncts have also been included, which normally suggest a higher level of epigraphic

Figure 29.2 Monument to Regina (*RIB* I.1065) (reproduced by permission of Arbeia Roman Fort and Museums, Tyne & Wear Archives & Museums).

awareness. It is possible that the Latin may have been incised by someone other than the composer and inscriber of the Palmyrene, though it is equally plausible that the Latin may have been inscribed by the same stonecutter, who, if trained in Palmyrene epigraphy, may well have been trained in Latin too; the linguistic evidence might support this option, as we shall see.

The content of the inscriptions themselves can help to reconstruct more of the story behind this stone. The female, Regina, is a Catuvellaunian, a native British woman, we can suppose, whose name Regina may have been chosen as a "cover name", i.e. it functions as both Celtic and Latin.[30] She is a freedwoman and wife of Barates, who may, or may not, be the same Palmyrene attested in another British inscription (*RIB* I.1171) from Corbridge, who is designated there as a *uexil(l)a(rius)* "standard-bearer".[31] Adams ((1998), (2003a) 254–255) discusses the linguistic detail of the Regina inscription, noting that the editors of *RIB* have mistakenly attributed *Regina, liberta, coniuge* and *Catuallauna* to the ablative case. He argues that the ablative would be impossible to construe syntactically, but that the nominative, dative or genitive, which are found expressing the dedicatee in Latin are not formally possible, even considering non-standard variants. Adams ingeniously suggests that the forms are actually accusatives (missing the final -*m* expected in standard Latin), and that this interference in the Latin inscription betrays information about the possible origins of the author. In Greek honorific inscriptions the accusative of the honorand is used, often accompanied by a statue. From this usage the accusative spread to Greek funerary inscriptions and some Latin inscriptions in Greek environments (Mednikarova (2003)). The accusative honorand is the standard form in the Greek of Palmyra and it seems that at South Shields, perhaps encouraged by the presence of the figure on this monument, the form of the Greek honorary inscriptions of Palmyra has influenced the creation of this Latin funerary text. Adams suggests "Barates was presumably bilingual in Aramaic and Greek, and he imitated here in Latin the Greek construction which he knew from his place of origin" ((2003a) 255). This would suggest that it is relatively likely that the Latin, the Palmyrene and the relief (as we shall see) have been produced by a Palmyrene, and probably Barates himself.

Barates specifically refers to himself as *Palmyrenus*. The addition of this ethnic origin, which can be paralleled elsewhere (e.g. at Rome *CIL* VI.19134), evidently impresses on the reader of the Latin the importance of this individual's ethnic identity. Palmyra is one of the few places in the Roman Empire where the non-Greek local language seems to have been used epigraphically late into the Empire in contexts where other communities would uniquely use Latin (e.g. in military inscriptions) or Greek, suggesting a strong link between ethnic identity and language at Palmyra. Perhaps this explains the addition of the Palmyrene section in this inscription. It serves to add nothing to the content of the Latin, and, as Adams notes, "there will never have been many Palmyrenes at South Shields capable of reading the Aramaic text (no Palmyrene unit of the Roman army is known from Britain)" ((2003a) 32). Yet, Barates clearly saw it as essential in representing his identity, and it is a neat example of Adams' claim that "a bilingual epitaph may be not only a means of imparting information about the deceased, but a form of display by the dedicator in which he expresses symbolically a feature of his identity or that of his referent" ((2003a) 32). The advantage of the foreignness of the Palmyrene script is that even illiterates would presumably be able to identify that there was something else on the stone that was not Latin.

This thought might lead us to investigate another piece of the puzzle which has not been fully considered by the linguists and epigraphers. The inscription should not be viewed separately from the iconography of the monument. Only around a quarter of the monument is actually taken up by the inscription. The more eye-catching aspect is, without doubt, the sculpted relief which depicts an archway supported by four columns under which is positioned the image of a seated woman, presumably Barates' wife, Regina. Though some of the detail has been lost through damage, it is clear that this sculpture is not typically Greco-Roman, nor Romano-Celtic.

The woman sits facing forward on a wicker chair, clasping a distaff and spindle in her left hand and holding open with her right hand a box which sits on the floor on her right. On the floor to her left is a basket filled with balls of wool. She is wearing a long-sleeved cloak over her tunic and has a necklace and bracelets of corded type. Behind her head is a circular object. Several of the elements fit with Western and Romano-British *comparanda*, for instance the positioning of the figure, architectural framing, chair and dress.[32] However, there are signs that this is a little out of the ordinary. The basket and chest can be paralleled by Palmyrene examples, and the hairstyle found here was worn almost without exception at Palmyra until around CE 170. But most importantly, the spindle and distaff held across the chest in the left hand is a feature almost unique to the iconography of Roman Syria. This monument has been created by a Palmyrene in a mixture of the preferred style of his native land and his new,[33] and, like the Palmyrene script, is a clear visual clue as to his duality of identity, even for illiterates.

Conclusions

In this introduction to Latin in contact with other languages, we have seen evidence for Latin interaction with Oscan, Gaulish, Greek and Palmyrene. Female slaves, a community of potters, an elite male and a man far from his homeland have all expressed themselves bilingually. However, this is a tiny fraction of the available material: evidence exists for dozens of other contact languages and many other communities and individuals. Even so, our highly restricted written evidence can never truly represent the multilingual complexity of the Roman world.

FURTHER READING

The most significant books concerning bilingualism and the Latin language are Adams (2003a) and Adams *et al.* (2002). Campanile *et al.* (1988), Bádenas de la Peña *et al.* (2004) and Neumann and Untermann (1980) are useful collections of papers on language contact in the ancient world. Recent work attempting interdisciplinary approaches includes Biville *et al.* (2008), Cotton *et al.* (2009), Mullen and James (forthcoming), Papaconstantinou (2010) and Wallace-Hadrill (2008) (which engages with bilingualism from an archaeological and historical perspective). Clackson and Horrocks (2007) and Horrocks (2010) provide general introductions to the Latin and Greek languages respectively, and include much of relevance to bilingualism. Adams (2007) has superseded previous scholarship on regional varieties of Latin. Other important treatments of aspects of bilingualism include: Biville (1990, 1995) on borrowings from Greek into Latin, Blanc and Christol (1999) on the lexicon, Brixhe (1998) on the *koiné* and contact languages, Dubuisson (1985) on Polybius, Kaimio (1979) on the Romans and Greek, Leiwo (1994) on Naples, Nicolas (1996) on calques, Rochette (1997) on Latin in the Greek world, Wenskus (1998) on code-switching. The literature on modern bilingualism is vast, and is summarized effectively by Adams (2003a). A key transitional text between historical linguistics and modern bilingualism theory is Thomason and Kaufman (1988). Some good general introductions to modern bilingualism include Hamers and Blanc (2000), Myers-Scotton (2006), Romaine (1995), Thomason (2001) and Winford (2003). Important, but more focused, studies include Ferguson (1959) on diglossia,

Fishman (1964) on language shift and maintenance, (1965) on domains, (1967) on diglossia, and Gardner-Chloros (2009), Heller (1988), Jacobson (1998, 2001), Milroy and Muysken (1995), Muysken (2000), Poplack (1980) on code-switching. See Fögen 2003 for further bibliography on bi- and multilingualism in Greco-Roman Antiquity and the modern world.

NOTES

1 We might note that *bilinguis* never means "bilingual" in Latin, but rather has a pejorative connotation and refers to "a language that is mixed and corrupted" (Rochette (2010) 288).

2 See also Myers-Scotton (2006) 45–66, who notes that cities, border areas and trading centres are particularly multilingual.

3 See also Fishman (1967), Hudson (1992, 2002a, 2002b), Myers-Scotton (2006) 80–89. The varieties are of the same language in "classic diglossia" and of different languages in "extended diglossia".

4 Occasionally we find details of the production process, see Adams (2003a) 84–88.

5 We do not have the manuals used in the preparation of epitaphs, but know they must have existed from indirect inscriptional evidence (e.g. instances of miscopying or verbatim copying where grammatical agreements have been missed).

6 I differ slightly from Adams (2003a) as regards these categories in that I count texts displaying code-switching under the second category, and reserve for category three (*mixed-language texts*) those texts which are so mixed that the matrix language is difficult or impossible to identify.

7 For *integration* or *nativization*, see Clyne (2003) 142–152, Myers-Scotton (2006) 219–226. Other possible markers of integration are syntactic, semantic, prosodic, tonemic and graphemic. There are, of course, exceptions, see Hock and Joseph (1996) 270 for "hyper-foreignization" of loanwords.

8 For loan-shifts, see Adams (2003a) 461–468. Adams states this is often a high-class feature, but he also presents evidence from non-technical, lower-class discourse. No full-length, systematic discussion as yet exists.

9 Syntactic interference is common in texts, see Adams (2003a) 496–520. There are other options, e.g. *tonemic interference*, see Clyne (2003) 76–79, but only the most pertinent to the material from the Classical world are mentioned.

10 Interference can affect "balanced bilinguals", particularly when their minds are for any reason not at full capacity, though this is not generally mentioned. Indeed, interference in the speech of balanced bilinguals in code-alternation situations seems to support this (Thomason (2003) 697–699).

11 See Adams (2003a) 108–110, 419 for phonetic features, 419–422 for morphology, 422–424 for syntax; though some of these examples are probably better classed as borrowings.

12 See Biville (1990) 31 for definitions.

13 For a discussion of the literary evidence for Oscanisms in Latin, see Adams (2003a) 116–123. The evidence is far from copious.

14 See Wallace-Hadrill (2008) 82.

15 Wallace-Hadrill (2008) 83 notes that of the non-Greek contact languages only Etruscan and Punic have "limited respect" from the Romans.

16 For some evidence of the education of local elites, see Adams (2003a) 691–693.

17 See Marichal (1988), *RIG* II.2 L-29–48 for the graffiti; for comments on linguistic and related aspects, see Adams (2003a) 687–724, (2007) 281–289, 701–702, Bémont (2004) and Flobert (1992).

18 For the possible meaning of *tuθos*, see Adams (2003a) 696, Delamarre (2003) 304, Marichal (1988) 97.

19 The categorization set up by Adams is followed here ((2003a) 21–25) and should be utilized as far as possible by Classicists to avoid the confusing proliferation of terms, overlap in uses of terms and conflicting uses of terms found in modern bilingualism theory. For instance, scholars still do not agree as to how the term code-switching should be employed: some use code-switching to refer to inter-sentential switching, and code-mixing for intra-sentential switching, see Muysken (2000) 1.

20 In the absence of the exact cognate in the Continental Celtic *corpus*, *extra* as Gaulish cannot be totally excluded (indeed Lambert ((2008) 106 argues that "*extra* est ici un mot gaulois"). However, reconstruction of the proposed Gaulish form suggests **ek(s)t(e)ro vel sim.*, so it is likely that *extra* marks a code-switch into Latin. On the presence or absence of -*s*-, see Russell (1988) 118–123. For *ex*-, *exs*-, see Delamarre (2003) 169–172. The Insular Celtic cognates (Old Irish *echtar* Middle Welsh *eithr*) do not help to reconstruct the quality of the final vowel.

21 The line between tag-switching and inter-sentential switches is very thin, and modern bilingual studies often regard tag-switching as a sub-category of inter-sentential switching.

22 For *paraxidi*, and the possibility that it may be an internal Latin development, see Adams (2003a) 438–440.

23 See Adams (2003a) 710. For the I-longa, see Flobert (1992) 106, Marichal (1988) 60–65. The theory that the scribes at La Graufesenque attended schools in the Gallo-Roman countryside is unconvincing; it seems much more likely that they would have been trained "on the job" by a scribe employed for this purpose.

24 Adams notes that Latin names with Latin inflections are used for the stamps on pots destined for sale beyond the potting community and that the Celtic names found in the firing lists are "virtually eliminated" ((2003a) 705, 755). Since the publication of Hartley and Dickinson (2008—), it has been possible to demonstrate that whilst the names are indeed nearly all inflected in the Latin way, Celtic names remain in roughly the same proportion as in the firing lists.

25 Poplack's code-switching subjects are Puerto-Rican residents of the stable Spanish–English bilingual community of El Barrio (New York City). Her analysis is somewhat general due to the small number of informants.

26 For the Greek in Cicero's letters, see also Baldwin (1992), Dunkel (2000), Steele (1900).

27 See also Cicero's comment at *Off.* 1.111.

28 All the translations are from Shackleton Bailey (1965–1970, 2001), whose careful treatment of the code-switches sometimes involves a code-switch from English into French or Latin.

29 See Plutarch *Caes.* 23.3.

30 The same name in Gaul is cited as Celtic by Evans ((1967) 247).

31 The inscription reads *[D(is)] M(anibus) | [..]rathes · Pal | morenus · uexil(l)a(rius) | uixit · an(n)os · LXVIII* "To the spirits, -rathes, the Palmyrene, a standard-bearer, lived 68 years". See *RIB* I p. 386 for the question of whether this is the same Barates.

32 See Colledge (1976) *passim*, but especially 231–233 and Phillips (1977) 90–91.

33 Due to signs of Palmyrene influence, Colledge argues that *RIB* I.1064 is also by the same sculptor, though he admits that there are some differences, namely that Regina's monument is more "crudely carved" and that some of the letters differ ((1976) 233). It must, of course, be remembered that the inscription may not be incised by the sculptor of the relief.

CHAPTER 30

Language Policies in the Roman Republic and Empire

Bruno Rochette (translated by James Clackson)

Introduction

The Romans exhibited an enormous capacity for adaptation and a great flexibility in many areas, including their use of language. Latin was never imposed by force as the official language in the regions Rome conquered. Cities in the Greek-speaking half of the Roman Empire continued to use Greek as they had in the past. Wherever there was a Roman presence, Latin existed alongside languages already spoken, and was not put in their place; the Romans preferred the initiative to come from the conquered peoples. Latin was imposed *per pacem societatis* ("through a pact of society"), following St Augustine's phrase (August. *C.D.* 19.7.18, Petersmann (1998) 94). In the speech Virgil gives to Jupiter in the first book of the *Aeneid*, it is *mores* ("customs") (*A.* 1.264) and *iura* ("laws") (*A.* 1.293) that the Romans give to the conquered peoples, not language. In contrast with Alexander the Great, who had wanted to extend Greek as the language of administration to his whole empire (Plut. *Alex.* 47.6), the Romans did not consider that the spread of their language was linked to their conquests (Petersmann (1994) 7). All the same, it is impossible to deny that Latin could represent Roman identity and power, as is shown by Virgil in a different speech given to Jupiter: *sermonem Ausonii patrium moresque tenebunt … faciamque omnis uno ore Latinos* (*A.* 12.834 and 837) "Ausonia's sons shall keep their father's speech and way … and I will make all to be Latins of one tongue" (trans. Rushton Fairclough).

The Republic and Early Principate

After the death of Alexander, Greek was spoken in the various successor kingdoms, but local languages were allowed to continue in use (Harris (1989) 175–190; Lewis (1993, 2001); Millar (1998a)). Roman power increased progressively in the West, but the

A Companion to the Latin Language, First Edition. Edited by James Clackson.
© 2011 Blackwell Publishing Ltd. Published 2011 by Blackwell Publishing Ltd.

Romanisation of the eastern half of the Mediterranean was preceded by its inverse, the Hellenisation of Rome: *Graecia capta ferum uictorem cepit* "Greece, conquered, has conquered its wild victor" (Hor. *Ep.* 2.1.156). Although they had gained the political upper hand over *capta* Greece, the Romans made no alteration to the existing customs of language use in the administration of the East. While Latin spread in the western half of the empire, Greek remained the major administrative language in the eastern half, at least until the time of Diocletian (Corbier (2008) 37).

Valerius Maximus 2.2.2

The fundamental text on language use and its circumstances in the Republic is a passage of Valerius Maximus (2.2.2). The strict rule explicitly states that Roman magistrates should only reply to foreign ambassadors in Latin, whether in the Senate or outside Rome (Kaimio (1979) 94–111; Ferrary (1988) 559–560; Gruen (1992) 235–236; Wallace-Hadrill (1998) 80–83; Clackson and Horrocks (2007) 188–189). This was a way to preserve their own *maiestas* "majesty" and that of the people of Rome.

The passage of Valerius has long been wrongly interpreted to mean that Latin was the only official language of the *Imperium Romanum* and that Latin was obligatory everywhere in the administration. It is true that some examples of linguistic behaviour in the Republic agree perfectly with the rule presented by Valerius. From the second century BCE the Romans demanded that ambassadors of foreign nations express themselves in Latin when they had to speak on official terms, or, if they were unable to do so, that they make use of interpreters. This was the case during the embassy of the three philosophers of 156–155 BCE (Gel. 6.14.9; Plut. *Cat. Mai.* 22.4). Since Carneades did not know Latin, his remarks were translated for the Senate by the senator C. Acilius (Kaimio (1979) 104–105; Petersmann (1998) 91). Around a hundred years later, in 81 BCE, Apollonios Molon of Rhodes, who did not understand Roman language (Plut. *Cic.* 4.6) and came on an embassy to Rome, was the first to be allowed to address the Senate directly in Greek without an interpreter (V. Max. 2.2.3). But, according to Cicero (Cic. *Fin.* 5.89), when an audience was given to Greek-speaking envoys in the Senate, there was always someone who demanded an interpreter. At that time, Greek was already well established at Rome and had long been used in the eastern provinces as a *lingua franca*. The importance of Greek was yet further increased in the first and second centuries CE, to the extent that Juvenal complained that Rome was becoming a Greek city (3.60–61; 6.187–188).

The use of interpreters to translate Latin proclamations into Greek was of great importance for the Romans during the Republic in order to demonstrate their power. They employed interpreters to underline their superiority in regions where they had enforced military domination. During the Isthmian games of 196 BCE, after his victory over Philip V at Cynoscephalae, the consul T. Quinctius Flamininus proclaimed the liberation of Macedonia not in Greek but in Latin (Livy, 33.32.5, Petersmann (1998) 96). Some years later, in 191 BCE, Cato, as military tribune in Athens, was not willing to address the Athenians in Greek (although able to do so), but instead he delivered his speech in Latin and had it translated in Greek (Plutarch indicates that the translation was much longer than the original, Plut. *Cat. Mai.* 12.5, Kaimio (1979) 98–99; Gruen (1992) 64–65, 68–69, 237). L. Aemilius Paulus, in 168 BCE, questioned the Macedonian king Perseus (who clearly did not know Latin) in Greek, before conversing with his own men in Latin. Then, in 167 BCE, after his decisive victory over the Macedonians, he announced the new order to be installed in Greece. He made the proclamation in Latin, and left it to an interpreter to translate into Greek. The interpreter was the praetor Cn. Octavius: *Paulus Latine, quae senatui, quae sibi ex consilii sententia uisa essent, pronuntiauit. Ea Cn. Octauius praetor – nam et ipse aderat – interpretata sermone Graeco referebat* (Livy, 45.29.3) ("Paulus announced in Latin the decisions of the senate, as well as his own, made by the advice of the council. This announcement was translated into Greek and repeated by Gnaeus Octavius the praetor – for he too was present" (trans. Schlesinger)).

The events of 191 and 167 follow analogous scenarios. In both cases, the Roman superior speaks in Latin before an assembly who do not understand. The translation is made after the Latin speech, and is made by a Roman subordinate, not by a Greek translator. In this way, two goals are met: the Greek translation transmits the information to Greek speakers and the preceding Latin proclamation, which cannot be understood by the audience, assumes a symbolic value – it is intended to stress the superiority of Rome, the *princeps populus*. Aemilius Paulus thus behaved in the manner of the official representative of victorious Roman power, even though he was a supporter of Greek culture. Note also that he had his victory over King Perseus and the Macedonians recorded in an inscription in Latin (*ILLRP* 323, Ferrary (1988) 556–558), just as Octavian/Augustus did, when he commemorated his victory at the Battle of Actium (Ehrenberg and Jones (1955) 57, n. 12). In the words of Levick ((1995) 396), "using Latin was not just using one language rather than another, but making a claim to status or authority".

Other magistrates did not always appear to be aware of the rule that was given by Valerius Maximus, but used Greek directly. Indeed, this is what Aemilius Paulus did when negotiating privately with King Perseus in Greek during the Macedonian campaign (see above). The recourse to Greek, the language of the conquered, was far from being a concession, but could also appear as a sign of power. After the death of King Attalus III in 133 BCE, when he bequeathed his kingdom of Pergamum to come under Roman rule, P. Licinius Crassus came to Asia in 131 and announced *decreta* not in Latin, but in Greek without a translator, and, what is more, in all the Greek dialects spoken in the kingdom (V. Max. 8.7.6; Quint. *Inst.* 11.2.50). The use of Greek in this case doubtless reflects the fact that the territory had not been conquered by military force, but had come into Roman control directly through Attalus' will.

In fact, Greek preserved its status through its use by Roman magistrates in the Greek-speaking parts of the Roman Empire. Kaimio (1979) has shown that the rule that is given by Valerius Maximus is in fact confirmed neither by the literary sources nor by epigraphy. Greek is the official language used alongside Latin by the Roman administration in the eastern part of the empire. It seemed logical to address Greeks in Greek, as Tiberius Sempronius Gracchus, the father of the Gracchi, did before the Rhodians (Cic. *Brut.* 79). This attitude could meet with objections: Cicero was criticised for having addressed the Syracusan senate in Greek (Cic. *Ver.* 2.4.147), on the grounds that it was inappropriate for a Roman to speak Greek before a Greek public (Adams (2003c) 198; Clackson and Horrocks (2007) 188). But there had been precedents. Appian (App. *Sam.* 7.2) recounts that the Roman ambassadors to Tarentum in 282 communicated in Greek. Indeed, this episode may explain the rule which is given by Valerius, since several paragraphs after he gives the rule, Valerius mentions the humiliation of one of the members of this delegation, L. Postumius Megellus, who had attempted to negotiate in Greek with the Tarentines (Kaimio (1979) 96; Gruen (1992) 229–230), and whose Greek was so bad that his speech provoked the derision of the city's inhabitants – an insult serious enough to justify a declaration of war against Tarentum. One way to explain the role that Valerius assigns to Latin, the language of Roman dignity, is to consider it a response to the humiliation of Postumius.

The first Julio-Claudians

Valerius Maximus 2.2.2 appears to imply that the rule governing the official use of Latin was no longer observed during his time, the reign of Tiberius, and it should be reinstated. He echoes a point of view current at the time of Tiberius, who, as Augustus had done before him, took up the defence of a pure Latinity as a force to unite the Empire by expunging hellenisms (Dubuisson (1986) 109–117). The linguistic scruples that Valerius attributed to a former age, may actually reflect those of the emperor Tiberius himself. Indeed, Suetonius records the care with which Tiberius controlled the correction of official texts (Suet. *Tib.* 71, Petersmann (1998) 97; Clackson and Horrocks (2007) 189).

Tiberius places a point of honour on the maintenance of the linguistic purity of the highest official mouthpiece of Rome, the Senate. Indeed, there are other reasons to think that the usage of Greek had become widespread at the beginning of the Empire, even in official circumstances: Augustus had his own texts translated into Greek, since his own knowledge of the language was not good enough to do it himself (Suet. *Aug.* 89, Best (1977)). On several occasions Tiberius took steps to restrict the use of Greek in official life. The text of Suetonius (*Tib.* 71) describes Tiberius' refusal to allow a soldier to reply except in Latin. However, Cassius Dio (57.15.3) reveals that Tiberius himself eventually agreed to hear a trial in which one of the parties spoke in Greek (Kaimio (1979) 106). Following Tiberius, the political defence of Latin seems to have diminished. Claudius, himself a fluent bilingual, also attempted to limit Greek, but did not show the same rigour. He responded to Greek ambassadors speaking Greek in the Senate with a coherent speech. Suetonius (Suet. *Claud.* 42) attributes to him a phrase which shows that he considered the two languages equally (*utraque lingua* "in both languages"). Addressing a stranger who conversed in both Greek and Latin he said to him "then you have our two languages". But, on the other hand, he did not hesitate to strike from a list of jurors one of the leading citizens of the province of Greece who did not know Latin, and removed his civic rights (Suet. *Claud.* 16, Kaimio (1979) 134–136; Dubuisson (1982) 189 and 207–208; (1986); Inglebert (2002) 242–243; Bérenger-Badel (2004) 46–47). Likewise, Claudius removed Roman citizenship from a Lycian who did not understand Latin (Cassius Dio, 60.17.4).

Latin eventually was imposed not through law, but thanks to the prestige of the conquerors. Under the Republic, the use of Latin in the public domain was presented as true privilege which the Romans gave out sparingly. In 180 BCE, the town of Cumae, which had always used Oscan as its official language, asked Rome for permission to employ Latin in public life (Livy, 40.42.13, Petersmann (1989) 423; Adams (2003a) 188–189;

Clackson and Horrocks (2007) 81–82): *Cumanis eo anno petentibus permissum, ut publice Latine loquerentur et praeconibus Latine uendendi ius esset* "The Cumaeans that year asked and were granted the privilege of using the Latin language officially, and the auctioneers that of conducting their sales in Latin" (trans. E.T. Sage and A.C. Schlesinger). Rome agreed to this demand, and the concession of the *ius Latii* in 180 sanctioned the process of Romanisation. It is clear that the Cumaeans considered Latin the language of prestige, and that Cumae attempted to tighten its links with Rome through its language policy (Adams (2003a) 113–114, 122, 148, 152, 657).

The importance of Greek in the eastern provinces

Epigraphy confirms the importance of Greek in the eastern provinces. Even after the Roman conquest, the publication of official Roman documents (*senatusconsulta*, edicts, imperial rescripts, letters from emperors and magistrates) were made in Greek, with only a few exceptions (Kaimio (1979) 85–86). The use of Greek in documents addressed to Greek cities is easy to comprehend: the chief goal was to be understood (Dubuisson (1982) 192). The Romans had a pragmatic concern for effective communication. In setting up a bilingual empire, the Romans put in place an effective communication system, based on the most widespread language in the Mediterranean basin, Greek. However, the latinisms and errors in Greek which are found in these Roman documents show that the originals were mostly in Latin (Lewis (1986)).

The Roman administration employed Latin in the East as the *internal* language of communication, whereas Greek was the *external* (Adamik (2006) 22–23). The Roman Empire can be characterised by what Kaimio ((1979) 129–130; 319–320) calls a "bilateral monolingualism" (Adamik (2006) 24–28); it was divided into two parts, one Latin-speaking, the other Greek-speaking, by a linguistic frontier passing through the Balkan peninsula (Gerov (1980), Rizakis (1995)). This bilateral monolingualism was reinforced by a conscious linguistic policy, which was, however, never fixed in writing. The only attestation for this policy is indirect evidence, such as the coinage of Magna Graecia, which shows that this region passed from the Greek zone to the Latin zone between the reigns of Augustus and Claudius (Kaimio (1979) 68–74, 112–114). The establishment of this system can be located probably to the reign of Claudius, since it is at that moment that the post of *ab epistulis* "secretary" is divided between two distinct offices: *ab epistulis Graecis* "Greek secretary" and *ab epistulis Latinis* "Latin secretary" (Kaimio (1979) 117, 319–320; Millar (1977) 224–226; Petersmann (1989) 409; Mourgues (1995) 106, 120). In 53 CE, the young Nero, in the presence of Claudius, delivered a Latin speech for the inhabitants of Bononia and a Greek speech for the inhabitants of Rhodes and Ilion (Suet. *Ner.* 7.2).

A recently published documentary archive enables the role played by Greek in administrative practice in the East to be measured: the Babatha Archive, comprising 60 papyri dated between 93/94 CE and August 132 CE. Babatha was a Jewish woman resident in the province of Arabia who took refuge with her family in a cave in the Judaean desert to escape Roman reprisals after the revolt of Bar-Kokhba in 132 BCE. The mother tongue of the scribes of documents in the archive is Aramaic, the common language of the population of that area. However, the documents are written in Greek showing some Semitic and also some Latin influences (Lewis *et al.* (1989) 16–19). The petition which Babatha addressed in 124 to Iulius Iulianus, the governor of Arabia, is in Greek (*P.Yadin* 13). It is therefore possible to see that the official language, Greek or Latin (depending on where you were), was used to address a governor. The other languages play no official role. Palmyra is the only city in the East that displays its bilingualism in public documents (Kaizer (2007)).

Language use in the public domain

In the western provinces, Latin was widespread with the extension of the *ciuitas Romana* (Polomé (1983)), although, in certain regions, local languages were retained for a fairly long time. If no law obliged the subject people to take up the language of the conquerors, Latin offered concrete advantages that could allow the conquered to obtain their own status. Latin was the language of the army and the law-courts.

In the eastern provinces, the situation was more complicated owing to the prestige of Greek and its long-rooted history (Zgusta (1980); Schmitt (1983)). It is possible to distinguish several different scenarios:

1 Greek is the language used for the composition of documents intended for Greek towns (*senatusconsulta*, edicts, imperial rescripts, letters from emperors and magistrates (Sherk (1969); Oliver (1989); Kokkinia (2003)). With regard to these official texts, it is reasonable to ask whether they were written in Greek at first, or whether they are translations of Latin originals. The most likely hypothesis is the second (Kaimio (1979) 120; Martín (1982) 322–326; Lewis (1986, 1996), although one cannot exclude the possibility that some of them were composed directly in Greek (Martín (1982) 327–336). The Greek of these texts is in general an inelegant jargon in which traces of the original Latin can be detected. It can be conceived of as a language of power, a government *koiné*, of which the underlying thought is Latin (Mourgues (1995) 116). Some official texts are full of formulae which belong to the Roman legal language (Mason (1974)), to the extent that the Latin text can be read behind the Greek, almost as a watermark on the paper. Consider, for example, the inscription known as the "Edict of Nazareth" concerning tomb violations (Oliver (1989), no. 2; Boffo (1994) 319–333 (no. 39), esp. 331–332, n. 23); the text is replete with Latinisms, so much so that it is possible to conclude that this is a faithful and competent translation of a Latin document (Giovannini and Hirt (1999) 112). On the other hand, publication in two languages is exceptional (Kaimio (1979) 319): among the seventy-seven inscriptions collected in Sherk (1969), only three are bilingual. The edict of Sextus Sotidius Strabo Libuscidianus, governor of Galatia under Tiberius, also gives a bilingual text (*SEG* XXVI 1392 = *AE* (1976) 653, Mitchell (1976); Corbier (2008), 34–35): the Latin version is intended for the Roman officials, whereas the Greek version is addressed to the inhabitants of Sagalassos (Levick (1995) 395–396). Indeed, it was important for the local inhabitants to know their obligations. Augustus' *Res Gestae* was also published in two languages, but the Latin version had only a symbolic value in the Greek world; the Greek translation gave Greek speakers access to the text. Moreover, the Greek of the *Res Gestae* is not

a word-for-word translation, but an adaptation which allows the text of Augustus to be made more accessible to a Greek public, who were unfamiliar with certain Roman concepts (Wigtil (1982)). Even the Roman army, whose official language was Latin, used Greek in its dealings with the local administration (Kaimio (1979) 153–154; Adams (2003a) 599–600).

There are several surviving examples of inscriptions or papyri where the Greek text is followed by a Latin *subscriptio* of the governor which authorises the promulgation of the Greek version (*P.Oxy.* X 1271 = *Sel. Pap.* 204 = *CPL* 179 [AD 246]; *AE* (1975) 805 = *SEG* XXVI 1353, Lewis (1991–1992)). Indeed, if the governor was not constrained by any rule, in general he chose to express himself in Greek, in order to be understood by the local population. The emperor himself might choose Greek. In 216, Caracalla was petitioned by the Goharieni while crossing Syria, who accused a certain Avidius Hadrianus of having usurped the priesthood of a temple at Dmeir. An inscription discovered at Dmeir in (1934) (*AE* (1947) 182 = *SEG* XVII 759) reproduces the protocol of the trial, which took place in Antioch on 27 May 216. Caracalla intervened in Greek, in the same way as the prosecution and defence lawyers (Lewis (1978); Millar (1977) 38, 42, 121, 233, 455, 535–536).

Similar conclusions can be drawn with regard to inscriptions including a local language: note, for example, the administrative documents from the Judaean desert (Cotton (1999)). Latin is nothing more than the language of the administration and the Roman army in Palestine, and is not integrated into the sociolinguistic fabric of the provincial population (Cotton (1999) 220). The Romans thus used Greek in their dealings with the local population (Millar (1995)).

A letter of Septimus Severus and Caracalla from the year 204 sets up a slightly unusual case. In this letter the two emperors let it be known that a *senator populi Romani* is not obliged to accept a guest at his house against his will. There are at least eight copies of this *sacrae litterae*, found at various towns in the provinces of Asia and Galatia (Eck (2009) 24). A Greek version has also been found in three places. The use of Latin can be explained here by the fact that these inscriptions were engraved for the benefit of travelling Roman officials and above all of soldiers, i.e. for Latin speakers (Drew-Bear *et al.* (1977) 363).

More straightforward is the epigraphic material from Perge, the capital of the province of Lycia-Pamphilia, studied by Eck ((2000); (2009) 29–32), which gives a good example of the political reality in the Greek world. The town of Perge and its leaders used Latin when the political circumstances demanded it. Greek was sufficient for the expression of personal opinions, even under Roman domination.

2 In autonomous Greek towns, as well as towns founded by Roman emperors, the administration took place exclusively in Greek.

3 In the administration of the Greek East, the use of Latin was limited to correspondence between the central administration, i.e. the emperors, and the Roman magistrates in post in the province. The correspondence between Pliny the Younger, governor of Bithynia, and Trajan is the clearest example. Latin is also used in communication between Roman magistrates and Roman colonies, and in the administration of the Roman colonies (Kaimio (1979) 75; Sartre (2001) 142–144). To some extent, Latin is used also in official dealings with *ciues Romani* (Kaimio (1979) 129; Adams (2003a) 562–571).

In summary, it is noteworthy that although Latin was the language of the Roman governors, the army and the law-courts, Greek continued to hold a very important place, owing to its prestige and its spread following the Hellenistic monarchies. A Roman emperor, when he was in the Greek world, could use Greek directly, as Nero did when he proclaimed the freedom of the Greeks (*IG* VII 2713 = *ILS* II 8794 = *SIG*³ II 814, Millar (1977) 430), or he could use Latin, the official language, but with a Greek translation. Hence Septimius Severus, on his visit to Egypt, gave judgments in Latin, which were then translated into Greek (*P.Oxy.* LI 3614).

Language use in the private domain

Epigraphy also allows us to detail the use of languages in the private domain. There are numerous surviving examples of bilingual inscriptions in the broad sense of the term, that is to say cases where two languages are used on the same inscription for different texts without any repetition. In some cases, there are several switches from Greek to Latin within the same text. In the East inscriptions are found which are largely in Latin, but in which brief Greek phrases have been inserted. One inscription of this type is an epitaph from Ephesus, from the second half of the second century CE, set up by Marcellus for his son (Kearsley and Evans (2001) no. 75; Levick (1995) 393–402 (399 and n. 21); Kearsley (1999) 77–88). This inscription was erected by an imperial freedwoman, Philoumene, for her husband and son. She records their lives in Greek in lines 4–17, and follows with a threat in Latin against tomb robbers in lines 18–22. The Latin part, written directly in Latin and not adapted from Greek, also mentions that the tomb will be defended by men from the chancellery of Ephesus, the colleges of her late husband. The epitaph ends in Greek (lines 23–24), with a short clause recording that Philoumene had the monument erected from her own funds. Levick (1995) has interpreted this text and others of the same genre in terms of communicative need: the Latin and Greek parts are directed at different audiences.

Latin, language of prestige

Soldiers recruited into the Roman army from different regions of the empire were proud of their recently acquired Roman identity, and expressed this feeling by their use of Latin. The only exception to this is that the soldiers who came originally from Palmyra retained their language. When Palmyrene soldiers were commemorated in an epitaph, Palmyrene appeared alongside Latin. For all the other ethnic groups, Latin was considered a prestige language. In Egypt, Greek is the dominant language everywhere in inscriptions, except for soldiers' epitaphs. It is possible to see clearly the role of the two languages in a text such as *CIL* III.125: Κλ. Κλαυδιανὸς οὐετ(ερανὸς) Θεοφάνου *leg(atus) p(ro) p(raetore) ex leg(ione) III K(yrenaica)* ἐποίησεν τὴν στήλην ἰδίαις αὐτοῦ δαπάναις "Claudius Claudianus, son of Theophanes, veteran, legate *pro praetore* from the III Kyrenaica Legion, set up this stele at his own private expense." The epitaph is in Greek, but the soldier's rank and unit are in Latin. The soldier was without doubt a Greek speaker, but he wanted his position in the Roman army to be recorded in Latin

(Adams (2003a) 200). A similar conclusion can be drawn with regard to a series of three inscribed stones from Caesarea Mazaca in Cappadocia (*AE* (1984) 893): a centurion is commemorated with a Latin epitaph by his wife and son, although the wife and son are in turn commemorated in Greek by the surviving daughter. The family language was Greek, but a Latin epitaph was needed to convey the *romanitas* of the centurion (Levick (1995) 398; Adams (2003a) 200).

The prestige of the Latin language can also be seen from monolingual documents. A good example can be found in a Latin marriage contract from Philadelphia (second century CE) (*P.Mich.* VII 434 and *P.Ryl.* IV 612 = *ChLA* IV 249, Leiwo and Halla-aho (2002); Adams (2003a) 623–629). This text was produced by Greek speakers who had only an imperfect command of the Latin language; the document is filled with linguistic interferences from Greek. The use of Latin is exceptional in this type of document; and the text may have been composed in a social milieu of soldiers and veterans, for whom Latin was a prestige language.

The attitude toward local languages

The Roman Empire comprised a mosaic of different peoples, and is impossible to say how many languages were spoken within it. In this extremely diverse setting, the Roman emperors resorted to Latin as the language of power. Latin was linked, as under the Republic, with the *maiestas* of the Roman people. Inscriptions which record the emperor's victories are written in Latin, even in regions where Greek was the official language. Military milestones are similarly all in Latin; the only exceptions are direction signs in Greek that needed to be understood by everyone (*ILS* II 5841; *AE* (1971) 471, Eck (2004) 6). Coin legends comprise another means by which the Romans could identify themselves as the conquerors. In Syria, even after its constitution as a Roman province, Latin coin legends are fairly numerous, although there is some representation of local languages (Burnett (2002) 118–120).

Therefore, the Romans can be seen to have a two-fold approach to language (Eck (2004) 5–6): on one hand, they wanted to reaffirm their superiority through language use; on the other, they kept a practical view of retaining the common language of the eastern half of the empire, Greek, the language which was understood by the largest number. Did the Romans used local languages in the same way? The realities of provincial government left little space for the language of the local population. In Egypt, the Egyptian language was hardly used: the only Demotic documents known from the Roman period are tax receipts issued on ostraca (Lewis (1993, 2001); Adams (2003c) 198). However, these dwindle in number to almost nothing around 235 CE, which clearly demonstrates that the Romans had no wish to continue them in use and that they thought Greek could be used, even if the local population did not understand it. In the whole of the Roman Empire, there are only two inscriptions which display Greek, Latin and a local language: the *Titulus Crucis* (inscription on the Cross), which John the Evangelist (19: 19) described as written Ἑβραϊστί, Ῥωμαϊστί, Ἑλληνιστί "in Hebrew [probably meaning Aramaic], Latin and Greek," and the trilingual inscription of Cornelius Gallus, the first Prefect of Egypt, which was set up on 17 April 29 CE and discovered in 1896 (*IGPhilae* II 128 = *CIL* III.14147 = *ILS* III

8995 = *OGI* II 654 = *SB* V 8894, Adams (2003a) 637–641; Costabile (2001)). How can these two special cases be explained? In the case of the *Titulus Crucis*, it is possible to contemplate that Pontius Pilate had made exceptional use of the local language to reach the populace directly, who were responsible for Jesus' condemnation. The Gallus inscription is completely different, since this is a commemorative inscription and the hieroglyphic version is unrelated to the text in Greek and Latin, so this is not a true trilingual text. Moreover, the Greek version of the Gallus inscription is not a literal translation of the Latin, but an adaptation with regard to the different sensibilities of the intended audience (Adams (2003a) 637–641; Costabile (2001) 299), in the same way as the Greek version of Augustus' *Res gestae*.

The limited use made of local languages in the Roman Empire appears not to have been paralleled in other ancient empires: the Persians made use of local languages (Esther 1: 22), as did the Ptolemies (note the Canopus decrees (*OGI* I.56) and the Rosetta stone (*OGI* I.90)), the Carthaginians (Livy, 28.46.16) and, in later times, Sapor I (240–271 CE) whose exploits were published in Persian, Parthian and Greek (*Res gestae Divi Saporis*; Rubin (2002); see also, for other examples, Millar (1998a) 159). However, Eck (2004) considers that the local languages played a greater role in the Romans' relations with their subject people than the surviving documentation shows. Indeed, he sees it possible that many of the trilingual documents, such as the *Titulus Crucis*, have not been preserved since they were written on perishable materials. Furthermore, the presence of interpreters shows that the Romans did pay attention to local languages. They had regular recourse to their services for commercial transactions (Pliny *Nat.* 6.15; Wiotte-Franz (2001) 111 and 139), in the army and in diplomacy (Peretz (2006)). In civic administration, interpreters were also active: papyri from Egypt give several examples of their intervention in law-courts and in other contexts (Peremans (1983)). There is much less evidence for interpreters outside of Egypt (Wiotte-Franz (2001) 111–119); most of the attestations belong to the military sphere and concern legions stationed on the Rhine and the Danube (Henar Gallego Franco (2003)).

In every province of the empire, there must have been structures that permitted provincials who only knew their own language to have access to Roman institutions; such flexibility would have made communication easier. While Latin and Greek were the official languages of the empire, the Romans must have taken other languages into consideration with the aim of maintaining the peace of local populations. A document in the Babatha archive shows the respective roles played by Greek, Latin and the local language (*P. Yadin* 16, Eck (2009) 18). In it, Babatha makes a declaration of her estate for a provincial census ordered by the Roman governor; the text is in Greek, Babatha's subscription is translated from Aramaic and Priscus' attestation of receipt is translated from Latin (Cotton (1999) 228–231).

The prescriptions of the jurists

The Roman jurists set down explicit prescriptions for the language required for several legal processes. They mention not just Latin and Greek, but also local languages, such as Punic, Gaulish and Aramaic (Manthe (1999)). Ulpian, the jurist who is most concerned with linguistic issues, gives a rule regarding *fideicommissa*: they can be given not only in Latin and Greek, but also in Punic or Gaulish or even the language of another people (Lib. 2 *fideicommissorum* [*Dig.* 32.1.11], Millar (1968) 130; Honoré (1982) 19–20; Polomé (1983) 529; Bürge (1999) 57). A specifically Roman procedure of concluding a transaction with a verbal question-and-answer affirming the satisfaction of the declarant party (*stipulatio*) was also discussed by the jurists, who wondered whether languages other than Latin could be used. The answer was that they could, at least according to Gaius (*Inst.* 3.93), who held that *stipulationes* made in Greek were also valid, but he does not mention any other languages. Ulpian (Lib. 48 *ad Sabinum* [*Dig.* 45.1.1.6], Bürge (1999) 57; Manthe (1999)) and Tribonian (*Inst. Iust.* 3.15.1) examine the issue from another angle, in considering the interaction of two parties speaking different languages (Wenskus (1995–1996)): if the question was asked in Latin and the response given in Greek, according to them, the *stipulatio* remained valid (for further references see Wacke (1993)).

Strengthening of the position of Greek after the third century

As Latin became general in the West, in the eastern half of the empire Greek did not stop gaining strength. However, the rules for language use seem to have remained unfixed. It is possible to find some indications of the position of Greek in bequests in the Gnomon of the Idios Logos (Egypt; around 150 CE): paragraph 8 forbids a Roman citizen from composing a will in Greek, although paragraph 34 makes an allowance for veteran soldiers. A further indirect piece of evidence comes from a will of 235 CE (*SB* I.5294) with a reference to a ruling (unknown from elsewhere) of Severus Alexander (222–235 CE), who authorises Roman citizens to leave wills in Greek (no doubt this is a consequence of the *Constitutio Antoniniana* of 212, cf. Beaucamp (1998) and Rochette (2000)). In terms of language use, the third century appears to have been the transition period between the Principate and the Dominate. Greek wins ground in different domains: it is used on milestones in Eastern provinces such as Thrace and Asia Minor, where earlier bilingual inscriptions or ones with Greek numbers are found to indicate distances. Kaimio ((1979) 83–85) has explained the tendency to use Greek in milestones as a symptom of the blurring of the dichotomy between the Latin West and the Greek East. From the beginning of the third century onwards, the linguistic split of the empire became weakened following cultural and political changes. The Greek-speaking elite were obliged to insist that provincial governors sent out to the East knew how to speak Greek, something which had earlier gone without saying; this is demonstrated by an anecdote which probably records the linguistic situation during the reign of Caracalla, in Philostratus' *Life of Apollonios of Tyana* (5.36) (Bérenger-Badel (2004) 51–52).

The Dominate

The official usage of languages in the Roman Empire altered after the accession of Diocletian in 284 CE (Rochette (1997) 118–119). The imperial administration in the East, which, until that point, had entirely used Greek, began to employ a large amount of Latin for decrees, edicts and imperial rescripts. This increased importance of Latin in the East has been explained by a new linguistic policy with which Diocletian and his successors replaced the tolerant and passive policy that had characterised the previous period. However, specialists have increasingly begun to doubt whether there was in fact such a new approach to language: Turner (1961) demonstrated the vitality of Greek and the very narrow limits within which Diocletian sought to impose the authority of Latin, in his examination of two papyrological dossiers published in 1960, *P.Panopolis* and the archive of Aurelius Isidorus. More recently, Adams ((2003a) 635–637, 758) has energetically challenged the idea of a language reform under Diocletian, and has stressed the need for a fresh appraisal of the evidence.

A new linguistic policy?

The constitutions of the Tetrarchs were promulgated in Latin (Feissel (1995) 34; Corcoran (1996) 246). Diocletian's Price Edict of 301 (Feissel (1995) no. 3) is not a bilingual text, but was drawn up in Latin and promulgated exclusively in Latin (Corcoran (1996) 230). There are local Greek versions (which differ from city to city) of the annexe of tariffs to the edict from Achaia and a Greek résumé in the form of an edict of the governor of Phrygia-Caria from Aizanoi (*AE* (1975) 805 = *SEG* XXVI 1353, Lewis (1991–1992)). From this period we only have a few Greek imperial constitutions, all of which are translations of Latin originals. The change of policy can also be seen in the legal transcriptions of court cases found on papyrus. Although the language of the hearings and the judgment is Greek, the language of the officials is Latin (Kaimio (1979) 127–128, 143–147; Adams (2003a) 383–390). In local administration, however, Greek is dominant, as in the earlier period. The importance of Latin, which the Greek elite referred to as ἡ κρατοῦσα διάλεκτος "the language of power" (Dagron (1969)), can be seen by the frequency of latinisms in documentary Greek papyri (Dickey (2003)).

The traditional view of a change in policy rests on the interpretation of a text of Libanius (Marrou (1965) 374–388). In his *Autobiography* (*Or.* 1.234), the rhetorician of Antioch reveals his deep disquiet over the future of Greek rhetoric. Libanius holds Roman law and the Latin language responsible for the decline of his school. But, a close reading of the text shows that he also stresses that no legal measure has been taken to impose Latin at the expense of Greek (γράμματα μὲν οὖν καὶ νόμος τοῦτο οὐκ ἔπραττεν "it is not law or edicts that have brought this about"). It is the honour and power linked to the knowledge of Latin that justifies the importance of the language of Rome. Arguments *e silentio* are always hazardous, but, if a systematic language policy had existed, there is a strong chance that Libanius, as the champion of Greek culture and language, would have mentioned it and would have argued against it in explicit terms.

If the establishment of the Tetrarchy did modify the tradition of official language use in the Roman Empire, this is not the result of a conscious change of linguistic policy, but more the consequence of a slow and complex evolution, in which several factors are concerned, including the move of the official imperial residence to the East.

Constantine the Great

Constantine's language policy can be illustrated by the *Vita Constantini* attributed to Eusebius: the emperor demanded that his soldiers understand Latin (Eus. *Vit. Const.* 4.19), and the influence of the language in the army was at its peak at the beginning of the fourth century. During the ecumenical council of Nicaea, in 325, the emperor regularly addressed the assembled Eastern bishops in Latin, and his words were translated into Greek by an interpreter (*Vit. Const.* 3.13, Wiotte-Franz (2001) 265). At the same council, Constantine wrote a speech in Latin, and then gave it to professional interpreters to translate into Greek (*Vit. Const.* 4.32, Millar (1977) 205; Wiotte-Franz (2001) 104). Having given his speech in Latin, he was then able to debate with the Greek-speaking bishops in Greek, in his attempt to find common ground (*Vit. Const.* 3.13). However. Constantine needed to have the theological tracts which were sent to him by Eusebius translated into Latin (*Vit. Const.* 4.35). Latin and Greek therefore appear to have had different roles: Latin was the official language, which Constantine had perfect mastery over, and Greek was used for spontaneous conversation, not as a written language. This approach is confirmed by the fragmentary protocol to a trial that includes several sentences spoken respectively by a party in the case and by the emperor (*Cod. Theod.* 8.15.1, Corcoran (1996) no. 5, 259–260). Here Constantine addresses a certain Agrippina, the plaintiff, always in Latin, and she always responds in Greek, without an interpreter; this implies that the two sides could understand each other.

Theodosius II

The empire of Theodosius II (408–450) was Roman: all the laws in *Codex Theodosianus* are in Latin; all the correspondence composed by the administration was also written in Latin (Millar (2006) 84–85, n. 2). A passage of John the Lydian (2.12.1–2 = 3.42.1–2, Trahman (1951) 53; Petersmann (1989) 409) alludes to an oracle given to Romulus, the founder of Rome, known through an antiquarian called Fonteius: if Rome forgets the language of her fathers, she will lose her Τύχη "good fortune". The man held responsible for the loss of Latin was an Egyptian, Cyrus, the Praetorian Prefect between 439 and 441, who may have been the first to produce decrees in Greek. The first indication of the abandoning of Latin was however a law of 9 January, 397, which authorised judges to give sentences in Greek as well as in Latin (*Cod. Iust.* 7.45.12, Petersmann (1989) 410). A novella of Theodosius II, dated to the 12 September 439 (*Nov. Theod.* 16.8), recognised the validity of wills drawn up in Greek, a ruling which is given even more clearly at *Cod. Iust.* 6.23.21.6. The custom of writing wills in Greek, as we have seen above, must however already have existed from well before this date, according to a decision of Severus Alexander. In the empire of Theodosius II, Greek remained very important; dealings with occupants of official posts took place in Greek (Millar (2006) 23, n. 51). The papyri show that the use of Latin was limited to official proceedings, whereas the governor expressed himself in Greek (*P.Oxy.* XVI 1879 = *CPL* 434, no. 11 and *CPR* XIV, no. 12, Millar (2006) appendix B no. 10 et 11).

Justinian

The reign of Justinian (527–565) opens a new epoch in the history of language policy in the Roman Empire. The emperor attempted to reaffirm the priority of Latin as the language of law. All the legal texts had to be written in Latin: *decreta a praetoribus Latine interponi debent* "the decrees must be issues by the praetors in Latin" (*Dig.* 42.1.48) and *legata Graece scripta non ualent* "legacies written in Greek are not valid" (Gaius *Inst.* 2.281). In the East, where Latin was no longer understood, texts had to be first read out in Latin before they could be translated into Greek or other languages (*Cod. Iust.* 7.45.12). With the help of the jurist Tribonian, the emperor Justinian published, between 528 and 529, his law code (*Corpus iuris ciuilis*) first in Latin, which he called πάτριος φωνή "paternal language", and only afterwards in Greek (*Nov.* 7.30 [535 CE], Petersmann (1989) 409; Yaron (1995) 663). In his attempts to keep Latin as the official language of legislation, Justinian battled against the incomprehension of the official Latin text. In order to preserve the original shape as much as possible, he authorised a word-by-word translation: this is the κατὰ πόδα(ς) "step by step" translation (*Constitutio Tanta, Cod. Iust.* 1.17.2.21, Fögen (1995) 254). However, during the reign of Justinian, Latin became a dead language even for the jurists. This is why the emperor was eventually forced to accept as valid wills which had not been written in Latin (*Cod. Iust.* 5.28.8).

Language policy under Justinian could be summed up as a conflict between Tribonian, supporter of Latin, and the unpopular John of Cappodocia, supporter of Greek, who eventually prevailed (Honoré (1978) 134–137). The programme for the reinstatement of Latin, which was promoted by Tribonian, was not continued for long, since the inconveniences created by the ancient practices became clear. Justinian, who already used Greek for religious matters, intervened to order the return to Greek as the language of law of the Eastern empire. In studying the relationship between the language of the codes and their intended audience, Adamik (2003) has shown that, in order to reconstruct the unity of the empire, Justinian intended to re-establish, after 535 (the date of the promulgation of the code), the bilateral monolingualism that had been characteristic of the Republic and the Principate (Kaimio (1979) 319–320). However, the practice after 535 contrasts with that before 284. Whereas, under the Principate, the distinction was between West and capital (Rome) = Latin, and East = Greek, after 534 the scheme was as follows: East and capital (Constantinople) = Greek, and West = Latin. With the return to bilateral monolingualism, Justinian had found a way to make Greek definitively the official language of the empire: in Byzantium, ῥωμαΐζω meant "speak Greek" (Inglebert (2002) 256–257).

Conclusion

While Latin can be considered as the unifying link across the whole Roman Empire, the Romans never established an official language policy ensuring that the subjects of the empire had to learn Latin, which would have been doomed to fail. The complete story of language use during Roman history can be summed up as a compromise between Latin and Greek, while leaving space for other languages, even if there is rarely sufficient evidence to specify the details. Although the Romans wanted their subjects to take an interest in Latin, they had to recognise that, in the eastern half of the empire, Greek had enough strength to impose itself. However, the conception that Latin was one of the criteria of *romanitas* was embedded in the Roman mindset. Latin had a symbolic value as the language of conquest and the language of prestige, especially in certain social contexts, such as the army.

It is difficult to say if the attitude to language use changed from one Emperor to another (Adams (2003a) 758). It is possible to distinguish, however, two different periods. The first, from roughly the second century BCE to 284 CE is characterised by the spread of Latin in the West and the use of Latin in the East confined to four domains: (1) official communication between the imperial administration and the provincial administration; (2) communication between governors and the Roman colonies; (3) the administration of colonies themselves; and (4) to some degree, the administration as it affected Roman citizens. The second period (284–439) saw the usage of Latin at every level in the West. In the East, the situation was more complex: Latin was used at the highest level for imperial administration, Greek as the language of communication and both languages in provincial administration. Finally, Justinian developed a policy to return to the situation of the first period, which had the consequence of the definitive triumph of Greek in the East.

CHAPTER 31

Latin Inside and Outside of Rome

Giovanbattista Galdi

Introduction

One of the most interesting and debated problems in the study of the Latin language is related to its regional diversification. The discussion has been less on the existence of local varieties (which can hardly be denied) than on their diatopic and diachronic distribution – in Italy as in the rest of the empire – during Roman times. The main aspect which has both attracted and puzzled Latin and particularly Romance philologists for over a hundred years is the contrast between what we would reasonably expect to find in ancient texts and what we have actual evidence for. On the one hand, a number of factors such as the influence of the languages with which Latin came into contact (both substrate and superstrate), the differing chronologies and types of Romanisation, metalinguistic evidence and the birth of Romance languages (which, as noticed by Väänänen, cannot have arisen "overnight"[1]), strongly hint at a regional diversification of the language much before the end of the Empire.[2] On the other hand, the extant Latin of ancient sources at first sight scarcely displays any local features but presents itself as a unitary system.[3] This phenomenon, usually traced back to unifying factors such as the spread of rhetorical training in schools and the influence of Classical models,[4] characterises also the later imperial literature where it occurs not only in more "traditional" texts and authors (for instance Augustine or Symmachus) but also in those which certainly draw on the spoken language, such as the *Peregrinatio Aetheriae*.[5] Even the language of sub-literary, particularly epigraphic, sources has been considered by several scholars as basically uniform on the grounds that Vulgar Latin features which emerge, say, in Spanish inscriptions are very likely to be found also in distant areas such as Britain or Pannonia and hence can hardly reflect local variation.[6] As a result of all this, after the initial enthusiasm accompanying Sittl's work (1882) on the peculiarities of African Latin (*Africitas*) and its

A Companion to the Latin Language, First Edition. Edited by James Clackson.
© 2011 Blackwell Publishing Ltd. Published 2011 by Blackwell Publishing Ltd.

justified criticism by Wilhelm Kroll (1897), Latinists have generally shown great scepticism towards the possibility of detecting local variations in ancient Latin sources, at least until the end of Late Antiquity.[7] A radical change of perspective appeared in the recent monograph by Adams (2007) who submitted the whole problem to a very accurate and wide-ranging analysis. This book, which represents the first attempt at "a systematic account of the whole field" (p. 8), collects and discusses all sort of material bearing witness to a regional diversification of the language, from Latin and Italic inscriptions of the earliest period (third century BCE) up to different categories of text from the end of the Empire (seventh/eighth century CE). One of the main findings reached therein is that "the language always showed regional as well as social, educational and stylistic variations" and thus regional diversity "can be traced back at least to 200 BCE and was not a new development of the Empire" (p. 684). On the other hand, the evidence we can collect from the sources mostly applies to lexicon and phonology and also the interest of ancient *testimonia* is basically confined to these two fields: "morphological features are hardly ever noted as regional … and … regional syntax, if it existed, is passed over in complete silence" (p. 727).

In this chapter we shall offer a survey of some of the evidence for regional diversity in Latin, from the early Republic until the end of the Empire. Together with lexical and phonological items we shall discuss selected syntactical and morphological features. A main distinction will be drawn between the republican and the imperial material, the former subdivided into explicit evidence (i.e. linguistic comments from ancient authors), and implicit evidence (i.e. usages that modern scholars regard as regionalisms),[8] the latter into western and eastern regions. Specifically, due to Adams's extensive treatment of western regions (including Italy and Africa), a particular focus shall be the East.[9]

The Republic

Implicit evidence

Latin inscriptions constitute the main source to detect regional variation in early times (from the third century onwards). Particularly significant is the investigation of non-Roman inscriptions: since these all come from areas where other Italic languages (especially Oscan and Faliscan) were in use,[10] several studies have suggested that the language of the documents[11] and more generally the Latin of the corresponding area has undergone a substrate influence, at the phono-morphological and orthographic level, from the local idiom. All inscriptional (and secondary) material has now been subjected to a rigorous examination by Adams ((2007) 37–187). Adams points, *inter alia*, to the crucial importance of two widely overlooked elements in establishing the regional nature of a linguistic feature from the early period: (1) the amount of inscriptions (notably of religious dedications) coming from Rome is poor and often much smaller than in other areas: thus, the comparison of evidence from inside and outside the city turns out often to be misleading; (2) numerous alleged dialectal features occur on religious inscriptions and should thus be considered as fossilised religious archaisms (that is, a mark of a register, not of a region).[12] The consistent application of these basic principles reveals that many of the features which have been earlier suggested as non-Roman Latin do not stand up to scrutiny. So for instance the genitive ending -*us* with third-declension words, the use of the digraph -*oi* for -*u* and the feminine dative -*a* instead of -*ae* (all attested on numerous republican inscriptions) turn out to be merely religious or legal archaisms.[13] There remains, however, a handful of phono-morphological cases which appear to reveal regional variation, although none of them can be directly traced back to Italic influence. These are: (a) the loss of final -*r* or its replacement by -*d* in Faliscan territory, (b) the opening of *i* to *e* in hiatus before a vowel in Praeneste and Falerii, (c) the early monophthongisation *ae/ai* > *e* and (d) the vocalism *e* arising from *ei* rather than Classical Latin *i*.[14] Interestingly enough, the first three phenomena occur in Faliscan territory, thus suggesting the existence of a local dialect which may have been in use until the end of the Republic. Besides, (c) and (d) also took place in the Latin of Rome either at an earlier (*ei* > *e* > *i*) or at a later stage (*ai/ae* > *e* was generalised in imperial times): they show how regional variation (in both the republican and imperial periods) is frequently not the result of a substrate influence, as often assumed in scholarly literature, but rather a matter of chronology, since the same linguistic phenomenon took place at different times in different places.[15]

Explicit evidence

A quick look at linguistic comments by ancient authors confirms the impression given by inscriptions about the non-uniformity of late republican Latin and the existence of linguistic variation, notably in some areas close to Rome. The territory about which we are best informed is Praeneste, a few kilometres east of Rome. Already in Plautus' comedies we read that people from Praeneste said *conea* for *ciconia* "stork" (*Truc.* 691) and use the expression *tam modo* ("just now", maybe in place of simple *modo*) (*Trin.* 609) and later *testimonia* by Lucilius (line 1130), Pompeius Festus (cf. Paul. *Fest.* p. 157.14 and Fest. p. 488.7) and others confirm the existence of what appeared to Roman ears a local dialect.[16] Further places which generate special linguistic comments in Varro are either around Rome (*e.g.* Lanuvium, Formiae) or at a more remote distance (the Sabine territory, Campania, Cisalpine Gaul and Baetica).[17] As for the individual dialectal features, it is mainly vocabulary that attracts the interest of the authors. In this respect, Adams stresses the significance of those words (he calls them "strong dialectical forms") that had synonyms in the standard language (or in other regions) and whose use cannot be simply traced back to a deficiency of Roman Latin: to this group belongs the use of *pellicula* for *scortum* "hide" (Varro *L.* 7.84), *iubilare* for *clamare* "shout" (Varro *L.* 6.67–68), etc.[18] Particularly relevant in diachronic perspective is the employment of *quando* with a temporal (instead of the Classical causal) value: this feature, ascribed by Varro to the people of Formiae and Fundi (cf. Charisius p. 143.4–9 Barwick), appears to have been alive for several centuries at lower social levels in areas around Rome (although its use in the city cannot be ruled out *a priori*)[19] and will later survive in nearly all Romance idioms (cf. the use of Italian and Portuguese *quando*, Spanish *cuando*, etc.). Turning to the phonetic remarks, it is interesting to observe that the non-Roman character of three of the four inscriptional features listed above (namely *e* for *i* in hiatus, *e* for *i* from *ei* and *e* for *ae*) receives further support from ancient *testimonia*.

The above mentioned passage of Plautus (*Truc.* 691) testifies, for instance, to the opening of *i < e* before a vowel in Praenestine territory (*conea* for *ciconia*). Besides, at *de Oratore* 3.46 Cicero considers the use of *e plenissimum* instead of *i* as a feature one would expect from reapers (*messores*) rather than from *oratores*, and Varro mentions the forms *speca* for *spica* "ear of corn" and *uella* for *uilla* "rural estate" (*R.* 1.2.14 and 1.48.2) as peculiar to the *rustici*.[20] The confusion between *eiram* "anger" and *eram* "mistress" made by the *agrestis* Truculentus in Plautus (*Truc.* 262–264) points in the same direction.[21] Similarly, Lucilius (1130) does not want Caecilius to become a rustic praetor, whereby his *rusticitas* is "exemplified" through the forms *Cecilius* and *pretor* (*Cecilius pretor ne rusticus fiat*), and Varro mentions the monophthongisation *ae > e* among rustics (cf. *L.* 7.96 *in pluribus uerbis A ante E alii ponunt, alii non … ac rustici Pappum Mesium, non Maesium*).[22] As far as morphology is concerned, Cicero's often quoted reference to the omission of final -*s* between a short vowel and a consonant as a *subrusticum* feature (*Orat.* 161) hints at the further resistance of this phenomenon in rural areas during his lifetime, whereas plenty of evidence shows that in Rome the phoneme had been fully restored around the first century BCE, both at a written and spoken level.[23]

The Empire

The regional diversity observed in the republican period continued and increased during the Empire, when Latin was spoken over a much larger territory and came into contact with a variety of languages. There is a reference to the poets of Corduba in Spain as *pingue quiddam sonantibus atque peregrinum* "sounding rather thick and foreign" already in Cicero (*Arch.* 10) and some years later Quintilian mentions the existence of certain sounds which allow one to recognise people of particular nations (*Inst.* 1.5.33 *sunt … proprii quidam et inenarrabiles soni, quibus nonnumquam nationes deprehendimus* "there are certain peculiar and inexpressible sounds for which we sometimes fault other peoples", 11.3.31 *nam sonis homines ut aera tinnitu dinoscimus* "for we recognise men by their voices as we recognise bronze from its ring").[24] Further *testimonia* refer more specifically to lexical differences in the regions. Columella, for instance, discussing the different types of vines raised in Italy, observes that each region or sub-region has its own denomination and sometimes plants changed name by changing location.[25] In the following centuries dialectal variation became, as expected, even more marked so that in the fourth century Jerome could make a general explicit statement about the diachronic and diatopic change of the language: (*Commentarii in epistulam Pauli apostoli ad Galatas* 357A *PL* 26) *cum … et ipsa Latinitas et regionibus quotidie mutetur et tempore* "Latin itself changes constantly according to region and through time".[26] This phenomenon, which eventually led to the birth of the Romance languages, can be traced back to several factors, such as the influence of the substrate languages (in the form of interference or through the intrusion of loanwords), the coinage of local terms, the retention of words that fell out of use in other areas (and thus developed to be dialectal terms),[27] etc.

Unlike in the archaic period, a wide range of primary sources helps us to reconstruct the variety of the language during the Empire: there are on the one hand different types of sub-literary sources, notably inscriptions on stone, papyri, writing tablets on wood, ostraca and curse tablets, and on the other hand several literary texts that picked up local forms or expressions from spoken usage. This is true, however, only for most of the western regions (including Italy) and Africa, whereas for eastern Latin, inscriptions are almost the only source of our knowledge. For this reason we shall proceed by a preliminary distinction between these two major areas.[28]

Western regions and Africa

Gaul

Ancient sources refer to the Latin of Gaul (or, more often, of certain Gallic regions) as characterised by local linguistic features. Again, we are best informed about vocabulary. Some of the earliest testimonies are found in Columella's work: in connection to the above-mentioned regional denominations of vines (see n. 25), he observes that the *incolae Galliarum* use the word *marcus* to designate a special type of helvennacan vine (3.2.25) and in another passage he says that *candetum* defines for the Gauls an area of 100 feet (or of 150 feet in rural areas). Noteworthy is a passage of Suetonius (*Vit.* 18) according to which Antonius Primus, who originated from Toulouse, bore in his childhood the cognomen *beccus* which in that region meant *gallinacei rostrum* "hen's beak": the parallel evidence of Gallic inscriptions, in which however *Beccus* only occurs as a personal name (*e.g. CIL* XIII.5381) and of the Gallo-Romance languages, where *beccus* largely survives in the meaning of "beak", shows that this word has to be regarded as a dialectalism of Gaul. According to Servius, even Virgil (who was born in Gallia Cisalpina) was not free from provincialisms: commenting on a verse of the *Georgics* (1.104 *quid dicam, iacto qui semine comminus arua/insequitur* "why should I speak of the one who immediately makes for the field when the seed has been sown?"), the grammarian notices that *comminus* here bears a temporal instead of the usual local meaning ("close at hand") and that this feature is peculiar to Gallia Cisalpina, where people used to say *uado ad eum, sed comminus* "I am on my way to him, but straightaway": although Servius' comment is most likely anachronistic, it again testifies to the existence of regional terms in Gaul.[29] This situation is well-supported from literary texts, mainly from the late period. The overwhelming majority of examples are found with substantives referring to flora and fauna.[30] The catalogue of fish in Ausonius' *Mosella* (16.75–149) deserves a special mention here: Adams has shown that fourteen of the fifteen fish names listed survive in Gallo-Romance and four are exclusively attested there. Thus, even if we were not informed about the origin of the author, "this list could be assigned to Gaul on statistical grounds" ((2007) 464).[31]

It appears that in the phonetic domain also Gallic Latin exhibited certain specific features compared with other areas. The best evidence can be found in the corpus of over 14,000 local inscriptions, almost all of which date from the imperial period.[32] Their language has been investigated, since Pirson's pioneering monograph (1901), in several studies which chiefly deal with phonetic features of the Christian period.[33] One of the most important results that has emerged is a substantial difference between the treatment of consonants and vowels on inscriptions from the fourth to seventh centuries CE. On the one hand, it has been shown that the confusion B/V (*biuus, Silbanus* for *uiuus, Siluanus*, etc.), frequently attested in other areas (notably in central and southern Italy and in the Balkans), is hardly found in Gallic inscriptions.[34] On the other hand, a high frequency of the confusion between the vowels $\bar{e}/\bar{\imath}$ appears here, which, as is well known, will eventually spread to nearly all Romance languages:[35] specifically, based on Gaeng's results (1968), Adams concludes that in Lugdunensis and Narbonensis *e* for $\bar{\imath}$ occurs in 30 per cent of the cases in which one would expect $\bar{\imath}$ and the statistics are even higher if restricted to inscriptions from the sixth and seventh centuries.[36] A confusion in the treatment of vowels is also indicated by a passage of the late grammarian Consentius (fifth century CE) according to which Gauls pronounce the letter *i* in a different way from Greek and Romans: in particular, he refers to the long initial *i* (occurring for instance in the word *ite*) which has in Gaul a somewhat "richer" (*pinguiorem*) sound, intermediate between *e* and *i*,[37] and which he opposes to the moderation of the Roman language that pronounces the same vowel in a "thin" way (*exilis*). This passage raises several difficult questions related to the obscure terminology (it is impossible to determine the exact meaning of the adjectives *pinguis* and *exilis*) and to the total absence of evidence of this phenomenon in the Romance languages as well as in Gallic inscriptions, where the confusion *i/e* solely affects short *i* (see above). However, the significance of Consentius' remark remains, which attempts to describe a phonetic (and not, as in most of the cases, lexical) feature that he considers specific of the Gallic Latin of his times and thus distinguishable from standard Latin.[38]

An interesting morphological item, in which a substrate influence may have encroached upon a general Vulgar Latin feature, is the nominative plural -*as* with feminine names. Due to its early appearance in inscriptions from Oscan areas (Pisaurum, Minturna) and in two debated passages of Pomponius (fragments 141 and 150 Ribbeck), the ending has been often traced back to Oscan influence.[39] This explanation is weakened by late republican instances both in Roman inscriptions and in Cato's work (*Agr.* 134.1).[40] In imperial times this morpheme is frequently attested on inscriptions from Italy, Africa, the Balkans and other countries, especially in the later period (from the fourth century onwards). Several factors hint at the diffusion of *as*-nominatives in the spoken language, or rather in some spoken varieties of substandard Latin. These are: the diversity of documents involved (inscriptions, graffiti, curse tablets); the low level of correctness of many of them (in about 40 per cent of the cases the text exhibits at least one further "deviating" feature); the diachronic and diatopic distribution (which prevents us from considering the form as a regional feature); and its probable survival in some Romance languages (French, Spanish and maybe even Italian).[41] As for Gaul, the usual claim that, in contrast with the later development of the language, *as*-nominatives are not found in local documents,[42] is contradicted by two early epigraphic examples in Narbonensis,[43] by the ostraca at La Graufesenque (see below) and by late literary evidence (Anthimus, sixth century). It is true, however, that for the period during which most epigraphic occurrences appear over the rest of the empire (second to fifth centuries CE) there are no examples from Gaul at our disposal. A possible reason for this phenomenon can be found in the pottery records at La Graufesenque. These documents, which are mostly dated to the time of Nero, exhibit several regionalisms, some of which appear to be due to Gaulish influence (notably the terms *canastrum*, *panna* and the spelling *ps* for *x*).[44] A feature which often emerges in the texts (twenty times) is the use of the feminine *as*-ending in contexts where nominatives were normally employed. Although a syntactic explanation cannot be ruled out (accusative of lists), it appears more reasonable to assume for these special cases an influence from Gaulish morphology where the nominative plural of feminine names ended in -*as*. By accepting this solution, the rare appearance of *as*-nominatives in this territory (and more generally in Gaul) may find an explication: it is possible, as suggested by Adams, that "because of its Gaulish association"[45] the ending -*as* was generally "stigmatised" in local Latin and consequently avoided either at both the spoken and written level or in writing alone.[46]

Spain

For the study of regional varieties in Spanish Latin we have less literary and sub-literary evidence at our disposal in comparison with Gaul. A feature which often emerges in Latin commentators is the existence of a special accent or way of speaking by which people from the Iberian peninsula could be easily recognised. The attribution to Spanish poets of a "thick and foreign" sound was made already by Cicero (*Arch.* 10; see above) and the *Historia Augusta* refers to a rustic pronunciation exhibited by Hadrian (who originated from Spain) while delivering a speech.[47] Even more explicit evidence comes from Seneca the Elder who mentions that Messala, after hearing a speech of the Spanish declaimer Latro, commented: "he is eloquent in his own language."[48] However, the characteristic that has been most discussed in modern scholarship in connection with the Latin of Spain is its alleged conservatism. This theory was suggested at the end of nineteenth century by Wölfflin and Lindsay and later met a large consensus, especially in the studies of Tovar.[49] Following this theory, Spanish Latin exhibits several conservative or archaic features which would correspond to current usage of Latin during the late third and early second centuries BCE, owing to the early date of occupation and Romanisation of the territory (*c.* 206 BCE).[50] In particular, proceeding on the assumption that many soldiers came from southern Italian areas, some scholars have claimed the existence of Oscan features in Spanish Latin. Adams' recent examination of all alleged archaisms has clearly shown that the great majority of them do not bear scrutiny and hence must be disregarded. Specifically, he stresses the importance of two aspects:

1 It is possible that some features entered the Latin of Spain in the second century BCE and survived there until the birth of Ibero-Romance, but in most of the cases these items were in use also elsewhere and only centuries later were they "restricted" to Spain. To this category belongs for instance the use of *fabulor* ("speak"; cf. Spanish *hablar*, Portuguese *falar*, etc.), *uaciuus* (in the meaning of *uacuus* "empty") and *percontari* "interrogate".[51]
2 Certain alleged archaisms cannot be traced back to republican times but arose in the late period. This is probably the case of *demagis* "furthermore" (the form turns up once in Lucilius and is scarcely evident in the later development of the language[52]), *rostrum* in the meaning of "human face", *baro* "blockhead" and others.[53]

More generally, there are very few extant lexical features which can be considered peculiar to Iberian Latin. These are found almost exclusively in literary sources[54] and most of them are due to innovation, not conservatism or archaism. Only in two cases can one assume a continuous use since the Roman occupation, namely the frequentative *incepto* "begin" (cf. early Spanish *encentar*) and the adjective *cuius, -a, -um* "whose" (cf. Spanish *cuyo*).

Turning to phonology and morphology, all the items mentioned by scholars in connection to Iberian Latin are usually traced back to an Oscan influence: these are the two word-internal assimilations *nd* > *n(n)* and *mb* > *m(m)*, and, in second-declension nouns, the nominative singular *-i* for *-ius* and the nominative plural *-eis* (also *-is*, *-es*) for *-i*. However, on closer inspection these forms cannot be considered regionalisms nor do they appear to be related to Oscan.[55]

Britain

In the near total absence both of explicit evidence from ancient authors and of local literary texts, our only source for investigating dialectal variation in British Latin is non-literary documents. Luckily enough, so many of them (notably the Vindolanda writing tablets and the Bath curse tablets) have come to light in the last two decades that among all imperial provinces "Britain is perhaps the most richly endowed with Latin of the sort that might be called "non-literary"".[56] Leaving aside one or two cases, all the regionalisms we have evidence of in these texts are to be ascribed to an interaction with the Celtic language.[57] In particular, a thorough analysis of these items reveals the existence of linguistic contacts between Britain and Gaul due both to the geographical vicinity and the common Celtic background.[58] These contacts are clearly identifiable in a group of Celtic loanwords that appear in Britain and Gaulish texts (or in Gallo-Romance), such as *souxtum* "type of pot" (both in Vindolanda and in a potter's account at Vayres), *popia* "ladle" (occurring in a curse tablet from Brandon and surviving solely in Gallo-Romance) and the Germanic borrowing *baro* "man" (in British curse tablets as well as in Frankish law codes). The evidence is not confined to vocabulary. A Gaulish feature figuring in the ostraca at La Graufesenque is the replacement of Latin *ps/pt* through *xs/xt* with the first element indicating a velar spirant (e.g. Greco-Latin *paropsides* "types of dish" > *paraxidi*): this development must have been known also in Britain where it affected the form of certain Latin loanwords in British Celtic (as in Latin *captiuus* "prisoner" > Welsh *ceithiw*). Another common phonetic trait is probably the spelling *diuus* for *deus* "god" attested twice in Britain (in *RIB* I.306 and on a curse tablet from Ratcliffe-on-Soar) and once in the *Vita Symphoriani Augustodunensis*, a late literary text from Gaul: owing to its context, the form can hardly be explained as an archaic or poetic feature, but it rather accounts for a switch into Celtic, where *diuus* was the normal equivalent of Latin *deus*.[59]

Africa

Much explicit and implicit evidence hints at the existence of regional varieties in African Latin and helps to reconstruct some of their features. The oldest source of information is represented by ancient *testimonia* referring both to lexical and phonetic features of the *Afri*. So already Pliny (*Nat.* 35.169) writes that the walls made out of earth are called *formacei* in Africa and Spain[60] and Nonius Marcellus provides some further (although uncertain) evidence about vocabulary.[61] On the other hand, some writers mention (as seen above for Spain) an undefined but yet recognisable African accent (for example in a passage of the *Historia Augusta* referring to the African emperor Septimius Severus[62]) and they occasionally mention specific phonetic traits of local Latin.[63] In modern research, even after the criticism following Sittl's study (1882), some scholars have attempted to find an African colour (*Africitas*) in literary works of local writers, arguing *inter alia* that as a result of the early contact with the Romans the language would bear traces of the *sermo priscus*.[64] This approach has recently been criticised by Adams who observed that, due to the existence of marked social variation in African Latin, literature can hardly provide indications about regional features of the language: even if we find a peculiar usage in, say, Apuleius, Tertullian or Augustine "such would be not regionalism of African Latin but modish artificial mannerism" ((2007) 519). One has rather to look at those texts whose authors belonged to a lower social or educational level and are thus more likely to have admitted local usages in their Latin. Specifically, Adams turns his attention to three types of sub-literary sources: medical texts and writers (Mustio, Cassius Felix, Dioscorides, and the *Liber Tertius*[65]), the *Tablettes Albertini* (written around 493–496 CE and providing information on agricultural language) and the Bu Njem ostraca (dated to the third century CE and accounting for the military register). This analysis produces unequivocal evidence for the presence of regional features in African Latin, notably in the lexical field where over thirty new dialectal words emerge, all of the "strong" type (that is with corresponding terms in the standard language). As observed for Britain, two sorts of items can be distinguished: (a) loanwords from a sub-strate language (in this case Punic): this is the largest group, including terms as *ginga* "henbane" and *boba* "mallow" in Mustio's translation and *girba* "mortar" and *gelela* "inner flesh of a gourd" in Cassius Felix; (b) native Latin words or forms showing no correspondences elsewhere, such as *baiae* in the meaning of "baths", *dulcor* meaning a sweet drink or liquid and *centenarium* which occurs in the *Tablettes Albertini* alone and perhaps indicates a grain store.[66] A peculiar morphological feature is the use of the voca-tive ending instead of the nominative with Latin names in *-us* and *-ius*. This usage occurs in a few African inscriptions (e.g. *CIL* VIII.8670 *D.M.S. Egnati Gem(i)ne uixit anos LXXXXV*),[67] notably characterising a small group of bilingual (Punic-Latin) texts from Sirte. Two explanations have been suggested for its origin: (a) Punic people usually heard Latin speakers calling each other in the vocative form and thus considered it as the "normal" form for Latin names: on this view, the Latin vocative ending would have "erro-neously" entered the Punic speaking community;[68] (b) the two morphemes *-e* and *-i* are the result of an adaptation of the Latin suffixes to Punic orthography: by this solution the form would be a Punicised ending attached to Latin names.[69] In either case, the morpheme is most likely to be traced back to interference between the two languages but owing to the scant number of examples it cannot be regarded as a characteristic of African Latin in general.

A further relevant aspect which emerges from the study of African texts is the pos-sible existence of a linguistic link between the local Latin and that of Sardinia. It is well known that these two areas had connections long before the Roman expansion and kept continuous trading relations during the Empire. Traces of this association can possibly be found in vocabulary where certain terms are attested in African Latin alone and which later turn up in Sardinian. Particularly interesting is the case of the words *spanus*, indicating a colour of a horse and *pala* "shoulder-blade" as well as of the feminine use of *acina* "grape", which were all to survive almost exclusively in Sardinia.[70] The phonological analysis of the Latin inscriptions from Africa leads to analogous con-clusions. Several studies, notably those of Barbarino, Gaeng and Omeltchenko, have shown that, in contrast to the rather frequent confusion of B and V, alternations between E and I and between O and U occur very seldom on African inscriptions.[71]

These results, which are exactly inverse to those observed for Gaul, have been confirmed by Adams' examination of the Bu Njem ostraca and the *Tablettes Albertini*.[72] Besides, they are perfectly consistent with some extant *testimonia* dealing with spoken features of African Latin which do not mention any confusion of distinct vocalic timbres but refer to a loss of the phonemic opposition of vowel quantity. Augustine, for instance, argues that, due to the incapacity of *Afrae aures* "African ears" to distinguish between short and long vowels, teachers should not have any regrets about using the word *ossum* for *ŏs* ("bone") in order to keep it distinct from *ōs* "mouth".[73] Similarly, Consentius observes that the lengthening of the accented *ĭ* in *pĭper* "pepper" and the shortening of unaccented *ō* in the first syllable of *ōrator* constitute vices peculiar to Africans.[74] This picture shows a close analogy with that emerging from Sardinia: on the one hand, local inscriptions display a correct treatment of vowels, with relatively infrequent confusions of E with I and O with U; on the other hand the later development of Sardinian is characterised by the lack of the near panromanic changes *ē* > *i* and *ō* > *u* and by the merger of each of the five long vowels with the corresponding short ones (*ĭ* with *ī*, *ŭ* with *ū* etc.).[75]

The eastern provinces

Among all imperial regions the eastern ones are certainly those we are worst informed about. Latin commentators show no interest in the linguistic peculiarities of these areas: all we have is a passage of the historian Velleius Paterculus (first century CE) according to which Pannonians possessed a knowledge both of Roman training and language and many of them were acquainted with literary culture.[76] As for the implicit evidence, the number of Latin writers originating from here is extremely small and can barely account for dialectal features.[77] Therefore, in nearly total absence of other types of sub-literary texts, inscriptions on stone (which amount approximately to 25,000[78]) remain our only source of knowledge of local Latin.[79] Linguistic studies devoted to this subject have shown that, with due caution, it is possible to detect certain specific features or tendencies (in the lexical, phono-morphological and syntactical domain), some of which are explainable through the contact with Greek.

A term peculiar to these territories is *brutes* meaning "daughter-in-law" or "young married woman": it has originally a Germanic root (cf. Old High German *brut*) and will later survive in several western and eastern idioms (cf. French *bru*, Engadine *brüt*, Friulan *brut*, etc.). In Roman times all occurrences of the word are confined to six inscriptions from Moesia (three), Noricum, Pannonia and Aquileia. This evidence along with the existence in standard Latin of another word with approximately the same meaning (*nurus*) makes it likely that *brutes* represented a "strong" dialectal term of eastern regions. Besides, in later times the word appears to have become quite common in this territory, finding its way in Greek texts (where it oscillates between the first and third declination) and even being glossed in the Suda.[80]

Another lexeme of Germanic origin attested only on funerary inscriptions is *socerio* or *suecerio* meaning the brother (or sister) of the wife (or husband). The few extant examples are almost entirely restricted to eastern regions (Noricum twice, Raetia and Aquileia) and refer to families of military men:[81] it is thus possible, as suggested by Adams, that

"Germanic speakers who had learnt Latin in the army may have been responsible for the introduction of the term to Latin" ((2007) 677).

Phonetic features of eastern European inscriptions have been the object of several articles by Herman who concentrated, through a "microtechnique" of linguistic geography, on the material found on both sides of the Adriatic (from modern Apulia up to southern Dalmatia) and in the interior provinces (Pannoniae and Dacia). Herman observes that, as far as vowels are concerned, Dalmatia and the Regio X belong to the same linguistic area by displaying an analogous high frequency of confusion within the palatal ($\bar{e}$ and $\breve{\imath}$) and velar ($\bar{o}$ and $\breve{u}$) series (in stressed as in unstressed syllables), which corresponds to the future developments in most of the Romance languages (see above). In Pannonia these changes are also attested but with less frequency (Herman refers to it as a sort of "prolongation" of the Italian-Dalmatic area).[82] Dacia, instead, "constitue une unité qui se sépare assez nettement de cette région 'adriatico-pannonienne'": its vocalism is very conservative and resembles that of southern Italy.[83]

A morphological feature which is often found in eastern regions is the use of *-es* and *-aes* in the genitive singular of feminine names. The two endings are found also elsewhere in the empire (notably in Rome) but they appear with remarkable frequency in the east[84] and might have spread in Greek communities under the influence of -ης.[85]

Several interesting phono-morphological and syntactical traits are attested in the province of Moesia Inferior, between the Danube and the Thracian mountains. In this area, notably in Scythia Minor region, there is evidence for the existence of Latin-speaking communities, basically consisting of soldiers and traders (as well as their families), surrounded by a much larger Greek speaking population.[86] The two languages must have coexisted here for a period of about 300 years (from the first to the fourth century CE) and the investigation of local inscriptions (especially of the Latin ones) shows that there may have been a reciprocal influence. As I have dealt extensively with this subject elsewhere I will confine myself here to a summary of the main results.[87] Two patterns which appear with remarkable frequency in Moesian inscriptions are *pro salutem* "for well-being" and *ex uotum* "from a vow" in place of the corresponding ablative constructions. The first one appears nineteen times (fourteen in Scythia Minor alone) and can be more generally regarded as characteristic of the eastern provinces where it globally occurs thirty-eight times.[88] These figures assume a special relevance if compared to those from other regions of the empire: for instance, *pro salutem* is attested only five times in over 40,000 Latin inscriptions from Rome and a further five times in African inscriptions (amounting to about 30,000).[89] Even more restricted are the figures for *ex uotum*: this formula is found seven times in Moesia Inferior (three with loss of final *-m*, and once with final *-n*), three times in Dacia, very close to the northern border of Moesia, and once in Epirus.[90] As for the rest of the Empire, Diehl ((1899) 32) noted two examples on Roman inscriptions "quorum auctores sunt Moesiae inferioris", and one in Spain. Now, prudence is required in judging the linguistic significance of both phrases (as, in general, with any recurring epigraphic pattern): they should probably be regarded as "inscriptional" regionalisms, in that they do not directly reflect a local variety of speech but are rather bound to the specialised written register of certain stonemasons' workshops.[91] However, considering that *pro salute* and *ex uoto* belong to the most common inscriptional formulae all over the empire, it is unsatisfactory to ascribe the relatively high concentration of their anomalous variants (both involving an erroneous use of the accusative) in a quite small territory to a mere epigraphic cliché: the more so since inscriptions from the same area exhibit a general tendency to employ the accusative in place of the ablative, mostly after preposition.[92] There are at least two factors that may be responsible for this phenomenon in Moesia: (a) the high frequency of omission of final -*m* in local inscriptions (which has possibly fostered its hypercorrect use);[93] (b) the contact with Greek: due to the absence of the ablative in this language, a general tendency may have arisen among Latin speakers to replace this case with the accusative, which was in Latin the only other prepositional case.[94]

Another feature of Moesian inscriptions that appears related to the contact with Greek is the pattern *uiuo suo*. This sepulchral formula, corresponding to the more common *se uiuo*, is usually found on inscriptions of the second to fourth centuries CE whose authors and/or dedicatees appear to be connected with a Greek environment:[95] there are fifteen instances all over the empire, of which twelve are in Moesia Inferior, one in Moesia Superior (very close to the western border) and once each in inscriptions from Mediolanum and Aquileia which reveal a connection with eastern Europe.[96] I have elsewhere suggested that the origin of the pattern can be ascribed to an interference with the Greek pronominal system. The common use here of the genitive of the reflexive pronoun ἑαυτοῦ as a personal adjective (thus in the meaning of Latin *suus*) might have produced among the Latin speakers a confusion between the reflexive pronoun and the adjective and a consequent tendency to loss of the former (which in fact occurs very rarely on Moesian stones). Traces of this process can be found in local inscriptions where both the genitive *sui* (corresponding to Greek ἑαυτοῦ) is occasionally employed instead of *suus* (as in Greek)[97] and the ablative *se* is replaced by *suo* in the formula *uiuo suo*.[98]

A syntactical pattern which occasionally turns up on eastern inscriptions and is barely known from other areas of the empire is the use of the genitive after prepositions. Of special interest are the examples with *a* (nine times), *de* (twice) and *ex* (six times), *e.g.* *AE* (1936) 51 [*ui*]*am a Dyrrachi usque Acontisma … curauit* (Macedonia, 112), *CIL* III.6109 *M. Iulius Sabinianus miles ex clas. praetoriae Misenesis* (Achaia). Since all instances are basically confined to bilingual or Greek-speaking areas (Moesia Inferior, Achaia, Macedonia and Asia Minor[99]), it is very likely that, although possibly fostered by some special factors – such as the confusion between the two types (a) preposition + ablative and (b) genitive – these constructions are primarily due to interference with the corresponding Greek patterns ἀπό and ἐξ + genitive.[100]

A final noteworthy pattern of eastern regions is the use of the dative instead of the genitive to indicate possess or belonging (so called possessive dative or *datiuus adnominalis*). This feature occasionally emerges in Latin literature, notably in technical or poetic texts, but it appears quite spread in eastern European inscriptions where it globally involves seventy words.[101] Particularly frequent is its use on Christian epitaphs from Dalmatia within the sepulchral formula "*arca* + name of the dedicatee", *e.g.* *CIL* III.6405 *arca Viforini et Sextilite fratribus germanis*.[102] Herman (1965) assumed that the origin of this phenomenon is to be found in local factors. Whenever Illyrian names entered the Latin morphological system they could be inflected according either to the third or to the second declension (that is *Pletor*, -*ris* or *Pletorius*, -*ri*). Therefore, with this type of names the ending -(*i*)*i* could express either a dative or a genitive: as Herman notes, this may have caused a "sentiment d'incertitude générale, surtout dans le cas des noms propres" and a consequent oscillation in the use of the two cases.

NOTES

1   Cf. Väänänen (1983) 481: "Les langues romanes ne sont pas nées du jour au lendemain. On s'accorde aujourd'hui pour postuler que la 'langue mère', le latin, à mesure qu'elle s'est répandue, n'a pas tardé à se diversifier. Mais l'accord ne va guère au-delà de cet axiome."

2   On these and other possible causes of regional diversifications in Latin, see particularly Löfstedt (1959) 39, Väänänen (1983) 502, Herman (1985a) 64 and Adams (2007) 711 ff.

3   See Adams (2007) 2: "The attentive reader of Latin texts written between 200 BCE and CE 600 ... will probably have a sense that the language changes in time, but no sense that texts could be assigned a place of composition on linguistic evidence alone."

4   Cf. Löfstedt (1959) 39.

5   See Herman (1985a) 65.

6   See for instance Mihaescu's conclusions (1978) 327 and their discussion in Herman (1985a) 66, (1983a) 176.

7   Symptomatic is Löfstedt's pessimism on the possibility of locating a late text geographically by using linguistic features (1959) 39 ff. One of the few exceptions to this general tendency is represented by Herman's various contributions which, by means of detailed small-case comparisons in Latin inscriptions ("microtechnique"), postulated the existence of distinct linguistic areas. Some of his findings will be mentioned below.

8   For reasons of space we have included in this last group the evidence derived both from literary and non-literary sources, particularly inscriptions.

9   Note that, since a huge amount of evidence is collected in Adams' book, we shall often refer to its findings.

10 It is important to recall that most of these texts have been written before the language had been standardised by grammarians: therefore "linguistically significant spelling variations may be identified" (Adams (2007) 39).

11 Worth mentioning in this respect are the works of Blümel (1972) and Coleman (1990). For full bibliographical details cf. Adams (2007) 39 ff.

12 Adams (2007) 108, 691.

13 For further pseudo-regionalisms see Adams (2007) 108.

14 More uncertain is the explanation of the misspelling *u* for long *o* in the ending *Herc(o)lo*. The few relevant instances appear on mixed-language text and might result from an imperfect learning of Latin. Cf. Adams (2007) 72–79, 95–96, 110–111).

15 On this important point see Adams (2007) 110, 186.

16 For a discussion of these and other passages, see Adams (2007) 79, 120 ff. with further literature.

17 See Adams (2007) 184–185 with references. The criticism by Asinius Pollio of Livy's *Patauinitas* reported in a famous passage of Quintilian (*Inst.* 1.5.56) is very difficult to inter-pret and seems to refer to speech rather than to writing. Whatever is to be made of it, it gives us further evidence on regional variation. See Adams (2007) 153, 184.

18 Cf. Adams (2007) 185. See also pp. 12–13 on the distinction between weak and strong dialect forms.

19 See Adams (2007) 158–160.

20 Cf. Adams (2007) 137–139, 183 with further references.

21 For an interpretation of this passage, which presupposes a visualisation of the word *e(i)ram* in his written form, see Adams (2007) 52–54, Müller (2001) 31 n. 3 and Leumann (1977) 64 with literature.

22 "In many words some speakers pronounce *ae*, others *e*, as the rustics say Pappus Mesius, not Maesius." See also *L.* 5.96 where we are informed about the pronunciation *hedus* (instead of *haedus*) *in Latio rure*.

23 See Adams (2007) 140–141 with further references. On the whole question concerning final *-s* see particularly Proskauer (1909).

24 For a discussion of these passages see Adams (2007) 117, 135–136, Russell (2001) I.141 n. 42 and Herman (1985a) 71–72.

25 See Col. 3.2.30 *uniuersae regiones regionumque paene singulae partes habent propria uitium genera, quae consuetudine sua nominant; quaedam etiam stirpes cum locis uocabula mutauerunt; … ideoque in hac ipsa Italia, ne dicam in tam diffuso terrarum orbe, **uicinae etiam nationes nominibus earum discrepant, uariantque uocabula**.* Cf. Adams (2007) 213–214.

26 Probably the most explicit remark on the existence of lexical variation in the empire is found in a later passage of Consultus Fortunatianus (fifth century CE): *gentilia uerba quae sunt? quae propria sunt quorundam gentium, sicut Hispani non cubitum uocant, sed Graeco nomine ancona, et Galli facundos pro facetis, et Romani uernaculi plurima ex neutris masculino genere potius enuntiant, ut hunc theatrum et hunc prodigium* (*Ars rhet.* 3.4 *RLM* p. 123). Cf. Adams (2007) 220–222.

27 Cf. Adams (2007) 368–369. On the last mentioned phenomenon cf. Adams (2007) 31–32 who refers to it as "shrinkage".

28 For reasons of space I will leave aside the regional diversification in Italy during the Empire, for which I refer to Adams (2007) 188–230, 435–515.

29 A similar remark is found in connection to *A.* 7.705. On both passages see Adams (2007) 250–251 with further literature.

30 Among the exceptions to this general tendency we must recall the expression *ab oculis* in the sense "blind" which is solely attested in the *Actus Petri cum Simone* (fifth to sixth century CE) and will later survive only in Gallo-Romance *aveugle* (and the Old Italian borrowing *avocolo*). For a discussion see Adams (2007) 338 ff.

31 See also Adams (2007) 304–311 and Green (1991) 472 ff. For further evidence of lexical variation in Gaul see Adams (2007) 276 ff.

32 On the quantity of Gallic inscriptions see particularly the study of Herman (1983b). Herman's methodology (which mainly addressed phonological problems, as the confusions *e/i* and *o /u*) consisted of calculating the frequency of an error on the inscriptions as a proportion of the total number of errors or as a percentage of another error. For a discussion of the problem cf. Adams (2007) 629 ff., Herman (1985a) 69 ff. and Väänänen (1983) 500–501 with further bibliographical references.

33 See particularly Gaeng (1968), Barbarino (1978) and Herman (1983b).

34 Gauthier (1975) 76 regards this as a Gallic characteristic. See also Barbarino (1978) 91 ff. and Adams (2007) 638–640 with further references. More generally, Herman mentions in Gaul "l'absence pratiquement complète d'altérations consonantiques présentes ailleurs" (1983b) 159 and refers, *inter alia*, to the greater stability of final *-t*. Besides, he observes in most of the imperial provinces a "complementarity" in the treatment of (a) *b/u* and (b) *i/e* and *o/u*: "Il est intéressant de constater que l'ensemble des régions 'actives' du point de vue du flottement B ~ V est presque strictement complémentaire de la région 'novatrice' dans la réorganisation du système vocalique" (1985a) 80.

35 An exception is found in Sardinian and Romanian. Cf. Väänänen (1981) 30.

36 Cf. Adams (2007) 640–641 based on Gaeng (1968) and Pirson (1901). It is noteworthy that the confusion *e/i* occurs without significant differences both on unaccented and accented vowels, whereas the latter are more resistant to confusion in other territories. Cf. Herman (1983b) 158. The writing of *o* for *ŭ* is found, according to Herman, "dans les proportions attendues d'après la fréquence de ces voyelles", that is, less frequently than *e/i* but more so than *b/u*.

37 Cf. Consentius, *GL* V.394.11–22: *Galli hac* [sc. *i littera*] *pinguius utuntur, ut cum dicunt ite, non expresse ipsam proferentes, sed inter e et i pinguiorem sonum nescio quem ponentes.*

38 For the possible explanations of Consentius' passage see particularly Adams (2007) 244–250.

39 See for instance Löfstedt (1942–1956) II.330 ff.; Norberg (1943) 26 ff.; Mohl (1899) 205 ff.

40 Cf. Adams (2003a) 118–119. For different explanations of the form see Galdi (forthcoming); (2004) 59–67.

41 In literary texts this form, which was certainly widespread in common usage along with many others, was filtered out by the conservative character of the language. The first certain examples (apart from the few republican ones) go back to the fourth century CE. For a detailed discussion of these data see Galdi (forthcoming).

42 See on this point Adams (2007) 675.

43 Caldelli and Vismara (2001) 39–40. *Viuont Ddei Man[es] sacrum umani T. Vettius P. f. Pap. Loripes summae rudi P. Vettius T. f. Pap. Martialis duas Vettias T. l. Suauis et Vtilis* (first century CE).

44 Cf. Adams (2007) 281–289; (2003a) 438–440 and see p. 538 of this volume.

45 See Adams (2007) 675.

46 This second solution would appear more suitable in view of the later development of French morphology. It is important to recall, in this respect, that the possible or even probable existence of a special phenomenon in the spoken usage does not necessarily imply its emergence in sub-literary texts.

47 SHA *Hadr.* 3.1 (Hadrianus) *cum orationem imperatoris in senatu agrestius pronuntians risus esset.*

48 Sen. *Con.* 2.4.8 *"sua lingua disertus est". ingenium illi concessit, sermonem obiecit.*

49 For a bibliography to the question, see Adams (2007) 372 ff. and n. 15. Directly connected to this theory is the more general view that the date of occupation of an area is a determining factor of its Latin (and its later development). Cf. Adams (2007) 372–373.

50 Two basic conditions of this theory are (1) that Latin-speaking communities existed in Spanish territory from the start so that the language had been in continuous use there until the birth of Ibero-Romance and (2) that this regional variety was scarcely exposed to the changes affecting Latin in other parts of the empire. This view also has relevance for Romance philologists because, according to it, the conservatism of the Latin of Spain would be reflected in Ibero-Romance. Cf. Adams (2007) 373.

51 Cf. Adams (2007) 383 ff., 392–393, 394.

52 Cf. Spanish *demás*, Portuguese *demais*, Catalan *demés*.

53 For a discussion of these and other items see Adams (2007) 374 ff. *Baro* belongs to a group of words (as *circius*, *patres*, etc.) that also occur in Gallic Latin (and Gallo-Romance) and that reveal the existence of a common lexical area between Spain and Gaul, comparable to that between both Britain and Gaul and Sardinia and Africa. Cf. also Adams' conclusions (2007) 705 ff.

54 As for non-literary texts, there is one single regionalism (*paramus* = "plateau") attested on Spanish inscriptions. The special words occurring in the *Lex Metalli Vipascensis* are all of technical nature and hence constitute a matter of register rather than of dialect. See in particular Adams (2007) 428 ff.

55 Adams (2007) 406–421.

56 Adams (2007) 622. As a consequence of these discoveries, Smith's "pioneer" paper (1983), which classified and discussed various types of deviations mainly occurring in British inscriptions on stone, is to be considered outdated. Cf. Adams (2007) 582.

57 As for the "pure" Latin words attested only or almost exclusively in Britain, a distinction must be made between (a) those which will survive in the Continent (their absence from written records appears to be a matter of chance, e.g. *uectura*, *braciarius*), (b) the term *excussorium* in the meaning "threshing-floor" which is later attested in British medieval Latin and can thus be considered a local regionalism. Cf. Adams (2007) 604 ff., 622–623.

58 It is to Adams's credit to have discovered and explained the existence of these shared linguistic features. See in particular (2007) 596 ff. with further references.

59 The presence in Latin texts of these and further features resulting from a Celtic background provides strong evidence for the spread of Latin among the Celtic population. See the extensive discussion in Adams (2007) 597 ff.

60 Cf. Adams (2007) 237–238.

61 Cf. Adams (2007) 546–549 and Contini (1987).

62 SHA *Sept. Sev.* 19.9 *canorus uoce, sed Afrum quiddam usque ad senectutem sonans.* A clearly negative connotation of this accent is found in a passage of Jerome's *Epistula aduersus Rufinum* (27) which mentions a man who, although being taught by a very well-prepared African grammarian, was only able to imitate the hissing of his teacher's speech and the vices of his pronunciation (*stridorem linguae eius et uitia tantum oris*). On both passages see Adams (2007) 260, 268 ff.

63 Consentius (*GL* V.286.34–287.6) refers to *labdacismus*, that is the substitution of dark *l* with clear *l* or vice versa, as a phenomenon characteristic of African people. For a discussion of this controversial testimony see Adams (2007) 265 ff. Augustine mentions certain quantity changes in the vocalic system to which we will return below.

64 For bibliographical details cf. Adams (2007) 518 ff.

65 It should be noticed that, apart from Cassius Felix, the geographical origin of these texts is uncertain. Adams, however, ascribes them to Africa on linguistic grounds (2007) 528.

66 These and further lexical items are extensively discussed in Adams (2007) 528 ff. See also his conclusions (pp. 540 ff., 565–566, 573 ff.).

67 For further examples see Adams (2003a) 512 ff.

68 Cf. Adams (2003a) 512 ff.; (2007) 570–571.

69 So Amadasi Guzzo (1995).

70 *Spanus* and *pala* are unique to Sardinia and Africa, whereas feminine *acina* for *acinus/acinum* is also found in some southern Italian dialects. Cf. Adams (2007) 576, 707.

71 Barbarino's study (1978) considers exclusively the alternation between B and V, whereas those of Gaeng (1968) and Omeltchenko (1977) are more generally devoted to vocalic changes. It was Herman who first related the two phenomena together. For detailed references see Herman (1985a) 74 ff. and Adams (2007) 642 ff.

72 Adams (2007) 644 ff.

73 *Doct. Christ.* 4.10.24 *cur pietatis doctorem pigeat imperitis loquentem ossum potius quam os dicere, ne ista sillaba non ab eo, quod sunt ossa, sed ab eo, quod sunt ora, intellegatur, ubi Afrae aures de correptione uocalium uel productione non iudicant?*

74 *GL* V.392.3 *ut quidam dicunt "piper" producta priore syllaba, cum sit breuis, quod uitium Afrorum familiare est* and 11 *ut si quis dicat "orator" correpta priore syllaba, quod ipsum uitium Afrorum speciale est.* Cf. the remarks of Herman (1982) 219–220. More sceptical is the view of Adams who believes that the vices described by Consentius were probably also spread outside Africa (2007) 263 ff.

75 See particularly Herman (1985b) and Omeltchenko (1977) 196, 466–467. Even more explicit is Adams' conclusion (2007) 648: "I suggest ... that African Latin had the same type of vowel system as Sardinian ... and that there was a regional distinction in this respect between Africa and, say, Gaul". On the different vocalic systems in Romance cf. Väänänen (1981) 30 ff.

76 2.110.5 *omnibus ... Pannoniis non disciplinae tantummodo, sed linguae quoque notitia Romanae, plerisque etiam litterarum usus et familiaris animorum erat exercitatio.* Velleius' statement probably does not refer to the entire Pannonia, but only to a limited territory. Cf. Herman (1983a) 172.

77 A full list of the eastern Latin authors is given in Mihaescu (1978) 4 ff. A writer sometimes mentioned by scholars in connection with eastern Latinity is the late historian Jordanes (sixth century). However, due to the literary aims of his works and to the frequent employment of sources (which he often copies word for word), he can hardly provide evidence for regional variation.

78   On the approximate amount of eastern Latin inscriptions cf. Galdi (2004) xxv ff.; Herman (1983a) 170 and Mihaescu (1978) 168.

79   Apart from inscriptions, there is a very small number of extant sources such as the *tabulae ceratae* in Dacia and a few curse tablets. The study of the Latin elements surviving in Albanian, Dalmatian, the southern Slavic languages, Greek and, above all, Romanian can also help to reconstruct certain aspects of local Latinity, but are often difficult to classify and to date. See Herman (1983a) 167–168 and Mihaescu (1978) 17 ff.

80   It must be noticed, however, that in Greek sources the word bears a more general meaning and in the Suda is explained as "something similar to the sibyls and the prophets". A full list of the occurrences is given and discussed in Boïadjiev (2000) 93–116. See also Adams (2007) 678 and Mihaescu (1978) 292.

81   Details about the occurrences and forms of the term are collected by Adams (2007) 678; see also Adams (2003a) 447–448 and Mihaescu (1978) 293.

82   The linguistic connection between Pannonia, Dalmatia and northern Italy is stressed by Herman (1961) also in connection with the use and distribution of the two forms *posit* and *posuit*. These results have been subjected to criticism by Adams (2007) 670 ff.

83   Cf. Herman (1983a) 178–179; (1968) 118–119. Already Löfstedt referred to the conservatism of the Latin of Dacia and compared it with that of Spain (1959) 5. For a criticism of Herman's results see Adams (2007) 668 ff.

84   For details cf. Galdi (2004) 14–22, 272, 364 with further references.

85   Cf. Adams (2007) 674 suggesting that both morphemes "are not regionalism in the strict sense but forms which developed in Greek communities and were liable to be heard wherever there were Greeks using Latin".

86   For details on the proportion of Greek and Latin inscriptions in Scythia Minor see Galdi (2009) 54–56.

87   Cf. Galdi (2008, 2009, 2006) and (2004) particularly the conclusions at pp. 354 ff.

88   Cf. Galdi (2008) 152; (2009) 65. The total figure of thirty-seven given in Galdi (2004) 222, 360, (2003) 508 has to be revised in the light of a further occurrence recently found in Pannonia Superior.

89   According to Carnoy (1906) 269 there are only two occurrences in Spain. Pirson (1901) 206–207 mentions no cases in Gaul. For further evidence see Diehl (1899) 47–48.

90   Cf. Galdi (2004) 122–123,133, 135; (2003) 508.

91   On inscriptional or (pseudo-) regionalisms and their linguistic relevance cf. Adams (2007) 678–679.

92   From my analysis of all eastern inscriptions (including the extra-European ones) it results that 67 of 168 erroneous usages of the accusative instead of other cases (that is about 40 per cent) come from Moesia Inferior, which ranges only at the seventh place for total number of inscriptions. Cf. Galdi (2004) 360.

93   For details see Galdi (2004) 360; (2003). It is significant that, apart from the frequent omission of -*m*, several "Vulgar Latin" features, such as the change -*um* > -*o* in the accusative singular of the second declension or the opening -*i* > -*e* in the ablative singular of the third declension, are often attested in Moesian inscriptions at a relatively early date as compared to other regions. These traits cannot necessarily be regarded as local dialectalisms (they were probably common in the spoken Latin of other areas as well), but do certainly reflect a generally low educational level of the writers. For a discussion of this phenomenon see Galdi (2008) 151 ff.; (2009) 63 ff.

94   See Galdi (2008) 153; (2009) 152–153.

95   It is noteworthy that, as in the case of *pro salutem* and *ex uotum*, the pattern *uiuo suo* affects one of the most common epigraphic formulae of the empire (*se uiuo*).

96 e.g. *CIL* III.12490 *G. Iul. Sergis uiuo suo posuit sibi et conigi suae The. Agenia.* In one case (*CIL* III.7496) the feminine form *uiua sua* is attested. For details on the single occurrences see Galdi (2000) 78 ff.

97 e.g. *Inscriptiones Latinae Bulgariae* 67 *sibi et Qyriae coiugi sui, uiuo suo, memoria dedicauit.*

98 For further details see Galdi (2000) 87 ff. In a single case (not included in the global figures) the pattern is transferred to the first person singular: *CIL* III.7552 *D.M. Val. Valens uet.* [*classis*] *Fl. Moesie me*[*moriam feci ui*]*uo meo mi et* [*dulcissi*]*me coiugi me*[*ae*].

99 The only exceptions are found in Noricum: *AE* (1987), 799 *a Celeie m(ilia) p(assuum) III* (201), *CIL* III.5728 *a Viruni m(ilia) p(assuum) XV* (218), *CIL* III.4839 *Bellicius Statutus de alae I Thrac(um).*

100 Cf. Galdi (2002). Similarly, the construction *in Thuscae* found on a Syrian stone (*AE* (1991), 1572) may reflect the Greek type ἐν + dative. Further features of eastern inscriptions possibly due to Greek influence are discussed in Galdi (2006, 2005).

101 Cf. Adams (2007) 675–676, Galdi (2004) 432–435 and Herman (1965) with further bibliography.

102 This special construction is barely attested in other regions. Cf. Herman (1965) 377–378.

References

Adamik, B. 2003. "Zur Geschichte des offiziellen Gebrauchs der lateinischen Sprache. Justinians Reform." *AAntHung* 43: 229–241.

Adamik, B. 2006. "Offizielles Kommunikationssystem und Romanisierung." In C. Arias Abellán, ed., *Latin vulgaire – latin tardif VII. Actes du VIIème Colloque international sur le latin vulgaire et tardif (Séville, 2–6 septembre 2003)*. Seville: 17–29.

Adams, J.N. 1971. "A type of hyperbaton in Latin prose." *PCPhS* 17: 1–16.

Adams, J.N. 1972. "The language of the later books of Tacitus' *Annals*." *CQ* 22: 350–373.

Adams, J.N. 1973. 'The vocabulary of the speeches in Tacitus' historical works.' *BICS* 20: 124–144.

Adams, J.N. 1976. *The Text and Language of a Vulgar Latin Chronicle (Anonymus Valesianus II)*. London.

Adams, J.N. 1977. *The Vulgar Latin of the Letters of Claudius Terentianus*. Manchester.

Adams, J.N. 1980. "Anatomical terminology in Latin epic." *BICS* 27: 50–62.

Adams, J.N. 1981. "A type of sexual euphemism in Latin." *Phoenix* 35: 120–128.

Adams, J.N. 1982a. *The Latin Sexual Vocabulary*. London.

Adams, J.N. 1982b. "Anatomical terms transferred from animals to humans in Latin." *IF* 87: 90–109.

Adams, J. N. 1982c. "Anatomical terms used *pars pro toto* in Latin." *Proceedings of the African Classical Association* 16: 37–45.

Adams, J.N. 1983. "Words for 'prostitute' in Latin." *RhM* 126: 321–358.

Adams, J.N. 1984. "Female speech in Latin comedy." *Antichthon* 18: 43–77.

Adams, J.N. 1990. "The Latinity of C. Novius Eunus." *ZPE* 82: 227–247.

Adams, J.N. 1991. "Some neglected evidence for Latin *habeo* + infinitive: The order of the constituents." *TPhS* 89: 131–196.

Adams, J.N. 1992. "The text, interpretation and language of the Bath curse tablets." *Britannia* 23: 1–26.

Adams, J.N. 1994a. "Latin and Punic in contact? The case of the Bu Njem ostraca." *JRS* 84: 87–112.

Adams, J.N. 1994b. *Wackernagel's Law and the Placement of the Copula* esse *in Classical Latin* [*PCPhS* Supplementary volume no. 18]. Cambridge.

A Companion to the Latin Language, First Edition. Edited by James Clackson.
© 2011 Blackwell Publishing Ltd. Published 2011 by Blackwell Publishing Ltd.

Adams, J.N. 1994c. "Wackernagel's law and the position of unstressed personal pronouns in Classical Latin." *TPhS* 92: 103–178.

Adams, J.N. 1995a. *Pelagonius and Latin Veterinary Terminology in the Roman Empire*. Leiden.

Adams, J.N. 1995b. "The language of the Vindolanda writing tablets: An interim report." *JRS* 85: 86–134.

Adams, J.N. 1996. "Interpuncts as evidence for the enclitic character of personal pronouns in Latin." *ZPE* 111: 208–210.

Adams, J.N. 1998. "Two notes on *RIB*." *ZPE* 123: 235–236.

Adams, J.N. 1999a. "The poets of Bu Njem: Language, culture and the centurionate." *JRS* 89: 109–134.

Adams, J.N. 1999b. "Nominative personal pronouns and some patterns of speech in republican and Augustan poetry." In Adams and Mayer, eds., 1999: 97–133.

Adams, J.N. 2003a. *Bilingualism and the Latin Language*. Cambridge.

Adams, J.N. 2003b. "Petronius and new non-literary Latin." In J. Herman and H. Rosén, eds., *Petroniana: Gedenkschrift für Hubert Petersmann*. Heidelberg: 11–23.

Adams, J.N. 2003c. "'Romanitas' and the Latin language." *CQ* 53: 184–205.

Adams, J.N. 2003d. "The new Vindolanda writing-tablets." *CQ* 53: 530–575.

Adams, J.N. 2005a. "Neglected evidence for female speech in Latin." *CQ* 55: 582–596.

Adams, J.N. 2005b. "The accusative + infinitive and dependent *quod-/quia*-clauses: The evidence of non-literary Latin and Petronius." In S. Kiss, L. Mondin and G. Salvi, eds., *Latin et langues romanes. Études de linguistique offertes à József Herman à l'occasion de son 80ème anniversaire*. Tübingen: 195–206.

Adams, J.N. 2005c. "The *Bellum Africum*." In Reinhardt, Lapidge and Adams, eds., 2005: 73–96.

Adams, J.N. 2007. *The Regional Diversification of Latin 200 BC–AD 600*. Cambridge.

Adams, J.N., and R.G. Mayer, eds. 1999. *Aspects of the Language of Latin Poetry* [Proceedings of the British Academy 93]. Oxford.

Adams, J.N., and S. Swain. 2002. "Introduction." In Adams, Janse and Swain, eds. 2002: 1–20.

Adams, J.N., M. Janse and S. Swain, eds. 2002. *Bilingualism in the Ancient World: Language Contact and the Written Text*. Oxford.

Adger, D. 2003. *Core Syntax: A Minimalist Approach*. Oxford.

Agostiniani, L. 1982. *Le "iscrizioni parlanti" dell' Italia antica*. Florence.

Ahlquist, H. 1909. *Studien zur spätlateinischen Mulomedicina Chironis*. Uppsala.

Albrecht, J. 1995. "Terminologie und Fachsprachen." In M. Beyer, H.J. Diller, J. Kornelius, E. Otto and G. Stratmann eds., *Anglistik und Englischunterricht Band 55/56: Realities of Translating*. Heidelberg: 111–161.

Allen, W.S. 1973. *Accent and Rhythm: Prosodic Features of Latin and Greek. A Study in Theory and Reconstruction*. Cambridge.

Allen, W.S. 1978. *Vox Latina: A Guide to the Pronunciation of Classical Latin*. 2nd edn. Cambridge.

Amadasi Guzzo, M.G. 1995. "More on the Latin personal names ending with -*us* and -*ius* in Punic." In Z. Zevit, S. Gitin and M. Sokoloff, eds., *Solving Riddles and Untying Knots: Biblical, Epigraphic, and Semitic Studies in Honor of Jonas C. Greenfield*. Winona Lake, IN: 495–504.

Anderson, R.D., P.J. Parsons and R.G.M. Nisbet. 1979. 'Elegiacs by Gallus from Qaṣr Ibrîm.' *JRS* 69: 125–155.

André, J. 1967. *Les noms d'oiseaux en latin*. Paris.

André, J. 1971. *Emprunts et suffixes nominaux en latin*. Geneva and Paris.

André, J. 1978. *Les mots à redoublement en latin*. Paris.

André, J. 1985. *Les noms de plantes dans la Rome antique*. Paris.

André, J. 1991. *Le vocabulaire latin de l'anatomie*. Paris.

Arena, V. 2007. "Roman oratorical invective." In Dominik and Hall, eds., 2007: 149–160.

Aronoff, M. 1994. *Morphology by Itself, Stems and Inflectional Classes*. Cambridge, MA.

Ash, R. 2007. *Tacitus, Histories Book II.* Cambridge.

Audollent, A. 1904. *Defixionum tabellae quotquot innotuerunt tam in Graecis orientis quam in totius occidentis partibus, praeter Atticas in corpore inscriptionum Atticarum editas.* Paris.

Auer, P. 1998. "Introduction. *Bilingual conversation* revisited." In P. Auer, ed., *Code-Switching in Conversation: Language, Interaction and Identity.* London and New York: 1–24.

Aumont, J. 1996. *Metrique et stylistique des clausules dans la prose latine: De Ciceron à Pline le Jeune et de César à Florus.* Paris.

Axelson, B. 1945. *Unpoetische Wörter. Ein Beitrag zur Kenntnis der lateinischen Dichtersprache.* Lund.

Ayres-Bennett, W. 1996. *A History of the French Language through Texts.* London.

Bacci, Cardinal A. 1963. *Lexicon vocabulorum quae difficilius Latine redduntur.* 4th edn. Rome.

Bader, F. 1962. *La formation des composés nominaux du latin.* Paris.

Bagnall, R., ed. 2009. *The Oxford Handbook of Papyrology.* Oxford.

Bádenas de la Peña, P., S. Torallas Tovar, E.R. Luján and M. Ángeles Gallego, eds. 2004. *Lenguas en contacto. El testimonio escrito.* Madrid.

Baier, T. 2001. "Lucilius und die griechischen Wörter." In Manuwald, ed., 2001: 37–50.

Baker, R. 1980. "Caesar's puerile wars." In R. Baker, *So This Is Depravity.* New York: 27–29.

Bakker, E.J., ed. 2010. *A Companion to the Ancient Greek Language.* Malden, MA and Oxford.

Bakkum, G.C.L.M. 2009. *The Latin Dialect of the Ager Faliscus: 150 Years of Scholarship.* Amsterdam.

Baldi, P., and P. Cuzzolin, eds. 2009. *New Perspectives on Historical Latin Syntax* [Trends in Linguistics: Studies and Monographs 180.1]. Berlin and New York.

Baldwin, B. 1992. "Greek in Cicero's letters." *Acta Classica* 35: 1–17.

Baratin, M. 1989. *La naissance de la syntaxe à Rome.* Paris.

Barbarino, J.L. 1978. *The Evolution of the Latin /b/–/u/ Merger: A Quantitative and Comparative Analysis of the B–V Alternation in Latin Inscriptions* [University of North Carolina Studies in the Romance Languages and Literatures 182]. Chapel Hill, NC.

Barnett, F.J. 2007. "The sources of the Appendix Probi: A new approach." *CQ* 57: 701–736.

Barsby, J. 2007. "Native Roman rhetoric: Plautus and Terence." In Dominik and Hall, eds., 2007: 38–53.

Bartoněk, A., and G. Buchner. 1995. "Die ältesten griechischen Inschriften von Pithekoussai." *Die Sprache* 37: 129–237.

Battisti, C. 1949. *Avviamento allo studio del latino volgare.* Bari.

Bausinger, H. 1971. "Subkultur und Sprachen." In H. Moser, ed., *Sprache und Gesellschaft. Jahrbuch des Instituts für deutsche Sprache 1970.* Düsseldorf: 45–62.

Beard, M. 2002. "Ciceronian correspondences: Making a book out of letters." In T.P. Wiseman, ed., *Classics in Progress: Essays on Ancient Greece and Rome.* Oxford: 103–144.

Beare, W. 1957. *Latin Verse and European Song.* London.

Beaucamp, J. 1998. "Tester en grec à Byzance." In *Eupsychia. Mélanges offerts à Hélène Ahrweiler,* I. Paris: 97–107.

Becker, A.S. 2004. "*Non oculis sed auribus:* The ancient schoolroom and learning to hear the Latin hexameter." *CJ* 99: 313–322.

Beckmann, G.A. 1963. *Die Nachfolgekonstruktionen des instrumentalen Ablativs im Spätlatein und im Französischen* [Beihefte zur Zeitschrift für Romanische Philologie 106]. Tübingen.

Beeson, C.H. 1925. *A Primer of Medieval Latin.* Chicago.

Beier, R. 1979. "Zur Syntax in Fachtexten." In W. Mentrup, ed., *Fachsprachen und Gemeinsprache. Jahrbuch des Instituts für deutsche Sprache 1978.* Düsseldorf: 276–301.

Belke, H. 1973. *Literarische Gebrauchsformen.* Düsseldorf.

Bémont, C. 2004. "L'écriture à La Graufesenque (Millau, Aveyron). Les vaisselles sigillées inscrites comme sources d'information sur les structures professionnelles." In M. Feugère and P.-Y. Lambert, eds., *L'écriture dans la société gallo-romaine.* Paris: 103–131.

Benedetti, M. 1988. *I composti radicali latini. Esame storico e comparativo.* Pisa.

Bennett, C.E. 1910–1914. *Syntax of Early Latin.* 2 vols. Boston and Leipzig.

Benveniste, E. 1958. "La phrase relative, problème de syntaxe générale." *Bulletin de la Société de Linguistique* 53: 39–54.

Benveniste, E. 1969. *Le vocabulaire des institutions indo-européennes.* Paris.

Bérard, F., D. Feissel, N. Laubry, P. Petitmengin, D. Rousset, M. Sève, *et al.* 2010. *Guide de l'épigraphiste. Bibliographie choisie des épigraphies antiques et médiévales.* 4th edn. Paris.

Bérenger-Badel, A. 2004. "Formation et compétences des gouverneurs de province dans l'Empire romain." *DHA* 30: 35–56.

Bergs, A. 2004. "Letters: A new approach to text typology." *Journal of Historical Pragmatics* 5: 209–227.

Berry, D. 2005. "Oratory." In Harrison, ed., 2005: 257–269.

Bers, V. 2009. *Genos Dikanikon: Amateur and Professional Speech in the Courtrooms of Classical Athens.* Washington, DC.

Bertocchi, A. 2001. "The scalar interpretation of the restrictive adverb *modo*." In A. Bertocchi, M. Maraldi and A.M. Orlandini, eds., *Papers on Grammar 7. Argumentation and Latin.* Bologna: 87–111.

Best, E.E. 1977. "Suetonius: The use of Greek among the Julio-Claudian emperors." *CB* 53: 39–45.

Bettini, M. 1984. "Arcaismi." In Della Corte, ed. 1984–1991, I: 287–291.

Bietti Sestieri, A.-M., and A. De Santis. 2000. *The Protohistory of the Latin Peoples. Museo Nazionale Romano, Terme di Diocleziano.* Milan.

Birley, A. R. 1999. *Tacitus* Agricola *and* Germany. Oxford.

Bischoff, B. 1990. *Latin Palaeography: Antiquity and the Middle Ages.* Trans. D.Ó. Cróinin and D. Ganz. Cambridge.

Biville, F. 1990–1995. *Les emprunts du latin au grec: approche phonétique.* 2 vols. I: *Introduction et consonantisme.* II: *Vocalisme et conclusions.* Louvain and Paris.

Biville, F. 2005. "Aspects populaires de la composition nominale en latin." In Moussy, ed., 2005: 55–70.

Biville, F. 2008. "Situations et documents bilingues dans le monde gréco-romain." In Biville, Decourt and Rougemont, eds., 2008: 35–53.

Biville, F., J.-C. Decourt and G. Rougemont, eds. 2008. *Bilinguisme gréco-latin et épigraphie. Actes du colloque organisé à l'Université Lumière-Lyon 2 Maison de l'orient de la Méditerranée-Jean Pouilloux UMR 5189 Hisoma et JE 2409 Romanitas, les 17, 18 et 19 mai 2004* [Collection de la Maison de l'Orient et de la Méditerranée (CMO 37), Série littéraire et philosophique 11]. Lyon.

Blaise, A. 1955. *Manuel du latin chrétien.* Turnhout = 1994. *A Handbook of Christian Latin: Style, Morphology, and Syntax.* Trans. G.C. Roti. Washington, DC.

Blanc, A., and A. Christol, eds. 1999. *Langues en contact dans l'Aantiquité. Aspects lexicaux. Actes du colloque Rouenlac III, Mont-Saint-Aignan, 6 février 1997.* Nancy.

Blank, D. 2005. "Varro's anti-analogist." In D. Frede and B. Inwood, eds., *Language and Learning: Philosophy of Language in the Hellenistic Age.* Cambridge: 210–238.

Blass, F., A. Debrunner and F. Rehkopf, 1976. *Grammatik des neutestamentlichen Griechisch.* 14th edn. Göttingen.

Blatt, F. 1977. "Die letzte Phase der lateinischen Sprache." *ALMA* 40: 65–75.

Blomgren, S. 1937. *De sermone Ammiani Marcellini quaestiones uariae.* Uppsala.

Blümel, W. 1972. *Untersuchungen zu Lautsystem und Morphologie des vorklassischen Lateins.* Munich.

Bo, D. 1960. *De Horati poetico eloquio. Indices nominum propriorum, metricarum rerum prosodiacarum grammaticarumque.* Turin.

Bodel, J., ed. 2001. *Epigraphic Evidence: Ancient History from Inscriptions.* London.

Bodelot, C. 1987. *L' interrogation indirecte en latin.* Paris.

Boffo, L. 1994. *Iscrizioni greche e latine per lo studio della Bibbia.* Brescia.

Boïadjiev, D. 2000. *Les relations ethno-linguistiques en Thrace et en Mésie pendant l'époque romaine.* Sofia.

Boldrini, S. 2004. *Fondamenti di prosodia e metrica latina.* Rome.

Bolkestein, A.M. 1995. "Questions about questions." In *Bibliothèque des cahiers de l'institut de linguistique de Louvain 70: De Vsu, Études de syntaxe Latin offertes à Marius Lavency.* Louvain-la-Neuve: 59–70.

Bolkestein, A.M. 1998. "Between brackets: (Some properties of) parenthetical clauses in Latin. An investigation of the language of Cicero's letters." In R. Risselada, ed., *Latin in Use. Amsterdam Studies in the Pragmatics of Latin.* Amsterdam: 1–17.

Bolkestein, A.M. 2000. "Discourse organization and anaphora in Latin." In S.C. Herring, P. van Reenen and L. Schøsler, eds., *Textual Parameters in Older Languages.* Amsterdam and Philadelphia: 107–137.

Bömer, F. 1969. *P. Ovidius Naso Metamorphosen: Buch 1–111.* Heidelberg.

Bömer, F. 1976. *P. Ovidius Naso Metamorphosen: Buch VI–VII.* Heidelberg.

Bonaria, M. 1965. *Romani Mimi.* Rome.

Bonner, S.F. 1949. *Roman Declamation in the Late Republic and Early Empire.* Liverpool.

Bonnet, M. 1890. *Le latin de Grégoire de Tours.* Paris.

Booth, J., ed. 2007. *Cicero on the Attack: Invective and Subversion in the Orations and Beyond.* Swansea.

Bourgain, P. 2005. *Le latin médiéval.* Turnhout.

Bourova, V. 2005. "À la recherche du 'conditionnel latin'. Les constructions '*Infinitif*+ forme de *habere*' examinées à partir d'un corpus électronique." In C.D. Pusch, J. Kabatek and W. Raible, eds., *Romanistische Korpuslinguistik* II: *Korpora und diachrone Sprachwissenschaft.* Tübingen: 303–316.

Bourova, V., and L. Tasmowski. 2007. "La préhistoire des futurs romans. Ordre des constituants et sémantique." *Cahiers Chronos* 19: 25–41.

Bowman, A.K., and J.D. Thomas. 1983. *Vindolanda: The Latin Writing-Tablets (Tabulae Vindolandenses I).* London.

Bowman, A.K., and J.D. Thomas. 1994. *The Vindolanda Writing Tablets (Tabulae Vindolandenses II).* London.

Bowman, A.K., and J.D. Thomas. 2003. *The Vindolanda Writing Tablets (Tabulae Vindolandenses III).* London.

Bowman, A.K., R.S.O. Tomlin and K.A. Worp. 2009. "*Emptio bovis frisica*: The 'Frisian ox sale' reconsidered." *JRS* 99: 156–170.

Boyce, B. 1991. *The Language of the Freedmen in Petronius' Cena Trimalchionis.* Leiden.

Boyd, B.W., ed. 2002. *Brill's Companion to Ovid.* Leiden.

Bradley, K. 2010. "Freedom and slavery." In A. Barchiesi and W. Scheidel, eds., *The Oxford Handbook of Roman Studies.* Oxford: 624–636.

Bradner, L. 1940. *Musae Anglicanae: A History of Anglo-Latin Poetry, 1500–1925.* New York.

Brink, C.O. 1971. *Horace on Poetry.* II. *The Ars Poetica.* Cambridge.

Briscoe, J. 2005. "Fragmentary republican historians." In Reinhardt, Lapidge and Adams, eds., 2005: 53–72.

Briscoe, J. 2010. "The fragments of Cato's *Origines.*" In Dickey and Chahoud, eds., 2010: 154–160.

Brixhe, C., ed. 1998. *La koiné grecque antique.*III: *Les contacts.* Nancy.

Brown, P., and S. Levinson 1987. *Politeness: Some Universals in Language Usage.* Cambridge.

Brown, S.F. 1996. "Theology and philosophy." In Mantello and Rigg, eds, 1996: 267–287.

Bruun, C. 1999. "Methodisches zu den Spitznamen der Antike und des Mittelalters (am Beispiel Notkers des Stammlers)." *AKG* 81: 259–282.

Buck, C.D. 1899. "Notes on Latin orthography." *CR* 13: 116–119, 156–167.

Buck, C.D. 1955. *The Greek Dialects.* Chicago.

Bülow-Jacobsen, A., H. Cuvigny and J-L. Fournet. 1994. "The identification of Myos Hormos: New papyrological evidence." *BIFAO* 94: 27–42.

Bürge, A. 1999. "Sprachenvielfalt und Sprachengruppen im Rechtleben der Stadt Rom – Gedanken zu D. 14.3.11.3 und zum Umgang mit Fremdsprachen im heutigen Buergerlichen Recht." In J.-F. Gerkens, P. Trenk-Hinterberger, H. Peter, and R. Vigneron, eds., 1999. *Mélanges F. Sturm. Droit romain, histoire du droit, droit civil, droit comparé, droit international privé*, I. Liège: 53–63.

Buridant, C. 2000. *Grammaire nouvelle de l'ancien français*. Paris.

Burnett, A. 2002. "Syrian coinage and Romanisation from Pompey to Domitian." In C. Augé and F. Duyrat, eds., *Les monnayages syriens. Quel apport pour l'histoire du Proche-Orient hellénistique et romain? Actes de la table ronde de Damas, 10–12 novembre 1999*. Beirut: 115–122.

Burton, P. 2000. *The Old Latin Gospels: A Study of Their Texts and Language*. Oxford.

Burton, P. 2007. *Language in the* Confessions *of Augustine*. Oxford.

Burton, P. 2008. "Revisiting the Christian Latin *Sondersprache* hypothesis." In H.A.G. Houghton and D.C. Parker, eds., *Textual Variation: Theological and Social Tendencies*. Piscataway, NJ: 149–171.

Butterfield, D.J. 2008a. "On the avoidance of *eius* in Latin poetry." *RhM* 151: 151–167.

Butterfield, D.J. 2008b. "Sigmatic ecthlipsis in Lucretius." *Hermes* 136: 188–205.

Calboli, G. 2009. "Latin syntax and Greek." In Baldi and Cuzzolin, eds., 2009: 65–193.

Calcante, C.M. 2000. *Genera dicendi e retorica del sublime*. Pisa and Rome.

Caldelli, M.L., and C. Vismara 2001. *Epigrafia anfiteatrale dell'occidente romano*. V: *Alpes Maritimae, Gallia Narbonensis, Tres Galliae, Germaniae, Britannia*. Rome.

Callebat, L. 1968. *Sermo cotidianus dans* Les Métamorphoses *d'Apulée*. Caen.

Callebat, L. 1990. "Langages techniques et langue commune." In G. Calboli, ed., *Latin vulgaire – latin tardif II: Actes du IIème Colloque international sur le latin vulgaire et tardif*. Tübingen: 45–56.

Callebat, L.J., ed. 1995. *Latin vulgaire – latin tardif IV*. Hildesheim.

Campanile, E. 1971. "Due studi sul latino volgare." *L'Italia dialettale* 34: 1–64 = Campanile 2008: I.337–383.

Campanile, E. 2008. *Latina e Italica. Scritti minori sulle lingue dell'Italia antica*. Ed. P. Pocetti. 2 vols. Pisa and Rome.

Campanile, E., G.R. Cardona and R. Lazzeroni, eds. 1988. *Bilinguismo e biculturismo nel mondo antico. Atti del colloquio interdisciplinare tenuto a Pisa il 28 e 29 settembre 1987*. Pisa.

Cann, R. 1993. *Formal Semantics: An Introduction*. Cambridge.

Carnoy, A.J. 1906. *Le latin d'Espagne d'après les inscriptions*. Brussels.

Cassio, A.C. 1991–1993. "La più antica iscrizione greca di Cuma e *tin(n)umai* in Omero." *Die Sprache* 35: 187–207.

Casson, L., and E.L. Hettich. 1950. *Excavations at Nessana*. II: *Literary Papyri*. Princeton, NJ.

Castagna, L., and E. Lefèvre, eds. 2003. *Plinius der Jüngere und seine Zeit*. Munich and Leipzig.

Catterall, J.L. 1938. "Variety and inconcinnity of language in the first decade of Livy." *TAPhA* 69: 292–318.

Cavallo, G. 2009. "Greek and Latin writing in the papyri." In Bagnall, ed., 2009: 101–148.

Ceccarelli, L. 1991. "Prosodia e metrica latina arcaica 1956–1990." *Lustrum* 33: 227–400.

Celle, A. and R. Huart, eds. 2007. *Connectives as Discourse Landmarks* [Pragmatics and Beyond New Series 161]. Amsterdam and Philadelphia.

Cencetti, G. 1956–1957. "Ricerche sulla scrittura Latina nell'eta arcaica." *Archivio Paleografico Italiano, Istituto de paleografia dell'Università di Roma* 213: 175–205.

Chahoud, A. 2004. "The Roman satirist speaks Greek." *Classics Ireland* 11: 1–46.

Chahoud, A. 2007. "Alterità linguistica, *latinitas* e ideologia tra Lucilio e Cicerone." In R. Oniga, ed., *Plurilinguismo letterario*. Udine: 39–56.

Chahoud, A. 2010. "Idiom(s) and literariness in Classical literary criticism." In Dickey and Chahoud, eds., 2010: 42–64.

Chambers, J.K. 2002. "Patterns of variation including change." In J.K. Chambers, P. Trudgill and N. Schilling-Estes, eds., *The Handbook of Language Variation and Change*. Oxford: 349–372.

Chaplin, J.D. 2000. *Livy's Exemplary History*. Oxford.

Chausserie-Laprée, J.-P. 1969. *L'expression narrative chez les historiens latins*. Paris.

Cheeseman, C. 2009. "Names in -*por* and slave naming in Republican Rome." *CQ* 59: 511–531.

Cheshire, J. 2002. "Sex and gender in variationist research." In J.K. Chambers, P. Trudgill and N. Schilling-Estes, eds., *The Handbook of Language Variation and Change*. Oxford: 423–443.

Clackson, J.P.T. 2004. "Latin." In R.D. Woodard, ed., *The Cambridge Encyclopedia of the World's Ancient Languages*. Cambridge: 789–811.

Clackson, J.P.T. 2007. *Indo-European Linguistics: An Introduction*. Cambridge.

Clackson, J.P.T. Forthcoming. "Language maintenance and language shift in the Mediterranean world during the Roman Empire." In Mullen and James, eds., forthcoming.

Clackson, J.P.T., and G.C. Horrocks. 2007. *The Blackwell History of the Latin Language*. Malden, MA, and Oxford.

Clarke, K. 1999. *Between Geography and History: Hellenistic Constructions of the Roman World*. Oxford.

Clarke, M.L. 1996. *Rhetoric at Rome: A Historical Survey*. 3rd rev. edn. Ed. Dominic Berry. London.

Classen, C.J. 1988. "Satire – the elusive genre." *SO* 63: 95–121.

Clausen, W.W., ed. 1959. *A. Persi Flacci et D. Iuni Iuuenalis Saturae*. Oxford.

Clyne, M. 2003. *Dynamics of Language Contact*. Cambridge.

Coffey, M. 1976. *Roman Satire*. London.

Cole, T. 1969. "The Saturnian verse." In C.M. Dawson and T. Cole, eds., *Studies in Latin Poetry*. [*YClS* 21]. Cambridge: 1–73.

Coleman, R.G.G. 1971. "The origin and development of Latin *habeo* + infinitive." *CQ* 21: 215–232.

Coleman, R.G.G. 1975. "Greek influence on Latin syntax." *TPhS* 74: 101–156.

Coleman, R.G.G. 1976. "Patterns of syncretism in Latin." in A.M. Davies, and W. Meid, eds. *Studies in Greek, Italic and Indo-European Linguistics Offered to Leonard R. Palmer*. Innsbruck: 47–56.

Coleman, R.G.G. 1977. *Vergil: Eclogues*. Cambridge.

Coleman, R.G.G. 1987. "Vulgar Latin and the diversity of Christian Latin." In J. Hermann, ed., *Latin vulgaire – Latin tardif: Actes du 1er Colloque International sur le latin vulgaire et tardif, Pécs, 2–5 septembre 1985*. Tübingen: 37–52.

Coleman, R.G.G. 1989a. "The formation of specialized vocabularies in philosophy, grammar and rhetoric: Winners and losers." In Lavency and Longrée, eds., 1989: 77–89.

Coleman, R.G.G. 1989b. "The rise and fall of absolute constructions: A Latin case history." In G. Calboli, ed., *Subordination and Other Topics in Latin: Proceedings of the Third Colloquium on Latin Linguistics, Bologna, 1–5 April 1985*. Amsterdam: 353–374.

Coleman, R.G.G. 1990. "Dialectal variation in Republican Latin, with special reference to Praenestine." *PCPhS* 36: 1–25.

Coleman, R.G.G. 1993. "Vulgar Latin and proto-Romance: Minding the gap." *Prudentia* 25: 1–14.

Coleman, R.G.G. 1998. "Accent and quantity in Latin versification: Continuities and disconti-nuities." In B. García-Hernández, ed., *Estudios de lingüística latina. Actas del IX. Coloquio Internacional de Lingüística Latina, Universidad Autonóma de Madrid, 14–18 de abril de 1997*. 2 vols. Madrid: 1087–1100.

Coleman, R.G.G. 1999. "Poetic diction, poetic discourse and the poetic register." In Adams and Mayer, eds., 1999: 21–93.

Colledge, M.A.R. 1976. *The Art of Palmyra*. London.

Collins, J.F. 1985. *A Primer of Ecclesiastical Latin*. Washington, DC.

Colonna, G. 1980. "Graeco more bibere. L'iscrizione della tomba 115 dell'Osteria dell'Osa." *Archaeologia laziale* 3: 51–55.

Colonna, G. 1996. "Rivista di epigrafica italica. Part II. Riletture. Lazio. Ancora sul *lapis Satricanus.*" *Studi Etruschi* 60: 298–301.

Colonna, G., and A.J. Beijer. 1993. "Rivista di epigrafia italica. Part I. Lazio. Satricum. Un' iscrizione latina di VII secolo da Satricum." *Studi Etruschi* 58: 316–320.

Colvin, S. 1999. *Dialect in Aristophanes.* Oxford.

Conrad, F. 1931. "Die Deminutiva im Altlatein." *Glotta* 19: 127–148.

Conte, G.B. 2007. *The Poetry of Pathos: Studies in Virgilian Epic.* Oxford.

Contini, A.M.V. 1987. "Nonio Marcello e l'*Africitas.*" *Studi noniani* 12: 17–26.

Conway, R.S., A.E. Housman, W.H.D. Rouse, J.P. Postgate and S.E. Winbolt. 1905. "Latin orthography: An appeal to scholars." *CR* 19: 6–7.

Corbier, M. 2008. "Rome. Un empire bilingue." In L. Villard, ed., *Langues dominantes, langues dominées.* Rouen: 29–55.

Corcoran, S. 1996. *The Empire of the Tetrarchs: Imperial Pronouncements and Government* AD *284–324.* Oxford.

Costabile, F. 2001. "Le *Res Gestae* di C. Cornelius Gallus nella trilingue di Philae. Nuove letture e interpretazioni." *Minima epigraphica et papyrologica* 6: 297–330.

Cotton, H.M. 1984. "Greek and Latin epistolary formulae: Some light on Cicero's letter writing." *AJPh* 105: 409–425.

Cotton, H.M. 1985. "*Mirificum genus commendationis*: Cicero and the Latin letter of recommendation." *AJPh* 106: 328–334.

Cotton, H.M. 1999. "The languages of the legal and administrative documents from the Judean desert." *ZPE* 125: 219–231.

Cotton, H.M., R.G. Hoyland, J.J. Price and D.J. Wasserstein, eds. 2009. *From Hellenism to Islam: Cultural and Linguistic Change in the Roman Near East.* Cambridge.

Courtney, E. 1980. *A Commentary on the Satires of Juvenal.* London.

Courtney, E. 1999. *Archaic Latin Prose* [American Classical Studies 42]. Atlanta.

Courtney, E. 2003. *The Fragmentary Latin Poets.* Rev. edn. Oxford.

Courtney, E. 2004. "The Greek accusative." *CJ* 99: 425–431.

Cousin, J. 1943. "Les langues spéciales." In *Mémorial des Études Latines. Offert par la Société des Études Latines à son fondateur Jules Marouzeau.* Paris: 37–54.

Craig, C.P. 1993. *Form as Argument in Cicero's Speeches: A Study of Dilemma.* Atlanta.

Crawford, M. 1974. *Roman Republican Coinage.* Cambridge.

Crawford, M. 1996. *Roman Statutes.* 2 vols. [BICS Supplement 64]. London.

Cristofani, M. 1972. "Sull'origine e la diffusione dell'alfabeto etrusco." *ANRW* 1.2: 466–489.

Cristofani, M. 1978a. "L'alfabeto etrusco." In A.L. Prosdocimi, ed., *Popoli e civiltà dell'Italia antica.* VI: *Lingue e dialetti dell'Italia antica.* Rome: 401–428.

Cristofani, M. 1978b. "Rapporto sulla diffusione della scrittura nell'Italia antica." *Scrittura e Civiltà* 2: 5–33.

Cristofani, M. 1984. "Iscrizioni e beni suntuari." *Opus* 3: 319–324.

Cristofani, M. 1996. *Due testi dell'Italia preromana.* Rome.

Crusius, F. 1967. *Römische Metrik: Eine Einführung.* 8th rev. edn. Munich.

Cugusi, P. 1983. *Evoluzione e forme dell'epistolografia latina nella tarda repubblica e nei primi due secoli dell'impero con cenni sull'epistolografia preciceroniana.* Rome.

Cugusi, P. 1992. *Corpus Epistularum Latinarum papyris tabulis ostracis servatarum.* 2 vols. Florence.

Cugusi, P. 1998. "L'epistola ciceroniana. Strumento di comunicazione quotidiana e modello letterario." *Ciceroniana* 10: 163–189.

Cuzzolin, P. 1994. *Sull'origine della costruzione* dicere quod. *Aspetti sintattici e semantici.* Florence.

Cuzzolin, P., and G. Haverling. 2009. "Syntax, sociolinguistics and literary genres." In Baldi and Cuzzolin, eds., 2009: 19–64.

Dagron, G. 1969. "Aux origines de la civilisation byzantine. Langue de culture et langue d'État." *RH* 249: 23–56. Reprinted 1984 in G. Dagron, *La romanité chrétienne en Orient: Héritages et mutations.* London: n° 1.

Dalziell, A.C. 1955. "Asinius Pollio and the early history of public recitation at Rome." *Hermathena* 86: 20–28.

Dammann, G. 1910. "Cicero quo modo in epistulis sermonem hominibus, quos appellat, et rebus, quas tangit, accommodaverit." PhD dissertation. Greifswald.

Danese R.M. and F. Gori, eds. 1990. *Metrica classica e linguistica. Atti del Colloquio di Urbino (3–6 ottobre 1988).* Urbino.

Daube, D. 1956. *Forms of Roman Legislation.* Oxford.

Daube, D. 1969. *Roman Law: Linguistic, Social and Philosophical Aspects.* Edinburgh.

Daviault, A. 1981. *Comoedia togata. Fragments; texte établi, traduit et annoté.* Paris.

de Melo, W.D.C. 2006. "If in doubt, leave it in: Subject accusatives in Plautus and Terence." In *Oxford University Working Papers in Linguistics, Philology and Phonetics* 11, 5–20.

de Melo, W.D.C. 2007a. "Latin prohibitions and the origins of the *u/w*-perfect and the type *amāstī.*" *Glotta* 83: 43–68.

de Melo, W.D.C. 2007b. *The Early Latin Verb System: Archaic Forms in Plautus, Terence, and Beyond.* Oxford.

de Melo, W.D.C. 2007c. "The present tense with future meaning in the accusative and infinitive construction in Plautus and Terence." *TPhS* 105: 105–125.

de Melo, W.D.C. 2007d. "Zur Sprache der republikanischen *carmina Latina epigraphica*: Satzumfang, Satzkomplexität und Diathesenwahl." In P. Kruschwitz, ed., *Die metrischen Inschriften der römischen Republik.* Berlin and New York: 97–120.

de Melo, W.D.C. 2009. "*Scies*(*Mil.* 520) e *scibis*(*Mil.* 1365). Variazione accidentale?" In R. Raffaelli and A. Tontini, eds., *Lecturae Plautinae Sarsinates XII: Miles gloriosus (Sarsina, 27 settembre 2008).* Urbino: 41–52.

de Melo, W.D.C. 2010. "Possessive pronouns in Plautus." In Dickey and Chahoud, eds., 2010: 71–99.

De Meo, C. 2005. *Lingue tecniche del latino.* 3rd edn. Bologna.

De Nonno, M. 1990. "Ruolo e funzione della metrica nei grammatici latini." In Danese and Gori, 1990: 453–494.

De Pretis, A. 2003. "'Insincerity', 'facts', and 'epistolarity': Approaches to Pliny's Epistles to Calpurnia." *Arethusa* 36: 127–146.

de Vaan, M. 2008. *Etymological Dictionary of Latin and the Other Italic Languages.* Leiden.

Delamarre, X. 2003. *Dictionnaire de la langue gauloise. Une approche linguistique du vieux-celtique continental.* 2nd edn. Paris.

Delatte, L., E. Evrard, S. Govaerts and J. Denooz. 1981. *Dictionnaire fréquentiel et index inverse de la langue latine.* Liège.

Della Corte, F., ed. 1984–1991. *Enciclopedia virgiliana.* 7 vols. Rome.

Deufert, M. 2007. "Terenz und die altlateinische Verskunst. Ein Beitrag zur Technik des Enjambements in der Neuen Komödie." In P. Kruschwitz, W.-W. Ehlers and F. Felgentreu, eds., *Terentius Poeta.* Munich: 51–71.

Devine, A.M., and L.D. Stephens. 1977. *Two Studies in Latin Phonology.* Saratoga, CA.

Devine, A.M., and L.D. Stephens. 1980. "Latin prosody and meter: *Brevis brevians.*" *CPh* 75: 142–157.

Devine, A.M., and L.D. Stephens. 1994. *The Prosody of Greek Speech.* New York and Oxford.

Devine, A.M., and L.D. Stephens. 2006. *Latin Word Order: Structured Meaning and Information.* Oxford.

Dickey, E. 2000. "*O egregie grammatice.* The vocative problems of Latin words ending in *-ius.*" *CQ* 50: 548–562.

Dickey, E. 2002. *Latin Forms of Address from Plautus to Apuleius.* Oxford.

Dickey, E. 2003. "Latin influence on the Greek of documentary papyri: An analysis of its chronological distribution." *ZPE* 145: 249–257.

Dickey, E., and A. Chahoud, eds. 2010. *Colloquial and Literary Latin*. Cambridge.

Diehl, E. 1899. *De m finali epigraphica*. Leipzig.

Diggle, J., and F.R.D. Goodyear, eds. 1972. *The Classical Papers of A.E. Housman*. 3 vols. Cambridge.

Diggle, J., J.B. Hall and H.D. Jocelyn, eds. 1989. *Studies in Latin Literature and Its Tradition in Honour of C.O. Brink*. [Cambridge Philological Society Supplementary 15]. Cambridge.

Dinkova-Bruun, G. 2004. *Alexandri Essebiensis Opera poetica* [Corpus Christianorum Continuatio Mediaevalis 188A]. Turnhout.

Dinkova-Bruun, G. 2005. *The Ancestry of Jesus: Excerpts from* Liber generationis Iesu Christi filii David filii Abraham *(Matthew 1:1–17)* [Toronto Medieval Latin Texts 28]. Toronto.

Dixon, R.M.W. 1994. *Ergativity*. Cambridge.

Dominik, W., and J. Hall, eds. 2007. *A Companion to Roman Rhetoric*. Malden, MA and Oxford.

Draeger, A. 1882. *Ueber Syntax und Stil des Tacitus*. 3rd edn. Leipzig.

Dressler, W. 1973. "Pour une stylistique phonologique du latin à propos des styles négligents d'une langue morte." *BSL* 68: 129–145.

Drew-Bear, T., P.W. Herrmann and W. Eck. 1977. "Sacrae Litterae." *Chiron* 7: 355–383.

Drexler, H. 1967. *Einführung in die römische Metrik*. Darmstadt.

Drexler, H. 1969. *Die Iambenkürzung*. Hildesheim.

Dubuisson, M. 1981. "Utraque lingua." *AC* 50: 274–286.

Dubuisson, M. 1982. "Y a-t-il une politique linguistique romaine?" *Ktèma* 7: 187–210.

Dubuisson, M. 1985. *Le latin de Polybe. Les implications historiques d'un cas de bilinguisme*. Paris.

Dubuisson, M. 1986. "Purisme et politique. Suétone, Tibère et le grec au Sénat." In *Mélanges J. Veremans* [Collection Latomus 193]. Brussels: 109–117.

Dubuisson, M. 1989. "Le contact linguistique gréco-latin. Problèmes d'interférences et d'emprunts." In *LALIES. Actes des sessions de linguistique et de littérature* 10: 91–109.

Dubuisson, M. 1992. "Le grec à Rome à l'époque de Cicéron. Extension et qualité du bilinguisme." *Annales. Histoire, Sciences Sociales* 47: 187–206.

Duckworth, G.E. 1952. *The Nature of Roman Comedy*. Princeton, NJ.

Dugan, J. 2009. "Rhetoric and the Roman Republic." In E. Gunderson, ed., *The Cambridge Companion to Ancient Rhetoric*. Cambridge: 178–193.

Dunkel, G.E. 2000. "Remarks on code-switching in Cicero's letters to Atticus." *MH* 57: 122–129.

Dutsch, D.M. 2008. *Feminine Discourse in Roman Comedy: On Echoes and Voices* [Oxford Studies in Classical Literature and Gender Theory]. Oxford and New York.

Eck, W. 2000. "Latein als Sprache politischer Kommunikation in Städten der östlichen Provinzen." *Chiron* 30: 641–660.

Eck, W. 2004. "Lateinisch, Griechisch, Germanisch …? Wie sprach Rom mit seinen Untertanen?" In L. De Ligt, E.A. Hemelrijk and H.W. Singor, eds., *Roman Rule and Civic Life: Local and Regional Perspectives. Proceedings of the Fourth Workshop of the International Network Impact of Empire (Roman Empire, c. 200 BC–AD 476), Leiden, June 25–28, 2003*. Amsterdam: 3–19.

Eck, W. 2009. "The presence, role and significance of Latin in the epigraphy and culture of the Roman Near East." In Cotton *et al.*, eds., 2009: 15–42.

Edwards, C. 2005. "Epistolography." In Harrison, ed., 2005: 270–283.

Egger, C. 2003. *Lexicon recentis Latinitatis*. Rome.

Ehrenberg, V., and A.H.M. Jones. 1955. *Documents Illustrating the Reigns of Augustus and Tiberius*. 2nd edn. Oxford.

Eichner, H. 1985. "Das Problem des Ansatzes eines urindogermanischen Numerus 'Kollektiv' ('Komprehensiv')." In B. Schlerath, ed., *Grammatische Kategorien: Funktion und Geschichte*.

Akten der VII. Fachtagung der Indogermanischen Gesellschaft. Berlin, 20–25. Februar 1983. Wiesbaden: 134–169.

Eichner, H. 1995. "Zu frühlateinischen Wortformen auf dem Forumscippus *CIL* I², 1." *Studia Onomastica et Indogermanica: Festschrift für Fritz Lochner von Hüttenbach zum 65. Geburtstag,* Graz: 65–73.

Elcock W.D. 1975. *The Romance Languages.* Rev. edn. London.

Ernout, A. 1946–1965. *Philologica* I–III. Paris.

Ernout, A. 1947. "Le vocabulaire poétique." *RPh* 21: 55–70 = Ernout 1946–1965, II: 66–86.

Ernout, A. 1954. *Aspects du vocabulaire latin.* Paris.

Ernout, A. 1957. *Recueil de textes latins archaïques.* Paris.

Ernout, A., and A. Meillet. 1979. *Dictionnaire étymologique de la langue latine.* 4th rev. edn. Paris.

Eska, J.F., and R.E. Wallace. Forthcoming. *Script and Language at Voltino.*

Evans, D.E. 1967. *Gaulish Personal Names. A Study of Some Continental Celtic Formations.* Oxford.

Farrell, J. 2001. *Latin Language and Latin Culture: From Ancient to Modern Times.* Cambridge.

Feissel, D. 1995. "Les Constitutions des Tétrarques connues par l'épigraphie. Inventaire et notes critiques." *AntTard* 3: 33–53.

Ferguson, C.A. 1959. "Diglossia." *Word* 15: 325–340.

Ferrary, J.-L. 1988. *Philhellénisme et impérialisme. Aspects idéologiques de la conquête romaine du monde hellénistique, de la seconde guerre de Macédoine à la guerre contre Mithridate* [BEFAR 271]. Paris.

Ferri, R., ed. 2003. *Octavia: A Play Attributed to Seneca* [Cambridge Classical Texts and Commentaries 41]. Cambridge.

Ferri, R., and P. Probert. 2010. "Roman authors on colloquial language." In Dickey and Chahoud, eds., 2010: 12–41.

Filliettaz, L., and E. Roulet. 2002. "The Geneva model of discourse analysis: An interactionist and modular approach to discourse organization." *Discourse Studies* 4: 369–393.

Fischer, K., ed. 2006. *Approaches to Discourse Particles* [Studies in Pragmatics 1]. Amsterdam.

Fishman, J.A. 1964. "Language maintenance–language shift as a field of inquiry." *Linguistics* 9: 32–70.

Fishman, J.A. 1965. "Who speaks what language to whom and when?" *La linguistique* 2: 67–88.

Fishman, J.A. 1967. "Bilingualism with and without diglossia; diglossia with and without bilingualism." *Journal of Social Studies* 23: 29–38.

Fleck, F. 2008. *Interrogation, coordination et subordination. Le latin* quin. Paris.

Fletcher, J.M. 1993. "The vocabulary of administration and teaching at Merton College, Oxford, at the close of the Middle Ages." In O. Weijers, ed., *Vocabulaire des colleges universitaires (XIIIe–XVIe siècles): Actes du colloque de Leuven 9–11 avril 1992* [Études sur le vocabulaire intellectuel du moyen age (CIVICIMA) 6]. Turnhout: 46–58.

Flobert, P. 1978. "La composition verbale en latin." In *Étrennes de septantaine. Travaux de linguistique et de grammaire comparée offerts à Michel Lejeune par un groupe de ses élèves.* Paris: 85–94.

Flobert, P. 1991. "L'apport des inscriptions archaïques à notre connaissance du latin prélittéraire." *Latomus* 50: 521–543.

Flobert, P. 1992. "Les graffites de La Graufesenque. Un témoignage sur le gallo-latin sous Néron." In Iliescu and Marxgut, eds., 1992: 103–114.

Fluck, H.-R. 1996. *Fachsprachen. Einführung und Bibliographie.* 5th edn. Tübingen.

Fögen, M.-T. 1995. "Diritto bizantino in lingua Latina." *Index* 23: 251–259.

Fögen, T. 2000. "*Patrii sermonis egestas*: *Einstellungen lateinischer Autoren zu ihrer Muttersprache. Ein Beitrag zum Sprachbewußtsein in der römischen Antike.* Munich and Leipzig.

Fögen, T. 2002. "Fachsprachen in der Antike. Zur Analyse metasprachlicher Dokumente am Beispiel der philosophischen Schriften Senecas." In B. Kovtyk and G. Wendt, eds., *Aktuelle Probleme der angewandten Übersetzungswissenschaft. Sprachliche und außersprachliche Faktoren der Fachübersetzung.* Frankfurt am Main: 10–35.

Fögen, T. 2003. "*Utraque lingua*": *A Bibliography on Bi- and Multilingualism in Graeco-Roman Antiquity and in Modern Times.* Essen.

Fögen, T. 2004. "Gender-specific communication in Greco-Roman antiquity: With a research bibliography." *Historiographia Linguistica* 31: 199–276.

Fögen, T. 2005. "The transformation of Greek scientific knowledge by Roman technical writers: On the translating of technical texts in antiquity." *Antike Naturwissenschaft und ihre Rezeption* 15: 91–114.

Fögen, T. 2007. "Pliny the Elder's animals. Some remarks on the narrative structure of *Nat. hist.* 8–11." *Hermes* 135: 184–198.

Fögen, T. 2009. *Wissen, Kommunikation und Selbstdarstellung. Zur Struktur und Charakteristik römischer Fachtexte der frühen Kaiserzeit.* Munich.

Fögen, T. 2010. "Female speech." In Bakker, ed., 2010: 311–326.

Fontaine, M. 2010. *Funny Words in Plautine Comedy.* Oxford.

Foolen, A. 1996. "Pragmatic particles." In J. Verschueren, J.-O. Östmann, J. Blommaert and C. Bulcaen, eds., *Handbook of Pragmatics.* Amsterdam: 1–24.

Fordyce, C.J. 1978. *Catullus: A Commentary.* Rev. edn. Oxford.

Fortson, B.W. IV. 2003. "Linguistic and cultural notes on the Roman calendar: *Mēnsis Iūnius* and related topics." In M.R.V. Southern, ed., *Indo-European Perspectives.* Washington, DC: 61–77.

Fortson, B.W. IV. 2008. *Language and Rhythm in Plautus : Synchronic and Diachronic Studies.* Berlin and New York.

Fortson, B.W. IV. 2010. *Indo-European Language and Culture: An Introduction.* 2nd edn. Malden, MA.

Foucher, A. 2000. Historia proxima poetis. *L'influence de la poésie épique sur le style des historiens latins de Salluste à Ammien Marcellin.* [Collection Latomus 255]. Brussels.

Fox, W.S. 1912. "The Johns Hopkins *Tabellae Defixionum.*" *AJPh* 33: 1–68.

Fraenkel, E. 1928. *Iktus und Akzent im lateinischen Sprechvers.* Berlin.

Fraenkel, E. 1951. "The pedigree of the Saturnian metre." *Eranos* 49:170–1.

Fraenkel, E. 1957. "Some notes on Cicero's letters to Trebatius." *JRS* 47: 66–70.

Fraenkel, E. 2007. *Plautine Elements in Plautus.* Trans. T. Drevikovsky and F. Muecke. Oxford = 1922 *Plautinisches im Plautus.* Berlin = 1960 *Elementi Plautini in Plauto* (+ Italian addenda). Florence.

Frassinetti, P. 1967. *Atellanae fabulae.* Rome.

Fredouille, J.-C. 1996. "'Latin chrétien' ou 'latin tardif?'" *Recherches augustiniennes* 29: 5–23.

Frere, S.S., M.W.C. Hassall and R.S.O. Tomlin. 1989. "Roman Britain in 1988." *Britannia* 20: 257–345.

Freudenburg, K., ed. 2005. *The Cambridge Companion to Roman Satire.* Cambridge.

Frischer, B. 1996. "How to do things with words per strong stop: Two studies on the *Historia Augusta* and Cicero." In H. Rosén, ed., *Aspects of Latin: Papers from the Seventh International Colloquium on Latin Linguistics, Jerusalem, April 1993.* Innsbruck: 585–599.

Fruyt, M. 1989. "Etude sémantique des 'diminutifs' latins. Les suffixes *-ulus, -culus, -ellus, -illus …* dé-substantivaux et dé-adjectivaux." In Lavency and Longrée, eds., 1989: 127–138.

Fruyt, M. 2002. "Constraints and productivity in Latin nominal compounding." *TPhS* 100: 259–287.

Fruyt, M. 2006. "La lexicalisation et la conceptualisation de la couleur dans les textes techniques et scientifiques latins." In C. Thomasset, ed., *L'écriture du texte scientifique au Moyen Âge.* Paris: 13–47.

Fruyt, M., and C. Nicolas, eds. 2000. *La création lexicale en latin.* Paris.

Fruyt, M., and A. Orlandini. 2008. "Some cases of linguistic evolution and grammaticalisation in the Latin verb." In Wright, ed., 2008: 230–237.

Gabba, E. 1981. "True history and false history in Classical Antiquity." *JRS* 71: 50–62.

Gaeng, P.A. 1968. *An Inquiry into Local Variations in Vulgar Latin, as Reflected in the Vocalism of Christian Inscriptions* [University of North Carolina Studies in the Romance Languages and Literatures 77]. Chapel Hill, NC.

Gaide, F. 1992. "Les substantifs 'diminutifs' latins en -*lus*, -*la* ou -*lum*." *RPh* 66: 15–27.

Gaide, F. 2002. "Les dérivés 'diminutifs' en -*lus*, -*la*, -*lum*." In Kircher-Durand, ed., 2002: 111–123.

Galdi, G. 2000. "Reflexive and possessive pronouns in Greek and Latin inscriptions of the Empire (Moesia Inferior)." In G. Calboli, ed., *Papers on Grammar* 5. Bologna: 73–94.

Galdi, G. 2002. "On the Latin genitive: Some special usages." In G. Calboli, ed., *Papers on Grammar* 8: 101–121.

Galdi, G. 2003. "The grammar of Latin inscriptions of east Roman Empire: Some morphological questions." In H. Solin, M. Leiwo and H. Halla-aho, eds., *Latin vulgaire – Latin tardif. Actes du 6ᵉ colloque international sur le latin vulgaire et tardif, Helsinki, 29 août–2 septembre 2000*. Hildesheim: 501–511.

Galdi, G. 2004. *Grammatica delle iscrizioni latine dell'impero (province orientali). Morfosintassi nominale*. Rome.

Galdi, G. 2005. "Sprachliche Beobachtungen am Formular lateinischer *Kaiser-Inschriften* des Osten." In *Papers from the 12th International Colloquium on Latin Linguistics*. Rome: 57–69.

Galdi, G. 2006. "Some remarks on the use of the ablative in the eastern inscriptions." In C. Arias Abellán, ed., *Latin vulgaire – latin tardif VII. Actes du VIIème Colloque international sur le latin vulgaire et tardif (Séville, 2–6 septembre 2003)*. Seville: 283–293.

Galdi, G. 2008. "Aspects du bilinguisme gréco-latin dans la province de la Mésie inférieure." In Biville, Decourt and Rougemont, eds., 2008: 141–154.

Galdi, G. 2009. "Beobachtungen zum griechisch-lateinischen Sprachverhältnis an der Schwarzmeerküste." *AAntHung* 49: 51–67.

Galdi, G. Forthcoming. "Again on feminine *as*-nominatives: An update to the problem." In M. Leiwo, H. Halla-aho and M. Vierros, eds., *Variation and Change in Greek and Latin. Problems and Methods*. Helsinki.

Gamberini, F. 1983. *Stylistic Theory and Practice in the Younger Pliny*. [Altertumswissenschaftliche Texte und Studien, Band XI]. Hildesheim, Zürich and New York.

Garcea, A. 2002. "L'interaction épistolaire entre dialogue *in absentia* et *in praesentia* chez Cicéron." In A.M. Bolkestein, C.H.M. Kroon, H. Pinkster, H.W. Remmelink and R. Risselada, eds., 2002. *Theory and Description in Latin Linguistics. Selected Papers from the XIth International Colloquium on Latin Linguistics (Amsterdam, June 24–29 2001)*. Amsterdam: 123–138.

Garcea, A. 2003. "Rispondere con ordine alle lettere. Una funzione di quod nell'epistolario di Cicerone." In Garcea, ed., 2003: 73–99.

Garcea, A., ed. 2003. *Colloquia absentium. Studi sulla communicazione epistolare in Cicerone*. Turin.

García de la Fuente, O. 1994. *Latín bíblico y latín cristiano*. Málaga.

Gardner-Chloros, P. 2009. *Code-switching*. Cambridge.

Gauthier, N. 1975. *Première belgique. Recueil des inscriptions chrétiennes de la Gaule antérieures à la Renaissance carolingienne I*. Paris.

Gay, P. 1974. *Style in History*. New York.

Geffcken, K.A. 1973. *Comedy in the* Pro Caelio. [Mnemosyne Supplement 30]. Leiden.

Gelsomino, R. 1958. "I grecismi di Augusto. Atti e documenti pubblici." *Maia* 10: 148–156.

Gerov, B. 1980. "Die lateinisch-griechische Sprachgrenze auf der Balkanhalbinsel." In Neumann and Untermann, eds., 1980: 147–165.

Gerschner, R. 2002. *Die Deklination der Nomina bei Plautus*. Heidelberg.

Giacomelli, G. 1963. *La lingua falisca*. Florence.

Giacomelli, G. 1973. "A problem in Praenestine palaeography." *JIES* 1: 309–315.

Gibson, R.K., and A.D. Morrison 2007. "Introduction: What is a letter?" In R. Morello and A.D. Morrison, eds., *Ancient Letters: Classical and Late Antique Epistolography*. Oxford: 1–16.

Gignac, F.T. 1976. *A Grammar of the Greek Papyri of the Roman and Byzantine Periods*. I: *Phonology*. Milan.

Gildersleeve, B.L. and G. Lodge. 1894. *Gildersleeve's Latin Grammar*. New York and Boston.

Gilleland, M.E. 1979. "Linguistic differentiation of character type and sex in the comedies of Plautus and Terence." PhD thesis. University of Virginia.

Gilleland, M.E. 1980. "Female speech in Greek and Latin." *AJPh* 101: 180–183.

Gilmartin, K. 1975. "A rhetorical figure in Latin historical style: The imaginary second person singular." *TAPhA* 105: 99–121.

Giovannini, A.-M., and M. Hirt 1999. "L'inscription de Nazareth. Nouvelle interprétation." *ZPE* 124: 107–132.

Gipper, H. 1979. "Fachsprachen in Wissenschaft und Werbung. Erkenntnisgewinn und Irreführung." In W. Mentrup, ed., *Fachsprachen und Gemeinsprache. Jahrbuch des Instituts für deutsche Sprache 1978*. Düsseldorf: 124–143.

Gläser, R., ed. 1996. *Eigennamen in der Fachkommunikation*. Frankfurt am Main.

Goodyear, F.R.D. 1972. *Tacitus. The Annals, Books 1–6. Edited with a commentary*. I: Annals *I. 1–54*. Cambridge.

Goold, G.P. 1965. "Amatoria critica." *HSCPh* 69: 1–107.

Göpferich, S. 1995. *Textsorten in Naturwissenschaften und Technik. Pragmatische Typologie – Kontrastierung – Translation*. Tübingen.

Gordon, A.E. 1971. "The letter names of the Latin alphabet." *Visible Language* 5: 221–228.

Gordon, A.E. 1983. *An Illustrated Introduction to Latin Epigraphy*. Berkeley, CA.

Görler, W. 1985. "Eneide: la lingua." In Della Corte, ed., 1984–1991. II: 262–278.

Gotoff, H.C. 1979. *Cicero's Elegant Style*. Urbana, IL.

Goullet, M., and M. Parisse. 1996. *Apprendre le latin médiéval. Manuel pour grands commençants*. Paris.

Goullet, M., and M. Parisse. 2003. *Traduire le latin médiéval. Manuel pour grands commençants*. Paris.

Gowers, E. 1993. *The Loaded Table: Representations of Food in Roman Literature*. Oxford.

Gradenwitz, O., B. Kubler and E.T. Schulze. 1903. *Vocabularium iurisprudentiae romanae iussu Instituti Savigniani compositum*. 5 vols. Berlin.

Graesse, J.H.G., F. Benedict and H. Plechl. 1972. *Orbis Latinus. Lexikon lateinischer geographischer Namen des Mittelalters und der Neuzeit*, 3rd edn. 3 vols. Brunswick.

Grafton, A. 1983. *Joseph Scaliger: A Study in the History of Classical Scholarship*. I: *Textual Criticism and Exegesis*. Oxford.

Gratwick, A.S. 1971. "Hanno's Punic speech in the *Poenulus* of Plautus." *Hermes* 99: 25–45.

Gratwick, A.S. 1982a. "Drama." In Kenney and Clausen, eds., 1982: 77–137.

Gratwick, A.S. 1982b. "The satires of Ennius and Lucilius." In Kenney and Clausen, eds., 1982: 162–171.

Gratwick, A.S. 1993. *Plautus Menaechmi*. Cambridge.

Green, R.P.H. 1991. *The Works of Ausonius*. Oxford.

Greenough, J.B., *et al.* eds. 1903. *Allen and Greenough's New Latin Grammar for Schools and Colleges: Founded on Comparative Grammar*. Boston and London.

Griffin, M.T. 1997. "The Senate's story." *JRS* 87: 249–263.

Grube, G.M.A. 1965. *The Greek and Roman Critics*. London.

Gruen, E.S. 1992. *Culture and National Identity in Republican Rome* [Cornell Studies in Classical Philology 52]. Ithaca, NY.

Gruppe, O.F. 1838. *Die römische Elegie*. I. Leipzig.

Guardì, T. 1985. *Titinio e Atta: Fabulae togatae; i frammenti: introduzione, testo, traduzione e commento*. Milan.

Guillemin, A.-M. 1929. *Pline et la vie littéraire de son temps*. Paris.

Habinek, T.N. 1985. *The Colometry of Latin Prose*. Berkeley.

Hadas-Lebel, J. 2004. *Le bilinguisme étrusco-latin. Contribution à l'étude de la romanisation de l'Etrurie*. Louvain and Paris.

Haffter, H. 1934. *Untersuchungen zur altlateinischen Dichtersprache*. Berlin.

Hahn, W. von 1983. *Fachkommunikation. Entwicklung – Linguistische Konzepte – Betriebliche Beispiele*. Berlin and New York.

Haines, C.R. 1920. *The Correspondence of Marcus Cornelius Fronto with Marcus Aurelius Antoninus, Lucius Verus, Antoninus Pius, and Various Friends*. Cambridge, MA.

Hakamies, R. 1951. *Étude sur l'origine et l'évolution du diminutif latin et sa survie dans les langues romanes*. Helsinki.

Hale, W.G., and C.D. Buck. 1903. *A Latin Grammar*. Boston.

Hall, J. 1998. "Cicero to Lucceius (*Fam.* 5.12) in its social context." *CPh* 93: 308–321.

Hall, J. 2005. "Politeness and formality in Cicero's letter to Matius (*Fam.* 11.27)." *MH* 62: 193–213.

Hall, J. 2009. *Politeness and Politics in Cicero's Letters*. Oxford.

Hall, L.G.M. 1998. "*Ratio* and *Romanitas* in the *Bellum Gallicum*." In K. Welch and A. Powell, eds. *Julius Caesar as Artful Reporter*. Swansea: 11–43.

Hall, R.A. Jr. 1974. *External History of the Romance Languages*. New York.

Hall, R.A. Jr. 1976. *Proto-Romance Phonology*. New York.

Halla-aho, H. 2009. *The Non-Literary Latin Letters: A Study of Their Syntax and Pragmatics*. Helsinki.

Halle, M., and B. Vaux. 1998. "Theoretical aspects of Indo-European nominal morphology: The nominal declensions of Latin and Armenian." In J. Jasanoff, H.C. Melchert and L. Olivier, eds., *Mír Curad: Studies in Honor of Calvert Watkins*. Innsbruck: 223–240.

Halliday, M.A.K. 2004. *An Introduction to Functional Grammar*. 3rd edn. rev. by Christian Matthiessen. London.

Halporn, J.W. 1963. *The Meters of Greek and Latin Poetry*. Indianapolis.

Halporn, J.W., M. Ostwald and T.G. Rosenmeyer. 1994. *The Meters of Greek and Latin Poetry*. 2nd rev. edn. Indianapolis.

Hamers, J.F., and M.H.A. Blanc. 2000. *Bilinguality and Bilingualism*. 2nd edn. Cambridge.

Hand(ius), F. 1829–1845. *Tursellinus seu de particulis Latinis commentarii*. 4 vols. Leipzig. Repr. 1969. Amsterdam.

Handley, E.W. 1968. *Menander and Plautus: A Study in Comparison. An Inaugural Lecture Delivered at University College London, 5 February 1968*. London.

Hansen, M. Mosegaard. 1998. *The Function of Discourse Particles: A Study with Special Reference to Spoken French*. Amsterdam.

Hansen, M. Mosegaard. 2006. "A dynamic polysemy approach to the lexical semantics of discourse markers (with an exemplary analysis of French *toujours*)." In Fischer, ed., 2006: 21–41.

Happ, H. 1967. "Die lateinische Umgangssprache und die Kunstsprache des Plautus." *Glotta* 45: 60–104.

Harries, J. 2006. *Cicero and the Jurists*. London.

Harrington, K.P. 1925. *Medieval Latin*. Chicago and London.

Harris, M., and N. Vincent, eds. 1988. *The Romance Languages*. London.

Harris, W.V. 1989. *Ancient Literacy*. Cambridge, MA, and London.

Harris-Northall, R. 1990. *Weakening Processes in the History of Spanish Consonants*. London.

Harrison, S.J. 1991. *Vergil:* Aeneid *10*. Oxford.

Harrison, S.J., ed. 2005. *A Companion to Latin Literature*. Malden, MA, and Oxford.

Harrison, S.J., and S.J. Heyworth. 1998. "Notes on the text and interpretation of Catullus." *PCPhS* 44: 85–109.

Hartley, B., and B. Dickinson. 2008–. *Names on Terra Sigillata: An Index of Makers' Stamps and Signatures on Gallo-Roman Terra Sigillata (Samian Ware)*. London.

Hartmann, M. 2005. *Die frühlateinischen Inschriften und ihre Datierung. Eine linguistisch-archäologisch-paläographische Untersuchung* [Münchner Forschungen zur historischen Sprachwissenschaft, Band 3]. Bremen.

Harvey, R.A. 1981. *A Commentary on Persius*. Leiden.

Hasenohr, C. 2007. "Les italiens à Délos. Entre romanité et hellénisme." *Pallas* 73: 221–232.

Hasenohr, C. 2008. "Le bilinguisme dans les inscriptions des *magistri* de Délos." In Biville, Decourt and Rougemont, eds., 2008: 55–70.

Haugen, E. 1950. "The analysis of linguistic borrowing." *Language* 26: 210–232.

Häusler, S. 2000. "Parenthesen im Lateinischen am Beispiel der Pliniusbriefe." *Glotta* 76: 202–231.

Heine, R.E. 2004. "The beginnings of Latin Christian literature." In F. Young, L. Ayres and A. Louth, eds., *The Cambridge History of Early Christian Literature*. Cambridge: 131–141.

Heller, M., ed. 1988. *Codeswitching: Anthropological and Sociolinguistic Perspectives*. Berlin and New York.

Henar Gallego Franco, M. del. 2003. "Intérpretes militares en el 'limes' de Danubio." *Aquila legionis* 4: 27–43.

Hendrikson, G.L. 1927. "Satura tota nostra est." *CPh* 22: 46–60.

Hengeveld, K., and J.L. Mackenzie. 2008. *Functional Discourse Grammar: A Typologically-Based Theory of Language Structure*. Oxford: 367–400.

Hengeveld, K., and J.L. Mackenzie. 2010. "Functional discourse grammar." In B. Heine and H. Narrog, eds., 2010. *The Oxford Handbook of Linguistic Analysis*. Oxford.

Henry, J. 1873. *Aeneidea; or, Critical, Exegetical, and Aesthetical Remarks on the* Aeneis. London.

Heraeus, W. 1902. "Die römische Soldatensprache." *ALL* 12: 255–280.

Heraeus, W. 1904. "Die Sprache der römische Kinderstube." *ALL* 13: 149–172.

Heraeus, W. 1937. "Zur römischen Soldatensprache (Nachträge)." In W. Heraeus, *Kleine Schriften*. Ed. J.B. Hofmann. Heidelberg: 151–157.

Herman, J. 1961. "*Posit* (= *posuit*) et questions connexes dans les inscriptions pannoniennes. Essai de géographie linguistique." *AAntHung* 9: 321–331 = Herman 1990: 94–104.

Herman, J. 1963. *La formation du système roman des conjonctions de subordination*. Berlin.

Herman, J. 1965. "Le datif possessif dans la latinité balkanique." In I. Iordan, ed., *Omagiu lui Alexandru Rosetti*. Bucarest: 375–378 = Herman 1990: 315–320.

Herman, J. 1968. "Latinitas Pannonica. Vue d'ensemble des caractéristiques de la latinité pannonienne: un essai." *Filológiae Közlöny* 14: 364–376 = Herman 1990: 105–120.

Herman, J. 1982. "Un vieux dossier réouvert: les transformations du système latin des quantités vocaliques." *BSL* 77; 285–302 = Herman 1990: 217–231.

Herman, J. 1983a. "Le latin dans les provinces danubiennes de l'empire romain. Problèmes et perspectives de la recherche." *ANRW* II.29.2: 1089–1106 = Herman 1990: 164–182.

Herman, J. 1983b. "La langue latine dans la Gaule romaine." *ANRW* II.29.2: 1045–1060 = Herman 1990: 147–163.

Herman, J. 1985a. "La différenciation territoriale du latin et la formation des langues romanes." In *Actes du XVIIe Congrès international de linguistique et philologie romanes II*. Aix-en-Provence: 15–62 = Herman 1990: 62–92.

Herman, J. 1985b. "Témoignage des inscriptions latines et préhistoire des langues romanes. Le cas de la Sardaigne." In M. Deanović, ed., *Mélanges de linguistique dédiés à la mémoire de Petar Skok* (1881–1956). Zagreb: 207–216 = Herman 1990: 183–194.

Herman, J. 1989. "Accusativus cum infinitivo et subordonée à *quod, quia* en latin tardif. Nouvelles remarques sur un vieux problème." In G. Calboli, ed., *Subordination and Other Topics in Latin*

(Proceedings of the Third Colloquium on Latin Linguistics, Bologna, 1–5 April 1985). Amsterdam and Philadelphia: 133–152.

Herman, J. 1990. *Du latin aux langues romanes. Études de linguistique historique*. Tübingen.

Herman, J., ed. 1994. *Linguistic Studies on Latin: Selected Papers from the 6th International Colloquium on Latin Linguistics (Budapest, 23–27 March 1991)*. Amsterdam and Philadelphia.

Herman, J. 2000. *Vulgar Latin*. Trans. R. Wright. University Park, PA.

Hettrich, H. 1988. *Untersuchungen zur Hypotaxe im Vedischen*. Berlin and New York.

Heyworth, S.J., ed. 2007a. *Sexti Properti Elegi*. Oxford.

Heyworth, S.J. 2007b. *Cynthia: A Companion to the Text of Propertius*. Oxford.

Highet, G. 1954. "Survey." In G. Highet, *Juvenal the Satirist: A Study*. Oxford: 161–178 = Plaza, ed., 2009: 278–304.

Hillen, M. 1989. *Studien zur Dichtersprache Senecas. Abundanz, Explikativer Ablativ, Hypallage*. Berlin and New York.

Hilton, J. 1999. "The role of discourse and lexical meaning in the grammaticalisation of temporal particles in Latin." *Glotta* 74: 198–210.

Hock, H.H., and B.D. Joseph. 1996. *Language History, Language Change, and Language Relationship: An Introduction to Historical and Comparative Linguistics*. Berlin.

Hodgman, A.W. 1902. "Noun declension in Plautus." *CR* 16: 294–305.

Hoffmann, F., M. Minas-Nerpel and S. Pfeiffer. 2009. *Die dreisprachige Stele des C. Cornelius Gallus. Übersetzung und Kommentar*. Berlin.

Hoffmann, L. 1987. *Kommunikationsmittel Fachsprache. Eine Einführung*. 3rd edn. Tübingen.

Hoffmann, L., H. Kalverkämper and H.E. Wiegand, eds. 1998–1999. *Fachsprachen. Ein internationales Handbuch zur Fachsprachenforschung und Terminologiewissenschaft [HSK 14.1 and 14.2]*. Berlin and New York.

Hofmann, J.B. 1951/2003. *Lateinische Umgangssprache*. 3rd edn. Heidelberg = 2003. *La lingua d'uso latina*. Trans. and augmented L. Ricottilli. Bologna.

Hofmann, J.B., and M. Leumann 1965–1979. *Lateinische Grammatik [Handbuch der Altertumswissenschaft, II 2.1, 2.2, 2.3]*. Munich.

Hofmann, J.B., and A. Szantyr 1965. *Lateinische Syntax und Stilistik [Lateinische Grammatik II = Handbuch der Altertumswissenschaft, II 2.2]*. 3rd edn. Munich.

Holford-Strevens, L. 1981. "Review of Vincenzo Loi, *Origini e caratteristiche della latinità cristiana*." *CR* 31: 230–233.

Holford-Strevens, L. 2003. *Aulus Gellius: An Antonine Scholar and His Achievement*. Rev. edn. Oxford.

Holloway, R.R. 1994. *The Archaeology of Early Rome and Latium*. London.

Holtz, L. 1981. *Donat et la tradition de l'enseignement grammatical. Études sur l'Ars Donati et sa diffusion (IVe–IXe siècle) et édition critique*. Paris.

Honoré, T. 1978. *Tribonian*. London.

Honoré, T. 1982. *Ulpian*. Oxford.

Horrocks, G. 2010. *Greek: A History of the Language and Its Speakers*. 2nd edn. Oxford.

Horsfall, N.M. 1994. "Prefazione." In G. Bonfante, *La lingua parlata in Orazio*. Venosa: 9–19.

Horsfall, N.M. 1999. "The legionary as his own historian." *Ancient History* 29: 107–117.

Horsfall, N.M. 2000a. *A Companion to the Study of Virgil*. 2nd edn. Leiden.

Horsfall, N.M. 2000b. "Language, metre, style." In N. Horsfall, ed., *A Companion to the Study of Virgil*: Leiden: 217–248.

Housman, A.E. 1888. "Emendationes Propertianae." *JPh* 16: 1–35 = Diggle and Goodyear, eds., 1972, I: 29–54.

Housman, A.E. 1893. "The Manuscripts of Propertius (cont'd)." *JPh* 21: 161–197 = Diggle and Goodyear, eds., 1972, I: 277–304.

Housman, A.E. 1894. "Schulze's edition of Baehrens' Catullus." *CR* 8: 251–7 = Diggle and Goodyear, eds., 1972, I: 305–313.

Housman, A.E. 1907. "Luciliana [II]." *CQ* 1: 148–159 = Diggle and Goodyear, eds., 1972, II: 685–697.

Housman, A.E. 1910. "Greek nouns in Latin poetry from Lucretius to Juvenal." *JPh* 31: 236–266 = Diggle and Goodyear, eds., 1972, II: 817–839.

Housman, A.E. 1930. "The Latin for ass." *CQ* 24: 11–13 = Diggle and Goodyear, eds., 1972, III: 1163–1165.

Hoven, R. and L. Grailet. 2006. *Lexique de la prose latine de la Renaissance.* 2nd revised edn. English trans. by C. Maas, revised by K. Renard-Jadoul. Leiden.

Hudson, A. 1992. "Diglossia: A bibliographical review." *Language in Society* 21: 611–674.

Hudson, A. 2002a. "Diglossia, bilingualism and history: Postscript to a theoretical discussion." *International Journal of the Sociology of Language* 157: 151–165.

Hudson, A. 2002b. "Outline of a theory of diglossia." *International Journal of the Sociology of Language* 157: 1–48.

Humphreys, M.W. 1879. "Influence of accent in Latin dactylic hexameters." *TAPhA* 9: 39–58.

Hutchinson, G.O. 1998. *Cicero's Correspondence: A Literary Study.* Oxford.

Huxley, A. 1963. *Literature and Science.* London.

Ijsewijn, J. 1998. *A Companion to Neo-Latin Studies.* 2 vols. Leuven.

Iliescu, M. and W. Marxgut, eds. 1992. *Latin vulgaire – latin tardif III.* Tübingen.

Inglebert, H., 2002. "Citoyenneté romaine, romanités et identités romaines sous l'empire." In H. Inglebert, ed., *Idéologies et valeurs civiques dans le monde romain. Hommage à Claude Lepelley.* Paris: 241–260.

Isaac, B. 2009. "Latin in cities of the Roman Near East." In Cotton *et al.*, eds., 2009: 43–72.

Jacobson, R., ed. 1998. *Codeswitching Worldwide.* Berlin and New York.

Jacobson, R., ed. 2001. *Codeswitching Worldwide II.* Berlin and New York.

Janko, R., ed. 2001. *Philodemus. On Poems. I.* Oxford.

Jannaris, A.N. 1897. *An Historical Greek Grammar Chiefly of the Attic Dialect.* London.

Janson, T. 1964. *Latin Prose Prefaces: Studies in Literary Conventions.* Stockholm.

Janson, T. 2002. *Speak: A Short History of Languages.* Oxford.

Janson, T. 2004. *A Natural History of Latin.* Oxford.

Janssen, H.H. 1941/1988. *De kenmerken der Romeinsche dichtertaal.* Nijmegen and Utrecht = Italian trans. with additions in Lunelli, ed., 1988: 69–130.

Jebb, R.C. 1881. *Bentley.* London.

Jocelyn, H.D. 1979. "Vergilius Cacozelus." *PLLS* 2: 67–142.

Jocelyn, H.D. 1980. "Eupla laxa landicosa (*CIL* 4.10004)." *LCM* 5: 153–154.

Jocelyn, H.D. 1999. "Code-switching in the *Comoedia Palliata*." In G. Vogt-Spira and B. Rommel, eds., *Rezeption und Identität. Die kulturelle Auseinandersetzung Roms mit Griechenland als europäisches Paradigma.* Stuttgart: 169–195.

Johnston, H.W. 1897. *A Collection of Examples Illustrating the Metrical Licenses of Vergil.* Chicago.

Joseph, B.D., and R.E. Wallace. 1992. "Socially determined variation in ancient Rome." *Language Variation and Change* 4: 105–119.

Kabell, A. 1960. *Metrische Studien. II: Antiker Form sich nähernd.* Uppsala.

Kaimio, J. 1979. *The Romans and the Greek Language* [Commentationes Humanarum Litterarum 64]. Helsinki.

Kaizer, T. 2007. "Palmyre, cité grecque? A question of coinage." *Klio* 89: 39–60.

Kalb, W. 1888. *Das Juristenlatein. Versuch einer Charakteristik auf Grundlage der Digesten.* 2nd edn. Nuremberg = 1961. Repr. Aalen.

Kalverkämper, H. 1982. "Fachsprachen und Textsorten." In J. Høedt, L. Lundquist, H. Picht and J. Qvistgaard, eds., *Proceedings of the 3rd European Symposium on LSP. "Pragmatics and LSP"*. Copenhagen: 105–168.

Kalverkämper, H. 1983. "Gattungen, Textsorten, Fachsprachen. Textpragmatische Überlegungen zur Klassifikation." In E.W.B. Hess-Lüttich, ed., *Textproduktion und Textrezeption*. Tübingen: 91–103.

Kalverkämper, H. 2005. "Fachkommunikation zwischen Tradition und Innovation. Ein kultur-historisches Phänomen der alten und modernen Gesellschaften." In T. Fögen, ed., *Antike Fachtexte – Ancient Technical Texts*. Berlin and New York: 319–361.

Kalverkämper, H., and K.-D. Baumann, eds., 1996. *Fachliche Textsorten. Komponenten, Relationen, Strategien*. Tübingen.

Kapp, E. 1941. "Bentley's *Schediasma* 'de metris Terentianis' and the modern doctrine of ictus in Classical verse." *Mnemosyne* 9: 187–194.

Karakasis, E. 2005. *Terence and the Language of Roman Comedy*. Cambridge.

Karlsen, E. 2001. *The* Accusativus cum infinitivo *and* Quod-*clauses in the "Revelationes" of St. Bridget of Sweden*. Bern.

Kaser, M. 1951. "Zum Ediktsstil." In *Festschrift F. Schulz*. II. Weimar: 21–70.

Kaster, R.A., 1995. *Suetonius* De Grammaticis et Rhetoribus. Oxford.

Kauer, R., and W.M. Lindsay. 1926. *P. Terenti Afri Comoediae*. Oxford = 1958. Repr. with additions by O. Skutsch. Oxford.

Keane, C. 2006. *Figuring Genre in Roman Satire*. Oxford.

Kearsley, R.A. 1999. "A bilingual epitaph from Ephesos for the son of a *tabularius* in the *Familia Caesaris*." In P. Scherrer, H. Taeuber and H. Thür, eds., *Steine und Wege. Festschrift für D. Knibbe zum 65. Geburtstag* [Sonderschriften. Österreichisches Archäologisches Institut]. Vienna: 77–88.

Kearsley, R.A., and T.V. Evans. 2001. *Greeks and Romans in Imperial Asia: Mixed Language Inscriptions and Linguistic Evidence for Cultural Interaction until the End of AD III*. Bonn.

Keitel, E.E. 2010. "The art of losing: Tacitus and the disaster narrative." In C.S. Kraus, J. Marincola and C. Pelling, eds., *Ancient Historiography and Its Contexts*. Oxford: 331–352.

Kelly, G. 2008. *Ammianus Marcellinus: The Allusive Historian*. Cambridge.

Kennedy, G.A. 1972. *The Art of Rhetoric in the Roman World: 300 BC–AD 300*. Princeton, NJ.

Kennedy, G.A. 1998. *Comparative Rhetoric: An Historical and Cross-Cultural Introduction*. New York and Oxford.

Kenney, E.J. 1974. *The Classical Text: Aspects of Editing in the Age of the Printed Book*. Berkeley, CA.

Kenney, E.J. 1986. "Prodelided *est*: A note on orthography." *CQ* 36: 542.

Kenney, E.J. 2002. "Ovid's language and style." In Boyd, ed., 2002: 27–89.

Kenney, E.J., and W.V. Clausen. 1982. *The Cambridge History of Classical Literature*. II: *Latin Literature*. Cambridge.

Kent, R.G. 1945. *The Sounds of Latin*. Baltimore.

Kircher-Durand, C., ed. 2002. *Création lexicale. La formation des noms par dérivation suffixale* [Grammaire ondamentale du Latin IX]. Louvain and Paris.

Kirchner, R. 2007. "*Elocutio*: Latin prose style." In Dominik and Hall, eds., 2007: 181–194.

Kiss, S. 1972. *Les transformations de la structure syllabique en latin tardif*. Debrecen.

Klein, H.-W. 1958. "Zur Latinität des *Itinerarium Egeriae* (früher *Peregrinatio Aetheriae*). Stand der Forschung und neue Erkenntnismöglichkeiten." In H. Lausberg and H. Weinreich, eds., *Romanica. Festschrift für Gerhard Rohlfs*. Halle (Saale): 243–258.

Kleve, K. 1990. "Ennius in Herculaneum." *Cronache ercolanesi* 20: 5–16.

Kleve, K. 1994. "An approach to the Latin papyri from Herculaneum." In U. Albini, ed., *Storia, poesia e pensiero nel mondo antico. Studi in onore di Marcello Gigante*. Naples: 313–320.

Knox, B.W. 1950. "The serpent and the flame." *AJPh* 70: 379–400.

Koch P. 1995. "Une langue comme toutes les autres. Latin vulgaire et traits universels de l'oral." In Callebat, ed., 1995: 125–144.

Kokkinia, C. 2003. "Letters of Roman authorities on local dignitaries: The case of Vedius Antonius." *ZPE* 142: 197–213.

Konjetzny, G. 1908. "De idiotismis syntacticis in titulis latinis urbanis (*CIL* Vol. VI.) conspicuis." *ALL* 15: 297–351.

Kooreman, M. 1995. "The expression of obligation and necessity in the works of Tertullian: The use of *habere* + infinitive, -*urus esse*, and the gerundive." In Callebat, ed., 1995: 383–394.

Korfmacher, W.C. 1934–1935. "Grecizing in Lucilian satire." *CJ* 30: 453–462.

Kramer, J. 1976. *Literarische Quellen zur Aussprache des Vulgärlateins.* Meisenheim an Glan.

Kramer, J. 2007. *Vulgärlateinische Alltagsdokumente auf Papyri, Ostraka, Täfelchen und Inschriften* [Archiv für Papyrusforschung und verwandte Gebiete Beiheft 23]. Berlin and New York.

Kraus, C.S. 1992. "How (not?) to end a sentence: The problem of -*que*." *HSCPh* 94: 321–329.

Kraus, C.S. 1994. *Livy* Ab urbe condita *Book VI*. Cambridge.

Kraus, C.S. 2005. "Hair, hegemony and historiography: Caesar's style and its earliest critics." In Reinhardt, Lapidge and Adams, eds., 2005: 97–115.

Krebs, C. 2008a. "Catiline's ravaged mind: *vastus animus* (Sall. *Cat.* 5.5)." *CQ* 58: 682–686.

Krebs, C. 2008b. "The imagery of the way in the proem to Sallust's *Bellum Catilinae* (1–4)." *AJPh* 129: 581–594.

Kroll, W. 1897. "Das afrikanische Latein." *RhM* 52: 569–590.

Kroll, W. 1924. "Die Dichtersprache." In W. Kroll, *Studien zum Verständnis der römischen Literatur*. Stuttgart: 247–279 = Lunelli, ed., 1988: 3–66.

Kroon, C. 1989. "Causal connectors in Latin: The discourse function of *nam, enim, igitur* and *ergo*." *CLL* 15.1–4: 231–243.

Kroon, C. 1995. *Discourse Particles in Latin. A Study of* nam, enim, autem, vero *and* at. Amsterdam.

Kroon, C. 1998. "A framework for the description of Latin discourse markers." *Journal of Pragmatics* 30: 205–223.

Kroon, C. 2004. "Scales of involvement and the use of Latin causal connectives." In A. López Eire and A. Ramos Guerreira, eds., *Registros lingüísticos en las lenguas clásicas* [Classica Salmanticensia III]. Salamanca: 65–86.

Kroon, C. 2005. "The relationship between grammar and discourse: Evidence from the Latin particle *quidem*." In G. Calboli, ed., *Latina Lingua!* [Papers on Grammar IX.2]. Rome: 577–590.

Kroon, C. 2009. "Latin linguistics between grammar and discourse: Units of analysis, levels of analysis." In E. Rieken and P. Widmer, eds., *Pragmatische Kategorien. Form, Funktion und Diachronie*. Wiesbaden: 143–158.

Kruschwitz, P. 2002. *Carmina Saturnia Epigraphica, Einleitung, Text und Kommentar zu den Saturnischen Versinschriften*. Stuttgart.

Kruschwitz, P. 2010a. "*Romanes eunt domus*. Linguistic aspects of the sub-literary Latin in Pompeian wall inscriptions." In T.V. Evans and D.D. Obbink, eds., *The Language of the Papyri*. Oxford: 156–170.

Kruschwitz, P. 2010b. "Writing on trees: Restoring a lost facet of the Graeco-Roman epigraphic habit." *ZPE* 173: 45–62.

Kruschwitz, P., and H. Halla-aho. 2007. "The Pompeian wall-inscriptions and the Latin language: A critical reappraisal." *Arctos* 41: 31–49.

Krylová, B. 2001. "Die Partikeln *ergo* und *igitur* bei Ammianus Marcellinus. Ein textologischer Beitrag zur Diskussion um Ammians Sprachkompetenz." In G. Thome and J. Holzhausen, eds., *Es hat sich viel ereignet, Gutes wie Böses. Lateinische Geschichtsschreibung der Spät- und Nachantike.* Munich and Leipzig: 57–79.

Krylová, B. 2003. "*Ergo* als Konsensus-Partikel in lateinischen narrativen Texten. Eine Untersuchung an Prosatexten historischer Thematik von Caesar bis Sueton." *Graecolatina Pragensia* 18: 63–94.

Krylová, B. 2006. "Consensus suggested and demanded: The use and role of *enim* and *ergo* in conflict management." *Graecolatina Pragensia* 20: 95–107.

Kübler, B. 1893. "Die lateinische Sprache auf afrikanischen Inschriften." *ALL* 8: 161–202.

Kühnast, L. 1872. *Die Hauptpunkte der livianischen Syntax.* Berlin.

Kühner, R., C. Stegmann and A. Thierfelder 1976. *Ausführliche Grammatik der lateinischen Sprache Teil II: Satzlehre.* 2 vols. I: *Elementar-, Formen- und Wortlehre.* II: *Satzlehre.* 5th rev. edn. Hanover.

Kuntze, A. 1892. *Sallustiana.* 3 vols. Leipzig.

Laird, A. 1999. *Powers of Expression, Expressions of Power: Speech Presentation and Latin Literature.* Oxford.

Lakoff, G. and M. Johnson. 1980. *Metaphors We Live By.* Chicago.

Lambert, P.-Y. 2008. "*RIG* II, 2: notes de compléments." *Études Celtiques* 36: 103–113.

Landgraf, G. 1914. *Kommentar zu Ciceros Rede Pro Sex. Roscio Amerino.* 2nd edn. Leipzig and Berlin.

Langslow, D.R. 1989. "Latin technical language: Synonyms and Greek words in Latin medical terminology." *TPhS* 87: 33–53.

Langslow, D.R. 2000a. "Latin discourse particles, 'Medical Latin' and 'Classical Latin'." *Mnemosyne* 53: 537–560.

Langslow, D.R. 2000b. *Medical Latin in the Roman Empire.* Oxford.

Langslow, D.R. 2002. "Approaching bilingualism in corpus languages." In Adams, Janse and Swain, eds., 2002: 23–51.

Langslow, D.R. 2005. "'Langues réduites au lexique?' The languages of Latin technical prose." In Reinhardt, Lapidge and Adams, eds., 2005: 287–302.

Latham, R.E. 1965. *Revised Medieval Latin Word-List.* Oxford.

Laughton, E. 1964. *The Participle in Cicero.* Oxford.

Lausberg, H. 1990. *Handbuch der literarischen Rhetorik.* 3rd edn. Stuttgart.

Lavency, M. 1998. *La proposition relative* [Grammaire fondamentale du latin, tome V, volume 2]. Louvain and Paris.

Lavency, M. 2002. "L'ablatif de modalité dans les *Lettres* de Pline le Jeune." In P. Defosse, ed., *Hommages à Carl Deroux.* II. *Prose et linguistique, Médecine* [Collection Latomus 267]. Brussels: 240–251.

Lavency, M., and D. Longrée, eds., 1989. *Actes du 5e colloque de Linguistique latine.* [Cahiers de l'Institut de Linguistique de Louvain 15]. Louvain-la-Neuve.

Laws, J., and S. Laws. 2003. "Iudicium Legum." *Ad Familiares: The Journal of Friends of Classics* 26: 11–13.

Leclerc, P., E.M. Morales and A. de Vogüé. 2007. *Jérôme: Trois vies de moines (Paul, Malchus, Hilarion).* Paris.

Lee, R.W. 1956. *The Elements of Roman Law.* London.

Leeman, A.D. 1963. Orationis Ratio: *The Stylistic Theories and Practice of the Roman Orators, Historians, and Philosophers.* 2 vols. Amsterdam.

Lehmann, C. 1979. "Der Relativsatz vom Indogermanischen bis zum Italienischen." *Die Sprache* 25: 1–25.

Leiwo, M. 1994. *Neapolitana. A Study of Population and Language in Graeco-Roman Naples.* Helsinki.

Leiwo, M., and H. Halla-aho. 2002. "A marriage contract: Aspects of Latin–Greek language contact (*P.Mich* VII 434 and *P.Ryl.* IV 612 = *ChLA* IV 249)." *Mnemosyne* 55: 560–580.

Lejeune, M. 1957. "Notes de linguistique italique: XIII. Sur les adaptations de l'alphabet étrusque aux langues indo-européennes d'Italie." *REL* 34: 88–105.

Lejeune, M. 1962. "Notes de linguistique italique: XVII. La bilingue étrusco-latine de Pesaro." *REL* 40: 160–166.

Lejeune, M. 1966. "Notes de linguistique italique: XXI. Les notations de F dans l'Italie ancienne." *REL* 44: 141–181.

Lendon, J.E. 1999. "The rhetoric of combat: Greek military theory and Roman culture in Julius Caesar's battle descriptions." *CA* 18: 273–329.

Leo, F. 1895–1896. *Plauti Comoediae*. 2 vols. Berlin.

Leo, F. 1905. *Der saturnische Vers*. Berlin.

Leo, F. 1912. *Plautinische Forschungen zur Kritik und Geschichte der Komödie*. 2nd edn. Berlin.

Leumann, M. 1944. "Gruppierung und Funktionen der Wortbildungssuffixe des Lateins." *MH* 1: 129–151 = Leumann 1959: 84–107.

Leumann, M. 1947. "Die lateinische Dichtersprache." *MH* 4: 116–139 = Leumann 1959: 131–156 = Lunelli, ed., 1988: 134–178.

Leumann, M. 1959. *Kleine Schriften*. Zürich and Stuttgart.

Leumann, M. 1977. *Lateinische Laut- und Formenlehre*. 5th edn. Munich.

Levene, D.S. 2000. "Sallust's *Catiline* and Cato the Censor." *CQ* 50: 170–191.

Levene, D.S. and D.P. Nelis, eds. 2002. *Clio and the Poets: Augustan Poetry and the Traditions of Ancient Historiography*. [Mnemosyne Supplements 224]. Leiden.

Levick, B. 1995. "The Latin inscriptions of Asia Minor." In Solin *et al.*, eds., 1995: 393–402.

Lewis, C.T. and C. Short. 1879. *A Latin Dictionary Founded on Andrew's Edition of Freund's Latin Dictionary. Revised, Enlarged and in Great Part Rewritten*. Oxford.

Lewis, N. 1978. "The imperial apokrima." *RIDA* 25: 261–278.

Lewis, N. 1986. "The process of promulgation in Rome's eastern provinces." In R.S. Bagnall and W.V. Harris, eds., *Studies in Roman Law in Memory of A. Arthur Schiller*. Leiden: 127–139.

Lewis, N. 1991–1992. "The governor's edict at Aizanoi." *Hellenica* 42: 15–20.

Lewis, N. 1993. "The demise of the demotic document: When and why." *JEA* 79: 276–281.

Lewis, N. 1996. "On Roman imperial promulgation in Greek." *SCI* 15: 208–211.

Lewis, N. 2001. "The demise of the Aramaic document in the Dead Sea region." *SCI* 20: 179–181.

Lewis, N., Y. Yadin and J.C. Greenfield. 1989. *The Documents from the Bar Kokhba Period in the Cave of Letters*. Jerusalem.

Liechtenhan, E. 1963. *Anthimi De obseruatione ciborum ad Theodoricum regem Francorum epistula*. Berlin.

Lindner, T. 1996. *Lateinische Komposita. Ein Glossar vornehmlich zum Wortschatz der Dichtersprache*. Innsbruck.

Lindner, T. 2002. *Lateinische Komposita. Morphologische, historische und lexikalische Studien*. Innsbruck.

Lindsay, W.M. 1904–1905. *T. Macci Plauti Comoediae*. 2 vols. Oxford.

Lindsay, W.M. 1907. *Syntax of Plautus*. Oxford.

Lindsay, W.M. 1922. *Early Latin Verse*. Oxford.

Lintott, A.W. 1999. *The Constitution of the Roman Republic*. Oxford.

Lloyd, G.E.R. 1983. "The development of Greek anatomical terminology." In G.E.R. Lloyd, *Science, Folklore and Ideology: Studies in the Life Sciences in Ancient Greece*. Cambridge: 149–167.

Lloyd, G.E.R. 1987. *The Revolutions of Wisdom: Studies in the Claims and Practice of Ancient Greek Science*. Berkeley and London.

Lodge, R.A. 1993. *French: From Dialect to Standard*. London.

Löfstedt, B. 1961. *Studien über die Sprache der langobardischen Gesetze. Beiträge zur frühmittelalterlichen Latinität*. Uppsala.

Löfstedt, E. 1907. *Beiträge zur Kenntnis der späteren Latinität*. Stockholm.

Löfstedt, E. 1908. *Spätlateinische Studien*. Uppsala.

Löfstedt, E. 1911. *Philologischer Kommentar zur Peregrinatio Aetheriae*. Uppsala = 2007 Italian trans. P. Pieroni, *Commento filologico all Peregrination Aetheriae: Ricerche sulla storia della lingua latina*. Bologna.

Löfstedt, E. 1942–1956. *Syntactica. Studien und Beiträge zur historischen Syntax des Lateins*. I: *Über einige Grundfragen der lateinischen Nominalsyntax*. II: *Syntaktisch-stilistische Gesichtspunkte und Probleme*. 2nd edn. Lund.

Löfstedt, E. 1959. *Late Latin*. Oslo.

Loporcaro, M. 2008. "La tendenza alla sillaba chiusa in latino tardo." In Wright, ed., 2008: 336–345.

Louis, P. 1956. "Observations sur le vocabulaire technique d'Aristote." In *Mélanges de philosophie grecque offerts à Mgr. Diès*. Paris: 141–149.

Lowe, N.J. 1988. "Sulpicia's syntax." *CQ* 38: 193–205.

Luce, T.J. 1971. "Design and structure in Livy: 5.32–55." *TAPhA* 102: 265–302.

Lunelli, A., ed. 1988. *La lingua poetica latina*. 3rd edn. Bologna.

Lyne, R.O.A.M. 1989. *Words and the Poet: Characteristic Techniques of Style in Vergil's* Aeneid. Oxford.

Lyons, J. 1977. *Semantics*. II. Cambridge.

Mackay, C.S. 1999. "Expressions to indicate goal of motion in the colloquial Latin of the early empire." *ZPE* 126: 229–239.

Magariños, A. 1939. "Peperci – parsi." *Emérita* 7: 136–145.

Maiden, M. 1995. *A Linguistic History of Italian*. London and New York.

Malcovati, H. 1969. *Imperatoris Caesaris Augusti Operum Fragmenta*. 5th edn. Turin.

Malherbe, A.J. 1988. *Ancient Epistolary Theorists*. Atlanta, GA.

Mallory, J.P., and D.Q. Adams. 2006. *The Oxford Introduction to Proto-Indo-European and the Proto-Indo-European World*. Oxford.

Maltby, R. 1975. "A comparative study of the language of Plautus and Terence." PhD thesis. Cambridge University.

Maltby, R. 1979. "Linguistic characterisation of old men in Terence." *CPh* 74: 136–147.

Maltby, R. 1985. "The distribution of Greek loan-words in Terence." *CQ* 35: 110–123.

Maltby, R. 1991. *A Lexicon of Ancient Latin Etymologies*. Leeds.

Maltby, R. 1995. "The distribution of Greek loan-words in Plautus." In R. Brock and A.J. Woodman, eds., *PLLS* 8: 31–69.

Mancini, M. 2001. "Agostino, i grammatici e il vocalismo del latino d'Africa." *Rivista di Linguistica* 13: 309–338.

Mantello, F.A., and A.G. Rigg, eds. 1996. *Medieval Latin: An Introduction and Bibliographical Guide*. Washington, DC.

Manthe, U. 1999. "*Assyrius sermo*: Ulp. D.45.1.16." In J.-F. Gerkens, P. Trenk-Hinterberger, H. Peter and R. Vigneron, eds., *Mélanges F. Sturm. Droit romain, histoire du droit, droit civil, droit comparé, droit international privé*, I. Liège: 357–364.

Manuwald, G., ed. 2001. *Der Satiriker Lucilius und seine Zeit*. Munich.

Marache, R. 1956. *Mots nouveaux et mots archaïques chez Fronton et Aulu-Gelle*. Rennes.

Marchesi, I. 2008. *The Art of Pliny's Letters: A Poetics of Allusion in the Private Correspondence*. Cambridge.

Marichal, R. 1988. *Les graffites de La Graufesenque*. Paris.

Marincola, J. 1997. *Authority and Tradition in Ancient Historiography*. Cambridge.

Marincola, J. 2007a. "Odysseus and the historian." *Syllecta Classica* 18: 1–79.

Marincola, J. 2007b. "Speeches in Classical historiography." In J. Marincola, ed., *A Companion to Greek and Roman Historiography*. Malden, MA and Oxford: 118–132.

Marinetti, A. 1985. *L' iscrizioni sudpicene: Testi*. Florence.

Mariotti, I. 1960. *Studi luciliani*. Florence.

Mariotti, S., ed. 1996–1998. *Enciclopedia oraziana*. 3 vols. Rome.

Markland, J. 1827. *P. Papinii Statii Libri quinque Silvarum*. Repr. of 1st 1728 edn. Dresden.

Marouzeau, J. 1921. "Pour mieux comprendre les textes latins. Essai sur la distinction des styles." *RPh* 45: 149–193.

Marouzeau, J. 1946. *Traité de stylistique latine.* 2nd edn. Paris.

Marouzeau, J. 1949. *Quelques aspects de la formation du latin littéraire.* Paris.

Marouzeau, J. 1953. *L'ordre des mots en latin.* Paris.

Marouzeau, J. 1959. "Sur deux aspects de la langue du droit." In *Droits de l'Aantiquité et sociologie juridique.* [*Mélanges Henri Lévy-Bruhl*]. Paris: 435–444.

Marouzeau, P. 1932. "Compte-rendu de J. Schrijnen: *Charakteristik des altchristlichen Latein.*" *REL* 10: 241–243.

Marrou, H.-I. 1965. *Histoire de l'éducation dans l'Antiquité.* 6th edn. Paris.

Marshall, P.K., ed. 1990. *A. Gellii* Noctes Atticae, II: *Libri XI–XX.* 2nd rev. edn. Oxford.

Martin, E.A., ed. 1990. *A Concise Dictionary of Law.* Oxford.

Martín, F. 1982. *La documentación griega de la cancillería del emperador Adriano.* Pamplona.

Marx, F. 1904–1905. *C. Lucilii carminum reliquiae.* Leipzig.

Marx, F. 1909. "Die Beziehungen des Altlateins zum Spätlatein." *Neue Jahrbücher für das klassische Altertum, Geschichte und deutsche Literatur* 12: 434–448.

Mason, H.J. 1974. *Greek Terms for Roman Institutions: A Lexicon and Analysis.* Toronto.

Matthews, P.H. 1972. *Inflectional Morphology: A Theoretical Study Based on Aspects of Latin Verb Conjugation.* Cambridge.

Matthews, P.H. 1994. "Greek and Latin linguistics." In G. Lepschy, ed., *History of Linguistics.* II: *Classical and Medieval Linguistics.* London and New York: 1–133.

Mattingly, H. and E.A. Sydenham. 1923–. *The Roman Imperial Coinage.* London. 2nd revised edn 1984– ed. C.H.V. Sutherland and R.A.G. Carson. London.

Maurach, G. 1989. *Enchiridion poeticum.* Darmstadt.

May, J.M. and J. Wisee. 2001. *Cicero On the Ideal Orator (*De Oratore*).* Oxford.

Mayer, R.G. 1999. "Grecism." In Adams and Mayer, eds., 1999: 157–182.

Mayer, R.G. 2001. *Tacitus* Dialogus de Oratoribus. Cambridge.

Mayer, R.G. 2003. "Pliny and *gloria dicendi.*" *Arethusa* 36: 227–234.

Mayser, E. 1934. *Grammatik der griechischen Papyri aus der Ptolemäerzeit* II.2: *Satzlehre.* Berlin and Leipzig.

Mazzini, I. 1978. "Il greco nella lingua tecnica medica latina." *Annali della facoltà di lettere e filosofia dell'Università di Macerata* 11: 543–556.

McDonald, A.H. 1957. "The style of Livy." *JRS* 47: 155–172.

McKie, D.S. 1989. "Salutati, Poggio and Codex M of Catullus." In Diggle, Hall and Jocelyn, eds.,1989: 66–86.

Mednikarova, I. 2003. "The accusative of the name of the deceased in Latin and Greek epitaphs." *ZPE* 143: 117–134.

Meiser, G. 1998. *Historische Laut- und Formenlehre der lateinischen Sprache.* Darmstadt.

Meister, K. 1916. *Lateinisch-griechische Eigennamen.* I: *Altitalische und römische Eigennamen.* Leipzig and Berlin.

Melzani, G. 1992. "Elementi della lingua d'uso nelle lettere di Plinio il Giovane." In P.V. Cova, R. Gazich, G.E. Manzoni and G. Melzani, eds., *Letteratura latina dell'Italia settentrionale. Cinque studi.* Milan: 197–244.

Mendell, C.W. 1917. *Latin Sentence Connection.* New Haven, CT.

Mercado, A.O. 2006a. "The Latin Saturnian and Italic verse." PhD thesis. University of California Los Angeles.

Mercado, A.O. 2006b. "Towards Proto-Indo-European metrics: The Italic saturnian reinterpreted." In G.-J. Pinault and D. Petit, eds., *La langue poétique indo-européenne. Actes du Colloque de travail de la Société des Études Indo-Européennes (Indogermanische Gesellschaft/ Society for Indo-European Studies), Paris, 22–24 octobre 2003.* Leuven and Paris: 299–316.

Mercado, A.O. 2008. "Italic and Celtic: Problems in the comparison of metrical systems." Paper presented at the XIII Fachtagung der Indogermanischen Gesellschaft, Salzburg.

Migliorini, B., and T. Gwynfor Griffith. 1984. *The Italian Language*. 2nd edn. London.

Mihaescu, H. 1978. *La langue latine dans le sud-est de l'Europe*. Bucarest and Paris.

Millar, F.G.B. 1968. "Local cultures in the Roman Empire: Libyan, Punic and Latin in Roman Africa." *JRS* 58: 126–134.

Millar, F.G.B. 1977. *The Emperor in the Roman World (31 BC–AD 337)*. London.

Millar, F.G.B. 1995. "Latin in the epigraphy of the Roman Near East." In Solin *et al.*, eds., 1995: 403–419.

Millar, F.G.B. 1998a. "Ethnic identity in the Roman Near East, 325–450: Language, religion and culture." *MedArch* 11: 159–176.

Millar, F.G.B. 1998b. *The Crowd in Rome in the Late Republic*. Ann Arbor, MI.

Millar, F.G.B. 2006. *A Greek Roman Empire: Power and Belief under Theodosius II (408–450)*. Berkeley, CA.

Miller, J.F. and A.J. Woodman, eds. 2010. *Poetry in the Early Empire: Generic Interactions*. [Mnemosyne Supplements 321]. Leiden.

Milroy, L., and P. Muysken, eds. 1995. *One Speaker, Two Languages: Cross-Disciplinary Perspectives on Code-Switching*. Cambridge and New York.

Mitchell, S. 1976. "Requisitioned transport in the Roman Empire: A new inscription from Pisidia." *JRS* 66: 106–131.

Mohl, F.G. 1899. *Introduction à la chronologie du latin vulgaire. Étude de philologie historique*. Paris.

Möhn, D. 1980. "Sondersprachen." In H.P. Althaus, H. Henne and H.E. Wiegand, eds., *Lexikon der Germanistischen Linguistik*. 2nd edn. Tübingen: 384–390.

Möhn, D., and R. Pelka. 1984. *Fachsprachen. Eine Einführung*. Tübingen.

Mohrmann, C. 1958–1977. *Études sur le latin des chrétiens*. 4 vols. I: 1958. *Le latin des chrétiens*. II: 1961. *Latin chrétien et médiéval*. III: 1965. *Latin chrétien et liturgique*. IV: 1977. *Latin Chrétien et latin médiéval*. Rome.

Money, D.K. 1998. *The English Horace: Anthony Alsop and the Tradition of British Latin Verse*. Oxford.

Moore, T.J. 2008. "When did the *tibicen* play? Meter and musical accompaniment in Roman comedy." *TAPhA* 138: 3–46.

Morello, R. 2003. "Pliny and the art of saying nothing." *Arethusa* 36: 187–209.

Mørland, H. 1932. *Die lateinischen Oribasiusübersetzungen*. [Symbolae Osloenses Fasc. Supplet. 5]. Oslo.

Morpurgo Davies, A. 1987. "The Greek notion of dialect." *Verbum* 10: 7–28.

Morstein-Marx, R. 2004. *Mass Oratory and Political Power in the Late Roman Republic*. Cambridge.

Morwood, J. 1991. "Aeneas, Augustus and the theme of the city." *G&R* 38: 212–223.

Mosci Sassi, M.G. 1992. *Il linguaggio gladiatorio*. Bologna.

Mosci Sassi, M.G. 1983. *Il "sermo castrensis."* Bologna.

Moser, H. 1959–1961. "'Umgangssprache.' Überlegungen zu ihren Formen und ihrer Stellung im Sprachganzen." *Zeitschrift für Mundartforschung* 27: 215–232.

Mourgues, J.-L. 1995. "Écrire en deux langues. Bilinguisme et pratique de chancellerie sous le Haut-Empire." *DHA* 21: 105–129.

Moussy, C., ed. 2005. *La composition et la préverbation en latin*. Paris.

Muecke, F. 2007. "The Satires." In S.J. Harrison, ed., *The Cambridge Companion to Horace*. Cambridge: 105–120.

Mullen, A. and P. James, eds. Forthcoming. *Multilingualism in the Graeco-Roman Worlds*. Cambridge.

Müller, A. 1905. 'Militaria aus Ammianus Marcellinus.' *Philologus* 18: 573–632.

Müller, R. 2001. *Sprachbewusstsein und Sprachvariation im lateinischen Schrifttum der Antike*. Munich.

Müller, R. 2007. "*Pura oratio* und *Puri sermonis amator.*" In P. Kruschwitz, W.-W. Ehlers and F. Felgentreu, eds., *Terentius Poeta.* [Zetemata Monographien zur klassischen Altertumswissenschaft 127]. Munich: 111–125.

Müller-Lancé, J. 1992. "Die Funktion vulgärlateinischer Elemente in den *Satiren* des Horaz am Beispiel von Sat. 2.5." In Iliescu and Marxgut, eds., 1992: 243–254.

Mundt, F. 2004. "Ciceros 'Commentarioli belli *Ciliciensis*'. *Fam.* 15.4 und andere Briefe aus Kilikien." *Philologus* 148: 255–273.

Muysken, P. 1997. "Code-switching processes." In M. Pütz, ed., *Language Choices.* Amsterdam: 361–380.

Muysken, P. 2000. *Bilingual Speech: A Typology of Code-Mixing.* Cambridge.

Myers-Scotton, C. 2006. *Multiple Voices: An Introduction to Bilingualism.* Malden, MA.

Mynors, R.A.B., ed. 1958. *C. Valerii Catulli Carmina.* Oxford.

Mynors, R.A.B. 1966. *Catullus Carmina. Codex Oxoniensis bibliothecae Bodleianae Canonicianus class. Lat. 30.* Leiden.

Nabrings, K. 1981. *Sprachliche Varietäten.* Tübingen.

Nauta, R.R. 2002. *Poetry for Patrons: Literary Communication in the Age of Domitian.* Leiden.

Neue, F., and C. Wagener. 1892–1905. *Formenlehre der lateinischen Sprache.* 4 vols. Berlin and Leipzig. Repr. 1985. Hildesheim.

Neumann, G., and J. Untermann, eds. 1980. *Die Sprachen im römischen Reich der Kaiserzeit.* Cologne and Bonn.

Nevalainen, T. 2004. "Letter writing." *Journal of Historical Pragmatics* 5: 181–191.

Nicholas, B. 1988. *An Introduction to Roman Law.* Oxford.

Nicholson, E.W.B. 1904. *Vinisius to Nigra: A Fourth Century Christian Letter Written in South Britain and Discovered at Bath.* London.

Nicolas, C. 1996. Utraque lingua. *Le calque sémantique: domaine gréco-latin.* Leuven and Paris.

Nisbet, R.G.M. 1963. "Persius." In J.P. Sullivan, ed., 1963. *Critical Essays on Roman Literature: Satire.* London: 39–71.

Nisbet, R.G.M. 1999. "Word order in Horace's *Odes.*" In Adams and Mayer, eds., 1999: 135–154.

Norberg, D. 1943. *Syntaktische Forschungen auf dem Gebiete des Spätlateins und des frühen Mittellateins.* Uppsala.

Norberg, D. 1944. *Beiträge zur spätlateinischen Syntax.* Uppsala.

Norberg, D. 1968. *Manuel pratique de latin médiéval.* Paris.

Norden, E. 1927. *P. Vergilius Maro* Aeneis *Buch VI.* Leipzig.

Noreña, C.F. 2007. "The social economy of Pliny's correspondence with Trajan." *AJPh* 128: 239–277.

Oakley, S.P. 1997. *A Commentary on Livy Books VI–X.* I: *Introduction and Book VI.* Oxford.

Oakley, S.P. 1998. *A Commentary on Livy. Books VI–X.* II: *Books VII and VIII.* Oxford.

Oakley, S.P. 2009. 'Style and language.' In A.J. Woodman, ed., *The Cambridge Companion to Tacitus.* Cambridge: 195–211.

Oates, J.F., R.S. Bagnall, S.J. Clackson, A.A. O'Brien, J.D. Sosin, T.G. Wilfong and K.A. Worp. *Checklist of Greek, Latin, Demotic and Coptic Papyri, Ostraca and Tablets.* http://scriptorium.lib.duke.edu/papyrus/texts/clist.html (accessed February 2011). 5th print edn. 2001, Oakville, CT, and Oxford.

Oberhelman, S.M. 1987. 'The provenance of the style of Ammianus Marcellinus.' *QUCC* 27: 79–89.

Odelman, E. 1972. *Études sur quelques reflets du style administratif chez César.* Stockholm.

Ogilvie, R.M. 1970. *A Commentary on Livy Books 1–5.* 2nd edn. Oxford.

Oliver, J.H. 1989. *Greek Constitutions of Early Roman Emperors from Inscriptions and Papyri.* [Memoirs of the American Philosophical Society 178]. London and New York.

Oliver, R.P. 1949. "The Claudian letter Ⱶ." *AJA* 53: 249–257.

Oliver, R.P. 1966. "Apex and Sicilicus." *AJPh* 87: 129–170.

Omeltchenko, S. 1977. *A Quantitative and Comparative Study of the Vocalism of the Latin Inscriptions of North Africa, Britain, Dalmatia, and the Balkans* [University of North Carolina Studies in the Romance Languages and Literatures 180]. Chapel Hill, NC.

Oniga, R. 1988. *I composti nominali latini. Una morfologia generativa.* Bologna.

Oniga, R. 1995. *Sallustio e l'etnografia.* [Biblioteca di 'Materiali e discussioni per l'analisi dei testi classici' 12]. Pisa.

Orlandini, A. 1995. "De la connexion. Une analyse pragmatique des connecteurs latins *atqui* et *immo.*" *Lalies* 15: 259–269.

Orlandini, A. 1997. "Adverbes d'énoncé et adverbes d'énonciation en latin: *forte, fortasse.*" *Lalies* 17: 251–260.

Österreicher, W. 1995. "'L'oral dans l'écrit'. Essaie d'une typologie à partir des sources du latin vulgaire." In Callebat, ed., 1995: 145–157.

Palmer, L.R. 1954. *The Latin Language.* London.

Papaconstantinou, A. 2010. *The Multilingual Experience in Egypt: From the Ptolemies to the Abbasids.* Farnham.

Parkes, M.B. 1993. *Pause and Effect: An Introduction to the History of Punctuation in the West.* Berkeley, CA.

Parsons, J. 1999. "A new approach to the Saturnian verse and its relation to Latin prosody." *TAPhA* 129: 117–137.

Pascucci, G. 1968. "Aspetti del latino giuridico." *SIFC* 40: 3–43.

Patzner, F. 1910. *De parataxis usu in Ciceronis epistulis praecipuo.* [Dissertationes philologae Vindobonenses 9.2]. Vienna: 119–184.

Penny, R. 2000. *Variation and Change in Spanish.* Cambridge.

Penny, R. 2002. *History of the Spanish Language.* 2nd edn. Cambridge.

Peremans, W. 1983. "Les ἑρμηνεῖς dans l'Égypte gréco-romaine." In *Das römisch-byzantinische Ägypten. Akten des internationalen Symposions 26.-30. September 1978 in Trier* [Aegyptiaca Treverensia 2]. Mainz: 11–17.

Peretz, D. 2006. "The Roman interpreter and his diplomatic and military roles." *Historia* 55: 451–470.

Perini, G.B. 1983. "Le 'riforme' ortografiche latine di età repubblicana." *AION (sez. linguistica)* 5: 141–169.

Perl, G. 1971. "Die Einführung der griechischen Buchstaben Y und Z in das lateinischen Alphabet." *Philologus* 115: 196–233.

Perrot, J. 1961. *Les dérivés latins en* -men *et* -mentum. Paris.

Peruzzi, E. 1963. "L' iscrizione di Vendia." *Maia* 15: 89–92.

Petersmann, H. 1989. "Die Urbanisierung des römischen Reiches im Lichte der lateinischen Sprache." *Gymnasium* 96: 406–428.

Petersmann, H. 1994. "De linguae Latinae origine atque de eius in Imperio Romano uso publico." In S. Albert, J. Kramer, and W. Schweickard, eds., *Miscellanea ad linguam Latinam linguasque recentiores attinentia.* Veitshöchheim: 5–10.

Petersmann, H. 1998. "Zur Sprach- und Kulturpolitik in der Klassischen Antike." *SCI* 17: 87–101.

Petersmann, H. 1999. "The language of early Roman satire: Its functions and characteristics." In Adams and Mayer, eds., 1999: 289–310.

Petersmann, H. 2002–2003. "Bedeutung und Gebrauch von lateinisch *fui*. Eine soziolinguistische Analyse." *Die Sprache* 43: 94–103.

Petersmann, H., and R. Kettemann eds. 1999. *Latin vulgaire – Latin tardif V. Actes du Ve Colloque international sur le latin vulgaire et tardif (Heidelberg, 5–8 septembre 1997).* Heidelberg.

Phillips, E.J. 1977. *Corpus signorum imperii Romani. Corpus of Sculpture of the Roman World. Great Britain.* I, fasc. I: *Corbridge, Hadrian's Wall East of the North Tyne.* Oxford.

Pighi, G.B. 1964. *Lettere latine d'un soldato di Traiano; P.Mich 467–472. Nuova edizione critica e commento con la traduzione latina di P.Mich, 465–466, 473–481, 485–487*. Bologna.

Pinkster, H. 1972. *On Latin Adverbs*. Amsterdam.

Pinkster, H. 1987. "The strategy and chronology of the development of future and perfect tense auxiliaries in Latin." In M. Harris and P. Ramat, eds., *Historical Development of Auxiliaries*. Berlin: 193–223.

Pinkster, H. 1990a. *Latin Syntax and Semantics*. London and New York.

Pinkster, H. 1990b. "The development of cases and adpositions in Latin." In H. Pinkster and I. Genee, eds., *Unity in Diversity: Papers Presented to Simon C. Dik on his 50th Birthday*. Dordrecht: 195–209.

Pinkster, H. 2004. "Attitudinal and illocutionary satellites in Latin." In H. Aartsen, M. Hannay and R. Lyall, eds., *Words in Their Places. A Festschrift for J. Lachlan Mackenzie*. Amsterdam: 191–198.

Pinkster, H. 2010. "Notes on the language of M. Caelius Rufus." In Dickey and Chahoud, eds., 2010: 189–205.

Pirson, J. 1901. *La langue des inscriptions latines de la Gaule*. Brussels.

Pirson, J. 1906. "*Mulomedicina Chironis*. La syntaxe du verbe." *Festschrift zum XII. Allgemeinen Deutschen Neuphilologentage*. Erlangen: 390–431.

Plass, P. 1988. *Wit and the Writing of History: The Rhetoric of Historiography in Imperial Rome*. Madison.

Plaza, M., ed. 2009. *Oxford Readings in Classical Studies: Persius and Juvenal*. Oxford.

Poccetti, P. 2005. "Notes de linguistique italique. 2: En marge de la nouvelle attestation du *perfectum* falisque *faced/facet*: le latin de Préneste *vhevhaked* et le falisque *fifiked*." *REL* 83: 27–35.

Poccetti, P. 2010. "Greeting and farewell expressions as evidence for colloquial language: between literary and epigraphical texts." In Dickey and Chahoud, eds., 2010: 100–126.

Poccetti, P., D. Poli and C. Santini. 1999. *Una storia della lingua latina. Formazione, usi, comunicazione*, Rome.

Polanyi, L., and R. Scha 1983. "On the recursive structure of discourse." In K. Ehlich and H. van Riemsdijk, eds., *Connectedness in Sentence, Discourse and Text*. Tilburg: 141–178.

Politzer, R.L. 1952. "On *b* and *v* in Latin and Romance." *Word* 8: 211–215.

Polomé, E.C. 1983. "The linguistic situation in the western provinces of the Roman Empire." *ANRW* II.29.2: 509–553.

Poplack, S. 1980. "Sometimes I'll start a sentence in Spanish Y TERMINO EN ESPAÑOL: toward a typology of code-switching." *Linguistics* 18.7–8: 581–618.

Portalupi, F. 1989. "Umgangssprache e Kunstsprache in Frontone." *Civiltà classica e cristiana* 10: 147–167.

Powell, J.G.F. 1988. *Cicero, Cato Maior de Senectute, Edited with an Introduction and Commentary*. [Cambridge Classical Texts and Commentaries 28]. Cambridge.

Powell, J.G.F. 1990. *Cicero: On Friendship and* The Dream of Scipio *(Laelius de amicitia et somnium Scipionis)*. Warminster.

Powell, J.G.F. 1999. "Stylistic registers in Juvenal." In Adams and Mayer, eds., 1999: 311–334.

Powell, J.G.F. 2001. "'Juvenal's style.' Review of H.J. Urech, *Hoher und niederer Stil in den Satiren Juvenals*, Bern 1999." *CR* 51: 43–44.

Powell, J.G.F. 2005a. "Cicero's adaptation of legal Latin in the *De legibus*." In Adams, Reinhardt and Lapidge, eds., 2005: 117–150.

Powell, J.G.F. 2005b. "Dialogues and treatises." In Harrison, ed., 2005: 223–240.

Powell, J.G.F. 2007a. "A new text of the *Appendix Probi*." *CQ* 57: 687–700.

Powell, J.G.F. 2007b. "Invective and the orator: Ciceronian theory and practice." In Booth, ed., 2007: 1–23.

Powell, J.G.F., ed. 2007c. *Logos: Rational Argument in Classical Rhetoric* [BICS Supplement 96]. London.

Powell, J.G.F. 2010. "Hyperbaton and register in Cicero." In Dickey and Chahoud, eds., 2010: 167–188.

Powell, J.G.F. Forthcoming. "Cicero's style." In C. Steel, ed., *The Cambridge Companion to Cicero*. Cambridge.

Proskauer, C. 1909. *Das auslautende -s auf den lateinischen Inschriften*. Strasbourg.

Pryor, J.H. 1996. "Commerce." In Mantello and Rigg, eds., 1996: 307–314.

Puelma, M. 1980. "Cicero als Platon-Übersetzer." *MH* 37: 137–178.

Pulgram, E. 1975. *Latin–Romance Phonology: Prosodics and Metrics*. Munich.

Questa, C. 1995. *Titi Macci Plauti Cantica*. Urbino.

Questa, C. 2007. *La metrica di Plauto e di Terenzio*. Urbino.

Ramminger, J. 2009. *Neulateinische Wortliste 1300–1700* (http://www.lrz-muenchen. de/~ramminger/).

Ramsey, J. 2007. "Roman senatorial oratory." In Dominik and Hall, eds., 2007: 122–135.

Raven, D.S. 1965. *Latin Metre: An Introduction*. London.

Rawson, E. 1979. "L. Cornelius Sisenna and the early first century BC." *CQ* 29: 327–346.

Redard, G. 1956. "Le rajeunissement du texte de Plaute." In *Hommages à Max Niedermann* [Collection Latomus 23]. Brussels: 296–306.

Rees, R. 2007. "Panegyric." In Dominik and Hall, eds., 2007: 136–148.

Regula, M. 1951. "Besonderheiten der lateinischen Syntax und Stilistik als Vorspiele romanischer Ausdrucksweisen." *Glotta* 31: 158–198.

Reinhardt, T., M. Lapidge and J.N. Adams, eds. 2005. *Aspects of the Language of Latin Prose* [Proceedings of the British Academy 129]. Oxford.

Reynolds, L.D., ed. 1983. *Texts and Transmission*. Oxford.

Reynolds, L.D., and N.G. Wilson, eds. 1991. *Scribes and Scholars: A Guide to the Transmission of Greek and Latin Literature*. 3rd edn. Oxford.

Reynolds, S. 1990. "*Ad Auctorum Expositionem*: Syntactic theory and interpretative practice in the twelfth century." *Histoire épistémologie langage* 12: 31–51.

Ribbeck, O., ed. 1897–1898. *Scaenicae Romanorum poesis fragmenta*. 2 vols. 3rd edn. Leipzig.

Rice-Holmes, T. 1911. *Caesar's Conquest of Gaul*. 2nd edn. Oxford.

Ricottilli, J. 2003. "La lingua d'uso in Orazio." In J.B. Hofmann, *La lingua d'uso latina*. Bologna: 465–509.

Ridgway, D. 1992. *The First Western Greeks*. Cambridge and New York.

Riemann, O. 1885. *Études sur la langue et la grammaire de Tite-Live*. 2nd edn. Paris.

Rigg, A.G. 1986. "Latin language." In J.R. Strayer, ed., *Dictionary of the Middle Ages*, VII. New York: 350–359.

Riggsby, A.M. 1991. "Elision and hiatus in Latin prose." *CA* 10: 328–343.

Risch, E. 1979. "Zur altlateinischen Gebetssprache." *Incontri linguistici* 5: 43–53 = 1981. A. Etter and M. Looser, eds., *Ernst Risch: Kleine Schriften zum siebzigsten Geburtstag*. Berlin and New York: 633–643.

Risselada, R. 1993. *Imperatives and Other Directive Expressions in Latin: A Study in the Pragmatics of a Dead Language*. Amsterdam.

Risselada, R. 1994. "*Modo* and *sane*, or what to do with particles in Latin directives." In Herman, ed., 1994: 319–343.

Risselada, R. 1996. "And now for something completely different? Temporal discourse markers: Latin *nunc* and English *now*." In R. Risselada, J.R. de Jong, and A.M. Bolkestein, eds., *On Latin. Linguistic and Literary Studies in Honour of Harm Pinkster*. Amsterdam: 105–125.

Risselada, R. 1998. "The discourse functions of *sane*: Latin marker of agreement in description, interaction and concession." *Journal of Pragmatics* 30: 225–244.

Rix, H. 1992. "Zur Entstehung des lateinischen Perfektparadigmas." In O. Panagl and T. Krisch, eds., *Latein und Indogermanisch. Akten des Kolloquiums der Indogermanischen Gesellschaft, 23.–26. September 1986.* Innsbruck: 221–240.

Rizakis, A. 1995. "Le grec face au latin. Le paysage linguistique dans la péninsule balkanique sous l'Empire." In Solin *et al.*, eds., 1995: 373–391.

Rochette, B. 1997. *Le latin dans le monde grec. Recherches sur la diffusion de la langue et des lettres latines dans les provinces hellénophones de l'Empire romain* [Collection Latomus 233]. Brussels.

Rochette, B. 2000. "La langue des testaments dans l'Égypte du IIIe s. ap. J. C." *RIDA* 47: 449–461.

Rochette, B. 2010. "Greek and Latin bilingualism." In Bakker, ed., 2010: 281–293.

Roelcke, T. 1999. *Fachsprachen.* Berlin.

Rohlfs, G. 1969. *Grammatica storica della lingua italiana et dei suoi dialetti. III: Sintassi e formazione delle parole.* Turin.

Romaine, S. 1995. *Bilingualism.* 2nd edn. Oxford.

Rönsch, H. 1869. *Itala und Vulgata. Das Sprachidiom der urchristlichen Itala und der katholischen Vulgata.* Marburg.

Rosén, H. 1994a. "*Demum*: A message-articulating particle." In J. De Clerq and P. Desmet, eds., *Florilegium historiographiae linguisticae. Études d'historiographie de la linguistique et de grammaire comparée à la memoire de Maurice Leroy.* Louvain-la-Neuve: 173–184.

Rosén, H. 1994b. "The definite article in the making, nominal constituent order and related phenomena." In Herman, ed., 1994: 129–150.

Rosén, H. 1999. Latine Loqui: *Trends and Directions in the Crystallization of Classical Latin.* Munich.

Rosén, H. 2009. "Coherence, sentence modification and sentence-part modification: the contribution of particles." In Baldi and Cuzzolin, eds., 2009: 301–424.

Ross, A.S.C. 1954. "Linguistic class-indicators in present-day English." *NphM* 55: 113–149.

Roulet, E. 2006. "The description of text relation markers in the Geneva model of discourse organization." In Fischer, ed., 2006: 115–131.

Roulet, E., A. Auchlin, M. Schelling, J. Moeschler and C. Rubattel. 1985. *L'articulation du discours en français contemporain.* Bern.

Roulet, E., L. Filliettaz, A. Grobet and M. Burger. 2001. *Un modèle et un instrument d'analyse de l'organisation du discours.* Bern.

Rouse, W.H.D. 1935. *Scenes from Sixth-Form Life.* Oxford.

Rubin, Z. 2002. "*Res gestae divi saporis*: Greek and Middle Iranian in a document of Sassanian anti-Roman propaganda." In Adams, Janse and Swain, eds., 2002: 267–297.

Rubinstein, L. 2003. "Volunteer prosecutors in the Greek world." *Dike* 6: 88–113.

Rudd, N. 1960. "Horace on the origins of *satura*." *Phoenix* 14: 36–44.

Rudd, N. 1976. "Association of ideas in Persius." In N. Rudd, *Lines of Enquiry.* Cambridge: 54–83 = Plaza, ed., 2009: 107–137.

Rudd, N. 1987. *Horace, Satires and Epistles. Persius, Satires.* Harmondsworth.

Rudd, N. 1991. *Juvenal: The Satires. A New Translation.* Oxford.

Rushton Fairclough, H. 1918. *Virgil, II. Aeneid VII–XII. The Minor Poems.* [Loeb Classical Library]. London and New York.

Russell, D.A. 1990. *An Anthology of Latin Prose.* Oxford.

Russell, D.A. 2001. *Quintilian: The Orator's Education.* 5 vols. [Loeb Classical Library]. Cambridge, MA.

Russell, D.A.F.M. 1964. *'Longinus' On the Sublime.* Oxford.

Russell, P. 1988. "The Celtic preverb 'uss and related matters." *Ériu* 39: 95–126.

Russell, P. Forthcoming. "*An habes linguam Latinam? Non tam bene sapio:* views of multilingualism from the early-medieval west." In Mullen and James, eds., forthcoming.

Rutledge, S.H. 2007. "Oratory and politics in the empire." In Dominik and Hall, eds., 2007: 109–121.

Sabbadini, R. 1885. *Storia del ciceronianismo e di altre questioni letterarie nell'età della rinascenza.* Turin.

Sage, E.T., and A.C. Schlesinger. 1938. *Livy, XII. Books XL–XLII.* [Loeb Classical Library]. London and Cambridge, MA.

Sager, J.C., D. Dungworth and P.F. McDonald. 1980. *English Special Languages: Principles and Practice in Science and Technology.* Wiesbaden.

Saller, R. 2001. "The family and society." In J. Bodel, ed., *Epigraphic Evidence: Ancient History from Inscriptions.* London and New York: 95–117.

Salonius, A.H. 1920. *Vitae Patrum: Kritische Untersuchungen über Text, Syntax und Wortschatz der spätlateinischen Vitae Patrum (B. III, V, VI, VII).* Lund.

Sampson, G. 1985. *Writing Systems.* Stanford, CA.

Santini, C., N. Scivoletto and L. Zurli, eds., 1990–1998. *Prefazioni, prologhi, proemi di opere tecnico-scientifiche latine.* 3 vols. Rome.

Sartre, M. 2001. "Les colonies romaines dans le monde grec." *Electrum* 5: 111–152.

Savory, T.H. 1967. *The Language of Science.* Rev. edn. London.

Scafuro, A.C. 1989. "Livy's comic narrative of the Bacchanalia." *Helios* 16: 119–142.

Scappaticcio, M.C. 2009. "Virgilio, allievi e maestri a Vindolanda. Per un'edizione di nuovi documenti dal forte britannico." *ZPE* 169: 59–70.

Schaad, D., and M. Genin. 2007. *La Graufesenque (Millau, Aveyron).* 2 vols. Pessac.

Scheidel, W. 2005. "Human mobility in Roman Italy, II: The slave population." *JRS* 95: 64–79.

Schenkeveld, D.M. 1988. "From particula to particle: The genesis of a class of words." In I. Rosier, ed., *L'heritage des grammairiens latins de l'Aantiquité aux lumières.* Louvain-la-Neuve: 81–93.

Schifko, P. 1992. "Morphologische Interferenzen im Bereich des fachsprachlichen Wortschatzes." In J. Albrecht and R. Baum, eds., *Fachsprache und Terminologie in Geschichte und Gegenwart.* Tübingen: 295–301.

Schironi, F. 2010. "Technical languages: Science and medicine." In Bakker, ed., 2010: 338–353.

Schlesinger, A.C. 1951. *Livy, XIII. Books XLIII–XLV* [Loeb Classical Library]. London and Cambridge, MA.

Schlicher, J.J. 1915. "The historical infinitive. III: Imitation and decline." *CPh* 10: 54–74.

Schmitt, R. 1983. "Die Sprachverhältnisse in den östlichen Provinzen des römischen Reiches." *ANRW* II.29.2: 554–586.

Schrickx, J. In press. *Lateinische Modalpartikeln:* nempe, quippe, scilicet, videlicet *und* nimirum. Leiden.

Schrijnen, J. 1932. *Charakteristik des altchristlichen Latein.* Nijmegen.

Schulz, F. 1951. *Classical Roman Law.* Oxford.

Sciarrino, E. 2007. "Roman oratory before Cicero: The Elder Cato and Gaius Gracchus." In Dominik and Hall, eds., 2007: 54–66.

Sedgwick, W.B. 1930. "The dating of Plautus' plays." *CQ* 24: 102–6.

Sedley, D. 1999. "Lucretius' use and avoidance of Greek." In Adams and Mayer, eds., 1999: 227–246.

Shackleton Bailey, D.R. 1965–1970. *Cicero's Letters to Atticus I–VII.* [Cambridge Classical Texts and Commentaries 3–9]. Cambridge.

Shackleton Bailey, D.R. 1977. *Cicero: Epistulae ad Familiares I–II.* [Cambridge Classical Texts and Commentaries 16–17]. Cambridge.

Shackleton Bailey, D.R. 1978. *Cicero's Letters to His Friends 1–2.* Harmondsworth.

Shackleton Bailey, D.R. 1980. *Cicero: Epistulae ad Quintum Fratrem et M. Brutum.* [Cambridge Classical Texts and Commentaries 22]. Cambridge.

Shackleton Bailey, D.R. 2000. *Valerius Maximus. Memorable Doings and Sayings.* 2 vols. [Loeb Classical Library]. London and Cambridge, MA.

Shackleton Bailey, D.R. 2001. *Cicero. Letters to Friends.* II [Loeb Classical Library]. London and Cambridge, MA.

Sheerin, D. 1996. "The liturgy." In Mantello and Rigg, eds., 1996: 157–182.

Sherk, R.K. 1969. *Roman Documents from the Greek East:* Senatus Consulta *and* Epistulae *to the Age of Augustus.* Baltimore, MD.

Sherwin-White, A.N. 1966. *The Letters of Pliny: A Historical and Social Commentary.* Oxford.

Shipp, G.P. 1953. "Greek in Plautus." *WS* 66: 105–112.

Shipp, G.P. 1955. "Plautine terms for Greek and Roman things." *Glotta* 34: 139–152.

Shipp, G.P. 1979. *Modern Greek Evidence for the Ancient Greek Vocabulary.* Sydney.

Sidwell, K. 1995. *Reading Medieval Latin.* Cambridge.

Sihler, A.L. 1995. *New Comparative Grammar of Greek and Latin.* Oxford and New York.

Sinclair, P. 1995. *Tacitus the Sententious Historian: A Sociology of Rhetoric in* Annals *1–6.* University Park, PA.

Sittl, K. 1882. *Die lokalen Verschiedenheiten der lateinischen Sprache mit besonderer Berücksichtigung des afrikanischen Lateins.* Erlangen.

Sjögren, H. 1906. *Zum Gebrauch des Futurums im Altlateinischen.* Uppsala.

Skutsch, O. 1985. *The Annals of Quintus Ennius.* Oxford.

Smith, C.C. 1983. "Vulgar Latin in Roman Britain: Epigraphic and other evidence." *ANRW* II.29.2: 893–948.

Smith, M.S. 1975. *Petronii Arbitri Cena Trimalchionis.* Oxford.

Solin, H. 1996. *Die stadtrömischen Sklavennamen. Ein Namenbuch I–III.* [Forschungen zur antiken Sklaverei, Beiheft 2]. Stuttgart.

Solin, H., O. Salomies and U.-M. Liertz, eds. 1995. *Acta Colloquii Epigraphici Latini, Helsinki 3–6 September* [Commentationes Humanarum Litterarum, 104]. Helsinki.

Solodow, J.B. 1978. *The Latin Particle* quidem. Boulder, CO.

Solodow, J.B. 1979. "Livy and the story of Horatius 1.24–26." *TAPhA* 109: 251–268.

Sommer, F. and R. Pfister. 1977. *Handbuch der lateinischen Laut- und Formenlehre.* 4th rev. edn. Heidelberg.

Sörbom, G. 1935. *Variatio sermonis Tacitei aliaeque apud eundem quaestiones selectae.* Uppsala.

Soubiran, J. 1966. *L' élision dans la poésie latine.* Paris.

Soubiran, J. 1988. *Essai sur la versification dramatique des Romains. Sénaire iambique et septénaire trochaïque.* Paris.

Spevak, O. 2006. "*Tamen.* Essai de description syntaxique." *Glotta* 82: 221–248.

Spilman, M. 1932. *Cumulative Sentence Building in Latin Historical Narrative.* Berkeley.

Steel, C. 2003. "Cicero's *Brutus:* The end of oratory and the beginning of history?" *BICS* 46: 195–211.

Steel, C. 2006. *Roman Oratory* [Greece and Rome New Surveys in the Classics 36]. Cambridge.

Steel, C. 2007. "Lost orators of Rome." In Dominik and Hall, eds., 2007: 237–249.

Steele, R.B. 1891. *Chiasmus in Sallust, Caesar, Tacitus and Justinus.* Northfield.

Steele, R.B. 1900. "The Greek in Cicero's Epistles." *AJPh* 21: 387–410.

Steele, R.B. 1901. "Anaphora and chiasmus in Livy." *TAPhA* 32: 154–185.

Stefenelli, A. 1962. *Die Volkssprache im Werk des Petron im Hinblick auf die romanischen Sprachen.* Vienna.

Stephens, L. 1985. "Indirect questions in Old Latin: Syntactic and pragmatic factors conditioning modal shift." *Illinois Classical Studies* 10: 195–214.

Stevenson, J. 2005. *Women Latin Poets: Language, Gender, and Authority, from Antiquity to the Eighteenth Century.* Oxford.

Stibbe, C.M., G. Colonna, C. de Simone and H.S. Versnel. 1980. *Lapis Satricanus: Archaeological, Epigraphical, Linguistical and Historical Aspects of the New Inscription from Satricum.* The Hague.

Stotz, P. 1996–2004. *Handbuch zur lateinischen Sprache des Mittelalters.* 5 vols. Munich.

Strecker, K. 1929/1957. *Introduction to Medieval Latin.* Trans. R.B. Palmer. Dublin.

Stroh, W. 1979. "Der deutsche Vers und die Lateinschule." *Antike und Abendland* 25: 1–19.

Stroh, W. 1990. "Arsis und Thesis, oder: Wie hat man lateinische Verse gesprochen?" In M. von Albrecht and W. Schubert, eds., *Musik und Dichtung: Neue Forschungsbeiträge, Viktor Pöschl zum 80. Geburtstag gewidmet.* Frankfurt am Main: 87–116.

Sturtevant, E.H. 1919. "The coincidence of accent and ictus in the Roman dactylic poets." *CPh* 14: 373–385.

Sturtevant, E.H. 1923. "Harmony and clash of accent and ictus in the Latin hexameter." *TAPhA* 54: 51–73.

Sturtevant, E.H. 1940. *The Pronunciation of Greek and Latin.* 2nd edn. Philadelphia.

Susini, G. 1973. *The Roman Stonecutter. An Introduction to Latin Epigraphy.* Oxford.

Svennung, J. 1932. *Wortstudien zu den spätlateinischen Oribasiusrezensionen.* Uppsala.

Svennung, J. 1935. *Untersuchungen zu Palladius und zur lateinischen Fach- und Volkssprache.* Lund.

Svennung, J. 1936. *Kleine Beiträge zur lateinischen Lautlehre.* Uppsala.

Swain, S. 2002. "Bilingualism in Cicero? The evidence of code-switching." In Adams, Swain and Janse, eds., 2002: 128–167.

Swain, S. 2004. "Bilingualism and biculturalism in Antonine Rome." In L. Holford-Strevens and A. Vardi, eds., *The Worlds of Aulus Gellius.* Oxford: 3–40.

Syme, R. 1939. *The Roman Revolution.* Oxford.

Syme, R. 1958. *Tacitus.* Oxford.

Szantyr, A. 1963. *Lateinische Syntax und Stilistik.* Munich.

Tamerle, E. 1926. *Der lateinische Vers ein akzenturierender Vers.* Innsbruck.

Tamm, D. 1997. *Roman Law and European Legal History.* Copenhagen.

Tarrant, R.J. 1998. "Parenthetically speaking (in Virgil and other poets)." In P.E. Knox and C. Foss, eds., *Style and Tradition: Studies in Honor of Wendell Clausen.* Stuttgart: 141–157.

Taylor, D.J. 1974. Declinatio: *A Study of the Linguistic Theory of Marcus Terentius Varro.* Amsterdam.

Thielmann, P. 1885. "*Habere* mit dem Infinitiv und die Entstehung des romanischen Futurums." *ALL* 2: 48–89, 157–202.

Thomas, R.F. 1982. *Lands and Peoples in Roman Poetry.* Cambridge.

Thomas, R.F. 2010. "Grist to the mill: The literary uses of the quotidian in Horace, *Satire* 1.5." In Dickey and Chahoud, eds., 2010: 255–265.

Thomason, S.G. 2001. *Language Contact: An Introduction.* Edinburgh.

Thomason, S.G. 2003. "Contact as a source of language change." In B.D. Joseph and R.D. Janda, eds., *The Handbook of Historical Linguistics.* London: 687–712.

Thomason, S.G., and T. Kaufman. 1988. *Language Contact, Creolization, and Genetic Linguistics.* Berkeley, Los Angeles and Oxford.

Thompson, E.M. 2008. *An Introduction to Greek and Latin Palaeography.* Rev. edn. of 1912 edn. Richmond.

Thomson, D.F.S. 1986. "On the Latin style of some French humanists." In C.M. Grisé and C.D.E. Tolton, eds. *Crossroads and Perspectives: French Literature of the Renaissance. Studies in Honour of Victor E. Graham.* Geneva: 77–100.

Thomson, D.F.S. 2003. *Catullus. Edited with a Textual and Interpretative Commentary* [Phoenix Supplementary Volume 34]. Rev. edn. Toronto.

Thulin, C. 1906. *Italische sakrale Poesie und Prosa: Eine metrische Untersuchung.* Berlin.

Tichy, E. 2006. *A Survey of Proto-Indo-European.* Trans. J.E. Cathey. Bremen.

Tomlin, R.S.O. 1993. "Votive objects: The inscribed lead tablets." In A. Woodward and P. Leach. *The Uley Shrines: Excavation of a Ritual Complex on West Hill, Uley, Gloucestershire, 1977–79.* London: 113–130.

Tomlin, R.S.O. 1994. "Vinisius to Nigra: Evidence from Oxford of Christianity in Roman Britain." *ZPE* 100: 93–108.

Tomlin, R.S.O., R.P. Wright and M.W.C. Hassall. 2009. *Roman Inscriptions of Britain. III: Inscriptions on Stone, Found or Notified between 1 January 1955 and 31 December 2006.* Oxford and Oakville, CT.

Touratier, C., ed. 2005. *Essais de phonologie latine.* Aix-en-Provence.

Tournoy, G., and T.O. Tunberg, 1996. "On the margins of Latinity? Neo-Latin and the vernacular languages." *HLov* 45: 134–175.

Trahman, C.R. 1951. "The attitude of the Roman administration toward Latin and Greek." *CB* 27: 51–53; 56–57.

Trappes-Lomax, J.M. 2007. *Catullus: A Textual Reappraisal.* Swansea.

Trisoglio, F. 1984. "La lettera di raccomandazione nell'epistolario ciceroniano." *Latomus* 43: 751–775.

Tunberg, T.O. 1997. "Ciceronian Latin: Longolius and others." *HLov* 46: 13–61.

Turner, E.G. 1961. "Latin versus Greek as a universal language: The attitude of Diocletian." In *Language and Society: Essays Presented to A.M. Jensen on his Seventieth Birthday.* Copenhagen: 165–168.

Tyrrell, R.Y., and L.C. Purser. 1904. *The Correspondence of M. Tullius Cicero, Arranged According to Its Chronological Order; With a Revision of the Text, a Commentary and Introductory Essays.* Dublin and London. Repr. 1969. Hildesheim.

Uddholm, A. 1953. Formulae Marculfi. *Études sur la langue et le style.* Uppsala.

Ullmann, R. 1927. *La technique des discours dans Salluste, Tite-Live et Tacite. La matière et la composition.* Oslo.

Untermann, J. 2000. *Wörterbuch des Oskisch-Umbrischen.* Heidelberg.

Urbanova, D. 1999. "La paleografia delle iscrizioni latine arcaiche." *Atti del XI congresso internazionale di epigrafia greca e Latina; Roma, 18–24 settembre 1997.* Rome: 477–492.

Utard, R. 2004. *Le discours indirect chez les historiens latins: Écriture ou oralité?* Louvain/Paris.

Väänänen, V. 1965. *Étude sur le texte et la langue des* Tablettes Albertini [Annales Academiae Scientiarum Fennicae B 141:2]. Helsinki: 26–57.

Väänänen, V. 1966. *Le latin vulgaire des inscriptions pompéiennes.* 3rd edn. Berlin.

Väänänen V. 1981. *Introduction au latin vulgaire.* 3rd edn. Paris.

Väänänen, V. 1983. "Le problème de la diversification du latin." *ANRW* II.29.1: 480–506.

Väänänen, V. 1987. *Le journal-épître d'Égérie (Itinerarium Egeriae). Étude linguistique.* Helsinki.

Väänänen, V. 2003. *Introduzione al latino volgare.* Ed. A. Limentani, trans. A. Grandesso Silvestri. 4th edn. Bologna.

Vainio, R. 1999. *Latinitas and Barbarisms According to the Roman Grammarians.* Turku.

Vairel-Carron, H. 1975. *Exclamation, ordre et défense. Analyse de deux systèmes syntaxiques en latin.* Paris.

van den Hout, M.P.J. 1999. *A Commentary on the Letters of M. Cornelius Fronto.* [Mnemosyne Supplement 190]. Leiden.

van Gils, L. 2003. "Narrative techniques compared in discourse and correspondence." In Garcea, ed., 2003: 47–72.

van Oorde, W. 1929. *Lexicon Aetherianum.* Amsterdam.

Ventura, I. 2007. *Bartholomaeus Anglicus: De proprietatibus rerum,* VI. Turnhout.

Vielliard, J. 1927. *Le latin des diplômes royaux et chartes privées de l'époque mérovingienne.* Paris.

Viljamaa, T. 1983. *Infinitive of Narration in Livy: A Study in Narrative Technique.* [Annales Universitatis Turkuensis Ser. B, t. 162]. Turku.

Vincent, N. 1997. "Synthetic and analytic structures." In M. Maiden and M. Parry, eds., *The Dialects of Italy.* London and New York: 99–105.

Vine, B. 1993. *Studies in Archaic Latin Inscriptions.* Innsbruck.

Vine, B. 1998. "Remarks on the Archaic Latin 'Garigliano Bowl' inscription." *ZPE* 121: 257–262.

Vollgraff, C.W. 1917. "De tabella emptionis aetatis Traiani nuper in Frisia reperta." *Mnemosyne* 45: 341–352.

Vollmer, F. 1898. *P. Papinii Statii Silvarum Libri.* Leipzig.

von Albrecht, M. 1989. *Masters of Roman Prose.* Trans. N. Adkin. Leeds.

von Albrecht, M. 2003. *Cicero's Style: A Synopsis* [Mnemosyne Supplement 245]. Leiden and Boston.

Voss, B.-R. 1963. *Der pointierte Stil des Tacitus.* Münster.

Waarsenburg, D.J. 1997. "*Lapis Satricanus minor.* New light on an old photograph of the *Lapis Satricanus.*" *Mededelingen van het Nederlands Instituut te Rome* 56: 197–200.

Wachter, R. 1987. *Altlateinische Inschriften. Sprachliche und epigraphische Untersuchungen zu den Dokumenten bis etwa 150 v. Chr.* Bern.

Wachter, R. 1989. "Zur Vorgeschichte des griechischen Alphabets." *Kadmos* 28: 19–78.

Wacke, A. 1993. "Gallisch, Punisch, Syrisch oder Griechisch statt Latein? Zur schrittweisen Gleichberechtigung der Geschäftssprachen im Römischen Reich." *ZSS* 110: 14–59.

Wackernagel, J. 2009. *Lectures on Syntax: With Special Reference to Greek, Latin, and Germanic.* Ed. and trans. D.R. Langslow. Oxford.

Walde, A., and J.B. Hofmann. 1938–1956. *Lateinisches etymologisches Wörterbuch.* 3rd edn. Heidelberg.

Wallace, R. 1989. "The origins and development of the Latin alphabet." In W.M. Senner, ed., *The Origins of Writing.* Lincoln, NE: 121–135.

Wallace, R. 2005. *An Introduction to Wall Inscriptions from Pompeii and Herculaneum.* Wauconda, IL.

Wallace, R.W. 2006. "Law and rhetoric: Community justice in Athenian courts." In K.H. Kinzl, ed., *A Companion to the Classical Greek World.* Malden, MA and Oxford: 416–431.

Wallace-Hadrill, A. 1998. "To be Roman, go Greek: Thoughts on hellenization at Rome." In M. Austin, J. Harries and C. Smith, eds., Modus operandi. *Essays in honour of Geoffrey Rickman* [BICS Supplement 71]. London: 79–81.

Wallace-Hadrill, A. 2008. *Rome's Cultural Revolution.* Cambridge.

Walsh, P.G. 2006. *Pliny the Younger: Complete Letters. Translated with an Introduction and Notes.* Oxford.

Ward-Perkins, B. 2005. *The Fall of Rome and the End of Civilization.* Oxford.

Warmington, E.H. 1938. *Remains of Old Latin III: Lucilius. Laws of the XII Tables.* [Loeb Classical Library]. London and Cambridge, MA.

Warmington, E.H. 1940. *Remains of Old Latin IV: Archaic Inscriptions.* [Loeb Classical Library]. London and Cambridge, MA.

Watkins, C. 1976. "Observations on the "Nestor's Cup" inscription." *HSCPh* 80: 25–40.

Watkins, C. 1995a. "Greece in Italy outside Rome." *HSCPh* 97: 35–50.

Watkins, C. 1995b. *How to Kill a Dragon: Aspects of Indo-European Poetics.* Oxford.

Watson, P. 1985. "Axelson revisited: The selection of vocabulary in Latin poetry." *CQ* 35: 430–448.

Weijers, O. 1987. *Terminologie des universités au XIIIe siècle.* Rome.

Weijers, O., ed. 1988–2003. *Études sur le vocabulaire intellectuel du moyen age* (CIVICIMA), I–X. Turnhout.

Weiss, M. 2009. *Outline of the Historical and Comparative Grammar of Latin.* Ann Arbor, MI.

Wenskus, O. 1995–1996. "Codewechsel bei der *Stipulatio.* Eine Bemerkung zur Sprachwandel im römischen Recht." *Glotta* 73: 116–117.

Wenskus, O. 1998. *Emblematischer Codewechsel und Verwandtes in der lateinischen Prosa. Zwischen Nähesprache und Distanzsprache.* Innsbruck.

West, D. 1982. *Greek Metre.* Oxford.

Westerburgh, U. 1956. *Chronicon Salernitanum: A Critical Edition with Studies on Literary and Historical Sources and on Language.* [Studia Latina Stockholmiensia 3]. Stockholm.

Wharton, D.B. 1997. "Tacitus' Tiberius: The state of the evidence for the emperor's *ipsissima verba* in the *Annals.*" *AJPh* 118: 119–125.

Whitney, W.D. 1881. "On mixture in language." *TAPhA* 12: 1–26.

Wierzbicka, A. 1986. "Introduction." *Journal of Pragmatics* 10: 519–534.

Wiese, I. 1984. *Fachsprache der Medizin. Eine linguistische Analyse*. Leipzig.

Wigtil, D.N. 1982. "The translator of the Greek *Res Gestae.*" *AJPh* 103: 189–195.

Wilcox, A. 2005. "Sympathetic rivals: Consolation in Cicero's letters." *AJPh* 126.2: 237–255.

Wilkinson, L.P. 1940. "The Augustan rules for dactylic verse." *CQ* 34: 30–43.

Wilkinson, L.P. 1963. *Golden Latin Artistry*. Cambridge.

Willi, A. 2003. *The Languages of Aristophanes: Aspects of Linguistic Variation in Classical Attic Greek*. Oxford.

Willi, A. 2010. "Campaigning for *utilitas*: Style, grammar and philosophy in C. Iulius Caesar." In Dickey and Chahoud, eds., 2010: 229–242.

Williams, G. 1968. *Tradition and Originality in Roman Poetry*. Oxford.

Williams, G. 1992. "The genesis of poetry in Rome." In Kenney and Clausen, eds., 1992: 53–59.

Wills, J. 1996. *Repetition in Latin Poetry: Figures of Allusion*. Oxford.

Wilson, A. Forthcoming. "Neo-Punic and Latin inscriptions in Roman North Africa: Function and display." In Mullen and James, eds., forthcoming.

Wilss, W. 1977. *Übersetzungswissenschaft. Probleme und Methoden*. Stuttgart.

Wilss, W. 1979. "Fachsprache und Übersetzen." In H. Felber, F. Lang and Gernot Wersig, eds., *Terminologie als angewandte Sprachwissenschaft. Gedenkschrift für Univ.-Prof. Dr. Eugen Wüster*. Munich: 177–191.

Winford, D. 2003. *An Introduction to Contact Linguistics*. Oxford.

Winterbottom, M. 1964. "Quintilian and the *vir bonus.*" *JRS* 54: 90–97.

Winterbottom, M. 1989. "Cicero and the middle style." In Diggle, Hall and Jocelyn, eds., 1989: 125–131.

Wiotte-Franz, C. 2001. *Hermeneus und Interpres. Zum Dolmetscherwesen in der Antike* [Saarbrücker Studien zur Archäologie und Alte Geschichte 16]. Saarbrücken.

Wiseman, T.P. 1998. *Roman Drama and Roman History*. Exeter.

Wisse, J. 2002. "The intellectual background of the rhetorical works." In J.M. May, ed., *Brill's Companion to Cicero: Oratory and Rhetoric*. Leiden: 331–374.

Wisse, J. 2007. "The riddle of the *Pro Milone*: The rhetoric of rational argument." In Powell, ed., 2007c: 35–68.

Witke, C. 1970. *Latin Satire: The Structure of Persuasion*. Leiden.

Witte, K. 1910. "Über die Form der Darstellung in Livius Geschichtswerk." *RhM* 65: 270–305, 359–419.

Wölfflin, E. 1884. "Zu den lateinischen Kausalpartikeln." *ALL* 1: 161–176.

Wölfflin, E. 1886 "Der substantivierte Infinitiv." *ALL* 3: 70–91.

Wölfflin, E. 1900. "Zum Asyndeton bei Sallust." *ALL* 11: 27–35.

Wölfflin, E. 1933. *Ausgewählte Schriften*. Leipzig.

Wolski, W. 1998. "Fachtextsorten und andere Textklassen. Probleme ihrer Bestimmung, Abgrenzung und Einteilung." In L. Hoffmann, H. Kalverkämper and H.E. Wiegand, eds., *Fachsprachen. Ein internationales Handbuch zur Fachsprachenforschung und Terminologiewissenschaft*. Berlin and New York: 457–468.

Woodcock, E.C. 1959. *A New Latin Syntax*. London.

Woodman, A.J. 1979. "Self-imitation and the substance of history: Tacitus, *Annals* 1.61–5 and *Histories* 2.70, 5.14–15." In D. West and T. Woodman, eds., *Creative Imitation and Latin Literature*. Cambridge: 143–156.

Woodman, A.J. 1988. *Rhetoric in Classical Historiography*. London.

Woodman, A.J. 1992. "Nero's alien capital: Tacitus as paradoxographer (*Annals* 15.36–7)." In T. Woodman and J. Powell, eds., *Author and Audience in Latin Literature*. Cambridge: 173–188.

Woodman, A.J. 1998. *Tacitus Reviewed*. Oxford.

Woodman, A.J. 2004. *Tacitus* The Annals. Indianpolis and Cambridge.

Woodman, A.J. 2006. "Tiberius and the taste of power: The year 33 in Tacitus." *CQ* 56: 175–189.

Woodman, A.J. 2007. *Salust* Catiline's War, The Jugurthine War, Histories. London.

Woodman, A.J. 2010a. "*Aliena facundia*: Seneca in Tacitus." In D.H. Berry and A. Erskine, eds., *Form and Function in Roman Oratory*. Cambridge: 294–307.

Woodman, A.J. 2010b. "Community health: Metaphors in Latin historiography." *PLLS* 14: 43–61.

Wright, R. 1982. *Late Latin and Early Romance in Spain and Carolingian France*. Liverpool.

Wright, R. 1989. *Latín tardío y romance temprano*. Madrid.

Wright, R., ed. 1996. *Latin and the Romance Languages in the Early Middle Ages*. 1st pub. London 1989. University Park, PA.

Wright, R. 2002. *A Sociophilological Study of Late Latin*. Turnhout.

Wright, R., ed. 2008. *Latin vulgaire – latin tardif VIII. Actes du VIIIe colloque international sur le latin vulgaire et tardif, Oxford 6–9 septembre 2006*. Hildesheim.

Yardley, J.C. 2003. *Justin and Pompeius Trogus: A Study of the Language of Justin's* Epitome *of Trogus*. Toronto.

Yaron, R. 1995. "The competitive coexistence of Latin and Greek in the Roman Empire." In R. Feenstra, A.S. Hartkamp, J.E.S. Pruit, P.J. Sijpestein and L.C. Winkel, eds., Collatio iuris Romani. *Études dédiées à Hans Ankum à l'occasion de son 65e anniversaire*. Amsterdam: II. 657–664.

Zeleny, K. 2008. *Itali modi: Akzentrhythmen in der lateinischen Dichtung der augusteischen Zeit*. Vienna.

Zetzel, J.E.G. 1981. *Latin Textual Criticism in Antiquity*. New York.

Zgusta, L. 1980. "Die Rolle des Griechischen im römischen Kaiserreich." In Neumann and Untermann, eds., 1980: 121–145.

Zimmermann, J.-L. 1986. "La fin de *Falerii veteres*: un témoignage archéologique." *The J. Paul Getty Museum Journal* 14: 37–42.

Zimmermann, M. Forthcoming. "Discourse particles." In C. Maienborn, K. von Heusinger and P. Portner, eds., *Semantics: An International Handbook of Natural Language Meaning*. Berlin.

Zinsser, J.P. 2009. "Why believe me? Narrative authority in biography." *Journal of Women's History* 21: 164–166.

Zucchelli, B. 1969a. *Studi sulle formazioni latine in -lo- non diminutive e sui loro rapporti con i diminutivi*. Parma.

Zucchelli, B. 1969b. "Sull' origine della funzione diminutiva del suffisso *-lo-* in latino." In *Studi linguistici in onore di V. Pisani*. Brescia: 1075–1100.

Index Locorum

Literary Texts

Accius *praet.* 16 261
Afranius *com.* 233 330; 383 337
Ammianus Marcellinus 15.9.1 415; 16.10 421;
    16.10.10 413; 17.11.1 412; 19.6.12 420;
    19.8.5–12 424; 23.4.7 463n; 26.10.19
    411; 29.3.8 270; 31.2 421; 31.16.9 424
Anthimus p. 10.12 168
Appendix Probi 136 521; 207 518–519
Apuleius *Met.* 5.19 178; 9.39 261
Asellio 1–2 412
Augustine *C.D.* 12.2 458; 19.7.18 549
  de Musica 2.1.1 274
  Doct. Christ. 2.13 486; 4.10 486;
    4.10.24 275
  Enarrationes in Psalmos 50.19.1 493
  Epistulae 17.5 496
  Quaest. Hept. 7.56 454
  Trin. 5.2 458
Aulus Gellius 1.10.4 238; 2.25.9 116, 238; 2.26
    460; 2.26.5 151; 6.3.36–39 391;
    6.3.52–53 393; 6.14.9 550; 10.3.3 391;
    10.9.1 453; 11.6 509; 13.6.3 515, 519;
    13.13.4 54–55; 13.14.1 53–54; 13.26.4 53;
    13.30.6 280; 17.2.19–20 244; 17.20.4 154
Ausonius *Mosella* 16.75–149 568

Bellum Africanum 48.3 522
Bellum Hispaniense 22 522; 23.3 415; 25.2
    413; 31.7 415; 36.1 281
Bible: Genesis 39:11–14 360
  Numbers 19:9 499
  Deuteronomy 28:59 490
  2 Regnorum 16:7 489; 22:6 497
  Esther 1:22 558
  Psalms 31:10 490; 17:6 497; 39:2 488;
    95:2 490; 138:15 487
  Proverbs 21:6 497; 28:6 497
  Ecclesiastes 7:30 493
  Daniel 9:23 489
  Habbakuk 2:3 488
  Matthew 24:42 498
  Luke 22:15 488
  John 19:19 557
  Acts 5:28 488
  Titus 1:7 491
  Revelation 3:13 490; 22:18–19 41
  apocryphal *Actus Petri cum Simone* 267

Caecilius *com.* 130 325; 263 327–328; 273 335
Caelius Aurelianus *Celeres Passiones* 1.2 462n;
    1.114 456; 2.56 457
  Tardae Passiones 1.60 452; 2.79 457; 3.33
    456; 3.68 451; 4.32 456

A Companion to the Latin Language, First Edition. Edited by James Clackson.
© 2011 Blackwell Publishing Ltd. Published 2011 by Blackwell Publishing Ltd.

Inscriptions and Papyri

Index

A Companion to the Latin Language, First Edition. Edited by James Clackson.
© 2011 Blackwell Publishing Ltd. Published 2011 by Blackwell Publishing Ltd.